Everyone's an Author

WITH READINGS

THIRD EDITION

ANDREA LUNSFORD
STANFORD UNIVERSITY

MICHAL BRODY

LISA EDE
OREGON STATE UNIVERSITY

BEVERLY J. MOSS
THE OHIO STATE UNIVERSITY

CAROLE CLARK PAPPER

KEITH WALTERS
PORTLAND STATE UNIVERSITY

W. W. NORTON & COMPANY

Independent Publishers Since 1923

W. W. Norton & Company has been independent since its founding in 1923, when William Warder Norton and Mary D. Herter Norton first published lectures delivered at the People's Institute, the adult education division of New York City's Cooper Union. The firm soon expanded its program beyond the Institute, publishing books by celebrated academics from America and abroad. By midcentury, the two major pillars of Norton's publishing program—trade books and college texts—were firmly established. In the 1950s, the Norton family transferred control of the company to its employees, and today—with a staff of five hundred and hundreds of trade, college, and professional titles published each year—W. W. Norton & Company stands as the largest and oldest publishing house owned wholly by its employees.

Editor: Erica Wnek
Project Editor: Christine D'Antonio
Assistant Editor: Edwin Jeng
Managing Editor, College: Marian Johnson
Managing Editor, College Digital Media: Kim Yi
Production Managers: Jane Searle, Brad Abromaitis
Media Editors: Samantha Held, Joy Cranshaw
Media Project Editor: Cooper Wilhelm
Media Editorial Assistant: Katie Bolger
Ebook Manager: Michael Hicks

Marketing Manager, Composition: Michele Dobbins
Design Director: Rubina Yeh
Designer: Lissi Sigillo
Director of College Permissions: Megan Schindel
Permissions Specialist: Elizabeth Trammell
Photo Editor: Ted Szczepanski
Photo Research: Elyse Rieder
Composition: Six Red Marbles
Manufacturing: Transcontinental—Beauceville

Permission to use copyrighted material is included in the credits section of this book, which begins on p. 1099.

The Library of Congress has catalogued another edition as follows:

Names: Lunsford, Andrea A., 1942- author. | Brody, Michal, author. | Ede, Lisa S., 1947- author. | Moss, Beverly J., author. | Papper, Carole Clark, author. | Walters, Keith, author.
Title: Everyone's an author / Andrea Lunsford, Michal Brody, Lisa Ede, Beverly J. Moss, Carole Clark Papper, Keith Walters.
Description: Third edition. | New York : W. W. Norton & Company, [2020] | Includes bibliographical references and index.
Identifiers: LCCN 2019044442 | **ISBN 9780393680850** (paperback)
Subjects: LCSH: English language—Rhetoric. | Report writing. | Authorship. | College readers.
Classification: LCC PE1408 .L874 2020 | DDC 808/.0427—dc23
LC record available at https://lccn.loc.gov/2019044442

ISBN 978-0-393-88561-3 (pbk.)

W. W. Norton & Company, Inc., 500 Fifth Avenue, New York, NY 10110
wwnorton.com
W. W. Norton & Company Ltd., 15 Carlisle Street, London W1D 3BS

3 4 5 6 7 8 9 0

For our students, authors all.

Preface

 **VERYONE'S AN AUTHOR** grew out of a growing concern for the mismatch we perceived between the kinds of writing students were asked to do in school and the kinds of writing they were doing everywhere else. They were doing more writing than ever as they tweeted, texted, blogged, and posted to all manner of social media—venturing well beyond "just words" to include photos, drawings, maps, sound, video, and visuals of all kinds. In addition, they were clearly aware that they could reach an audience far beyond their classrooms. In short, we were responding to a sea change we saw in students as they entered enthusiastically into what media scholar Henry Jenkins refers to as our "participatory culture."

So we set out to create a text that would introduce students to the joy and power and responsibility of authorship, that would present writing as it really is today—multimodal, multimedia, multilingual, and deeply digitized—and that would show students how the basic insights of rhetoric are applicable to writing in any media, any genre, any language. Our book's title argues that today, *everyone* with access to the internet can become an author who can reach broad audiences. And it aims to speak to every student who will use it: we want all students to see themselves in the pages of this book.

So these have been the overarching goals for our text. We aim to connect to students where they are, with the kinds of reading and writing they do *outside* the classroom; to acknowledge the communities they belong to; and to show respect for their linguistic and cultural diversity. We've included examples of language at work (and play) everywhere, from *YouTube* videos to ads, from hip-hop to classical genres, from pick-up basketball to the Olympics. In the pages of our book, students meet a community college student working two jobs while attending school full-time; a man who walks 21 miles every day to work; an ex-con who became a successful college student and published author; and many more. On every page, we try to show that *every* student has important ideas and significant things to say, and that we stand ready to help them do so.

Everyone's an Author thus acknowledges the primacy of writing and verbal communication in today's world, echoing the findings of Deborah Brandt and other researchers who demonstrate that writing has surpassed reading as the most significant literate practice of our time. For teachers of writing and rhetoric everywhere, this is good news indeed. But there's also an underbelly of bad news: as writing has exploded exponentially through social media, the ability to spread untrustworthy, mean-spirited, and dangerous ideas has also exploded.

We came to work on this third edition of *Everyone's an Author*, then, with a sense of urgency. Could we find ways to help students resist the lure of clickbait and misinformation, help them rev up their critical-thinking engines and become hardheaded fact-checkers who are not taken in by misleading and false stories? Could we do this while at the same time helping students remain open to ideas that differ from theirs and to people with different backgrounds and convictions? These two issues—being open to new and different ideas yet capable of critical skepticism—are two sides of the same "ethos" coin perhaps captured best in the Russian proverb: "Trust, but verify." We hope this edition answers "yes, we can, and yes, we did" to these questions—primarily in two new chapters.

Chapter 2, **"Engaging Respectfully with Others,"** provides concrete guidance to help students listen actively and respectfully so they can really hear what others are saying and can understand, as much as possible, why they are saying it.

But even as students practice empathy and look for common ground, they also must be strong critical thinkers. So in Chapter 8, **"Distinguishing Facts from Misinformation,"** students learn first to look closely at their own beliefs and values—questioning where those beliefs came from and considering whether to uphold those ideas or let them go—and then learn practical steps for reading *defensively*.

Knowing how to find and verify what media critic Howard Rheingold calls "the good stuff" calls for strong reading abilities, and that's one reason we have included a new part on **"Reading Processes"** (now Part 2) in this edition. This part comprises three chapters that provide advice for active, engaged reading; annotating texts; writing summary/response essays; and much more.

This edition continues to see students as resourceful writers and readers who bring strengths to the work they do in college. One such strength is linguistic versatility. Students are coming to college today with multiple languages and the abilities that go along with them. In addition, all students bring with them some regional, ethnic, occupational, or other dialects. A new chapter, **"Mixing Languages and Dialects,"** recognizes this fact of contemporary life and shows students how to put their linguistic versatility to work in college and beyond. Throughout, this chapter encourages students to draw on their own home languages and dialects to connect to audiences and to present their messages most effectively.

And, as always, this third edition of *Everyone's an Author* is grounded in rhetoric, which we define as "the art, theory, and practice of ethical communication." Of course rhetoric can be (and often is) used for nefarious, harmful, even evil purposes: in fact, as our book rolls off the presses, the use of rhetoric to humiliate and belittle, to confuse and distract, to distort and mislead is on the rise. But giving in to these misuses would mean giving up on rhetoric as ethical communication. And that we cannot do. Never has it been more important for teachers to embrace and practice ethical communication and to pass it on to their students. Teachers of writing everywhere have an urgent obligation to help students understand the pervasive forces appealing to people's worst instincts and build tools capable of revealing these negative and destructive forces for what they are. This means providing students with the rhetorical knowledge and strategies that can lead to true, honest, honorable, and good communication.

We believe that the third edition of *Everyone's an Author* embodies these aims and ideals and that teachers and students will respond to its message and become authors who are always—always!—ethical communicators.

Other Highlights

- *NEW advice on developing academic habits of mind* now appears in Chapter 4, "Meeting the Expectations of Academic Writing."

- *A NEW chapter on "Editing the Errors That Matter"* covers 14 errors that teachers identified as ones that undermine a writer's authority and explains why these errors matter, how to spot them in a draft, and how to edit them out. InQuizitive activities give students more practice editing the same errors online.

- *NEW readings and examples* students will relate to. From a rhetorical analysis of smart speakers with female voices and a student's narrative about growing up in his family's nail salon business to a review of *Black Panther* and an argument for deleting social media accounts, we hope that all students will find examples and images that will make them smile—and inspire them to read and write.

- *On the need for rhetoric.* From Chapter 1 on "Thinking Rhetorically" to the many prompts throughout the book that help students reflect on their own rhetorical situations and choices, this book makes students aware of the importance of rhetoric and shows them the power of understanding and using it.

- *On research.* The challenge today's students face is not gathering data but making sense of massive amounts of information and using it effectively in support of their own arguments. Chapters 20 to 29 cover all stages of research, from finding and evaluating sources to citing and documenting them. Guidelines for evaluating sources have been updated to help students judge accuracy and avoid misinformation.

- *On argument.* Chapter 12 covers "Arguing a Position," Chapter 18 covers "Analyzing and Constructing Arguments," and Chapter 19 offers "Strategies for Supporting an Argument."

- *On writing in multiple modes.* Chapter 35 provides practical advice on writing illustrated essays, blogs, wikis, audio and video essays, and posters, and Chapter 36 covers oral presentations. The companion *Tumblr* site provides a regularly updated source of multimodal readings.

- *On social justice.* Minimum wages, safe drinking water, Black Lives Matter, safety at school: many of the examples in this book demonstrate how people use writing in ways that strive to create "a more perfect union," a society that is just and equitable for all its members. We don't always agree on how to go about reaching those goals, and that's why rhetoric and civic discourse matter.

- *Menus, directories, documentation templates, and a glossary / index* make the book easy to use—and to understand.

Everyone's an Author is available in two versions, with and without an anthology of 32 readings. Readings are arranged alphabetically by author, with menus indexing the readings by genre and theme. And the book is formatted as two books in one, rhetoric in front and readings in the back. You can therefore center your course on either the rhetoric or the readings, since links in the margins will help you draw from the other part as you wish to.

What's Online

Ebooks, available for both versions of the text, provide an enhanced reading experience at a fraction of the cost of a print textbook. Norton ebooks allow students to access the entire book, highlight, bookmark, and take notes with ease, allowing students to practice active reading as it's modeled in *Everyone's an Author.* The ebooks can be viewed on—and synced between—all computers and mobile devices and include links to online multimodal examples referenced in the text. Ebook access comes free with all new copies of this textbook. See the bind-in card in the front of this book for more information.

InQuizitive for Writers delivers a game-like approach to practicing sentence editing and working with sources. After practicing with InQuizitive, students will be better prepared to find and edit errors in their own writing, and they will approach research projects with more focus and confidence. The activities are adaptive so students receive additional practice in the areas where they need more help. And explanatory feedback offers advice precisely when it's needed. The learning objectives covered in InQuizitive for Writers align with the "Editing the Errors That Matter" chapter in *Everyone's an Author.* InQuizitive for Writers access comes free with all new copies of this textbook. See the bind-in card in the front of this book for more information.

Everyonesanauthor.tumblr.com, a dynamic collection of online media curated by book author Michal Brody, provides a rich, regularly updated source of readings—including articles, speeches, advertisements, and more—for inspiration, analysis, and response. Readings are sortable by theme, genre, and medium, and each reading is accompanied by a headnote and prompts that guide students to evaluate, reflect, and develop arguments. "Conversation" clusters pair multiple readings with diverse viewpoints on contemporary topics. Find a chapter-by-chapter menu of the online examples in this book by clicking "Links from the Book." See you and your students at *everyonesanauthor.tumblr.com!*

Resources for your LMS. You can easily add high-quality Norton digital resources to your online, hybrid, or lecture course. All activities can be accessed within your existing learning management system, and many components are customizable. The *Everyone's an Author* coursepack files include reading comprehension quizzes for every chapter and reading in the book; assignable short-answer prompts and discussion questions that ask students to apply skills discussed in the text, some tied to "Think Beyond Words" and "Reflect" prompts from the book; model student papers; quizzes and exercises on grammar and research; documentation guidelines; revision worksheets, and more.

Author videos. Andrea Lunsford, Lisa Ede, Beverly Moss, Carole Clark Papper, and Keith Walters answer questions they're often asked by other instructors: about fostering collaboration, teaching multimodal writing, taking advantage of the writing center, teaching classes that include both L1 and L2 students, and more. View the videos at *everyonesanauthor.tumblr.com*.

The Guide to Teaching *Everyone's an Author*

Written by the book's authors, the *Everyone's an Author* Instructor's Guide includes specific advice for teaching every chapter and reading in the text and general advice for teaching first-year writing. It now includes new suggested classroom activities and writing assignments; more sample syllabi; and new coverage of teaching reading, maintaining a respectful classroom environment, and teaching facts versus misinformation. Available online and in print.

Find all of the resources at **wwnorton.com/instructors**.

Acknowledgments

We are profoundly grateful to the many people who have helped bring *Everyone's an Author* into existence. Indeed, this text provides a perfect example of what an eighteenth-century German encyclopedia meant when it defined *book* as "the work of many hands." Certainly this one is the work of many hands, and among those hands none have been more instrumental than those of Marilyn Moller: the breadth of her vision is matched by her meticulous attention to detail, keen sense of style and design, and ability to get more work done than anyone we have ever known. Throughout the process of conceiving and composing this text, she has set the bar high for us, and we've tried hard to reach it. For this edition, we have been graced with the editorial wisdom, wit, generosity, and organizational acumen of Erica Wnek, who has guided us in all the best ways and managed to keep us on track throughout this complex process of group revision. A big thank-you as well to Marian Johnson for making time to read and respond to many of the chapters in the first edition.

We are similarly grateful to many others who contributed their talents to this book, especially Christine D'Antonio and Jane Searle, for all they did to produce this book (no small undertaking). Thanks as well to Elizabeth Trammell for her work clearing the many text permissions and to Ted Szczepanski and Elyse Rieder for their work finding and clearing permissions for the many images. Last but certainly not least, we thank Edwin Jeng for undertaking countless tasks large and small with efficiency, conscientiousness, and smarts.

Everyone's an Author is more than just a print book, and we thank Sam Held as well as Joy Cranshaw, Katie Bolger, Cooper Wilhelm, and Michael Hicks for producing the superb resources that support the text, including the ebook, InQuizitive, LMS resources, and instructor's guide. And we again want to thank Cliff Landesman for his work in imagining and creating the fantastic *Tumblr* site.

The design of this book is something we are particularly proud of, and for that we offer very special thanks to several amazing designers. Stephen Doyle created the spectacular cover that embodies a key message of our book: that we live in a world made of words and images. Carin Berger created the illuminated alphabet, also made of text, that opens every chapter. JoAnne Metsch and Lissi Sigillo did the lovely interior design. And Debra Morton-Hoyt, Rubina Yeh, and Michael Wood oversaw the whole thing as well as adding their own elegant—and whimsical!—touches inside and out. Best thanks to all of them.

Special thanks to the fabled Norton Travelers, who have worked so hard to consult with teachers across the country about what *Everyone's an Author* can offer them. And a big thank-you to Michele Dobbins, Elizabeth Pieslor, Emily Rowan, and Lib Triplett for helping us keep our eye on our audience: teachers and students at colleges where rhetorics of this kind are assigned. Finally, we are grateful to Roby Harrington, Julia Reidhead, Steve

Dunn, and Mike Wright, who have given their unwavering support to this project for more than a decade now. We are fortunate indeed to have had the talent and hard work of this distinguished Norton team.

An astute and extremely helpful group of reviewers has helped us more than we can say: we have depended on their good pedagogical sense and advice in revising every chapter of this book. Special thanks to Forster Agama, Tallahassee Community College; Jacob Babb, Indiana University Southeast; Edward Baldwin, College of Southern Nevada; Brooke Ballard, Lone Star College–CyFair; Nancy Barendse, Charleston Southern University; Dawn Bergeron, St. Johns River State College; J. Andrew Briseño, Northwestern State University; Paul Cook, Indiana University Kokomo; Adrienne J. Daly, University of Rhode Island; Christine Davis, Northern Arizona University; James M. Decker, Illinois Central College; Sara DiCaglio, Texas A&M University; Beth Ebersbaker, Lee College; Michael Emerson, Northwestern Michigan College; Michael Faris, Texas Tech University; Wioleta Fedeczko, Utah Valley University; Bill FitzGerald, Rutgers University–Camden; Stephanie Freuler, Valencia State College; Jennifer Holly-Wells, Montclair State University; Debra Knutson, Shawnee State University; Lynn C. Lewis, Oklahoma State University; Cathy Mahaffey, University of North Carolina, Charlotte; Sadeem El Nahhas, Northwestern State University; Nicole F. Oechslin, Piedmont Virginia Community College; Kate Pantelides, Middle Tennessee State University; Jerry Petersen, Utah Valley University; Mary Jo Reiff, University of Kansas; Thomas Reynolds, Northwestern State University; Janice Rieman, University of North Carolina, Charlotte; Mary Elizabeth Rogers, Florida Gateway College; Pamela Saunders, Suffolk University; Emerson Schroeter, Northern Arizona University; Shawna Shapiro, Middlebury College; Kaia Simon, University of Wisconsin–Eau Claire; Kristen Snoddy, Indiana University Kokomo; Daniel Stanford, Pitt Community College; Shannon C. Stewart, Coastal Carolina University; Emily Suh, Texas State University; Edwin Turner, St. Johns River State College; Verne Underwood, Rogue Community College; Melanie Verner, Lee College; Courtney Wooten, George Mason University; Craig Wynne, Hampton University; and Vershawn Ashanti Young, University of Waterloo.

We'd also like to thank those reviewers who helped us to shape the previous editions: Stevens Amidon, Indiana University–Purdue Fort Wayne; Georgana Atkins, University of Mississippi; Michelle Ballif, University of Georgia; Larry Beason, University of South Alabama, Mobile; Kristen Belcher, University of Colorado, Denver; Samantha Bell, Johnson County Community College; Cassandra Bishop, Southern Illinois University; Kevin Boyle, College of Southern Nevada; Erin Breaux, South Louisiana Community College; Elizabeth Brockman, Central Michigan University; Stephen Brown, University of Nevada, Las Vegas; Ellie Bunting, Edison State College; Vicki Byard, Northeastern Illinois University; Maggie Callahan, Louisiana State University; Laura Chartier, University of Alaska, Anchorage; Tera Joy Cole, Idaho State University; Beth Daniell, Kennesaw State University; Anne-Marie Deitering, Oregon State University; Nancy DeJoy, Michigan State University; Debra Dew, Valparaiso University; Robyn DeWall, Idaho State University; Ronda Dively, Southern Illinois University, Carbondale; Patrick Dolan Jr., University of Iowa; Douglas Downs, Montana State University; Suellynn Duffey, University of Missouri, St. Louis; Anne Dvorak, Longview Community College; Maryam El-Shall, Jamestown Community College; Patricia Ericsson, Washington State University; Frank Farmer, University of Kansas; Casie Fedukovich, North Carolina State University; Lindsay Ferrara, Fairfield University; Lauren Fitzgerald, Yeshiva University; Maureen Fitzpatrick, Johnson County Community College; Kitty Flowers, University of Indianapolis; Robin Gallaher, Northwest Missouri State University; Diana Grumbles, Southern Methodist University; Ann Guess, Alvin Community College; Michael Harker, Georgia State University; Samuel Head, Idaho State University; Tara Hembrough, Southern Illinois University; Charlotte Hogg, Texas Christian University; Emma Howes, Coastal Carolina University; Melissa Ianetta, University of Delaware; Joyce Inman, University of Southern Mississippi; Jordynn Jack, University of North Carolina, Chapel Hill; Sara Jameson, Oregon State University; David A. Jolliffe, University of Arkansas; Ann Jurecic, Rutgers University; Connie Kendall, University of Cincinnati; William Lalicker, West Chester University; Michelle S. Lee, Daytona State College; Sonja Lynch, Wartburg College; Phillip Marzluf, Kansas State University; Richard Matzen, Woodbury University; Moriah McCracken, The University of Texas, Pan American; Mary Pat McQueeney, Johnson County Community College; Clyde Moneyhun, Boise State University; Chelsea Murdock, University of Kansas; Whitney Myers, Texas Wesleyan University; Carroll Ferguson Nardone, Sam Houston State University; Jessie Nixon, University of Alaska, Anchorage; Rolf Norgaard, University of Colorado, Boulder; Katherine Durham Oldmixon, Huston-Tillotson University; Matthew Oliver, Old Dominion University; Gary Olson, Idaho State University; Paula Patch, Elon University; Scott Payne, University of Central Arkansas; Albert Rouzie, Ohio University; Alison Russell, Xavier University; Kathleen J. Ryan, University of Montana; Matthew Schmeer, Johnson County Community College; Emily Robins Sharpe, Penn State University; John Sherrill, Purdue University;

Mary Lourdes Silva, Ithaca College; Marc Simoes, California State University, Long Beach; Eddie Singleton, The Ohio State University; Allison Smith, Middle Tennessee State University; Susan Smith, Georgia Southern University; Tracie Smith, University of Indianapolis; Paulette Swartzfager, Rochester Institute of Technology; Deborah Coxwell Teague, Florida State University; Jason Tham, St. Cloud State University; Tom Thompson, The Citadel; Jennifer Vala, Georgia State University; Rex Veeder, St. Cloud State University; Emily Ward, Idaho State University; Matthew Wiles, University of Louisville; Lauren Woolbright, Clemson University; and Mary Wright, Christopher Newport University.

Collectively, we have taught for over 150 years: that's a lot of classes, a lot of students—and we are grateful for every single one of them. We owe some of the best moments of our lives to them—and in our most challenging moments, they have inspired us to carry on. In *Everyone's an Author*, we are particularly grateful to the student writers whose work adds so much to this text: Ade Adegboyega, Rutgers University; Crystal Aymelek, Portland State University; Halle Edwards, Stanford University; Ryan Joy, Portland State University; Julia Landauer, Stanford University; Larry Lehna, University of Michigan, Dearborn; Melanie Luken, The Ohio State University; David Pasini, The Ohio State University; Walter Przybylowski, Rutgers University; Melissa Rubin, Hofstra University; Shuqiao Song, Stanford University; Katryn Sheppard, Portland State University; Katherine Spriggs, Stanford University; Manisha Ummadi, University of California, Berkeley; Saurabh Vaish, Hofstra University; Yuliya Vayner, Hunter College; and Kameron Wiles, Ball State University.

Each of us also has special debts of gratitude. Andrea Lunsford thanks her students and colleagues at the Bread Loaf Graduate School of English and in the Program in Writing and Rhetoric at Stanford, along with her sisters Ellen Ashdown and Liz Middleton, editor and friend Marilyn Moller, friends and life supporters Shirley Brice Heath, Betty Bailey, Cheryl Glenn, Beverly Moss, Marvin Diogenes, and Adam Banks; and especially—and forever—her grandnieces Audrey and Lila Ashdown, already compelling authors.

Michal Brody would like to thank her two wonderful families in the United States and Yucatán who so graciously support (and endure) her crazy and restless transnational life. Her conversations with each and all of those loved ones provide the constant impetus to reach for clarity and honesty of expression. She also thanks her students in both countries, who remind her every day that we are all teachers, all learners.

Lisa Ede thanks her husband, Greg Pfarr, for his support, for his commitment to his own art, and for their year-round vegetable garden. Thanks as well to her siblings, who have stuck together through thick and thin: Leni Ede Smith, Andrew Ede, Sara Ede Rowkamp, Michele Ede Smith, Laurie Ede Drake, Robert Ede, and Julie Ede Campbell. She also thanks her colleagues in the Oregon State School of Writing, Literature, and Film for their encouragement and support.

Beverly Moss thanks her parents, Harry and Sarah Moss, for their love, encouragement, and confidence in her when her own wavered. In addition, she thanks her Ohio State and Bread Loaf students, who inspire her and teach her so much about teaching. She also wants to express gratitude to her colleagues in Rhetoric, Composition, and Literacy at Ohio State for their incredible support. Finally, she thanks two of her own former English teachers, Dorothy Bratton and Jackie Royster, for the way they modeled excellence inside and outside the classroom.

Carole Clark Papper would like to thank her husband, Bob, and wonderful children—Dana, Matt, Zack, and Kate—without whose loving support little would happen and nothing would matter. In addition, she is grateful for the inspiration and support over the years of teachers, colleagues, and students at Ohio State, Ball State, and Hofstra, but especially for Beverly Moss and Andrea Lunsford for launching her on this journey.

Keith Walters thanks his partner of thirty-seven years and husband of fourteen, Jonathan Tamez, for sharing a love of life, language, travel, flowers, and beauty. He is also grateful to his students in Tunisia, South Carolina, Texas, Oregon, and Palestine who have challenged him to find ways of talking about what good writing is and how to do it.

Finally, we thank those who have taught us—who first helped us learn to hold a pencil and print our names, who inspired a love of language and of reading and writing, who encouraged us to take chances in writing our lives as best we could, who prodded and pushed when we needed it, and who most of all set brilliant examples for us to follow. One person who taught almost all of us—about rhetoric, about writing, and about life—was Edward P. J. Corbett. We remember him with love and with gratitude

—Andrea Lunsford, Michal Brody, Lisa Ede,
Beverly Moss, Carole Clark Papper, Keith Walters

CONTENTS

PART II Reading Processes   65

19 Strategies for Supporting an Argument   *451*

PART VI Research   *475*

20 Starting Your Research / Joining the Conversation   *477*

21 Finding Sources / Online, at the Library, in the Field   *486*

PART VIII Design and Delivery 755

Readings *821*

*New to the third edition

*New to the third edition

Is Everyone an Author?

**E'VE CHOSEN A PROVOCATIVE TITLE** for this book, so it's fair to ask if we've gotten it right, if everyone is an author. Let's take just a few examples that can help to make the point:

- A student creates an *Instagram* account, which immediately finds a large audience of other interested people.

- A visitor to the United States sends an email to a few friends and family members in Slovakia—and they begin forwarding it. The message circles the globe in a day.

- A professor assigns students in her class to work together to write a number of entries for *Wikipedia*, and they are surprised to find how quickly their entries are revised by others.

- An airline executive writes a letter of apology for unconscionable delays in service and publishes the letter in newspapers, where millions will read it.

- A small group of high school students who are keen on cooking post their recipe for Crispy Candy Cookies on their *Cook's Corner* blog and are overwhelmed by the number of responses to their invention.

- Five women nominated for the Academy Award for Best Actress prepare acceptance speeches: one of them will deliver the speech live before an international audience.

- You get your next assignment in your college writing class and set out to do the research necessary to complete it. When you're finished, you turn in your twelve-page argument to your instructor and classmates for their responses—and you also post a short excerpt from it on *Twitter*.

All of these examples represent important messages written by people who probably do not consider themselves authors. Yet they illustrate what we mean when we say that today "everyone's an author." Once upon a time, the ability to compose a message that reached wide and varied audiences was restricted to a small group; now, however, this opportunity is available to anyone with access to the internet.

The word *author* has a long history, but it is most associated with the rise of print and the ability of writers to claim what they have written as property. The first copyright act, in the early eighteenth century, ruled that authors held the primary rights to their work. And while anyone could potentially be a writer, an author was someone whose work had been published. That rough definition worked pretty well until recently, when traditional copyright laws began to show the strain of their 300-year history, most notably with the simple and easy file sharing that the internet makes possible.

In fact, the web has blurred the distinction between writers and authors, offering anyone with access to the internet the opportunity to publish what they write. If you have access to the internet (at school, at a library, at home), you can publish what you write and thus make what you say available to readers around the world.

Think for a minute about the impact of blogs, which first appeared in 1997. When this book was first published, there were more than 156 million public blogs, and as this new edition goes to press, there are more than 478 million blogs on *Tumblr* alone. Add to blogs the rise of *Twitter, YouTube, Instagram, Facebook,* and other social networking sites for even more evidence to support our claim: today, everyone's an author. Moreover, twenty-first-century authors just don't fit the image of the Romantic writer, alone in a garret, struggling to bring forth something unique. Rather, today's authors are part of a huge, often global, conversation; they build on what others have thought and written, they create mash-ups and remixes, and they practice teamwork at almost every turn. They are authoring for the digital age.

Redefining Writing

If the definition of *author* has changed in recent years, so has our understanding of the definition, nature, and scope of *writing*.

Writing, for example, now includes much more than words, as images and graphics take on an important part of the job of conveying meaning. In addition, writing now includes sound, video, and other media. Perhaps more important, writing now often contains many voices, as information from the internet is incorporated into the texts we write with ease. Finally, as we noted above, writing today is almost always part of a larger conversation. Rather than rising mysteriously from the depths of a writer's original thoughts, a stereotype made popular during the Romantic period, writing almost always responds to some other written piece or to other ideas. If "no man [or woman] is an island, entire of itself," then the same holds true for writing.

Writing now is also often highly collaborative. You work with a team to produce an illustrated report, the basis of which is used by members of the team to make a key presentation to management; you and a classmate carry out an experiment, argue over and write up the results together, and present your findings to the class; a business class project calls on you and others in your group to divide up the work along lines of expertise and then to pool your efforts in meeting the assignment. In all of these cases, writing is also performative—it performs an action or, in the words of many students we have talked with, it "makes something happen in the world."

Perhaps most notable, this expanded sense of writing challenges us to think very carefully about what our writing is for and whom it can and might reach. Email provides a good case in point. In the aftermath of the September 11 attacks, Tamim Ansary, a writer who was born in Afghanistan, found himself stunned by the number of people calling for bombing Afghanistan "back to the Stone Age." He sent an email to a few friends expressing his horror at the events, his condemnation of Osama bin Laden and the Taliban, and his hope that those in the United States would not act on the basis of gross stereotyping. The few dozen friends to whom Ansary wrote hit their forward buttons. Within days, the letter had circled the globe more than once, and Ansary's words were published by the Africa News Service, the *Philippine Daily Inquirer,* the *Evening Standard* in London, the *San Francisco Chronicle* and many other papers in the United States, as well as on many websites.

Authors whose messages can be instantly transported around the world need to consider those who will receive those messages. As the example of Tamim Ansary shows, no longer can writers assume that they write only to a specified audience or that they can easily control the dissemination of their messages. We now live not only in a city, a state, and a country but in a global community as well—and we write, intentionally or not, to speakers of many languages, to members of many cultures, to believers of many creeds.

Everyone's a Researcher

Since all writing responds to the ideas and words of others, it usually draws on some kind of research. Think for a moment of how often you carry out research. We're guessing that a little reflection will turn up lots of examples: you may find yourself digging up information on the pricing of new cars, searching *Craigslist* or the want ads for a good job, comparing two new smartphones, looking up statistics on a favorite sports figure, or searching for a recipe for tabbouleh. All of these everyday activities involve research. In addition, many of your most important life decisions involve research—what colleges to apply to, what jobs to pursue, where to live, and more. Once you begin to think about research in this broad way—as a form of inquiry related to important decisions—you'll probably find that research is something you do almost every day. Moreover, you'll see the ways in which the research you do adds to your credibility—giving you the authority that goes along with being an author.

But research today is very different from the research of only a few decades ago. Take the example of the concordance, an alphabetized listing of every instance of all topics and words in a work. Before the computer age, concordances were done by hand: the first full concordance to the works of Shakespeare took decades of eye-straining, painstaking research, counting, and sorting. Some scholars spent years, even whole careers, developing concordances that then served as major resources for other scholars. As soon as Shakespeare's plays and poems were in digital form—voilà!—a concordance could be produced automatically and accessed by writers with the click of a mouse.

To take a more recent example, first-year college students not too long ago had no access to the internet. Just think of how easy it is now to check temperatures around the world, track a news story, or keep up to the minute on stock prices. These are items that you can google, but you may also have many expensive subscription databases available to you through your school's library. It's not too much of an exaggeration to say that the world is literally at your fingertips.

What has *not* changed is the need to carry out research with great care, to read all sources with a critical eye, and to evaluate sources before depending on them for an important decision or using them in your own work. What also has not changed is the sheer thrill research can bring: while much research work can seem plodding and even repetitious, the excitement of discovering materials you didn't know existed, of analyzing information in a new way, or of tracing a question through one particular historical period brings its own reward. Moreover, your research adds to what philosopher Kenneth Burke calls "the conversation of humankind," as you build on what others have done and begin to make significant contributions of your own to the world's accumulated knowledge.

Everyone's a Student

More than 2,000 years ago, the Roman writer Quintilian set out a plan for education, beginning with birth and ending only with old age and death. Surprisingly enough, Quintilian's recommendation for a lifelong education has never been more relevant than it is in the twenty-first century, as knowledge is increasing and changing so fast that most people must continue to be active learners long after they graduate from college. This explosion of knowledge also puts great demands on communication. As a result, one of your biggest challenges will be learning how to learn and how to communicate what you have learned across wider distances, to larger and increasingly diverse sets of audiences, and using an expanding range of media and genres.

When did you first decide to attend college, and what paths did you take to achieve that goal? Chances are greater today than at any time in our past that you may have taken time off to work before beginning college, or that you returned to college for new training when your job changed, or that you are attending college while working part-time or even full-time. These characteristics of college students are not new, but they are increasingly important, indicating that the path to college is not as straightforward as it was once thought to be. In addition, college is now clearly a part of a process of lifetime learning: you are likely to hold a number of positions—and each new position will call for new learning.

Citizens today need more years of education and more advanced skills than ever before: even entry-level jobs now call for a college diploma. But what you'll need isn't just a college education. Instead, you'll need an education that puts you in a position to take responsibility for your own learning and to take a direct, hands-on approach to that learning. Most of us learn best by *doing* what we're trying to learn rather than just being told about it. What does this change mean in practice? First, it means you will be doing much more writing, speaking, and researching than ever before. You may, for instance, conduct research on an economic trend and then use that research to create a theory capable of accounting for the trend; you may join a research group in an electrical engineering class that designs, tests, and implements a new system; you may be a member of a writing class that works to build a website for the local fire department, writes brochures for a nonprofit agency, or makes presentations before municipal boards. In each case, you will be doing what you are studying, whether it is economics, engineering, or writing.

Without a doubt, the challenges and opportunities for students today are immense. The chapters that follow try to keep these challenges and opportunities in the foreground, offering you concrete ways to think about yourself as a writer—and yes, as an author; to think carefully about the rhetorical situations you face and about the many and varied audiences for your work; and to expand your writing repertoire to include new genres, new media, and new ways of producing and communicating knowledge.

PART I

The Need for Rhetoric and Writing

CLOSE YOUR EYES and imagine a world without any form of language—no spoken or written words, no drawings, no mathematical formulas, no music—no way, that is, to communicate or express yourself. It's pretty hard to imagine such a world, and with good reason. For better or worse, we seem to be hardwired to communicate, to long to express ourselves to others. That's why philosopher Kenneth Burke says that people are, at their essence, "symbol-using animals" who have a basic need to communicate.

We can look across history and find early attempts to create systems of communication. Think, for instance, of the

Horses in prehistoric art: Uffington White Horse, Oxfordshire, England (approx. 3,000 years old); Chauvet Cave, near Vallon-Pont-d'Arc, France (approx. 30,000 years old); rock paintings, Bhimbetka, India (approx. 30,000 years old).

chalk horses of England, huge figures carved into trenches that were then filled with white chalk some 3,000 years ago. What do they say? Do they act as maps or road signs? Do they celebrate, or commemorate, or tell a story? Whatever their original intent, they echo the need to communicate to us from millennia away.

Cave paintings, many of them hauntingly beautiful, have been discovered across Europe, some thought to be 30,000 years old. Such communicative art—all early forms of writing—has been discovered in many other places, from Africa to Australia to South America to Asia.

While these carvings and paintings have been interpreted in many different ways, they all attest to the human desire to leave messages. And we don't need to look far to find other very early attempts to communicate— from makeshift drums and whistles to early pictographic languages to the symbols associated with the earliest astronomers.

As languages and other symbolic forms of communication like our own alphabet evolved, so did a need for ways to interpret and organize these forms and to use them in effective and meaningful ways. And out of these needs grew rhetoric—the art, theory, and practice of communication. In discussing rhetoric, Aristotle says we need to understand this art for two main reasons: first, in order to express our own ideas and thoughts, and second, to protect ourselves from those who would try to manipulate or harm us. Language, then, can be used for good or ill, to provide information that may help someone—or to deliberately mislead.

We believe the need for understanding rhetoric may be greater today than at any time in our history. At first glance, it may look as if communication has never been easier. We can send messages in a nanosecond, reaching people in all parts of the world with ease. We can broadcast our thoughts, hopes, and dreams—and invectives—in emails, *YouTube* videos, status updates, tweets, text messages, and a plethora of other ways.

So far, perhaps, so good. But consider the story of the Tower of Babel, told in different ways in both the Qur'an and the Bible. When the people sought to build a tower that would reach to the heavens, God responded to their hubris by creating so many languages that communication became impossible and the tower had to be abandoned. Like the languages in Babel, the means of communication are proliferating today, bringing with them the potential for miscommunication. From the struggle to sift through the amount of information created in a day—more than was previously created in several lifetimes—to the difficulty of trying to communicate across vast differences in languages and cultures, we face challenges that our parents and grandparents never did.

Pieter Brueghel the Elder, *Tower of Babel*, 1563.

"The need for rhetoric" translated from English to Japanese.

In a time when new (and sometimes confusing) forms of communication are available, many of us are looking for help with making our messages known. *Google Translate* and *Bing Translator*, for example, are attempts to offer instant translation of texts from one language to another.

Such new technologies and tools can certainly help us as we navigate twenty-first-century global villages. But they are not likely to reduce the need for an art and a theory that can inform the conversations we have there—that can encourage thoughtfulness, empathy, and responsible use of such technologies. Rhetoric responds to this need. Along with writing, which we define broadly to include speaking and drawing and performing as well as the literal inscription of words, rhetoric offers you solid ground on which to build both your education and your communicative ability and style. The chapters that follow will introduce you more fully to rhetoric and writing—and engage you in acquiring and using their powers.

ONE

Thinking Rhetorically

The only real alternative to war is rhetoric.

—WAYNE BOOTH

**ROFESSOR WAYNE BOOTH** made this statement at a conference of scholars and teachers of writing held only months after 9/11, and it quickly drew a range of responses. Just what did Booth mean by this stark statement? How could rhetoric—the art and practice of persuasion—act as a counter to war?

A noted critic and scholar, Booth explored these questions throughout his career, identifying rhetoric as an ethical art that begins with intense listening and that searches for mutual understanding and common ground as alternatives to violence and war. Put another way, two of the most potent tools we have for persuasion are language—and violence: when words fail us, violence often wins the day. Booth sees the careful and ethical use of language as our best approach to keeping violence and war at bay.

Over the past several years, Booth's words echoed again, as the Myanmar army renewed attacks that killed and maimed legions of Rohingyas, forcing hundreds of thousands to flee. In the United States, demonstrators used signs and chants—"Black Lives Matter!" and "3 shots to the back—how do you justify that?"—to demand justice for African Americans killed at the hands of police. Following the 2018 shooting in Parkland, Florida, young activists took to social media using #NeverAgain, held "March for Our Lives" protests, and founded a movement devoted to preventing gun violence. And as this book goes to press, people across the country are protesting the treatment of immigrant children and families. All these

Protesters use posters, raised fists, and more to communicate their positions.

We didn't burn
down buildings. . . .
You can do a lot
with a pen and pad.
            —ICE CUBE

groups are using dramatic, memorable statements as rhetorical strategies to capture and hold the attention of millions of people.

Note that while Booth speaks of rhetoric as an "ethical art," rhetoric can also be used for unethical purposes, as Hitler and other dictators have done; in fact, rhetoric used in unethical ways can itself lead to violence. That's why Aristotle cautioned that people need to understand rhetoric—both to get their own ethical messages across *and* to be able to recognize and resist unethical messages that others attempt to use against them. We take Aristotle's point and focus in this book on how to think rhetorically both as readers and writers. In addition, we define rhetoric as the art, theory, and practice of ethical communication—the ethical language use that Booth speaks of.

So how can you go about developing your own careful, ethical use of language? Our short answer: by learning to think and act rhetorically, that is, by developing habits of mind that begin with listening and searching for understanding before you decide what you yourself think, and by thinking hard about your own beliefs before trying to persuade others to listen to and act on what you say.

Learning to think rhetorically can serve you well as you negotiate the complexities of life today. In many everyday situations, you'll need to communicate successfully with others in order to get things done, and done in a responsible and ethical way. On the job, for example, you may need to bring coworkers to consensus on how best to raise productivity when there

Students use posters and conversation to protest the low wages paid to campus workers.

is little, if any, money for raises. Or in your college community, you may find yourself negotiating difficult waters.

When a group of students became aware of how little the temporary workers on their campus were paid, for example, they met with the workers and listened to gather information about the issue. They then mounted a campaign using flyers, speeches, and sit-ins—in other words, using the available means of persuasion—to win attention and convince the administration to raise the workers' pay. These students were thinking and acting rhetorically, and doing so responsibly and ethically. Note that these students, like the protesters from Parkland, worked together, both with the workers and with each other. In other words, none of us can manage such actions all by ourselves; we need to engage in conversation with others and listen hard to what they say. Perhaps that's what philosopher Kenneth Burke had in mind when he created his famous "parlor" metaphor:

> Imagine that you enter a parlor. You come late. When you arrive, others have long preceded you, and they are engaged in a heated discussion, a discussion too heated for them to pause and tell you exactly what it is about. . . . You listen for a while, until you decide that you have caught the tenor of the argument; then you put in your oar.
>
> —KENNETH BURKE, *The Philosophy of Literary Form*

In this parable, each of us is the person arriving late to a room full of animated conversation; we don't understand what is going on. Yet instead of butting in or trying to take over, we listen closely until we catch on to what people are saying. Then we join in, using language and rhetorical strategies to engage with others as we add our own voices to the conversation.

This book aims to teach you to *think and act rhetorically*—to listen carefully and respectfully and then to "put in your oar," join conversations about important issues, and develop strong critical and ethical habits of mind that will help you engage with others in responsible ways. This chapter will help you develop the habit of thinking rhetorically.

First, Listen

> We have two ears and one mouth so we may listen more and talk less.
> —EPICTETUS

Thinking rhetorically begins with listening, with being willing to hear the words of others in an open and understanding way. It means paying attention to what others say before and even *as a way* of making your own contributions to a conversation. Think of the times you are grateful to others for listening closely to you: when you're talking through a conflict with a family member, for instance, or even when you're trying to explain to a salesperson what you're looking for. On those occasions, you want the person you're addressing to really *listen* to what you say.

This is a kind of listening that rhetorician Krista Ratcliffe dubs "rhetorical listening," opening yourself to the thoughts of others and making the effort not only to hear their words but to take those words in and fully understand what people are saying. It means paying attention to what others say as a way of establishing good will and acknowledging the importance of their views. And yes, it means taking seriously and engaging with views that differ, sometimes radically, from your own.

Rhetorical listening is what middle school teacher Julia Blount asked for in a *Facebook* post following the 2015 riots in Baltimore after the death of Freddie Gray, who suffered fatal spinal injuries while in police custody:

> Every comment or post I have read today voicing some version of disdain for the people of Baltimore—"I can't understand" or "They're destroying their own community"—tells me that many of you are not listening. I am not asking you to condone or agree with violence. I just need you

to listen. . . . If you are not listening, not exposing yourself to unfamiliar perspectives . . . not engaging in conversation, then you are perpetuating white privilege. . . . It is exactly your ability to *not* hear, to ignore the situation, that is a mark of your privilege.

—JULIA BLOUNT, "Dear White *Facebook* Friends: I Need You to Respect What Black America Is Feeling Right Now"

Hear What Others Are Saying—and Think about Why

When you enter any conversation, whether academic, professional, or personal, take the time to understand what is being said rather than rushing to a conclusion or a judgment. Listen carefully to what others are saying and consider what motivates them: where are they coming from?

Developing such habits of mind will be useful to you almost every day, whether you are participating in a class discussion, negotiating with friends over what movie is most worth watching, or studying a local ballot issue to decide how you'll vote. In each case, thinking rhetorically means being flexible and fair, able to hear and consider varying—and sometimes conflicting—points of view.

In ancient Rome, Cicero argued that considering alternative points of view and counterarguments was key to making a successful argument, and it is just as important today. Even when you disagree with a point of view—perhaps especially when you disagree with it—allow yourself to see the issue from the viewpoint of its advocates before you reject their positions. You may be skeptical that hydrogen fuel will be the solution to global warming—but don't reject the idea until you have thought hard about others' perspectives and carefully considered alternative solutions.

Thinking hard about others' views also includes considering the larger context and how it shapes what they are saying. This aspect of rhetorical thinking goes beyond the kind of reading you probably learned to do in high school literature classes, where you looked very closely at a particular text and interpreted it on its own terms, without looking at secondary sources. When you think rhetorically, you go one step further and put that close analysis into a larger context—historical, political, or cultural, for example—to recognize and consider where the analysis is "coming from."

In analyzing the issue of gun control, for instance, you would not merely consider your own thinking or do a close reading of texts that address the issue. In addition, you would look at the whole debate in context by

See how carefully Brent Staples considers the positions and reasoning that he is opposing on p. 1039.

considering its historical development over time, thinking about the broader political agendas of both those who advocate for and those who oppose stricter gun control, asking what economic ramifications adopting—or rejecting—new gun restrictions might have, examining the role of constitutional rights in the debate, and so on. In short, you would try to see the issue from as many different perspectives and in as broad a context as possible before you formulate your own stance. When you write, you draw on these sources—what others have said about the issue—to support your own position and to help you consider counterarguments to it.

⌇⌇⌇ *REFLECT. Go to* everyonesanauthor.tumblr.com *and read "The 'Other Side' Is Not Dumb" by blogger Sean Blanda, who warns that many of us gravitate on social media to those who think like we do, which often leads to the belief that we are right and that those with other worldviews are "dumb." He argues that we need to "make an honest effort to understand those who are not like us" and to remember that "we might be wrong." Look at some of your own recent posts. How many different perspectives do you see represented? What might you do to listen—and think—more rhetorically?*

What Do You Think—and Why?

Examining all points of view on any issue will engage you in some tough thinking about your own stance—literally, where you are coming from on an issue—and why you think as you do. Such self-scrutiny can eventually clarify your stance or perhaps even change your mind; in either case, you stand to gain. Just as you need to think hard about the motivations of others, it's important to examine your own motivations in detail, asking yourself what influences in your life lead you to think as you do or to take certain positions. Then you can reconsider your positions and reflect on how they relate to those of others, including your audience—those you wish to engage respectfully in conversation or debate.

In your college assignments, you probably have multiple motivations and purposes, one of which is to convince your instructor that you are a serious and hardworking student. But think about additional purposes as well: What could you learn from doing the assignment? How can doing it help you attain goals you have?

Examining your own stance and motivation is equally important outside the classroom. Suppose you are urging fellow members of a campus group to lobby for a rigorous set of procedures to deal with accusations of sexual harassment. On one level, you're alarmed by the statistics showing a steep increase in cases of rape on college campuses and you want to do something about it. But when you think a bit more, you might find that you have additional motivations. Perhaps you've long wanted to become a leader of this group. You may have just seen *The Hunting Ground*, a documentary about rape on US college campuses, and found it deeply upsetting—and persuasive. These realizations shouldn't necessarily change your mind about what action you want your group to take, but examining what you think and why will help you to challenge your own position—and to make sure that it is fair and appropriate.

Do Your Homework

Rhetorical thinking calls on you to do some homework, to find out everything you can about what's been said about your topic, to **ANALYZE** what you find, and then to **SYNTHESIZE** that information to inform your own ideas. To put it another way, you want your own thinking to be aware and deeply informed, to reflect more than just your own opinion.

To take an everyday example, you should do some pretty serious thinking when deciding on a major purchase, such as a new car. You'll want to begin by considering the purchase in the larger context of your life. What motivates you to buy a car? Do you need one for work? Do you want it in part as a status symbol? Are you concerned about the environment and want to switch to an electric vehicle? Who besides you might be affected by this decision? A thoughtful analysis of the context and your specific motivations and purposes can guide you in drawing up a preliminary list of cars to consider.

Then you'll need to do some research, checking out product reviews and reports on safety records, efficiency, cost, and so on. Sometimes it can be hard to evaluate such sources: how much should you trust the mileage statistics provided by the carmaker, for example, or one particular reviewer's evaluation? For this reason, you should consult multiple sources and check them against one another.

You will also want to consider your findings in light of your priorities. Cost, for instance, may not be as high on your priority list as fuel efficiency. Such careful thinking will help you come to a sound decision, and then to explain it to others. If your parents, for instance, are helping you buy the car,

**THINK
BEYOND
WORDS**

⬀ *TAKE A LOOK at the 2011 Super Bowl Chrysler ad at* <u>everyonesanauthor.tumblr</u> <u>.com</u>. *You'll see many scenes from Detroit and hear a voiceover say, "What does this city know about luxury? What does a town that's been to hell and back know about the finer things in life? I'll tell you, more than most." What kind of rhetorical thinking did the ad writers do? Who was their target audience, and how did they go about appealing to them? This was an award-winning ad—but how successful do you think it was as an ad? In other words, do you think it sold a lot of cars? If you were looking to buy a car, what would this ad tell you about Chryslers—and what would you have to find out from other sources?*

you'll want to consider what their responses to your decision will be, antici-pating questions they may ask and how to respond.

    Doing your homework also means taking an analytic approach, focus-ing on *how* various rhetorical strategies work to persuade you. You may have been won over by a funny car commercial you saw on Super Bowl Sunday. So what made that advertisement so memorable? To answer that question, you'll need to study the ad closely, determining just what qualities—a clever script? memorable music? celebrity actors? cute animals? a provocative message?—made the ad so persuasive. Once you've determined that, you'll want to consider whether the car will actually live up to the advertiser's promises. This is the kind of analysis and research you will do when you engage in rhetorical thinking.

Give Credit

As part of engaging with what others have thought and said, you'll want to give credit where credit is due. Acknowledging the work of others will help build your own ethos, or character, showing that you have not only done your homework but that you want to credit those who have influenced you. The great physicist Isaac Newton famously and graciously gave credit when he wrote to his rival Robert Hooke in 1676, saying:

> What Descartes did was a good step. You have added much in several ways, and especially in taking the colours of thin plates into philosophical consideration. If I have seen a little further it is by standing on the shoulders of giants.   —ISAAC NEWTON, letter to Robert Hooke

In this letter, Newton acknowledges the work of Descartes as well as of Hooke before saying, with a fair amount of modesty, that his own advancements were made possible by their work. In doing so, he is thinking—and acting—rhetorically.

You can give credit informally, as Newton did in this letter, or you can do so formally with a full citation. Which method you choose will depend on your purpose and context. Academic writing, for instance, usually calls for formal citations, but if you are writing for a personal blog, you might embed a link that connects to another's work—or give an informal shout-out to a friend who contributed to your thinking. In each case, you'll want to be specific about what ideas or words you've drawn from others, as Newton does in referring to Hooke's consideration of the colors of thin plates. Such care in crediting your sources contributes to your credibility—and is an important part of ethical, careful rhetorical thinking.

Be Imaginative

Remember that intuition and imagination can often lead to great insights. While you want to think carefully and analytically, don't be afraid to take chances. A little imagination can lead you to new ideas about a topic you're studying and suggest how to approach it in a way that will interest others. Such insights and intuitions can often pay off big-time. One student athlete we know was interested in how the mass media covered the Olympics, and he began doing research on the coverage in *Sports Illustrated* from different periods. So far, so good: he was gathering information and would be able to write an essay showing that the magazine had been a major promoter of the Olympics.

While looking through old issues of *Sports Illustrated*, however, he kept feeling that something he was seeing in the early issues was different from what he saw in current issues of the magazine . . . something that felt important to him though he couldn't quite articulate it. This hunch led him to make an imaginative leap, to study that difference even though it was outside of the topic he had set out to examine. Excited that he was on to something, he returned to his chronological examination of the magazine. On closer inspection, he found that over the decades, *Sports Illustrated* had slowly but surely moved from focusing on teams to depicting *only* individual stars.

This discovery led him to make an argument he would never have made had he not followed his creative hunch—that the evolution of sports from a focus on the team to a focus on individual stars is perfectly captured

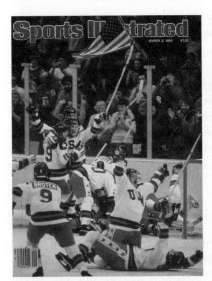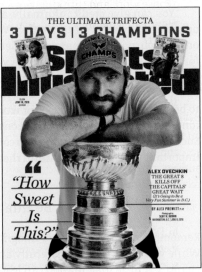

Two *Sports Illustrated* covers depicting hockey players. The cover on the left, from the 1980 Winter Olympics, showcases the US team's "miracle on ice" victory over the heavily favored USSR team. The one on the right, from 2018, pictures Washington Capitals captain Alexander Ovechkin, who was named MVP in the Stanley Cup play-offs for leading the team to victory against the Vegas Golden Knights.

in the pages of *Sports Illustrated*. It also helped him write a much more interesting—and more persuasive—essay, one that captured the attention not only of his instructor and classmates but of a local sports newsmagazine, which reprinted his essay. Like this student, you can benefit by using your imagination and listening to your intuition. You could stumble upon something exciting.

Put In Your Oar

So rhetorical thinking offers a way of entering any situation with a tool kit of strategies that will help you understand it and "put in your oar." When you think rhetorically, you ask yourself certain questions:

- How do you want to come across to your audience?
- What can you do to represent yourself as knowledgeable and credible?
- What can you do to show respect both for your audience and for those whose work and thinking you engage with?
- How can you show that you have your audience's best interests at heart?

This kind of rhetorical thinking will help ensure that your words will be listened to and taken seriously.

We can find examples of such a rhetorical approach in all fields of study. Take, for instance, the landmark essay by James Watson and Francis Crick on the discovery of DNA, published in *Nature* in 1953. This essay shows Watson and Crick to be thinking rhetorically throughout, acutely aware of their audience (major scientists throughout the world), including competitors who were simultaneously working on the same issue.

Here is Wayne Booth's analysis of Watson and Crick's use of rhetoric:

In [Watson and Crick's] report, what do we find? Actually scores of *rhetorical* choices that they made to strengthen the appeal of their scientific claim. (Biographies and autobiographies have by now revealed that they did a lot of conscientious revising, not of the data but of the mode of presentation; and their lives were filled, before and after the triumph, with a great deal of rhetoric-charged conflict.) We could easily compose a dozen different versions of their report, all proclaiming the

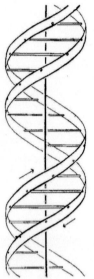

The original sketch showing the structure of DNA that appeared in Watson and Crick's article.

same scientific results. But most alternatives would prove less engaging to the intended audience. They open, for example, with

> "*We wish to suggest* a structure" that has "*novel* features which are of *considerable* biological *interest*." *(My italics, of course)*

Why didn't they say, instead: "We shall here demonstrate a *startling, totally new structure* that will *shatter* everyone's conception of the biological world"? Well, obviously their rhetorical choice presents an ethos much more attractive to most cautious readers than does my exaggerated alternative. A bit later they say

> "We have made the *usual chemical assumptions,* namely . . ."

Why didn't they say, "*As we all know*"? Both expressions acknowledge reliance on warrants, commonplaces within a given rhetorical domain. But their version sounds more thoughtful and authoritative, especially with the word "chemical." Referring to Pauling and Corey, they say

> "They *kindly* have made their manuscript available."

Okay, guys, drop the rhetoric and just cut that word "kindly." What has that got to do with your scientific case? Well, it obviously strengthens the authors' ethos: we are nice guys dealing trustfully with other nice guys, in a rhetorical community.

And on they go, with "*In our opinion*" (rather than "We proclaim" or "We insist" or "We have miraculously discovered": again ethos—we're not dogmatic); and Fraser's "*suggested*" structure is "*rather ill-defined*" (rather than "his structure is stupid" or "obviously faulty"—we *are* nice guys, right?).

And on to scores of other such choices.

—WAYNE BOOTH, *The Rhetoric of Rhetoric*

Booth shows in each instance that Watson and Crick's exquisite understanding of their rhetorical situation—especially of their audience and of the stakes involved in making their claim—had a great deal to do with how that claim was received. (They won the Nobel Prize!)

As the example of Watson and Crick illustrates, rhetorical thinking involves certain habits of mind that can and should lead to something—often to an action, to making something happen. And when it comes to taking action, those who think rhetorically are in a very strong position. They have listened attentively, engaged with the words and ideas of others, viewed their topic from many alternate perspectives, and done their homework. This kind of rhetorical thinking will set you up to contribute to conversations—and will increase the likelihood that your ideas will be heard and will inspire real action.

Indeed, the ability to think rhetorically is of great importance in today's global world, as professors Gerald Graff and Cathy Birkenstein explain:

> The ability to enter complex, many-sided conversations has taken on a special urgency in today's diverse, post-9/11 world, where the future for all of us may depend on our ability to put ourselves in the shoes of those who think very differently from us. Listening carefully to others, including those who disagree with us, and then engaging with them thoughtfully and respectfully . . . can help us see beyond our own pet beliefs, which may not be shared by everyone. The mere act of acknowledging that some-one might disagree with us may not seem like a way to change the world; but it does have the potential to jog us out of our comfort zones, to get us thinking critically about our own beliefs, and perhaps even to change our minds.   —GERALD GRAFF AND CATHY BIRKENSTEIN, *"They Say / I Say"*

In the long run, if enough of us learn to think rhetorically, we just might achieve Booth's goal—to use words (and images) in thoughtful and constructive ways as an alternative to violence and war.

🖋 *REFLECT. Read Margaret Mead's words below, and then think of at least one historical example in which a "small group of thoughtful citizens" has changed the world for the better. Then think about your own life and the ways in which you have worked with others to bring about some kind of change. In what ways were you called upon to think and act rhetorically in order to do so?*

> Never doubt that a small group of thoughtful
>
> committed citizens can change the world;
>
> indeed, it's the only thing that ever has.
>
> —MARGARET MEAD

TWO

Engaging Respectfully with Others

IN THE LATE spring of 2017, Oprah Winfrey, standing before a cheering crowd of graduating students at Agnes Scott College in Atlanta, urged them to learn to engage respectfully with others. She told the assembled crowd that "two weeks after the election last year" she had invited a group of women voters—half on the right and half on the left, politically—to join her at a diner for "great croissants with jam." But none of the women wanted to come, saying they'd "never sat this close" to someone from the other side and didn't want to start now. Winfrey eventually prevailed and brought the women together, even though they came in "all tight and hardened." As she goes on to tell it in her speech,

> After two and a half hours . . . the women were sitting around the table, listening to each other's stories, hearing both sides, and by the end they were holding hands, exchanging emails and phone numbers, and singing "Reach Out and Touch." . . . Which means it's possible; it can happen. So I want you to work in your own way to change the world in respectful conversations with others. And I want you to enter every situation aware of its context, open to hear the truths of others and most important open to letting the process of changing the world change you.
>
> —OPRAH WINFREY, Agnes Scott College
> Commencement Address, 2017

The goal of this chapter is to encourage and guide you as you engage with others: respectfully listening to their stories, their truths, and contributing to a process that may, indeed, change the world. Here are some steps you can take to realize this goal.

Get to Know People Different from You

It's a commonplace today to point out that we often live and act in "silos" where we encounter only people who think like we do, who hold the same values. While the internet has made the whole world available to us, we increasingly choose to interact with like-minded people—online and in person. We are in what some call "filter bubbles" or "echo chambers," where we hear our views echoed back to us from every direction. In such an atmosphere, it can be easy—and comforting—to think this is the real world, but it's not!

Beyond your own bubble of posts and tweets and conversations lie countless other people with different views and values.

So one of the big challenges we face today is finding ways to get out of our own echo chambers and get to know people who take different positions, hold different values. But simply encountering people who think differently is just the start. Breaking out of our bubbles calls for making the effort to understand those different perspectives, to listen with openness and empathy, and to hear where others are coming from. As Winfrey notes in her commencement address, even the first step is hard: she had to work to convince the women simply to meet one another, and then she had to persuade them to listen, as she says, with respect. Once they did, things changed: they realized that it's not as easy to dislike or dismiss someone when you are sitting face-to-face.

That's certainly what one Canadian student found when she spent a semester in Washington, DC. Shauna Vert had expected the highlights of her semester to be visiting places like the museums of the Smithsonian Institution or the Library of Congress, but her greatest experience, as she describes it in a blog post, turned out to be an "unexpected gift: While in DC, I became close, close friends with people I disagree with on almost everything." As she got to know these people, she found that they were:

> funny, smart, and kind. We all really liked music. . . . We even lived together. We ate dinner together, every single night. So I couldn't look down on them. I couldn't even consider it. And when you can't look down on someone who fundamentally disagrees with you, when you're busy breaking bread, sharing your days, laughing about the weather . . . well.
>
> —SHAUNA VERT, "Making Friends Who Disagree with You (Is the Healthiest Thing in the World)"

Read Shauna Vert's blog by visiting everyonesanauthor.tumblr.com.

During a conversation with one of her housemates, a deeply conservative Christian from Mississippi, Vert mentioned that she was "pro-choice," realizing as she did so that this was "dangerous territory." To her surprise, she met not resistance or rebuke but curiosity:

> She wanted to know more. Her curiosity fueled my curiosity, and we talked. We didn't argue—we debated gently, very gently. . . . We

laughed at nuance, we self-deprecated, we trusted each other. And we liked each other. Before the conversation, and after the conversation. To recap: Left-wing Canadian meets Bible Belt Republican. Discusses controversial political issues for over an hour. Walks away with a new friend.

This kind of careful, responsible, respectful exchange seems hard in today's highly polarized society, where anger and hate are fueled by incendiary messages coming from social media and highly partisan news organizations. Just finding people outside our silos to talk with can be hard. But like Vert, some people have taken up the challenge of finding ways to bring people with different views together.

One group aiming to create conversation rather than conflict is the Living Room Conversations project, which offers guidelines for engaging in meaningful discussions on more than eighty specific topics—free speech on campus, the opportunity gap, privacy and security, climate change, and more. The founders want these conversations between people who disagree to "increase understanding, reveal common ground and allow us to discuss possible solutions." Visit livingroomconversations.org to find the resources to start a "living room" conversation yourself.

The point is that it's worth making the time to try to find and engage with those who hold different ideas and values than you do. And this means becoming familiar with sources other people read, too. Get out of your comfort zone and look beyond the sources you know; look carefully at what the "the other side" is reading. Sites like *AllSides* can help. It's time to shut down the echo chambers and seek out people outside of our silos.

Practice Empathy

The examples in this chapter suggest the power of empathy, the ability to share the feelings of someone else. Dylan Marron is someone who directly addresses empathy and shows how it works. As the creator and host of several popular video series on controversial social issues, Marron has gained quite a bit of attention and, he says, "a lot of hate." Early on, he tried to ignore hateful comments, but then he got interested and began visiting commenter profiles to learn about the people behind them. Doing so, he said, led him to realize "there was a human on the other side of the screen"—and prompted him to call some of these people on the phone, conversations he shares on his podcast *Conversations with People Who Hate Me*.

In one of these talks, Marron learned that Josh, who in a comment had called Marron a "moron" and said that being gay was a sin, had recently graduated from high school. When Marron asked him, "How was high school for you?" Josh replied that "it was hell" because he'd been bullied by kids who made fun of him for being "bigger." Marron shared his own experiences of being bullied too, and as the conversation progressed, empathy laid the groundwork that helped them relate to each other.

At the end of another conversation, a man who had called Marron a "talentless hack" reflected on the ubiquitous comment fields where such statements are often made, saying "the comment sections are really a way to get your anger at the world out on random strangers"—an insight "that made me rethink the way I interact with people online."

Marron's work shows that comment sections are used to release anger—and often hate, the very opposite of the kind of empathy that can bring people together. More than that, his work demonstrates the power of practicing empathy and how it can help us to see one another as human, even in the most negative and nasty places. In a 2018 TED talk, Marron again stressed the importance of empathy, noting, however, that "empathy is not endorsement" and doesn't require us to compromise our deeply held values but rather to acknowledge the views of "someone raised to think

↪ Watch Marron's TED talk and listen to his podcast by visiting everyonesanauthor .tumblr.com.

Dylan Marron, creator and host of *Conversations with People Who Hate Me*, a podcast featuring conversations between people who disagree.

very differently" than we do. That's the power and the promise of practicing empathy.

Demonstrate Respect

"R-E-S-P-E-C-T." That spells respect. If you've never heard Aretha Franklin belt out these lyrics, take time to look her up on *YouTube*. Franklin added this now-famous line to her 1967 rendition of Otis Redding's original song, inspiring millions to expect and to demand R-E-S-P-E-C-T.

Franklin's message is still a timely one today, when *dis*respect seems common, especially between those who don't agree. But respect is a two-way street: if we need to stand up and ask for the respect of others, we also need to respect them. Moreover, we need to invite (and deserve!) respect. Easy to say, but harder to do. So just how can you demonstrate respect for others? Not surprisingly, the first tip for showing respect is listening, open-mindedly and generously, without interrupting or making snap judgments. You should also strive to:

Aretha Franklin performs onstage in 1968.

- Be helpful and cooperative.
- Be sincere, and remember to say "thank you."
- Be on time: even something as simple as that is a sign of respect.
- Follow through and do what you say you'll do. Keep your promises!
- Be careful to represent other people's views fairly and generously—and acknowledge their accomplishments whenever you can.
- Ask questions rather than issuing orders or challenges.
- Apologize if you say or do something you regret. We all make mistakes.

If you respect others in these ways, you will invite their respect for you. As the French philosopher Voltaire is reported to have said, "I may disapprove of what you say, but I will defend to the death your right to say it."

Search for Common Ground

Coal miners and mine owners have often engaged in bitter struggles. Still, they have a lot in common, as Carolyne Whelan's report from West Virginia relates. Read it on p. 1086.

Even children learn early on that digging in to opposing positions doesn't usually get them far: "No, you can't!" "Yes, I can!" can go on forever, without going anywhere. Rhetoricians in the ancient world understood this very well and thus argued that for conversations to progress, it's necessary to establish some **COMMON GROUND**, no matter how small. If "No, you can't!" moves on to "Well, you can't do that in this particular situation," then maybe a conversation can begin.

This is a strategy musician Daryl Davis discovered in his high-stakes work researching the Ku Klux Klan, a white supremacist group that's terrorized African Americans. Davis decided to try to meet some Klansmen, listen to them, and engage with what they said. As he says, finding common ground is essential:

> Look for commonalities. You can find something in five minutes, even with your worst enemy. And build on those. Say I don't like you because you're white and I'm black. . . . And so our contention is based upon our races. But if you say "How do you feel about all these drugs on the street" and I say "I think the law needs to crack down on things that people can get addicted to very easily" . . . and you say "Well, yeah, I agree with that" . . . You might even tell me your son started dabbling in drugs. So now I see

Daryl Davis with former KKK member Scott Sheperd. Because Davis was willing to listen to, respect, and talk with him, Sheperd listened, respected, and talked with Davis, a process that led to his leaving the KKK.

that you want what I want, that drugs are affecting your family the same way they affect my family. So let's focus on that. And as we focus more and more and find more things in common, things we have in contrast, such as skin color, matter less and less.

—DARYL DAVIS, "How to Argue"

So Davis urges us to seek out areas of agreement and then areas of compromise, all the while listening carefully and respectfully to one another. He reminds us that argument doesn't need to be abusive, insulting, or condescending—stances that usually only make things worse. But he notes as well that looking for areas of compromise doesn't mean giving in to ideas you know are not right. As Davis says, "you're going to hear things that you know are absolutely wrong. You will also hear opinions put out as facts." In such cases, Davis suggests offering facts or other **EVIDENCE** that disprove the opinion being put forward. Then, if the other person still holds to the opinion, try saying something like "I believe you are wrong, but if you think you're right, then bring me the data." Such a response invites the person to supply information that may actually carry the conversation forward.

So when you hear things you believe to be wrong, try to respond in a civil way, showing data that refute what other people say or asking them to show you evidence that *you* are wrong—with the hope of continuing the conversation based on evidence.

REFLECT. Some would say it's pointless or even wrong to try to find common ground with people whose views they find hateful or dangerous. Daryl Davis might disagree. Based on your own experiences, what do you think—and why?

Invite Response

All the examples we've provided in this chapter feature dialogue and conversation: the road to understanding is never a one-way street. That's why long speeches often have little effect on anyone who doesn't already agree with you. But tuning out is a lot harder in "live" conversations. So if

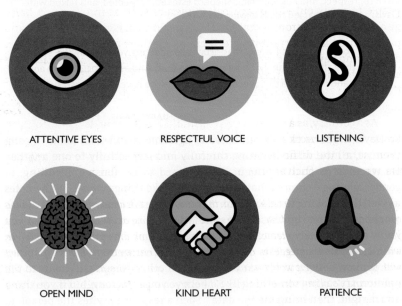

ATTENTIVE EYES   RESPECTFUL VOICE   LISTENING

OPEN MIND   KIND HEART   PATIENCE

Graphic from a website devoted to helping children learn to communicate respectfully.

you want to engage successfully with people who think differently from you, then inviting them to respond is a good way forward.

To invite response, you have to make time for it. Rather than rushing forward or talking over others, make a space for others to chime in: pause, make eye contact, even ask for response directly: "How do you feel about what I've just said?" You can also invite response online, turning commenting features on, for example, and even explicitly asking for responses to social media posts—and then responding respectfully to those who leave comments for you. In doing so, you are showing that you are open to what others think and that you really want to understand their views.

Join the Conversation: Collaborate! Engage! Participate!

Especially in times of deep societal divisions, it may be tempting to retreat, to put our heads in the sand and hope that, somehow, things will get better. But don't give in to that temptation. Your voice is important, your thoughts are important, and you can best make them heard if you engage and join with other people. That may mean working with groups of like-minded people to speak out—for or against—on issues such as immigration bans, gun control, or environmental policies. That kind of civic engagement and participation is important in a democracy. But there are smaller ways, too, like looking beyond those who think as you do, seeking to collaborate with them, listening with empathy, understanding their reasons for thinking as they do—and then looking hard for a shared goal that you can work toward together.

As a country, as a world, we have a lot riding on our willingness to reach across barriers, work together for the common good, and keep on trying even in the most difficult circumstances. And as writers, readers, and thinkers, we all have much to offer in this endeavor. So let's get going!

REFLECT. Look back through the examples in this chapter of people working out disagreements or finding ways to empathize with one another. Then think about your own experiences interacting with people who think differently than you do or with whom you disagree. How did you handle those encounters? Were you satisfied with the results? What would you do differently if you could replay them? What will you try and do differently next time? How can you apply this advice when engaging with the ideas of others in writing?

THREE

Rhetorical Situations

S PART OF A COLLEGE APPLICATION, a high school student writes a personal statement about what she plans to study, and why. A baseball fan comments on an article that analyzes data to show why a beloved New York Yankees pitcher probably won't be elected to the Hall of Fame. Eighty-seven readers respond, some praising his analysis, others questioning his conclusions and offering their own analyses. The officers of a small company address the annual shareholders' meeting to report how the firm is doing, using *PowerPoint* slides to call attention to their most important points. They take questions afterward, and two people raise their hands. The student in our first example takes a deep breath and logs in to the website of the college she wants to attend to see if she's been accepted. Good news: she's in. Come September she's at the library, working on an essay for her first-year composition course—and texting her friends as she works.

In each of these scenarios, an author is writing (or speaking) in a different set of specific circumstances—addressing certain audiences for a particular purpose, using certain technologies, and so on. So it is whenever we write. Whether we're texting a friend, outlining an oral presentation, or writing an essay, we do so within a specific rhetorical situation.

Three different rhetorical situations: a lone writer texting (*top left*); a student giving an oral presentation in class (*right*); and members of a community group collaborating on a project (*bottom left*).

We have a purpose, an audience, a stance, a genre, a medium, a design—all of which exist in some larger context. This chapter covers each of these elements and provides prompts to help you think about some of the choices you have as you negotiate your own rhetorical situations.

Every rhetorical situation presents its own unique constraints and opportunities, and as authors, we need to think strategically about our own situation. Adding to a class discussion thread presents a different challenge from writing an in-class essay exam, putting together a résumé and cover letter for a job, or working with fellow members of a campus choir to draft a grant proposal to the student government requesting funding to go on tour. A group of neighbors developing a proposal to present at a community meeting will need to attend to both the written text they will submit and the oral arguments they will make. They may also need to create slides or other visuals to support their proposal.

The workplace creates still other kinds of rhetorical situations with their own distinctive features. Reporters, for instance, must always consider their deadlines as well as their ethical obligations—to the public, to the persons or institutions they write about, and to the story they are reporting. A reporter working for six months to investigate corporate wrongdoing faces different challenges from one who covers local sports day to day. The medium—print, video, radio, podcast, social media feed, or some combination of these or other media—also influences how reporters write their stories.

Think about Your Own Rhetorical Situation

Jose Antonio Vargas risked everything by revealing his status as an undocumented immigrant. See how he navigated that rhetorical situation on p. 1069.

It is important to start thinking about your rhetorical situation early in your writing process. As a student, you'll often be given assignments with very specific guidelines—to follow the conventions of a particular genre, in a certain medium, by a specific date. Nevertheless, even the most fully developed assignment cannot specify every aspect of any particular rhetorical situation.

Effective writers—whether students, teachers, or journalists—know how to analyze their rhetorical situations. They may conduct this analysis unconsciously, drawing on the rhetorical common sense they have developed as writers, readers, speakers, and listeners. Particularly when you are writing in a new genre or discipline—a situation that you'll surely face in college—it can help to analyze your rhetorical situation more systematically.

THINK ABOUT YOUR GENRE

- *Have you been assigned a specific genre?* If not, do any words in the assignment imply a certain genre? *Evaluate* may signal a review, for example, and *explain why* could indicate a causal analysis.

- *If you get to choose your genre,* consider your PURPOSE. If you want to convince readers to recycle their trash, you would probably write an argument. If, however, you want to explain how to recycle food waste into compost, your purpose would call for a process analysis.

- *Does your genre require a certain organization?* A process analysis, for instance, is often organized CHRONOLOGICALLY, whereas a visual analysis may be organized SPATIALLY—and an annotated bibliography is almost always organized alphabetically.

- *How does your genre affect your TONE?* A lab report, for example, generally calls for a more matter-of-fact tone than a film review.

- *Are certain DESIGN features expected in your genre?* You would likely need to include images in a review of an art show, for instance, or be required to use a standard font for a research paper.

THINK ABOUT YOUR AUDIENCE

- *Who is your intended audience?* An instructor? A supervisor? Classmates? Members of a particular organization? Visitors to a website? Who else might see or hear what you say?

- *How are members of your audience like and unlike you?* Consider demographics such as age, gender, religion, income, education, occupation, and political attitudes.

- *What's your relationship with your audience?* An instructor or supervisor, for example, holds considerable authority over you. Other audiences may be friends, coworkers, or even strangers. What expectations about the text might they have because of your relationship?

- *If you have a choice of MEDIUM,* which one(s) would best reach your intended audience?

- *What do you want your audience to think or do* as a result of what you say? Take your ideas seriously? Reflect on their beliefs? Respond to you? Take some kind of action? How will you signal to them what you want?

- *Can you assume your audience will be interested* in what you say, or will you need to get them interested? Are they likely to resist any of your ideas?

- *How much does your audience know about your topic?* How much background information do they need? Will they expect—or be put off by—the use of technical jargon? Will you need to define any terms?

- *Will your audience expect a particular GENRE?* If you're writing about Mozart for a music class, you might analyze a piece he composed; if, however, you're commenting on a music video posted on *YouTube,* you'd be more likely to write some kind of review.

To quote further from People's Exhibit A, your Twitter feed, "@holdupguy82 I'm in the getaway vehicle with the money and hostages. Where R U?"

- *What about audience members you don't or can't know?* It goes without saying that you won't always know who could potentially read your writing, especially if you're writing on a site that anyone can access. The ability to reach hundreds, even thousands of readers is part of the internet's power, but you will want to take special care when your writing might reach unknown audiences. Remember as well that anything posted on the internet may easily be shared and read out of context, as the above cartoon shows!

THINK ABOUT YOUR PURPOSE

- *How would you describe your own motivation for writing?* To fulfill a course assignment? To meet a personal or professional commitment? To express your ideas to someone?

- *What is your primary goal?* To inform your audience about something? To persuade them to think a certain way? To call them to action? To entertain them? Something else?

- *How do your goals influence your choice of genre, medium, and design?* For example, if you want to persuade neighbors to recycle, you may choose to make colorful posters for display in public places. If you want to inform a corporation about what recycling programs accomplish, you may want to write a report using charts and data.

THINK ABOUT YOUR STANCE

- *What's your attitude toward your topic?* Objective? Strongly support-ive? Mildly skeptical? Amused? Angry?

- *What's your relationship with your AUDIENCE ?* Do they know you, and if so, how? Are you a student? a friend? a mentor? an interested commu-nity member? How do they see you, and how do you want to be seen?

- *How can you best convey your stance in your writing?* What TONE do you want it to have?

- *How will your stance and tone be received by your audience?* Will they be drawn in by it?

THINK ABOUT THE LARGER CONTEXT

- *What else has been said about your topic,* and how does that affect what you will say? What would be the most effective way for you to add your voice to the conversation?

- *Do you have any constraints?* When is this writing due and how much time and energy can you put into it? How many pages (or minutes) do you have to deliver your message?

- *How much independence do you have as a writer* in this situation? To what extent do you need to meet the expectations of others, such as an instructor or a supervisor? If this writing is an assignment, how can you approach it in a way that makes it matter to you?

THINK ABOUT YOUR MEDIUM AND DESIGN

- *If you get to choose your medium,* which one will work best for your audience and purpose? Print? Spoken? Digital? Some combination?

- *How will the medium determine what you can and cannot do?* For example, if you're submitting an essay online, you could include video, but if you were writing the same essay in print, you'd only be able to include a still shot from the video.

- *Does your medium favor certain conventions?* Paragraphs work well in print, but *PowerPoint* presentations usually rely on images or bulleted phrases instead. If you are writing online, you can include links to sources and background information.

- *What's the most appropriate look for your writing given your* RHETORICAL SITUATION*?* Plain and serious? Warm and inviting? What design elements will help you project that look?

- *Should you include visuals?* Would any part of your text benefit from them? Will your audience expect them? What kind would be appropriate—photographs? videos? maps? Is there any statistical data that would be easier to understand as a table, chart, or graph?

- *If you're writing a spoken or digital text,* should you include sound? still images? moving images?

REFLECT. *Make a list of all the writing that you remember doing in the last week. Be sure to include everything from texts and posts to more formal academic or work-related writing. Choose three examples that strike you as quite different from one another and analyze the rhetorical situation you faced for each one, drawing upon the guidelines in this chapter.*

FOUR

Meeting the Expectations of Academic Writing

"It's Like Learning a New Language"

LLEN MacNAMARA ARRIVED AT COLLEGE excited but also anxious. She had grown up in a small town far from the college, had not taken calculus, and had never written more than a five-paragraph essay. So when she got her first college writing assignment—in a political science class, to write a ten-page essay on how the relationship among the three branches of the US government has evolved—she felt a little panic. She had read all her assignments and done some research, and she had even met with her instructor during office hours. She had quite a bit of material. But her first attempts at writing just didn't sound right. She wasn't sure what college writing sounded like, but this wasn't it.

Following her instructor's advice, MacNamara studied several of the political science articles on her course reading list. Compared to her usual writing, they were much more formal, full of complicated sentences. What she eventually came up with wasn't a particularly good essay (and she knew it), but it served its purpose: it had gotten her thinking about college-level writing. Looking back at the work she had done to get this far, she thought, "Wow, this is almost like learning a new language."

MacNamara had a point. Many students have experiences similar to hers, especially multilingual students who've grown up in other cultures. One Romanian student we know put it this way:

In my country we care very much about the beauty of what we write. Even with academic and business writing, we try to make our texts poetic in some way. When I got to the U.S.A., I discovered that writing that I thought was beautiful struck my teachers as wordy and off-task. I was surprised about this.

This student, like Ellen MacNamara, needed to set about learning a new language—in this case, the language of US academic writing.

Habits of Mind for Academic Success

Learning the language of US academic writing is key to succeeding in college. Luckily, you don't need to guess at what strategies will lead to success. In *Framework for Success in Postsecondary Writing*, researchers and scholars have identified several key habits characteristic of students who do well in college—and beyond. Practice these habits in your coursework and you'll be "approaching learning from an active stance." In other words, you'll be on the path to succeed as an active, engaged writer and thinker.

- *Be curious.* Inquire, investigate, poke and pry until you find answers to questions you have or until you discover or create something new. Without curiosity, you'll miss much of what is really going on around you—in the courses you take and the sources you read. You can practice curiosity by asking questions: Why are the dorms on your campus so far away from the academic buildings? Who makes such decisions? How does the distance affect students who don't have bikes, for instance, or those with physical disabilities?

- *Be open & flexible.* Look at all sides of an issue. Consider fairly ideas that at first seem strange, foreign, or incorrect. Don't simply gather sources that agree with your position; instead, look for opposing views. And don't accept easy answers or those that occur to you first. In a discussion about campus safety, for example, listen and try to put yourself in the position of people with different perspectives—perhaps a young woman visitor, an older faculty member, or a student who works in a lab late at night.

- *Be engaged.* Grapple with the ideas of others, responding to them and finding connections between them. And don't give in to boredom—seek out something that really interests you in each course and assignment. A student we know was taking a course on ancient religious texts, primarily to fulfill a requirement, but when he read the Samson and Delilah story in different traditions, he used his interest in comics to create a graphic narrative of his favorite version. A topic that didn't draw him in at first became one he was excited about.

- *Be creative.* Try a new method or approach. Use a different medium for representing an idea. Take a risk investigating an idea or topic outside your comfort zone. If you think for a minute or two about your most successful school endeavors, you'll probably find that creativity played an important role: that geology project you created and presented that was unlike anything anyone else had done; the decision you made to create hip-hop lyrics to illustrate a point in a history essay.

- *Be persistent.* Keep at it. Follow through. Take advantage of opportunities to redo and improve. Keep track of what's challenging or hard for you—and look for ways to overcome those specific obstacles. You've probably already seen the positive effects of persistence in your life: they will count double (or triple) in college. Successful students don't give up but keep on keeping on. A student searching for information on a distant relative who had played a role in the civil rights movement kept coming up empty-handed and was about to give up on the project. But she decided to try one last lead on an ancestry website—and came up with a crucial piece of information that led to a big breakthrough and a sense of personal satisfaction. Persistence pays off!

- *Be responsible.* You're in control of your own learning—own it. Hold yourself responsible for making the most of your education. And be a responsible participant in the academic conversation by both incorporating and acknowledging the words and ideas of others in your own work.

- *Think about your own thinking.* Reflect on how you learn and think—and develop a habit of doing so often. Several major studies identify this kind of purposeful reflection as instrumental to becoming well educated. Many students find that keeping an informal journal to write about what they are learning, how they are learning it, and how they are learning to overcome obstacles leads to better comprehension and better success.

It's no coincidence that these habits of mind overlap with what it means to think and act rhetorically. The same practices that make us careful, ethical, and effective communicators (listen, search for understanding, put in your oar) also lead to success in college. You'll have opportunities to practice and develop these habits in your college writing. And doing so means you'll be well on your way to learning the "new language" of academic writing Ellen MacNamara described.

REFLECT. Think about a writing task you've recently been assigned or you're working on now. Which of the habits of mind have you used? And which ones are missing? Which habits of mind seem to come most naturally to you and which do you need to develop? Is there a habit you could put to better use? How will you do so next time?

So Just What Is Edited Academic Writing?

Academic writing is the kind of writing you do for school (and sometimes for work). It follows a set of conventions, such as using fairly formal edited English, following patterns of organization, and providing support for the points you make. But academic writing is also rather flexible, reaching beyond the classroom: it's used in many journals, newspapers, and books as well as online, especially on sites that address serious topics like politics, research, or cultural analysis. So "academic writing" is a broad category, one flexible enough to accommodate differences across disciplines, for example, while still remaining recognizably "academic." This chapter considers some of the assumptions that lie behind academic writing in the United States and describes some of the most common characteristics of that writing.

Tressie McMillan Cottom opens her essay with a startling statement made in a nonacademic variety of English. Check out how effective her opening is on p. 975.

We're giving so much attention to academic writing for a couple of important reasons. First, becoming fluent in it will be of great help to you both in college and well beyond; and second, it poses challenges to both native and nonnative speakers of English. We want to acknowledge these challenges without making them seem difficult to overcome. Instead, we want to demystify some of the assumptions and conventions of academic writing and get you started thinking about how to use them to your advantage.

Though edited academic English is used in most academic and professional situations in the United States, the multilingual nature of our society often leads writers to bring other dialects of English and other languages into their writing and to take what Professors Jerry Won Lee and Christopher Jenks refer to as "translingual dispositions." This term refers to a pretty simple concept: those who adopt such a way of thinking are open and receptive to language differences, including differences among varieties of any language. Taking such a flexible approach to language difference is now characteristic of many college writing programs as well as much of the best writing occurring today. This mindset recognizes that there's usually more than one effective way to say or write something. And while edited academic English is one way (and a very common one in academic writing), it's not objectively better or worse than other ways. Ultimately, your audience and purpose should always inform your language choices.

Joining US Academic Conversations

If you are new to college, you'll want to learn to "talk the talk" of academic writing so that you can join the conversations in progress all around you. Doing so calls for understanding some common expectations that most of your instructors likely hold.

You're expected to respond. One important assumption underlying the kind of writing expected in American colleges is that reading and writing are active processes in which students not only absorb information but also respond to and even question it. Not all educational systems view reading and writing in this way. In some cultures, students are penalized if they attempt to read established texts critically or disagree with authorities or insert their own views. If you are from such a background, you may find it difficult to engage in this kind of active reading and writing. It may feel rude, disrespectful, or risky, particularly if you would be reprimanded for such engagement in your home culture.

Remember, however, that the kind of engagement your instructors want is not hostile or combative; it's not about showing off by beating down the ideas of others. Rather, they expect you to demonstrate your active engagement with the texts you read—and an awareness that in doing so you are joining an academic conversation, one that has been going on for a long time and that will continue. It's fine to express strong opinions, but it's also important to remember—and acknowledge—that there is value in perspectives other than your own.

You're expected to ask questions. Because US culture emphasizes individual achievement, students are expected to develop authority and independence, often by asking questions. In contrast to cultures where the best students never ask questions because they have already studied the material and worked hard to learn it, students in American academic contexts are expected and encouraged to voice their questions. In other words, don't assume you have to figure everything out by yourself. Do take responsibility for your own learning whenever possible, but it's fine to ask questions about what you don't understand, especially specific assignments.

You're expected to say what _you_ think. American instructors expect that students will progress from relying on the thoughts of others to formulating ideas and arguments of their own. One important way to make that move is to engage in dialogue with other students and teachers. In these dialogues, teachers are not looking for you to express the "right" position; instead, they're looking for you to say what _you_ think and provide adequate and appropriate support for that point of view.

You're expected to focus from the start. In contrast to many cultures, where writers start with fairly general background information, American academic writing immediately focuses in on the topic at hand. Thus, even in the introduction of an essay, you begin at a relatively focused level, providing even greater detail in the paragraphs that follow. The point is not to show how much you know but instead to provide the information your audience needs to understand the point easily.

Because American academic writers generally open their discussions at a fairly specific level, you wouldn't want to begin with a sentence like "All over the world and in many places, there are families," a thesis statement in an essay one of us once received from a native speaker of Arabic. (Translated into Arabic, this would make a beautiful sentence and an appropriate opening statement for an essay.) Students educated in Spanish or Portuguese and, to an even greater extent, those educated in Arabic are accustomed to providing a great deal more background information than those educated in English. If you are from one of these cultural backgrounds, do not be surprised if your instructor encourages you to delete most of the first few pages of a draft, for example, and to begin instead by addressing your topic more directly and specifically.

Academic writers at work in (*clockwise from top left*) India, Chile, Burkina Faso, the United States, Thailand, and Italy.

You're expected to state your point explicitly. In US academic English, writers are usually expected to provide direct and explicit statements that lead readers, step by step, through the text—in contrast to cultures that value indirectness, circling around the topic rather than addressing it head-on. A Brazilian student we knew wasn't inclined to state the point of an essay up front and explicitly. From his cultural perspective, it made more sense to develop an argument by building suspense and stating his position only at the end of the essay. As he said, "It took a lot of practice for me to learn how to write the very direct way that professors in the USA want."

All these expectations suggest that American academic discourse puts much of the burden for successful communication on the author rather than on members of the audience. So with these expectations in mind, let's take a close look at eight common characteristics of US academic writing.

CHARACTERISTIC FEATURES

No list of characteristics can describe all the kinds of texts you'll be expected to write in college, particularly given the differences among disciplines. But there are certain things you're expected to do in college writing:

- Use edited academic English.
- Use clear and recognizable patterns of organization.
- Mark logical relationships between ideas.
- State claims explicitly and provide appropriate support.
- Present your ideas as a response to others.
- Express your ideas clearly and directly.
- Be aware of how genres and conventions vary across disciplines.
- Document sources using the appropriate citation style.

Use Edited Academic English

Academic writing usually follows the conventions of **EDITED ACADEMIC ENGLISH** in terms of spelling, grammar, and punctuation. In addition, it is often more rather than less formal. Thus, the kinds of abbreviations and other shortcuts you use while texting or posting to social media usually aren't appropriate in academic writing: you'll have to write out "in my opinion" rather than "IMHO," and you'll also want to avoid emojis. Likewise, slang isn't usually appropriate. In some contexts, you'll discover that even contractions aren't appropriate—although we use them in this book because we're aiming for a conversational tone, one that is formal to some degree but not stuffy.

Thinking about the term itself—edited academic English—will give you some insights into the goal you are trying to accomplish. In general, this **DIALECT** of language, like its counterpart in many other cultures, is the one used in formal contexts, including academic ones, by educated people.

There is a logic behind using such an academic dialect: if everyone can agree on and follow the same basic conventions, whether for spelling or subject-verb agreement, we should all be able to communicate successfully with a broad range of people. It's helpful but not perfect, since as you know if you have been to Canada or the United Kingdom or Australia, academic English varies from country to country. *Edited* reminds you that this variety of English is one that has been looked at very carefully. Most writers, especially those who grew up speaking other varieties of English and those whose first language is not English, re-read their writing several times with great care. This is also, of course, the role that good editors play: they read someone else's work and make suggestions about how to improve the quality, whether at the level of the sentence, the paragraph, or the text as a whole. Few of us pay such careful attention to our writing when we tweet or text—but we *all* need to do so with our academic writing, even if it's in the form of email.

Use Clear and Recognizable Patterns of Organization

Academic writing is often organized in a way that's clear and easy for readers to recognize. In fact, writers generally describe the pattern explicitly early in a text by including a **THESIS** sentence that states the main point and says how the text is structured.

At the paragraph level, the opening sentence generally serves as a **TOPIC SENTENCE**, which announces what the paragraph is about. Readers of academic writing expect such signals for the text as a whole and within each paragraph, even in shorter texts like essay exams. Sometimes you'll want to include headings to make it easy for readers to locate sections of text.

Readers of academic writing look for organization not only to be clear but also to follow some kind of logical progression. For example:

- Beginning with the simplest ideas and then moving step by step to the most complex ideas
- Starting with the weakest claims or evidence and progressing to the strongest ones
- Treating some topics early in the text because readers must have them as background to understand ideas introduced later
- Arranging the text chronologically, starting with the earliest events and ending with the latest ones

Some academic documents in the sciences and social sciences require a specific organization known as **IMRAD** for its specific headings: introduction, methods, results, and discussion. Although there are many possible logical patterns to use, readers will expect to be able to see that pattern with little or no difficulty. Likewise, they generally expect the **TRANSITIONS** between sections and ideas to be indicated in some way, whether with words like *first*, *next*, or *finally*, or even with full sentences like "Having considered three reasons to support this position, I will now present some alternative positions."

Finally, remember that you need to conclude your text by somehow reminding your readers of the main point(s) you want them to take away. Often, these reminders explicitly link the conclusion back to the thesis statement or introduction.

Mark Logical Relationships between Ideas

Academic writers usually strive to make clear how the ideas they present relate to one another. Thus, in addition to marking the structure of the text, you need to mark the links between ideas and to do so explicitly. If you say in casual conversation, "It was raining, and we didn't go on the picnic," listeners will interpret *and* to mean *so* or *therefore*. In academic writing, however, you have to help readers understand how your ideas are related to one another. For this reason, you'll want to use **TRANSITIONS** like *therefore*, *however*, or *in addition*. Marking the relationships among your ideas clearly and explicitly helps readers recognize and appreciate the logic of your arguments.

State Claims Explicitly and Provide Appropriate Support

One of the most important conventions of academic writing is to present **CLAIMS** explicitly and support them with **EVIDENCE**, such as examples or statistics, or by citing authorities of various kinds. Notice the two distinct parts: presenting claims clearly and supporting them appropriately. In academic writing, authors don't generally give hints; instead, they state what is on their minds, often in a **THESIS** statement. If you are from a culture that values indirection and communicates by hinting or by repeating proverbs or telling stories to make a point, you'll need to check to be sure that you have stated your claims explicitly. Don't assume that readers will be able to understand what you're saying, especially if they do not have the same cultural background knowledge that you do.

Qualify your statements. Note that being clear and explicit doesn't mean being dogmatic or closed-minded. You'll generally want to moderate your claims by using qualifying words like *frequently, often, generally, sometimes,* or *rarely* to indicate how strong a claim you are making. Note as well that it is much easier to provide adequate support for a qualified claim than it is to provide support for a broad unqualified claim.

Choose evidence your audience will trust. Whatever your claim, you'll need to use **EVIDENCE** that will be considered trustworthy and persuasive by your audience. And keep in mind that what counts as acceptable and appropriate evidence in academic writing often differs from what works in other contexts. Generally, for example, you wouldn't cite sacred religious texts as a primary source for academic arguments. In addition, writers today need more than ever to act as fact-checkers, making certain that their sources are accurate and credible rather than based on misinformation or lies.

Consider multiple perspectives. You should be aware that your readers may have a range of opinions on any topic, and you should write accordingly. Thus, citing only sources that reflect one perspective won't be sufficient in most academic contexts. Be sure to consider and acknowledge **COUNTER-ARGUMENTS** and viewpoints other than your own.

Organize information strategically. One common way of supporting a claim is by moving from a general statement to more specific information.

When you see words like *for example* or *for instance*, the author is moving from a more general statement to a more specific example.

In considering what kind of evidence to use in supporting your claims, remember that the goal is not to amass and present large quantities of evidence but instead to sift through all the available evidence, choose the evidence that will be most persuasive to your audience, and arrange and present it all strategically. Resist the temptation to include information or **ANECDOTES** that do not contribute to your argument. Your instructor may see these as digressions and encourage you to delete them.

Present Your Ideas as a Response to Others

Strong academic writers do more than just make well-supported claims. They present their ideas as a response to what else has been said (or might be said) about their topic. One common pattern, introduced by professors Gerald Graff and Cathy Birkenstein, is to start with what others are saying and then to present your ideas as a response. If, as noted earlier in this chapter, academic writing is a way of entering a conversation—of engaging with the ideas of others—you need to include their ideas with your own.

Gerald Graff himself provides a good example, on p. 929, of beginning with another's idea and then responding with his own.

In fact, providing support for your claims will often involve **SYNTHESIS**: weaving the ideas and even the words of others into the argument you are making. And since academic arguments are part of a larger conversation, all of us are always responding to and borrowing from others, even as we are developing our own individual ideas.

Express Your Ideas Clearly and Directly

Another characteristic of academic writing is clarity. You want to be sure that readers can understand exactly what you are writing about. Have you ever begun a sentence by writing "This shows . . ." only to have your teacher ask, "What does this refer to?" Such a comment is evidence that the reader isn't sure what the author—you—is referring to: this argument? this evidence? this analysis? Be specific in your language. You'll also want to **DEFINE** terms you use, both to be sure readers will not be confused and to clarify your own positions—much as we defined "edited academic English" earlier in this chapter.

Clarity of expression in academic writing also means being direct and concise. Academic writers in the United States avoid highly elaborate sentence structures or flowery language, and they don't let the metaphors and similes they use get the best of them either, as this author did:

> Cheryl's mind turned like the vanes of a wind-powered turbine, chopping her sparrowlike thoughts into bloody pieces that fell onto a growing pile of forgotten memories.

In fact, this sentence was the winner of an annual "bad writing" contest in which writers try to write the worst sentence they can. It's easy to see why this one was a winner: it has way too much figurative language—chopping wind turbines, bleeding sparrows, thoughts in a pile, forgotten memories—and the metaphors get in the way of one another. Use metaphors carefully in academic writing, making sure they add to what you're trying to say. Here's one way the prize-winning sentence might be revised to be clearer and more direct: "Cheryl's mind worked incessantly, thought after thought piling up until she couldn't keep track of them all."

Be Aware of How Genres and Conventions Vary across Disciplines

While we can identify common characteristics of all academic writing, some genres and conventions vary across disciplines. Thus, an analytic essay in psychology is similar to one in a literature class, but it is also different in crucial ways. The same will be true for lab reports or position papers in various fields. In this regard, different disciplines are like different cultures, sharing many things but unique in specific ways. Therefore, part of becoming a biologist or an engineer—or even an electrical engineer instead of a civil engineer—is learning the discipline's particular rules and rituals as well as its preferred ways of presenting, organizing, and documenting information.

You'll also find that some rhetorical moves vary across genres. In the humanities, for example, writers often use a quotation to open an essay, as a way of launching an argument—or to close one, as a way of inspiring the audience. Such a move occurs far less often in the sciences or social sciences.

Despite these differences in genres across academic disciplines, you'll also find there are some common rhetorical moves you'll make in much of the academic writing you do. You'll find that short essays and research articles generally open with three such moves:

- First, you give the **CONTEXT** or general topic of whatever you are writing; frequently, you will do this by discussing the existing research or commentary on the topic you are writing about.

- Second, you point out some aspect of this topic that merits additional attention, often because it is poorly understood or because there is a problem that needs to be solved—that is, you'll show there is a problem or gap of some kind in our understanding.

- Finally, you'll explain how your text addresses that problem or fills that gap. This explanation often happens within the first paragraph or two of the text.

Document Sources Using the Appropriate Citation Style

Finally, academic writers credit and **DOCUMENT** all sources carefully. Understanding how Western academic culture defines intellectual property and **PLAGIARISM** is complicated. Although you never need to provide a source for common knowledge that no one disputes (for example, that the US Declaration of Independence was approved by Congress on July 4, 1776, in Philadelphia), you will need to document words, information, or ideas that you get from others, including, of course, any content (words or images) you find on the internet.

What else do you need to learn about academic writing? While we hope this chapter gives you a good idea of the major features of academic writing in the United States, you may still find yourself asking questions. What kinds of evidence are necessary to support a claim sufficiently? How much documentation is needed? Should a review of literature primarily describe and summarize existing research, or should it go one step further and critique this research? You will begin to learn the answers to these questions in time, as you advance through college, and especially when you choose your major. But don't be surprised that the immediate answer to questions like these will very often be "It depends." And "it" will always depend on your purpose for writing and on the audience you wish to reach.

In the meantime, even as you work to become fluent in US academic writing, it's worth returning to a note we have sounded frequently in this chapter: the US way of writing academically is not the only way. Nor is it a better way. Rather, it is a different way. As you learn about other cultures and languages, you may have an opportunity to learn and practice the conventions those cultures use to guide their own forms of academic writing. When you do so, you'll be learning yet another "new" language, just as you have learned the "academic writing" language of the United States.

FIVE

Writing and Rhetoric in the Workplace

LASH FORWARD FIVE OR TEN YEARS. You've graduated from college, maybe from graduate or professional school as well; you're on the job. And whatever that job is, one thing is certain: your ability to communicate— through writing, speaking, and other means—will be crucial to your success. If you're an engineer, you'll likely be writing **PRO-POSALS**, specifications, and directions and maybe giving presentations to prospective clients. If you're a teacher, you'll be writing lesson plans and student **EVALUATIONS**. If you're a health-care practitioner, you'll be writing medical **NARRATIVES** and patient charts and speaking with patients and their families. If you're an accountant, you'll be **ANALYZING** data. If you're a sales representative, you'll be writing **REPORTS** as well as presenting pitches to customers. So strong is the demand for good communicators that virtually every survey of employers reports that the ability to write and speak well is the skill they value most.

Becoming a strong writer, speaker, and presenter isn't rocket science or a gift from the gods: it's a product of careful choices, hard work, and lots of practice. This chapter offers advice on some of the writing and speaking you'll need to do for work, first to get hired and then to succeed once you're on the job.

Strong writing and speaking skills are essential in the workplace—from finding a job to performing the tasks that job will require.

Consider Your Rhetorical Situation

Whether you have a job or are searching for one, you'll be communicating with many different audiences for many different purposes—and so you should get in the habit of thinking systematically about your rhetorical situation. Here are some questions that can guide you:

- *What's your* **PURPOSE**? Are you seeking information? an interview? a specific job? Are you asking someone to do something for you? Are you discussing a possible job, plan, or project? Are you presenting a proposal? asking for a raise?

- *Who's your* **AUDIENCE**? Someone you know or have been referred to? A human resources director? A colleague? A person you would report to? Someone you know nothing about? What can you assume about someone you don't know—and what can you find out by looking on a company website? If you don't know whose desk your message will land on, or if it's likely to be read by multiple people, err on the side of caution: it's better to come across as too formal than too casual.

- *What* **GENRES** *should you use?* Are you writing a letter? composing a résumé? reporting information? arguing a position or proposing some kind of action? reviewing someone's work (or being reviewed)? Thinking about genre can help you know what is expected in any of these instances.

- *What's your* **STANCE**? How do you want to present yourself—as eager? curious? confident? knowledgeable? professional? friendly? earnest? If you're looking for a job, what experience do you bring—and how can you demonstrate what you could contribute?

- *What's the* **CONTEXT**? Are you responding to an ad? writing a cover letter to go with an application or a proposal? presenting to a large group? If you're applying for a job, what can you find out about the organization online?

- *What* **MEDIA** *will you use?* If you're sending a letter or résumé, should you use email or snail mail? Or are you required to upload your application to a website? If you're participating in a discussion or interview, will it be face-to-face? on the phone? in a webinar? If you're giving a presentation, should you include slides or handouts?

Be Professional

The words you choose, the sentences you write, the way you design a letter or résumé, even your email address create an impression for prospective employers—and you want it to be a good one. The impression you make is even more important once you're on the job, for then you'll be representing both yourself and the organization you work for. Careless errors that might result in a few points off a grade at school can have greater consequences in the working world, from not getting an interview to not winning a contract to actually losing a job or a promotion. Whether you're on the job or applying for one, every word is crucial for making your goals clear and establishing credibility with employers, colleagues, or clients.

Job Letters

Letters are an important part of a job search. You will almost certainly write letters to gather information or ask about possible positions, to apply for specific jobs, and to thank those with whom you have interviewed. For all the job-related letters you'll write, here are some tried-and-true tips:

- Be direct and brief. Say what you want, and why. Assume that your readers will be scanning for just the information they need; make it easy for them to find it.

- Focus more on how you can help the company or organization than on why working there would be good for you. Be careful not to start too many sentences with I.

- State your interest and qualifications in a way that makes your readers want to speak with you—and hire you.

- Design letters carefully, making sure they look neat and professional. Use a single typeface—Times New Roman or **Arial** are always appropriate. Remember that the look of your letters says a lot about you.

- Use capitalization and punctuation the way you would in an academic essay. Don't include emojis or too many exclamation points.

- Address readers by name and title (Dear Ms. Willett) or by first name and last if you're not sure about the correct title (Dear Mary Helen

Willett). If an advertisement lists only an office, use that in your saluta-tion (Dear Office of Human Resources). If you can't find a person or an office to use, check the company's website—or make a call to the company headquarters to find out more about whom you should address.

• Proofread, proofread, proofread! Make sure that nothing is misspelled.

Inquiry letters. Sometimes you may want to send a letter looking for information about a position, an industry, an organization, or something else. If you admire someone's work or are interested in a particular company, do some research. You can probably find contact information online and some specific names on *LinkedIn*. Write to ask if they would speak with you.

Inquiry letters should be brief. Introduce yourself, and explain your interest in the organization or the person's work. Be enthusiastic but direct about what you're asking for—information about an organization? an opportunity to meet with someone? Remember to include your contact information.

Shuqiao Song read a book on designing presentations that she liked very much and that helped her improve her own presentation skills. When she noticed in the book that the author had a business near her college, Song sent the following email:

From: Shuqiao Song <ssong@gmail.com>

Date: Sunday, May 26, 2019 8:28 PM

To: Nancy Duarte <nduarte@presentations.com>

Subject: Interested in communications design

Dear Ms. Duarte:

I'm a sophomore at Stanford, where I recently took a rhetoric course in which we studied your book *slide:ology* for examples of successful presentations. I loved your book and was inspired to incorporate your suggestions and model my own presentation and slides on the advice you give.

The words and images in the graphic novel that I analyzed in my presentation interact in unusual and fascinating ways. My research on this topic led me to some insights about the way that speech, written text, and images could interact in my presentation. I've attached a video file of the presentation, which I hope you'll find interesting. My performance is far from perfect, but reading your book changed the way I thought about presenting and helped me analyze the elements of good (and bad) presentations.

Your book also made me aware of the field of communications design, and I'm interested to learn more about it. Would you be willing to meet with me to tell me about your work and how I can learn more about the field?

Thank you so much for considering this request. I hope to have the opportunity to speak with you.

Sincerely yours,
Shuqiao Song
650-555-5555

Application letters. When you're writing to apply for a job, a grant, or something else, you'll usually need to write an application letter. This kind of letter is ordinarily sent along with a résumé, so it should be relatively short and to the point, saying what you are applying for and why you are interested in it. Most important of all, try to show readers why they should consider your application—and here you need to focus on why hiring you would be good for them, not for you. Finally, identify anything you are including with your letter: your résumé, a writing sample, and so on.

Ade Adegboyega saw an advertisement for a summer internship at a ticket sales and service company. He was majoring in exercise science and sport management and had some experience in ticket sales and related services, so he was quick to apply. See the letter he sent on the next page.

An Application Letter

89 Laurel Ave.
Irvington, NJ 07111
April 14, 2019

Frank Miller, Sales Manager
The ASR Group
3120 Industrial Blvd.
Suite A200
Atlanta, GA 30318

Dear Mr. Miller:

I am writing in response to your Teamworkonline.com posting for a summer intern in ticket sales and services. I believe that I have skills and experience that would enable me to contribute to your organization, and I am interested in this position.

I am a sophomore at Rutgers University, majoring in exercise science and sport management, graduating in May 2021. The enclosed résumé provides details of my skills, education, and work experience. One item that may be of particular interest to you is my work in the ticket sales department at the Prudential Center. This experience taught me how to analyze sales patterns and meet sales quotas and promotional objectives. I've also worked as an office assistant and would also be able to contribute to the production of reports. All my jobs have helped me learn to communicate effectively with both colleagues and vendors.

I would welcome the opportunity to put my experience and abilities to work for the ASR Group sport management department and to discuss the position further with you. I can be reached at 862-555-5555 or ade.adegbo@gmail.com. Thank you for considering my application.

Sincerely,

Ade Adegboyega

Ade Adegboyega

Thank-you letters. Send a thank-you letter to anyone you speak with or who helps you when you're looking for a job. Whether you talk to people in person, on the phone, or in an email, you should thank them in writing. Doing so is a sign of respect and demonstrates your seriousness and your ability to follow through. When you're writing to someone who's interviewed you, try to reference something discussed in the interview, to raise a new question that might extend the conversation, and to provide additional thoughts about why the position would be an excellent match for your abilities and interests. And be sure to send a thank-you promptly, within a day or two of your interview. A handwritten note is a nice touch, but it's perfectly appropriate to send the thank-you via email, especially if the employer will be making a decision soon. When Scott Williams was looking for a job, he was careful to write thank-you emails like this one after every interview.

From: Scott Williams <sjwilliams@optonline.net>

Date: Friday, March 23, 2018 4:35 PM

To: Yuri Davison <davisony@graceco.com>

Subject: Thank You

Dear Mr. Davison,

Thank you for meeting with me yesterday and for taking so much time to explain the work your firm does. My studies as an economics major were mostly theoretical, so I was especially interested to hear about the day-to-day work at a private equity firm.

It's exciting to know that Grace & Company might be looking for a junior analyst in the near future, and I'm pleased to attach a sample of my writing, as you requested. It's an analytical paper I wrote about the music of Franz Liszt.

Thank you again for your time and consideration. I hope you'll keep me in mind if you do decide you need a junior analyst.

Sincerely,
Scott Williams
203-555-5555

Résumés

Your résumé provides an overview of your education and work experience—and thus is usually your most important chance to create a strong and favorable impression. While busy employers may not take time to read all the materials you send them, they will certainly take a close look at your résumé. For that reason, you'll need to write and design it carefully. As a piece of writing that represents you, your résumé should look good and be easy to read. Keep it to one page—just enough to showcase your experience and to present yourself thoughtfully. The sample résumé on the next page lists experience in chronological order, but you might consider using reverse-chronological order if your recent experiences relate directly to the kind of job you'd like to attain.

Format. Be prepared to submit your document in a variety of ways: Word, rich text format (RTF) or plain text, PDF, or HTML. Because browsers or company systems can translate files in different ways, having a clean, simple setup will prevent your résumé from being relegated to the "toss pile" because it has defaulted to something that's difficult to read. If you're submitting your résumé online, check how it looks once uploaded. If a company you're applying to wants résumés in a particular format, be sure you deliver yours that way.

Design. Use headings to organize your information and highlight key information with bullets. Make your design as simple as possible: fonts and indents won't always carry over, and simpler can often be more readable. Many companies rely on scanning technology to filter résumés for a specific position. A simple design means your résumé will be easy for automatic scanners to read. These systems search keywords to find candidates with the most appropriate experience, so mention skills, qualities, and qualifications listed in the job description when detailing your own experience.

If you have a specific job objective, you might list that objective at the top, just under your name and contact information. Be sure to mention any courses and experience that are relevant to that objective. If you're applying to be a teaching assistant at an elementary school, for example, you'll want to list any substitute teaching or babysitting experience and your CPR certification. And you might want to put experience that is most relevant to your goals first, as Ade Adegboyega did on the résumé he sent in for an internship at a ticket sales and service company.

A Print Résumé

Ade Adegboyega   •—————————
89 Laurel Ave.
Irvington, NJ 07111
862-555-5555
ade.adegbo@gmail.com

OBJECTIVE
To obtain an internship related to the field of sport management

EDUCATION
Rutgers University, New Brunswick, NJ (2017–present)
- School of Arts and Science
- Major: Exercise Science and Sport Management •————— *Headings and bullets used to highlight information.*
- Minor: Economics
- Bachelor of Science expected May 2021

EXPERIENCE
Prudential Center, Newark, NJ (Oct. 2015–Sept. 2017) •——— *Experience directly relevant to the job listed first; other experience in chronological order.*
Ticket Sales Associate
- Responded to inbound sales calls and inquiries, and provided information and/or follow-up materials as requested
- Maintained knowledge of ticket plan programs and ticket holder preferences

Answer, Rutgers University Center for Applied Psychology, Piscataway, NJ (Sept. 2017–present)
Office Assistant at national organization for sex education
- Oversee database management for quality assurance
- Assist staff with administrative duties as requested
- Compile statistical information for program coordinators
- Distribute incoming mail and prepare outgoing mail

Rutgers Recreation, New Brunswick, NJ (Jan. 2018–present)
Intramural Referee
- Look for violations of rules during play
- Impose penalties on players as necessary
- Explain the rules governing a specific sport

COMPUTER SKILLS
Microsoft Office, Adobe InDesign, HTML coding

ACTIVITIES
Intramural soccer
Rutgers Brazilian Jiu Jitsu Club   •—————————— *Length kept to one page.*

References

Often prospective employers will ask for references—professors or supervisors who can speak about your work and your work ethic. Your first step is to develop relationships with teachers and others who might serve as references. Start early in your college career; visit your teachers during office hours, discuss your goals with them—and keep in touch. When you feel comfortable enough, ask if they would be willing to be a reference for you.

When it comes time to apply for a specific job, be sure to provide your references with helpful information: a description of the position, your résumé and cover letter, and samples of your work. Give ample notice—never less than a week or two to write a letter. If the letter will be mailed, be sure to provide stamped, addressed envelopes. Remember to thank your references at every step: when they agree to be a reference, after they recommend you, and when you get the position!

Writing Samples

You may be asked to submit a writing sample or even a **PORTFOLIO** of your work. For some positions, you may want to choose writing that relates in some way to the position you're seeking, but often you'll just need to show something that demonstrates your writing ability. Include a brief cover note with your sample explaining what it is, why you are proud of it, and why you've chosen to submit it. Label the sample with your name and contact information, and take care with its presentation: place it in a folder if you're delivering it in person or make sure it's a neatly designed document if you're sending it via email.

When Elizabeth Sanders interviewed for a position as a student events coordinator for a campus research institute that specified "experience organizing and publicizing campus events" as a qualification, she was asked to bring a portfolio of her work along. She chose work that showcased writing that would matter for that job—two brochures she wrote, designed, and produced; an interview she'd conducted with a visiting speaker; and a press release—and then wrote a cover statement listing what was in her portfolio and describing how each item addressed the job she was applying for.

Job Interviews

When it comes time to interview, you'll need to prepare. Review the job description and plan how you will talk about your experiences. Research the department and organization that you'd be working for. Make a list of questions you can imagine being asked and come up with answers to each. Prepare your own list of questions that you'd like to ask. You may even want to ask a friend to do a mock interview with you for practice.

The day of the interview, be on time, dress appropriately, and bring extra copies of your résumé, cover letter, references, and any other materials that were requested. Of course you'll be nervous, but be sure to *listen*—and to think before responding. And remember to smile! Here are a few questions that interviewers might ask that you can use to practice and build your own list of potential questions:

- Why are you interested in this industry or field?
- What interests you about this specific position?
- What do you know and like about our organization?
- What is your greatest strength? weakness?
- Can you describe a time that you successfully collaborated on a project?

Participating in a video interview. Many employers today use *Skype* or other videoconferencing technologies to conduct interviews. If you're asked to do an interview of this kind, here's some advice:

- Practice speaking over video chat with a friend.
- Dress appropriately and in clothing that is easy to move around in: you may be asked to stand, or sit, or both.
- Avoid using overhead lighting, which can appear harsh on camera; try for natural light if at all possible.
- Make sure that you have a reliable internet connection.
- Remember to look and speak directly into the camera in order to come as close as possible to establishing eye contact with your interviewers.
- Be sure to speak carefully, enunciating each word in case the connection is less than ideal.
- Make sure that the area around you is neat—and that your dog isn't barking!

Remember to focus on the camera, rather than the screen, during a videoconference.

Writing on the Job

The fact is that almost any job you take will call for writing—and for speaking and presenting as well. Regardless of what job you do, you will surely be writing email. You will also likely be composing **EVALUATIONS** as well as letters of recommendation for others and carrying out **ANALYSES** of all kinds. Many jobs will call on you to write a whole range of **REPORTS** and to give presentations incorporating handouts or slides.

As rhetorician Deborah Brandt points out, most of those working in the United States today spend part of their day writing:

> A large majority of Americans . . . now make their living in the so-called information economy, people who produce, distribute, process, manipulate or vend mostly written work during a significant percentage of the workday. At the turn of the 20th century, information workers represented 10 percent of all employees. By 1959, they had grown to more than 30 percent; by 1970, they were at 50 percent and now are 75 percent of the employed population. . . . As the nature of work in the

United States has changed—toward making and managing information and knowledge—intense pressure has come to bear on the productive side of literacy, the writing side, made all the more intense . . . with the wide distribution of communication technologies that enable writing, that put keyboards and audiences readily at hand.

—DEBORAH BRANDT, "Writing at Work"

So writing will probably be a key part of your day-to-day work, as well as a key to your future success. And the greatest success comes to those who present themselves effectively, develop a strong work ethic, and seek mentorship and constructive criticism—literally writing and speaking their way to success. Remember that getting—and keeping—a job depends on some basic rhetorical principles that will never go out of style:

- Become a strong and proactive team player who collaborates well with others.

- Know your **AUDIENCE**, and make the effort to meet them more than halfway, with respect and a willingness to listen and learn from them.

- Clarify your goals and **PURPOSES**, and stick to them—but also know when and how to compromise.

- Consider the **RHETORICAL SITUATION** of any task you face, and make sure that what you are doing is appropriate in that context.

- Know your own strengths and weaknesses, and strive to build on the former and minimize the latter.

- Learn from your mistakes.

REFLECT. Think back to the jobs you've held recently. Whether you were a volunteer at your local hospital or animal shelter, a cashier, a barista, a tutor, or a summer intern, chances are that rhetoric, writing, and collaboration played a role in the work you did. Make some notes about how a particular job required you to use writing or rhetorical strategies. How do you think you might use these skills in future jobs or workplaces?

PART II

Reading Processes

DO YOU REMEMBER the first word you learned to read? For many people, that first word is their own name: you learn to print it and you do this over and over again and—suddenly, as if by magic—you can read it! Those first reading moments are miraculous because they open up entire new worlds to us. And as this example suggests, writing and reading are reciprocal processes: writing evokes reading and reading evokes writing, as if they two are intertwined in a seamless dance.

Like writing, many of us take reading for granted: it's something we have been able to do for so long that it seems run-of-the-mill, almost like breathing. But reading turns out to be a complicated process, and one with a long history. The word comes down to us from Old English, *rædan*: to advise, counsel, guess, learn by reading—and, as early as 1610, "to make out the character of a person." Sojourner Truth, a former slave and abolition advocate who was thought to be illiterate, surely knew this definition of "read" when she said, "I don't read such small things as letters; I read men and nations." This early sense of the word *read* is still with us: we "read" situations, we "read" people, we "read" images, and so on. We also read with eyes, ears, and fingers: those with low vision read by listening or by tracing braille, for example, while people who are hard of hearing use closed captions while watching television.

One aim of the following chapters is to do what ethnographers recommend to spark new ideas: make the familiar strange. We want to make the processes and practices of everyday, commonplace reading "strange" in order to call attention to them, to get you to look at them with fresh and creative eyes, and to think carefully—about what you are doing when you read, about different ways of reading, and about the processes that reading demands of you.

The chapters that follow will introduce you to the concept of reading rhetorically—that is, reading a text with clear intention and attention and putting that text, whether written, oral, visual, or digital, in its context. This kind of reading will help you read and understand the texts you encounter during your college career and well beyond. In addition, we'll focus on particular processes of reading, from annotating and summarizing a text to the point where reading meets writing in the responses you compose to what you have read. And last but certainly not least, we'll focus on drawing careful distinctions among facts, misinformation, and lies—and provide ways in which you can identify, understand, and engage productively with each category, practicing what we call "defensive reading."

Reading is a profoundly social act: it connects us to other people and places and times and at its best can be an act of empathy, helping us to walk in other people's shoes. As novelist Jean Rhys says, "Reading makes immigrants of us all. It takes us away from home, but more important, it finds homes for us everywhere." Or, in the inimitable words of Dr. Seuss: "The more that you read, the more things you will know. The more you learn, the more places you'll go!"

SIX

Reading Rhetorically

CHANCES ARE, YOU READ MORE than you think you do. You read print texts, of course, but you probably also read regularly on a phone, tablet, or computer. Reading is now, as perhaps never before, a basic necessity. In fact, if you think that reading is something you learned once and for all in the first or second grade, think again.

Reading calls for strategic effort. As media critic Howard Rheingold sees it, literacy today involves at least five interlocking abilities: attention, participation, collaboration, network awareness, and critical consumption. Of these, attention is first and foremost. In short, you need to work at paying attention to what you read. In his book *The Economics of Attention*, rhetorician Richard Lanham explains: "We're drowning in information. What we lack is the human attention needed to make sense of it all."

When so many texts are vying for our attention, which ones do we choose? In order to decide what to read, what to pay attention to, we need to practice what Rheingold calls *infotention*, a word he came up with to describe a "mind-machine combination of brain-powered attention skills and computer-powered information filters." Rheingold is talking primarily about reading online, but we think that infotention is important for reading any kind of text because it calls for synthesizing and thinking rhetorically about the enormous amount of information available to us

So many texts vying for our attention!

in both print and digital sources. And while some of us can multitask (fighter pilots are one example Rheingold gives), most of us are not good at it and must learn to focus our attention when we read.

In other words, we need to learn to read rhetorically. Reading rhetorically means attending carefully and intentionally to a text. It means being open-minded to that text. And it means being an active participant in understanding and thinking about and responding to what is in the text. As Nobel laureate Toni Morrison says, "The words on the page are only half the story. The rest is what you bring to the party."

So how do you learn to read rhetorically and to practice infotention? Some steps seem obvious: especially for high-stakes reading, like much of what you do for school, you need to find space and time in which you can really focus—turn off social media and put down your phone. Beyond such obvious steps, though, you can improve your reading by approaching texts systematically. This chapter and the chapter that follows will guide you in doing so, beginning with tips for considering your rhetorical situation and motivating yourself to engage actively with texts.

THINKING ABOUT YOUR RHETORICAL SITUATION

Before jumping into a text, consider your rhetorical situation; doing so will help you get straight where the author—and you—are coming from. Following are some questions to consider when approaching a text:

- What's the **PURPOSE** for your reading? To learn something new? To fulfill an assignment? To prepare for a test?

- Who's the intended **AUDIENCE**? What words or images in the text make you think so? Are you a member of this group? If not, there may be unfamiliar terms or references that you'll need to look up.

- What's the **GENRE**? An argument? Report? Review? Proposal? Knowing the genre will tell you something about what to expect.

- How might the **MEDIUM** affect how you will read the text? Is it a written print text? An oral text? A visual or multimedia text, such as an infographic? How will you go about attending carefully to these different media?

- What do you know about the larger **CONTEXT** of the text? What do you know about the topic? What do you need to find out? What resources can you draw on for the information you will need?

- What is your own **STANCE** on the topic? Are you an advocate? a critic? an impartial observer?

Getting your rhetorical situation straight begins your first job as a reader: making sure you understand what you read. Chapter 7 offers guidance on other essential strategies for understanding texts: previewing, annotating, and summarizing. The rest of this chapter focuses on how to be a motivated, engaged, and persistent reader.

BECOMING AN ACTIVE, ENGAGED READER

"Engagement" is one of the habits of mind scholars see as crucial to success in college, and it's certainly crucial to any reading you do there. You're "engaged" in reading when you are invested in the text. Sounds good in theory, right? But just how can you get yourself "invested" in something you've been assigned to read, especially if it's a text you wouldn't choose to read otherwise? There's no magic wand you can wave to make this happen, but we can offer some advice for staying engaged while reading:

- *Find your comfort zone,* someplace where you're most likely to be able to concentrate. A comfy lounge chair? A desk chair with back support? Starbucks? Some students tell us they like to be a little *uncomfortable* because it keeps them on their mental toes.

- *Choose a device that helps you focus.* Some like print texts best for taking notes, while others like reading on a Kindle or other device without internet distractions.

- *Make it social.* In the case of difficult texts, two heads are usually better than one—and discussing text with someone else will help you both to engage with it. Try to explain something in the text to a friend or classmate; if you can get across the major points, you've surely understood it!

- *Start with what's easy, then tackle what's difficult.* The introduction may be easy to read, so begin there and make sure you understand before moving on to more difficult material. If the text is short, read it all the way through once, marking the hard parts. Then return to the tricky parts without spending too much time; you'll probably find they are easier to understand once you've read through the entire text once.

- *Annotate as you read.* The following chapter will give you guidelines for using annotation to understand, engage, and respond to what you read.

FAST—AND SLOW—READING

Do you feel like you are always rushing? Running to the next thing, and the next, and the next? We seem to like everything fast—fast cars, fast videos, fast food—and often, fast reading. We're not talking about speed reading, which advocates claim can allow you to read up to 1,500 words a minute, but rather about the kind of skimming and scanning that most of us do online.

And there are good reasons to skim texts, particularly when you are looking for specific information. You can skim across passages looking for keywords that signal information you need, or you can read the first sentence of a paragraph to get the gist of whether what follows is relevant for your purposes. Reading expert Louise Rosenblatt calls this kind of reading "efferent," reading that's aimed at getting into a text and extracting key information in the swiftest and most effective way possible. She uses the example of a parent whose child has swallowed a dangerous substance: the parent is looking for the antidote and needs only one piece of information—fast!

The opposite of such fast reading is, logically enough, slow reading. There are lots of "slow" movements with loyal participants today: slow travel, slow media, slow fashion, and even slow reading. Some colleges now offer courses in slow reading; we know of one in a literature department where students are allowed to read only five pages a night. In his book *The Art of Slow Reading*, English professor Tom Newkirk describes six "slow" practices we believe are helpful for the kind of reading you're expected to do in college:

- *Perform.* Imagine the text you're reading is a drama, one that can be played out before an audience. Thinking of the content as a story—a narrative with low points and climaxes—can help you engage with and understand the text.

- *Make a mark.* Annotate what you notice as key parts of a text, what stands out to you as central or important to remember.

- *Find problems.* Stop to note a problem or confusion in the text and try to come up with a strategy for solving it. Such problem finding can work especially well if you are reading with someone else, someone you can talk with about the problem or confusion.

- *Read like a writer,* asking yourself about the decisions or moves the writer is making: Why shift topics here? Why introduce a particular piece of evidence at this point? Why choose this word rather than another?

- *Elaborate,* going beyond the text by comparing and contrasting it with other texts or drawing out unstated implications from the text.

- *Memorize key passages.* Learning key terms and bits of text by heart can help you understand and remember what you are reading. This can be especially helpful for reading literature, though less applicable in other fields and disciplines.

Slow reading, then, doesn't refer simply to speed. Rather it's about attending carefully to the text, taking responsibility for your reading practices.

READING UNFAMILIAR OR DIFFICULT TEXTS

You'll surely encounter subject matter and texts that are hard to understand. Most often these will be texts that you're reading not for pleasure but to learn something. You'll want to slow down with such texts, to stop and think—and you might find this easier to do with print texts, where paragraphs and headings and highlighted features help you see the various parts and find key information. Here are some other tips for making your way through difficult texts:

- On your first reading, read for what you can understand, and simply mark places that are confusing or where you don't understand.

- Then choose a modest amount of material to read—a chapter, say, or even part of a chapter. Look it over to figure out how it is organized and see its main points—look at headings, for example, as well as any **THESIS** and **TOPIC SENTENCES**.

- Check to see if there's a summary at the beginning or end of the text. If so, read it very carefully.

- Re-read the hard parts. Slow down, and focus.

- Try to make sense of the parts: "this part offers evidence," "that paragraph summarizes an alternative view," "here's a signal about what's coming next."

- If the text includes visuals, what do they contribute to the message?

- Resist highlighting: better to take notes in the margins or on digital sticky notes.

READING ON-SCREEN AND OFF

Once upon a time "reading" meant attending to words on paper. But today we often encounter texts that convey information in images and in sound as well—and they may be on- or off-screen. When you approach such texts, think carefully about how the medium of delivery may affect your understanding, engagement, and response.

Researchers have found that we often take shortcuts when we read online, searching and scanning and jumping around in a text or leaping from link to link. This kind of reading is very helpful for finding answers and information quickly, but it can blur our focus and make it difficult to attend to the text carefully and purposefully. Here are a few tips to help you when you're reading on-screen:

- Be clear about your purpose for reading. If you need to understand and remember the text, remind yourself to read carefully and avoid skimming or skipping around.
- Close *YouTube* and other pages that may distract you from reading.
- Learn how to take notes in PDFs and Word documents. Then you can make notes as you read on-screen, just as you would when reading a print text. Or take notes on paper.
- Look up unfamiliar terms as you read, making a note of definitions you may need later.
- For really high-stakes readings, consider printing out the text to read.

The pervasiveness of reading on-screen may suggest that many readers prefer to read that way. But current research suggests that most students still prefer to read print, especially if the reading is important and needs to be internalized and remembered. Print texts, it's worth remembering, are easy to navigate—you can tell at a glance how much you've read and how much you still have to go, and you can move back and forth in the text to find something important.

In addition, researchers have found that students reading on-screen are less likely to reflect on what they read or to make connections and synthesize in ways that bind learning to memory. It's important to note, however, that studies like these almost always end with a caveat: reading practices are changing and technology is making it easier to read on-screen.

It's important to note that online texts often blend written words with audio, video, links, charts and graphs, and other elements that you can attend to in any order you choose. In reading such texts, you'll need to make decisions carefully. When exactly should you click on a link, for example? The first moment it comes up? Or should you make a note to check it out later since doing so now may break your concentration—and you might not be able to get back easily to what you were reading. Links are useful in that they lead to more information, but following them can interrupt your train of thought. In addition, scrolling seems to encourage skimming and to make us read more rapidly. In short, reading on-screen can make it harder to stay on task. So you may well need to make a special effort with digital texts—to read them attentively and to pay close attention to what you're reading.

We are clearly in a time of flux where reading is concerned, so the best advice is for you to think very carefully about why you are reading. If you need to find information quickly, to follow a conversation on *Twitter*, or to look for online sources on a topic you're researching, reading on-screen is the way to go. But if you need to fully comprehend and retain the information in a text, you may want to stick with print.

Reading Visual Texts

Take a look at the excerpt from Alison Bechdel's graphic novel on p. 859. You could read only the words in the narrative boxes and get a good sense of the story she tells about her father, but how much more deeply do you understand her narrative from viewing the drawings?

Visual texts present their own opportunities and challenges. They have become so familiar and pervasive that "reading" them may seem just natural. But reading visual texts with a critical eye takes time, patience, and attention.

Take a look at the advertisement for a Shinola watch on the next page. You may know that Shinola is a Detroit-based watchmaker proud that its watches are "made in America"; if not, a quick look at the company's website will fill in this part of the ad's CONTEXT. But there's a lot more going on in terms of its particular rhetorical situation. The ad first ran in 2015, when it was clearly talking back to smart watches in general and to the launch of the Apple watch in particular, with its full panoply of futuristic bells and whistles. "Hey," the ad writers are saying to the smart watch crowd, "our watch is just smart enough."

Thinking through the rhetorical situation tells you something about the ad's purpose and audience. Of course its major PURPOSE is to sell watches, but one other goal seems to be to poke a little fun at all the high-tech, super-smart watches on the market. And what about its AUDIENCE: who do you think the ad addresses most directly? Perhaps Americans who think of themselves as solid, "no frills" folks?

Reading a visual begins, then, with studying the purpose, audience, message, and context. But there's a lot more you can do to understand a visual. You can look closely, for instance, at its DESIGN. In the Shinola ad, the stark, high-contrast, black-and-white image takes center stage, drawing our eyes to it and its accompanying captions. There are no other distracting elements, no other colors, no glitz. The simplicity gives the watch a retro look, which is emphasized by its sturdy straps, open face, and clear numerals, its old-fashioned wind-up button and second hand.

You'll also want to take a close look at any words. In this case, the Shinola ad includes a large headline centered above the image, three lines of all-caps, sans serif type that match the simplicity and straightforwardness of the image itself. And it's hard to miss the mocking TONE: "A WATCH SO SMART THAT IT CAN TELL YOU THE TIME JUST BY LOOKING AT IT." The small caption below the image underscores this message: "THE RUNWELL. IT'S JUST SMART ENOUGH." Take that, Apple!

A WATCH SO SMART
THAT IT CAN TELL YOU THE TIME
JUST BY LOOKING AT IT.

THE RUNWELL. IT'S JUST SMART ENOUGH.™

SMART ENOUGH THAT YOU DON'T NEED TO CHARGE IT AT NIGHT. SMART ENOUGH THAT IT WILL NEVER NEED
A SOFTWARE UPGRADE. SMART ENOUGH THAT VERSION 1.0 WON'T NEED TO BE REPLACED NEXT YEAR,
OR IN THE MANY DECADES THAT FOLLOW. BUILT BY THE WATCHMAKERS OF DETROIT TO LAST
A LIFETIME OR LONGER UNDER THE TERMS AND CONDITIONS OF THE SHINOLA GUARANTEE.

SHINOLA
DETROIT

Where American is made.™

NEW YORK 177 FRANKLIN ST.
DETROIT • MINNEAPOLIS • CHICAGO • WASHINGTON DC • LOS ANGELES • LONDON

SHINOLA.COM

Reading Print Texts

Print texts may consist mostly of sentences and paragraphs that (should) follow logically from one to the next, with a clear beginning, middle, and end. For these texts, the familiar practice of reading left to right, top to bottom (at least in English) will carry you through the text, though you may occasionally need to pause to look up the meaning of a word, to take notes, or just to reflect on what you're reading.

"Reading" Spoken Texts

Spoken texts need to be "read" in a different way, by listening to what speakers are saying while you view images they project on a screen or have put in a handout. If the presentation is a really good one, these elements will complement each other, joining together to get their message across. Still, you may need to learn to split your attention, making sure you are not focusing so much on any slides or handouts that you're missing what the speaker is saying—or vice versa. Remember, too, that you'll be a better audience member if you look at the speaker and any visuals, rather than staring at your laptop or looking down at the desk.

READING ACROSS GENRES

Genres affect how we read and can help guide our reading. Knowing the characteristic features of a genre, therefore, can help you read more attentively and more purposefully. When you read REPORTS, for example, you expect information you can trust, and you look for signs that the authors know what they are writing about and have cited authoritative sources. When you read a REVIEW, you expect to find some judgment, along with reasons and evidence to support that judgment. And you know to question any ARGUMENT that fails to acknowledge likely counterarguments. In other words, what you know about common genres can help you as a reader. Knowing what features to expect will help you read with a critical eye, and just recognizing a genre can help you adjust your reading as need be (reading directions more slowly, for example).

READING ACROSS ACADEMIC DISCIPLINES

Differences in disciplines can make for some very difficult reading tasks, as you encounter texts that seem almost to be written in foreign languages. As with most new things, however, new disciplines and their texts will become familiar to you the more you work with them. So don't be put off by texts in fields like psychology or physics that seem hard to read: the more you read such texts, the more familiar they will become until, eventually, you will be able to "talk the talk" of that discipline yourself.

Pay attention to terminology. It's especially important to read rhetorically when you encounter texts in different academic fields. Take the word *analysis*, for instance. That little word has a wide range of definitions as it moves from one field to another. In philosophy, analysis has traditionally meant breaking down a topic into its constituent parts in order to understand them—and the whole—more completely. In the sciences, analysis often involves the scientific method of observing a phenomenon, formulating a hypothesis about it, and experimenting to see whether the hypothesis holds up. And in business, analysis usually refers to assessing needs and finding ways to meet them. In literary studies, on the other hand, analysis usually calls for close reading in order to interpret a passage of text. When you're assigned to carry out an analysis, then, it's important to know what the particular field of study requires you to do and to ask your instructors if you aren't sure.

Know what counts as evidence. Beyond attending to what particular words mean from field to field, you should note that what counts as effective **EVIDENCE** can differ across academic disciplines. In literature and other fields in the humanities, textual evidence is often the most important: your job as a reader is to focus on the text itself. For the sciences, you'll most often focus on evidence gathered through experimentation, on facts and figures. Some of the social sciences also favor the use of "hard" evidence or data, while others are more likely to use evidence drawn from interviews, oral histories, or even anecdotes. As a strong reader, you'll need to be aware of what counts as credible evidence in the fields you study.

Be aware of how information is presented. Finally, pay attention to the way various disciplines format and present their information. You'll probably find that articles and books in the fields of literature and history present their information in paragraphs, sometimes with illustrations. Physics texts present much important information in equations, while those in psychology and polit-ical science rely more on charts and graphs and other visual representations of quantitative data. In art history, you can expect to see extensive use of images, while much of the work in music will rely on notation and sound.

So reading calls for some real effort. Whether you're reading words or images or bar graphs, literary analysis or musical notation, in a print book or on a screen, you need to read rhetorically—attentively and intentionally and with an open mind. And on top of all that, you need to be an active partici-pant with what you read, just as Toni Morrison says: "The words on the page are only half the story. The rest is what you bring to the party."

REFLECT. The next time you're assigned to read a text online, pay attention to your process. Take some notes on just how you read: Do you go straight through, or do you stop often? Do you take notes? Do you take breaks while reading to attend to something else? What do you do if you don't understand a passage? How long can you read at a stretch and maintain full concentration? Then answer the same questions the next time you're assigned to read a print text. What differences do you notice in the way you read each text? What conclusions can you draw about how to be a more effective reader, both on- and off-screen?

SEVEN

Annotating, Summarizing, Responding

**OW DO YOU** read when the stakes are high, when you really need to understand and remember what you're reading? One student we know, who chooses to read hard copy whenever possible, keeps a highlighter and a stack of sticky notes on hand in order to talk back to the text. Another student makes comments using *Acrobat Reader*. And still another takes photos of lecture slides and annotates them in a *Google Doc* while in class. These students are all using strategies they've developed for reading purposely and attentively, strategies that suit their own needs.

Like these students, you've likely already developed reading strategies that work for you and the kinds of reading you do, and you'll surely be developing new strategies as you encounter new kinds of texts and disciplines, from reports in a plant science course to executive summaries in business management. This chapter offers guidance on three key strategies that will help you engage actively and productively with all kinds of texts. *Annotating*—the process of taking notes, underlining important information, and marking key aspects of a text that strike you as important—helps you focus and attend carefully to what you read. *Summarizing* helps you synthesize the ideas in what you are reading, consolidate your understanding, and remember important points. And *responding* gives you an opportunity to engage the text directly, talking back and joining the conversation.

"We may have the same books, but we highlight entirely different passages."

Each of these strategies marks a point where reading and writing intersect: reading leads to writing (annotating, summarizing, responding), and writing about what you've read often leads you to re-read.

ANNOTATING

Annotating might sound simple: you just mark up the text as you read, right? Keep in mind, however, that what you annotate should be driven by your purpose for reading. Whatever that purpose, annotating will help you read actively—thinking, questioning, and responding as you go. Like Hansel and Gretel sprinkling bread crumbs in the forest, it's also a way of leaving a trail you can revisit later if you need to review concepts for an exam or find a quote for an essay. Taking the following steps will help you annotate purposefully and productively.

Think about your purpose for reading. If you're reading a biology textbook to prepare for an exam, you might highlight key concepts, summarize theories to be sure you understand them, and respond to the chapter's review questions. When reading a treatise by Aristotle to prepare for discussion in a philosophy class, however, you may mark passages that are hard to understand, write out questions to ask in class, and highlight statements to remember. Consider the following questions:

- *Why are you reading this text?* As a model for writing you'll be expected to do? So that you'll learn about a certain topic?

- *What do you need to be able to do with this text?* Apply concepts? Respond to the author's argument? Cite it in something you're writing?

Preview the text. Rather than plunging right in, skim the text first to get a sense of what it's about and how it's organized. Jot down what you notice.

- *What do you already know (and think) about the topic?* Do you have any personal experience with the subject? What do you want or expect to learn?

- *Who are the authors or sponsors?* Where do you think they're coming from? Might they have a particular agenda or purpose?

- *Who published the text,* and what does that tell you about its intended audience and purpose?

- *What does the title tell you?* If there's a subtitle, does it indicate the author's argument or stance?

- *If there's an abstract,* read it. If not, read the introduction. What new information do you learn?

- *Scan any headings* to see what's covered, and look at any text that's highlighted. How will the design help you read the text?

- *What is your initial response* to the text based on your preview of it?

Annotate as you read. Annotate the text as a way of talking back to it—marking *what* the author is saying, *how* the author is getting their message across, and how *you* are reacting to what you're reading.

WHAT'S THE TEXT SAYING?

- What claims does the text make? Underscore the THESIS statement. If there's no explicit thesis, what key questions and issues does the text address?

- What REASONS and EVIDENCE does the author provide? Are they sufficient?

- Does anything surprise you or make you feel skeptical? Mark any facts or statements that seem questionable.

- Note any COUNTERARGUMENTS. Does the author represent and respond to them fairly? Are any other perspectives missing?

- Identify any key terms (and look them up if necessary). This can be especially important if you're reading a text in an unfamiliar discipline. Define important terms and concepts in your own words.
- Do you understand graphs, charts, or other visual elements? These often play an important role in the sciences and social sciences.

WHO'S THE INTENDED AUDIENCE?

- Who do you think the author is addressing? Students like you? Other scholars? The general public? Mark words that make you think so. Are you included in that group? If not, does that affect your response?
- What do you know about the audience's values? Highlight words that suggest what the author thinks the audience cares about.

WHAT DO YOU KNOW ABOUT THE AUTHOR?

- Who wrote the text? Is the author credible and reliable? What makes you believe that this is the case? Note places in the text where the author demonstrates **AUTHORITY** to write on the topic. Is the author a scholar? a popular commentator? Do a search to learn what sources you trust say about the author.
- What is the author's **STANCE**? Objective? Passionate? Something else? Mark words that indicate the author's stance.
- How would you describe the author's **STYLE** and **TONE**? Formal? Casual? Serious? Humorous? Mark any words or passages that establish that style and tone.

HOW IS THE TEXT DESIGNED?

- How does the design affect the way you understand the text?
- Note headings, sidebars, or other design features that add emphasis.
- If the text includes visuals, what do they contribute to the message?

WHAT ARE YOUR REACTIONS?

- Mark places in the text where you agree, disagree, or both. Note why.
- Note any claims, facts, or other things you find surprising—and why.
- Note any passages you find confusing or difficult to understand. What questions do you have?

- Jot down any possible counterarguments or conflicting evidence that you need to check out.

- If a passage reminds you of a past experience, memory, or strong emotion, note it.

If you're reading a particularly important text, read it more than once, paying attention to different elements each time. For example, to prepare for a class discussion you might first focus on the argument and then re-read focusing on how the writer supports that argument. With long or dense texts, you may want to annotate by summarizing paragraphs or sections as you go.

Since you likely read on-screen often, take the time to learn one of the many free programs that make it easy to annotate digital texts. *Hypothesis* and *Adobe Acrobat Reader* are two programs that allow you to add notes, highlight, insert URLs and images, and more. In fact, the ebook version of this book includes annotation tools to mark up what you're reading right now!

So annotating keeps you active and helps you engage more deeply with what you read. Annotating also helps you approach reading as a social activity, bringing you into conversation with writers, engaging them and their ideas actively. Sometimes, especially for a research project, you'll be assigned to write formal annotations in the form of an **ANNOTATED BIBLIOGRAPHY**. That's a reading (and writing) situation with its own characteristic features. For now, focus on making annotating a habit—especially when you read academic texts.

↪ To read—and annotate—a digital version of this book, visit digital.wwnorton.com/everyone3r.

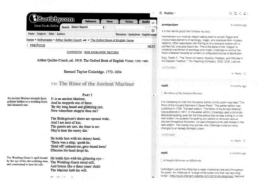

Online or on a printed page, there are many methods and tools for annotating as you read. Try a few to find the ones that work best for you.

A Sample Annotated Text

Here's the opening of an essay on shopping locally, along with annotations by YULIYA VAYNER, a Hunter College student who read and annotated this piece for a summary/response essay assignment.

AMERICANS TODAY CAN eat pears in the spring in Minnesota, oranges in the summer in Montana, asparagus in the fall in Maine, and cranberries in the winter in Florida. In fact, we can eat pretty much any kind of produce anywhere at any time of the year. But what is the cost of this convenience? In this essay, I will explore some answers to this question and argue that we should give up a little bit of convenience in favor of buying local.

Thesis statement

"Buying local" means that consumers choose to buy food that has been grown, raised, or produced as close to their homes as possible ("Buy Local"). Buying local is an important part of the response to many environmental issues we face today (fig. 1). It encourages the development of small farms, which are often more environmentally sustainable than large farms, and thus strengthens local markets and supports small rural economies. By demonstrating a commitment to buying local, Americans could set an example for global environmentalism.

I wonder what she means exactly by "buying local."

This paragraph states her stance: strongly in favor of sustainable farming and buying local.

In 2010, the international community is facing many environmental challenges, including global warming, pollution, and dwindling fossil fuel resources. Global warming is attributed to the release of greenhouse gases such as carbon dioxide and methane, most commonly emitted in the burning of fossil fuels. It is such a pressing problem that scientists estimate that in the year 2030, there will be no glaciers left in Glacier National Park ("Global Warming Statistics"). The United States is especially guilty of contributing to the problem, producing about a quarter of all global greenhouse gas emissions, and playing a large part in pollution and shrinking world oil supplies as well ("Record Increase"). According to a CNN article published in 2000, the United States manufactures more than 1.5 billion pounds of chemical pesticides a year that can pollute our water, soil, and air (Baum). Agriculture is particularly interconnected with all of these issues. Almost three-fourths of the pesticides produced in the United States are used in agriculture (Baum). Most produce is

But what about people who don't have access to locally produced food or who can't afford to buy it?

Here comes some evidence. Looks like she's done research to inform her argument.

I want to check out this source: I'm a little suspicious of what she says here.

Fig. 1. Shopping at a farmers' market is one good way to support small farms and strengthen the local economy. Timothy Mulholland. *Dane County Farmers Market on the Square Madison Wisconsin*. 2008, *Alamy*.

Farmers' markets are expensive. Many people—including me!—can't afford to shop at them.

shipped many miles before it is sold to consumers, and shipping our food long distances is costly in both the amount of fossil fuel it uses and the greenhouse gases it produces.

She's serious about this issue and is making a strong case. Including these researched facts lends credibility, but I'm waiting to see if she acknowledges the fact that many people can't afford or easily get to locally grown food.

✐ REFLECT. *Find something you've read and annotated recently. What kinds of annotations did you make? Calling out keywords, ideas, and claims? Strategies the writer used? Areas of confusion? Points you agree or disagree with? Your own personal connections? Try highlighting your annotations in different colors for a visual breakdown by type. What do these annotations tell you about your reading process? Looking back at the prompts in this section, are there types of annotations that you didn't make but would have proved useful? Re-read the text and add them!*

SUMMARIZING

Summarizing a text helps you understand and engage with it—and internalize and remember what you read. When you summarize, you're boiling a text down to its central ideas, claims, and theories in your own words. One student we know writes summaries in the margins as a strategy for making sure she understands the most important concepts, especially in textbooks. These summaries, along with additional annotations throughout the chapters, help her prepare for exams. Besides helping you understand what you read, summarizing is also essential for weaving the viewpoints of others into your own writing. Both at work and at school, you'll be expected to summarize something—the plot of a short story, the results of a scientific study, takeaways from a meeting. The following advice will help you craft strong summaries in academic and professional writing.

Read the text carefully—and annotate. Read the text to figure out its main message, idea, or argument. Annotate as you read, marking key ideas and claims as well as supporting points such as anecdotes, supporting evidence, and counterarguments. When you identify a sentence or paragraph that states a main point, try restating it in your own words. A pair of highlighters can help; try using different colors to distinguish the main ideas from the supporting points.

When you summarize something other than a printed text—a music video, a printed advertisement, a speech—practice the same careful reading. Observe your subject and take note of the main message as well as the supporting details that lead you to draw this conclusion.

Take a look at how Nicholas Carr incorporates brief summaries of several research reports (and an op-ed) in his essay on p. 875.

Be brief, stating the main points while leaving out minor supporting details. Summaries are generally brief, stating the main ideas while leaving out the supporting evidence and anecdotes that aren't necessary for understanding. A summary serves as a stand-in for readers who aren't familiar with the full text, so your aim is to get readers up to speed on the main points without getting lost in the details.

Be fair and accurate, using neutral language. Think of a summary as stating the facts, not sharing your opinion. Use neutral language to present the author's main ideas with evenhandedness and respect, not judgment or criticism. Imagine the author reading your summary of their work. Would they find it accurate? Have you left out an important point? Would the writer find it fair? Have your opinions snuck in?

Use SIGNAL PHRASES to present what the author says as distinct from what you say—and use quotations in moderation. Summarizing calls for boiling down information and presenting it in your own words and sentence structure. Use signal phrases such as *she concludes* or *the report states* to indicate that you're summarizing someone else's ideas and claims, not your own. At the start of a summary, state the author's name, credentials, and the title of the work so it's clear what you're referring to. While you may quote notable phrases or key terms, your summary should be made up of mostly your own unique language and sentence structure. And any text you summarize should be documented in a list of works cited or references.

Consider visuals. Not all summaries are written text: summaries can also be presented visually. In scientific, technical, or social science writing, charts and graphs often summarize key information and data from other sources. For example, in the following infographic from a sociology textbook, the author summarizes data from a 2010 study analyzing college students'

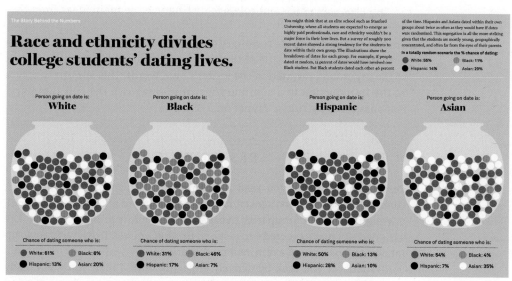

An infographic from a sociology textbook summarizes the results of a Stanford University social science study so that the main takeaway is clear: Stanford students "show a strong tendency to date within their own [racial and ethnic] group."

dating habits by race and ethnicity. The colorful visuals summarize the data so it's easier to understand than if the same results were presented using only words and statistics.

A Sample Summary

Here is a summary of Katherine Spriggs's essay "On Buying Local" (see her full essay on p. 177):

> In her essay "On Buying Local," college student Katherine Spriggs argues that consumers should purchase food grown locally whenever possible. After demonstrating the environmental and practical reasons for doing so, Spriggs shows that buying local can offer an alternative to destructive mass farming, help small farmers and their families, build sustainable agricultural models, reduce the cost of shipping food from faraway places, and avoid the exploitation of workers, especially in third-world countries. In spite of a few drawbacks (local food may be more expensive, and seasonal variation may reduce the number of choices available), she concludes that shopping local is an easy lifestyle change that will make a big difference to our environment.

This is a fair and accurate summary of Spriggs's essay. It begins by stating the author's name and the title of the work and includes only the main points of the argument, restated in the writer's own words. This summary serves as the introduction to a summary/response essay (see the full summary/response essay by Yuliya Vayner on p. 93).

RESPONDING

Responding to what you read is nothing new—it's what you do when commenting on a friend's *Instagram* post, replying to an instructor's email, or weighing in on a group text. In college and in many professions, you'll be assigned—or just expected—to respond to what you read, in a written document, a discussion, an exam, or a presentation.

Whenever you read by actively engaging with a text, you are already responding—annotating to talk back to it, question it, assess its claims, and come to conclusions about whether or not you accept them. Looking over your annotations will help you generate ideas when you're assigned to respond formally. Do your annotations reveal any patterns? Maybe you disagreed with many of the author's claims, jotted down a related experience, or noted the author's use of emotional appeals. As you take stock of your annotations, consider which of the following ways you'll respond to what you've read: argue with what the text says, analyze the way it says it, or reflect on its ideas.

Respond to what a text says, agreeing or disagreeing with its position—or both. However you respond, you'll be making an **ARGUMENT** for what you say. Before you come to any final conclusions, keep an open mind by saying "yes," "no," and "maybe" to the text. First say "yes" by making an effort to understand the way the author sees the topic and where they're coming from. Doing so can be especially important if you find yourself strongly disagreeing with the author's position. Then say "maybe" to any passages that seem confusing or poorly supported—and consider why. Finally, look for anything to which you feel obligated to say "no," and think about why it seems unacceptable or just plain wrong. Here are some questions to consider when you're responding to what a text says:

- What does the text **CLAIM**, and what **REASONS** and **EVIDENCE** does the author provide?
- Do you agree or disagree with the author's position? Why?
- Does the author acknowledge any other positions? If so, are they treated fairly? What other perspectives should be addressed?
- Has the author overlooked anything?
- Is it clear why the topic matters, why anyone should care?
- What's the larger **CONTEXT**? How does the text fit into the larger conversation on the topic? Is the author's point corroborated by what others have said, or is it a claim that hardly anyone else agrees with?

Analyze the way a text is written to figure out how it works, what makes it tick. Here are some questions to consider when you're analyzing how a text is written:

- What does the text **CLAIM**? Is it stated explicitly—and if not, should it be? Has it been carefully qualified—and if not, does it need to be?

- Look for and assess the **REASONS** and **EVIDENCE** provided in support of the claim. Are you persuaded? If not, what other kinds of evidence would help?

- Does the author use emotional, ethical, or logical appeals? Do you notice any logical **FALLACIES**?

- Has the writer mentioned any **COUNTERARGUMENTS** or alternative points of view? If so, are they described respectfully and fairly? And how does the writer respond—by acknowledging that other writers have a point? Refuting what they say?

- How has the author established **AUTHORITY** to write on this topic? Do you think the text is trustworthy and fair?

- What design elements help convey the text's main message?

Reflect on a text's ideas by drawing connections to your own personal experiences, beliefs, or ways of thinking. Maybe the text leads you to see a topic in a new light, question your assumptions and biases, or wonder about how your beliefs influenced your reaction. Here are some questions to consider when you're reflecting on a text's ideas:

- What impact has the reading had on you—as a student, scholar, citizen, and researcher? What are the big takeaways for you personally?

- Did any parts of the text make you feel uneasy, laugh, or cry? Investigate why.

- Which past experiences or memories did you recall while reading the text? Can you relate to anything in the text? Why or why not?

- Does the text challenge or uphold any of your beliefs? Or cause you to question some of your assumptions and biases?

- What other texts, images, videos, recordings, etc., does the text remind you of?

- What lessons, insights, or ideas has the text taught you? How might you apply those lessons in your own writing or thinking?

SUMMARY/RESPONSE ESSAYS

A summary/response essay demonstrates that you have engaged with a text, understand its main message, and have something to say as a result. This assignment is common in first-year writing classes because of the focus on critical reading and supporting a position with evidence. Unless the assignment names other requirements, your summary/response should cover the following ground.

A Fair, Accurate, and Concise Summary

A fair and objective summary of the text to which you are responding is essential. To make your subject crystal clear, begin by stating the author, title, and author's credentials. And keep the following points in mind:

- Include the main claims and primary supporting points of the text, and exclude examples or supporting ideas that aren't essential to the text's main message.

- Use an even and objective **TONE**. Would the author of the text find your summary fair and accurate?

- Be concise. Most summaries of full texts are 100 to 125 words, giving readers enough information to understand what you're responding to without unnecessary details.

- Make it clear that you are summarizing someone else's text by using **SIGNAL PHRASES** like "according to X." Words such as "asserts," "argues," and "examines" are also good signals—just be sure they are neutral. Include quotations only when keywords and phrases are central to the overall argument.

A Clear Response, Supported by Evidence

Your response is the meat of a summary/response essay. There's more than one way to respond to a text. See if you're being asked to respond in a particular way—for example, to "assess the author's argument and take a stance" or "analyze how effectively the text addresses its intended audience." If the assignment isn't specific, think about what you're most interested in doing: responding to what the text says, analyzing how the text works, reflecting on the text's ideas, or some combination. No matter how you respond, support your position with evidence.

- If you're responding to what the text says, take a position—agreeing, disagreeing, or both. State your position explicitly in a **THESIS STATEMENT**.

Support your position with evidence from the text and from outside sources, if necessary. Facts, statistics, anecdotal evidence, and textual evidence can serve as support. Think about and address any **COUNTER-ARGUMENTS** to your position.

- If you're analyzing how the text works, you'll describe both what the text is saying and the strategies used to convey the message. You might analyze a text's organization, **DICTION**, use of appeals, design, or other elements. Include evidence from the text to demonstrate the features or strategies you're analyzing. Be sure you state your main takeaway in an explicit thesis statement. Why did you choose to analyze what you did and why does it matter?

- If you're reflecting on the text's ideas, you'll likely explain some way in which the text impacted you personally or evoked a particular emotion, memory, or idea. Passages from the text that prompted your response should be cited as evidence. And your own beliefs, experiences, or emotions might serve to support and explain your personal response. Boil down your main point in a thesis statement—even a reflection should tell readers what you're saying and why it matters.

A Logical Organization

A summary/response can be organized in different ways, and your assignment may ask for a specific structure. Here are some general ways of structuring a summary/response to help you get started:

- Summarize first, and then respond: Introduce and summarize the text first, then state your thesis (this might all fall in the first paragraph). Then respond to the text, providing supporting points for your thesis. End by summing up your response and its implications.

- Summarize and respond point-by-point: Introduce the text and state your thesis. Then summarize a claim or strategy from the text and respond to it. Do this for as many supporting points as you have to develop and defend your thesis. End by summing up your response and its implications.

YULIYA VAYNER, a Hunter College student, summarizes and responds to Katherine Spriggs's essay "On Buying Local" in the following example. You can read Spriggs's full essay on page 177. Vayner primarily responds to what the text says—taking a position that both agrees and disagrees with Spriggs's argument. This essay is organized around several counterarguments that Vayner says Spriggs does not address.

The Higher Price of Buying Local

YULIYA VAYNER

IN HER ESSAY "On Buying Local," Katherine Spriggs argues that consumers should purchase food grown locally whenever possible. After demonstrating the environmental and practical reasons for doing so, Spriggs shows that buying local can offer an alternative to destructive mass farming, help small farmers and their families, build sustainable agricultural models, reduce the cost of shipping food from faraway places, and avoid the exploitation of workers, especially in third-world countries. Though Spriggs acknowledges that buying local can be inconvenient (local food may be more expensive, and seasonal variation may reduce the number of choices available), she argues that the benefit outweighs the inconvenience and concludes that shopping local is an easy lifestyle change that will make a big difference to our environment.

Begins with a concise summary

But is buying local truly an "easy step" that "everyone can take"? Is inconvenience the only drawback? There are at least two

Articulates a key question that motivates and grounds the analysis.

A thesis statement offers a clear position.

additional challenges to buying local that Spriggs doesn't acknowledge in her analysis: cost and access. It's clear that buying locally grown food benefits the environment, but because cost and access limit some people from being able to buy local, it is not a habit everyone is equally able to practice.

Agrees with part of Spriggs's argument and explains why.

Spriggs makes a convincing argument that giving up a bit of convenience in return for a healthier environment is a worthy trade. In discussing polyculture farming (producing a variety of crops from the same land—an approach small farms tend to prefer), Spriggs juxtaposes personal convenience and environmental benefits. She concedes that being unable to buy whatever produce we want whenever we want is less convenient than most consumers are used to but suggests this sacrifice would allow farmers to harvest from healthier soil and foster a healthier environment.

Summarizes Spriggs's argument in her own words.

Quotes specific details from Spriggs's essay.

Spriggs explains that while monoculture farms (producing a small number of single crops—the approach large mass-production farms use) provide the convenience of year-round access to produce, they do so by resorting to "modern fertilizers, herbicides, and pesticides [that] allow farmers to harvest crops from even unhealthy land" (181). By giving up the convenience of eating strawberries at any time of year, Americans could begin to rely less on chemical treatments that damage the environment

Quotes a key term and defines it in her own words.

and more on natural resources through what Spriggs calls "dual usage"—like using pigs to plow blueberry fields and putting cows to pasture in last year's cornfields. Considering the environmental damage that large-scale farming causes, sacrificing convenience is a small price to pay for a healthier land and atmosphere.

Notes an argument that Spriggs does not address: how will people who live in food deserts access locally produced foods?

However, Spriggs doesn't acknowledge that some people would be giving up more than just evergreen strawberries in an attempt to buy local. For many, lack of access to any fresh produce at all is an issue, making the sacrifice of buying produce that's locally sourced unaffordable. According to a recent report by the US Department of Agriculture's Economic Research Service, an estimated 1 in 8 Americans or 40 million people experienced food insecurity, which is defined as "a lack of consistent access to enough food for an active, healthy life" in 2017 ("What Is Food Insecurity?"). So when Spriggs argues that there's little reason to ship strawberries from California all over the United

States when they can easily be grown closer to the customers who want to eat them, she fails to acknowledge that there are areas that can't readily access or grow fresh produce (181). These areas are sometimes called food deserts: areas that have limited access to affordable and nutritious food, forcing residents to rely on food sold at convenience stores or fast-food chains, which is often highly processed and of limited nutritional value ("Why Low-Income and Food-Insecure People"). These food deserts exist overwhelmingly in low-income areas, and studies have shown that "both poverty and race matter when it comes to having healthy food options" (Brooks). So, although Spriggs does not mention these issues, buying local is also a question of access—which is impacted by race and income level rather than being purely one about convenience and ease.

Time becomes an issue of access as well: for some a long drive to a grocery store is merely inconvenient. For others, there simply aren't enough hours in a day to make an extended trip for fresh, local produce. People living below the poverty line tend to work multiple jobs (Sherman); in addition, they may also be responsible for household errands and family care. Lower-income families are not only less likely to have places nearby that sell locally grown food, they are also less likely to have the time and the means to visit them ("Why Low-Income and Food-Insecure People"). Even when locally grown food can be found within a reasonable distance, it may still be out of reach for those living on a limited income.

Here's another argument Spriggs doesn't cover.

This adds yet another aspect to the challenge of buying local that Spriggs doesn't address: low-income individuals are significantly less likely to be able to afford the extra expense of locally sourced food, which Spriggs explains as only slightly pricier. Yet, "slightly more expensive than 'industrially grown' food" (Spriggs 183) is subjective. Not only would buying local potentially strain the budgets of those struggling to get by, it could also make it more difficult to make use of government assistance, especially since farmers' markets have struggled to obtain the necessary equipment to process SNAP, a government assistance program that provides a monthly supplement for purchasing nutritious foods (Andrews). So for many, buying local is not just an

A third counterargument Spriggs doesn't cover: the financial expense of buying local.

inconvenience, it's not a financial possibility. Furthermore, the price gap seems wider than Spriggs admits; a journalist for *The Washington Post* reports that in 2016 "cage-free eggs, cheese, mushrooms, salad mix and both organic and conventional strawberries" came to be $64.62 at the local market in Richmond, Virginia—"I could have bought them all from Kroger for $31.37" (Hise). At nearly double the price, this difference is far from Spriggs's claim that buying local is only "slightly more expensive" (183). The price increase that comes with buying local is not a mere inconvenience but rather a question of affordability for many.

Concludes by summarizing her own argument in response to Spriggs.

While Spriggs succeeds in showing that buying local can contribute to a healthier environment, in addressing the obvious drawback of inconvenience she considers only one aspect of a complex issue involving race, income level, and access. The inconvenience of buying local comes at a much higher price for some people, a fact Spriggs leaves out. People who are struggling to make ends meet cannot always afford this social and economic privilege, nor do they always have access to this privilege. To many, industrially grown food is a necessity rather than, as Spriggs suggests, a convenience.

Works Cited

Andrews, Michelle. "Technical Difficulties May Jeopardize Food
    Stamps at Farmers Markets." *NPR*, 5 Nov. 2018, www.npr
    .org/sections/thesalt/2018/11/05/662322655/technical
    -difficulties-may-jeopardize-food-stamps-at-farmers
    -markets.
Brooks, Kelly. "Research Shows Food Deserts More Abundant
    in Minority Neighborhoods." *Johns Hopkins Magazine*,
    10 Mar. 2014. *The Hub*, Johns Hopkins U, hub.jhu.edu
    /magazine/2014/spring/racial-food-deserts/.
Hise, Phaedra. "Why Does a Strawberry Grown Down the Road
    Cost More than One Grown in California?" *The Washington
    Post*, 21 June 2016, www.washingtonpost.com/lifestyle
    /food/why-local-food-costs-more-a-strawberry-case
    -study/2016/06/20/c7177c56-331f-11e6-8ff7-7b6c1998b7a0
    _story.html.
Sherman, Erik. "More People Probably Work Multiple Jobs than
    the Government Realizes." *Forbes*, 22 July 2018, www
    .forbes.com/sites/eriksherman/2018/07/22/more-people
    -probably-work-multiple-jobs-than-the-government-realizes.
Spriggs, Katherine. "On Buying Local." *Everyone's an Author*, by
    Andrea Lunsford et al., W. W. Norton, 2020, pp. 177–85.
"What Is Food Insecurity in America?" *Hunger and Health*,
    Feeding America, hungerandhealth.feedingamerica.org
    /understand-food-insecurity/.
"Why Low-Income and Food-Insecure People Are Vulnerable to
    Poor Nutrition and Obesity." *Food Research & Action
    Center*, www.opportunityhome.org/wp-content/uploads
    /2018/04/frac_org.pdf.

ᴗᴗ *REFLECT. Think about something you were recently assigned to read. What was your purpose for reading? What strategies from this chapter, if any, did you use to achieve that purpose? Re-read the text again, this time preparing to write a brief 250- to 500-word summary/response. Practice annotating, summarizing, and responding using the guidelines in this chapter. How did reading in preparation to respond change your reading process? What did you find challenging—and not so challenging—about writing a brief summary/response?*

EIGHT

Distinguishing Facts from Misinformation

POPE FRANCIS Says 'God Has Instructed Me to Revise the Ten Commandments.'" "Palestinians Recognize Texas as Part of Mexico." "Canada Bans Beyoncé after Her Superbowl Performance." Really? Well, actually, no. While these are actual headlines, none is anywhere near the truth. But being false hasn't kept them from being widely shared—and not as jokes but as facts. With people spreading misinformation, unsubstantiated claims, and even outright lies today, it can be hard to know whom and what to trust or whether to trust anything at all. The good news is that you don't have to be taken in by such misinformation. This chapter provides strategies for navigating today's choppy waters of news and information so that you can make confident decisions about what to trust—and what not to.

Defining Facts and Misinformation

Some say we are living in a "post-truth" era, when the loudest voices take up so much airtime that they can sometimes be seen as telling the truth no matter what they say. A 2018 study by MIT scholars examined tweets about every major contested news story in English across the ten years of *Twitter*'s existence and came to the conclusion that satirist Jonathan Swift was right: "the truth simply can't compete with hoax and rumor."

In fact, the study says, "fake news and false rumors reach more people, penetrate deeper into the social network, and spread much faster than accurate stories."

It's worth asking why misinformation outperforms real news. While it is notoriously difficult to establish airtight cause-and-effect relationships, these researchers suspect that several reasons account for the "success" of false stories. First, they're often outlandish and novel in a way that attracts attention. Second, the content of such stories is often negative and tends to arouse strong emotions. Third, they use language that evokes surprise or disgust, as compared to accurate tweets, which, the researchers found, use words associated with trust or sadness rather than surprise or disgust: as they note, "the truth simply does not compete." For all these reasons, misinformation tends to attract attention and spread quickly.

Lies and misinformation are nothing new. What's new is that anyone with an internet connection can post whatever they think (or want others

Politico cartoonist Matt Wuerker paints a picture of a pollution-filled media landscape.

to think) online, where it can easily reach a wide audience. And unlike traditional newspapers and other publications, it can go out without being vetted by editors or fact-checkers.

Perhaps it's time to step back, take a deep breath, and attend to some basic definitions. Just what is a "fact"? What's "misinformation"? And what about "fake news"? In the most straightforward terms, *misinformation* is false or inaccurate information that is intended to deceive. *Fake news* is a kind of misinformation made to look like authentic news. Often it's used to spread conspiracy theories or deliberate hoaxes, the more bizarre the better: "Obama Signs Executive Order Banning the Pledge of Allegiance in Schools Nationwide." In addition, some people simply dismiss anything they don't like or agree with as fake news. *Facts*, on the other hand, can be verified and backed up by reliable evidence: Robert F. Kennedy was murdered on June 6, 1968; the Washington Capitals won the 2018 Stanley Cup; consumption of soft drinks in the United States has declined in the last five years. Unlike claims about what God has instructed Pope Francis to do, these statements can be verified and checked; we can then trust them.

Think about Your Own Beliefs

It's one thing to be able to spot unsubstantiated claims and exaggerations in the words of others, but it's another thing entirely to spot them in your own thinking and writing. So you need to take a good look at your own assumptions and biases (we all have them!).

Attribution bias is the tendency to think that your motives for believing, say, that the Environmental Protection Agency (EPA) is crucially important for keeping our air and water clean are objective or good while the motives of those who believe the EPA is not at all necessary are dubious or bad. We all have this kind of bias naturally, tending to believe that what we think must be right. When you're thinking about an argument you strongly disagree with, then, it's a good idea to ask yourself why you disagree—and why you believe you're right. What is that belief based on? Have you considered that your own bias may be keeping you from seeing all sides of the issue fairly, or at all?

Confirmation bias is the tendency to favor and seek out information that confirms what we already believe and to reject and ignore information that contradicts those beliefs. Many studies have documented this phenomenon.

For example, a Stanford University experiment gathered 48 students, half of whom favored capital punishment and thought it was a deterrent to crime and half of whom thought just the opposite. Researchers then asked students to respond to two studies: one provided data that supported capital punishment as a deterrent to crime; the other provided data that called this conclusion into question. Sure enough, the students who were in favor of capital punishment rated the study that showed evidence that it was a deterrent as "more highly credible," while the students who were against capital punishment rated the study that showed evidence that it did not deter crime as "more highly credible"—in spite of the fact that both studies had been made up by the researchers. Moreover, by the end of the experiment, each side had doubled down on its original beliefs.

That's confirmation bias at work, and it works on all of us. It affects the way we search for information and what we pay attention to, how we interpret it, and even what we remember. So don't assume information is trustworthy just because it confirms what you already think. Ask yourself if you're seeing what you want to see. And look for confirmation bias in your sources; do they acknowledge viewpoints other than their own?

Read Defensively and Find the Good Stuff

Well over two thousand years ago, the philosopher Aristotle said that one reason people need rhetoric is self-defense, for making sure that we aren't being deceived, manipulated, or lied to. Today, the need for such caution may be more important than ever when false stories often look authentic and appear right next to accurate, factual information online. These times call, then, for what we think of as defensive reading—the kind of reading that doesn't take things at face value, that questions underlying assumptions, that scrutinizes claims carefully, and that does not rush to judgment. This is the kind of reading that media and technology critic Howard Rheingold calls "crap detection." Crap, he says sardonically, is a "technical term" he uses to describe information "tainted by ignorance or deliberate deception." He warns us not to give in to such misinformation:

> Some critics argue that a tsunami of hogwash has already rendered the web useless. I disagree. We are indeed inundated by online noise pollution, but the problem is soluble. The good stuff is out there if you know how to find and verify it.
>
> —HOWARD RHEINGOLD, "Crap Detection 101"

As Rheingold and many others note, there is no single foolproof way to identify misinformation. But we can offer some advice, along with some specific strategies.

Triangulate—and use your judgment. Find three different ways to check on whether a story can be trusted. Google the author or the sponsor. Check *FactCheck.org* or *Snopes.* Look for other sources that are reporting the same story, especially if you first saw it on social media. If it's true and important, you should find a number of other reputable sources reporting on it. But however carefully you check, and whatever facts and evidence you uncover, it's up to you to sort the accurate information from the misinformation— and to use your own judgment.

Before reading an unfamiliar source, determine whether it's trustworthy. History professor Sam Wineburg and his research team have found that professional fact-checkers don't even start to read an unfamiliar website until they've determined that it's trustworthy. Here are some ways to do so:

- Do a search about the author or sponsor. What's the author's expertise? Be wary if there's no author. Does the author belong to any organizations you don't know or trust? Look up any unfamiliar organizations to see what reliable sources have to say. And do a search about the site's sponsor. If the website is run by an organization you've never heard of, find out what it is—and whether it actually exists. What do reliable sources say about it? Read the site's About page, but check up on what it says. As Wineburg says, "If an organization can game what they are, they can certainly game their About page!"

- Check any links to see who sponsors the site and whether they are trustworthy sources. Do the same for works cited in print sources.

- Be careful of over-the-top headlines, which often serve as clickbait to draw you in. Check to see that the story and the headline actually match. Question any exaggerated words like "amazing," "epic," "incredible," or "unbelievable." (In general, don't believe anything that's said to be unbelievable!)

- Pay attention to design. Be wary if it looks amateurish, but don't assume that a professional-looking design means the source is accurate or trustworthy. Those who create fake news sites often design them to look like real news sites.

- Recognize satire! Remember that some authors make a living by writing satirical fake news articles. Here's one: "China Slaps Two-Thousand-Per-Cent Tariff on Tanning Beds." This comes from Andy Borowitz, who writes political satire in *The New Yorker*, which tips us off not to take it seriously by the label "not the news." *The Onion* is another source that pokes fun at gullible readers. Try this: "Genealogists Find 99% of People Not Related to Anyone Cool." This one's silly enough that it can't possibly be true. But if you're not sure, better check.

Ask questions, and check evidence. Double-check things that too neatly support what you yourself think.

- What's the **CLAIM**, and what **EVIDENCE** is provided? What motivates the author to write, and what's their **PURPOSE**—to provide information? make you laugh? convince you of something?

- Check facts and claims using nonpartisan sites that confirm truths and identify lies. *FactCheck.org*, *Snopes*, and *AllSides* are three such sites. Copy and paste the basics of the statement into the search field; if it's information the site has in its database, you'll find out whether it's a confirmed fact or lie. If you use *Google* to check on a stated fact, keep in mind that you'll need to check on any sources there—and that even if the statement brings up many hits, that doesn't make it accurate.

Jia Tolentino's review of *Coco* on p. 1043 was originally published in *The New Yorker*, a magazine with an excellent reputation for fact-checking. But for some practice, go ahead and do some fact-checking of the statements and facts Tolentino includes about the movie.

- If you think a story is too good to be true, you're probably right to be skeptical. And don't assume that it must be true because no one could make up such a story. They can. Do research on stories that are so outrageous that you don't believe them; if they are true, they will be widely reported. On the other hand, double-check stories that confirm your own beliefs; that might well be **CONFIRMATION BIAS** at work.

- Look up any research that's cited. You may find that the research has been taken out of context or misquoted—or that it doesn't actually exist. Is the research itself reliable? Pay close attention to quotations: who said it, and when? Is it believable? If not, copy and paste the quotation into *Google* or check *FactCheck.org* to verify that it's real.

- Check the comments. If several say the article sounds fake, it may well be. But remember that given the presence of trolls and people with malicious intent, comments too can't be taken at face value.

A still from *The Day After Tomorrow* shows fictional tidal waves battering the Statue of Liberty, but when Hurricane Sandy hit in 2012 this image spread as a warning for a real storm's strength. The fake local news banner lends (false) credibility.

Fact-Check Photos and Videos

Is a picture really worth a thousand words? In some cases, yes—but only if the picture is an accurate depiction. It's never been easier to falsify photographs. Take the often repurposed and exaggerated stories of flooding and damage beyond belief whenever a natural disaster strikes like the image on the previous page. When so-called Superstorm Sandy hit New York City in 2012, a photo of waves nearly as tall at the Statue of Liberty—seemingly captured by a live local news broadcast—circulated online. But some were quick to notice a problem. It was an image of Lady Liberty taking on water all right, but one from the science fiction movie *The Day After Tomorrow*, where fictional catastrophic climate events wreak havoc.

And here's one other photo that went viral in 2017, showing President Donald Trump, President Vladimir Putin of Russia, and others in conversation. A little investigation, however, showed that Putin had been photoshopped into the image; he wasn't actually at the table with other world leaders. Again, there are no simple, foolproof ways to identify doctored photos, but experts in digital forensics recommend various steps we can take. Here's advice from Hany Farid, a computer science professor at the University of California at Berkeley:

- Do a reverse image search, using *Google Images* or *Tin Eye* to see if an image has been recirculated or repurposed from another website. Both sites allow you to drag an image or paste a link to an image into a search bar to learn more about the image's source and see where the image appears online.

World leaders gathered during the 2017 G20 leaders' summit. Russian president Vladimir Putin was not in attendance despite what it looks like in the fake photo on the left.

- Check *Snopes*, where altered images are often identified, by typing a brief description of the image into the *Snopes* search box.
- Look carefully at shadows: an image may have been altered if you find shadows where you don't expect them or don't see them where you do expect them.

Farid goes on to say that the best defense against fabricated photos is "to stop and think about the source"—especially before you share it with others. After a shooter killed seventeen people at a Florida school in 2018, an altered photo of Emma González, one student survivor who advocated for stronger gun laws, went viral, showing her tearing up a page of the US Constitution. In fact, she was actually tearing up a shooting target as part of her advocacy for gun control.

The same advice holds true for researching suspicious video, which is also easy to falsify. Videos that flicker constantly or that consist of just one short clip are often questionable, as are videos of famous people doing things that are highly suspicious. How likely is it that NBA all-star Kobe Bryant could jump over a speeding Aston Martin? Not very—but a lot of us were fooled by a fake video made for Nike.

Kobe Bryant is a world-class athlete, but can he really clear a speeding Aston Martin? Nike's ad tries to make us think so.

Such fabricated videos and deepfakes proliferate, especially on *YouTube*. The *Guardian* warns that "advances in artificial intelligence and computer graphics . . . allow for the creation of realistic looking footage of public figures appearing to say, well, anything." Using the fact-finding and defensive-reading strategies described in this chapter, we hope you'll become able to sort out fact from fiction and determine with confidence who and what you can trust in all the kinds of reading you do—from keeping up with the news and scanning your friends' social media posts to conducting research for a project at school or work.

PART III

Writing Processes

IMAGINE THAT YOU are living in the Middle Ages and that you know how to write (a rare skill at that time). Now imagine the processes you have to engage in to do that writing. You might well begin by making the surface you need to write on, probably parchment or vellum made from animal skins—a process that takes several days.

Once you have something to write on, you make lines across the page to "rule" it and guide your writing. When at last you're ready to begin to write, you do so with a quill pen crafted out of a feather that had its end sharpened into a "nib" with a slit in the middle through

The medieval equivalent to a blank *Word* document: writers began by making their own writing surfaces, first soaking animal skins to remove the fur, then stretching and scraping them until they were the right thickness.

which the ink flows onto the parchment. Woe to you if you make a mistake, for correction is exceedingly difficult—or impossible. And once the writing is done, you still might not be finished if you need to illustrate the manuscript, as in the "illuminated" page from *The Canterbury Tales* on the facing page.

Because the process was so complicated, writing often demanded a team approach. In fact, *book* is defined in an early German encyclopedia as a "work of many hands."

With the advent of the printing press and subsequent technological developments, such material aspects of the writing process became easier, so much so that they became somewhat invisible: writers simply *wrote*. The focus, especially in schools, shifted to the final product, one composed by individual students; any concern with the process, as well as with writing's collaborative aspects, disappeared entirely. And so for many years, the emphasis on the final or "published" piece kept us from seeing the many other processes of writing, from generating ideas to hypothesizing, drafting, revising, and more. Writing involves far more than putting words down on

The Knight. An illuminated page from *The Canterbury Tales*, circa 1410.

a page and checking punctuation. For any important piece of writing, the author must think the message through in many ways to understand and communicate it to an audience. As researcher Janet Emig has concluded, writing is a unique form of learning, and understanding it calls for understanding the complex processes involved.

In studying just how those processes work, researchers have lately returned to the medieval notion that a piece of writing is the "work of many hands," recognizing that almost all writing is highly social, created by one or more writers in conversation with many others, from those who have influenced us in the past to those who read and respond to our work. By the end of the twentieth century, the popular image of a writer as a solitary figure (almost always a man) holed up in a tiny room struggling to create an individual work of great genius began to give way to that of a writer as part of an elaborate network, what author Steven Johnson called "connected minds."

The kind of networking now available through the internet and especially through social media surely does involve "connected minds." John Donne's insight that no one "is an island, apart from the main" has never been more true than it is today, as writers around the globe collaborate on everything from a *Google Doc* to a flash mob to a protest movement like Black Lives Matter.

The chapters that follow invite you to think hard about the processes you engage in when you write and about how those processes involve other writers (those you write with and those you write to). We hope that such thinking will not only make you more aware of how, when, and where you write, but also help to make your writing processes more efficient—and more fun!

NINE

Managing the Writing Process

**THINK OF SOMETHING YOU LIKE TO DO**: ride a bike, play a certain video game, do Sudoku. If you think about it, you'll see that each of these activities involves learning a process that took some effort to get right when you first started doing it. But eventually, the process became familiar, and now you do it almost automatically.

Writing is much the same. It, too, is a process: a series of activities that takes some effort to do well. At some level, everyone who writes knows this—from a child who draws a picture and then erases part of it, thinking, "That tree just doesn't look right," to the college student working over an extended period of time on a research paper.

And as with any process, you can manage the writing process by approaching it in parts. This chapter introduces the various stages of the writing process—from generating ideas and coming up with a topic to drafting and revising—and provides strategies that will help you make the most of the many writing demands you'll encounter at school, at work, and elsewhere.

One important aspect of becoming comfortable with the writing process is figuring out what works best for you. No single process works for every author or every writing task, so work instead to develop a repertoire of strategies that will enable you to become an efficient, productive, and effective writer.

Writing involves complex processes and often the "work of many hands."

Develop writing habits that work for you. Think about how you usually approach a writing task. Do you draw up extensive outlines? Do you organize visually or use note cards? Do you write best at a particular time of the day? Do you write best with solitude and quiet—or do you like to have music playing? Think carefully about what habits seem to help you produce your best work. But be careful: if you think you do your best work while multitasking, think again. Research increasingly challenges that assumption!

WRITING PROCESSES / A Roadmap

Whatever processes you find most productive, following are some tips that provide general guidance. If and when you decide on a particular genre, you'll find genre-specific guidance in the Roadmaps in Chapters 12–17.

Understand your assignment. If you're writing in response to an assignment, make sure you understand what it asks you to do. Does it specify a topic? a theme? a genre? Look for words like *argue*, *evaluate*, and *analyze*—words that specify a **GENRE** and thus point you to approach your topic in a certain way. An assignment that asks you to analyze, for example, lets you know that you should break down your topic into parts that can then be examined closely. If your assignment doesn't name a genre, think about which genre will best suit your rhetorical situation.

Come up with a topic. If you get to choose your topic, think of things you are particularly interested in and want to know more about—or something that puzzles you or poses a problem you'd like to solve or that gets you fired up. A topic you're passionate about is more likely to interest your audience and to keep you engaged as you research and write. If your topic is assigned, try to find an aspect or angle that interests you. Looking for a particular angle on a topic can help you to narrow your focus, but don't worry if the topic you come up with right now isn't very specific: as you do research, you'll be able to narrow and refine it. Coming up with a broad topic that interests you is just the starting point.

Consider your RHETORICAL SITUATION. Whether you're writing an argument or a narrative, working alone or with a group, you'll have an audience, a purpose, a stance, a genre, a medium and design, and a context—all things that you should be thinking about as you write.

- *Audience.* Whom are you addressing? What do they likely know or believe about your topic? What do you want them to think or do in response to your writing?

- *Purpose.* What is your goal in writing? What has motivated you to write, and what do you wish to accomplish?

- *Stance*. What is your attitude toward your topic? What perspective do you offer on it? What's your relationship with your audience, and how do you want to be seen by them?

- *Genre*. Have you been assigned a specific genre? If not, which genre(s) will best suit your purpose and audience?

- *Medium and design*. What medium or media will best suit your audience, purpose, and message? What design elements are possible (or required) in these media?

- *Context*. Consider the conversation surrounding your argument. What has been said about your topic, and how does that affect what you say? What about your immediate context—when is your writing due, and are there any other requirements or constraints?

Schedule your time. Remember that you must fit any writing project into your schedule, so think about how to use your time most wisely. However you keep yourself on track, taking a series of small steps is easier than doing it all at once. So schedule periodic goals for yourself: meeting them will build your confidence and reinforce good writing habits.

Generate ideas. Most of us find that writing can help us explore a topic and can even lead us to new ideas. Here are some activities that can help you sort out what you already know about your topic—and come up with new ideas about it:

- *Brainstorming* is a way to generate ideas without worrying about whether they're useful or not. Take a few minutes to focus on your topic or thesis (or a broad idea you want to develop into a specific topic or thesis) and list, using words or phrases, everything that occurs to you about this subject. Then review what you have written, looking for ideas that seem promising and relationships that you can develop. Remember: there are no right answers at this point!

- *Clustering* is a strategy for generating and processing ideas visually. Take a sheet of paper and write a word or phrase that best summarizes or evokes your topic. Draw a circle around this word. Now fill in the page by adding related words and ideas, circling them and connecting them to the original word, forming clusters. Then look at all the clusters to see what patterns you can find or where your ideas seem to be leading.

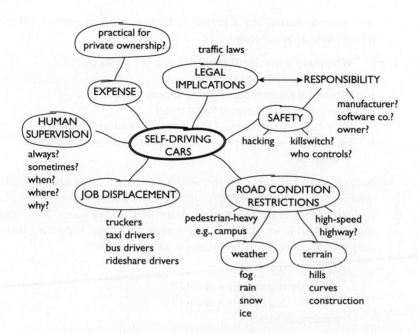

- *Freewriting* is a strategy for writing ideas down quickly, without stopping. To freewrite, simply write about whatever comes into your head in relation to a particular idea or topic for five to ten minutes. Be careful not to censor yourself: let your ideas flow as freely as possible. You may be surprised at the complexity and power of the ideas that you can develop through this process.

- *Looping* is an extended and more focused kind of freewriting. Begin by establishing a subject and then freewrite for five to ten minutes. Look at what you've written. Identify the most important or interesting or promising idea and write a sentence summarizing it. Use this sentence to start another "loop" of freewriting. Repeat this process as many times as necessary.

- *Drawing or sketching a picture of your topic* can help spark and guide your thinking about it. Drawing it may lead to a creative breakthrough. See if creating a series of sketches can help you figure out the structure of an essay you're writing.

- *Questioning* is an especially good way of exploring a topic. Starting with questions can help you discover what you already know about your topic—and, just as importantly, what you don't know and need to learn. Try starting with the questions *Who? What? Where? When? Why? How?*

> Who was / is involved? What can you say about them?
> What happened / happens?
> Where did / does it occur? What should you describe?
> When did / does it occur? What time?
> Why did / does it happen? What caused / causes it to occur?
> How did / does it happen? Was / is there a process you should describe?

- *Outlining* can help you see connections between ideas and organize information, especially if you're writing about a complex subject. Begin by listing your main ideas in an order that makes sense. Then add supporting evidence or details under each main idea, indenting these subpoints to mark the different levels, as shown below:

> First main idea
> 　Supporting evidence or detail
> 　Supporting evidence or detail
> Second main idea
> 　Supporting evidence or detail
> 　Supporting evidence or detail

Do some RESEARCH. You may want or need to do some research to better understand your topic, learn more about it, and decide what aspects of it you want to explore further. This could mean reading about your topic, INTERVIEWING experts about it, conducting surveys, observing something firsthand, or some combination of those methods. Learning what others have said about a topic is an important step to figuring out what you want to say—and to joining the conversation.

Come up with a tentative THESIS, a statement that identifies your topic and the point you want to make about it. You'll rarely, if ever, have a final thesis when you start writing, but establishing a tentative one will help focus your thinking and any research you may do. Here are some prompts to get you started.

1. ***What point do you want to make about your topic?*** Try writing it out as a promise to your audience: *In this essay, I will present reasons for limiting use of social media.*

2. ***Try plotting out a tentative thesis in two parts,*** the first stating your topic, the second making some claim about the topic:

    ┌─────── TOPIC ──────────┐┌──────── CLAIM ──────────┐
    Limiting your social media time will improve your concentration, provide
    ┌───┐
    real-life social opportunities, and reduce vulnerability to hacking.

3. ***Ask some questions about what you've written.*** Will it engage your intended audience? What's your claim? Is it debatable? There's no point in staking a claim that is a fact, or one that no one would disagree with.

4. ***Do you need to narrow or*** **QUALIFY** ***your thesis?*** Can you do what you say you will, given the time and resources available? You don't want to overstate your case—or make a claim that you'll have trouble supporting. Adding words such as *could, might, likely,* or *potentially* can qualify what you say: *Limiting your social media time provide social opportunities will <u>likely</u> improve concentration, <u>might</u>, and <u>could potentially</u> reduce vulnerability to hacking.*

5. ***Is the thesis clear and focused?*** Will it tell readers what's coming? And will it help keep you (and your readers) on track?

Keep in mind that at this point in your process, this is a tentative thesis, one that could change as you research, write, and revise. Continue to explore your topic. Don't stop until you feel you've reached a full understanding of your topic. As you learn more about it, you may well find that you want to revise your thesis.

Once you're satisfied that your thesis makes a clear claim that you can support, and one that will interest your readers, gather together the notes from your research. This is the information you'll draw from as support for your thesis.

ORGANIZE your ideas. Whether you like to write out an outline or prefer to do most of your planning on note cards or sticky notes (or in your head!), you'll want to think about how best to organize your text before beginning to write. Writing about events generally works best when told in **CHRON-OLOGICAL ORDER**. And facts, data, and other **EVIDENCE** are usually most effective when stated in order of importance, starting with the information that's most crucial to your argument before stating the less important information. If you're describing something, you might organize your information SPATIALLY, beginning at one point and moving from left to right, or top to bottom. As you see, there's no one way to organize your writing; the order in which you present your points will depend on many things, including the topic and what you have to say about it.

Write out a draft. Keep your tentative thesis statement and any other notes and outlines close at hand as you start writing. A complete draft will include an introduction, a body, and a conclusion, though you may not necessarily draft them in that order.

- *The* INTRODUCTION is often the most difficult part to write, so much so that some authors decide to write it last. But just as a well-crafted opening can help guide your readers, it can also help you get started writing. A good introduction should grab readers' attention, announce your topic and your claim, and indicate how you plan to proceed. A provocative question, an anecdote, a startling claim: these are some of the ways you might open an essay.

- *The body* of an essay is where you will develop your argument, point by point, paragraph by paragraph. Strategies such as COMPARISON, DESCRIPTION, NARRATION, and others can help you develop paragraphs to present EVIDENCE in support of your THESIS.

- *The* CONCLUSION should sum up your argument in a way that readers will remember. You might end by restating your claim, discussing the implications of your argument, calling for some action, or posing further questions—all ways of highlighting the significance of what you've said.

Be flexible, and make changes if you need to. Even the most well-planned writing doesn't show its true shape until you've written a full draft, so don't be surprised if you find that you need to reorganize, do additional research, or otherwise rethink your argument as you go. Be flexible! Rather than sticking stubbornly to a plan that doesn't seem to be working, use each draft and revision as an opportunity to revisit your plan and to think about how you can strengthen your argument or your appeal.

The ancient Greeks had a word for thinking about the opportunities presented by a particular rhetorical situation. They called it *kairos,* and it referred to the ability to seize an opportune and timely moment. Kairos was the ancient Greek god of opportunity and perfect timing, qualities every author needs. He was often depicted as a young man running, and it was said that you must seize the forelock of his hair as he passes by; once he's passed, there's nothing to cling to because the back of his head is completely bald—you've missed your opportunity.

This is a concept that can be especially helpful when you're drafting—and that can also help you revise. As you work, think of each paragraph and sentence as an opportunity to add (or eliminate) detail, to reorganize, or to improve your point in some other way. Think about how your sentences and paragraphs might be received by your audience—and about how you can get readers to pay attention to and value what you say.

Kairos

Get response from others—from your instructor, a classmate, a writing center tutor. Be sure to tell them about any questions or concerns you have about the draft, and ask for their advice. But remember: you don't have to take all the advice you get, just what you consider helpful. You're the author!

Look at your draft with a critical eye and revise. You'll find genre-specific guidelines for reading a draft carefully and revising in the chapters on **ARGUMENTS**, **NARRATIVES**, **ANALYSES**, **REPORTS**, **REVIEWS**, and **PROPOSALS**. For more general advice, following are some prompts to help you read over a draft, either your own or one you're peer-reviewing for a fellow writer.

- How does the **INTRODUCTION** capture readers' attention and make them want to read on? Does it indicate that (or why) the topic matters? How else might it begin?

- How do you as the author come across—as well-informed? passionate? serious? something else?

- Is it clear what motivated you to write? Consider the larger **CONTEXT**: what else has been said about the topic, and have you considered perspectives other than your own?

- Is there an explicit **THESIS**? If not, does there need to be? If so, does it make clear what you are claiming about the topic?

- Is there sufficient support for the thesis? What **REASONS** and **EVIDENCE** do you provide? Will they be persuasive for the intended audience?

- Is the draft organized in a way that is easy to follow? Check to see how each paragraph supports the thesis, and whether it is developed fully enough to make its point. Are there headings—and if not, should there be? Is there any information that would be easier to follow if set off as a list? Are there explicit TRANSITIONS to help readers follow the text—and if not, are they needed?

- How does the text CONCLUDE? What does it leave readers thinking? How else might it conclude?

- Is there a title? If so, does it tell readers what your topic is and make them want to read on? If not, think in terms of KAIROS: the title is your first opportunity to indicate that this is a text about something that matters and that readers should care about.

Edit and proofread. Now's the time to pay close attention to the details: to check your paragraphs, your sentences, your words, and your punctuation. Think about the STYLE of your writing: is it appropriate for your purpose and audience? And don't forget to check for common mistakes. Finally, take the time to proofread. Read with an eye for typos and inconsistencies. Make sure all your sentences are complete. Run a spell checker, but be aware that it is no substitute for careful proofreading.

Approach Your Writing Pragmatically

Gerald Graff's essay on p. 929 might help you appreciate that you already have a lot of everyday skills that you can apply to your own writing process.

Even if you have a writing process that works well for you, that doesn't mean you complete all writing tasks the same way—or that you should. It's just common sense that you spend more time and take more care with your writing process for a fifteen-page research paper that counts for 40 percent of your final grade than you do for a much briefer essay that counts for 10 percent of that grade. Approach your writing pragmatically: consider how important your task is, what time constraints you face, what else you may have to do, what the nature of the task itself requires, and how well prepared you feel to complete it. Then, make *realistic* decisions. What do you *need* to do to complete an assignment effectively—and what *can* you do?

REFLECT. Take some time to think about your writing process. What works well? What tends to be a struggle? What do you want to try to do differently? Think about the various ways and places in which you've been able to do good writing. Are you able to make them a regular part of your writing process?

TEN

The Need for Collaboration

"Here Comes Everybody!"

ERE COMES EVERYBODY is the title of NYU professor Clay Shirky's book about "what happens when people are given the tools to do things together, without needing traditional organizational structures" to do them. Put another way, Shirky's book is about how technology has led to connectivity and how connectivity has led to easy and innovative collaborations. Here's what we mean:

- A group of students creates a *Wikipedia* entry devoted to manga, a genre of Japanese comic books. Within hours, others from around the world have joined in, helping to expand and refine the entry.

- A budding essayist uses the blogging platform *Medium* to publish her writing and interact with readers and other writers. She finds that the online community is full of authors who want to collaborate and discuss their ideas.

- Assigned to write an essay about the dangers faced by independent war journalists, a student starts by researching what has been written on this topic (reading current news magazines, online news sites, and *Twitter* feeds and blogs kept by the journalists themselves). When he writes the essay, he weaves the views of others (carefully cited) in with his own, adding his voice to the conversation about that topic.

- Fans of the TV mystery-drama *Veronica Mars* keep the show alive by writing and sharing fanfiction for years after the series ends. The fan base remains so strong that a *Kickstarter* campaign to fund a *Veronica Mars* movie raises over $5 million. The movie hit theaters in 2014, its fans walking down the red carpet alongside the stars.

Even the student mentioned above, researching alone at his computer, depends on others. In short, writers seldom—if ever—write alone. Collaboration has always been inevitable and essential, and our digital connectivity makes working together easier—and more interesting—than ever. This chapter will help you think about the role that collaboration plays in your life, and especially how it affects the work you do as an author and a reader.

In *Powers of Two*, Joshua Wolf Shenk argues that the real genius of the Beatles and their best work grew out of the collaborative nature of the Lennon-McCartney partnership.

∾_REFLECT. Think about reading and writing that you do regularly online—status updates, blog posts, articles, comments—everything. In what ways are you an author, and in what ways are you a member of an audience? To what extent does each activity involve collaboration with others, and how would it be different if there were no collaboration at all?_

What Collaboration Means for Authors—and Audiences

The examples above show some of the ways that authors collaborate—and how they sometimes even trade places with their audiences. Readers of the *Wikipedia* entry on manga can take on the role of editors or authors; the student writer using *Medium* becomes an audience for her readers' suggestions and ideas; the student reading and writing about independent war reporters is an audience for those authors whose work he reads and then an author when he responds to their views in his own essay. Authors and audiences shift roles and collaborate constantly—there's hardly any way to avoid doing so.

Once upon a time, newspapers reported information and events; today, they maintain social media accounts and blogs that serve as forums for discussing, challenging, and updating information. Readers who were once passive consumers of the news can now be active participants in responding to and sharing that information with others. As media professor Henry Jenkins puts it, ours is "a world where no one knows everything, but everyone knows something." Putting those somethings together is what happens when we collaborate.

To take another familiar example, players of the first video games were an audience for stories that were written by the games' designers. That's not the case in many of today's games, however, in which the players / audience customize their characters and write their own story—very often in collaboration with other players. Consider, for example, multiplayer online games such as *Fortnite*, in which a large number of people play as a group, or the more serious video game *World without Oil*, in which almost 2,000 individuals from twelve countries collaborated over the course of a month to imagine how to deal with a global oil crisis. Such games don't merely offer opportunities for collaboration; it's actually impossible for any one player to play alone.

Collaboration is an everyday matter. We collaborate for fun, as when a flash mob suddenly appears and starts dancing to Queen or singing the

**THINK
BEYOND
WORDS**

↪ *TAKE A LOOK at some favorite flash mobs at* everyonesanauthor.tumblr.com. *Some promote a cause, others sell a product, still others celebrate something or someone. The picture above is from a flash mob in the Netherlands to raise awareness of the exploitation of women. Inspired by One Billion Rising, performances like this one take place around the world every February to shine light on violence against women and to demand change. We think you'll agree that in addition to fulfilling various purposes, flash mobs can be great fun. What ideas do you have for an effective flash mob? In what ways would a flash mob accomplish your goal better than a piece of writing?*

"Hallelujah Chorus" and then just as suddenly disappears. And we collaborate for more serious purposes, as when many people contribute over time to develop a *Wikipedia* entry or when people in countries as far-flung as the United States, Malaysia, Germany, Nigeria, and dozens more collaborate on a dance project such as One Billion Rising or when musicians sprinkled throughout the world play together virtually through Playing for Change. In his book *Net Smart*, digital communications scholar Howard Rheingold argues that collaboration is today's tool for social engagement: "Knowing the importance of participation and how to participate has suddenly become not only an individual survival skill but a key to large-scale social change." For these and other purposes, collaboration is a necessity.

What Collaboration Means for You as a Student

As a student, you'll have many occasions to collaborate, from a simple class discussion to a full-fledged team project to research and write a report, carry out and write up an experiment, or build a website.

As a writer, you'll be in constant collaboration with others, from teachers and classmates who read and respond to your drafts to the audience you're addressing—and don't forget those whose work you read and cite. Academic writing in particular calls on you to engage with the ideas of others—to listen to and think about what they say, to respond to views you don't agree with, and to weave the ideas of others (those you agree with and those you don't) into your own arguments. Very often you'll want to present your own views as a direct response to what others say—in fact, when you think about it, the main reason we make arguments at all is because someone has said or done something that we want to respond to. And one reason we make academic arguments is to add our voices to conversations about topics that we're studying, things that matter to us.

And consider your nonacademic writing, particularly the writing you do online. Whether you're posting or following others on *Instagram,* viewing or contributing to *Wikipedia* or *YouTube* these kinds of writing assume and make possible a back-and-forth—a collaboration. You might be an author, an audience, or both. These are all ways that we regularly communicate—and collaborate—with others.

〰️ *REFLECT. Go to* Wikipedia *and work with several classmates to choose an entry that interests you and then revise or add to it. Or, if you don't find what you're looking for, create a new entry yourselves. Revisit in a few days to see what others may have added (or removed). For tips on writing for* Wikipedia, *see pages 785–86.*

Collaboration with a Writing Tutor

Speaking of collaboration in your academic writing, have you heard of your school's writing center? Most schools have one, and it's a place where you can go (online or physically) to consult with a trained tutor on any aspect of a class assignment. All writers need good readers, and a tutor can work with you at any stage of the process—brainstorming ideas, organizing the sequence of information, polishing, clarifying, documenting your sources.

And the good news is that the writing center probably doesn't charge a cent for what it offers. Or rather, you've already paid for it as part of your tuition and fees, so you might as well take advantage.

Here's something we know for sure: the more prepared you are for your writing center session, the more you'll get out of it. First, figure out what you'd like to accomplish in your session and share that information with your tutor early. Discuss your ideas, goals, doubts, and questions. Your tutor may suggest a different focus for your session; be open and flexible to such suggestions and reasoning. Let the session be a collaboration. A lot of ideas and information will be discussed during your session, so it's important that you take good notes in order to be able to remember it all. You may want to sit down immediately after your session and add more details while your memory is still fresh. Finally, write out a plan of action for what you'll do next; this plan will guide you when you get back to your assignment. We also recommend that you schedule your next appointment before leaving the writing center. Doing it promptly will improve your chances of getting a preferred day and time, and having an appointment can be a soft deadline for advancing your project.

Collaboration at Work

The collaborative projects described by Taté Walker deal with agriculture rather than writing, but think about the level of good, clear communication that each project requires. Read the report on p. 1079.

Collaboration almost certainly plays a role in your work life. Indeed, teamwork is central to most businesses and industries. Engineers work in teams to design power plants; editors and designers work together to publish books and magazines; businesses from Best Buy to Google rely on teams to develop and market new products. Whatever work you do—whether it is that of an engineer, health-care worker, bookstore owner, chemist, or teacher—you will find yourself continually communicating with others. The effectiveness of these communications will depend to a large extent on your ability to collaborate effectively.

Today's global culture can raise particular challenges for communication. Increasing numbers of workers are telecommuting—spending time working at home rather than at a desk in an office with other workers. Even when they are working from a centralized office, workers often need to communicate with colleagues elsewhere in the world and in other

At public relations agency ID's headquarters in Los Angeles, CEO Kelly Bush Novak leads a videoconference with members of her New York staff.

time zones. Digital humanities professor Cathy Davidson describes how one company holds global conference calls:

> Everyone chats using Sametime, IBM's internal synchronous chat tool, and has a text window open during the conversation. Anyone can be typing in a comment or a question (backchatting) while any other two people are speaking. Participants are both listening to the main conversation between whichever two people happen to be talking while also reading the comments, questions, and answers that any of the other participants might be texting. The conversation continues in response to both the talk and the text.
>
> —CATHY DAVIDSON, *Now You See It: How the Brain Science of Attention Will Transform the Way We Live, Work, and Learn*

A dizzying scenario to be sure—and an excellent reminder of both the challenges and the opportunities that the future holds for all who wish to make our voices heard in today's global culture. As a student in college, you are well positioned to prepare yourself for this future—which is in fact not the future at all but our present moment. In fact, you're most likely already using remote communication skills by taking courses online. Rather than taking your online writing for granted as "just for fun," learn from it. Take advantage as well of the opportunities that your school provides to learn with and from people with diverse cultural backgrounds. Such collaborative interactions are intrinsically satisfying, and they can also help you practice communicating effectively in the twenty-first century.

Some Tips for Collaborating Effectively

Sometimes your class collaborations will be fleeting and low risk—for example, to work with a group to respond to questions about a reading and then to share the group's ideas with the class. Other collaborations are more extended and high risk, as when you pick lab partners for the whole term or have a major group project that will count for a significant percentage of everyone's final grade.

Extended collaborative assignments can be a challenge. Members of the group may have differing goals—for instance, two members will accept nothing less than an A and others are just hoping for a C. Domineering members of the team may try to run the show; others won't participate at all. And the logistics of collaborating on a major project can be a challenge. Here are some tips that can help ensure efficient, congenial, and productive team relationships when you are working on an extended collaborative project.

- *Find ways of recognizing everyone.* For example, all group members could talk about a strength that they can contribute to the project.

- *Listen carefully*—and respectfully—to every group member.

- *Establish some ground rules.* Whether online or face-to-face, the way your group runs its meetings can make or break your collaborative effort. Spend part of your first meeting exploring your assignment and figuring out how often the group will meet, the responsibilities of each member, and the general expectations you have of each other.

- *Make an effort to develop trust and group identity.* To get started, members could share some pertinent information, such as their favorite spots for writing or their typical writing processes. Remember, too, that socializing can play an important role in the development of group identity. Sharing a pizza while brainstorming can pay off down the road. However, remember to stay focused on the project.

- *Get organized.* Use an agenda to organize your meetings, and be sure that someone takes notes. Don't count on anyone's memory, and don't leave all the note-taking to one person! You may want to take turns developing the agenda, reminding everyone of upcoming meetings via email or text message, maintaining written records, and so on.

- *Develop nonthreatening ways to deal with problems.* Rather than stating that a member's ideas are unclear, for instance, you might say, "I'm having trouble making the connection between your suggestion and my understanding of what we're discussing." Just a simple shift from *your* to *my* can defuse difficult situations. And remember that tact, thoughtfulness, and a sense of humor can go a long way toward resolving any interpersonal issues.

- *Build in regular reality checks* to nip any potential problems in the bud—for example, reserve some time to discuss how the group is working and how it could be better. Try not to criticize anyone; instead, focus on what's working and what could be improved.

- *Encourage the free play of ideas,* one of the most important benefits of working collaboratively. Think carefully about when your group should strive for consensus and when you should not. You want to avoid interpersonal conflicts that slow you down, yet remain open and consider everyone's ideas.

- *Expect the unexpected.* Someone's computer may crash, interlibrary loan materials may arrive later than expected, someone may be sick on the day when she was supposed to write a key section of the text. Try to build in extra time for the unexpected, and help each other out when extra teamwork is needed.

- *Be flexible about how you meet.* If getting together in person poses problems, use video chat or *Google Docs* to meet and work. Use your school's course management system for discussion forums, wikis, and file-sharing folders—all of which will prove helpful for collaborative work.

Remember that when you engage in group work, you need to attend to both the task and the group. And keep in mind that each member of the group should be valued equally and that the process should be satisfying to all.

PART IV

Genres of Writing

WHEN YOU WERE A KID, did you have certain kinds of clothes you liked to wear? Six-year-old Lila describes her wardrobe this way: "I have school clothes—they're okay, I guess. And I have dress-up clothes, like for when I go to the *Nutcracker* or a birthday party. But my favorites are my make-believe clothes: Snow White, Alice in Wonderland, and Princess Anna from *Frozen*. She's my favorite!" What Lila displays here is a fairly sophisticated sense of *genres*, ways that we categorize things. You see genres everywhere—in literature (think poetry, fiction, drama), in movies (Westerns, film noir, documentaries), and in music (rap, country, classical). And when we talk about writing, we often talk in terms of genres too: narratives, lab reports, project proposals, movie reviews, argument essays, and so on. Like all genres, those associated with writing are flexible: they expand and change over time as writers find new ways to communicate and express themselves.

In the ancient world, for example, personal communication involved carving symbols into clay tablets or, a bit later, having a scribe record your message on papyrus. For communicating with speed, couriers memorized letters and raced to deliver them orally. Once paper was available and letters were less costly and easier to produce, they evolved into multiple subgenres: the business letter, the personal letter, the condolence letter, the thank-you letter, and so on. Today, letters have further evolved into electronic forms— emails, *Instagram* messages, texts. It's hard to predict how these genres of communication will evolve in the future, but when they do, we know they will stretch to accommodate new modes and new media, as genres always do. In short, genres reflect current expectations while also shaping—and sometimes even changing—them.

Instructors will often ask you to use particular genres, most likely including the ones taught in this book: arguments, narratives, analyses, reports, reviews, and proposals. You may need to write a rhetorical analysis of a speech, for instance, or to analyze the causes of the increased frequency of wildfires in California. In either case, knowing the characteristic features of an analysis will be helpful. And you may want or need to combine genres—to introduce an analysis with a short narrative or to conclude it with a proposal of some kind.

Of course, you may not always be assigned to write in a particular genre. Your instructor may give you a topic to write about in whatever way you choose. In this case, you'll need to think carefully about what genre will be most appropriate for addressing that topic—and Chapter 11 will help you choose a genre when the choice is yours.

The chapters that follow introduce most of the genres you'll be assigned to do in college. Each chapter explains the genre's characteristic features; discusses how, when, where, and why you might use the genre most appropriately; provides a roadmap to the process of writing in that genre; and includes several example essays. We hope that you'll use these chapters to explore these common academic genres—and to adapt them as needed to your own purposes and goals.

Communication throughout the ages, from clay tablets to couriers delivering messages to tweets and texts.

ELEVEN

Choosing Genres

COMICS HAVE MANGA, superheroes, and fantasy. Music has hip-hop, country, and folk. Video games? Think shooters, simulation, or role-playing. How about restaurants? Try Italian, Vietnamese, Tex-Mex, vegan, or southern soul food. Or movies: sci-fi, thrillers, drama, anime. These are all genres, and they are one important way we structure our world.

Genres are categorizations, ways of classifying things. The genres this book is concerned with are kinds of writing, but you'll find genres everywhere you look.

In fact, rhetorician and researcher Carolyn Miller has been tracking the use of the word *genre* and has found it everywhere, including on many of the sites you visit every day. *Netflix* lists nineteen film genres, from action and drama to sports and thrillers—and many subgenres within each of these. The video game review site *GameSpot* sorts games into sixty-eight genres, and *Spotify* lists forty-three kinds of music and nine categories of podcasts as this book goes to press. You can even see new genres developing on *YouTube*, including microgenres like "cute babies" or "cats being mean." Indeed, there is now such a proliferation of genres that they've become the subject of parody, with comedians mixing musical genres to make new ones, like honky tonk and techno to make "honky techno" or folk and dubstep to make "folk step." To get a sense of the result, just take a look at the cartoon on the next page.

In this cartoon, Roz Chast comes up with her own new movie genres: sci-fi/Western, musical/self-help, sports/horror, and documentary/romance.

What You Need to Know about Genres of Writing

Genres are kinds of writing that you can use to accomplish a certain goal and reach a particular audience. As such, they have well-established features that help guide you in your writing. However, they're not fill-in-the-blank templates; you will adapt them to address your own rhetorical situations.

Genres have features that can guide you as a writer and a reader. Argument essays, for instance, take a position supported by reasons and evidence, consider a range of perspectives, and so on. These features help guide you as an author in what you write—and they also set up expectations for you as a reader, affecting the way you interpret what you read. If something's called a report, for instance, you are likely to assume that it presents information—that it's in some way factual.

This book covers those genres that are most often assigned in school—**ARGUMENTS, ANALYSES, REPORTS, NARRATIVES, REVIEWS, PROPOSALS,** and **ANNOTATED BIBLIOGRAPHIES** —and some subgenres: **VISUAL ANALYSES, PROFILES, LITERACY NARRATIVES, LITERATURE REVIEWS,** and **PROJECT PROPOSALS** . These are kinds of writing that have evolved over the years as a useful means of creating and sharing knowledge. As you advance in a major, you will become familiar with the most important genres and subgenres in that field. Especially when you are new to a genre, its features can serve as a kind of blueprint, helping you know how to approach an assignment. Knowing these features helps you organize a text and guides your choices in terms of content.

Genres are flexible. Keep in mind that genres can be both enabling and constraining. Sometimes you'll have reason to adapt genre features to suit your own goals. One student who was writing an analysis of a sonnet, for example, wanted to bend the analysis genre just a little to include a sonnet of his own. He checked with his teacher, got approval, and it worked. You probably wouldn't want to stretch a lab report in this way, however. Lab reports follow a fairly set template, covering purpose, methods, results, summary, and conclusions to carry out the goals of the scientific fields that use them; they would not be appropriate (or effective) in a creative writing class.

See how Dana Canedy's narrative about a conversation with her son makes an argument on p. 870.

You may also have occasion to combine genres—to tell a story in the course of arguing a position or to conclude a report with a proposal of some kind. If you ever decide to adapt or combine genres, think hard about your rhetorical situation: what genres will help you achieve your purpose? reach the audience you're addressing? work best in the medium you're using?

Genres evolve. While it is relatively easy to identify some characteristic genre features, such features are not universal rules. Genres are flexible, and they evolve across time and in response to shifting cultural contexts. Letters, for example, followed certain conventions in medieval Europe (they were handwritten, of course, and they were highly formal); by the twentieth century, letters had developed dozens of subgenres (thank-you notes, letters to the editor, application letters). Then, in the 1990s, letters began to morph into email, adapting in new ways to online situations. Today, text messages, tweets, and posts to *Instagram* may be seen as offshoots of the letter genre.

And as with all genres and subgenres, letters, email, text messages, and *Instagram* posts have developed their own conventions and features, ones that guide you as a writer and a reader.

REFLECT. Think about a favorite song, movie, or game, and then decide what genre it is. How do you know? List the features that help you identify it as belonging to a particular genre. What do you know about that genre? Name a few other examples of that genre, and then think about what features they have in common.

Deciding Which Genres to Use

Sometimes you'll be assigned to write in a particular genre. If that's the case, think about what you know about the genre, about what it expects of you as a writer, and turn to the appropriate chapter in this book for guidance. But other times your assignments won't make the genre perfectly clear. The following advice can help determine which genre(s) to use when the choice is yours. In all cases, remember to consider your **PURPOSE** for writing and the **AUDIENCE** you want to reach in deciding which genres would be most appropriate.

Look for clues in the assignment. Even without a clearly assigned genre, your assignment should be your starting point. Are there any keywords that suggest one? *Discuss*, for example, could indicate a **REPORT** or an **ANALYSIS**. And you might also need to consider how such a keyword is used in the discipline the assignment comes from—*analyze* in a philosophy assignment doesn't likely mean the same thing as in a literature assignment. In either case, you should ask your instructor for clarification.

Consider this assignment from an introductory communications course: "Look carefully at letters to the editor in one newspaper over a period of two weeks, and write an essay describing what you find. Who are the letter writers? What issues are they writing about? How many different perspectives are represented?" Though this assignment doesn't name a genre, it seems to be asking students for a report: to research a topic and then report on what they find.

But what if this were the assignment: "Look carefully at letters to the editor in one newspaper over a period of two weeks, and write an essay describing what you find. Who are the letter writers? What issues are they writing about? How many different perspectives are represented? What rhetorical strategies do the writers use to get their points across? Draw some conclusions based on what you find." This assignment also asks students to research a topic and report on what they find. But in asking them to draw some conclusions based on their findings, it is also prompting them to do some analysis. As you look at your own assignments, look for words or other clues that will help you identify which genres are expected.

If an assignment doesn't give any clues, here are some questions to ask in thinking about which genre may be most appropriate:

- *What discipline is the assignment for?* Say you're assigned to write about obesity and public health. If you're writing for a journalism course, you might write an op-ed essay **ARGUING** that high-calorie sodas should not be sold in public schools. If, on the other hand, you're writing for a biology class, you might **REPORT** on experiments done on eating behaviors and metabolic rates.

- *What is the topic?* Does it call for a specific genre? If you are asked, for example, to write about the campaign speeches of two presidential candidates, that topic suggests that you're being asked to **ANALYZE** the speeches (and probably **COMPARE** them). On the other hand, if you're writing about an experiment you conducted, you're probably writing a **REPORT** and should follow the conventions of that genre.

- *What is your purpose in writing?* If you want to convince your readers that they should "buy local," for example, your purpose will likely call for an **ARGUMENT**. If, however, you want to explain what buying local means, your purpose will call for a **REPORT**.

- *Who is the audience?* What interests and expectations might they have? Say you're assigned to write about the collective-bargaining rights of unions for a first-year seminar. There your audience would include other first-year students, and you might choose to write a **NARRATIVE** about the father of a friend who lost his job as a high school teacher. Imagine, however, writing on the same topic for a public policy course; there you would be more likely to write an essay **ANALYZING** the costs and benefits of unionized workers in the public sector.

- *What medium will you use?* Are there certain genres that work well— or not—in that medium? If you are assigned to give an oral presentation, for example, you might consider writing a **NARRATIVE** because listeners can remember stories better than they are able to recall other genres. Even if you decide to write an analysis or a report, you might want to include some narrative.

If the assignment is wide open, draw on what you know about genres. Sometimes you may receive an assignment so broad that not only the genre but even the topic and purpose are left up to you. Consider, for example, a prompt one of the authors of this book encountered in college: in an exam for a drama class, the professor came into the room, wrote "Tragedy!" on the blackboard, and said, "You have an hour and a half to respond." We hope you don't run into such a completely open-ended assignment, especially in a timed exam. But if you do, your knowledge of genre can help out. If this assignment came in a Shakespeare course, for example, you might **ARGUE** that *Hamlet* is Shakespeare's most powerful tragedy. Or you could perhaps **ANALYZE** the role of gender in one of his tragedies.

Luckily, such wide-open assignments are fairly rare. It's more likely that you will encounter an assignment like this one: "Choose a topic related to our course theme and carry out sufficient research on that topic to write an essay of eight to ten pages. Refer to at least six sources and follow MLA citation style." In this instance, you know that the assignment calls for some kind of research-based writing and that you need a topic and thesis that can be dealt with in the length specified. You could write an **ARGUMENT**, taking a position and supporting it with the research you have done. Or you could write a **REPORT** that presents findings from your research. At this point, you would be wise to see your instructor to discuss your choices. Once you have decided on a genre, turn to the appropriate chapter in this book (Chapters 12–17) to guide your research and writing.

When an assignment is wide open, try using what you know about genres as a way to explore your topic:

- What are some of the **POSITIONS** on your topic? What's been said or might be said? What controversies or disagreements exist? What's your own perspective?
- What stories—**NARRATIVES**—could you tell about it?
- How might you **ANALYZE** your topic? What are its parts? What caused it—or what effects might it have? Does it follow a certain process?
- What information might be important or interesting to **REPORT** on?
- How can your topic be evaluated, or **REVIEWED**?
- What problems does your topic present for which you can **PROPOSE** a solution?

REFLECT. Look at three writing assignments you have been given for any of your classes. Did the assignments specify a genre? If so, what was it? If not, what genres would you say you were being asked to use—and how can you tell?

TWELVE

"This Is Where I Stand"
Arguing a Position

SO WHAT'S YOUR POSITION ON THAT?" This familiar phrase pops up almost everywhere, from talk radio to social media, from political press conferences to classroom seminars. In fact, much of the work you do as an author responds, in some way, to this question.

After all, taking a position is something you do many times daily: you visit your advisor's office to explain in person your reasons for dropping a course; you text a friend the reasons she should see a certain film with you; in an economics class discussion, you offer your own position on consumer spending patterns in response to someone else's; you survey research on fracking and then write a letter to the editor of your local newspaper advocating (or protesting) a ban on fracking. In all these cases, you're doing what philosopher Kenneth Burke calls "putting in your oar," taking and supporting positions of your own in conversation with others around you.

Look around, and you'll see other positions being articulated all over the place. Here's one we saw recently on a T-shirt:

Work to eat.

Eat to live.

Live to bike.

Bike to work.

The central argument here is clear: bike to work. One of the reasons it's so effective is the clever way that the last sentence isn't quite parallel to the others. (In the first three, *to* can be replaced by *in order to*; in the last case, it can't.) Another reason it works well is the form of the argument, which is a series of short commands, each beginning with the same word that the previous sentence ends with.

This chapter offers guidelines for writing an academic essay that takes a position. While taking a position in an academic context often differs in crucial ways from doing so in other contexts, many of the principles discussed will serve you well when stating a position generally.

REFLECT. Stop for a moment and jot down every time you remember having to take a position on something—anything at all—in the last few days. The list will surely soon grow long if you're like most of us. Then take an informal survey, noting and writing down every time in one day someone around you takes a position. This informal research should convince you that the rhetorical genre of taking a position is central to many of your daily activities.

Across Academic Disciplines

Position papers are written in many fields, and a number of disciplines offer specific guidelines for composing them. In *philosophy*, a position paper is a brief persuasive essay designed to express a precise opinion about some issue or some philosopher's viewpoint. In *computer science*, a position paper considers a number of perspectives on an issue before finally offering the writer's own position. In *political science*, a position paper often critiques a major argument or text, first summarizing and analyzing its main points and then interpreting them in the context of other texts. Many college courses ask students to take a position in response to a course reading, specifying that they state their position clearly, support it with evidence and logical reasons, and cite all sources consulted. So one challenge you'll face when you're asked to write a position paper in various disciplines will be to determine exactly what is expected of you.

Across Media

Different media present different resources and challenges when it comes to presenting your position. Setting up a *website* that encourages people to take action to end animal abuse gives you the ability to link to additional information, whereas writing a traditional *essay* advocating that position for a print magazine requires that you provide all the relevant evidence and reasons on the page. It is very easy to incorporate color images or video clips in the webpage, but the magazine's budget may not allow for color at all. If you make the same argument against animal abuse in an *oral presentation*, you'll mostly be talking, though you may use *PowerPoint* slides to help your listeners follow the structure of your comments, to remind them of your main points, and to show graphs or photos that will appeal to their sense of reason or their emotions. Finally, if your marketing class is designing a fund-raising *TV commercial* for a nonprofit organization that works to stop animal abuse, you'll likely be able to use images and even music to drive home your point, but you might have only thirty seconds to get the message across.

THINK BEYOND WORDS

☛ *TAKE A LOOK at the website of Mutt Love Rescue, a dog adoption organization in Washington, DC, where you can see photos of available dogs, find out about fostering a dog, and more. Click on "Saving a Life" to see the organization's appeal for donations, along with photos of some of the "lucky pups." How compelling do you find the organization's argument? How does the use of words and images contribute to its appeal—is one more important? How would you revise this site to make it more effective—add video? audio? statistics? testimonials? more written information (or less)? Go to everyonesanauthor.tumblr.com to access the site.*

Remember that persuasion is always about connecting with an audience, meeting them where they are, and helping them see why your position is one they should take seriously or even adopt. To achieve that goal, you have to convey your position in a medium your audience will be receptive to—and can access. Different media serve different purposes, and you will want to consider your own goals as well as your audience's expectations.

Across Cultures and Communities

Taking a position in cultures or communities other than your own poses special challenges. Advertising—a clear case of taking a position—is full of humorous tales of cross-cultural failure. When Pepsi first sought to break into the Chinese market, for example, its slogan, "Pepsi Brings You Back to Life," got mangled in translation, coming out as "Pepsi Brings Your Ancestors Back from the Grave."

Far more problematic than questions of translation are questions of STANCE. When taking a position in American academic contexts, you're almost always expected to state your position explicitly while showing your awareness of other possible positions. In contrast, in some cultures and communities, you would generally avoid stating your opinion directly; rather, you would hint at it. In yet others, you would be expected to state your mind forthrightly, paying little attention to what others think about the issue or to how your words might make them feel.

Equally important, how people are expected to frame positions they take varies within a community, depending on their place in the social hierarchy as supervisor or employee, teacher or student, ruler or governed. To complicate matters, the expectations with respect to outsiders are almost always different from those for the locals. Most people might be quick to criticize their own government among friends, but they don't necessarily grant outsiders the same privilege. A word to the wise: humility is in order, especially when taking a position in communities or cultures of which you're not a member. Don't assume that what works at home will work elsewhere. A safe first step is to listen and observe carefully when in a new context, paying special attention to how people communicate any positions they are taking.

Across Genres

Arguing a position, as we've pointed out, is something that we do, in small ways or large, almost every day—and even across a range of genres. You might, for instance, write a letter to the editor of your local newspaper lamenting the closure of the local library—and setting forth your **POSITION** that it must be kept open at all costs. Similarly, a company's annual **REPORT** would likely set out its position that collective bargaining with suppliers will improve the company's bottom line. After taking in a highly anticipated film, you might tweet a brief **REVIEW**, arguing that it wasn't as good as you'd expected. In each case, the text states a position.

➦ See how video game publisher Activision-Blizzard states its position on esports in its 2017 annual report. Go to everyonesanauthor .tumblr.com and scroll to p. 15 of the report.

✍ *REFLECT. Look to see where and how positions are expressed around you, considering posters, editorials, songs,* Instagram *postings, blog entries, and so on. Then choose one that most interests you—or that most irritates you—and spend some time thinking about how it presents its position. How does it appeal to you—or why does it fail to appeal? What kinds of words, images, or sounds does it offer as support for its position? If you were going to revise it for a different audience, what would you do? If you were going to create it in another medium, how would it be different?*

CHARACTERISTIC FEATURES

Given the many different forms of writing that take a position, no one-size-fits-all approach to composing them is possible. We can, however, identify the following characteristic features common to writing in which the author is arguing a position:

- An explicit position
- A response to what others have said or done
- Appropriate background information
- A clear indication of why the topic matters
- Good reasons and evidence
- Attention to more than one point of view
- An authoritative tone
- An appeal to readers' values

An Explicit Position

Stating a position explicitly is easier said than done, since the complexity of most important issues can make it hard to articulate a position in a crystal-clear way. But it's very important to do so insofar as possible; nothing will lose an audience faster than hemming and hawing or drowning your position in a sea of qualifications. At the same time, in most academic contexts (as well as many others), a position stated baldly with no qualifications or nuances may alienate many readers.

In a syndicated column from 2009, just as the severity of the financial downturn was finally sinking in, *New York Times* columnist Thomas Friedman, writing for an American audience, explained:

> Let's today step out of the normal boundaries of analysis of our economic crisis and ask a radical question: What if the crisis of 2008 represents something much more fundamental than a deep recession? What if it's telling us that the whole growth model we created over the last 50 years is simply unsustainable economically and ecologically and that 2008 was when we hit the wall—when Mother Nature and the market both said: "No more."
>
> We have created a system for growth that depended on our building more and more stores to sell more and more stuff made in more and more factories in China, powered by more and more coal that would cause more and more climate change but earn China more and more dollars to buy more and more U.S. T-bills so Americans would have more and more money to build more and more stores and sell more and more stuff that would employ more and more Chinese. . . .
>
> We can't do this anymore.
>
> —THOMAS FRIEDMAN, "The Inflection Is Near?"

Friedman's position is clear and explicit: Americans' assumptions about their country's economic relationship with China and the behavior growing out of these assumptions must change. Although such a strong position may alienate some readers, all readers have a clear understanding of where Friedman stands.

There are times, however, when you will want to **QUALIFY** your position by using words like *many, some,* or *maybe*—or writing *could* rather than *will.* Not every position you take can be stated with absolute certainty, and a qualified claim is generally easier to support than an unqualified one. When LeBron

James announced that he would leave the Cleveland Cavaliers to join the Los Angeles Lakers, many argued that this move would be a great boon to the LA economy. See how one writer for *Fortune* was careful to qualify that position:

> LeBron James' move to Los Angeles is expected to have more than just an impact on the Lakers—a once-dominant team that has sagged in recent years. His move might also boost the local economy. According to a study conducted by legal document website FormSwift in February, LeBron James will likely have a positive economic impact on the food and drink industries in Los Angeles based on data from the previous cities he's called home, including Cleveland and Miami, before and after he left.
>
> —SARAH GRAY, "Why LeBron James' Move to Los Angeles Could Boost the City's Economy"

Gray's position is clear—LeBron James's move to Los Angeles will have a positive effect on the economy—but she is careful to qualify that claim so as not to overstate it. Note that she says James's move is *expected* to have an impact, *might* improve the LA economy, and *will likely* add growth to the local food and drink industries.

Keep in mind that while it may be useful, even necessary, to qualify a statement, you should be careful not to overdo it. You don't want to sound unsure of your position.

A Response to What Others Have Said or Done

Crucially, position papers respond to other positions. That is, they are motivated by something that has been said or done by others—and are part of an ongoing conversation. In the *New York Times* example, Thomas Friedman explicitly questions a popular position—namely that despite the current economic downturn, Americans and people around the world will eventually be able to continue the patterns of consumption they have created over the past few decades. His response is a rejection of this position, signaled with his emphatic "we can't do this anymore."

In some cases, the position the author is responding to becomes part of the argument. The music video "Immigrants (We Get the Job Done)," produced by Lin-Manuel Miranda and released in the aftermath of the 2016 presidential election, uses this strategy. Viewed more than

5 million times on *YouTube*, the video features four well-known rappers from around the world responding to the vilification of immigrants by making a case for how much immigrants contribute to the United States. The video begins by acknowledging the debate and the lyrics are punctuated throughout by a chorus with a clear position: "Immigrants, we get the job done. Look how far I come." The video's argument is an explicit response to those who think that *immigrant* is a "bad word." In fact, Lin-Manuel Miranda even described the video as "musical counterweight" to the xenophobia and criticism of immigrants at the time it was written.

Later in this chapter, you will meet Katherine Spriggs, who staked out a position on "buying local" in an essay written for one of her college courses. In this brief excerpt from her essay, she responds directly to those who say buying local will have negative environmental effects:

> It has also been argued that buying locally will be detrimental to the environment because small farms are not as efficient in their use of resources as large farms. This is a common misconception and actually depends on how economists measure efficiency. Small farms are less efficient than large farms in the total output of one crop per acre, but they are more efficient in total output of all crops per acre (McCauley).
>
> —KATHERINE SPRIGGS, "On Buying Local"

In a short space, Spriggs identifies an argument that others have made about the position she is taking and then responds to it explicitly. In academic position papers, authors are expected to acknowledge and address other positions directly in this way. That is often not the case when you take a position in other contexts and in some cultures. In online writing, for instance, it's not unusual for authors to simply provide a brief mention with a link to refer readers to another position within an ongoing conversation.

REFLECT. Think about your writing as part of a larger, ongoing conversation. Examine something that you have recently written—an email, a tweet, an essay for a class—that expresses a position about an issue that matters to you. Check to see whether it makes clear your motivation for writing and the position(s) to which you were responding. If these aren't clear, try revising your text to make them more explicit.

HAMILTON ★ MIXTAPE

☛ *WATCH THE VIDEO of "Immigrants (We Get the Job Done)." Consider how the medium—video, with the addition of music by diverse performers, a radio voice-over at the start, and images of immigrant experiences—contributes to the power of the argument. Find the link to view the full video at everyonesanauthor.tumblr.com.*

Appropriate Background Information

The amount of background information needed—historical background, definitions, contextual information—will vary widely depending on the scope of your topic, your audience, and your medium. If you are preparing a position paper on the effects of global warming for an environmental group, any background information provided will represent extensive, often detailed, and sometimes highly technical knowledge. If, on the other hand, you are preparing a poster to display on campus that summarizes your position on an increase in tuition, you can probably assume your audience will need little background information—for which you will have only limited space anyway.

The "Immigrants (We Get the Job Done)" video, as a music video partly intended to entertain, provided no background information other than the radio voice-over that sounds like a news broadcast indicating "you know, and it gets into this whole issue of border security" and "we've got the House and the Senate debating this issue." The video's creators assume the viewers will know about the context of the video's message—how immigrants and refugees were being talked about and treated in the United States when the video was made. In online writing, links can often do much of the work of filling readers in on background information; they are especially convenient because readers have the option of clicking on them or not, depending on how much information they need or want.

In academic contexts, writers are generally expected to provide a great deal of background information to firmly ground their discussion of a topic. When the president of Rensselaer Polytechnic Institute, Shirley Ann Jackson, spoke at a 2011 symposium celebrating women in science and engineering, she argued that while the number of women graduating with degrees in STEM fields has increased, major obstacles still stand in the way of women academics in the sciences at research universities. To make this argument, she first provided background information about the number of women PhDs leaving the research science track:

> Writing for the *New York Times*, Steven Greenhouse noted that, based on a University of California, Berkeley, study, "Keeping Women in the Science Pipeline," women are far more likely than men to " 'leak' out of the research science pipeline before obtaining tenure at a college or university." After receiving a PhD, married women with young children are 35 percent less likely to enter a tenure-track position in science than are married men with young children and PhDs in science. According to the report from the University of California, "women who had children after becoming postdoctoral scholars were twice as likely as their male counterparts to shift their career goals away from being professors with a research emphasis—a 41 percent shift for women versus 20 percent for men." And a 2005 report from Virginia Tech found a disproportionate share of women made up "voluntary departures" from the faculty. Although women represented one-fifth of the faculty, they accounted for two-fifths of departures.
>
> At every step along the way—from entering college as a science or engineering major to graduating with a technical degree, from entering graduate school to exiting successfully, to getting a postdoc, to succeeding as faculty, to attaining tenure—we need to provide women with bridges to the next level. As is clear from the studies I mentioned, the unequal burden of family life turns the gaps in the road into chasms. Help

with childcare, which has been provided at MIT, and the establishment of parental childbirth leave, which has been provided at Rensselaer, can help. But there is more to be done.

—SHIRLEY ANN JACKSON, "Leaders in Science and Engineering: The Women of MIT"

Hearing about specific research studies helps Jackson's audience see that a disproportionately high number of women scientists are "shift[ing] their career goals away from being professors with a research emphasis"—and supports her argument that universities must do more to ease the "unequal burden of family life" that young women scientists bear.

Background information is not always statistical and impersonal, even in academic contexts. In an essay written for *Academe*, a publication of the American Association of University Professors, Randall Hicks, a professor of chemistry at Wheaton College, argues that it is harder for working-class students to become professors than it is for children of

Many women are earning degrees in STEM fields, and universities need to do more to help young women scientists balance the demands of family life and scientific research.

college-educated parents. The background information he provides is startlingly personal:

> "I'll break his goddamned hands," my father said. I wonder if he remembers saying it. Nearly twenty-five years later, his words still linger in my mind. My father had spent the entire day in the auto body shop only to come home and head to the garage for more work on the side. I may have finished my homework, and, tired of roughhousing with my brother, gone out to help him scrape the paint off his current project, some classic car that he was restoring. "It's okay for a hobby, but if somebody tells me that he's thinking of doing it for a living, I'll break his goddamned hands." Although we had no firm plans and little financial means to do so, he was telling me that he expected me to get an education.
>
> —RANDALL HICKS

Note how this story provides readers with important background information for Hicks's argument. Immediately, we learn relevant information about him and the environment that shaped him. Thus, we understand part of his passionate commitment to this topic: he learned, indirectly, from his father to put a high value on education, since doing so in his father's view would allow Hicks to get a job that would be better than something that is just "okay for a hobby."

A Clear Indication of Why the Topic Matters

No matter the topic, one of an author's tasks is to demonstrate that the issue is real and significant—and thus to motivate readers to read on or listeners to keep listening. Rarely can you assume your audience sees why your argument matters.

As a student, you'll sometimes be assigned to write a position paper on a particular topic; in those cases, you may have to find ways to make the topic interesting for you, as the writer, although you can assume the topic matters to the person who assigned it. On other occasions, you may take it upon yourself to write about something you care deeply about, in which case you will need to help your audience understand why they should care as well.

See how Mellody Hobson, president of an investment firm and a board member of Starbucks, JPMorgan Chase, and other prominent companies, begins her 2014 TED talk with a personal story that is meant to illus-

Mellody Hobson calls on businesses "not to be color blind but to be color brave."

trate why Americans need to talk about race—and why that conversation matters:

> So it's 2006. My friend Harold Ford calls me. He's running for U.S. Senate in Tennessee, and he says, "Mellody, I desperately need some national press. Do you have any ideas?" So I had an idea. I called a friend who was in New York at one of the most successful media companies in the world, and she said, "Why don't we host an editorial board lunch for Harold? You come with him."
>
> Harold and I arrive in New York. We are in our best suits. We look like shiny new pennies. And we get to the receptionist, and we say, "We're here for the lunch." She motions for us to follow her. We walk through a series of corridors, and all of a sudden we find ourselves in a stark room, at which point she looks at us and she says, "Where are your uniforms?"
> Just as this happens, my friend rushes in. The blood drains from her face. There are literally no words, right? And I look at her, and I say, "Now, don't you think we need more than one black person in the U.S. Senate?"
> —MELLODY HOBSON, "Color Blind or Color Brave?"

By sharing this story about how she and Ford were assumed to be kitchen staff on the basis of their race, Hobson establishes in a vivid and distressing way why her topic matters—and she uses the fact that this story makes people uncomfortable to show precisely why it is so important that we talk about race. She then goes on to cite statistics about how few people of color hold board seats in corporate America, driving home for her audience the need for this conversation in concrete terms. Like many writers of academic arguments, Hobson uses personal, statistical, and historical data to demonstrate why her argument matters.

The creators of the "Immigrants (We Get the Job Done)" video certainly believed immigrants matter, as demonstrated in the values they appealed to and the range of people they included in the video. Similarly, Thomas Friedman certainly thinks America's response to the economic downturn that began in 2008 is important. When he writes that the 2008 crisis might be "something much more fundamental than a deep recession" and "the whole growth model . . . is simply unsustainable," his tone in these broad assertions conveys a sense of urgency. In all these cases, the writers share the conviction that what they're writing about matters not just to them but to us all, and they work hard to make that conviction evident.

~~_REFLECT. Examine something you've written that takes a strong position. Catalog the specific ways you make clear to your readers that the topic matters to you—and that it should matter to them._

Good Reasons and Evidence

See how Barbara Ehrenreich went about getting first-hand information in order to write about low-wage workers in Florida, p. 889.

Positions are only as good as the reasons and evidence that support them, so part of every author's task in arguing a position is to provide the strongest possible reasons for the position, and evidence for those reasons. Evidence may take many forms, but among the most often used, especially in academic contexts, are facts; firsthand material gathered from observations, interviews, or surveys; data from experiments; historical data; examples; expert testimony (often in the form of what scholars have written); precedents; statistics; and personal experience.

In an essay from the *New York Times* op-ed page, Jennifer Delahunty, dean of admissions at Kenyon College, seeks to explain to her own daughter why one of her daughter's college applications had been rejected.

Delahunty's explanation—the position her essay takes—is that the rejection was due at least in part to the fact that young women, even accomplished ones, face particular challenges in getting into prestigious colleges:

> She had not . . . been named a National Merit Finalist, dug a well for a village in Africa or climbed to the top of Mount Rainier. She is a smart, well-meaning, hard-working teenage girl, but in this day and age of swollen applicant pools that are decidedly female, that wasn't enough. . . .
>
> Had she been a male applicant, there would have been little, if any, hesitation to admit. The reality is that because young men are rarer, they're more valued applicants. Today, two-thirds of colleges and universities report that they get more female than male applicants, and more than 56 percent of undergraduates nationwide are women.
>
> —JENNIFER DELAHUNTY, "To All the Girls I've Rejected"

Delahunty offers two related reasons that her daughter had not been admitted. First, for all her daughter's accomplishments, they were not as impressive as those of other applicants. Here she provides specific evidence (her daughter was not a National Merit finalist, nor had she "dug a well for a village in Africa or climbed to the top of Mount Rainier") that makes the reason memorable and convincing.

The second reason focuses on the fact that male applicants in general have a better chance than female applicants of getting into many schools. This time her evidence is of a different sort; she uses statistics to show that "young men are rarer" and therefore "more valued applicants." Note that Delahunty expects readers to share her knowledge that something seen as valuable takes on additional value when it is rare.

The scientific community typically takes the long view in terms of gathering evidence in support of the positions it takes. Certainly that was true in the case of smoking, when decades of research paved the way for a statement on the relationship between smoking and cancer. The 1964 surgeon general's report on the health consequences of smoking notes:

> The U.S. Public Health Service first became officially engaged in an appraisal of the available data on smoking and health in June, 1956, when, under the instigation of the Surgeon General, a scientific Study Group on the subject was established jointly by the National Cancer Institute,

the National Heart Institute, the American Cancer Society, and the American Heart Association. After appraising sixteen independent studies carried on in five countries over a period of eighteen years, this group concluded that there is a causal relationship between excessive smoking of cigarettes and lung cancer.

—*Smoking and Health: Report of the Advisory Committee of the Surgeon General of the Public Health Service*

In this case, the surgeon general's study group analyzed evidence gathered over eighteen years from a range of research conducted by multiple scholars before reaching its conclusion.

Attention to More than One Point of View

Considering multiple, often opposing, points of view is a hallmark of any strong position paper, particularly in an academic context. By showing that you understand and have carefully evaluated other viewpoints, you show respect for the issue's complexity and for your audience, while also showing that you have done your homework on your topic.

In a journal article on human-caused climate change, Naomi Oreskes takes a position based on a careful analysis of 928 scientific articles published in well-known and respected journals. Some people, she says, "suggest that there might be substantive disagreement in the scientific community about the reality of anthropogenic climate change. This is not the case." Yet in spite of the very strong consensus on which Oreskes bases her claim, she still acknowledges other possible viewpoints:

Admittedly, [some] authors evaluating impacts, developing methods, or studying paleoclimatic change might believe that current climate change is natural. . . . The scientific consensus might, of course, be wrong. If the history of science teaches anything, it is humility, and no one can be faulted for failing to act on what is not known.

—NAOMI ORESKES, "Beyond the Ivory Tower: The Scientific Consensus on Climate Change"

Oreskes acknowledges that the consensus she found in the articles she examined might be challenged by other articles she did not consider and that any consensus, no matter how strong, might ultimately prove to be wrong. Thus does she remain respectful of those members of the scientific community who may hold other views.

Sometimes you'll want to both acknowledge and reply to other viewpoints, especially if you can answer any objections persuasively. Here is college admissions officer Jennifer Delahunty, noting—and ruling out—the possible criticism that college admissions officers do not give careful consideration to all applicants:

> Rest assured that admissions officers are not cavalier in making their decisions. Last week, the 10 officers at my college sat around a table, 12 hours every day, deliberating the applications of hundreds of talented young men and women. While gulping down coffee and poring over statistics, we heard about a young woman from Kentucky we were not yet ready to admit outright. She was the leader/president/editor/captain/lead actress in every activity in her school. She had taken six advanced placement courses and had been selected for a prestigious state leadership program. In her free time, this whirlwind of achievement had accumulated more than 300 hours of community service in four different organizations.
>
> Few of us sitting around the table were as talented and as directed at age 17 as this young woman. Unfortunately, her test scores and grade point average placed her in the middle of our pool. We had to have a debate before we decided to swallow the middling scores and write "admit" next to her name.
>
> —JENNIFER DELAHUNTY, "To All the Girls I've Rejected"

Delahunty provides evidence from a specific case, demonstrating persuasively that the admissions officers at her college take their job seriously.

Even bumper stickers can subtly acknowledge more than one position, as does this one from late 2008:

> I Support Our Troops / I Question Our Policies

This bumper sticker states two positions that initially might seem contradictory, arguing that supporting the country's troops and questioning our government's foreign policies are not mutually exclusive.

An Authoritative Tone

Nicholas Carr isn't a neuroscientist, but he writes with authority about how using GPS devices changes our brains. See how he does it on p. 875.

Particularly in academic contexts, authors make a point of taking an authoritative tone. Even if your goal is to encourage readers to examine a number of alternatives without suggesting which one is best, you should try to do so in a way that shows you know which alternatives are worth examining and why. Likewise, even if you are taking a strong position, you should seek to appear reasonable and rational. The 1964 surgeon general's report on the consequences of smoking does not waver: smoking causes cancer. At the same time, in taking this position, it briefly outlines the history of the issue and the evidence on which the claim is logically based, avoiding emotional language and carefully specifying which forms of smoking ("excessive" cigarettes) and cancer (lung) the claim involves.

Jennifer Delahunty establishes her authority in other ways. Her description of ten admissions officers putting in twelve-hour days going through hundreds of applications and "poring over statistics" backs up her forthright assertion, "Rest assured that admissions officers are not cavalier in making their decisions." Later in the essay, acknowledging her own struggles to weigh issues of fairness to highly qualified young women against the need to maintain gender balance in incoming classes, Delahunty not only demonstrates that she knows what she is writing about but also invites readers to think about the complexity of the situation without offering them any easy answers. In short, she is simultaneously reasonable and authoritative.

An Appeal to Readers' Values

Implicitly or explicitly, authors need to appeal to readers' values, especially when taking a strong position. The creators of the "Immigrants (We Get the Job Done)" video clearly appealed to a number of cultural values Americans hold dear, such as work ethic and opportunity (with references to the demanding kinds of work immigrants do to survive—picking oranges, sewing textiles, nursing the ill, constructing buildings) as well as equality, justice, and hope (depictions of harrowing migration journeys and confrontations with border agents). The refrain "Immigrants, we get the job done" is itself a strong appeal to the audience's sense of fairness and democratic ideals.

Freeman A. Hrabowski III, president of the University of Maryland, Baltimore County, appeals to similar values of opportunity, equality, and democracy in a 2015 essay in *Inside Higher Ed*. His essay responds to the riots in Baltimore that spring, sparked by the death of a black man, Freddie Gray, while in police custody, but which also aired the grievances of a community with a long history of poverty and little opportunity.

> As one of my students said to me recently, the Baltimore story—which is the American story—should remind us that issues related to poverty and inequality, crime and opportunity are not about "those people." They are about us—all of us. How we react to events like those in Baltimore speaks volumes about our values. We know we must do much better, especially for people who have not had a chance to thrive in our society. Americans—not just in Baltimore but across the country—have an opportunity now to ask difficult questions and take long-term action. . . . Historically, one of America's greatest strengths has been our ability to look squarely at our problems and to make hard changes. To do so often requires struggle, and we have a responsibility to embrace that struggle. To do so is a fundamental part of the learning and growing process—and it is fundamental to changing issues of systemic injustice and inequality that are neither new nor isolated.
>
> —FREEMAN A. HRABOWSKI III, "After the Cameras Leave"

Hrabowski appeals to readers' patriotic values of unity and democracy, saying that these issues aren't just about certain communities in Baltimore, but "about us—all of us." He goes on to call for universities to engage with underprivileged communities, upholding the American ideal of hard work and "struggle" that has led the nation to face difficult problems throughout its history. Writing for *Inside Higher Ed*, Hrabowski was addressing a vast audience of educators—and his text appeals to a wide set of values he can assume his readers to hold: the spirit of the American nation.

Online contexts are particularly interesting for considering appeals to values since you can rarely be sure who your actual readers are, and you certainly can't control who will see a text you create. Yet appealing to values is no less important in online situations and may, in fact, take on a greater role in arguing positions effectively. In this case, writers often seek to create their ideal audience through the words and images they choose. Online environments remind us that as writers, we are always imagining who our audience is and appealing to what we imagine their values to be.

RUSSEL HONORÉ wrote this essay for *This I Believe,* a not-for-profit organization that sponsors "a public dialogue about belief, one essay at a time." The essay was later broadcast on *NPR's Weekend Edition* on March 1, 2009. Honoré is a retired lieutenant general in the US Army who has contributed to response efforts to Hurricanes Katrina and Rita in 2005 and other natural disasters.

Work Is a Blessing

RUSSEL HONORÉ

I GREW UP IN Lakeland, Louisiana, one of 12 children. We all lived on my parents' subsistence farm. We grew cotton, sugarcane, corn, hogs, chickens and had a large garden, but it didn't bring in much cash. So when I was 12, I got a part-time job on a dairy farm down the road, helping to milk cows. We milked 65 cows at 5 in the morning and again at 2 in the afternoon, seven days a week.

Background information.

In the kitchen one Saturday before daylight, I remember complaining to my father and grandfather about having to go milk those cows. My father said, "Ya know, boy, to work is a blessing."

A position taken in response to another position.

I looked at those two men who'd worked harder than I ever had—my father eking out a living on that farm and my grandfather farming and working as a carpenter during the Depression. I had a feeling I had been told something really important, but it took many years before it sunk in.

Admitting his own slowness to understand what his father meant contributes to his authoritative tone.

Going to college was a rare privilege for a kid from Lakeland, Louisiana. My father told me if I picked something to study that I liked doing, I'd always look forward to my work. But he also added, "Even having a job you hate is better than not having a job at all." I wanted to be a farmer, but I joined the ROTC program to help pay for college. And what started out as an obligation to the Army became a way of life that I stayed committed to for 37 years, three months and three days.

Citing his father, Honoré shows his attention to more than one point of view about work.

In the late 1980s, during a visit to Bangladesh, I saw a woman with a baby on her back, breaking bricks with a hammer. I asked a Bangladesh military escort why they weren't using a machine, which would have been a lot easier. He told me a machine would put that lady out of work. Breaking those bricks meant she'd earn enough money to feed herself and her baby that day. And as bad as that woman's job was, it was enough to keep a small family alive. It reminded me of my father's words: To work is a blessing.

Reasons and evidence for how the author came to see work as a blessing.

Serving in the United States Army overseas, I saw a lot of people like that woman in Bangladesh. And I have come to believe that people without jobs are not free. They are victims of crime, the ideology of terrorism, poor health, depression and social unrest. These victims become the illegal immigrants, the slaves of human trafficking, the drug dealers, the street gang members. I've seen it over and over again on the U.S. border, in Somalia, the Congo, Afghanistan and in New Orleans. People who have jobs can have a home, send their kids to school, develop a sense of pride, contribute to the good of the community, and even help others. When we can work, we're free. We're blessed.

Specific examples indicate why the topic matters and show the author's awareness of his audience's values.

I don't think I'll ever quit working. I'm retired from the Army, but I'm still working to help people be prepared for disaster. And I may get to do a little farming someday, too. I'm not going to stop. I believe in my father's words. I believe in the blessing of work.

The author concludes by stating his position explicitly.

Listen to the audio essay at everyonesanauthor.tumblr.com. You'll hear someone who sounds like he grew up on a farm in Louisiana, a fact that contributes to Honoré's authority: this guy knows what he's talking about.

REFLECT. *Choose a short piece of writing on a website such as* Salon *that takes a position on an issue you care about. Look at the list of characteristic features on page 147 and annotate your text to point out the ones that are represented in it, using Honoré's essay as a model. Make a list of any features that are not included as well. (While not every effective position paper will include all of the characteristic features, many of them will.) Then consider whether including those features might have improved the text—and if so, how.*

ARGUING A POSITION / A Roadmap

Choose a topic that matters—to you, and to others

If you get to select your topic, begin by examining your own interests and commitments in light of the context you are writing for. Global warming might be an appropriate topic for a course in the life sciences or social sciences, but it's probably not going to serve you well in a course in medieval history unless you can find a direct link between the two topics. You might consider focusing on some issue that's being debated on campus (Are those new rules for dropping classes fair?), a broader political or ethical issue (Is eating meat by definition unethical?), or an issue in which you have a direct stake (Does early admission penalize those who need financial aid?).

Lynda Barry thinks arts education is really important. See how she makes us think the same in "The Sanctuary of School," p. 853.

If you've been assigned a topic, do your best to find an aspect of it that interests you. (If you're bored with your subject, you can be sure your readers will be.) If, for example, you're assigned to write about globalization in a required international studies course, you could tailor that topic to your own interests and write about the influence of American hip-hop on world music.

Be sure that your topic is one that is arguable—and that it matters. Short of astounding new evidence, it's no longer worth arguing that there is no link between smoking and lung cancer. It's a fact. But you can argue about what responsibility tobacco companies now have for tobacco-related deaths, as recent court cases demonstrate.

One sure way to find out whether a topic is arguable is to see if it *is* being debated—and that is a good first step as you explore a topic. You can probably assume that any topic that's being widely discussed matters—and of course you'll want to know what's being said about it in order to write about it. Remember that your essay is part of a larger conversation about your topic: you need to become familiar with that conversation in order to contribute to it.

Be careful to keep an open mind. A good, arguable topic will surely trigger at least several different points of view. Keeping an open mind and considering those points of view fairly and carefully at the start is always a good idea. And it will make your argument stronger by showing that you can be trusted to consider all sides of an issue, especially those you may not agree with.

Consider your rhetorical situation

Looking at your audience, your purpose, and other aspects of your rhetorical situation will help you to think carefully about how to achieve your goals.

Focus on your AUDIENCE. Who are you trying to reach, and what do you hope to persuade them to think or do?

- What are they likely know about your topic, and what background information will you need to provide?

- How are they like or unlike you—and one another? Consider such things as age, education, gender, abilities and disabilities, cultural and linguistic heritage, and so on. How will such factors influence the way you make your argument?

- What convictions might they hold about the topic you're addressing— and how sympathetic are they likely to be to your position?

If you're trying to convince your fellow business majors of the virtues of free-market capitalism, your task is quite different than if you're trying to convince members of the campus socialist organization. In the first case, you would almost surely be preaching to the choir, whereas in the second, you would likely face a more skeptical audience.

Keep in mind that there's always danger in speaking only to those who already agree with you; if you keep audiences with differing values and viewpoints in mind, you will be more likely to represent all views fairly and hence encourage others to consider your position seriously. Keeping your audience in mind, then, means thinking in terms of who may respond to your position, how they will likely respond, and why.

Think hard about your PURPOSE. Why are you arguing this position? What has motivated you to write on this topic? What do you hope to learn by writing about it? What do you want to convince your audience to think or do? How can you best achieve your purpose or purposes?

Think about your STANCE. Start by asking yourself where you are coming from in regard to this topic. What about the topic captured your interest, and how has that interest led you to the position you expect to take on it? Why do you think the topic matters? How would you describe your attitude toward the topic: are you an advocate, a critic, an observer, an apologist, or something else? How do you want to be seen as an author—as forceful? thoughtful? curious? How can you establish your own authority in writing on this topic?

Consider the larger CONTEXT. What are the various perspectives on the issue? What have others said about it? If you're writing about the use of ethanol as a fuel source, for instance, you'll need to look at what circumstances led to its use, at who's supported and opposed it (and why), and at the economic ramifications both of producing ethanol for fuel and of not doing so. As you come to understand the larger context, you'll become aware of various positions you'll want to consider, and what factors will be important to consider as you develop your position.

Consider your **MEDIUM**. Will your writing take the form of a print essay? Will it appear as an editorial in a local paper? on a website? as an audio essay to be broadcast on a local radio station or posted as a podcast? as an oral or multimedia presentation for a class you are taking? The medium you choose should be one that suits both your purpose and your audience.

Consider matters of **DESIGN**. Think about the "look" you want to achieve and how you can format your text to make it easy to follow. Do you need headings? illustrations? any other graphics? color? Does the discipline you're writing in have any conventions you should follow? Does your medium allow for certain elements such as audio or video links that will help you achieve your purpose?

Research your topic

Begin exploring the topic by looking at it from different points of view. Whatever position you take will ultimately be more credible and persuasive if you can show evidence of having considered other positions.

Begin by assessing what you know—and don't know—about the topic. What interests you about the topic, and why? What more do you want or need to find out about it? What questions do you have about it, and where might you go for answers? To answer these questions, you might try **BRAIN-STORMING** or other activities for **GENERATING IDEAS**.

What have others said? What are some of the issues that are being debated now about your topic, and what are the various positions on these issues? What other **POSITIONS** might be taken with respect to the topic? Remember, too, to seek out sources that represent a variety of perspectives.

Where should you start your research? Where you start and what sources you consult depend upon your topic and what questions you have about it. If you are focusing on a current issue, turn to news media and to websites, listservs, *Twitter*, or other online groups devoted to the issue. If you are investigating a topic from the distant past, be sure to look for both older sources and more recent scholarship on the topic. For some issues, you might want to interview experts or conduct other sorts of **FIELD RESEARCH**.

Do you need to cut your topic down to size? Few among us know enough to make strong general claims about global warming. While that fact does not and should not keep us from having opinions about the issue, it suggests that the existence of global warming is much too broad a topic to be appropriate for a five-page essay. Instead, you'll need to focus on some aspect of that topic for your essay. What angle you take will depend on the course you're writing for. For a geology class, you might focus on the effects of rising temperatures on melting glaciers; for an international relations course, you could look at climate shift and national security debates. Just remember that your goal is to take an informed position, one that you can support well.

Formulate an explicit position

Once you have sufficient information about your topic and some understanding of the complexity of the issue, you'll need to formulate a position that you can state explicitly and support fully. Let's say you decide to take a position on a current controversy among scientists about climate change. Here's how one author formulated a position:

> Many scientists have argued that climate change has led to bigger and more destructive hurricanes and typhoons. Other researchers, however, have countered by saying that climate change is not linked causally to an increase in hurricane strength. After reviewing both sides of this debate, I see two strong reasons why changes in our climate have not necessarily led to more severe hurricanes.
> —SOFI MINCEY, "On Climate Change and Hurricanes"

These three sentences articulate a clear position—that climate change is not necessarily to blame for bigger hurricanes—and frame that position as a response to an existing debate. Notice also how the writer qualifies her claim: she does not claim definitively that climate change has not led to bigger hurricanes; rather, she promises to present reasons that argue for this view.

By arguing only that the claims of many scientists *may* be wrong, she greatly increases the likelihood that she can succeed in her argument, setting a reasonable goal for what she must achieve. Note that her position still requires support: she needs to present reasonable evidence to challenge the claim that climate change has "necessarily" led to bigger hurricanes.

State your position as a tentative THESIS. Once you formulate your position, try stating it several different ways and then decide which one is most compelling. Make sure the position is stated explicitly—no beating around the bush. Your statement should let your audience know where you stand and be interesting enough to attract their attention.

Then think about whether you should QUALIFY your position. Should you limit what you claim—is it true only sometimes or under certain circumstances? On the other hand, does it seem too weak or timid and need to be stated more forcefully?

Remember that a good thesis for a position paper should identify your specific topic and make a CLAIM about that topic that is debatable. The thesis should also give your audience some idea of your reasons for making this claim. Consider the following thesis statement from two scholars at a public policy institute:

> The case against raising the minimum wage is straightforward: A higher wage makes it more expensive for firms to hire workers.
> —KEVIN A. HASSET AND MICHAEL R. STRAIN,
> "Why We Shouldn't Raise the Minimum Wage"

Hasset and Strain's claim about raising the minimum wage is explicitly stated (they are "against" it), as is a major reason for that position.

Come up with REASONS and EVIDENCE. List all the reasons supporting your position that you discovered in your research. Which ones will be most persuasive to your audience? Then jot down all the evidence you have to support those reasons—facts, quotations, statistics, examples, testimony, visuals, and so on. Remember that what counts as evidence varies across audiences and disciplines. Some are persuaded by testimonials, while others want statistical data. Finally, look for any FALLACIES or weak reasons or evidence, and decide whether you need to do further research.

Identify other positions. Carefully consider COUNTERARGUMENTS and other points of view on the topic and how you will account for them. At the very least, you need to acknowledge other positions that are prominent in

the larger conversation about the topic and to treat them fairly. If you disagree with a position, you need to offer reasons why and to do so respectfully.

Organize and start writing

Once you have a fair sense of how you will present your position, it's time to
write out a draft. If you have trouble getting started, it might help to think
about the larger conversation about the topic that's already going on—and
to think of your draft as a moment when you get to say what *you* think.

Be guided by your THESIS. As you begin to organize, type it at the top of
your page so that you can keep looking back to it to be sure that each part of
your text supports the thesis.

Give REASONS for your position, with supporting EVIDENCE. Determine an
order for presenting your reasons, perhaps starting with the one you think
will speak most directly to your audience.

Don't forget to consider COUNTERARGUMENTS. Acknowledge positions
other than your own, and respond to what they say.

Draft an OPENING. Introduce your topic, and provide any background
information your audience may need. State your position clearly, perhaps as
a response to what others have said about your topic. Say something about
why the issue matters, why your audience should care.

Draft a CONCLUSION. You might want to end by summing up your position
and by answering the "so what" question: why does your topic matter—and
who cares? Make sure you give a strong takeaway message. What are the
implications of your argument? What do you want readers to remember or
do as a result of reading what you've written?

Look critically at your draft, get response—and revise

Go through your draft carefully, looking critically at the position you stake
out, the reasons and evidence you provide in support of it, and the way you
present them to your audience. For this review, play the "doubting game"

with yourself by asking "Who says?" and "So what?" and "Can this be done better?" at every point.

Being tough on yourself now will pay off by showing you where you need to shore up your arguments. As you work through your draft, make notes on what you plan to do in your revision.

Next, ask some classmates or friends to read and respond to your draft. Here are some questions that can help you or others read over a draft of writing that takes a position.

- *Is the position stated explicitly?* Is there a clear THESIS sentence—and if not, is one needed? Does it need to be qualified, or should it be stated more strongly?

- *What positions are you responding to?* What is the larger conversation?

- *Is it clear why the topic matters?* Why do you care about the topic, and why should your audience care?

- *How effective is the* OPENING*?* How does it capture your audience's interest? How else might you begin?

- *Is there sufficient background information?* What other information might the audience need?

- *How would you describe the* STANCE *and* TONE —and are they appropriate to your audience and purpose? Does the tone seem both authoritative and reasonable?

- *What* REASONS *do you give for the position, and what* EVIDENCE *do you provide for those reasons?* What are the strongest reasons and evidence given? the weakest? What other evidence or reasons are needed to support this position?

- *How trustworthy are the sources you've cited?* Are QUOTATIONS, SUMMARIES, and PARAPHRASES smoothly integrated into the text—and is it clear where you are speaking and where (and why) you are citing others?

- *What other positions do you consider, and do you treat them fairly?* Are there other COUNTERARGUMENTS you should address as well? How well do you answer possible objections to your position?

- *How is the draft organized?* Is it easy to follow, with clear TRANSITIONS from one point to the next? Are there headings—and if not, would they help? What about the organization could be improved?

- *Is the* **STYLE** *appropriate to the audience and purpose?* Could the style— choice of words, kinds of sentences—be improved in any way?

- *How effective is your text* **DESIGN**? Have you used any visuals to support your position—and if so, have you written captions that explain how they contribute to the argument? If not, what visuals might be appropriate? Is there any information that would be easier to follow if it were presented in a chart or table?

- *How does the draft* **CONCLUDE**? Is the conclusion forceful and memorable? How else might you conclude?

- *Consider the title.* Does it make clear what the text is about, and does it make a reader want to read on?

- *What is your overall impression of the draft?* Will it persuade your audience to accept the position—and if not, why? Even if they don't accept the position, would they consider it a plausible one?

Revise your draft in light of your own observations and any feedback from others—keeping your audience and purpose firmly in mind, as always.

⟋⟍◎ *REFLECT. Once you've completed your essay, let it settle for a while before you look back at it with a critical eye. How well did you argue your point? What additional revisions would you make if you could? Research shows that such reflections help "lock in" what you learn for future use.*

Delete Your Social Media Accounts Right Now

JARON LANIER

Lᴇᴛ's sᴛᴀʀᴛ ᴡɪᴛʜ cats.
Cats are everywhere online. They make the memiest memes and the cutest videos.

Why cats more than dogs?

Dogs didn't come to ancient humans begging to live with us; we domesticated them. They've been bred to be obedient. They take to training and they are predictable. They work for us. That's not to say anything against dogs. It's great that they're loyal and dependable.

Cats are different. They came along and partly domesticated themselves. 5
They are not predictable. Popular dog videos tend to show off training, while the most wildly popular cat videos are the ones that capture weird and surprising behaviors.

Cats are smart, but not a great choice if you want an animal that takes to training reliably. Watch a cat circus online, and what's so touching is that the cats are clearly making their own minds up about whether to do a trick they've learned, or to do nothing, or to wander into the audience.

JARON LANIER, often referred to as the "father of virtual reality," is a scientist, musician, and writer who focuses on virtual reality and advocates for sustainable economics in a digital world. He is the author of *Who Owns the Future* and *You Are Not a Gadget*. His book *Dawn of the New Everything* was named one of the best books of 2017 by the *Wall Street Journal* and the *Economist*. This piece is from his 2018 book, *Ten Arguments for Deleting Your Social Media Accounts Right Now*.

Cats have done the seemingly impossible: They've integrated themselves into the modern high-tech world without giving themselves up. They are still in charge. There is no worry that some stealthy meme crafted by algorithms and paid for by a creepy, hidden oligarch has taken over your cat. No one has taken over your cat; not you, not anyone.

Oh, how we long to have that certainty not just about our cats, but about ourselves! Cats on the internet are our hopes and dreams for the future of people on the internet.

Meanwhile, even though we love dogs, we don't want to *be* dogs, at least in terms of power relationships with people, and we're afraid Facebook and the like are turning us into dogs. When we are triggered to do something crappy online, we might call it a response to a "dog whistle." Dog whistles can only be heard by dogs. We worry that we're falling under stealthy control.

This is about how to be a cat. How can you remain autonomous in a world 　10 where you are under constant surveillance and are constantly prodded by algorithms run by some of the richest corporations in history, which have no way of making money except by being paid to manipulate your behavior? How can you be a cat, despite that?

Something entirely new is happening in the world. Just in the last five or ten years, nearly everyone started to carry a little device called a smartphone on their person all the time that's suitable for algorithmic behavior modification. A lot of us are also using related devices called smart speakers on our kitchen counters or in our car dashboards. We're being tracked and measured constantly, and receiving engineered feedback all the time. We're being hypnotized little by little by technicians we can't see, for purposes we don't know. We're all lab animals now.

Algorithms gorge on data about you, every second. What kinds of links do you click on? What videos do you watch all the way through? How quickly are you moving from one thing to the next? Where are you when you do these things? Who are you connecting with in person and online? What facial expressions do you make? How does your skin tone change in different situations? What were you doing just before you decided to buy something or not? Whether to vote or not?

All these measurements and many others have been matched up with similar readings about the lives of multitudes of other people through massive spying. Algorithms correlate what you do with what almost everyone else has done.

The algorithms don't really understand you, but there is power in numbers, especially in large numbers. If a lot of other people who like the foods you like were also more easily put off by pictures of a candidate portrayed in a pink border instead of a blue one, then you *probably* will be too, and no one needs to know why. Statistics are reliable, but only as idiot demons.

Are you sad, lonely, scared? Happy, confident? Getting your period? Experiencing a peak of class anxiety? 15

So-called advertisers can seize the moment when you are perfectly primed and then influence you with messages that have worked on other people who share traits and situations with you.

I say "so-called" because it's just not right to call direct manipulation of people advertising. Advertisers used to have a limited chance to make a pitch, and that pitch might have been sneaky or annoying, but it was fleeting. Furthermore, lots of people saw the same TV or print ad; it wasn't adapted to individuals. The biggest difference was that you weren't monitored and assessed all the time so that you could be fed dynamically optimized stimuli—whether "content" or ad—to engage and alter you.

Now everyone who is on social media is getting individualized, continuously adjusted stimuli, without a break, so long as they use their smartphones. What might once have been called advertising must now be understood as continuous behavior modification on a titanic scale.

Please don't be insulted. Yes, I am suggesting that you might be turning, just a little, into a well-trained dog, or something less pleasant, like a lab rat or a robot. That you're being remote-controlled, just a little, by clients of big corporations. But if I'm right, then becoming aware of it might just free you, so give this a chance, okay?

A scientific movement called behaviorism arose before computers were 20 invented. Behaviorists studied new, more methodical, sterile, and nerdy ways to train animals and humans.

One famous behaviorist was B. F. Skinner. He set up a methodical system, known as a Skinner box, in which caged animals got treats when they did something specific. There wasn't anyone petting or whispering to the animal, just a purely isolated mechanical action—a new kind of training for modern times. Various behaviorists, who often gave off rather ominous vibes, applied this method to people. Behaviorist strategies often worked, which freaked everyone out, eventually leading to a bunch of creepy "mind control" sci-fi and horror movie scripts.

An unfortunate fact is that you can train someone using behaviorist techniques, *and the person doesn't even know it*. Until very recently, this rarely happened unless you signed up to be a test subject in an experiment in the basement of a university's psychology building. Then you'd go into a room and be tested while someone watched you through a one-way mirror. Even though you knew an experiment was going on, you didn't realize *how* you were being manipulated. At least you gave consent to be manipulated in *some* way. (Well, not always. There were all kinds of cruel experiments performed on prisoners, on poor people, and especially on racial targets.)

What has become suddenly normal—pervasive surveillance and constant, subtle manipulation—is unethical, cruel, dangerous, and inhumane. Dangerous? Oh, yes, because who knows who's going to use that power, and for what? . . .

I realize that we live in a world of stunning inequality, and not everyone has the same options. Whoever you are, I hope you have options to explore what your life might be, especially if you are young. You need to make sure your own brain, and your own life, isn't in a rut. Maybe you can go explore wilderness or learn a new skill. Take risks. But whatever form your self-exploration takes, do at least one thing: detach from the behavior-modification empires for a while—six months, say? Note that I didn't name [my] book *Arguments for Deleting Your Social Media Accounts Right Now and Keeping Them Deleted Forever*. After you experiment, you'll know yourself better. Then decide.

See Lanier's TED talk in which he makes a case that we need to remake the internet at everyonesanauthor.tumblr.com.

Author's Note, March 2018

This book was written primarily during the final months of 2017, but events in 2018 turned out to be explosively relevant. The manuscript was done, done, done—headed to the printer—when the sorry revelations of the Cambridge Analytica scandal fueled a sudden, grassroots movement of people deleting Facebook accounts.

Unfortunately, not all public figures and thought leaders handled the moment with the courage that was required. There were pundits who tried to quit but could not. There were others who pointed out that not everyone is privileged enough to quit, so it felt cruel to leave the less fortunate behind. Others said it was irrelevant to quit because the thing that mattered was pressuring governments to regulate Facebook. Overall, the attitude of professional commentators regarding account deleters was smug and dismissive. And dead wrong.

C'mon people! Yes, being able to quit is a privilege; many genuinely can't. But if you have the latitude to quit and don't, you are not supporting the less fortunate; you are only reinforcing the system in which many people are trapped. I am living proof that you can have a public life in media without social media accounts. Those of us with options must explore those options or they will remain only theoretical. Business follows money, so we who have options have power and responsibility. You, you, you have the affirmative responsibility to invent and demonstrate ways to live without the crap that is destroying society. Quitting is the only way, for now, to learn what can replace our grand mistake.

Thinking about the Text

1. Why does Lanier open his argument with an **ANALOGY** between cats and dogs—and people? How effective do you find this opening strategy and why?

2. Lanier says that he is "living proof that you can have a public life in media without social media accounts." Take a few minutes to look up Lanier and read about his career; do you find that he really has "a public life in media without social media"? How does having a public life, without media, affect his **CREDIBILITY** as an author?

3. Lanier argues that social media train us (like you can train a dog) and that as a result we are losing free will. While Lanier doesn't take up **COUNTERARGUMENTS** in this section of his book, what counterarguments can you offer to his major claim?

4. How would you describe Lanier's **STANCE** and **TONE**? What particular words and phrases lead you to that description?

5. At the end of his book, Lanier makes a final plea: "But whatever form your self-exploration takes, do at least one thing: detach from the behavior-modification empires for a while—six months, say?" Try accepting Lanier's challenge and avoid your accounts—for a week, or even just 24 hours. Then write a few paragraphs describing what you discovered about yourself during this experiment and take a **POSITION** of your own in response in Lanier.

On Buying Local

KATHERINE SPRIGGS

AMERICANS TODAY can eat pears in the spring in Minnesota, oranges in the summer in Montana, asparagus in the fall in Maine, and cranberries in the winter in Florida. In fact, we can eat pretty much any kind of produce anywhere at any time of the year. But what is the cost of this convenience? In this essay, I will explore some answers to this question and argue that we should give up a little bit of convenience in favor of buying local.

"Buying local" means that consumers choose to buy food that has been grown, raised, or produced as close to their homes as possible ("Buy Local"). Buying local is an important part of the response to many environmental issues we face today (fig. I). It encourages the development of small farms, which are often more environmentally sustainable than large farms, and thus strengthens local markets and supports small rural economies. By demonstrating a commitment to buying local, Americans could set an example for global environmentalism.

In 2010, the international community is facing many environmental challenges, including global warming, pollution, and dwindling fossil fuel resources. Global warming is attributed to the release of greenhouse gases such as carbon dioxide and methane, most commonly emitted in the burning of fossil fuels. It is such a pressing problem that scientists estimate that in the year 2030,

KATHERINE SPRIGGS wrote this essay for a writing course she took in her first year at Stanford University.

Fig. 1. Shopping at a farmers' market is one good way to support small farms and strengthen the local economy. Timothy Mulholland. *Dane County Farmers Market on the Square Madison Wisconsin*. 2008, *Alamy*.

there will be no glaciers left in Glacier National Park ("Global Warming Statistics"). The United States is especially guilty of contributing to the problem, producing about a quarter of all global greenhouse gas emissions, and playing a large part in pollution and shrinking world oil supplies as well ("Record Increase"). According to a CNN article published in 2000, the United States manufactures more than 1.5 billion pounds of chemical pesticides a year that can pollute our water, soil, and air (Baum). Agriculture is particularly interconnected with all of these issues. Almost three-fourths of the pesticides produced in the United States are used in agriculture (Baum). Most produce is shipped many miles before it is sold to consumers, and shipping our food long distances is costly in both the amount of fossil fuel it uses and the greenhouse gases it produces.

A family friend and farmer taught me firsthand about the effects of buying local. Since I was four years old, I have spent every summer on a 150-acre farm in rural Wisconsin, where my family has rented our 75 tillable acres to a farmer who lives nearby. Mr. Lermio comes from a family that has farmed the area for generations. I remember him sitting on our porch at dusk wearing his blue striped overalls and dirty white T-shirt, telling my parents about all of the changes in the area since he was a kid. "Things sure are different around here," he'd say. He told us that all the farms in that region used to milk about 30 head of cattle each. Now he and the other farmers were selling their herds to industrial-scale farms milking 4,000 head each. The shift came when milk started being processed on a large scale rather than at small local cheese factories. Milk is now shipped to just a few large factories where it is either bottled or processed into cheese or other dairy products. The milk and products from these factories are then shipped all across the country. "You see," Mr. Lermio would tell us, "it's just not worth shipping the milk from my 20 cows all the way to Gays Mills. You just can't have a small herd anymore." Farming crops is also different now. Machinery is expensive and hard to pay off with profits from small fields. The Lermio family has been buying and renting fields all around the area, using their tractors to farm hundreds of acres. Because they can no longer sell locally, Mr. Lermio and many other rural farmers have to move towards larger-scale farming to stay afloat.

　　Buying local could help reverse the trend towards industrial-scale farming, ₅ of which the changes in Wisconsin over Mr. Lermio's lifetime are just one

Fig. 2.　A small polyculture farm. *Crops Growing on a Farm.* 2013, *iStock.*

example. Buying local benefits small farmers by not forcing them to compete with larger farms across the country. For example, if consumers bought beef locally, beef cattle would be raised in every region and their meat would be sold locally rather than shipped from a small number of big ranches in Texas and Montana. Small farms are often polycultures—they produce many different kinds of products (fig. 2). The Lermios' original farm, for example, grew corn, hay, oats, and alfalfa. They also had milking cattle, chickens, and a few hogs. Large farms are often monocultures—they raise only one kind of crop or animal (fig. 3). The Lermio family has been moving towards becoming a monoculture; they raise only three field crops, and they don't have any animals. Buying local, as was common in the first half of the twentieth century, encourages small polyculture farms that sell a variety of products locally (McCauley).

For environmental purposes, the small polyculture farms that buying local encourages have many advantages over industrial-scale monoculture farms because they are more sustainable. Small farmers tend to value local natural resources more than industrial-scale farmers do and are therefore more conscientious in their farming methods. Small farms are also intrinsically more sustainable. As mentioned, small farms are more likely to be polycultures—to

Fig. 3. A large monoculture farm. *Aerial Mid-Summer Farm Surrounded by Cornfields.* 2013, *iStock.*

do many different things with the land—and using a field for different purposes does not exhaust the soil the way continually farming one crop does. Rotating crops or using a field alternately for pasture and for crops keeps the land "healthy." On small farms, sometimes a farmer will pasture his cattle in the previous year's cornfield; the cattle eat some of the stubble left from last year's crop and fertilize the field. The land isn't wasted or exhausted from continuous production. I've even seen one organic farmer set up his pigpen so that the pigs plow his blueberry field just by walking up around their pen. This kind of dual usage wouldn't be found on a large monoculture farm. Most big farms use their fields exclusively either for crops or for pasture. Modern fertilizers, herbicides, and pesticides allow farmers to harvest crops from even unhealthy land, but this is a highly unsustainable model. Farming chemicals can pollute groundwater and destroy natural ecosystems.

   Not only are small farms a more sustainable, eco-friendly model than big commercial farms, but buying local has other advantages as well. Buying local, for example, would reduce the high cost of fuel and energy used to transport food across the world and would bring long-term benefits as well. It is currently estimated that most produce in the United States is shipped about fifteen-hundred miles before it is sold—it travels about the distance from Nebraska to New York ("Why Buy Local?"). Eighty percent of all strawberries grown in the United States are from California ("Strawberry Fruit Facts"). They are shipped from California all around the country even though strawberries can be grown in Wisconsin, New York, Tennessee, and most other parts of the United States. No matter how efficient our shipping systems, shipping food thousands of miles is expensive—in dollars, in oil, and in the carbon dioxide it produces (fig. 4). One of the main reasons that produce is shipped long distances is that fruits and vegetables don't grow everywhere all year around. Even though strawberries grow in a lot of places during the early summer, they grow only in Florida in the winter, or in California from spring to fall (Rieger). Americans have become accustomed to being able to buy almost any kind of produce at any time of the year. A true commitment to buying local would accommodate local season and climate. Not everything will grow everywhere, but the goal of buying local should be to eliminate all unnecessary shipping by buying things from as close to home as possible and eating as many things in season as possible.

   Some argue that buying local can actually have negative environmental effects; and their arguments add important qualifiers to supporting small local farms. Alex Avery, the director of research and education at the Center for

Fig 4. Interstate trucking is expensive financially and ecologically. *Interstate Traffic with Trucks.* 2012, *iStock.*

Global Food Issues, has said that we should "buy food from the world region where it grows best" (qtd. in MacDonald). His implication is that it would be more wasteful to try to grow pineapples in the Northeast than to have them shipped from the Caribbean. He makes a good point: trying to grow all kinds of food all over the world would be a waste of time and energy. Buying local should instead focus on buying *as much as possible* from nearby farmers. It has also been argued that buying locally will be detrimental to the environment because small farms are not as efficient in their use of resources as large farms. This is a common misconception and actually depends on how economists measure efficiency. Small farms are less efficient than large farms in the total output of one crop per acre, but they are more efficient in total output of all crops per acre (McCauley). When buying locally, the consumer should try to buy from these more efficient polyculture farms. Skeptics of buying local also say that focusing food cultivation in the United States will be worse for the environment because farmers here use more industrial equipment than farmers in the third world (MacDonald). According to the Progressive Policy Institute, however, only thirteen percent of the American diet is imported ("98.7 Percent"). This is a surprisingly small percentage, especially considering that seafood is one of the top imports. It should also be considered that as countries around the world become wealthier, they will industrialize, so exploiting manual labor in the third world would only be a temporary solution (MacDonald). The environmental benefits now, and in the long run, of buying local outweigh any such immediate disadvantages.

Critics have also pointed to negative global effects of buying local, but buying local could have positive global effects too. Speaking with the *Christian Science Monitor*, John Clark, author of *Worlds Apart: Civil Society and the Battle for Ethical Globalization*, argues that buying local hurts poor workers in third world countries. He cites the fact that an estimated fifty thousand children in Bangladesh lost their jobs in the garment industry because of the 1996 Western boycott of clothing made in third world sweatshops (qtd. in MacDonald). It cannot be denied that if everyone buys locally, repercussions on the global market seem unavoidable. Nonetheless, if the people of the United States demonstrated their commitment to buying local, it could open up new conversations about environmentalism. Our government lags far behind the European Union in environmental legislation. Through selective shopping, the people of the United States could demonstrate to the world our commitment to environmentalism.

Arguments that decentralizing food production will be bad for the national 10 economy also ignore the positive effects small farms have on local economies. John Tschirhart, a professor of environmental economics at the University of Wyoming, argues that buying locally would be bad for our national economy because food that we buy locally can often be produced more cheaply somewhere else in the United States (qtd. in Arias Terry). This seems debatable since most of the locally grown things we buy in grocery stores today aren't much more expensive, if at all, than their counterparts from far away. In New York City, apples from upstate New York are often cheaper than the industrial, waxed Granny Smiths from Washington State or Chile; buying locally should indeed save shipping costs. Nonetheless, it is true that locally grown food can often be slightly more expensive than "industrially grown" food. Probably one of the biggest factors in the difference in price is labor cost. Labor is cheap in third world countries, and large U.S. farms are notorious for hiring immigrant laborers. It is hard to justify the exploitation of such artificially cheap labor. While the case for the economic disadvantages of buying local is dubious, buying local has clear positive economic effects in local communities. Local farms hire local workers and bring profits to small rural communities. One study of pig farmers in Virginia showed that, compared to corporate-owned farms, small farms created ten percent more permanent local jobs, a twenty percent higher increase in local retail sales, and a thirty-seven percent higher increase in local per capita income (McCauley).

Buying locally grown and produced food has clear environmental, social, and economic advantages. On the surface it seems that buying local could constitute a big personal sacrifice. It may be slightly more expensive, and it wouldn't allow us to buy any kind of produce at any time of the year, a change that would no doubt take getting used to. But perhaps these limitations would actually make food more enjoyable. If strawberries were sold only in the summer, they would be more special and we might even enjoy them more. Food that is naturally grown in season is fresher and also tends to taste better. Fresh summer strawberries are sweeter than their woody winter counterparts. Buying local is an easy step that everyone can take towards "greener" living.

Works Cited

Arias Terry, Ana. "Buying Local vs. Buying Cheap." *Conscious Choice: The Journal of Ecology and Natural Living*, Jan. 2007, www.alternet.org /story/342/buying_local_vs._buying_cheap. Accessed 27 Apr. 2011.

Baum, Michele Dula. "U.S. Government Issues Standards on Organic Food." *CNN*, 20 Dec. 2000, www.cnn.com/FOOD/specials/2000 /organic.main/story.html. Accessed 25 Apr. 2011.

"Buy Local." *Sustainable Table*. Grace Communications Foundation, Jan. 2007, www.sustainabletable.org. Accessed 27 Apr. 2011.

"Global Warming Statistics." *Effects of Global Warming*, 2007, www .effectofglobalwarming.com/global-warming-statistics.html.

MacDonald, G. Jeffrey. "Is Buying Local Always Best?" *Christian Science Monitor*, 24 July 2006, www.csmonitor.com/2006/0724/p13s02-lifo.html.

McCauley, Marika Alena. "Small Farms: The Optimum Sustainable Agriculture Model." *Oxfam America*, 2007, oxfamamerica.org /whatwedo/where_we_work/united_states/news_publications /food_farm/art2570.html. Accessed 27 Apr. 2011.

"98.7 Percent of Imported Food Never Inspected." *Progressive Policy Institute*, 7 Sept. 2007, www.ppionline.org/ppi_ci.cfm?knlgAreaID=85&subsecID =108&contentID. Accessed 25 Apr. 2011.

"Record Increase in U.S. Greenhouse Gas Emissions Reported." *Environment News Service*, 18 Apr. 2006, ens-newsire.com/ens/apr2006/2006-04 -18-02.asp.

Rieger, Mark. "Strawberry—*Fragaria X ananassa*." *Mark's Fruit Crops*, 2006, fruit-crops.com/strawberry-fragaria-x-ananassa.

"Strawberry Fruit Facts Page." *Grown in California*, Gourmet Shopping
    Network, grownincalifornia.com/fruit-facts/strawberry-facts.html.
    Accessed 25 Apr. 2011.
"Why Buy Local?" *LocalHarvest*, localharvest.org/buylocal.jsp. Accessed
    23 Apr. 2011.

Thinking about the Text

1. It's clear that this is a topic that matters to Katherine Spriggs. Has she
   convinced you that it matters—and if so, how? How does Spriggs establish the importance of her topic?

2. What **COUNTERARGUMENTS** or positions other than her own does
   Spriggs consider—and how does she respond in each case?

3. Choose a section of Spriggs's essay that you find especially effective or
   ineffective. Referring to the genre features listed on page 147, describe
   what makes this part of her argument persuasive—or not.

4. Spriggs includes several photos in her essay. How do they contribute to
   her argument?

5. Consider your own response to Spriggs's position. Write an essay in
   response to one of the issues she raises. State your **POSITION** explicitly,
   and be sure to consider arguments other than your own.

THIRTEEN

"Here's What Happened"

Writing a Narrative

**O, TELL ME WHAT HAPPENED."** Anytime we ask someone about an incident at work or an event at school, we are asking for a narrative: tell us about what happened. Narratives are stories, and they are fundamental parts of our everyday lives. When we tell someone about a movie we've seen or a basketball game we played in, we often use narrative. When we want someone to understand something that we did, we might tell a story that explains our actions. When we post to *Instagram*, we often write about something we've just done or seen.

If you wrote an essay as part of your college applications, chances are that you were required to write a narrative. Here, for instance, are instructions from two colleges' applications:

> Describe a meaningful event or experience and how it has changed or affected the person you are today.　　　　—HOFSTRA UNIVERSITY

> Describe a personal moral or ethical dilemma and how it impacted your life.　　　　—HAMPTON UNIVERSITY

Each of these prompts asks applicants to write a narrative about some aspect of their lives. In each case they need to do more than just tell a good story; they need to make a clear point about why it matters.

Narrative is a powerful way to get an audience's attention. Telling a good story can even help establish your authority as a writer. Take a look, for example, at the opening paragraphs from an obituary for the "Queen of Soul," Aretha Franklin, from the *Guardian*:

> On a crisp, sparkling day in January 2009, Aretha Franklin stood on the steps of the Capitol in Washington, an ample figure swathed in a spectacular ensemble of coat and hat in two shades of grey, singing "My Country, 'Tis of Thee" to her new president. All around her, and down the full length of the National Mall, the vast audience included African Americans with tears in their eyes, celebrating the inauguration of Barack Obama. She was facing west, as hundreds of thousands of slaves had done when they landed on a bitter shore at the conclusion of their portage from Africa. "Let freedom ring," she sang, in the anthem's famous exhortation, and many millions watching on television around the world could not help but share the resonance of a historic moment.
>
> Franklin, who has died aged 76, sounded exalted that day. She almost always did, even when handcuffed to unsympathetic material. Her voice could scald or soothe, singing with equal intimacy and intensity to her God or a faithless lover.
>
> —RICHARD WILLIAMS, "Aretha Franklin Obituary"

Author Richard Williams could have opened this obituary the way he ended it: "Aretha Louise Franklin, singer, pianist and songwriter, born 25 March 1942; died 16 August 2018." However, that statement doesn't draw readers in the way that opening with a story of Franklin singing at Barack Obama's 2009 inauguration does. With vivid and fascinating details, he piques our interest. We want to keep reading about an artist whose "voice could scald and soothe."

Images, too, can tell stories, as the cartoon of Franklin on the following page shows. Artist Jamaal Rolle captures Franklin in mid-song, with eyes closed and microphone in hand, showing us the artist. Surrounding her are the titles of some of her biggest hits. These titles, familiar to Franklin's fans, and the image of a singing Franklin tell the story of the memories her songs invoke, their place in American culture, and the powerful and successful singer that Aretha Franklin was.

Think about some of the powerful personal narratives you've read, perhaps the *Narrative of the Life of Frederick Douglass* or Anne Frank's *Diary of*

One cartoonist's tribute to Aretha Franklin.

a Young Girl. We could, of course, read about their lives on *Wikipedia*, but a good narrative provides more than just the facts; it gives us a well-told story that captures not only our attention but also our imagination.

So what exactly is a narrative? For our purposes, narrative is a kind of writing that presents events in some kind of time sequence with a distinct beginning, middle, and ending (but not necessarily in strict chronological order) and that is written for the purpose of making a point. That is, to write a narrative it is not enough to simply report a sequence of events ("this happened, then that happened"), which is often what children do when they tell stories. Narrative essays, especially in college, are meaningful ways of making sense of our experiences, of what goes on around us—and of illustrating a point, making an argument, or writing about the lives of others.

REFLECT. Think about some stories that are told in your favorite songs or music videos, that you hear in sermons, or that your grandma tells. Make a list of the stories that you hear, read, see, or tell in one day and the subjects of those stories. You'll begin to see how narratives are an important way that we communicate with each other.

Across Academic Disciplines

The narrative essay is a common assignment in the humanities and increasingly in other academic fields as well. In a *composition* class, you may be asked to write a literacy narrative about how you learned to read or write or a personal narrative about an important person or experience in your life. In a *history* class, you may be asked to take data from archives and construct a narrative about a particular historical event. (Some think that historians focus on dates and facts about incidents from the past, but actually they are generally piecing together narratives that provide a context for interpreting what those dates and facts mean.) In *medicine*, patient accounts and medical histories play a key role in diagnosis and treatment and provide important documentation for insurance companies. In the *sciences*, lab reports tell the story of how researchers conducted an experiment and interpreted the data they collected. Since narratives take different forms across disciplines, one challenge you'll face will be to determine which narrative elements are valued or even required in a particular situation.

Visit the Digital Archive of Literacy Narratives (thedaln .org), a site sponsored by Ohio State and Georgia State where you can read literacy narratives as well as post your own.

Across Media

The medium you use makes a big difference in the way you tell a story. *Video*, for example, presents a wide range of possibilities. TV broadcasts of football games cut between shots of players, coaches, and fans. Commentators review key plays in slow motion or from multiple angles, diagram plays on the screen, and pull up player statistics—all of which combine to tell the story of what's happening on the field. These same stories will be told differently in *print*, with written words, still photos, and tables of statistics to show how the players performed.

Analysts circle players and draw arrows to show those watching the game on TV what just happened.

When you're writing a narrative, you'll want to think about what media will best suit your audience and purpose. But you won't always have a choice. If you're assigned to work in a specific medium, think about whether a narrative would help get your message across. Well-told stories are a good way to engage your audience's attention in an *oral presentation*, for instance, and to help them remember what you say.

REFLECT. *Compare narratives in different media. From the many kinds of narratives you encounter in one day—in books or magazines, on* YouTube *or in video games, in textbooks or conversations with friends—choose two narratives on the same topic from different media that you find most interesting. Think about the similarities and differences between the ways the two stories are told. What would change about each narrative if it were presented in a different medium?*

Across Cultures and Communities

What makes a good story often depends on who's telling the story and who's listening. Not only is that the case for individuals, but different communities and cultures also tell stories in unique ways and value particular things in them.

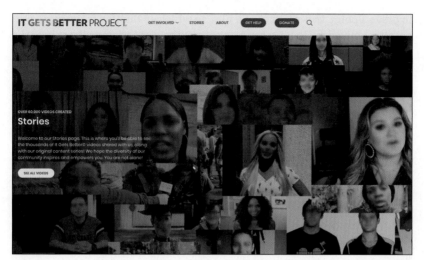

➤ *GO TO itgetsbetter.org, the award-winning site of the It Gets Better Project, begun in 2010 to show LGBTQ+ youths that life will get better "if they can just get through their teen years." There you'll find thousands of videos, including many personal narratives from adults who tell how their lives got better. There's also a button to add your story, in video or writing. Watch some of the videos and read some of the written stories. Which do you find more powerful, and why?*

Many *Native American tribes* consider narrative an important tradition and art form, so much so that storytellers hold a place of honor. In much of *West Africa*, the griots are the official storytellers, entrusted with telling the history of a village or town through recitation and song. And in many *Appalachian communities*, storytelling functions as a way to pass down family and community history. As in West Africa, good storytellers enjoy high status in Appalachia.

In many cultures and communities, stories are the way that history is passed down from generation to generation. Think about the ways that family histories are passed down in your family or community—through oral stories? photo albums? home videos?

Across Genres

Narrative is often a useful strategy for writers working in other genres. For example, in an essay **ARGUING A POSITION**, you may use a narrative example to prove a point. In a **REVIEW** of a film, in which evaluation is the main purpose, you may need to tell a brief story from the plot to demonstrate how the film meets (or does not meet) a specific evaluative criterion. These are only two of the many ways in which narrative can be used as part of a text.

CHARACTERISTIC FEATURES

There is no one way to tell a story. Most written narratives, however, have a number of common features, revolving around the following characteristics and questions:

- A clearly identified event: What happened? Who was involved?
- A clearly described setting: When and where did it happen?
- Vivid, descriptive details: What makes the story come alive?
- A consistent point of view: Who's telling the story?
- A clear point: Why does the story matter?

A Clearly Identified Event:
What Happened? Who Was Involved?

Narratives are based on an event or series of events, presented in a way that makes audiences want to know how the story will turn out. Consider this paragraph by Mike Rose, in which he narrates how he, as a marginal high school student with potential, got into college with the help of his senior-year English teacher, Jack MacFarland:

> My grades stank. I had A's in biology and a handful of B's in a few English and social science classes. All the rest were C's—or worse. MacFarland said I would do well in his class and laid down the law about doing well in others. Still the record for my first three years wouldn't have been acceptable to any four-year school. To nobody's surprise, I was turned down flat by USC and UCLA. But Jack MacFarland was on the case. He had received his bachelor's degree from Loyola, so he made calls to old professors and talked to somebody in admissions and wrote me a strong letter. Loyola finally accepted me as a probationary student. I would be on trial for the first year, and if I did okay, I would be granted regular status. MacFarland also intervened to get me a loan, for I could never have af-

forded a private college without it. Four more years of religion classes and four more years of boys at one school, girls at another. But at least I was going to college. Amazing.

—MIKE ROSE, *Lives on the Boundary*

As inspiring as it is to learn of someone with lots of C's (or worse) getting into college, it's not the actual facts that make this narrative worth reading; rather, it's the way the facts are presented—in other words, the way the story is told.

The narrator grabs our attention with his first sentence ("My grades stank"), then lays out the challenges he faced ("turned down flat by USC and UCLA"), and ends with a flourish ("Amazing"). He could have told us what happened much more briefly—but then it would have been just a sequence of facts; instead, he told us a story. As the author of a narrative, you'll want to be sure to get the facts down, but that won't be enough. Your challenge will be to tell about "what happens" in a way that gets your audience's attention and makes them care enough to keep on reading.

A Clearly Described Setting:
When and Where Did It Happen?

Narratives need to be situated clearly within time and space in order for readers to understand what's going on. For that reason, you will generally arrange your story in **CHRONOLOGICAL ORDER** starting at the beginning and moving straight ahead to the end. There are times, though, when you may choose to present a narrative in reverse chronological order, starting at the end and looking back at the events that led up to it—or with a flashback or flash-forward that jumps back to the past or ahead to the future. Whether you tell your story in chronological order or not, the sequence of events needs to be clear to your audience.

Also important is that your audience get a clear idea of the place(s) where the events occur. Time and space work together to create a scene that your audience can visualize and follow, as they do in the following example from student Minh Vu's essay "Dirty Nails," which documents growing up in his family's nail salon.

I was born in my family's nail salon. It was in the waxing room, and my first swaddle was made up of giant waxing strips. Normally, they're used to tear the hair off people. For me, they were warmth and protection.

I was raised within glass doors kept shiny with diluted Windex, among towering boxes of acetone, and atop giant pedicure thrones. Such was my childhood kingdom. Alphabet blocks were replaced by white Arial stickers I used to spell out "JEL MANICURE" and "BIKIKNEE WAX" on the price board. Instead of bicycles I rode bumper cars with the pedicure stools. And the rest of my time I spent trying to fit my toddler toes into the pastel foot separators that looked like mini combs. . . . The pallor of peeling plaster was rolled over with a deep textured azure, like the ocean [my grandma] immigrated across in the 1970s. Dim overhead lights were torn down and replaced with a crystal chandelier that, albeit fake, brought illumination in a time of immigrant loneliness. And red leather diner stools from the space's past life were refurbished into sleek manicure chairs.

The nail salon was my world. It was where all of life existed.

—MINH VU, "Dirty Nails"

Minh Vu establishes the setting by providing vivid, descriptive language of the nail salon that makes up the center of his story. His first statement— "I was born in my family's nail salon"—establishes the setting of the story, but it's the details that come after that that paint a picture for readers: "glass doors kept shiny with diluted Windex," "giant pedicure thrones," "bumper cars with the pedicure stools," "pastel foot separators," and "red leather diner stools . . . refurbished into sleek manicure chairs." These details help readers, especially those who have been to nail salons, visualize where and how the writer grew up.

Vivid, Descriptive Details:
What Makes the Story Come Alive?

A report about agricultural use of antibiotics could be boring, but Tom Philpott brings the topic to life by detailing the sights, sounds, and smells of the poultry facilities he visits. Check it out on p. 997.

You may remember English teachers telling you that good writers "show rather than tell." It's an old adage that applies to narratives in particular. Vivid, descriptive detail makes the people, places, and events in a narrative come alive for an audience, helping them see, hear, smell, taste, and feel "what happened." See how the following example from *ESPN Magazine* provides colorful detail that shows us Steph Curry's brilliant technique:

Without ever taking his eyes off the rim, Curry moves to finish his shot. From his toes through his torso to the top of his head, his body is so

Steph Curry elevates for a shot during the 2018 NBA finals.

vertical, he looks as if he's coming down from the ceiling, not jumping toward it. His shooting elbow passes shoulder height, still at a perfect 90-degree angle. And when his arms are straight and extended over-head—elbow over eye, shooters call it—the left hand opens. The path of the ball, like the elbow, stays clean and true, riding the beginning of a Vitruvian arc; it doesn't hitch backward over the crown of his head or veer to the side.

Now the wrist begins its flection. The ball lifts off the tip of his index finger, then off the tip of his middle finger. His palm falls, his fingers now extended to the floor. The left arm stays perfectly still. The head never moves. . . .

Before the game, boyish smile on his face, Curry had laughed, shrug-ging his shoulders and saying, yeah, he knows the second the ball leaves his hands. As his shot now begins its descent toward the rim, he drops both arms behind his back, palms up, chest out, like a bullfighter. Yeah, he knows. "There's a difference between shooters and shot makers," says [Jerry] West. "This kid is a shot maker."

—DAVID FLEMING, "Sports' Perfect 0.4 Seconds"

Notice how the author slows down the action to show us each step in intricate detail—steps we can't possibly see or understand in the lightning-fast action of real time. With two powerful similes ("his body is so vertical, he looks as if he's coming down from the ceiling," "palms up, chest out, like a bullfighter"), Fleming's text brings Curry to life for readers.

Think about how much detail and what kind of detail your narrative needs to "come to life" for your audience. Remember that you are likely writing for readers (or listeners) unfamiliar with the story you are telling. That means that you need to choose details that help them get a vivid picture of the setting, people, and events in the narrative. When deciding whether to include direct quotations or dialogue, ask yourself if doing so would paint a scene or create a mood more effectively than a summary would.

A Consistent Point of View: Who's Telling the Story?

A good narrative is generally told from one consistent point of view. If you are writing about something that happened to you, then your narrative should be written from the first-person point of view (*I, we*). First person puts the focus on the narrator, as Georgina Kleege does in the following example, which recounts the opening moments of one of her classes:

> I tell the class, "I am legally blind." There is a pause, a collective intake of breath. I feel them look away uncertainly and then look back. After all, I just said I couldn't see. Or did I? I had managed to get there on my own—no cane, no dog, none of the usual trappings of blindness. Eyeing me askance now, they might detect that my gaze is not quite focused. My eyes are aimed in the right direction but the gaze seems to stop short of touching anything. But other people do this, sighted people, normal people, especially in an awkward situation like this one, the first day of class. An actress who delivers an aside to the audience, breaking the "fourth wall" of the proscenium, will aim her gaze somewhere above any particular pair of eyes. If I hadn't said anything, my audience might understand my gaze to be like that, a part of the performance. In these few seconds between sentences, their gaze becomes intent. They watch me glance down, or toward the door where someone's coming in late.

I'm just like anyone else. Then what did I actually mean by "legally blind"? They wait. I go on, "Some people would call me 'visually challenged.'" There is a ripple of laughter, an exhalation of relief. I'm making a joke about it. I'm poking fun at something they too find aggravating, the current mania to stick a verbal smiley-face on any human condition which deviates from the status quo. Differently abled. Handicapable. If I ask, I'm sure some of them can tell jokes about it: "Don't say 'bald,' say 'follicularly challenged.'" "He's not dead, he's metabolically stable." Knowing they are at least thinking these things, I conclude, "These are just silly ways of saying I don't see very well."　　　　　　—GEORGINA KLEEGE, "Call It Blindness"

Notice how the first-person point of view—and the repetition of *I*—keep our attention focused on Kleege. Like the students in her class, we are looking right at her.

If your narrative is about someone else's experience or about events that you have researched but did not witness, then the narrative should probably be written in third person (*he, she, it, they*). Unlike a first-person narrative, a third-person narrative emphasizes someone or something other than the narrator. Historical and medical narratives are usually written in third person, as are newswriting and sportswriting. Look at the following account of the on-field actions leading up to the moment in 1985 when quarterback Joe Theismann was tackled by Lawrence Taylor, suffering a devastating, career-ending broken leg.

From the snap of the ball to the snap of the first bone is closer to four seconds than to five. One Mississippi: The quarterback of the Washington Redskins, Joe Theismann, turns and hands the ball to running back John Riggins. He watches Riggins run two steps forward, turn, and flip the ball back to him. . . . Two Mississippi: Theismann searches for a receiver but instead sees Harry Carson coming straight at him. It's a running down—the start of the second quarter, first and 10 at midfield, with the score tied 7–7—and the New York Giants' linebacker has been so completely suckered by the fake that he's deep in the Redskins' backfield. Carson thinks he's come to tackle Riggins but Riggins is long gone, so Carson just keeps running, toward Theismann. Three Mississippi: Carson now sees that Theismann has the ball. Theismann notices Carson coming straight at him, and so he has time to avoid him. He steps up and to the side and Carson flies right on by and out of the

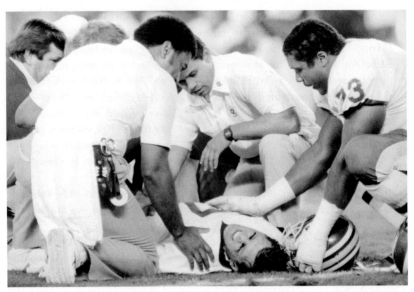

Athletic trainers surround Joe Theismann after a tackle by Lawrence Taylor broke Theismann's leg.

play. The play is now 3.5 seconds old. Until this moment it has been defined by what the quarterback can see. Now it—and he—is at the mercy of what he can't see.

—MICHAEL LEWIS, *The Blind Side*

The opening sentence takes us right into the game, with "the snap of the ball." The repetition of "one Mississippi . . . two Mississippi . . ." marches us one excruciating second (and sentence) at a time through the actions that led to an injury that became the lead story on every sports broadcast that evening and for days to come. The photograph and caption tell the story of how that play ended for Theismann.

Compare the points of view of Georgina Kleege's first-person narrative and Michael Lewis's third-person one. Notice that there is one consistent point of view in each example. As an author, you will have to determine whether your narrative is most effective told from the first-person or third-person point of view. No matter what you may have been taught in high school, the first person is acceptable in many (though not all) academic contexts. Whatever point of view you use, however, do so consistently. That is, if you refer to yourself in the narrative, do not switch between first (*I*, *we*) and third (*he, she, they*) person. (Rarely is a narrative told from a second-person—*you*—point of view.)

Part of maintaining a consistent point of view is establishing a clear time frame. Notice Michael Lewis's use of present-tense verbs in the example from *The Blind Side*. By consistently narrating the actions in the game in the present tense, the narrator, much like a play-by-play announcer, places the reader in the moment of the story being told. Using a consistent verb tense situates the actions of the event within a clear time frame.

A clear time frame does not mean that every verb in the narrative has to be in the same tense, only that the writer establishes one primary tense—usually present or past—for the main action of the story. In the example by Mike Rose on page 1015, most of the verbs are in the past tense: *said, made, talked*. But other tenses are used to indicate events that, in relation to the main action of the narrative, occurred earlier (*He had received his bachelor's degree from Loyola*) or might occur later (*I would be granted regular status*).

A Clear Point: Why Does the Story Matter?

Good narratives tell stories that matter. In academic writing in particular, narratives are told to make a point. Whether they begin by stating the point explicitly in a thesis or build toward a point that is expressed at the end, the purpose of the narrative needs to be clear to the audience. Nothing irritates an audience more than reading or listening to a story that has no point. Even if a story is interesting or entertaining, it will most likely be deemed a failure in an academic context if it does not make clear why the events matter. Consider how author and English professor bell hooks makes a point about learning to value work:

See how Zeynep Tufekci's personal narrative gives an ordinary trip to the post office a whole new perspective on p. 1065.

> "Work makes life sweet!" I often heard this phrase growing up, mainly from old black folks who did not have jobs in the traditional sense of the word. They were usually self-employed, living off the land, selling fishing worms, picking up an odd job here and there. They were people who had a passion for work. They took pride in a job done well. My Aunt Margaret took in ironing. Folks brought her clothes from miles around because she was such an expert. That was in the days when

using starch was common and she knew how to do an excellent job. Watching her iron with skill and grace was like watching a ballerina dance. Like all the other black girls raised in the fifties that I knew, it was clear to me that I would be a working woman. Even though our mother stayed home, raising her seven children, we saw her constantly at work, washing, ironing, cleaning, and cooking (she was an incredible cook). And she never allowed her six girls to imagine we would not be working women. No, she let us know that we would work and be proud to work.

—BELL HOOKS, "Work Makes Life Sweet"

Hooks opens with her main point, that "work makes life sweet!" In the sentences that follow, she explains how she learned this lesson from "old black folks who did not have jobs in the traditional sense." Through specific examples, she illustrates how they "took pride in a job done well" and passed on this pride in their work to hooks and her sisters. The explicit restatement of the point in the final sentence—that hooks and her six sisters learned from their mother that they would "work and be proud to work"— recasts the notion of "working woman" in a unique and engaging way.

In contrast to bell hooks, author and activist Roxane Gay, in a speech to publishers, withholds her main point even after announcing to the audience that she had anticipated what topic she would be asked to address:

When I received the invitation to speak at Winter Institute, I knew, even before I got the details, that I would be asked to talk about diversity in some form or fashion. This is the state of most industries, and particularly contemporary publishing. People of color are not asked about our areas of expertise as if the only thing we are allowed to be experts on is our marginalization. We are asked about how white people can do better and feel better about diversity or the lack thereof. We are asked to offer "good" white people who "mean well," absolution from the ills of racism.

—ROXANE GAY, speech to *Publishers Weekly*'s Winter Institute, 2017

Rather than announcing her main point right away, Gay provides a bit of context on the word *diversity,* including the current state of discussions about diversity. After giving this background and making a bold admission, she *then* states her main point:

> The word diversity has of late become so overused as to be meaningless. In a 2015 article for *The New York Times Magazine,* Anna Holmes wrote about the dilution of the word diversity, attributing its loss of meaning to "a combination of overuse, imprecision, inertia, and self-serving intentions."
>
> The word diversity is, in its most imprecise uses, a placeholder for issues of inclusion, recruitment, retention and representation. Diversity is a problem, seemingly without solutions. We talk about it and talk about it and talk about it and nothing much ever seems to change. And here we are today, talking about diversity yet again.
>
> I am so very tired of talking about diversity.
> Publishing has a diversity problem. This problem extends to absolutely every area of the industry. I mean, look at this room, where I can literally count the number of people of color among some 700 booksellers. There are not enough writers of color being published. When our books are published, we fight, even more than white writers, for publicity and reviews. People of color are underrepresented editorially, in book marketing, publicity, and as literary agents. People of color are underrepresented in bookselling. On and on it goes.

Gay states her main point—"Publishing has a diversity problem"—and provides further clarification and evidence of the problem. She makes the main point even more visible by focusing on the lack of diversity in the audience. In contrast to hooks, Gay moves more slowly toward her main point, describing her reaction both to the speaking invitation and the topic she was asked to cover before offering her main message outright: "People of color are underrepresented in bookselling."

As an author, don't assume that your readers will recognize the point you're trying to make. No matter how interesting you think your story is, they need to know why they should care. Why is the story important? State your main point as bell hooks and Roxane Gay do.

≋ *REFLECT. Look at a narrative in a newspaper or magazine article or on a blog or other website to see what main point it makes and how it does so. Is the main point explicitly stated in a thesis, or is it only implied? Does the narrative make clear to readers why the story is important or why they should care about it?*

WRITING A NARRATIVE / An Annotated Example

RAYA ELFADEL KHEIRBEK is an associate professor at the George Washington University School of Medicine and Health Sciences in Washington, DC, and a physician at the Veterans Affairs (VA) Medical Center in the city. This 2017 essay was originally published in *Health Affairs*, an American journal about national and global health policy and research issues.

At the VA, Healing the Doctor-Patient Relationship

RAYA ELFADEL KHEIRBEK

The title suggests what the narrative is about: resolving a conflict between doctor and patient.

Opens with an attention-grabbing quote and introduction to a central person in the story. And the author sets the scene—the Veterans Affairs (VA) Medical Center.

THE MAN'S VOICE over the phone was angry: "The VA provides terrible care!" I had promised the Veterans Affairs (VA) Medical Center's Patient Advocate office that I would connect with the man, Mr. Davis, who had called three times before to complain about his care. I was warned beforehand that he was displeased, to say the least.

With him on the line, I took a deep breath and began to look up his records. "I am sorry to hear this, Mr. Davis," I said. "Would you please tell me specifically what is bothering you? I am covering for your doctor and will do my best to help."

The author provides details about Mr. Davis's medical condition, necessary background information for readers.

Mr. Davis needed to have an MRI for his right shoulder, as was recommended by his military doctor before he separated from the service. He also was having back pain and wasn't exercising enough. He had gained twenty pounds in six months and asked if we offered liposuction.

He had met his primary care clinician, Dr. Kumar, for the first time a couple of weeks earlier and was very uncomfortable when he saw her. To him, there was great insensitivity in the VA's decision to assign him a doctor who he believed was originally from the Middle East.

"Those people wanted to kill me," he remarked to me on the phone, "and I do not appreciate having a doctor who is one of them."

Even more details that contribute to making Mr. Davis a compelling character.

"If you had a woman who was subjected to repeated rape, would you let her be examined by a male doctor?" he continued.

I knew that our policy would allow him to switch doctors, but I had no idea what to say. I had been practicing medicine for a couple of decades and naturally had encountered many types of unusual behavior. Yet I had never heard this type of comment from a patient. I composed myself and quietly explained to Mr. Davis that Dr. Kumar's family came from India. Dr. Kumar herself was born and raised in Pennsylvania and had no connection to the Middle East whatsoever.

A consistent point of view. The story is told through the author's eyes—with lots of dialogue between her and Mr. Davis.

But Mr. Davis was insistent on having a doctor who looked like him.

And he was angry.

"I am not your typical patient," he fired back. "I am smart, educated, and highly trained. I do not need your opinion. I have lived in my body for three decades. I know what I want, and your job is to deliver."

Direct quotes support the author's claims.

I told him that I wanted to meet with him to help resolve these issues and blocked off an hour the following week to meet during my administrative time. He was excited that I would be able to see him quickly, given what he referred to as the long wait time to get an appointment in the VA. He added that, based on our conversation, I seemed to be a good doctor.

While I was determined to meet and help Mr. Davis, a potential challenge loomed. I am of Middle Eastern origin. I wondered if I should reveal this information after coordinating his care and give him another opportunity to seek a different clinician. My colleagues advised me to stand tall and not give him that choice. To them, his views represented bigotry.

The author provides important details about herself.

A Veteran Affairs health care center in Phoenix, Arizona—similar to the one where Mr. Davis and Dr. Kheirbek met.

Yet Mr. Davis was not the only one struggling with the past. For me, encountering Mr. Davis brought back painful memories and forced me to stop and reflect on my years of service in the VA, my belief system, and my biases. I wondered if his "bigotry" was really so alien to the human nature in us all.

An Occupational Hazard

Details about the author's experience move the story along.

As a primary care physician working in the VA, I have heard countless stories from soldiers reliving their experiences in war zones. As an Arab American immigrant, I had followed the Iraqi war and—later—the promising start of the Arab Spring and then watched them both spiral into the chaos of death and destruction, including a civil war in my native country, Syria. I felt privileged to be a physician and an American, especially as violence took hold overseas. I could have been back home, along with everyone I worried about. I could be dead. Feeling powerless, I forced myself to watch and listen to the news. The least I could do was to be aware.

Meeting Mr. Davis

I introduced myself to Mr. Davis on a Tuesday in March 2017, less than a week after our initial phone conversation. A white man in his early thirties, he was tall and well built, with a rectangular face; a defined, slightly pointed chin; and a sturdy jaw line. He had light brown hair, small blue eyes, and a straight nose. The jacket he wore over his broad shoulders had neatly polished buttons and was slightly frayed in places. Part of his right hand was missing. He glanced at me with a smile. I am a white woman with green eyes and brown hair.

Reestablishing the timeline makes the progression of events clear.

Vivid details paint a picture of Mr. Davis's physical appearance.

"I am very happy you were able to make it to this meeting," I said with a big smile.

He nodded in silence and avoided making eye contact.

"I had a chance to review your chart. I think I can help with your physical needs," I added. "But I am also suspecting there are mental health issues that might need to be addressed."

Given his sentiments about Middle Eastern doctors, I thought he had a plausible PTSD diagnosis. When I began to suggest as much, he cut me off.

"This is all stereotyping," he asserted. "I did what I was supposed to do. I will heal through going back to work and being productive."

Dialogue makes us feel as if we're witnessing the conversation.

I caught him looking at my name badge.

"I understand," I said. "Thank you for clarifying."

I asked how he had ended up in the military. He said he'd signed up simply because college was "so damn expensive." He was not a "military brat" and didn't enlist out of a sense of obligation. He was not angry or in need of some form of revenge. It's not that he felt enlisting was brave or important.

Mr. Davis had been in three combat deployments—Iraq in 2010 and Afghanistan in 2011 and 2013—as a member of the US Army Special Forces. He'd been involved in multiple close-range blasts, traumatic jumps, and firefights. Many of the people he had served with had been killed. Since his return to the United States, he had been having constant pain in his right shoulder. He had nightmares one or two times a week, and recently they'd become more frequent.

Details establish the intensity of Mr. Davis's combat experiences.

"What kept you going during all the deployments?" I asked.

A turning point signals the growing bond between doctor and patient.

"I closed my eyes while hiding from fire and remembered family trips skiing with my little sister and laughing on the slopes of Jackson Hole." He looked up and smiled. I saw a glimpse of the little boy in his face and knew he was in pain. I wanted to reach out and touch his hand, but I was afraid he would not welcome my gesture.

I asked if he'd had any good experiences in Iraq. Yes, he said. It touched him to see families with young children walking for many miles to collect American parachutes to help build houses. The local people found something useful to do with even the trash that Americans had left. All his memories, however, were haunted by the killings he had witnessed and the poverty of the places he had been.

I felt it was then time to address his comments about Dr. Kumar. I said: "You know, Mr. Davis, you are a man of tremendous courage. It is not easy to share your experiences with someone else, especially experiences of this nature."

He looked out the window.

"You mentioned to me in our phone conversation last week that you were uncomfortable with a doctor from the Middle East."

I paused, then continued. "I want you to be comfortable, and I am very happy we met today. I want to thank you for allowing me into your life and for the opportunity to help. I owe to you the knowledge that I was born and raised in Syria."

The few seconds of silence that ensued felt like an eternity.

Then Mr. Davis abruptly got to his feet and raised his severed hand. "I am so sorry I was being a jerk. I would really like you to be my physician—unless you do not feel comfortable caring for me, based on my earlier comments."

I stood up and extended my hand to him. "It was important for us to talk. Please keep doing so, as it's the only way for us to deal with such emotions."

A resolution follows a tense moment.

His face broke out into a wide smile. He was absolutely thrilled at the prospect of us working together. I was, too.

Healing Takes Time

Though I have served in the VA for many years and in different
roles, my focus has always been on patients. The sacred time
spent with patients in an exam room is the only lasting truth in
medicine. In this large bureaucratic system, all else can wait. Yet
many priorities compete for our attention during a single visit. It
might not be possible to spend the needed time on each important issue. While a slew of mandatory screenings for diseases has
improved our medical care, it is equally crucial to take the time to
develop a relationship with the patient, exploring his or her service history and the lived experiences that may come with that. It
is not always easy. In my work, I know what it is like to be discriminated against, and what it is like to have stereotypes of my own.
Yet an admission of our own vulnerability and opening the door to
a conversation about self-care, compassion, understanding, and
human connection is how we attend to all aspects of our patients'
suffering—and perhaps some of our own.

> *The conclusion tells the significance of the two meeting, why the story matters.*

REFLECT. *Analyze a short nonfiction narrative that you find in a magazine or on a website. Look at the list of five characteristic features of narratives on page 192 and annotate the essay to point out these features, using Kheirbek's essay as a model. Then look at your annotations and the parts of the text they refer to and evaluate how well your chosen narrative illustrates the characteristic features. For example, is the setting clearly described? How vivid are the details?*

LITERACY NARRATIVES

Literacy narratives focus on meaningful experiences involving some kind of reading or writing: stories, music, computer code, learning a foreign language, and so on. The focus on learning and literacy makes this sort of narrative a common assignment in first-year writing classes. Professional writers also use the genre to reflect on their craft. Literacy narratives can serve various purposes, but they generally have the following characteristic features.

A Well-Told Story

Whether you're writing about how you learned to do something (or struggled to do so) or why you've always loved a certain book or song, there are some tried-and-true storytelling techniques that can help your literacy narrative interest readers. If you write about something you struggled to learn, for instance, readers will want to know how your struggle turned out, how the story ends. And whatever your topic, make sure your narrative has a clear arc, from a beginning that engages your audience to a conclusion that leaves them understanding why the experience you wrote about matters to you.

A Firsthand Account,
Often (but Not Always) about Yourself

You'll want to write about an experience that you know firsthand, not one that you've only read about. Writing about your own experience is the most common way of achieving this close perspective, but you may also reflect on the experiences of others. Perhaps you've observed or had a hand in helping someone else learn to read or write and are able to speak about it firsthand. This, too, could be a productive topic for a literacy narrative.

An Indication of the Narrative's Significance

Readers quickly lose patience with stories that seem to have no point, so you need to make clear what significance your narrative has for those involved. Sometimes you may have an explicit THESIS that makes the point clear from the start; other times, you may prefer to let the narrative play out before explaining its significance.

MELANIE LUKEN was a senior French and English major at The Ohio State University when she wrote this literacy narrative for an English course in which she was being trained to be a writing tutor.

Literacy: A Lineage

MELANIE LUKEN

IT WOULD BE IMPOSSIBLE to discuss my path to literacy without talking about my literary guardian, the person who inspired and encouraged my love for reading and writing: my father. I spent a lot of time with my dad as a child, but one of the most important experiences we shared was our Sunday afternoon bike rides. We nearly always took the same route, down to the bike path by the river, circling around, and breaking at Carillon Park under the bell tower. We would just sit, rest, and think under the bells. Etched at the bottom of the bell tower was part of a poem by Henry Wadsworth Longfellow:

> It was as if an earthquake rent
> The hearth-stones of a continent,
> And made forlorn
> The households born
> Of peace on earth, good-will to men!
> And in despair I bowed my head;
> "There is no peace on earth," I said;
> "For hate is strong,

The author makes her point clear from the start: her father played a large role in her love of reading and writing.

And mocks the song
Of peace on earth, good-will to men!"
Then pealed the bells more loud and deep:
"God is not dead; nor doth he sleep;
The Wrong shall fail,
The Right prevail,
With peace on earth, good-will to men." (lines 21–35)

My dad would inevitably read it aloud, but we both knew it by heart; it is one of the many poems that have come to mean something to me. As I got older, my dad didn't come riding as often with me. He was older and more tired, but I still went by myself. Each time I arrived under the bells, I would recite the poem to myself, even when the weather was cold and my breath made the air foggy. It had become part of me, this poem, this tradition of riding and reading and thinking. In the same way, my passion for reading and writing developed in me through the influence of my father, who has a deep love of literature himself. For this reason, my definition of literacy involves more than the ability to read and write; for me, it is also a tradition, an inheritance I received from my father, and an ability to appreciate language because of him and because of many other writers who came before me.

Engaging details draw readers into the story.

You could define my dad as a jack-of-all-trades artist. He has dabbled in almost every art: novel-writing, poetry-writing, song-writing, painting, sculpture, and acting. He was originally in graduate school for English with hopes of becoming a professor. After a couple of years, however, he tired of academia. His tendencies towards creativity and individuality did not mix well with the intense analysis and structure of university life. Eventually, he ended up as a stay-at-home dad, *my* stay-at-home dad, who continues to this day to work on his art and writing. Although our relationship has not always been simple and easy, I benefited greatly from having such an intelligent and imaginative father as my primary caretaker.

For my whole life, my father has quoted the "greats," the "classics," or at least the authors that he admired, in normal conversation. It has become a joke among me and my brothers because we can all recite from memory his favorite lines of books and his favorite poems. Because of him I can quote, "If you can keep your

head when all about you / Are losing theirs and blaming it on you"
(Kipling, lines 1–2), "And early though the laurel grows / It withers
quicker than the rose" (Housman, lines 11–12), "I grow old . . .
I grow old . . . / I shall wear the bottoms of my trousers rolled"
(Eliot, lines 120–21), and of course, "Call me Ishmael" (Melville 3),
among many others. Sometimes he will quote things far out of context, and yet I understand and enjoy it because these quotes evoke
intense feelings of tradition and love. My father's love of literature
pervaded my young mind the way it must pervade his own, and it
has stayed with me.

Vivid details and classic lines from literature bring the story to life.

From the time I could read and write, I wrote and acted out princess stories all on my own. I read voraciously, and I loved being told
stories. I attribute all of this to my father, who taught me to read and
to write, who put *Little Women* in my hands when I was ten years
old, and who continued to introduce me to his favorite authors as
I got older. The only reason I picked up books like *The Heart Is a
Lonely Hunter* or Capote's *Other Voices, Other Rooms* is because he
suggested them or handed them to me. I realize that I did not have
a particularly normal American childhood in terms of my relationship with books and literature (most of my friends preferred playing
sports or watching TV to reading), but I am blessed to have a father
who sees art in language and stories and who passed this gift to me.
I have a greater understanding of the diversity of books, authors,
and the ways in which language is used because of my father. He
always pushed me to read literature other than what I read in school
and particularly encouraged me to read female writers like Carson
McCullers, Zora Neale Hurston, and Flannery O'Connor to empower me as a young girl and to expand my perspective. Now, everything I read is within this tradition that he and I have established.

A firsthand account, told from a first-person point of view.

Another thing that I vividly remember as a child is spending quite
a bit of time in public libraries. My brothers, my dad, and I would
visit the library at least once a week, and more often in the summer when we were out of school. We were never allowed to play
video games or watch much TV, so our entertainment consisted of
what we could create ourselves or what we could gain from books.
Our ability to use and understand language proficiently was very
important to my father. Although I am the only child who has displayed a penchant for creative writing, I think my father has always

held on to the hope that each of his children will spring into novel-writers. Since we were about twelve or thirteen, he has consistent-ly demanded that we each write a story for him at Christmastime rather than buy him a gift. His favorite is a story I wrote for him in high school; it was my own personal version of *A Christmas Carol*.

I began seriously writing creatively towards the end of high school. I have kept journals since I was eight or nine, but in high school, I discovered my true capacity for poetry. I wrote poetry for English classes and for our high school literary magazine. When I got to college, I naturally began taking creative writing classes. I have taken Beginning Poetry, Intermediate Poetry twice, and the Honors 598 seminar with a creative writing component. I improve constantly, and with each class my relationship to language chang-es and grows. Anyone who has taken a workshop knows that in these courses you have to be able to stand criticism and to pick out which suggestions are beneficial and which are not. It was my father, the constant in my literacy narrative, who encouraged me through all of these classes, telling me that no matter what any-body thought, I was a poet, a better poet than he had ever been.

I believe that my choice to major in French is also rooted in this tradition of language and literature. Studying a foreign language can, at times, be just like learning how to read and write as a child. Studying French intensely became for me the perfect, impossible challenge: to read and write French like I read and write English. However, it seems that as long and hard as I study French, I will never be quite so comfortable nor quite so capable of understand-ing it or placing it within a context. I believe that this is partially because tradition plays no role in my study of French. It has noth-ing to do with my family or my background, and it cannot move me emotionally to the extent that English language can. Unlike French, I have a tradition of reading, speaking, and writing English, and I have a much vaster appreciation for English literature in general.

Because of my father and our shared love of literature, my defi-nition of literacy is intimately linked to the idea of tradition. In a way, my literacy is part of my lineage, part of the legacy of my father. My love for literature and writing, my poetic tendencies, my passion for language are all gifts from him. I think that I tend to have more of an imagination than my peers, and I also love to write and create using words. The reason for these qualities is that my father once

A clear indication of why this story matters to the author.

inspired in me his own creativity and instructed me on the under-standing of human experience through writing. In turn, this literacy experience is something I want to pass on to my children someday.

Literacy is generally known as the ability to read and write. My definition of literacy is: the ability to read, write, and understand within a tradition. For me, this is a familial tradition that has per-meated my literacy experience. Parents have an incredible power to influence their children through their own behaviors and at-titudes, and it is certainly true that my father has impressed upon me his own attitudes towards literacy and literature. Now, every time we talk he asks me, "What are you reading? What do you think about it?" We talk about what each of us is reading, as well as our thoughts and impressions. In this way, the tradition continues.

Some daughters inherit a certain amount of money from their fathers. Some inherit a car or a house. Others inherit jewelry. My father will never have much money or a nice car or many mate-rial goods at all. I have, however, received something from him that will last my whole life and will continue to give me joy as long as I live. He has passed on to me his love of language and litera-ture. It is within this tradition that I understand literacy, a tradition that causes me to sometimes think "God is not dead; nor doth he sleep" (Longfellow, line 32) when I hear bells ringing.

The author concludes with a strong statement about why this story is so meaningful.

Works Cited

Eliot, T. S. "The Love Song of J. Alfred Prufrock." *Poets.org*, Academy of American Poets, www.poets.org/poem /love-song-j-alfred-prufrock.

Housman, A. E. "To an Athlete Dying Young." *Poets.org*, Academy of American Poets, www.poets.org/poem /athlete-dying-young.

Kipling, Rudyard. "If——." *Poets.org*, Academy of American Poets, www.poets.org/poem/if.

Longfellow, Henry Wadsworth. "Christmas Bells." *Poets.org*, Academy of American Poets, www.poets.org/poem /christmas-bells.

Melville, Herman. *Moby-Dick*. Penguin Books, 1988.

REFLECT on your own experiences as a writer or reader. Identify one person who played a key role in your developing literacy. What did they teach you, and how? Whatever it was, what impact has it had on your life?

WRITING A NARRATIVE / A Roadmap

Choose a topic that matters—to you, and to others

Whether you write a narrative for personal reasons or in response to an assignment, choose your own topic or work with an assigned topic, try to write about something that matters to you—and try to make sure that it will matter to your audience as well.

If you are writing a personal narrative, choosing a topic can be difficult because you are deciding to share something personal about yourself or someone you know. You will need to choose an experience or event that you feel comfortable sharing, in some detail, with an audience. Be sure that the experience is not only important to you but also of enough general interest to engage your audience.

If your narrative is not a personal one, you still want it to be compelling. Narratives that aren't personal are often part of a larger conversation about an event, or some topic that the event represents, which gives the story significance. For example, if you are writing a narrative about how specific students' academic performances changed when they enrolled in a charter school, you need to recognize that such stories are part of an ongoing educational and political debate about the effectiveness of charter schools as an alternative to traditional public schools. You may need to do some research to understand this debate and how your narrative fits into it.

Consider your rhetorical situation

Whenever you write a narrative (or anything, for that matter), you need to consider the following elements of your rhetorical situation:

Think about your AUDIENCE. Who will be reading what you write, and what's your relationship with them?

- Will your audience have any knowledge about your topic? Will you need to explain anything or provide any background information?
- How are they like or unlike you? Consider age, gender, income, cultural heritage, political beliefs, and so on. How will such factors affect how you tell the story?

- Can you assume they'll be interested in what you write? How can you get them interested?
- How are they likely to react to your narrative? What do you want them to think or do as a result of reading what you say?

Think about your PURPOSE. Why are you writing this narrative? What is the significance of this story, and what do you hope it will demonstrate to your readers? Remember that your narrative needs to do more than just tell an engaging story; it needs to make a point of some kind.

Think about your STANCE. Are you telling a story that is very personal to you, or is it one you have some distance from? How do you want to present yourself as the narrator? Do you want to come across as witty and amusing, if you're telling a humorous family story? As knowledgeable but impersonal, if you're recounting historical events for a political science essay? Whatever your stance, how can you make your writing reflect that stance?

Consider the larger CONTEXT. What broader issues are involved in your narrative? What else has been said and written about this topic? Even if your narrative is personal, how might it speak to some larger topic—perhaps a social or political one? Considering the larger context for your narrative can help you see it from perspectives different from your own and present it in a way that will interest others.

Consider your MEDIUM. If you have a choice, think about which medium best suits your goals and audience. The kinds of details you include, the language you use, the way you present materials from sources, and many other things depend on the medium. The conventions of a print essay, for instance, in which you can use written words and images, differ markedly from those of an audio essay (in which you can use sounds but no written words or images).

Consider matters of DESIGN. Does your narrative need headings? Is there anything in the story that could be conveyed better with a photograph than with words alone? Will embedded audio or video clips help you engage your audience? Often in academic writing, you may be expected to use a specific font and type size or to structure headings a certain way. If you can determine the look of your text, though, remember that design has a powerful impact on the impression your narrative makes.

Explore your topic and do any necessary research

If you are writing a personal narrative, write down all that you remember about your topic. Using **FREEWRITING** or other activities for **GENERATING IDEAS**, write down as many specific details as you can: sounds, smells, textures, colors, and so on. What details will engage your audience? Not all the details that you jot down in this exploratory stage will make it into your essay. You'll need to choose the ones that will engage your audience and support your main point. In addition to sensory details, try to write down direct quotations or dialogue you can remember that will help bring your story to life.

If your narrative is not a personal one, you'll likely need to conduct **RESEARCH** so that you can provide accurate and sufficient details about the topic. Whether your research takes you to sources in the library or online, or into the community to conduct interviews, it's important to get the what, when, and where of the narrative right, and consulting sources will help you do that.

Decide on a point of view

The subject that you choose to write about will usually determine the point of view from which you write. If you're telling a story in which you are a central participant, you will usually use the first person (*I, we*). In some academic disciplines, however, or if you're narrating a story that is not personal, the third person (*he, she, they*) may be more appropriate.

Also think about what verb tense would be most effective for establishing the point of view in your narrative. Most personal narratives that are arranged in chronological order are written in the past tense ("When I *was* twelve, I *discovered* what I *wanted* to do for the rest of my life"). However, if you want readers to feel like they are actually experiencing an event, you may choose to use the present tense, as Georgina Kleege and Michael Lewis do in examples earlier in this chapter.

Organize and start writing

Once you've chosen a subject and identified your main point, considered your rhetorical situation, come up with enough details, and decided on a point of view (not necessarily in this order), it's time to think about how to organize your narrative.

Keep your main point in mind. As you begin to draft, type out that point as a tentative THESIS and keep your eye on it as you write; you can decide later whether you want to include it in your text.

Organize your information. What happened? Where? When? Who was there? What details can you describe to make the story come alive? Decide whether to present the narrative in CHRONOLOGICAL ORDER, in reverse chronological order, or in some other order.

Draft an OPENING. A good introduction draws your audience into the story and makes them want to know more. Sometimes you'll need to provide a context for your narrative—to describe the setting and introduce some of the people before getting on with what happened. Other times you might start in the middle of your story, or at the end—and then circle back to tell what happened.

Draft a CONCLUSION. If you organize your narrative chronologically, you'll likely conclude by telling how the story ends. But make sure your readers see the point of your story; if you haven't made that clear, you might end by saying something about the story's significance. Why does it matter to you? What do you want readers to take away—and remember?

Look critically at your draft, get response—and revise

Read your draft slowly and carefully. Try to see it as if for the first time: Does the story grab your attention, and can you follow it? Can you tell what the point is, and will your audience care? If possible, get feedback from others. Following are some questions that can help you or others examine a narrative with a critical eye:

- *How does the OPENING capture the audience's interest?* Is it clear why you're telling the story, and have you given readers reason to want to find out what happened? How else might the narrative begin?

- *Who's telling the story?* Have you maintained a consistent **POINT OF VIEW**?

- *Is the setting of your story clear?* Have you situated the events in a well-described time and place?

- *Is the story easy to follow?* If it's at all confusing, would **TRANSITIONS** help your audience follow the sequence of events? If it's a lengthy or complex narrative, would headings help?

- *Are there enough vivid, concrete details?* Is there an appropriate balance of showing and telling? Have you included any dialogue or direct quotations—and if not, would adding some help the story come alive?

- *Are there any visuals?* If not, would adding some help bring the narrative to life?

- *How do you establish* **AUTHORITY** *and credibility?* How would you describe the **STANCE** and **TONE**—and are they appropriate for your audience and purpose?

- *Does the story have a clear point?* Is the point stated explicitly—and if not, should it be? If the main point is implied rather than stated, is the significance of the narrative still clear?

- *How satisfying is the* **CONCLUSION**? What does it leave the audience thinking? How else might the narrative end?

- *Does the title suggest what the narrative is about,* and will it make an audience want to read on?

Revise your draft in light of any feedback you receive and your own critique, keeping your purpose and especially your audience firmly in mind.

REFLECT. Once you've completed your narrative, let it settle for a while and then take time to reflect. How well did you tell the story? What additional revisions would you make if you could? Research shows that such reflections help "lock in" what you learn for future use.

Bathtime

CONNOR COYNE

THE BATH DELIGHTS her.

When it's 6:45 in the evening—dark or getting darker—and we ask her, "You ready to go night-night?" Ruby toddles over toward the stairs, muttering: "Bobble, Eejee." A bottle of milk. Geegee, her stuffed giraffe. She is one year old.

Her eyes light up when we carry her into the bathroom. We drop the plug and press down the plastic mat—you don't want little babies slipping and banging their heads on the hard porcelain—and fill the small room with the silver sound of falling water.

She gives us a big smile as the lukewarm bath surges up around her sides. She laughs brightly when she sees she can make waves by slapping her hands down against the water. She feels buoyed by the bubbles between her toes, the fine mist that catches in her light, pixie hair. She grabs for floating foam letters, a plastic turtle, a rubber duckie. This is one of the happiest moments of her day, and it's good that she is happy before we ask her to keep calm in the darkness, to let her brain slip into sleep, to stop moving for a while. Bath as benediction. A sacred quietness that slips between the Flinty clatter of distant train wheels rolling. The familiar thrill of train whistles. A reminder of her baptism.

CONNOR COYNE, a fiction writer, grew up in Flint, Michigan. After leaving to attend college in Chicago, Coyne eventually moved back to Flint with his wife to raise a family, and he lives there still. His narrative essay "Bathtime" was originally published in the 2018 edited collection *Voices from the Rust Belt*.

For Ruby, the bath is an immersive experience, and so she tries to dip a   5
plastic cup in the water and take a big gulp. Little kids are immune to parental
squeamishness. They do this all over the world, or at least anywhere little kids
take baths in porcelain bathtubs. Squeamish parents cringe and say, "No, no,
we don't do that. We don't drink water from the tub."

In Flint, though, our reaction is more severe. We lurch forward, our faces
pale. It's like catching your toddler tottering at the top of a flight of stairs. It's like
seeing a preschooler running headlong toward a busy street in pursuit of a plastic ball. You feel it, visceral in your gut, like someone sucker punched you and
you want to puke. They might be making themselves sick from something much
worse than suds and whatever scum has been washed away by the day's play.

*　*　*

My wife isn't from Flint.

I am.

Well, I grew up in the city until I was twelve, when my parents moved out to
Flushing, a picturesque suburb that finally got its own coffee shop in 1997. That
was the year I graduated high school. But even though I had a Flushing address,
I auditioned for every play at Flint Youth Theatre and went to the Flint Central
High School prom. I always considered myself a Flintstone and spent as much
time as I could in the city. When I went away to college in Chicago, I always
hoped to come back home. To me, Flint was a place of youthful energy and risk,
frisson and connection. I was aware that I was the salmon swimming upstream,
against the current of all the other people eager to leave, but I didn't care.

When I met my eventual wife a few years later, I regaled her with all the   10
stories of my friends and their . . . lives. The insane intensity of life in Flint. The
city had been abandoned, I said. Physically abandoned by the company that
built and nurtured it, and then again by half of its people left struggling in the
wake of deindustrialization . . .

For my wife, practical concerns edged out my visionary rants.

I wanted to go back to the place she said seemed to break everyone I knew. . . .

"I got this," I said.

I actually felt—and I'm not [BSing] here—more able to deliver that happy,
stable childhood in Flint than anywhere else. See, in Flint, I knew the rules. It
isn't chaos. There are rules. There are especially rules if you're 1) middle-class,
2) white, and 3) educated. And the college education supplied by my father's
almost forty years at GM under UAW-earned contracts got me there. My
kids would have friends here. They would live in a stable neighborhood and
go to a good school. They would have educational opportunities, we'd keep

an eye on them, and it wouldn't be any more difficult or risky than a life in Chicago, or New York, or New Orleans, or San Francisco. It would be safer, less risky, because I knew how Flint worked. I didn't know how those other cities worked. I didn't know their rules. I had the tools to control a child's experience of Flint. Anything else, I'd be learning from scratch.

I said this with a lot of arrogance and a fair amount of truth, but hubris 15 always lands the punch line.

When our first daughter was born, we decided to leave Chicago and move to Flint. Because of the fallout from the 2008 housing meltdown, we could afford a house south of Court Street, just east of downtown. When I grew up, this was one of Flint's most exclusive neighborhoods. Now, a family on a single income could land a beautiful 1930s Tudoresque house for a down payment less than that of the tiniest Chicago bungalow, in the middle range of five figures. We could use the money we saved to choose any school for our daughter we wanted. We were close to my parents. We were close to friends. I planted a garden in our backyard and put up a swing set and a fort. The front yard was filled with dappled sunlight that streamed through the maple leaves each summer, enough shade to cool off, and enough sun to nourish the petunias, iridescent in their violet summer glory.

It was cool.

I knew the rules.

* * *

I didn't know the rules.

The rules were [BS].

I was thinking about classroom sizes and museums and violent crime and 20 copper scrappers. I was thinking about street violence and friends from broken homes and arson and unemployment. Too many guns and too little supervision. These were the problems I was trying to puzzle out. Meanwhile, the city went under state receivership and started drawing water from the Flint River instead of the Great Lakes by way of Detroit. The rest is a sad story told across the world by now: the river water wasn't treated properly; it leached lead and other junk from the pipes into tap water. A lot of people drank that water. A lot of people got very sick. Government officials tried to cover up the catastrophe, leading to more sickness, more delays, more damage.

I had never banked on the water going bad.

In all my youthful exuberance, my desire to bring my girls up here, in my community, my pride, my home, I thought I had covered all of the bases, but water is fundamental, the number-two necessity for humans after breathable air. A place that tries to damage you with its water is damaging in the most basic way. And so, I stayed alert each night, watching Ruby bathe, conscious that this isn't right, that this is supposed to be safe, that she would only be safe, for sure, through our unfailing vigilance.

* * *

Ruby doesn't know that the water in this city is bad. Dangerous.

Mary, her five-year-old sister, understands it in a straightforward way, like Darth Vader, like busy traffic, a risk to be avoided. She knows that she shouldn't drink the water just like she shouldn't talk to strangers in strange cars. This loss of innocence and the anonymous lies that prompted it make me sad and angry. Sometimes, it keeps me up at night, thinking of all the injury, the hurt, the real hurt, physical, mental; the loss of trust, the enormity of that loss, the immensity of betrayal; the contempt of those officials who have treated us—treated our children—like expendable animals. Lab rats. Numbers and statistics that might be converted into a political liability, and what a pain in the ass we are for that reason. I've dreamed about it more than once. What if the tests the city conducted on our household water were wrong? What if we didn't act quickly enough? What was this place going to look like in fifteen years? Who was going to be left?

Mary is a bright five-year-old. She is old enough to understand some of this. Not old enough to feel the outrage, but old enough to notice the contradiction and confusion. "It's expensive," we tell her. "Why can't we drink it?" she asks. "Well," I tell her, "you can wash your hands in it, but don't drink it. Don't you drink it. Even if it's the middle of the night and you're thirsty, come and wake me up. I'll get you a glass. You're right. The world isn't right and the world isn't fair."

Some of these are conversations every father expects to have with his child, but not so soon, and certainly not about the unsafe tap water that costs you $130 each month. Not in the first state to light its darkened city streets with streetlamps. Not in the U.S. state that put the world on wheels and taught it to move with speed.

Ruby isn't even two yet. She doesn't see the confusion or the contradiction. For Ruby, the confusion is much simpler: she likes to dip the plastic cup in her bathwater and take a drink when she can. We freak out, lunge forward, snatch up that cup, and toss it to the floor. Ruby yells in surprise and disappointment, at the loud noise, our worried faces, the brief chaos of moving hands and water spray.

She'll relax again, in a few moments, when we soothe her with a song, or give her something else to play with.

We'll relax, too, when the last of the water has finally vanished down the drain. 30

Thinking about the Text

1. How does Coyne use his daughter's bathtime to make an **EMOTIONAL APPEAL** to his readers? Point to specific words and passages. How effective is this appeal?

2. Coyne's memories of his childhood in Flint help establish the **SETTING**. How else does Coyne set a clear scene?

3. Note how Coyne **COMPARES AND CONTRASTS** his five-year-old daughter Mary's behavior with that of one-year-old Ruby's behavior. How does this comparison contribute to the story? Where else in the story does Coyne compare and contrast people, opinions, and places to make a point?

4. "Bathtime" is about Coyne's fatherhood as much as it is about his daughter's bathtime—his **POINT OF VIEW** as a father is important. How would the story be different if it were told from a different perspective—for example, that of Flint's mayor? A child who's lived through the water crisis? A person who grew up in Flint and didn't move back to raise a family?

5. Coyne's decision to move his family back to Flint is based on his childhood memories and his expectation that Flint would offer his family a good life. His expectations were challenged by the water crisis. Write a **NARRATIVE** about an experience in your life that did not live up to your expectation—describing in detail the anticipated event, the outcome, and why it matters to you and potentially to others, too.

The Look
LARRY LEHNA

IFEAR THAT I CARRY FAR MORE BAGGAGE than the typical college student. Unlike Frank Sinatra, regrets I have more than "a few," and even if I do not mention them they weigh heavily upon me. I sometimes regret my wasted life. Then I stop and wonder if it was really wasted. There are so many things I did not accomplish. However, I helped to raise a fine son and he was almost through college before my downfall. My step-daughters were seven and sixteen when I was sent to prison. Yet they both wrote to me for the full eleven years. At different times they have both told me that I am the only real father they have known. Each of them now has children of her own whom I dote upon. So even among the regrets is a modicum of satisfaction.

Always present are my scars, both physical and mental. Mine was not an easy life. I carry many memories. The burning pain of bullet wounds (they really do burn). The agony of stitches going into a fresh knife wound. The nearly immobilizing ache of broken ribs. But most of all I carry emotions. The anguish of being arrested. The despair over lost loves. The disappointment of unfulfilled dreams. I am an emotional cauldron. There is a reason for this.

LARRY LEHNA is a writer whose work has been published in the *Detroit Metro Times* and *Quail Bell Magazine*, an online feminist magazine that publishes "real and unreal stories." Lehna was a student at University of Michigan–Dearborn at the time that he wrote this essay for a narrative journalism class, and he now volunteers on campus to support nontraditional students striving for a chance through education like he once was.

For eleven years I could not show any emotion. When you go to prison you put on a mask called a "Marquette," the name of Michigan's toughest prison. The look says, "I'm tough, I like to fight, and I would just love to hurt you. So mess with me if you dare." When I was in jail awaiting my sentencing I spent hours glaring into the mirror trying to perfect the look, but what gazed back at me was a look that said instead, "I'm constipated." I concluded I would never achieve that look. Little did I know that it would come naturally.

When I was sentenced to ten to thirty years in prison I was stunned. I wanted to cry. I wanted to be hugged. I wanted my mommy. I wanted to hurt someone, but I knew I should not show any emotion. That is when the look appeared on my face. When I got back to the cell-block I noticed a new-found wariness from the other prisoners. They kept their distance. When I went to the bathroom I glanced in the mirror. There it was: the look I would wear for over eleven years, the look that acted like a stopper in the bottle of my emotions. Nothing could faze me, and nothing did. It was more than a look; it was an attitude that was much more severe than mere stoicism. No emotions in, no emotions out.

Over the course of my first year that attitude became ingrained. Part of it 5 was always expecting the worst. I learned to never anticipate anything good from my fellow prisoners or from the institution. When they denied my first attempt at parole, after ten years, I received the information with the same deadpan expression as if they were handing me a pair of socks.

When I finally received my parole I wore the same look. I assumed they would take my parole away, and they did postpone it six months because I had once assaulted a thieving bunkmate. Another bit of news that had no visible effect. I no longer had to try to hide my feelings; I no longer felt any.

When I was released I was sent to a halfway house in Pontiac, one of the few cities in the country in worse shape than Detroit. There were absolutely no job prospects. Add to this the fact that a minimum of three days a week I had to report to either parole, or one of their programs, such as their Job Shop. What a joke. They acted as if they actually spoke with the people offering the jobs. They never did. They found the ads online and printed them. It did not bother these people to send us miles away to apply only to find out that the employer would not even consider a felon. Meanwhile, the amount they spent on counseling and other programs was enormous. It would have been enough to offer a parolee a fresh start, with a car and an apartment and a little bit of a chance at success. But let's not cloud this issue with logic.

The programs, too, were miles away in different directions. It was winter when I was released. I plodded through the snow wearing my cheap state shoes and the look. Whatever they got, I could take it. I only had 90 days to make something happen, and then I had to leave the halfway house. With less than a week left I told my parole officer that I had nowhere to go. When she suggested the homeless shelter, I took her response with a simple nod of my head and the look. With one day to spare I found a place where I could work for my room and board; I was glad to avoid the shelter, but I don't recall a feeling of happiness.

Once ensconced in my palatial new digs, I found my room was actually smaller than my prison cell, but it was all mine. No bunkie for me, but otherwise I continued on as I had done for the past eleven years. I was existing. I had learned that if I applied for a FAFSA [Free Application for Federal student Aid] educational grant they would pay for my schooling and give me whatever was left over in a check. I applied, was accepted and I made an appointment to see a counselor at Oakland Community College. I expected resistance, having experienced nothing but rejection for the last eleven years. The Secretary of State made it almost impossible to get a driver's license once they saw my prison ID card. Society did not like me; they too had a look when they learned of my past. That was just fine; I didn't like them in return. The pressure was building up like Mount St. Helens.

I arrived for my appointment at OCC less than two weeks before classes 10 were to begin. They ushered me into the office of a woman named Noreen Ruehs. I was fully prepared for her to adopt the look and I was ready to set the counselor straight about how little I cared about her and her fancy college job.

When I told her about my past she raised her eyebrows, nodded and said, "Well, you have some catching up to do. Let's see what kind of degree would suit you best." She proffered a few small pamphlets and suggested I look over the one for General Studies. She asked if I knew about computers. When I admitted my ignorance she recommended a Computer Literacy class. She asked about my typing skills and suggested a keyboarding class. We soon had my whole schedule full and all of it at very convenient times. Her kindness had a remarkable effect. There were times when I had to look at the floor and blink several times before I could speak. Kindness was unexpected and I got choked up. I was starting to believe that I could do this. She asked how I planned to pay for college. I told her about my Pell grant. When she said it could be too late for the summer semester, I know she saw my disappointment.

The counselor picked up the phone. "Have you got a minute or two right now? It's important," she said into the handset. Together we walked to the financial aid office and went straight to the supervisor. Noreen asked the woman if she could rush my paperwork through to get me into the coming semester, adding, "Please do this as a personal favor to me."

"Okay, I will handle this myself," said the supervisor. As we left the office I couldn't speak. I just nodded dumbly. The same thing happened in the enrollment office—straight to the supervisor. The problem was that my financial aid had not been processed and I did not have my transcripts from the 1960's at Henry Ford Community College.

Noreen also asked this woman for a personal favor. "Please, just get him enrolled and make sure he gets these classes," she said. "I guarantee the financial aid will come through and we will have his transcripts in here tomorrow." My eyes were blinking like a strobe light to keep the tears at bay. This woman had spent two hours helping me pick my classes and asking for personal favors on my behalf.

"Well, you're all set. Now it is up to you," she said. I reached out to shake   15 her hand, but she gave me a hug instead and went in to counsel the next student. I was unprepared for a physical demonstration of warmth. I had not been hugged by a woman in eleven years. I walked to the parking structure in a daze. It was darker inside with very few people. By the time I got to my car tears were streaming down my cheeks. When someone walked by I would duck down in the seat. After twenty minutes I managed to slap my mask back on.

But when I walked into my room the mask slipped again. It didn't just slip, the damn thing fell off. This time it was not just tears. My body convulsed in guttural sobs. I fell on the bed, and all of the anguish of the lost years came pouring out. I gagged and gasped and howled. It lasted a good thirty minutes, until I cried myself to sleep. When I woke up an hour later the pillow was wet with tears and drool, and my mustache was stuck to it with dried snot. I got up and washed my face, and afterward I felt remarkably good. I knew I would excel at school. That counselor had given me a new outlook on life. I knew from then on things would change, and they did. But one lingering symptom has refused to go away.

When something good happens to me I get choked up. When someone gives me a compliment I get choked up. While typing this I have used two paper towels just from remembering the counselor's kindness. I blubber through any movie or TV show. It's the same with books. It does not have to be a heart-wrenching scene. If someone succeeds I get tears. If anything good happens I get tears. I sometimes tear up just thinking about good things in my life. There is no returning to what was once my emotional normal. I have turned into a real wuss. Even so, I believe I am a better person now. My look has vanished, but I still get the opposite looks on occasion from people who know about my past. Those looks are the least of my worries; you can't argue with the ignorant.

Noreen Ruehs called Susan Cushner at the University of Michigan—Dearborn and helped me transfer there. I'll graduate in a few weeks with "high distinction" and one of the five Chancellor's Medallions that are awarded to the best in the class. I have tried to thank Noreen but she says that I am the one who did all the work. She has no idea what she did for me. Of course I am wiping tears now.

Thinking about the Text

1. What is Larry Lehna's point in telling this story? Where does he make that point clear?

2. How would you describe the organization of Lehna's narrative? Chronological? Reverse chronological? Some other order? Where does the story start and end, and how effective is this structure?

3. Lehna talks about a look he sometimes receives from "people who know about my past," a look that tells him that "society did not like me" and that people doubted his character. We're willing to bet you feel quite differently after reading his story. How does Lehna connect with his **AUDIENCE** in this piece and establish his **CREDIBILITY**?

4. This essay was written for a course in narrative journalism, a genre that uses individual stories to illuminate public issues. Imagine that Lehna told this story as part of an essay on the need for prison reform for a political science course. How might the essay be different for that **PURPOSE**?

5. Identify an experience from your own life that sheds light on a social, political, cultural, or economic issue. Perhaps you were bullied in middle school, for instance—a deeply personal experience that has broader significance. Write a **NARRATIVE** essay in which you bring your own experience to life while also making the broader significance clear.

FOURTEEN

"Let's Take a Closer Look"
Writing Analytically

**NALYSIS IS A NECESSARY STEP** in much of the thinking that we do, and something that we do every day. What should you wear today? T-shirt and flip-flops? A sweatshirt? Your new red sweater? You consider the weather forecast, what you will be doing, the people you will be with (and might want to impress, or not), and then decide based on those factors. You may not consciously think of it as analysis, but that's what you've done.

When you analyze something, you break it down into its component parts and think about those parts methodically in order to understand it in some way. Since our world is awash in information, the ability to read it closely, examine it critically, and decide how—or whether—to accept or act on it becomes a survival skill. To navigate this sea of information, we rely on our ability to analyze.

Case in point: you want a new set of headphones, but do you want earbuds? over-the-ear? noise canceling? Bluetooth? wireless? As you consider your options, your analysis will be driven by a number of questions: What's most important to you—sound quality? comfort? price? brand or look? When will you most often be wearing your headphones—at the gym? on your daily bus commute? while playing video games? You could ask your music-loving friends for their opinions, or you might check websites like *CNET*, which provide expert analysis as well as price comparisons. You might test out different styles and designs at your local

Best Buy store. These are some of the ways you might analyze the various options, first to understand what they offer and then to decide which one you want to buy.

You have probably analyzed literary texts in English classes. In many college classes, you'll be expected to conduct different kinds of analyses—of texts, and also of events, issues, arguments, and more. Analysis is critical to every academic discipline, useful in every professional field, and essential to everyday decision making. This chapter provides guidelines for conducting an analysis and writing analytically, with specific advice for rhetorical, causal, discourse, process, data, and visual analysis.

REFLECT. Think about your own use of analysis. How many decisions—large and small—have you made in the last week? in the last month? in the last year? From small (what to have for breakfast) to major (which college to attend), make a chart listing a representative sample of these decisions and what areas of your life they affected. Then note the information you gathered in each case before you came to a final decision. What does this chart tell you about your interests, activities, and priorities? You've just completed an analysis.

Across Academic Disciplines

Some form of analysis can be found in every academic discipline. In a *history* class, you may be asked to analyze how Russia defeated Napoleon's army in 1812. In *biology*, you might analyze how the body responds to exercise. In *economics*, you might analyze the trade-off between unemployment and inflation rates. In a *technical communication* course, you might analyze a corporate website to understand how it appeals to various audiences. In your *composition* course, you'll analyze your own writing for many purposes, from thinking about how you've appealed to your audience to deciding how you need to revise a draft. So many courses require analysis because looking closely and methodically at something—a text, a process, a philosophy—helps you discover connections between ideas and think about how things work, what they mean, and why.

Across Media

Your medium affects the way you present your analysis. In *print*, you'll be writing mostly in paragraphs, and you might include photos, tables, graphs, diagrams, or other images to make your analysis clear. If you're making an *oral presentation*, you might show some information on slides or handouts. A *digital text* allows you to blend words, images, and audio—and you can embed these elements directly in your text or link to more information elsewhere. See how the following analysis from *Examiner.com* links to a *YouTube* video of Serena Williams practicing her serve to let readers see for themselves the process the author is analyzing. Had he been writing for a print publication, he might have included a still image like the one below.

Most casual tennis fans may think Williams simply hits the ball harder than any other female on the planet, but the fact of the matter is that Serena Williams' service mechanics are textbook perfect and allow her to maximize every ounce of energy and power she possesses to its fullest extent—all without trying to bash the felt off the ball.

If you watch Williams' entire service motion from beginning to end, you'll see that she has every part of her body working toward one goal, powering up—and through—the tennis ball.

First, Williams gets that familiar "rocking motion" of hers, shifting back and then forward as she begins her swing take-back. Next, the younger tennis-playing Williams sister begins her service toss motion as

Serena Williams serving at Wimbledon, 2015.

her body weight begins moving toward the net. Williams then brings her feet together and takes a fantastic knee bend that all players need to copy whether male or female. With her weight shifted and her knees bent significantly and left arm still pointing up, Williams literally explodes upward toward the ball while her racquet head drops as her right elbow stretches up toward the heavens.

Now, with her body launched in the air, Williams reaches up for the ball and just before striking it, she pronates her wrist, arm and racquet as she powers through the ball as only she can.

—ERIC WILLIAMS, "Five Things All Tennis Players
Can Learn from Serena Williams"

**THINK
BEYOND
WORDS**

↪ *WATCH THE VIDEO of a TED talk by statistician Nate Silver on whether race affects voting. Silver includes slides with lists, bar graphs, photos, and maps. How do the visuals contribute to his analysis? A space below the posted video invites viewers to comment. Write a comment about something Silver said in his talk that you find thought-provoking: your challenge will be to frame your comment in response to Silver while adding your own perspective. Go to* everyonesanauthor.tumblr.com *to view the video.*

Across Cultures and Communities

Communicating with people from other communities or cultures challenges us to examine our assumptions and think about our usual ways of operating. Analyzing and understanding beliefs, assumptions, and practices that we are not familiar with may take extra effort. We need to be careful not to look at things only through our own frames of reference.

Sheikh Jamal Rahman, Pastor Don Mackenzie, and Rabbi Ted Falcon put in this extra effort in writing their book, *Getting to the Heart of Interfaith: The Eye-Opening, Hope-Filled Friendship of a Pastor, a Rabbi and a Sheikh.* In this book they take on the challenge of working toward interfaith understanding, saying that religion today "seems to be fueling hatred rather than expanding love" and that in order to heal the divisions between us, we must "find ways of entering into conversation with those different from us." And they say that analysis—what they call "inquiring more deeply"—is essential to their ongoing journey toward understanding issues central to each faith.

All three agree that it is critical to discuss the difficult and contentious ideas in faith. For the minister, one "untruth" is that "Christianity is the only way to God." For the rabbi, it is the notion of Jews as "the chosen people." And for the sheikh, it is the "sword verses" in the Koran, like "kill the unbeliever," which when taken out of context cause misunderstanding.

Their book embodies cultural sensitivity and describes the process of creating a text that's respectful of their different faiths. Reading a sentence that the sheikh had written about the security wall in Israel, the rabbi responded, "If that line is in the book, I'm not in the book." Then they analyzed and discussed the sentence, and Sheikh Rahman revised the wording to be "respectful of [both] their principles."

Having respect for the principles, values, and beliefs of others means recognizing and being sensitive to differences among cultures. The best way to demonstrate cultural sensitivity is to use precise language that avoids negative words or stereotypes about gender, religion, race, ethnicity, and such—in short, by carefully selecting the words you use.

Across Genres

Seldom does any piece of writing consist solely of one genre; in many cases, writers draw on multiple genres as the situation demands. Analysis is a crucial step in writing for many purposes. To **ARGUE A POSITION** on an issue, you'll need to analyze that issue before you can take a stand on it. To compose a **REPORT**, you sometimes have to first analyze the data or the information that the report will be based on. And a **REVIEW**—whether it's of a film, a website, a book, or something else—depends on your analyzing the material before you evaluate it. Likewise, you might use a short **NARRATIVE** as an introductory element in a process or causal analysis.

REFLECT. Look for analysis in everyday use. Find two consumer-oriented websites that analyze something you're interested in—laptops, cell phones, sneakers, places you might like to go, things you might like to do. Study the analyses and decide which one is more useful. Then try to figure out what makes it better. Is it the language? the images? the amount of detail? the format? Keep these observations in mind as you write and design your own analyses.

CHARACTERISTIC FEATURES

While there are nearly as many different kinds of analysis as there are things to be analyzed, we can identify five common elements that analyses share across disciplines, media, cultures, and communities:

- A question that prompts you to take a closer look
- Some description of the subject you are analyzing
- Evidence drawn from close examination of the subject
- Insight gained from your analysis
- Clear, precise language

A Question That Prompts You to Take a Closer Look

Kneeling is an ordinary human activity, suitable to various purposes, but when athletes kneel during the national anthem, their action is considered controversial. Jeremy Adam Smith and Dacher Keltner wondered why, and they analyzed the topic from the viewpoint of psychology. See how they present their findings on p. 1033.

If you look at the examples cited earlier in this chapter, you'll note that each is driven by a question that doesn't have a single "right" answer. What should you wear today? Which set of headphones best meets your needs? How can we begin to achieve interfaith understanding? Each question requires some kind of analysis. While an author may not explicitly articulate such a question, it will drive the analysis—and the writing that presents the analysis. In an essay examining our two-party political system, see how *New York Times* journalist David Brooks starts by posing two questions, the second building on the first.

> Is there room for a third party? If some independent mounted a presidential bid, would that person have a chance? . . .
>
> There is no evidence that there are enough centrists or "pragmatists" to threaten the two-party duopoly. To have a chance, the third-party candidate would have to emerge as the most radical person in the race. That person would have to argue that the Republicans and Democrats are just two sides of a Washington-centric power structure that has ground to a halt. That person would have to promise to radically redistribute power across American society . . .
>
> [T]oday, the country is diverse, trust in big institutions is low, the federal government is immobilized by partisanship and debt. Now, state and local governments are more effective across many overlapping domains.
>
> It's no wonder that so many, especially millennials (the most diverse generation of voters in our history), have become disillusioned with federal action. . . .
>
> All recent presidential candidates have run against Washington, but on the premise that they could change Washington. Today, a third-party candidate would have to run on creating different kinds of power structures at different levels.
>
> Across the country, power is being most effectively wielded by civic councils—organically formed groups of local officials, business leaders, neighborhood organizations. The members may have different racial, class and partisan identities, but they have one shared identity—love of their community. My colleague Thomas Friedman wrote about one such council in Lancaster, Pa. If you want to see others you probably don't have to travel far—Winston-Salem, Indianapolis, Detroit, Kalamazoo, Denver, Grand Rapids. Power in these places is not just wielded at the ballot box; it is wielded by movements and collaboratives in a thousand ways. According to a 2015 Heartland Monitor poll, 66 percent of Americans believe that their local area is moving in the right direction. . . . A third-party candidate who shifted attention to local people actually getting stuff done might lose, but he or she would begin to define a new and more plausible version of American greatness.
>
> —DAVID BROOKS, "Third-Party Option"

To answer his opening questions, Brooks lays out the conditions he believes are necessary for a third-party or an independent candidate to get traction. Then he takes a closer look, providing a succinct analysis of those conditions. You might not always start an analytical essay as Brooks does, by asking an explicit question, but your analysis will always be prompted by a question of some kind.

Some Description of the Subject You Are Analyzing

To be sure your audience fully understands your analysis, you need to first describe what you are analyzing. How much description you need depends on your subject, your audience, and the medium in which you present your piece. For example, if you are analyzing tropes in George R. R. Martin's *A Song of Fire and Ice* series for your fantasy literature class, you can assume most of your audience will be familiar with your subject. However, if you are analyzing the success of the TV series based on Martin's novels for your marketing class, you will have to describe the elements that make it HBO's most popular series ever. See how Ken Tucker does so in a piece on the British website *BBC Culture* that tackles that question: "Why is *Game of Thrones* so popular?"

> The return of *Game of Thrones*, back for a fourth season of sword fighting, bed hopping and mud flinging, reminds us once again what a clever gamble HBO took in squeezing this massive production through our TV and laptop screens. Yes, George R. R. Martin's *A Song of Fire and Ice* novels, on which the series is based, were bestsellers. But the size of the audience for epic fantasy fiction is a fraction of what is needed to make a profit on television. Martin's forest-dense family trees of characters—knights in dented armour, damsels in bodice-bursting distress, and a nest of dragons imported from fairy tales—could not have been an easy sell. Legend has it that writer-producer Vince Gilligan sold *Breaking Bad* to TV network AMC with the pithy phrase "Mr. Chips becomes Scarface." One imagines the folks peddling *Game of Thrones* to HBO calling it "The Sopranos with swords."
>
> —KEN TUCKER, "Why Is *Game of Thrones* So Popular?"

Writing for this site, Tucker rightly assumes that some in his audience may know little or nothing about the series and thus he includes descriptions

Daenerys Targaryen, mother of dragons in HBO's *Game of Thrones*.

that help readers understand what the series is about—and what draws so many viewers to it week after week. Vivid language detailing the show's characters ("knights in dented armour, damsels in bodice-bursting distress, and a nest of dragons imported from fairy tales") and typical plotlines ("sword fighting, bed hopping and mud flinging") gives readers a sense of the epic fantasy fiction genre, and does so in a way that highlights the show's most thrilling and scandalous aspects.

In a similar situation, when you're composing a text that will be read by an audience that may not know your topic well, you'll also need to provide necessary description and details. You might also include an image, embed a video, or include a link to a site offering more information on your subject if the medium you're writing in allows it.

Evidence Drawn from Close Examination of the Subject

Examining the subject of your analysis carefully and in detail and then thinking critically about what you find will help you discover key elements, patterns, and relationships in your subject—all of which provide you with the evidence on which to build your analysis. For example, if you are analyzing a poem, you might examine word choice, rhyme scheme, figurative language, repetition, and imagery. If you are analyzing an ad in a magazine, you might look at the use of color, the choice of fonts, and the placement of figures or logos. Each element contributes something significant to the whole; each carries some part of the message being conveyed. The kinds of elements you examine and the evidence you draw from them will depend on the nature of your subject as well as the kind of analysis you are conducting. Following are discussions and examples of five common kinds of analysis: rhetorical analysis, discourse analysis, process analysis, causal analysis, and data analysis.

Rhetorical analysis. This kind of analysis can focus on a written text, a visual text, an audio text, or one that combines words, images, and sound. All of these are rhetorical analyses; that is, they all take a close look at how authors, designers, or artists communicate a message to an audience. Whether they are using words or images, adjusting font sizes or colors, they all are trying to persuade a particular audience to have a particular reaction to a particular message—theirs.

See how the following example from an article published on *Branding Strategy Insider*, a blog about brand strategy and management, analyzes Nike's thirtieth anniversary Just Do It campaign and the company's choice to feature Colin Kaepernick, a former NFL quarterback who sat and knelt during the national anthem at 49ers games in the 2016 season as a protest against the oppression of people of color:

> Is the new Kaepernick 30th Anniversary Just Do It Campaign a smart move for the Nike brand? . . . Perhaps the first question to ask about this campaign from a brand planner's perspective is: *What is it about Colin Kaepernick's character that Nike finds so important to attach it to the Nike brand?*
>
> Developing brand character has many things in common with screenwriting and the attempt to develop relatable characters for film and TV. Relatable characters are . . . sympathetic heroes on a mission to achieve worthy goals. They're often created as original, attractive, intelligent and provocative, and definitely not cliché, predictable or superficial. They have a definite point of view and a convincing way of getting it across. . . . Above all, relatable characters get people talking about them.
>
> In Nike's current campaign, Kaepernick has certainly demonstrated that he has character, conviction about his beliefs, concern for social justice and he certainly has people talking about him. But, is he really

a sympathetic hero? To segments of society struggling with [or sympathetic to] experiences of social injustice he definitely is. . . . [T]o [others]
. . . he carries strong and negative emotional associations.

Risk or Reward? In launching this new campaign Nike is risking alienat-
ing a huge segment of its U.S. consumer base, perhaps as much as half.
Why would they do that? Perhaps they are thinking that it will tighten the
tribe with millennials, who tend to be involved in protest movements,
particularly when political leaders and other authority figures are not
aligned with their feelings and values. They see Kaepernick as a champion
of individual rights, fighting for a sense of social justice. . . .

[T]his campaign will [also] scatter parts of the Nike tribe. . . . These
people see not standing for the national anthem at a sporting event as
an outward sign of disrespect for the idea of America and all the sacrifices made in the name of the nation. They see the gestures taken by
Colin Kaepernick as a sign of questionable character. They see his public
gestures as inappropriate and out of place.

—JEROME CONLON, "Analyzing Nike's Controversial
Just Do It Campaign"

In the rest of the article, Conlon goes on to analyze how two different
and opposing audiences are likely to react to the ad: those who will
"like that Nike is supporting individual athlete rights, acts of moral conscience, conviction and protest," and those who will see the choice as
disrespectful to the American values they embrace. As a former director of marketing for Nike, Conlon also analyzes the advertisement—and
its likely impact—by looking at the history of the Just Do It campaign,
which was designed to celebrate "the joy of all kinds of sports and fitness
activities . . . for everyone, pro sports athletes to fitness amateurs, young
and old, men and women, people in America, people around the world.
No one was excluded."

To see Nike's
Just Do It
campaign videos
and posters, go to
everyonesanauthor
.tumblr.com.

Conlon concludes with a prediction and wider implications of the ad:
"Short-term pain for Nike's brand, but long-term gain. The social discussion around the campaign will elevate public understanding of the greatness of America and the need for more respect and regard for all people,
of all colors and classes." Note how the author begins with a question and
then presents evidence by analyzing the ad's tone, stance, context, and
how all of these elements will play with two specific audiences.

Nike's 2018 Just Do It ad campaign featuring former football quarterback Colin Kaepernick. About his controversial gesture, Kaepernick explained, "I am not going to stand up to show pride in a flag for a country that oppresses black people and people of color."

In the following example from her study of a literacy tradition in African American churches, rhetorician Beverly Moss uses direct quotations from her field notes to illustrate a key rhetorical pattern she noticed in one preacher's sermons.

> One of the patterns that leapt out at me as I sat in the pew during all the sermons and as I listened to tapes and reviewed fieldnotes was the high level of participation in the sermons by the congregation. . . . It is a pattern that almost any discussion of African American preaching addresses. Just as in the three churches highlighted [earlier], in this church, the congregation and Reverend M. engaged in a call-and-response dialogue. At times during the revival sermons, the feedback

from the congregation was so intense that it was impossible to separate speaker from audience.

Consider the following exchange. . . .

When you shout before the battle is over (Preach!)
It puts things in a proper perspective (Yeah!)
It puts you in a posture of obedience (Yeah!)
And it puts things in a proper perspective
But finally
When you shout before the battle is fought
It puts the enemy in confusion (Yeah! That's right!)

The parenthetical expressions, responses from the congregation, do not appear on separate lines because there was little or no pause between the minister's statement and the congregation's response. Often, the congregation's response overlapped with the minister's statement. This type of feedback was typical in the sermons Reverend M. preached to this congregation, as was applause, people standing, cheering, and so on. Practically every sermon Reverend M. preached ended with the majority of the congregation on their feet clapping and talking back to Reverend M.

—BEVERLY MOSS, *A Community Text Arises*

Members of a congregation move and shout in response to the preacher's words.

Moss analyzes and presents evidence from a spoken text. Because she was writing a print book, she could not include the actual audio of the sermon, but still she presents evidence in a way that demonstrates a key point of her analysis: that the closeness of the preacher's "call" and the congregation's "response" made it almost "impossible to separate speaker from audience." This quoted evidence shows a specific example of how the congregation's response becomes a part of the sermon, filling the church with "applause, people standing, cheering."

Discourse analysis. This kind of analysis can focus on any spoken or written language used in a particular social context. Discourse analysis often entails analyzing the communication practices of a specific community—people who share basic values, beliefs, practices, and goals. For example, a community of scholars such as the teachers at your school all likely value education, believe in helping students grow intellectually, and practice their profession by providing instruction to enable students to learn and achieve their goals. You've probably noticed that most of your teachers—especially those in a particular discipline or department—share a specific vocabulary. This holds true for any field, any profession, any group of people with shared interests; they develop ways of interacting and communicating most effectively with each other. In order to analyze how a specific group communicates, you'll examine that community's values, beliefs, goals, and practices, an effort that requires careful observation and even immersion when possible.

Discourse analysis might even scrutinize elements as tiny as periods and commas. Check out Jessica Wildfire's examination of online punctuation on p. 1093.

Look at the following example by Alberta Negri, a student at the University of Cincinnati, that analyzes the communication practices of a local group of bikers. Note how the introduction draws you in with a brief narrative and specific sensory details before offering background information. The author moves from common misperceptions of bikers to her specific subject, a group of bikers she refers to as the "Shell Station Squad." Note that Negri gives a rationale for focusing on this specific group; she tells readers why it matters.

> It's 8:56 p.m. on a Tuesday evening, and from my third-floor dorm room, I can once again hear the aggressive growls of 600-pound motorcycles as they roll into the parking lot of the Shell station across the street. The riders meet every night around 9:00 and face the usual apprehensive looks from bystanders. . . . Few investigations have been done from within the

biking community; even fewer have examined the inner workings of the communication among members. In his ethnography *A Brotherhood of Outlaw Bikers*, Daniel Wolf points out the realization that most bike-related media content continues to portray motorcyclists in the same negative light. . . . The following research makes the effort to peek into this unexplored group and discuss the less action-packed qualities, including its status as a discourse community, the process of club enculturation, and how a member's new identity can complicate their previous social roles.

—ALBERTA NEGRI, "Underneath the Leather Jackets and Chrome Pipes: Research into a Community of Local Bikers"

Negri goes on to explain the methods used to conduct her research— including first-hand observation—and then she begins her analysis:

What do these men have in common? The riders of the Shell Station Squad have separate personal lives: full-time gunsmith, engineering firm representative, college student and *Call of Duty* gamer among them, but they all plan to meet every night and anticipate their 9 p.m. ride all day. Their passion to ride is often their only unifying characteristic. There is no need for them to begin each ride with a preface, stating the goals for the ride for the night, or what they hope to accomplish as a team. There is a simple, unspoken understanding that if you pull into that gas station parking lot, you're there for the chance to revel in the thrill of weaving through streets on a motorcycle, while flocking as a group to make the experience a little safer for all involved. . . .

Their primary mode of correspondence is *Facebook*; they use social media to create a private group for discussing matters such as driving routes and safety updates. . . . [T]here is no clear pecking order. The peer-appointed leader never dominated the discourse. More often, he would push for more interaction from those who were recently recruited: addressing questions to them to get individual opinions and inviting them to special weekend rides. [This leader] went as far as directly introducing new riders, saying, "Guys: new kid with us tonight. Thomas is a student at [the university], new rider, let's make sure to make him feel welcome tonight, alrite? Good kid, i think" [sic] (Lucius). His digital diction was a tad gentler in these interactions compared to his brash joking with the more experienced riders.

Negri analyzes the shared motivations and passions that build kinship among the group members—"the thrill of weaving through streets on a motorcycle"—and acknowledges what sets them apart from one another, too: their personal lives outside of biking. She goes on to examine the group's way of communicating and building community, in person and online, in order to understand how the community operates. To conduct her analysis, Negri relies on interviews with group members and a recent recruit as well as "primary texts": texts, *Facebook* group posts, and hand signals.

Visit everyones anauthor.tumblr .com for a link to Negri's complete analysis.

Process analysis. Analyzing a process requires you to break down a task into individual steps and examine each one to understand how something works or how something is done. Thus there are two kinds of process analyses: **INFORMATIONAL**, showing how something works; and **INSTRUCTIONAL**, telling how something is done. An analysis of the chemistry that makes a cake rise would be informational, whereas an analysis of how to make a cake would be instructional.

The following example analyzes the process of how skaters make high-speed turns. This is the most critical element in speed skating, for being able to consistently make fast turns without slipping and losing ground can be the difference between winning and losing. This analysis from *Science Buddies*, a website for students and parents, closely examines the key steps of the process. Note how the author provides some information about the basic physics of speed and turns and then systematically explains how each element of the action—speed, angle, push-back force from the surface—contributes to the total turn.

Whether it's ice, wood, or a paved surface, the science that governs a skater's ability to turn is essentially the same. It's based on a couple of basic laws of physics that describe speed and the circular motion of turns. The first is Newton's *law of inertia* that says a body in motion will stay in motion unless there is some outside force that changes it. To skaters hoping to make a turn after they speed down the straightaway, that means the force of inertia would tend to keep them going straight ahead if there wasn't a greater force to make them change direction and begin turning.

The force that causes the change in direction comes from the skater's blades or wheels as they cross over at an angle in front of the skater leaning to make a turn. Newton's *law of reaction* explains

Skating for the finish line in the women's 1,000-meter short-track speed skating finals at the 2018 Winter Olympics in Pyeongchang.

that the push from the skater's skates generates an equal but opposite push back from the ice or floor. This push back force draws the skater in towards the track and is described as a "center seeking" or *centripetal* type of force. It's the reason why turns are possible in any sport. The wheels of a bicycle, for example, also angle into the road surface when the cyclist leans to begin a turn. As the road pushes back on both bike and rider, it supplies the inward centripetal force to generate the turning motion.

The more a skater leans into a turn, the more powerful the push from the skate, and the greater centripetal force produced to carry the skater through the turn. Leaning in also creates a smaller arc, or tighter turn, making for a shorter distance and a faster path around the turn. However, there's a catch. As the skater leans more and more into the track, the balancing point of the body, or the skater's *center of gravity*, also shifts more and more to the side. If it shifts too far, the skater no longer can maintain balance and ends up splayed out onto the rink rather than happily heading round the turn to the finishing line.

So success in turns, especially fast ones, means skaters must constantly find their center of gravity while teetering on the edge of their skates. To make the turn at all requires that the skater push the skates against the ice with sufficient power to generate enough inward centripetal force to counter the inertia of skating straight ahead. And to keep up speed in a race, a skater must calculate and execute the shortest, or tightest, turns possible around the track.

—DARLENE JENKINS, "Tightening the Turns in Speed Skating: Lessons in Centripetal Force and Balance"

To read the full analysis, go to everyonesanauthor .tumblr.com.

This kind of close examination of the subject is the heart of analysis. Darlene Jenkins explains the key elements in the process of making a high-speed turn—speed, angle, push-back force—and also examines the relationships among these elements as she describes what happens in minute detail, revealing how they all combine to create the pattern of movement that leads to a successful high-speed turn. By including a photograph that shows skaters leaning into a turn, blades and bodies angled precariously, Jenkins shows what the process entails, and readers can actually see what's being described.

Causal analysis. Why is the Arctic ice pack decreasing in volume? What causes extreme droughts in California? These and other questions about why something occurs or once occurred call on you to analyze what caused a certain event, but a causal analysis can also investigate the possible effects of an event, or the links in a chain of connected events. Put most simply, causal analyses look at why something happened or will happen as a result of something else.

Go to everyones anauthor.tumblr .com to link to the full article, "The Cry Embedded within the Purr."

Behavioral ecologist Karen McComb, who studies communication between animals and humans, wanted to understand why cat owners so often respond to purring cats by feeding them. To answer this question, McComb and a team recorded a number of domestic cats in their homes and discovered what the team termed "solicitation purring"—an urgent high-frequency sound, similar to an infant's cry, that is embedded within the cats' more pleasing and low-pitched purring and that apparently triggered an innate nurturing response in their owners. In an article presenting their findings, the team provided quantitative data about the pitch and frequency of different kinds of purring to support their conclusion about what the data showed: that the similarities in pitch and frequency to the cries of human infants "make them very difficult to ignore."

Using data like these to support an analysis is common in science class-es, while in the humanities and social sciences, you're more likely to write about causes that are plausible or probable than ones that can be measured. In a literature class, for example, you might be asked to analyze the influ-ences that shaped F. Scott Fitzgerald's creation of Jay Gatsby in *The Great Gatsby*—that is, to try to explain what caused Fitzgerald to develop Gatsby the way he did. In a sociology class, you might be asked to analyze what fac-tors contributed to a population decline in a certain neighborhood. In both cases, these causes are probabilities—plausible but not provable.

Data analysis. Some subjects will require you to examine data. **QUANTITA-TIVE** analysis looks at numerical data; **QUALITATIVE** analysis looks at data that's not numerical.

When Beverly Moss analyzed the rhetoric of three ministers, she worked with qualitative data: transcripts of sermons, personal testimonies, her own observations from the church pews. Her data came mostly in the forms of words and text, not statistics.

Now see how blogger Will Moller analyzes the performances of ten major-league baseball pitchers using quantitative data—baseball statistics, in this case—to answer the question of whether New York Yankees pitcher Andy Pettitte is likely to get into baseball's Hall of Fame.

I prefer to look at Andy versus his peers, because simply put, it would be very odd for 10 pitchers from the same decade to get in (though this number is rather arbitrary). Along that line, who are the best pitchers of Andy's generation, so we can compare them?

	Wins	Win%	WAR	ERA+	IP	K	K/BB	WAR/9IP
Martinez	219	68.7%	89.4	154	2827	3154	4.15	0.28
Clemens	354	65.8%	145.5	143	4917	4672	2.96	0.27
Johnson	303	64.6%	114.8	136	4135	4875	3.26	0.25
Schilling	216	59.7%	86.1	128	3261	3116	4.38	0.24
Maddux	355	61.0%	120.6	132	5008	3371	3.37	0.22
Mussina	270	63.8%	85.6	123	3563	2813	3.58	0.22
Smoltz	213	57.9%	82.5	125	3473	3084	3.05	0.21
Brown	211	59.4%	77.2	127	3256	2397	2.66	0.21
Pettitte	240	63.5%	66.9	117	3055	2251	2.34	0.20
Glavine	305	60.0%	67.1	118	4413	2607	1.74	*0.14*

The above table tells the story pretty well. I've bolded the numbers that are particularly absurd, and italicized one in particular which should act as a veto. Though I imagine most of the readers of this blog know full well what these statistics mean at this point, for those of you who don't, a primer:

WAR stands for Wins Above Replacement, and is a somewhat complicated equation which estimates the true value of a pitcher, taking into account league, ERA, park effects, etc. For instance, a pitcher that wins a game but gives up 15 earned runs has probably lost value in their career WAR, even though they get the shiny addition to their win-loss record. We like WAR around these parts.

ERA+ is a normalized version of ERA centered on 100, basically showing how much better or worse a pitcher was compared to their league average (by ERA). 110, for example, would indicate that the pitcher's ERA was 10% better than average. 95, on the other hand, would be roughly 5% worse than average. This is a good statistic for comparing pitchers between different time periods—a 4.00 ERA in 2000 doesn't mean the same thing as a 4.00 ERA in 1920, for example.

K/BB is how many strikeouts a pitcher had per walk. More is better, less is worse.

As you can see, the above table doesn't do Andy any favors. He's 6th in wins and 5th in winning percentage, but he's 9th in ERA+ and dead last in WAR. His K/BB beats only Tom Glavine, who comes off looking pretty bad on this list. The only thing he has going for him is his playoff record—and frankly, the team he was on won a whole bunch of playoff games while he was on the team, even when he wasn't pitching. Besides, we're pretty much past the point of taking W/L record as a good indication of pitcher skill—why is it that when we slap the word "postseason" onto the statistic, we suddenly devolve 10 years to when such things seemed to matter?   —WILL MOLLER, "A Painful Posting"

Moller's guiding question, "Should Andy Pettitte be in the Hall of Fame?" is unstated in this excerpt, but it is made clear earlier in the piece. He presents the data in a table for readers to see—and then walks us through his analysis of that data. It's critical when using numerical data like these not only to present the information but also to say what it means. That's a key part of your analysis. Using a table to present data is a good way to include numerical evidence, but be careful that you don't just

Andy Pettitte pitching against the Kansas City Royals in April 2009.

drop the table in; you need to explain to readers what the data mean and to explain any abbreviations that readers may not know, as Moller does. Though he does not state his conclusions explicitly here, his analysis makes clear what he thinks.

Insight Gained from Your Analysis

One key purpose of an analysis is to offer your audience some insight on the subject you are analyzing. As you examine your subject, you discover patterns, data, specific details, and key information drawn from the subject—which will lead you to some insight, a deeper understanding of the subject you're analyzing. The insight that you gain will lead you to your thesis. When the sheikh, pastor, and rabbi mentioned earlier in this chapter analyzed a sentence in their book that offended the rabbi, each gained insight into the others' principles that led them to further understanding. In "Third-Party Option," David Brooks makes clear the insights he derived from his analysis of the national political climate and especially the community conditions he believes would need to be considered for a third-party option to be viable:

> We also need a national leader to tell a different national story. During the 20th century, a superpower story emerged. In that story, the nation moved as one, and a ridiculous amount of attention got focused on the supposed superhero in the White House. A third-party candidate who shifted attention to local people actually getting stuff done might lose, but he or she would begin to define a new and more plausible version of American greatness.   —DAVID BROOKS, "Third-Party Option"

Brooks makes it clear that the major change represented by a third-party option would require fresh perspectives on the part of both politicians and voters, especially a willingness to shift the focus from what he calls "the supposed superhero in the White House" to one recognizing the importance of accomplishing positive changes in local communities.

Summarizing the study of the way humans react to a cat's purr, Karen McComb and her team note parallels between the isolation cry of domestic cats and the distress cry of human infants as a way of understanding why the "cry embedded within the purr" is so successful in motivating owners to feed their cats. They conclude that the cats have learned to communicate their need for attention in ways that are impossible to ignore, ways that prompt caring responses from people. Thus, their work suggests that much can be learned by studying animal-human communication from both directions, from animals to humans as well as the reverse.

Remember that any analysis you do needs to have a purpose—to discover how cats motivate their owners to provide food on demand, to understand how partisan misperceptions create roadblocks in government, to explain why a favorite baseball player's statistics probably won't get him into the Hall of Fame. In writing up your analysis, your point will be to communicate the insight you gain from the analysis.

Clear, Precise Language

Since the point of an analysis is to help an audience understand something, you need to pay extra attention to the words you use and the way you explain your findings. You want your audience to follow your analysis easily and not get sidetracked. You need to demonstrate that you know what you are talking about. You've studied your subject, looked at it closely, thought about it—*analyzed* it; you know what to say about it and why. Now you have to craft your analysis in such a way that your readers will follow that analysis and understand what it shows. Andy Pettitte doesn't just rank low by his statistics; "he's 9th in ERA+ and dead last in WAR." Political conditions in the United States aren't just in bad shape; "the federal government is immobilized by partisanship and debt." Like Moller and Brooks, you should be precise in your explanations and in your choice of words.

Analyzing an intricate process or a complicated text requires you to use language that your audience will understand. The analysis of speed skating turns earlier in this chapter was written for an audience of young people and their parents. The language used to describe the physics that govern the process of turning is appropriate for such an audience—precise but not technical. When the author refers to Newton's law of inertia, she defines *inertia* and then explains what it means for skaters. The role of centripetal force is explained as "the more a skater leans into a turn, the more powerful the push from the skate." Everything is clear because the writer uses simple, everyday words—"tighter turn," "teetering on the edge of their skates"—to convey complex science.

Look also at the analysis of baseball statistics presented earlier in this chapter; even though it was written for a blog targeting Yankees fans, the author includes a "primer" for those readers who may not understand the kinds of statistics he presents.

You need to consider what your audience knows about your topic and what information you'll need to include to make sure they'll understand what you write. You'll also want to be careful to state your conclusions explicitly—in clear, specific language.

EAMONN FORDE, a British journalist, wrote this article in 2014, analyzing the phenomenal success of "Happy" by Pharrell Williams. It was published in *The Big Issue*, a magazine written by professional journalists and sold by homeless and unemployed people in Great Britain and nine other nations.

"Happy" by Pharrell Williams: Why This Song Has Grabbed the Nation

EAMONN FORDE

In its online version, the article links to a site showing an audience of retirees "clapping and grooving."

Y OU KNOW WHEN a song has gone that one step further and connects with people of all ages when it gets <u>the crowd at the World Indoor Bowls Championships in Great Yarmouth clapping and grooving along</u>. "Happy" by Pharrell Williams did exactly that.

The author begins by describing the song's success.

"Happy" has sold more than 650,000 copies so far in the UK, was being played more than 5,500 times a week on British radio at its peak, and has become a viral *YouTube* hit (notably a girl dancing down the street to it like it was a Northern Soul classic), but getting an audience reaction like that at the bowls—that's proper success. It now unashamedly sits in the very heart of the mainstream, capturing the hearts and ears of the nation and making everyone who hears it, well, happy.

Here's the insight that the analysis will explain.

Not bad going for a song that was never supposed to be released as a single. Its history is a curious one and drips in serendipity, showing how something in an age of over-marketing can take on a life of its own and pull off the near impossible by appealing to people of all ages.

Pharrell Williams at the 2015 Pinkpop Festival in the Netherlands.

It was originally released back in June last year, tucked away as track four on the *Despicable Me 2* soundtrack album, released by the Back Lot Music label. Pharrell had signed to Sony Music and the track was considered a "possible" to appear on his new album, which is due out later this year but has no official release date yet. Then dance and urban station Capital Xtra started playing it. Pluggers, as is the norm in radio promotion, had not been knocking on its door. They just decided they liked it and put it on heavy rotation.

> Background information provides context for those unfamiliar with how the music industry works.

This coincided with the DVD release of *Despicable Me 2* and the launch of the 24hoursofhappy.com site that featured, as its name suggests, a 24-hour-long video for the song featuring cameos from Jamie Foxx, Steve Carell and others. RCA hadn't even decided what the lead track from the album would be but quickly swung into action, and it was released as a single by the label.

"Happy" went to number one in the UK at the end of December, selling 107,000 copies in its first week. It dropped to number two the next week but was back at number one the following week, then dipping to number two a week later. RCA is confident it will sell one million copies and has weeks, if not months, in the top 10 to come.

A specific question that drives the analysis.

A precise term, "ear-worms," is used for a key concept—and carefully defined.

The author provides evidence for his analysis by quoting experts about some elements that make "Happy" so catchy.

So what is it about the song that has made it so ubiquitous without it becoming irritating?

"It's a very poppy tune and it transcends a few different genres, so maybe people are more open to it," suggests Dr. Lauren Stewart, a reader in psychology at Goldsmiths in London, who has done lengthy research into "earworms"—those songs that burrow into your brain and are difficult to dislodge. "It made me think of that OutKast song 'Hey Ya!,' which had a similar quality to it and seemed to be everywhere."

Key to its success is its musical reiteration and the instructional nature of its lyrics, according to Dr. Elizabeth Margulis, director of the Music Cognition Lab at the University of Arkansas and author of *On Repeat: How Music Plays the Mind.* "That's a pretty repetitive song," she says of "Happy." "There is a catchy bit that expressly invites you to clap along. It is literally inviting you." In that sense, "Happy" is basically an update of "If You're Happy and You Know It (Clap Your Hands)" or "Don't Worry, Be Happy."

She adds, "The thing repetition really does is it captures the motor circuitry of the brain, so you have this sense the music is really pulling you along. It can make people feel really happy. There is something about having a song that is literally about being happy that is using this technique that makes people happy. It just feels good."

But repetition and irritation are often bedfellows, so it is very tricky to pull off just the right amount of recurrence in a song. "If something is really simple and just does all the ordinary things you'd expect it to do . . . repetition can seem really annoying," says Margulis. "If it has enough sparks of new and interesting things going on in there—and not too many to make it overwhelmingly complex—it can get into that sweet spot where you can just listen to it again and again and again and it doesn't seem to get tired."

Margulis says that listening can be tightly defined by age or subculture, so being appealing to one often means being unappealing to another. "So often music is a marker of group identity," she says. "So when a song can do that [cross age boundaries], that's really powerful and unusual."

Pharrell had, of course, been on the two biggest hits of last year in the UK—"Get Lucky" (1.28 million sales) and "Blurred

Lines" (1.47 million sales), both of which relied heavily on repetition—so things were clearly in place for him with whatever song he put out, allowing him to step up as the focal point rather than play a side role as guest vocalist. "Happy" has gone that bit further and has pan-generational appeal.

"For an artist to sell a significant amount of music in this day and age you need to be applicable to more than one demographic," says Neil Hughes, the director of promotions at RCA. "The most recent one I can think of that worked in this way was 'Get Lucky,' which was also a Pharrell track. 'Get Lucky' was an event record, but the difference with that was there was an awful lot of clever build-up before they launched the project, whereas this is very much a slow-burner."

> More evidence to explain the song's great success.

"Happy" is going to be everywhere for months to come, lifting spirits and putting springs in steps. Just as he defined the sound of 2013, Pharrell looks set to provide the soundtrack to 2014—but this time with him in the spotlight and, happily, all on the song's own terms.

REFLECT. *Find a short analytical article in a newspaper or magazine. Look at the list of five characteristic features of analysis on page 234 and, using Forde's essay as a model, annotate the article to point out these features. Then evaluate how successful the article's analysis is. For example, can you identify the question that drove the analysis? Has the author provided enough description for you to follow the analysis? Is the language clear and precise? Has the author clearly stated the insight the analysis led to? Does the author provide evidence to support that insight?*

VISUAL ANALYSIS

Photos, cartoons, ads, movies, *YouTube* videos—all are visual texts, ones that say something and, just like words alone, make some kind of claim that they hope we will accept. When you analyze a visual, you ask the same questions you would of any text: How does it convey its message? How does it appeal to audiences? To answer such questions for a visual text, you'd begin by considering each of its elements—its use of color, light, and shadow; its perspective; any words or symbols; and its overall composition. Visual analysis takes various forms, but it generally includes the following features:

A Description of the Visual

Include an image of the visual in your analysis, but if that's not possible—in a print essay analyzing a video, for instance—you'll need to describe it. Your description should focus on the most important elements and those you'll point to in your analysis. What draws your eye first, and why? What's most interesting or seems most important? Does any use of contrast affect what you see? Consider the cartoon below. Your eyes were probably first drawn to the white speech balloons, because they stand out against the dark background, and they then bring your attention down to the two phones.

Some Contextual Information

You'll need to provide contextual information about your subject. What's its purpose, and who's the target audience? Is there any historical, political, or cultural context that's important to describe? Such factors are important to think about—and to describe in your analysis. The political cartoon about texting, for instance, was published in the *Atlanta Journal-Constitution* in 2009 and made a point about the need for laws prohibiting the use of hand-held cell phones while driving.

Attention to Any Words

If the visual includes any words, what do they add to its message? Whatever the words—the name of a sculpture, a caption beneath a photo, a slogan in an ad, the words in a speech balloon—you'll want to discuss how they affect the way we understand the visual. The same is true of the typography: words in boldface are likely ones the author wants to emphasize; the fonts affect the tone. If you were analyzing the cartoon about texting, for instance, you might point out that the words themselves are in textese ("Im txtng") and that they say something ridiculous (why would the driver send a text saying he's texting?)—demonstrating that texting while driving is not only dangerous but often stupid.

Close Analysis of the Message

What elements are most important in conveying the message? In the cartoon about texting, for instance, the split screen focuses attention on the contrasts between the two sides—bright colors on one side, dark ones on the other; a busy life, the lone figure of Death. And the words make the point clear: when it comes to texting while driving, Death gets the last laugh. Color, contrast, words, focus, the way it's all framed—these are all details that combine to convey a message, ones that you'll want to consider in analyzing what a visual text "says."

Insight into What the Visual "Says"

Your analysis of the visual will lead you to an understanding of what it's saying. The cartoon about texting argues that doing so while driving could be fatal. Athletic shoe ads try to persuade us to buy something—and those featuring stars like Rihanna suggest that we too can be as fierce and cool as a pop music icon: all we need are shoes like hers. How does the photo or painting or whatever you're analyzing make you feel? What does it suggest that you think or do? What techniques does it use to make you feel, think, or act in these ways?

Precise Language

It's especially important to use precise words in writing about a visual. Saying that the cartoonist uses "different colors in the driver's panel than in the one about Death" doesn't say much. Better: "the bright colors of the driver's panel—red and yellow against a purple background—present a vivid contrast to the tan and black in Death's panel." When you write about a visual, you need to use language that will help readers see the things that matter.

THINK BEYOND WORDS

↪ *TAKE A LOOK at "Paradise, Paved," a photo essay about travelers spending the night in Walmart parking lots. Click through the images and read the surrounding text. Then pick one image to analyze. How are the people in the image portrayed? How is the image itself composed? If this photo essay had a thesis, what would it be? Go to* everyonesanauthor.tumblr.com *to access the entire piece.*

VISUAL ANALYSIS / An Annotated Example

SOMINI SENGUPTA writes about technology and the law for the *New York Times*. She posted this article in 2012 on *Bits*, a *Times* blog about the technology industry.

Why Is Everyone Focused on Zuckerberg's Hoodie?
SOMINI SENGUPTA

WHO COULD HAVE THOUGHT a hoodie could mean so much? Over the last two days, there has been a great deal of mudslinging and hand-wringing about the significance of what Mark Zuckerberg, 27, the chief executive of Facebook, wore when he went courting would-be investors in New York.

> *Contextual information about the subject of the analysis.*

On the first stop of the Facebook public offering road show, Mr. Zuckerberg wore a hoodie. The only thing I remember thinking, when I first saw the footage, was that it was not a spring color. It was a dark, drab gray. That made me cringe.

> *Description of the hoodie that's being analyzed.*

Mr. Zuckerberg, of course, often wears a hoodie. Perhaps he thinks it's fetching. Perhaps, he wears it because it is his trademark, much like the Issey Miyake custom-made black turtlenecks that Steve Jobs, one of Mr. Zuckerberg's executive idols, wore during his public appearances. (Mr. Jobs had hundreds of them made, and he told his biographer, Walter Isaacson, that he had enough of them to wear every day for the rest of his life.)

Hoodies, like black turtlenecks, appear casual, like you just threw on the first thing you could find dangling on a hook behind the door. In fact, it carries a lot of meaning. It signifies the opposite of a Hermès tie, the favored accoutrement of Wall Street.

> *Analysis of what a hoodie signifies, and of the statement that Zuckerberg was making by wearing one when meeting with investors.*

Mark Zuckerberg in New York during Facebook's road show.

It signifies that you're busy making things that are really, really important to the world, which is what Silicon Valley believes, and hey—you don't really care what you look like.

Right.

Mr. Zuckerberg is nothing if not a master of optics. Like Mr. Jobs' black turtleneck, the hoodie is his anti-fashion statement.

The hoodie in Manhattan prompted, as Mr. Zuckerberg may have expected, a gush of approval and disdain. Hoodiegate, it came to be called, and it began to show signs of a culture war between the two coasts—Wall Street versus Silicon Valley.

His critics saw it as a sign of immaturity and disrespect for those whom he expected to finance his company. An equities research analyst, Michael Pachter, said it would have been more fitting had he put on a blazer over a T-shirt. Mr. Pachter, incidentally, is so bullish on Facebook he thinks it's worth more than what the company estimates to be its value. But would Mr. Zuckerberg dress like that at church, Mr. Pachter, wearing a pinstripe suit, wondered aloud on a television program.

Naturally, a Twitter hashtag emerged to take up the cause: #zuckerbergshoodie.

His defenders said the hoodie signified Silicon Valley ethos: a brash, youthful self-confidence.

Clear and precise language presents the two opposing perceptions of the hoodie: as a sign of "immaturity and disrespect" or of "brash, youthful self-confidence."

"Mark Zuckerberg really doesn't give a damn about you," Henry Blodget wrote in *Business Insider*. Mr. Blodget continued, in case New York wanted to listen: "I don't mean to be rude, Wall Street, but Mark Zuckerberg is actually wise not to care much about you. First, as discussed, he controls the company. But second, most of you don't do much to deserve much attention from CEOs."

Quotes from business and technology professionals show what they think of Zuckerberg's hoodie.

Om Malik, founder of the GigaOm technology blog, opined that Mr. Pachter "is smoking stuff that's outside the realm of legality." The dapper blogger went on to conclude: "Now if you were looking for a problem with Zuckerberg's hoodie, then you should see it for what it really is: a fashion abomination."

On Thursday, Mr. Zuckerberg's sister, Randi, posted on Twitter a link to a pinstripe hoodie that a clothing label had unveiled immediately after hoodiegate began. A post in the *Atlantic Wire* surmised that the hoodie gave Mr. Zuckerberg the magical powers that he—and his investors—would need to keep spinning gold.

The to and fro over hoodiegate of course has been largely about what wealthy and, by and large, white men wear in Silicon Valley and on Wall Street.

The author's insight: what she thinks the ruckus about Zuckerberg's hoodie means.

But a hoodie is not just a hoodie, except when it's just a hoodie.

A teenage boy named Trayvon Martin was wearing a hoodie the night that he was killed in a gated townhouse community in Sanford, Fla., outside Orlando. His killer, an armed neighborhood watch volunteer, told police he appeared "real suspicious."

The hoodie became a symbol of solidarity in the days after the boy's death. Many people I know took pictures of themselves wearing hoodies. Naturally, they posted their pictures on *Facebook*.

An unexpected insight: that those fretting about Zuckerberg's hoodie are focusing on the wrong things.

Trayvon's hoodie is a reminder that neither Wall Street nor Silicon Valley is terribly representative of our country.

REFLECT. *How surprised were you by the way Somini Sengupta concluded her post? What do you think her main point was in writing this piece? Look again at her title: what do you think it means? Keeping in mind that she posted this piece on a blog read by people in the technology business, what do you think she was saying to them?*

WRITING ANALYTICALLY / A Roadmap

Find a topic that matters—to you, and to others

Whether you can choose your topic or have to respond to a specific assignment, find an angle that appeals to you—and to your audience. Write about something that you care about, that engages you. No audience will want to hear about something that you are not interested in writing about.

If you can choose your topic, begin by considering your interests. What do you like to do? What issues do you care about? Do you have a favorite book? If you've read and re-read the Harry Potter books, you might analyze J. K. Rowling's storytelling style or the causes behind the books' ongoing popularity. An interest in sports could lead you to analyze statistical data on a favorite athlete (as Will Moller does) or to analyze the process of doing something in a particular sport (as Darlene Jenkins does).

If you've been assigned a topic, say to conduct a rhetorical analysis of the Gettysburg Address, find an angle that interests you. If you're a history buff, you might research the particular occasion on which Lincoln spoke and look at how his words were especially appropriate to that audience and event. Or perhaps your interests lie more in current politics, in which case you might compare Lincoln's address to the speeches politicians make today.

Make your topic matter to your audience. Some topics matter to everyone, or nearly everyone; you might be able to identify such topics by checking the media for what's being debated and discussed. But when you're writing about something that may not automatically appeal to a wide audience, it's your responsibility as the writer to tell them why they should care about it. Somini Sengupta does this in her piece about Mark Zuckerberg's hoodie by showing the powerful assumptions we make about people based on their dress—assumptions that, for a different young man wearing a similar hoodie, determined life and death.

Consider your rhetorical situation

Keep in mind the elements of your particular situation—your audience, your specific purpose, your stance, and so on—and how they will or should influence the choices you make in your writing.

Identify your AUDIENCE. Who do you want to reach, and how can you shape your analysis so that you get through to them? Karen McComb's analysis of cat purring was for an audience of scientific peers, whereas Ken Tucker wrote about *Game of Thrones* for BBC's *Culture* site, which is written for the general public. Very different audiences, very different purposes—very different analyses. You, too, should think carefully about whom you are trying to reach.

- What do you know about them—their age, gender, cultural and linguistic background?
- What are they likely to know about your subject, and what background information will you need to provide?
- How might they benefit from the analysis and insight you offer?
- Will your subject matter to them—and if not, how can you make them care about it?

If you are writing for the internet, you will likely reach a broad audience whose characteristics you can't predict, so you need to assume a range of readers—just as Will Moller does in his blog post about Andy Pettitte. Even though his primary audience is Yankees fans, he knows that some readers won't know much about statistics, so he provides the definitions they need to understand his analysis.

Articulate your PURPOSE. Even if you're writing in response to an assignment, here are some questions that can help you narrow your focus and articulate some more specific purposes:

- What are you analyzing? A text? A community? A process? Causes? Data? A visual?
- What's motivated you to write? Are you responding to some other text or author?
- What do you want to accomplish by analyzing this subject? How can you best achieve your goals?
- What do you want your audience to take away from your analysis?

Think about your STANCE. How do you want to come across as an author? How can your writing reflect that stance? If your subject is surfing and you're writing on a surfers' blog about how to catch a wave for an audience of beginners, your stance might be that of an experienced surfer or a former beginner. Your language would probably be informal, with little or no surfing jargon. If, on the other hand, you're writing an article for *Surfing Magazine* analyzing the process Laird Hamilton developed to ride fifty-foot waves, your stance might be that of an objective reporter, and your language would need to be more technical for that well-informed audience. No matter what your stance or target audience, you need to consider what kind of language is appropriate, what terms need to be defined, and how you can establish your authority as an author.

Consider the larger CONTEXT. If you are analyzing an ad for a composition class, you will want to look at relevant information about its original context. When was the ad created, and who was the target audience? What were the social, economic, and political conditions at the time? All of that is contextual information. If you are preparing a load analysis for an engineering class, you'll need to consider factors such as how, when, and where the structure will be used. Other contextual information comes from what others have said about your subject, and your analysis adds to the conversation.

Consider MEDIA. Will your analysis be delivered in print? on a website? in an oral presentation? Are you writing for an online class? a blog? your campus newspaper? If you get to choose your medium, the choice should depend on how you can best present your subject and reach your intended audience. Do you need to be able to incorporate visuals, or audio or video, or to speak directly to your audience in person? Whether you have a choice or not, the media you use will affect how you design and deliver your analysis.

Consider matters of DESIGN. Think about how to best present your information and whether you need to follow any disciplinary conventions. Does your analysis include data that is easiest to understand in a chart or graph? Would headings help readers follow your analysis? Would illustrations make your point clearer?

Analyze your subject

What kind of analysis is needed for your subject and purpose? You may be assigned to conduct a certain kind of analysis, or you may be inspired by a question, as Will Moller was in analyzing data to determine whether Andy Pettitte is likely to be elected to the Hall of Fame. But sometimes you may be asked simply to "analyze x"—an ad, a game, a historical event, profiles of several companies—in which case you'll need to determine what kind of analysis will work best. The kind of analysis you need to do—*rhetorical analysis, discourse analysis, process analysis, causal analysis, data analysis, visual analysis*—will determine the way you study your subject.

If you're analyzing rhetoric, you need to look at what the text you're examining says and how it supports its claims.

- What question are you asking about this text? What specifically are you looking for?
- What CLAIM is the text making—and what REASONS and EVIDENCE does the author provide for the claim? Do they convince you?
- Does the writer acknowledge or respond to COUNTERARGUMENTS or other opinions? If so, are they presented fairly?
- Are there any words that indicate what the author thinks—or wants you to think?
- How does the author establish AUTHORITY to address the topic?
- Does the text use any EMOTIONAL APPEALS? If so, how?

If you're analyzing a discourse community, you're trying to understand the community whose language practices you are focusing on. And you'll want to be clear about both your reasons for choosing a particular community and the questions you're striving to answer about your subject.

Are you primarily concerned with how a given community creates cohesion through its discourse practices? Or are you interested in narrowing your focus to a particular type of exchange, focusing on vocabulary choices, figurative language, rhetorical elements, or preferred types of argument? Are you interested in understanding how the community establishes its social relationships through language? Or do you want to chart this particular community's similarities to and differences from other groups? Or perhaps you want to focus on how a given individual manages the discourses of multiple communities: an engineering student who is also a birder and a church choir member. Enacting one's identity in multiple communities requires using language at least somewhat differently in each. The following questions can guide your research and analysis:

- Why have you chosen this particular community? Or this specific discourse?

- What questions are you trying to answer about your subject?

- What existing texts—written, visual, recorded—can you draw on for background information?

- What kinds of research will you need to do to observe your subject's communication practices? Textual analysis? Data collection? Interviews?

- Do you observe any patterns or habits? Does what you observe match your expectations or surprise you?

- Can you observe your subject firsthand? Who might help you access the community you're interested in? Will you need permissions from your subjects or your university?

If you're analyzing a process, you'll need to decide whether your analysis will be **INFORMATIONAL** (how something works) or **INSTRUCTIONAL** (how to do something). Writing about how solar panels convert sunshine to energy would be informational, whereas writing about how to install solar panels would be instructional—and would need to explicitly identify all materials needed and then tell readers step-by-step exactly how to carry out the process. Once you've determined the kind of analysis, you might then consider questions like these:

- What question is prompting your analysis?

- If the process is instructional, what materials are needed?

- What are the steps in the process? What does each step accomplish?

- What order do the steps follow? Whether a process follows a set order (throwing a curveball, parallel parking a car) or not (playing sudoku), you'll need to present the steps in some order that makes sense.

If you're analyzing causes, you're looking for answers to why something happened. Why, for instance, have crime rates fallen in a particular city over the past few decades? Is it because police are more actively patrolling neighborhoods? Or because poverty has dropped in some parts of the city? Or because prison programs have expanded?

Questions about causes can rarely be answered definitively, so you'll usually be **ARGUING** that certain causes are the most plausible or the *primary* ones, and that others are less likely or *secondary*. In addition, although an *immediate cause* may be obvious, less obvious *long-term causes* may also have contributed. You'll need to consider all possible causes and provide evidence to support the ones you identify as most plausible.

As you determine which causes are more or less likely, be careful not to confuse coincidence with causation. That two events—such as a new police-patrol policy in a city and a drop in the crime rate—occurred more or less simultaneously, or even that one event preceded the other, does not prove that one *caused* the other.

You'll often need to do some **RESEARCH** to understand all the possible causes and whether they are primary or contributing, immediate or long-term causes. The following questions can guide your research and analysis:

- What question is prompting your analysis?
- List all the causes you can think of. Which seem to be the primary causes and which are contributing or secondary causes? Which are immediate causes and which are long-term causes?
- Might any of the causes on your list be merely coincidences?
- Which causes seem most plausible—and why?
- What research do you need to do to answer these questions?

If you're analyzing data, you're trying to identify patterns in information that you or someone else has gathered in order to answer a question or make an argument. The information collected by the US Census is data. Social scientists looking for patterns to help them make arguments or predictions about population trends might analyze the data on numbers of families with children in urban areas.

In his blog post on Andy Pettitte, Will Moller provides numerical data on ten pitchers' performances, which he then analyzes to determine whether Pettitte is likely to get into the Hall of Fame. His analysis explicitly states his guiding question—"Should Andy Pettitte be in the Hall of Fame?"—and then answers it by considering each element of the data as it relates to Pettitte's performance.

Although the mathematical nature of analyzing **QUANTITATIVE** data can often make it more straightforward than other kinds of analysis, identifying statistical patterns and figuring out their significance can be challenging. Finding and interpreting patterns in **QUALITATIVE** data can also be tricky, especially as the data is more free-form: words, stories, photographs, and so on. Here are some questions to consider when analyzing data:

- What question are you trying to answer?
- Are there any existing data that can help answer your question? If so, will they provide sufficient information, or do you need to conduct any RESEARCH of your own to generate the data you need?
- If you're working with existing data, who collected the data, using what methods, and why? How do the data relate to the analysis you're conducting?
- Do the data show the full picture? Are there other data that tell a different story?
- Can you identify patterns in the data? If so, are they patterns you expected, or are any of them surprising?

If you're analyzing a visual, how do specific visual elements convey a message or create an effect?

- What draws your eye first, and why? What seems most interesting or important?
- What's the PURPOSE of this visual, and who's its target AUDIENCE?
- Is there any larger historical, cultural, or political CONTEXT to consider?
- Are there any words, and what do they tell you about the message?
- What's the overall ARGUMENT or effect? How do you know?

Determine what your analysis shows

Once you've analyzed your subject, you need to figure out what your analysis shows. What was the question that first prompted your analysis, and how can you now answer that question? What have you discovered about your subject? What have you found that interests you—and how can you make it matter to your audience?

State your insight as a tentative THESIS. Once you've determined what insight your analysis has led to, write it out as a tentative thesis, noting what you've analyzed and why and what conclusions or insights you want to share. Your thesis introduces your point, what you want to say about your subject. Let's say you're writing a rhetorical analysis of the Gettysburg Address. Here's how you might introduce an analysis of that speech:

> Following Edward Everett's two-hour oration, President Lincoln spoke eloquently for a mere two minutes, deploying rhetorical devices like repetition, contrast, and rhythm in a way that connected emotionally with his audience.

This sentence tells us that the writer will describe the event, say something about the length of the speech, and explain how specific words and structures resulted in an eloquently simple but profoundly moving speech.

As you formulate your thesis, begin by thinking about your **AUDIENCE** and how you can make your analysis most compelling to them. What aspects of your analysis will they care most about? How might it apply to them? Does your analysis have important implications beyond the immediate subject, as Somini Sengupta's analysis of a simple hoodie does?

Then list the evidence you found that supports your analysis—examples, quotations, significant data points, and so forth. What of all your evidence will best support your point, and what will your audience find most persuasive?

Organize and start writing

Start with your tentative thesis, being sure that it identifies what you're analyzing, what insights you have to offer, and why it is significant. As you write, be sure you're supporting your thesis—and that it's working. That said, don't hesitate to revise it if you have difficulty supporting it.

Give EVIDENCE that supports your thesis. Depending on the kind of analysis, evidence could include examples, statistics, quotations, definitions, and so on.

Cite other sources, but remember that this is *your* analysis. Your audience wants to hear your voice and learn from your insights. At the same time, don't forget to acknowledge other perspectives.

Draft an OPENING. You might begin by describing what you're analyzing and why, explaining what question prompted you to take a closer look at your topic. Provide any background information your audience might need. State your thesis: what are you claiming about your subject?

Draft a **CONCLUSION**. You might reiterate what you've learned from your analysis and what you want your audience to understand about your subject. Make sure they know why your analysis matters, to them and to you.

Look critically at your draft, get response—and revise

Read your draft slowly and carefully to see whether you've made your guiding question clear, described your subject sufficiently, offered enough evidence to support your analysis, and provided your audience with some insight about your subject.

Then ask others to read and respond to your draft. If your school has a writing center, try to meet with a tutor, bringing along any questions you have. Here are some questions that can help you or others read over a draft of analytic writing:

- *Is the question that prompted your analysis clear?* Is it a question worth considering?

- *How does the* **OPENING** *capture the audience's interest?* Does it indicate why this analysis matters? How else might you begin?

- *Is the point of your analysis clear?* Have you stated the point explicitly in a **THESIS** —and if not, do you need to?

- *Is the subject described in enough detail for your audience?* Is there any other information they might need in order to follow your analysis?

- *What* **EVIDENCE** *do you provide to support your point?* Is it sufficient?

- *What insights have you gained from the analysis?* Have you stated them explicitly? How likely is it that readers will accept your conclusions?

- *If you've cited any sources, are they credible and convincing?* Have you integrated them smoothly into your text—is it clear what you are saying yourself and where (and why) you are citing others? And have you **DOCUMENTED** any sources you've cited?

- *Have you addressed other perspectives?* Do you need to acknowledge possible **COUNTERARGUMENTS** ?

- *How would you describe the* TONE, and does it accurately convey your STANCE? Is the tone appropriate for your audience and purpose?

- *How is the analysis organized?* Is it easy to follow, with clear TRANSITIONS from one point to the next? Are there headings—and if not, would adding them help? If you're analyzing a process, are the steps in an order that your audience will be able to follow easily?

- *Consider* STYLE. Look at the choice of words and kinds of sentences—are they appropriately formal (or informal) for the audience and purpose? Could the style be improved in any way?

- *How effective is the* DESIGN? Have you included any images or other visual elements—and if so, how do they contribute to the analysis? If not, is there any information that might be easier to understand if presented in a table or chart or accompanied by an image?

- *How does the draft* CONCLUDE? Is the CONCLUSION forceful and memorable? How else might the analysis conclude?

- *Consider the title.* Does it make clear what the analysis is about, and will it make your audience interested in reading on?

Revise your draft in light of your own observations and any feedback you get from others, keeping your audience and purpose firmly in mind. But remember: *you* are the analyst here, so you need to make the decisions.

REFLECT. Once you've completed your analysis, let it settle for a while and then take time to reflect. How well did you analyze your subject? What insights did your analysis lead to? What additional revisions would you make if you could? Research shows that such reflections help "lock in" what you learn for future use.

Google Home vs Alexa:
Two Simple User Experience Design Gestures That Delighted a Female User

JOHNA PAOLINO

A YEAR AGO, MY BOYFRIEND got an Amazon Echo. I remember first using the product, dazzled at its ability to process requests from across the room. *Alexa, play us some music.*

As the year progressed, the wow factor faded quickly.

The product features continued working to their full effect, but I felt very unsettled. I found myself constantly agitated as I observed my boyfriend bark commands at this black cylinder.

Alexa, turn off the lights. Alexa, set my alarm for 8am.

This declarative speech was so incongruous with how he interacts with me, with how he interacts with any human.

Was it how he was asking? Was it that she was female? Was I jealous?

As a user experience designer, I am constantly questioning the emotional effect technology has on me. Perhaps I was taking too much of my day job into my

---

JOHNA PAOLINO is a senior product designer at the *New York Times,* where she designs digital tools to make the newsroom more efficient. She also writes about user experience and design. This piece was published on *Medium* in 2017.

personal life. I decided to mute this awareness until this holiday season when I unwrapped my very own Google Home. I configured the device, hesitantly looking forward to some of the features my apartment had been missing over the past year.

Ok Google, play NPR news. Hey Google, set my alarm for 8am.

Why did these interactions suddenly feel so natural? They felt appropriate. In fact, I was delighted by my new Google Home.

Although product features differ slightly, the root cause of my emotional shift had nothing to do with these capabilities. All the feelings I had for Alexa came down to two simplistic user experience design differences.

The Naming of the Products

I've learned throughout my career that the most significant UX performance 5 gains often come down to microcopy. This could not be more true here. Amazon is the name of a pioneering e-commerce platform and revolutionary cloud computing company. Echo is its product name, first to market of its kind. Alexa? Alexa is just the name of a female that performs personal tasks for you in your home.

Apple and Siri set a precedent for this. Was there a need to rename the voice component of these products? Why isn't it Echo or Amazon? Why not Apple? By doing this, we've subconsciously constrained the capabilities of a female. With the Echo, we've even gone as far as to confine her to a home.

The voice component of the Google Home, however, is simply triggered with "Google." Google, a multinational, first-of-its-kind technology company. Suddenly a female's voice represents a lot more. This made me happy.

Conversational Triggers

Alexa responds to her name only. Google's product must be triggered with a "hey Google" or "ok Google." By requiring these introductory words as triggers, Google has forced an element of conversation. The experience difference here is huge! When I return to Alexa now I feel authoritative.

The advancement of feminism requires awareness from both genders. It isn't isolated to how men treat women, but extends to how women treat each other. I am constantly making an effort to change my behaviors towards other women, and in this effort certainly prefer how I am asked to greet Google.

The smallest of user experience details matter. My entire emotional experience   10
between these products can be boiled down to: "Hey," "Ok," and a name. I want to thank Google. Thank you for paying closer attention to the details, and to the female users.

We have a responsibility as designers and technologists. We can make these systems model how we want the world to be—let's take steps forward not backward.

Thinking about the Text

1. With her title, Johna Paolino immediately establishes that this will be a contest: Google Home against Alexa. How does she establish her **AUTHORITY** to write on this topic?

2. Where does Paolino indicate the question driving her analysis?

3. Who is Paolino's **AUDIENCE**? Point to specific places where she uses language to establish a connection with readers. How would you describe her **TONE**?

4. Since Paolino doesn't include any photographs or audio clips (just her own original drawing of her subjects), the analysis largely depends on her **DESCRIPTION** of the two smart speakers. What **EVIDENCE** does Pao-

lino provide to support her stance? What details or evidence might you add to make her argument even stronger?

5. Following the guidelines in this chapter, write an **ANALYSIS** of two competing tech products you have experience using—perhaps an Android phone and an iPhone, two fitness tracking apps, or competing social media platforms. Be sure to state the question you're exploring, the insight you gain, and the evidence supporting your stance.

Advertisements R Us

MELISSA RUBIN

ADVERTISEMENTS ARE WRITTEN to persuade us—to make us want to support a certain cause, buy a particular car, drink a specific kind of soda. But *how* do they do it? How do they persuade us? Since the beginning of modern consumer culture, companies have cleverly tailored advertisements to target specific groups. To do so, they include text and images that reflect and appeal to the ideals, values, and stereotypes held by the consumers they wish to attract. As a result, advertisements reveal a lot about society. We can learn a great deal about the prevailing culture by looking closely at the deliberate ways a company crafts an ad to appeal to particular audiences.

This ad that appeared in the August 1950 *Coca-Cola Bottler* magazine, a trade magazine for Coca-Cola bottlers (fig. 1), features a larger-than-life red Coca-Cola vending machine with the slogan "Drink Coca-Cola—Work *Refreshed*" (Advertisement for Coca-Cola). Set against a bright blue sky with puffy white clouds, an overlarge open bottle of Coke hovers just to the right and slightly above the vending machine, next to the head of "Sprite Boy," a pixie-ish character and onetime Coke symbol, who sports a bottle cap for a hat. Sprite Boy's left hand gestures past the floating Coke bottle and toward a crowd congregating before the vending machine. The group, overwhelmingly male and apparently all white, includes blue-collar workers in casual clothing, servicemen in

MELISSA RUBIN wrote this analysis when she was a student at Hofstra University using an early draft of this chapter. She now teaches creative writing and composition at Hofstra University and Touro College.

Fig. 1. 1950 ad from *Coca-Cola Bottler* magazine. Advertisement for Coca-Cola.

uniform, and businessmen in suits in the foreground; the few women displayed are in the background, wearing dresses. The setting is industrialized and urban, as indicated by the factory and smokestacks on the far left side of the scene and by the skyscrapers and apartment building on the right.

Practically since its invention, Coca-Cola has been identified with mainstream America. Born from curiosity and experimentation in an Atlanta pharmacy in 1886, Coke's phenomenal growth paralleled America's in the industrial age. Benefiting from developments in technology and transportation, by 1895 it was "sold and consumed in every state and territory in the United States" ("Coca-Cola Company"). In 2010, Diet Coke became the second-most-popular carbonated drink in the world . . . behind Coca-Cola (Esterl). In the immediate postwar world, Coke became identified with American optimism and energy, thanks in part to the company's wartime declaration that "every man in uniform gets a bottle of Coca-Cola for 5 cents, wherever he is, and whatever it costs the Company" ("Coca-Cola Company"). To meet this dictate, bottling plants were built overseas with the result that many people other than Americans first tasted Coke during this war that America won so decisively, and when peace finally came, "the foundations were laid for Coca-Cola to do business overseas" ("Coca-Cola Company").

Given the context, just a few years after World War II and at the beginning of the Korean War, the setting clearly reflects the idea that Americans experienced increased industrialization and urbanization as a result of World War II. Factories had sprung up across the country to aid in the war effort, and many rural and small-town Americans had moved to industrial areas and large cities in search of work. In this advertisement, the buildings surround the people, symbolizing a sense of community and the way Americans had come together in a successful effort to win the war.

The ad suggests that Coca-Cola recognized the patriotism inspired by the war and wanted to inspire similar positive feelings about their product. In the center of the ad, the huge red vending machine looks like the biggest skyscraper of all—the dominant feature of the urban industrial landscape. On the upper right, the floating face of Coca-Cola's Sprite Boy towers above the scene. A pale character with wild white hair, hypnotic eyes, and a mysterious smile, Sprite Boy stares straight at readers, his left hand gesturing toward the red machine. Sprite Boy's size and placement in the ad makes him appear godlike, as if he, the embodiment of Coca-Cola, is a powerful force uniting—and refreshing—hardworking Americans. The placement of the vending machine in the center of the ad and the wording on it evoke the idea that drinking

Coca-Cola will make a hardworking American feel refreshed while he (and apparently it was rarely she) works and becomes part of a larger community. The text at the bottom of the ad, "A welcome host to workers—*Inviting you to the pause that refreshes with ice-cold Coca-Cola*"—sends the same message to consumers: Coke will refresh and unite working America.

The way that Coca-Cola chooses to place the objects and depict men and women in this ad speaks volumes about American society in the middle of the twentieth century: a white, male-dominated society in which servicemen and veterans were a numerous and prominent presence. The clothing that the men in the foreground wear reflects the assumption that the target demographic for the ad—people who worked in Coca-Cola bottling plants—valued hard workers and servicemen during a time of war. White, uniformed men are placed front and center. One man wears an Army uniform, the one next to him wears a Navy uniform, and the next an Air Force uniform. By placing the servicemen so prominently, Coca-Cola emphasizes their important role in society and underscores the value Americans placed on their veterans at a time when almost all male Americans were subject to the draft and most of them could expect to serve in the military or had already done so. The other men in the foreground—one wearing a blue-collar work uniform and the other formal business attire—are placed on either side of and slightly apart from the soldiers, suggesting that civilian workers played a valuable role in society, but one secondary to that of the military. Placing only a few women dressed in casual day wear in the far background of the image represents the assumption that women played a less important role in society—or at least in the war effort and the workforce, including Coke's.

The conspicuous mixture of stereotypical middle-class and working-class attire is noteworthy because in 1950, the US economy had been marked by years of conflict over labor's unionization efforts and management's opposition to them—often culminating in accommodation between the two sides. The ad seems to suggest that such conflict should be seen as a thing of the past, that men with blue-collar jobs and their bosses are all "workers" whom Coca-Cola, a generous "host," is inviting to share in a break for refreshments. Thus all economic classes, together with a strong military, can unite to build a productive industrial future and a pleasant lifestyle for themselves.

From the perspective of the twenty-first century, this ad is especially interesting because it seems to be looking backward instead of forward in significant ways. By 1950, the highly urban view of American society it presents was starting to be challenged by widespread movement out of central cities to the suburbs, but nothing in the ad hints at this profound change. At the time, offices and factories were still located mostly in urban areas and associated in Americans' minds with cities, and the ad clearly reflects this perspective. In addition, it presents smoke pouring from factory smokestacks in a positive light, with no sign of the environmental damage that such emissions cause, and that would become increasingly clear over the next few decades.

Another important factor to consider: everyone in the ad is white. During the 1950s, there was still a great deal of racial prejudice and segregation in the United States. Coca-Cola was attuned to white society's racial intolerance and chose in this ad to depict what they undoubtedly saw as average Americans, the primary demographic of the audience for this publication: Coca-Cola employees. While Coke did feature African Americans in some ads during the late 1940s and early 1950s, they were celebrity musicians like Louis Armstrong, Duke Ellington, Count Basie, or Graham Jackson (the accordion player who was a huge favorite of Franklin Delano Roosevelt) or star athletes like Marion Motley and Bill Willis, the first men to break the color barrier in NFL football ("World"). The contrast between these extremes underscores the prejudice: "ordinary" people are represented by whites, while only exceptional African Americans appear in the company's ads.

In 1950, then, the kind of diversity that Coke wanted to highlight and appeal   10 to was economic (middle-class and working-class) and war-related (civilian and military). Today, such an ad would probably represent the ethnic diversity missing from the 1950 version, with smiling young people of diverse skin colors and facial features relaxing with Cokes, probably now in cans rather than bottles. But the differences in economic, employment, or military status or in clothing styles that the 1950 ad highlighted would be unlikely to appear, not because they no longer exist, but because advertisers for products popular with a broad spectrum of society no longer consider them a useful way to appeal to consumers.

While initially the ads for Coca-Cola reflected the values of the time, their enormous success eventually meant that Coke ads helped shape the American identity. In them, Americans always appear smiling, relaxed, carefree, united in their quest for well-deserved relaxation and refreshment. They drive convertibles, play sports, dance, and obviously enjoy life. The message: theirs is a life to be envied and emulated, so drink Coca-Cola and live that life yourself.

Works Cited

Advertisement for Coca-Cola. *Vintage Ad Browser*, 1950, www
　　.vintageadbrowser.com/coke-ads-1950s/6#adjjm2v0hc7efog6.
"The Coca-Cola Company Heritage Timeline." *Coca-Cola History*, Coca-Cola
　　Company, www.coca-colacompany.com/history/.
Esterl, Mike. "Diet Coke Wins Battle in Cola Wars." *The Wall Street Journal*,
　　17 Mar. 2011, p. B1.
"The World of Coca-Cola Self-Guided Tour for Teachers. Highlights: African
　　American History Month." *World of Coca-Cola*, www.worldofcoca-cola
　　.com/wp-content/uploads/sites/3/2013/10/aahhighschool.pdf.

Thinking about the Text

1. What insight does Melissa Rubin offer about the Coca-Cola ad she analyzes, and what **EVIDENCE** does she provide to support her analysis? Has she persuaded you to accept her conclusions? Why or why not?

2. What historical **CONTEXT** does Rubin provide, and what does that information contribute to her analysis?

3. Rubin's analysis is driven by this question: what can we learn about the culture in which a given ad is created by closely examining how that ad appeals to particular audiences? What other questions might you try to answer by analyzing an ad?

4. Rubin looks closely at the men and women in this ad and makes certain assumptions about them. What sorts of details does she point out to identify who these people are? Do you think she's represented them accurately? If not, how might you identify them differently, and why?

5. Write an **ANALYSIS** of a current ad, looking specifically at how it reflects American values in the twenty-first century. Be sure to include the ad in your essay.

FIFTEEN

"Just the Facts"
Reporting Information

**S**OME **AMERICANS ASSOCIATE THE LINE** "Just the facts, ma'am" with *Dragnet*, a 1950s TV crime drama, and more specifically with Sgt. Joe Friday, played by Jack Webb, who used this phrase when interviewing women during investigations. The first radio show to jump to TV, *Dragnet* was produced in close collaboration with the LAPD. How close? Police Chief William Parker had veto power over every scene in exchange for the use of real LAPD case files. The show was even often filmed in police headquarters. Parker and Webb brought their law-and-order worldview to the series along with its 1950s view of race differences and gender roles.

This story can be seen as a kind of very short report, and it demonstrates an important aspect of reports: they present information to audiences made up of people with varying degrees of knowledge. Perhaps you've heard the phrase "Just the facts, ma'am" but had no idea where it came from. Perhaps you've never heard of *Dragnet*. Now you have, and you know a few things about it. Even if you were familiar with both the program and the expression, you now likely have a new bit of information: the show that defined the genre of police procedurals was a PR vehicle for the LAPD. Thus, this very short report demonstrates how reports are written with a range of readers in mind.

A meme using a photo of actor Jack Webb in his most famous role as Sgt. Joe Friday with his most famous line from the program *Dragnet* at the top, along with a more modern addition below.

Reports are built of information that is factual in some way. As you no doubt realize, separating what is factual from what is opinion can be a challenge, especially when the topic is controversial.

The primary goal of a report is to present factual information to educate an audience in some way. The stance of those who write reports is generally objective rather than argumentative. Thus, newspaper and television reporters—note the word—in the United States have traditionally tried to present news in a neutral way. Writers of lab reports describe as carefully and objectively as they can how they conducted their experiments and what they found. Perhaps even more than authors in other genres, therefore, writers of reports aim to create an ETHOS of trustworthiness and reliability.

This chapter offers guidelines for composing reports, including profiles, a kind of report often assigned in college. As you'll see, writing effective reports requires you to pay careful attention to your purpose, audience, and stance as well as to whatever facts you're reporting.

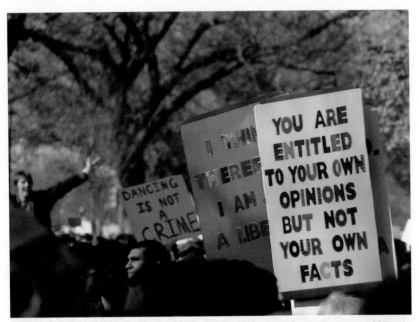

A 2010 rally sign quoting a statement attributed to Daniel Patrick Moynihan (1927–2003), who served as a US senator from New York, advisor to President Richard Nixon, ambassador to India, and UN ambassador.

REFLECT. Think about reports you've read, heard, seen, or written recently, and make a list of them. Your list may include everything from a lab report for a biology class, to a documentary film, to a PowerPoint *presentation you and several classmates created for a course. What features do these reports share—and how do they differ?*

Across Academic Disciplines

Reports are found everywhere in academic life. You're certainly familiar with book reports, and you're probably familiar with lab reports from science courses. Students and practitioners in most fields in the *physical sciences, social sciences,* and *applied sciences* regularly write reports, generally based on experiments or other kinds of systematic investigation.

Many scientific reports share a common format—often labeled IMRAD (introduction, methods, results, and discussion)—and a common purpose: to convey information. The format mirrors the stages of inquiry: you ask a question, describe the materials and methods you used to try to answer it, report the results you found, and discuss what they mean in light of what you and others already know.

Another kind of report students often write, especially in courses that focus on contemporary society in some way, is the profile, a firsthand report on an individual, a group, an event, or an institution. A profile of a person might be based on an interview, perhaps with an American soldier who served in Afghanistan, for example, or the first female professor to receive tenure in your college's economics department. Similarly, a profile of an institution might report on the congregation of a specific house of worship, an organization, or a company; such reports often have a specific audience in mind, whether it is donors, investors, members, or clients.

Across Media

When reporting information, you'll find that different media offer you radically different resources. Throughout this chapter, we'll refer to reporting by the *New York Times* on the "double-full-full-full," an especially challenging aerial skiing maneuver involving a triple back flip and four body twists. Just before the 2010 Winter Olympics, the *Times* reported on this jump in three media. It was the subject of a *news article* by Henry Fountain that appeared in the Science section in print and online. It was also the basis of a *video* feature on the *Times* website in which Fountain explains the physics of the flip, as demonstrated by US Olympic skier Ryan St. Onge. Finally, it was the focus of part of a science *podcast* featuring interviews with both St. Onge and Fountain. Two of these reports use images, two use spoken words, and one relies primarily on written words.

In studying these three reports, you'll get a clear idea of how medium influences not only how information is reported but also what kinds of information can be covered. For example, consider *Twitter*: imagine what Fountain could have reported about the double-full-full-full in 280 characters.

Across Cultures and Communities

Wherever you find formal organizations, companies, and other institutions, you'll find reports of various kinds. For example, a school board trying to improve safety measures in a time of shrinking budgets will surely rely on information in reports written by *parents' organizations, community groups,*

WATCH THE VIDEO of US Olympic skier Ryan St. Onge performing a double-full-full-full, a triple back flip with four body twists. Then read the article on the physics of aerial skiing. Pay attention to how some of the technical terms are defined (and keep in mind that in the video, definitions may include images as well as words). Describe the double-full-full-full using words alone. Then add an image. Do you need to alter your original description once you add the image? Go to everyonesanauthor .tumblr.com to access the video and article.

teachers' unions, or *outside consultants.* Odds are that the reports from each of these groups would differ in focus and tone. Some of these reports might be based primarily on statistical data while others might feature personal testimonies. Those created by outside consultants would likely be very formal and data-driven and might include a *PowerPoint* presentation to the school board followed by a question-and-answer period. In contrast, a report from a parents' group could include a homemade video consisting primarily of conversations with students.

As a student, you'll be working in various academic communities, and you will need to pay attention to the way information is reported across disciplines—and to what is expected of you in any reports that you write.

Across Genres

While reports are a common genre of writing, you'll also have occasion to report information in other genres. **NARRATIVES**, **ANALYSES**, **REVIEWS**, **ARGUMENTS**, and many other kinds of writing contain factual information often presented as neutrally as possible—and you will often report factual evidence to support your claims.

On the other hand, some documents that are called reports present more than "just the facts" and cross the line to **ANALYZE** or interpret the information presented, to make a **PROPOSAL**, and so on. For example, a report on economic development in Austin, Texas, concludes with recommendations for the future. Those recommendations follow many pages of carefully reported information (as well as considerable analysis of that information). When you're assigned to write a report, you will want to determine exactly what the person who assigned it has in mind: a text that only reports information or one that is called a report but that also requires you to analyze the information, make some kind of argument, and so on.

Josh Trujillo and Levi Hastings incorporate numerous elements of a report in their graphic argument about blood donation rules in the United States. See how they've used maps, statistics, and more on p. 1048.

❄ *REFLECT. Analyze the purposes of the reports that you listed (see p. 284). Who is the intended audience for each? To what degree does each simply report information, and to what degree does it use information to serve some larger goal, for example, to take a position on an issue? Can you distinguish clearly between a report that only presents information and one that presents information and also argues a point?*

CHARACTERISTIC FEATURES

While you can expect differences across media and disciplines, most of the reports you will write share the following characteristics:

- A topic carefully focused for a specific audience
- Definitions of key terms
- Trustworthy information
- Appropriate organization and design
- A confident, informative tone

A Topic Carefully Focused for a Specific Audience

The most effective reports have a focus, a single topic that is limited in scope by what the audience already knows and what the author's purpose is. For example, in 2016, Liveable City, a nonprofit organization that works to protect the quality of life in Austin, Texas, released a report on affordability in Austin. The report's executive summary frames the issue and outlines the organization's activities.

> Austin residents are feeling the burden of rising household costs. Prices for many goods and services . . . are escalating even as incomes for most households remain relatively stagnant. . . . This report examines the seven basic cost categories that significantly impact household budgets. . . . [W]e focus on specific local actions that can influence these [categories] of living costs. We especially emphasize local policy and initiatives that promise to limit cost pressures across multiple elements of household budgets, especially for middle- and lower-income households.
> —LIVEABLE CITY, "Reclaiming Affordability in Today's Austin"

Notice how the authors focus their report on household budgets and issues of affordability, items that, at first glance, may not appear to be local in scope. The authors are careful, however, to emphasize that their recommendations and proposals are intended to be accomplished locally by involved Austin residents along with local government bodies.

Three iconic Austin images from Liveable City's website that depict Austin's vibrant character.

The authors assume that they are writing for people who care about Austin (notice that they refer to specific local actions). The intended readers would have included members of the board of Liveable City as well as individual and corporate donors. Because such reports are often cited in news stories and opinion pieces in the local media, we can assume that the intended readers also included Austinites more broadly. But the authors are also writing for audiences beyond Austin, especially those interested in improving the economic outcomes for working families. Although the report was distributed as a print document, probably to local members of the intended audience, it is also available to anyone with internet access.

In their 2018 annual report for Oakland Promise, a nonprofit group striving to ensure that all children in Oakland, California, graduate from high school with access to the resources required to succeed in college, the authors have a different focus with three clear purposes. First, they aim to showcase the successes over the past year by using attractive infographics detailing the number of children and families served in the organization's programs. Second, the authors inform readers of the short- and medium-range goals of each program through more infographics. Third, the authors demonstrate the ample and enthusiastic community support the initiative receives by including a long list of elected officials, institutions both public and private, and individuals who advise, volunteer, and donate. The report is sprinkled with photos showing the activities and success stories of the programs. These images add life to what might otherwise be a dry recitation of names and numbers; the photos connect to the readers' emotions and ethics in reminding them of Oakland Promise's mission as well as its success.

In composing this report, the authors were obviously thinking about their primary audience: those who have participated in and donated to Oakland Promise in the past and those who might do so in the future, and who want to be informed about the work the initiative does—what it accomplishes and how economically it does so.

TODAY

150+
babies have a $500
BB college savings account

70%
of BB families participate in
financial coaching

80%
of BB parents believe
their child is college bound

From the Oakland Promise annual report, the year's acccomplishments of the Brilliant Baby (BB) program.

"When we visited UC Berkeley, the whole idea of college became real. We could actually picture the campus and see ourselves there. Everything changed!"

—K2C Parent

2018 goals
50
elementary schools implementing K2C
8,000
elementary students awarded $100 early college scholarships
500
families have opened their own college savings account with K2C support
80%
of K2C students and families report a strong college-bound identity
500+
students and families visit a college as part of K2C

 ## 2025 targets
ALL
Oakland public elementary schools implementing K2C
40,000
elementary students awarded $100 early college scholarships
5,000
families have opened their own college savings account with K2C support
80%
of ALL Oakland elementary students and families
report strong college-bound identity

From the Oakland Promise annual report, a photo of a college visit (top) and the short- and medium-range goals of the Kindergarten to College (K2C) program (bottom).

In both the Liveable City and Oakland Promise reports, the topic is carefully focused, and the authors approach their task with a keen eye toward the intended audiences and their organization's goals. You'll want to do the same in the reports that you write: to consider carefully whom you're addressing, what they know about your topic, and what information they expect.

Definitions of Key Terms

Effective reports always define key terms explicitly. These definitions serve several functions. Some audience members may not understand some of the technical terms. And even those familiar with the terms pay attention to the definitions for clues about the writer's stance or assumptions. Here's an example of a definition from Liveable City's 2016 report:

> *Support legislation to establish a "circuit breaker" provision for property tax payments.* A circuit breaker provision directs the state to reimburse taxpayers if their total property tax bills exceed a specified percentage of their income. Similar provisions currently exist in 21 states.

Here, the term "circuit breaker" is introduced as a recommendation for change at the state level, where property tax laws are set. Notice how the term is defined in very general terms as soon as it is introduced. Information about other states' use of such a strategy lends authority and confidence to the concept. Another concept in Liveable City's discussion of how affordability is affected by the taxing structure is the term "regressive":

> [T]he chief reason that tax burdens have reduced affordability is that the structure of virtually all taxes paid by residents is highly regressive. Sales taxes, gas taxes, . . . and property taxes are the key revenue sources for state and local governments in Texas. For each of these . . . , the higher your income, the lower share of your income you pay toward these taxes. Conversely, the lower your income, the higher the share of your income you pay. Thus the tax burden hits low- and moderate-income households the hardest, and remains relatively light for the higher-income residents of the city.

Notice how the report doesn't call particular attention to the term "regressive" with italics or any other marking, but the explanation of the term comes immediately along with examples of the relevant tax categories (sales tax, gas tax, etc.) and reasons why such taxes are undesirable.

In the *New York Times* article on aerial skiing mentioned on page 285, Henry Fountain uses a number of strategies to provide readers with definitions they might need. As a newspaper journalist, Fountain writes for a general audience, and he can safely assume that some readers of the Science section will have a great deal of knowledge about physics. He can likewise assume that some readers will know something about aerial skiing, but he also anticipates that other readers will know little about either. Here's one definition Fountain offers:

> The first time you watch skiers hurtle off a curved ramp at 30 miles per hour, soaring six stories in the air while doing three back flips and up to five body twists, you can't help but think: These people are crazy. . . .
> Freestyle aerialists, as these athletes are known, are not actually throwing caution, along with themselves, to the wind.
> —HENRY FOUNTAIN, "Up in the Air, and Down, with a Twist"

Here the short phrase "as these athletes are known" refers back to the skiers Fountain has described earlier, and this description explains the term "freestyle aerialists."

A few paragraphs later, Fountain explains *torque*, the concept in physics that allows freestyle aerialists to do somersaults, without explicitly defining it:

> "The forces are pretty simple," said Adam Johnston, a physics professor at Weber State University in Ogden, Utah. . . . "There's the force of the ramp on his skis, and the force of gravity on him," Dr. Johnston said, after Ryan St. Onge, the reigning world champion in men's aerials and a member of the Olympic team, zipped down a steep inrun, leaned back as he entered the curved ramp until he was nearly horizontal and flew off at a 70-degree angle. "That's all there is."
> But it is enough to create torque that sends Mr. St. Onge somersaulting backward as he takes to the air, arcing toward a landing on a steep downslope that the skiers and coaches have chopped and fluffed for safety.

Later in the article, Fountain writes: "In this training jump, Mr. St. Onge adds a full twist in both the second and third flips—a lay-full-full in the language of the sport." Here Fountain provides a technical term used by experts—a "lay-full-full"—immediately after explaining what the term means. In a subsequent paragraph, Fountain uses another strategy, providing a definition of a "double-full-full-full" in a **SUBORDINATE CLAUSE** (italicized here): "And when doing a double-full-full-full, *which requires four full twists, including two in the first flip,* he will use all three methods at takeoff." Note that none of the definitions shown here quote a dictionary, nor do they use the formula "the definition of X is Y"—and that each of the experts offers memorable examples that help readers understand the subject.

Trustworthy Information

Dennis Baron provides a lot of historical facts that likely would not be in the general knowledge of most people, but he presents the information in a matter-of-fact manner and backs it up with detailed references to his sources. See how he does it on p. 846.

Effective reports present information that readers can trust to be accurate. In some cases, writers provide documentation to demonstrate the verifiability of their information, including citations of published research, the dates of interviews they have conducted, or other details about their sources.

In a report for a writing class at Chapman University, Kelley Fox presents information in ways that lead readers to trust the details she presents and, ultimately, the author herself. The report describes how Griffin, Simon, and Andy, three roommates in Room 115 of her dorm, create their identities. Beginning with Muhammad Ali's line "Float like a butterfly, sting like a bee," which is the caption on a large poster of Ali on Griffin's wall, Fox seeks to characterize Griffin as someone who floats at "the top of the pecking order" and who seems "invincible":

> In a sense, Griffin is just that: socially invincible. A varsity basketball athlete, Griffin has no shortage of friends, or of female followers. People seem to simply gravitate toward him, as if being around him makes all their problems trivial. Teammates can often be found in his room, hanging out on his bed, watching ESPN. Girls are certainly not a rarity, and they usually come bearing gifts: pies, CDs, even homework answers. It happens often, and I have a feeling this "social worship" has been going on for a while, although in myriad other forms. Regardless, the constant and excessive positive attention allows Griffin to never have to think about his own happiness; Griffin always seems happy. And it is because of this that, out of the three roommates, it is easiest to be Griffin.
>
> —KELLEY FOX, "Establishing Identities"

Fox's description demonstrates to readers that she has spent considerable time in or around Room 115 and that she knows what she is writing about. Her use of specific details convinces us that Griffin is real and that the things she describes in fact occur—and on a regular basis.

In a report on early language development in children written for a linguistics class at Portland State University, Katryn Sheppard demonstrates the trustworthiness of her information differently, citing both published research and her own primary research on a speech transcript of one-year-old Allison.

> One feature of Allison's utterances that did adhere to what is expected for a typical child at this age was related to her use of negatives. Although she used only one negative word—"no"—the word was repeated frequently enough to be the fourth most common category in the transcript. Her use of "no" rather than any other negative conformed to Brown's (1973) finding that other forms of negation like "not" and "don't" appear only in later stages (Santelmann, 2014). In Allison's very early stage of linguistic development, the reliance on "no" alone seems typical.
>
> —KATRYN SHEPPARD, "Early Word Production"

By citing both published research and examples from her own primary research, Sheppard demonstrates that she has spent considerable time researching her topic and can thus make informed observations about Allison's speech. These citations not only let readers know that Sheppard can support her claims, they also indicate where readers can go to verify the information if they so choose; both strategies demonstrate trustworthiness.

Although Fox and Sheppard use different techniques, both of them convince readers that the information being presented and the writers themselves can be trusted.

For the full text of Katryn Sheppard's report, go to p. 647.

Appropriate Organization and Design

There is no single best strategy for organizing the information you are reporting. In addition to **DEFINING** (as Henry Fountain does), you'll find yourself **DESCRIBING** (as Kelley Fox does), offering specific **EXAMPLES** and data (as the report from Oakland Promise does), **ANALYZING CAUSES AND EFFECTS** (as Liveable City does), and so on. The specific organizational strategies you'll use will depend on the information you want to report.

In many cases, you'll want to include visuals of some sort, whether photographs, charts, figures, or tables. See, for example, the pie chart from the Liveable City annual report. The information conveyed would be harder to understand and thus far less effective if it were presented in a paragraph or even as a table. And as noted on page 290, Oakland Promise also uses color photos to make the report more interesting and appealing. Similarly, see on page 286 the way that Henry Fountain uses images in his discussion of aerial skiing.

Sometimes the way in which you organize and present your information will be prescribed. If you're writing a report following the **IMRAD** format, you will have little choice in how you organize and present information. Everything from the use of headings to the layout of tables to the size of fonts may be dictated.

Some disciplines specify certain format details. Students of *psychology*, for example, are expected to follow **APA STYLE**. On the other hand, a report

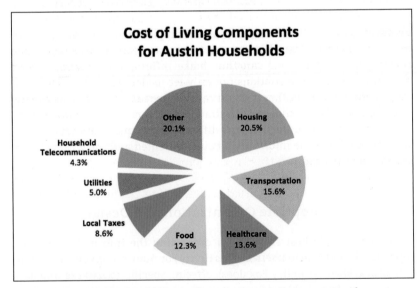

Pie chart from Liveable City 2016 annual report showing the categories of expenditures for Austin households.

for a *composition* class may have fewer constraints. For example, you may get to decide whether you will need headings and whether to use personal examples.

A Confident, Informative Tone

Effective reports have a confident tone that assumes the writer is presenting reliable information rather than arguing or preaching. The authors of the Liveable City report and Henry Fountain both sound like they know what they're writing about. In both these cases, we as readers are by and large getting just "the facts," though it is clear that Liveable City has strong convictions about what the city of Austin should be doing in the future and that Fountain delights in both the beauty and the science of what freestyle aerialists can achieve.

The line between informing and arguing can become fuzzy, however. If you read reports on any number of hot-button issues—climate change, the economy, transgender rights, abortion—you'll find that they often reflect some kind of position or make recommendations that betray a position. But the authors of such reports usually try to create an informative tone that avoids indicating their own opinions.

You may sometimes find yourself struggling with this line, working to present information while stopping short of telling readers what to think about or how to feel about a topic. Here we can offer two pieces of advice. First, keep in mind that you're aiming to explain something to your audience clearly and objectively rather than to persuade them to think about it a certain way. You'll know you've succeeded here if someone reading a draft of your report can't tell exactly what your own opinion about the topic is. Second, pay special attention to word choice because the words you use give subtle and not-so-subtle clues about your stance. Referring to "someone who eats meat" is taking an objective tone; calling that person a "carnivore" is not.

WIKIPEDIA, the free online encyclopedia that "anyone can edit," has become one of the most-visited sites on the internet since its launch in 2001. Like any encyclopedia, the primary purpose of *Wikipedia* is to report information. Below is an example from the entry on gender, as it appeared on July 19, 2018. This article demonstrates how authors negotiate the challenges of reporting information fairly and from an unbiased perspective. *Wikipedia* provides many examples of reporting on controversial topics, and the site has explicit policies and guidelines for authors to follow. Documenting the sources of information is an important tool for maintaining the reliability of information; this lengthy article, for example, has 163 citations, principally from academic journals in the physical and social sciences.

Gender

WIKIPEDIA

A definition of the term followed by several ways that the term may be applied.

GENDER IS THE range of characteristics pertaining to, and differentiating between, masculinity and femininity. Depending on the context, these characteristics may include biological sex (i.e., the state of being male, female, or an intersex variation), sex-based social structures (i.e., gender roles), or gender identity.[1][2][3] People who do not identify as men or women or with masculine or feminine gender pronouns are often grouped under the umbrella terms non-binary or genderqueer. Some cultures have specific gender roles that are distinct from "man" and "woman," such as the hijras of South Asia. These are often referred to as third genders.

The tone is confident and informative and avoids indicating a specific stance or opinion.

Sexologist John Money introduced the terminological distinction between biological sex and gender as a role in 1955. Before his work, it was uncommon to use the word gender to refer to anything but grammatical categories.[1][2] However, Money's meaning of the word did not become widespread until the 1970s, when feminist theory embraced the concept of a distinction between biological sex and the social construct of gender. Today the distinction is strictly followed in some contexts, especially the social sciences[4][5] and documents written by the World Health Organization (WHO).[3]

Underlining signals links to more information in Wikipedia entries.

In other contexts, including some areas of social sciences, gender includes sex or replaces it.[1][2] For instance, in non-human animal research, gender is commonly used to refer to the biological sex of the animals.[2] This change in the meaning of gender can be traced to the 1980s. In 1993, the US Food and Drug Administration (FDA) started to use gender instead of sex.[6] Later, in 2011, the FDA reversed its position and began using sex as the biological classification and gender as "a person's self representation as male or female, or how that person is responded to by social institutions based on the individual's gender presentation."[7] . . .

Notice the overall organization of the entry: definition and explanation first, brief historical context of the term's application, and an amplification of the categories that the term encompasses.

Globally, communities interpret biological differences between men and women to create a set of social expectations that define the behaviors that are "appropriate" for men and women and determine women's and men's different access to rights, resources, power in society and health behaviors.[26] Although the specific nature and degree of these differences vary from one society to the next, they still tend to typically favor men, creating an imbalance in power and gender inequalities within most societies.[27] Many cultures have different systems of norms and beliefs based on gender, but there is no universal standard to a masculine or feminine role across all cultures.[28] Social roles of men and women in relation to each other are based on the cultural norms of that society, which lead to the creation of gender systems. The gender system is the basis of social patterns in many societies, which include the separation of sexes, and the primacy of masculine norms.[27] . . .

Traditionally, most societies have only recognized two distinct, broad classes of gender roles, masculine and feminine, that correspond with the biological sexes of male and female. When a baby is born, society allocates the child to one gender or the other, on the basis of what their genitals resemble.[31] However, some

Go to everyones
anauthor.tumblr
.com to link to
the full *Wikipedia*
article.

*Footnotes link to evidence
that demonstrates the
trustworthiness of the
information.*

societies explicitly incorporate people who adopt the gender role opposite to their biological sex; for example, the two-spirit people of some indigenous American peoples. Other societies include well-developed roles that are explicitly considered more or less distinct from archetypal female and male roles in those societies. In the language of the sociology of gender, they comprise a third gender,[34] more or less distinct from biological sex (sometimes the basis for the role does include intersexuality or incorporates eunuchs).[35] One such gender role is that adopted by the hijras of India and Pakistan.[36][37] Another example may be the muxe (pronounced ['muʃe]), found in the state of Oaxaca, in southern Mexico.[38] The Bugis people of Sulawesi, Indonesia have a tradition that incorporates all the features above.[39]

REFLECT. Analyze a Wikipedia _entry on a topic of your choice to see how focused the information is, how key terms are defined, and how the entry is organized. How trustworthy do you find the information—and what makes you trust it (or not)? How would you characterize the tone—informative? informative but somewhat argumentative? something else? Point to words that convey that tone._

PROFILES

Profiles provide firsthand accounts of people, places, events, institutions, or other things. Newspapers and magazines publish profiles of interesting subjects; college websites often include profiles of the student body; investors may study profiles of companies before deciding whether or not to buy stock. If you're on *Instagram* or *LinkedIn*, you have likely created a personal profile saying something about who you are and what you do. Profiles take many different forms, but they generally have the following features.

A Firsthand Account

In creating a profile, you're always writing about something you know firsthand, not merely something you've read about. You may do some reading for background, but reading alone won't suffice. You'll also need to talk with people or visit a place or observe an event in some way. Keep in mind, however, that while a profile is a firsthand account, it should not be autobiographical. In other words, you can't profile yourself. In his 2002 *New Yorker* profile of soul singer James Brown, Philip Gourevitch describes Brown's performance as he saw it firsthand as a member of the audience.

> There he is: arms out from his sides as if to welcome an embrace, dentistry blazing in a beatific grin, head turning slowly from side to side, eyes goggle-wide—looking down-right blown away to find himself the focus of such a rite of overwhelming acclamation. He lingers thus for several seconds, then, throwing his head back, he lets out a happy scream and rips into the song "Make It Funky." Within seconds, he has sent his microphone stand toppling toward the first row of orchestra seats, only to snatch the cord and yank it back, while spinning on the ball of one foot in a perfect pirouette, so that his mouth returns to the mike and the mike to his mouth in the same instant. He howls. The crowd howls back.
>
> —PHILIP GOUREVITCH, "Mr. Brown"

Here the author gives readers information about Brown's performance that he could only have gathered from seeing him live, and it's those details of Brown's actions on stage that make the profile come to life.

Detailed Information about the Subject

Profiles are always full of details—background information, descriptive details (sights, sounds, smells), anecdotes, and dialogue. Ideally, these details help bring the subject to life—and persuade your audience that whatever you're writing about is interesting, and worth reading about. What makes the *New Yorker* piece so successful is the kind of details about Brown that the author provides. We can almost see him "spinning on the ball of one foot in a perfect pirouette." Here's another example with different but similarly detailed information about Brown's early musical training (or lack thereof).

> He claims to have mastered the harmonica at the age of five, blowing "Lost John," "Oh, Susannah," and "John Henry," and one afternoon, when he was seven, he taught himself to play the organ by working out the fingering of "Coonshine Baby." Before long, he was picking up guitar licks to such songs as "(Honey) It's Tight Like That" from the great blues-man Tampa Red, who was dating one of Aunt Honey's girls. By the time he was twelve, the young prodigy was fronting his own group.

Much of this information comes from the interviews that Gourevitch conducted while following Brown on tour and visiting his childhood home. The specific details, from the names of songs he sang to the ages when he sang them, go a long way toward establishing Gourevitch's credibility as a writer—and make his profile of Brown even more believable.

Another way that writers of profiles bring their subjects "to life" is by including photos, letting readers see their subjects in action. In the photo on the next page, James Brown seems larger than life, performing with soulful passion, letting us see what Gourevitch describes.

An Interesting Angle

The best profiles present a new or surprising perspective on whatever is being profiled. In other words, a good profile isn't merely a description; rather, it captures something essential about its subject from an interesting angle, much as a memorable photo does. When you plan a profile, try to come up with an angle that will engage readers. That angle will dictate

James Brown performing at the Newport Jazz Festival, 1969.

what information you include. One thing that makes Gourevitch's profile of James Brown so interesting is the angle that he takes on Brown's life and career, starting with his improbable musical genius.

> He was a middle-school dropout, with no formal musical training (he could not read a chart, much less write one), yet from early childhood he had realized in himself an intuitive capacity not only to remember and reproduce any tune or riff he heard but also to hear the underlying structures of music, and to make them his own.

PROFILE / An Annotated Example

BILL LAITNER covers local news for the *Detroit Free Press*, specializing in social and political issues and human interest stories like the one below. The following profile, published in the *Free Press* in January 2015, inspired a nationwide response.

Heart and Sole:
Detroiter Walks 21 Miles in Work Commute
BILL LAITNER

The profile opens with descriptive details that introduce readers to the subject—and make us want to read on.

LEAVING HOME IN DETROIT at 8 a.m., James Robertson doesn't look like an endurance athlete.

Pudgy of form, shod in heavy work boots, Robertson trudges almost haltingly as he starts another workday.

But as he steps out into the cold, Robertson, 56, is steeled for an Olympic-sized commute. Getting to and from his factory job 23 miles away in Rochester Hills, he'll take a bus partway there and partway home. And he'll also walk an astounding 21 miles.

Five days a week. Monday through Friday.

It's the life Robertson has led for the last decade, ever since his 1988 Honda Accord quit on him.

Every trip is an ordeal of mental and physical toughness for this soft-spoken man with a perfect attendance record at work. And every day is a tribute to how much he cares about his job,

James Robertson commutes 23 miles to and from his job every day—most of it on foot.

his boss and his coworkers. Robertson's daunting walks and bus rides, in all kinds of weather, also reflect the challenges some metro Detroiters face in getting to work in a region of limited bus service, and where car ownership is priced beyond the reach of many.

> *Placing Robertson's challenging commute in the context of the struggles faced by other Detroiters gives it an interesting and meaningful angle.*

But you won't hear Robertson complain—nor his boss.

"I set our attendance standard by this man," says Todd Wilson, plant manager at Schain Mold & Engineering. "I say, if this man can get here, walking all those miles through snow and rain, well I'll tell you, I have people in Pontiac 10 minutes away and they say they can't get here—bull!"

> *Another interesting angle: Robertson's extraordinary work ethic in spite of the challenging circumstances.*

As he speaks of his loyal employee, Wilson leans over his desk for emphasis, in a sparse office with a view of the factory floor. Before starting his shift, Robertson stops by the office every day to talk sports, usually baseball. And during dinnertime each day, Wilson treats him to fine Southern cooking, compliments of the plant manager's wife.

> *Interviews with Robertson and his co-workers provide detailed firsthand information.*

"Oh, yes, she takes care of James. And he's a personal favorite of the owners because of his attendance record. He's never missed a day. I've seen him come in here wringing wet," says Wilson, 53, of Metamora Township.

With a full-time job and marathon commutes, Robertson is clearly sleep deprived, but powers himself by downing 2-liter bottles of Mountain Dew and cans of Coke.

"I sleep a lot on the weekend, yes I do," he says, sounding a little amazed at his schedule. He also catches zzz's on his bus rides. Whatever it takes to get to his job, Robertson does it.

"I can't imagine not working," he says.

"Lord, Keep Me Safe"

The sheer time and effort of getting to work has ruled Robertson's life for more than a decade, ever since his car broke down. He didn't replace it because, he says, "I haven't had a chance to save for it." His job pays $10.55 an hour, well above Michigan's minimum wage of $8.15 an hour but not enough for him to buy, maintain and insure a car in Detroit.

As hard as Robertson's morning commute is, the trip home is even harder.

At the end of his 2-10 p.m. shift as an injection molder at Schain Mold's squeaky-clean factory just south of M-59, and when his coworkers are climbing into their cars, Robertson sets off, on foot—in the dark—for the 23-mile trip to his home off Woodward near Holbrook. None of his coworkers lives anywhere near him, so catching a ride almost never happens.

Instead, he reverses the 7-mile walk he took earlier that day, a stretch between the factory and a bus stop behind Troy's Somerset Collection shopping mall.

"I keep a rhythm in my head," he says of his seemingly mechanical-like pace to the mall.

At Somerset, he catches the last SMART bus of the day, just before 1 a.m. He rides it into Detroit as far it goes, getting off at the State Fairgrounds on Woodward, just south of 8 Mile. By that time, the last inbound Woodward bus has left. So Robertson foots it the rest of the way—about 5 miles—in the cold or rain or the mild summer nights, to the home he shares with his girlfriend.

"I have to go through Highland Park, and you never know what you're going to run into," Robertson says. "It's pretty dangerous. Really, it is dangerous from 8 Mile on down. They're not the type of people you want to run into.

"But I've never had any trouble," he says. Actually, he did get mugged several years ago—"some punks tuned him up pretty good," says Wilson, the plant manager. Robertson chooses not to talk about that.

So, what gets him past dangerous streets, and through the cold and gloom of night and winter winds?

"One word—faith," Robertson says. "I'm not saying I'm a member of some church. But just before I get home, every night, I say, 'Lord, keep me safe.' "

The next day, Robertson adds, "I should've told you there's another thing: determination."

A Land of No Buses

Robertson's 23-mile commute from home takes four hours. It's so time-consuming because he must traverse the no-bus land of rolling Rochester Hills. It's one of scores of tri-county communities (nearly 40 in Oakland County alone) where voters opted not to pay the SMART transit millage. So it has no fixed-route bus service.

> *Detailed information about Robertson's commute, including a graphic with time stamps, helps readers understand it more clearly—and why it's so incredible.*

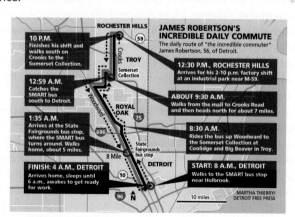

Buses provide sparse service on Robertson's long work commute, leaving him to walk most of the way on foot.

Once he gets to Troy and Detroit, Robertson is back in bus country. But even there, the bus schedules are thin in a region that is relentlessly auto-centric.

"The last five years been really tough because the buses cut back," Robertson says. Both SMART and DDOT have curtailed service over the last half decade, "and with SMART, it really affected service into Detroit," said Megan Owens, executive director of Transportation Riders United.

The local angle on this story as an example of the struggles many face in Detroit leads Laitner to include information about the city's transportation services.

Detroit's director of transportation said there is a service Robertson may be able to use that's designed to help low-income workers. Job Access and Reverse Commute, paid for in part with federal dollars, provides door-to-door transportation to low-income workers, but at a cost. Robertson said he was not aware of the program.

Still, metro Detroit's lack of accessible mass transit hasn't stopped Robertson from hoofing it along sidewalks—often snow-covered—to get to a job.

At Home at Work

Robertson is proud of all the miles he covers each day. But it's taking a toll, and he's not getting any younger.

"He comes in here looking real tired—his legs, his knees," says coworker Janet Vallardo, 59, of Auburn Hills.

But there's a lot more than a paycheck luring him to make his weekday treks. Robertson looks forward to being around his coworkers, saying, "We're like a family." He also looks forward to the homemade dinners the plant manager's wife whips up for him each day.

"I look at her food, I always say, 'Excellent. No, not excellent. Phenomenal,' " he says, with Wilson sitting across from him, nodding and smiling with affirmation.

Although Robertson eats in a factory lunchroom, his menus sound like something from a Southern café: Turnip greens with smoked pork neck bones, black-eyed peas and carrots in a brown sugar glaze, baby-back ribs, cornbread made from scratch, pinto beans, fried taters, cheesy biscuits. They're the kind of meal that can fuel his daunting commutes back home.

Though his job is clearly part of his social life, when it's time to work this graduate of Northern High School is methodical. He runs an injection-molding machine the size of a small garage, carefully slicing and drilling away waste after removing each finished part, and noting his production in detail on a clipboard.

Strangers Crossing Paths

Robertson has walked the walk so often that drivers wonder: Who is that guy? UBS banker Blake Pollock, 47, of Rochester, wondered. About a year ago, he found out.

Pollock tools up and down Crooks each day in his shiny black 2014 Chrysler 300.

"I saw him so many times, climbing through snow banks. I saw him at all different places on Crooks," Pollock recalls.

Last year, Pollock had just parked at his office space in Troy as Robertson passed. The banker in a suit couldn't keep from asking the factory guy in sweats, what the heck are you doing, walking out here every day? They talked a bit. Robertson walked off and Pollock ruminated.

From then on, Pollock began watching for the factory guy. At first, he'd pick him up occasionally, when he could swing the time. But the generosity became more frequent as winter swept in. Lately, it's several times a week, especially when metro Detroit sees single-digit temperatures and windchills.

"Knowing what I know, I can't drive past him now. I'm in my car with the heat blasting and even then my feet are cold," Pollock says.

Other times, it's 10:30 or 11 p.m., even after midnight, when Pollock, who is divorced, is sitting at home alone or rolling home from a night out, and wondering how the man he knows only as "James" is doing in the frigid darkness.

On those nights, Pollock runs Robertson all the way to his house in Detroit.

"I asked him, why don't you move closer" to work. "He said his girlfriend inherited their house so it's easy to stay there," Pollock said.

On a recent night run, Pollock got his passenger home at 11 p.m. They sat together in the car for a minute, outside Robertson's house.

"So, normally you'd be getting here at 4 o'clock (in the morning), right?" the banker asks. "Yeah," Robertson replies. Pollock flashes a wry smile. "So, you're pretty early, aren't you?" he says. Robertson catches the drift.

> Laitner notes details such as Pollock's "wry smile" and "sheepish laugh" that signal that he is providing details from conversations he heard, adding credibility to his writing.

"Oh, I'm grateful for the time, believe me," Robertson says, then adds in a voice rising with anticipation: "I'm going to take me a bath!"

After the door shuts and Pollock pulls away, he admits that Robertson mystifies him, yet leaves him stunned with admiration for the man's uncanny work ethic and determination.

"I always say to my friends, I'm not a nice guy. But I find myself helping James," Pollock says with a sheepish laugh. He said he's picked up Robertson several dozen times this winter alone.

Has a Routine

At the plant, coworkers feel odd seeing one of their team numbers always walking, says Charlie Hollis, 63, of Pontiac. "I keep telling him to get him a nice little car," says Hollis, also a machine operator.

> The conclusion brings up another interesting angle to Robertson's story, how he connects his walking to a strong work ethic he inherited from his parents.

Echoes the plant manager Wilson, "We are very much trying to get James a vehicle." But Robertson has a routine now, and he seems to like it, his coworkers say.

"If I can get away, I'll pick him up. But James won't get in just anybody's car. He likes his independence," Wilson says.

Robertson has simple words for why he is what he is, and does what he does. He speaks with pride of his parents, including his father's military service.

"I just get it from my family. It's a lot of walking, I know."

REFLECT. Bill Laitner profiles an ordinary person whose extraordinary commute brought nationwide attention to the challenges of getting to work without a car or public transportation. Think about someone you know whose story might prove significant in this way. If you were to profile this person, what details would bring the person to life and what angle would make their story matter to others?

REPORTING INFORMATION / A Roadmap

Choose a topic that matters—to you, and to others

If you get to select your topic, begin by considering topics that you know something about or are interested in learning more about. Whatever your topic, be sure it's one you find intriguing and can be objective about. If you're a devout Catholic and believe that the church is wrong—or right—in its stance on birth control, you're likely to have trouble maintaining the "just the facts" stance necessary for writing a good report.

The more controversial the topic, the more challenging it may be to report fairly and accurately on it because the facts themselves likely will be the subject of controversy. So if you're going to write about a controversial topic, you might consider reporting on the controversy itself: the major perspectives on the issue, the kinds of evidence cited, and so on.

If you've been assigned a topic, find an aspect of it that is both interesting and focused. Unless you've been specifically instructed to address a broad topic (for example, the consequences of World Bank policies for third-world economies), focus on a narrower aspect of the topic (take a single developing country that interests you and report on the consequences of World Bank policies for that economy). Even when you are asked to report on a broad topic, see if it is possible to start out with a specific case and then move to the broader issue.

Consider your rhetorical situation

Analyzing your audience, purpose, and other elements of your rhetorical situation will help you to make the decisions you'll face as you write.

Address your AUDIENCE appropriately. If you're writing a report for an audience you know—your classmates, your instructor—you can sometimes assume what they will and won't know about your topic. But if you're writing for a broader audience—all students on campus, readers of a blog—you'll probably be addressing people with different levels of knowledge. Your challenge will be to provide enough information without including irrelevant details. For example, Henry Fountain didn't explain what skiing is or waste his readers' time by including information not directly relevant to his topic. Here are some questions that might guide you in considering your audience:

- What do you know about your audience? To what extent are they like or unlike you—or one another?
- What background information will your audience need on your topic? Will their knowledge of it vary?
- What terms need to be defined or illustrated with examples? What sorts of examples will be most effective for your audience?
- What interest does your audience have in your topic? If they're not already interested in it, how can you get them interested—or at least to see that it matters?

Be clear about your PURPOSE. Consider why you are writing a report on this topic for this particular audience. Odds are that you want your report to do more than merely convey information. If you're writing it for a course, you want to learn something and to get a good grade. If the report is part of a large project—a campaign to encourage composting on campus, for example—a lot may be riding on the quality of your work. What short-term goals do you have in writing, and do they relate to any longer-term goals?

Consider your STANCE. Think about your own attitudes toward your topic and your audience: What about this topic captured your interest? Why do you think it matters—or should matter—both in general and to your audience? How can you establish your authority on the topic and get your audience to trust you and the information you provide? How do you want them to see you? As a fair, objective reporter? As thoughtful? serious? curious? something else?

Consider the larger CONTEXT. What are the various perspectives on the topic, and what else has been said about it? What larger conversations, if any, is this topic a part of? For a report that's part of a campaign to encourage composting on campus, for example, you'd need to become familiar with how such programs have been conducted at other schools, and what the main challenges and arguments have been.

Think about MEDIA. As the three reports on aerial skiing make clear, the medium you use to say something plays a big role in determining the message you convey. If you have a choice, will your text be presented in print? online? as an oral report? Which will be most effective for your subject and audience? If you've got audio of an interview, can you embed it in an online report or incorporate it into an oral report? If your report will be in print, can you summarize or quote from the interview? If your report will be oral, should you prepare slides to help your audience follow your main points?

Think about DESIGN. Consider what design elements are available to you and will help you convey your information in the clearest, most memorable way. For example, much of the effectiveness of Oakland Promise's annual report comes from the large color photos and testimonials from students, parents, and teachers. Think about whether your report will include any elements that should be highlighted. Do you need headings? Would photos, charts, tables, or other visuals help you convey information more effectively than words alone? Do you have the option of using color in your text—and if so, what colors will set the right tone?

Research your topic

Your goal in researching your topic is first to get a broad overview of what is known about it and second to develop a deeper understanding of the topic. While most high school reports discuss the research of others, those you write in college may call on you to gather data yourself and then write about the data in light of existing research.

LAB REPORTS, for example, describe the results of experiments in engineering and the natural sciences, and reports based on ethnographic observation are common in the social sciences. And whatever your topic or field, reading SECONDARY SOURCES will help you see how your findings relate to what people already know.

Thus, your first task is to read broadly enough to get a feel for the various issues and perspectives on your topic so that you know what you're talking about and can write about it authoritatively.

Begin by assessing what you know—and don't know—about the topic. What aspects of your topic do you need to learn more about? What questions do you have about it? What questions will your audience have? To answer these questions, you might try BRAINSTORMING or other activities for **GENERATING IDEAS**. Such activities may help you focus your topic and also discover areas you need to research further.

Find out what others say. You can research others' **POSITIONS** and perspectives in many different ways. If your topic is a local one, such as alcohol use at your college, you may want to conduct a student survey, interview administrators or counselors who deal with campus drinking problems, or do a search of local newspapers for articles about alcohol-related incidents. But it would also be a good idea to look beyond your own community, in order to gain perspective on how the situation at your school fits into national patterns. You could consult books and periodicals, databases, websites, or online forums devoted to your topic. If your topic doesn't have a local focus, you will likely start out by consulting sources like these. You may also interview people at your school or in the community who are experts on your topic.

Decide whether you need to narrow your topic. What aspect of your topic most interests you, and how much can you cover given the constraints of your assignment? If your political science professor has assigned a five-minute oral report on climate-change legislation, for example, you will need to find a more specific focus than you would for a twenty-page written report on the same general topic.

Organize and start writing

Once you've narrowed your topic and have some sense of what you want to say about it, you need to think about how you can frame your topic to appeal to your audience and how you can best organize the information you have collected. As you draft, you may discover that you need to do some additional research as new questions and ideas arise. But for now, just get started.

Come up with a tentative thesis. State your topic and the gist of what you have to say about it in a tentative **THESIS** statement, trying to make it broad enough to cover the range of information you want to share with your audience but limited enough to be manageable—and keeping in mind that your goal is to report information, not to argue a position.

Organize your information. Make a list of the information you want to convey, and think about what details you want to include. You'll find that you need various strategies for presenting information—**DESCRIPTION**, **DEFINI-TION**, **ANALYSIS**, **EXAMPLES**, and so on.

Then consider how to arrange your material. Some topics call for a **CHRONOLOGICAL** structure, moving from past to present, maybe even projecting into the future, as the report on economic development in Austin does. Or you may find that a **SPATIAL ORGANIZATION** works well—if you're reporting on the design of a new building, for instance—moving from exterior to interior or from top to bottom. There are any number of ways to organize a report in addition to these; you'll just need to work out a structure that will help your audience understand your topic in a systematic way.

Don't be surprised if you find that you do not need to use all of the information that you have collected. Authors often gather far more information than they finally use; your task is to choose the information that is most relevant to your thesis and present it as effectively as possible.

Draft an **OPENING**. Why do you care about your topic, and how can you get your audience interested in it? You will want to open by announcing your subject in a way that makes your audience want to know more about it. Consider opening with an intriguing example or a provocative question. Perhaps you have a memorable anecdote. It's usually a good idea also to include the thesis somewhere in the introduction so that your audience can follow from the outset where your report is heading and don't have to figure it out for themselves.

Draft a **CONCLUSION**. What do you want your audience to take away from your report? What do you want them to remember? You could end by noting the implications of your report, reminding them why your topic matters. You could summarize your main points. You could even end with a question, leaving them with something to think about.

Look critically at your draft, get response—and revise

Try re-reading your draft several times from different perspectives and imagining how different readers will experience your text. Will readers new to the topic follow what you are saying? Will those who know about the topic think that you have represented it accurately and fairly? If possible, get feedback from a classmate or a tutor at your school's writing center. Following are some questions that can help you and others examine a report with a critical eye:

- *How does the report* OPEN*?* Will it capture your audience's interest? How else might it begin?

- *Is the topic clear and well focused?* Are the scope and structure of the report set out in its opening paragraphs? Is there an explicit THESIS statement—and if not, would it help to add one?

- *Is it clear why the topic matters*—why you care about it and why others should?

- *How does the draft appeal to your* AUDIENCE*?* Will they be able to understand what you say, or do you need to provide more background information or define any terms?

- *How do you establish your* AUTHORITY *on the topic?* Does the information presented seem trustworthy? Are the sources for your information credible, and have you provided any necessary DOCUMENTATION?

- *Is the* TONE *appropriate for your audience and purpose?* If it seems tentative or timid, how could you make it more confident? If it comes across as argumentative, how could you make it focus on "just the facts"?

- *How is the information organized?* Past to present? Simple to complex? Some other way? Does the structure suit your topic and MEDIUM? What strategies have you used to present information— COMPARISON, DESCRIPTION, NARRATION?

- *What* MEDIA *will the report be presented in,* and how does that affect the way it's written? You might consider including photos in a print report, for example, videos and links in an online report, or slides to go along with an oral presentation.

- *Is the report easy to follow?* If not, try adding TRANSITIONS or headings. If it's an oral report, you might put your main points on slides.

- *If you've included illustrations,* are there captions that explain how they relate to the written text? Have you referred to the illustration in your text? Is there information in your text that would be easier to follow in a chart or table?

- *Is the* STYLE *appropriate for your audience and purpose?* Consider choice of words, level of formality, and so on.

- *How effective is your* CONCLUSION *?* How else might you end?

- *Does the title tell readers what the report is about,* and will it make them want to know more?

Revise your draft in response to any feedback you receive and your own analysis, keeping in mind that your goal is to present "just the facts."

⮺ REFLECT. Once you've completed your report, let it settle for a while and then take time to reflect. How well did you report on your topic? How successful do you think you were in making the topic interesting to your audience? What additional revisions would you make if you could? Research shows that such reflections help "lock in" what you learn for future use.

Selling the Farm
BARRY ESTABROOK

Last Friday, for the first time in 144 years, no one at the Borland family farm got out of bed in the pre-dawn hours—rain, shine, searing heat, or blinding blizzard—to milk the cows. A day earlier, all of Ken Borland's cattle and machinery had been auctioned off. After six generations on the same 400 acres of rolling pastures, lush fields, and forested hillsides tucked up close to the Canadian border in Vermont's remote Northeast Kingdom, the Borlands were no longer a farm family.

It was not a decision they wanted to make. A fit, vigorous 62-year-old, Borland could have kept working. His son, who is 35 and has two sons of his own, was once interested in taking over. But the dismal prices that dairy farmers are receiving for their milk forced the Borlands to sell. "We've gone through hard times and low milk prices before," said Borland's wife, Carol, a retired United Methodist minister. "This time there doesn't seem to be any light at the end of the tunnel. There's no sense working that hard when you're 62 just to go into debt."

For several months I'd been reading headlines and following the statistics behind the current nationwide dairy crisis. The math is stark. Prices paid to farmers per hundredweight (about 12 gallons) have fallen from nearly $20 a

BARRY ESTABROOK, a journalist who concentrates on food politics, writes for the *New York Times*, the *Washington Post*, and a variety of other publications. This article appeared in *Gourmet* magazine in August 2009.

year ago to less than $11 in June. Earlier this month, the Federal government raised the support price by $1.25, but that is only a drop in the proverbial bucket. It costs a farmer about $18 to produce a hundredweight of milk. In Vermont, where I live, that translates to a loss of $100 per cow per month. So far this year, 33 farms have ceased operation in this one tiny state.

Meanwhile, the price you and I pay for milk in the grocery store has stayed about the same. Someone is clearly pocketing the difference. Perhaps that explains why profits at Dean Foods—the nation's largest processor and shipper of dairy products, with more than 50 regional brands—have skyrocketed. The company announced earnings of $75.3 million in the first quarter of 2009, more than twice the amount it made during the same quarter last year ($30.8 million). (Dean countered that "current supply and demand is contributing to the low price environment.")

But rote statistics have a way of masking reality. So last week, I drove up to the village of West Glover for a firsthand look at the human side of the dairy crisis by attending the Borland auction. "You will be witnessing what is going to be the fate of all heritage farms," Carol Borland told me.

It was a breathtakingly clear morning in one of the most stunning settings imaginable. The Northeast Kingdom is an undulating patchwork of fields, woodlots, streams, lakes, barns, and white clapboard houses, set against the jagged, blue-gray backdrop of distant mountaintops. I didn't need a sign to direct me to the Borland place: For more than a mile before I crested a hill and saw the barns and silos, the gravel road leading to the farm was lined with dusty, mud-splattered pickup trucks. A crowd of close to 900 had gathered, in part because a country auction is always a major social event, a festive excuse for bone-weary farmers to take a day off, bring the kids, catch up with the gossip, and grumble about the weather, costs, and prices. That made it easy to overlook the sad, serious nature of the business at hand: selling off every last item there (and with any luck, providing the Borlands with a retirement nest egg). Among other things to go on the auction block was a massive amount of equipment, much of which had been shared with neighbors in loose, mutually beneficial arrangements stretching back generations. The demise of one family farm can affect similar small operators for miles in all directions. The auctioneer had to sell a half-dozen tractors, a dump truck, a couple of pickup trucks, manure spreaders, hay balers, wagons, seeders, mowers, milking machines, and assorted antique farm implements. There was feed that Borland had harvested but would no longer have any use for, 50 tons of shelled corn, 800 bales of hay. And, last in the photocopied catalogue, 140 prime Holsteins,

Nearly 900 farmers attended the auction that marked the end of the 144-year-old Borland family farm.

a herd known for its excellence, having earned Borland 16 quality awards over the previous two decades. Unlike the cows that pass their lives in complete confinement on the factory farms that are replacing farms like his, Borland's cows went out on those hilly pastures every day, strengthening their bodies and feeding on grass. Borland worried that with most other farmers as financially strapped as he was, or worse, the cows might not sell. "I didn't spend my whole life breeding up a good herd to see them beefed" (meaning slaughtered for hamburger meat), he said.

Items were sold at a nerve-rattling pace as the auctioneer chanted his frenzied, mesmerizing, "I've got five. Give me ten, ten, ten. Five, gimme ten, ten, ten. A ten dollar bill. Five gimme ten, ten ten." Three "ringmen" worked the crowd, waving their canes to cajole bids, and whooping when the price rose. A John Deere tractor started at $25,000 and was dizzily bid up to $30,000, $40,000, $50,000, and finally $60,000, in a matter of three minutes. Lesser machines sometimes sold in half that time. All morning long, there was no let-up.

Just after the Deere was sold, I asked Borland's son Nathan how he thought things were going. "Online, that tractor would be listed for $75,000, if you can find one half that good, which you can't," he said. "But I guess you can't complain, given how hard it is for everybody."

Making maple syrup a century ago at the sugarhouse built by Ken Borland's great-grandfather in 1898.

After attending college and working out of state for a few years, Nathan came home and joined his father on the farm. But he left to become a paramedic. "I like the work, but it got so bad financially that I felt guilty taking a paycheck," he said. "My sons, they're young. It'd be nice if they wanted to farm one day, but there's not a living to be made in dairy farming."

Carol, who was beside us, added, "The reality of farming is that as a parent, even if you'd like to and they want to, you can't encourage a child to go into something where he won't be able to earn a decent living." 10

Once the last piece of machinery was gone, the throng moved to folding chairs set up around a fenced ring inside the barn. Borland, who had been taciturn and shy most of the day, stood before the crowd to deliver a short speech. After thanking everybody for coming and expressing his gratitude for the efforts of the auction crew, he said, "I just want to say that these are a good bunch of cows. This auction wasn't their fault. They've always done their part. They have produced well."

Then he told a sad joke. "There was this farmer's son who left the farm and found work as a longshoreman in the city. The first ship that came in carried a cargo of anvils. To impress his new workmates, the boy picked up two anvils, one under each arm. But the gangplank snapped under the weight. He fell

The Borlands still sugar the old-fashioned way, insisting it makes for better-tasting maple syrup.

into the water and sank. He came up one time and shouted for help. No one moved. He went down and came up a second time. Still no help. The third time he came up he hollered, 'If you guys don't help me soon, I'm going to have to let go of one of these anvils.' "

There was nervous laughter. Borland went on, "That's what farming's been these last six months, trying to stay afloat with anvils. This is the day that I let go of mine."

The herd sold well. As an emotional bonus, 20 went to local farmers and would still be grazing on nearby pastures. Borland and Carol were pleased with the overall proceeds of the auction, and doubly pleased because they had been fortunate enough to find a buyer for the property and buildings who would take good care of the land that had supported their family through the generations. The Borlands severed off a piece of land where they will build a house. In the spring, they still plan to tap some maples. The sap will be boiled in the sugarhouse that Borland's great-grandfather built in 1898.

Before the auction, Borland had told his son that he planned to sleep until ₁₅ noon the day afterwards. Fat chance. He was up at 3:30 in the morning, as always. A few cows that had been sold had yet to be picked up, and cows, even ones that now belong to another man, need to be milked. He finished that chore and drove the full milk cans over to a neighbor who was still in the business and had a cooling tank. Borland offered him a lift back to a hayfield he wanted to cut that day. As they rode along in the cab of the truck with the early morning sun streaming over the mountains, the neighbor said, "Ken, do you know how many farmers around here would give anything to be in your shoes? We have to keep struggling. You had a way out."

Thinking about the Text

1. How does Barry Estabrook make this profile of the Borland auction interesting? What details does he provide to show the "human side of the dairy crisis"?

2. "Selling the Farm" is a profile, a firsthand account written for *Gourmet* magazine. How would Estabrook's AUDIENCE, readers interested in food and wine, have affected the details he included?

3. How does Estabrook establish his AUTHORITY to write on this topic? How does he convince readers that the information he's providing is trustworthy?

4. Imagine Estabrook had written about the Borland auction for a newspaper, as an objective REPORT rather than a profile. How would it have been different?

5. Write a PROFILE of a person or event, following the guidelines on pages 301–03. To come up with an interesting angle for your profile, it might help to identify the audience you want to reach: what angle would probably interest them?

The Right to Preach on a College Campus

RYAN JOY

FREE SPEECH ON college campuses has recently become a hotly contested issue in both the popular press and academic circles. The question of whether incendiary speech abides by university guidelines and constitutional protections raises important and fraught questions for both students and the administrators who arbitrate disputes over what qualifies as protected free expression.

Last month, in an area of campus on Park Avenue called the Park Blocks, a street preacher aggressively ministered to the students of Portland State University (PSU) in service to his religious beliefs. On a number of occasions over about a week, he harangued passersby, even instigating verbal altercations with students. The man seems to have been unaffiliated with any student group or organization.

In seeking to understand the significance of such an event, we come to a better comprehension of the larger issue of how college administrators seek to foster a safe and secure environment for students without running afoul of laws protecting the right to freedom of expression.

The question of whether informal public preaching falls within the First

RYAN JOY graduated from Lewis and Clark College with a degree in religious studies and went on to study economics at Portland State University. A version of this article was first published in 2015 in the *Portland Spectrum*, a student magazine at Portland State.

Amendment's definition of protected religious speech becomes more complicated when considering a few of the comments this preacher made to specific people. For example, he is purported to have called one woman a "slut" and to have asked others intrusive, personal questions.

When deciding on issues of free speech, administrators must balance the competing interests of a student's right to attend class free of harassment with someone else's right to voice his or her views unimpeded. Indeed, it is often the most objectionable views that require the most steadfast protection. Generally, the Supreme Court disallows speech restrictions that discriminate on the basis of content, and religious speech has been notoriously difficult to proscribe.

Legal precedent has something to say on the subject: in *McGlone v. Cheek, et al.,* a 6th U.S. Circuit Court of Appeals decided against the school after the administration sought to bar an itinerant preacher from speaking publicly on campus. Although the preacher, John McGlone, appears to have been moderately respected in the community (the PSU preacher struck many observers as unstable at best), the precedent set by the *McGlone* decision starkly illustrates how our courts balance rival interests in such disputes.

In *McGlone*, the preacher successfully reversed a lower court ruling and affirmed his right to preach on the basis of a rule known as the "vagueness doctrine," a legal test founded in the due process clause of the Fifth and Fourteenth Amendments that requires that laws must be clearly comprehensible and allow for uniform enforcement ("Vagueness Doctrine"). The judge who wrote the opinion in *McGlone* remarked that First Amendment cases must apply the vagueness doctrine stringently. Thus, since John McGlone contends that the university gave him conflicting information about his right to preach on campus, the 6th Circuit Court overturned the lower court's decision to uphold the university's rule barring public speech absent formal permission from a registered student organization or a current student.

Extrapolating from this court's decision, one may wonder whether a clear, unambiguous rule banning unaffiliated speakers would pass constitutional muster if instituted at PSU. As it stands, the university has no restrictions against people wandering onto campus and expounding on their topic of choice. While it is true that PSU has instituted and assiduously promoted its safety guidelines, PSU's codes of conduct stay largely silent on the type of on-campus conflicts that might occur between a student and those unaffiliated with the university— the types of conflicts that are abundant on a downtown college campus.

In response to an emailed list of questions concerning whether PSU might successfully restrict the presence of such visitors, Phillip Zerzan, PSU's chief of campus public safety, confirmed that "the ability to regulate or control speech in the Park Blocks is guided by the First Amendment" and that while the preacher appears to have harassed students, such "non-physical, generally directed harassment speech is still protected speech."

"There is much case law confirming [that the regulation of speech] must be content neutral," Zerzan added, recognizing that speech restrictions are difficult if not impossible to institute when they restrict speech on a certain topic, especially religion. Even religiously motivated hate-speech enjoys the same protections as more benign forms of expression. "The preachers are a common event on campus, and we encourage students to engage in this conversation in a constructive manner, or otherwise ignore the speech," Zerzan concluded. 10

David Johns, a PSU professor of political science, corroborates this reading of the law as it applies to the preacher, who technically was preaching on public, city-owned property. According to Johns, as long as someone in the Park Blocks is not drawing noise complaints, engaging in disorderly conduct, or specifically threatening students, "they can pretty much say what they want."

To be sure, there are categories of speech that courts have exempted from First Amendment protections. Speech that presents an imminent danger to public health, for instance, and that which intends to do harm enjoy no legal immunity. In the landmark 1942 Supreme Court case *Chaplinsky v. New Hampshire*, the "fighting words" doctrine limited the First Amendment's protection of certain types of speech, including "the lewd and obscene, the profane, the libelous, and the insulting or 'fighting' words—those which by their very utterance inflict injury or tend to incite an immediate breach of the peace" (United States, Supreme Court).

This category may not apply to street preachers, however, regardless of the illicit questions they might pose to students. And while the courts may have once been sympathetic to the notion that large categories of speech deserved little in the way of First Amendment protections, as of the late twentieth century, courts have begun to roll back such exemptions and have granted First Amendment protection to all types of speech. As Johns notes, "although *Chaplinsky* has never been overturned directly . . . its effect has been considerably reduced."

The current Supreme Court seems more inclined than ever to give preference to those claiming immunity under the First Amendment, often invoking the reasoning that more speech equals more freedom. PSU, for one, is in no danger of stifling freedom of expression. Recently, PSU has witnessed a flourishing display of ideas, and while certain visitors may strike some as unworthy of careful consideration, it is the principle that allows them to continue that many consider worthy of protection.

Works Cited

United States, Court of Appeals for the Sixth Circuit. *McGlone v. Cheek, et al.* Docket no. 12-5306, 2 Aug. 2013. *United States Court of Appeals for the Sixth Circuit,* www.ca6.uscourts.gov/opinions.pdf/13a0710n-06.pdf. PDF download.

United States, Supreme Court. *Chaplinsky v. State of New Hampshire.* 9 Mar. 1942. *Legal Information Institute,* Cornell Law School, www.law.cornell.edu/supremecourt/text/315/568.

"Vagueness Doctrine." *Legal Information Institute,* Cornell Law School, www.law.cornell.edu/wex/vagueness_doctrine.

Thinking about the Text

1. A good report generally does not take sides on an issue and instead presents a balanced discussion of the major viewpoints in play. What key positions does Ryan Joy identify in the controversy over the rights of the campus preacher? How fairly does he represent each side?

2. Examine the way that Joy introduces the issue in the first few paragraphs of his report. What kind of background information does he provide? Do you think he should have provided any additional background information or definitions—and if so, why?

3. Joy wrote this report for the *Portland Spectrum*, a student publication about campus issues, yet he addresses a controversy that has wide significance. How does Joy make his report applicable to **AUDIENCES** beyond the Portland State community?

4. What types of **EVIDENCE** does Joy rely on to develop his discussion of the two sides of this issue? How does the range of evidence affect Joy's **CREDIBILITY** as an author?

5. Choose an important campus issue that you want to explore. Research the issue by reading what others have written, speaking to people in your campus community, conducting a survey, or some other method of gathering information. Write a **REPORT** that presents a balanced view of all sides of the issue. Consider submitting the report to a school publication.

SIXTEEN

"Two Thumbs Up"

Writing a Review

RESTAURANTS, **CELL PHONES, BOOKS**, movies, TV shows, cars, toaster ovens, employees—just about anything can be reviewed. Many people don't buy a new product or try a new restaurant without first checking to see what others have said about it online—and even posting their own thoughts on it afterward.

You've probably given casual reviews of this sort yourself. If a friend asks what you think of the TV series *The Handmaid's Tale*, your response would probably constitute a brief review: "It mostly lived up to the hype. The acting was really impressive, but sometimes the plot lagged. I guess I'll keep watching since so many people are talking about it." Even this offhand opinion includes two basic elements of all reviews: a judgment ("impressive," "lagged") and the criteria you used to arrive at that judgment, in this case the quality of the performances, the script, and the show's popularity.

Reviews can vary a good deal, however, as you can see in these examples from other reviews of *The Handmaid's Tale*.

Gilead may be the creation of religious patriarchy grown monstrous, but "The Handmaid's Tale" is a creation shaped by the female gaze. Reed Morano, who directed the first three episodes, establishes

A still from *The Handmaid's Tale*.

a visual language that plays as important a role in this series as the dialogue. Her lush cinematography latches onto the hazy nightmarishness of Offred's tenuous existence.

Gilead is a place of shadowed interiors, where costume designer Ane Crabtree's creations remind us with elegant subtlety of the place's sinister caste system. The aquamarine dress of the commander's wife pops into the fore in dim hallways, the dove gray worn by the Marthas and Aunts demarcates the border between light and shadow, and the handmaids' scarlet dresses mark them as targets as well as silent, compliant objects of desire. . . .

And [Elizabeth] Moss' acting style works in concert with Morano's direction. She devastatingly conveys Offred's seething exasperation with shock darting through slightly widened eyes or tiny curls of defiance dancing around the edge of her lips. Those milliseconds of honesty make the viewer's adrenaline spike along with the character's.

—MELANIE McFARLAND, "'The Handmaid's Tale': A Dystopian Tale of
Female Subjugation That Hits Close to Home"

Melanie McFarland's review, published on *Salon*, makes clear her criteria: the show's cinematic qualities, on the one hand, and its actors' performances, on the other. McFarland is able to elaborate on these criteria with vivid examples like the costumes and acting methods she describes above.

On the other hand, *Metacritic.com* gives ratings by gathering numerical scores from multiple sources and calculating an average—92 out of 100 in the case of this series, on the high end of "Universal Acclaim." The site also provides excerpts and links to full reviews, and lets visitors add their own reviews. On *Metacritic.com*, everyone can be a reviewer.

This chapter provides guidelines for writing reviews—whether an academic book review for a political science class, a product review on *Amazon*, or a review of the literature on a topic you're researching.

REFLECT. Think about reviews you've read. All reviews evaluate something and they do so using relevant criteria. Someone reviewing a movie, for instance, would generally consider such factors as the quality of the script, acting, directing, and cinematography. Think about a product you are familiar with or a performance you have recently seen. Develop a list of criteria for evaluating it, and then write an explanation of why these criteria are appropriate for your subject. What does this exercise help you understand about the process of reviewing?

Across Academic Disciplines

Reviews are a common genre in all academic disciplines. As a student, you will often be assigned to write a review of something—a book, a work of art, a musical performance—as a way of engaging critically with the work. While students in the *humanities* and *social sciences* are often asked to write book reviews, students in the *performing arts* may review a performance. In a *business* course, you may be asked to review products or business plans.

In each of these cases, you'll need to develop appropriate criteria for your evaluation and to support that evaluation with substantial evidence. The kind of evidence you show will vary across disciplines. If you're evaluating a literary work, you'll need to show evidence from the text (quotations, for example), whereas if you are evaluating a proposed tax policy for an economics class, you're probably going to be required to show numerical data demonstrating projected outcomes.

↪ LOOK AT this photo of artist Alex Da Corte's Rubber Pencil Devil, *an art installation that features videos playing inside the neon-lit frame of a house. The photo was included in an online review of the 57th Carnegie International, an exhibition held at Pittsburgh's Carnegie Museum of Art in 2018. The review, which you can see at* <u>everyonesanauthor.tumblr.com</u>, *includes a digital gallery of art from the exhibit. How else could a review designed specifically for the internet take advantage of the medium—with maps? music? video? interviews? What else?*

Across Media

Reviews can appear in many media—from print to digital, online to television and radio. Each medium offers different resources and challenges. A *television* film critic reviewing a new movie can intersperse clips from the film to back up her points, but her own comments will likely be brief. A different critic, writing about the same film for a *print magazine*, can develop a fuller, more carefully reasoned review, but will be limited to still images rather than video clips.

The same choices may be available to you when you are assigned to review something. For instance, if you give an *oral presentation* reviewing an art show, you might create slides that show some of the art you discuss.

Perhaps your review could be a *video* that includes not only images of the art but also footage of viewers interacting with it. If you get to choose media, you'll need to think about which one(s) will allow you to best cover your subject and reach your audience.

Across Cultures and Communities

Conventions for reviewing vary across communities and cultures. In most US academic contexts, reviews are quite direct, explicitly stating whether something is successful or unsuccessful and why. Especially on the internet, reviews are often very honest, even brutal. In other contexts, reviewers have reason to be more guarded. When the *Detroit News* reviews a new car, for instance, its writers have to keep in mind the sensitivities of the community, many of whom work in the auto industry, and of the company that produces that car, which may be a major advertiser in the newspaper. *Consumer Reports* might review the same car very differently, since it is supported not by advertisers but by subscribers who want impartial data and information that will help them decide whether or not to purchase that car.

A very different sort of review occurs in most workplaces, where employees receive annual performance reviews by their supervisors. There are often explicit criteria for evaluating workers, but these vary across professional communities and institutions: the criteria for someone who works at a hospital (a *medical community*) will be different from those for college instructors (an *academic community*).

Across Genres

Evaluation is often used as a strategy in other genres. **PROPOSALS** offer solutions to problems, for example, and in that process they must consider—and review—various other solutions. Evaluation and **ANALYSIS** often go hand in hand as well, as when *Consumer Reports* analyzes a series of smartphones in order to evaluate and rank them for its readers.

∿ℂ_REFLECT. Look for several reviews of a favorite movie. You're likely to find many reviews online, but try also to find reviews in print sources or online versions of print publications. How do the reviews differ from one medium to the next? What, if anything, do the online reviews have that the print versions do not? Then check out some fan sites or Twitter about the same movie. How does the medium affect the decisions that a reviewer makes about content, length, style, and design?_

CHARACTERISTIC FEATURES

Whatever the audience and medium, the most successful reviews share most of the following features:

- Relevant information about the subject
- Criteria for the evaluation
- A well-supported evaluation
- Attention to the audience's needs and expectations
- An authoritative tone
- Awareness of the ethics of reviewing

Geoffrey Pullum's essay on emoji use is more a rebuttal than a review, but notice how his essay employs many of the same characteristic features. Read what he has to say about "the stupidest story about language this week" on p. 1011.

Relevant Information about the Subject

The background information needed in a review may entail anything from items on a restaurant menu to a description of the graphics of a video game to the plot summary of a novel or movie. What information to include—and how much—depends on your rhetorical situation. In the case of an academic review, your instructor may specify a length, which will affect how much information you can provide. What's needed in nonacademic reviews varies depending on the audience and publication. Someone reviewing a new album by an indie group for _Rolling Stone_ may not need to provide much background information since readers are already likely to be familiar with the group. This would not be the case, however, if the same author were writing a review for a more general-interest magazine, such as _Time_.

See how a review of the Nintendo Switch device opens with background information to help readers appreciate its portability and convenience:

Nintendo Switch

> When you're deep in a video game, the last thing you want to do is leave home. If only you could take the game with you for your commute to work or your bus ride to school, or to liven up your lunch hour.
>
> Nintendo's new Switch console tries to address that by letting you play it anywhere. You simply yank the Switch out of its docking station. It functions as a tablet with a built-in display, so you don't have to worry about finding a TV. Games typically work without a persistent internet connection. Once you're back home, just slide it back into the docking station to play games on a big-screen TV.
>
> The Switch works like a traditional game console when you want that; it offers portability when you need that. Over the past week, I've played the new "Legend of Zelda" game at home, outside, in a laundromat and in a mechanic's waiting room. The game picks right up wherever I left off.
>
> The big question, as it so often is with Nintendo, is whether it will be able to deliver enough games.
>
> —LOU KESTEN, "Review: Nintendo Switch Is Impressive, but Needs More Games"

This example comes from a 2017 review written for the *Associated Press News*; the author assumes that his readers have some familiarity with video games but that they may not have paid much attention to the particulars of gaming consoles.

Reviews of films (and other narratives) often provide background information about the story, as does the following example from a newspaper review of *Walk the Line,* the film about the singer Johnny Cash:

> Arkansas, 1944. Two brothers walk the long, flat corridor of earth between one corn field and another. Jack Cash, the elder, is memorizing the Bible. His little brother prefers the music of the hymnals and worries that Jack's talent for stories is the nobler enterprise. Jack wants to be a preacher. "You can't help nobody," he explains, "if you don't tell them the right story." Yet we already know it is his little brother, Johnny, who will grow up to tell the memorable stories, the kind you sing, the kind that matter most. In their own generic way, musical biopics are always the right story: the struggle towards self-actualization. With songs. They

Joaquin Phoenix as Johnny Cash in *Walk the Line* (2005).

are as predictable and joyful as Bible stories: the Passion of Tina Turner, the Ascension of Billie Holiday. It is a very hard-hearted atheist indeed who does not believe that Music Saves.　　　　　—ZADIE SMITH

This review was written for the *Daily Telegraph*, a British newspaper, by the novelist Zadie Smith. She opens with a summary of the story as the film begins and quotes some dialogue that catches our interest—but she also tells us something about "biopics," the film's genre. In short, this review's opening gives us information we will need, and that makes us want to read on.

Criteria for the Evaluation

Underlying all good reviews are clear criteria. As an author, then, you'll need to establish the criteria for any review you write. Sometimes, the criteria are obvious or can be assumed: criteria for reviewing cars, for example, would almost assuredly include price, style, comfort, performance, safety, gas mileage, and so on. Often, however, you may want to shape the criteria for specific purposes and audiences. See how a reviewer of a performance of Handel's vocal music focuses on two criteria as the basis for her evaluation: expressive and technical abilities.

> Forsythe was unquestionably the star of the evening. Her tone was like toasted caramel and her expressiveness and vocal control were astounding. Her embellishments sounded spontaneous and effortless, pinpoint clear and fiendishly twisty but never gratuitous; every display of vocal fireworks had an expressive purpose. I've heard coloratura sopranos with expressive or technical abilities equal to Forsythe's, but almost none so rich in both.　　　—KATIE TAYLOR, "Handel in Good Hands"

If you were posting a quick review of the same concert on *Twitter*, you might be able to assume that your followers are familiar with these criteria and skip straight to the evaluation. In fact, one tweet about this concert said it simply: "Heart-stopping Handel." No need to name criteria—the author assumed her followers know what it takes for a soprano to stop hearts.

Many reviews combine both **QUANTITATIVE** and **QUALITATIVE** criteria. For example, one well-known source for evaluating colleges and universities is the annual rankings published by *U.S. News & World*

Report, whose criteria are mostly quantitative. Here's how Texas A&M University, College Station fared in this ranking system in 2019, coming in at number 66:

Tuition	Total Enrollment Fall 2019	Acceptance Rate	6-year Graduation
In-state: $10,968 Out of state: $36,636	67,580	70%	80%

In addition, *U.S. News & World Report* often includes brief reviews written by students that rely on qualitative criteria:

> I love Texas A&M for all of its quirks and traditions. There is no other school this large where you will not feel like just another number to the faculty and staff. In fact, I rarely notice that the school is big at all. I love that everything seems to have a tradition to go along with it. While it takes a while to learn them all, and a lot of them seem kind of hokey, the traditions will enrich your college experience, and make you feel a kinship with your fellow schoolmates. Everyone you meet on campus is not a stranger, but merely a friend you've yet to meet! It's so true. Aggies are the friendliest bunch you will encounter.   —K'LEE, senior at Texas A&M

K'Lee uses qualitative criteria such as the campus atmosphere ("you will not feel like just another number") and values ("everything seems to have a tradition to go along with it") to give readers a sense of the school that they don't get from just seeing the numbers.

A Well-Supported Evaluation

The foundation of every review is a clear evaluation, a claim that something is good or bad, right or wrong, useful or not. Whatever you're reviewing, you need to give reasons for what you claim and sufficient evidence to support those reasons. And because rarely is anything all good or all bad, you also need to acknowledge any weaknesses in things you praise and any positives in things you criticize. Also, remember to anticipate and acknowledge reasons that others might evaluate your subject differently than you do. In other words, you need to consider other possible perspectives on whatever you're reviewing.

Journalist Amy Goldwasser approached a number of passengers on a New York subway and asked them for impromptu reviews of what they were reading. She then collaborated with the illustrator Peter Arkle to compose graphic reviews for the *New York Times Book Review*. Here's what two readers had to say:

MARIAH ANTHONY, 18, high school senior, on p.133 of **THE KITE RUNNER**, by Khaled Hosseini (paperback)

I read every day. Every. Day. I'm not a novel-reader. I'm more self-help and psychology. But this is an *amazing* book. You should read it. The author went way into depth. Where I'm at, the main character's 18. He and his father moved to San Francisco from Kabul...they were **refugees** who had to be smuggled into the States. He had to travel *inside an oil tank* to be here. I don't think I can exactly relate, but it's about how people go through things. It's **beautiful**.

DON SHEA, 70, fiction writer, on p. 214 of **LIT**, by Mary Karr (paperback)

This is her third book. I've read the first two. She's a poet.... I've been struck by the **wonderful** metaphors. I'm always surprised when poets really write superb prose. It gets a little draggy in the rehab part. She just keeps **slipping and slipping.** But it's good—all her stuff is good.

Both readers clearly stated what they thought of the books they were reading ("an amazing book," "it's good"). And then they gave reasons ("the author went way into depth," "all her stuff is good") and evidence to support those reasons ("he had to travel *inside an oil tank* to be here," "wonderful metaphors"). Note as well that one of the readers, Don Shea, acknowledges one weakness in Mary Karr's book ("It gets a little draggy in the rehab part").

When you're writing a review for a college class, you'll need to be more systematic and organized than these off-the-cuff reviews—with an explicitly stated evaluation, for one thing. See how a more formal review opens with a clear evaluation of a documentary film about a cave in southern France that contains paintings thought to have been done more than 30,000 years ago:

> What a gift Werner Herzog offers with *Cave of Forgotten Dreams*, an inside look at the Cave of Chauvet-Pont d'Arc—and in 3-D too.
>
> —MANOHLA DARGIS, "Herzog Finds His Inner Man"

The reviewer states her evaluation explicitly: the film is so good it is "a gift." As the review continues, she gives her readers background information on the cave and provides good reasons for her evaluation: "It's a blast . . . to see these images, within 3-D grabbing reach"; "Herzog is an agreeable, sometimes . . . funny guide, whether showing you the paintings or talking with

A still from *Cave of Forgotten Dreams* (2010).

the men and women who study them"; and he "also has a talent for tapping into the poetry of the human soul." At the same time, she acknowledges that the film has some shortcomings, though nothing that changes her overall assessment:

> *Cave of Forgotten Dreams* is . . . an imperfect reverie. The 3-D is sometimes less than transporting, and the chanting voices in the composer Ernst Reijseger's new-agey score tended to remind me of my last spa massage. Yet what a small price to pay for such time traveling!

In addition, the reviewer provides an image from the film, visual evidence of the "inside look" *Cave of Forgotten Dreams* offers. This review appeared in the *New York Times*; the print version includes the photo shown here, but the online version also includes four video clips from the film, along with several reviews posted by readers.

Attention to the Audience's Needs and Expectations

All authors need to consider what their audience expects from them. But this consideration plays a particularly important role in the case of reviews. In many situations, some audience members will be familiar with what you're reviewing, whereas others will need a detailed summary or description; some will need an explicit statement of the criteria for the evaluation, while others will know what the criteria are without being told.

Audience considerations can also influence the criteria that reviewers identify as most crucial for their evaluation. Consider, for instance, reviews of video games. Gamers might expect one set of criteria, perhaps focusing on the games' playability and entertainment value. Parents and teachers might want entirely different criteria, ones that call attention instead to any violence and strong language.

Here, for instance, is the introduction to a review of *Minecraft: Play-Station 4 Edition* from *GameSpot*, a website for news and reviews serving the gaming community. This review was clearly written for an audience concerned with what this game lets them explore and create.

> To say that *Minecraft* is a game about digging and building huts to protect you from zombie attacks is to only scratch the surface of its immense depth. *Minecraft* has evolved considerably since its release to PC more than five years ago. Its boundaries have been tested by its community, which has birthed stunning castles and cities, as well as music machines, calculators, and tender homages to popular television shows and film. While the game eventually made a home on consoles, the aging hardware of the <u>Xbox 360</u> and <u>PlayStation 3</u> kept *Minecraft*'s voxel world restrained by an invisible border.
>
> *Minecraft: PlayStation 4 Edition* shatters that barrier, allowing you to fully experience seemingly endless worlds in which to explore and create. The stretching horizon, combined with better performance and sharper aesthetics, do not only make this version of *Minecraft* the best you can find on modern consoles. The boundless delight in creation, coupled by challenging exploration, all shouldered by supreme accessibility, makes *Minecraft: PlayStation 4 Edition* one of the best games to own on PlayStation 4. —CAMERON WOOLSEY, "Blocky Empires"

Woolsey also assumes his readers are familiar with other gaming systems (Xbox 360, PlayStation 3) and know the language of gamers; later in this review he uses terms like "tooltips" and "four-player cooperative split-screen play" without taking the time to define them. More general audiences would have appreciated it if he had paused to explain, but defining terms his audience already knows would position him as an outsider to the gaming community and thus diminish his credibility with readers of *GameSpot*. Instead, he signals respect for his readers by addressing them as knowledgeable gamers and focusing on issues they will care about.

REFLECT. Find two reviews of the same subject (a movie, a band, whatever) from two different sources: Yelp *and* Travel + Leisure, *perhaps, or* Salon *and* Time. *Look over each source, considering both articles and ads, and decide what kind of audience each one addresses. Young? Affluent? Intellectual? A general audience? Then study each review. How much prior knowledge does each one expect of its readers? How much space is devoted to describing the subject and how much to evaluating it? Do the two reviews use the same criteria—and if not, what might account for the difference? What does this analysis suggest about the role that audience plays in the way reviews are written?*

An Authoritative Tone

Authors of reviews have multiple ways of establishing their authority and credibility, and introductions are often crucial to doing so. Here, for instance, is the first paragraph of a lengthy review of several histories of American whaling that appeared in the *New Yorker*:

> If, under the spell of *Moby-Dick*, you decided to run away to the modern equivalent of whaling, where would you go? Because petroleum displaced whale oil as a source of light and lubrication more than a century ago, it might seem logical to join workers in Arabian oil fields or on drilling platforms at sea. On the other hand, firemen, like whalers, are united by their care for one another and for the vehicle that bears them, and the fireman's alacrity with ladders and hoses resembles the whaler's with masts and ropes. Then, there are the armed forces, which, like a nineteenth-century whaleship, can take you around the world in the company of people from ethnic and social backgrounds unfamiliar to you. All these lines of work are dangerous but indispensable, as whaling once was, but none seems perfectly analogous. Ultimately, there is nothing like rowing a little boat up to a sixty-ton mammal that swims, stabbing it, and hoping that it dies a relatively well-mannered death.
> —CALEB CRAIN, "There She Blew: The History of American Whaling"

"Moby Dick swam swiftly round and round the wrecked crew."

The series of arresting examples not only captures readers' attention but also demonstrates how thoroughly and carefully the reviewer knows his subject, thus making readers trust him and want to hear what he has to say.

Here is the introduction to an essay published in *Harper's Magazine* reviewing a number of works by Egyptian novelists Albert Cossery and Sonallah Ibrahim:

> Egypt is hard on its novelists. Their audience is tiny, their rewards few, their risks considerable. This is true in most if not all Arab countries, but Egypt is notable in having a long and astonishingly varied novelistic tradition, some of which is now becoming available in translation.
>
> —ROBYN CRESWELL, "Undelivered"

The broad generalizations at the start of this review make clear that this reviewer has considerable knowledge about Egyptian novels and Arabic literature more generally.

Finally, here is the introduction to a review of *Spider-Man: Into the Spider-Verse* written by Orange Coast College student Areyon Jolivette and published in the *Daily Californian*, the independent student-run newspaper of the University of California, Berkeley.

> Sony's most recent production of Spider-Man, *Spider-Man: Into the Spider-Verse*, is a dramatic departure from the Spider-Man audiences have seen time and time again. If you've ever rolled your eyes at the massive catalog of Spider-Men on screen, this one's for you. The film is incredibly self-aware, making a point to acknowledge some of the most infamous moments cemented in the canon of the superhero. *Spider-Verse* doesn't shy away from making fun of itself; instead, the animated feature embraces the multitude of memes and pop culture tropes to come out of the superhero's long run both on-screen and off.
>
> —AREYON JOLIVETTE, "*Spider-Man: Into the Spider-Verse* Is as
> Extraordinary as It Allows Its Audience to Be"

This introduction shows that the reviewer is knowledgeable about previous Spider-Man movies and also about the conventions of the superhero genre.

If you get to choose your subject, be sure to select a topic that you know (and care) about, and share some of what you know in your introduction. Telling your audience something interesting about your subject and giving some sense that it matters will help establish your credibility and make them want to know more.

The many faces of the iconic superhero in *Spider-Man: Into the Spider-Verse* (2018).

Awareness of the Ethics of Reviewing

Depending on context and purpose, a review can have substantial—or minimal—consequences. When the late, widely syndicated film reviewer Roger Ebert gave a Hollywood movie a thumbs-up or thumbs-down, his judgment influenced whether the movie was shown in theaters across America or went immediately to DVD. Those reviewing Broadway plays for publications like the *New York Times* hold similar powers. And reviews in *Consumers Reports* significantly influence the sale of the products they evaluate.

By comparison, a review of a local high school musical will not determine how long the musical will run or how much money it will make, but an especially negative review, particularly if it is unjustified, will certainly wound the feelings of those involved in the production. And a movie review on the *Internet Movie Database* (*IMDb*) that gives away key elements of a plot without including a "spoiler alert" will ruin the film for some of the audience. So an ethical reviewer will always keep in mind that a review has power—whether economic, emotional, or some other kind—and take care to exercise that power responsibly.

Considering the likely effect of your review on those who created whatever you're reviewing is part of the ethics of reviewing as well. It's one thing to criticize the latest episode of *The Handmaid's Tale* (the creators of that series can likely afford to laugh all the way to the bank) but quite another when you're reviewing a new restaurant in town. It's not that you should hold back criticism (or praise) that you think the subject deserves, but you do need to think about the effect of your judgments before you express them.

How you express them is also important. In academic contexts, remember this responsibility especially when reviewing other students' drafts. Don't avoid mentioning problems just because you might make the writer feel bad, but be sure that any criticisms are constructive. Be sure to mention strengths as well as weaknesses and offer suggestions and encouragement for overcoming those weaknesses if you can.

WRITING A REVIEW / An Annotated Example

TIM ALAMENCIAK is studying ecological restoration at the University of Waterloo. He previously wrote for the *Toronto Star*, Canada's most widely read newspaper, where this book review was published in 2015.

Monopoly: The Scandal Behind the World's Favorite Board Game

TIM ALAMENCIAK

SOMETIMES THE IRONIES OF THE WORLD are stranger than fiction. That a game based on wheeling and dealing was born of wheeling and dealing writ large is a prime example of this.

Mary Pilon's *The Monopolists* unearths and charts the fascinating history of the popular board game Monopoly and the court battle fought by Ralph Anspach, a quixotic professor trying to save his own game. It's a story rife with controversy and scandal.

The book hitches its narrative on the tale of Anspach, the professor who took umbrage with Monopoly's capitalist focus and created Anti-Monopoly. His move so rankled Parker Brothers, the then-owner of the original game, they started a legal action that unfolded over decades of hearings and appeals.

Once thought to be the brainchild of a man named Charles Darrow, who profited immensely from the game's success, the history is much more complicated than that.

A woman named Elizabeth Magie originally invented "The Landlord's Game" to teach students about Henry George's "single tax" concept—a notion that all land should be owned by

Opening with a mysterious but clever statement that turns out to be about a game many readers will know establishes an authoritative tone; the promise of a good story makes us want to read on.

[345]

the public and simply rented by the occupants. She patented it in 1903—three decades before Darrow attempted to sell the game.

Magie was a prolific advocate for the rights of women but remained hidden for decades—overshadowed by the story Parker Brothers included with every game about Darrow, a down-on-his-luck man during the depression who invented a game for his kids.

Magie made waves in other ways after inventing the game. Finding it difficult to support herself on a stenographer's wage and frustrated with the way things were, she took out an ad in the paper offering herself for sale as a "young woman American slave." The satirical ad spread like wildfire and Magie was eventually hired as a newspaper reporter.

Meanwhile, her game had taken on a life of its own and was being passed around from family to family across the country. While still obscure, its fans were devoted and eager to teach it to others.

The board went through some transformations as others picked up the game and copied it for themselves. The original game was anti-capitalist, with an alternate set of rules to teach the difference. Pilon meticulously charts the path the design took from Magie's hands to Atlantic City, where Quakers penned the famous street names that exist to this day, then to the living room of Darrow.

The book is a compelling look at history through the lens of Monopoly. Pilon paints Magie as a heroine long forgotten who contributed more than just a game but also then-rebellious writing that advanced the cause of women.

Pilon's book is full of interesting historical info, but rather than unfolding as a cohesive narrative that follows Anspach's quest to keep Anti-Monopoly alive, it reads more like a book divided into two parts. The reader is provided the true biography of Monopoly and then is asked to accompany Anspach as he uncovers the revelations that were just delivered.

More could have been done to weave the two together and bring the reader with Anspach throughout the text.

That said, Pilon's writing is on-point and the historical information she's uncovered is fascinating. She is not writing about Monopoly; she is writing about American history intertwined with games.

"Games aren't just relics of their makers—their history is also told through their players," writes Pilon. "And like Lizzie's original innovative board, circular and never-ending, the balance between winners and losers is constantly in flux."

This is not just a book for Monopoly fans. It's a great read for anyone who likes to know the quirky, interesting history of board games in twentieth century America. Even discussions on trademarks and brands—which are frequent in the book—are made interesting by Pilon's well-reported examples.

She chronicles the fight by Parker Brothers to keep the sport of ping-pong known as Ping-Pong, their brand name, rather than table tennis. In 1933, the United States Table Tennis Association was formed to oversee the sport.

"It's hard to say just how much money Parker Brothers lost after control of the game slipped out of its grasp, meaning it now produced the game alongside a fleet of competitors," writes Pilon.

This is a great book for anyone who likes a good historical read. It moves quickly and provides lots of interesting bits of history, wrapped together in a fascinating package that tells the true story of Monopoly.

Quotes and specific examples from the book provide evidence for Alamenciak's claims.

Alamenciak concludes by stating his overall evaluation of the book in a way that is useful to his audience.

REFLECT. Study a review on a subject that interests you and evaluate it, using the list of characteristic features of reviews on page 333. Annotate the text you have chosen, noting which of the features are included and which are not. For any features you find missing, consider whether including them might have improved the review.

LITERATURE REVIEWS

When instructors refer to "the literature" on a certain topic, they probably aren't talking about poetry or other literary texts. Rather, "literature" in this case means published research on a given topic, and a literature review is a common assignment that asks you to survey, synthesize, and evaluate that research. You may be assigned to write a full essay reviewing a body of research, or to write a literature review as part of a report on research you've conducted. In either case, a literature review contains these features.

A Survey of Relevant Research on a Carefully Focused Topic

The literature you review should be credible, relevant academic sources related to your topic. When the choice is yours, a narrower topic is best: a review of what historians have learned about colonies and postcolonialism could easily run to thirty or more pages, whereas a review of what's been said about just one aspect of one of those topics would be more manageable. If your review is part of a research report, the literature you review will be guided by your RESEARCH QUESTION and should cover all the sources your study is based on. In some fields, you may be expected to cite only the most recent research, while in others you would likely begin with foundational studies and then trace the research that's followed. Keep in mind your assignment and the discipline you're working in to determine what kinds of sources are appropriate and how many are required in your review.

An Objective Summary of the Literature

Once you've collected the sources you'll review, you'll need to SYNTHESIZE them, looking for significant connections, trends, and themes that have emerged in the scholarship over time. Summarizing the themes and trends shows that you understand how the pieces in your review relate to one another and provides readers with an overview of their significance. In addition, you'll want to look for any ways that sources diverge or disagree. A synthesis of important trends might begin something like this: "Researchers writing about X have generally taken one of three perspectives on it," followed by a section discussing each perspective and what it has contributed to our understanding of the topic.

An Evaluation of the Literature

Like all reviews, literature reviews include an evaluation. The criteria for your evaluation will depend on your purpose for reviewing and the discipline you're writing in. If you're reviewing research as background for a report, its relevance to your project will be a key criterion. In all cases, you will also be looking at whether the research considers important questions and offers new insights—and at the **EVIDENCE** it provides. Your evaluation might point out strengths and weaknesses, as well as any limitations in what the research covers. Are there any important questions that are ignored? Claims for which little evidence exists? Gaps that future research might address?

An Appropriate Organization

It may be easiest to march through your sources one by one, but this sort of organization is hardly the most effective—and may end up reading like an annotated bibliography. When organizing sources for a literature review, think about how the sources relate to one another logically. Do they follow a clear progression that makes a chronological organization the most logical? Do they group by theme? by the authors' perspectives? by research methods? by trends in the results? Looking for ways in which your sources connect with one another will help you both synthesize the information and organize it in a way that helps readers see any significant patterns and trends.

Careful, Accurate Documentation

Be sure to follow carefully any disciplinary conventions for **CITING** and **DOCUMENTING** sources. For guidelines on following MLA and APA style, see Chapters 28 and 29.

CRYSTAL AYMELEK wrote the following literature review as part of a research report for a course in experimental psychology at Portland State University. To frame her research question, she first reviews literature on the nature of memory, then hones in on her topic with research on the effects of stress on memory, on mindfulness meditation and its potential benefits, and on the reported benefits of exercise. Evaluating this literature helps establish how her study attempts to add to our present knowledge of the topic. Her review includes a long list of the sources she reviews, which we've abbreviated here to save space.

The Effects of Mindfulness Meditation and Exercise on Memory

CRYSTAL AYMELEK

ACCORDING TO INFORMATION PROCESSING THEORY (Atkinson & Shiffrin, 1968; Baddeley & Hitch, 1974), human memory comprises three interconnected systems: sensory, working, and long-term memory. Information is initially detected and processed by sensory memory. The quality or quantity of information processed by the senses is determined by one's level of attention. Once information enters the working memory, its ability to be encoded and stored in long-term memory depends on the efficiency by which initial connections are made. Together these systems process information in response to stimuli through encoding, storage, and retrieval.

The opening paragraph establishes the research topic and gives background information about the workings of human memory.

Research has shown that high levels of stress both impede the ability to focus attention and interfere with working memory during the acquisition of information (Al'Absi et al., 2002; Aronen et al., 2005; Hadwin et al., 2005; Owens et al., 2012). The effects of stress on brain structure have been connected to decreases in gray matter similar to those typically associated with age (Hedden & Gabrieli, 2004). Such changes occur when an excess of cortisol inhibits the production of neurotrophic proteins responsible for the growth of new neurons and synapses. Consequently, this process prevents regions of the brain associated with memory, such as the hippocampus and amygdala, from modulating effectively (Cahill & McGaugh, 1996; Roozendaal et al., 2009).

Over the last 30 years, mindfulness meditation has acquired popularity in the West thanks to its success in effectively reducing stress (Grossman et al., 2004). Moreover, it is increasingly applied in psychotherapeutic programs for the treatment of anxiety and depression (Hofmann et al., 2010; Salmon et al., 1998). Meditation is the practice of training mental attention to achieve a state of mindfulness. Mindfulness is commonly defined as "paying attention in a particular way: on purpose, in the present moment, and non-judgmentally" (Kabat-Zinn, 1994, p. 4). It is cultivated during meditation and extends beyond the time of formal practice. The major components of mindfulness, awareness and acceptance of both internal (e.g., cognitive-affective-sensory) and external (e.g., social-environmental) experiences in the present moment, are considered effective agents against psychological malaise (Keng et al., 2011). The benefits of meditation for anxiety and depression are thought to depend partially on the development of greater attentional control and executive functioning (Baer, 2003). That is, attention and energy previously allocated towards negative stimuli are redirected to more neutral or positive stimuli. The most well known meditation treatment program is Mindfulness-Based Stress Reduction (MBSR; Kabat-Zinn, 1990), which provides comprehensive training in mindfulness meditation.

Recently, meditation has been correlated with improvements in memory, cognition, and brain composition (Jha et al., 2007, 2010; Ortner et al., 2007; Slagter et al., 2007; Zeidan et al., 2010). A study

Summarizes a major research finding and cites the relevant sources. Parenthetical citations follow APA style.

Aymelek organizes her literature review by topic; here she surveys literature on mindfulness and meditation.

Such a statement, along with the numerous citations, helps demonstrate Aymelek's awareness of the relevant research literature.

by Hölzel et al. (2011) used the Five Facet Mindfulness Question-naire (FFMQ; Baer et al., 2006) and magnetic resonance imaging (MRI) to measure subjective mindfulness and neurological chang-es in participants of the MBSR program. They found that partici-pation in MBSR was associated with increased concentrations of gray matter in the left hippocampus and other regions of the brain connected to learning and memory processes as well as emotion regulation. Regular meditation has also been shown to strengthen one's ability to control impulses and maintain attention with less utilization of the brain's resources (Kozasa et al., 2012). In addition, Pagnoni and Cekic (2007) used voxel-based morphometry (VBM; Ashburner & Friston, 2000) and a computerized neuropsycholog-ical test to determine if gray matter in older populations would be more substantial in experienced meditators versus inexperienced meditators. They discovered increases in gray matter volume in the putamen, an area of the brain implicated in attentional pro-cesses, in experienced meditators but not in controls.

The benefits of exercise for physical health and stress manage-ment have been well documented (Penedo & Dahn, 2005). Cur-rent research suggests that frequent exercise may also enhance brain structure and cognition (Griffin et al., 2011; Hillman et al., 2008). A controlled, longitudinal study by Erickson et al. (2011) aimed to determine if aerobic exercise could promote growth in the hippocampus of healthy older adults. They used an MRI to measure volume in the hippocampus at baseline, at 6 months, and at 1 year, and found that the exercise group demonstrated an increase in the left and right hippocampus by 2.12% and 1.97%, re-spectively, while the control group showed a 1.40% and 1.43% de-crease in hippocampal volume. Furthermore, physical activity has been reported potentially to enhance cognitive capacity through the production of brain-derived neurotrophic factors (BDNF), which support the growth of neurons and synapses (Tyler et al., 2002). Griffin et al. (2011) measured cognition and blood levels of BDNF in sedentary young males following acute and chronic ex-ercise. To assess cognition, they used a face-name task previously demonstrated by MRI to engage the hippocampus and medial-temporal lobes. Griffin et al. found increases in BDNF concentra-

Summarizes a recurring research finding, citing the findings of several studies.

tion in both acute and chronic exercise groups that corresponded with improved scores on the face-name task.

Although both meditation and exercise have been associated with enhancements in cognition and memory, it is important to note some of the limitations of past research. For example, many studies on meditation did not randomly assign participants and/or used small sample sizes (Eberth & Sedlmeier, 2012). In addition, studies frequently used clinical populations, and participants with prior interest in or experience with meditation (Chiesa et al., 2011; Hofmann et al., 2010). Likewise, many previous studies on exercise have not controlled and/or randomized designs. Additionally, subjects have often been limited to animals, human adult males, and older populations (Lambourne & Tomporowski, 2010; Smith et al., 2010).

Evaluates earlier research, acknowledging some of its limitations.

Despite these limitations, the above findings provide evidence that prolonged practice of tasks such as meditation and exercise induce positive changes in anatomical plasticity reflected in both subjective and objective measures of cognition. Based on the success of meditation and exercise in decreasing inhibitory stress levels that interfere with cognition and thus memory function, I hypothesize that: (1) practicing mindfulness meditation over not practicing mindfulness meditation will improve memory function; (2) practicing exercise over not practicing exercise will improve memory function; (3) the effects of mindfulness meditation on memory function will be greater in the exercise group versus the non-exercise group as measured by the Wechsler Memory Scale, fourth edition, adult version (WMS-IV; Wechsler, 2009).

Aymelek concludes by stating her hypotheses, which represent the research questions she will investigate and are clearly based on her review of existing research.

References

Al'Absi, M., Hugdahl, K., & Lovallo, W. R. (2002). Adrenocortical stress responses and altered working memory performance. *Psychophysiology, 39*(1), 95–99. https://doi.org/cjz8bh

Aronen, E. T., Vuontela, V., Steenari, M. R., Salmi, J., & Carlson, S. (2005). Working memory, psychiatric symptoms, and academic performance at school. *Neurobiology of Learning and Memory, 83*(1), 33–42. https://doi.org/dpwf55

Ashburner, J., & Friston, K. J. (2000). Voxel-based morphometry: The methods. *Neuroimage, 11*(6), 805–821. https://doi.org/brt2cb

Atkinson, R. C., & Shiffrin, R. M. (1968). Human memory: A proposed system and its control processes. *The Psychology of Learning and Motivation: Advances in Research and Theory, 2,* 89–195. https://doi.org/dnbb7v

Baddeley, A. D., & Hitch, G. J. (1974). Working memory. *The Psychology of Learning and Motivation, 8,* 47–89. https://doi.org/d4vgnk

Baer, R. A. (2003). Mindfulness training as a clinical intervention: A conceptual and empirical review. *Clinical Psychology: Science and Practice, 10*(2), 125–143. https://doi.org/fjq9qc

Baer, R. A., Smith, G. T., Hopkins, J., Krietemeyer, J., & Toney, L. (2006). Using self-report assessment methods to explore facets of mindfulness. *Assessment, 13*(1), 27–45. https://doi.org/dj5sc9

Cahill, L., & McGaugh, J. L. (1996). Modulation of memory storage. *Current Opinion in Neurobiology, 6*(2), 237–242. https://doi.org/bqn28r

Chiesa, A., Calati, R., & Serretti, A. (2011). Does mindfulness training improve cognitive abilities? A systematic review of neuropsychological findings. *Clinical Psychology Review, 31*(3), 449–464. https://doi.org/fhj9jp

. . .

Penedo, F. J., & Dahn, J. R. (2005). Exercise and well-being: A review of mental and physical health benefits associated with physical activity. *Current Opinion in Psychiatry, 18*(2), 189–193. https://doi.org/cfcxb2.

Roozendaal, B., McEwen, B. S., & Chattarji, S. (2009). Stress, memory and the amygdala. *Nature Reviews Neuroscience, 10*(6), 423–433. https://doi.org/b95m9c

Salmon, P. G., Santorelli, S. F., & Kabat-Zinn, J. (1998). Intervention elements promoting high adherence to mindfulness-based stress reduction programs in the clinical behavioral medicine setting. In S. A. Shumaker, E. B. Schron, J. K. Ockene, & W. L. McBee (Eds.), *Handbook of health behavior change* (2nd ed., pp. 239–266). Springer.

Slagter, H. A., Lutz, A., Greischar, L. L., Francis, A. D., Nieuwenhuis, S., Davis, J. M., & Davidson, R. J. (2007). Mental training affects distribution of limited brain resources. *PLOS Biology, 5*(6), e138. https://doi.org/cw46zf

Smith, P. J., Blumenthal, J. A., Hoffman, B. M., Cooper, H., Strauman, T. A., Welsh-Bohmer, K., Browndyke, J. N., & Sherwood, A. (2010). Aerobic exercise and neurocognitive performance: A meta-analytic review of randomized controlled trials. *Psychosomatic Medicine, 72*(3), 239–252. https://doi.org/d7vvcj

Tyler, W. J., Alonso, M., Bramham, C. R., & Pozzo-Miller, L. D. (2002). From acquisition to consolidation: On the role of brain-derived neurotrophic factor signaling in hippocampal-dependent learning. *Learning & Memory, 9*(5), 224–237. https://doi.org/cdnzhq

Wechsler, D. (2009). *WMS-IV: Wechsler Memory Scale administration and scoring manual* (4th ed). Pearson.

Zeidan, F., Johnson, S. K., Diamond, B. J., David, Z., & Goolkasian, P. (2010). Mindfulness meditation improves cognition: Evidence of brief mental training. *Consciousness and Cognition, 19*(2), 597–605. https://doi.org/fdvb4r

REFLECT. Find an article in a scholarly journal in a field you're interested in, perhaps your major. Locate the literature review section of the article (it may or may not be explicitly labeled as such) and analyze it in terms of the genre features on page 333. What kinds of sources does the author review? What aspects are discussed? How is the review organized? What is the author's evaluation of the literature, and how does that set up the rest of the article?

WRITING A REVIEW / A Roadmap

Choose something to review and find an interesting angle

If you get to choose your topic, pick a subject you're interested in and know something about. Perhaps you're an avid fan of Harry Potter. Reviewing the final novel in the series might be a good choice. Or maybe you love mountain biking: you could review three best-selling bikes. Remember that many things can be reviewed—shoes, appliances, restaurants, books, music. Choose a topic you want to learn more about.

If your topic is assigned, try to tailor it to your interests and to find an angle that will engage your audience. For instance, if your assignment is to review a specific art exhibit, see if you can focus on some aspect of the work that intrigues you, such as the use of color or the way the artist represents nature. If you are assigned to review a particular book, try to center your review on themes that you find compelling and that might interest your audience.

Consider your rhetorical situation

Once you have a tentative topic, thinking about your audience and the rest of your rhetorical situation will help you focus on how you can best address it.

Think about what your AUDIENCE knows and expects. If your review is for an assignment, consider your instructor to be your primary audience (unless they specifies otherwise) and know what's expected of a review in your discipline. If, however, you're writing for a specific publication or another audience, you'll have to think about what's appropriate or expected in that situation. Here are some things to consider:

- Who are you trying to reach, and why?
- In what ways are they like or unlike you? Are they likely to agree with you?
- What do they probably know about your subject? What background information will you need to provide?
- Will the subject matter to your audience? If not, how can you persuade them that it matters?
- What will they be expecting to learn from your review? What criteria will they value?

Think about your PURPOSE. Why are you writing this review? If it's for a class, what motivations do you have beyond getting a good grade? To recommend a book or film? evaluate the latest smart device? introduce your classmates to a new musical group? What do you expect your audience to do with the information in your review? Do you want them to go see something? buy something (or not)? just appreciate something? How can you best achieve your purpose?

Consider your STANCE. Think about your overall attitude about the subject and how you want to come across as an author. Are you extremely enthusiastic about your subject? firmly opposed to it? skeptical? lukewarm? How can you communicate your feelings? Think also about how you want your audience to see you as author. As well informed? thoughtful? witty? How can your review reflect that stance?

Think about the larger CONTEXT. What, if any, background information about your subject should you consider—other books on the same subject or by the same author? movies in the same genre? similar products made by different companies? What else has been said about your subject, and how will you respond to it in your review?

Consider MEDIA. Whether or not you have a choice of medium—print, spoken, or electronic—you need to think about how your medium will affect what you can do in your review. If you're presenting it online or to a live audience, you may be able to incorporate video and audio clips of a film or a concert. If your review will appear in print, can you include still photos? And most important of all: if you get to choose your medium, which one will best reach your audience?

Consider matters of DESIGN. If you are writing for an academic assignment, be sure to follow the format requirements of the discipline you're writing in. If you're writing for a particular publication, you'll need to find out what design options you have. But if you have the option of designing your text yourself, think about what will help readers understand your message. Should you include illustrations? Are you including any information that would be best presented in a list or a graph? Product reviews, for example, often display data in a table so that readers can compare several products.

Evaluate your subject

Think about your own first impressions. What about the subject got your interest? What was your first reaction, and why? What is the first thing you would tell someone who asked your opinion on this subject?

Examine your subject closely. If you're reviewing a performance, take notes as you're watching it; if you're reviewing a book, read it more than once. Look for parts of your subject that are especially powerful, or weak, or unexpected to mention in your review.

Do any necessary RESEARCH. Your subject will be your primary source of information, though you may need to consult other sources to find background information or to become aware of what else has been written about your subject. Would learning more about a book's author or a film's director help you evaluate your subject? If you're writing an academic review, do you need to find out what else has been said about your subject?

Determine the CRITERIA for your evaluation. Sometimes these are obvious: film reviews, for instance, tend to focus on criteria like acting, directing, script, and so forth. At other times, you'll need to establish the criteria that will guide your review. If you're unsure what criteria are most appropriate for your subject, look up reviews others have written on a similar topic. What criteria do those models use effectively?

Make a judgment about your subject. Based on the criteria you've established, evaluate your subject. Remember that few things are all good or all bad; you will likely find some things to praise, and others to criticize. Whatever you decide, use your criteria to examine your subject carefully, and look for specific EVIDENCE you can cite—lines or scenes from a movie, particular features of a product, and so on.

Anticipate other points of view. Not everyone is going to agree with your evaluation, and you need to acknowledge COUNTERARGUMENTS to what you think. Even if you don't persuade everyone in your audience to accept your judgment, you can demonstrate that your opinion is worth taking seriously by acknowledging and responding respectfully to those other perspectives.

Think about your mix of DESCRIPTION or SUMMARY and EVALUATION. You need to describe or summarize your subject enough so that readers will understand it, but remember that your primary goal is to evaluate it. The balance will depend on your purpose. Some reviews are expected to give a simple star rating, or a thumbs-up (or down). Others require more complex judgments.

Organize and start writing

Once you've determined your overall evaluation of your subject, compiled a list of its strengths and weaknesses, and assembled EVIDENCE you can draw upon to support that evaluation, it's time to organize your materials and start writing. To organize your review, think about what you want to tell readers about your subject, what your evaluation of it is, and why.

Come up with a tentative THESIS. What major point do you want to make about your subject? Try writing this point out as a tentative thesis. Then think about whether the thesis should be stated explicitly or not. Also consider whether to put the thesis toward the end of your introduction or save it for the conclusion.

DESCRIBE or SUMMARIZE the subject you're reviewing, and provide any background information your audience may need.

Evaluate your subject. Using the CRITERIA you identified for your review, present your subject's strengths and weaknesses, generally in order of importance. Provide REASONS and specific EVIDENCE to back them up. Don't forget to acknowledge other points of view.

Draft an OPENING. Introduce your subject in a way that makes clear what you're reviewing and why your audience should care about it—and shows that you know what you're talking about!

Draft a CONCLUSION. Wrap up your review by summarizing your evaluation. If you have any recommendations, here's where to make them known.

Look critically at your draft, get response—and revise

Once you have a complete draft, read it over carefully, focusing on your evaluation, the reasons and evidence you provide as support, and the way you appeal to your audience. If possible, ask others—a writing center tutor, classmate, or friend—for feedback. Be sure to give your readers a clear sense of your assignment or purpose and your intended audience. Here are some questions that can help you or others respond:

- *Is the evaluation stated explicitly?* Is there a clear **THESIS** —and if not, is one needed?

- *How well does the introduction capture the audience's interest?* How well does it establish your **AUTHORITY** as a reviewer? Does it make clear what the review is about? How will it engage your audience's interest? How else might it begin?

- *Is the subject* **DESCRIBED** *or* **SUMMARIZED** *sufficiently* for your audience? Is any additional description or background information needed?

- *How much of the review is* **DESCRIPTION** *and how much is* **EVALUATION** —and does the balance seem right for the subject and purpose?

- *What are the* **CRITERIA** *for the evaluation?* Are they stated explicitly— and if not, should they be? Do the criteria seem appropriate for the subject and audience? Are there other criteria that should be considered?

- *What good* **REASONS** *and* **EVIDENCE** *support the evaluation?* Will your audience be persuaded?

- *What other viewpoints do you consider,* and how well do you respond to these views? Are there other views you should consider?

- *How would you describe the* **STANCE** *and* **TONE**? Are they appropriate and authoritative? What words or details create that impression?

- *How is the draft organized?* Is it easy to follow, with clear **TRANSITIONS** from one point to the next?

- *What about* **DESIGN**? Should any material be set off as a list or chart or table? Are there any illustrations—and if not, should there be?

- *Is the* **STYLE** —choice of words, kinds of sentences, level of formality— appropriate for the intended audience?

- *How does the draft* CONCLUDE *?* Is the conclusion decisive and satisfying? How else might it conclude?

- *Is this a fair review?* Even if readers do not agree with the evaluation, will they consider it fair?

～◎ *REFLECT. Once you've completed your review, let it settle for a while and then take time to reflect. How well did you argue for your evaluation? How persuasive do you think your readers will find your review? Will those who do not agree with your evaluation consider it fair? What additional revisions would you make if you could? Research shows that such reflections help "lock in" what you learn for future use.*

Black Panther Gets So Much Right and One Crucial Thing Wrong

MARC BERNARDIN

THERE'S A MOMENT early on in *Black Panther* that took my breath away. T'Challa (Chadwick Boseman), not yet a king, is riding in his hovercraft shuttle with spy and former paramour Nakia (Lupita Nyong'o) and General Okoye (Danai Gurira), leader of the Dora Milaje, the Panther's personal honor guard. We follow the craft as it makes its way through the holographic barrier that conceals Wakanda from the outside world, and you can see the thrusters that propel it—and in the energy bloom, you can make out African symbols, shifting, pulsing, morphing.

Someone had to design that (namely, production designer Hannah Beachler). Someone had to approve it. Hundreds of thousands of dollars had to be spent to render something that, in any other movie, would just be "space blue."

It's as if everyone enlisted to bring the project to life understood the magnitude of what *Black Panther*, the first comic-based studio movie with a black hero at the center since 1998's *Blade*, would represent: The chance to fill every corner of their fictional Wakanda with the same level of craft and detail

---

MARC BERNARDIN, former film critic for the *L.A. Times*, has written comic books, television shows, and podcasts in addition to his work for *Entertainment Weekly* and the *Hollywood Reporter*. In 2018, Bernardin won a Comic-Con Ink Pot award for those who make a significant contribution to the worlds of "comics, science fiction/ fantasy, film, television, animation, and fandom services." This review appeared on *Nerdist.com* in 2018.

usually reserved for British-star-studded period pieces; an opportunity to tell a story about black lives, which matter and are not defined by their pain but, instead, by their glory; an answer to a culture's question, "When will it be our time in the sun?"

As such, it can be hard to separate what *Black Panther* means from what it is. What it means is *everything*, especially to any kid who has never put the words "African" and "king" together in the same sentence. Or to any young woman who was ever discouraged from chasing a life in science and technology. To anyone who was ever told "you fight like a girl."

As for what it is? *Black Panther* is like the most delicious cake you've ever tasted in your entire life, but which isn't quite cooked all the way through. 5

Black Panther picks up where *Captain America: Civil War* left off: With T'Challa still grieving the death of his father, even on the eve of his ascendance to the throne. In short order, we see the web of relationships that bind T'Challa to Wakanda. His love for his widowed mother, Queen Ramonda (the resplendent Angela Bassett), who invests in her son all the dreams of a happy future curtailed. His respect for Zuri (Forest Whitaker), his father's boon companion and Wakanda's spiritual leader. His playful bond with his younger sister Shuri (Letitia Wright), a tech wizard whose inventions kick Tony Stark's and James Bond's to a distant curb. His trust in Okoye, who has the rare

A still shows Black Panther T'Challa with two characters who support his fight to hold onto power—Nakia, a Wakandan spy, and Okoye, head of the Wakandan special forces.

Shuri, T'Challa's sister, engineers an arsenal of gadgets to protect and equip her brother.

pleasure of both serving the throne of Wakanda and liking the man who sits upon it. And his affection for Nakia, one of Wakanda's spies-at-large who thinks it might be time for her nation to share its tremendous gifts with a world that needs them.

Into that web wanders Ulysses Klaue (Andy Serkis), a South African arms dealer and mercenary who has been caught and branded for stealing the miraculous metal Vibranium from Wakanda, the only place in the world it can be mined.

And then there's the sinewy Erik Killmonger (Michael B. Jordan), an American veteran who is crazy about Wakanda, Wakandans, and the new King T'Challa. The minute he strides on screen, you can't take your eyes off of him—partially because he's played by the unfairly charismatic Jordan, partially because his attire is all Dwyane Wade-meets-Big Boi funky. As his story develops and deepens, we understand why he's a villain, what broke him as a child, and how he never healed right. We understand who he is and exactly what he wants.

In fact, every character's wants and needs are clearly defined, with one exception: T'Challa's. When the film opens, he wants to be king. Ten minutes and one ceremonial duel with rival tribe-leader M'Baku (Winston Duke) later, he's king. After that, he wants to maintain the status quo: Preserve the Wakandan way of life. But the status quo, by definition, is static, and stasis isn't drama. His romance with Nakia never exceeds nascence; by the time the film ends, you might've forgotten they had ever been "a thing." For too much of *Black Panther*, the Black Panther has everything he wants.

Chadwick Boseman as King T'Challa in *Black Panther*.

On top of this, he is also almost entirely devoid of flaws. He's a deadly 10 martial artist, a stalwart friend, well-educated, even-tempered, quick to smile, and, despite all that, he's humble. Flaws are the grooves, the nocks that add depth. Perfection in fiction, unlike in life, can be boring. I mean, even Indiana Jones was afraid of snakes.

The movie leaps to its feet when T'Challa, Nakia, and Okoye find themselves in Busan, South Korea, hot on the heels of the criminal Klaue. For a hot 15 minutes, *Black Panther* becomes the best Bond movie you'll ever see, partially because, here, the Panther wants something—to kill or capture Klaue. But this can also be thanked to the bone-crushing, wall-smashing action executed to perfection by director Ryan Coogler, who takes to it like an artist in love with the ways human bodies can cause destruction. Quickly, the sequence morphs into a car chase that feels as inspired by anime as it does by John Frankenheimer's *Ronin*.

Then, *Black Panther* settles back into its groove, in which everything on the periphery is awesome (especially the Dora Milaje . . . my gods, the Dora Milaje), but the center does not hold. Though Boseman pivots from dignity to delight on a dime, the screenplay (by Coogler and Joe Robert Cole) has trouble finding ways to emotionally engage with the character, all the way through to an action climax whose humanity is outweighed by its CGI.

The film does deal head-on with issues of race, subjugation, and oppression in ways both heartbreaking and hilarious. The final coda is as direct an address to the xenophobia at home in our current administration as that which you'll find in any film this year, let alone any giant Marvel movie. As a nerd and as a black man, I've been waiting for this movie for my entire life, whether I knew it or not. The fact that *Black Panther* gets so much right, but one crucial thing wrong, is both thrilling and maddening.

What it is. And what it means.

There are a few scenes set in Oakland, California—Coogler's hometown. 15 At one point, a young black boy in a rundown apartment dismisses the idea of Wakanda itself: What good is "a kid in Oakland, running around believing in fairy tales"? Coogler is that kid and this is his fairy tale—a fairy tale for other kids who rarely get them, and never like this.

What it means.

Thinking about the Text

1. Write a one-paragraph **SUMMARY** of Bernardin's review, being sure to identify his criteria for evaluation and the extent to which he claims the movie did or did not satisfy them.

2. Do you find Bernardin's **TONE** authoritative? Why or why not? How does Bernardin establish his own **AUTHORITY** and **CREDIBILITY**—or fail to do so? Point to specific parts of the text to support your response.

3. What assumptions does Bernardin make about his **AUDIENCE** and the things they are familiar with? How do you know? You might start by considering the vocabulary he uses and the topics he mentions as he discusses the film.

4. How does Bernardin frame his review? In other words, how does the review open, and how does Bernardin use this **OPENING** to make a crucial point about the significant achievement of *Black Panther*?

5. Bernardin states that he has two main criteria for reviewing *Black Panther*: "what it is" and "what it means." Think of a movie, book, television show, concert—anything—that represents an important milestone, either for you personally or to the larger culture it impacted. Write a **REVIEW** in which you evaluate not just what this significant thing "is" but also what it "means." Be sure to state your **CRITERIA** clearly and use **EVIDENCE** to support your claims.

Indie Gem *Please Knock on My Door* Expertly Captures Mental Illness

MANISHA UMMADI

FOR SOMEONE WHO NEVER personally experienced the crippling effects of mental illness, the idea of climbing into the complex mind of an afflicted individual may seem like a daunting experience. But as Swedish indie developer Michael Levall proves through his new story-driven, top-down adventure game *Please Knock on My Door*, investigating depression and anxiety at a personal level may be the key to understanding the inner mechanisms of our own minds.

Built around Levall's own experiences with depression, *Please Knock on My Door* gives the player control over the daily life of an individual navigating depression and social anxiety—the player takes on the responsibility of getting the unnamed protagonist through the routine of eating, working, sleeping, and tending to his other needs as he progresses through the workweek. Yet what begins as an inconsequential life simulator quickly escalates to an emotionally grueling daily battle against both time and the darker voices in the protagonist's head.

MANISHA UMMADI is an undergraduate student at the University of California, Berkeley, where she is studying molecular and cell biology. Ummadi is also a staff writer for the *Daily Californian*, an independent, student-run newspaper, for which she wrote this review in 2017.

Please Knock on My Door features a thoughtfully minimalistic art style reminiscent of an old-school, two-dimensional, top-down game—even the game's protagonist is depicted as a simple Minecraft-esque being, devoid of any detail except for his expressive eyes. Yet the game uses extensive narration and written text in the form of text boxes and journal entries to construct a thorough narrative that delves into the deep roots of the protagonist's most vulnerable feelings.

Consistent with its art style, most of the game takes place in the protagonist's darkened apartment, which contains only a limited number of objects, such as his bed or computer, that can be interacted with. Throughout the game, the player is also led to make decisions that determine the protagonist's interpersonal relationships and job performance each workday.

But embedded in these deceivingly simple daily interactions is a robust system   5
of rewards and consequences that factors the player's every decision into the protagonist's mental well-being and physical health—making the decision to forsake sleep or work in order to appease the protagonist's all-encompassing thoughts affect his emotional engagement and the end result of his journey.

As the game progresses and the protagonist increasingly falls victim to his own headspace, completing even the simplest sequence of tasks within the limited time frame each day becomes a near-impossible challenge. Learning from the player's decisions, the game attempts to push and pull the protagonist against the will of the player, leaving the player to painfully fight the game itself to just survive through each increasingly difficult day.

Yet despite the inevitably heavy subject matter that *Please Knock on My Door* tackles, the game manages to approach mental illness with a sense of realistic optimism—for every isolating interaction the protagonist experiences within his own headspace, the game presents a support system in the form of friends and coworkers, each with a particular personality, that reminds both the protagonist and the player that healing is as much an aspect of mental illness as the symptoms themselves. In fact, Levall adds an utterly human dimension to the gameplay by using the game's unique endings to explore the direct effects of reaching out and seeking help in the face of even the most debilitating mental challenges.

A unique experience from start to finish, *Please Knock on My Door* uses its quirky gameplay to masterfully radiate an unwavering sense of authenticity as it conducts an exploration into the emotions associated with mental illness. The game's basis in Levall's own struggle with depression undoubtedly feeds into its hauntingly realistic nature, developing the game itself into an extremely personal journey of varying interpretation depending on the player. Indeed, no two playthroughs of the game are remotely identical to one another, adding to the game's replay value.

As the protagonist perpetually struggles through the symptoms of depression and anxiety that cloud his days, the player cannot help but reciprocate his raw feelings of helplessness and frailty. Placing the player in the darkest corner of the protagonist's mind, *Please Knock on My Door* manages to do the unthinkable and force the player into not just observing but experiencing the indescribable effects of mental illness. Through every aspect of the game, Levall showcases his prowess as an interactive storyteller, affirming that video games as a genre can be used to tell rich stories that carry emotional weight, rather than being confined to a series of mind-numbing shooters. *Please Knock on My Door* undeniably cements itself as an indie gem bent on changing the way in which narratives are delivered to the player, making the experience of interacting with a game a highly personal matter.

While the player's takeaway from the taxing journey of *Please Knock on My* 10 *Door* ultimately depends on the real-life experiences that the player enters with, the game undoubtedly bestows a level of profound insight upon all— some may experience a mind-shattering introspective epiphany by the end of the game, some may not—but at the very least, the player will walk away with a more nuanced understanding of mental illness.

Thinking about the Text

1. How does Manisha Ummadi establish her **AUTHORITY** and credibility as a reviewer? How does her **INTRODUCTION**, for instance, contribute to her credibility? How would you describe her **TONE**? Point to specific words and passages that contribute to that tone.

2. What is Ummadi's **EVALUATION** of this video game, and what evidence does she offer in support of her views? How persuasive do you find her evaluation? What **CRITERIA** do Ummadi use as a basis for her evaluation? How does she make these criteria clear? Point out specific passages from the text that support your response.

3. Mental illness is an unusual subject for a video game to address, and it poses challenges for those reviewing the video game as well. What strikes you as particularly helpful and relevant in Ummadi's comments

on mental illness in the review? How does Ummadi work to build her **AUDIENCE**'s interest on this topic?

4. Imagine that you, like Ummadi, wanted to tell your classmates about a book, performance, game, podcast, or artist that you like—or don't like—in a piece that will be published in your campus newspaper. Write a **REVIEW** to persuade other students to check it out—or not. Take care to introduce your subject, establish criteria for your evaluation, and show evidence from the subject to support what you say.

SEVENTEEN

"Here's What I Recommend"
Making a Proposal

 ILL YOU MARRY ME? There is no clearer proposal than the one this question represents. It proposes something that at least one person thinks ought to occur. Proposals are just that: recommendations that something be done, often to bring about some kind of change or to solve a problem. You'll likely have occasion to write proposals for various purposes; and if you're reading this chapter now, you've probably been assigned to write one for a composition class.

You might propose better financial aid options, a new way of disposing of excess cafeteria food, a possible solution to the childhood obesity crisis. Like a marriage proposal, each suggests change; unlike a marriage proposal, however, each of these cases addresses a problem and calls for careful analysis of several possible courses of action. While it may be obvious to your beloved that you are the one, it's less obvious how a more flexible borrowing plan can ease the burden of student debt, how composting can create a more sustainable food system, or how school lunch programs can help end childhood obesity. Proposals of this kind argue for clear solutions to specific problems; and as with any argument, they build a convincing case that what they recommend should be considered—and even acted on.

This chapter provides guidelines for writing proposals that will be taken seriously, ones that say, "Here's what I recommend—and why you should take my advice."

REFLECT. Proposals are part of daily life, but some are more compelling than others. Find a proposal that interests you, perhaps an op-ed on a social issue such as homelessness or inequality or a GoFundMe campaign. How does the proposal convince or fail to convince you that it's important and that the recommended solution is worth your support?

Across Academic Disciplines

If you've been assigned to write a research paper, chances are your instructor has asked you to present a proposal before you begin researching and drafting the paper. Such proposals ensure that your topic and plan of action are appropriate for the assignment. You'll likely have occasion to write these and other kinds of proposals in many courses. For a *biology* course, you may be asked to propose an experiment, explaining why it's important and hypothesizing what you expect to find. In a *public policy* course, you might work with a group to analyze a specific policy—perhaps your city's policy of providing incentives to encourage the use of solar power—and to propose changes. In each case, you'll need to think about what's expected, given the topic and the discipline.

Across Media

Authors of proposals often use multiple media to present their recommendations. Crowdfunding sites like *Kickstarter* may use *video* to show their projects in action or bring audiences face-to-face with their cause. Op-ed columnists writing for *print* newspapers rely on carefully crafted words to make their points, but online versions of the papers include links to supporting materials. If you're presenting a proposal in an *oral presentation*, slides can help illustrate what you're recommending—and you may be asked to provide a print document to elaborate on what you propose.

Across Cultures and Communities

Proposals of various sorts are common in the United States. At your school, for example, students might band together to propose more effective campus

↪ *CROWDFUNDING SITES are filled with proposals. Take a look at the proposal that former flight attendant Robin Wearly created on Kickstarter for a disabled passenger transfer sling (ADAPTS) that permits air travelers who use wheelchairs to get off the plane quickly and safely in case of evacuation. It states a problem and proposed a solution. Go to everyonesanauthor.tumblr.com to see the full proposal. Note how the campaign page uses written text, images, and videos. Imagine how Wearly might present this proposal in a meeting with potential investors. What information would be best presented as speech, on slides, as an embedded video, or in a handout? What additional information might investors want that the website does not contain?*

policies to prevent sexual assault. In business, many companies encourage employees at all levels to share ideas for improving the company's products or services. And in many states, voters can propose a ballot initiative to change existing laws.

Proposals are common in cultures and industries that thrive on open discussion and innovation, but not every community is receptive to input from just anyone. Many governments, organizations, and households around the world value the judgment of authorities and community leaders, and proposals from others may be seen as disrespectful. So be aware of the situation you're writing in and the audience you are speaking to, not just to avoid offending someone but to determine how best to present your ideas.

Across Genres

Proposals occur in many kinds of writing. **REVIEWS** sometimes end with proposals for how something could be improved, and many **REPORTS**, especially those on pressing social issues, conclude by proposing a course of action to address the issue.

A fully developed proposal is based on an **ANALYSIS** of a problem or situation in great detail. It requires **REPORTING** trustworthy information, and often involves **NARRATING** one or more past events as part of that reporting.

REFLECT. Find two proposals that address the same issue, perhaps one students are currently debating on your campus. How does each proposal define the issue, what solutions does each of them offer, and what evidence does each provide to show that its solutions will work? Which of the two proposals do you find more persuasive, and why?

CHARACTERISTIC FEATURES

Although there will be variation depending on the topic, you'll find that nearly all strong proposals share the following characteristics:

- A precise description of the problem
- A clear and compelling solution to the problem
- Evidence that your solution will address the problem
- Acknowledgment of other possible solutions
- A statement of what your proposal will accomplish

A Precise Description of the Problem

The goal of all proposals is to offer a solution for some problem, so most of them begin by explicitly stating the problem and establishing that it is serious enough that it needs a solution. Some problems are obvious—that there's a water shortage in California, for instance, or few women majoring in engineering—so you won't have to say much to convince your audience that they matter. In other cases, though, you'll need to describe the problem in detail and provide data, examples, and other evidence to convince readers that it's serious enough to require a solution.

The title of a controversial article by journalist David Freedman identifies a problem and proposes a possible solution: "How Junk Food Can End Obesity." But in the following passage from that article, Freedman describes a specific problem in the wide debate about obesity that his proposal then responds to.

> If the most-influential voices in our food culture today get their way, we will achieve a genuine food revolution. Too bad it would be one tailored to the dubious health fantasies of a small, elite minority. And too bad it would largely exclude the obese masses, who would continue to sicken and die early. Despite the best efforts of a small army of wholesome-food heroes, there is no reasonable scenario under which these foods could become cheap and plentiful enough to serve as the core diet for most of the obese population—even in the unlikely case that your typical junk-food eater would be willing and able to break lifelong habits to embrace kale and yellow beets. And many of the dishes glorified by the wholesome-food movement are, in any case, as caloric . . . as anything served in a Burger King.
>
> Through its growing sway over health-conscious consumers and policy makers, the wholesome-food movement is impeding the progress of the one segment of the food world that is actually positioned to take effective, near-term steps to reverse the obesity trend: the processed-food industry.   —DAVID FREEDMAN, "How Junk Food Can End Obesity"

Not only does Freedman say that the views of many well-known food writers are wrong (that there wouldn't be so much obesity if only we all ate more "wholesome food"); he also argues that their "growing sway" over consumers and policy makers is actually "impeding the progress" of one group that might be able to do something to "reverse the obesity trend." In other words, he identifies them as part of the problem.

Robin Wearly, author of the *Kickstarter* proposal illustrated on page 373, begins her proposal by stating the problem in terms that appeal to readers' emotions and logic in a culture that values individual responsibility and thinking ahead: "Emergencies happen. What if you or a loved

Kale and beets are part of the problem? Read David Freedman's full proposal on p. 903 where he explains why.

one rely on a wheelchair? What's the plan?" She then provides a series of brief but vivid scenarios that confront readers with the reality of the problem:

> Wheelchairs are checked in cargo on airplanes. Elevators are shut down in hotel emergencies. So did you ever wonder how wheelchair travelers escape a burning airplane, a derailed train, a bus accident, a cruise ship disaster, or hotel room when told to evacuate? What if they can't wait for rescue personnel and their only hope is the crew or kindness of strangers? What if you have less than 90 seconds to make it to an emergency exit? Will a trapped person leave both your lives in peril? Here's how ADAPTS comes to the rescue!
>   —"ADAPTS, the First Evacuation Sling for Wheelchair Users"

These descriptions remind readers, especially able-bodied ones, of things that can go wrong and the consequences of such situations for wheel-chair users. These high-stakes scenarios define the problem that the proposal will then address.

In any proposal, it's important to identify the problem clearly and in a way that sets up the solution you'll be recommending. Defining the problem precisely can also help make your solution realistic: preventing emergencies that endanger individuals with various mobility impairments is a tall order, while creating a tool that helps people with physical disabilities get to safety more easily in an emergency seems doable.

A Clear and Compelling Solution to the Problem

Successful proposals offer a compelling solution to the problem at hand. That is, it isn't sufficient merely to have a good idea; in a proposal, you'll have to convince readers that your idea squarely addresses the problem as you've defined it.

You'll want to explain the solution succinctly but in enough detail to make a clear and confident case for it. See how the Interdisciplinary Group on Preventing School and Community Violence offers a research-based proposal to respond to gun violence in schools and communities. While acknowledging the need for security measures—a common response to such acts of violence, the group proposes a more focused solution: "a change in mindset and policy," that is, focusing on preventing such events in the first place. They frame the issue as a public health problem and detail specific steps to achieve the needed shift in mindset and policy:

> A public health approach to protecting children as well as adults from gun violence involves three levels of prevention: (1) universal approaches promoting safety and well-being for everyone; (2) practices for reducing risk and promoting protective factors for persons experiencing difficulties; and (3) interventions for individuals where violence is present or appears imminent.
> —INTERDISCIPLINARY GROUP ON PREVENTING SCHOOL AND
> COMMUNITY VIOLENCE, "Call to Action to Prevent Gun Violences"

In the paragraphs that follow, the group then explains what each level of prevention would require of various stakeholders—from Congress and social service agencies to students and parents. The number and detail of the proposed actions along with logical appeals make a strong and clear case why, if the country carried out these actions, gun violence in schools and communities would be greatly reduced.

Now consider a proposal for a policy that would provide more affordable housing in Portland, Oregon, from an article by a member of that city's city council written for *Street Roots*, a weekly newspaper often sold by people who are experiencing homelessness:

> We can't require developers to build affordable housing; state law prevents it. But we can encourage those who want to build here to be part of the solution. . . . The city currently provides "density bonuses" to developers for including certain public benefits in their projects— meaning they can build taller buildings or get more floor space than would normally be allowed in exchange for including features like eco-roofs or bicycle parking.
>
> Now is the time to restructure our density bonus regulations to prioritize affordable housing development. . . .
>
> Under a proposal that will go before the council on July 9, developers seeking a density bonus must either provide affordable housing within their development or pay a fee into a fund for the creation and preservation of affordable housing. This proposal . . . would require them to contribute to the creation of affordable housing in order to receive the maximum density that our zoning currently allows.
> —DAN SALTZMAN, "Incentive for Developers
> Would Spur Affordable Housing"

Saltzman's proposal describes a solution that addresses the problem clearly: to build the largest permissible buildings (and hence make more money), developers will have to include affordable units in the development *or* contribute to a fund for creating affordable housing. In return for something a developer wants, the city gets something it wants: more affordable housing.

Evidence That Your Solution Will Address the Problem

A proposal is convincing when the evidence it provides shows that the solution being proposed will, in fact, address the problem. The kind of evidence that will be convincing will vary depending on what it is you're proposing and to whom. If you're pitching a new business venture to potential investors, your evidence would include numbers showing the projected returns on investment. If you're proposing a new honor code at your school, your evidence would likely include testimonies and examples of how it would improve the learning environment. In his article on the Portland affordable housing proposal, Dan Saltzman provides data projecting what the proposal could accomplish:

> This "affordable housing incentive zoning proposal" could result in as many as 60 additional units of affordable housing a year on top of those already being developed by the city, or it could mean an additional $120 million to $200 million in funds for affordable housing over the next 20 years.
>
> This proposal alone will not solve our affordable-housing crisis but is a critical step to ensuring more affordable housing in our city.

By acknowledging that this proposal will not totally solve the problem of affordable housing but demonstrating its potential benefits—more affordable housing or funds to create such housing—Saltzman limits his solution to one that Portland will be able to address at the time, thus making a persuasive case that what he is suggesting is feasible.

Another example comes from Appleton, Wisconsin, a city facing the challenge of redesigning its streets and transit systems to accommodate pedestrians and bicyclists. In an eighty-page proposal laying out a twenty-year plan to improve such access, the city's designers offer plenty of evidence to support their ideas: diagrams showing how specific roads will be reconfigured to include bike lanes, charts of costs and funding sources, and a timetable for completing the project over the twenty-year construction period. Some of this evidence illustrates that the proposed changes will achieve the city's goal; other evidence shows that they will do so in a feasible manner.

Acknowledgment of Other Possible Solutions

Part of crafting a persuasive proposal is making it clear that your solution is the best course of action—and hence better than other options. To do so, you need to account for other possible solutions and demonstrate the comparative advantages of the solution you're suggesting.

English has a pronoun problem, according to Dennis Baron. See how he calmly explains all of the proposed solutions (including the status quo) before arguing for his preferred course of action on p 846.

In his article proposing that junk food has the best potential to end obesity, David Freedman describes in detail what those in the "wholesome food" camp suggest—and then points out why what they advocate is not so good after all. Here he visits his local Whole Foods store, where he finds many "wholesome" items:

> One that catches my eye . . . is Vegan Cheesy Salad Booster . . . whose package emphasizes the fact that it is enhanced with spirulina, chlorella, and sea vegetables. The label also proudly lets me know that the contents are raw—no processing!—and that they don't contain any genetically modified ingredients. What it does contain, though, is more than three times the fat content per ounce as the beef patty in a Big Mac . . . and four times the sodium.
>
> —DAVID FREEDMAN, "How Junk Food Can End Obesity"

Later in his article, he does acknowledge that some of the arguments on behalf of "wholesome food" are accurate:

> For the purpose of this article, let's simply stipulate that wholesome foods are environmentally superior. But let's also agree that when it comes to prioritizing among food-related public-policy goals, we are likely to save and improve many more lives by focusing on cutting obesity—through any available means—than by trying to convert all of industrialized agriculture into . . . small organic farms.

Notice that in each case Freedman first describes something others have proposed (or might propose)—and then points out its shortcomings.

Other situations call for proposals that consider several possible solutions at the same time, as in the case of the one for creating bicycle and pedestrian access in Appleton, Wisconsin. Because there's no one-size-fits-all solution that will work for every street in the city, the authors of this proposal suggest several possible configurations, including those shown on the following page in Figures 17.a and 17.b.

Bike lanes, which are meant only for cyclists, and shared lanes, which are shared by bicycles and cars, are two of the possible road configurations the authors explore. They provide detailed information about each option, describing its purpose, listing its advantages and disadvantages, and including a diagram. By presenting multiple design options, the authors address the full range of situations that exist. In situations that call for multiple solutions, considering all possibilities shows that you have fully considered the problems' complexity.

A Statement of What Your Proposal Will Accomplish

So what if readers decide to follow your proposal? What can they expect it to accomplish? The strongest proposals answer that question explicitly. Given that your goal is to persuade readers to agree with what you suggest and perhaps to take some kind of action, you need to help them understand the likely outcomes. Many proposals end by making clear what's to be gained, what outcomes large and small they might bring about.

Megan Hopkins, a former teacher with Teach For America (TFA), concludes her proposal calling for changes in that program by making clear how her suggestions—a longer commitment period, a full year of training, more incentives to continue teaching—will help TFA realize its mission.

> While these proposals would require substantial redesign of the TFA model, the results are likely to be worth the investment. Teach For America has the potential to effect large-scale change in the field of education. It recruits highly qualified, motivated corps members who appreciate the importance of equal education opportunities, and many go on to devote their lives to this mission. However, these bright individuals are not as effective in the classroom as they could be, and their students do not perform as well as students in classrooms where teachers have more formal training. Corps members who are given a full year to learn effective instructional practices and to fully prepare to work

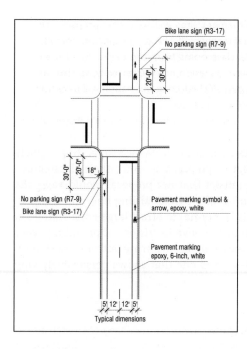

Fig. 17.a BIKE LANE

Description/Purpose: Marked space along length of roadway for exclusive use of cyclists. Bike lanes create separation between cyclists and automobiles.

Advantages
- Provides bicycle access on major through streets
- Clarifies lane use for motorists and cyclists
- Increases cyclists' comfort through visual separation

Disadvantages
- Space requirements may preclude other possible uses like parking or excess travel lane width

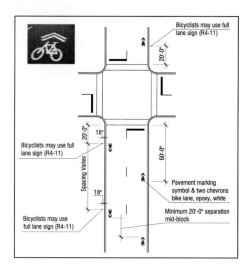

Fig. 17.b SHARED LANE

Description/Purpose: Shared roadway pavement markings, or "sharrows," are markings used to indicate a shared lane environment for bicycles and automobiles. Sharrows identify to all road users where bicycles should operate on a street where a separated facility is not feasible.

Advantages
- Helps cyclists position themselves in lanes too narrow for a motor vehicle and a bicycle to travel side by side
- Provides pavement markings where bike lanes are not possible

Disadvantages
- Maintenance requirements
- Not as effective as a separated bicycle facility

—WISCONSIN DEPARTMENT OF TRANSPORTATION, *City of Appleton On-Street Bike Plan*

within the context of their placement sites will be better prepared to enter their classrooms as skilled teachers. If TFA can prepare its recruits to be more successful in their classrooms from the beginning of their service, it may be able to achieve its vision more effectively, so that, as the TFA mission states, "One day, all children in this nation will have the opportunity to attain an excellent education."

—MEGAN HOPKINS, "Training the Next Teachers for America"

Hopkins states one immediate result of the reforms she's suggesting, namely that corps members will be "better prepared to enter their classrooms." However, to highlight the true impact that her proposal would have, she starts and ends her summary of results by explaining how these adjustments would help TFA realize its "potential to effect large-scale change in the field of education" and thereby "achieve its vision" of providing every child in America with a good education—an inspiring outcome most audiences would happily stand behind, and one that shows persuasively why this proposal matters.

WRITING A PROPOSAL / An Annotated Example

In response to the deadly 2018 shooting at Marjory Stoneman Douglas High School in Parkland, Florida, this proposal was issued by a group of nationally recognized experts across fields whose research focuses on violence prevention. More than 4,000 individuals, 80 national organizations, and 170 other state and local organizations signed in support. This proposal relies on the credibility of the authors instead of a great deal of documented evidence for the claims presented. This approach keeps the proposal brief—one page exactly in the version posted online—and therefore more likely to be read, understood, and ultimately enacted by a wide general audience.

See the complete list of authors and signatories by visiting everyonesanauthor.tumblr.com.

Call for Action to Prevent Gun Violence in the United States of America

INTERDISCIPLINARY GROUP ON PREVENTING SCHOOL AND COMMUNITY VIOLENCE

SCHOOL SHOOTINGS AND widespread community gun violence are far greater in the United States than other nations. America cannot be great and realize its promise of life, liberty, and the pursuit of happiness if our children are not safe from gun violence.

A direct statement of the problem. Words from the Declaration of Independence establish a serious tone.

Although security measures are important, a focus on simply preparing for shootings is insufficient. We need a change in mindset and policy from reaction to prevention. Prevention entails more than security measures and begins long before a gunman comes to school. We need a comprehensive public health approach to gun violence that is informed by scientific evidence and free from partisan politics.

Acknowledgement of a common response—and an argument why it's inadequate.

The authors are clear about what kinds of evidence their solution is based on: scientific evidence unaffected by political affiliation.

A public health approach to protecting children as well as adults from gun violence involves three levels of prevention: (1) universal approaches promoting safety and well-being for everyone; (2) practices for reducing risk and promoting protective factors for persons experiencing difficulties; and (3) interventions for individuals where violence is present or appears imminent.

A proposed three-point solution to the problem.

On the first level we need:

1. A national requirement for all schools to assess school climate and maintain physically and emotionally safe conditions and positive school environments that protect all students and adults from bullying, discrimination, harassment, and assault;
2. A ban on assault-style weapons, high-capacity ammunition clips, and products that modify semi-automatic firearms to enable them to function like automatic firearms.

On the second level we need:

3. Adequate staffing (such as counselors, psychiatrists, psychologists, and social workers) of coordinated school- and community-based mental health services for individuals with risk factors for violence, recognizing that violence is not intrinsically a product of mental illness;
4. Reform of school discipline to reduce exclusionary practices and foster positive social, behavioral, emotional, and academic success for students;
5. Universal background checks to screen out violent offenders, persons who have been hospitalized for violence towards self or others, and persons on no-fly, terrorist watch lists.

On the third level we need:

6. A national program to train and maintain school- and community-based threat assessment teams that include mental health and law enforcement partners. Threat assessment programs should include practical channels of communication for persons to report potential threats as well as interventions to resolve conflicts and assist troubled individuals;
7. Removal of legal barriers to sharing safety-related information among educational, mental health, and law enforcement agencies in cases where a person has threatened violence;
8. Laws establishing Gun Violence Protection Orders that allow courts to issue time-limited restraining orders requiring that firearms be recovered by law enforcement when there is evidence that an individual is planning to carry out acts against others or against themselves.

Congress and the executive branch must remove barriers to gun violence research and institute a program of scientific research on gun violence that encompasses all levels of prevention. We contend that well-executed laws can reduce gun violence while protecting all Constitutional rights.

It's time for federal and state authorities to take immediate action to enact these proposals and provide adequate resources for effective implementation. We call on law enforcement, mental health, and educational agencies to begin actions supporting these prevention efforts. We ask all parents and youth to join efforts advocating for these changes, and we urge voters to elect representatives who will take effective action to prevent gun violence in our nation.

Response to major barriers and potential objections to acting on these proposals.

Reiterating what the proposed solutions can accomplish.

A call to action that proposes everyone can—and should—be a part of the solution.

~~~ *REFLECT. Find a proposal in a campus publication or local newspaper. Read it first to see if you find it persuasive. If not, why not? Then annotate it as we've done with the proposal of the Interdisciplinary Group on Preventing School and Community Violence to see if it includes all the features listed on page 374. If not, would it be improved by adding any of the features it's lacking or by elaborating on any it doesn't demonstrate well?*

PROJECT PROPOSALS

You may be asked to write a project proposal to explain your plans for a large or long-term assignment: what you intend to do, how you'll go about doing it, and why the project is important. Like any proposal, a project proposal makes an argument, demonstrating that the project is worth doing and feasible given the available time and resources. Unless the assignment names other requirements, your proposal should cover the following ground:

An Indication of Your Topic and Focus

Explain what your topic is, giving any necessary background information. In some cases, you might be required to do some background research and to include a LITERATURE REVIEW summarizing what you find, including any issues or controversies you want to investigate. Say what your research focus will be, with the RESEARCH QUESTION you plan to pursue and a tentative THESIS. Finally, say why the topic matters—so what, and who cares?

An Explanation of Why You're Interested in the Topic

Briefly explain what you already know about your topic and why you've chosen to pursue this line of inquiry. You might describe any coursework, reading, or experience that contributes to your knowledge and interest. Also note what you don't yet know but intend to find out.

A Plan

Explain how you will investigate your research question. What types of sources will you need, and what will your research methods be? If you plan to do FIELD RESEARCH, how will you conduct your study? And what GENRE and MEDIUM will you use to present your findings? What steps will be required to bring it all together into the final document?

A Schedule

Break your project into tasks and make a schedule, taking into account all the research, reading, and writing you'll need to do. Include any specific tasks your instructor requires, such as handing in a draft or an ANNOTATED BIBLIOGRAPHY. Be sure also to leave yourself time to get feedback and revise.

PROJECT PROPOSAL / An Annotated Example

DAVID PASINI wrote this project proposal for a first-year writing course at The Ohio State University on the theme of sports in contemporary American society.

The Economic Impact of Investing Public Funds in Sports Franchises

DAVID PASINI

SINCE THE 1960S, local governments have provided increased funding and subsidies for professional sports franchises. Taxpayer money has gone toward facilities like stadiums and arenas, and many cities have offered tax exemptions and other financial incentives to keep a team in town that has threatened to relocate. Proponents of public funding for privately owned sports franchises argue that cities gain more from the arrangement—namely jobs, status, and tourist dollars—than they lose. Opponents argue that using public funds for these purposes results in long-term financial drains on local governments and point out that many communities have been abandoned by teams even after providing substantial benefits, leaving the city or state holding the proverbial debt-heavy bag.

Writing in *The New York Times*, Ken Belson gives an example of one such government-funded project: "The old Giants Stadium, demolished to make way for New Meadowlands Stadium, still carries about $110 million in debt, or nearly $13 for every New Jersey resident, even though it is now a parking lot" (Belson). The image

The introduction announces the topic and summarizes a controversy the project will focus on.

Fig. 1. Left to right: The governor of New Jersey, William T. Cahill; the owner of the Giants, Wellington Mara; and chairman of the New Jersey sports authority, Sonny Werblin, admire a drawing of Giants Stadium. Neal Boenzi. Photograph of William T. Cahill, Wellington Mara, and Sonny Werblin. 1971. "As Stadiums Vanish, Their Debt Lives On," by Ken Belson. *The New York Times*, 8 Sept. 2010, p. A1.

included here shows the governor of New Jersey looking over a drawing of the Giants Stadium, which was completed in 1976 and destroyed in 2010 (fig. 1).

Given the high stakes involved—and particularly the use of taxpayer dollars—it seems important, then, to ask what these sports franchises contribute (or do not contribute) to their cities and wider metropolitan areas. Do these teams "generate positive net economic benefits for their cities," or do they "absorb scarce government funds" that would be better spent on programs that have "higher social or economic payoff" (Noll and Zimbalist 55)? My research project will investigate these questions.

An explicit statement of his research questions.

The question of public funding for sports is important to any resident of a community that has a professional sports franchise or is trying to lure one, as well as to any citizen, sports fan or not, who is interested in the economic and political issues surrounding this topic. I am in the latter group, a nonfan who is simply interested in how public monies are being used to support sports, and whose knowledge about the issues is primarily in the economic domain. At this point in the research process, I am neither a proponent

A statement of why this topic matters, and to whom.

Pasini explains his interest in the topic and his current knowledge of it.

nor an opponent of investing in sports, but I think that it's important to consider just how—and how much—professional sports contribute to the economic well-being of the government that funds them. How much of the money that teams generate supports local businesses, school districts, or other important entities that benefit all citizens? How much of it stays in the owners' pockets? Do the franchises "give back" to their communities in any other tangible or intangible ways? The franchises themselves should consider these questions, since the communities that helped to provide them with the amenities they require to be successful sports teams have a right to expect something in return.

More focused research questions, leading to a tentative thesis statement.

To learn more about investment in sports teams and the teams' economic impact, I will consult business and sports management journals and appropriate news sources, both print and digital. I will also interview stakeholders on both sides of the debate as well as experts on this topic. In my research, I will consider the many factors that must be taken into account, such as the benefits of tourism and the costs of "creating extra demand on local services" (Crompton 33). As a result of my research, I hope to offer insight on whether public funds are in fact put to good use when they are invested in major sports franchises.

A research plan, including kinds of sources he'll consult and field research he plans to conduct.

The conclusion restates why this research matters.

Proposed Schedule

Do library and internet research	April 6–20
Submit annotated bibliography	April 20
Schedule and conduct interviews	April 21–25
Turn in first draft	May 10
Turn in second draft	May 18
Turn in final draft	May 25

A schedule that allows time for research, writing, and revising—and lists assignment deadlines.

Preliminary Works Consulted

Belson, Ken. "As Stadiums Vanish, Their Debt Lives On." *The New York Times*, 8 Sept. 2010, p. A1.

Crompton, John L. "Economic Impact Analysis of Sports Facilities and Events: Eleven Sources of Misapplication." *Journal of Sport Management*, vol. 9, no. 1, 1995, pp. 14–35.

Pasini uses MLA style for a preliminary list of works consulted.

Noll, Roger G., and Andrew Zimbalist, editors. *Sports, Jobs, and Taxes: The Economic Impact of Sports Teams and Stadiums.* Brookings Institution Press, 1997.

Robertson, Robby. "The Economic Impact of Sports Facilities." *The Sport Digest,* vol. 16, no. 1, 2008, www.thesportdigest .com/archive/article/economic-impact-sports-facilities.

REFLECT. *If you're reading about project proposals, you've probably been assigned to write one. Analyze what your assignment is asking for, comparing it with the features listed on page 374. What does this exercise help you appreciate about how such a proposal works? What you can learn from doing one?*

WRITING A PROPOSAL / A Roadmap

Think of a problem you can help solve

If you get to select the topic, identify an issue you know something about. You'll find it easiest—and most rewarding—to tackle an issue on which you can have some real impact. Try choosing a topic you have authority to speak on and one that is narrowly focused or local enough that your suggestions may be heard. You can't expect to solve all the problems of America's food system, but you may well be able to propose a more healthy and sustainable campus dining option.

If you've been assigned a topic, consider ways that you can make it interesting to you and your readers. This may mean finding an interesting angle on the topic you've been assigned, or, if the assignment is framed in general terms, finding a specific aspect that you can address with a specific solution.

Consider your rhetorical situation

Once you have a topic, thinking about your rhetorical situation will help you focus on how to proceed.

Think about your AUDIENCE. Who do you want your proposal to reach, and why? If you're proposing changes to a campus policy, you would do so differently if you're writing to school administrators in charge of that policy than if you're writing a piece for the newspaper. Here are some things to consider:

- What do you know about your audience? In what ways are they like or unlike you—and one another?
- What will they likely know about your topic? What background information will you have to provide?
- What interest or stake are they likely to have in the situation you're addressing? Will you need to convince them that the problem matters—and if you do, how can you do so?
- What sorts of evidence will they find most convincing?
- How likely are they to agree with what you propose?

Be clear about your PURPOSE. Odds are that you'll have multiple purposes— everything from getting a good grade to demonstrating your understanding of a situation to making your community a better place for everyone. The more you understand your own motivations, the clearer you can be with your audience about what is at stake.

Be aware of your STANCE. What is your attitude about your topic, and how do you want to come across to your audience? How can your choice of words help convey that stance? When David Freedman refers to those he disagrees with as the "let-them-eat-kale" crowd, his dismissive language tells us as much about him as it does about those he is criticizing.

Examine the larger CONTEXT. What do you know about the problem you're tackling? What might you need to learn? How have others addressed it? What solutions have they proposed and how well have they worked?

Think about MEDIA. If the choice is yours, what medium will best reach your audience and suit your purpose? If you're assigned to use a particular medium, how can you use it best? If, for example, you're giving an oral presentation, *PowerPoint* slides can help your audience follow the main points of your proposal, especially if you're presenting quantitative data.

Think about DESIGN. If you have the option of designing your proposal, think about what it needs. If it's lengthy or complex, should you use headings? Is there anything in your proposal that would be hard to follow in a paragraph—and easier to read in a chart or a graph?

Study the situation

Whatever the problem, you have to understand it in all its complexity and think about the many ways different parties will likely understand it.

Begin by thinking about what you know about the situation. What interests you about the issue, and why do you care? What more do you need to find out about it? To answer these questions, try BRAINSTORMING or other activities for GENERATING IDEAS.

Be sure you understand the problem. To do so, you'll surely need to do some RESEARCH. What CAUSED this problem, and what are its EFFECTS?

How serious is it? Who cares about it? What's been said about it? What efforts have already been made to address the problem, and how have they succeeded? How have similar problems been handled, and what insights can you gain from studying them?

Consider how you can best present the problem for your AUDIENCE. If they're aware of the problem, how much do they care about it? Does it affect them? If they're not aware of it, how can you make them aware? What kind of evidence can you provide to make them recognize the potential consequences? Why do you think the issue matters, and how can you persuade others to take it seriously?

For example, if you were writing about the need for a program to raise awareness of the effects of hate speech on campus, you might open with an anecdote about hateful things that have been said about others to make those not otherwise concerned with the topic aware of the issue. And you could then appeal to their goodwill and concern for fellow students to understand why it's a problem that needs to be tackled.

Determine a course of action

Once you've got a thorough understanding of the problem and what others think about it, you can start thinking about possible solutions.

Come up with some possible solutions. Start by making a list of options. Which ones seem most feasible and most likely to solve the problem? Is there one that seems like the best approach? Why? Will it solve the problem entirely, or just part of it?

If, for example, you're proposing a program to raise awareness about hate speech on campus, what are the options? You could suggest an open forum, or a teach-in. Maybe you could get an outside speaker to visit campus.

Decide on the best solution. Determine which of the options would be feasible and would work the best. Then think about how far it would go toward actually solving the problem. Hate speech is not easily solved, so this might well be a case when you can realistically only raise awareness of the problem.

These are some of the questions you'll need to ask and answer as you determine the best solution to propose.

Organize and start writing

Once you've clearly defined the problem, figured out a viable solution, and identified evidence to support your proposal, it's time to organize your materials and start drafting.

Come up with a tentative THESIS that identifies the problem that it proposes a solution. Use this statement to guide you as you write.

Provide EVIDENCE showing that the problem in fact exists, that it is serious enough to demand a solution, and that your proposed solution is feasible and the best among various options.

Acknowledge other possible solutions. Decide how and at what point in your proposal you will address other options. You might start with them and explain their shortcomings, as David Freedman does in "How Junk Food Can End Obesity." Or you could raise them after presenting your own solution, comparing your solution with the others as a way of showing that yours is the most feasible or the most likely to solve the problem.

Draft an OPENING. Identify and describe the problem, making clear why the issue matters—and why the problem needs a solution.

Draft a CONCLUSION. Reiterate the nature of the problem and the solution you're proposing. Summarize the benefits your proposal offers. Most of all, remind readers why the issue matters, why they should care, and why they should take your proposal seriously (and perhaps take action).

Look critically at your draft, get response—and revise

Once you have a complete draft, read it over carefully, focusing on how you define the problem and support the solution you propose—and the way you appeal to your audience. If possible, ask others to read it over as well. Here are some questions to help you or others read over the draft with a critical eye:

- *How does the proposal OPEN?* Will it capture readers' interest? Does it make clear what problem will be addressed and give some sense of why it matters? How else might it begin? Does the title tell readers what the proposal is about, and will it make them want to know more?

- *Is the problem* DESCRIBED *in enough detail?* Will any readers need more information to understand that it's a problem that matters? Have you said anything about its CAUSES and consequences—and if not, do you need to?

- *Is the proposed solution explicit and compelling?* Have you provided enough EVIDENCE to show that it's feasible and will address the problem—and that it's better than other possible solutions? Is there an explicit statement of what it will accomplish?

- *Have other possible solutions been acknowledged fairly?* How well have you responded to them? Are there any other solutions to be considered?

- *Is the proposal easy to follow?* If not, try adding TRANSITIONS or headings.

- *How have you established your* AUTHORITY *to write on this topic?* Does the information seem trustworthy? How do you come across as an author—passionate? serious? sarcastic?—and how does this tone affect the way the proposal comes across to readers?

- *How would you characterize the* STYLE *?* Is it appropriate for your intended audience? Consider the choice of words, the level of formality, and so on.

- *How about* DESIGN *?* Are there any illustrations—and if so, how do they contribute to the proposal? If not, is there any information that would be easier to show with a photo or in a chart? What about the font: is it appropriate for a proposal of this kind? Is the design appropriate for the MEDIUM ?

- *How does the proposal* CONCLUDE *?* Will it inspire the change or action you're calling for? How else might it conclude?

Revise your draft in response to any feedback you receive and your own analysis.

REFLECT. Once you've completed your proposal, let it settle for a while and take time to reflect. How well did you define the problem? How thoroughly did you support your proposed solution? How persuasively have you demonstrated the feasibility of your solution? How fairly did you acknowledge and respond to other possible solutions? Research shows that such reflections help "lock in" what you learn for future use.

Speaking While Female

SHERYL SANDBERG AND ADAM GRANT

YEARS AGO, while producing the hit TV series *The Shield*, Glen Mazzara noticed that two young female writers were quiet during story meetings. He pulled them aside and encouraged them to speak up more.

Watch what happens when we do, they replied.

Almost every time they started to speak, they were interrupted or shot down before finishing their pitch. When one had a good idea, a male writer would jump in and run with it before she could complete her thought.

Sadly, their experience is not unusual.

We've both seen it happen again and again. When a woman speaks in a pro-   5
fessional setting, she walks a tightrope. Either she's barely heard or she's judged as too aggressive. When a man says virtually the same thing, heads nod in appreciation for his fine idea. As a result, women often decide that saying less is more.

Some new studies support our observations. A <u>study</u> by a Yale psychologist, Victoria L. Brescoll, found that male senators with more power

---

SHERYL SANDBERG serves as the chief operating officer of *Facebook*; she is also founder of *LeanIn.org*, inspired by her bestselling book of the same name. ADAM GRANT teaches at the Wharton School of Business at the University of Pennsylvania; he is the author of *Originals: How Non-Conformists Move the World* (2016). This essay was the second in a series of four on women in the workplace that Sandberg and Grant wrote for the *New York Times* in 2015. Go to <u>everyones anauthor.tumblr.com</u> to access the links (underscored here) as you read.

(as measured by tenure, leadership positions and track record of legislation passed) spoke more on the Senate floor than their junior colleagues. But for female senators, power was not linked to significantly more speaking time.

Suspecting that powerful women stayed quiet because they feared a backlash, Professor Brescoll looked deeper. She <u>asked</u> professional men and women to evaluate the competence of chief executives who voiced their opinions more or less frequently. Male executives who spoke more often than their peers were rewarded with 10 percent higher ratings of competence. When female executives spoke more than their peers, both men and women punished them with 14 percent lower ratings. As this and other research shows, women who worry that talking "too much" will cause them to be disliked are not paranoid; they are often right.

One of us, Adam, was dismayed to find similar patterns when studying a <u>health care company</u> and advising an international bank. When male employees contributed ideas that brought in new revenue, they got significantly higher performance evaluations. But female employees who spoke up with equally valuable ideas did not improve their managers' perception of their performance. Also, the more the men spoke up, the more helpful their managers believed them to be. But when women spoke up more, there was no increase in their perceived helpfulness.

This speaking-up double bind harms organizations by depriving them of valuable ideas. A University of Texas researcher, Ethan Burris, conducted an <u>experiment</u> in which he asked teams to make strategic decisions for a bookstore. He randomly informed one member that the bookstore's inventory system was flawed and gave that person data about a better approach. In subsequent analyses, he found that when women challenged the old system and suggested a new one, team leaders viewed them as less loyal and were less likely to act on their suggestions. Even when all team members were informed that one member possessed unique information that would benefit the group, suggestions from women with inside knowledge were discounted.

Obviously, businesses need to find ways to <u>interrupt</u> this gender bias. Just 10 as orchestras that use blind auditions <u>increase the number of women who are selected</u>, organizations can increase women's contributions by adopting practices that focus less on the speaker and more on the idea. For example, in <u>innovation tournaments</u>, employees submit suggestions and solutions to problems anonymously. Experts evaluate the proposals, give feedback to all participants and then implement the best plans.

Since most work cannot be done anonymously, leaders must also take steps to encourage women to speak and be heard. At *The Shield*, Mr. Mazzara, the show runner, found a clever way to change the dynamics that were holding those two female employees back. He announced to the writers that he was instituting a no-interruption rule while anyone—male or female—was pitching. It worked, and he later observed that it made the entire team more effective.

The long-term solution to the double bind of speaking while female is to increase the number of women in leadership roles. (As we noted in our previous article, research shows that when it comes to leadership skills, although men are more confident, women are more competent.) As more women enter the upper echelons of organizations, people become more accustomed to women's contributing and leading. Professor Burris and his colleagues studied a credit union where women made up 74 percent of supervisors and 84 percent of front-line employees. Sure enough, when women spoke up there, they were more likely to be heard than men. When President Obama held his last news conference of 2014, he called on eight reporters—all women. It made headlines worldwide. Had a politician given only men a chance to ask questions, it would not have been news; it would have been a regular day.

As 2015 starts, we wonder what would happen if we all held Obama-style meetings, offering women the floor whenever possible. Doing this for even a day or two might be a powerful bias interrupter, demonstrating to our teams and colleagues that speaking while female is still quite difficult. We're going to try it to see what we learn. We hope you will, too—and then share your experiences with us all on Facebook or in the comments section.

Thinking about the Text

1. What specific problem do Sheryl Sandberg and Adam Grant seek to solve in this essay? What sorts of **EVIDENCE** do they offer to show that the problem exists?

2. What specific solutions do they suggest? Consider both the short- and long-term solutions that they raise. How practical or compelling do you find these solutions?

3. The problem Sandberg and Grant describe extends beyond women's frustrations in their workplaces. What is the ultimate significance of the problem, and how do these authors make it clear? In other words, what meaningful outcomes do they argue their proposal can ultimately bring about?

4. How did the **AUDIENCE** for this piece, the readers of a major US newspaper, likely affect this essay? How might it have been different had it been written for an audience of male executives? of female employees?

5. Sandberg and Grant tackle a persistent problem of some magnitude, one that is clearly important to them. Choose a problem that matters to you and offer a **PROPOSAL** that addresses some aspect of that problem. You might start by observing issues you see around you, but you'll likely find that you need to do some research to precisely define the problem and propose a solution. Use the genre features listed on page 374 as a guide as you construct your proposal.

Snowflakes and Free Speech on Campuses

SHAWNA SHAPIRO

OVER THE PAST FEW YEARS, we have seen a <u>growing concern in public discourse</u> about free speech on college campuses in the United States. The familiar narrative labels college-aged students "snowflakes" who <u>don't like discomfort</u> and therefore expect colleges to be intellectual "safe spaces" in which their <u>ideological bubbles</u> are left intact.

This, the story goes, is creating a <u>crisis of free speech</u> in American higher education. The proposed solution for that crisis, according to many critics, is to bring <u>high-profile, controversial speakers to campuses</u> to somehow break through the echo chambers—an ideological "exposure therapy" of sorts.

Often missing in that narrative are the voices of students themselves. That absence became increasingly salient for me after <u>Charles Murray's visit to my campus last year.</u>* As I spoke with my students in the fallout from those events,

SHAWNA SHAPIRO teaches writing and linguistics at Middlebury College, directs the college's Writing & Rhetoric Program, and has published and edited works focused on international student success. This essay was published in *Inside Higher Ed,* an online publication about issues related to colleges and universities, in 2018. Go to <u>everyonesanauthor.tumblr.com</u> to access the links underscored in the version printed here.

*Charles Murray, a political scientist and writer whose work has been accused of scientific racism, was invited to speak on Middlebury's campus by a student-run club. Prior to Murray's lecture, college administrators reminded students they were permitted to protest but not to disrupt a campus event. Yet more than 100 students began chanting during the talk, causing Murray and the moderating professor to relocate their discussion to a private studio. The college disciplined sixty-seven students for disruptive behavior, but several masked individuals who assaulted Murray and the faculty moderator outside the lecture hall were not identified.

I found that many of them had complex reactions that didn't fit the simplistic "free speech vs. inclusion/diversity" dichotomy that has <u>become dominant</u> in such discussions.

In response, since last summer, I have been working with undergraduate researchers on a study entitled "Middlebury Students Engaging Across Difference." We developed an online survey that was completed by 80 undergraduates, from first years through seniors. We then drew from those findings to develop a protocol for more in-depth, one-on-one interviews with 19 students.

Here's some of what we've found thus far: 5

Students want to engage with ideological difference. As many as 89 percent of all survey participants, including 83 percent of left-leaning students (who made up 71 percent of the sample), said that it was "important" or "very important" to them to have conversations about controversial issues with people who have a viewpoint distinct from their own. A number of participants talked about the relationship between engaging across difference and their personal growth. As one explained, "It's important to value putting in the effort to know someone whose values are different from yours. If you are stuck in a bubble, there is no room to grow as a person." Students who were "neutral" about the importance of such conversations cited concerns about lack of purpose or productivity for the conversation rather than a disinterest in engaging other viewpoints.

Many students (58 percent) are having such conversations on at least a weekly basis. We asked those we surveyed to note all of the locations where such interactions tend to occur. They reported that they are more prevalent over a meal (78 percent) or in the residence halls (65 percent) than in classrooms (53 percent) or at public lectures (38 percent).

The majority (almost 80 percent) reported that such conversations, when they do occur, can be difficult to navigate. Many survey participants said the discussion too quickly devolves into a debate where, as one put it, "We're talking *at* people instead of *with* them." An interviewee said it's easy to forget to "see the person as a person and not just a clump of ideas." Students expressed a keen desire for interactions centered on empathy—not just "being right." Many said they don't feel heard, but they also admitted that they struggle to listen fully to others as well.

One prevalent barrier to productive interaction is confusion about goals and responsibilities. Many students indicated that they have absorbed some confusing messages about speaking and silence. They have been taught that in some situations—for instance, as a bystander to bullying—silence equals complicity. As a result, they worry that simply listening, without offering a rebuttal, might be interpreted as tacit support for a particular viewpoint. Hence, while they may want to "just listen," they feel tremendous pressure to "speak out."

Some participants acknowledged that this pressure to speak hinders empathy and understanding. One admitted that at times, feeling empathy with someone who has a view that is "crazy, absurd, mean or hateful . . . scares me because I feel like I am agreeing with this hateful thing." Another said, "Calling people out does need to happen, but [I'm] also realizing that that's not the solution every time."

A further complication is that fear of social marginalization is pervasive, particularly on a small, residential campus like ours. "The fear of ostracization is terrifying . . . of being the only one and a social outcast," one interviewee explained. Some students claimed that this fear created a dynamic of "band-wagoning" in which "many people just seem to agree with one another for the sake of having the correct opinion." One student framed the situation as "rhetorical gymnastics."

Unsurprisingly, some students decide only to engage in these conversations with close friends, recognizing that probably limits the range of perspectives represented since "friend groups . . . often have similar ideas and opinions [as] mine." Others feel differently: "I do not want to create a conflict with friends," one said, adding, "It is also difficult to be in a relationship with someone when you disagree on most things political." Students in this latter group expressed a preference for conversations in a more structured environment like the classroom.

Perhaps some readers will see these findings as nothing more than a confirmation of the "snowflake" narrative. But I see much more going on: students want to engage deeply and productively with ideological difference, and many are aware of the barriers to that sort of engagement. Our first step as educators must be to acknowledge that these challenges exist and to talk about them openly with students and colleagues.

What else can be done? This research suggests that our institutional resources should be invested not just in the *what* of ideological difference but in the *how*. Perhaps some of the money and energy spent on bringing high-profile speakers to campus should be devoted to creating opportunities for more small-group dialogue about those speakers' ideas and students' reactions to them. We also need to see empathetic listening as a skill set to be taught, not just as a disposition students are expected to develop on their own. One central component of that skill set is the capacity for self-questioning: What do I hope to gain from this conversation? What assumptions am I bringing? How can I respect the humanity of the people with whom I am in dialogue? Of course, we as educators are often lacking in this area, as can be attested by anyone who has taken part in a highly contentious faculty meeting. Faculty members need not only professional development in how to create the conditions for productive dialogue: we also need to consider how we might engage differing viewpoints more productively among ourselves.

In recent years, my institution has been piloting a number of initiatives aimed at cultivating the skills necessary for engaging across difference. All our first-year students are required to attend a daylong workshop in which they discuss "race and other difficult topics." We have begun offering occasional meals in which students, staff and faculty engage in "deliberative dialogue." We are also exploring ways to bring restorative practices into student life.

Those efforts have not yet been integrated systematically into the classroom, however—nor are they prioritized (yet) in the academic curriculum. We need a comprehensive approach to creating a community of thoughtful listeners who are willing and prepared to engage productively with ideological difference. That could include courses or workshops on topics such as civil dialogue, empathetic listening and intercultural competence. Faculty members could form professional learning communities in which they share strategies and resources for engaging students in difficult conversations. The administration could request—or even require—that major co-curricular events (keynotes, symposia and the like) be accompanied by opportunities for small-group discussion and/or personal reflection before or after the event.

Of course, our students will also be able to tell us what they need, if given the opportunity. We must make "engaging across difference" an explicit pedagogical focus, if we wish to achieve the ideal of free speech in higher education.

Thinking about the Text

1. What problem has Shapiro defined, and what solutions does she **PROPOSE** to solve that problem? What specific actions does Shapiro propose be taken on college campuses as part of the solution?

2. Shapiro's **AUDIENCE** is college and university faculty and administrators. How does Shapiro establish her **CREDIBILITY** and tailor her proposal for her audience? How might this proposal be different if it were written instead for a student newspaper?

3. What **COUNTERARGUMENTS** does Shapiro acknowledge? What other objections could she address to make her proposal more convincing? Raise and respond to additional objections you come up with yourself.

4. What **EVIDENCE** does Shapiro offer to demonstrate that her proposal will address the actual problem she defines? Why is it important to her to avoid the common "free speech vs. inclusion/diversity" dichotomy that frames most discussions of these issues?

5. What's your reaction to Shapiro's proposal? Write an essay to respond—agreeing, disagreeing, or both, raising any questions you think need to be considered or offering suggestions about how to carry out or adapt Shapiro's proposal on your campus.

PART V

The Centrality of Argument

CHANCES ARE THAT your first attempt to communicate was an argument. Your first cry, that is, argued that you were hungry or sleepy or wanted to be held. Later, you could use words to say what you wanted: "More!" "No!" "Candy!" All arguments. So if you think that argument is just about disputes or disagreements, think again. In rhetorical terms, argument refers to any way that human beings express themselves to try to achieve a particular purpose—which, many would say, means any way that people express themselves at all.

If you think about the kinds of writing covered in this book, for example, it is easy to understand that an op-ed taking a position on a political issue or a TV critic's rave review of a new series is "arguing" for or against something. An editorial cartoon about the issue or an ad for the movie is making an obvious argument, too. But even when you post on *Instagram* about something you just did, you're implicitly arguing that it will be intriguing or important or perhaps amusing to your audience, those who follow you on *Instagram*. Even when you write a lab report, you'll describe and interpret the results of an experiment, arguing that your findings have certain implications.

In fact, you are immersed in argument. Try counting the number of arguments you either make or encounter in just one day, starting with the argument you have with yourself over what to wear, moving on to the barrage of posters asking you to support certain causes or attend various concerts, to a biology lecture where the professor explains the conflicting arguments about climate change, then the flood of claims and arguments you scroll through in your social media feed, and ending only when you and a friend agree to disagree about who's better, Michael Jordan or LeBron James. We bet you'll be surprised by how many arguments you encounter in a day.

The point we want to make is simple: you are the author of many arguments and the target of many more—and you'll be a better reader and writer of your own arguments if you understand how they work.

It's important to mention as well that arguments today most often consist of more than just words, from the signs admonishing you to fasten your seat belt, to a big "thumbs up," to an ad for McDonald's. These familiar images demonstrate how words and images can make strong visual arguments.

Words, graphics, and images can be combined to make strong visual arguments.

It's also worth noting that arguments today are more seductive than ever. A fifteen-second sound bite sways millions of voters; a song you loved as a twelve-year-old now boosts sales of soft drinks; celebrities write op-ed essays on issues they care about. Even your school mounts arguments intended to attract prospective students—and, later, to motivate alumni to give generously. Check out your school's homepage, and you'll find appeals intended to attract applications and contributions.

Perhaps you think that such arguments are somewhat manipulative, intended to trick you into buying a product or contributing to a cause. But arguments are always trying to achieve some purpose, so it is up to you both as a reader and as a writer to distinguish the good from the bad. And arguments can, of course, be used for good (think of the powerful arguments for human rights) or ill (think of Hitler's hypnotic arguments). They can be deceptive, even silly—does that gorgeous woman holding a can of cleanser really mean to claim that if you buy the cleanser, you'll look just like her?

In fact, argument is about many things and has many purposes. Of the many purposes we might name, here are just a few:

to explore

to understand

to find consensus

to make decisions

to convince or persuade

Keep in mind, however, that arguments are always embedded in particular contexts—and that what is persuasive can vary from one context to another, or from one culture to another. The most persuasive evidence in one community might come from religious texts; in another, from personal testimony; in another, from facts or statistics. Especially now that arguments so often take place online, reaching people all around the world, it's important to be aware of such differences.

When two brothers attacked the Paris offices of the satiric journal *Charlie Hebdo* in 2015, leaving twelve people dead and eleven others wounded, the entire world was caught up in the story. Why attack a journal that publishes satirical comics? As we later learned, the brothers were acting on their belief that the artists at *Charlie Hebdo* were guilty of (mis)representing the Prophet Mohammed in cartoons and thus of violating the traditions of Islam as they understood them. Condemnations of the attacks echoed around the world, from Europe to Australia and Japan, arguing that murder is never an appropriate act and that the brothers had struck not only at *Charlie Hebdo* but at a bedrock principle of the Western world: freedom of speech. Yet others disagreed, arguing that the cartoonists' satires had gone too far, that their work was insulting and destructive of another culture's beliefs; while they did not condone the bloodshed, these critics argued that the cartoonists' work had been deliberately inflammatory. Still others argued that the attack was justified, that the brothers were heroes and martyrs to their faith. Not surprisingly, these opinions varied from culture to culture. Especially when their message spreads online, writers, speakers, cartoonists, and activists must remember that their intended arguments will be interpreted variably, depending on audience and context. The poster below illustrates a French-language slogan, "I am Charlie," that quickly spread around the world as supporters of free speech rallied. Clearly, not everyone who saw the poster agreed with its sentiments.

Posters often make powerful arguments—and those who disagree sometimes argue back on the poster itself.

During his lifetime, Martin Luther King Jr. did not have the benefit of the internet, but the arguments he made eventually reverberated around the world. In his "Letter from Birmingham Jail," King was responding to a statement written in 1963 by eight white Alabama clergymen who had urged him to stop his campaign of civil disobedience to protest racial discrimination. This particular context—the US South at the height of the civil rights struggle—informs his argument throughout. And while King's argument remains the same, having been republished countless times, its interpretation varies across time and cultures. When the letter first appeared, it responded point by

Martin Luther King Jr. in a jail cell in Birmingham, Alabama.

point to the statement by the eight clergymen, and it was read as an answer to their particular charges. Today, however, it is read as a much more general statement about the importance of civil rights for all people. King's famous conclusion to this letter sums up his argument and consciously addresses an audience that extends far beyond the eight clergymen:

> Let us all hope that the dark clouds of racial prejudice will soon pass away and the deep fog of misunderstanding will be lifted from our fear-drenched communities, and in some not too distant tomorrow the radiant stars of love and brotherhood will shine over our great nation with all their scintillating beauty.   —MARTIN LUTHER KING JR., "Letter from Birmingham Jail"

As with all arguments, the effectiveness of King's letter has always varied according to the context in which it is read and, especially, the audience that is reading it. In most of his letter, King addresses eight specific people, and they are clearly part of his primary audience. But his use of "us" and "our" in the passage above works to broaden that audience and reaches beyond that time and place to many other readers and listeners.

Because arguments are so central to our lives, it's important to understand how they work—and to learn how to make effective arguments of your own, remembering that you can do so only by paying very careful attention to your purpose, your intended audience, and the rest of your rhetorical situation. The next two chapters focus on how good arguments work and on strategies for supporting the arguments that you make.

EIGHTEEN

Analyzing and Constructing Arguments
Those You Read, Those You Write

HE CLOTHES YOU CHOOSE TO WEAR argue for your own sense of style; the courses your college requires argue for what educators consider important; the kind of transportation you take, the food you eat (or don't eat)— almost everything represents some kind of argument. So it is important to understand all these arguments, those you encounter and those you create. Consider a couple of everyday examples.

What's in a social media handle? An email address? You may not have thought much about the argument that these chosen titles make, but they certainly do make a statement about you. One student we know chose the email address 2hot2handl@gmail.com. But when it came time to look for meaningful employment, he began to think about what that address said about him. As a result, he chose an address he felt was more appropriate to the image he wanted to convey: DavidLopez494@gmail.com.

If you need to think about what arguments you may be making yourself, it's also important to understand the arguments that come from others. Take a look, for example, at the two images on the next page, both of which appeared after the 2012 shootings at Sandy Hook Elementary School. The first image shows signs that make the argument that gun control will protect our loved ones; the second takes a very different approach, showing gun rights activists invoking their constitutional right to bear arms. These two images make radically different arguments

Protesters' signs make decidedly different arguments about guns in America.

about the role guns should play in US society, arguments that call on us to think very carefully before we respond. Crucially, they demonstrate that arguments always exist in a larger context, that they always involve more than just the person or group making the argument.

Arguments, in short, don't appear out of thin air: every argument begins as a response to some other argument—a statement, an event, an image, or something else. From these images we see how important it is to analyze any argument you encounter—and consider the other side—before deciding where you yourself stand. That goes for arguments you read and for ones you write. Either way, all arguments are part of a larger conversation. Whether you're responding to something you've read, discussing a film you've seen, or writing an essay that argues a position, you enter into a dialogue with the arguments of others.

This chapter will help you analyze the arguments you encounter and compose arguments of your own.

You can tell by the brevity and the directness of his language that Brent Staples is jumping right into an ongoing conversation. See what he's done on p. 1039.

WHERE'S THE ARGUMENT COMING FROM?

As a reader, you need to pay special attention to the source of an argument—literally to where it is coming from. It makes a difference whether an argument appears in the *New York Times* or a school newspaper, in *Physics Review* or on someone's *Twitter* feed you know nothing about, in an impromptu speech by a candidate seeking your vote or in an analysis of that speech done by the nonpartisan website *FactCheck.org*. And even when you know who's putting forward the argument, you need to dig deeper to find out where—what view of the world—that source itself is "coming from."

For example, here's the homepage of the website of Public Citizen, a nonprofit organization founded in 1971 by consumer advocate and social critic Ralph Nader. So what can we tell about where this argument is coming from? We might start with the image in the upper-left corner of Lady Liberty holding up her torch right next to the headline "PUBLIC CITIZEN Protecting Health, Safety and Democracy." Below that is the menu bar and an example of the kind of analysis Public Citizen is known for:

> As Medicare-for-all gains popularity with the public and lawmakers, opponents like Big Pharma are already pushing false claims. What's fact and what's fiction?

Based on its website and its stated goal of "defending democracy and resisting corporate power," we can surmise, then, that Public Citizen supports the rights of ordinary citizens and liberal democratic values and opposes the

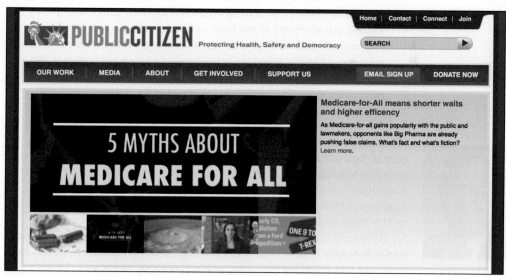

The homepage of Public Citizen's website.

influence of corporations on government. Indeed, if we look a bit further, to the About page, we will find the following statement:

> Public Citizen is a nonprofit consumer advocacy organization that champions the public interest—your interests—in the halls of power. Since our founding in 1971, we have defended democracy, resisted corporate power and worked to ensure that government works for the people—not for big corporations.

Together, these images and statements tell us a lot about Public Citizen's stance, where the organization is coming from. And other trustworthy sources confirm it, calling Public Citizen a "progressive" and "liberal" organization that practices "lobbying and advocacy." As savvy readers, we then have to assess the claims Public Citizen makes on its website and elsewhere in light of this knowledge: knowing where an organization is coming from and how it is seen by others affects how willing or skeptical we are to accept what it says.

Or consider a more lighthearted example, this time from political pundit David Brooks:

> We now have to work under the assumption that every American has a tattoo. Whether we are at a formal dinner, at a professional luncheon, at a sales conference or arguing before the Supreme Court, we have to assume that everyone in the room is fully tatted up—that under each suit, dress or blouse, there is at least a set of angel wings, a barbed wire armband, a Chinese character or maybe even a fully inked body suit. We have to assume that any casual anti-tattoo remark will cause offense, even to those we least suspect of self-marking.
>
> —DAVID BROOKS, "Nonconformity Is Skin Deep"

David Brooks

What can we know about where Brooks is coming from? For starters, it's easy to find out that he is a conservative journalist whose work appears in many publications across the political spectrum and who often appears as a television commentator on the *PBS NewsHour*. We also know that this passage comes from one of his op-ed columns for the *New York Times*. His photo on the *Times* website presents him as a professional, in jacket and tie.

What more can we tell about where he's coming from in the passage itself? Probably first is that Brooks is representing himself here as somewhat old-fashioned, as someone who's clearly an adult and a member of what might be called "the establishment" in the United States (note his off-handed assumption that "we" might be "at a formal dinner" or "arguing before the Supreme Court"). He's someone who almost certainly does not have a tattoo himself. He's also comfortable using a little sarcasm ("everyone in the room is fully tatted up") and exaggeration ("every American has a tattoo") to make a humorous point. Finally, we can tell that he is a self-confident—and persuasive—author and that we'll need to be on our toes to understand the argument that he's actually making.

As an author, you should always think hard about where *you* are coming from in the arguments you make. What's your STANCE, and why? How do you want your audience to perceive you? As reasonable? knowledgeable? opinionated? curious? something else?

How can you convey your stance? Through your choice of words, of course—both *what* you say and *how* you say it—but also through any images you include and the way you design your text. The words you choose not only convey your meaning, they reveal a lot about your attitude—toward your subject and your audience. Introducing a quotation with the words "she insists" indicates a different attitude than the more neutral "she says."

WHAT'S THE CLAIM?

You run into dozens of claims every day. Your brother says the latest Spiderman film is the best one ever; your news feed says that Kentucky will be in the Final Four; a friend texts to say it's a waste of time and money to eat at Power Pizza. Each of these statements makes a claim and argues implicitly for you to agree. The arguments you read and write in college often begin with a claim, an arguable statement that must then be supported with good reasons and evidence.

The *New Yorker* cover on the next page titled "Moment of Joy" shows *Sesame Street* character Bert with his arm around Ernie's shoulder as they watch the 2013 Supreme Court ruling overturning the Defense of Marriage Act, which had denied federal benefits to same-sex couples. The cover immediately sparked debate. The creator of the image saw it as portraying a celebratory moment, saying, "It's amazing to witness how attitudes on gay rights have evolved in my lifetime. This is great for our kids, a moment we can all celebrate." But others read the image differently, saying that using puppets rather than actual people trivialized the issue; still others claimed

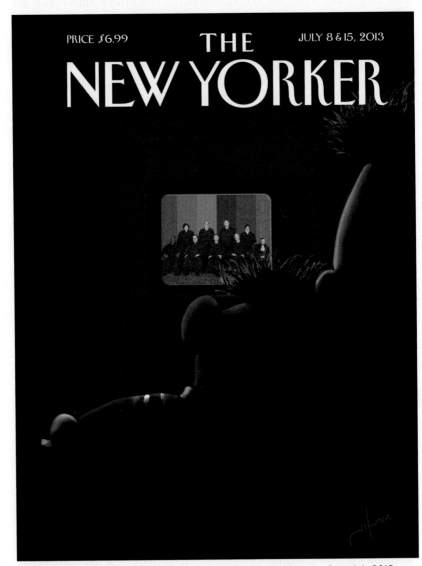

Sesame Street characters Bert and Ernie are featured on this cover from July 2013 marking the Supreme Court's decision to grant federal benefits to same-sex couples.

that the image inappropriately sexualized the much-loved children's show. Images can make powerful arguments that often spark debate.

The easiest claims to identify are those that are stated directly as an explicit **THESIS**. Look, for instance, at the following paragraph from a journal article by civil rights activist W. E. B. Du Bois in 1922. As you read each sentence, ask yourself what Du Bois's claim is.

> Abraham Lincoln was a Southern poor white, . . . poorly educated and unusually ugly, awkward, ill-dressed. He liked smutty stories and was a politician down to his toes. Aristocrats—Jeff Davis, Seward and their ilk—despised him, and indeed he had little outwardly that compelled respect. But in that curious human way he was big inside. He had reserves and depths and when habit and convention were torn away there was something left to Lincoln—nothing to most of his contemners. There was something left, so that at the crisis he was big enough to be inconsistent—cruel, merciful; peace-loving, a fighter; despising Negroes and letting them fight and vote; protecting slavery and freeing slaves. He was a man—a big, inconsistent, brave man.
>
> —W. E. B. DU BOIS, "Abraham Lincoln"

We think you'll find that the claim is difficult to make out until the last sentence, which lets us know in an explicit thesis that the contradictions Du Bois has been detailing are part of Lincoln's greatness, part of what made him "big" and "brave." Take note as well of where the thesis appears in the text. Du Bois holds his claim for the very end.

Here is a very different example, from a newspaper column about legendary dancer Judith Jamison. Note that it begins with an explicit thesis stating a claim that the rest of the passage expands on—and supports:

> Judith Jamison is my kind of American cultural icon. . . . She has many accolades and awards—among them the National Medal of Arts, the Kennedy Center Honors and an Emmy. . . .
>
> But when I met her . . . she said with a huge smile, "Yes, honey, but you know I still have to do the laundry myself, and no one in New York parts the sidewalk 'cause I am comin' through!"
>
> I like icons who are authentic and accessible. I think our country benefits from that. It can only serve to inspire others to believe that they can try to do the same thing.
>
> —MARIA HINOJOSA, "Dancing Past the Boundaries"

Judith Jamison dancing with the Alvin Ailey Dance Theater.

Notice that although Hinojosa's claim is related to her own personal taste in American cultural icons, it is not actually about her taste itself. Her argument is not about her preference for cultural icons to be "authentic and accessible." Instead, she's arguing that given this criterion, Judith Jamison is a perfect example.

As an author making an argument of your own, remember that a claim shouldn't simply express a personal taste: if you say that you feel lousy or that you hate the New York Yankees, no one could reasonably argue that you don't feel that way. For a claim to be *arguable*—worth arguing—it has to take a **POSITION** that others can logically have different perspectives on. Likewise, an arguable claim can't simply be a statement of fact that no one would disagree with ("Violent video games earn millions of dollars every year"). And remember that in most academic contexts, claims based on religious faith alone often cannot be argued since there are no agreed-upon standards of proof or evidence.

In most academic writing, you'll be expected to state your **CLAIM** explicitly as a **THESIS**, announcing your topic and the main point(s) you are going to make about that topic. Your thesis should help readers follow your train of thought, so it's important that it state your point clearly. A good thesis will also engage your audience's interest—and make them want to read on.

Be careful, however, not to overstate your thesis: you may need to **QUALIFY** it with words like *some*, *might*, or *possible*—for example, that "Recent studies have shown that exercise has a *limited* effect on a person's weight, so eating less *may be* a better strategy for losing weight than exercising more." By saying that dieting "may be" more effective than exercise, the author of this thesis has limited her claim to one she will be able to support.

In most US academic contexts, authors are expected to make claims directly and get to the point fairly quickly, so you may want to position the thesis near the beginning of your text, often at the end of the introduction or the first paragraph. When your claim is likely to challenge or surprise your audience, though, you may want to build support for it more gradually and hold off stating it explicitly until later in your argument, as Du Bois does. In other situations, you may not need to make a direct statement of your claim at all. But always make sure in such cases that your audience has a clear understanding of what the claim is.

bell hooks begins her essay with a simple, direct statement of her thesis. See how much impact her opening has on p. 935.

WHAT'S AT STAKE?

Figuring out the answer to this question takes you to the heart of the argument. Rhetoricians in ancient Rome developed what they called *stasis theory*, a simple system for identifying the crux of an argument—what's at stake in it—by asking four questions in sequence:

1. What are the facts?
2. How can the issue be defined?
3. How much does the issue matter, and why?
4. What actions should be taken as a result?

Together these questions help determine the basic issues at stake in an argument. A look at the arguments that swirled around Hurricane Katrina and its effects can illustrate how these questions work.

What are the facts? Certainly the hurricane hit the Gulf Coast squarely, resulting in almost unimaginable damage and loss of life, especially in New Orleans, where levees failed along with the city's evacuation plan. Many arguments about the disaster had their crux (or stasis) here, claiming that the most important aspect of "what happened" was not the hurricane itself but the lack of preparation for it and the response to it.

How can the issue be defined? In the case of Katrina, the question of definition turned out to be crucial for many arguments about the event: it was easy enough to define the storm itself as a "category 4 hurricane" but much more difficult to classify the disaster beyond that simple scientific tag. To what extent was it a national disaster or a local one? A natural disaster or a man-made one? Was it proof of corruption and incompetence on the part of local and state officials? of FEMA and the Bush administration? Something else?

How much does the issue matter, and why? In addition to questions of fact and definition, ones about how serious the event was also produced many arguments in the wake of Katrina. In the first week or so after the storm hit, the mayor of New Orleans argued that it was the most serious disaster ever to strike that city and that up to 10,000 lives would be lost. Others argued that while the storm represented a huge setback to the people of the region, they could and would overcome their losses and rebuild their cities and towns.

What actions should be taken as a result? Of all the stasis questions, this one was the basis for the greatest number of arguments. From those arguing that the federal government should be responsible for funding reconstruction, to those arguing that the government should work with insurance agencies and local and state officials, to those arguing that the most damaged neighborhoods should not be rebuilt, thousands of proposals were offered and debated.

Such questions can help you understand what's at stake in an argument—to help you figure out and assess the arguments put forth by others, to identify which stasis question lies at the heart of an argument—and then to decide whether or not the argument answers the question satisfactorily.

As an author, you can use these questions to identify the main point you want to make in an argument of your own. In the Katrina example, for instance, working through the four stasis questions would help you see the disaster from a number of different perspectives and then develop a cogent argument related to them. In addition, these questions may help you decide just what **GENRE** of argument you want to make: a question of fact might lead you to write a **NARRATIVE**, explaining what happened, while the question of what action(s) should be taken might lead you to compose a **PROPOSAL**.

MEANS OF PERSUASION: EMOTIONAL, ETHICAL, AND LOGICAL APPEALS

Aristotle wrote that good arguments should make use of "all the available means" of persuading an audience and named three in particular, which he labeled *emotional* appeals (to the heart), *ethical* appeals (about credibility or character), and *logical* appeals (to the mind).

Emotional Appeals

Emotional appeals (also referred to as *pathos*) stir feelings and often invoke values that the audience is assumed to hold. The paragraph on Lincoln on page 417, for example, offers a strong appeal to readers' emotions when it represents Lincoln as "big" and "brave," invoking two qualities Americans traditionally value. Images can make especially powerful appeals to our emotions, such as the ones below from the Ebola outbreak in West Africa.

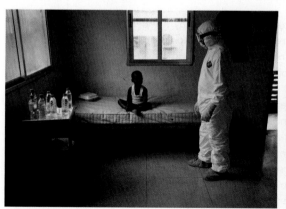

#ENDEBOLA. DONATE TO CARE.

Halt a global outbreak by fighting Ebola in the hardest-hit communities.

These images pull at our heartstrings, leading us both to empathize with the plight of children facing Ebola and to support efforts to end the epidemic.

The first image appeals directly to our hearts, showing a young boy suspected of having Ebola, a table of medications on one side and a healthcare worker in full protective gear on the other. In the second image, from the international relief agency CARE, the message is clear and simple: donate now and help halt the outbreak. As the first example shows, images can appeal very strongly to emotions. But words too can make a powerful emotional appeal, as in the second example. As a reader, you'll want to consider how any such emotional appeals support an author's claim.

As an author, you should consider how you can appeal to your audience's emotions and whether such appeals are appropriate to your claim, your purpose, and your audience. And whatever you decide, be careful not to overdo emotional appeals, pulling at the heartstrings so hard that your audience feels manipulated.

Ethical Appeals

Ethical appeals (also referred to as *ethos*) invoke the credibility and good character of whoever is making the argument. See how the website for the Interfaith Youth Core, a nonprofit organization building common ground between people with different beliefs, includes information intended to establish founder Eboo Patel's credibility and integrity. Here is part of Patel's "bio" page from the site:

> [Eboo] is inspired to build this bridge by his identity as an American Muslim navigating a religiously diverse social landscape.
>
> For over 15 years he has worked with governments, social sector organizations, and college and university campuses to help make interfaith cooperation a social norm. Named by *U.S. News & World Report* as one of America's Best Leaders of 2009, Eboo served on President Obama's Inaugural Faith Council and is the author of *Acts of Faith, Sacred Ground, Interfaith Leadership: A Primer,* and *Out of Many Faiths: Religious Diversity and the American Promise.* He holds a doctorate in the sociology of religion from Oxford University, where he studied on a Rhodes scholarship.
>
> These days, Eboo spends most of his time on the road, doing what he loves: meeting students, educators, and community leaders to talk about the complex landscape of religious diversity and the power of interfaith cooperation in the 21st century.   —INTERFAITH YOUTH CORE, "Eboo Patel"

Interfaith leader Eboo Patel delivering a talk on religious diversity and the American promise at Dickinson University.

All of this information, including Patel's numerous degrees and publications and his position advising the US president helps establish his credibility and helps readers decide how much stock they can put in his words and the work of the organization he founded.

Citing scholarly achievements and national positions of influence is only one way of establishing credibility. Here Patel uses another approach during a *PBS NewsHour* interview when he responds to a question about "hostile racial divisions" on campus:

> I'm on 25 college campuses a year. I have probably visited something like 130 in the past eight or 10 years. It's not like things don't ever get tense, but what I read about in the news on college campuses is foreign to me, right, which is to say it is by definition sensational.
>
> How am I not going to be optimistic, really? . . . The beautiful thing is, there's lots of us that feel this way. There's this whole growing network of college student interfaith leaders on American campuses basically saying, where's the divide? Let me bridge it. That's the future of America, or we have no future at all.
>
> —EBOO PATEL, *PBS NewsHour* Interview, "To Narrow Toxic Divides, Students Build Bridges between Faiths"

In his comments, Patel lets listeners know that he is basing his claim on a lot of personal experience. And his informal tone suggests that he has a simple, direct message to give to his audience. His extensive experience gives him confidence to talk with conviction about why he's optimistic in the face of deep differences.

Building common ground. Patel's use of simple, everyday language helps establish credibility in another way: by building common ground with his audience. He is not "putting on airs" but speaking directly to them; the concerns so many feel, he seems to say, are his concerns. He also uses **ANALOGIES**, invoking universally respected figures, that few people will disagree with: "I think that the great lesson of Lincoln and Jane Addams and King and Mandela is, for every stitch of hate or distrust that you put into the fabric now, you're going to have to unstitch at a later point." Given Patel's goals and the aims of the organization he founded, it's no surprise that he seeks to build common ground with his audience.

➔ Visit everyones
anauthor.tumblr
.com to find Patel's
full interview.

While building common ground cannot ensure that your audience is "on your side," it does show that you respect your audience and their views and that you've established, with them, a mutual interest in the topic. Both parties care about the issues that you are addressing. Thus, building common ground is a particularly important part of creating an effective argument. Especially if you are addressing an audience unlikely to agree with your position, finding some area of agreement with them, some common ground you can all stand on, can help give the argument a chance of being heard.

No global leader in recent history has been more successful in building common ground than Nelson Mandela, who became the first black president of South Africa in 1994 after the country's harsh apartheid system of racial segregation ended. In *Playing the Enemy: Nelson Mandela and the Game That Made a Nation*, the basis for the 2009 film *Invictus*, author John Carlin recounts hearing Mandela say that "sport has the power to change the world . . . the power to unite people in a way that little else does" and that "It is more powerful than governments in breaking down racial barriers." Carlin uses this quotation as an example of Mandela's singular ability to "walk in another person's shoes" and to build common ground even where none seems possible. He goes on to detail the ways in which Mandela used white South Africans' love of rugby to build common ground between them and the country's black majority, which had long seen the almost all-white national rugby team, the Springboks, as a symbol of white supremacy:

He explained how he had . . . used the 1995 Rugby World Cup as an instrument in the grand strategic purpose he set for himself during his five years as South Africa's first democratically elected president: to reconcile blacks and whites and create the conditions for a lasting peace. . . . He told me, with a chuckle or two, about the trouble he had persuading his own people to back the rugby team. . . . Having won over his own people, he went out and won over the enemy.

—JOHN CARLIN, *Playing the Enemy*

Mandela understood, in short, that when people were as far apart in their thinking as black and white South Africans were when apartheid ended, the only way to move forward, to make arguments for the country's future that both groups would listen to, was to discover something that could bring them together. For Mandela—and for South Africa—rugby provided the common ground. His personal meetings with the Springboks players and his support for the team paid off to such an extent that when they won a stunning upset victory in the 1995 World Cup final in Johannesburg, the multiracial crowd chanted his name and the country united in celebration. And establishing that common ground contributed to Mandela's extraordinary ethical appeal—which he put to good use in the difficult arguments he had to make in the transition to a post-apartheid South Africa.

In all the arguments you encounter, you'll want to consider how much you can trust the author. Do they seem knowledgeable? represent opposing positions fairly (or at all)? do anything to build common ground?

As an author, you need to establish your own **AUTHORITY**: to show that you know what you're talking about by citing trustworthy sources; to demonstrate that you're fair by representing other positions even-handedly and accurately; and to establish some kind of common ground with your audience.

Logical Appeals

Appeals to logic (also referred to as *logos*) have long been regarded as the most important of all the appeals, following Aristotle's definition of humans as rational animals. Recent research has made it increasingly clear, however, that people seldom make decisions based on logic alone and that emotion often plays a larger role in our decision making than does logic. Nevertheless, in academic contexts, logical appeals count for a lot. When we

President Nelson Mandela, wearing a Springboks cap and shirt, presents the Rugby World Cup to South African captain Francois Pienaar in June 1995.

make an argument, we need to provide **REASONS** and **EVIDENCE** to support our claims. Such evidence may include facts and statistics, data from surveys and questionnaires, direct observations, interviews, testimony, experiments, personal experience, visuals, and more.

Facts and statistics. Facts and statistics are two of the most commonly used kinds of evidence. Facts are claims that have been proven to be true—and that an audience is likely accept without further proof. Statistics are research-based numerical data. Here *Men's Health* editor David Zinczenko offers facts and statistics as support for an argument in the *New York Times* about the effects of fast foods on Americans:

> Before 1994, diabetes in children was generally caused by a genetic disorder—only about 5 percent of childhood cases were obesity-related, or Type 2 diabetes. Today, according to the National Institutes of Health, Type 2 diabetes accounts for at least 30 percent of all new childhood cases of diabetes in this country.
>
> Not surprisingly, money spent to treat diabetes has skyrocketed, too. The Centers for Disease Control and Prevention estimate that diabetes accounted for $2.6 billion in health care costs in 1969. Today's number is an unbelievable $100 billion a year.
>
> Shouldn't we know better than to eat two meals a day in fast-food restaurants? That's one argument. But where, exactly, are consumers—particularly teenagers—supposed to find alternatives? Drive down any thoroughfare in America, and I guarantee you'll see one of our country's more than 13,000 McDonald's restaurants. Now, drive back up the block and try to find someplace to buy a grapefruit.
>
> —DAVID ZINCZENKO, "Don't Blame the Eater"

The facts about the proliferation of fast-food chains compared to the relative lack of healthier options will be obvious to Zinczenko's readers, and most of his statistics come from respected health organizations whose authority adds to the credibility of his argument. Statistics can provide powerful support for an argument, but be sure they're accurate, current, from reliable sources—and relevant. And if you base an argument on facts, be sure to take into account all the relevant information. Realistically, that's hard to do—but be careful not to ignore any important available facts. The advice in chapter 8 will further help you distinguish facts from misinformation.

Surveys and questionnaires. You have probably responded to a number of surveys or questionnaires, and you will often find them used as evidence in support of arguments. When a college student wondered about the kinds of reading for pleasure her dormmates were doing, she decided to gather information through a survey and to present it in a pie chart.

What Genres Students Are Reading

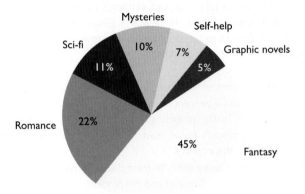

The information displayed in the chart offers evidence that fantasy is the most-read genre, followed by romance, sci-fi, mysteries, self-help, and graphic novels. Before accepting such evidence, however, readers might want to ask some key questions: How many people were surveyed? What methods of analysis did the student use? How were particular works classified? (For example, how did she decide whether a particular book was a "romance" or a "mystery"?) Whether you're reacting to survey data in an essay or a lecture, or conducting a survey of your own, you need to scrutinize the methods used and findings. Who conducted the survey, and why? (And yes, you need to think about that even if you conducted it.) Who are the respondents, how were they chosen, and are they representative? What do the results show?

Observations. A 2011 study reported in *Science News* demonstrates the way direct observations can form the basis for an argument. In this study, researchers in Uganda observed the way young chimpanzees play, and their findings support arguments about the relative importance of biology and socialization on the way boys and girls play.

A young chimp holds a stick in imitation of a mother caring for her child.

A new study finds that young females in one group of African chimpanzees use sticks as dolls more than their male peers do, often treating pieces of wood like a mother chimp caring for an infant. . . .

Ape observations, collected over 14 years of field work with the Kanyawara chimp community in Kibale National Park, provide the first evidence of a nonhuman animal in the wild that exhibits sex differences in how it plays, two primatologists report in the Dec. 21 *Current Biology*. This finding supports a controversial view that biology as well as society underlies boys' and girls' contrasting toy preferences.

—BRUCE BOWER, "Female Chimps Play with 'Dolls'"

As this study suggests, observations carried out over time are particularly useful as evidence since they show that something is not just a onetime event but a persistent pattern. As a college student, you probably won't have occasion to spend 14 years observing something, but in most cases you'll need to observe your subject more than once.

Interviews. Reporters often use information drawn from interviews to add authenticity and credibility to their articles. For an article on the danger concussions cause to athletes and the number of such unreported injuries, Kristin Sainani, a professor of health policy, interviewed Stanford neuroscientists conducting research on concussions as well as one athlete who had suffered several. Here is basketball star Toni Kokenis describing the effects her concussions had on her:

> I felt withdrawn from everything. It was like I was there, but in slow motion. I didn't feel comfortable shooting three-pointers because I couldn't focus on the basket long enough to know that the ball was actually going to go near the hoop.　　　—KRISTIN SAINANI, "Damage Control"

Sainani also cites information she learned from researcher David Camarillo, whose lab is at work on understanding concussions—a science, he says, that is still in its infancy. Preventing concussions won't be possible, he tells us, until we understand them. Camarillo then goes on to describe, in everyday language, what happens during a concussion: "You've got this kind of gelatinous blob in a fluid floating in a sealed pressure vessel. A concussion occurs when the brain is sloshed and bounced around in this fluid."

Unfortunately, he tells Sainani, wearing a helmet does little to prevent concussions, and so his lab is conducting research to "change the industry standards" for protective equipment.

Throughout this article, Sainani uses evidence drawn from interviews to engage readers and convince them that equipment to protect against concussions "needs to be better." As an author, be sure that anyone you interview is an authority on your subject whom your audience will consider trustworthy.

Good testimony doesn't have to come from experts. See how Barbara Ehrenreich uses the testimony of coworkers in her essay about blue-collar working conditions, on p. 889.

Testimony. Most of us depend on reliable testimony to help us accept or reject arguments: a friend tells us that *This Is Us* is a great TV show, and likely as not we'll watch it at least once. Testimony is especially persuasive evidence when it comes from experts and authorities on a topic. When you cite authorities to support an argument, you build your own credibility as an author; readers know that you've done your homework and are aware of the different perspectives on your topic. In the example on pages 428–29 about gender-linked behavior among chimpanzees, for example, the *Science News* report notes testimony from the two scientists who conducted the research.

Experiments. Evidence based on experiments is especially important in the sciences and social sciences, where data is often the basis for supporting a claim. In arguing that multitaskers pay a high mental price, Clifford Nass, a professor of communications, based his claims on a series of empirical studies of college students who were divided into two groups, those identified as "high multitaskers" and those identified as "low multi-taskers." In the first studies, which measured attention and memory, Nass and his fellow researchers were surprised to find that the low multitaskers outperformed high multitaskers in statistically significant ways. Still not satisfied that low multitaskers were more productive learners, the researchers designed another test, hypothesizing that if high multitask-ers couldn't do well in the earlier studies on attention and memory, maybe they would be better at shifting from task to task more quickly and effec-tively than low multitaskers.

> Wrong again, the study found.
>   The subjects were shown images of letters and numbers at the same time and instructed what to focus on. When they were told to pay atten-tion to numbers, they had to determine if the digits were even or odd. When told to concentrate on letters, they had to say whether they were vowels or consonants.
>   Again, the heavy multitaskers underperformed the light multitaskers.
>   "They couldn't help thinking about the task they weren't doing," the researchers reported. "The high multitaskers are always drawing from all the information in front of them. They can't keep things separate in their minds."   —ADAM GORLICK, "Media Multitaskers Pay Mental Price"

As Gorlick notes, these researchers had evidence to support their hypoth-esis. Nevertheless, they realized the dangers of generalizing from one set of students to all students. Whenever you use data drawn from experiments, you need to be similarly cautious not to overgeneralize.

Personal experience can provide powerful support for an argument since it brings "eyewitness" evidence, which can establish a connection between author and audience. In an *Atlantic* article about Cesar Chavez, Caitlin Flanagan—who grew up where Chavez's United Farm Workers movement began—recounts her mother's personal experience to support the argu-ment that Chavez had a "singular and almost mystical way of eliciting not just fealty but a kind of awe."

> Of course, it had all started with Mom. Somewhere along the way, she had met Cesar Chavez, or at least attended a rally where he had spoken,

Cesar Chavez

and that was it. Like almost everyone else who ever encountered him, she was spellbound. "This wonderful, wonderful man," she would call him, and off we went to collect clothes for the farmworkers' children, and to sell red-and-black UFW buttons and collect signatures.

—CAITLIN FLANAGAN, "The Madness of Cesar Chavez"

In your own writing, make sure that any personal experience you cite is pertinent to your argument and will be appropriate to your purpose.

Charts, images, and other visuals. Visuals of various kinds often provide valuable evidence to support an argument. Pie charts like the one showing the literary genres favored in a college dorm, photographs like the one of the female chimpanzee cradling a stick, and many other kinds of visuals—including drawings, bar and line graphs, cartoons, screenshots, videos, and advertisements—can often make it easier for an audience to see certain kinds of evidence. Imagine how much more difficult it would be to take in the information shown in the pie chart about the genres read by students in the dorm had the data been presented in a paragraph. Remember, though, that visual evidence usually needs to be explained—photos need captions, and any visuals need to be referenced in the accompanying text.

As an author, keep in mind that the MEDIUM you're using affects the kind of EVIDENCE you choose and how you present it. In a print text, evidence has to be in the text itself; in a digital medium, you can link directly to statistics, images, and other information. In a spoken text, any evidence needs to be said or shown on a slide or a handout—and anything you say should be simple, direct, and memorable (your audience can't rewind what you say). In every case, any evidence drawn from sources needs to be fully DOCUMENTED.

Are There Any Problems with the Reasoning?

Some kinds of appeals use faulty reasoning, or reasoning that some may consider unfair, unsound, or demonstrating lazy or simpleminded thinking. Such appeals are called *fallacies,* and because they can often be very powerful and persuasive, it's important to be alert for them in arguments you encounter—and in your own writing. Here are some of the most common fallacies.

Begging the question tries to support an argument by simply restating it in other language, so that the reasoning goes around in circles. For example, the statement "We need to reduce the national debt because the government owes too much money" begs the question of whether the debt is actually too large, because what comes before and after *because* say essentially the same thing.

Either-or arguments, also called *false dilemmas,* argue that only two alternatives are possible in a situation that actually is more complex. A candidate who declares, "I will not allow the United States to become a defenseless, bankrupt nation—it must remain the military and economic superpower of the world," ignores the many possibilities in between.

Ad hominem (Latin for "to the man") arguments make personal attacks on those who support an opposing position rather than address the position itself: "Of course council member Acevedo doesn't want to build a new high school; she doesn't have any children herself." The council member's childlessness may not be the reason for her opposition to a new high school, and even if it is, such an attack doesn't provide any argument for building the school.

Faulty causality, the mistaken assumption that because one event followed another, the first event caused the second, is also called *post hoc, ergo propter hoc* (Latin for "after this, therefore because of this"). For example, a mayor running for reelection may boast that a year after her administration began having the police patrol neighborhoods more frequently, the city's crime rate has dropped significantly. But there might be many other possible causes for the drop, so considerable evidence would be needed to establish such a causal connection.

Bandwagon appeals simply urge the audience to go along with the crowd: "Join the millions who've found pain relief through Weleda Migraine Remedy." "Everybody knows you shouldn't major in a subject that doesn't lead to a job." Such appeals often flatter the audience by implying that making the popular choice means they are smart, attractive, sophisticated, and so on.

Slippery slope arguments contend that if a certain event occurs, it will (or at least might) set in motion a chain of events that will end in disaster, like a minor misstep at the top of a slick incline that causes you to slip and then slide all the way to the bottom. For example, opponents of physician-assisted suicide often warn that making it legal for doctors to help people end their lives would eventually lead to an increase in the suicide rate, as people who would not otherwise kill themselves find it easier to do so, and even to an increase in murders disguised as suicide. Slippery slope arguments are not always wrong—an increasingly catastrophic chain reaction does sometimes grow out of a seemingly small beginning. But the greater the difference is between the initial event and the predicted final outcome, the more evidence is needed that the situation will actually play out in this way.

Setting up a straw man misrepresents an opposing argument, characterizing it as more extreme or otherwise different than it actually is, in order to attack it more easily. The misrepresentation is like an artificial figure made of straw that's easier to knock down than a real person would be. For example, critics of the 2010 Affordable Care Act often attacked it as a "federal takeover of health care" or a "government-run system." In fact, although the legislation increased the government's role in the health-care system, it still relied primarily on private systems of insurance and health-care providers.

Hasty generalizations draw sweeping conclusions on the basis of too little evidence: "Both of the political science classes I took were deadly dull, so it must be a completely boring subject." "You shouldn't drink so much coffee— that study that NPR reported on today said it causes cancer." Many hasty generalizations take the form of stereotypes about groups of people, such as men and women, gays and straights, and ethnic or religious groups. It's difficult to make arguments without generalizing, but they always need to be based on sufficient evidence and appropriately qualified with words like *most, in many cases, usually, in this state, in recent years*, and so on.

Faulty analogies are comparisons that do not hold up in some way crucial to the argument at hand. Accusing parents who homeschool their children of "educational malpractice" by saying that parents who aren't doctors wouldn't be allowed to perform surgery on their children, so parents who aren't trained to teach shouldn't be allowed to teach their children makes a false analogy. Teaching and surgery aren't alike enough to support an argument that what's required for one is needed for the other.

WHAT ABOUT OTHER PERSPECTIVES?

In any argument, it's important to consider perspectives other than those of the author, especially those that would not support the claim or would argue it very differently. As a reader, you should question any arguments

Camels ad, 1946.

that don't acknowledge other positions, and as a writer, you'll want to be sure that you represent—and respond to—perspectives other than your own. Acknowledging other arguments, in fact, is another way of demonstrating that you're fair and of establishing your credibility—whereas failing to consider other views can make you seem close-minded or lazy, unfair or manipulative. Think of any advertisements you've seen that claim, "Doctors recommend drug X."

The cigarette ad included here is one of the most infamous of such advertising arguments. Of course, this ad doesn't claim that all doctors smoke Camels, but it implies that plenty of them do and that what's good for a doctor is good for other consumers. But what if the ad had been required to consider other viewpoints? The result would have been a more honest and more informative, though perhaps a less successful, argument. Today, cigarette ads are required to carry another point of view: a warning about the adverse effects of smoking. So if an argument does not take other points of view into consideration, you will be right to question it, asking yourself what those other viewpoints might be and why they were not taken into account.

Compare the misleading Camels ad to the following discussion of contemporary seismology:

Jian Lin was 14 years old in 1973, when the Chinese government under Mao Zedong recruited him for a student science team called "the earthquake watchers." After a series of earthquakes that had killed thousands in northern China, the country's seismologists thought that if they augmented their own research by having observers keep an eye out for anomalies like snakes bolting early from their winter dens and erratic well-water levels, they might be able to do what no scientific body had managed before: issue an earthquake warning that would save thousands of lives.

In the winter of 1974, the earthquake watchers were picking up some suspicious signals near the city of Haicheng. Panicked chickens were squalling and trying to escape their pens; water levels were falling in wells. Seismologists had also begun noticing a telltale pattern of small quakes. "They were like popcorn kernels," Lin tells me, "popping up all over the general area." Then, suddenly, the popping stopped, just as it had before a catastrophic earthquake some years earlier that killed more than 8,000. "Like 'the calm before the storm,' " Lin says. "We have the exact same phrase in Chinese." On the morning of February 4, 1975, the seismology bureau issued a warning: Haicheng should expect a big earthquake, and people should move outdoors.

At 7:36 p.m., a magnitude 7.0 quake struck. The city was nearly leveled, but only about 2,000 people were killed. Without the warning, easily 150,000 would have died. "And so you finally had an earthquake forecast that did indeed save lives," Lin recalls. . . .

Lin is now a senior scientist of geophysics at Woods Hole Oceanographic Institution, in Massachusetts, where he spends his time studying not the scurrying of small animals and fluctuating electrical current between trees (another fabled warning sign), but seismometer readings, GPS coordinates, and global earthquake-notification reports. He and his longtime collaborator, Ross Stein of the U.S. Geological Survey, are champions of a theory that could enable scientists to forecast earthquakes with more precision and speed.

Some established geophysicists insist that all earthquakes are random, yet everyone agrees that aftershocks are not. Instead, they follow certain empirical laws. Stein, Lin, and their collaborators hypothesized that many earthquakes classified as main shocks are actually aftershocks, and they went looking for the forces that cause faults to fail.

Their work was in some ways heretical: For a long time, earthquakes were thought to release only the stress immediately around them; an earthquake that happened in one place would decrease the possibility of another happening nearby. But that didn't explain earthquake sequences like the one that rumbled through the desert and mountains east of Los Angeles in 1992. . . .

Lin and Stein both admit that [their theory] doesn't explain all earthquakes. Indeed, some geophysicists, like Karen Felzer, of the U.S. Geological Survey, think their hypothesis gives short shrift to the impact that dynamic stress—the actual rattling of a quake in motion—has on neighboring faults.

—JUDITH LEWIS MERNIT, "Seismology: Is San Francisco Next?"

As this excerpt shows, Lin and Stein's research supports the claim that earthquakes can be predicted some of the time, but they—and the author of the article about them—are careful not to overstate their argument or to ignore those who disagree. The author responds to other perspectives in three ways. She *acknowledges* the "all random" theory held by "[s]ome established geophysicists"; she provides evidence (not shown here) to *refute* the idea that "earthquakes release only the stress immediately around them." And in the last paragraph she *accommodates* other perspectives by qualifying Lin and Stein's claim and mentioning what some critics see as a weakness in it.

As an author, remember to consider what other perspectives exist on your topic—and what **COUNTERARGUMENTS** someone might have to your position. You may not agree with them, but they might lead you to **QUALIFY** your thesis—or even change your position. Whatever you think about other viewpoints, be sure to **ACKNOWLEDGE** them fairly and respectfully—and to accommodate or refute them as possible. And carefully investigate your reactions to opposing positions to be sure you aren't falling prey to **CONFIRMATION BIAS** or **ATTRIBUTION BIAS**. They will help you to sharpen your own thinking, and your writing can only improve as a result.

WAYS OF STRUCTURING ARGUMENTS

You can organize arguments in several ways. You may decide to approach a controversial or surprising argument slowly, *building up to the claim* but withholding it until you have established plenty of evidence to support it, as in this introductory paragraph from an essay about sports injuries:

> The flood of media attention highlighting damaged brains, dementia, and suicides in retired NFL players has made concussions synonymous with football. That attention was greatly needed: the debilitating consequences of brain injuries in football players of all ages has been severely overlooked. But the focus of this controversy has been far too narrow. It's true that young players need better equipment and stricter safety standards on the gridiron. But in many of the most popular sports, boys aren't the ones most likely to be afflicted by concussions. Girls are.
>
> —MARJORIE A. SNYDER, "Girls Suffer Sports Concussions at a Higher Rate than Boys. Why Is That Overlooked?"

On the other hand, you may choose to *start right off with the claim* and then build support for it piece by piece by piece, as in this opening from a 2011 essay in *Wired* on the power of product tie-ins.

> Cartoon characters permeate every aspect of our children's existences. We serve them Transformers Lunchables and have them brush with SpongeBob-branded toothpaste. We tuck them in on branded sheets, fix their owies with branded bandages, and change their branded diapers because we know, or at least we think, that the characters will make them happy. Whether our kids are sleeping, bleeding, or pooping, Spider-Man is there. Even if you operate one of those rarefied TV-free households, the brands will penetrate, assuming your children go to preschool, have friends, or eat food.
>
> —NEAL POLLACK, "Why Your Kids Are Addicted to *Cars*"

Another common way to begin is to *note what others have said* about your topic and then to present your own ideas—your claim—as a response. Whether you agree, disagree, or both, this is a way of adding your voice to the larger conversation. See how libertarian journalist Radley Balko uses this technique to begin an essay on government policies on obesity:

This toy store display argues that if you loved the movies, you should buy Minions-themed products.

> This June, *Time* magazine and ABC News will host a three-day summit on obesity [that] promises to be a pep rally for media, nutrition activists, and policy makers—all agitating for a panoply of government anti-obesity initiatives. . . . In other words, bringing government between you and your waistline. . . .
>
> This is the wrong way to fight obesity. Instead of manipulating or intervening in the array of food options available to American consumers, our government ought to be working to foster a sense of responsibility in and ownership of our own health and well-being.
>
> —RADLEY BALKO, "What You Eat Is Your Business"

Whatever the approach, arguments are inherently social, involving an author and an audience. They always have certain purpose(s) and make of debatable claims that the author presents as true or beneficial. In addition, they all provide reasons and evidence as support for their claims, though what counts as good evidence varies across fields and communities. And finally, arguments almost always rely on assumptions that may not be explicitly stated but that the audience must agree with in order to accept the argument. For example:

> *Claim*: Colleges should not rely on standardized tests for admission.
>
> *Reason*: Such tests are socioeconomically biased.
>
> *Evidence*: The disparity in test scores among various groups has been linked to cultural biases in the types of questions posed on such tests.
>
> *Assumption*: Questions that favor any group are inherently unfair.

Now let's consider four ways of approaching and structuring an argument: **CLASSICAL**, **TOULMIN**, **ROGERIAN**, and **INVITATIONAL**.

Classical Arguments

Originating in the ancient Greek law courts and later refined by Roman rhetoricians, the classical system of argumentation is still favored by writers in different fields. Throughout a classically structured argument, you'll rely on **ETHICAL**, **EMOTIONAL**, and **LOGICAL** appeals to your audience. Ethical appeals (those that build your credibility) are especially effective in the introduction, while logical and emotional appeals are useful anywhere.

The introduction engages the interest and attention of its audience by establishing the importance of the issue, establishing **COMMON GROUND** with the audience and showing how they are affected by the argument, and establishing the author's **CREDIBILITY**. To engage the audience, you might begin with an anecdote, ask a provocative question, or state the issue explicitly. Most writers taking a classical approach state the **CLAIM** in the introduction; students making an academic argument do so in an explicit **THESIS** statement.

The body of the argument provides any necessary background information, followed by **REASONS** and **EVIDENCE** in support of the claim. In addition, this section should make clear how the argument you're making is in the best interests of the audience. Finally, it should acknowledge possible **COUNTERARGUMENTS** and alternative points of view, presenting them fairly and respectfully and showing how your own argument is preferable.

The conclusion may summarize your argument, elaborate on its implications, and make clear what you want those in your audience to do in response. Just as it's important to open in a way that will engage their attention, you'll want to close with something that will make them remember your argument—and act on it in some way.

Let's suppose you've been assigned the topic of free speech on campus, and you believe that free speech must always be protected. That's a fairly broad topic, so eventually you decide to focus on the trend at many colleges to withdraw invitations to speakers holding controversial viewpoints. You might begin your introduction with a provocative statement, followed by some facts that will get your readers' attention (both ways of appealing to emotions) and culminating in a statement of your claim:

> Our most cherished American freedom is under attack—and not from abroad. On numerous campuses in recent years, an increasing number of invited speakers have been disinvited or driven to decline because various members of the campus community find it offensive to hear from people who hold beliefs or positions that they or others disagree with. However, true freedom of speech requires us to encounter ideas and even language we don't like, don't agree with, or find offensive. As students, we need to wrestle with ideas that challenge us, that make us think beyond our personal beliefs and experiences, and that educate us in and out of the classroom.

You might then introduce some background information about this issue, identifying points you'll develop later as support for your claim. Here you might note examples of disinvitation campaigns. Using specific examples will make your argument more credible:

> According to the Foundation for Individual Rights in Education (FIRE), 192 college campus speakers have been disinvited between 1999 and 2014, and most often conservative speakers. As noted by Isaac Chotiner in the New Republic, such campaigns indicate "rising levels of liberal intolerance, which is good for neither university campuses nor the truly shun-worthy people in our midst."

And then you might provide support for your claim by noting specific instances when invitations to speak have been withdrawn or speeches have been derailed by hecklers and giving reasons that free speech applies to everyone:

Former Secretary of State Condoleezza Rice, Director of the International Monetary Fund Christine Lagarde, New York Police Commissioner Ray Kelly, and former U.C. Berkeley Chancellor Robert Birgeneau: each was silenced by hecklers as they attempted to speak or even before they had the opportunity to speak on campus. If we accept only speakers whose political philosophies are ones no one would disagree with, free speech becomes "free only if you agree with me" speech. And then we may as well give up the notion of independent thought.

Acknowledging and responding to counterarguments or other viewpoints strengthens your argument by showing you to be well informed, fair, and open-minded:

On the other hand, some resistance may well be justified, as when some students and faculty at Brown University protested a speech by Ray Kelly, arguing that it took such a "disruption" to have their voices heard.

And then in your conclusion you might reiterate the major points of your argument and rephrase your claim:

See how Shawna Shapiro enters the debate on campus free speech on p. 400.

We should strive to accept diverse voices and viewpoints on campus. Our conversations should challenge us to question our own long-held beliefs and closely examine those of others. We can do so only if we protect and truly embrace the right to freedom of speech—for one and all.

Toulmin Arguments

Philosopher Stephen Toulmin developed a detailed model for analyzing arguments, one that has been widely used for writing arguments as well.

The introduction presents a **CLAIM**, one that others will find debatable. If need be, you'll want to carefully **QUALIFY** this claim using words like *often* or *it may be* that limit your argument to one you'll be able to support.

The body of the argument presents good **REASONS** and **EVIDENCE** (which Toulmin calls "grounds") in support of the claim and explains any underlying assumptions (Toulmin calls these "warrants") that your audience needs to agree with in order to accept your argument. You may need to provide further evidence (which Toulmin calls "backing") to illustrate the assumptions. Finally, you'd acknowledge and respond to any **COUNTERARGUMENTS**.

The conclusion restates the argument as strongly and memorably as possible. You might conclude by discussing the implications of your argument, saying why it matters. And you'll want to be clear about what you want readers to think (or do).

For example:

> *Claim*: Our college should ban the smoking of e-cigarettes.
>
> *Qualification*: The ban should be limited to public places on campus.
>
> *Good reasons and evidence*: E-cigarettes contain some of the same toxins as cigarettes; research shows that they are a hazard to health.
>
> *Underlying assumptions*: Those who work and study here are entitled to protection from the harmful acts of others; the US Constitution calls for promoting "the general welfare" of all citizens.
>
> *Backing for the assumptions*: Other colleges and even some cities have banned e-cigarettes; highly respected public health advocates have testified about their ill effects.
>
> *Counterarguments*: E-cigarettes are less harmful than traditional cigarettes; smokers have rights too. However, this argument limits the ban to public spaces, which means smokers can still use e-cigarettes in their homes and other private places.
>
> *Conclusion*: Our school should ban the use of e-cigarettes in public places to protect the health of all who work and study here.

Now let's see how an argument about free speech on campus would work using Toulmin's model. You'd begin with your claim, carefully qualified if need be. The italicized words in the following example are qualifiers:

> To be successful as college students, to truly develop into independent thinkers, we need to wrestle with ideas that challenge us and that make us think beyond our personal beliefs and experiences, both in and out of the classroom. Such intellectual challenges are being diminished at *many* colleges as *some* on campus decide that ideas they or others disagree

with are more threatening than educational. On numerous campuses in recent years, a number of invited speakers have been disinvited or driven to decline because some on campus find it offensive to hear from those who hold beliefs different from theirs.

You would then follow that claim with the reasons and evidence that support your claim:

> Education requires exposure to multiple points of view, at least according to Aristotle and Martin Luther King Jr. Aristotle notes in his Metaphysics that "It is the mark of an educated mind to be able to entertain a thought without accepting it." More than two thousand years later, King defined the purpose of education as enabling a person to "think incisively and to think for one's self . . . [and not to] let our mental life become invaded by legions of half truths, prejudices, and propaganda."

Then you would make clear the assumptions on which you base your claim:

> Considering a variety of viewpoints is a hallmark of intelligent thinking. Freedom of speech is the right of every American.

And you'd add backing to support your assumptions:

> Freedom of speech requires us to encounter ideas, language, or words we don't like, don't agree with, or find offensive. To truly protect our own right to free speech, we need to protect those rights for everyone.

Next you'd acknowledge and respond to counterarguments and other views, showing yourself to be well-informed, fair, and open-minded:

> Sometimes, supporting free speech calls for just the kind of protests that have led to disinviting speakers. For example, students and faculty at Brown University protested a speech by New York Police Commissioner Ray Kelly, arguing that it took a disruption to have their voices heard.

Finally, in your conclusion you'd remind your readers of your claim, reiterate why it matters, and let them know what you want them to think or do.

> Free speech is a bedrock value of American life. It's up to all of us to protect it—for ourselves as well as for others.

Rogerian Arguments

Noting that people are more likely to listen to you if you show that you are really listening to them, psychologist Carl Rogers developed a series of nonconfrontational strategies to help people involved in a dispute listen carefully and respectfully to one another. Rhetoricians Richard Young, Alton Becker, and Kenneth Pike developed an approach to argument based on Rogers's work as a way to resolve conflict by coming to understand alternative points of view. Rogerian argument aims to persuade by respectfully considering other positions, establishing COMMON GROUND, encouraging discussion and an open exchange of ideas, and seeking mutually beneficial compromise. Success depends on a willingness to listen and to try to understand where others are coming from.

The introduction identifies the issue and DESCRIBES it as fully and fairly as possible. It then acknowledges the various viewpoints on the issue, using nonjudgmental language to show that you respect the views of others.

The body of the argument discusses the various POSITIONS respectfully and in neutral language, presenting REASONS and EVIDENCE showing how each position might be acceptable in certain circumstances. Then state your own position, also using neutral language. You'll want to focus on the commonalities among the various positions—and if at all possible, show how those who hold other positions might benefit from the one you propose.

The conclusion proposes some kind of resolution, including a compromise if possible and demonstrating how it would benefit all parties.

Now let's take a look at how you'd approach the topic of free speech on campus using Rogerian methods. You could begin by identifying the issue, noting that there are a number of different viewpoints, and describing them respectfully:

> On many campuses today, reasonable people are becoming increasingly concerned about the unwillingness of some students and others to listen to people with viewpoints they disagree with—or even to let them speak. As Americans, we can all agree that our right to speak freely is guaranteed by the US Constitution. Yet this principle is being tested at

many colleges. Some say that controversial figures should not be invited to speak on campus; others have even argued that certain people who've been invited to speak should be disinivited.

Next you'd discuss each position, showing how it might be reasonable. Then explain your position, being careful to use neutral language and to avoid seeming to claim the moral high ground:

> Some speakers may bring messages based on untruths or lies or hate. If such speakers represent a threat to campus life and safety, it seems reasonable that they be disinvited or simply not invited in the first place. Others feel that speakers who hold extreme or radical positions— on either the right or the left—should not be invited to speak on our campuses. In some cases, this position might be justified, especially if the speaker's position is irrelevant to higher education. Except in such extreme circumstances, however, a very important part of a college education involves exposure to multiple points of view. Such great thinkers as Aristotle and Martin Luther King Jr. have expressed this better than I can: in the *Metaphysics*, Aristotle notes that "It is the mark of an educated mind to be able to entertain a thought without accepting it," and more than two thousand years later, King defined the purpose of education as enabling a person to "think incisively and to think for one's self."

Try to conclude by suggesting a compromise:

> Speakers who threaten campus life or safety may be best left uninvited. But while controversial figures may sometimes cause disruption, our community can learn from them even if we disagree with them. Rather than disinviting such speakers, let's invite discussion after they speak— and make it open to all of the interested parties.

Invitational Arguments

Feminist scholars Sonja Foss and Cindy Griffin have developed what they call "invitational" arguments, using an approach that aims to foster conversation instead of confrontation. Rather than trying to convince an audience to accept a position, invitational argument aims to get people to work together toward understanding. This approach begins with demonstrating to your audience that you understand and respect their position, setting the stage for discussion and collaboration in which all parties can benefit.

As you can see, invitational arguments have much in common with the Rogerian approach. One important difference, however, lies in the emphasis on openness and the focus on a shared goal. Rather than presenting the audience with a predetermined position that you then attempt to convince them to accept, an invitational argument starts out by assuming that both author and audience are open to changing their minds.

The introduction presents the topic, acknowledges that there are various **POSITIONS** and perspectives on it, and makes clear that the goal is to understand each viewpoint so that readers can decide what they think.

In the body of the argument, you'd **DESCRIBE** each perspective fairly and respectfully. If you can, **QUOTE** those who favor each viewpoint—a way of letting them speak for themselves.

The conclusion looks for **COMMON GROUND** among the various perspectives, calling on readers to consider each carefully before making up their minds.

Using an invitational approach to the subject of disinvitations and free speech on campus, you could begin by focusing on the complexity of the issue, noting the ways that well-meaning people can have strong differences of opinion but still aim for a common goal:

> On many campuses today, well-meaning people are increasingly concerned about a tendency to reject others' viewpoints out of hand, without even listening to them. This trend has led to such acts as disinviting speakers to campus or preventing them from speaking, once there. This issue might seem to pit freedom of speech against the right to resist speakers whose views may be harmful in certain ways. Yet looking only at this dichotomy ignores the many other possible perspectives people hold on this issue. The goal of this essay is to bring the major perspectives on free speech on campus together in order to understand each one thoroughly, to identify any common ground that exists among the perspectives, and to provide readers with the information they need to make informed decisions of their own.

Next, you would discuss each perspective fairly and openly, showing its strengths and weaknesses.

There seem to be at least four perspectives on the issue of free speech on our campus. First, there are those who believe that the principle of free speech is absolute and that anyone should be able to speak on any issue—period. A second perspective holds that free speech is "free" in context; that is, the right to free speech goes only so far and when it verges on harming others, it is "free" no more. Still a third perspective argues that universities must accept the role of "in loco parentis" and protect students from speech that is offensive, even if it potentially offends only a small group of students. Finally, some hold that universities are indeed responsible for maintaining a safe environment—physically, mentally, and emotionally—and that they can do so while still honoring free speech in most circumstances.

You could then look in detail at the four perspectives, allowing proponents of each to speak for themselves when possible (through quoted and cited passages) and exploring each respectfully and fairly. Following this discussion, you could identify any commonalities among the perspectives:

Each perspective on this issue has good intentions. Let us use that common ground as the starting point for further exploration, seeing if we can develop guidelines for protecting free speech on campus while also keeping our campus safe. It may well be that considering these perspectives carefully, honestly, and fairly will lead some to change their minds or to come together in certain areas of agreement. I hope that readers of this essay will do just that before taking a position on this issue.

REFLECT. Look for an argument you've read recently that caught your attention and re-read it with an eye for the argumentative strategies it uses. Does it use one particular approach—classical? Toulmin? Rogerian? invitational?—or does it mix strategies from more than one approach? Is the argument persuasive? If not, try revising it using strategies from one of these approaches.

MATTERS OF STYLE

An argument's style usually reinforces its message in as many ways as possible. The ancient Roman orator Cicero identified three basic styles, which he termed "high," "middle," and "low." Today, we can see a wider range of styles, from the highly formal language of US Supreme Court opinions to the informal style of everyday written communication such as memos and email, to the colloquial style of spoken language and the casual shorthand of texts and tweets.

You can learn a lot by looking closely at the stylistic choices in an argument—the use of individual words and figurative language, of personal pronouns (or not), of vivid images (verbal and visual), of design and format. In 2005, the *Los Angeles Times* announced an experiment it called its "Wikitorial," in which the newspaper cautiously invited readers to log on to its website and rewrite editorials:

> Plenty of skeptics are predicting embarrassment; like an arthritic old lady who takes to the dance floor, they say, the *Los Angeles Times* is more likely to break a hip than to be hip. We acknowledge that possibility.

The skeptics turned out to be right, and after three days the paper ended the experiment, saying:

> Unfortunately, we have had to remove this feature, at least temporarily, because a few readers were flooding the site with inappropriate material. Thanks and apologies to the thousands of people who logged on in the right spirit.

Savvy readers will be alert to the power of stylistic choices in these messages. The description of closing down "Wikitorial" as "unfortunate" and the equally careful choice of "a few readers," "flooding," and "inappropriate material" mark this as a formal and judicious message that stands in sharp contrast to the slightly self-deprecating style of the first announcement, with its casual use of "plenty of " and its play on "hip." How does the sober style of the second announcement influence your response? How different might your response be if the paper had declared, "We're pulling the plug on this page since a few creeps loaded it with a bunch of crap"?

Now let's look at a visual argument. The spoof ad on the next page was created by Adbusters, whose website identifies it as a "global network of artists, activists, writers, pranksters, students, educators and entrepreneurs" whose aim is "to topple existing power structures and forge a major shift in the way we will live in the twenty-first century." The ad satirizes the assumption that drugs can simply "wash your blues away," like laundry

Adbusters spoof ad.

detergent. Note especially the retro style, which evokes the "happy house-wife" of the 1950s.

As an author, you will need to make such important stylistic choices, beginning—as is almost always the case—with the overall effect you want to create. Try to identify that overall effect in a word or phrase (for instance, concern, outrage, sympathy, or direct action), and then use it to help you choose specific words, images, and design elements that will create that effect and convey it most powerfully to your audience.

NINETEEN

Strategies for Supporting an Argument

RGUMENTS ARE ONLY AS STRONG as the evidence that supports them. Just as a house built on weak foundations is likely to crumble, so it is with arguments. As an author arguing a point, then, you will need to provide good, strong, reliable evidence to support your position. Ancient Greek rhetoricians developed strategies for finding such support, strategies that continue to serve us well today. This chapter introduces you to those strategies, arranged alphabetically from analogy to reiteration.

Analogy

Analogies are comparisons that point out similarities between things that are otherwise very different. Authors often use them to create vivid pictures in a reader's mind and make abstract ideas more concrete. Analogies can be especially powerful in an **ARGUMENT**, demonstrating that what is true in one case is true in another, usually more complicated, case. Here Annie Dillard draws an analogy between a writer's words and various tools:

> When you write, you lay out a line of words. The line of words is a miner's pick, a wood-carver's gouge, a surgeon's probe. You wield it, and it digs a path you follow. Soon you find yourself deep in new

territory. Is it a dead end, or have you located the real subject? You will know tomorrow, or this time next year.

—ANNIE DILLARD, *A Writing Life*

Dillard uses this analogy to suggest that writers can use words as tools for exploring a topic—to "probe" or "dig a path" into their subject.

Now see how Malala Yousafzai uses an analogy in a speech to the United Nations to support her argument that education is the best means of overcoming poverty and injustice:

> We will continue our journey to our destination of peace and education for everyone. No one can stop us. We will speak for our rights and we will bring change through our voice. We must believe in the power and the strength of our words. Our words can change the world because we are all together, united for the cause of education. And if we want to achieve our goal, then let us empower ourselves with the weapon of knowledge and let us shield ourselves with unity and togetherness.
>
>   Dear brothers and sisters, we must not forget that millions of people are suffering from poverty, injustice, and ignorance. We must not forget that millions of children are out of schools. We must not forget that our sisters and brothers are waiting for a bright, peaceful future.

Malala Yousafzai addressing the United Nations in 2013.

So let us wage a global struggle against illiteracy, poverty, and terrorism and let us pick up our books and pens. They are our most powerful
weapons.   —MALALA YOUSAFZAI, 2013 Speech at the United Nations

Yousafzai, a Pakistani activist for girls' education and Nobel Prize winner, builds her argument on an analogy that compares "the power and strength of our words" to the power of weapons used by the Taliban and others who would deny women education. She draws this analogy throughout her speech, calling upon us to use knowledge to "empower," unity to "shield," and books and pens to "wage a global struggle" against illiteracy, poverty, and terrorism. If these are our weapons, she says, then "no one can stop us." As an author, when you use an analogy, check to be sure it isn't a faulty analogy. In other words, compare things that are alike enough to support your claim; compare apples to apples, not apples to oranges.

Cause / Effect

When we analyze causes, we're trying to understand and explain why something happened. Why did the Virgin Galactic spaceship come apart in mid-air seconds after its launch? Why has there been so much extreme weather in recent years? Why did your chocolate chip cookies all run together on the cookie sheet? And when we think about effects, we speculate about what might happen. How will recent weather patterns affect crop yields? Will the cookies still run if you let the cookie sheet cool between batches?

Authors of **LITERARY NARRATIVES** could focus on teachers or books that caused them to love (or hate) reading, whereas someone writing a **PROPOSAL** may argue that a specific solution will have a particular effect. And in a **NARRATIVE**, you might use cause-and-effect reasoning to explain an event.

Arguing about causes and effects can be tricky, because often it's almost impossible to link a specific cause to one specific effect. That's why it took decades of research to establish a strong enough link between cigarette smoking and cancer to label tobacco products with a warning: researchers had to be able to discount many other possible causes. For the past several decades, astrophysicists have tried to photograph the black hole at the center of the Milky Way in order to test two dominant (but thought to be conflicting) theories of the nature of matter. Using data recently collected with an Event Horizon Telescope, they believe they will be able to support one theory or the other—or to reconcile the two.

Tressie McMillan Cottom is careful not to claim a direct link between display-ing status symbols and receiving certain treatment, but hinting at the effect is all that it takes. Read her essay on p. 975.

Given the many variables involved, the researchers will likely discuss the behavior of the black hole in terms of *probable* or *possible* causes of observed phenomena. Claiming definite causes will take much longer, and it may never be possible to do so.

Exact effects are similarly difficult to determine. In 2014, the United Nations released a report on climate change, stating the possible environmental effects if we continue to burn fossil fuels. Notice how the report's authors qualify their statements by noting what effects greenhouse emissions "could" cause to happen:

- The risks of climate change could reverse years of progress against poverty and hunger if greenhouse emissions continue at their present pace.
- The emission of greenhouse gases could cause dangerous warming and long-lasting changes in the climate system, severely impacting people and ecosystems.
- Failure to reduce emissions . . . could cause food shortages, flooding of cities and even nations and a dangerous climate during the hottest times of the year.

— *Climate Change 2014: Synthesis Report*

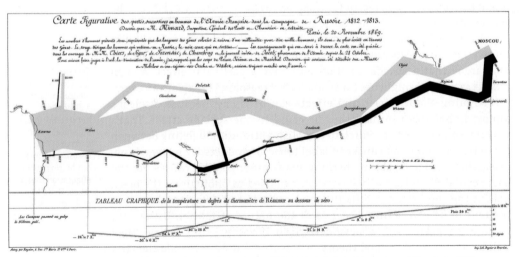

A map showing Minard's analysis of Napoleon's failed invasion of Russia in 1812.

Often when you write about causes and effects, then, you can only argue that they are likely or probable, not proven. This is just one reason that you'll want to QUALIFY what you say: to add words like "might" or "should" that limit your claim.

Causal analysis can sometimes be easier to understand in a chart or graph than in words alone. See an especially famous example in the history of information graphics on the facing page, a map created in 1869. It depicts the horrific loss of life resulting from Napoleon's decision to march on Moscow in 1812. Its creator, Charles Joseph Minard, plotted information about troop numbers and locations, dates, direction and distances traveled, longitude and latitude, and the temperatures as soldiers retreated from Moscow. He used the width of the tan line to show the troops going into Russia (initially 680,000) and the much narrower black line to show those retreating (27,000). His causal argument was clear as he linked the dropping temperatures to the retreat: the colder the temperature, the fewer soldiers who survived.

Classification

When you classify, you group items into categories according to similarities. Tomatoes, for example, can be classified according to their varieties: cherry, plum, grape, heirloom, and so on. Authors frequently turn to classification in order to organize and elaborate on a topic. Writers of REVIEWS often use classification when focusing on more than one work, as Adam Gopnik does in evaluating a number of books about the internet by categorizing the authors into groups.

> The Never-Betters believe that we're on the brink of a new utopia, where information will be free and democratic, news will be made from the bottom up, love will reign, and cookies will bake themselves. The Better-Nevers think that we would have been better off if the whole thing had never happened, that the world that is coming to an end is superior to the one that is taking its place, and that, at a minimum, books and magazines create private space for minds in ways that twenty-second bursts of information don't. The Ever-Wasers insist that at any moment in modernity something like this is going on, and that a new way of organizing data and connecting users is always thrilling to some and chilling to others—that something like this is going on is exactly what makes it a modern moment. One's hopes rest with the Never-Betters; one's head

with the Ever-Wasers; and one's heart? Well, twenty or so books in, one's heart tends to move toward the Better-Nevers, and then bounce back toward someplace that looks more like home.

—ADAM GOPNIK, "How the Internet Gets Inside Us"

Classification is an essential feature of all websites, one that makes accessible the enormous amount of information available on a site. Take a look at the homepage on the National Weather Service site at weather.gov and you'll find various kinds of classification, starting with the horizontal menu bar at the top that categorizes the information on the site into commonly consulted topics: Forecast, Safety, News, and so on. Hovering your mouse over "Forecast" opens a drop-down menu that classifies forecasts into various categories: Aviation, Marine, Hurricanes, Fire Weather, and so on.

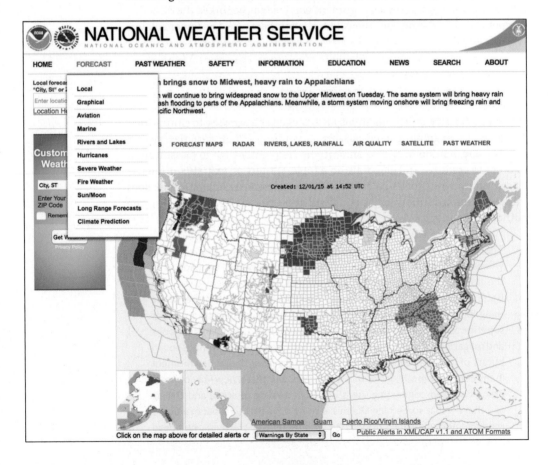

Comparison / Contrast

When you compare things, you focus on their similarities, and when you contrast them, you look at their differences. Both strategies can be very useful in developing an argument, helping to explain something that is unfamiliar by comparing (or contrasting) it with something more familiar. In a book **REVIEW**, for example, you might compare the Hunger Games trilogy to the Harry Potter series, or in a **REPORT** on Brexit, the prespectives of those who support it with those opposing it.

There are two ways you can organize a comparison: block and point by point. Using the *block* method, you present the subjects you're comparing one at a time, as in the following paragraphs:

> Most men, I believe, think of themselves as average-looking. Men will think this even if their faces cause heart failure in cattle at a range of 300 yards. Being average does not bother them; average is fine, for men. This is why men never ask anybody how they look. Their primary form of beauty care is to shave themselves, which is essentially the same form of beauty care that they give to their lawns. If, at the end of his four-minute daily beauty regimen, a man has managed to wipe most of the shaving cream out of his hair and is not bleeding too badly, he feels that he has done all he can, so he stops thinking about his appearance and devotes his mind to more critical issues, such as the Super Bowl.
>
> Women do not look at themselves this way. If I had to express, in three words, what I believe most women think about their appearance, those words would be: "not good enough." No matter how attractive a woman may appear to be to others, when she looks at herself in the mirror, she thinks: woof. She thinks that at any moment a municipal animal-control officer is going to throw a net over her and haul her off to the shelter.   —DAVE BARRY, "Beauty and the Beast"

Or you can organize your comparison *point by point*, discussing your subjects together, one point at a time, as David Sedaris does in the following paragraph comparing his own childhood in Raleigh, North Carolina, with that of his partner Hugh, a diplomat's son who grew up in Africa:

> Certain events are parallel, but compared with Hugh's, my childhood was unspeakably dull. When I was seven years old, my family moved to North Carolina. When he was seven years old, Hugh's family moved to the Congo. We had a collie and a house cat. They had a monkey and

two horses named Charlie Brown and Satan. I threw stones at stop signs. Hugh threw stones at crocodiles. The verbs are the same, but he definitely wins the prize when it comes to nouns and objects. An eventful day for my mother might have involved a trip to the dry cleaner or a conversation with the potato-chip deliveryman. Asked one ordinary Congo afternoon what she'd done with her day, Hugh's mother answered that she and a fellow member of the Ladies' Club had visited a leper colony on the outskirts of Kinshasa. No reason was given for the expedition, though chances are she was staking it out for a future field trip.

—DAVID SEDARIS, "Remembering My Childhood on the
Continent of Africa"

Here's Ashley Highfield, managing director of Microsoft UK, drawing a comparison in a 2005 speech to the Royal Television Society of Britain to illuminate an argument that the "digital revolution is only just beginning":

I was reading an article the other day called "The Dangers of Wired Love," about a teenage girl called Maggie, who helped her dad run a newspaper stand in Brooklyn. Business was booming, so Maggie's dad, George McCutcheon, decided to get wired up, to help him process electronic orders. Being a total technophobe, Mr. McCutcheon got Maggie to operate the thing, but soon found out she was using it to flirt with a number of men, particularly one married man she had met online called Frank. Breaking all the known rules of cyber dating, she invited Frank to visit her in the real world, and of course he accepted. McCutcheon found out, went mad and forbade his daughter to meet up with Frank. But Maggie nevertheless continued to meet him in secret. Her furious father found out and one day followed her to one of the couple's rendezvous. He threatened to blow her brains out. She later had him arrested and charged with threatening behaviour.

An everyday story of modern times maybe? McCutcheon's fathering skills perhaps a bit severe, and Maggie perhaps a little naive? The striking thing about this story is that it was published in a magazine called *Electrical World* in 1886. The Victorian network that McCutcheon got wired to, and Maggie got hooked on, was of course the telegraph.

Those of us in technology like to think we're breaking new ground, that we're creating history through the latest revolution, when we're quite clearly not, as the very modern Maggie McCutcheon illustrates. The telegraph and the internet are perhaps more evolution than revolution: but in a way that means the seismic shifts in society that they cause creep up on us unnoticed. But these cycles of change come round again and again—and people tend to see them as momentous and more often than not scary.   —ASHLEY HIGHFIELD, "Why the Digital Revolution Is Only Just Beginning"

Comparisons of data can often be easier to understand in a chart or graph than in paragraphs. Why spend pages describing changes in demographics over the last fifty years, for example, when a bar graph can make the comparison in a half page? See how the graph below, from an article in the *Atlantic,* compares the number of college graduates in fourteen American cities, helping to support the article's argument that "America's educated elite is clustering in a few cities—and leaving the rest of the country behind."

The Uneven Fortunes of America's Cities

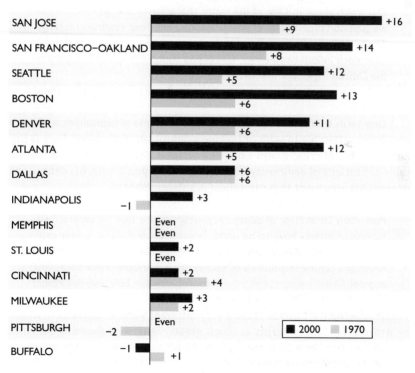

Number of college graduates per 100 people, relative to the national average.
    —RICHARD FLORIDA, "Where the Brains Are"

Definition

Mike Rose takes on the way intelligence is defined and demonstrated in our culture. Check out what he says on p. 1015.

Definitions often lie at the heart of an argument: if readers don't agree with your definition of "the good life," for example, they aren't likely to take your advice on how to achieve one. As such, definitions themselves are rhetorical choices, especially in the case of controversial topics. Whether you're writing an **ANALYSIS**, a **REPORT**, or using some other genre, you'll often have reason to include definitions. Good definitions provide clear explanations of a word, concept, or idea, often by listing its characteristic features, noting distinguishing details, and perhaps providing an illustration as well. A good definition tells readers what something is—and sometimes what it is not.

In a humorous essay about what it means to be a guy, Dave Barry starts out by noting one thing that guys are not:

> And what, exactly, do I mean by "guys"? I don't know. I haven't thought that much about it. One of the major characteristics of guyhood is that we guys don't spend a lot of time pondering our deep innermost feelings. There is a serious question in my mind about whether most guys actually have deep innermost feelings, unless you count, for example, loyalty to the Detroit Tigers, or fear of bridal showers.
>
> —DAVE BARRY, "Guys vs. Men"

One term that is the focus of many arguments is *capitalism,* and such arguments often begin with or include a definition of the word. Here is linguist and social critic Noam Chomsky weighing in with brief but memorable definitions of *democracy* and *capitalism.* As you'll note, his definitions support his argument that capitalism is antidemocratic:

> Personally I'm in favor of democracy, which means that the central institutions of society have to be under popular control. Now, under capitalism, we can't have democracy by definition. Capitalism is a system in which the central institutions of society are in principle under autocratic control.   —NOAM CHOMSKY, *Language and Politics*

Theologian Michael Novak takes a very different view of capitalism, which he defines in glowing terms at much greater length by focusing on what capitalism *does,* in a keynote address to an international conference on economies and nation-states in 2004:

Finally, capitalism instills in tradition-bound populations a new and in some respects a higher personal morality. It demands transparency and honest accounts. It insists upon the rule of law and strict observance of contracts. It teaches hard work, inventiveness, initiative, and a spirit of responsibility. It teaches patience with small gains, incremental but steady and insistent progress. During the 19th century, Great Britain achieved an average of one-and-a-half percent of GDP growth every year, with the happy result that the average income of the ordinary laborer in Britain quadrupled in a single century. The moral habits of invention, discovery, hard work, persistence, saving, investment, and moral seriousness brought about the single greatest transformation in the condition of the poor of all time—the greatest advances in hygiene, medicine, longevity, and physical well-being in all recorded history.

Capitalism brings in its train immense transformation, and the root of this transformation is moral. Those peoples and nations that neglect the moral ecology of their own cultures will not enjoy the fruits of such a transformation—or, having tasted them, will fall into rapid decline.

—MICHAEL NOVAK, "The Spirit of Capitalism"

Visuals can help in making arguments that hinge on definition. Below is a case in which the way the word *capitalism* is designed argues for yet another definition of that word. What argument(s) do you find in this illustration?

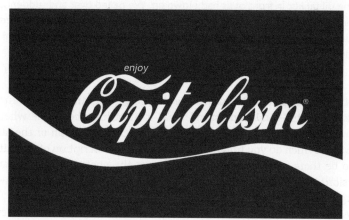

Image from *Daily Wallpapers* blog.

Description

When you describe something, you explain how it looks (or sounds, smells, tastes, or feels). Good descriptions focus on distinctive features and concrete details that add up to some **DOMINANT IMPRESSION** and help readers or listeners imagine what you are describing. You'll have occasion to use description in most of the writing you do—in a **PROFILE** of a neighborhood, you might describe the buildings and people; in a **NARRATIVE**, you'll likely describe people, places, and events.

In writing about atomic testing in Utah in her 1991 book *Refuge: An Unnatural History of Family and Place,* writer and activist Terry Tempest Williams uses description to set the scene for the facts she then presents about the high incidence of breast cancer there. She tells her father of a recurring dream she has, of a flash of light in the desert. Hearing this story, he has a sudden realization:

> "You did see it," he said.
>
> "Saw what?"
>
> "The bomb. The cloud. We were driving home from Riverside, California. You were sitting on [your mother's] lap. . . . In fact, I remember the day, September 7, 1957. We had just gotten out of the Service. We were driving north, past Las Vegas. It was an hour or so before dawn, when this explosion went off. We not only heard it, but felt it. I thought the oil tanker in front of us had blown up. We pulled over and suddenly, rising from the desert floor, we saw it, clearly, this golden-stemmed cloud, the mushroom. The sky seemed to vibrate with an eerie pink glow. Within a few minutes, a light ash was raining on the car."
>
> —TERRY TEMPEST WILLIAMS, "The Clan of One-Breasted Women"

Williams's description lets readers see the "golden-stemmed cloud" and feel the sky "vibrate"—and understand what it must have been like when the bomb exploded. Compare her description with a photograph of the atomic bomb test. Which do you find more powerful—the description of what it was like to be there when the bomb exploded or the photograph of the actual explosion? Would adding the photo have made Williams's description—and her argument—even more forceful?

Williams eventually testified before Congress about the effects of nuclear testing and has also worked as an environmental advocate. In 1995, aghast at a federal wilderness bill that would protect only a tiny fraction of

Utah's wilderness areas, she spoke at a public hearing. In this passage from an interview, see how her description of the hearing helps her make the case that the governmental officials were openly dismissive of her arguments:

> Congressman Jim Hansen and his colleagues sat on a riser above us. I remember how his glasses were perched on the end of his nose, how when I began to speak he was shuffling his papers, yawning, coughing, anything to show his boredom and displeasure. I was half-way through reading the citizens' testimonies—speaking on behalf of those who were at the Indian Walk-In Center the night before. He wasn't even listening—that was clear. Finally, I stopped mid-sentence and said something to the effect, "Congressman Hansen, I have been a resident of Utah all of my life. Is there anything I could say to you that will in some way alter your perspective so that you might consider wilderness in another way?"
>
> What I remember is how he leaned over his elbows and looked down on me over the tops of his glasses and said simply, "I'm sorry, Ms. Williams, there is something about your voice I cannot hear." It was chilling—personal. I don't think he was referring to the quality of the microphone. And then, it was over.
>
> —TERRY TEMPEST WILLIAMS, interview with David Sumner

Fiery mushroom cloud rising above Nevada atomic bomb test site, 1957.

Williams could have simply told us who said what and what was decided, but her description helps us picture the congressman "shuffling his papers" and "yawning," hear him "coughing," and sense "his boredom and displeasure."

Examples

If a picture is sometimes worth a thousand words, then a good example runs a close second: examples can make abstract ideas concrete and provide specific instances to back up a claim. See how novelist Gretel Ehrlich uses two examples to support her **ANALYSIS** of courage in a cowboy context:

> In a rancher's world, courage has less to do with facing danger than with acting spontaneously—usually on behalf of an animal or another rider. If a cow is stuck in a boghole, he throws a loop around her neck, takes his dally (a half hitch around the saddle horn), and pulls her out with horsepower. If a calf is born sick, he may take her home, warm her in front of the kitchen fire, and massage her legs until dawn.
>
> —GRETEL EHRLICH, "About Men"

You can sometimes draw on personal experience for powerful examples, provided that the experience you cite is pertinent to your point. In a commencement address to Stanford University's graduating class of 2005, Apple founder Steve Jobs used the example of his own experience with cancer in **ARGUING** that the graduates should make the most of every moment:

Steve Jobs

> About a year ago I was diagnosed with cancer. . . . The doctors told me this was almost certainly a type of cancer that is incurable, and that I should expect to live no longer than three to six months. My doctor advised me to go home and get my affairs in order, which is doctor's code for prepare to die. . . .
>
> I lived with that diagnosis all day. Later that evening I had a biopsy. . . . I was sedated, but my wife, who was there, told me that when they viewed the cells under a microscope the doctors started crying because it turned out to be a very rare form of pancreatic cancer that is curable with surgery. . . .

Your time is limited, so don't waste it living someone else's life. Don't be trapped by dogma—which is living with the results of other people's thinking. Don't let the noise of others' opinions drown out your own inner voice. And most important, have the courage to follow your heart and intuition. They somehow already know what you truly want to become. Everything else is secondary.

—STEVE JOBS, Stanford University commencement address

Examples can also be presented visually. See how the following *Twitter* post from someone who attended Fyre Festival includes a minimum of words but uses an image to show what the event really amounted to.

Humor

Comedian John Oliver uses humor to stake his claims. See an example by visiting everyones anauthor.tumblr .com.

Humor can often be used to good effect to support an argument—as long as the humor is appropriate to the context and audience. Of course, humor comes in many forms, from a self-deprecating story to a gentle parody or satire, from biting ridicule to a tired joke. While few of us are talented enough to write an argument based entirely on humor, it's possible to learn to use it judiciously. Doing so can help you to connect with your audience, provide some relief from a serious topic, or just vary the tone of your argument.

In today's world, however, you'll want to make sure that most members of your audience will understand the humor. Jokes are notoriously difficult to translate, and what's funny in one language rarely comes through the same way in another. Sometimes attempts to translate advertisements into various languages are a source of humor themselves, as when Kentucky Fried Chicken's "finger lickin' good" came out in Chinese as "eat your fingers off"! And cultural context can also determine if something will be funny at all—if it will fall flat, or worse, offend. For example, a story beginning "two cows walked into a bar" might seem like a humorous way to introduce an argument about overproduction of beef in the United States, but it probably wouldn't sit too well in India, where cows are sacred.

The late journalist Molly Ivins was famous for using humor in arguing serious positions. In the following interview on *Nightline*, Ivins is arguing in favor of gun regulation, but she uses humorous exaggeration—and a bit of real silliness—to help make her point:

Humor isn't only a matter of ha-ha jokes. A writer's tone can also convey humor. Jessica Wildfire's essay on p. 1093 has a delightfully snarky tone that helps to support her argument.

I think that's what we need: more people carrying weapons. I support the [concealed gun] legislation but I'd like to propose one small amendment. Everyone should be able to carry a concealed weapon. But everyone who carries a weapon should be required to wear one of those little beanies on their heads with a little propeller on it so the rest of us can see them coming.
—MOLLY IVINS

We're all familiar with the way cartoons use humor to make arguments—as in the one on the facing page, which argues that perhaps airport security has gone just a little overboard.

The 5ᵗʰ Wave   **By Rich Tennant**

©RICHTENNANT

AIRPORT SECURITY

"They won't let me through security until I remove the bullets from my Word document."

The Onion is a satirical news website that regularly uses humor to make its arguments. This article makes an indirect argument that at too many colleges and universities, athletics outweigh academics:

SARASOTA, FL—Bowing to pressure from alumni, students, and a majority of teaching professors of Florida State University, athletic director Dave Hart Jr. announced yesterday that FSU would completely phase out all academic operations by the end of the 2010 school year in order to make athletics the school's No. 1 priority. "It's been clear for a while that Florida State's mission is to provide the young men and women enrolled here with a world-class football program, and this is the best way to cut the fat and really focus on making us No. 1 every year," Hart said. "While it's certainly possible for an academic subsidiary to bring a certain amount of prestige to an athletic program, the national polls have made it clear that our non-athletic operations have become a major distraction." FSU's restructuring program will begin with the elimination of the College of Arts and Sciences, effective October 15.

—*THE ONION*, "Florida State University to Phase Out Academic Operations"

Narration

A good story well-told can engage your audience and help to support an argument. Both writers and speakers use narratives often—in **REPORTS**, **MEMOIRS**, and many other genres. Be sure, however, that any story you tell supports your point and that it is not the only evidence you offer. In most academic contexts, you shouldn't rely only on stories to support an argument, especially personal stories.

In the following example, author Bich Minh Nguyen writes about her experiences becoming "the good immigrant student." In this essay, she uses narration to capture the tension she felt between wishing to fit in and wanting to rebel as well as to document the racist behavior she endured.

> More than once, I was given the assignment of writing a report about my family history. I loathed this task, for I was dreadfully aware that my history could not be faked: it already showed on my face. When my turn came to read out loud the teacher had to ask me several times to speak louder. Some kids, a few of them older, in different classes, took to pressing back the corners of their eyes with the heels of their palms while they chanted, "Ching-chong, ching-chong!" during recess. This continued until Anh [Nguyen's sister], who was far tougher than me, threatened to beat them up.
>
> I have no way of telling what tortured me more: the actual snickers and remarks and watchfulness of my classmates, or my own imagination, conjuring disdain. My own sense of shame. At times I felt sickened by my obedience, my accumulation of gold stickers, my every effort to be invisible.   —BICH MINH NGUYEN, "The Good Immigrant Student"

Advertisements use narrative to appeal to viewers, as in this ad campaign for animal adoption. With three frames and eight words, the cartoon below tells a story to make an argument.

Narrative is often used to **OPEN** an argument. A good story can get an audience's attention and make them interested in the argument that follows. In arguing for the need to take global warming seriously by rethinking our dependence on fossil fuels, Naomi Klein opens with this narrative:

> A voice came over the intercom: would the passengers of Flight 3935, scheduled to depart Washington, D.C., for Charleston, South Carolina, kindly collect their carry-on luggage and get off the plane.
>
> They went down the stairs and gathered on the hot tarmac. There they saw something unusual: the wheels of the US Airways jet had sunk into the black pavement as if it were wet cement. The wheels were lodged so deep, in fact, that the truck that came to tow the plane away couldn't pry it loose. . . . Someone posted a picture: "Why is my flight cancelled? Because DC is so damn hot that our plane sank 4 inches into the pavement." —NAOMI KLEIN, *Capitalism vs. the Climate*

Problem / Solution

Most **PROPOSALS** articulate a problem and then offer a solution that addresses that problem. The following passage from a National Institutes of Health press release sets out a clear problem (drinking among college students) and identifies three elements that must be addressed in any solution:

> The consequences of college drinking are larger and more destructive than commonly realized, according to a new study supported by the National Institute on Alcohol Abuse and Alcoholism (NIAAA). Commissioned by the NIAAA Task Force on College Drinking, the study reveals that drinking by college students age 18–24 contributes to an estimated 1,400 student deaths, 500,000 injuries, and 70,000 cases of sexual assault or date rape each year. It also estimates that more than one-fourth of college students that age have driven in the past year while under the influence of alcohol. . . .
>
> "Prevention strategies must simultaneously target three constituencies: the student population as a whole; the college and its surrounding environment; and the individual at-risk or alcohol-dependent drinker," says [task force co-chair Dr. Mark] Goldman. "Research strongly supports strategies that target each of these factors."
>
> —"College Drinking Hazardous to Campus Communities: Task Force Calls for Research-Based Prevention Programs"

Children in sub-Saharan Africa who have lost parents to AIDS.

Often writers open with a statement of the problem, as Rhoi Wangila and Chinua Akukwe do in their article on HIV and AIDS in sub-Saharan Africa:

> Simply stated, Africans living with H.I.V./AIDS and the millions of others at high risk of contracting H.I.V. are not benefiting significantly from current domestic, regional, and international high profile remedial efforts.
>
> —RHOI WANGILA AND CHINUA AKUKWE,
> "H.I.V. and AIDS in Africa: Ten Lessons from the Field"

Wangila and Akukwe's article includes a photograph of African children affected by AIDS, which enhances their statement of the problem. The remainder of their essay then tackles the staggering complexities involved in responding to this problem.

Infographics are often used to present problems and solutions. Here's the final panel of an infographic that Chloe Colberg created about saving rhinos from illegal poaching. It identifies three ways of helping solve the problem: "get informed," "spread the word," and "support a campaign." The same information could be communicated in a paragraph or a bulleted list, but the large bold type makes the message much more visible.

What can you do to make a difference?
There are a number of different ways to get involved.

GET INFORMED	SPREAD THE WORD	SUPPORT A CAMPAIGN
Continue to educate yourself on this issue. Visit the WWF website to learn more specifics and details about the rhino crisis.	The more people that know about this issue, the better! Let your colleagues, friends and families know about this serious problem.	Support the WWF and other organizations' campaigns by learning about their efforts and considering a financial contribution.

SOURCES:
http://www.bbc.co.uk/news/uk-england-11477508
http://www.cites.org/eng/news/pr/2013/20131106_forensics.php
http://www.savetherhino.org/rhino_info/poaching_statistics
http://www.savetherhino.org/rhino_info/thorny_issues/
http://www.worldwildlife.org/species/rhino

DESIGNED FOR:
World Wildlife Fund
Chloe Colberg
December 2013

Reiteration

A form of repetition, reiteration helps support an argument through empha-sis: like a drumbeat, the repetition of a keyword, phrase, image, or theme can help drive home a point, often in very memorable ways. Reiterating is especially powerful in presentations and other spoken texts—think "Yes, we can!" and Sojourner Truth's "Ain't I a Woman?" Martin Luther King Jr. was a master of effective repetition, as is evident in the famous speech he deliv-ered on the steps of the Lincoln Memorial in 1963. Just think for a moment what would be lost in this speech without the power of that repeated phrase, "I have a dream."

> I have a dream that one day this nation will rise up and live out the true meaning of its creed: "We hold these truths to be self-evident, that all men are created equal." I have a dream that one day on the red hills of Georgia, the sons of former slaves and the sons of former slave owners will be able to sit down together at the table of brotherhood. I have

a dream that one day even the state of Mississippi, a state sweltering with the heat of injustice, sweltering with the heat of oppression, will be transformed into an oasis of freedom and justice. I have a dream that my four little children will one day live in a nation where they will not be judged by the color of their skin but by the content of their character.

I have a dream today!

I have a dream that one day, down in Alabama, with its vicious racists, with its governor having his lips dripping with the words of "interposition" and "nullification"—one day right there in Alabama little black boys and black girls will be able to join hands with little white boys and white girls as sisters and brothers.

I have a *dream* today!

I have a dream that one day every valley shall be exalted, and every hill and mountain shall be made low, the rough places will be made plain, and the crooked places will be made straight; "and the glory of the Lord shall be revealed and all flesh shall see it together."

This is our hope, and this is the faith that I go back to the South with.

—MARTIN LUTHER KING JR., "I Have a Dream"

Reiteration also works in visual texts and is a hallmark of graphic novelist Marjane Satrapi's work. Born and raised in Iran before being sent abroad in 1984 to escape what became the country's Islamic revolution, Satrapi recounts her childhood in *Persepolis I*, arguing implicitly that repressive regimes squelch individuality. In the frame shown here, Satrapi depicts a class of female students, using reiteration to make her point: all these girls are dressed exactly the same.

Part of a frame from *Persepolis*.

A little reiteration can go a long way. In an article published in *Ebony* magazine about the future of Chicago, see how it drives an argument that Chicago is still a home of black innovation and creativity:

> [Chicago]'s the place where organized Black history was born, where gospel music was born, where jazz and the blues were reborn, where the Beatles and the Rolling Stones went up to the mountaintop to get the new musical commandments from Chuck Berry and the rock 'n' roll apostles.   —LERONE BENNETT JR., "Blacks in Chicago"

Here the reiteration of "where" and the parallel clauses help establish a rhythm of forward movement that drives the argument.

⟁ *REFLECT. Choose an example in this chapter that's all words. Think about whether the same argument could be made visually—in a chart, with a photo and caption, and so on. If that doesn't seem possible, how might you illustrate the example?*

PART VI

Research

RESEARCH IS AN EVERYDAY MATTER. You gather information from reliable sources all the time to help you make decisions, support arguments, solve problems, become more informed, and for a host of other reasons. Filling out a March Madness basketball bracket? You probably review team records, player profiles, and statistics to help decide which teams you think will win. Going out for dinner and a movie? You probably look up reviews on *Yelp* and the *Internet Movie Database* before deciding where to go. Need directions to the theater? Arguing that this film is better and more critically acclaimed than another? In each case you'd probably do some research—to know what route to take, to locate information, to support an argument. Research helps you do all those things, and you do them all the time.

When you do research, you engage in a process of inquiry: that is, you are guided by questions for which you want answers. You might use a variety of methods—fieldwork, lab experiments, *Google* searches; and you'll find information in a variety of sources—books, articles, news reports, databases, websites, letters, photographs, historical records. However you approach it, research is more than simply a matter of compiling information; the most meaningful research is a process of discovery and learning.

As a student, you'll engage in research in many of the courses you take and in a variety of disciplines. Research is likely to be part of your work life as well. People working in business, government, and industry all need to follow research in order to make important decisions and keep up with new developments in their fields. Restaurant owners need to do research, for instance, to discover how to maximize profits from menu options and portion sizes. Engineers constantly do research to find equipment and suppliers. When a group of US senators argued for a federal ban on texting while driving, they cited research from a Virginia Tech study as evidence showing the dangers of allowing distracted drivers on the road.

Artists too rely on research for inspiration and also to gather information and materials to use in their artwork. As photographer Laurie Simmons said, "Artists are always doing research on their own behalf and for their work. For some artists, it's reading. For some, it's shopping. For some, it's traveling. And I think that there's always this kind of seeking quality that artists have where they're looking for things that will jog them and move them in one direction or another."

When you do academic research, you'll likely be studying a topic that scholars before you have examined. You'll want to start by learning what has been written about your topic and then thinking carefully about questions you want to pursue. In this way, you'll be engaging with the ideas of others and participating in discussions about topics that matter—and adding your own insights and discoveries. You'll be joining the larger academic conversation. The following chapters can help you do so.

REFLECT. Think about questions you've had in the past few weeks that have led you to do research to find an answer. List the different kinds of information you've sought and the ways you went about finding it. How did you then use the information or data that you gathered?

TWENTY

Starting Your Research

Joining the Conversation

 **HAT DO YOU FIND MOST DIFFCULT** about doing research? Gathering data? Writing it up? Documenting sources? For most students, the hardest part is just getting started. Researchers from Project Information Literacy, a nonprofit research institute conducting ongoing national studies of college learning practices in the digital age, report that US students doing course-related research have the most difficulty with three things: getting started, defining a topic, and narrowing a topic. This chapter will help you tackle these tricky first steps, identify specific questions that will drive your research, and make a schedule to manage the many tasks involved in a research project.

At the same time, we aim to show you that doing research means more than just finding sources. College-level research is a discovery process: it's as much about the search for knowledge and answers as it is about managing sources. When we search, we go down expected and unexpected paths to answer interesting questions, to discover solutions to problems, and to come to new perspectives on old issues. Doing research means learning about something you want to know more about. It means finding out what's been said about that topic, listening to the variety of perspectives (including those that differ from your own)—and then adding your own ideas to that larger conversation when you write about that topic.

While this chapter suggests a sequence of activities for doing research, from finding a topic to coming up with a research question to establishing a schedule, keep in mind that you won't necessarily move through these stages in a fixed order. As you learn more about your topic, you may want to reexamine or change your focus. But first, you have to get started.

Find a Topic That Fascinates You

At its best, research begins as a kind of treasure hunt, an opportunity for you to investigate a subject that you care or wonder about. So finding that topic might be the single most important part of the process.

If you've been assigned a topic, study the instructions carefully so that you understand exactly what you are required to do. Does the assignment give you a list of specific topics to choose from or a general topic or theme to address? Does it specify the research methods? number and kinds of sources? a GENRE in which to write up your findings? Even if you've been assigned a particular topic and told how to go about researching it, you'll still need to decide what aspect of the topic you'll focus on. Consider the following assignment:

> Identify a current language issue that's being discussed and debated nationally or in your local community. Learn as much as you can about this issue by consulting reliable print and online sources. You may also want to interview experts on the issue. Then write a 5- to 7-page informative essay following MLA documentation style. And remember, your task is to report on the issue, not to pick one side over others.

This assignment identifies a genre (a report), research methods (interviews and published sources), a documentation style (MLA), and a general topic (a current language issue), but it leaves the specific issue up to the author. You might investigate how your local school district handles bilingual education for immigrants, for example, or you could research the debate about how texting and social media affect writing habits.

While this particular assignment is broad enough to allow you to choose a particular issue that interests you, even assignments that are more specific can be approached in a way that will make them interesting to you.

Is there some aspect of the topic related to your major that you'd like to look into? For example, a political science major might research court cases about the issue.

If you get to choose your topic, think of it as an opportunity to learn about something that intrigues you. Consider topics related to your major, or to personal or professional interests. Are you a hunter who is concerned about legislation that impacts gun rights in your hometown? Are you into binge-watching *Netflix* or *Hulu* shows, but frustrated by streaming services' restrictions and limitations so you want to learn why and how they operate? Maybe you're an environmentalist interested in your state's policies on fracking.

For ideas and inspiration, visit TED.com, a site devoted to "ideas worth spreading." While there, check out Steven Johnson's talk, "Where Good Ideas Come From."

In addition to finding a topic that interests you, try to pick one that has not been overdone. Chances are, if you're tired of hearing about an issue—and if you've heard the same things said repeatedly—it's not going to be a good topic to research. Instead, pick a topic that is still being debated: the fact that people are talking about it will ensure that it's something others care about as well.

Think about doing research as an invitation to explore a topic that really matters to you. If you're excited about your topic, that excitement will take you somewhere interesting and lead you to ideas that will in turn inform what you know and think.

Consider Your Rhetorical Situation

As you get started, think about your rhetorical situation, starting with the requirements of the assignment. You may not yet know your genre, and you surely won't know your stance, but thinking about those things now will help you when you're narrowing your topic and figuring out a research question.

- **AUDIENCE**. Who will be reading what you write? What expectations might they have, and what are they likely to know about your topic? What kinds of sources will they consider credible?

- **PURPOSE**. What do you hope to accomplish by doing this research? Are you trying to report on the topic? argue a position? analyze the causes of something? something else?

- **GENRE**. Have you been assigned to write in a particular genre? Will you **ARGUE A POSITION**? **NARRATE** a historical event? **ANALYZE** some kind of data? **REPORT** information? something else?

- **STANCE**. What is your attitude toward the topic—and toward your audience? How can you establish your authority with them, and how do you want them to see you? As a neutral researcher? an advocate for a cause? something else? Check your biases—is **CONFIRMATION** or **ATTRIBUTION BIAS** keeping you from considering all sides fairly?

- **CONTEXT**. Does the assignment have any length requirements? When is the due date? What other research has been done on your topic, and how does that affect the direction your research takes?

- **MEDIA**. Are you required to use a certain medium? If not, what media will be most appropriate for your audience, your topic, and what you have to say about it? Will you want or need to include links to other information? audio? video?

- **DESIGN**. Will you include photographs or other illustrations? present any data in charts or graphs? highlight any parts of the text? use headings or lists? Are you working in a discipline with specific format requirements?

Don't worry if you can't answer all of these questions at this point or if some elements change along the way. Just remember to keep these questions in mind as you work.

Narrow Your Topic

A good academic research topic needs to be substantive enough that you can find adequate information but not so broad that you become overwhelmed by the number of sources you find. The topic "women in sports," for example, is too general; a quick search on *Google* will display hundreds of subtopics, from "Title IX" to "women's sports injuries." One way to find an aspect of a topic that interests you is to scan the subtopics listed in online search results. Additionally, online news sites like *Google News* and *NPR Research News* can give you a sense of current conversations related to your topic. Your goal is to move from a too-general topic to a manageable one, as shown on the facing page:

General topic: women in sports

Narrower topic: injuries among women athletes

Still narrower: injuries among women basketball players

Even narrower: patterns of injuries among collegiate women basketball players compared with their male counterparts

Notice how the movement from a broad topic to one with a much narrower focus makes the number of sources you will consult more manageable. But just as a topic that is too broad will yield an overwhelming number of sources, one that is too narrow will yield too little information. The topic "shin splints among women basketball players at the University of Tennessee," for example, is so narrow that there is probably not enough information available.

Another way of narrowing a topic is to think about what you already know. Have you had any experiences related to your topic? read about it? heard about it? talked with friends about it? Suppose you have been asked to investigate a current health debate for a public health class. You think of the US opioid crisis that's affected families in your hometown. Maybe you've seen news stories in which doctors explained the positive pain management provided by opioids but caution about the addiction potential, while law enforcement officials and the families of people who suffer from addiction attest to the human cost. These are all things that can help you to narrow a topic.

Whatever your topic, write down what you know about it and what you think. Do some **BRAINSTORMING** or some of the other activities for **GENERATING IDEAS**. And if it's an issue that's being debated, you could search online to find out what's being said—just be sure to analyze what you find to ensure it's not **MISINFORMATION**. Exploring your topic in this way can give you an overview of the issue and help you find a focus that you'd like to pursue.

REFLECT. Review your research assignment. Make a list of three topics that you're considering and jot down what you already know about each. Review those notes. What do they suggest to you about your interest in these topics? Finally, narrow each one to a specific, manageable research topic. Which of the three now seems most promising?

Do Some Background Research

Becoming familiar with some existing research on your topic can provide valuable background information and give you an overview of the topic before you dive into more specialized sources. It can also help you discover issues that have not been researched—or perhaps even identified. At this point, your goal should be to see your topic in a larger context and to begin formulating questions to guide the rest of your research.

You may want to take a look at some encyclopedias, almanacs, and other REFERENCE WORKS, which can provide an overview of your topic and point you toward specific areas where you might want to follow up. Subject-specific encyclopedias provide more detail, including information about scholarly books to check out.

If you don't have access to a university library, see what information you can find online. Though free online encyclopedias such as *Wikipedia* may not be considered appropriate to cite as authoritative sources, such sites can be helpful in the early stages of research because they link to additional sources and will often summarize any controversies around a topic.

Finally, you might begin your background research by reading articles in popular newsmagazines or newspapers to get a sense of who's talking about the topic and what they're saying.

Articulate a Question Your Research Will Answer

Once you have sufficiently narrowed your topic, you will need to turn it into a question that will guide your research. Start by asking yourself what you'd like to know about your topic. A good research question should be simple and focused, but require more than a "yes" or "no" answer. "Yes" or "no" questions are not likely to lead you anywhere—and often obscure the complexity of an issue. Instead, ask an open-ended question that will lead you to gather more information and explore multiple perspectives on your topic. For example:

Topic: injuries among women soccer players

What you'd like to know: What are the current trends in injuries among women soccer players, and how are athletic trainers responding?

Kansas defender Stacy Leeper is tended to after suffering a game-ending injury.

This is a question that's focused, complex, and meaningful. Before settling on a research question, you should consider why the answer to that question matters. Why is it worth looking into and writing about? And why will others want to read about it? Answering the above question, for instance, can help athletic trainers see if their approach can be improved.

Keep your rhetorical **CONTEXT** in mind as you work to be sure your research question is manageable in the time you have and narrow or open enough to address in the number of pages you plan to write. Consider also any **GENRE** requirements. If you're assigned to argue a position, for example, be sure your research question is one that will lead to an argument. Notice how each question below suggests a different genre:

A question that would lead to a **REPORT**: What are the current trends in injuries among women soccer players?

A question that would lead to an ANALYSIS : Why do women soccer players suffer specific types of injuries during training?

A question that would lead to an ARGUMENT : At what age should young girls interested in soccer begin serious athletic training to minimize the chance of injury?

Once you've settled on a research question, your next step is to do some more research. Keeping your question in mind will help you stay focused. Your goal at this point is to look for possible answers to your question—to get a sense of the various perspectives on the issue and to start thinking about where you yourself stand.

REFLECT. Write a research question for your narrowed topic that would lead to a report, one that would lead to an analysis, and one that would lead to an argument. Remember, try to avoid "yes" or "no" questions.

Plot Out a Working Thesis

Once you've determined your research question and gathered more information, you should begin to think about what answers are emerging—in sources you consult and in your own mind. When you think you've found the best possible answer, the next step is to turn it into a working thesis. Basically, a working thesis is your hypothesis, your best guess about the claim you will make based on your research thus far.

Your working thesis will not necessarily be your final thesis. As you conduct more research, you may find more support for it or new information that prompts you to rethink your position. Consider one working thesis on the question about why women soccer players experience so many injuries during training:

Female soccer players sustain more injuries than their male counterparts during training because they use training methods that were developed for men; developing training methods to suit female physiology would reduce the incidence of injuries.

This working thesis makes a clear, arguable claim and provides reasons for that position.

Keep in mind that your working thesis may well change as you learn more about your topic; stay flexible—and expect to revise it as your ideas develop. The more open your mind, the more you'll learn.

Establish a Schedule

A research project can seem daunting if you think of it as one big undertaking, rather than as a series of gradual tasks. Establishing a schedule will help you break your research into manageable steps, stay organized, and focus on the task at hand. The following template can help you make a plan:

Working title:

Working thesis:

	Due date
Choose a topic.	_____
Analyze your rhetorical situation.	_____
Do some preliminary research.	_____
Narrow your topic and decide on a research question.	_____
Plot out a working thesis.	_____
Do library and web research.	_____
Start a working bibliography.	_____
Turn in your research proposal and annotated bibliography.	_____
Plan and schedule any field research.	_____
Do any field research.	_____
Draft a thesis statement.	_____
Write out a draft.	_____
Get response.	_____
Do additional research, if needed.	_____
Revise.	_____
Prepare your list of works cited.	_____
Edit.	_____
Write your final draft.	_____
Proofread.	_____
Turn in the final draft.	_____

TWENTY-ONE

Finding Sources
Online, at the Library, in the Field

IF YOU'VE SEEN *The Amazing Race*, a reality show that sends teams of contestants to overcome challenges as they race around the world, then you know what has kept it winning Emmys for more than a decade. Each season, we see the teams learning about cultural traditions in small Italian villages, famous art in German museums, and social practices in little-known regions of the world—all during their wild race to the finish line.

What we don't see is the research on those locations and cultures conducted by the 2,000 crew members who explore potential sites, interview residents and town officials, read histories, pore over maps, and seek information from as many sources as they can before sending the contestants out on their quests.

Like the *Amazing Race* crew, student researchers today have access to a vast number of resources. And with so much information out there, housed in libraries, archives, museums, and online, you too face the challenge of sifting through a lot of information to find the sources you're looking for. A daunting task, perhaps, but much like finding your way to an unfamiliar location, finding sources is a process of exploration that will lead to new discoveries.

Luckily, you have access to a number of resources to ease the journey.

This chapter will teach you how to use these resources, from library catalogs and reference works to online search engines and social media as research tools. The following sections introduce you to different types of sources by explaining what's out there, where to find it, how to access it, and how to use it. Finally, this chapter teaches methods of conducting field research firsthand, for examining uncharted territory.

Starting with *Wikipedia* or Social Media

You've probably been told you must use reliable sources, and you may have been steered away from *Wikipedia* or *Google*. But today, these and other casual sources like *YouTube* can offer good starting points for your research. Indeed, you might even begin with social media. Of course, whenever you use online sources like these, it's crucial to read defensively—checking out the information you find to be sure it's trustworthy.

One student we know saw a *YouTube* review of a video game developed by Native Alaskans. Curious, she googled the game and found links to information about its origins and artwork, along with a statement about the purpose of the project: "We want to take back our culture out of the museum . . . to share who we are with the world." This statement got our student thinking about how Native Alaskans were representing their own culture in this game compared to how museums were representing it in exhibitions. So she searched the internet for more information about the game, visited her campus library for books and articles on Native Alaskan culture, and perused museum websites to investigate their presentation of it. She checked out her sources along the way, especially those turned up by *Google* searches. A *YouTube* video led this student all the way to the Smithsonian! That's how research often develops: curiosity and the questions that grow out of it lead to valuable and relevant sources.

As this example also demonstrates, the questions that emerge as you examine sources will determine the kinds of information you will seek out. Do you need to learn the history of a group of people or an event? Do you need to research different perspectives on an issue? Do you need statistical data? personal narratives? Once you've determined the types of information that will best address your questions, you will need to figure out where to find this information—what sources you will need to locate or what studies you will need to conduct.

WHAT KIND OF SOURCES DO YOU NEED?

The decisions you make about what types of sources you seek, where you look for them, and how authoritative you need them to be will be guided not only by the requirements of your assignment, but also by your **PURPOSE**, **AUDIENCE**, and other elements of the **RHETORICAL SITUATION**. For the research you do in college, an important part of that rhetorical situation may be the discipline you are working in; for example, scientists tend to value research done through observation and experimentation whereas historians tend to value research done in libraries and archives.

You may not always be able to anticipate who will read your writing, especially if you're posting online, but you can analyze other aspects of your rhetorical situation to determine what types of sources you'll need. For instance, if your purpose is to convince voters of a political candidate's honesty, what information will be most persuasive and where will you find it? If you're writing about this candidate for a website, what kinds of sources do other writers cite on that site? Who's the site's primary audience? Will you find what you need in the library, online, or will you need to go out and talk to voters? Or will you need to use a variety of sources?

For academic research, you'll also want to keep several other distinctions in mind: the differences between primary and secondary sources, scholarly and popular sources, and older and more current sources.

Primary and secondary sources. Primary sources are original documents or materials, firsthand accounts, or field research like interviews or observations. Secondary sources are texts that analyze and interpret primary sources; they offer background and context that can help you gain perspective on your topic. Secondary sources on a subject might include scholarly books and journal articles about the topic, magazine and newspaper reviews, government research reports, or annotated bibliographies. The student who researched the video game that drew on Native Alaskan culture conducted primary research when she analyzed the game itself and secondary research when she turned to articles about the game's development and books about the politics surrounding the representation of Native Alaskans.

Whether a particular source is considered primary or secondary often depends on what the topic is. If you are analyzing an artistic work, say a film, then the film itself is a primary source, while A. O. Scott's review of the

Research sources vary by topic and discipline: interviews, observations (both in the outdoors and in the lab), library databases and printed resources, and archives can all prove valuable to your research project.

film is a secondary source. But if you are researching Scott's work as a critic, then his review would be a primary source.

Scholarly and popular sources. For most academic assignments, you'll want to consult scholarly sources: articles, books, conference papers, and websites written by authorities in a given field. Such sources have usually been peer-reviewed, evaluated by experts in the field before publication. Because they are written for a knowledgeable audience, scholarly texts go into more depth than popular sources do, citing research and including detailed documentation.

Popular sources, by contrast, are written by journalists and writers for a general audience. They may be fact-checked, but they are not likely to be evaluated by experts before publication. Popular magazine articles and websites can play an important role at the start of a research project. Popular magazines can be a good source of information on current issues since they're published so frequently. Like scholarly sources, they often cite research, but rarely do they document those citations. Make sure that any such sources you use serve your subject and purpose. If, for instance, you're writing about fashion, *Vogue* might be a useful source—but its brief reviews of new books would not be appropriate sources in a literary analysis.

DETERMINING IF A SOURCE IS SCHOLARLY

- *What are the author's credentials* to write on the topic? Look authors up to confirm they are who they say they are.

- *Who's the publisher or sponsor?* Look for academic presses, professional or academic organizations, or government sources. And see what others say about the source to ensure it's legitimate.

- *What's the URL,* if it's an online source? Colleges and universities use *edu,* and government agencies use *gov.*

- *Does the source include original research* or interpret research by others that it cites?

- *Does it provide documentation?* Look for a list of works cited or references at the end and parenthetical documentation within the text. Check out a few cited sources to see that they're reputable.

- *Does the text seem authoritative?* Most scholarly texts use FORMAL language and provide evidence that shows the author can be trusted.

- *Does the text look academic?* Scholarly texts tend to use conservative fonts and often include tables and charts. Popular texts are more likely to include color photos and to highlight certain things in sidebars.

- *Are there ads?* Scholarly texts have few, if any, ads; popular articles and sites have many ads.

Considering these questions can help you distinguish between sources such as the two on the following page, one from the popular magazine *National Geographic*, the other from the scholarly *American Journal of Human Genetics*. While both sources address the legacy of Genghis Khan, note the differences in focus and design. Famous for its photographs, *National Geographic* displays on its cover a striking image of the Khan's face; the article's first pages feature large and colorful photographs, and the typography and layout include some decorative elements. The visuals attract readers' attention. In contrast, the journal's cover includes only its name (which tells us it's a *journal*) and publication information and a picture of a former president of the American Society of Human Genetics. The article looks like serious scholarship; the first page includes its genre (report), its title ("The Genetic Legacy of the Mongols"), the authors' names and credentials, and an abstract.

While the questions above can help you judge whether a source is scholarly and appropriate for your research project, keep in mind that some sources are designed to look, act, and feel scholarly, but aren't. You'll need to be vigilant about checking out all the sources you consult—even those that seem scholarly—to ensure you aren't relying on MISINFORMATION. For example, some predatory publishers pose as legitimate even while they publish anything someone pays to have published—without conducting any peer review. These predatory journals have names, websites, and published works that look and seem scholarly. READING DEFENSIVELY by checking out what others say about the source will help you steer clear of these unreliable sources.

Older and more current sources. You will need to determine whether older or more current sources are most appropriate for your topic, purpose, and

Popular source

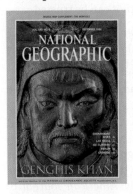
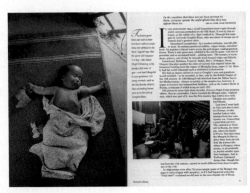

Scholarly source

Report

The Genetic Legacy of the Mongols

Tatiana Zerjal,[1] Yali Xue,[1,2] Giorgio Bertorelle,[3] R. Spencer Wells,[1] Weidong Bao,[1,5] Suling Zhu,[1] Raheel Qamar,[1,6] Qasim Ayub,[1] Aisha Mohyuddin,[6] Songbin Fu,[5] Pu Li,[5] Nadira Yuldasheva,[1] Ruslan Ruzibakiev,[7] Jiujin Xu,[8] Qunfang Shu,[8] Ruofu Du,[8] Huanming Yang,[8] Matthew E. Hurles,[1,4] Elizabeth Robinson,[1,4] Tudevdagva Gerelsaikhan,[9] Bumbein Dashnyam,[9] S. Qasim Mehdi,[6] and Chris Tyler-Smith[1]

[1]Department of Biochemistry, University of Oxford, Oxford; [2]Department of Medical Biology, Harbin Medical University, Harbin, China; [3]Dipartimento di Biologia, Università di Ferrara, Ferrara, Italy; [4]Wellcome Trust Centre for Human Genetics, University of Oxford, Headington, United Kingdom; [5]Institute of Genetics, Chinese Academy of Sciences, Beijing; [6]Biomedical and Genetic Engineering Labs, Islamabad; [7]Institute of Immunology, Academy of Sciences, Tashkent, Uzbekistan; [8]McGonald Institute, University of Cambridge, Cambridge, United Kingdom; and [9]Institute of Biotechnology, Mongolian Academy of Sciences, Ulaanbaatar, Mongolia

We have identified a Y-chromosomal lineage with several unusual features. It was found in 16 populations throughout a large region of Asia, stretching from the Pacific to the Caspian Sea, and was present at high frequency: ~8% of the men in this region carry it, and it thus makes up ~0.5% of the world total. The pattern of variation within the lineage suggested that it originated in Mongolia ~1,000 years ago. Such a rapid spread cannot have occurred by chance; it must have been a result of selection. The lineage is carried by likely male-line descendants of Genghis Khan, and we therefore propose that it has spread by a novel form of social selection resulting from their behavior.

The patterns of variation found in human DNA are usually considered to result from a balance between neutral processes and natural selection. Among the former, mutation, recombination, and migration increase variation, whereas genetic drift decreases it. Natural selection can act to remove deleterious variants (purifying selection), maintain polymorphism (balancing selection), or produce a trend (directional selection). Clear examples of the latter are rare in humans, but probable cases, such as those associated with resistance to malaria (Hamblin and Di Rienzo 2000) or unidentified pathogens (Stephens et al. 1998), can be recognized by the "signature" they leave in the genome. The rapid increase in frequency of the selected allele and its linked sequences results in a haplotype that is found at higher frequency than would be expected from its degree of variation. We have now

Received September 27, 2002; accepted for publication November 23, 2002; electronically published January 17, 2003.
Address for correspondence and reprints: Dr. Chris Tyler-Smith, Department of Biochemistry, University of Oxford, South Parks Road, Oxford OX1 3QU, UK. E-mail: chris@bioch.ox.ac.uk
* Present affiliations: Combinatorx, Boston
† Present affiliation: National Institute of Dental and Craniofacial Research, National Institutes of Health, Bethesda.

identified such a haplotype on the Y chromosome, but we suggest that its spread results not from a biological advantage, but from human activities recorded in history.

In surveys of DNA variation in Asia, we typed 2,123 men with >12 markers to produce a Y haplotype for each man; these included 1,116 individuals described elsewhere (Qamar et al. 2002; Zerjal et al. 2002). Over 90% of the haplotypes showed the usual pattern (Mohyuddin et al. 2001): most males had a unique code; and the few haplotypes present in more than one individual were generally found within the same population. However, we also saw some patterns that was novel in two respects. First, there was a high frequency of a cluster of closely related lineages, collectively called the "star cluster" (fig. 1, shaded area). Second, star-cluster chromosomes were found in 16 populations throughout a large geographical area extending from Central Asia to the Pacific (fig. 2); thus, they do not result from an event specific to any single population. We can deduce that the most likely time to the most recent common ancestor (TMRCA) and place of origin of this unusual lineage from the observed genetic variation. To do this, it is first necessary to distinguish star-cluster chromosomes from the remainder. For this, we used the criterion that haplotypes linked to the central one in the shaded area of the network without gaps would be included (fig. 1).

717

AJHG
Volume 97
Number 4
October 1, 2015
The American Journal of Human Genetics
www.ajhg.org

Maimon M. Cohen, Ph.D.
ASHG President, 1994

Published by Cell Press
for The American Society of Human Genetics

Cell PRESS

audience. Although you will always want to investigate the latest news and research about your topic, sometimes older works will serve as sources of essential information. Your research question and your discipline may dictate the balance between using older or more current sources. In scientific and technological fields, the most current scholarly sources are usually favored, since change is occurring so rapidly, while in history or literature, older sources that have stood the test of time may offer the best and most appropriate information.

Remember that your professors may expect—or require—certain kinds of sources. They may, for instance, want you to use only scholarly books and articles. Most projects, however, call for information drawn from many types of sources. For a report on the impact of recent floods on small local farms, for example, you may need to conduct primary research by interviewing local farmers affected; carry out secondary research online for news reports, photographs, and videos that document the floods; and use library sources to document flood conditions in the past.

TYPES OF SOURCES—AND WHERE TO FIND THEM

Reference Works

General reference sources include general encyclopedias (*Encyclopaedia Britannica, Columbia Encyclopedia*), dictionaries (*Merriam-Webster's, Oxford English Dictionary*), almanacs (*The World Almanac and Book of Facts*), and atlases (*The National Atlas of Canada*), among others. Besides brief overviews of your topic, such sources can be helpful for gathering background information, defining core concepts and terms, and understanding the larger context of your topic—or narrowing it if need be—as well as for getting leads to more specific sources. Your library may have print versions of some of these resources and online subscriptions to others. Still other dictionaries and encyclopedias, such as *Wikipedia*, are online only and free to access.

Specialized encyclopedias and wikis can give information that is more specifically related to your topic or discipline than general reference works. Through your library or the library website you'll find subject-specific resources ranging from the *Encyclopedia of Ethics* to the *Encyclopedia Latina* and many more. Specialized wikis put similar information online in groups of pages about health and medicine, or philosophy, or comic book superheroes of the Marvel universe. Wikis can connect you to information and communities online, but keep in mind that their open, collaborative authoring policy means that anyone can edit the information on a page.

So be sure to evaluate the source carefully and use the information only as a starting point.

Bibliographies, also called references or works cited, are lists of publications that appear at the end of books or scholarly articles and can lead you to further sources on a topic. If you've located a useful source, check its bibliography to find additional sources related to your topic. Your library may also have compiled longer, standalone bibliographies for popular or widely researched subjects; ask your librarian about availability. Many bibliographies also include descriptive annotations for sources that can help you determine if a source will be useful to you.

Books

If you're looking for a print book, the first place you think to go is probably the library. But before you venture into the library stacks, you'll want to search a topic or title in the library catalog, accessible through the library website, to see what your library has in its holdings and where a book you're looking for is physically located. The catalog can also tell you if a title is available as an ebook.

In addition to the thousands of print books available through your campus library, you can also access many books online. *Project Gutenberg* makes freely available over 57,000 ebooks and digitized texts that are in the public domain. *Google Books* also provides free digital access to books in the public domain, and it makes these texts searchable.

Rarely will an entire book be relevant to your specific topic, so you'll need to be selective. Reading the table of contents, skimming chapter headings and sections, and examining the list of keywords and topics in the book's catalog or database entry can tell you whether all or part of a book is relevant to your research.

Periodicals

Articles from newspapers, magazines, and scholarly journals are available online through news sites, academic search engines, journal websites, and open-access databases. In addition to these, many more articles may be available to you in your library in print or online or both, depending on the library and the periodical; you can locate such articles through indexes and databases to which the library subscribes. If you can't access an index electronically through your library, ask a reference librarian to help you locate the print version on the library shelves.

Journal articles can be found online through academic search engines such as *Google Scholar* and *JURN*, which yield results from electronic journals and works from academic publishers. *Google Scholar* tends to produce more results in the sciences than in the humanities, while *JURN* focuses on humanities and the arts. You may come across a site that offers an abstract but charges to unlock the full text. In such cases, see whether your library gives you access to the journal. Your campus library may also give you access to subscription-only articles that simply don't turn up on *Google Scholar* and *JURN*, which find a portion of the scholarly texts available online but can miss content held behind paywalls. For this reason, library databases are a good place to go when searching for articles from scholarly journals.

Magazine and news articles are available online through news organizations' websites that provide searchable access to current and archived articles, photos, podcasts, videos, and streaming broadcasts. Some sites, like that of the *New York Times*, provide only limited access or require subscriptions, but much is available for free online. News aggregators like *Google News* are also useful for searching news on specific subjects, turning up articles from a range of international or local news sources; often you can personalize such aggregators to track news on specific subjects.

For newspapers that do not archive their articles online, and for older or historical articles that have not been digitized, you can turn to your library's indexes and databases. To find articles published before 1980, you'll most likely need to search print indexes such as *The Readers' Guide to Periodical Literature*, *Magazine Index*, and *National Newspaper Index*. Like the index of this book, print indexes list articles by topic and point you to issues and pages where relevant articles can be found. Many databases also include newspaper as well as journal articles and might give you access to articles not openly available online. Remember to carefully scrutinize and evaluate news sources you encounter so that you aren't duped by FAKE NEWS or material that seems trustworthy but isn't based on facts.

Government and Legal Documents

Official reports, legislative records, laws, maps and photos, census data, and other information from federal, state, and local governments are available for free online. Check the websites of government departments and agencies for these resources; you can access such resources for the US government through *USA.gov*. The Library of Congress website provides a large archive of photographs, maps, and other US historical and cultural materials.

Primary and Historical Documents

Most university libraries include among their holdings rare and unique materials—books, photographs, fine art, cultural artifacts, maps, and other material—held in the library's archives or special collections. These materials are usually searchable through the library's main catalog, but because the items are often rare and hard, if not impossible, to replace, you'll need to contact your library for access.

Some libraries also house digital images of rare documents in online archives; this is one way of viewing documents held by another institution

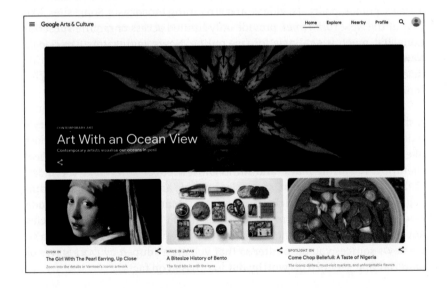

that you cannot access in person. Many museums, cultural institutions, and historical societies also make their holdings available for viewing through their own online archives—you can explore many rooms of the Smithsonian this way—or through open-access archives like *Google Arts and Culture*.

RESEARCH SITES:
ON THE INTERNET, IN THE LIBRARY

Many researchers turn to the internet first for answers to all sorts of questions, and understandably so; you can quickly and easily use it to locate an array of sources. Convenient and powerful the internet may be, but given the prevalence of false and misleading information, using this vast resource requires extra caution in order to verify the accuracy of what you uncover. At the same time, academic libraries still provide access to a wealth of reliable resources, from reference works to bibliographies to **PRIMARY SOURCES** and **SECONDARY SOURCES**. Most college libraries provide online access to electronic resources such as indexes, databases, and the library catalog remotely. The following sections introduce you to some tools for finding sources on the internet and in the library; knowing how to use these tools effectively will help you take advantage of all that these sites have to offer.

Search sites. You're likely already familiar with search engines like *Google* and *Bing*. These powerful tools help you locate information on general sites like *Wikipedia*, government information sites like the Library of Congress, and social media sites like *Twitter* or *Instagram*, as well as public sites for colleges and professional organizations. Through them, you can also access local, national, and international news sites, though some will require you to subscribe in order to access their materials. One drawback to reading information on public sites found from an internet search is that you'll often need to disregard distracting advertisements and pop-ups.

General search sites like these are a good starting point, but you can find more specialized sources on your topic by identifying which sites will be most relevant to your search. For academic searches, try *Google Scholar* or *JURN*. *Google Scholar* locates peer-reviewed articles, books, abstracts, and technical reports by searching the websites of academic publishers, professional societies, and universities. A variety of search sites are useful for specific types of searches, including those devoted to maps or image searches (*Google Maps, Flickr*), news aggregators (*Google News, NewsNow*), and so on.

As you use search terms to further your research, move from general concepts to more specific ones by configuring short, increasingly narrowed combinations of keywords. Most search sites also allow advanced searches that help you limit results by date, type of source, or other criteria; check the site's search tips for guidelines that are specific to the search engine you're using.

Keep in mind that some search sites allow websites to pay for higher placement or ranking in search results, which means that what comes up first in a search may not be the most useful or relevant to your topic. And we know that many search engines collect information on us each time we search, which impacts what we see in future searches. So don't take search results at face value—go beyond the first few results and see what multiple search engines produce, not just one. You can also seek out search engines that don't track users, like *DuckDuckGo*.

Social media may be something you search unconsciously as you scroll through your personal feeds. Sites like *Twitter, Instagram, YouTube*, and *Facebook* are useful as "sources of sources," where you can connect with people who share your interests to find and share information and sources about those interests. *Twitter* especially has become a popular site for sharing information, following other people, and staying on top of the latest news and trends. Many journalists break big stories on *Twitter* before they reach official news sites. With so many prominent people tweeting, the site can also provide you with primary source material. By following experts in the field you're researching, you can find relevant quotes or introductions to a larger discussion.

Online forums, groups, and discussion lists can also connect you with people who share an interest or expertise in specific topics. Many forums and discussion lists archive past posts and threads that you can search to see if your topic has come up in the discussion before; you can also join current discussions and post questions or requests for information.

While social media let you see what others are reading and allow them to recommend sources you might otherwise miss, recent research tells us that people tend to follow like-minded individuals from similar social circles; that is, the view from your feed may not be truly representative of a larger reality. And we know that social media sites are where **FAKE NEWS** and **MISINFORMATION** spread most quickly. So be sure to evaluate every source: Is the person you are quoting actually an expert? Can you confirm the information in the tweet and follow it to a larger discussion? Have you checked sites like *Snopes* and *FactCheck.org* to be sure you aren't relying on something phony?

Libraries. College libraries are often large and spread across many wings, so it's a good idea to sign up to take a tour of yours. You'll learn the location of key materials and spaces, including the library stacks, special collections, computer rooms, computers designated for searching databases or the catalog, screening and other media rooms, study areas, meeting rooms, and so on. If there are no guided tours available, pick up a library map at the information desk and spend a little time exploring on your own.

Librarians are especially valuable resources. All college libraries are staffed with reference librarians whose major responsibility is to help faculty and students with their research inquiries. While they will not do the research for you, reference librarians can be enormously helpful in showing you where you can find materials specific to your research question or topic and how you can search for them most efficiently. Their advice can save you considerable time and frustration.

In addition to reference librarians, many libraries have specialists in specific academic disciplines. Discipline (or subject) librarians work closely with academic departments to make sure that the relevant journals, databases, and books for that discipline are available to students and faculty.

Schedule a meeting with a reference or discipline librarian, and come to the meeting prepared to discuss your research question or topic. This is also your chance to ask about library resources available on your topic or any specific kinds of sources you're looking for.

Library websites. In addition to information about hours, location, and holdings, library websites often provide useful guides or tutorials to using the library. College libraries often provide online research guides that list databases, references, websites, organizations, and other discipline- or subject-specific resources. The image on the following page shows the homepage of the College of Southern Nevada library. Note the links that allow you to search in various ways and access specific services, including getting help from research librarians. In addition to multiple libraries on campus and special collections, many universities offer research guides

by discipline. If you're conducting research in a particular discipline, these guides can help you understand conventions and search for books, journals, and articles in that field.

Library catalogs. Most libraries have electronic catalogs that account for all their holdings. Searching the catalog is the best method for locating books and other materials, such as audio and video recordings, that you can access through the library. The record for each item includes the author, title, and publication information; a physical description of the item; and sometimes a summary or overview of the contents. The electronic catalog also provides a call number that tells you where the item is physically located in the library stacks (or a networked library), and whether or not it is currently available.

You can search a library catalog by author, title, series, subject, or keyword—or some combination of those in an advanced search. The image on the following page shows the initial search terms for a paper in an introduction to biology course. The student researcher, intrigued by the conflicting stories they had heard about the impact of caffeine on the human body, searched by selecting filters (subject terms include "caffeine," "effects," and "humans"), limited the type of source (articles only), selected a specific language (English), and specified a date range (the last 10 years).

These search criteria turned up 184 results in the College of Southern Nevada library catalog. All the results yielded peer-reviewed articles, so the student knows they can trust them. Analyzing the results reveals a variety of ways the researcher could narrow their focus. For example, several of the articles examine the effects of combining caffeine with energy drinks or

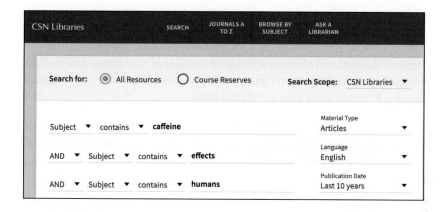

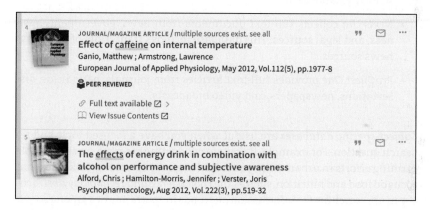

alcohol or high-calorie foods; others look at behavioral effects at a variety of consumption levels. The point is that doing the initial search of a library's full catalog, depending on your findings, can help you focus—or broaden—your scope and identify more specific databases that include works relevant to your topic.

Databases organize and provide access not only to listings (bibliographic citations) of journal and news articles but also, in many cases, to abstracts and full texts. A variety of open-access databases, such as the *Directory of Open Access Journals*, allow you to search research journals that are freely available online. Your library probably also has subscriptions to a number of databases that you can access through its website.

General databases that cover a range of disciplines and topics and include scholarly articles, popular magazines, and news stories may be a good place to start. Here are a few that are widely used:

- *Academic Search Complete* (EBSCO) includes the full text of many periodicals from the humanities, arts, and sciences—the majority of which are peer-reviewed—and provides abstracts for others.

- *JSTOR* makes available scanned copies of scholarly journals from many disciplines. It includes issues from further back in time than most other scholarly databases.

- *Nexis Uni* collects full-text documents from news, government, business, and legal sources. This database includes transcripts of broadcast news sources.

- *ProQuest One* provides full-text articles from journals, periodicals, dissertations, newspapers, and video broadcasts.

Subject-specific databases are useful when you have a focused topic and research question. For example, if you are conducting research on sustainable farming efforts in urban areas, you might begin by searching databases that focus on food and nutrition, such as the *Food Science and Technology Abstracts*. If you are searching for information on trends in sports injuries among soccer players, you might search a sports research database like *SPORTDiscus*. Below are some examples of subject-specific databases; ask a subject or reference librarian to direct you to those most relevant to your topic.

- *CAB Abstracts* provides bibliographic information, abstracts, and some limited full text for a range of agricultural sources including peer-reviewed journals, technical reports, and conference proceedings.

- *IEEE Xplore* provides access to full-text documents in computer science, electronics, and electrical engineering.

- *PsycINFO* provides indexes and abstracts for peer-reviewed sources in psychology and the behavioral sciences.

- *MLA International Bibliography* indexes scholarly books and articles on literature, languages, linguistics, and folklore from around the world.

- *ERIC* (Educational Resources Information Center) provides bibliographies for journal articles, books, and other materials related to education.

- *SocINDEX*, a sociology-specific research database provided by EBSCO, includes bibliographic records, a sociology-specific thesaurus, author profiles, indexing, and abstracts of journal articles.

RUNNING SEARCHES

Whether you're looking for sources online or in the library, the search typically starts with a website and an open search bar. Most academic libraries offer multiple options for searches available through the library's website. Remember to meet the reference/research librarians—they are an invaluable resource as you search for sources. The following sections cover some basic tips for using search sites, library catalogs, and electronic databases.

Keyword Searches

Keyword searches allow you to use words and phrases, including author names, titles, and descriptions, to locate sources—but keep in mind that you may need to adjust your keywords or use synonyms if your initial searches don't yield useful results. If searching for *women's sports injuries* doesn't yield much, try *female athlete injuries*. You may also need to try broader keywords (*women sports medicine*). If your search returns too many results, try narrowing your term (*women's sports injuries soccer*).

Following are some advanced search techniques that can help you focus your search. *Google* and many search sites provide their own advanced search options—allowing you to limit searches, for example, to items published only during a particular time period.

Quotation marks can be used around terms to search for an exact phrase, such as "International Monetary Fund" or "obesity in American high schools." Using quotation marks may exclude useful results, however—for example, searching for "factory farms" may omit results with "factory farming" in a library search.

Wildcard searches allow you to insert a special symbol (usually ? or *) in the middle or at the end of a word to retrieve multiple forms of that word. For example, typing in *wom?n* would retrieve both *woman* and *women*.

Truncation allows the symbols ? or * to stand in for one or more missing letters at the end of a word; for example, typing in *ethnograph** would retrieve *ethnography*, *ethnographic*, *ethnographer*, and so on.

Boolean operators (AND, OR, and NOT) let you refine your search by combining keywords in different ways to include or exclude certain terms. Using AND narrows a search to include all terms joined by AND; using OR broadens a search to include items with any of the terms joined by OR; and using NOT limits a search to exclude items with any term preceded by NOT. For example, if you're researching solar energy, typing in *alternative energy* will bring up many more options than *alternative energy AND solar*, which reduces the number to only those that include the term *solar*. Typing in *alternative energy NOT wind* narrows the search to results that exclude the term *wind*.

Parentheses allow you to combine Boolean searches in a more complex way. For example, a search for *alternative energy AND (solar OR wind)* yields only those items that contain both *alternative energy* and *solar* or both *alternative energy* and *wind*. *Alternative energy NOT (solar OR wind)* yields only items that contain *alternative energy* but do not contain either *solar* or *wind*; this kind of search might be useful, for example, if you are specifically researching forms of alternative energy other than solar or wind energy.

Plus and minus signs are used by some search sites instead of AND and NOT. Using a plus sign (+) in front of words and phrases indicates that those exact words must appear, so +*"alternative energy"* +*solar* will bring up results that include both terms. The minus sign (a hyphen) excludes results, so +*"alternative energy"* -*solar* brings up sources in which *alternative energy* is included but *solar* is not. Searching for +*"alternative energy"* -*solar* -*biofuel* excludes results with both *solar* and *biofuel*.

Author, Title, and Subject Searches

Most library catalogs and many databases are searchable by author, title, and subject as well as by keyword. Using the author and title fields allows you to go directly to a source when you know its title or author. Subject searches allow an overview of your library's holdings on a topic. To do an effective subject search, it helps to know what cataloging system the library uses—most commonly the Library of Congress Subject Headings (LCSH) or the National Library of Medicine's Medical Subject Headings (MeSH). Subject heading searches use what is called "left-hand truncation," which means that you can access a list of headings by entering the first term. These types of searches require terms that are specific to their lists. For example, if you're searching for material on the American Civil War, and you search for the subject *civil war*, you'll get a long list that begins with your term and branches to the right, like this:

Num	Mark	Subjects (1-50 of 870)	Year	Entries 10000 Found
1		Civil War -- See Also the narrower term <u>Insurgency</u>		1
2	☐	Civil War		41
3	☐	Civil War 43 31 B C Rome History		5
4	☐	Civil War 43 31 B C Rome History Drama		7
5	☐	Civil War 49 45 B C Rome History		12
6	☐	Civil War 49 45 B C Rome History Literature And The War		4
7	☐	Civil War 68 69 Rome History		2

These results are not on your topic. If you then go back to the subject search page and type in *American Civil War*, you'll get this suggestion:

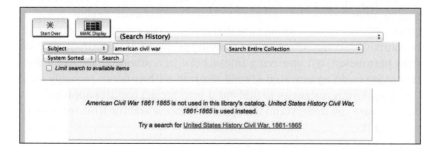

Once you know that the LCSH list uses "United States History Civil War 1861–1865" to begin subject headings on this topic, you'll be on the right track and will get the following search result:

Num	Mark	Subjects (1-50 of 432)	Year	Entries 10000 Found
1		United States History Civil War 1861 1865 -- 2 Related Subjects		2
2	☐	United States History Civil War 1861 1865		1079
3	☐	United States History Civil War 1861 1865 19th Century		3
4	☐	United States History Civil War 1861 1865 Abstracts Periodicals	1984 -	1
5	☐	United States History Civil War 1861 1865 Aerial Operations		2
6	☐	United States History Civil War 1861 1865 Aerial Operations Juvenile Fiction		2
7	☐	United States History Civil War 1861 1865 Aerial Operations Juvenile Literature : Jarrow, Gail.	2010	1

CONDUCTING FIELD RESEARCH

Journalists who interview eyewitnesses, researchers who spend months observing the behavior of a particular population, historians who gather oral histories, and pollsters who conduct surveys on the general public's attitudes about current government policies are all engaging in field research. Depending on your research question, you may need to go "into the field" to conduct research, using data-gathering methods that rely on firsthand accounts. The three most common discovery methods for field research are observation, interviews, and surveys or questionnaires.

Keep in mind that conducting field research on human subjects may require prior approval from your college's Institutional Review Board, a group responsible for making sure that a study will not harm research participants. Observing what kinds of clothing people wear to the mall may not need permission, but observing interactions in a private space like a doctor's office or doing any kind of field research with children probably will. Check with your instructor to find out if your project requires approval. If it does, be sure you understand the approval process and the time required to complete it.

Observations

Observation as a field research method calls for a lot more than casual "people watching." It involves taking careful notice of environments and behaviors, with a clear sense of your purpose and of how your observations will help you answer your research question. Many disciplines use observation to collect data about individuals and communities in order to answer questions about how and why they organize, relate to, or interact with one another and the world around them. In many cases, observation is the best and often the only means of gathering field data.

When reference librarian Linda Bedwell and graduate student Caitlin Banks wanted to find out how the study areas in Canada's Dalhousie University Library were being used, they observed students there, noting behaviors and paying attention to how they themselves used the spaces. Bedwell and Banks were conducting **PARTICIPANT OBSERVATION**, which operates on the principle that researchers can learn by doing as well as by watching. In non-participant observation, on the other hand, researchers focus on the actions of others but do not participate in the situations they're observing.

The process (and resulting information) will differ significantly depending on the type of observation, and you should choose the type most appropriate to the situation and for addressing your research topic and question. If you're studying the winning strategies of video gamers, you might choose to do participant observation if you're an expert gamer yourself and if playing the games would result in more insightful data. If you are researching careers in medicine and want to learn about the typical day of a nurse, participant observation would not be an option—unless you have the credentials, training, and legal standing to provide patient care.

Keep your research question clearly in mind when conducting observations and carefully record what you see. Following are some additional tips for conducting effective observations.

Ryan Kohls uses participant observation to report on the cleaning staff of a large stadium. Go to p. 947 to see how his employee status gave him access and a unique perspective.

- *Determine your purpose and method for observing.* Is participant observation the appropriate method to pursue your research question? Or do you need to focus only on the actions of others—and not to participate yourself? How do you expect to use the data?

- *Plan ahead.* Decide where you will observe and what materials you'll need—and make sure your equipment is ready and working. Determine whether you'll need permission to observe, photograph, and/or record; if so, secure appropriate permissions ahead of time. Keep in mind that it may not be appropriate to take photographs or record video in some sites—at a church service, for instance.

- *Record your observations.* Take detailed descriptive notes, even if you are also recording audio or video; your notes will add necessary texture. Note who is present, the activities they engage in, where they're situated, and pertinent details about the setting such as the physical design of the space. Be sure to record the date, time, and location. As you observe, focus on recording and describing; save the interpretation and analysis for later, when you review your notes and recordings.

- *Be guided by your purpose for observing,* but don't let that purpose restrain you. Be open to whatever you see. Sometimes in the process of looking for one thing, you may find something else that is equally interesting or important. And don't look only for extraordinary behavior. The goal of observation is generally to look for the routine and for patterns, things that are important because they happen regularly.

- *After your observation,* take a moment to flesh out what you've recorded with notes about any additional thoughts or reflections you have.

- *Review your observation notes* and any audio or videotapes, looking for patterns that emerge. Look for actions that recur, for topics that are repeatedly addressed, for individual participants who seem to play important roles. Also note when deviations from patterns occur and what seems to prompt the deviation. You should also consider whether those you observe have changed their behavior because they are being observed and, if so, how these changes may affect your data. You won't be able to correct for these effects, but you can consider and acknowledge them in your analysis. Your goal at this point is to start to analyze and look for an answer to your research question.

Interviews

You may find that the best way to answer your research question is to interview people who have a valuable perspective on your topic, such as experts, witnesses, or key participants in an event. Interviews can provide information that may not be available elsewhere; they can also complement other research and data-gathering methods, such as observations and library research. Just as with observations, you'll need to consider your purpose for conducting an interview and how the information you gain from it will speak to your research question.

You'll also need to decide who to interview. Will one interview provide the needed information, or will you need several? And how qualified are those you're considering to address your research question? As a veteran of the war in Afghanistan, a friend may not be the most credible source for a detailed analysis of the history of US involvement in the region; print sources may be a better starting place for that type of background information. But your friend or relative probably *would* be a valuable, reliable source for a firsthand account of the combat experience and could probably provide details that you would never get from a book.

In any case, remember to ask your interviewees for their written consent to the interview, especially if your work will be published online or elsewhere. Following are additional tips for conducting successful interviews.

- *Plan to conduct your interviews early in your research* in case you have to do follow-up interviews. Contact interviewees well before your research project is due to set up appointments.

- *Do some background research* on your topic before the interview so that you can ask informed questions.

- *Write out a list of questions* that you will ask in the interview. These questions should be directly related to your research. Avoid questions that are too general that lead to one-word answers like "yes" or "no." For example, don't ask, "Do you like music?" when you want specific details. Try asking "What kind of music do you like?" instead. Also avoid leading questions, ones that prompt answers that you want. The question "Don't you think his campaign tactics were dishonest?" allows the interviewee to disagree, but it still suggests a particular response. A better question would be "What is your opinion on the candidate's campaigning methods?" This question is specific enough to provide a focus yet open enough to let the interviewee answer freely.

- *Decide how you'll record the interview.* Will you rely solely on note taking, or will you combine it with audio or video recording? Remember to ask permission before you tape any part of an interview.

- *If your interview requires any electronic equipment,* test it before the interview to make sure that it is working. And have a back-up plan; there's nothing more frustrating than finding out that you've lost the data from a wonderful interview because batteries died.

- *Be polite.* Remember that the person you're interviewing is doing you a favor by agreeing to speak with you.

- *Record the date, time, and location* of every interview that you conduct, and write down contact information for the interviewee.

- *Send a thank-you note* to anyone you interview.

- *Check facts, dates, and other information* the interviewee provides, especially about anything controversial. If any of the information seems questionable, try to interview others who can corroborate it or provide another perspective.

Surveys and Questionnaires

You've probably been asked to participate in marketing surveys that review products or services, or maybe you've completed questionnaires for course evaluations. Such surveys and questionnaires can be useful in soliciting information from a large number of people. Most often they aren't meant to poll an entire population; rather, they usually target a *representative sample*, a selected subset of a group that accurately reflects the characteristics of the whole group. The most reliable way to select such a group is by *random sampling*. A true random sample is one in which every member of the target population has the same chance of being selected to participate. Say you want to survey the first-year students in your school. You could try to track down each one—not a problem in a tiny school, but what if there are 5,000? Not feasible. Or you could acquire a list of names from the registrar, assign each name a number (you can use Excel to assign random numbers), and then select a certain percentage of these people.

    Unlike interviews, most surveys or questionnaires do not solicit detailed information; generally, researchers use them to gauge trends and opinions on a rather narrow topic. Following are some tips for deciding when to use surveys and how to design and administer them.

Consider your PURPOSE. Will a survey be an effective way to collect the information you need to address your research question? If you are trying to find out how first-year medical residents negotiate the challenges of their demanding schedule, a survey is not likely to provide you with the level of detail you will need; interviews might be more effective. However, if you are researching how the residents account for their time in a typical day, a survey would likely be your best method.

Once you've decided that a survey is the practical way to proceed, think about how you will use the results. Will the results provide essential support for your argument or anecdotal details to make your discussion more interesting and concrete? These considerations will determine the number of people you survey and what sorts of questions you ask them.

Determine your sample. Unless you are only after anecdotal information, you should aim to survey a representative sample, a randomly selected subset of a group that reflects the characteristics of the whole group. If you want to discover your college community's level of satisfaction with campus dining services, for example, you'll need to solicit a sample that represents all those who use the services—students, faculty, administrative staff, and visitors—and also reflects the range of ages, genders, ethnicities, and so on. Including only students who eat breakfast in the dining halls on weekends is not likely to give you a viable sample. Most important, decide how many people you will contact; generally, the more of the target population you sample, the more reliably you will be able to claim that your results represent trends in that population.

Choose your distribution method. Will you administer the survey over the phone or face-to-face? send a written survey through email? Or will you use an online service like *Qualtrics*, *SurveyMonkey*, or *Google Forms*? Most universities provide access to one of these tools; check with the Office of Research on campus. And don't expect a 100 percent response rate. Researchers often distribute surveys multiple times to get as many people in their targeted population to respond as they can.

Write the questions and an introduction, and test the survey. Respondents tend not to complete long or complicated surveys, so the best surveys include only a few questions and are easy to understand. Sequence questions from simple to complex unless there is a good reason not to do so. Also decide what kinds of questions are most likely to yield the information you're after. Here are examples of four common kinds of survey questions: open-ended, multiple-choice, agreement scale, and rating scale.

Open-ended

What genre of books do you like to read?

Where is your favorite place to read?

Multiple-choice

Please select your favorite genre of book (check all that apply):
__ fiction __ autobiography __ self-help __ histories __ biography

Please indicate your favorite location for reading (check one):
__ coffee shop __ library __ home __ office __ other

Agreement scale

Indicate your level of agreement with the following statements:

	Strongly Agree	Agree	Strongly Disagree	Disagree
The library should provide both ebooks and print books.	☐	☐	☐	☐

Rating scale

How would you rate your campus library?
__ Excellent __ Good __ Fair __ Poor

Your questions should focus on specific topics related to your research question. For example, undergraduate researcher Steven Leone believed that solar energy provided by thin-film solar cells could be an alternative to fossil fuels as an energy source, but he knew many homeowners resist expensive solar installations. His project, "The Likelihood of Homeowners to Implement Thin-Film Solar Cells," was designed to discover the relationship between homeowners' socioeconomic status and their attitudes about alternative energy sources in order to gauge how likely they are to adopt this new technology. These are the questions he asked in a survey of homeowners. Notice that some call for short answers while others ask for detailed responses.

1. What is your combined annual household income?

2. What is the highest level of education you have completed?
   __ high school   __ some college   __ college   __ graduate school

3. How is your home currently heated?

4. How much are you currently spending each year on home energy costs?

5. Which is more important to you—saving money or going green? Why?

6. Have you considered using solar energy as your home energy source? Why or why not?

7. Thin-film solar cells cost significantly less than conventional solar instal- lations and offer an energy-cost payback that is twice as fast. How much more likely does this information make it that you will implement this technology?
   __ very likely   __ somewhat likely
   __ somewhat unlikely   __ very unlikely

8. Thin-film solar cells will increase the resale value of your home. How much more likely does this information make it that you will implement the technology?
   __ very likely   __ somewhat likely
   __ somewhat unlikely   __ very unlikely

Leone's questions provided him with data that he then analyzed to deter- mine patterns (education, income, lifestyle) of attitudes on his topic.

Once you're satisfied with your questions, write a brief introductory statement that will let participants know the purpose of the survey and what they can expect, including an estimate of how long it will take to complete.

Manage your results. When you are done collecting data, be sure to careful- ly record and store your responses. If you are using a print survey, one simple method is to use a blank survey and tally responses next to each question. You can also use a spreadsheet to track your findings. If your survey includes open-ended questions, you may want to choose some responses to quote from when you present your results.

ANALYZE your results. After you have tallied up the results, you need to analyze them, looking for patterns that reveal trends and explaining what those trends may mean. Data from survey results do not speak for themselves. You need to analyze the data by looking for similar responses to questions you've asked. Group those that are similar, and label them accordingly. What does that pattern or trend in responses indicate about your research question? When you move from describing the patterns and trends to discussing what they mean, you are interpreting your results. For example, suppose you survey 200 classmates about a recent increase in student fees for using the on-campus fitness center and find that the students, by a significant majority, think the fees are cost-prohibitive. Based on your survey results, your interpretation is that the fee increase is likely to lead to decreased use of the fitness center. You didn't just report the results; you interpreted them as well.

REFLECT on how well the survey worked. When you present your results, be sure to acknowledge any limitations of your survey. What topics were not covered? What populations were not surveyed? Was your sample truly representative?

Information today lives everywhere: in traditional libraries, on the internet, and out "in the field." Your research question and your rhetorical situation—including who will read your research—dictate what kinds of sources you consult and cite. But ultimately, research should be a voyage of discovery, driven by *your* questions based on *your* desire to find out something you didn't know before.

REFLECT. Now that you have thought more about your topic and questions, done some preliminary research, decided on methods, and located some sources, review the types of sources that you've consulted. How did each of those sources help you answer your research question? What other sources do you still need to consult?

TWENTY-TWO

Keeping Track

Managing Information Overload

RESEARCH HAS ALWAYS been a complex, often messy process, but in an age of information overload, it can spiral out of control. Where did you save those notes you took? Did that piece of information come from the book you read or somewhere online? Researchers today have so much information at their fingertips that just managing it has become tough. This chapter aims to help you organize potential chaos by offering tips for keeping track of your sources, taking notes, and maintaining a working bibliography.

Keep Track of Your Sources

The easiest way to keep track of your sources is to save a copy of each one. Especially when your research is spread out over several days or weeks, and when it turns up dozens of potential sources, don't rely on your memory.

Electronic sources. Download and save files, or print them out. Make copies of materials on the web, which can change or even disappear: print out what you might use, or take a screenshot and save the image. Some subscription database services let you save, email, or print citations and articles. You might also want to use one of the free online tools, like

Zotero or *Mendeley*, that allow you to organize, store, analyze, and share articles, images, and even audio/video files.

Once you've got copies of your sources, the challenge is to keep them all organized and easy to find. Store all the files for a single project together in one folder, and use a consistent file-naming system so each item is easy to identify. The following example uses the author's last name and keywords from the source's title. All of the sources are saved in a folder under the course title and assignment.

> ENG1102_ResearchProject
>   Ehrenreich_ServingFL
>   hooks_TouchingEarth
>   Kohls_CleanSweep
>   McMillanCottom_LogicOfPoor

You should note the author(s), title, URL, and date of access on each item—and record all the other information needed in a **WORKING BIBLIOGRAPHY**. And be sure to back up your files regularly.

Print sources. Make photocopies, printouts, or scans of everything you think will be useful to your research. Keep a copy of the title and copyright pages of books and of the table of contents or front page of periodicals. Label everything with the author(s), title, and page numbers, and file related materials together in a clearly marked folder.

Take Notes

We cannot stress enough the importance of taking notes systematically *as you go*. But this doesn't mean you should write down everything; carefully select what details you note to be sure they are pertinent to your project. **ANNOTATING** as you read sources will help you understand and synthesize important information.

Take notes in your own words, and be sure to enclose any words taken directly from a source in quotes. Label anything you **QUOTE**, **PARAPHRASE**, or **SUMMARIZE** as such so that you'll remember to acknowledge and document the original source if you use it—and so that you don't accidentally **PLAGIARIZE**. Consider this example:

Lyon, G. Reid. "Learning Disabilities." *The Future of Children: Special Education for Children with Disabilities*, vol. 6, no. 1, spring 1996, pp. 54–76. JSTOR, https://doi.org/10.2307/1602494.

Summary: Focuses on problems with reading skills but cautions that early intervention with reading won't address all manifestations of LD.

- Lyon is chief of Child Development and Behavior in the National Institute of Child Health and Human Development at the NIH.
- LD is several overlapping disorders related to reading, language, and math (paraphrase, p. 54).
- Lyon: "[L]earning disability is not a single disorder, but is a general category of special education composed of disabilities in any of seven specific areas: (1) receptive language (listening), (2) expressive language (speaking), (3) basic reading skills, (4) reading comprehension, (5) written expression, (6) mathematics calculation, and (7) mathematical reasoning" (direct quotation, p. 55).

Comment: Lyon breaks down LD into more precise categories. Defines each category. Will help me define LD.

Notice the specific information included in these notes—all details that will help the researcher later on if she decides to reference this article in her own writing: a full MLA-style citation, a brief summary of the article, and notes about how the source might relate to her research. And notice too that she's indicated when she's paraphrased and quoted from the text, with page numbers in each case. If she does end up citing this source in her own work, she'll already have all the documentation information she'll need.

Label notes with full citation information—the author(s) and title, publication information, page numbers, and DOI or URL.

SUMMARIZE the main point and any other important points you want to remember in a sentence or two. Be very careful to write your summary using your own words and sentence patterns.

If you copy any passages by hand, take care to do so accurately, paying attention to both words and punctuation and enclosing the entire passage in quotation marks. If you cut and paste any text from electronic sources, put quotation marks around it.

Record your own questions or reactions as you go. Do you see anything that addresses your research question? anything you want to know more about? Consider what role this source might play in your own writing. Does it provide evidence? represent perspectives show why the topic matters?

Maintain a Working Bibliography

It might seem easiest to keep track only of the sources that you know you will cite. But what if your research takes an interesting twist and you need to include some of the sources that you discarded earlier? Rather than having to stop and search for those earlier sources, you could access the source information right away if you keep a working bibliography—a list of all the sources that you consult.

Unlike a final works-cited or reference page, a working bibliography constantly changes as you find more sources to add to it. Keep it on a computer or individual note cards for easy updating. As you update, note for each source whether you have already used it, rejected it, or are still thinking about it. You may even want to annotate your working bibliography with a summary of each source. Eventually this information will become your list of works cited or references, so follow whatever DOCUMENTATION style you plan to use. See Chapters 28 and 29 for information on MLA and APA style.

Consider the working bibliography entries below:

Ellcessor, Elizabeth. *Restricted Access: Media, Disability,* and *the Politics of Participation.* NYU P, 2016.

> Drawing on multiple examples from participant observation in blogs and websites, Ellcessor exposes the myth of digital media accessibility to the disabled. Support for my central claim re: "participatory culture"?

Brueggemann, Brenda. Personal interview. 10 July 2019.

> Professor Brueggemann is one of the world's leading scholars in the field of disability studies. This interview focused on the growth of that field.

WHAT TO PUT IN YOUR WORKING BIBLIOGRAPHY

For books

- Author(s), editors, or translators
- Title
- Edition or volume number
- Publisher, year published

For periodicals

- Author(s)
- Title and subtitle of article
- Name of periodical
- Volume and issue numbers, date
- Page numbers
- URL and date accessed (for online sources)

Additional items for articles accessed via database

- Name of database
- DOI, if there is one, or URL if not

For web sources

- Author(s) and any editors
- Title and subtitle of source
- Name of site
- Date published, posted, or last updated
- Publisher or sponsor of site (if different from name or site)
- Page or paragraph numbers, if any
- URL
- Date accessed

REFLECT. Review your system for organizing and tracking your sources. Are your sources organized in a way that lets you go back to them easily? Have you recorded the necessary bibliographic information? If you answered "no," take the time now to set up a system that helps you keep track of your sources.

TWENTY-THREE

Evaluating Sources

 **OUR RESEARCH QUESTION:** Is it important to address the loss of sea ice in the Arctic? If so, what actions should be taken? To research this topic, rather than merely giving your opinion, you would need to consult reliable sources. Which do you trust more: official reports from the National Aeronautics and Space Administration (NASA), the *Wikipedia* page on the issue, or a post on the website *JunkScience.com*? Is it possible that they could all be useful? How will you know?

Your integrity as an author rests to some degree on the quality of the sources you cite, so your sources need to be appropriate and reliable. You can probably trust that an article or website recommended by a known expert on your topic is a credible source of information.

But in the absence of such advice, and given the overwhelming amount of information available—not to mention *mis*information, it can be difficult to know which sources will be useful, appropriate, and relevant. Or, as media expert Howard Rheingold puts it, the unending stream of information on the internet calls for some serious "crap detection": we have to know how to separate the credible sources from the questionable ones. This chapter provides advice for determining which sources are appropriate for your purposes and then for reviewing those sources with a critical eye.

Is the Source Worth Your Attention?

A database search turns up fifty articles on your topic. The library catalog shows hundreds. *Google?* Thousands. So how do you decide which sources are both reliable and worth your time and attention? Professional fact-checkers don't start to read a new source and judge its relevance until they've determined it's trustworthy—so the two processes should go hand-in-hand. Being a skeptical, defensive reader is never a bad idea, but it's most important when sifting through sources from an internet search. Sources you uncover in library catalogs or databases, on the other hand, are generally already vetted for credibility. Here are some questions to consider as you first scan your search results.

What's the title? Does it sound relevant to your topic? Does it sound serious? humorous? Is it too good to be true or extreme? Do the title and the content of the source match up? What does the title tell you about the source's purpose?

Who are the authors? Do a search to check that they are who they say they are. Are they experts on your topic? journalists? staff writers? Are they affiliated with any institution that would indicate their expertise—or affect their viewpoints? Check the source for biographical information, and confirm any pertinent information you find there by looking elsewhere—at other reliable sources.

If, for example, you were researching brain injuries among NFL players, you might run across the opinions of two medical experts, Dr. Ann McKee and Dr. Elliott Pellman, each offering very different evidence about the long-term effects of concussions. Looking into their credentials and affiliations, you'd learn that McKee is a neurologist who specializes in brain injuries, while Pellman is a rheumatologist who specializes in the body more than the brain—and chairs a medical committee in the NFL—information that tells you something about each one's STANCE.

Who's the publisher or sponsor? Is it an academic press? a news organization? a government agency or nonprofit? a business or individual? What do other reliable sources say about it? Read the source's "about" page online and follow up on what you find to confirm it's accurate. Knowing the publisher or sponsor can tell you whether the content has been peer-reviewed by experts, as is typical for scholarly works and government publications, or fact-checked,

Which would you trust more: official reports with data from NASA, the *Wikipedia* page on the issue, or a clip from ABC's *Nightline* found on *YouTube*?

"On the Internet, nobody knows you're a dog."

as news organizations typically require. Consider also whether the publication or its sponsor has a particular agenda, especially if it presents the opinions of an individual.

What's the URL? A site's URL can tell you something about what kind of organization is sponsoring the site: generally, *com* is used by commercial organizations, *edu* by colleges and universities, *org* by nonprofits, *gov* by government agencies. If it's a site you've never heard of, do an internet search of the source's URL to be sure it checks out.

When was it published or last updated? Does your topic call for the most current sources or for older historical ones? Even if you're researching a current issue, you may still want to consult older sources to get a sense of the larger context. Likewise, if your topic calls for older sources, you may also want to read the current research on it. And if your source is on a website, check to see that the site itself and any links are still active.

What's the genre? Pay particular attention to whether it's REPORTING information or ARGUING some kind of claim. You'll have reason to look for both, but for those that make an argument, you'll need to find multiple sources expressing a number of different perspectives. And double-check facts, claims, and evidence that too neatly support what you already think or seem too good to be true. Sites like *Snopes* and *FactCheck.org* can help.

Is it cited in other works? Are there links to it in other online sources? Has it been referenced or reposted? You can determine this by searching for the author and title using *Google Scholar*. For instance, if you enter *Susan Miller "Textual Carnivals,"* the search page returns information letting you know the work has been cited in 541 related articles. If many other writers refer or respond to this author's work, you can probably assume they find it credible.

Let's say you are conducting preliminary research on climate change and a *Google* search turns up an article titled "On the Linearity of Local and Regional Temperature Changes from 1.5°C to 2°C of Global Warming." You've heard that small temperature increases are significant and the title uses academic language, so this article sounds promising. Following the guidelines above will help you determine whether it'll be worth your attention.

Before you read the article itself, check out the author and source to be sure they're reliable. Written by seven international scholars, this report is hosted on the American Meteorological Society's page and was published in the *Journal of Climate*. Clicking on each author's name provides their individual publishing history which helps verify their expertise. Googling each of the authors' names plus "climate science" further confirms their identities and expertise by uncovering university faculty bios and *Google Scholar* pages listing when their works have been cited by others. Now look at the source itself; the American Meteorological Society's "about" page says it was established in 1919, has more than 13,000 members, and "is the nation's premier scientific and professional organization promoting and disseminating information about the atmospheric, oceanic, and hydrologic sciences." This information paints a picture of a trustworthy source, but don't stop there. Doing an internet search of the society's name turns up other trustworthy sources (such as *Forbes* and *JSTOR*) that confirm its mission and stature.

Now that you've confirmed the report comes from a credible source, look more closely to see if it is relevant to your research topic. While the title suggests the article will focus on local and regional temperature change, the abstract gives a summary of why the research was conducted, what research methods were used, and the implications of the findings—all important moves for laying out a researched argument. Given your topic, you're likely to encounter many more research reports, so this one seems like a good start for understanding how to read and analyze them. In addition, it lists keywords that seem relevant to your research ("climate models," "temperature") and lists of additional scholarly articles. Finally, note that the date of publication is September 2018, so it's recent enough to be useful.

Given all that you know about this source, is it worth your attention? We would say so. The report seems to provide valuable information in addition to giving you an example of how climate science research is conducted and analyzed. And even if you don't end up citing the findings of this paper, it still offers links to additional related research published in a source you've already verified as reliable.

That said, you should be mindful to research other relevant perspectives on your topic—especially those outside of the sources that confirm what you already think. In this case, clicking on the keyword "climate change" at the end of the abstract turns up a list of additional papers, including one offering a different point of view titled "'We Have Seen It with Our Own Eyes': Why We Disagree about Climate Change Visibility." The title indicates this article will present opposing positions on something called "climate change visibility." In the abstract and article that follow, the author summarizes and investigates positions held by opposing sides in the debate on whether climate change can be witnessed firsthand. Now things are getting interesting; this article introduces a more human, even personal, element to the debate, suggesting that even scientists disagree on how—even if—people experience climate change firsthand. If this human element sparks your interest, then this article is definitely relevant to your research and worth your attention. It might even help you focus your research question. As you go further in your research, you should seek out other credible sources arguing from different sides of the issue.

⁓ℰ REFLECT. Read the Popular Science *article titled* "What you should know about the new climate change report" *on* everyonesanauthor.tumblr.com. *Underlined words are linked to sources—open a few of these sources and evaluate them, using the questions earlier in this chapter, to determine if they would be credible sources for research on this topic. What are the sources' strengths and weaknesses?*

Reading Sources with a Critical Eye

Once you've determined that a source is credible and appropriate, you'll need to read it closely, thinking carefully about the author's position, how (and how well) it's supported, and how it affects your understanding of the topic as a whole. As you read your sources, approach each one with a critical eye and practice READING DEFENSIVELY. The following questions can help you do so.

Consider your own RHETORICAL SITUATION. Will the source help you achieve your **PURPOSE**? Look at the preface, abstract, or table of contents to determine how extensively and directly it addresses your topic. Will your **AUDIENCE** consider the source reliable and credible? Are they expecting you to cite certain kinds of materials, such as historical documents or academic journals? Does the source confirm what you already believe or expose you to new considerations?

What is the author's STANCE? Does the title indicate a certain attitude or perspective? How would you characterize the **TONE**? Is it objective? argumentative? sarcastic? How does the author's stance affect its usefulness for your project?

Who is the AUDIENCE for this work? Is it aimed at the general public? members of a field? policy makers? Sources written for a general audience may provide useful overviews or explanations. Sources aimed at experts may be more authoritative and provide more detail—but they can be challenging to understand.

What is the main point, and what has motivated the author to write? Is the author responding to some other argument? What's the larger conversation on this issue? Is it clear why the topic matters?

What REASONS and EVIDENCE does the author provide as support? Are the reasons fair, relevant, and sound? Is the evidence drawn from credible sources? Is the kind of evidence (statistics, facts, examples, expert testimony, and so on) appropriate to the point it's supporting? How persuasive do you find the argument? Check facts and claims you're skeptical of by using nonpartisan sites (*Snopes* and *FactCheck.org*) that confirm truths and identify lies or misinformation.

Does the author acknowledge and respond to other viewpoints? Look for mention of multiple perspectives, not just the author's own view. And be sure to consider how fairly any **COUNTERARGUMENTS** are represented. The most trustworthy sources represent other views and information fairly and accurately, even (especially) those that challenge their own. Check out the people and ideas cited to be sure they are reliable themselves. The sources and ideas an author is in conversation with can help you uncover more information about the author's own purpose, stance, and bias.

Have you seen ideas given in this source in any other sources? Information found in multiple sources is more reliable than information you can find in only one place. Do other credible sources challenge this information? If so, is

We know seas are rising and we know why. The urgent questions are by how much and how quickly.

243.5 mm
2017

SEA LEVEL RISE: 1880 - 2017

Sea levels have risen about **8 inches** since the beginning of the 20th century. The ocean is projected to rise by as much as **3 feet or more** by the end of this century.

Earth's climate history shows there have been times when ice sheets rapidly changed and created multiple meters of sea level rise in a century. As Earth's ice sheets continue to change, a key question facing scientists now is: Could human-caused global warming be pushing us toward one of those times?

0 mm

1880

CSIRO, updated Church and White (2011)
GSFC (2017); Global Mean Sea Level Trend from Integrated Multi-Mission Ocean Altimeters. Ver. 4

THINK
BEYOND
WORDS

SUPPOSE YOU'RE RESEARCHING climate change and come across NASA's site sealevel.nasa.gov. Checking out what others say about the source tells you that NASA stands for National Aeronautics and Space Administration, and it is an agency of the US government that employs thousands of scientists and publishes information on natural-science topics. If you were writing an essay about how climate change impacts coastal communities, what kinds of information from this site would you consider citing? How does the way information is presented make it seem more or less credible? For instance, compare the site's report "Melting Ice, Warming Ocean" with the infographic shown above. Is one source easier to vet than the other? Does one seem more appropriate to cite than the other—and if so, why?

what's said in this source controversial or is it flat out false? Copy and paste the basics of the questionable statement into a search engine and see what reliable sources say. Even if a search brings up many hits, that doesn't make the information accurate—look for sources you trust to weigh in.

How might you use this source? Source materials can serve a variety of purposes in both your research and your writing. You might consult some sources for background information or to get a sense of the larger context for your topic. Other sources may provide support for your claims—or for your credibility as an author. Still others will provide other viewpoints, ones that challenge yours or that provoke you to respond. Most of all, they'll give you some sense of what's been said about your topic. Then, in writing up your research, you'll get your chance to say what *you* think—and to add your voice to the conversation.

REFLECT. Choose three or four different sources on your chosen topic— possibly one from a government source, one from an academic journal, one from a popular source, and one from a website. Evaluate each of the sources according to the guidelines laid out in this chapter. Explain what makes each source credible (or not).

TWENTY-FOUR

Annotating a Bibliography

**HEN WE ASSIGN RESEARCH PROJECTS**, we often require our students to annotate a bibliography as part of the research process. Instructors do this for a variety of reasons: to ensure that you read sources carefully and critically, summarize useful information about them, and think about how and why you expect to use particular ones. The rhetorical purpose of the annotated bibliography is to inform—and you are part of the audience. Conscientiously done, annotating a bibliography will help you gain a sense of the larger conversation about your topic and think about how your work fits into that conversation.

In a formal annotated bibliography, you **DESCRIBE** each of the sources you expect to consult and state what role each will play in your research. Sometimes you will be asked to **EVALUATE** sources as well—to assess their strengths and weaknesses in one or two sentences.

Characteristic Features

Annotations should be brief, but they can vary in length from a sentence or two to a few paragraphs. They also vary in terms of style: some are written in complete sentences; others consist of short phrases. And like a works-cited or references list, an annotated bibliography is arranged in alphabetical order. You'll want to find out exactly what your instructor expects, but most annotated bibliographies include the following features.

Complete bibliographic information, following whatever documentation style you'll use in your essay— MLA, APA, or another style. This information will enable readers to locate your sources—and can also form the basis for your final list of works cited or references.

A brief SUMMARY or DESCRIPTION of each work, noting its topic, scope, and STANCE. If a source reports on research, the research methods may also be important to summarize. Other details you include will depend on your own goals for your project. Whatever you choose to describe, however, be sure that it represents the source accurately and objectively.

Evaluative comments. If you're required to write evaluative annotations, you might consider how AUTHORITATIVE the source is, how up-to-date, whether it addresses multiple perspectives, and so on. Consider both its strengths and its limitations.

Some indication of how each source will inform your research. Explain how you expect to use each source. Does it present a certain perspective you need to consider? report on important new research? include a thorough bibliography that might alert you to other sources? How does each source relate to the others? How does each source contribute to your understanding of the topic and to your research goals? Or if you find that it isn't helpful to your project, explain why you won't use it.

A consistent and concise presentation. Annotations should be presented consistently in all entries: if one is written in complete sentences, they all should be. The amount of information and the way you structure it should also be the same throughout. And that information should be written concisely, summarizing just the main points and key details relevant to your purpose.

Following are two annotated bibliographies, the first descriptive and the second evaluative.

A Descriptive Annotated Bibliography

Renewable and Sustainable Energy in Rural India

SAURABH VAISH

"Renewable Energies." Deutsche Energie-Agentur GmbH (dena), www.dena.de/en/topics-projects/renewable-energies/. The German Energy Agency provides information on energy efficiency, renewable energy sources, and intelligent energy systems. The website contains some useful databases, including ones of energy projects in Germany and of recent publications. It is a useful source of information on the manufacturing and production of alternative energy systems.

    Though this site does not provide statistical data and covers only a limited number of projects and publications, it includes links to much useful information. It's a great source of publications and projects in both Germany and Russia, and so it will help me broaden my research beyond the borders of the United States.

Complete bibliographic information for this source, following MLA style.

Summarizes and describes the source.

Explains how this source will inform his project.

SAURABH VAISH was a management and entrepreneurship major at Hofstra University when he wrote this descriptive annotated bibliography for a research project on renewable and sustainable energy in rural India. We then adapted two entries to demonstrate evaluative annotations.

Moner-Girona, Magda, editor. *A New Scheme for the Promotion of Renewable Energies in Developing Countries: The Renewable Energy Regulated Purchase Tariff.* European Commission Joint Research Centre, 2008, https://doi.org/10.2790/11999.

> This report on a study by the PhotoVoltaic Technology Platform discusses how to promote the use of renewable energy in developing countries. The report proposes a new tariff scheme to increase the flow of money where it is most needed, suggests several business models, and estimates the potential success or failure of each. The detailed information it provides about business models, supply-chain setups, and financial calculations will be useful in my analysis, especially in the part of my project that deals with photovoltaic cells.

United States, Energy Information Administration. *Renewable & Alternative Fuels Reports.* U.S. Dept. of Energy, 1998–2010, www.eia.gov/renewable/reports.cfm.

> This site reports statistical and graphical data on energy production and consumption, including all major alternative energies. It provides access to numerous databases on energy consumption across the world. This website provides most of the statistical data I will need to formulate conclusions about the efficiency of alternative energies. Its data are reliable, current, and easy to understand.

An Evaluative Annotated Bibliography

Moner-Girona, Magda, editor. *A New Scheme for the Promotion of Renewable Energies in Developing Countries: The Renewable Energy Regulated Purchase Tariff.* European Commission Joint Research Centre, 2008, https://doi.org/10.2790 /11999.

> This report on a study by the PhotoVoltaic Technology Platform discusses how to promote renewable energy in developing countries. The report proposes a new tariff scheme to increase the flow of money where it is needed, suggests several business models, and estimates the potential success or failure of each.
>
> The detailed information about business models, supply-chain setups, and financial calculations will be useful, especially in the part of my project that deals with photovoltaic cells. One potential drawback is that this report makes premature assumptions: the proposed business plan is probably not implementable for twenty years. Even so, this report contains useful data and models, including graphs and charts, that will support my claims.

Evaluates the source, acknowledging a potential weakness—but explains why it is still useful.

United States, Energy Information Administration. *Renewable & Alternative Fuels Reports.* U.S. Dept. of Energy, 1998–2010, www.eia.gov/renewable/reports.cfm.

> This website reports statistical and graphical data on energy production and consumption, including all major alternative energies. It provides access to numerous databases on energy consumption across the world.
>
> This site provides most of the statistical data I will need to formulate conclusions about the efficiency of alternative energies. Its data are reliable, current, and easy to understand. I see no potential weakness in this source because the data it presents are non-biased statistics and supporting graphics pertaining to alternative energies. Using such data will allow me to shape my own opinions regarding the research I undertake.

TWENTY-FIVE

Synthesizing Ideas

Moving from What Your Sources Say to What You Say

**T'S SUPER BOWL SUNDAY**, just before kickoff and just after the teams have been introduced. The broadcast cuts back from a commercial set to DJ Schmolli's "Super Bowl Anthem" and returns to the stadium where Idina Menzel is singing "The Star-Spangled Banner." So you've just heard two anthems. But what else, if anything, do these tunes have in common? Answer: each is a mash-up—a combination of material from a number of different sources. "The Star-Spangled Banner" combines a poem written by Francis Scott Key with the music of an old British drinking song. DJ Schmolli's effort combines clips from more than a dozen popular stadium anthems, from Madonna's "Celebration" to Queen's "We Will Rock You." And each smoothly integrates its sources into one seamless whole. In academic terms, the authors of these mash-ups have effectively engaged in **SYNTHESIS**, bringing together material from various sources to create something new.

Like a good mash-up artist, you don't just patch together ideas from various sources when you do research. Instead, you synthesize what they say to help you think about and understand the topic you're researching—to identify connections among them and blend them into a coherent whole that at the same time articulates *ideas of your own*. This chapter will help you blend ideas from sources with your own ideas smoothly and effectively—just like a really great mash-up.

An unlikely mash-up: Jane Austen's *Pride and Prejudice* and . . . zombies! With 85 percent Austen's original text and 15 percent zombie gore, *Pride and Prejudice and Zombies* became an instant best-seller, setting off a slew of literary monster mash-ups.

Synthesizing the Ideas in Your Sources

Here are some questions to help you synthesize information as you work with your sources. Try **ANNOTATING** sources with these questions in mind:

- What issues, problems, or controversies do your sources address?
- What else do your sources have in common? Any ideas? facts? examples? statistics? Are any people or works cited in more than one source?
- What significant differences do you find among sources? Different stances? positions? purposes? kinds of evidence? conclusions?
- Do any of your sources cite or refer to one another? Does one source provide details, examples, or explanations that build on something said in another? Does any source respond specifically to something said in another?

Your goal is to get a sense of how the information from your various sources fits together—how the sources speak to one another and what's being said about your topic.

One function of a synthesis is to establish **CONTEXT** and set the scene for what you yourself have to say. See how the following example from an academic article on high-stakes testing brings together information from a number of sources about the history of testing as context for the discussion of trends in school testing today.

> Although the practice of high-stakes testing gained a prominent position in educational reform with the passage of the No Child Left Behind Act (NCLB) of 2002, its use as a lever for school change preceded NCLB. Tests have been used to distribute rewards and sanctions to teachers in urban schools since the mid 1800s (Tyack, 1974) and for most schools throughout the United States since at least the 1970s (Haertel & Herman, 2005). New York state in particular has led the United States in test-based accountability efforts, "implementing state-developed (1965) and mandated minimal competency testing (MCT) before most other states (1978) and disseminating information to the media about local district performance on the state assessments before it became routinely popular (1985)" (Allington & McGill-Franzen, 1992, p. 398).
>
> —SHARON NICHOLS, GENE GLASS, AND DAVID BERLINER,
> "High-stakes Testing and Student Achievement"

Look now at this dramatic opening to a magazine article on actor-comedian Robin Williams's death by suicide:

> If you were keeping an eye on Robin Williams' *Twitter* feed these past few months—along with his 875,000 followers—you would have noticed nothing the least bit worrying about the 63-year-old actor-comedian's state of mind. On June 6, he uploaded a photo of himself visiting the San Francisco Zoo, where one of the monkeys had been named after him ("What an honor!"). On July 30, he posted a plug for his December movie, *Night at the Museum: Secret of the Tomb* ("I hope you enjoy it!"). And then, on July 31, in what would turn out to be his last public comment, he tweeted his daughter Zelda a birthday message ("Quarter of a century old today but always my baby girl").
>
> Eleven days later, he was discovered dead at his home in Marin County, California.—BENJAMIN SVETKEY, "Robin Williams Remembered
> by Critics, Close Friends"

By synthesizing multiple sources—in this case, Williams's *Twitter* posts—and presenting them as one cohesive whole, Svetkey paints a picture of a seemingly happy man.

While these two examples are quite different—one cites academic sources in an academic publication, the other cites social media sources in a popular magazine—they both synthesize information to give readers context for what the authors go on to say. For all writers, including you, that's the next step.

REFLECT. Try your hand at synthesizing the sources you've consulted so far for something you're writing. What patterns do you see? What's being said about your topic?

Moving from What Your Sources Say to What You Say

As a researcher, you'll always be working to synthesize the ideas and information you find in your research, to see the big picture and make sense of it all. At the same time, you'll be striving to connect the data you gather to your own ideas and to your research goals. You'll be learning a lot about what many others have discovered or said about your topic, and that will surely affect what you yourself think—and write—about it. Here are some questions that can help you move from the ideas you find in your sources to the ideas that you'll then write about:

- How do the ideas and information in your sources address your **RESEARCH QUESTION**? What answers do they give? What information do you find the most relevant, useful, and persuasive?

- How do they support your tentative **THESIS**? Do they suggest reasons or ways that you should expand, qualify, or otherwise revise it?

- What viewpoints in your sources do you most agree with? disagree with? Why?

- What conclusions can you draw from the ideas and information you've learned from your sources? What discoveries have you made in studying these sources, and what new ideas have they led you to?

- Has your research changed your own views on your topic? Do any of your sources raise questions that you can pursue further?

- Have you encountered any ideas that you would like to build on— or challenge?
- From everything you've read, what is the significance of the topic you're researching? Who cares, and why does it matter?

When you work with your sources in this way, you can count on your ideas to grow and change. As we've been saying, research is an act of learning and inquiry, and you never know where it will lead. But as soon as you sit down and write, no matter what you say or how you say it, you will be, as Kenneth Burke says, "putting in your oar," adding your voice *and your ideas* to the very conversation you've been researching.

**THINK
BEYOND
WORDS**

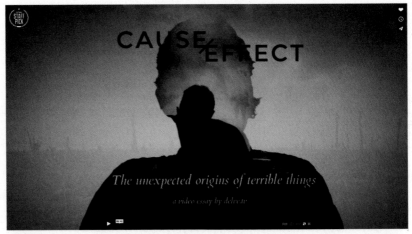

📤 *WATCH* Cause/Effect: The Unexpected Origins of Terrible Things, *a video essay by Adam Westbrook that makes a fascinating argument about what caused World War I. (You'll find it at* <u>everyonesanauthor.tumblr.com</u>.) *As you'll see, Westbrook synthesizes many kinds of sources and information—history books, maps, cartoons, newspapers, archival photographs and video, data from public records, and more—to build a case for his argument. How does he synthesize all these sources in a video? How does he go about introducing each one and weaving them together with his own ideas?*

Entering the Conversation You've Been Researching

Once you've thought carefully about what others have said about your topic, you can add your own voice to the conversation. Look at the following example from the introduction to an essay tracing the changes in political cartoons in the United States between World War II and the Iraq War. See how the writer synthesized ideas from her research into her writing in a way that set up her own questions and thoughts.

> A cartoon shows carolers at the White House door making a choral argument to then president George W. Bush that "we gotta get out of this place," referring to America's involvement in the war in Iraq (fig. 1). Bush appears completely oblivious to their message.
>
> First published in 2006, this cartoon offered a critique of America's continued presence in Iraq by criticizing the president's actions and attitudes towards the war, exemplifying how political cartoons have long been, and continue to be, a prominent part of wartime propaganda.

Fig. 1. Gary Markstein. Cartoon. *Copley News Service*, 9 Dec. 2006.

Combining eye-catching illustrations with textual critique, such cartoons do more than merely convey messages about current events. Rather, political cartoons serve as a tool for shaping public opinion. In fact, since the 1500s, political cartoons have used satirical critiques to persuade the general public about matters large and small (McCloud 16–17).

In the United States, the political (or editorial) cartoon is a form of editorializing that began as "scurrilous caricatures," according to Stephen Becker, author of *Comic Art in America*. Becker's book looks, in part, at the social history of political cartoons and states that it was only after "newspapers and magazines came to be published regularly . . . that caricatures, visual allegories, and the art of design were combined to form . . . modern editorial art" (15). As all-encompassing as that description of "modern editorial art" seems to be, it suggests several questions that remain unanswered: Do cartoonists use common themes to send their critical messages? As society and regulations change from generation to generation, do the style and content of political cartoons change as well? Have political cartoons become "modernized" since World War II? The essay that follows aims to answer as well as draw out the implications of these questions.   —JULIA LANDAUER, "War, Cartoons, and Society: Changes in Political Cartoons between World War II and the Iraq War"

Judith Newman puts two seemingly unrelated topics together when writing about her son: autism and Siri. Check out how she describes her autistic son's relationship with Apple's personal assistant on p. 981.

Landauer begins with a cartoon (a primary source) that illustrates a point she is making—that editorial cartoons are known for stinging political critiques. She then refers to a source (McCloud) to provide some background information and then another (Becker) to provide additional commentary on the "modern editorial art" she intends to examine in her essay. At that point, she raises questions "that remain unaddressed"—and says that answering them will be the work of her essay. Thus she uses ideas drawn from her sources to introduce her own ideas—and weave them all together into a strong introduction to her essay.

In your college writing, you will have the opportunity to come up with a research question and to dig in and do some research in order to answer it. That digging in will lead you to identify key sources already in conversation about your topic, to read and analyze those sources, and to begin synthesizing them with your own ideas. Before you know it, you won't be just listening in on the conversation: you'll be an active participant in it.

TWENTY-SIX

Quoting, Paraphrasing, Summarizing

HEN YOU'RE TEXTING or talking with friends, you don't usually need to be explicit about where you got your information; your friends trust what you say because they know you. In academic writing, however, it's important to establish your credibility, and one way to do so is by consulting authoritative sources. Doing so shows that you've done your homework on your topic, gives credit to those whose ideas you've relied on, and helps demonstrate your own authority as an author.

Your challenge in much academic writing is to integrate other voices with your own. How do you let your audience hear from expert sources while ensuring that their words don't eclipse yours? How do you pick and choose brief segments from long passages of text—or condense those passages into much briefer statements—without misrepresenting someone's ideas? How do you then introduce these segments and integrate them with your own words and ideas? This chapter provides guidelines on the three ways you can incorporate sources into your writing: quoting, paraphrasing, and summarizing.

A **QUOTATION** consists of someone's exact words, enclosed in quotation marks or set off as a block from the rest of your text. A **PARAPHRASE** includes the details of a passage in your own words and syntax. A **SUMMARY** contains the points of a passage that are important to your purpose, leaving out the other details.

Deciding Whether to Quote, Paraphrase, or Summarize

Quote

- Something that is said so well that it's worth repeating
- Complex ideas that are expressed so clearly that paraphrasing or summarizing could distort or oversimplify them
- Experts whose opinions and exact words help to establish your own **CREDIBILITY** and **AUTHORITY** to write on the topic
- Passages that you yourself are analyzing
- Those who disagree or offer **COUNTERARGUMENTS** —quoting their exact words is a way to be sure you represent their opinions fairly

Paraphrase

- Passages where the details matter, but not the exact words
- Passages that are either too technical or too complicated for your readers to understand

Summarize

- Lengthy passages when the main point is important to your argument but the details are not

Whatever method you use for incorporating the words and ideas of others into your own writing, be sure that they work to support what *you* want to say. You're the author—and whatever your sources say needs to connect to what you say—so be sure to make that connection clear. Don't assume that sources speak for themselves. Introduce any source that you cite, naming the authors and identifying them in some way if your audience won't know who they are. In addition, be sure to follow quotations with a comment that explains how they relate to your point.

And regardless of whether you decide to quote, paraphrase, or summarize, you'll need to credit each source. Even if what you include is not a direct quotation, the ideas are still someone else's, and failing to credit your source can result in plagiarism. Indicate the source in a **SIGNAL PHRASE** and include in-text documentation.

Nicholas Carr writes for a general audience, but some of his sources are very technical. See how he uses paraphrases in order not to lose his readers on p. 875.

Quoting

When you include a direct quotation, be sure to use the exact words of the original source. And while you don't want to include too many quotations—you are the author, after all—using the exact words from a source is sometimes the best way to ensure that you accurately represent what was said. Original quotations can also be an effective way of presenting a point, by letting other people speak in their own words. But be sure to frame any quotation you include, introducing it and then explaining why it's important to the point that you are making.

Enclose short quotations in quotation marks within your main text. Such quotations should be no longer than four typed lines (in MLA style) or forty words (in APA style).

> Programmer and digital media pioneer Jaron Lanier describes the problems resulting from "lock-in" (in which software becomes difficult to change because it has been engineered to work with existing programs), arguing that lock-in "is an absolute tyrant in the digital world" (8). He means that "lock-in" inhibits creativity as new development is constrained by old software.

In MLA style, short quotations of poetry—no more than three lines—should also be enclosed in quotation marks within the main text. Include slashes (with a space on either side) between each line of verse.

> In "When You Are Old," poet William Butler Yeats advises Maud Gonne, the radical Irish nationalist, that when she looks back on her youth from old age, she should consider "How many loved your moments of glad grace, / And loved your beauty with love false or true, / But one man loved the pilgrim soul in you" (lines 5–7). Yeats thus suggests that he is the "one man" who truly loved her so sincerely all these years.

Set off long quotations as a block by indenting them from the left margin. No need to enclose them in quotation marks, but do indent five spaces (or one-half inch) if you are using either MLA or APA style. Use this method for quotations that are more than four lines of prose or three lines of poetry (in MLA) or longer than forty words (in APA).

> In her 1976 keynote address to the Democratic National Convention, Texas congresswoman Barbara Jordan reflects on the occasion:

↪ Go to every onesanauthor .tumblr.com to listen to the full text of Barbara Jordan's speech.

>> Now that I have this grand distinction, what in the world am I supposed to say? . . . I could list the problems which cause people to feel cynical, angry, frustrated: problems which include lack of integrity in government; the feeling that the individual no longer counts; the reality of material and spiritual poverty; the feeling that the grand American experiment is failing or has failed. I could recite these problems, and then I could sit down and offer no solutions. But I don't choose to do that either. The citizens of America expect more. (189)

> In this passage, Jordan resists the opportunity to attack the opposing party, preferring instead to offer positive solutions rather than simply a list of criticisms and problems.

Notice that with block quotations, the parenthetical citation falls *after* the period at the end of the quotation.

Indicate changes to the text within a quotation by using brackets to enclose text that you add or change and ellipses to indicate text that you omit.

Use brackets to indicate that you have altered the original wording to fit grammatically within your text or have added or changed wording to clarify something that might otherwise be unclear. In this example, the author changed the verb *had* to *should have*:

> John Maeda, president of the Rhode Island School of Design, reacts to America's current emphasis on STEM education with the proposal that "just like STEM is made up of science, technology, engineering and math, we [should have] IDEA, made up of intuition, design, emotion and art—all the things that make us humans feel, well, human" ("On Meaningful Observation").

Read John Maeda's complete essay on p. 953.

Use ellipsis marks in place of words, phrases, or sentences that you leave out because they aren't crucial or relevant for your purpose. Use three dots, with a space before each one and after the last, when you omit only words and phrases within a sentence. If you leave out the end of a sentence or a whole sentence or more, put a period after the last word before the ellipsis mark. Note how a writer does both in the example below.

> Warning of the effects of GPS on our relationship to the world around us, Nicholas Carr concludes that "the automation of wayfinding . . . encourages us to observe and manipulate symbols on screens rather than attend to real things in real places. . . . What we should be asking ourselves is, *How far from the world do we want to retreat?*" (137)

When you use brackets or ellipses, make sure your changes don't end up misrepresenting the author's original point, which would damage your own credibility. Mark Twain once joked that "nearly any invented quotation, played with confidence, stands a good chance to deceive." Twain was probably right—it's quite easy to "invent" quotations or twist their meaning by taking them out of context or changing some keyword. You don't want to be guilty of this!

Set off a quotation within a quotation with single quotation marks. In the following passage, the author quotes Nicholas Carr, who himself quotes the writing of anthropologist Tim Ingold:

Nicholas Carr sums up the difference between navigating with and without a GPS device using two terms borrowed from Scottish anthropologist Tim Ingold. As Carr explains, Ingold "draws a distinction between two very different modes of travel: wayfaring and transport. Wayfaring, he explains, is 'our most fundamental way of being in the world'" (132). It is navigating by our observations and mental maps of the world around us, as opposed to blindly following GPS-generated directions from point A to point B—the mode Ingold and Carr call "transport."

Punctuate quotations carefully. Parenthetical documentation comes after the closing quotation mark, and any punctuation that is part of your sentence comes after the parentheses (except in the case of a block quote, where the parenthetical documentation goes at the very end).

See on p. 870 how Dana Canedy quotes dialogue in writing about a difficult conversation with her eight-year-old son.

- *Commas and periods* always go inside the closing quotation marks. If there's parenthetical documentation, however, the period goes after the parentheses.

  "Everybody worships," said David Foster Wallace in a 2005 commencement speech. "There is no such thing as not worshipping" (8).

- *Colons and semicolons* always go outside closing quotation marks.

  Wallace warned as well that there are "whole parts of adult American life that nobody talks about in commencement speeches": sometimes, he says, we'll be bored (4).

  He also once noted that when a lobster is put in a kettle of boiling water, it "behaves very much as you or I would behave if we were plunged into boiling water"; in other words, it acts as if it's in terrible pain (10).

- *Question marks and exclamation points* go inside closing quotation marks if they are part of the original quotation, but outside the quotation marks if they are part of your sentence.

Wallace opened his speech with a now famous joke about how natural it is to be unaware of the world: an old fish swims by two young fish and says, "Morning, boys. How's the water?" They swim on, and after a while one young fish turns to the other and asks, "What the hell is water?" (1)

So what, according to David Foster Wallace, is the "capital-T Truth about life" (9)?

Paraphrasing

When you paraphrase, you restate information or ideas from a source using your words, your sentence structure, your style. A paraphrase should cover the same points that the original source does, so it's usually about the same length—but sticking too closely to the sentence structures in your source could be plagiarizing. And even though you're using your own words, don't forget where the ideas came from: you should always name the author and include parenthetical documentation.

Here is a paragraph about the search for other life-forms similar to our own in the universe, followed by three paraphrases.

Original source

As the romance of manned space exploration has waned, the drive today is to find our living, thinking counterparts in the universe. For all the excitement, however, the search betrays a profound melancholy—a lonely species in a merciless universe anxiously awaits an answering voice amid utter silence. That silence is maddening. Not just because it compounds our feeling of cosmic isolation, but because it makes no sense. As we inevitably find more and more exo-planets where intelligent life *can* exist, why have we found no evidence—no signals, no radio waves—that intelligent life *does* exist?

    —CHARLES KRAUTHAMMER, "Are We Alone in the Universe?"

As the underlined words show, the following paraphrase uses too many words from the original.

Unacceptable paraphrase: wording too close to the original

Charles Krauthammer argues that finding our intelligent <u>counterparts</u> <u>in the universe</u> has become more important as the <u>romance of manned</u> <u>space exploration</u> has declined. Even so, the hunt for similar beings also suggests our sadness as a species waiting in vain for an acknowledgment that we aren't alone in <u>a merciless universe</u>. The lack of response, he says, just doesn't make sense because if we keep finding planets that *could* support life, then we should find evidence—like <u>radio waves or</u> <u>signals</u>—of intelligent life out there (A19).

While the next version uses original language, the sentence structures are much too similar to the original.

Unacceptable paraphrase: sentence structures too close to original

As the allure of adventuring into the unknown cosmos has diminished, the desire to discover beings like us out there has grown. There is a sadness to the search though—the calling out into empty space that brings no response. Nothing. Only a vast silence that not only emphasizes our solitary existence but increases our frustration. How can we continue to discover potentially hospitable planets that could sustain life like ours, yet find no evidence—no signs, no data—that such life exists (Krauthammer A19)?

When you paraphrase, be careful not to simply substitute words and phrases while replicating the same sentence structure. And while it may be necessary to use some of the key terms from the original in order to convey the same concepts, be sure to put them in quotation marks—and not to use too many (which would result in plagiarism).

Acceptable paraphrase

Syndicated columnist Charles Krauthammer observes that our current quest to discover other "intelligent life" in the universe comes just as the allure of exploring outer space is dimming. It's a search, he says, that reveals a deep sadness (that we may in fact be living in "cosmic isolation") and a growing frustration: if scientists continue to discover more planets where life like ours can be sustainable, why do we find no actual signs of life (A19)?

Summarizing

Like a paraphrase, a summary presents the source information in your words. However, a summary dramatically condenses the information, covering only the most important points and leaving out the details. Summaries are therefore much briefer than the original texts, though they vary in length depending on the size of the original and your purpose for summarizing; you may need only a sentence or two to summarize an essay, or you may need several paragraphs. In any case, you should always name the author and document the source. The following example appropriately summarizes Krauthammer's passage in one sentence:

> Charles Krauthammer questions whether we will ever find other "intelligent life" in the universe—or whether we'll instead discover that we do in fact live in "cosmic isolation" (A19).

This summary tells readers Krauthammer's main point and includes in quotation marks two key phrases borrowed from the original source. If we were to work the summary into an essay, it might look like this:

> Many scientists believe that there is a strong probability—given the vastness of the universe and how much of it we have yet to explore, even with advances like the Hubble telescope—that there is life like ours somewhere out there. In a 2011 opinion piece, however, syndicated columnist Charles Krauthammer questions whether we will ever find other "intelligent life" in the universe—or whether we'll instead discover that we do in fact live in "cosmic isolation" (A19).

Three ways a summary can go wrong are if it represents inaccurately the point of the original source, provides so many details that the summary is too long, or is so general that readers are left wondering what the source is about. Consider the following unsuccessful summaries of Krauthammer's passage:

Unacceptable summary: misrepresents the source

Pulitzer Prize–winning columnist Charles Krauthammer extols the virtues of space exploration.

This summary both misses the point of Krauthammer's questioning our troubled search for "intelligent life" beyond Earth and claims that the author praises space exploration when at no point in the passage does he do so.

Unacceptable summary: provides too many details

Award-winning columnist Charles Krauthammer suggests that while sending people into space is no longer as exciting to us as it once was, we are interested in finding out if there is life in the universe beyond Earth. He laments the feeling of being alone in the universe given that all signs point to the very real possibility that intelligent life exists elsewhere. Krauthammer wonders "why we have no evidence . . . of intelligent life" on other habitable planets. He finds this lack of proof confounding.

This summary is almost as long as the original passage and includes as many details. As a summary, it doesn't let readers know what points are most important.

Unacceptable summary: too general

Charles Krauthammer is concerned about the search for life on other planets.

While the statement above is not false, it does not adequately reflect Krauthammer's main point in a way that will help the reader get the gist of the original passage. A better summary would tell readers what precisely about the search for life concerns Krauthammer.

REFLECT. Return to the quotation from Barbara Jordan on page 544. First, write an appropriate paraphrase of the quotation; then write an appropriate summary.

Incorporating Source Material

Whether you quote, paraphrase, or summarize source material, you need to be careful to distinguish what you say from what your sources say, while at the same time weaving the two together smoothly in your writing. That is, you must make clear how the ideas you're quoting, paraphrasing, or summarizing relate to your own—why you're bringing them into your text.

Use **signal phrases** to introduce source materials, telling readers who said what and providing some context if need be. Don't just drop in a quotation or paraphrase or summary; you need to introduce it. And while you can always use a neutral signal phrase such as "he says" or "she claims," try to choose verbs that reflect the **STANCE** of those you're citing. In some cases, a simple "she says" does reflect that stance, but usually you can make your writing livelier and more accurate with a more specific signal verb.

Use a **SIGNAL PHRASE** and parenthetical documentation to clearly distinguish your own words and ideas from those of others. The following paraphrase introduces source material with a signal phrase that includes the author's name and closes with documentation giving the page number from which the information is taken.

> As Ernst Mayr explains, Darwin's theory of evolution presented a significant challenge to then-prevalent beliefs about humanity's centrality in the world (9).

If you do not give the author's name in a signal phrase, include it in the parenthetical documentation.

> Darwin's theory of evolution presented a significant challenge to then-prevalent beliefs about humanity's centrality in the world (Mayr 9).

Sometimes you'll want or need to state the author's authority or credentials in the signal phrase, lending credibility to your own use of that source.

> According to music historian Ted Gioia, record sales declined sharply during the Great Depression, dropping by almost 90 percent between 1927 and 1932 (127).

Choose verbs that reflect the author's stance toward the material—or your own stance in including it. Saying "she notes" means something different than saying "she insists" or "she implies."

> Because almost anyone can create a blog, most people assume that blogs give average citizens a greater voice in public dialogue. Political scientist Matthew Hindman questions this assumption: "Though millions of Americans now maintain a blog, only a few dozen political bloggers get as many readers as a typical college newspaper" (103).

Signal phrases do not have to come first. To add variety to your writing, try positioning them in the middle or at the end of a sentence.

> "Attracting attention," observes Richard Lanham, "is what style is all about" (xi).

> "We've got to stop the debates! Enough with the debates!" pleaded John McCain last Sunday on *Meet the Press* (31).

SOME USEFUL SIGNAL VERBS

acknowledges	concludes	observes
adds	declares	reports
asserts	implies	responds
claims	objects	suggests

Verb tenses. The verb tense you use when referring to a text or researcher in a signal phrase will depend on your documentation style. MLA style requires the present tense (*argues*) or the present perfect (*has argued*). Using MLA style, you might write, "In *Rhetoric*, Aristotle argues" or "In commenting on Aristotle's *Rhetoric*, scholars have argued." An exception involves sentences that include specific dates in the past. In this case, use the past tense: "In his introduction to the 1960 edition of Aristotle's *Rhetoric*, Lane Cooper argued."

The past tense is conventional in APA style. The present perfect is conventional when referring to an ongoing action that started in the past or to something that didn't occur at a specific time. You might write, "Anderson (1988) argued" or "In commenting on Aristotle's *Rhetoric*, scholars have argued." However, use the present tense when you refer to the results of a study ("the results of Conrad (2012) demonstrate") or when you make a generalization ("writing researchers agree").

Parenthetical documentation. If you're following **MLA**, you'll need to include page numbers for all quotations, paraphrases, and summaries from print sources in your parenthetical documentation. If you're using **APA**, page numbers are required for quotations; for paraphrases and summaries, they're optional—but it's always a good idea to include them whenever you can do so.

Incorporating Visual and Audio Sources

Sometimes you will want to incorporate visual or audio elements from sources that you cannot write into a paragraph. For example, you may include charts, photographs, or audio/video clips. Remember that any such materials that come from sources need to be introduced, explained, and documented just as you would a quotation. If you're following MLA or APA style, refer to Chapters 28 and 29 for specific requirements.

Tables. Label anything that contains facts or figures displayed in columns as a table. Number all tables in sequence, and provide a descriptive title for each one. Supply source information immediately below the table; credit your data source even if you've created the table yourself. If any information within the table requires further explanation (abbreviations, for example), include a note below the source citation.

Figures. Number and label everything that is not a table (photos, graphs, drawings, maps, and so on) as a figure and include a caption letting readers know what the image illustrates. Unless the visual is a photograph or drawing you created yourself, provide appropriate source information after the caption; graphs, maps, and other figures you produce based on information from other sources should still include a full credit. If the visual is referenced within your text, you can use an abbreviated citation and include full documentation in your list of **WORKS CITED** or **REFERENCES**.

Audio and video recordings. If your medium allows it, provide a link to any recorded element or embed a media player into the text. If you're working

Fig. I: The Guggenheim Museum, Spain.

in a medium that won't allow linking or embedding, discuss the recording in your text and provide a full citation in your list of **WORKS CITED** or **REFERENCES** so your readers can track down the recording themselves.

Captions. Create a clear, succinct caption for each visual or recording: "Fig. 1: The Guggenheim Museum, Spain." The caption should identify and explain the visual—and should reflect your purpose. In an essay about contemporary architecture in Spain, your caption might say "Fig. 1: The Guggenheim Museum, Bilbao. Designed by Frank Gehry."

Sizing and positioning visuals and recordings. Refer to every visual or embedded recording in your text: "(see fig. 1)," "as shown in Table 3," "in the *YouTube* video below." The element may be on the page where it's discussed, but it should not come before you introduce it to your readers. Think carefully about how you will size and position each visual to be most effective: you want to make sure that your visuals are legible and that they support rather than disrupt the text.

TWENTY-SEVEN

Giving Credit, Avoiding Plagiarism

**HO OWNS WORDS AND IDEAS?** Answers to this question differ from culture to culture. In some societies, they are shared resources, not the property of individuals. In others, using another person's words or ideas may be seen as a tribute or compliment that doesn't require specific acknowledgment. In the United States, however (as in much of the Western world), elaborate systems of copyright and patent law have grown up to protect the intellectual property (including words, images, voices, and ideas) of individuals and corporations. This system forms the foundation of the documentation conventions currently followed in US schools. And while these conventions are being challenged today by the open-source movement and others who argue that "information wants to be free," the conventions still hold sway in the academy and in the law. As a researcher, you will need to understand these conventions and to practice them in your own writing. Put simply, these conventions allow you to give credit where credit is due and thereby avoid plagiarism (the use of the words and ideas of others as if they were your own work).

But acknowledging your sources is not simply about avoiding charges of plagiarism (although you would be doing that too). Rather, it helps establish your own **CREDIBILITY** as a researcher and an author. It shows that you have consulted other sources of information about your topic and can engage with them in your own work. Additionally, citing and documenting your sources allows readers to locate them for their own purposes if they wish; in effect, it anticipates the needs of your audience.

There are some cases, however, in which you do not need to provide citations for information that you incorporate—for example, if the information is common knowledge. This chapter will help you identify which sources you must acknowledge, explain the basics of documenting your sources, and provide strategies for avoiding plagiarism.

Knowing What You Must Acknowledge

As a general rule, material taken from specific outside sources—whether ideas, texts, images, or sounds—should be **CITED** and **DOCUMENTED**. But there are some exceptions.

INFORMATION THAT DOES NOT NEED TO BE ACKNOWLEDGED

- *Information that is "common knowledge."* Uncontroversial information ("People today get most of their news and information from the internet"), well-known historical events ("Neil Armstrong was the first person to walk on the moon"), facts ("All mammals are warm-blooded"), and quotations (Armstrong's "That's one small step for man, one giant leap for mankind") that are widely available in general reference sources do not need to be cited.

You may not know when the astrolabe was invented or what it does, but Nicholas Carr knows you can find that information easily, so he didn't cite a source. See how he mentioned those instruments on p. 875.

- *Information well known to your audience.* Keep in mind that what is common knowledge varies depending on your audience. While an audience of pulmonary oncologists would be familiar with the names of researchers who established that smoking is linked to lung cancer, for a general audience you might need to cite a source if you give the names.

- *Information from well-known, easily accessible documents.* You do not need to include the specific location where you accessed texts that are available from a variety of public sources and are widely familiar, such as the United States Constitution.

- *Your own work.* If you've gathered data, come up with an idea, or generated a text (including images, multimedia texts, and so on) entirely on your own, you should indicate that to your readers in some way—but it's not necessary to include a formal citation, unless the material has been previously published elsewhere.

INFORMATION THAT MUST BE ACKNOWLEDGED

- *Direct quotations, paraphrases, and summaries.* Exact wording should always be enclosed in quotation marks and cited. And always cite specific ideas taken from another source, even when you present them using your own words.

- *Controversial information.* If there is some debate over the information you're including, cite the source so readers know whose version or interpretation of the facts you're using.

- *Information given in only a few sources.* If only one or two sources make this information available (that is, it isn't common knowledge widely accessible in general sources), include a citation.

- *Any materials that you did not create yourself*—including tables, charts, images, and audio or video segments. Even if you create a table or chart yourself, if it presents information from an outside source, that's someone else's work that needs to be acknowledged.

A word to the wise: it's always better to cite any information that you've taken from another source than to guess wrong and unintentionally plagiarize. If in doubt, err on the safe side and include a citation.

Fair Use and the Internet

In general, principles of fair use apply to the writing you do for your college classes. These principles allow you to use passages and images from the copyrighted work of others without their explicit permission as long as you do so for educational purposes and you fully cite what you use. When you publish your writing online, however, where that material can be seen by all, then you must have permission from the copyright owner in order to post it.

Students across the country have learned about this limitation on fair use the hard way. One student we know won a prize for an essay she wrote, which was then posted on the writing prize website. In the essay, she included a cartoon that was copyrighted by the cartoonist. Soon after the essay was posted, she received a letter from the copyright holder, demanding that she remove the image and threatening her with a lawsuit. Another student, whose essay was published on a class website, was stunned when his instructor got an angry email from a professor at another university, saying that the student writer had used too much of her work in the essay and that, furthermore, it had not been fully and properly cited. The student, who had intended no dishonesty at all, was embarrassed, to say the least.

Many legal scholars and activists believe that fair use policies and laws should be relaxed and that making these laws more restrictive undermines creativity. While these issues get debated in public forums and legal courts, however, you are well advised to be careful not only in citing and documenting all your sources thoroughly but in getting permission in writing to use any copyrighted text or image in anything you plan to post or publish online.

Avoiding Plagiarism

In US academic culture, incorporating the words, ideas, or materials of others into your own work without giving credit through appropriate citations and documentation is viewed as unethical and is considered plagiarism. The consequences of such unacknowledged borrowing are serious: students who plagiarize may receive failing grades for assignments or courses, be subjected to an administrative review for academic misconduct, or even be dismissed from school.

Certainly, the deliberate and obvious effort to pass off someone else's work as your own, such as by handing in a paper purchased online or written by someone else, is plagiarism and can easily be spotted and punished. More troublesome and problematic, however, is the difficulty some students have using the words and ideas of others fairly and acknowledging them fully. Especially when you're new to a field or writing about unfamiliar ideas, incorporating sources without plagiarizing can be challenging.

In fact, researcher Rebecca Moore Howard has found that even expert writers have difficulty incorporating the words and ideas of others acceptably when they are working with material outside their comfort zone or field of expertise. Such difficulty can often lead to what Howard calls **PATCHWRITING**: restating material from sources in ways that stick too closely to the original language or syntax.

But patchwriting can help you work with sources. Some call patchwriting plagiarism, even when it's documented, but we believe that it can be a step in the process of learning how to weave the words and thoughts of others into your own work. Assume, for example, that you want to summarize ideas from the following passage:

> Over the past few decades, scholars from a variety of disciplines have devoted considerable attention toward studying evolving public attitudes toward a whole range of LGBT civil rights issues including support for open service in the military, same-sex parent adoption, employment non-discrimination, civil unions, and marriage equality. In the last 10 years in particular, the emphasis has shifted toward studying the various factors that best explain variation in support for same-sex marriage including demographic considerations, religious and ideological predispositions, attitudes toward marriage and family, and social contact (Baunach 2011, 2012; Becker, 2012a, 2012b; Becker & Scheufele, 2009, 2011; Becker & Todd, 2013; Brewer, 2008; Brewer & Wilcox, 2005; Lewis, 2005, 2011; Lewis & Gossett, 2008; Lewis & Oh, 2008).
> —AMY BECKER, "Employment Discrimination, Local School Boards, and LGBT Civil Rights: Reviewing 25 Years of Public Opinion Data"

This passage includes a lot of detailed information in complex sentences that can be hard to process. See how one student first summarized it, and why this summary would be unacceptable in an essay of his own:

A patchwritten summary

For more than 20 years, scholars from many disciplines have committed their energies to examining changing public attitudes toward a variety of LGBT civil rights issues. These encompass things like open military service, same-sex parent adoption, equal employment opportunities, civil unions, and marriage equality. Since 2004, focus has moved toward examining those elements that best account for differences in public support for same-sex marriage like demographic considerations, religious and ideological predispositions, attitudes toward marriage and family, and social contact (Baunach 2011, 2012; Becker, 2012a, 2012b; Becker & Scheufele, 2009, 2011; Becker & Todd, 2013; Brewer, 2008; Brewer & Wilcox, 2005; Lewis, 2005, 2011; Lewis & Gossett, 2008; Lewis & Oh, 2008).

This is a classic case of patchwriting that would be considered plagiarism. The sentence structure looks very much like Becker's, and even some of the language is taken straight from the original article. While such a summary would not be acceptable in any writing you turn in, this sort of patchwriting can help you understand what a difficult source is saying.

And once you understand the source, writing an acceptable summary gets a lot easier. In the acceptable summary below, the writer focuses on the ideas in the long second sentence of the original passage, turning those ideas into two simpler sentences and using a direct quotation from the original.

Acceptable summary

Scholars studying changes in public opinion on LGBT issues have increasingly focused on the growing support for same-sex marriage. In looking at the question of why opinions on this issue differ, these scholars have considered factors such as "demographic considerations, religious and ideological predispositions, attitudes toward marriage and family, and social contact" (Becker 342).

An acceptable summary uses the writer's own language and sentence structures, and quotation marks to indicate any borrowed language. To write a summary like this one, you would need to be able to restate the source's main point (that same-sex marriage has gotten greater scholarly attention lately than other LGBTQ issues) and decide what information is most important for your purposes—what details are worth emphasizing with a quotation or a longer summary. Finally, notice that the citation credits Becker's article, because that is the source this writer consulted, not the research Becker cites. Chapter 26 offers you more guidelines on QUOTING, PARAPHRASING, and SUMMARIZING appropriately.

STEPS YOU CAN TAKE TO AVOID PLAGIARISM

Understand what constitutes plagiarism. Plagiarism includes any unacknowledged use of material from another source that isn't considered common knowledge; this includes phrases, ideas, and materials such as graphs, charts, images, videos, and so on. In a written text, it includes neglecting to put someone else's exact wording in quotation marks; leaving out in-text documentation for sources that you QUOTE, PARAPHRASE, or SUMMARIZE; and borrowing too many of the original sources' words and sentence structures in paraphrases or summaries. Check to see if your school has any explicit guidelines for what constitutes plagiarism.

Take notes carefully and conscientiously. If you can't locate the source of words or ideas that you've copied down, you may neglect to cite them properly. Technology makes it easy to copy and paste text and materials from electronic sources directly into your own work—and then to move on and forget to put such material in quotation marks or record the source. So keep copies of sources, note documentation information, and be sure to put any borrowed language in quotation marks and to clearly distinguish your own ideas from those of others.

Know where your information comes from. Because information passes quickly and often anonymously through the internet grapevine, you may not always be able to determine the origin of a text or image you find online. If you don't know where something came from, don't include it. Not only would you be unable to write a proper citation, chances are you haven't been able to verify the information either.

DOCUMENT sources carefully. Below you'll find an overview of the basics of documenting sources. More detail on using **MLA** and **APA** documentation is given in the next two chapters.

Plan ahead. Work can pile up in a high-pressure academic environment. Stay on top of your projects by scheduling your work and sticking to the deadlines you set. This way, you'll avoid taking shortcuts that could lead to inadvertent plagiarism.

Consult your instructor if necessary. If you're uncertain about how to acknowledge sources properly or are struggling with a project, talk with your instructor about finding a solution. Even taking a penalty for submitting an assignment late is better than being caught cheating or being accused of plagiarism that you didn't intend to commit.

Documenting Sources

When you document sources, you identify the ones you've used and give information about their authors, titles, and publication. Documenting your sources allows you to show evidence of the research you've done and enables your readers to find those sources if they wish to. Most academic documentation systems include two parts: **IN-TEXT DOCUMENTATION**, which you insert in your text after the specific information you have borrowed, and an end-of-text list of **WORKS CITED** or **REFERENCES**, which provides complete bibliographic information for every work you've cited.

This book covers two documentation systems—those of the Modern Language Association (**MLA**) and the American Psychological Association (**APA**). MLA style is used primarily in English and other humanities subjects, and APA is used mostly in psychology and other social sciences. Chances are that you will be required to use either MLA or APA style or both in your college courses. Note that some disciplines may require other documentation systems, such as CSE (Council of Science Editors) or *Chicago Manual of Style*.

MLA and APA both call for the same basic information; you'll need to give the author's name (or sometimes the editor's name or the title) in the in-text citation, and your end-of-text list should provide the author, title, and publication information for each source that you cite. But the two systems differ in some ways. In APA, for example, your in-text documentation always includes the date of publication, but that is not generally done in MLA. You'll find detailed guidance on the specifics of MLA in Chapter 28 and of APA in Chapter 29, with color-coded examples to help you easily distinguish where the author and editor, title, and publication information appear for each type of work you document. Each of these chapters also includes a student paper that uses that style of documentation.

REFLECT. Think about the kinds of information you'll need to give when writing about your research. For your topic and your intended audience, what would be considered common knowledge? What might not be common knowledge for a different audience? What do you know about your audience that can help you make that decision?

TWENTY-EIGHT

MLA Style

 **LA STYLE CALLS** for (1) brief in-text documentation and (2) complete bibliographic information in a list of works cited at the end of your text. The models and examples in this chapter draw on the ninth edition of the *MLA Handbook*, published by the Modern Language Association in 2021. For additional information, or if you're citing a source that isn't covered, visit style.mla.org.

A DIRECTORY TO MLA STYLE

In-Text Documentation   565

author   title   publication

Throughout this chapter, you'll find color-coded models and examples to help you see how writers include source information in their texts and in their lists of works cited: tan for author, editor, translator, and other contributors; yellow for titles; gray for publication information—publisher, date of publication, page number(s), DOIs, and other location information.

IN-TEXT DOCUMENTATION

Whenever you **QUOTE**, **PARAPHRASE**, or **SUMMARIZE** a source in your writing, you need to provide brief documentation that tells readers what you took from the source and where in the source you found that information.

You'll need to mention the author or title, either in a signal phrase—"as Toni Morrison writes"—or in parentheses—(Morrison). Name the author in either place but not in both places.

Shorten any lengthy titles or descriptions in parentheses by including the first noun with any preceding adjectives but without any initial articles (*Norton Field Guide* rather than *The Norton Field Guide to Writing*). Use the full title if it's short (*What's Your Pronoun?*).

The first examples below show basic in-text documentation of a work by one author. Variations on those examples follow. The examples illustrate the MLA style of using quotation marks around titles of short works and italicizing titles of long works.

1. Author named in a signal phrase

If you mention the author in a **SIGNAL PHRASE**, put only the page number(s) in parentheses. Do not write *page* or *p*. The first time you mention the author, use their first and last names. Omit any middle initials.

> David McCullough describes John Adams's hands as those of someone used to manual labor (18).

2. Author named in parentheses

If you do not mention the author in a signal phrase, put the last name in parentheses along with any page number(s). Do not use punctuation between the name and the page number(s).

> Adams is said to have had "the hands of a man accustomed to pruning his own trees, cutting his own hay, and splitting his own firewood" (McCullough 18).

Whether you use a signal phrase and parentheses or parentheses only, try to put the parenthetical documentation at the end of the sentence or as close as possible to the material you've cited—without awkwardly interrupting the sentence. Notice that in the example above, the parenthetical reference comes after the closing quotation marks but before the period at the end of the sentence.

author   title   publication

3. Two or more works by the same author

If you cite multiple works by one author, include the title of the work you are citing either in the signal phrase or in parentheses.

> Robert Kaplan insists that understanding power in the Near East requires "Western leaders who know when to intervene, and do so without illusions" (*Eastward to Tartary* 330).

Put a comma between author and title if both are in the parentheses.

> Understanding power in the Near East requires "Western leaders who know when to intervene, and do so without illusions" (Kaplan, *Eastward to Tartary* 330).

4. Authors with the same last name

Give the author's first and last names in any signal phrase, or add the author's first initial in the parenthetical reference.

> *Imaginative* applies not only to modern literature but also to writing of all periods, whereas *magical* is often used in writing about Arthurian romances (A. Wilson 25).

5. Two or more authors

For a work with two authors, name both. If you first mention them in a signal phrase, give their first and last names.

> Lori Carlson and Cynthia Ventura's stated goal is to introduce Julio Cortázar, Marjorie Agosín, and other Latin American writers to an audience of English-speaking adolescents (v).

For a work by three or more authors that you mention in a signal phrase, you can either name them all or name the first author followed by *and others* or *and colleagues*. If you mention them in a parenthetical reference, name the first author followed by *et al.*

> Phyllis Anderson and colleagues describe a thematic survey of American literature (A19-A24).

One popular survey of American literature breaks the contents into sixteen thematic groupings (Anderson et al. A19-A24).

6. Organization or government as author

In a signal phrase, use the full name of the organization: American Academy of Arts and Sciences. In parentheses, use the shortest noun phrase: American Academy. Omit any initial articles.

The US government warns, "If you are overpaid, we will recover any payments not due you" (Social Security Administration 12).

7. Author unknown

If you don't know the author, use the work's title in a signal phrase and a shortened version of the title in the parenthetical reference.

A powerful editorial in last week's paper asserts that healthy liver donor Mike Hurewitz died because of "frightening" faulty postoperative care ("Every Patient's Nightmare").

8. Literary works

When referring to common literary works that are available in many different editions, give the page numbers from the edition you are using, followed by information that will let readers of any edition locate the text you are citing.

Novels and prose plays. Give the page number followed by a semicolon and any chapter, section, or act numbers, separated by commas.

In *Pride and Prejudice*, Mrs. Bennet shows no warmth toward Jane and Elizabeth when they return from Netherfield (Austen 105; ch. 12).

Verse plays. Give act, scene, and line numbers, separated by periods.

Shakespeare continues the vision theme when Macbeth says, "Thou hast no speculation in those eyes / Which thou dost glare with" (*Macbeth* 3.3.96-97).

author | title | publication

Poems. Give the part and the line numbers (separated by periods). If a poem has only line numbers, use the word *line(s)* only in the first reference.

> Walt Whitman sets up not only opposing adjectives but also opposing nouns in "Song of Myself" when he says, "I am of old and young, of the foolish as much as the wise, / . . . a child as well as a man" (16.330-32).

> One description of the mere in *Beowulf* is "not a pleasant place" (line 1372). Later, it is labeled "the awful place" (1378).

9. Work in an anthology

Name the author(s) of the work, not the editor of the anthology.

> "It is the teapots that truly shock," according to Cynthia Ozick in her essay on teapots as metaphor (70).

> In *In Short: A Collection of Creative Nonfiction*, readers will find both an essay on Scottish tea (Hiestand) and a piece on teapots as metaphors (Ozick).

10. Encyclopedia or dictionary

For an entry in an encyclopedia or dictionary, give the author's name, if available. For an entry without an author, give the entry's title.

> According to *Funk and Wagnall's New World Encyclopedia*, early in his career Kubrick's main source of income came from "hustling chess games in Washington Square Park" ("Kubrick, Stanley").

11. Legal documents

For legal cases, give whatever comes first in the works-cited entry. If multiple entries in your works-cited list start with the same government author, give as much of the name as you need to differentiate the sources.

> In 2015, for the first time, all states were required to license and recognize the marriages of same-sex couples (United States, Supreme Court).

12. Sacred text

When citing a sacred text such as the Bible or the Qur'an for the first time, give the title of the edition as well as the book, chapter, and verse (or their equivalent), separated by periods. MLA recommends abbreviating the names of the books of the Bible in parenthetical references. Later citations from the same edition do not have to repeat its title.

> The wording from *The New English Bible* follows: "In the beginning of creation, when God made heaven and earth, the earth was without form and void . . ." (Gen. 1.1-2).

13. Multivolume work

If you cite more than one volume of a multivolume work, each time you cite one of the volumes, give the volume *and* the page number(s) in parentheses, separated by a colon and a space.

> Carl Sandburg concludes with the following sentence about those paying last respects to Lincoln: "All day long and through the night the unbroken line moved, the home town having its farewell" (4: 413).

If you cite an entire volume of a multivolume work in parentheses, give the author's last name followed by a comma and *vol.* before the volume number: (Sandburg, vol. 2). If your works-cited list includes only a single volume of a multivolume work, give just the page number in parentheses: (230).

14. Two or more works cited together

If you're citing two or more works closely together, you will sometimes need to provide a parenthetical reference for each one.

> Tanner (7) and Smith (viii) have looked at works from a cultural perspective.

If you are citing multiple sources for the same idea in parentheses, separate the references with a semicolon.

> Many critics have examined great works of literature from a cultural perspective (Tanner 7; Smith viii).

15. Source quoted in another source

When you are quoting text that you found quoted in another source, use the abbreviation *qtd. in* in the parenthetical reference.

> Charlotte Brontë wrote to G. H. Lewes, "Why do you like Miss Austen so very much? I am puzzled on that point" (qtd. in Tanner 7).

16. Work without page numbers

For works without page or part numbers, including many online sources, identify the source using the author or other information.

> Studies show that music training helps children to be better at multitasking later in life ("Hearing the Music").

If you mention the author in a signal phrase, or if you mention the title of a work with no author, no parenthetical reference is needed.

> Arthur Brooks argues that a switch to fully remote work would have a negative effect on mental and physical health.

If the source has chapter, paragraph, or section numbers, use them with the abbreviations *ch., par.,* or *sec.* ("Hearing the Music," par. 2). Don't count lines or paragraphs on your own if they aren't numbered in the source. For an ebook, use chapter numbers. For an audio or video recording, give the hours, minutes, and seconds (separated by colons) as shown on the player: (00:05:21-31).

17. An entire work or a one-page article

If you cite an entire work rather than a part of it, or if you cite a single-page article, there's no need to include page numbers.

> Throughout life, John Adams strove to succeed (McCullough).

NOTES

Sometimes you may need to give information that doesn't fit into the text itself—to thank people who helped you, to provide additional details, to refer readers to other sources, or to add comments about sources. Such information can be given in a *footnote* (at the bottom of the page) or an *endnote* (on a separate page with the heading *Notes* or *Endnotes* just before your works-cited list). Put a superscript number at the appropriate point in your text, signaling to readers to look for the note with the corresponding number. If you have multiple notes, number them consecutively throughout your paper.

Text

This essay will argue that giving student athletes preferential treatment undermines educational goals.[1]

Note

[1] I want to thank those who contributed to my thinking on this topic, especially my teacher Vincent Yu.

LIST OF WORKS CITED

A works-cited list provides full bibliographic information for every source cited in your text. See page 602 for guidelines on formatting this list and page 617 for a sample works-cited list.

Core Elements

MLA style provides a list of core elements for documenting sources, advising writers to list as many of them as possible in the order that MLA specifies. We've used these general principles to provide templates and examples for documenting 52 kinds of sources college writers most often need to cite. The following general guidelines explain how to treat each of the core elements.

Authors and Contributors

- An author can be any kind of creator—a writer, a musician, an artist, and so on.
- If there is one author, list the last name first: Morrison, Toni.

- If there are two authors, list the first author last name first and the second one first name first: Lunsford, Andrea, and Lisa Ede. Put their names in the order given in the work. For three or more authors, give the first author's name followed by *et al.*: Rose, Mike, et al.

- Include any middle names or initials: Heath, Shirley Brice; Toklas, Alice B.

- If the author is a group or organization, use the full name, omitting any initial article: American Psychological Association, United Nations.

- If an author uses a handle that is significantly different from their name, include the handle in square brackets after the name: Ocasio-Cortez, Alexandria [@AOC].

- If there's no known author, start the entry with the title.

- If you're citing an editor, translator, director, or other contributors, specify their role. For works with multiple contributors, put the one whose work you wish to highlight before the title, and list any others you want to mention after the title. If you don't want to highlight one particular contributor, start with the title and include any contributors after the title. For contributors named before the title, put the label after the name: Fincher, David, director. For those named after the title, specify their role first: Directed by David Fincher.

Titles

- Include any subtitles and capitalize all the words in titles and subtitles except for articles (*a, an, the*), prepositions (*to, at, from,* and so on), and coordinating conjunctions (*and, but, for, or, nor, yet*)—unless they are the first or last word of a title or subtitle.

- Italicize the titles of books, periodicals, websites, and other long works (*Pride and Prejudice, Wired*).

- Enclose in quotation marks the titles of articles and other short works: "Letter from Birmingham Jail."

- To document a source that has no title, describe it without italics or quotation marks: Letter to the author, Review of rap concert. For a short, untitled email, text message, tweet, or poem, you may want to include the text itself instead: Dickinson, Emily. "Immortal is an ample word." *American Poems,* www.americanpoems.com/poets/emilydickinson/immortal-is-an-ample-word.

Versions and Numbers

- If you cite a source that's available in more than one version, specify the one you consulted in your works-cited entry. Write ordinal numbers with numerals, and abbreviate *edition*: 2nd ed. Write out names of specific versions, and capitalize following a period or if the name is a proper noun: King James Version, unabridged version, director's cut.
- If you cite a book that's published in multiple volumes, indicate the volume number. Abbreviate *volume*, and write the number as a numeral: vol. 2.
- Indicate any volume and issue numbers of journals, abbreviating both *volume* and *number*: vol. 123, no. 4.
- If you cite a TV show or podcast episode, indicate the season and episode numbers: season 1, episode 4.

Publishers

- Write publishers', studios', and networks' names in full, but omit initial articles and business words like *Company* or *Inc.*
- For academic presses, use *U* for "University" and *P* for "Press": Princeton UP, U of California P. Spell out *Press* if the name doesn't include *University*: Running Press, MIT Press.
- If the publisher is a division of an organization, list the organization and any divisions from largest to smallest: Stanford U, Center for the Study of Language and Information, Metaphysics Research Lab.

Dates

- Whether to give just the year or to include the month and day depends on the source. In general, give the full date that you find there.
- For books, give the copyright date: 1948. If a book lists more than one date, use the most recent one.
- Periodicals may be published annually, monthly, seasonally, weekly, or daily. Give the full date that you find there: 2019, Apr. 2019, spring 2019, 16 Apr. 2019.
- Abbreviate the months except for May, June, and July: Jan., Feb., Mar., Apr., Aug., Sept., Oct., Nov., Dec.

author   title   publication

- For online sources, use the copyright date or the full date that you find in the source. If the source does not give a date, use the date of access: Accessed 6 June 2020. Give a date of access as well for online sources you think are likely to change, or for websites that have disappeared.

Location

- For most print articles and other short works, give a page number or range of pages: p. 24, pp. 24-35. For those that are not on consecutive pages, give the first page number with a plus sign: pp. 24+.
- If it's necessary to specify a particular section of a source, give the section name before the page numbers: Sunday Review sec., p. 3.
- Indicate the location of an online source by giving a DOI if one is available; if not, give a URL—and use a permalink if one is available. URLs are not always reliable, so ask your instructor if you should include them. DOIs should start with *https://doi.org/* but no need to include *https://* for a URL, unless you want the URL to be a hyperlink.
- For a location, give enough information to identify it: a city (Houston), a city and state (Provo, Utah), or a city and country (Itu, Brazil). For something seen in a museum or elsewhere, name the institution and its location: Olson House, Cushing, Maine.
- For performances or other live presentations, name the venue and its location: Mark Taper Forum, Los Angeles.

Punctuation

- Use a period after the author name(s) that start an entry (Morrison, Toni.) and the title of the source you're documenting (*Beloved*.).
- Use a comma between the author's last and first names: Morrison, Toni.
- Some URLs won't fit on one line. When necessary, we recommend breaking a URL before a punctuation mark. Do not add a hyphen or a space.
- Sometimes you'll need to provide information about more than one work for a single source—for instance, when you cite an article from a periodical that you access through a database. MLA refers to the periodical and database (or any other entity that holds a source) as

"containers." Use commas between elements within each container and put a period at the end of each container. For example:

Semuels, Alana. "The Future Will Be Quiet." *The Atlantic*, Apr. 2016, pp. 19-20. *ProQuest*, search.proquest.com/docview /1777443553?accountid+42654.

The guidelines below should help you document kinds of sources you're likely to use. The first section shows how to acknowledge authors and other contributors and applies to all kinds of sources—print, online, or others. Later sections show how to treat titles, publication information, location, and access information for many specific kinds of sources. In general, provide as much information as possible for each source—enough to tell readers how to find a source if they wish to access it themselves.

Sources Not Covered

These guidelines will help you cite a variety of sources, but there may be sources you want to use that aren't mentioned here. If you're citing a source that isn't covered, consult the MLA style blog at style.mla.org, or ask them a question at style.mla.org/ask-a-question.

Authors and Contributors

When you name authors and other contributors in your citations, you are crediting them for their work and letting readers know who's in on the conversation. The following guidelines for citing authors and contributors apply to all sources you cite: in print, online, or in some other medium.

1. One author

Author's Last Name, First Name. *Title*. Publisher, Date.

Anderson, Chris. *The Long Tail: Why the Future of Business Is Selling Less of More*. Hyperion, 2006.

2. Two authors

1st Author's Last Name, First Name, and 2nd Author's First and Last Names. *Title*. Publisher, Date.

author   title   publication

Lunsford, Andrea, and Lisa Ede. *Singular Texts/Plural Authors: Perspectives on Collaborative Writing*. Southern Illinois UP, 1990.

3. Three or more authors

1st Author's Last Name, First Name, et al. *Title*. Publisher, Date.

Sebranek, Patrick, et al. *Writers INC: A Guide to Writing, Thinking, and Learning*. Write Source, 1990.

4. Two or more works by the same author

Give the author's name in the first entry, and then use three hyphens in the author slot for each of the subsequent works, listing them alphabetically by the first word of each title and ignoring any articles.

Author's Last Name, First Name. *Title That Comes First Alphabetically*. Publisher, Date.

---. *Title That Comes Next Alphabetically*. Publisher, Date.

Kaplan, Robert D. *The Coming Anarchy: Shattering the Dreams of the Post Cold War*. Random House, 2000.

---. *Eastward to Tartary: Travels in the Balkans, the Middle East, and the Caucasus*. Random House, 2000.

5. Author and editor or translator

Author's Last Name, First Name. *Title*. Role by First and Last Names, Publisher, Date.

Austen, Jane. *Emma*. Edited by Stephen M. Parrish, W. W. Norton, 2000.
Dostoevsky, Fyodor. *Crime and Punishment*. Translated by Richard Pevear and Larissa Volokhonsky, Vintage Books, 1993.

Start with the editor or translator if you are focusing on their contribution rather than the author's. If there is a translator but no author, start with the title.

Pevear, Richard, and Larissa Volokhonsky, translators. *Crime and Punishment*. By Fyodor Dostoevsky, Vintage Books, 1993.
Beowulf. Translated by Stephen Mitchell, Yale UP, 2017.

6. No author or editor

When there's no known author or editor, start with the title.

> *The Turner Collection in the Clore Gallery.* Tate Publications, 1987.

> "Being Invisible Closer to Reality." *The Atlanta Journal-Constitution,*
>   11 Aug. 2008, p. A3.

7. Organization or government as author

> Organization Name. *Title.* Publisher, Date.

> Diagram Group. *The Macmillan Visual Desk Reference.* Macmillan, 1993.

For a government publication, give the name that is shown in the source.

> United States, Department of Health and Human Services, National
>   Institute of Mental Health. *Autism Spectrum Disorders.*
>   Government Printing Office, 2004.

When a nongovernment organization is both author and publisher, start with the title and list the organization only as the publisher.

> *Stylebook on Religion 2000: A Reference Guide and Usage Manual.*
>   Catholic News Service, 2002.

If a division of an organization is listed as the author, give the division as the author and the organization as the publisher.

> Center for Workforce Studies. *2005-13: Demographics of the U.S.
>   Psychology Workforce.* American Psychological Association, July
>   2015.

Articles and Other Short Works

Articles, essays, reviews, and other short works are found in journals, magazines, newspapers, other periodicals, and books—all of which you may find in print, online, or in a database. For most short works, you'll need to provide information about the author, the titles of both the short work and the longer work, any page numbers, and various kinds of publication information, all explained below.

Documentation Map (MLA) / Article in a Print Journal

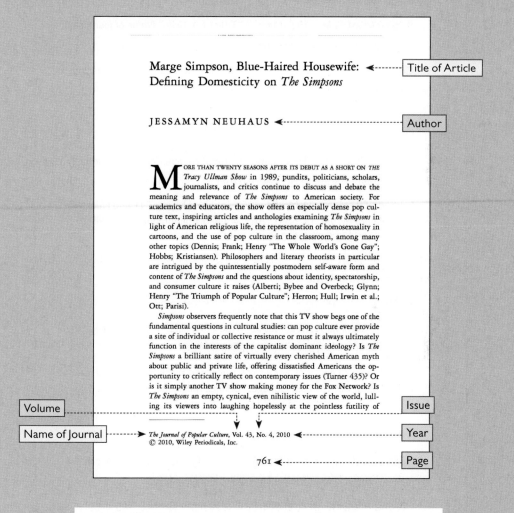

Marge Simpson, Blue-Haired Housewife: ◄-------- Title of Article
Defining Domesticity on *The Simpsons*

JESSAMYN NEUHAUS ◄-------------------------------- Author

MORE THAN TWENTY SEASONS AFTER ITS DEBUT AS A SHORT ON *THE Tracy Ullman Show* in 1989, pundits, politicians, scholars, journalists, and critics continue to discuss and debate the meaning and relevance of *The Simpsons* to American society. For academics and educators, the show offers an especially dense pop culture text, inspiring articles and anthologies examining *The Simpsons* in light of American religious life, the representation of homosexuality in cartoons, and the use of pop culture in the classroom, among many other topics (Dennis; Frank; Henry "The Whole World's Gone Gay"; Hobbs; Kristiansen). Philosophers and literary theorists in particular are intrigued by the quintessentially postmodern self-aware form and content of *The Simpsons* and the questions about identity, spectatorship, and consumer culture it raises (Alberti; Bybee and Overbeck; Glynn; Henry "The Triumph of Popular Culture"; Herron; Hull; Irwin et al.; Ott; Parisi).

Simpsons observers frequently note that this TV show begs one of the fundamental questions in cultural studies: can pop culture ever provide a site of individual or collective resistance or must it always ultimately function in the interests of the capitalist dominant ideology? Is *The Simpsons* a brilliant satire of virtually every cherished American myth about public and private life, offering dissatisfied Americans the opportunity to critically reflect on contemporary issues (Turner 435)? Or is it simply another TV show making money for the Fox Network? Is *The Simpsons* an empty, cynical, even nihilistic view of the world, lulling its viewers into laughing hopelessly at the pointless futility of

Volume -------
Name of Journal -------► *The Journal of Popular Culture*, Vol. 43, No. 4, 2010 ◄
© 2010, Wiley Periodicals, Inc.

Issue
Year

761 ◄-------------------------------- Page

Neuhaus, Jessamyn. "Marge Simpson, Blue-Haired Housewife: Defining Domesticity on *The Simpsons*." *The Journal of Popular Culture*, vol. 43, no. 4, 2010, pp. 761-81.

8. Article in a journal

Print

Author's Last Name, First Name. "Title of Article." *Name of Journal*,
        Volume, Issue, Date, Pages.

Cooney, Brian C. "Considering *Robinson Crusoe*'s 'Liberty of Conscience'
        in an Age of Terror." *College English,* vol. 69, no. 3, Jan. 2007,
        pp. 197-215.

Online

Author's Last Name, First Name. "Title of Article." *Name of Journal*,
        Volume, Issue, Date, DOI *or* URL.

Schmidt, Desmond. "A Model of Versions and Layers." *Digital Humanities
        Quarterly*, vol. 13, no. 3, 2019, www.digitalhumanities.org/dhq
        /vol/13/3/000430/000430.html.

9. Article in a magazine

Print

Author's Last Name, First Name. "Title of Article." *Name of Magazine*,
        Volume (if any), Issue (if any), Date, Pages.

Burt, Tequia. "Legacy of Activism: Concerned Black Students' 50-Year
        History at Grinnell College." *Grinnell Magazine*, vol. 48, no. 4,
        summer 2016, pp. 32-38.

Online

Author's Last Name, First Name. "Title of Article." *Name of Magazine*,
        Volume (if any), Issue (if any), Date, DOI *or* URL.

Brooks, Arthur C. "The Hidden Toll of Remote Work." *The Atlantic*,
        1 Apr. 2021, www.theatlantic.com/family/archive/2021/04
        /zoom-remote-work-loneliness-happiness/618473.

author   title   publication

Documentation Map (MLA) /
Article in an Online Magazine

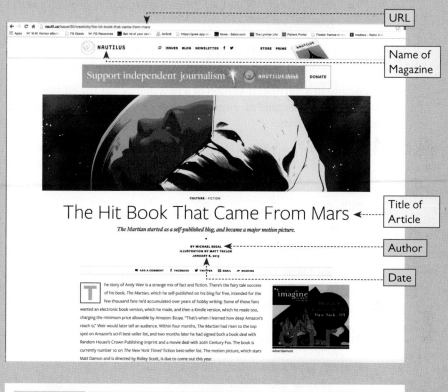

URL

Name of Magazine

Title of Article

Author

Date

Segal, Michael. "The Hit Book That Came from Mars." *Nautilus*, 8 Jan. 2015, nautil.us/issue/20/creativity/the-hit-book-that-came-from-mars.

10. Article in a news publication

Print

Author's Last Name, First Name. "Title of Article." *Name of Publication,*
   Date, Pages.

Saulny, Susan, and Jacques Steinberg. "On College Forms, a Question of
   Race Can Perplex." *The New York Times,* 14 June 2011, p. A1.

To document a particular edition of a newspaper, list the edition before the
date. If a section name or number is needed to locate the article, put that
detail after the date.

Burns, John F., and Miguel Helft. "Under Pressure, YouTube Withdraws
   Muslim Cleric's Videos." *The New York Times,* late ed., 4 Nov. 2010,
   sec. 1, p. 13.

Online

Author's Last Name, First Name. "Title of Article." *Name of Publication,*
   Date, URL.

Banerjee, Neela. "Proposed Religion-Based Program for Federal Inmates
   Is Canceled." *The New York Times,* 28 Oct. 2006, www.nytimes
   .com/2006/10/28/us/28prison.html.

11. Article accessed through a database

Author's Last Name, First Name. "Title of Article." *Name of Periodical,*
   Volume, Issue, Date, Pages. *Name of Database,* DOI *or* URL.

Stalter, Sunny. "Subway Ride and Subway System in Hart Crane's 'The
   Tunnel.'" *Journal of Modern Literature,* vol. 33, no. 2, Jan. 2010, pp.
   70-91. *JSTOR,* https://doi.org/10.2979/jml.2010.33.2.70.

12. Entry in a reference work

Print

Author's Last Name, First Name (if any). "Title of Entry." *Title of
   Reference Book,* edited by Editor's First and Last Names (if any),
   Edition number (if any), Volume (if any), Publisher, Date, Pages.

author   title   publication

Documentation Map (MLA) /
Journal Article Accessed through a Database

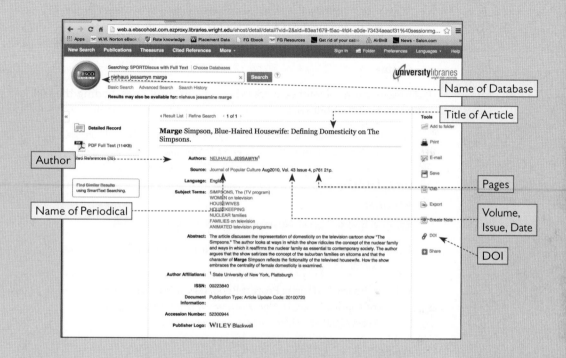

Author — NEUHAUS, JESSAMYN[1]

Name of Database — Title of Article

Name of Periodical

Pages

Volume, Issue, Date

DOI

Neuhaus, Jessamyn. "Marge Simpson, Blue-Haired Housewife: Defining
Domesticity on *The Simpsons*." *Journal of Popular Culture,* vol. 43,
no. 4, Aug. 2010, pp. 761-81. *EBSCOhost,* https://doi.org/10.1111
/j.1540-5931.2010.00769.x.

Fritz, Jan Marie. "Clinical Sociology." *Encyclopedia of Sociology*, edited by
    Edgar F. Borgatta and Rhonda J. V. Montgomery, 2nd ed., vol. 1,
    Macmillan Reference USA, 2000, pp. 323-29.

"California." *The New Columbia Encyclopedia*, edited by William H.
    Harris and Judith S. Levey, 4th ed., Columbia UP, 1975,
    pp. 423-24.

Online

Document online reference works the same as print ones, adding the URL
after the date of publication.

"Baseball." *The Columbia Electronic Encyclopedia,* edited by Paul Lagassé,
    6th ed., Columbia UP, 2012, www.infoplease.com/encyclopedia.

13. Editorial or op-ed

Editorial

Editorial Board. "Title." *Name of Periodical*, Date, Page *or* URL.

Editorial Board. "A New Look for Local News Coverage." *The Lakeville
    Journal*, 13 Feb. 2020, p. A8.

Editorial Board. "Editorial: Protect Reporters at Protest Scenes."
    Los Angeles Times, 11 Mar. 2021, www.latimes.com/opinion
    /story/2021-03-11/reporters-protest-scenes.

Op-ed

Author's Last Name, First Name. "Title." *Name of Periodical*, Date, Page
    or URL.

Okafor, Kingsley. "Opinion: The First Step to COVID Vaccine
    Equity Is Overall Health Equity." *The Denver Post*, 15 Apr. 2021,
    www.denverpost.com/2021/04/15/covid-vaccine-equity
    -kaiser.

If it's not clear that it's an op-ed, add a label at the end.

Balf, Todd. "Falling in Love with Swimming." *The New York Times*, 17 Apr.
    2021, p. A21. Op-ed.

author   title   publication

14. Letter to the editor

> Author's Last Name, First Name. "Title of Letter (if any)." *Name of Periodical*, Date, Page *or* URL.

> Pinker, Steven. "Language Arts." *The New Yorker*, 4 June 2012, p. 10.

If the letter has no title, include *Letter* after the author's name.

> Fleischmann, W. B. Letter. *The New York Review of Books*, 1 June 1963, www.nybooks.com/articles/1963/06/01/letter-21.

15. Review

Print

> Reviewer's Last Name, First Name. "Title of Review." *Name of Periodical*, Date, Pages.

> Frank, Jeffrey. "Body Count." *The New Yorker*, 30 July 2007, pp. 86–87.

Online

> Reviewer's Last Name, First Name. "Title of Review." *Name of Periodical*, Date, URL.

> Donadio, Rachel. "Italy's Great, Mysterious Storyteller." *The New York Review of Books*, 18 Dec. 2014, www.nybooks.com/articles/2014/12/18/italys-great-mysterious-storyteller.

If a review has no title, include the title and author of the work being reviewed after the reviewer's name.

> Lohier, Patrick. Review of *Exhalation*, by Ted Chiang. *Harvard Review Online*, 4 Oct. 2019, www.harvardreview.org/book-review/exhalation.

16. Comment on an online article

> Commenter's Last Name, First Name *or* Username. Comment on "Title of Article." *Name of Periodical*, Date posted, Time posted, URL.

> ZeikJT. Comment on "The Post-Disaster Artist." *Polygon*, 6 May 2020, 4:33 a.m., www.polygon.com/2020/5/5/21246679/josh-trank-capone-interview-fantastic-four-chronicle#comments.

Books and Parts of Books

For most books, you'll need to provide information about the author, the title, the publisher, and the year of publication. If you found the book inside a larger volume, a database, or some other work, be sure to specify that as well.

17. Basic entries for a book

Print

Author's Last Name, First Name. *Title*. Publisher, Year of publication.

Watson, Brad. *Miss Jane*. W. W. Norton, 2016.

Ebook

Author's Last Name, First Name. *Title*. Ebook ed., Publisher, Year of Publication.

Watson, Brad. *Miss Jane*. Ebook ed., W. W. Norton, 2016.

Concise Guide to APA Style. 7th ed., ebook ed., American Psychological Association, 2020.

On a website

Author's Last Name, First Name. *Title*. Publisher, Year of publication, DOI *or* URL.

Ball, Cheryl E., and Drew M. Loewe, editors. *Bad Ideas about Writing*. West Virginia U Libraries, 2017, textbooks.lib.wvu.edu/badideas /badideasaboutwriting-book.pdf.

18. Anthology or edited collection

Last Name, First Name, editor. *Title*. Publisher, Year of publication.

Kitchen, Judith, and Mary Paumier Jones, editors. *In Short: A Collection of Brief Creative Nonfiction*. W. W. Norton, 1996.

19. Work in an anthology

> Author's Last Name, First Name. "Title of Work." *Title of Anthology*, edited
> by First and Last Names, Publisher, Year of publication, Pages.

> Achebe, Chinua. "Uncle Ben's Choice." *The Seagull Reader: Literature*,
> edited by Joseph Kelly, W. W. Norton, 2005, pp. 23-27.

Two or more works from one anthology

Prepare an entry for each selection by author and title, followed by the anthology editors' last names and the pages of the selection. Then include an entry for the anthology itself (see no. 18).

> Author's Last Name, First Name. "Title of Work." Anthology Editors'
> Last Names, Pages.

> Hiestand, Emily. "Afternoon Tea." Kitchen and Jones, pp. 65-67.

> Ozick, Cynthia. "The Shock of Teapots." Kitchen and Jones, pp. 68-71.

20. Multivolume work

All volumes

> Author's Last Name, First Name. *Title of Work*. Publisher, Year(s) of
> publication. Number of vols.

> Churchill, Winston. *The Second World War*. Houghton Mifflin, 1948-53.
> 6 vols.

Single volume

> Author's Last Name, First Name. *Title of Work*. Vol. number, Publisher,
> Year of publication.

> Sandburg, Carl. *Abraham Lincoln: The War Years*. Vol. 2, Harcourt, Brace
> and World, 1939.

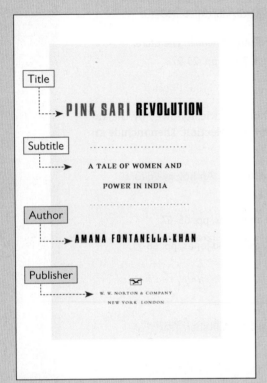

Title → **PINK SARI REVOLUTION**

Subtitle → A TALE OF WOMEN AND POWER IN INDIA

Author → **AMANA FONTANELLA-KHAN**

Publisher → W. W. NORTON & COMPANY NEW YORK LONDON

Year of Publication

For my parents and James, naturally

Copyright © 2013 by Amana Fontanella-Khan

All rights reserved
Printed in the United States of America
First published as a Norton paperback 2014

For information about permission to reproduce selections from this book,
write to Permissions, W. W. Norton & Company, Inc.,
500 Fifth Avenue, New York, NY 10110

For information about special discounts for bulk purchases, please contact
W. W. Norton Special Sales at specialsales@wwnorton.com or 800-233-4830

Manufacturing by Courier Westford
Book design by Barbara M. Bachman
Production manager: Anna Oler

Library of Congress Cataloging-in-Publication Data

Fontanella-Khan, Amana.
Pink sari revolution : a tale of women and power in India / Amana Fontanella-Khan.
—First Edition.
pages cm
Includes bibliographical references and index.
ISBN 978-0-393-06297-7 (hardcover)
1. Women—India—Social conditions. 2. Women's rights—India. 3. Feminism—India.
4. Pal, Sampat, 1961– I. Title.
HQ1743.F66 2013
305.4209594—dc23
2013018948

ISBN 978-0-393-34947-4 pbk.

W. W. Norton & Company, Inc.
500 Fifth Avenue, New York, N.Y. 10110
www.wwnorton.com

W. W. Norton & Company Ltd.
Castle House, 75/76 Wells Street, London W1T 3QT

1 2 3 4 5 6 7 8 9 0

Fontanella-Khan, Amana. *Pink Sari Revolution: A Tale of Women and Power in India.* W. W. Norton, 2013.

If the volume has its own title, include it after the author's name, and indicate the volume number and series title after the year.

> Caro, Robert A. *Means of Ascent*. Vintage Books, 1990. Vol. 2 of *The Years of Lyndon Johnson*.

21. Book in a series

> Author's Last Name, First Name. *Title of Book*. Edited by First and Last Names, Publisher, Year of publication. Series Title.

> Walker, Alice. *Everyday Use*. Edited by Barbara T. Christian, Rutgers UP, 1994. Women Writers: Texts and Contexts.

22. Graphic narrative or comic book

> Author's Last Name, First Name. *Title*. Publisher, Year of publication.

> Barry, Lynda. *One! Hundred! Demons!* Drawn and Quarterly, 2005.

If the work has more than one contributor you want to include, start with the one you want to highlight, and label the role of anyone who's not an author.

> Pekar, Harvey. *Bob and Harv's Comics*. Illustrated by R. Crumb, Running Press, 1996.

> Crumb, R., illustrator. *Bob and Harv's Comics*. By Harvey Pekar, Running Press, 1996.

To cite several contributors, you can also start with the title.

> *Secret Invasion*. By Brian Michael Bendis, illustrated by Leinil Yu, inked by Mark Morales, Marvel, 2009.

23. Sacred text

If you cite a specific edition of a religious text, you need to include it in your works-cited list.

> *The New English Bible with the Apocrypha*. Oxford UP, 1971.

The Torah: A Modern Commentary. W. Gunther Plaut, general editor,
Union of American Hebrew Congregations, 1981.

24. Edition other than the first

Author's Last Name, First Name. *Title.* Name or number of edition,
Publisher, Year of publication.

Smart, Ninian. *The World's Religions.* 2nd ed., Cambridge UP, 1998.

25. Republished work

Author's Last Name, First Name. *Title.* Year of original publication.
Current publisher, Year of republication.

Bierce, Ambrose. *Civil War Stories.* 1909. Dover, 1994.

26. Foreword, introduction, preface, or afterword

Part Author's Last Name, First Name. Name of Part. *Title of Book,* by
Author's First and Last Names, Publisher, Year of publication, Pages.

Tanner, Tony. Introduction. *Pride and Prejudice*, by Jane Austen, Penguin,
1972, pp. 7-46.

27. Published letter

Letter Writer's Last Name, First Name. "Title of letter." Day Month
Year. *Title of Book*, edited by First and Last Names, Publisher,
Year of publication, Pages.

White, E. B. "To Carol Angell." 28 May 1970. *Letters of E. B. White,*
edited by Dorothy Lobrano Guth, Harper and Row, 1976, p. 600.

28. Paper heard at a conference

Author's Last Name, First Name. "Title of Paper." Conference, Day
Month Year, Location.

author   title   publication

Hern, Katie. "Inside an Accelerated Reading and Writing Classroom."
Conference on Acceleration in Developmental Education, 15 June
2016, Sheraton Inner Harbor Hotel, Baltimore.

29. Dissertation

Author's Last Name, First Name. *Title*. Year. Institution, PhD
dissertation. *Name of Database*, URL.

Simington, Maire Orav. *Chasing the American Dream Post World War II:
Perspectives from Literature and Advertising*. 2003. Arizona State U,
PhD dissertation. *ProQuest*, search.proquest.com/docview
/305340098.

For an unpublished dissertation, end with the institution and a description
of the work.

Kim, Loel. *Students Respond to Teacher Comments: A Comparison of
Online Written and Voice Modalities*. 1998. Carnegie Mellon U,
PhD dissertation.

Websites

Many sources are available in multiple media—for example, a print periodical that is also on the web and contained in digital databases—but some
are published only on websites. A website can have an author, an editor, or
neither. Some sites have a publisher, and some do not. Include whatever information is available. If the publisher and title are essentially the same,
omit the name of the publisher. If the site is likely to change, if it has no date,
or if it no longer exists, include a date of access.

30. Entire website

Author's Last Name, First Name. *Title of Site*. Date (if any), URL.

Park, Linda Sue. *Linda Sue Park: Author and Educator*. 2021, lindasuepark
.com.

Editor's Last Name, First Name, role. *Title of Site*. Publisher (if any), Date
(if any), URL.

Documentation Map (MLA) / Work on a Website

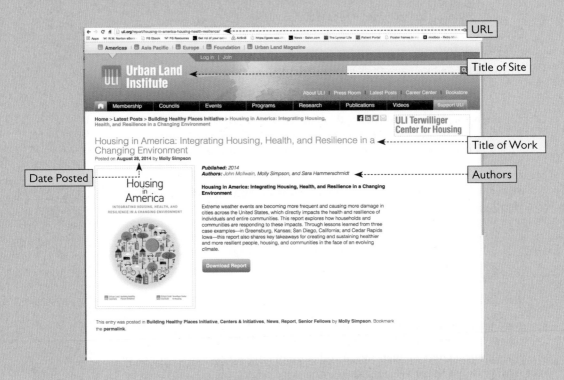

McIlwain, John, et al. "Housing in America: Integrating Housing, Health,
and Resilience in a Changing Environment." *Urban Land Institute*,
28 Aug. 2014, uli.org/report/housing-in-america-housing-health
-resilience.

Proffitt, Michael, chief editor. *The Oxford English Dictionary*. Oxford UP, 2021, www.oed.com.

If a site is likely to change or has no date, include a date of access.

Archive of Our Own. Organization for Transformative Works, archiveofourown.org. Accessed 23 Apr. 2021.

31. Work on a website

Author's Last Name, First Name (if any). "Title of Work." *Title of Site*, Publisher (if any), Date, URL.

Cesareo, Kerry. "Moving Closer to Tackling Deforestation at Scale." *World Wildlife Fund*, 20 Oct. 2020, www.worldwildlife.org /blogs/sustainability-works/posts/moving-closer-to-tackling -deforestation at scale.

32. Blog entry

Author's Last Name, First Name. "Title of Blog Entry." *Title of Blog*, Date, URL.

Hollmichel, Stefanie. "Bring Up the Bodies." *So Many Books*, 10 Feb. 2014, somanybooksblog.com/2014/02/10/bring-up-the-bodies.

Document a whole blog as you would an entire website (no. 30) and a comment on a blog as you would a comment on an online article (no. 16).

33. Wiki

"Title of Entry." *Title of Wiki*, Publisher, Date, URL.

"Pi." *Wikipedia*, Wikimedia Foundation, 28 Aug. 2013, en.wikipedia.org/ wiki/Pi.

Personal Communication and Social Media

34. Personal letter

Sender's Last Name, First Name. Letter to the author. Day Month Year.

Quindlen, Anna. Letter to the author. 11 Apr. 2013.

35. Email or text message

Sender's Last Name, First Name. Email *or* Text Message to First Name
Last Name *or* to the author. *Day Month Year.*

Smith, William. Email to Richard Bullock. 19 Nov. 2013.

Rombes, Maddy. Text message to Isaac Cohen. 4 May 2021.

O'Malley, Kit. Text message to the author. 2 June 2020.

You can also include the text of a short email or text message, with a label
at the end.

Rust, Max. "Trip to see the cows tomorrow?" 27 Apr. 2021. Email.

36. Post to *Twitter, Instagram*, or other social media

Author. "Title." *Name of Site*, Day Month Year, URL.

Oregon Zoo. "Winter Wildlife Wonderland." *Facebook*, 8 Feb. 2019,
www.facebook.com/80229441108/videos/2399570506799549.

If there's no title, you can use a concise description or the text of a short post.

Millman, Debbie. Photos of Roxane Gay. *Instagram*, 18 Feb. 2021, www
.instagram.com/p/CLcT_EnhnWT.

Obama, Barack [@POTUS44]. "It's been the honor of my life to serve
you. You made me a better leader and a better man." *Twitter*, 20
Jan. 2017, twitter.com/POTUS44/status/82244588224741376l.

Audio, Visual, and Other Sources

37. Advertisement

Print

Description of ad. *Title of Periodical*, Date, Page.

Advertisement for Grey Goose. *Wine Spectator*, 18 Dec. 2020, p. 22.

Video

"Title." *Name of Site*, uploaded by Company, Date, URL.

"First Visitors." *YouTube*, uploaded by Snickers, 20 Aug. 2020, www
.youtube.com/watch?v=negeco0b1L0.

38. Art

Original

Artist's Last Name, First Name. *Title of Art.* Year created, Location.

Van Gogh, Vincent. *The Potato Eaters.* 1885, Van Gogh Museum, Amsterdam.

In a Book

Artist's Last Name, First Name. *Title of Art.* Year created, Location.
Title of Book, by First and Last Names, Publisher, Year of
publication, Page.

Van Gogh, Vincent. *The Potato Eaters.* 1885, Scottish National Gallery.
*History of Art: A Survey of the Major Visual Arts from the Dawn of
History to the Present Day*, by H. W. Janson, Prentice-Hall /
Harry N. Abrams, 1969, p. 508.

Online

Artist's Last Name, First Name. *Title of Art.* Year created. *Name of
Site*, URL.

Warhol, Andy. *Self-portrait.* 1979. *J. Paul Getty Museum*, www
.getty.edu/art/collection/objects/106971/andy-warhol-self
-portrait-american-1979.

39. Cartoon

Print

Author's Last Name, First Name. Cartoon or "Title of Cartoon." *Name
of Periodical*, Date, Page.

Mankoff, Robert. Cartoon. *The New Yorker*, 3 May 1993, p. 50.

Online

Author's Last Name, First Name. Cartoon or "Title of Cartoon." *Title*
of Site, Date, URL.

Munroe, Randall. "Up Goer Five." *xkcd*, 12 Nov. 2012, xkcd.com/1133.

40. Supreme Court case

United States, Supreme Court. *First Defendant v. Second Defendant.* Date
of decision. *Name of Source Site,* Publisher, URL.

United States, Supreme Court. *District of Columbia v. Heller.* 26 June
2008. *Legal Information Institute,* Cornell U Law School, www.law
.cornell.edu/supct/html/07-290.

41. Film

Name individuals based on the focus of your project—the director, the
screenwriter, or someone else.

Title of Film. Role by First and Last Names, Production Company, Date.

Breakfast at Tiffany's. Directed by Blake Edwards, Paramount, 1961.

Online

Title of Film. Role by First and Last Names, Production Company,
Date. *Name of Site,* URL.

Interstellar. Directed by Christopher Nolan, Paramount, 2014. *Amazon*
Prime Video, www.amazon.com/Interstellar-Matthew
-McConaughey/dp/B00TU9UFTS.

42. TV show episode

Name contributors based on the focus of your project—director, writers,
actors, or others. If you don't want to highlight anyone in particular, don't
include any contributors.

Broadcast

"Title of Episode." *Title of Program,* role by First and Last Names (if any),
season, episode, Production Company, Date.

"The Storm." *Avatar: The Last Airbender*, created by Michael Dante
DiMartino and Bryan Konietzko, season 1, episode 12,
Nickelodeon Studios, 3 June 2005.

DVD

"Title of Episode." Broadcast Date. *Title of DVD*, role by First and Last
Names (if any), season, episode, Production Company, Release Date,
disc number. DVD.

"The Storm." 2005. *Avatar: The Last Airbender: The Complete Book
1 Collection*, created by Michael Dante DiMartino and Bryan
Konietzko, episode 12, Nickelodeon Studios, 2006, disc 3. DVD.

Streaming Online

"Title of Episode." *Title of Program*, role by First and Last Names (if any),
season, episode, Production Company, Date. *Title of Site*, URL.

"The Storm." *Avatar: The Last Airbender*, season 1, episode 12,
Nickelodeon Studios, 2005. *Netflix*, www.netflix.com.

Streaming on an App

"Title of Episode." *Title of Program*, role by First and Last Names (if any),
season, episode, Production Company, Date. *Name of* app.

"The Storm." *Avatar: The Last Airbender*, season 1, episode 12,
Nickelodeon Studios, 3 June 2005. *Netflix* app.

43. Online video

"Title of Video." *Title of Site*, uploaded by Uploader's Name, Day Month
Year, URL.

"Everything Wrong with *National Treasure* in 13 Minutes or Less."
YouTube, uploaded by CinemaSins, 21 Aug. 2014, www.youtube
.com/watch?v=1ul-_ZWvXTs.

44. Virtual presentation on *Zoom* or other platform

MLA doesn't give specific guidance on how to cite a virtual presentation, but this is what we recommend. See style.mla.org for more information.

> Author's Last Name, First Name. "Title." Sponsoring Institution, Day Month Year. *Name of Platform.*

> Budhathoki, Thir. "Cross-Cultural Perceptions of Literacies in Student Writing." Conference on College Composition and Communication, 9 Apr. 2021. *Zoom.*

45. Interview

If it's not clear that it's an interview, add a label at the end. If you are citing a transcript of an interview, indicate that at the end as well.

Published

> Subject's Last Name, First Name. "Title of Interview (if any)." Interviewed by First Name Last Name (if given). *Name of Publication*, Date, Pages *or* URL.

> Whitehead, Colson. "Colson Whitehead: By the Book." *The New York Times*, 15 May 2014, www.nytimes.com/2014/05/18/books /review/colson-whitehead-by-the-book.html. Interview.

Personal

> Subject's Last Name, First Name. Concise description. Day Month Year.

> Bazelon, L. S. Telephone interview with the author. 4 Oct. 2020.

46. Map

If the title doesn't make clear it's a map, add a label at the end.

> *Title of Map.* Publisher, Date.

> *Brooklyn.* J. B. Beers, 1874. Map.

author | title | publication

47. Musical score

Composer's Last Name, First Name. *Title of Composition.* Publisher, Year of publication.

Frank, Gabriela Lena. *Compadrazgo.* G. Schirmer, 2007.

48. Oral presentation

Presenter's Last Name, First Name. "Title of Presentation." Sponsoring Institution, Date, Location.

Cassin, Michael. "Nature in the Raw—The Art of Landscape Painting." Berkshire Institute for Lifelong Learning, 24 Mar. 2005, Clark Art Institute, Williamstown, Massachusetts.

49. Podcast

If you accessed a podcast online, give the URL; if you accessed it through an app, indicate that instead.

"Title of Episode." *Title of Podcast,* hosted by First Name Last Name, season, episode, Production Company, Date, URL.

"DUSTWUN." *Serial,* hosted by Sarah Koenig, season 2, episode 1, WBEZ / Serial Productions, 10 Dec. 2015, serialpodcast.org /season-two/1/dustwun.

"DUSTWUN." *Serial,* hosted by Sarah Koenig, season 2, episode 1, WBEZ / Serial Productions, 10 Dec. 2015. *Spotify* app.

50. Radio program

"Title of Episode." *Title of Program,* hosted by First Name Last Name, Station, Day Month Year.

"In Defense of Ignorance." *This American Life,* hosted by Ira Glass, WBEZ, 22 Apr. 2016.

51. Sound recording

If you accessed a recording online, give the URL; if you accessed it through an app, indicate that instead.

> Artist's Last Name, First Name. "Title of Work." *Title of Album*, Label, Date, URL.

> Beyoncé. "Pray You Catch Me." *Lemonade*, Parkwood Entertainment / Columbia Records, 2016, www.beyonce.com/album/lemonade -visual-album/songs.

> Simone, Nina. "To Be Young, Gifted and Black." *Black Gold*, RCA Records, 1969. *Spotify* app.

On a CD

> Artist's Last Name, First Name. "Title of Work." *Title of Album*, Label, Date. CD.

> Brown, Greg. "Canned Goods." *The Live One*, Red House, 1995. CD.

52. Video game

> *Title of Game.* Version, Distributor, Date of release.

> *Animal Crossing: New Horizons.* Version 1.1.4, Nintendo, 6 Apr. 2020.

FORMATTING A RESEARCH PAPER

Name, course, title. MLA does not require a separate title page, unless your paper is a group project. In the upper left-hand corner of your first page, include your name, your instructor's name, the course name and number, and the date. Center the title of your paper on the line after the date; capitalize it as you would a book title. If your paper is a group project, include all of that information on a title page instead, listing all the authors.

Page numbers. In the upper right-hand corner of each page, one-half inch below the top of the page, include your last name and the page number. If it's a group project and all the names don't fit, include only the page number. Number pages consecutively throughout your paper.

author   title   publication

Font, spacing, margins, and indents. Choose a font that is easy to read (such as Times New Roman) and that provides a clear contrast between regular text and italic text. Set the font between 11 and 13 points. Double-space the entire paper, including your works-cited list and any notes. Set one-inch margins at the top, bottom, and sides of your text; do not justify your text. The first line of each paragraph should be indented one-half inch from the left margin. End punctuation should be followed by one space.

Headings. Short essays do not generally need headings, but they can be useful in longer works. Use a large, bold font for the first level of heading, and smaller fonts and italics to signal lower-level headings. MLA requires that headings all be flush with the left margin.

First-Level Heading
Second-Level Heading
Third-Level Heading

Long quotations. When quoting more than three lines of poetry, more than four lines of prose, or dialogue between characters in a drama, set off the quotation from the rest of your text, indenting it one-half inch (or five spaces) from the left margin. Do not use quotation marks, and put any parenthetical documentation *after* the final punctuation.

> In *Eastward to Tartary*, Robert Kaplan captures ancient and contemporary Antioch for us:
>
> > At the height of its glory in the Roman-Byzantine age, when it had an amphitheater, public baths, aqueducts, and sewage pipes, half a million people lived in Antioch. Today the population is only 125,000. With sour relations between Turkey and Syria, and unstable politics throughout the Middle East, Antioch is now a backwater—seedy and tumbledown, with relatively few tourists. I found it altogether charming. (123)

> In the first stanza of Matthew Arnold's "Dover Beach," exclamations make clear the speaker is addressing someone who is also present in the scene:
>
> > Come to the window, sweet is the night air!
> > Only, from the long line of spray

> Where the sea meets the moon-blanched land,
>
> Listen! You hear the grating roar
>
> Of pebbles which the waves draw back, and fling. (lines 6-10)

Be careful to maintain the poet's line breaks. If a line does not fit on one line of your paper, put the extra words on the next line. Indent that line an additional quarter inch (or two spaces). If a citation doesn't fit, put it on the next line, flush with the right margin.

Tables and illustrations. Insert illustrations and tables close to the text that discusses them, and be sure to make clear how they relate to your point. For tables, provide a number (Table 1) and a title on separate lines above the table. Below the table, provide a caption with source information and any notes. Notes should be indicated with lowercase letters. For graphs, photos, and other figures, provide a figure number (*Fig. 1*) and caption with source information below the figure. If you give only brief source information, use commas between elements—Zhu Wei, *New Pictures of the Strikingly Bizarre #9*, print, 2004—and include full source information in your list of works cited. If you give full source information in the caption, don't include the source in your list of works cited. Punctuate as you would in the works-cited list, but don't invert the author's name: Berenice Sydney. *Fast Rhythm*. 1972, Tate Britain, London.

List of works cited. Start your list on a new page, following any notes. Center the title, *Works Cited*, and double-space the entire list. Begin each entry at the left margin, and indent subsequent lines one-half inch (or five spaces). Alphabetize the list by authors' last names (or by editors' or translators' names, if appropriate). Alphabetize works with no author or editor by title, disregarding *A*, *An*, and *The*. To cite more than one work by a single author, list them as in no. 4 on page 577.

SAMPLE RESEARCH PAPER

Walter Przybylowski wrote the following analysis for a first-year writing course. It is formatted according to the guidelines of the MLA (style.mla.org).

author   title   publication

1"

½"

Put your last name
and the page num-
ber in the upper-right
corner of each page.

Walter Przybylowski

Professor Matin

English 102, Section 3

4 May 2019

Center the title.

Holding Up the Hollywood Stagecoach:

The European Take on the Western

Double-space
throughout.

    The Western film has long been considered by film scholars and enthusiasts to be a distinctly American genre. Not only its subject matter but its characteristic themes originate in America's own violent and exciting past. For many years, Hollywood sold images of hard men fighting savages on the plains to the worldwide public; by ignoring the more complicated aspects of "how the West was won" and the true nature of relations between Native Americans and whites, filmmakers were able to reap great financial and professional rewards. In particular, the huge success of John Ford's 1939 film *Stagecoach* brought about countless imitations that led over the next few decades to American Westerns playing in a sort of loop, which reinforced the same ideas and myths in film after film.

1"

Indent paragraphs
5 spaces or ½".

    After the success of German-made Westerns in the 1950s, though, a new take on Westerns was ushered in by other European countries. Leading the Euro-Western charge, so to speak, were the Italians, whose cynical, often politically pointed Westerns left a permanent impact on an American-based genre. Europeans, particularly the Italians, challenged the dominant conventions of the American Western by complicating the morality of the characters, blurring the lines between

1"

good and evil, and also by complicating the traditional narrative, visual, and aural structures of Westerns. In this way, the genre motifs that *Stagecoach* initiated are explored in the European Westerns of the 1950s, 1960s, and early 1970s, yet with a striking difference in style. Specifically, Sergio Leone's 1968 film *Once upon a Time in the West* broke many of the rules set by the Hollywood Western and in the process created a new visual language for the Western. Deconstructing key scenes from this film reveals the demythologization at work in many of the Euro-Westerns, which led to a genre enriched by its presentation of a more complicated American West.

       Stagecoach is a perfect example of almost all the visual, sound, and plot motifs that would populate "classic" Hollywood Westerns for the next few decades. The story concerns a group of people, confined for most of the movie inside a stagecoach, who are attempting to cross a stretch of land made dangerous by Apache Indians on the warpath. Little effort is made to develop the characters of the Indians, who appear mainly as a narrative device, adversaries that the heroes must overcome in order to maintain their peaceful existence. This plot, with minor changes, could be used as a general description for countless Westerns. In his book *The Crowded Prairie: American National Identity in the Hollywood Western*, Michael Coyne explains the significance of *Stagecoach* to the Western genre and its influence in solidifying the genre's archetypes:

> [I]t was *Stagecoach* which . . . redefined the contours of the myth. The good outlaw, the whore with a heart of gold, the Madonna/Magdalene dichotomy between opposing female

Quotations of more than 4 lines are indented ½" (5 spaces) and double-spaced.

Przybylowski   3

leads, the drunken philosopher, the last-minute cavalry rescue, the lonely walk down Main Street—all became stereotypes from *Stagecoach*'s archetypes. *Stagecoach* quickly became the model against which other "A" Westerns would be measured. (18-19)

Coyne is not exaggerating when he calls it "the model": in fact, all of these stereotypes became a sort of checklist of things that audiences expected to see. The reliance on a preconceived way to sell Western films to the public—where you could always tell the good characters from the bad and knew before the film ended how each character would end up—led to certain genre expectations that the directors of the Euro-Westerns would later knowingly reconfigure. As the influential critic Pauline Kael wrote in her 1965 book *Kiss Kiss Bang Bang*, "The original *Stagecoach* had a mixture of reverie and reverence about the American past that made the picture seem almost folk art; we wanted to believe in it even if we didn't" (52).

There seemed to be a need not just in Americans but in moviegoers around the world to believe that there was (or had been) a great untamed land out there just waiting to be cultivated. More important, as Kael pointed out, Americans wanted to believe that the building of America was a wholly righteous endeavor wherein the land was free for the taking—the very myth that Europeans later debunked through parody and subversive filmmaking techniques. According to Theresa Harlan, author of works on Native American art, the myth was based on the need of early white settlers to make their elimination of American Indians

For a set-off quotation, the parenthetical reference follows the closing punctuation.

Verb in signal phrase is past tense because date of source is mentioned.

Parenthetical reference following a quotation within the main text goes before the closing punctuation of the sentence.

more palatable in light of the settlers' professed Christian beliefs. In her article "Adjusting the Focus for an Indigenous Presence," Harlan writes that

> Eurocentric frontier ideology and the representations of indigenous people it produced were used to convince many American settlers that indigenous people were incapable of discerning the difference between a presumed civilized existence and their own "primitive" state. (136)

Although this myth had its genesis long before the advent of motion pictures, the Hollywood Western drew inspiration from it and continued to legitimize and reinforce its message. *Stagecoach*, with its high level of technical skill and artistry, redefined the contours of the myth, and a close look at the elements that made the film the "classic" model of the Western is imperative in order to truly understand its influence.

The musical themes that underscore the actions of the characters are especially powerful in this regard and can be as powerful as the characters' visual representation on screen. In *Stagecoach*, an Apache does not appear until more than halfway through the movie, but whenever one is mentioned, the soundtrack fills with sinister and foreboding drumbeats. The first appearance of Indians is a scene without dialogue, in which the camera pans between the stagecoach crossing through the land and Apaches watching from afar. The music that accompanies this scene is particularly telling, since as the camera pans between stagecoach and Apaches, the music shifts in tone dramatically from a pleasant melody to a score filled with dread. When the heroes shoot and kill the Apaches, then, the viewer has already been subjected to specific film techniques to give the stagecoach riders moral certitude in their annihilation of the alien menace. This kind of score is powerful stuff to accompany an image and does its best to tell the viewers how they should react. When Europeans start to make Westerns, the line of moral certitude will become less distinct.

In her essay "Of Mother Nature and Marlboro Men: An Inquiry into the Cultural Meanings of Landscape Photography," Deborah Bright argues that landscape photography has reinforced certain formulaic myths about landscape, and the same can be said of the Hollywood Western during the 1940s and 1950s. For example, in *Stagecoach*, when the stagecoach finally sets out for its journey through Apache territory, a fence is juxtaposed against the vast wide-open country in the foreground. The meaning is clear—the stagecoach is leaving civilized society to venture into the wilds of the West, and music swells as the coach crosses into that vast landscape (fig. 1). Ford uses landscape in this way to engender in the audience the desired response of longing for a time gone past, where there was land free for the taking and plenty to go around. Yet Bright suggests that "[i]f we are to redeem landscape photography from its narrow self-reflexive project, why not openly question the assumptions about nature and culture that it has traditionally served and use our practice instead to criticize them?" (141). This is exactly what Europeans, and Italians in particular, seem to have done with the Western. When Europeans started to make their own

Figure number calls readers' attention to illustration.

Brackets show that the writer has changed a capital letter to lowercase to make the quotation fit smoothly into his own sentence.

Fig. 1. In *Stagecoach*, swelling music signals the coach's passage through the western landscape. Still from *Stagecoach*. *Internet Movie Database*, www.imdb.com/title/tt0031971/mediaviewer/rm1596567552.

Illustration is positioned close to the text to which it relates, with figure number, caption, and full source information.

Westerns, they took advantage of their outsider status in relation to an American genre by openly questioning the myths that have been established by *Stagecoach* and its cinematic brethren.

Sergio Leone's *Once upon a Time in the West* is a superior example of a European artist's take on the art form of the American Western. The "plot" of the film is flimsy, driven by the efforts of a mysterious character played by Charles Bronson to avenge himself against Henry Fonda's character, a lowdown gunfighter trying to become a legitimate businessman. Claudia Cardinale plays a prostitute who is trying to put her past behind her. The similarities to American Westerns, on paper at least, seem to be so great as to make *Once upon a Time* almost a copy of what had long been done in Hollywood, but a closer look at European Westerns and at this film in particular shows that Leone is consciously sending up the stereotypes. After all, he needs to work within the genre's language if he is to adequately challenge it.

During the opening of *Once upon a Time in the West*, the viewer is given a kind of audio and visual tour of Euro-Western aesthetics. Leone introduces three gunmen in typical Italian Western style, with the first presented by a cut to a dusty boot heel from which the camera slowly pans up until it reaches the top of the character's cowboy hat. During this pan, the gunman's gear and its authenticity—a major aspect of the Italian Western—can be taken in by the audience. A broader examination of the genre would show that many Euro-Westerns use this tactic of hyperrealistic attention to costuming and weaponry, which Ignacio Ramonet argues is intended to distract the viewer from the unreality of the landscape:

> Extreme realism of bodies (hairy, greasy, foul-smelling), clothes or objects (including mania for weapons) in Italian films is above all intended to compensate for the complete fraud of the space and origins. The green pastures, farms and cattle of American Westerns are replaced by large, deserted canyons. (32)

In the opening scene, the other two gunfighters are introduced by a camera panning across the room, allowing characters to materialize seemingly out of nowhere. Roger Ebert notes that Leone

> established a rule that he follows throughout . . . that the ability to see is limited by the sides of the frame. At important moments in the film, what the camera cannot see, the characters cannot see, and that gives Leone the freedom to surprise us with entrances that cannot be explained by the practical geography of his shots.

No page number given for online source.

It is these aesthetic touches created to compensate for a fraudulent landscape that ushered in a new visual language for the Western. The opening of *Once upon a Time in the West* undercuts any preconceived notion of how a Western should be filmed, and this is exactly Leone's intention: "The director had obviously enjoyed dilating the audience's sense of time, exploiting, in his ostentatious way, the rhetoric of the Western, and dwelling on the tiniest details to fulfill his intention" (Frayling 197). By using jarring edits with amplified sounds, Leone informs the audience not only that he has seen all the popular Hollywood Westerns, but that he is purposely not going to give them that kind of movie. The opening ten-minute scene would be considered needlessly long in a typical Hollywood Western, but Leone is not making a copy of a Hollywood Western. In fact, it is this reliance on the audience's previously established knowledge of Westerns that allows Euro-Westerns to subvert the genre. Leone and other directors of Euro-Westerns are asking the public to open their eyes, to not believe what

When no signal phrase is used to introduce a quotation, the author's name is included in the parenthetical citation.

Przybylowski   9

is shown; they are attempting to take the camera's power away by parodying its effect. When Leone has characters magically appear in the frame, or amplifies the squeaking of a door hinge on a soundtrack, he is ridiculing the basic laws that govern American Westerns. The opening of *Once upon a Time* can be read as a sort of primer for what is about to come for the rest of the film, and its power leaves viewers more attuned to what they are watching.

   Leone's casting also works to heighten the film's subversive effect. Henry Fonda, the quintessential good guy in classic Hollywood Westerns like *My Darling Clementine*, is cast as the ruthless Frank, a gunman shown murdering a small child early in the film. In a 1966 article on Italian Westerns in the *Saturday Evening Post*, Italian director Maurizio Lucidi gave some insight into the European perspective that lay behind such choices:

> We're adding the Italian concept of realism to an old American myth, and it's working. Look at Jesse James. In your country he's a saint. Over here we play him as a gangster. That's what he was. Europeans today are too sophisticated to believe in the honest gunman movie anymore. They want the truth and that's what we're giving them. (qtd. in Fox 55)

A citation of a source the writer found quoted in another source.

Leone knew exactly what he was doing, and his casting of Fonda went a long way toward confusing the audience's sympathies and complicating the simple good guy versus bad guy model of Hollywood films. For this reason, Fonda's entrance in the film is worth noting. The scene begins with a close-up of a shotgun barrel, which quickly explodes in a series

of (gun)shots that establish a scene of a father and son out hunting near
their homestead. Here, Leone starts to move the camera more, with pans
from father to son and a crane shot of their house as they return home
to a picnic table with an abundance of food: the family is apparently
about to celebrate something. Throughout this scene, crickets chirp on the
soundtrack—until Leone abruptly cuts them off, the sudden silence quickly
followed by close-ups of the uneasy faces of three family members. Leone
is teasing the audience: he puts the crickets back on the soundtrack until
out of nowhere we hear a gunshot. Instead of then focusing on the source
or the target of the gunshot, the camera pans off to the sky, and for a
moment the viewer thinks the shot is from a hunter. We next see a close-up
of the father's face as he looks off into the distance, then is rattled when he
sees his daughter grasping the air, obviously shot. As he runs toward her,
tracked by the camera in a startling way, he is quickly shot down himself.

The family has been attacked seemingly out of nowhere, with only
a young boy still alive. During the massacre, there is no musical score,
just the abstract brutality of the slayings. Then Leone gives us a long
camera shot of men appearing out of dust-blown winds, from nearby
brush. It is obvious to the viewer that these men are the killers, but there
is no clear sight of their faces: Leone uses long camera shots of their backs
and an overhead shot as they converge on the young boy. This is the
moment when Leone introduces Henry Fonda; he starts with the camera
on the back of Fonda's head and then does a slow track around until his
face is visible. At this point, audience members around the world would
still have a hard time believing Fonda was a killer of these innocent

people. Through crosscutting between the young boy's confused face
and Fonda's smiling eyes, Leone builds a doubt in the audience—maybe
he will not kill the boy. Then the crosscutting is interrupted with a close-
up of Fonda's large Colt coming out of its holster, and Ennio Morricone's
score, full of sadness, becomes audible. The audience's fears are realized:
Fonda is indeed the killer. This scene is a clear parody of Hollywood
casting stereotypes, and Leone toys with audience expectations by
turning upside down the myth of the noble outlaw as portrayed by John
Wayne in *Stagecoach*.

    During the late 1960s and the early 1970s, Europeans were at
odds with many of the foreign policies of the United States, a hostility
expressed in Ramonet's characterization of this period as one "when
American imperialism in Latin America and Southeast Asia was
showing itself to be particularly brutal" (33). Morton, the railroad baron
who is Frank's unscrupulous employer in *Once upon a Time in the
West*, can easily be read as a critique of the sometimes misguided ways
Americans went about bringing their way of life to other countries.
Morton represents the bringer of civilization, usually a good thing in the
classic Western genre, where civilization meant doctors, schools, homes
for everyone. But the Europeans question how this civilization was built.
Leone, in a telling quotation, gives his perspective: "I see the history of
the West as really the reign of violence by violence" (qtd. in Frayling 134).

    Instead of the civilizing myth and its representations, the concern
of *Once upon a Time*—and the Euro-Western in general—is to give voice
to the perspective of the marginal characters: the Native Americans,

Mexicans, and Chinese who rarely rated a position of significance in a
Hollywood Western. In *Once upon a Time*, Bronson's character, Harmonica,
pushes the plot forward with his need to avenge. Harmonica stands
in for all the racial stereotypes that populated the American Western
genre. When he and Frank meet in the movie's climactic duel, Frank is
clearly perplexed about why this man wants to fight him, but his ego
makes it impossible for him to refuse. They meet in an abandoned yard,
with Frank in the extreme foreground and Harmonica in the extreme
background (fig. 2). The difference between the two is thus presented
from both physical and ideological standpoints: Frank guns down
settlers to make way for the railroad (and its owner), whereas Harmonica
helps people to fend for themselves. Morricone's score dominates the
soundtrack during this final scene, with a harmonica blaring away
throughout. The costuming of Frank in black and Harmonica in white
is an ironic throwback to classic Hollywood costuming and one that
suggests Harmonica is prevailing over the racial stereotypes of American
Westerns. Leone milks the scene for all it's worth, with the camera circling
Harmonica as Frank looks for a perfect point to start the duel. Harmonica
never moves, his face steadily framed in a close-up. Meanwhile, Frank is
shown in mostly long shots; his body language shows that he is uncertain
about the outcome of the duel, while Harmonica knows the ending.

   As the two seem about to draw, the camera pushes into
Harmonica's eyes, and there is a flashback to a younger Frank walking
toward the camera, putting a harmonica into the mouth of a boy (the
young Harmonica), and forcing him to participate in Frank's hanging of

Przybylowski   13

Fig. 2. The climactic duel in *Once upon a Time in the West* challenges the casting and costuming stereotypes of the Hollywood Western. Still from *Once upon a Time in the West*. *Internet Movie Database*, www.imdb.com /title/tt0064116/mediaviewer/rm1124971008.

Complete source information provided along with the caption since this figure is not included in the works-cited list.

the boy's older brother. This brutal scene, in which Frank unknowingly seals his own destiny, is set in actual American locations and is taken directly from John Ford Westerns; Leone is literally bringing home the violence dealt to minorities in America's past. As soon as the brother is hanged, the scene returns to the present, and Frank is shot through the heart. As he lies dying, we see a look of utter disbelief on his face as he asks Harmonica, "Who are you?" At this moment, a harmonica is shoved into his mouth. Only then does recognition play over Frank's face; as he falls to the ground, his face in close-up is a grotesque death-mask not unlike the massacred victims of Morton's train. The idea of past misdeeds coming back to haunt characters in the present is a clear attempt to challenge the idea that the settlers had a moral right to conquer and destroy indigenous people in order to "win" the West.

The tremendous success of *Stagecoach* was both a blessing and curse for the Western genre. Without it, the genre would surely never have gained the success it did, but this success came with ideological and creative limitations. Both the popularity and the limitations of the American Western may have inspired European directors to attempt something new with the genre, and unlike American filmmakers, they could look more objectively at our history and our myths. Leone's demythologization of the American Western has proved a valuable addition to the Western genre. The effect of the Euro-Western can be seen in American cinema as early as *The Wild Bunch* in 1969—and as recently as the attention in *Brokeback Mountain* to types of Western characters usually marginalized. In this way, Italian Westerns forced a new level of viewing of the Western tradition that made it impossible to ever return to the previous Hollywood model.

Przybylowski   15

Works Cited

Bright, Deborah. "Of Mother Nature and Marlboro Men: An Inquiry into the Cultural Meanings of Landscape Photography." *The Contest of Meaning: Critical Histories of Photography*, edited by Richard Bolton, MIT Press, 1993, pp. 125-43.

Coyne, Michael. *The Crowded Prairie: American National Identity in the Hollywood Western*. I. B. Tauris, 1997.

Ebert, Roger. "The Good, the Bad and the Ugly." *Chicago Sun-Times*, 3 Aug. 2003, www.rogerebert.com/reviews/great-movie-the-good-the-bad-and-the-ugly-1968.

Fox, William. "Wild Westerns, Italian Style." *The Saturday Evening Post*, 6 Apr. 1968, pp. 50-55.

Frayling, Christopher. *Spaghetti Westerns: Cowboys and Europeans from Karl May to Sergio Leone*. St. Martin's Press, 1981.

Harlan, Theresa. "Adjusting the Focus for an Indigenous Presence." *Overexposed: Essays on Contemporary Photography*, edited by Carol Squiers, New Press, 1999, pp. 134-52.

Kael, Pauline. *Kiss Kiss Bang Bang*. Bantam Books, 1965.

Once upon a Time in the West. Directed by Sergio Leone, performances by Henry Fonda and Charles Bronson, Paramount, 1968.

Ramonet, Ignacio. "Italian Westerns as Political Parables." *Cineaste*, vol. 15, no. 1, 1986, pp. 30-35. *JSTOR*, www.jstor.org/stable/41686858.

Stagecoach. Directed by John Ford, United Artists, 1939.

List of works cited begins on a new page. Heading is centered.

Each entry begins at the left margin, with subsequent lines indented.

List is alphabetized by authors' last names or by title for works with no author.

TWENTY-NINE

APA Style

AMERICAN PSYCHOLOGICAL ASSOCIATION (APA) style calls for (1) brief documentation in parentheses near each in-text citation and (2) complete documentation in a list of references at the end of your text. The models in this chapter draw on the *Publication Manual of the American Psychological Association*, 7th edition (2020). Additional information is available at www.apastyle.org.

A DIRECTORY TO APA STYLE

Throughout this chapter, you'll find models and examples that are color-coded to help you see how writers include source information in their texts and reference lists: tan for author or editor, yellow for title, gray for publication information—publisher, date of publication, page number(s), DOI or URL, and so on.

IN-TEXT DOCUMENTATION

Brief documentation in your text makes clear to your readers precisely what you took from a source. If you are quoting, provide the page number(s) or other information that will help readers locate the quotation in the source. You are not required to give the page number(s) with a paraphrase or summary, but you may want to do so if you are citing a long or complex work.

PARAPHRASES and SUMMARIES are more common than QUOTATIONS in APA-style projects. See Chapter 26 for more on all three kinds of citation. As

author   title   publication

you cite each source, you will need to decide whether to name the author in a signal phrase—"as McCullough (2001) wrote"—or in parentheses—"(McCullough, 2001)." Note that APA requires you to use the past tense for verbs in **SIGNAL PHRASES**, or the present perfect if you are referring to an ongoing action that started in the past or to something that didn't occur at a specific time: "Moss (2019) argued," "Many authors have argued."

1. Author named in a signal phrase

Put the date in parentheses after the author's last name, unless the year is mentioned in the sentence. If you are including the page number, put it in parentheses after the quotation, paraphrase, or summary. Documentation information in parentheses should come *before* the period at the end of the sentence and *after* any quotation marks.

> McCullough (2001) described John Adams as having "the hands of a man accustomed to pruning his own trees, cutting his own hay, and splitting his own firewood" (p. 18).

> In 2001, McCullough noted that John Adams's hands were those of a laborer (p. 18).

> John Adams had "the hands of a man accustomed to pruning his own trees," according to McCullough (2001, p. 18).

If the author is named after a quotation, as in this last example, put the page number(s) after the date within the parentheses.

2. Author named in parentheses

If you do not mention an author in a signal phrase, put the name, the year of publication, and any page number(s) in parentheses at the end of the sentence or right after the quotation, paraphrase, or summary.

> John Adams had "the hands of a man accustomed to pruning his own trees" (McCullough, 2001, p. 18).

3. Authors with the same last name

If your reference list includes more than one person with the same last name, include initials to distinguish the authors from one another.

> Eclecticism is common in modern criticism (J. M. Smith, 1992, p. vii).

4. Two authors

Always mention both authors. Use *and* in a signal phrase, but use an ampersand (&) in parentheses.

> Carlson and Ventura (1990) wanted to introduce Julio Cortázar, Marjorie Agosín, and other Latin American writers to an audience of English-speaking adolescents (p. v).

> According to the Peter Principle, "In a hierarchy, every employee tends to rise to his level of incompetence" (Peter & Hull, 1969, p. 26).

5. Three or more authors

When you refer to a work by three or more contributors, name only the first author followed by "et al.," Latin for "and others."

> Peilen et al. (1990) supported their claims about corporate corruption with startling anecdotal evidence (p. 75).

6. Organization or government as author

If an organization name is recognizable by its abbreviation, give the full name and the abbreviation the first time you cite the source. In subsequent references, use only the abbreviation. If the organization does not have a familiar abbreviation, always use its full name.

First reference

The American Psychological Association (APA, 2020)

(American Psychological Association [APA], 2020)

Subsequent references

The APA (2020)

(APA, 2020)

author   title   publication

7. Author unknown

Use the complete title if it's short; if it's long, use the first few words of the title under which the work appears in the reference list. Italicize the title if it's italicized in the reference list; if it isn't italicized there, enclose the title in quotation marks.

> According to *Feeding Habits of Rams* (2000), a ram's diet often changes from one season to the next (p. 29).

> The article noted that one healthy liver donor died because of "frightening" postoperative care ("Every Patient's Nightmare," 2007).

8. Two or more works together

If you document multiple works in the same parentheses, place the source information in alphabetical order, separated by semicolons.

> Many researchers have argued that what counts as "literacy" is not necessarily learned at school (Heath, 1983; Moss, 2003).

Multiple authors in a signal phrase can be named in any order.

9. Two or more works by one author in the same year

If your list of references includes more than one work by the same author published in the same year, order them alphabetically by title, adding lowercase letters ("a," "b," and so on) to the year.

> Kaplan (2000a) described orderly shantytowns in Turkey that did not resemble the other slums he visited.

10. Source quoted in another source

When you cite a source that was quoted in another source, add the words *as cited in*. If possible, cite the original source instead.

> Thus, Modern Standard Arabic was expected to serve as the "moral glue" holding the Arab world together (Choueri, 2000, as cited in Walters, 2019, p. 475).

11. Work without page numbers

Instead of page numbers, some works have paragraph numbers, which you should include (preceded by the abbreviation *para.*) if you are referring to a specific part of such a source.

> Russell's dismissals from Trinity College at Cambridge and from City College in New York City have been seen as examples of the controversy that marked his life (Irvine, 2006, para. 2).

In sources with neither page nor paragraph numbers (e.g., many online journals), refer readers to a particular part of the source if possible, perhaps indicating a heading and the paragraph under the heading: (Brody, 2020, Introduction, para. 2).

12. An entire work

You do not need to give a page number if you are directing readers' attention to an entire work.

> Kaplan (2000) considered Turkey and Central Asia explosive.

When you are citing an entire website, give the URL in the text. You do not need to include the website in your reference list. To cite a webpage on a website, see no. 17 on page 633.

> Beyond providing diagnostic information, the website for the Alzheimer's Association (http://www.alz.org) includes a variety of resources for the families of patients.

13. Personal communication

Document emails, telephone conversations, personal interviews, personal letters, messages from nonarchived electronic discussion sources, and other personal texts as *personal communication,* along with the person's initial(s), last name, and the date. You do not need to include such personal communications in your reference list.

> L. Strauss (personal communication, December 6, 2013) told about visiting Yogi Berra when they both lived in Montclair, New Jersey.

author　　title　　publication

NOTES

You may need to use footnotes to give an explanation or information that doesn't fit into your text. To signal a content footnote, place a superscript numeral at the appropriate point in your text. Include this information in a footnote, either at the bottom of that page or on a separate page with the heading "Footnotes" in bold, after your reference list. If you have multiple notes, number them consecutively throughout your text. Here is an example from *In Search of Solutions: A New Direction in Psychotherapy* (2003).

Text with superscript

An important part of working with teams and one-way mirrors is taking the consultation break, as at Milan, BFTC, and MRI.[1]

Footnote

[1]It is crucial to note here that while working within a team is fun, stimulating, and revitalizing, it is not necessary for successful outcomes. Solution-oriented therapy works equally well when working solo.

REFERENCE LIST

A reference list provides full bibliographic information for every source cited in your text with the exception of entire websites, common computer software and mobile apps, and personal communications. See page 645 for guidelines on preparing such a list; for a sample reference list, see page 660.

Key Elements for Documenting Sources

APA style provides a list of four elements that should be used to document a source: author, date, title, and source. The kind of information that makes up each element can change slightly depending on the type of source. The following guidelines explain how to handle each of the key elements generally; refer to these guidelines and the section on "Authors and Other Contributors" if your specific kind of source isn't covered in the examples provided.

AUTHOR: Use the author's last name, but replace the first and middle names with initials and invert the order: Kinder, D. R. for Donald R. Kinder.

DATE: Include the date of publication, which will vary based on the type of work you are citing.

TITLE: Capitalize only the first word and proper nouns and adjectives in the title and subtitle of the work you are citing. Titles of periodicals and websites are capitalized differently, so refer to an example for specifics.

SOURCE: The source indicates where the work can be found. It includes the publisher, any additional information about the source (e.g., volume number, issue number, pages), and the DOI or URL if applicable.

DOI OR URL: Include a DOI (digital object identifier, a string of letters and numbers that identifies an online document) for any work that has one, regardless of whether you accessed the source in print or online. For a print work with no DOI, do not include a URL. For an online work with no DOI, include a URL unless the URL is no longer working or unless the work is from an academic database.

Authors and Other Contributors

This section provides general guidelines for documenting authors and other contributors across sources and in various kinds of media (in print, online, and in other media). Note that most of the examples in this section are books. If you are documenting a different kind of source, follow the appropriate formatting guidelines.

1. One author

Author's Last Name, Initials. (Year of publication). *Title of book.* Publisher. DOI *or* URL

Lewis, M. (2003). *Moneyball: The art of winning an unfair game.* W. W. Norton.

This book does not have a DOI, so that element does not appear in the reference entry.

author   title   publication

2. Two authors

First Author's Last Name, Initials, & Second Author's Last Name, Initials.
(Year of publication). *Title of book.* Publisher. DOI *or* URL

Montefiore, S., & Montefiore, S. S. (2016). *The royal rabbits of London.*
Aladdin.

3. Three or more authors

For three to 20 authors, include all names.

First Author's Last Name, Initials, Next Author's Last Name, Initials,
& Final Author's Last Name, Initials. (Year of publication). *Title of
book.* Publisher. DOI *or* URL

Greig, A., Taylor, J., & MacKay, T. (2013). *Doing research with children:
A practical guide* (3rd ed.). Sage.

For a work by 21 or more authors, name the first 19 authors, followed by
three ellipsis points, and end with the final author.

Gao, R., Asano, S. M., Upadhyayula, S., Pisarev, I., Milkie, D. E., Liu, T.-L.,
Singh, V., Graves, A., Huynh, G. H., Zhao, Y., Bogovic, J., Colonell, J.,
Ott, C. M., Zugates, C., Tappan, S., Rodriguez, A., Mosaliganti, K. R.,
Sheu, S.-H., Pasolli, H. A., . . . Betzig, E. (2019, January 18). Cortical
column and whole-brain imaging with molecular contrast and
nanoscale resolution. *Science, 363*(6424). https://doi.org/10.1126
/science.aau8302

4. Two or more works by the same author

If the works were published in different years, list them chronologically.

Lewis, B. (1995). *The Middle East: A brief history of the last 2,000 years.*
Scribner.
Lewis, B. (2003). *The crisis of Islam: Holy war and unholy terror.* Modern
Library.

If the works were published in the same year, list them alphabetically by title (ignoring *A*, *An*, and *The*), adding "a," "b," and so on to the year.

> Kaplan, R. D. (2000a). *The coming anarchy: Shattering the dreams of the post Cold War.* Random House.
> Kaplan, R. D. (2000b). *Eastward to Tartary: Travels in the Balkans, the Middle East, and the Caucasus.* Random House.

5. Author and editor

If a book has an author and an editor who is credited on the cover, include the editor in parentheses after the title. If the book is a republished version of an earlier book, include the year of publication of the version you are using as the date and the original publication year at the end.

> Author's Last Name, Initials. (Year of publication). *Title of book* (Editor's Initials Last Name, Ed.). Publisher. DOI *or* URL (Original work published Year)

> Dick, P. F. (2008). *Five novels of the 1960s and 70s* (J. Lethem, Ed.). Library of America. (Original works published 1964–1977)

6. Author and translator

> Author's Last Name, Initials. (Year of publication). *Title of book* (Translator's Initials Last Name, Trans.). Publisher. DOI *or* URL (Original work published Year)

> Hugo, V. (2008). *Les misérables* (J. Rose, Trans.). Modern Library. (Original work published 1862)

7. Editor

> Editor's Last Name, Initials (Ed.). (Year of publication). *Title of book.* Publisher. DOI *or* URL

> Jones, D. (Ed.). (2007). *Modern love: 50 true and extraordinary tales of desire, deceit, and devotion.* Three Rivers Press.

author   title   publication

8. Unknown or no author or editor

When there's no known author or editor, start with the title.

> *Title.* (Year of Publication). Publisher. DOI *or* URL

> *Feeding habits of rams.* (2000). Land's Point Press.

> Hot property: From carriage house to family compound. (2004, December). *Berkshire Living, 1*(1), 99.

> Clues in salmonella outbreak. (2008, June 21). *The New York Times*, A13.

If the author is listed as *Anonymous*, treat the reference list entry as if the author's name were Anonymous.

9. Organization or government as author

Sometimes an organization or a government agency is both author and publisher. If so, omit the publisher.

> Organization Name *or* Government Agency. (Year of publication). *Title of book.* DOI *or* URL

> Catholic News Service. (2002). *Stylebook on religion 2000: A reference guide.*

Articles and Other Short Works

Articles, essays, reviews, and other short works are found in periodicals and books—in print, online, or in a database. For most short works, provide information about the author, the titles of both the short work and the longer work, any volume and issue numbers, any page numbers, various kinds of publication information, and a DOI or URL if applicable.

10. Article in a journal

> Author's Last Name, Initials. (Year). Title of article. *Title of Journal, volume*(issue), page(s). DOI *or* URL

> Gremer, J. R., Sala, A., & Crone, E. E. (2010). Disappearing plants: Why they hide and how they return. *Ecology, 91*(11), 3407–3413. https://doi.org/10.1890/09-1864.1

If a DOI is long or complicated, it's acceptable to use a shortDOI. Create one by entering the DOI into the shortDOI service (https://shortdoi.org/). A URL can also be shortened using any online URL shortener, as long as the shorter URL leads to the correct work.

11. Article in a magazine

If a magazine is published weekly, include the day and the month. Include the volume number and issue number after the magazine title.

> Author's Last Name, Initials. (Year, Month Day). Title of article. *Title of Magazine, volume*(issue), page(s). DOI *or* URL

> Klump, B. (2019, November 22). Of crows and tools. *Science, 366*(6468), 965. https://doi.org/10.1126/science.aaz7775

12. Article in a newspaper

If page numbers are consecutive, separate them with an en dash. If not, separate them with a comma.

> Author's Last Name, Initials. (Year, Month Day). Title of article. *Title of Newspaper,* page(s). URL

> Schneider, G. (2005, March 13). Fashion sense on wheels. *The Washington Post,* F1, F6.

13. Article on a news website

Articles on CNN, HuffPost, Salon, Vox, and other news websites are documented differently from articles published in online newspapers and magazines. If an article is published in an online news source that is not a periodical or a blog, the article is treated as a stand-alone work, and the title should be italicized. Do not italicize the name of the website.

> Author's Last Name, Initials. (Year, Month Day). *Title of article.* Title of Site. URL

> Travers, C. (2019, December 3). *Here's why you keep waking up at the same time every night.* HuffPost. https://bit.ly/3drSwAR

author   title   publication

Documentation Map (APA) / Article in a Journal with DOI

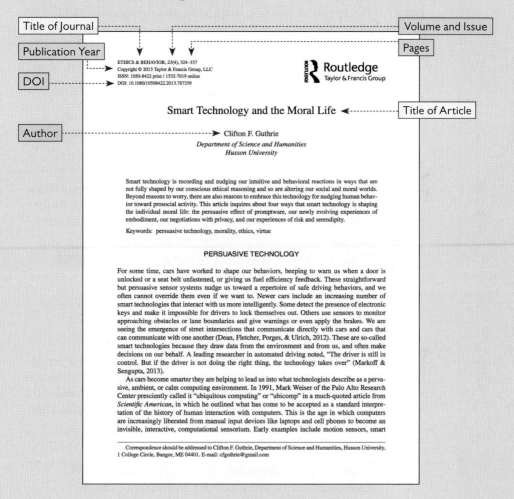

Title of Journal

Publication Year

DOI

Author

Volume and Issue

Pages

Title of Article

ETHICS & BEHAVIOR, 23(4), 324–337
Copyright © 2013 Taylor & Francis Group, LLC
ISSN: 1050-8422 print / 1532-7019 online
DOI: 10.1080/10508422.2013.787359

Routledge
Taylor & Francis Group

Smart Technology and the Moral Life

Clifton F. Guthrie

Department of Science and Humanities
Husson University

Smart technology is recording and nudging our intuitive and behavioral reactions in ways that are not fully shaped by our conscious ethical reasoning and so are altering our social and moral worlds. Beyond reasons to worry, there are also reasons to embrace this technology for nudging human behavior toward prosocial activity. This article inquires about four ways that smart technology is shaping the individual moral life: the persuasive effect of promptware, our newly evolving experiences of embodiment, our negotiations with privacy, and our experiences of risk and serendipity.

Keywords: persuasive technology, morality, ethics, virtue

PERSUASIVE TECHNOLOGY

For some time, cars have worked to shape our behaviors, beeping to warn us when a door is unlocked or a seat belt unfastened, or giving us fuel efficiency feedback. These straightforward but persuasive sensor systems nudge us toward a repertoire of safe driving behaviors, and we often cannot override them even if we want to. Newer cars include an increasing number of smart technologies that interact with us more intelligently. Some detect the presence of electronic keys and make it impossible for drivers to lock themselves out. Others use sensors to monitor approaching obstacles or lane boundaries and give warnings or even apply the brakes. We are seeing the emergence of street intersections that communicate directly with cars and cars that can communicate with one another (Dean, Fletcher, Porges, & Ulrich, 2012). These are so-called smart technologies because they draw data from the environment and from us, and often make decisions on our behalf. A leading researcher in automated driving noted, "The driver is still in control. But if the driver is not doing the right thing, the technology takes over" (Markoff & Sengupta, 2013).

As cars become smarter they are helping to lead us into what technologists describe as a pervasive, ambient, or calm computing environment. In 1991, Mark Weiser of the Palo Alto Research Center presciently called it "ubiquitous computing" or "ubicomp" in a much-quoted article from *Scientific American*, in which he outlined what has come to be accepted as a standard interpretation of the history of human interaction with computers. This is the age in which computers are increasingly liberated from manual input devices like laptops and cell phones to become an invisible, interactive, computational sensorium. Early examples include motion sensors, smart

Correspondence should be addressed to Clifton F. Guthrie, Department of Science and Humanities, Husson University, 1 College Circle, Bangor, ME 04401. E-mail: cfguthrie@gmail.com

Guthrie, C. F. (2013). Smart technology and the moral life. *Ethics & Behavior, 23*(4), 324–337. https://doi.org/10.1080/10508422.2013.787359

14. Editorial

Editorials can appear in journals, magazines, and newspapers. The following example is from an online newspaper. If the editorial is unsigned, put the title of the editorial in the author position.

> Author's Last Name, Initials. (Year, Month Day). Title of editorial
>   [Editorial]. *Title of Newspaper.* URL

> *The Guardian* view on local theatres: The shows must go on [Editorial].
>   (2019, December 6). *The Guardian.* https://bit.ly/2VZHIUg

15. Review

The following example is a book review in a newspaper; if you are citing a review that appears in print or online in a journal, magazine, or newspaper, use this general format, indicating in brackets what is being reviewed (a film, an app, etc.)

> Reviewer's Last Name, Initials. (Year, Month Day). Title of review
>   [Review of the book *Title of book,* by Author's Initials Last Name].
>   *Title of Newspaper.* DOI or URL

> Joinson, S. (2017, December 15). Mysteries unfold in a land of minarets
>   and magic carpets [Review of the book *The city of brass,* by S. A.
>   Chakraborty]. *The New York Times.* https://nyti.ms/2kvwHFP

For a review published on a website that is not associated with a periodical or a blog, italicize the title of the review and do not italicize the website name. If the review does not have a title, include the information about the work being reviewed in brackets immediately after the date of publication.

16. Comment on an online article or post

> Author's Last Name, Initials [username]. (Year, Month Day). Text of
>   comment up to 20 words [Comment on the article "Title of
>   article"]. *Title of Publication.* DOI or URL

> PhyllisSpecial. (2020, May 10). How about we go all the way again?
>   [Comment on the article "2020 Eagles schedule: Picking wins and
>   losses for all 16 games"]. *The Philadelphia Inquirer.* https://rb.gy/iduabz

Include a link to the comment if possible; if not, include the URL of the article.

17. Webpage on a website

Author's Last Name, Initials. (Year, Month Day). *Title of work*. Title of
    Site. URL

Pleasant, B. (n.d.). *Annual bluegrass*. The National Gardening Association.
    https://garden.org/learn/articles/view/2936/

If the author and the website name are the same, use the website name as
the author. If the content of the webpage is intended to change over time
and no archived version exists, use "n.d." as the date and include a retrieval
date.

Centers for Disease Control and Prevention. (2019, December 2). *When
    and how to wash your hands*. https://www.cdc.gov/handwashing
    /when-how-handwashing.html

Worldometer. (n.d.). *World population*. Retrieved February 2, 2020, from
    https://www.worldometers.info/world-population/

Books, Parts of Books, and Reports

18. Basic entry for a book

Author's Last Name, Initials. (Year of publication). *Title of book*.
    Publisher. DOI *or* URL

Print book

Schwab, V. E. (2018). *Vengeful*. Tor Books.

Ebook

Jemisin, N. K. (2017). *The stone sky*. Orbit. https://bit.ly/2DrGzKR

A print book and an ebook are documented in the same way. For an ebook,
do not include the format or platform you used (e.g., Kindle).

Documentation Map (APA) / Webpage on a Website

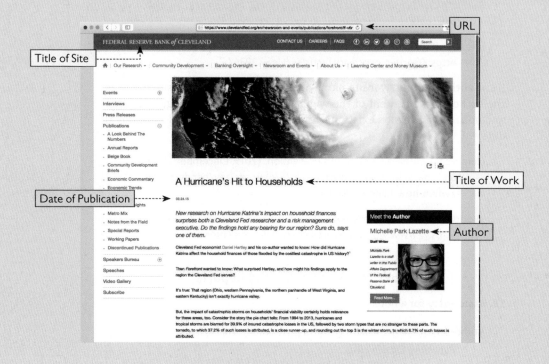

Lazette, M. P. (2015, February 24). *A hurricane's hit to households*. Federal
   Reserve Bank of Cleveland. https://www.clevelandfed.org
   /en/newsroom-and-events/publications/forefront/ff-v6n01/ff
   -20150224-v6n0107-a-hurricanes-hit-to-households.aspx

Documentation Map (APA) / Book

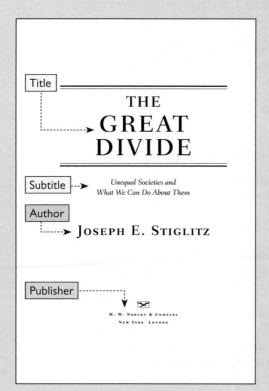

Stiglitz, J. E. (2015). *The great divide: Unequal societies and what we can do about them.* W. W. Norton.

19. Edition other than the first

Author's Last Name, Initials. (Year). *Title of book* (Name *or* number ed.). Publisher. DOI *or* URL

Burch, D. (2008). *Emergency navigation: Find your position and shape your course at sea even if your instruments fail* (2nd ed.). International Marine/McGraw-Hill.

20. Edited collection or anthology

Editor's Last Name, Initials (Ed.). (Year of edited edition). *Title of anthology* (number ed., Vol. number). Publisher. DOI *or* URL

Raviv, A., Oppenheimer, L., & Bar-Tal, D. (Eds.). (1999). *How children understand war and peace: A call for international peace education.* Jossey-Bass.

21. Work in an edited collection or anthology

Author's Last Name, Initials. (Year). Title of work. In Editor's Initials Last Name (Ed.), *Title of anthology* (number ed., Vol. number, pp. pages). Publisher. DOI *or* URL (Original work published Year)

Baldwin, J. (2018). Notes of a native son. In M. Puchner, S. Akbari, W. Denecke, B. Fuchs, C. Levine, P. Lewis, & E. Wilson (Eds.), *The Norton anthology of world literature* (4th ed., Vol. F, pp. 728–743). W. W. Norton. (Original work published 1955)

22. Entry in a reference work (dictionary, thesaurus, or encyclopedia)

If the entry has no author, use the name of the publisher as the author. If the reference work has no editor, do not include an editor. If the entry is archived or is not intended to change, use the publication date and do not include a retrieval date.

Author's Last Name, Initials. (Year). Title of entry. In Editor's Initials Last Name (Ed.), *Title of reference book* (Name *or* number ed., Vol. number, pp. pages). Publisher. URL

author   title   publication

Merriam-Webster. (n.d.). Epoxy. In *Merriam-Webster.com dictionary*.
Retrieved January 29, 2020, from https://www.merriam-webster
.com/dictionary/epoxy

23. Book in a language other than English

Author's Last Name, Initials. (Year). *Title of book* [English translation of
title]. Publisher. DOI *or* URL

Ferrante, E. (2011). *L'amica geniale* [My brilliant friend]. Edizione E/O.

24. One volume of a multivolume work

If the volume does not have a separate title, include the volume number in
parentheses after the title.

Author's Last Name, Initials. (Year). *Title of entire work* (Vol. number).
Publisher. DOI *or* URL

Spiegelman, A. (1986). *Maus* (Vol. 1). Random House.

If the volume does have a separate title, include the volume number and
title in italics after the main title (see no. 27 for an example from a religious
work).

25. Ancient Greek, Roman, or other classical work

Author's Name. (Year of publication). *Title of work* (Translator's Initials
Last Name, Trans.). Publisher. URL (Original work published Year)

Aristotle. (1994). *Nichomachean ethics* (W. D. Ross, Trans.). The Internet
Classics Archive. http://classics.mit.edu/index.html (Original
work published ca. 350 B.C.E.)

If the exact date is unknown, use "ca.," which stands for "circa."

26. Work by Shakespeare or other classical literature in English

Author's Last Name, Initials. (Year of publication). *Title of work* (Editor's Initials
Last Name, Ed.). Publisher. URL (Original work published Year)

Shakespeare, W. (2009). *Macbeth* (S. Barnes & A. Coleman, Eds.).
Insight Publications. (Original work published 1606)

27. Religious work

Do not include an author for most religious works. If you are citing an annotated version, include the editor and/or translator. If the date of original publication is known, include it at the end.

Unannotated

Title of work. (Year of publication). Publisher. URL (Original work
    published Year)

New American Bible. (2002). United States Conference of Catholic Bishops.
    http://www.vatican.va/archive/ENG0839/_INDEX.HTM (Original work
    published 1970)

Annotated

Editor's Last Name, Initials (Ed.). (Year of publication). *Title of work.* Publisher.
    URL (Original work published Year)

Marks, H. (Ed.). (2012). *The English Bible, The King James Version: Vol. 1. The Old
    Testament.* W. W. Norton. (Original work published 1611)

28. Report by a government agency or other organization

Author's Last Name, Initials. (Year, Month Day). *Title of report* (Report
    No. number). Publisher. DOI *or* URL

Centers for Disease Control and Prevention. (2009). *Fourth national
    report on human exposure to environmental chemicals.* US
    Department of Health and Human Services. https://www.cdc
    .gov/exposurereport/pdf/fourthreport.pdf

Omit the report number if one is not given. If more than one government department is listed as the publisher, list the most specific department as the author and the larger department as the publisher.

29. Published dissertation

Author's Last Name, Initials. (Year). *Title of dissertation* (Publication No.
    number) [Doctoral dissertation, Name of School]. Database *or*
    Archive Name. DOI *or* URL

Solomon, M. (2016). *Social media and self-examination: The examination of social media use on identity, social comparison, and self-esteem in young female adults* (Publication No. 10188962) [Doctoral dissertation, William James College]. ProQuest Dissertations and Theses Global.

If the thesis or dissertation is in a database, do not include a URL. Include a URL if the thesis or dissertation is published elsewhere online. If the dissertation is unpublished, use the name of the school as the source.

30. Paper or poster presented at a conference

Presenter's Last Name, Initials. (Year, Month First Day–Last Day). *Title of paper* or *poster* [Paper or Poster presentation]. Name of Conference, City, State, Country. URL

Dolatian, H., & Heinz, J. (2018, May 25–27). *Reduplication and finite-state technology* [Paper presentation]. The 53rd Annual Meeting of the Chicago Linguistic Society, Chicago, IL, United States. http://chicagolinguisticsociety.org/public/CLS53_Booklet.pdf

Audio, Visual, and Other Sources

If you are referring to an entire website, do not include the website in your reference list; simply mention the website's name in the body of your paper and include the URL in parentheses. Do not include email, personal communication, or other unarchived discussions in your list of references.

31. *Wikipedia* entry

Because *Wikipedia* has archived versions of its pages, give the date on which you accessed the page and the permanent URL of the archived page, which is found by clicking "View history."

Title of entry. (Year, Month Day). In *Wikipedia*. URL

List of sheep breeds. (2019, September 9). In *Wikipedia*. https://en.wikipedia.org/w/index.php?title=List_of_sheep_breeds&oldid=914884262

For a wiki that doesn't have permanent links to archived versions of its pages, include a retrieval date before the URL.

32. Online forum post

Author's Last Name, Initials [username]. (Year, Month Day). *Content of the post up to 20 words* [Online forum post]. Title of Site. URL

Hanzus, D. [DanHanzus]. (2019, October 23). *GETCHA DAN HANZUS. ASK ME ANYTHING!* [Online forum post]. Reddit. https://bit.ly /38WgmSF

33. Blog post

Author's Last Name, Initials [username]. (Year, Month Day). Title of post. *Title of Blog.* URL

gcrepps. (2017, March 28). Shania Sanders. *Women@NASA.* https:// blogs.nasa.gov/womenatnasa/2017/03/28/shania-sanders/

If only the username is known, do not use brackets.

34. Online streaming video

Uploader's Last Name, Initials [username]. (Year, Month Day). *Title of video* [Video]. Name of Video Platform. URL

CinemaSins. (2014, August 21). *Everything wrong with* National treasure *in 13 minutes or less* [Video]. YouTube. https://www.youtube.com /watch?v=1ul-_ZWvXTs

The person or group that uploaded the video is considered the author, even if someone else created the content. If only the username is known, do not use brackets. If there is another title within a title, put that other title in reverse italics.

35. Podcast episode

Host's Last Name, Initials (Host). (Year, Month Day). Episode title (No. episode number) [Audio podcast episode]. In *Podcast name.* Production Company. URL

Tamposi, E., & Samocki, E. (Hosts). (2020, January 8). The year of the broads [Audio podcast episode]. In *The broadcast podcast.* Podcast One. https://podcastone.com/episode/the-year-of-the-broads

author   title   publication

The host of the podcast, or the executive producer if known, is considered the author. Do not include an episode number if one isn't given.

36. Film

> Director's Last Name, Initials (Director). (Year). *Title of film* [Film]. Production Company. URL

> Jenkins, B. (Director). (2016). *Moonlight* [Film]. A24; Plan B; PASTEL.

> Cuarón, A. (Director). (2016). *Harry Potter and the prisoner of Azkaban* [Film; two-disc special ed. on DVD]. Warner Bros.

List the director as the author of the film. Indicate how you watched the film only if the format is important to the content.

37. Television series episode

> Writer's Last Name, Initials (Writer), & Director's Last Name, Initials (Director). (Year, Month Day). Title of episode (Season number, Episode number) [TV series episode]. In Executive Producer's Initials Last Name (Executive Producer), *Title of series*. Production Company. URL

> Siegal, J. (Writer), Morgan, D. (Writer), & Sackett, M. (Director). (2018, December 6). Janet(s) (Season 3, Episode 10) [TV series episode]. In M. Schur, D. Miner, M. Sackett, & D. Goddard (Executive Producers), *The good place*. Fremulon; 3 Arts Entertainment; Universal Television.

To document an entire series, use the executive producer as the author.

38. Song

> Artist's Last Name, Initials. (Year). Title of song [Song]. On *Title of album*. Label. URL

> Giddens, R. (2015). Shake sugaree [Song]. On *Tomorrow is my turn*. Nonesuch.

The recording artist or group is considered the author. Do not include a URL unless the song can be accessed only on one specific online platform.

39. Software, computer program, or mobile app

Include entries for software, programs, or mobile apps if they are uncommon or will not be known by your audience. Otherwise, just include the name (not italicized) and version number in the body of your text.

> Last Name, Initials. (Year). *Name of program* (Version number)
> [Computer software]. Publisher. URL

> Blount, K. (2018). *Scrivener for Windows* (Version 1.9.9.0) [Computer software].
> Literature & Latte. https://www.literatureandlatte.com/scrivener

Include a description of the content in brackets after the version number. For a mobile app, use "App Store" or wherever you accessed the app as the publisher. Use the year of publication of the version you accessed as the date.

40. *PowerPoint* slides or lecture notes

> Author's Last Name, Initials. (Year, Month Day). *Title of presentation*
> [Description of content]. Publisher. URL

> Pavliscak, P. (2016, February 21). *Finding our happy place in the internet of
> things* [PowerPoint slides]. Slideshare. https://bit.ly/3aOcfs7

If the lecture notes or slides do not have a title, describe the contents in brackets after the date.

41. Recording of a speech or webinar

> Author's Last Name, Initials. (Year, Month Day *or* Year). *Title* [Speech
> audio recording *or* Webinar]. Publisher. URL

> Kennedy, J. F. (1961, January 20). *Inaugural address* [Speech audio
> recording]. American Rhetoric. https://bit.ly/339Gc3e

For a speech, include the year, month, and day. For a webinar, include only the year.

42. Map

> Mapmaker's Last Name, Initials. (Year). *Title of map* [Map]. Publisher. URL

> Daniels, M. (2018). *Human terrain: Visualizing the world's population, in 3D*
> [Map]. The Pudding. https://pudding.cool/2018/10/city_3d/

author   title   publication

Google. (n.d.). [Google Maps directions for biking from Las Vegas,
    Nevada, to Los Angeles, California]. Retrieved January 30, 2020,
    from https://goo.gle/maps/9NdekwAkHeo4HM4N7

To cite a dynamic map, use "n.d." for the date and include a retrieval date. For
the title, include a description of the map in brackets.

43. Social media posts

Use the author's real name and include the social media handle in brackets.
If only the handle is known, do not use brackets. List any audiovisual content (e.g., a video, an image, a link) in brackets after the content of the post.
Replicate emoji if possible; if not, include a bracketed description. Follow the
spelling and capitalization of the original post.

Author's Last Name, Initials [@username]. (Year, Month Day). *Content
    of post up to 20 words* [Description of audiovisual content] [Type of
    post]. Platform. URL

Tweet

Baron, D. [@DrGrammar]. (2019, November 11). *Gender conceal: Did
    you know that pronouns can also hide someone's gender?* [Thumbnail
    with link attached] [Tweet]. Twitter. https://bit.ly/2vaCcDc

***Instagram* photograph or video**

Jamil, J. [@jameelajamilofficial]. (2018, July 18). *Happy Birthday to our
    leader. I steal all my acting faces from you. @kristenanniebell* [Face
    with smile and sunglasses emoji] [Photograph]. Instagram. https://
    www.instagram.com/p/BIYX5F9FuGL/

***Facebook* post**

Philadelphia Eagles. (2019, December 3). *"'We control our own destiny.'
    That's going to be the message moving forward to this football team."*
    #FlyEaglesFly [Thumbnail with link attached] [Status update].
    Facebook. https://bit.ly/39Ghjil

44. Data set

> Author's Last Name, Initials. (Year). *Title of data* set (Version number) [Data set]. Publisher. DOI *or* URL

> Pew Research Center. (2019). *Core trends survey* [Data set]. https://www.pewresearch.org/internet/dataset/core-trends-survey/

If the name of the author is the same as the name of the publisher, omit the publisher.

Sources Not Covered by APA

To document a source for which APA does not provide guidelines, look at models similar to the source you have cited. Give any information readers will need in order to find it themselves—author; date of publication; title; source, including DOI or URL (if applicable); and any other pertinent information. You might want to test your reference note to be sure it will lead others to your source.

FORMATTING A RESEARCH ESSAY

Title page. APA generally requires a title page. The page number should go in the upper right-hand corner. Center the full title of the paper in bold in the top half of the page. Center your name, the name of your department and school, the course number and name, the instructor's name, and the due date on separate lines below the title. Leave one line between the title and your name.

Page numbers. Place the page number in the upper right-hand corner. Number pages consecutively throughout.

Fonts, spacing, margins, and indents. Use a legible font that will be accessible to everyone, either a serif font (such as Times New Roman or Bookman) or a sans serif font (such as Calibri or **Verdana**). Use a sans serif font within figure images. Double-space the entire paper, including any notes and your list of references; the only exception is footnotes at the bottom of a page, which should be single-spaced. Leave one-inch margins at the top, bottom, and sides of your text; do not justify the text. The first line of each paragraph should be indented one-half inch (or five to seven spaces) from the left margin. APA recommends using one space after end-of-sentence punctuation.

Headings. Though they are not required in APA style, headings can help readers follow your text. The first level of heading should be bold, centered, and capitalized as you would any other title; the second level of heading should be bold and flush with the left margin; the third level should be bold, italicized, and flush left.

First Level Heading

Second Level Heading

Third Level Heading

Abstract. An abstract is a concise summary of your paper that introduces readers to your topic and main points. Most scholarly journals require an abstract; an abstract is not typically required for student papers, so check your instructor's preference. Put your abstract on the second page, with the word "Abstract" centered and in bold at the top. Unless your instructor specifies a length, limit your abstract to 250 words or fewer.

Long quotations. Indent quotations of forty or more words one-half inch (or five to seven spaces) from the left margin. Do not use quotation marks, and place the page number(s) or documentation information in parentheses *after* the end punctuation. If there are paragraphs in the quotation, indent the first line of each paragraph another one-half inch.

> Kaplan (2000) captured ancient and contemporary Antioch:
>
> > At the height of its glory in the Roman-Byzantine age, when it had an amphitheater, public baths, aqueducts, and sewage pipes, half a million people lived in Antioch. Today the population is only 125,000. With sour relations between Turkey and Syria, and unstable politics throughout the Middle East, Antioch is now a backwater—seedy and tumbledown, with relatively few tourists. (p. 123)
>
> Antioch's decline serves as a reminder that the fortunes of cities can change drastically over time.

List of references. Start your list on a new page after the text but before any endnotes. Title the page "References," centered and in bold, and double-space the entire list. Each entry should begin at the left margin, and subsequent lines should be indented one-half inch (or five to seven spaces). Alphabetize the list by authors' last names (or by editors' names, if appropriate). Alphabetize works that have no author or editor by title, disregarding *A, An,* and *The.* Be sure every source listed is cited in the text; do not include sources that you consulted but did not cite.

Tables and figures. Above each table or figure (charts, diagrams, graphs, photos, and so on), provide the word "Table" or "Figure" and a number, flush left and in bold (e.g., **Table 1**). On the following line, give a descriptive title, flush left and italicized. Below the table or figure, include a note with any necessary explanation and source information. Number tables and figures separately, and be sure to discuss them in your text so that readers know how they relate.

Table 1
Hours of Instruction Delivered per Week

	American classrooms	Japanese classrooms	Chinese classrooms
First grade			
Language arts	10.5	8.7	10.4
Mathematics	2.7	5.8	4.0
Fifth grade			
Language arts	7.9	8.0	11.1
Mathematics	3.4	7.8	11.7

Note. Adapted from "Peeking Out from Under the Blinders: Some Factors We Shouldn't Forget in Studying Writing," by J. R. Hayes, 1991, National Center for the Study of Writing and Literacy (Occasional Paper No. 25). National Writing Project website: http://www.nwp.org/

SAMPLE RESEARCH ESSAY

Katryn Sheppard wrote the following paper, "Early Word Production: A Study of One Child's Word Productions," for a linguistics course. It is formatted according to the guidelines of the *Publication Manual of the American Psychological Association,* 7th edition (2020).

1

Page numbers appear in the upper right corner.

The title is bold, centered, and placed in the upper half of the page.

Early Word Production: A Study of One Child's Word Productions

Katryn Sheppard

Your name is centered below the title, with one double-spaced line in between.

Department of Applied Linguistics, Portland State University

LING 437: First Language Acquisition

Dr. Lynn Santelmann

October 31, 2019

The school name and department, course number and name, professor's name, and due date of the paper are centered below your name.

Abstract begins on a new page. Heading is centered and bold. An abstract is not generally required for a student paper, so check with your professor.

Abstract text does not need a paragraph indent.

Use one space after each sentence.

250 words or fewer.

Abstract

Early word production, one of the initial stages of language development in children, plays an important role in the development of later language skills. This study identifies the word classes and number of words spoken in a recorded interaction (Bloom, 1973) by one normally developing child of sixteen months and analyzes aspects of the child's speech, with the goal of noting if the characteristics observed were supported by the existing research on early word production or if they deviated from those findings. The words that I analyzed fell into six categories: nouns, spatial terms, adjectives, negatives, social phrases, and verbs. Although the frequency with which the child used words from some of these categories reflected the expectations established by previous research, her use of words in other categories was less predictable. Noting word usage in the six categories led to an analysis of the functions that those categories served in the child's semantic communication at this early stage of language development.

3

Early Word Production: A Study of One Child's Word Productions • ————

Text starts on a
new page. Title is
centered and bold.

Each step in the course of language development and acquisition in
children provides a foundation for later skills and eventual mastery of
the language. Early word production, a stage of language development in
which children have only a few words in their vocabularies, provides the
foundation for later vocabulary building and language production and
has been shown to be closely linked to later language performance skills
(Walker et al., 1994). The early word production stage is therefore worthy
of examination, as it "signals that children have a new tool that will
enable them to learn about and participate more fully in their society"
(Uccelli & Pan, 2013, p. 95).

*Essay is double-
spaced.*

*Because this source
has more than two
authors, the in-text
documentation
begins with the
first author's name
followed by et al. The
year of publication
is included in the
reference.*

Because so few words are produced by children in this early stage,
the analysis of their word production focuses on the frequency of
particular word classes in speech. When examining typically developing
English-speaking children who have few words in their productive
vocabulary, Bates et al. (1994) found that the words produced were most
often nouns, while other categories more seldom appeared. These less
frequent categories included verbs and closed-class words. *Closed-class*
words are function words, categories to which new members cannot be
added: articles, conjunctions, numbers, pronouns, and prepositions.

*The signal phrase
uses past tense,
and the year of
publication is given in
parentheses.*

Reporting on the most common kinds of the nouns uttered in •————
early vocabularies, Nelson (1973) found that children "began by naming
objects exhibiting salient properties of change whether as the result
of the child's own action . . . or independent of it" (p. 1). In other words,

*Indent each
paragraph ½" (5–7
spaces).*

4

nouns that point to consistent, concrete objects are most prevalent in
early speech because "children learn to name and understand categories
that are functionally relevant to them" (Anglin, 1995, p. 165)—they learn
to name the objects they see and interact with day to day.

> The author, year, and page number are given in parentheses right after a quotation.

Although nouns make up the largest percentage of the words
produced by children in the earlier stages of language acquisition, other
word classes also appear. While occurring in children's first fifty words,
"verbs, adjectives, and function words each account for less than 10
percent" of total utterances (Uccelli & Pan, 2013, p. 96). Infrequent use
of these categories supports the idea that, while all word classes are
represented, nouns are expected to occur most often.

> Because the authors are not named in a signal phrase, their names are given in parentheses, with an ampersand rather than and between them. A page number is provided for a direct quotation.

Other lexical items found in the speech of children with limited
vocabulary are words indicating spatial relationships, how things
relate to one another in physical space. According to Bowerman (2007),
"children's earliest spatial words are topological forms like 'in' and
'on'" (p. 177). This observation supports the hypothesis that those
prepositions are among the first lexical items acquired (Brown, 1973;
Zukowski, 2013).

> The page number is provided in parentheses for a direct quotation when the author and year of the work are given earlier in the signal phrase.

> Multiple sources documented in the same parentheses are ordered alphabetically and separated by a semicolon.

Overall, the research on early word production in children just
beginning to acquire their first language has found that the majority of
words produced will be nouns that refer to concrete objects. According to
Pine (1992), children frequently use their early words to describe or label or
to do both. Pine concluded that "children are making referential statements
about the world with the kind of vocabulary items which they . . . have
available to them" (p. 53). That is, children try to comment on referents

> 1" margins

5

(the things that words stand for) in various ways using just the limited language skills that they possess in their early stage of development.

Taking into account prior research on the early words children produce, I analyzed the classes and categories of words appearing in a transcript of a young child speaking. I wanted to compare this particular child's speech with what is expected during this early stage of language development, knowing that research predicts a higher number of nouns than other word classes. I was interested to know whether nouns occur as frequently as the literature would have me believe and whether or not spatial terms appear in such early speech. Furthermore, I wanted to note whether verbs occur as infrequently as expected and, if so, what words the child used instead of verbs to convey action.

> *The first person is used when describing your own actions.*

Method

> *First-level headings are centered, bold, and capitalized.*

The transcript that I chose to analyze is one sample from a series of six recordings by Bloom (1973) of her daughter, Allison, a normally developing, English-speaking child. Allison's age in the samples ranged from 1 year 4 months and 21 days to 2 years and 10 months. The transcript that I analyzed was the earliest of these. Information about the socioeconomic status of Allison and her family was not available in the transcript or the North American English manual of the CHILDES database (MacWhinney, 2000), from which the transcript came. However, we can assume the family was from the professional class, as Bloom was a professor at Columbia University.

According to information in the CHILDES manual, the recordings occurred in the Audio-Visual Studio at Teachers College, Columbia

6

University, in a room containing some furniture and toys. The sessions were conducted with audio-recording devices alone; as a result, no videos were available. Each recording session lasted 40 minutes, for a total of four hours of recording. Bloom (1973) described her role as "more investigator than mother" (p. 11), but the interactions seem to have been more relaxed than one associates with investigators and not structured according to a test or other prearranged activity. Rather, the interactions were led by the child's actions in relation to her mother and objects in the room.

The date is placed right after the author's name; the page number in parentheses is as close to the quotation as possible.

The data are organized in six separate transcripts, arranged chronologically. They contain the actual utterances and morphological notation indicating the parts of speech being used. Bloom initially transcribed the recordings; later, Lois Hood, a fellow researcher, revised the transcript, which was revised again by a larger group of researchers. Each time, the researchers added notes to provide situational context. Each line of the transcript is numbered, and there was an attempt to divide the data to reflect "shift[s] in topic or focus" (Bloom, 1973, p. 11).

Data is treated as a plural noun; therefore, the verb (are) is plural.

Results

During the 40-minute exchange between Bloom and Allison, Allison produced a total of 362 occurrences of identifiable words. I did not distinguish between single- and multi-word utterances because that distinction was not relevant to the purpose of this study. Not all of Allison's turns in the conversation were intelligible; only intelligible words were included in my analysis. Altogether, I identified 27 different words (types) used by the subject, although there were many repetitions

The past tense is used to discuss the results of a study.

7

(tokens) of words. I assigned the 27 words to six categories: nouns, spatial terms, adjectives, negatives, social phrases, and verbs.

The category of nouns contained the largest number of distinct types as well as the largest number of tokens, as shown in Figure 1. Allison used a total of 12 nouns, and all reflected concrete concepts. These included household objects, nouns that referenced people, and the names of animals referring to toys in the recording room. The most frequently used noun was "baby" (n=25); "chair" was second (n=24). The total number of nouns represented 122 occurrences, or 34% of the total words uttered.

Figure 1 is referred to in the text.

Figure number is bold and flush left

Figure 1

Categories of Words Uttered by the Subject

Descriptive figure title is italicized and appears below the figure number.

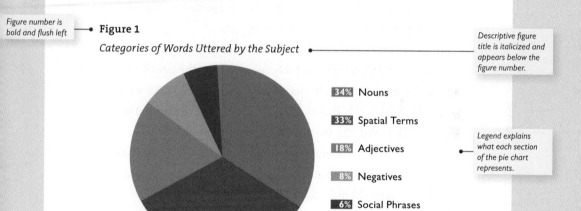

34% Nouns

33% Spatial Terms

18% Adjectives

8% Negatives

6% Social Phrases

1% Verbs

Legend explains what each section of the pie chart represents.

Description and source information are given in the figure note.

Words uttered by the subject, by word category (n=362), are shown. Data recorded in transcripts by L. Bloom (1973), accessed through the CHILDES database (MacWhinney, 2000).

The second most frequent category of words found in Allison's utterances was spatial terms. Five different spatial terms, or types, occurred, with "up" being the most common (n=48). All of the spatial terms Allison used referred to her immediate surroundings—for example, the chair that she wanted to climb "up" on or "down" from. Altogether, 120 of Allison's words were spatial words, accounting for 33% of her speech by word count.

The third most frequently used category of words in the data was adjectives, of which there were three types. Although "more" was the most frequently occurring adjective, "gone" was also often repeated. I will elaborate on the special role that adjectives played in Allison's speech in the discussion and conclusion section.

Negatives also appeared with some frequency in Allison's speech, although the category comprised only one type: "no." The word occurred 28 times (n=28). Sometimes it referred back to and negated other words that she had previously spoken; at other times it negated the word or words that followed. The level of emphasis Allison placed on the word varied. Sometimes her utterance was transcribed as "no"; at other times it was transcribed more emphatically, with an exclamation point, as "no!" This negative term accounted for 8% of her total words.

The remaining categories, social phrases and verbs, occurred less frequently. Social phrases—utterances that are appropriately used in specific social contexts—were present in the transcript in two different words: "uhoh" (n=20), and "oh" (n=3). Together, these add up to a total of 23 words.

9

The category of verbs was by far the least common in the subject's production. Four different verbs were used, three of which occurred only a single time. "Stop" was used twice, while "turn," "climb," and "sit" were used once each. A total of five tokens (n=5) were identified as verbs.

Discussion and Conclusion

Allison's single-word utterances fell into six identifiable categories, the frequency of which varied considerably. Some categories contained only a few items that were not repeated often while other words and categories of words showed up repeatedly. Allison's tendency to use words in certain categories matches the findings of the existing research literature on child language production. In other instances, Allison's use of words differed slightly from what might be expected.

As predicted, nouns made up a large portion of Allison's speech. Since researchers have found the majority of early words to be nouns, it was not surprising that Allison used the greatest number of different words within the noun category and likewise showed the greatest number of repeated tokens in this category. Furthermore, the kinds of nouns Allison used are also in line with the finding that children in the early stages of language acquisition focus on concrete concepts. All the nouns that Allison used referred to things in the recording room, mostly common objects that she could draw attention to. For instance, Allison used the noun "baby" when she wanted to communicate something to her mother about a doll she wanted to play with.

The category of spatial terms also accounted for a large percentage of the words Allison produced. The most frequently uttered word in

10

any category in the transcript was "up." That word, like other spatial terms, was often repeated and sometimes took the place of a more complex construction, as when the subject said "up" as she struggled to get up onto the chair and "down" when she wished to get back down. Allison's choice of words fits with the descriptions by Bowerman (2007) of children's first spatial terms: "early acquired spatial words revolve around relationships of . . . verticality (up, down)" (p. 180). This use of spatial terms contrasts with more complex spatial terms that appear in later development. However, the fact that Allison used five different words in the spatial word category could suggest that those terms play several important roles in her communication at this early stage.

As noted, adjectives like "gone" and "more" played important roles in Allison's speech when she wanted to convey something to her mother, as when she finished eating a cookie and repeatedly told her mother "more." This single word seemed to stand in for a more elaborate question or request Allison could not produce at this stage, such as "Give me more." "Gone" was also used repeatedly in the same context to refer to the cookie. The use of "gone" to describe what had happened to the cookie might be seen as evidence of the observation by Pine (1992) that children's early words are used to label and describe objects around them.

While the category of adjectives formed a smaller portion of Allison's speech than nouns or spatial words, adjectives composed a surprising 18% of total words in the transcript. Generally, adjectives and other word classes that are not nouns are expected to account for a much smaller percentage of words spoken in early word production (Bates et al., 1994).

Only the first author's last name is included in the signal phrase.

11

One feature of Allison's utterances that adhered to what is expected for a typical child at this age was her use of negatives. Although she used only one negative word—"no"—it was repeated frequently enough to be the fourth most common category. Her use of "no" rather than any other negative conformed to Brown's (1973) finding that forms of negation like "not" and "don't" appear only in later stages of development. In this very early stage, Allison's reliance on "no" alone seems typical.

Allison used "no" in varied contexts. In some cases, the word seemed to convey a lack of something, as when she uttered "cookie," looked around for the cookies, and then said "no." This sequence of events might indicate that Allison was conveying the lack of cookies to her mother. A similar exchange involved a picture of a girl: when Allison turned the picture over and found the other side blank, she said "no," evidently trying to convey that there was nothing on that side of the picture. On other occasions, "no" was produced as an answer to a question. In one example, Bloom asked Allison if the cup was for her (i.e., Bloom), to which the girl replied "no" and took the cup back. While adhering to the use of the single, simple form of negation that might be expected, Allison's utterances of "no" were varied in purpose and effective in communicating a range of ideas.

The remaining categories, social phrases and verbs, made up only a small percentage of Allison's words. Social words appeared infrequently and were sometimes attached to other words, as when the subject said "uhoh there." The infrequency of social phrases in Allison's speech reflects typical aspects of early vocabulary development. As

12

Because this source is a personal communication, it is cited in the text only and not documented in the list of references.

L. Santelmann (personal communication, 2014) explained, at this stage in a child's development, nearly all lexical items will be nouns and adjectives, with a limited number of social phrases.

True to previous research findings, verbs formed the least frequently used category in Allison's speech. Allison used four different verbs to describe what something was in the act of doing or what she intended to do. For example, she used "stop" to describe a toy car coming to a stop. The remaining three verbs were produced when Allison was performing an action herself, as when she said "turn" when turning the pages of a book, "climb" when trying to climb up onto the chair, and "sit" when going to sit on the chair. Although four different verbs showed up in Allison's speech, the total number of tokens from the verb category was much lower than for any other word category. This follows what researchers generally expect of children's early speech, which includes only a small percentage of verbs (Uccelli & Pan, 2013).

While Allison used these four verbs to communicate action, she often used other words to convey the same meaning. For example, Allison used "up" in two different contexts. The first was narrating an action she was performing, as when she said "up" while trying to get up onto the chair. The second was a request to Bloom to help her up. Allison also used the spatial term "down" to indicate similar intentions.

When not using spatial terms in place of more specific verbs, Allison used nouns to communicate intention and action. For example, one instance of her uttering "cookie" was to tell her mother that she wanted a cookie, indicating intention without using a verb. This

13

pattern occurred in other contexts, as when she used the concrete noun "chair" but not the verb "sit" to indicate that she wanted to get onto the chair. The use of nouns instead of verbs when communicating certain concepts is perhaps expected, given the established preponderance of nouns in early word production. It also supports the idea that children communicate using the tools at hand (Pine, 1992): since Allison frequently employed nouns and spatial terms, those are the tools that she had to rely on to convey whole hosts of meaning.

The results of my analysis of the transcript of Allison interacting with Bloom revealed aspects of the child's speech that were mostly in line with the established features of early word production. The frequency of the use of different word classes conformed to previous findings that concrete nouns are most common. Her choice of the spatial terms "up" and "down" and the simple negative "no" is also typical of children at this age. However, the uncommon frequency of adjectives in her speech indicates that they are important to how she communicated certain meanings; like spatial terms, they often filled in for verbs in cases where the actual verb was beyond her vocabulary. Her use of verbs, while predictably limited, showed how she conveyed meaning when she did not have the precise verbs available to her. Overall, Allison used a somewhat varied set of words to communicate a wide range of meanings even though she had only a limited vocabulary.

14

References

Entries are arranged alphabetically.

Anglin, J. M. (1995). Classifying the world through language: Functional relevance, cultural significance, and category name learning. *International Journal of Intercultural Relations, 19*(2), 161–181. http://doi.org/bg4cz3

Bates, E., Marchman, V., Thal, D., Fenson, L., Dale, P., Reznick, J. S., & Hartung, J. (1994). Developmental and stylistic variation in the composition of early vocabulary. *Journal of Child Language, 21*(1), 85–123. http://doi.org/fbjfz6

Bloom, L. (1973). *One word at a time: The use of single-word utterances before syntax*. Mouton.

Bowerman, M. (2007). Containment, support, and beyond: Constructing topological spatial categories in first language acquisition. In M. Aurnague, M. Hickmann, & L. Vieu (Eds.), *The categorization of spatial entities in language and cognition* (pp. 177–203). John Benjamins. http://doi.org/dffs

Brown, R. (1973). *A first language: The early stages*. Harvard University Press.

MacWhinney, B. (2000). *The CHILDES Project: Tools for analyzing talk* (3rd ed.). Lawrence Erlbaum Associates.

Nelson, K. (1973). Structure and strategy in learning to talk. *Monographs of the Society for Research in Child Development, 38*(1), 1–135. http://doi.org/fpfm6f

List of references begins on a new page. Heading is centered and bold.

All entries are double-spaced, and all lines except the first are indented ½" (5–7 spaces).

DOI given when one is available. Do not add a period at the end of a DOI or a URL.

Entry for a work found in an edited collection includes the editors' names, first initial followed by last name.

15

Pine, J. M. (1992). The functional basis of referentiality: Evidence from children's spontaneous speech. *First Language, 12*(1), 39–55. http://doi.org/d3769w

Uccelli, P., & Pan, B. A. (2013). Semantic development. In J. Berko Gleason & N. Bernstein Ratner (Eds.), *The development of language* (pp. 89–112). Pearson.

Walker, D., Greenwood, C., Hart, B., & Carta, J. (1994). Prediction of school outcomes based on early language production and socioeconomic factors. *Child Development, 65*(2), 606–621. http://doi.org/cb8pjs

Zukowski, A. (2013). Putting words together. In J. Berko Gleason & N. Bernstein Ratner (Eds.), *The development of language* (pp. 120–156). Pearson.

PART VII

Style

"How to Get and Hold Attention"

ONCE UPON A time—and for a very long time too—style in writing and speaking meant ornamentation, "dressing up" your language the way you might dress yourself up for a fancy party. In fact, ancient images often show rhetoric as a woman, Dame Rhetorica, in a gaudy, flowing gown covered with figures of speech—metaphors, similes, alliteration, hyperbole, and so on: her "stylish" ornaments. The influence of this view eventually led many writers to set aside issues of style, preferring to focus on substance, getting to the point and not worrying about making it fancy or pretty.

But not today. Not in a time of instant communication, of being inundated with notifications, news, advertisements—all of them coming at us with the force of a fire hose. In such

Dame Rhetorica, from Gregor Reisch's *Margarita Philosophica* (1504).

a time, scholars like Richard Lanham and Howard Rheingold argue, the most important task facing writers and speakers is making our messages so compelling that they will stand out from all the others. While pundits often claim we live in an information society, Lanham insists that, instead, "we're drowning in information" and that what we "lack is the human attention to make sense of it all." We would add, too, that we're missing the critical ability to know what to pay attention to and what to ignore.

How can we achieve this goal of getting and managing attention? Both Lanham and Rheingold, among others, answer with one word: **STYLE**. Just what do we mean by this simple-sounding word? When it comes to writing, most dictionaries offer something about word choice and how it differs from field to field or they will define style as "distinctiveness of expression." But style is not so much about *what* a message says as about *how* a message is presented—whether the message is in writing, in speech, includes (or is made up of) visuals, is delivered using formal language, and many more possibilities.

Wow. So style turns out to be all the elements that go into making a message (in any form) effective, memorable, compelling. Think, for instance, of a movie you really admire and that you think has real "style." Then make a list of all the things that go into creating its particular style: the "how" of its acting, directing, musical score, camera angles, editing, and so on. All these elements are at work in the film's style.

Style and substance are inseparable, and style is more crucially important to writers and speakers than ever before. Without close attention to style, to how our messages are presented, we are unlikely to attract an audience, much less hold its attention.

How can you create your own particular, powerful style in writing, speaking, and presenting? The chapters that follow aim to guide you in this task. But what we can say now is that you already have the primary tools that writers and speakers have always had for creating style: words—words that can create spellbinding images, rouse deep emotions, hammer home points, seize and hold attention. Choosing words (**DICTION**) and putting them in the best places (**SYNTAX**) still matter a lot in developing your style. But today you also have many other tools—visuals, video, sound, color, and more. All these elements are available as you choreograph the dance of your message, as you develop its style.

Getting and holding an audience's attention, however, is not the one single thing that matters when it comes to style. You want to get that attention in ways that are *appropriate* to your entire rhetorical situation. If you're dressing for an important job interview, you will probably choose clothes that are pleasing in a businesslike way (unless you're applying to be a lifeguard); if you're dressing for a championship basketball game or a religious service, however, you'll dress very differently.

It's hard (maybe impossible) to set hard-and-fast rules to be sure you're making the best choice for a particular situation. Consider a fascinating analogy from rhetorician Brent Simoneaux about the calculated choices baseball players have to make and the choices we as authors have to make:

> Imagine . . . the relationship between the pitcher and the batter. It's a complicated relationship forged in a complex calculus of the probable, yet unknown. I love those close-up shots on television of the batter studying the pitcher, waiting for the ball. The batter is poised, bat over shoulder, feet planted just so, ready to nimbly meet whatever comes. In that moment, the batter is both *at the mercy of* the pitcher, the rules of the game, the equipment, the umpire and also a *participant* and a *creator* of the game.
>
> The ball leaves the pitcher's hand.
>
> In that moment, the coach can't tell the batter exactly what to do at the plate. There's absolutely no way of knowing exactly where that ball is going to go. . . . The only thing the batter can do is to arrive at the plate poised and remain sensitive to the game unfolding.
>
> Of course, the coach can make a pretty good guess about what will happen. . . . The batter can guess as well. And they can both prepare accordingly. But in that utterly kairotic moment when the ball is flying through the air, everything is in flux. . . . And the coach's line has to be: *do the right thing.*
>
> That doesn't mean do whatever you want. It doesn't mean anything goes. Rather, it's an acknowledgment that . . . the terms of "rightness" are always shifting. . . . Do the *right* thing.
>
> —BRENT SIMONEAUX, "Do the Right Thing"

The same goes for authors. But that's part of the fun of writing with style. You get to analyze the situation before you and to think about how to seize the moment in order to get and hold the attention of your audience in the most appropriate ways. You even get something that the batter and pitcher don't have: you can take time to make your rhetorical decisions. The chapters that follow aim to help you achieve that goal.

THIRTY

What's Your Style?

"Style is all that matters."

—VLADIMIR NABOKOV

AKE A LOOK at the image on the following page: row after row of construction workers in identical outfits, interrupted by a stately figure—the queen of England—in bright turquoise. Our eyes are drawn to the queen because of her ensemble—hat, dress, and stockings—against a sea of men in orange jumpsuits: she stands out. This image could be captioned "Got style?" because it demonstrates that being like everyone or everything around you doesn't add up to a style that can get and hold attention. The same is true for writing; style helps you get readers to take notice—and listen—to what you have to say.

But style isn't just about getting attention: it's also about making choices that are appropriate to your particular situation, and all in an effort to achieve your purpose. You might wear shorts and running shoes to the gym but not to a job interview, a bathing suit to the beach but not to class. It's a delicate balance. Style in writing works the same way. How can the words, images, and sentence structures you use stand out (like the queen) while at the same time meeting your intended audience's expectations and giving you credibility? This chapter offers strategies for achieving this balance and shaping your own flexible style of writing.

Queen Elizabeth II of the United Kingdom sits for a photo with construction workers at the opening of a new rail station in Reading, England.

See how Roxane Gay's style decisions match her context—a book written for a general audience—on p. 923. Sentence fragments aren't always appropriate, but they certainly work for Gay's purpose and audience.

Appropriateness and Correctness

Making good stylistic choices, ones that strike the balance between getting attention and keeping readers with you, calls for considering what's appropriate to your particular situation. In the simplest terms, an "appropriate" writing style is one in which your words and the way you arrange them suits your topic, your purpose, and your audience. But making stylistic choices in writing can be tricky, especially because we don't have a set of hard-and-fast rules to follow. You may have "learned" that it isn't appropriate to start a sentence with *and* or *but* and never to end a sentence with a preposition. But those "rules" are far from universal, and they change over time. In fact, a lot of fine writing today bends and breaks these rules to good effect.

So it won't work to think about style simply as a matter of following rules. In fact, if you have to choose between being "correct" and being "appropriate," being appropriate almost always wins out. In 1966, in the original *Star Trek*, when Captain Kirk of the starship *Enterprise* announced

The crew of the USS *Enterprise* split infinitives boldly, and with emphasis.

its mission "to boldly go where no man has gone before," that split infinitive ("boldly" splits the two words of the infinitive "to go") wasn't absolutely "correct," but it created just the emphasis the writers were after. Moreover, it was an appropriate choice for the time (the 1960s) and place (a TV show). One mark of its stylistic appropriateness and effectiveness: it's still quoted, even in textbooks like this one. Making appropriate stylistic choices, then, will almost always depend on your RHETORICAL SITUATION.

Some contexts already have a defined style of communicating or a specific dialect that's considered most appropriate. In those situations, being aware of the conventional style will help guide your style decisions. For example, what some refer to as "edited academic English" is the DIALECT often thought of as appropriate for writing done in most school, government, and professional contexts. But like any other "standard," it has changed across time and will continue to change. If you read the stories of Flannery O'Connor, a twentieth-century American fiction writer and essayist, you'll notice she uses the words *man* and *he* to refer to people in general. Stylistic choices like this were completely appropriate at the time. But when many criticized the use of "he" to refer to all people—including women—conventions changed, and writers looked for more appropriate choices, including alternatives to the designation of all people as either male or female, *he and she,* or even *they,* the increasingly preferred option. Were O'Connor, who died in 1964, writing today, it's very likely she would make different choices when using personal pronouns.

But the fact that academic dialects of languages emerge and change over time and that the appropriate use of a language most often depends on context doesn't mean that stylistic choices are without any boundaries at all. Audiences often expect that writers will follow accepted conventions, and choosing to do so—or not—has consequences. When the choices you make ignore or defy audience expectations or when they push the envelope, you may be able to get an audience's attention, but you may not hold it for very long.

Take a look, for instance, at how linguist Geneva Smitherman pushes against the traditional "rules" of academic English and does so brilliantly. In fact, had she stuck to the traditional rules, the following paragraph would have been far less effective than it is.

> Before about 1959 (when the first study was done to change black speech patterns), Black English had been primarily the interest of university academics, particularly the historical linguists and cultural anthropologists. In recent years, though, the issue has become a very hot controversy, and there have been articles on Black Dialect in the national press as well as in the educational research literature. We have had pronouncements on black speech from the NAACP and the Black Panthers, from highly publicized scholars of the Arthur Jensen–William Shockley bent, from executives of national corporations such as Greyhound, and from housewives and community folk. I mean, really, it seem like everybody and they momma done had something to say on the subject!
>
> —GENEVA SMITHERMAN, *Talkin and Testifyin: The Language of Black America*

Geneva
Smitherman

Smitherman obviously knows the rules of edited academic English but breaks them to support her point and also to create a clear rhetorical stance, as a scholar, a skilled writer, and a proud African American. Writing in the late 1970s, she could assume that her readers would know that the NAACP is the National Association for the Advancement of Colored People, that the Black Panthers were a revolutionary social action group in the 1960s and 1970s, and that Arthur Jensen and William Shockley had made controversial claims about relationships between race and intelligence. She could also assume that readers of her book would expect her to write in edited academic English since the volume was published by a mainstream publisher and treated its subject from an academic perspective.

But Smitherman wasn't interested in writing a book about the language of African Americans using only edited academic English. After all, one of her claims was that the language practices of African Americans were influencing American culture and language in many ways. Notice how her stylistic choices support that claim. She not only talks the talk of edited academic English but walks the walk of African American English as well. When she switches in her final sentence from edited academic English to African American English, she simultaneously drives home her point—that everyone at that time seemed to have an opinion about the language of African Americans—while demonstrating membership in that community by using the language variety associated with it. In short, she makes sound and appropriate stylistic choices.

You'll find more on mixing dialects and languages in the following chapter. For now, remember that your style should be appropriate to your purpose, audience, and rhetorical situation, even—and especially—when you bend the rules.

Connecting with Audiences

In all your writing, you'll want to have a reasonably good sense of your intended **AUDIENCE** in order to make effective stylistic choices. Take a look at the image on the following page; it's the webpage for a supermarket in a small town in California that appeals directly to its local community. The writers set a friendly, informal tone right away, announcing that "we love good food" and appealing to their audience to "SHOP LOCAL." The emphasis on the local continues as they note that they've been "serving our community" for decades. They also invite readers to visit their *Facebook* page—and learn about "our sustainable fish program." The use of "our" emphasizes the community and establishes **COMMON GROUND** with readers. The bright colors and simple design add to the warm, inviting tone that underscores the overall message.

A student writing about this same topic for a class project must be more formal and would need to include the background and contextual information that an academic audience expects. For example, here is Katherine Spriggs arguing for the importance of "buying local":

The Surf Market in Gualala, California, welcomes customers to its webpage with a friendly, informal tone.

> "Buying local" means that consumers choose to buy food that has been grown, raised, or produced as close to their home as possible. Buying local is an important part of the response to many environmental issues we face today. It encourages the development of small farms, which are often more environmentally sustainable than large farms, and thus strengthens local markets and supports small rural economies. By demonstrating a commitment to buying local, Americans could set an example for global environmentalism.
>
> —KATHERINE SPRIGGS, "On Buying Local"

Rather than assuming that her audience already knows what "buying local" means, Spriggs begins with a careful definition—something the Surf Market webpage doesn't need to do—as a way of laying the groundwork for her argument and demonstrating that she is knowledgeable about her topic. She then starts to build her argument by linking the idea of buying local to environmental issues and community values. Her tone is serious; she gives practical reasons for why buying local is "important," noting that it "encourages the development of small farms" and "supports small rural economies." Like Surf Market and Spriggs do, you'll want to think about who will read what you write and make stylistic choices that help you connect with them.

Levels of Formality

Being appropriate also calls on writers to pay attention to the level of formality they use. In ancient Rome, Cicero identified three levels of style: low or plain style, used to teach or explain something; middle style, used to please an audience; and high or grand style, used to move or persuade an audience. Note that these classifications link style with a specific purpose and a likely audience.

On August 27, 2018, an aide to Senator John McCain shared a farewell statement McCain had written to America before his death two days earlier. Here is the opening of that letter:

> My fellow Americans, whom I have gratefully served for sixty years, and especially my fellow Arizonans,
>
> Thank you for the privilege of serving you and for the rewarding life that service in uniform and in public office has allowed me to lead. I have tried to serve our country honorably. I have made mistakes, but I hope my love for America will be weighed favorably against them.
>
> I have often observed that I am the luckiest person on earth. . . . Like most people, I have regrets. But I would not trade a day of my life, in good or bad times, for the best day of anyone else's.
>
> I owe that satisfaction to the love of my family. No man ever had a more loving wife or children he was prouder of than I am of mine. And I owe it to America. To be connected to America's causes—liberty, equal justice, respect for the dignity of all people—brings happiness more sublime than life's fleeting pleasures. Our identities and sense of worth are not circumscribed but enlarged by serving good causes bigger than ourselves.
> —JOHN MCCAIN, "Farewell Letter to America"

Writing in full awareness of his imminent death, McCain uses a solemn, deliberate, formal tone, writing in the grand style that seeks to inspire by both word and deed. Twice he uses balanced phrases to acknowledge weaknesses as well as strengths ("I have made mistakes, but I hope my love of America . . ." and "I have regrets. But I would not trade a day . . ."). And he expresses deep satisfaction at his connection to "America's causes—liberty, equal justice, respect for the dignity of all people," saying that this connection brings him happiness "more sublime than life's fleeting pleasures." In concluding his letter, McCain uses repetition and very brief sentences to punctuate this final message:

> Do not despair of our present difficulties but believe always in the promise and greatness of America, because nothing is inevitable here. Americans never quit. We never surrender. We never hide from history. We make history. Farewell, fellow Americans. God bless you, and God bless America.

The four short sentences that follow the longer opening sentence are like drumbeats, with their use of the repeated "we," calling Americans to attend to McCain and to be inspired by his example. McCain's style choices match his unique **RHETORICAL SITUATION**—and help his message land with impact.

Stance

Stance refers to the attitude authors take toward their topic and audience. For example, you might write about immigration as an impassioned advocate or critic, someone with strong opinions about the inherent good or evil of immigration. Or you might write as a dispassionate analyst, someone trying to weigh carefully the pros and cons of the arguments for and against a particular proposal. Either stance—and any possible stances in between—will affect what style you use.

If your audience changes, your language will likely shift, too. Debating immigration issues with close friends whose opinions you're fairly sure of will differ in crucial ways from debating them with people you know less well or not at all because you'll be able to take less for granted. That you will likely shift all aspects of your message—from word choice and sentence structure to amount of background information and choice of examples—doesn't make you a hypocrite or a flip-flopper; instead, it demonstrates your skill at finding the most effective rhetorical resources to make your point.

In a posting titled "Same Food Planet, Different Food Worlds," blogger Rod Dreher calls attention to the drastically different stances taken by two restaurant reviewers. Here's an excerpt from one, a review of a new Olive Garden restaurant in Grand Forks, North Dakota, by eighty-five-year-old Marilyn Hagerty:

It had been a few years since I ate at the older Olive Garden in Fargo, so I studied the two manageable menus offering appetizers, soups and salads, grilled sandwiches, pizza, classic dishes, chicken and seafood and filled pastas.

At length, I asked my server what she would recommend. She suggested chicken Alfredo, and I went with that. Instead of the raspberry lemonade she suggested, I drank water.

She first brought me the familiar Olive Garden salad bowl with crisp greens, peppers, onion rings and yes—several black olives. Along with it came a plate with two long, warm breadsticks.

The chicken Alfredo ($10.95) was warm and comforting on a cold day. The portion was generous. My server was ready with Parmesan cheese. . . .

All in all, it is the largest and most beautiful restaurant now operating in Grand Forks. It attracts visitors from out of town as well as people who live here.   —MARILYN HAGERTY, "Long-awaited Olive
Garden Receives Warm Welcome"

Hagerty's polite, unpretentious stance is evident in this review—and as it happens, the style of her writing attracted much attention when it went viral, with readers both celebrating and bashing that style.

Dreher contrasts Hagerty's stance with that of Dive Bar Girl (DBG), who writes for a newsletter in Baton Rouge, Louisiana. In fact, DBG starts right out by announcing her stance—she's going to be "mean," not "informative"—and so after saying "a few nice things" about her topic, a restaurant called Twin Peaks, she writes the review that she assumes her readers "want to read":

➦ Marilyn Hagerty. Read the *Los Angeles Times*' take on the controversy— and Hagerty's son's response in the *Wall Street Journal*—at everyones anauthor .tumblr.com.

Admit it, you like it when DBG is mean. You only send her fan mail when she's mean. She never gets mail for being informative. . . . So she is going to write about the positive things first and then write the review you want to read. The smokehouse burger was above average. The patio was a nice space. The staff, while scantily clad, was professional. The salads even looked good. The place was miles above Hooters.

Here is the review you want: Twin Peaks has to be the brainchild of two 14-year-old boys who recently cracked the parental controls on the home computer. Waitresses are known as "Lumber Jills." In case you are missing the imagery—each Lumber Jill has been endowed with an epic pair of Twin Peaks.   —CHERRYTHEDIVEBARGIRL

These two reviews could hardly be more different in stance: the first is low key and even-handed, well suited to Hagerty's stance as a modest and sincere reviewer. The second is highly opinionated and sarcastic, true to the brash, in-your-face stance of Dive Bar Girl. So both are written in styles that suit (and reflect) their respective stances.

But what happens when that stance doesn't fit well with a particular audience? That's what happened when Hagerty's review went viral: some writers immediately began making fun of her as inept and hopelessly out of it; others jumped in just as quickly to defend Hagerty's review, while still others read her review as an indirect parody of local restaurant reviews. Now imagine that Dive Bar Girl's review appeared in Hagerty's hometown newspaper. Chances are it would attract some hefty criticism as well.

The takeaway lesson here: as a writer, you need to consider whether your **STANCE** is appropriate not only to your topic and audience but also to your **MODE** of distribution.

Tone

All the writing you do, regardless of stance or level of formality, has a particular **TONE**. You may not think consciously about how to establish that tone, especially when commenting on a friend's *Instagram* post or writing a text message, but even in social media writing you are making choices about whether you want to convey a serious tone, a humorous tone, an exasperated tone. When you know that your readers are friends and family, your tone can probably be pretty casual, like this *Facebook* update posted by a student in Washington, DC, which is playful, critical, reasoned, and ironic:

> Note to self: avoid union station on weekday mornings. Hordes of angry commuters make getting to the train impossible? #notfun #DCMetro #rushhour #istheworst

Here the tone is one of frustration and exasperation, expressed in the hashtags the writer adds (#notfun, etc.). She is assuming her readers will not only know what she is talking about but also appreciate her playful tone.

For a report on commuters in Union Station for an urban studies class, the author establishes the more serious tone of a reporter or researcher:

> Walking into Union Station on a weekday morning can be like going against a herd of stampeding cattle. Riders rush from the trains, swinging briefcases and computer bags, knocking over anything or anyone in the way. Rush hour in this station, one of the busiest train stations in the country, is not enjoyable. Looking at some usage statistics and videos will show just how unpleasant this experience is and how it affects those who regularly ride the metro.

Here the tone is studied and serious. The writer opens by describing the scene in the congested station and then moves to introduce an analysis of usage statistics and videos. But even a serious tone doesn't need to result in a dull, boring style: note the lively description ("stampeding cattle"; "swinging briefcases"; "knocking over everything or anyone in the way"). Your **PURPOSE**, **AUDIENCE**, **STANCE**, and even **MEDIUM** will help determine an appropriate and effective tone.

Style across Media

You probably already find yourself using a variety of media to communicate every day and making intuitive choices about style: you post a message on *Twitter*, you make an oral presentation using *Prezi* for a class, you conduct research for an article that you submit in print and then "remediate" as part of a website. Each of these tasks calls for an appropriate medium, whether written, oral, or electronic. In each case, you have a good sense of your purpose and audience, and you use that knowledge to establish an appropriate style and choose the best medium to deliver your message. This is the same kind of rhetorical thinking you need to be doing consciously and analytically for the writing you do in school or work. So in all your writing across media—at home, at work, at school, wherever—you will want to make stylistic choices that are appropriate for your rhetorical situation, your audience, and your purpose.

You are no doubt familiar with the hashtag #BlackLivesMatter, which has generated over 50 million tweets since Alicia Garza, grieving over the death of Trayvon Martin and astonished that his killer was not convicted of any crime, logged onto *Facebook* in July 2013 and wrote "Black people, I love you. I love us. Our lives matter," and her good friend Patrissa Cullors wrote back, closing her post with "#blacklivesmatter." Note the stylistic choices that make these messages memorable: very short sentences; repetition; a serious and urgent tone. Garza, Cullors, and Opal Tometi—cofounders of the Black Lives Matter movement—used those same choices as they went on to create pages on *Tumblr*, *Twitter*, and *Facebook* to launch a rallying cry across the country.

Some writers post images to get their message across, such as this tweet which includes a photo taken after a protest against the separation of immigrant children from their parents during the summer of 2019:

RAICES ✔
@RAICESTEXAS

Follow ⌄

Today in NYC @Raicestexas protests the separation of children from their families. These cages represent the real living conditions of children caged at our border. Sharing is an act of protest. Follow @NoKidsInCagesUS for updates. #KeepFamiliesTogether #PassHR541 #NoKidsInCages

WE SAY NO.

NOKIDSINCAGES

9:32 AM - 12 Jun 2019

How would you describe the style and tone of this message and its accompanying images? How might the author adjust the style in writing an op-ed in the local newspaper instead? Or creating a *YouTube* video or brief podcast describing and analyzing the issue? Different media and platforms call for different style choices in order to grab attention and get your message across. And remember that grabbing attention is only half the battle—making sure your style is appropriate and effective is just as important. Especially online, it can be easy and tempting to use an over-the-top title or a startling image to grab attention (it's how clickbait works, after all), but they won't keep your readers with you beyond a flashy opening, so stick to style choices that strike the right balance.

REFLECT. Take some time to look carefully at some of your posts on social media. How informal or formal are they? What do they assume your audience will know about your topic? What are your purposes for writing—to share information? To ask for advice? What else? What kind of style does your audience respond best to? Do you use a mix of media—words, images, video? Then write a few sentences describing what you've noticed about your writing style on social media and how it differs from the other kinds of writing you do—at school, at work, at home.

Style across Disciplines

Making good choices is especially important when writing in different disciplines, where what's appropriate and effective often varies from field to field or workplace to workplace. Many fields have established conventions—reading published writing in a field or discipline can help you see what stylistic features are most common. Look for patterns—do writers use a particular verb tense? Active voice instead of passive voice? A specific organization or style of headings? Identifying what other successful writers have done in a field that's new to you is a good way to figure out what you'll try in order to be effective and appropriate.

One notable stylistic difference between fields is favoring the **ACTIVE VOICE** or the **PASSIVE VOICE**. For example, reports in the sciences usually call for the passive voice. Take a look at this passage from a 2017 article on whether long-distance running affects runners' ankles and feet in a way that's detectable by MRI (magnetic resonance imaging). The authors explain what methods they used to review existing research on their topic; notice that most of the verbs are passive:

> **Methods:** Scopus, Web of Science, Embase and Ovid Medline *were searched* using key terms in relation to MRI findings of the ankle and foot in response to long-distance running, published between 1990 and 2016. The final search *was conducted* on 19 September, 2016. Studies *were identified* using inclusion and exclusion criteria. Methodological quality *was assessed* using a modified Quality Index.

In scientific writing the passive is generally favored because it shouldn't matter who searched for the articles, applied the criteria, or assessed the quality using the stated criteria; in the end, the results should be the same. The passive voice also focuses the reader's attention on what was done, not on who did it. So although you may have been instructed in your writing classes to "avoid the passive," it is often the appropriate and effective choice in the sciences.

At the same time, there are many occasions when writers avoid the passive voice for good reason. For example, engineers often rely on information gathered by other firms or information they gather themselves from interviews. In contexts where they need to make clear who is responsible for observations, recommendations, or judgments, engineers use the active voice to locate responsibility. Thus, engineers would write "Our firm hired ABC Tech to conduct a geotechnical evaluation" rather than "A geotechnical evaluation was conducted" so that readers know the source of the data presented and analyzed. Voice is just one example of how style changes between disciplines—the point is you'll want to seek out reliable examples to learn what style works and is expected of you in a new field.

Thinking about Your Own Style

As you've seen, style is all about making appropriate choices, choices that inevitably depend on your topic and all the elements of your rhetorical situation, especially your STANCE, your PURPOSE, your GENRE, and your AUDIENCE. Have you written a review of something—a restaurant for the campus newspaper? a book on *Amazon*? your instructor on ratemyprofessor.com? If so, take a look at the choices you made in the review, and then compare them to those you made in an essay you wrote for class. You'll see right away that you have instinctively used different styles for these different occasions.

For an example of what we mean about making appropriate stylistic choices, take a look at a paragraph from this book, first as it appears on page 663 and then as it is revised as a tweet, a report, and a flyer.

Original text

Once upon a time—and for a very long time too—style in writing and speaking meant ornamentation, "dressing up" your language the way you might dress yourself up for a fancy party. In fact, ancient images often show rhetoric as a woman, Dame Rhetorica, in a gaudy, flowing gown covered with figures of speech—metaphors, similes, alliteration, hyperbole, and so on: her "stylish" ornaments.

Revised as a tweet

Writing style used to mean dressing up your words, like Cinderella getting ready for the ball. Not anymore. #rhetorictoday

Revised as a report

For more than 500 years, the definition of "style" held relatively stable. Style was a form of ornamentation that was added to texts in order to make them more pleasing or accessible to an audience. In ancient depictions, Rhetoric is often shown as a woman dressed in elegant attire and "ornamented" with dozens of stylish figures of speech.

Revised as a flyer

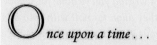

Once upon a time . . .

writing style was all about ornamentation.

ℰ𝒪 *Language* ℭℛ

in fancy dress

What do you know about writing style?

Join us in the Writing Center to learn how style has changed over time
and how your style can be *in* style.

Sterling C. Evans Library

Room 214

Note how the style changes to match each genre and audience: the tweet is short, of course, and very informal; it uses a sentence fragment and then uses a hashtag to link readers with others talking about rhetoric today. The report is much more formal and is written in edited academic English. The flyer uses a much more conversational style—ellipses to signal a pause, a sentence fragment, a question, and italics for emphasis—and announces an event (the purpose of a flyer).

We've tried in this chapter to emphasize how important the stylistic choices you make are to getting the attention of your audiences—and holding it; style really is the key to achieving that goal. And remember that, as an author, you get to call a lot of the stylistic shots. As you do so, of course, you'll want to think carefully about what styles are appropriate in particular situations and how you can meet an audience's expectations without "painting by the numbers" or writing dull, predictable prose. You're a lot better than that: you've got STYLE.

REFLECT. Think about a person who you think has style (a friend or family member, a public figure, a boss or teacher): how would you describe that style? What about this person and their style appeals to you—or doesn't? What choices has the person made that contribute to this particular style? If you can, look at a few examples of the person's style in language and writing (social media posts, for example, or captions on a T-shirt). How does their writing style align (or not) with the other parts of the person's style?

Now think about you: how would you describe your own style? What makes up your style? Finally, look at a few recent pieces of writing you've done for school or for your job: how well do they represent you? Do they align (or not) with your style? Do these pieces of writing sound like you—does your voice come through? What about these pieces of writing is memorable or vivid, and what makes them so? What is their level of formality? What is your stance in them and what tone do you take? How would you describe your writing style?

THIRTY-ONE

Mixing Languages and Dialects

OW MANY LANGUAGES do you know well enough to speak or write? Which languages would you like to know? The United States is often referred to as a monolingual country, one where English is the only language needed to get along. But that characterization has never been accurate. Languages other than English have always been present here. Today, the US Census Bureau estimates that approximately 20 percent of Americans report speaking a language other than English at home—Spanish, Chinese, and Tagalog are the three most common. And American Sign Language is probably the third most commonly used language (after Spanish), although the census doesn't ask about signed languages.

So the United States is a country of many languages. It is also a country of multiple dialects and, again, it always has been. *Dialects* are varieties of language that are spoken by people in a particular region, social class, or ethnic group—like the English spoken by residents of Appalachia or the Spanish spoken in Texas. *Registers* are varieties of language associated not with particular people but with a particular activity or occupation—like soccer or chemical engineering. Just listen closely to people you know or see on *YouTube*, and you will surely hear various dialects and registers, as well as distinctive vocabularies, at work.

Spend a day taking notice of all the languages, dialects, and registers you encounter around you—from conversations on campus to signs, billboards, and texts that convey information.

The languages, dialects, and registers you use make up your own unique way of speaking—a sort of linguistic fingerprint, called an *idiolect*. One of our grandmothers, who lived in the foothills of Tennessee's Smoky Mountains, referred to kitchen cabinets as "the upper division"—something we've never heard said by anyone else, in Tennessee or elsewhere! She also drew out the sound of vowels in words like "broil" so that the word sounded as if it had several syllables rather than one. These quirks—among others—made up her idiolect.

No matter how many languages you speak, you probably use a number of different dialects and registers. Is the way you speak at the dinner table different from the way you speak in class or at work? Is the way you write an *Instagram* post different from an email to an instructor? We bet that it is.

We also bet that you probably mix whatever languages, dialects, and registers you use, consciously or unconsciously. Language scholars have identified two ways in particular that people do so. **CODE-SWITCHING** is the practice of shifting from one language or dialect to another, whereas **CODE-MESHING** is a way of weaving together languages and dialects. Both are ways of mixing varieties of language for various purposes—to reflect a particular **STANCE**, for example, or to establish a connection with certain **AUDIENCES**. This chapter provides examples and guidelines to help you mix languages, dialects, and registers for various rhetorical situations.

REFLECT. Think for a few minutes about the varieties of language spoken where you grew up. What features of pronunciation and vocabulary can you identify? What groups do you belong to now that have a specialized way of communicating? Fans of one type of music? A religious community? An athletic team or social club? Write a paragraph describing what influences the way you speak; include specific examples.

Using Edited Academic English and Other Dialects

What some call **EDITED ACADEMIC ENGLISH** is actually a dialect—one that's used both in formal and informal contexts. For example, during a heated discussion about jobs and automation with a friend, you may say things in informal but effective ways that wouldn't work as well if you were writing up the same point in a formal report. Even within a single dialect there's almost always more than one appropriate way to say or write something; your audience and purpose inform your choices.

That is not to say that all dialects are regarded as equals. What we are calling edited academic English—and some have called "standard" English—has long held a prestigious position in the United States. But so-called standard languages have been challenged for centuries by vernacular dialects and languages. After all, English once challenged Latin and Greek as the languages of power, notably in Chaucer's *Canterbury Tales*. So it's no surprise that in the United States, many writers have challenged or even rejected the privileged dialect of edited academic English. This chapter provides a number of examples of writers mixing varieties of language—often beyond edited academic English—in ways that speak powerfully to their audiences. Such moves are increasingly common, but doing so doesn't always come risk-free. Keep your rhetorical situation front and center—what's your purpose? what's at stake? what does your audience consider appropriate?—when you make language choices that push against readers' expectations.

Connecting with Audiences

If you're a fan of popular music today, you can probably come up with examples of lyricists mixing languages to craft powerful messages. Here is the opening of Kenyan rapper Bamboo's remix of the song "Mama Africa," first written and sung by Jamaican reggae artist Peter Tosh. A love song to the African continent, which has in Bamboo's view too often been represented negatively, his remix connects to his international audience of hip-hop and pop music fans by moving between Swahili and English:

> *tunaishi vizuri*
> check out the way we be livin
> *na tunakula vizuri*
> we always eating the best
> *poteza yako kwa nini*
> why should you settle for less
> *TV haiwezi kuambia*
> they never show on your screen
> *kwa hivyo mi ntawaambia*
> so you can see what I mean
> *Africa maridadi*
> Africa's beautiful baby
>   —BAMBOO, "Mama Africa"

Bamboo uses hip-hop rhythms and dialect to connect with the listeners he wants to reach. By using both Swahili and English, he reaches more people than if he'd used just one language—and exposes those who speak just one of these languages to the other.

Sandra Cisneros, a Mexican American writer who's fluent in both English and Spanish, makes similar choices in a collection of short stories inspired by her experience growing up in the United States surrounded by Mexican culture. See how she mixes languages to speak to an audience that's likely to include both English and Spanish speakers:

> "¡Ay!" The true test of a native Spanish speaker. ¡Ay! To make love in Spanish, in a manner as intricate and devout as la Alhambra. To have a lover sigh *mi vida, mi preciosa, mi chiquitita,* and whisper things in that

language crooned to babies, that language murmured by grandmothers, those words that smelled like your house, like flour tortillas.

—SANDRA CISNEROS, *Woman Hollering Creek and Other Stories*

As writers and speakers, we have to think carefully about when mixing languages or dialects will help us connect with our audiences—and when it won't. In most cases, authors have a kind of informal contract with readers: while readers may need to work some to understand what a writer is saying, the writer in turn promises to consider the audience's expectations and abilities. The end goal is usually accessibility: will your message be understood by those you are trying to reach? If some members of your audience aren't likely to understand, should you provide a translation? Are you choosing not to translate so that readers experience what it's like to *not* understand?

Providing Translation

One way to stay true to a language or dialect you identify with while still reaching readers who may not understand is to provide a translation. Bamboo's example, which invites English-speaking listeners to think about Africa's rich culture in part by including Swahili, demonstrates how translation helps when you're mixing languages. When including translations, you will usually want to introduce the term that is being translated in its original language, followed by the translation, as in the poster on the following page announcing a conference taking place in the Navajo Nation.

Note that the designer places the Navajo title first—and in slightly larger and bolder text—to underscore the importance of the Navajo language at this conference.

For another example, see how sociolinguist Guadalupe Valdés uses translation in an ethnographic study of a family of Mexican origin that included a young boy named Saúl:

During his kindergarten year, . . . winning was important to Saúl. Of all the cousins who played together, it was he who ran the fastest and pushed the hardest. "*Yo gané, yo gané*" (I won, I won), he would say enthusiastically. . . . Saúl's mother, Velma, wished that he would win just a bit more quietly. . . . "*No seas peleonero*" (Don't be so quarrelsome),

Check out Michelle Obama's commencement address to City College of New York on p. 989. Her speech is mainly delivered in a formal tone appropriate to the occasion, but when she talks about her own story, her language becomes more conversational, more personal.

WINDOW ROCK, ARIZONA

HAZHÓ'Ó HÓLNE'
WRITING CONFERENCE

Come join writers, poets, and our youth leaders for a fun-filled
weekend learning the art of story telling in its many forms.

17-18. MAR. 2018 **9AM-5PM**

17TH at Navajo Nation Museum | 18TH at Dept. of Diné Education

Free and open to the public. Online Registration
For more information, contact Zunneh-bah Martin zunnehbah@gmail.com
Snacks will be provided, but lunch will be on your own

Sponsored by: Middlebury Bread Loaf School of English, Middlebury Bread Loaf Teacher
Network, Next Gen Leadership Network, La Casa Roja, Navajo Nation Museum,
Department of Diné Education, Community Outreach and Patient
Empowerment, Write to Change, Navajo Community Health Outreach

Conference poster announcing—in both Navajo and English—
a gathering of writers in Window Rock, the capital of Navajo
Nation.

she would say. "*Es importante llevarse bien con todos*" (It's important to
get along with everyone).
　　　　　　　—GUADALUPE VALDÉS, *Con Respeto: Bridging the Distances Between
Culturally Diverse Families and Schools*

Note especially that Valdés always puts the Spanish words first, as they were
spoken, and only then gives the English translation. She could have chosen
to put the English translation first, or to write only in English, but giving the
Spanish first puts the spotlight on her subjects' voices and their own words.
By including the English translation at all, Valdés acknowledges readers

who don't speak Spanish and makes sure they can understand what she's written. Like Bamboo and the Navajo writing conference poster, she translates to make sure her message is accessible to as many people as possible. Notice, too, that Valdés italicizes words in a language other than English, which is a common academic convention when mixing languages.

Illustrating a Point

Professional groups have their own specialized ways of speaking: people in economics and finance will have different vocabulary and style at work from people in medicine, engineering, or food service. Much has been written about what is often called "valley speak," a common way of speaking in Silicon Valley where tech giants like Google, Apple, and Twitter reside. In a book that aims to be a definitive guide to the language of Silicon Valley, authors Rochelle Kopp and Steven Ganz incorporate examples to illustrate their point:

> When we moved to Silicon Valley, we found it challenging to pick up the lingo. . . . Around here, people toss off sentences like "Everyone thought that [the] *semantic search startup* launched by those Stanford *whiz kids* was going to be the next *unicorn*, but now they are doing a *down round* and it's looking like they are candidates for an *acqui-hire*." It can be awkward if you're the only one who doesn't understand what people here are saying.
> —ROCHELLE KOPP AND STEVEN GANZ, *Valley Speak:*
> *Deciphering the Jargon of Silicon Valley*

By mixing in phrases like *semantic search startups* and *down round,* Kopp and Ganz illustrate valley speak while suggesting that the vocabulary of Silicon Valley startups may alienate any people who don't want to take the time to penetrate the jargon.

Professor Jamila Lyiscott mixes dialects to illustrate her point in a spoken-word essay called "Broken English" in which she "celebrates—and challenges—the three distinct flavors of English she speaks." Prompted by a "baffled lady" who seemed surprised to find that Lyiscott is "articulate," Lyiscott says:

> Pay attention
> 'Cause I'm "articulate"
> So when my father asks, "Wha' kinda ting is dis?"

My "articulate" answer never goes amiss
I say "Father, this is the impending problem at hand"
And when I'm on the block I switch it up just because I can
So when my boy says, "What's good with you son?"
I just say, "I jus' fall out wit dem people but I done!"
And sometimes in class
I might pause the intellectual sounding flow to ask
"Yo! Why dese books neva be about my peoples"
Yes, I have decided to treat all three of my languages as equals
Because I'm "articulate"

—JAMILA LYISCOTT, "Broken English"

In her performance, which has more than four million views online, Lyiscott uses what she calls "three tongues"—one each for "home, school, and friends"—to make the point that there are many different ways to be "articulate." And she's articulate, all right, in three different dialects.

THINK
BEYOND
WORDS

➤ *WATCH THE VIDEO of Jamila Lyiscott's TED talk by visiting everyonesanauthor .tumblr.com. Why do you think Lyiscott chose a spoken-word essay as her medium? How does watching and listening to her performance (versus reading words on a page) change the way you understand her message? Why do you think Lyiscott chose to mix dialects? How would it change her message if she chose just one dialect instead of mixing several?*

Drawing Attention

Here is Buthainah, a Saudi Arabian student writing a literacy narrative for an education class at an American college:

ومن يتهيّب صعود صعود الجبال ~~~   يعش ابد الدّهر بين الحفر

"I don't want to" was my response to my parents' request of enrolling me in a nearby preschool. I did not like school. I feared it. I feared the aspect of departing my comfort zone, my home, to an unknown and unpredictable zone. . . . To encourage me, they recited a poetic line that I did not comprehend as a child but live by it as an adult. They said, "Who fears climbing the mountains~~~ . . . Lives forever between the holes." As I grew up, knowledge became my key to freedom; freedom of thought, freedom of doing, and freedom of beliefs.

—BUTHAINAH, "Who Fears Climbing the Mountains
Lives Forever between the Holes"

In this instance, opening with the Arabic proverb (which also serves as the title of Buthainah's essay) draws readers' attention and announces the importance of Arabic in the author's journey to become the writer she is while also letting non-Arabic speakers feel a bit of what it's like to encounter a foreign language without an immediate translation. At the same time, she makes a point of translating the proverb for her readers as the essay progresses—"They said 'Who fears climbing the mountains ~~~ Lives forever between the holes.'" Buthainah's essay illustrates how switching to a different language or way of speaking can grab attention and show—instead of tell—your audience something that's important to you.

Quoting People Directly and Respectfully

If you are writing about a person or group of people you have interviewed or who have been interviewed by others, you will want to let those people speak for themselves. From 1927 to 1931, Zora Neale Hurston, the famed African American folklorist, cultural anthropologist, and novelist, interviewed Cudjo Lewis, one of the last known slaves to have made the journey across the Atlantic. Lewis's story, told from Hurston's perspective, appears in *Barracoon: The*

Story of the Last "Black Cargo," a book published after Hurston's death. Hurston takes care to let the subject of her interview speak his mind, and in his own words. She begins by documenting her initial interaction with Lewis, telling us, "I hailed him by his African name" (Oluale Kossula) which she had learned from others while conducting prior research. In the next paragraph, Lewis speaks:

> Oh Lor', I kno it *you* call my name. Nobody don't callee me my name from cross de water but you. You always callee me Kossula, jus' lak I in de Affica soil! —ZORA NEALE HURSTON, *Barracoon: The Story of the Last "Black Cargo"*

Hurston alternates between edited academic English and a representation of the actual speech of the person whose words she quotes. These quotations report what she heard, which helps build her **ETHOS** as a careful listener and researcher. Finally, the use of quotations appeals to her audience's emotions; we can *hear* Lewis's surprise and delight. Readers familiar with the varieties of English Lewis uses might sense kinship with him, while those who are not will be reminded that Hurston is writing about a context different from their experience—but in a way that is always respectful.

When you're quoting others, let them speak for themselves not only in their own words but also in their own language. Whenever possible, ask your subjects to review the quotations you use to ensure they find the representation accurate and respectful.

Evoking a Particular Person, Place, or Community

Using the language of a specific community or group is a good way to evoke the character and sounds of the place. In the following passage, journalist David Thompson is interviewing Lee A. Tonouchi, author of *Living Pidgin: Contemplations on Pidgin Culture*. Responding to a question about his work, Tonouchi uses Hawai'ian Pidgin to evoke family relationships in his particular Hawaiian community:

> [This book is] about finding humor in tragedy. It's about da relationship between one son and his uncommunicative faddah in da wake of da maddah's early passing. An den, it's also about da son's relationship with his grandmas as he discovers what it means for be Okinawan in Hawaii.
> —DAVID THOMPSON, "Lee Tonouchi: Pidgin Poet," *Honolulu Magazine*

Notice that Tonouchi mixes more academic English and Hawai'ian Pidgin within sentences and not just between them, bringing the two into even closer contact and familiarity. When using the language of a community or group you don't belong to yourself, take care to do so with respect. When possible, ask someone who does speak the language to provide feedback on what you've drafted to ensure it's accurate and respectful.

As we've tried to demonstrate, using your own idiolect and shifting between styles are powerful tools for communicating what you have to say. Consider the following questions as you think about mixing languages, dialects, and registers in your own writing:

- *Who's your target* **AUDIENCE**? Are there places where you can shift styles to connect with them? to get and keep their attention? to illustrate a point? What expectations does your audience have about language? Are you meeting or challenging those expectations?

- *What's the larger* **CONTEXT**? Are readers likely to find your language choices appropriate? Is anything at risk, like your credibility or clarity? What's your **PURPOSE** for taking such risks?

- *Are readers likely to understand your words?* Do you need to provide translations? If you're using a specific style, like **MLA** or **APA**, are there conventions—like italicizing non-English words in an English-language text—you need to follow?

- *Have you treated languages, dialects, and registers that are not your own with respect?* When quoting, have you let subjects speak for themselves? Have you solicited feedback from someone who speaks the language, dialect, or register to be sure your text is accurate and respectful?

〰️◎ *REFLECT. Think about one or two ways of speaking you encounter that are different from your own—in places you work, movies you watch, or groups you are familiar with but don't belong to. Then find out as much as you can about that way of speaking and gather examples of it in use. What can you determine about how widely the dialect is used, who uses it, when it's used, what characteristics define it, and how it's perceived by different audiences? Write a brief reflection summarizing what you've found.*

THIRTY-TWO

How to Craft Good Sentences

HEN A STUDENT asked author Annie Dillard, "Do you think I could become a writer?" Dillard replied with a question of her own: "Do you like sentences?" French novelist Gustave Flaubert certainly did, once saying that he "itched with sentences." Itching with sentences probably isn't something you've experienced—and liking or not liking sentences might not be something you've ever thought about—but we're willing to bet that you know something about how important sentences are. Anyone who has ever tried to write the perfect tweet or, better yet, the perfect love letter knows about choosing just the right words for each sentence and about the power of the three-word sentence "I love you"—or the even shorter sentence that sometimes follows from such declarations: "I do."

In his book *How to Write a Sentence*, English professor Stanley Fish declares himself to be a "connoisseur of sentences" and offers some particularly noteworthy examples. Here's one, written by a fourth grader in response to an assignment to write something about a mysterious large box that had been delivered to a school:

▶ I was already on the second floor when I heard about the box.

This sentence reminded us of a favorite sentence of our own, this one the beginning of a story written by a third grader:

▶ Today, the monster goes where no monster has gone before: Cincinnati.

Here the student manages to allude to the famous line from *Star Trek*—"to boldly go where no man has gone before"—while suggesting that Cincinnati is the most exotic place on earth and even using a colon effectively. It's quite a sentence.

Finally, here's a sentence that opens a chapter from a PhD dissertation on literacy among young people today:

▶ Hazel Hernandez struck me as an honest thief.

Such sentences are memorable: They startle us a bit and demand attention. They make us want to read more. Who's Hazel Hernandez? What's an honest thief, and what makes her one?

As these examples suggest, you don't have to be a famous author to write a great sentence. In fact, crafting effective and memorable sentences is a skill everyone can master with careful attention and practice. Sometimes a brilliant sentence comes to you like a bolt of lightning, and all you have to do is type it out. More often, though, the perfect sentence is a result of tweaking and tinkering during your revision stages. Either way, crafting good sentences is worth the effort it may take. You may not come up with a zinger like the famous sentence John Updike wrote about Ted Williams's fabled home run in his last at bat at Fenway Park—"It was in the books while it was still in the sky"—but you can come close.

Just as certain effects in film—music, close-ups—enhance the story, a well-crafted sentence can bring power to a piece of writing. So think about the kind of effect you want to create in what you're writing—and then look for the type of sentence that will fit the bill. Though much of the power of the examples above comes from being short and simple, remember that some rhetorical situations call for longer, complex sentences—and that the kind of sentence you write also depends on its context, such as whether it's opening an essay, summing up what's already been said, or something else. This chapter looks at some common English sentence patterns and provides some good examples for producing them in your own work.

FOUR COMMON SENTENCE PATTERNS

We make sentences with words—and we arrange those words into patterns. If a sentence is defined as a group of words that expresses a complete thought, then we can identify four basic sentence structures: a **SIMPLE SENTENCE** (expressing one idea); a **COMPOUND SENTENCE** (expressing more than one idea, with the ideas being of equal importance); a **COMPLEX SENTENCE** (expressing more than one idea, with one of the ideas more important than the others); and a **COMPOUND-COMPLEX SENTENCE** (with more than one idea of equal importance and at least one idea of less importance).

Simple Sentences: One Main Idea

Let's take a look at some simple sentences:

- ▶ Resist!

- ▶ Consumers revolted.

- ▶ Angry consumers revolted against new debit-card fees.

- ▶ A wave of protest from angry consumers forced banks to rescind the new fees.

- ▶ The growth of the internet and its capacity to mobilize people instantly all over the world have done everything from forcing companies to rescind debit-card fees in the United States to bringing down oppressive governments in the Middle East.

As these examples illustrate, simple sentences can be as short as a single word—or they can be much longer. Each is a simple sentence, however, because it contains a single main idea or thought; in grammatical terms, each contains one and only one **MAIN CLAUSE**. As the name suggests, a simple sentence is often the simplest, most direct way of saying what you want to say—but not always. And often you want a sentence to include more than one idea. In that case, you need to use a compound sentence, a complex sentence, or a compound-complex sentence.

Compound Sentences:
Joining Ideas That Are Equally Important

Sometimes you'll want to write a sentence that joins two or more ideas that are equally important, like this one attributed to former president Bill Clinton:

- ▶ You can put wings on a pig, but you don't make it an eagle.

In grammatical terms, this is a compound sentence with two main clauses, each of which expresses one of two independent and equally important ideas. In this case, Clinton joined the ideas with a comma and the coordinating conjunction *but*. But he had several other options for joining these ideas. For example, he could have joined them with only a semicolon:

▶ You can put wings on a pig; you don't make it an eagle.

Or he could have joined them with a semicolon, a conjunctive adverb like *however,* and a comma:

▶ You can put wings on a pig; however, you don't make it an eagle.

All of these compound sentences are perfectly acceptable—but which seems most effective? In this case, we think Clinton's choice is: it is clear and very direct, and if you read it aloud you'll hear that the words on each side of *but* have the same number of syllables, creating a pleasing, balanced rhythm—and one that balances the two equally important ideas. It also makes the logical relationship between the two ideas explicit: *but* indicates a contrast. The version with only a semicolon, by contrast, indicates that the ideas are somehow related but doesn't show how.

Using *and*, *but*, and other coordinating conjunctions. In writing a compound sentence, remember that different **COORDINATING CONJUNCTIONS** carry meanings that signal different logical relationships between the main ideas in the sentence. There are only seven coordinating conjunctions.

COORDINATING CONJUNCTIONS

and	for	or	yet
but	nor	so	

▶ China's one-child policy has slowed population growth, *but* it has helped create a serious gender imbalance in the country's population.

▶ Most of us bike to the office, *so* many of us stop at the gym to shower before work.

▶ The first two batters struck out, *yet* the Cubs went on to win the game on back-to-back homers.

See how the following sentences express different meanings depending on which coordinating conjunction is used:

▶ You could apply to graduate school, *or* you could start looking for a job.

▶ You could apply to graduate school, *and* you could start looking for a job.

Using a semicolon. Joining clauses with a semicolon only is a way of signaling that they are closely related without saying explicitly how. Often the second clause will expand on an idea expressed in the first clause.

▶ My first year of college was a little bumpy; it took me a few months to get comfortable at a large university far from home.

▶ The Wassaic Project is an arts organization in Dutchess County, New York; artists go there to engage in "art, music, and everything else."

Adding a **TRANSITION WORD** can make the logical relationship between the ideas more explicit:

▶ My first year of college was a little bumpy; *indeed,* it took me a few months to get comfortable at a large university far from home.

Note that the transition in this sentence, *indeed,* cannot join the two main clauses on its own—it requires a semicolon before it. If you use a transition between two clauses with only a comma before it, you've made a mistake called a **COMMA SPLICE**.

SOME TRANSITION WORDS

also	indeed	otherwise
certainly	likewise	similarly
furthermore	nevertheless	therefore
however	next	thus

REFLECT. Read through something you've written recently and identify compound sentences joined with and. *When you find one, ask yourself whether* and *is the best word to use: does it express the logical relationship between the two parts of the sentence that you intend? Would* but, or, so, for, nor, *or* yet *work better?*

Complex Sentences:
When One Idea Is More Important than Another

Many of the sentences you write will contain two or more ideas, with one that you want to emphasize more than the other(s). You can do so by putting the idea you wish to emphasize in the **MAIN CLAUSE**, and then putting those that are less important in **SUBORDINATE CLAUSES**.

▶ Mendocino County is a place in California *where you can dive for abalone.*

▶ *Because the species has become scarce,* abalone diving is strictly regulated.

▶ Fish and Wildlife Department agents *who patrol the coast* use sophisticated methods to catch poachers.

As these examples show, the ideas in the subordinate clauses (italicized here) can't stand alone as sentences: when we read "where you can dive for abalone" or "who patrol the coast," we know that something's missing. Subordinate clauses begin with words such as *if* or *because,* **SUBORDINATING WORDS** that signal the logical relationship between the subordinate clause and the rest of the sentence.

SOME SUBORDINATING WORDS

after	even though	until
although	if	when
as	since	where
because	that	while
before	though	who

Notice that a subordinate clause can come at the beginning of a sentence, in the middle, or at the end. When it comes at the beginning, it is usually followed by a comma, as in the second example. If the opening clause in that sentence were moved to the end, a comma would not be necessary: "Abalone diving is strictly regulated because the species has become scarce."

Grammatically, each of the three examples above is a complex sentence, with one main idea and one other idea of less importance. In writing you will often have to decide whether to combine ideas in a compound sentence, which gives the ideas equal importance, or in a complex sentence, which makes one idea more important than the other(s). Looking once more at our sentence about the pig and the eagle, Bill Clinton could have made it a complex sentence:

▶ Even though you can put wings on a pig, you don't make it an eagle.

Again, though, we think Clinton made a good choice in giving the two ideas equal weight because doing so balances the sentence perfectly—and tells us that both parts are equally important. In fact, neither part of this sentence is very interesting in itself: it's the balancing and the contrast that make it interesting and memorable.

Compound-Complex Sentences: Multiple Ideas—Some More Important, Some Less

When you are expressing three or more ideas in a single sentence, you'll sometimes want to use a compound-complex sentence, which gives some of the ideas more prominence and others less. Grammatically, such sentences have at least two **MAIN CLAUSES** and one **SUBORDINATE CLAUSE**.

               —— MAIN CLAUSE ——   ┌— SUBORDINATE CLAUSE
▶ We have experienced unparalleled natural disasters that have devastated

                     ——— MAIN CLAUSE ———
entire countries, yet identifying global warming as the cause of these

disasters is difficult.

            —— SUBORDINATE CLAUSE ——   —— MAIN CLAUSE
▶ Even after distinguished scientists issued a series of reports, critics continued

                  —— SUBORDINATE CLAUSE ——
to question the findings because they claimed results were falsified;

    —— MAIN CLAUSE ——
nothing would convince them.

As these examples show, English sentence structure is flexible, allowing you to combine groups of words in different ways in order to get your ideas across to your audience most appropriately and effectively. There's seldom only one way to write a sentence to get an idea across: as the author, you must decide which way works best for your **RHETORICAL SITUATION**.

WAYS OF EMPHASIZING
THE MAIN IDEA IN A SENTENCE

Sometimes, you will want to lead off a sentence with the main point; other times, you might want to hold it in reserve until the end. **CUMULATIVE SENTENCES** start with a main clause and then add on to it, "accumulating" details. **PERIODIC SENTENCES** start with a series of phrases or subordinate clauses, saving the main clause for last.

Cumulative Sentences: Starting with the Main Point

In this kind of sentence, the writer starts off with a **MAIN CLAUSE** and then adds details in phrases and **SUBORDINATE CLAUSES**, extending or explaining the thought. Cumulative sentences can be especially useful for describing a place or an event, operating almost like a camera panning across a room or landscape. The sentences below create such an effect:

▶ The San Bernardino Valley lies only an hour east of Los Angeles by the San Bernardino Freeway but is in certain ways an alien place: not the coastal California of the subtropical twilights and the soft westerlies off the Pacific but a harsher California, haunted by the Mojave just beyond the mountains, devastated by the hot dry Santa Ana wind that comes down through the passes at 100 miles an hour and whines through the eucalyptus windbreaks and works on the nerves.
　　　　　　　　—JOAN DIDION, "Some Dreamers of the Golden Dream"

▶ Public transportation in Cebu City was provided by jeepneys: refurbished military jeeps with metal roofs for shade, decorated with horns and mirrors and fenders and flaps; painted with names, dedications, quotations, religious icons, logos—and much, much more.

▶ She hit the brakes, swearing fiercely, as the deer leapt over the hood and crashed into the dark woods beyond.

▶ The celebrated Russian pianist gave his hands a shake, a quick shake, fingers pointed down at his sides, before taking his seat and lifting them imperiously above the keys.

These cumulative sentences add details in a way that makes each sentence more emphatic. Keep this principle in mind as you write—and also when you revise. See if there are times when you might revise a sentence or sentences to add emphasis in the same way. Take a look at the following sentences, for instance:

▶ China has initiated free-market reforms that transformed its economy from a struggling one to an industrial powerhouse. It has become the world's fastest-growing major economy. Growth rates have been averaging 10 percent over the last decade.

These three sentences are clearly related, with each one adding detail about the growth of China's economy. Now look what happens when the writer eliminates a little bit of repetition, adds a memorable metaphor, and combines them as a cumulative—and more emphatic—sentence:

▶ China's free-market reforms have led to 10 percent average growth over the last decade, transforming it from a paper tiger into an industrial dragon that is now the world's fastest-growing major economy.

Periodic Sentences: Delaying the Main Point until the End

In contrast to sentences that open with the main idea, periodic sentences delay the main idea until the very end. Periodic sentences are sometimes fairly long, and withholding the main point until the end is a way of adding emphasis. It can also create suspense or build up to a surprise or inspirational ending.

▶ In spite of everything, in spite of the dark and twisting path he saw stretching ahead for himself, in spite of the final meeting with Voldemort he knew must come, whether in a month, in a year, or in ten, he felt his heart lift at the thought that there was still one last golden day of peace left to enjoy with Ron and Hermione.   —J. K. ROWLING, *Harry Potter and the Half-Blood Prince*

▶ Unprovided with original learning, uninformed in the habits of thinking, unskilled in the arts of composition, I resolved to write a book.
                                          —EDWARD GIBBON, *Memoirs of My Life*

▶ In the week before finals, when my studying and memorizing reached a fever pitch, came a sudden, comforting thought: I have never failed.

Here are three periodic sentences in a row about Whitney Houston, each of which withholds the main point until the end:

▶ When her smiling brown face, complete with a close-cropped Afro, appeared on the cover of *Seventeen* in 1981, she was one of the first African-Americans to grace the cover, and the industry took notice. When she belted out a chilling and soulful version of the "Star-Spangled Banner" at the 1991 Super Bowl, the world sat back in awe of her poise and calm. And in an era when African-American actresses are often given film roles portraying them as destitute, unloving, unlovable, or just "the help," Houston played the love interest of Kevin Costner, a white Hollywood superstar.
—ALLISON SAMUELS, "A Hard Climb for the Girl Next Door"

These three periodic sentences create a drumlike effect that builds in intensity as they move through the stages in Houston's career; in all, they suggest that Houston was, even more than Kevin Costner, a "superstar."

Samuels takes a chance when she uses three sentences in a row that withhold the main point until the end: readers may get tired of waiting for that point. And readers may also find the use of too many such sentences to be, well, too much. But as the example above shows, when used carefully a sentence that puts off the main idea just long enough can keep readers' interest, making them want to reach the ending, with its payoff.

You may find in your own work that periodic sentences can make your writing more emphatic. Take a look at the following sentence from an essay on the use of animals in circuses:

▶ The big cat took him down with one swat, just as the trainer, dressed in khakis and boots, his whip raised and his other arm extended in welcome to the cheering crowd, stepped into the ring.

This sentence paints a vivid picture, but it gives away all the action in the first six words. By withholding that action until the end, the writer builds anticipation and adds emphasis:

▶ Just as the trainer stepped into the ring, dressed in khakis and boots, his whip raised and his other arm extended in welcome to the cheering crowd, the big cat took him down with one swat.

Lynda Barry begins her narrative on p. 853 with a compelling opening sentence. Check it out (and be prepared to keep reading; you won't want to stop).

OPENING SENTENCES

The opening sentences in your writing carry big responsibilities, setting the tone and often the scene—and drawing your readers in by arousing their interest and curiosity. Authors often spend quite a lot of time on opening sentences for this very reason: whether it's a business report or a college essay or a blog posting, the way the piece begins has a lot to do with whether your audience will stay with you and whether you'll get the kind of response you want from them. Here are three famous opening sentences:

▶ I am an invisible man.   —RALPH ELLISON, *Invisible Man*

▶ The sky above the port was the color of television, tuned to a dead channel.
       —WILLIAM GIBSON, *Neuromancer*

▶ They shoot the white girl first.   —TONI MORRISON, *Paradise*

Each of these sentences is startling, making us read on in order to find out more. Each is brief, leaving us waiting anxiously for what's to come. In addition, each makes a powerful statement and creates some kind of image in readers' minds: an "invisible" person, a sky the color of a "dead" TV channel, someone being shot. These sentences all come from novels, but they use strategies that work in many kinds of writing.

It usually takes more than a single sentence to open an essay. Consider, for example, how Michael Pollan begins a lengthy essay on animal liberation:

▶ The first time I opened Peter Singer's *Animal Liberation*, I was dining alone at the Palm, trying to enjoy a rib-eye steak cooked medium-rare. If this sounds like a good recipe for cognitive dissonance (if not indigestion), that was sort of the idea. Preposterous as it might seem to supporters of animal rights, what I was doing was tantamount to reading *Uncle Tom's Cabin* on a plantation in the Deep South in 1852.
       —MICHAEL POLLAN, "An Animal's Place"

The first sentence presents an incongruous image that holds our attention (he's eating a steak while reading about animal liberation). Then the rest of the paragraph makes this incongruity even more pronounced, even comparing the situation to someone reading the antislavery novel *Uncle Tom's Cabin* while on a slave-owning plantation. It's an opening that makes us read on.

Here is the opening of a blog posting that begins with a provocative question:

> ▶ Have you ever thought about whether to have a child? If so, what factors entered into your decision? Was it whether having children would be good for you, your partner and others close to the possible child, such as children you may already have, or perhaps your parents? For most people contemplating reproduction, those are the dominant questions. Some may also think about the desirability of adding to the strain that the nearly seven billion people already here are putting on our planet's environment. But very few ask whether coming into existence is a good thing for the child itself.
> —PETER SINGER, "Should This Be the Last Generation?"

Singer's question is designed to get the reader's attention, and he follows it up with two additional questions that ask readers to probe more deeply into their reasons for considering whether or not to reproduce. In the fifth sentence, he suggests that the answers people give to these questions may not be adequate ones, and in the last sentence he lays down a challenge: perhaps coming into existence is not always good for "the child itself."

Here's another example of an opening that uses several sentences, this one from a student essay about graphic memoirs:

> ▶ In 1974, before the Fall of Saigon, my 14-year-old father, alone, boarded a boat out of Vietnam in search of America. This is a fact. But this one fact can spawn multiple understandings: I could ask a group of students to take a week and write me a story from just this one fact, and I have no doubt that they would bring back a full range of interpretations.
> —BRANDON LY, "Leaving Home, Coming Home"

This opening passage begins with a vivid image of a very young man fleeing Vietnam alone, followed by a very short sentence that makes a statement and then a longer one that challenges that statement. This student writer is moving readers toward what will become his thesis: that memoirs can never tell "the whole truth, and nothing but the truth."

Finally, take a look at the opening of the speech Toni Morrison gave when she won the Nobel Prize for Literature:

> ▶ Members of the Swedish Academy, Ladies and Gentlemen:
> Narrative has never been mere entertainment for me. It is, I believe, one of the principal ways in which we absorb knowledge. I hope you will

understand, then, why I begin these remarks with the opening phrase of what must be the oldest sentence in the world, and the earliest one we remember from childhood: "Once upon a time . . ."

—TONI MORRISON, Nobel Prize acceptance speech

Morrison begins with a deceptively simple statement that narrative is for her not just entertainment. In the next sentences, she complicates that statement and broadens her claim that narrative is the way we understand the world, concluding with what she calls "the oldest sentence in the world."

You can use strategies similar to the ones shown here in opening your college essays. Here are just some of the ways you might begin:

- With a strong, dramatic—or deceptively simple—statement
- With a vivid image
- With a provocative question
- With an anecdote
- With a startling claim

Opening sentences online. If the internet lets us send messages to people all over the world, it also challenges us to get and keep their attention. And with limited space and time (small screens, readers in a hurry, scanning for what they need), writers need to make sure the opening sentences of any online text are as attention getting and informative as possible.

In email, for instance, first sentences often show up in auto-preview lines, so it's a good idea to write them carefully. Here's the first line of an email sent recently to everyone at W. W. Norton:

▶ A Ping-Pong table has been set up on the 4th floor in loving memory of Diane O'Connor.

This email was sent by O'Connor's colleagues, honoring her efforts to persuade Norton to have an annual company Ping-Pong tournament. It might have said less ("Ping-Pong on 4," "remembering Diane"), as email usually does—but there was more that they wanted to say.

And then there's *Twitter*. As if it weren't enough of a challenge to say what you want to say in 280 characters, you'd better begin with a sentence that will catch readers' attention. Here are two tweets that got ours:

▶ Steve Jobs was born out of wedlock, put up for adoption at birth, dropped out of college, then changed the world. What's your excuse?   —@JWMOSS

▶ It's so weird because Rush Limbaugh has been such an awesome human being until now.   —@BUCK4ITT

You'll want to think carefully about how you open any text that you post online—and to craft opening sentences that will make sense in a *Google* search list. Here are two that we like:

▶ Smith Women Redefine "Pearls and Cashmere."

This is the headline for an article in *Inside Higher Ed,* an online magazine read by educators, but it's also the line that comes up in a *Google* search. The article is about a controversy at Smith College—and we think you'll agree that the headline surely got the attention of those scanning the magazine's list of articles or searching *Google*.

▶ *The Art of Fielding* is a 2011 novel by former *n+1* editor Chad Harbach. It centers on the fortunes of shortstop Henry Skrimshander and his career playing college baseball with the Westish College Harpooners, a Division III (NCAA) team.

This is the start of the *Wikipedia* entry for a novel, which comes up in a *Google* search. As you can see, it identifies the book, says who wrote it, and gives a one-sentence description of the story. Safe to say, the authors of this entry were careful to provide this information in the very first sentences.

CLOSING SENTENCES

Sentences that conclude a piece of writing are where you have a chance to make a lasting impact: to reiterate your point, tell readers why it matters, echo something you say in your opening, make a provocative statement, issue a call for action.

Here's Joe Posnanski, wrapping up an essay on his blog arguing that college athletes should not be paid:

▶ College football is not popular because of the stars. College football is popular because of that first word. Take away the college part, add in money,

and you are left with professional minor league football. . . . See how many
people watch that.   —JOE POSNANSKI, "The College Connection"

These four sentences summarize his argument—and the last one's the zinger, one that leaves readers thinking.

Now take a look at the conclusion to a scholarly book on current neurological studies of human attention, the brain science of attention:

▶ Right now, our classrooms and workplaces are structured for success in the
last century, not this one. We can change that. By maximizing opportunities
for collaboration, by rethinking everything from our approach to work
to how we measure progress, we can begin to see the things we've been
missing and catch hold of what's passing us by.

  If you change the context, if you change the questions you ask, if you
change the structure, the test, and the task, then you stop gazing one way
and begin to look in a different way and in a different direction. You know
what happens next:

  Now you see it.   —CATHY DAVIDSON, *Now You See It: How the Brain Science
                        of Attention Will Transform the Way We Live, Work, and Learn*

Cathy Davidson uses two short paragraphs to sum up her argument and
then concludes with a final paragraph that consists of just one very short
four-word sentence. With this last sentence, she uses a tried-and-true strategy of coming full circle to echo the main idea of her book and, in fact, to
reiterate its title. Readers who have worked their way through the book will
take pleasure in that last sentence: *Now* they do see her point.

For another example, note how in the ending to a speech about language and about being able to use "all the Englishes" she grew up with, author Amy Tan closes with a one-sentence paragraph that quotes her mother:

▶ Apart from what any critic had to say about my writing, I knew I had
succeeded where it counted when my mother finished reading my book and
gave me her verdict: "So easy to read."   —AMY TAN, "Mother Tongue"

Tan's ending sums up one of her main goals as an author: to write so that
readers who speak different kinds of English will find her work accessible,
especially her mother.

Finally, take a look at how Toni Morrison chose to close her Nobel Prize
acceptance speech:

▶ It is, therefore, mindful of the gifts of my predecessors, the blessing of my sisters, in joyful anticipation of writers to come that I accept the honor the Swedish Academy has done me, and ask you to share what is for me a moment of grace.   —TONI MORRISON, Nobel Prize acceptance speech

In this one-sentence conclusion, Morrison speaks to the past, present, and future when she says she is grateful for those writers who came before her, for those who are writing now (her sisters), and for those yet to come. She ends the sentence by asking her audience to share this "moment of grace" with her and, implicitly, with all other writers so honored.

You may not be accepting a Nobel Prize soon, but in your college writing you can use all the strategies presented here to compose strong closings:

- By reiterating your point
- By discussing the implications of your argument
- By asking a question
- By referring back to your beginning
- By recommending or proposing some kind of action

REFLECT. Identify two memorable openings and closings from a favorite novel, comic book, film, or social media post. What makes them so good? Do they follow one of the strategies presented here?

VARYING YOUR SENTENCES

Read a paragraph or two of your writing out loud and listen for its rhythm. Is it quick and abrupt? slow and leisurely? singsong? stately? rolling? Whatever it is, does the rhythm you hear match what you had in mind when you were writing? And does it put the emphasis where you want it? One way to establish the emphasis you intend and a rhythm that will keep readers reading is by varying the length of your sentences and the way those sentences flow from one to the other.

A string of sentences that are too much alike is almost certain to be boring. While you can create effective rhythms in many ways, one of the simplest and most effective is by breaking up a series of long sentences with a shorter one that gives your readers a chance to pause and absorb what you've written.

Take a look at the following passage, from an article in the *Atlantic* about the finale of the *Oprah Winfrey Show*. See how the author uses a mix of long and short sentences to describe one of the tributes to Oprah, this one highlighting her support of black men:

▶ Oprah's friend Tyler Perry announced that some of the "Morehouse Men," each a beneficiary of the $12 million endowment she has established at their university, had come to honor her for the scholarships she gave them. The lights were lowered, a Broadway star began singing an inspirational song, and a dozen or so black men began to walk slowly to the front of the stage. Then more came, and soon there were a score, then 100, then the huge stage was filled with men, 300 of them. They stood there, solemnly, in a tableau stage-managed in such a way that it might have robbed them of their dignity—the person serenading them (or, rather, serenading Oprah on their behalf) was Kristin Chenoweth, tiniest and whitest of all tiny white women; the song was from *Wicked,* most feminine of all musicals; and each man carried a white candle, an emblem that lent them the aspect of Norman Rockwell Christmas carolers. But they were not robbed of their dignity. They looked, all together, like a miracle. A video shown before the procession revealed that some of these men had been in gangs before going to Morehouse, some had fathers in prison, many had been living in poverty. Now they were doctors, lawyers, bankers, a Rhodes Scholar—and philanthropists, establishing their own Morehouse endowment.

—CAITLIN FLANAGAN, "The Glory of Oprah"

The passage begins with three medium-length sentences—and then one very long one (seventy-two words!) that points up the strong contrast between the 300 black men filling the stage and the "whitest of white" singer performing a song from the "most feminine" of musicals. Then come two little sentences (the first one eight words long and the second one, seven) that give readers a chance to pause and absorb what has been said while also making an important point: that the men "looked, all together, like a miracle." The remainder of the passage moves back toward longer sentences, each of which explains just what this "miracle" is. Try reading this passage aloud and listen for how the variation in sentences creates both emphasis and a pleasing and effective rhythm.

The Morehouse Men surprise Oprah.

In addition to varying the lengths of your sentences, you can also improve your writing by making sure that they don't all use the same structure or begin in the same way. You can be pretty sure, for example, that a passage in which every sentence is a simple sentence that opens with the subject of a main clause will not read smoothly at all but rather will move along awkwardly. Take a look at this passage, for example:

> ▶ The sunset was especially beautiful today. I was on top of Table Mountain in Cape Town. I looked down and saw the sun touch the sea and sink into it. The evening shadows crept up the mountain. I got my backpack and walked over to the rest of my group. We started on the long hike down the mountain and back to the city.

There's nothing wrong with these sentences as such. Each one is grammatically correct. But if you read the passage aloud, you'll hear how it moves abruptly from sentence to sentence, lurching along rather than flowing smoothly. The problem is that the sentences are all the same: each one is a simple sentence that begins with the subject of a main clause (*sunset, I, I, evening shadows, I, we*). In addition, the use of personal pronouns at the beginning of the sentences (three *I*'s in only six sentences!) makes for dull reading. Finally, these are all fairly short sentences, and the sameness of the sentence length adds to the abrupt rhythm of the passage—and doesn't keep readers reading. Now look at how this passage can be revised by working on sentence variation:

▶ From the top of Cape Town's Table Mountain, the sunset was especially beautiful. I looked down just as the fiery orb touched and then sank into the sea; shadows began to creep slowly up the mountain. Picking up my backpack, I joined the rest of my group, and we started the long hike down the mountain.

This revision reduces the number of sentences in the passage from six to three (the first simple, the second compound-complex, the third compound) and varies the length of the sentences. Equally important, the revision eliminates all but one of the subject openings. The first sentence now begins with the prepositional phrase ("From the top"); the second with the subject of a main clause ("I"); and the third with a participial phrase ("Picking up my backpack"). Finally the revision varies the diction a bit, replacing the repeated word "sun" with a vivid image ("fiery orb"). Read the revised passage aloud and you'll hear how varying the sentences creates a stronger rhythm that makes it easier to read.

This brief chapter has only scratched the surface of sentence style. But we hope we've said enough to show how good sentences can be your allies, helping you get your ideas out there and connect with audiences as successfully as possible. Remember: authors are only as good as the sentences they write!

REFLECT. Take a look at a writing assignment you've recently completed. Read it aloud, listening for rhythm and emphasis. If you find a passage that doesn't read well or provide the emphasis you want, analyze its sentences for length (count the words) and structure (how does each sentence begin?). Revise the passage using the strategies presented in this chapter.

THIRTY-THREE

Editing the Errors That Matter

**N PREPARATION FOR** a 2018 Coachella performance, Beyoncé led her team through eleven-hour rehearsal days. LeBron James spends five to seven hours every day training in the gym (in addition to team practices). It takes a lot of hard work to make something look easy. Beyoncé rehearses, LeBron trains; what do authors do? We revise.

Take this book, for example. It was written by experienced authors—skilled teachers and professional writers, all. The page that you're reading right now—how many drafts and revisions did it go through before it reached you? We lose count after three or four. The point is, completing a draft is a great accomplishment, and at the same time, it's only the beginning.

One of the most important parts of your revision process is examining each sentence for structural errors. Don't be afraid of "errors"; we all make them, even the pros. Some of our errors are no big deal, barely noticeable, not worth mentioning. Others, however, are more serious—deal breakers, maybe—and we try hard to avoid them.

One of the great things about writing is that we can edit our work and fix our errors. Our team asked seventy-five writing instructors which errors really matter to them—which ones are most bothersome and do the most damage to a writer's credibility and ideas. Their responses covered a wide gamut, from sentence structure to punctuation. This chapter focuses on those errors that matter, showing how to spot them in a draft, explaining why they're so troublesome, and suggesting strategies for editing them out.

Throughout this chapter, you'll find opportunities for editing practice in adaptive activities called InQuizitive. For more information on how to get started with InQuizitive, see the access card at the front of your book or visit *digital.wwnorton.com/everyone3r.*

EDITING SENTENCES

Fragments, comma splices, fused sentences, and mixed constructions are all types of sentence-structure errors. Such sentences are usually comprehensible in context, so if readers can understand the message, why are they errors? Solid sentence structure matters for two reasons:

- The perception of your competence hangs on it: readers don't trust writers who write sloppy sentences.

- Even if a poorly structured sentence can be understood, your readers have to work a little harder to get there, and they may not want to put forth the effort. Your job is to make it easy for readers, to keep them reading smoothly all the way to the end.

Every sentence is composed of one or more CLAUSES, and every clause needs to have a SUBJECT, a VERB, and appropriate punctuation. Don't underestimate those little dots and squiggles; they often make all the difference in how a sentence is read and understood. Consider these two examples:

▶ Let's eat Grandma.

▶ Let's eat, Grandma.

Are you inviting your grandmother to eat a meal right now, or are you inviting someone else to eat *her*? That one little comma in the right place can save grandma's life (or at least make it clear to your readers that you aren't proposing to make a meal of her). The following advice will help you examine your writing with an eye to four common sentence-structure errors: fragments, comma splices, fused sentences, and mixed constructions.

Fragments

At first glance, a fragment looks like a complete sentence—it begins with a capital letter and concludes with end punctuation—but on closer examination, a key element, usually a **SUBJECT** or a **VERB**, is missing. For example: *Forgot to vote.* Who forgot to vote? We don't know; the subject is missing. *Two bottles of rancid milk.* Wow. That sounds interesting, but what about them? There's no verb, so we don't know. A fragment also occurs when a sentence begins with a **SUBORDINATING WORD** such as *if* or *because*, but the **SUBORDINATE CLAUSE** is not followed by a **MAIN CLAUSE**. *If the ball game is rained out.* Well, what happens if the ball game is rained out? Again, we don't know.

Checking for fragments

Sometimes writers use fragments for stylistic reasons, but it's best to avoid them in academic writing. To check your text for fragments, examine each sentence one by one, making sure there's both a subject and a verb. (It might take you a while to do this at first, but it will go much faster with practice, and it's worth the time.) Check also for subordinating words (see p. 699 for a list of common ones), and if there's a subordinate clause, make sure there's also a main clause.

Editing fragments

Let's look at some fragments and see what we can do about them.

NEEDS A SUBJECT

▶ The Centipedes were terrible last night. *Started late, played three songs, and left.*

Context makes it clear that it was the Centipedes who started late. Still, the italicized part is a fragment because there is no explicit subject. We have two good options here. One is to add a subject to the fragment in order to make the sentence complete; the other is to attach the fragment to a nearby sentence. Both strategies will work, and you can choose whichever sounds better to you.

▶ The Centipedes were terrible last night. ~~Started~~ *They started* late, played three songs, and left.

▶ The Centipedes were terrible last night/ *because they started* ~~Started~~ late, played three songs, and left.

In the first example, we've added a subject, *They*, which refers to the Centipedes. In the second, we've attached the fragment to the preceding sentence using a subordinating word, *because*, followed by an explicit subject, *they*.

NEEDS A VERB

▶ Malik heard a knock on the door. *Then a loud thud*.

The example makes sense: we know that Malik heard a loud thud after the knock. But the italicized part is a fragment because between the capital *T* at the beginning and the period at the end, there is no verb. Again, there are two strategies for editing: to add a verb to the fragment in order to make the sentence complete, or to incorporate the fragment into the previous sentence so that its verb can do double duty.

▶ Malik heard a knock on the door. Then a ^came^ loud thud.

▶ Malik heard a knock on the door~~.~~ /, ~~Then~~ ^followed by^ a loud thud.

NEEDS MORE INFORMATION

▶ Olga nearly missed her plane. *Because the line at security was so long*. She got flustered and dropped her change purse.

The italicized part of the example above does have a subject and a verb, but it can't stand alone as a sentence because it starts with *because*, a subordinating word that leads readers to expect more information. Did the long security line cause Olga to nearly miss her plane? Or did the long line fluster her? We can't be sure. How you edit this fragment depends on what you're trying to say—and how the ideas relate to one another. For example:

▶ Olga nearly missed her plane~~.~~ /~~Because~~ ^because^ the line at security was so long.

▶ Because the line at security was so long~~.~~ /, ~~She~~ ^she^ got flustered and dropped her change purse.

The first option explains why Olga nearly missed her plane, and the second explains why she got flustered and dropped her change purse.

Edit
The word *if* leads readers to expect a clause explaining what will happen. Consider the following example:

▶ If you activate the alarm.

This example is a fragment. We need the sentence to show the "what-if": what happens if you activate the alarm? Otherwise, we have an incomplete thought—and readers will be confused.

▶ The whole lab will be destroyed. If you activate the alarm.
  Spider-Man, you can avert the tragedy.

Will the lab be destroyed if Spider-Man activates the alarm? Or will activating the alarm avert the tragedy? There is no way for readers to know. This example needs to be edited! You try. Edit the example above for both possible interpretations.

➡ For more practice, complete the InQuizitive activity on **sentence fragments**.

Comma Splices

A comma splice looks like a complete sentence in that it starts with a capital letter, concludes with end punctuation, and contains two **MAIN CLAUSES**. The problem is that there is only a comma between the two clauses. Here's an example:

▶ It was the coldest day in fifty years, the marching band performed brilliantly.

Both clauses are perfectly clear, and we expect that they are connected in some way—but we don't know how. Did the band play well because of the cold or in spite of it? Or is there no connection at all? In short, comma splices can leave your readers confused.

Checking for comma splices
Writers sometimes use comma splices to create a certain stylistic effect, but it's best to avoid them in academic writing. To check your work for comma splices, look at each sentence one by one and identify the **VERBS**. Next, look for their **SUBJECTS**. If you find two or more sets of subjects and verbs that form **MAIN CLAUSES**, make sure they are connected appropriately.

Editing comma splices

What are the appropriate ways to connect two independent clauses? Let's look at some of the possibilities.

CHANGE THE COMMA TO A PERIOD

One of your options is to create two separate sentences by inserting a period (**.**) after the first clause and capitalizing the first letter of the following word.

▶ It was the coldest day in fifty years~~.~~ ~~the~~ *The* marching band performed brilliantly.

This might be your preferred choice if you want to write tersely, with short sentences, perhaps to open an essay in a dramatic way. Maybe there is a connection between the two sentences; maybe there's not. Readers will want to keep going in order to find out.

CHANGE THE COMMA TO A SEMICOLON

Another simple way to edit a comma splice is to insert a semicolon (**;**) between the two clauses.

▶ It was the coldest day in fifty years~~,~~*;* the marching band performed brilliantly.

The semicolon lets readers know that there is a definite connection between the weather and the band's brilliant performance, but they can't be certain what it is. The sentence is now correct, if not terribly interesting. You can make the connection clearer and even make the sentence more interesting by adding a **TRANSITION** (*nevertheless, still, in any event*; check the Glossary / Index for more examples).

▶ It was the coldest day in fifty years~~,~~*; nevertheless,* the marching band performed brilliantly.

ADD A COORDINATING CONJUNCTION

You can also insert a **COORDINATING CONJUNCTION** (*and, but, or, nor, so, for,* or *yet*) after the comma between the two clauses.

▶ It was the coldest day in fifty years, *but* the marching band performed brilliantly.

With this option, the two clauses are separated clearly, and the word *but* indicates that the band played brilliantly in spite of the cold weather.

ADD A SUBORDINATING WORD

Another way to show a relationship between the two clauses is with a **SUBORDINATING WORD** (*while, however, thus*; see p. 699 for more examples).

▶ ~~It~~ *Although it* was the coldest day in fifty years, the marching band performed brilliantly.

Here, the logical relationship between the two clauses is clear and explicit, and the band's performance becomes the important part of the sentence. But what if you wanted to suggest that the cold weather was responsible for the band playing so well? You could use the same clauses, but with a different subordinating word, as in the example below.

▶ ~~It~~ *Possibly because it* was the coldest day in fifty years, the marching band performed brilliantly.

You may also want to experiment with changing the order of the clauses; in many cases, that will cause the emphasis to change. Sometimes, too, changing the order will help you transition to the next sentence.

▶ ~~It~~ *The marching band performed brilliantly, even though it* was the coldest day in fifty years, ~~the marching band performed brilliantly~~. Fans huddled together under blankets in the stands.

Edit

Consider the following example:

> Transit officials estimate that the new light-rail line will be 20 percent faster than the express bus, the train will cost $1.85 per ride regardless of distance traveled.

Try editing this comma splice in two ways: one that emphasizes the speed of the train and another that emphasizes the cost.

↪ For more practice, complete the InQuizitive activity on **comma splices**.

Fused Sentences

A fused sentence looks like a complete sentence at first glance because it begins with a capital letter, concludes with end punctuation, and contains two **MAIN CLAUSES**. The reason it is problematic is that there is no explicit connection between the two clauses. A fused sentence will make sense to readers most of the time, but most of the time isn't quite often enough, and you don't want your readers to struggle to understand what you're saying. A sentence can contain more than one main clause, no problem, but if it does, there needs to be some signal indicating how the clauses relate to one another. That signal could be a punctuation mark, a word that shows how the clauses are related, or both.

Checking for fused sentences

To check your text for fused sentences, look at each sentence one by one and identify any that have more than one **MAIN CLAUSE**. Then see how the clauses are connected: is there a word or punctuation mark that indicates how they relate? If not, you've got a fused sentence.

Editing fused sentences

Let's look at a typical fused sentence and some ways it can be edited.

▶ The fire alarm went off the senator spilled her latte all over her desk.

Perfectly clear, right? Or did you have to read it twice to make sure? This example is a fused sentence because it contains two main clauses but offers no way of knowing where one stops and the next begins, and no indication of how the clauses relate to one another. Here are some options for editing this fused sentence.

ADD A PERIOD

One option is to make the fused sentence into two separate sentences by inserting a period after the first independent clause and capitalizing the first letter of the following clause.

▶ The fire alarm went off. ~~the~~ The senator spilled her latte all over her desk.

Now you have two complete sentences, but they are a little dry and lifeless. Readers may think the two events have nothing to do with one another, or they may think some explanation is missing. In some cases, you may want to choose this solution—if you are merely reporting what happened, for example—but it might not be the best one for this example.

ADD A SEMICOLON

Another option is to insert a semicolon (;) between the two clauses.

▶ The fire alarm went off; the senator spilled her latte all over her desk.

This is another simple way to deal with a fused sentence, although it still doesn't help readers know *how* the two clauses relate. The relationship between the clauses is fairly clear here, but that won't always be the case, so make sure the logical connection between the two clauses is very obvious before you use a semicolon. You can also add a **TRANSITION** (*nevertheless, still, in any event*; see the Glossary/Index for more examples) after the semicolon to make the relationship between the two clauses more explicit.

▶ The fire alarm went off; *as a result,* the senator spilled her latte all over her desk.

ADD A COMMA AND A COORDINATING CONJUNCTION
In order to clarify the relationship between the clauses a little more, you could insert a comma and a **COORDINATING CONJUNCTION** (*and, but, or, nor, so, for,* or *yet*) between the two clauses.

▶ The fire alarm went off, *and* the senator spilled her latte all over her desk.

Here the division between the two clauses is clearly marked, and readers will generally understand that the latte spilled right after (and the spill was possibly caused by) the fire alarm. With this solution, both clauses have equal importance.

ADD A SUBORDINATING WORD
One of the clearest ways to show the relationship between two clauses is by using a **SUBORDINATING WORD** (see p. 699 for more examples).

▶ ~~The~~ *When the* fire alarm went off, the senator spilled her latte all over her desk.

Adding the subordinating word *when* to the first clause makes it clear that the fire alarm caused the senator to spill her latte and also puts emphasis on the spilled coffee. Note that you need to add a comma after the introductory clause. You can also change the order of the two clauses; see how the emphasis changes slightly. Note, too, that in this case, you should not add a comma.

▶ The senator spilled her latte all over her desk *when* the fire alarm went off.

Edit
Using the editing options explained above, edit the following fused sentence in two different ways. Make one of your solutions short and snappy.

In the other solution, show that the banging and the shouting were happening at the same time.

> The moderator banged his gavel the candidates continued to shout at each other.

➤ For more practice, complete the InQuizitive activity on **fused sentences**.

Mixed Constructions

A **MIXED CONSTRUCTION** is a sentence that starts out with one structure and ends up with another one. Such a sentence may be understandable, but more often it leaves readers scratching their heads in confusion. There are many different ways to end up with a mixed construction, and this fact alone makes it difficult to identify one. Here is an example of one common type of mixed construction:

▶ Décollage is when you take away pieces of an image to create a new image.

The sentence is clear enough, but look again at the word *when*. That word locates an event in time—*I'll call* when *I get there. The baby woke up* when *the phone rang.* When *the armistice was signed, people everywhere cheered.* In the example above, there is no time associated with décollage; the sentence is simply describing the process. To edit the sentence, replace *when* with a more appropriate word, and adjust the rest of the sentence as needed.

▶ Décollage is ~~when you take~~ *the technique of taking* away pieces of an image to create a new image.

Checking for mixed constructions
Let's consider another example:

▶ Nutritionists disagree about the riskiness of eating raw eggs and also more healthful compared with cooked ones.

What? It's hard to even know where to start. Let's begin by identifying the **VERB(S)**. There's only one verb here, *disagree*. Next, let's identify the **SUBJECT**. Who disagrees? *Nutritionists*. Now we have a subject and a verb. What do nutritionists disagree about? It's clear enough that they disagree about *the riskiness of eating raw eggs,* but after that, it gets confusing. Consider the next words: *and also.* Also what? Do nutritionists also disagree that raw eggs are more nutritious than cooked eggs? Or is the writer claiming that raw eggs *are* more healthful? It's impossible to tell, which suggests that we have a mixed construction.

Editing mixed constructions
Let's look at a couple of ways we might edit the sentence about raw eggs. Here's one way:

▶ Nutritionists disagree about the riskiness of eating raw eggs and also
  about their healthfulness
  ~~more healthful~~ compared with cooked ones.

Notice that we added another *about,* which makes it clear that what follows is also something nutritionists disagree about. We also added the suffix *–ness* to *healthful* so that the word would be parallel to *riskiness.* Now the verb *disagree* applies to both *riskiness* and *healthfulness:* nutritionists disagree about the riskiness of eating raw eggs, and they also disagree about the healthfulness of raw eggs compared with cooked ones.

What if the writer's original intention was to claim that raw eggs are more healthful than cooked ones? Since the two parts of the sentence express two different ideas, an editor might choose to simply make the mixed construction into two separate sentences.

▶ Nutritionists disagree about the riskiness of eating raw eggs. ~~and also~~ *Raw eggs are*
  than
  more healthful ~~compared with~~ cooked ones.

Just considering sentence structure, now we have two good sentences, but even though they both focus on raw eggs, the two sentences are not clearly connected. And besides, who is saying that eating raw eggs is more healthful? The author or the nutritionists? Adding just a couple of words links the sentences together and helps readers follow the ideas.

▶ Nutritionists disagree about the riskiness of eating raw eggs. *Some claim raw* ~~Raw~~ eggs
  are more healthful than cooked ones.

Here we've added a new subject, *some* (which refers to nutritionists), and we've also given the second sentence a verb, *claim.* Now the two sentences have a logical sequence and are easier to read. Next, let's look at one other mixed construction:

▶ Because air accumulates under the eggshell is why an egg stands up underwater.

This sentence is more or less clear, but its parts don't fit together properly. What can we do about that? Same procedure as before—first, look for the verbs. This time, it's more complicated because there are three: *accumulates, is,* and *stands up*. Next, we look for the subject of each of the verbs. The first one is easy—*air* accumulates; the subject is *air*. The third one is also simple— *an egg* stands up; the subject is *an egg*. But what is the subject of *is*? That's not such an easy question with this sentence because its structure changes in the middle. So let's try a different approach.

What exactly is this sentence trying to say? It's clear that the point of this sentence is to explain why a submerged egg stands up, and we have two clauses: one that tells us that *an egg stands up underwater* and another that tells us that the egg stands up *because air accumulates under the eggshell*. Now we just have to put them together in an appropriate way.

▶ Because air accumulates under the eggshell, ~~is why~~ an egg stands up underwater.

Did you notice that this version is almost exactly the same as the original sentence? The main difference is the words *is why*—which turn out not to be necessary. We now have one **MAIN CLAUSE** (*an egg stands up underwater*) and one **SUBORDINATE CLAUSE** (*because air accumulates under the eggshell*), with a comma in between. If it sounds better to you, you can reverse the order of the clauses, and the meaning stays the same. Note that you should not use a comma with this option.

▶ An egg stands up underwater because air accumulates under the eggshell.

We can use the same approach for a sentence that starts with a prepositional phrase but changes its structure in the middle: figure out what the sentence is trying to say, identify the phrases and clauses, and edit as needed so that you can put them together in an appropriate way.

▶ *Parents*
  ~~For parents~~ of children with a peanut allergy depend on rules that prohibit
  nuts in school.

Edit

Try editing the following mixed construction in two ways. First, make one sentence that includes all of the information in the example. Next, present the same information in two separate sentences. Which way do you like better? Why?

> One or two months before mating, male and female eagles together build their nests can be four or five feet in diameter.

↪ For more practice, complete the InQuizitive activity on **mixed constructions**.

EDITING PRONOUNS

Pronouns are some of the smallest words in the language, so you might think they should be among the easiest. Well, no, they're often not. But the good news is that editing your work to make sure all your pronouns are used appropriately is not too complicated. The advise that follows gives you tools for editing three common pronoun issues: pronoun reference, pronoun-antecedent agreement, and pronoun case.

First, let's clarify the terms. **PRONOUNS**, as you probably know, are words that refer to other words or phrases (and occasionally even whole clauses). They're very useful precisely because they're small and they do a lot of work representing larger units. The words that they represent are their **ANTECEDENTS**. Most frequently, the antecedent is something or somebody that has already been mentioned, and English has very specific conventions for signaling to readers exactly what that antecedent is so that they won't be confused. We call that **PRONOUN REFERENCE**. Let's suppose this next example is the first sentence in a news report.

▶ The Procurement Committee meets today to review the submitted bids, and she will announce the winner tomorrow.

Wait. *She? She* who? It's not clear what *she* refers to, and readers are now lost.

Pronoun **AGREEMENT** is another important convention. Pronouns have to agree with their antecedents in number (*I, we*) and in some cases gender (*he, she, it*). *Mr. Klein misplaced her phone again.* If Mr. Klein is in the habit of losing a specific woman's phone, then perhaps the sentence makes sense. If it's his own phone that he misplaced again, then *her* doesn't agree with its antecedent, Mr. Klein, and readers will get confused.

PRONOUN CASE is a concept that you may never have encountered, but it's one that you use every day, probably appropriately and without giving it any thought. For example, you probably say *I bought ice cream* automatically—and are not likely to say *Me bought ice cream* or *Coach wants I to play shortstop.* Those two pronouns—*I* and *me*—refer to the same person, but they're not interchangeable. Still, most of the time we automatically choose the appropriate one for the specific context.

Pronoun Reference

Unclear pronoun reference occurs when readers can't be certain what a **PRONOUN** refers to. Usually this confusion arises when there are several possibilities in the same sentence (or sometimes in the previous sentence). Here's an example: *Andrew and Glen competed fiercely for the office of treasurer, but in the end, he won handily.* If Andrew and Glen are both men, the pronoun *he* could refer to either one of them, so who was it that won? We don't know.

Checking for unclear pronoun reference
To check for unclear pronoun reference, you need to first identify each pronoun and then make sure that it points very clearly to its **ANTECEDENT**. Often, the meanings of the words provide clues about what the pronoun refers to—but not always. Let's look at three sentences that have very similar structures.

▶ My grandparents ordered pancakes because *they* weren't very hungry.

First, we identify the pronouns: *my* and *they*. *My* clearly refers to the writer, but what about *they*? Although both *pancakes* and *grandparents* are possible antecedents for *they*, we know that the pronoun here has to refer to grandparents because pancakes don't get hungry. Now let's look at another sentence:

▶ My grandparents ordered pancakes because *they* weren't very expensive.

This sentence is almost identical to the first one and has the same pronoun, *they,* but this time, the antecedent has to be *pancakes* because there is no price on grandparents. Sorry to say, though, that antecedents aren't always so obvious. For example:

▶ My grandparents like playing cards with their neighbors because *they* aren't very competitive.

Wait. Who's not very competitive here? The grandparents or the neighbors? Or maybe all of them? We really can't be sure.

Editing unclear pronoun reference
Let's look again at the last example:

▶ My grandparents like playing cards with their neighbors because they aren't very competitive.

To edit this sentence, our best option may be to change the structure, and there are several possibilities:

▶ My grandparents like playing cards with their neighbors, ~~because they~~ *who* aren't very competitive.

This option makes clear that the neighbors are the ones who aren't very competitive.

▶ My grandparents, *who aren't very competitive,* like playing cards with their neighbors, *who are also not too* ~~because they aren't very~~ competitive.

Now we know that everybody mentioned here is noncompetitive. You may not think the sentence sounds as good as the original, but at least the meaning is clear. And of course there are usually other options.

The most important objective is to make clear what word or words each pronoun refers to. You don't want to leave your readers guessing. Here is one more example:

▶ After months of posturing and debate, those planning the expensive new football stadium suspended the project, which students loudly celebrated.

What is the antecedent for *which* in this example? You probably interpret this sentence to say that the students celebrated the suspension of the plans to build the stadium, but in fact, that's not really clearly established in the sentence. Another plausible interpretation is that the students celebrated the building of the stadium. Let's reword the sentence and remove *which* in order to make the meaning perfectly clear.

▶ After months of posturing and debate, those planning the expensive
new football stadium suspended the project, ~~which~~ *and* students loudly
celebrated, *the news*

Edit
The following sentence uses the words *it* and *which* to refer to . . . well, it's not exactly clear what they refer to.

A temperature inversion happens when a layer of warmer air is positioned above a layer of cooler air, which is not how it usually occurs.

You have several options here that would make this sentence better, but try this one: rewrite the sentence to eliminate the need for any pronoun at all.

For more practice, complete the InQuizitive activity on **unclear pronoun references**.

Pronoun-Antecedent Agreement

Pronoun-antecedent agreement means that every **PRONOUN** has to agree with its **ANTECEDENT** in gender (*he, she, it*) and number (singular or plural). Some sentences with pronouns that don't agree with their antecedents are relatively easy to understand, and usually readers can figure the meanings out, but they shouldn't have to do that extra work. For your academic writing, you need to make sure that all of your pronouns agree with their antecedents.

Checking for pronoun-antecedent agreement
To check for pronoun-antecedent agreement, you need to first identify the pronouns and their antecedents. Then you need to make sure each pronoun agrees with its antecedent in gender and number. Let's look at a couple of examples:

▶ Trombones might be very loud, but it was drowned out last night by the cheering of the crowd.

This sentence has only one pronoun: *it. Trombones* is the only noun that precedes *it*, so *trombones* has to be the antecedent. Do they agree? We don't have to think about gender in this example, but we do have to think about number. And that's a problem, because the numbers don't match: *trombones* is plural, but *it* is singular.

▶ The table is wobbly because one of her legs is shorter than the others.

In some languages, tables, chairs, and other inanimate objects have grammatical gender, but in English, they don't. The legs of a table are never referred to with masculine or feminine gender.

Editing for pronoun-antecedent agreement

In order to fix the trombone sentence, you can change either the antecedent or the pronoun to make them agree in number. In this case, it is clear that the first CLAUSE refers to trombones in general, and the second clause refers to a specific trombone at a specific event. Assuming that the more important part is the specific event, and that there was only one trombone, let's change the word *trombones* from plural to singular. We can do that easily in this case without really changing the meaning, although sometimes it might be more difficult to do so.

▶ *The trombone*
~~Trombones~~ might be very loud, but it was drowned out last night by the cheering of the crowd.

Both the pronoun and its antecedent are now singular; that is, they agree in number. Now let's consider several examples where gender is a factor. In the example about the table legs, we simply have to replace the feminine pronoun with the inanimate one.

▶ The table is wobbly because one of *Its* ~~her~~ legs is shorter than the others.

Remember that the gender of English pronouns matters only with *he, him, his; she, her, hers; it, its*. No other English pronouns specify gender. Some languages have more gender-specific pronouns, and some languages have fewer, but let's just stick to English right now.

▶ My mom and dad have an arrangement about sausage pizza—
he picks off the sausage, and *she* eats *it*.

This sentence has three pronouns—*he, she*, and *it*—and it's quite evident that *he* refers to *dad, she* refers to *mom*, and *it* refers to *sausage*. All the antecedents are clear. But what if we changed the cast of characters in the sentence to two men? It would be confusing to refer to each of them as *he*, so we need a different strategy. One possibility is to use *he* to represent one of the men and to refer to the other man by name. Will that work?

▶ Paul and *his* brother have an arrangement about sausage pizza—Paul picks off the sausage, and *he* eats it.

Who eats the sausage? Paul or his brother? It's still not clear. In this case, our best option is to eliminate the pronoun and refer to both men explicitly both times.

▶ Paul and *his* brother have an arrangement about sausage pizza—
Paul picks off the sausage, and ~~he~~ *his brother* eats it.

If you'd rather not repeat both phrases, and the arrangement itself is more important than which person eats all the sausage, you can try this option:

▶ Paul and *his* brother have an arrangement about sausage pizza—
~~Paul~~ *one of them* picks off the sausage, and ~~he~~ *the other one* eats it.

Now we've got it; everything is clear. As this last edit shows, making pronouns and antecedents agree sometimes requires reworking the structure of a sentence and occasionally even modifying what it says. Pronouns may be small words, but getting them right is hugely important; don't be afraid to make changes in your writing.

Now let's look at some other contexts where making pronouns agree in gender with their antecedents can be complicated. We'll start with one that's pretty straightforward.

▶ Trey noticed a sunflower growing along the path; *he* grabbed *his* phone and took a picture of *it*.

We know that Trey is a man or a boy—*he, his*—and the flower, of course, is inanimate—*it*. In academic writing, inanimate objects are always referred to as *it*, even though in casual speech, we may use gendered pronouns to refer to things such as cars, boats (almost always *she*), and others. What about animals? If you know the sex of an animal, then by all means, refer to it as *he* or *she*. If you don't know the sex, or if the sex isn't pertinent, just use *it*. Also, it is becoming more common for people to specify (or ask one another about) their pronouns—in person, in email signatures, in social media bios—a practice that is in response to increasing flexibility about gender identity. Some individuals opt to be referred to as *they*, a usage that transforms *they* from its conventional usage as plural to a singular pronoun of unspecified gender. Other people may use other pronouns, such as *ze/hir/hirs*. We recommend that, whenever possible, you use individuals' specified pronouns in your writing about them. And what if you're writing about a person whose sex or gender you don't know? That happens, and that's when it can get complicated. For example:

> ▶ Anyone who gets three speeding tickets in a year will lose *his* license.

What's wrong with this example? Plenty, unless only men have such a license. If what you are writing applies to both women and men, your pronouns should reflect that reality. One of the easiest solutions is to use plural nouns and pronouns because they do not specify gender:

> ▶ ~~Anyone~~ who ~~gets~~ three speeding tickets in a year will lose ~~his license~~.
>   Drivers   get   their licenses

You may need to tinker a bit with the structure, but the message can remain the same. Another option is to revise the sentence altogether. Here's one possibility:

> ▶ Getting three speeding tickets in a year will result in the driver's license being revoked.

Another possible solution is to write *his* or *her*:

> ▶ Anyone who gets three speeding tickets in a year will lose ~~his~~ license.
>   his or her

This last solution is fine, although if you have many such instances close together, the writing can start to feel awkward. Another possibility is to employ **SINGULAR THEY**, using *they*, *them*, *their*, or *theirs* with a singular antecedent.

> ▶ Anyone who gets three speeding tickets in a year will lose ~~his~~ license.
>   their

Pronouns are, in fact, a topic of debate. See Dennis Baron's take in his essay "What's Your Pronoun?" on p. 846.

Many of us use singular *they* this way in casual speech, and its use is becoming more and more accepted in some newspapers and magazines and other more formal contexts. Singular *they* is a very useful solution, but even though it's becoming ever more common, it's still not always accepted in academic writing. Before you use it in your class work, you might check with your instructor to be sure it will be acceptable in their class.

Edit

Edit the following sentence in two ways. First, make both the pronoun and its antecedent singular; second, make the pronoun and antecedent plural. Both ways are acceptable, but which way sounds better to you?

> Applicants must file the forms before the deadline and make sure that it's filled out correctly.

For more practice, complete the InQuizitive activity on **pronoun antecedent agreement**.

Pronoun Case

Pronoun CASE refers to the different forms a PRONOUN takes in order to indicate how it functions in a sentence. English pronouns have three cases: subject, object, and possessive. Most of the time, we choose the appropriate pronouns automatically, as in the following sentence:

> ▶ *I* texted *her*, and *she* texted *me*, but *we* didn't see *our* messages.

This sentence involves two people and six distinct pronouns. *I* and *me* refer to one person (the writer), *she* and *her* refer to the other person, and *we* and *our* refer to both people. Each of the three pronoun pairs has a distinct role in the sentence. *I, she*, and *we* are all subjects; *me* and *her* are objects; and *our* is possessive.

Checking for correct pronoun case

You would probably not ever say *Me saw her* because it wouldn't sound right. In casual speech, though, you might hear (or say) *Me and Bob saw her*. While you might hear or say that in informal conversation, it would not be acceptable in academic writing. Here is a simple and reliable technique for checking your work for case: check for compound subjects like *me and Bob* and cover up everything in the phrase but the pronoun. Read it out loud.

▶ Me ~~and Bob~~ saw her.

Does it sound good to you? Hope not. So how do you change it? Read on.

Editing for pronoun case

To edit for pronoun case, the first step is to identify the pronouns in each sentence. The following example has only one, *us*:

▶ Us first-year students are petitioning for a schedule change.

Remember that the way a pronoun functions in a sentence is the key and that there are three possibilities for case. Is *us* functioning as subject, object, or possessive? In order to answer that question, first we need to identify the verb: *are petitioning*. The subject tells us who (or what) is petitioning—in this sentence, *us first-year students*. If you're not sure if *us* is correct, try it by itself, without *first-year students*.

▶ Us are petitioning for a schedule change.

▶ $\overset{We}{\underset{\wedge}{\text{Us}}}$ are petitioning for a schedule change.

We changed *us* to *we* here because it's the subject of the sentence and thus needs to be in the subject case. For more advice on choosing the correct case, see the table below. Now let's look at two more examples: *Pat dated Cody longer than me. Pat dated Cody longer than I.* The only difference between the two sentences is the case of the pronoun, but that little word gives the sentences totally different meanings because the case lets readers know whether the person—*I* or *me*—is the subject or the object of the verb.

▶ Pat dated Cody longer than me.

Look carefully. There's only one verb, *dated*, and its subject is *Pat*. Now notice the pronoun: *me*. That's object case, right? So, according to the example, Pat dated Cody and also dated *me*. Try the next one.

▶ Pat dated Cody longer than I.

Here the pronoun is in subject case: *I*. Even though it's not followed by a verb, the pronoun tells us that Pat dated Cody and so did I.

Subject	Object	Possessive
I	me	my/mine
we	us	our/ours
you	you	your/yours
he/she/it	him/her/it	his/her/hers/its
they	them	their/theirs
who/whoever	whom/whomever	whose

Edit

Use the technique explained in this section to edit the following sentence for pronoun case.

> Iris was unhappy, but the judges called a tie and gave the award to she and Lu.

 For more practice, complete the InQuizitive activity on **pronoun case**.

EDITING VERBS

Verbs. Are any words more important—or hardworking? Besides specifying actions (*hop, skip, jump*) or states of being (*be, seem*), verbs provide most of the information about *when* (happening now? already happened? might happen? usually happens?), and they also have to link very explicitly to their subjects. That's a lot of work!

Because verbs are so important, verb problems are often easily noticed by readers, and once readers notice a verb problem in your work, they may question your competence as a writer. But if your readers can catch these problems, so can you. The following advice will help you edit your work for two of the most troublesome verb problems: subject-verb agreement and shifts in tense.

Subject-Verb Agreement

In English, every **VERB** has to agree with its **SUBJECT** in number and person. That may sound complicated, but it's really only third-person singular subjects—*runner, shoe, he, she, it*—that you have to look out for, and even then, only when the verb is in the simple present tense. Still, the third-person present tense is the most common construction in academic writing, so it matters. Take a look at this example:

▶ First the coach enters, then you enter, and then all of the other players enter.

The verb *enter* occurs three times in that sentence, but notice that when its subject is third-person singular—*coach*—an *-s* follows the base form of the verb, *enter*. In the other two cases, the verb has no such ending. What's so complicated about that? Well, there are two kinds of subjects that cause problems: indefinite pronouns, such as *everyone* and *many*, which may require a singular or plural verb even if their meaning suggests otherwise; and subjects consisting of more than one word, in which the word that has to agree with the verb may be hidden among other words.

Checking for subject-verb agreement
To check for subject-verb agreement, first identify the subjects and their verbs, paying careful attention to **INDEFINITE PRONOUNS** and subjects with more than one word. Then, check to make sure that every subject matches its verb in number and person.

Editing for subject-verb agreement
Let's look at a few common mistakes and see what we can do about them.

INDEFINITE PRONOUNS

Indefinite pronouns are words like *anyone, each, everything,* and *nobody.* When they're used as a subject, they have to agree with the verb. Sometimes that's tricky. For example:

▶ First the coach enters, then you enter, and then each of the other players enter.

We know that the subject of the first clause is *coach* and the subject of the second clause is *you*, but what about the third clause? Is the subject *each*? Or is it *players*? You might be tempted to choose *players* because that's the word closest to the verb *enter*, but that's not correct; the subject is *each*, an indefinite pronoun.

▶ First the coach enters, then you enter, and then each of the other
           enters
  players ~~enter~~.

That -*s* at the end of *enters* is necessary because the **SIMPLE SUBJECT** of the final clause is *each*, which is singular. The phrase *of the other players* is additional information. Now see what happens if we change *each* to *all*:

▶ First the coach enters, then you enter, and then ~~each~~ ^{all} of the other players ~~enters~~ _{enter}.

Even though the two phrases—*each of the other players* and *all of the other players*—have essentially the same meaning, the word *each* refers to the members of a group individually so it is always singular and requires the verb to have the -*s* ending. *All* is plural here because it refers to a plural noun, *players*. However, *all* is singular when it refers to a singular noun.

▶ *All* of the strawberries *were picked* today.

▶ *All* of the rhubarb *was picked* yesterday.

In the first sentence, *all* refers to *strawberries* all together, in plural form, while in the second sentence, *all* refers to *rhubarb*, a **NONCOUNT NOUN**, which requires the singular form of the verb. **INDEFINITE PRONOUNS** can be tricky. Most take a singular verb, even if they seem plural or refer to plural nouns. These include *anyone, anything, each, either, everyone, everything, neither, nobody, no one, one, somebody, someone,* and *something*. A few indefinite pronouns are always plural: *both, few, many, others, and several*. Some take a singular verb when they refer to a singular or noncount noun, but they take a plural verb when referring to a plural noun. These are *all, any, enough, more, most, none,* and *some*.

SUBJECTS CONSISTING OF MORE THAN ONE WORD
Sometimes a sentence has a subject with more than one word, so you need to determine which of the words is the one that the verb has to agree with and which words simply provide extra information. To do that, pull the subject apart to find which word is the essential one. Let's practice with this sentence:

▶ The guy with the mirrored sunglasses run in this park every morning.

The **COMPLETE SUBJECT** is *the guy with the mirrored sunglasses*, but who is it that does the running? It's the guy, and the fact that he has mirrored sunglasses is simply extra information. You could remove the phrase *with the mirrored sunglasses* and still have a complete sentence—it might not be very informative, but it's not incorrect.

To check for subject-verb agreement when a subject has more than one word, first locate the verb and then the complete subject. Then check each word in the subject until you find the one keyword that determines the form of the verb. Since the **SIMPLE SUBJECT** here—*guy*—is in the third-person singular, and the verb is in the present tense, the verb should also be in the third-person singular:

▶ The guy with the mirrored sunglasses ~~run~~ *runs* in this park every morning.

Let's try one more problem sentence:

▶ The neighbor across the hall from the Fudds always sign for their packages.

First, find the verb: *sign*. The complete subject is *the neighbor across the hall from the Fudds*. What part of that subject indicates who does the signing? *Neighbor*. Everything else is extra. Since it's just one *neighbor*, the subject is singular, and since a third-person singular subject requires a present tense verb to have an *-s* ending, the edited sentence will be:

▶ The neighbor across the hall from the Fudds always ~~sign~~ *signs* for their packages.

Edit

The sentence below has four subjects and four verbs. One (or more) of the subjects is singular, so its verb should have an *-s* ending. Edit and make any necessary changes.

> All of the boxes need to be stacked neatly, and every box need to be labeled; the red box with the taped edges fit on top, and each of the boxes need its own lid.

In casual speech, you may not use the *-s* ending, or it may be hard to hear, so you may not be able to rely on your ear alone to edit this sentence.

☞ For more practice, complete the InQuizitive activity on **subject-verb agreement**.

Shifts in Tense

We live in the present moment; our ideas and our feelings are happening right now. Often, though, our present thoughts—and comments—are responses to things that happened in the past or that haven't happened yet. In conversation, we usually shift our verb tenses smoothly and automatically to account for actions that take place at different times, as in the following example of something you might hear or say:

▶ Flor *is* upset because Justin *informed* her that he *will not be able to come* to her graduation.

In writing, however, we need to take extra care to ensure that our tenses are clear, consistent, and appropriate to what we're describing. In contrast to face-to-face conversation—in which tone of voice, facial expressions, and hand gestures help create meaning—writing has to rely on carefully chosen words. Verb tenses work hard to put complex sequences of events into appropriate context. The previous example has three clauses, each in a different tense: Flor *is* upset (right now); because Justin *informed* her (in the past); that he *will not be able to come* (to an event in the future).

Checking for shifts in tense

In academic writing, you'll often need to discuss what other authors have written, and the different disciplines have different conventions and rules for doing that (see p. 552). In classes that require you to use **MLA** style, for example, you'll rely heavily on the simple present tense:

MLA Morton argues that even though Allende's characters are not realistic, they're believable.

Notice how *argues*, *are not*, and *they're* all use the simple present tense even though Morton's article and Allende's novel were both written in the past. If you mention the date when something was written, however, the verb should be in the past tense. In contrast, disciplines that follow **APA** style require that references to published sources and research results be stated in the past tense (or the present perfect, if the research isn't from one specific time in the past):

APA Azele (2010) reported that 59% of the subjects showed high gamma levels.

Notice here that the two verbs in the sentence—*reported* and *showed*—are both in the past tense because both Azele's research and the report were done in the past. Be careful, though, because your sources may be writing about current or future conditions. If that's the case, be sure to preserve the tense of the original in your work, as the following example does.

APA Donnerstag and Jueves (2019) predicted that another Jovian moon will soon be discovered.

Regardless of what class you're writing for, however, the most important thing about verb tenses is consistency—unless you have a reason to shift tense.

Editing confusing shifts in tense

Much of the editing that you do calls for sentence-by-sentence work, but checking for confusing shifts in tense often requires that you consider several sentences together.

Starting at the beginning, mark every **MAIN VERB**, along with any **HELPING VERBS**, in every sentence (remembering that there may be more than one clause in each sentence). Don't make any changes yet; just mark the verbs. Next, go back to the beginning and notice what tense you used each time. Examine each tense one by one, and when you notice a shift to a different tense, read carefully what you have written and look for a reason for the shift. If you can explain why the shift makes sense, leave it alone. Then move on to the next verb. Is it in the original tense or the new tense? Can you explain why? Continue all the way through your text, examining every verb tense and making sure that any shifts you find can be explained. Let's practice with two examples:

▶ Bates underestimated the public when she writes disparagingly about voters' intelligence.

First, we mark the verbs—*underestimated*, *writes*—and we notice that the first is in past tense while the second is in present. Is there a clear explanation for the shift? No, not really. If you are using **MLA** style, you'll want to put both verbs in the present: *underestimates* and *writes*. In **APA** style, past tense is more appropriate for both: *underestimated* and *wrote*. In any case, there is no reason to use two different tenses in the sentence. Here is another example, this time a little more complicated:

► All of the guests ate the stew, but only two showed symptoms of food poisoning.

It's true that the events (*ate, showed*) in both clauses of the example occurred in the past, but can we be certain that the symptoms were a result of eating the stew? Could the guests have had the symptoms already? The sentence isn't really clear.

► All of the guests ~~ate~~ *had eaten* the stew, but only two showed symptoms of food poisoning.

By changing the verb tense in the first clause to the past perfect (the tense used to indicate that an action was completed before another action in the past began), we show clearly that the stew was eaten before the food poisoning occurred. (We may never know what caused the illness, but at least we know the sequence of events.)

Edit
Edit the following sentence to eliminate any confusing shifts in tense. Assume that the writing has to follow **APA** format for verb tenses.

Levi (2013) notes that the trade deficit decreases from 2005 to 2015, but he warns that the improvement may be reversed because the new treaty will go into effect in 2020.

For more practice, complete the InQuizitive activity on **verb tense**.

EDITING QUOTATIONS

In academic writing, you are required not only to express your own ideas, but also to incorporate the ideas of other authors. In a way, you are engaging in a conversation with your sources, whether you draw from Aristotle, Toni Morrison, or a classmate. Your success as a writer has a lot to do with how well you weave your sources' ideas in with your own without your readers ever having to wonder who said what. Editing your work for citation and documentation issues therefore involves two main tasks:

• incorporating any words of others that you quote into your text so that everything flows smoothly

- making sure the punctuation, capitalization, and other such elements are correct

The conventions for citing and documenting sources in academic writing are very precise—every period, every comma, every quotation mark has its job to do, and they must be in exactly the right place.

Incorporating Quotations

Whenever we quote something someone else has said, we need to structure the sentences that contain the quoted material so that they read as smoothly as any other sentence. As writers, we need to master our use of language in much the same way that musicians have to master their instruments, and in both cases, it's not easy. Just as musicians playing together in an orchestra (or a garage band) have to coordinate with one another in tempo, key, and melody, you have to make sure that your words and those of others that you quote fit together smoothly.

Checking to see that quotations are incorporated smoothly
One good way to begin checking a draft to see how well any quotations have been incorporated is to read it aloud, or better yet, get someone else to read it aloud to you. If the reader (you or someone else) stumbles over a passage and has to go back and read the sentence again, you can be fairly certain that some changes are necessary. We can practice with some sentences that quote the following passage from a 2013 *Atlantic* article about fast food:

> Introduced in 1991, the McLean Deluxe was perhaps the boldest single effort the food industry has ever undertaken to shift the masses to healthier eating.
>
> —DAVID FREEDMAN, "How Junk Food Can End Obesity"

Assume that you might not want or need to quote the entire passage, so you incorporate just one part of Freedman's sentence into one of your sentences, as follows:

▶ Freedman refers to a failed McDonald's menu item "the McLean Deluxe was perhaps the food industry's boldest single effort to shift the masses to healthier eating."

If you read the sentence aloud, you should be able to notice that it is awkwardly structured and even hard to understand. Also, do you notice that the quoted section doesn't exactly match the author's words? Some of the words from the original are missing and some others have been added. Changing an author's words in a quoted section is only allowed if the original meaning is not altered in any way. Also, you need to indicate to your readers that you've modified the author's words. Let's see how we can go about fixing these things.

Editing sentences that include quotations
There are two ways of smoothly incorporating quoted material. One strategy is to adjust your own words to accommodate the quoted material; another is to lightly modify the quoted material to fit your sentence. Here's one way we might edit our sentence by adjusting our own words:

> ▶ ~~Freedman refers~~ *Referring* to a failed McDonald's menu item, *Freedman notes that* "the McLean Deluxe was perhaps the food industry's boldest single effort to shift the masses to healthier eating."

Let's look at what we did. First, we changed the first two words. The meaning didn't change; only the structure did. Then, we added a SIGNAL PHRASE (*Freedman notes that*) to introduce the quoted words.

So far so good. But what about the places where we changed the author's words? If you modify an author's words, you need to signal to your readers what changes you've made, and there are precise conventions for doing that.

Enclose anything you add or change within the quotation itself in square brackets (**[ ]**), and insert ellipses (**. . .**) to show where any content from the original has been omitted.

> ▶ Referring to a failed McDonald's menu item, Freedman notes that "the McLean Deluxe was perhaps the [food industry's] boldest single effort . . . to shift the masses to healthier eating."

With minimal changes, the sentence now has all the necessary parts and reads smoothly. Note the two things we've done to modify the quotation. We've enclosed the words we added—*food industry's*—in square brackets, and we've inserted ellipses in place of the six words that were omitted from Freedman's sentence. It's worth repeating here that it is only permissible to add or delete words if the meaning of the quotation isn't substantially altered.

Edit

Here is another sentence based on the Freedman passage:

> Freedman talks about an earlier effort the McLean Deluxe by McDonald's
> was perhaps the boldest try to shift the masses to healthier eating.

First, you'll have to make a few changes to help the sentence read smoothly.
There are several ways to do that, but try to make as few changes as possible.
Once the sentence reads smoothly, compare it with the original passage to
see where you might need square brackets (for added material) or ellipses
(to show where words have been removed). By the way, you don't have to
put *McLean Deluxe* in quotation marks because it was not a term coined by
Freedman.

For more practice, complete the InQuizitive activity on **incorporating
quotations**.

Punctuating Quotations

Citation conventions exist to help us clearly distinguish our words from the
words of our sources, and one way we do that is by punctuating quotations
carefully. When you quote someone's exact words, you need to attend to four
elements: quotation marks, capitalization, commas, and end punctuation.
These elements let your readers know which words are yours and which are
the words of someone else.

Checking to see how any quoted material is punctuated

Here is another sentence taken from the *Atlantic* article about fast food; let's
use it in a variety of ways in order to show how to capitalize and punctuate
sentences that quote from this passage.

> A slew of start-ups are trying to find ways of producing fresh, local, unpro-
> cessed meals quickly and at lower cost.
>
> —DAVID FREEDMAN, "How Junk Food Can End Obesity"

You might write a sentence such as this one:

▶ It may one day be possible to get fast food that is healthy and affordable
since a slew of start-ups are trying to find ways, according to David
Freedman.

Structurally, the sentence is fine, but it includes a direct quotation from Freedman without letting readers know which words are his and which are yours. Even if you used Freedman's exact words accidentally, it would still be **PLAGIARISM**, which may carry a stiff penalty. The sentence needs to be edited.

Editing quotations to indicate who said what

There are numerous ways to edit the above sentence to make clear who said what. Here is one option:

> ▶ It may one day be possible to get fast food that is healthy and affordable. ~~since~~ slew of start-ups are trying to find ways. ~~according to Freedman.~~
>
> *According to David Freedman,* "A ~~slew of start-ups are trying to find ways~~/. "

What changed? First, we added quotation marks to enclose Freedman's exact words. Second, we broke the sentence into two and started the second one with the signal phrase *According to Freedman*, followed by a comma. Third, we capitalized the first letter of the quotation. Since *A* was capitalized in the original quotation, no brackets are necessary. Finally, notice the period. The sentence ends with the quoted material, so the period goes inside the quotation marks. Now let's look at how you might go about editing another sentence.

> ▶ Freedman asserts that many new businesses are working to develop fresh, local, unprocessed meals quickly and at lower cost.

Check your four elements. First, insert any necessary quotation marks; make sure they enclose Freedman's exact words. Second, is any additional capitalization necessary? If so, capitalize the appropriate word(s). Third, if there's a **SIGNAL PHRASE** before the quoted material, does it need to be followed by a comma? Finally, make sure any end punctuation is in the right place. Try editing the sentence yourself before you look at the following revision.

> ▶ Freedman asserts that many new businesses are working to develop "fresh, local, unprocessed meals quickly and at lower cost."

The quoted portion is not a complete sentence, and we placed it in the middle of ours, so no capitalization was necessary. We didn't insert a comma because his words flow smoothly within the larger sentence. Since the sentence ends with the quoted material, we put the period inside the quotation marks.

Depending on the documentation style that you are using, you may need to provide parenthetical information at the end of any sentences that include quoted material. Some styles require that you name the author(s) if you haven't named them earlier in the sentence, along with the page number(s) where their words appeared. Here's how you would do so in MLA and APA style requirements.

MLA   Freedman asserts that many new businesses are working to develop "fresh, local, unprocessed meals quickly and at lower cost" (82).

APA   Freedman asserted that many new businesses are working to develop "fresh, local, unprocessed meals quickly and at lower cost" (2013, p. 82).

One more important point: notice that with parenthetical documentation, the final period of the sentence is no longer inside the quotation marks; it is after the parentheses.

Edit

The following sentences cite the passage from Freedman's essay; they need to be formatted properly in order to read smoothly and also to show more clearly which words are the writer's and which are Freedman's. Remember the four elements: quotation marks, capitalization, commas, and end punctuation.

> Healthy and affordable fast food may not be a reality yet, but we may not have too long to wait. As Freedman explains a slew of start-ups are trying to find ways to bring such meals to market.

It is possible to edit the sentence using only the four elements and not adding, subtracting, or changing any words. Try it.

➡ For more practice, complete the InQuizitive activity on **punctuating quotations**.

EDITING COMMAS

Ideas are made out of words, right? So why should we care about commas? Well, here's why—they help those words make more sense. Nobody wants to have to read the same sentence two or three times in order to get it. Well-placed commas can make your sentence clear and easy to read—and can keep the words (and ideas) correctly grouped together. Read this next sentence out loud:

▶ The boxer exhausted and pounded on wearily left the ring.

Did you start off expecting to read about the boxer's opponent who was getting "exhausted and pounded on"? Did you have to go back and start over? Bet you did. Well-placed commas would have immediately pointed us all in the right direction—like this:

▶ The boxer, exhausted and pounded on, wearily left the ring.

There are a lot of ways to err with commas. You might omit one that's necessary or place one where it doesn't belong. Even professional writers sometimes have trouble deciding where (and where not) to put a comma, and it's not always a big deal. The advice that follows won't make you a comma superstar, but it will show you how to edit your work for two of the comma problems that matter most to instructors and other readers: the commas that set off introductory information and the commas that distinguish between essential and nonessential information.

Introductory Information

English sentences generally begin with a **SUBJECT**. Without ever really thinking about it, those of us who read and write in English have an expectation that the first thing we read in a sentence will be its subject. Often, however (like right now), we begin a sentence in a different way. In academic writing especially, we might vary the structure of our sentences just to make our writing interesting. One way we vary our sentences is by starting some of them with introductory words, phrases, or even clauses. And usually we use a comma to set off those introductory words. That comma signals to readers that they haven't gotten to the subject yet; what they are seeing is additional information that is important enough to go first. For example:

▶ In Georgia, Lee's book jumped quickly to the top of the best-seller list.

Without the comma, readers might think the author's name was Georgia Lee, and they would get very lost in the sentence. Introductory words don't always cause so much confusion; in fact, some authors omit the comma if the introductory element is very short (one, two, or three words). Still, adding the comma after the introductory information is never wrong and demonstrates the care you take with your work.

Checking for commas after introductory information

▶ Initially the council proposed five miles of new bike paths; they later revised the proposal.

To check for introductory information, you should first identify the **VERB** —in this case, *proposed*. Now what's the subject? (In other words, who or what *proposed*?) The subject here is *the council*. Everything that goes before the subject is introductory information, so the comma goes between that information and the subject.

▶ Initially, the council proposed five miles of new bike paths; they later revised the proposal.

In the example above, the introductory element is only one word, and the comma could have been omitted, but its presence adds a little extra emphasis to the word *initially*, and in fact, that emphasis is probably why the author chose to put that word at the beginning, before the subject. The comma definitely helps. And sometimes, introductory elements can cause confusion:

▶ Tired and discouraged by the unsuccessful search for the fugitive Sgt. Drexler the detective and her squad returned to headquarters.

In this example, the introductory information is much longer, and without an appropriate comma, readers have no way of knowing if Sgt. Drexler is the name of the fugitive, the name of the detective, or someone else entirely. Let's imagine that Drexler is the fugitive. With one well-placed comma, the sentence is now perfectly clear.

▶ Tired and discouraged by the unsuccessful search for the fugitive Sgt. Drexler, the detective and her squad returned to headquarters.

Editing for commas after introductory information

Let's take a look at a few examples to see how we can figure out where to put commas with introductory elements. The following sentence needs a comma; where should it go?

▶ For the first three scoreless innings Clark struggled to stay awake.

How do you know where to put the comma? Let's follow the steps described in this chapter. First, identify the verb: *struggled*. Next, identify the subject—in other words, who or what struggled? The subject here is *Clark*, and everything that precedes it is introductory information.

▶ For the first three scoreless innings, Clark struggled to stay awake.
                                    ^

Here is one more example. Follow the same procedure to determine where to put the comma.

▶ In the chaotic final episode of season 2 the shocking plot twists left viewers breathless.

In this example, the comma should go after *2*; the verb in the sentence is *left*, and the **COMPLETE SUBJECT** is *the shocking plot twists*. Everything that goes before the subject is introductory information, so the comma falls between that information and the subject:

▶ In the chaotic final episode of season 2, the shocking plot twists left viewers breathless.
                                          ^

Edit

Try editing the following sentence by inserting a comma after the introductory information. Remember the technique: first, find the verb; second, find the subject. The comma goes before the subject because everything that precedes it is introductory information.

Behind the parade marshal and the color guard the sponsors' convertible carrying the Founders' Day Queen will proceed along Cunningham Street.

↪ For more practice, complete the InQuizitive activities on **commas**.

Essential and Nonessential Information

What do we mean by **ESSENTIAL** and **NONESSENTIAL** information? The simplest way to explain the difference is with examples.

▶ My sister Jamilah graduates on Saturday.

If the writer has more than one sister, the name *Jamilah* tells us which one; that's important to know because we don't want to congratulate the wrong sister. Therefore, her name is essential information. When the information is essential, it should not be set off with commas. But if the writer has only one sister, writing her name there is simply extra information; it's not essential. When the information is nonessential, we set it off with commas:

▶ My sister, Jamilah, graduates on Saturday.

Checking for essential and nonessential information
To check your work for these kinds of commas, read over what you've written and identify the **NOUNS**. When a noun—*stadium, achievement, amino acids*, whatever—is followed immediately by additional information about it, ask yourself if the information is essential: does it tell you which stadium, which achievement, which amino acids? If so, it shouldn't be set off with commas. If, however, the information is nonessential, and the sentence would still be fine without that information, it should be set off with a pair of commas. Let's examine two examples:

▶ The neighbors, who complained about parking, called a meeting to discuss the problem.

▶ The neighbors who complained about parking called a meeting to discuss the problem.

In these examples, the noun *neighbors* is followed by additional information. Which sentence talks about a situation where all of the neighbors complained? Which one describes a situation where only some of them did? Remember that the commas set off information that is extra and not essential. In the first sentence, the commas indicate that the information *who complained about parking* is extra, nonessential; it doesn't tell us which neighbors, so we can safely conclude that all of the neighbors complained. In the second sentence, the absence of commas lets us know that the information is essential; the clause *who complained about parking* tells us which neighbors called the meeting—only the ones who complained.

Editing commas with essential and nonessential information
Here is an example to practice with:

▶ Vitamins, such as B and C, are water-soluble and easily absorbed by the body; excess amounts are eliminated in the urine.

In order to edit the example, you will need to know if the phrase *such as B and C* is essential or if it's only additional information. In order to save you from looking it up, here it is: not all vitamins are water-soluble; some are fat-soluble and are stored in the body rather than quickly eliminated. Now, is the phrase *such as B and C* essential information? And if it is, should this sentence have commas? Here is the edited version:

▶ Vitamins/ such as B and C/ are water-soluble and easily absorbed by the body; excess amounts are eliminated in the urine.

Edit
The two sentences below are nearly identical; the difference is that one has essential information about its subject, while the other one's subject has extra information. Put commas in the appropriate places.

Missy Elliott who will perform in the opening act will do her sound check at 5:30.

The backup singers who will perform in the opening act will do their sound check at 5:30.

▶ For more practice, complete the InQuizitive activity on **commas**.

EDITING WORDS THAT ARE OFTEN CONFUSED

English has more than a million words, and any one of them could be used appropriately—or inappropriately—in a variety of ways, so no book could possibly help you edit all of the "wrong words" that might turn up in your writing. A few basic strategies, however, can help you with many of those problems. Here you'll find tips for identifying a few of those in your own work—and then editing as need be. Although there are countless ways to get a word wrong, many such problems can be traced back to two causes: words that sound like other words (homophones) and apostrophes (which don't have any sound at all). Here's an example:

▶ Joe should of told them to buy there TV there because its cheaper and its screen is bigger.

Read that sentence out loud and it sounds exactly as the writer intended it; the meaning is perfectly clear. But your writing can't just "sound" right—it has to look right, too. In other words, the written words have to be correct. There are three wrong words in that sentence: *of*, *there*, and *its*. Let's look at each one.

Of/Have

The useful little word *of*, which is a preposition, sounds a lot like another very useful and common word, the verb *have*, especially in rapid or casual speech. The two are often confused when *have* is used as a HELPING VERB with the MODALS *can*, *could*, *may*, *might*, *must*, *should*, *will*, or *would*—especially in contractions, such as *could've* or *should've*. How do you know if the appropriate word is *of* or *have*? Try reframing your sentence as a question. That should tell you right away which one is the right choice.

▶ Should Joe of told them?

▶ Should Joe have told them?

You can probably tell right away that *have* is the better choice. When you're editing, develop the habit of noticing whenever you use a modal, and make sure the words that follow it are appropriate. *Have* can be written out in its full form or combined with the preceding word to form a contraction—*should've*, *would've*. Try it without the modal. *Have you told them?* That's good. *Of you told them?* Not so good. That's because *have* is a helping verb, and *of* is not.

There/Their/They're

There is a common and useful word that sounds exactly like another common word, *their*, and those two sound the same as a third common word, *they're*, the contracted form of *they are*. So not only do we have three homophones, but each of the three words is used very frequently in both speech and writing. That leads to a large number of wrong word problems. For example:

▶ For security screening, passengers must put all cell phones in the trays, and now *there* required to put *there* shoes *there*, too.

You'll notice three instances of *there* in the example, and two of them are "wrong words." The sentence should have one each of *they're*, *their*, and *there*, so let's take a closer look at each use of *there*.

THEY'RE

Let's start with the first one. That part of the sentence is trying to say that the passengers—*they*—are required to do something, so the appropriate word would be the contraction of *they are*: *they're*. The word *they're* has only that one meaning, so using it is very simple. Just see if you can substitute "they are" for the word in question and still have the meaning you intended. If not, you'll need to make a change.

THEIR

Now let's look at the second instance of *there*: *there shoes*. That part of the sentence is talking about the shoes that belong to the passengers, so the appropriate word would be a possessive: *their*. The word *their* has only that one uncomplicated meaning—it always indicates possession, as in the following examples:

▶ *Their* feet were swollen and *their* toes were numb, but the hikers were determined to reach Vogelsang before dark.

▶ The birds are squawking because the wind blew *their* nest down.

▶ Both of the radios still work, but *their* clocks are wrong.

When you're trying to decide if *their* is the right word, try asking if the word you are using is intended to show possession. In the examples above, *their* is correct because it indicates possession: Whose feet and toes? *Their* (the hikers') feet and toes. Whose nest? *Their* (the birds') nest. Whose clocks? *Their* (the radios') clocks.

THERE

That leaves us with the final instance of *there* in our example sentence. That *there* is correct. Most of the time, as in our example, *there* simply indicates a place, telling *where* something is: Where's my phone? It's *there*, on the table. Sometimes, though, *there* is used to introduce information that's provided later in the sentence. For example:

► Whenever *there* was a big snowstorm, the neighbors all helped clear the street.

► *There* are three candidates in the race, but only one has the right experience.

That meaning of *there* simply indicates the existence of something—*a big snowstorm, three candidates*. Here's an example that uses both meanings:

► *There* is a coatrack behind the door; you can hang your jacket *there*.

To check whether *there* is the appropriate word, ask whether the word indicates either the existence of something or a place. If the word indicates either of those two things, *there* is the correct choice.

When editing your own work, check each instance of *there*, *their*, and *they're* to make sure that you've written the one you really mean. That may sound tedious, but here's a handy shortcut: use the Find function in your word processing program to search for each instance of *there*, *their*, and *they're*. That way, you won't miss any.

Now let's revise our original example sentence. Try it yourself before you look at the edited version below.

► For security screening, passengers must put all cell phones in the trays,
      they're   *their*
and now ~~there~~ required to put ~~there~~ shoes there, too.

It's / Its

It's and *its* make for many "wrong word" problems. Although they're pronounced exactly the same, they really are two distinct words with distinct uses: *its* is the possessive form of *it*, and *it's* is a contraction of *it is*. That difference makes it easy to know which one is appropriate for your sentence. Let's look at one problematic sentence:

► When my phone fell, *its* screen shattered, but luckily, *its* still working.

There are two instances of *its* in the sentence, but one of them should be *it's*. How can you tell which is which? Check to see which one can be replaced by *it is*. The second one—*it is* still working. The one without the apostrophe, *its*, is the possessive form of *it*: the screen that belongs to *it* (the phone). So here's how you'd edit this sentence:

>   *it's*
> ▶ When my phone fell, its screen shattered, but luckily, ~~its~~ still working.

Wait. Haven't you been told to use an apostrophe to indicate possessives, as in *the priest's robe, the frog's sticky tongue*? So how can it be that the version *without* the apostrophe is the possessive one? *It* is a **PRONOUN**, along with *he, I, she*, and *you*, for example. What are the possessive forms of those pronouns? *His. My. Her. Your.* Do you notice that those possessives don't have an apostrophe? Neither does *its*.

If you know or suspect that you have problems confusing *it's* and *its* in your work, you can check for them using the Find function of your word processor. Search your text for each of the two words, and make sure that the possessive *its* has no apostrophe and that the contracted form of *it is* always appears as *it's*.

Edit

Return now to the first problem sentence at the top of page 751, and try editing it using all of the techniques discussed above:

> Joe should of told them to buy there TV there because its cheaper and its screen is bigger.

➤ For more practice, complete the InQuizitive activity on **words often confused**.

PART VIII

Design and Delivery

ASKED TO NAME the three most important parts of rhetoric, the famous Greek statesman and orator Demosthenes is said to have replied: "Delivery, delivery, delivery." Not too many years ago, that assessment might have seemed overdone: Delivery, more important than content? Delivery, more important than the inventiveness of the message? Delivery, more important than style? But those were the years when print texts still claimed pride of place, when what was most important was "put in writing," and when most messages came to us in black print on white pages. In these instances, the message was carried by words alone, and those words were "delivered" in print texts. Period.

But today, Demosthenes is right on target. With messages of every imaginable sort packaged in ever more alluring garb vying for our attention, just how those messages are delivered matters—a lot. So just what do we mean by "delivery"? For the purposes of this book, we have two senses of the word in mind.

The first refers to how the message is communicated: in what *mode* and through what *medium*. Mode refers to what makes up the message and communicates its meaning: words, sounds, gestures, still and moving images, or some combination of those. Medium is the form in which the audience receives it: these days, that's print, oral, or digital. So a political candidate delivering a campaign speech (the medium) might use words, gestures, and a series of images (the modes) to make a vivid and personal appeal to her audience.

But there's another important sense of the word "delivery," one that comes down to us through the history of human communication. This sense of the word refers to the *performance* of a text and captures the speaker's tone, pacing, and quality of voice as well as a full range of facial and bodily gestures and movements. In Demosthenes's time, such delivery was of paramount importance in connecting to an audience and gaining its assent, approval, or understanding. And given the ubiquity of television, film, and video (not to mention *YouTube* and *Instagram*), these elements of communication are taking on greater significance.

Savvy authors understand that messages today don't just lie there on the page and wait for readers to discover them. Rather, it's up to you as author to capture and hold the attention of your audience. For authors of texts in all media, that means paying careful attention to *design*. A text's design— whether it be the use of color and fonts in a print text, the choice of music and moving images in a video, or the slides and handouts in an oral presentation—often determines your audience's first and lasting impressions. An effective design can draw the notice of your audience, keep their attention on your message, and help you achieve your purpose.

This section of *Everyone's an Author* aims to get *your* attention and to focus it on what delivery can mean for you as an author. The chapters that follow will ask you to consider the choices you'll need to make as an author who is designing texts, and how those choices affect the delivery and reception of your messages. In addition, we will examine the role of delivery in successful oral presentations, multimodal compositions, and portfolios. And last but not least, we'll urge you to deliver some of your ideas to audiences by way of publication, proving once again that, today, everyone's an author.

THIRTY-FOUR

Designing
What You Write

ESIGN. IT'S A WORD YOU HEAR ALL THE TIME, one you use without thinking about it. "Meghan Markle walked down the aisle in a wedding dress designed by Clare Waight Keller for Givenchy." "Have you seen the design for Stephen Colbert's new book?" "Frank Gehry's design of the Disney Concert Hall astonished critics with its waves of gleaming stainless steel." "My essay was designed to get the attention of the college admissions committee."

Fashion, technology, architecture, toys: everything is designed, and that includes everything you write. A slide presentation, a *YouTube* video, an essay—you design it, whether you are conscious of doing so or not. You select a medium and tools: a lined notebook and a pencil, a text message and a smartphone, white paper and black printer ink. You choose fonts and colors: big red capital letters for a poster, 12-point black Times New Roman for an essay, your neatest cursive for a thank-you note. You think about including visuals: a bar graph on a slide, a cartoon in a blog, a photo in an essay. You consider whether to use multiple columns, bullet points, numbered lists—and where to leave some white space. You decide what you want readers to notice first and how to make it catch their eye.

This chapter discusses several key design elements: typography, color, visuals, and layout. Whatever fonts or images you choose, though, remember that they are not mere decoration. However you design a text, you need to be guided by your purpose, your audience, and the rest of your rhetorical situation.

THINKING RHETORICALLY ABOUT DESIGN

Researchers point out that being able to design your writing gives you more control over your message than writers had in the past, when they had fewer options and tools at their disposal. That's because your design choices can play a big role in the way your audience receives your message and whether your text achieves its purpose. Look, for example, at the different ways that Coca-Cola was advertised in 1913 and in 2014.

In 1913, Coke was relatively new, and its ads relied on words to introduce it to an audience that was not yet familiar with the drink, telling them it had "character" and was "delicious," "refreshing," and "thirst-quenching." The ad shown here was designed so that these words would pop and be easy to read.

To reach today's audiences, however, advertisers use multiple media—in the case of this 2014 ad aired just before the World Cup in Brazil, print as well as video. Coca-Cola knew the world would be watching the World Cup, and this ad launched a special celebration of the event: mini bottles featuring designs inspired by the flags of World Cup host nations past, present, and future. The message: Coca-Cola is global, reaching potential customers all over the world.

A print ad for Coca-Cola in Georgia Tech's 1913 yearbook and a video ad presented during the telecast of the 2014 FIFA World Cup.

One thing the two ads have in common, though, is the logo. Whether it's in black ink on white paper or red and white pixels on a screen, the Coca-Cola logo was *designed* to be instantly recognizable.

In designing what you write, think about how you can best reach your audience and achieve your purpose. Given the deluge of words, images, and other data, readers today are less likely than they once were to read anything start to finish. Instead, they may scan for just the information they need. So as an author, you need to design your documents to be user-friendly: easy to access, to navigate, to read—and to remember.

Considering Your Rhetorical Situation

- *Who is your* **AUDIENCE**, and are there any design elements they expect or need? Large type? Illustrations? Are there any design elements that might not appeal to them—or cause them to question your authority?

- *What is your* **PURPOSE**, and what design elements can help you achieve that purpose? If you're trying to explain how to do something, would it help to set off the steps in a numbered list? Is there anything that would work against your goals—using a playful typeface in a business letter, for example?

- *What's your* **GENRE**, and does it have any design requirements?

- *What's your* **STANCE** *as an author,* and how do you want to come across to your audience? Do you want to seem businesslike? serious? ironic? practical and matter-of-fact? How can your use of fonts, color, images, and other design elements reflect that stance?

- *Consider the larger* **CONTEXT**. Does your assignment specify any design requirements? What design elements are possible with the technology you have available?

- *What* **MEDIA** *will you use*—print? digital? spoken?—and what kinds of **DESIGN** elements are appropriate (or possible)? A print essay, for example, could include photographs but not video.

CHOOSING FONTS

Authors today have hundreds of fonts to choose from, and the choices you make affect the message your readers receive—so it's important to think carefully about what's most appropriate for the particular rhetorical situation.

Serif fonts (fonts with small decorative lines, called serifs, added to the ends of most letters) such as Times New Roman or Bodoni have a traditional look, whereas sans serif fonts (those without serifs) such as Arial or Futura give a more modern look. Your instructors may require you to use a specific font, but if you get to choose, you'll want to think about what look you want for your text—and what will be most readable. Some readers find serif fonts easier to read in longer pieces of writing. Sans serif, on the other hand, tends to be easier to read in slide presentations. Save novelty or decorative fonts such as **Impact** or *Allegro* for your nonacademic writing—and even there, use them sparingly, since they can be difficult (or annoying!) to read.

Most fonts include **bold**, *italics*, and underlining options, which you can use to highlight parts of a text. In academic writing, bold is generally used for headings, whereas italics or underlining is used for titles of books, films, and other long works. If you're following MLA, APA, or another academic style, make sure that your use of fonts conforms to the style's requirements.

Readability matters. For most academic and workplace writing, you'll want to use 10-to-12-point type, and at least 18-point type for most presentation slides. Academic writing is usually double-spaced; letters and résumés are single-spaced.

ADDING HEADINGS

Brief texts may need no headings at all, but for longer texts, headings can help readers follow the text and find specific information. Some kinds of writing have set headings that authors are required to use— IMRAD reports, for instance, require introduction, methods, research, and discussion headings. When you include headings, you need to decide on wording, fonts, and placement.

Wording. Make headings succinct and parallel. You could make them all nouns ("Energy Drinks," "Snack Foods"), all gerund phrases ("Analyzing the Contents of Energy Drinks," "Resisting Snack Foods"), or all questions ("What's in Energy Drinks?" and "Why Are Snack Foods So Hard to Resist?").

Fonts. If you've chosen to divide your text further using subheadings, distinguish different level headings from one another typographically by using bold, italic, underlining, and capitalization. For example:

First-Level Heading
Second-Level Heading
Third-Level Heading

When you get to choose, you may want to make headings larger than the main text or to put them in a different font or color (as we do throughout this book). But if you're following MLA or APA styles, be aware that they require headings to be in the same font as the main text.

Placement. You can center headings or set them flush left above the text, or place them to the left of the text; but whatever you do, treat each level of heading consistently throughout the text. If you're following MLA style, set all headings flush left. If you're following APA style, center first-level headings.

USING COLOR

Sometimes you'll be required to write in black type on a white background, but many times you'll have reason to use colors. In some media, color will be expected or necessary—on websites or presentation slides, for instance. Other times it may be inappropriate—in a thank-you note following a job interview at a law firm or in an application essay to business school. As with any design element, color should be used to help you get a message across and appeal to an audience, never just to decorate your text.

Be aware that certain colors can evoke specific emotional reactions: blue, like the sky and sea, suggests spaciousness and tranquillity; red invokes fire and suggests intense energy and emotions; yellow, the color of our sun, generates warmth and optimism. Also remember that certain colors carry different associations across cultures—to Westerners, white suggests innocence and youth, but in China white is traditionally associated with death (which is why Chinese brides wear red).

Especially if you use more than one color in a text, you'll want to consider how certain colors work together. Look at the color wheel on the next page to see how the colors are related. *Primary colors* (red, blue, and yellow) create

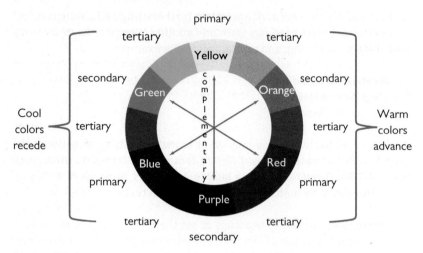

A color wheel.

an effect of simplicity and directness. The more *secondary* and *tertiary colors* you use, the more sophisticated the design. *Complementary colors*, located opposite each other on the color wheel, look brighter when placed next to each other but can sometimes clash and look jarring. (Black and white are also considered complementary colors.) Cool and dark colors appear to recede, whereas warm and bright colors seem to advance. So using both cool and warm colors can create a feeling of movement and energy.

Remember that any color scheme includes the type, the background, and any images or graphics that you use. If colorful photos are an important part of your website, they'll stand out most strongly on a white background and with black type—both of which you may want to use for that reason alone. If you're writing a report that includes multicolored pie charts and want to have color headings, you wouldn't want to use primary colors in the headings and pastels in the charts. In short, if you use colors, make sure they work well with all the other design elements in the text.

Using color to guide readers. Like bold or italic type, color can help guide readers through a text. In fact, that's the way color is used in this book. The headings are all red to make them easy to spot, and keywords are color-coded a pale orange to signal that they're defined in the glossary/index. In addition, we've color-coded parts of the book—roadmaps are on yellow pages, readings are light blue, research chapters are green, style chapters are lavender, design and delivery chapters are aqua—to help readers find them easily.

Color is an important navigational element on websites as well, sometimes used to indicate links and to highlight headings. For such uses of color, it's important to choose colors that are easy to see.

Considering legibility. Using color can make your writing easier—or harder—to read. Use type and background colors that are compatible. Dark type on a light background works best for lengthy pieces of writing, while less text-heavy projects can use a light text on a dark background for visual effect. In either case, be sure that the contrast is dramatic enough to be legible. Keep in mind that some people can't see or distinguish certain colors (notably, red and green).

USING VISUALS

Authors today write with more than just words. Photos, charts, tables, and videos are just some of the visual elements you can use to present information and to make your writing easier or more interesting to read. Would a photo slideshow help listeners see a scene you're describing in an oral presentation? Would readers of a report be able to compare data better in a table or chart than in a paragraph? Would a map or diagram help readers see how and where an event you're describing unfolded? These are questions you should be asking yourself as you write.

Be sure that any visuals you use are relevant to what you have to say—that you use them to support your point, not just to decorate your text. And remember that even the most spectacular images do not speak for themselves: you need to refer to them in your text and to explain to readers what they are and how they support what you're saying.

Kinds of Visuals

You may be assigned to include certain kinds of visuals in your writing—but if not, a good way to think about what sorts of visuals to use (or not) is by considering your rhetorical situation. What visuals would be useful or necessary for your topic and purpose? What visuals would help you reach

A photo of street art in a Texas parking lot demonstrates the layering effect of graffiti in a way that would be difficult to do with words alone.

your audience? What kinds of visuals are possible in your medium—or expected in your genre?

Photographs can help an audience envision something that's difficult to describe or to explain in words. A good photo can provide powerful visual evidence for an argument and can sometimes move readers in a way that words alone might not. Think of how ads for various charities use photos of hungry children to appeal to readers to donate.

Photos can be useful for many writing purposes, letting readers see something you're **DESCRIBING** or **ANALYZING**, for instance, or even something you're **REPORTING** on. (See how Melissa Rubin needed to include a photo of the ad that she analyzes on p. 276, and how Katherine Spriggs included photos of two different kinds of farms in her argumentative essay on p. 177.) You can take your own photos or use ones that you find in other sources. Remember, however, to provide full documentation for any photos that you don't take yourself and to ask permission before photographing people and using their image in your writing.

Videos are useful for demonstrating physical processes or actions and for showing sequences. Your medium will dictate whether you can include videos in a text. The print version of a newspaper article about aerialist skiers, for instance, includes a still photo of a skier in mid-jump, whereas the same article on the newspaper's website and on a TV news report features videos showing the skier in action. Your topic and genre will affect whether or not you have reason to include video if you can. If you were writing a PRO-CESS ANALYSIS to teach a skier how to perform a certain aerial maneuver, a video would be far more useful than the still photo you might include if you were writing a PROFILE of a professional skier.

Graphs, charts, and tables. Numerical and statistical data can be easier both to describe and to understand when they are presented visually. See the fantasy sports graphics on this page, for example—and imagine trying to present that data in a paragraph. You'll often have occasion to present data in graphs or charts, in bar graphs, pie charts, and the like, especially in REPORTS and ANALYSES. In many cases, you'll be able to find tables and graphs in your research and then incorporate them into your own writing. You can also use templates found in *Excel, Word, PowerPoint,* and other programs to create charts and tables yourself. Whether you find or create them, be sure to indicate in your text where the information comes from and how they support your argument.

Line graphs are useful for illustrating trends and changes over time—how unemployment fluctuates over a period of years, for instance. By using more than one line, you can compare changes in different variables, such as unemployment for those with a college education and those with only a high school education. When comparing more

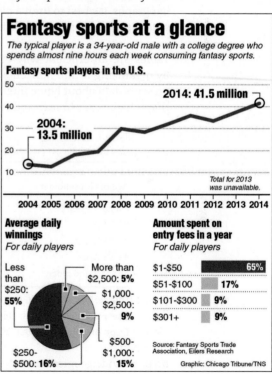

A line graph shows the rising number of fantasy sports players over a period of 10 years; a pie chart and a bar graph break down average winnings and entry fees.

than one variable, the lines should be in two different colors so that readers can easily see the comparison.

Bar graphs are useful for comparing quantitative data, such as for different age groups or different years. In the example about fantasy sports, the bars make it easy to see how much most players spend to participate in fantasy sports leagues. It would be easy enough to convey this same information in words alone—but more work to read and harder to remember.

Pie charts give an overview of the relative sizes of parts to a whole, such as what share of a family budget is devoted to food, housing, entertainment, and so on. Pie charts are useful for showing which parts of a whole are more or less significant, but they are less precise (and harder to read) than bar graphs. It's best to limit a pie chart to six or seven slices, since when the slices become too small, it's difficult to see how they compare in size.

Tables are an efficient way of presenting a lot of information concisely by organizing it into horizontal rows and vertical columns. Table 1 below presents data about home internet access in the United States, information that is made easy to scan and compare in a table.

Table I
US Home Internet Access by Age Group, 2009

Age of Householder	No In-Home Internet (%)	In-Home Internet (%)
Under 25 years	33.0	67.0
25-34 years	25.8	74.2
35-44 years	22.2	77.8
45-55 years	24.2	75.8
55 years and older	41.8	58.2

Source: United States Dept. of Commerce, Census Bureau; "Internet Use in the United States: October 2009," Current Population Survey; US Dept. of Commerce, Oct. 2009; Web; 11 June 2012; table 1.

Maps provide geographic context, helping to orient your audience to places mentioned in your text. A report on the 2011 earthquake in New Zealand, for example, includes the maps on the facing page showing where the earthquake was centered and where the most damage was done. Include a map when location is important to your point.

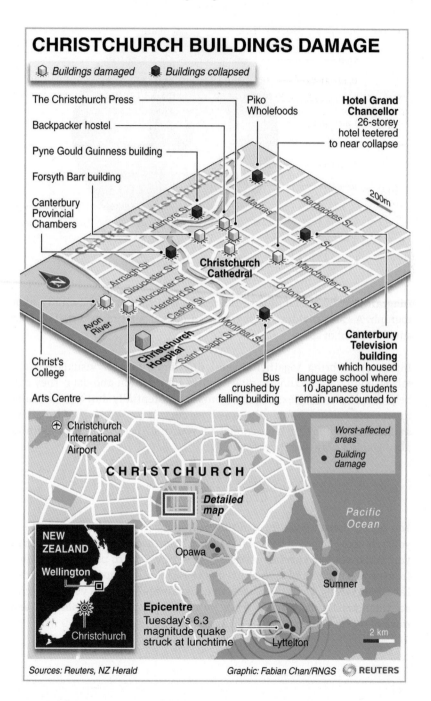

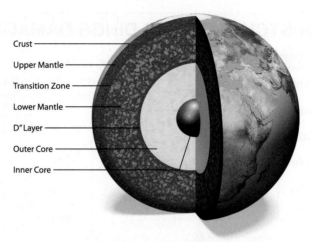

Crust
Upper Mantle
Transition Zone
Lower Mantle
D" Layer
Outer Core
Inner Core

A diagram of the earth's internal structure shows the various layers.

Diagrams are useful for illustrating details that cannot be shown in a photograph. A carefully drawn diagram can deliver a lot of information in a small amount of space.

Infographics bring together several different types of visuals—charts, tables, photos, and so on—to give detailed information and data. They can help simplify a complex subject—or make a potentially dull topic visually interesting. Because infographics can be so densely packed with information, make sure that they are large enough for your audience to be able to read and arranged in a way that they can follow.

Creating Visuals

You can find visuals online, scan them from print sources, or create them yourself using basic software or a camera. If you come across an illustration you think would be useful, make or save a copy. Scan or photocopy visuals from print sources, and save a link or take a screen grab from digital sources. Label everything clearly. Be aware that visuals and any data you use to create them need to be **DOCUMENTED** in a **CAPTION** or source note—so keep track of where you found everything as you go.

- *Photographs and videos.* If you plan to print an image, save each file in as high a resolution as possible. If a photo is only available in a very small size or low resolution, try to find a more legible option. Be careful about cropping, adjusting color, and altering images or videos in other ways that could change the meaning; straying too far from the original is considered unethical.

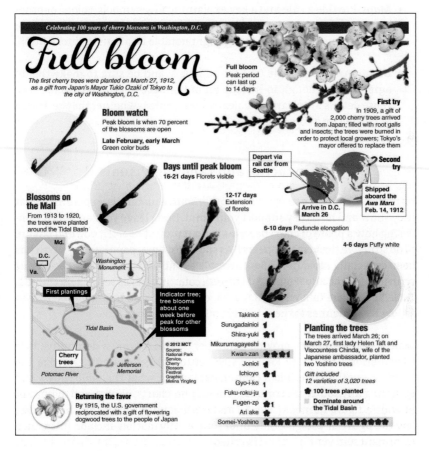

This infographic on the cherry blossom season in Washington, DC, includes photos, diagrams, maps, and a bar chart.

- *Graphs, charts, and tables.* Be consistent in your use of fonts and colors, especially if you include more than one graph, chart, or table. Be sure that the horizontal (*x*) and vertical (*y*) axes are labeled clearly. If you use more than one color, add labels for what each color represents. When you have many rows or columns, alternating colors can make categories easier to distinguish.

- *Maps.* Provide a title and a key explaining any symbols, colors, or other details. If the original is missing these elements, add them. If you create the map yourself, be sure to highlight notable locations or information.

- *Diagrams.* Use a single font for all labels, and be sure to make the diagram large enough to include all of the necessary detail. Make sure these details are clearly and neatly represented, whether they're drawn or created on a computer.

Introducing and Labeling Visuals

Introduce visuals as you would any other source materials, explaining what they show and how they support your point. Don't leave your audience wondering how a photo or chart pertains to your project—spell it out, and be sure to do so *before* the visual appears ("As shown in fig. 3, population growth has been especially rapid in the Southwest"). Number visuals in most academic writing sequentially (Figure 1, Figure 2), counting tables separately (Table 1, Table 2). If you're following MLA, APA, or another academic style, be sure to follow its guidelines for how to label tables and figures.

MLA STYLE. For tables, provide a number ("Table 1") and a descriptive title ("Population Growth by Region, 1990–2010") on separate lines above the table; below the table, add a caption explaining what the table shows and including any source information. For graphs, charts, photos, and diagrams, provide a figure number ("Fig. 1") and caption with source information below the figure. If you give only brief source information, include full source information in your list of works cited.

APA STYLE. For tables, charts, diagrams, graphs, and photos, provide a number ("Table 1" or "Figure 1") and a descriptive title on separate lines above the table or figure; below the table or figure, include a note explaining any elements whose meanings are not apparent in the table or figure and providing source information if the table or figure is adapted or reprinted from another source.

PUTTING IT ALL TOGETHER

Once you've chosen fonts, colors, and visuals, you need to think about how they all come together as a text. Look, for instance, at the homepage of TED, a nonprofit group dedicated to disseminating "ideas worth spreading." It's easy to read with a sans serif font and minimal text. The logo draws your eye because it's large, red, capitalized, and positioned in the upper left corner of the screen. The soft gray "ideas worth spreading" complements the red and leads your eye to the bold black text below—"Riveting talks by remarkable people, free to the world"—which defines the group's purpose and

audience. Each of the images is a link to a specific TED talk. Note how white space separates the parts and makes the page easy to read. No surprise that this site won a Webby Award, the online equivalent of an Oscar.

You may not have occasion to design anything as large or complex as the TED site, but the same design principles will apply for all the writing you do. Whether you're designing a report, a photo essay, or a slide presentation, chances are you'll be working with some combination of words, images, graphs, and other graphic elements that you'll need to put on paper or screen in order to reach a certain audience to achieve a certain purpose.

Look beyond the details and think about what you want your design to accomplish. Do you want it to help your audience grasp a message as fast as possible? convey your identity as a creative author? conform to the requirements of a certain academic style? be appealing yet simple enough to implement by an approaching deadline? Thinking about what you want your design to do can help you determine how to put it all together in a way that achieves your end goal.

Keep it simple. Sometimes you'll need to follow a prescribed organization and layout, but if you get to decide how to design your document, here's a piece of advice: don't make your design any more complex than it has to be. Readers want to be able to find the information they need without having to spend time deciphering a complex hierarchy of headings or an intricate navigational system.

Think about how to format your written text. Should it all be in paragraphs, or is there anything that should be set off as a list? If so, should it be a bulleted list to make it stand out, or a numbered list to put items in a sequence? If your text includes numerical data, should any of it be presented in a graph, chart, or table to make it easier for readers to understand? Is there any information that's especially important that you'd like to highlight in some way?

Notice how we've placed the visual elements here in your textbook. In the Barlett and Steele reading, for example, all of the photos are at the top of their respective pages, making the essay easier to follow on the page. Check it out on p. 823.

Position visuals carefully. Keep in mind how they will look on a page or screen. Placing them at the top or bottom of a print page will make it easier to lay out pages. If your text will be online, you have more freedom to put visuals wherever you wish. Reproduce visuals at a large enough size so that readers will be able to see all the pertinent detail, but be aware that digital images become fuzzier when they are enlarged. Reduce large image files by saving them in compressed formats such as JPEGs or GIFs; you don't want readers to have problems loading the image. And once everything is in place, look over your text carefully to be sure that nothing is too small or blurry to read.

Use white space to separate the parts of your text. Add some extra space above headings and around lists, images, graphs, charts, and tables. This will keep your text from looking cluttered and make everything easier to find and read.

Organize the text. Whether your text is a simple five-page report or a full website, readers will need to know how it's organized and how to find the information they're looking for. In a brief essay, you might simply indicate that in a sentence in your introduction, but in lengthier pieces, you may need headings, both to structure your text and to make it easy for readers to navigate.

If you're creating a website, you'll need to figure out how you're dividing materials into pages and to make that clear on the site's homepage. Most homepages have a horizontal navigation bar across the top indicating and linking to the main parts and often another navigation menu going down the left side of the screen, with links to specific materials on the site. These menus should appear in the same position on every page of the site—and every page should include a link to take readers back to the homepage. Take a look at the examples from *National Geographic* on the following page and you'll see the consistent elements that help readers navigate the site: navigation bars at the top, links to popular information in bulleted lists, ads in the bottom right corner, consistent colors and fonts on all the pages.

GETTING RESPONSE TO YOUR DESIGN

Whether you're composing a report, an illustrated essay, or a blog post, try to get response to the design. Enlist the help of friends or classmates, asking them what they think of the "look" of your text, how easy it is to read, and so on. Following are some specific things they (and you) should consider:

- Is the design appropriate to the text's **PURPOSE**, **AUDIENCE**, **GENRE**, and **MEDIUM**? Consider the fonts and any use of color: do they suit your rhetorical situation?

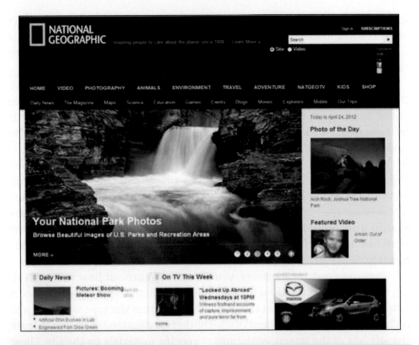

Examples from the *National Geographic* website.

- Does the design make the main parts of your text easy to see? If not, would it help to add headings?

- Is there any information that should be set off as a list?

- Does the text include any data that would be easier to follow in a chart, table, or graph?

- If you've included images, what purpose do they serve? How do they support the point of your text? If some are only decorative, should you delete them?

- Does the overall "look" of your text suit the message that you want to convey?

Remember: your design is often the first impression readers get, and it can make all the difference in getting your message across. There may be a lot at stake in the simple choice of a font or color or image, so make these choices carefully—and make your design work for you.

〰️⟳ *REFLECT. Find a design that you think is attractive (or not)—a book cover, a magazine spread, a brochure, a poster, a blog, a website, whatever.* **ANALYZE** *its use of fonts, colors, and visuals. What works, and what doesn't? How would you revise the design if you could?*

THIRTY-FIVE

Writing in Multiple Modes

Ever since the days of illustrated books and maps, texts have included visual elements for the purpose of imparting information. The contemporary difference is the ease with which we can combine words, images, sound, color, animation, and video . . . so that they are part of our everyday lives.

—NCTE ON MULTIMODAL LITERACIES

He National Council of Teachers of English made this statement more than a decade ago, and in the years that have passed, multimodal literacies have indeed become part of the "everyday lives" of students everywhere. Take a look at the cartoon on the next page, for example.

The little boy in this cartoon illustrates the NCTE statement perfectly: he lies in bed, listening to his dad read him a story. But the boy does more than just listen: he compliments his dad on his reading ("darn good job") and offers to record him reading and then "podcast" him on his website. Multimodal, indeed.

Defining Multimodal Writing

So just what are these multimodal texts? Put most simply, they are texts that draw on more than words, bringing in still or moving images, sound, and so on. Researcher Cynthia Selfe identifies five modes writers can use to convey their messages: linguistic (that's words, written or spoken); visual (colors, fonts, images, and so on); audio (tone of voice, music, and

"You know, Dad, you do a darn good job.
You should let me record you sometime, and
I'll podcast you on my website. Just a thought."

other sounds); gestural (body language and facial expression); and spatial (the way elements are arranged on a page or screen).

For hundreds of years, writers have relied primarily on two of these modes, the linguistic and the visual. In this sense, all writing uses multiple modes, so multimodality is nothing new. And just like traditional print texts, more complex multimodal ones call for careful attention to the same conventions of good writing, research, and argument expected of all college writing.

But today writers have easy access to all five modalities and can produce texts that convey meaning not only through words but also through sounds, moving and still images, animations, and more—delivered through print, spoken, and digital media. For you as a writer, that opens up an infinite number of options. This chapter offers some tips for deciding among those options and for making best use of the various technologies available for writing in multiple modes.

REFLECT. *Make a list of writing assignments you've done this term and of any writing projects you have worked on out of class. How many of them rely on printed words on a page? How many use multiple modes—and what are they? On the basis of this exercise, write (or draw, or record) a reflection about yourself as a writer of multimodal texts. Then consider the next piece of writing you're preparing to do. How might you use sounds, images, and other modes to get your message across?*

Considering Your Rhetorical Situation

Writing in multiple modes calls for the same close attention to rhetorical principles that all writing does. Whatever your topic, the following questions can help you think about your purpose, audience, and the rest of your rhetorical situation:

Consider your PURPOSE. Why are you creating this project? What are your purposes or goals? No doubt one purpose is to fulfill an assignment—and do a good job of it. But you may have other purposes as well: to raise awareness about a problem on campus; to convince someone to support a project you have in mind; to provide information. Consider the message you want to communicate. What do you want to see happen as a result of what you write?

Think about your AUDIENCE. Whom are you aiming to reach, and how can you best reach them? If you're writing to all members of your campus community, you'll probably want to post your message online, but if you're writing to neighbors about a lost dog, posters might work better. If your intended audience is limited to people you know (such as on a website accessible only to students at your school), you may make some assumptions about them and how they're likely to respond. But remember that most projects you put online may well be accessible to the public—that is, to people you don't and can't know. In this case, it's important not to make assumptions about what they know and to be respectful of the diverse audience that may read what you write.

Think about your STANCE. What is your attitude toward your topic, and how do you want to present yourself as an author—as well-informed? outraged? perplexed? How can you convey that stance? Certain fonts look serious while others look silly; same thing with colors. If you're including music, that too affects the tone. If you're giving an oral presentation, your facial expression and gestures can signal something about your stance.

Choose your GENRE. The kind of writing you're doing can sometimes determine the form that your multimodal project will take. If you're **REPORTING** information, a wiki might be an appropriate choice. But if you're delivering a **PROPOSAL** asking for funding for an event, a print text may be most appropriate. And if afterward you want to create a **NARRATIVE** documenting the event, a video essay might capture the experience most vividly.

Consider the larger CONTEXT. How much time do you have, and is your topic narrow enough that you can do a good job in that amount of time? Do you have access to whatever technology you will need? If you'll need to learn new software, remember to build in time for that. Does your campus offer any services (perhaps at a writing center) where you can get help?

Consider MEDIA. What media will best serve your audience, purpose, and topic? If you're writing about Bollywood films, you might create a blog, which would enable you to embed video clips and to reach a community of fans. If you want to inform fellow students about ways to save water, you might create an infographic to post in restrooms around campus.

KINDS OF MULTIMODAL PROJECTS

A wide range of multimodal projects have made their way into classrooms at colleges and universities across the country. The most prevalent and popular of these projects are illustrated essays, blogs, wikis, audio essays, video essays, and posters. Following are some tips for composing each of these kinds of writing.

Illustrated Essays

Probably the simplest and most likely multimodal assignment you will encounter is an essay in which you're asked to embed illustrations—photos, drawings, maps, graphs, charts, and so on. Illustrated essays offer you a chance for creativity and for getting your point across in multiple ways; in fact, such writing is a staple in all newspapers and most magazines today. So there's no reason why your college assignments should be words only, not when you have so many other elements to work with.

> In Trujillo and Hastings's graphic essay, the words and the drawings are woven together so well that neither element could stand alone. See how they've done it on p. 1048.

　　See how one student used images in an essay about how Japanese video games are no longer being "localized," that is, remade so as to better appeal to foreign audiences.

Even companies like Nintendo, which had previously relied on the denationalized nature of their characters for international success, have begun capitalizing on uniquely Japanese concepts. For example, the Tanooki Suit is an item introduced with *New Super Mario Bros. 3* that allows Mario to

Fig. 1. The box art for *Super Mario Bros. 3* prominently featured Raccoon Mario . . .

Fig. 2. . . . while art for later releases focused on Tanooki Mario, who, although present in *Super Mario Bros. 3*, was not nearly as prominent as in *3D Land* or *3D World*.

transform into a tanuki, or Japanese raccoon dog. In the original release of *Super Mario Bros. 3*, Tanooki Mario was de-emphasized in favor of Raccoon Mario, which was prominently featured on the cover art, since Americans were more likely able to identify a raccoon rather than a tanuki (see figure 1). However, with the release of *Super Mario 3D Land*, which some consider to be a spiritual successor to *Super Mario Bros. 3* (Sterling), Nintendo fully embraced the Tanooki power-up and made it the primary focus both in their advertising and in-game, with many enemies gaining Tanooki tails. This newly realized proliferation of Tanooki extended into its sequel, *Super Mario 3D World* (see figure 2) and related games, such as *Mario Kart 7*. By embracing their cultural heritage rather than disguising it, Nintendo helps introduce Western gamers to elements of Japanese culture they may otherwise not be aware of, no longer fearful of culture shock.

—RUIZHE (THOMAS) ZHAO, "Word for Word: Culture's Impact on the Localization of Japanese Video Games"

Notice how Zhao has carefully incorporated the two images into his argument, labeling them with figure numbers, referring to them in the text, and providing captions for each one. Though it's not shown here, he also included documentation information in a works-cited list. Far from being mere decoration, these images provide essential support for his argument.

Some Tips for Writing Illustrated Essays

- Make sure all illustrations help communicate your message. You never want to use illustrations as mere decoration.
- Refer to each illustration in the text and position each one carefully so that it appears near the text where it's discussed.
- Give each illustration a figure number and a caption that tells readers what it is.
- Provide documentation for any illustrations that you don't create yourself, either in a caption or in a works-cited list.

Blogs

Blogs—an abbreviation of "weblogs"—are regularly updated sites on which writers post reflections, ideas, information, and arguments. They often include images, embedded audio or video clips, and links to other sites. Some blogs focus on a single topic (Deb Perelman's *Smitten Kitchen* blog focuses on home cooking; Nate Silver's *FiveThirtyEight* analyzes politics, economics, and sports), but those run by newspapers, advocacy organizations, or other institutions cover a wide range of topics (the *Huffington Post* hosts dozens of blogs by politicians, academics, celebrities, and many ordinary folks who have something to say). Almost all blogs allow readers to comment and thus function as sites where people share and discuss information and ideas. Blogs are a part of the everyday landscape of the web: as of May 2019, the blogging platform *Tumblr* hosted well over 467 million blogs—including *everyonesanauthor.tumblr.com*, the companion site to this book.

Blogs are frequently assigned in college classes. You may have been assigned to post responses to one, or maybe you have a blog yourself. Check out the following excerpt from a blog posting in the *Huffington Post* by Julia Landauer, who was a college student as well as a NASCAR driver when she wrote this post:

The Lady Up Front

"Boogity boogity boogity, let's just go racing!" screams Darrell Waltrip from the booth. That's when you know the green flag has flown and the Daytona 500 is under way.

Julia Landauer,
NASCAR driver.

Normally Waltrip says, "Boogity boogity boogity, let's go racing, boys!" But from here on out his trademark phrase will have to be slightly altered to include the sole lady racer, Danica Patrick.

I was thrilled when Danica qualified on pole [won the number one starting position by having the fastest qualifying time] for the 55th running of the Daytona 500. Yes, I wanted to be the first woman to do that, but women in racing is bigger than me. In the effort to draw in more female racers, crewmembers and race/safety officials to the sport, Danica's history-making pole was a huge contribution. Hopefully this contribution will help catapult more women into the sport.

People will critique it, saying that a pole on a super speedway (oval tracks that are over 2 miles long, such as Daytona or Indy) is irrelevant to the rest of the season, so Danica's accomplishment is not a big deal. How wrong! The fact is that success is success and if people consider super speedway poles and wins to be "easy accomplishments," then they should be taken out of the schedule. Or people shouldn't make a big deal about other racers finding success on them. But clearly there is a prestige that goes along with setting pole and winning at Daytona, which can't be taken away from Danica.

The big picture is that Danica showed that women can run up front at the highest levels of racing. There were concerns as to whether she'd

Danica Patrick's race car.

be able to stay up front, and she did; she was in the top five for the ma-jority of the race and even became the first woman to lead laps at the Daytona 500.

Despite finishing 8th, which is still quite respectable, Danica did a great job and set the stage for the future of women in racing. Lyn St. James, retired racer and first female to win the Indianapolis 500 Rookie of the Year award, stated in an interview with CNN, "[Danica] did ev-erything right for the whole race . . . she learned a lot and earned respect from so many people that it was a terrific start of the season and a posi-tive example for women everywhere."

To piggyback off of Lyn's comment, my favorite result from Danica winning the pole comes in something Ella Gordon, Jeff Gordon's daugh-ter, finally realized. As the *Atlantic* pointed out, Danica's pole brought widespread publicity to the fact that women can be racecar drivers too, something that 4-year-old Ella hadn't previously understood to be a pos-sibility. Now think of what all the other little girls who grow up around racing are thinking! We can do it too.

—JULIA LANDAUER, "The Lady Up Front"

Note that the photo of Landauer is one she includes on the blog, in racing gear—a personal touch that helps to build her readership, especially among the women she wants to see join this sport. Her title, "The Lady Up Front," gives a clue about the topic and is meant to intrigue any readers who as-sume that racing is a man's sport. In providing detailed information about a Daytona 500 race, she quotes from CNN and includes a link to an article in the *Atlantic*. Landauer's writing is informal and friendly, and her point is clear: girls "can do it too."

While you may create a blog of your own, you'll probably also find yourself responding to other people's posts or being assigned to do so for a class. See one response to a post on the *Web of Language* blog run by linguis-tics professor Dennis Baron. The response is to a posting he wrote in 2010, "Should Everybody Write?"

shon.bacon@ttu.edu Mar 9, 2010 12:08 am

Nice post. This makes me think about a question I've had for a while now with participatory culture and everyone being a producer—pro-ducer and user. With the internet and social media, the idea of "audi-ence" has blurred quite a bit considering, as this post notes, that anyone can create content. The idea of a participatory culture, of everyone having a voice, sounds great in theory, but I'm not sure how beneficial it is to have all voices create a cacophony instead of a well-blended harmony. I guess this is my longwinded way of answering your question. My short version: "Yes, but . . ."

Note that the author of this response raises a question of his own that relates to Baron's post, about the blurring of the line between author and audience. He builds on what Baron has written and then concludes by answering Baron's original question about whether everyone should write: "Yes, but . . . "

Some Tips for Posting to a Blog

- Blog posts are usually fairly brief and to the point because bloggers assume that their readers are reading for specific information. With this in mind, make sure your posts have a point—and that you make that point clear.
- Blogs tend to be written in fairly informal, conversational language.
- Many readers scan blogs for information, so use lists, headings, italics, and other design elements to make your text easy to scan.
- When appropriate, include images or embed audio or video clips to help make your message clear.
- Include links to guide your readers to additional information.
- Invite feedback: ask questions so that readers will naturally want to comment and respond.
- Give your post a compelling title, one that will make readers want to read on. Try to use keywords that will help your post turn up on a search site.

Wikis

Wikis are collaborative websites that invite readers to add and edit content, allowing them to make changes to an existing page, link to other pertinent pages, or even create new pages. Wikis serve as running records of information that is shared within online communities of various kinds: doctors, gamers, students and staff of a college—or, in the case of *Wikipedia*, the entire internet.

You're no doubt familiar with *Wikipedia,* the "free encyclopedia that anyone can edit." Since it started in 2001, it has grown from a site that many were suspicious of (Can you trust the information is correct?) into the first place many people go when looking for information. *Wikipedia* now contains over 5.8 million entries in its English version alone, the majority of which, it turns out, are reliable. And it has set a precedent for just how effective collaboration can be in creating and sharing knowledge. Here is part of *Wikipedia*'s entry on "wiki," showing how this particular web format works.

> A **wiki** is a website on which users collaboratively modify content and structure directly from the web browser. In a typical wiki, text is written using a simplified markup language and often edited with the help of a rich-text editor.[1]   —WIKIPEDIA.ORG, "Wiki"

This entry gives readers options to click for more information. Highlighted terms indicate links to pages about key concepts, and clicking on the numbers takes you to a list of references. The entry also includes—in true multimodal fashion—a video interview with Ward Cunningham, inventor of the wiki.

Some instructors use wikis to collect and add to class notes, creating a collaborative record of what is taught and said in class during the term. Maybe you've been assigned to contribute to an entry on *Wikipedia* or to a wiki for a class.

Whether you build a wiki or add to an existing one, you should think carefully about what community it serves. Wikis are never private sites—they're meant to be collaborative and shared! So in contributing to a wiki, you potentially become part of a huge collaborative project.

Some Tips for Contributing to a Wiki

- Be sure any information you present is authoritative and credible. Information should come from reliable sources, and you should check multiple sources before presenting it as fact.

- Remain fair and be respectful, both in your choice of topic and in what you say about it. Some wikis have rules for what content is allowed, and remember that while you may write whatever you wish, other editors can choose to delete it.

- Anticipate a broad audience. Don't assume others have background knowledge of your subject. Explain terms or events that may be unfamiliar, or link to pages on those topics.

- Offer information that will be useful to others. Write about something others will want to learn about!

- Add links, references, and citations that lead to reliable sources for more information.

- If you are adding links to a wiki entry, be sure that you have correctly coded the links so that they work, and make sure that the pages linked to actually exist.

- Remember that wikis are usually sites for shared revision. You will need to think carefully and respectfully before editing or changing other authors' contributions.

Audio Essays

The University of Wisconsin's Design Lab defines audio essays as ones that "explore topics using spoken text, audio interviews, archival recordings, music, environmental sounds, and/or sound effects" and notes that they "can make unfamiliar materials more accessible to new audiences and/or reveal new perspectives on familiar subjects."

↪ Russel Honoré's essay on p. 162 was written for *This I Believe*. Read it, and then listen to the audio version at everyonesanauthor .tumblr.com. What does he do differently for those listening to his text?

National Public Radio has helped popularize audio essays with its *This I Believe* and *This American Life* series. One of NPR's most popular pieces is humorist David Sedaris's readings from his "Santaland Diaries," which chronicle his experiences working as a department store elf one holiday season. Listen to the audio at everyonesanauthor.tumblr.com, paying attention to how the piece is structured in 45-to-50-second segments and how that structure affects the way you follow the story. Here's one segment of Sedaris's tale:

Twenty-two thousand people came to see Santa today, and not all of them were well-behaved. Today I witnessed fistfights and vomiting and magnificent tantrums. The back hallway was jammed with people. There was a line for Santa and a line for the women's bathroom. And one woman, after asking me a thousand questions already, asked, "Which is the line for the women's bathroom?" And I shouted that I thought it was the line with all the women in it. She said, "I'm going to have you fired."

I had two people say that to me today: "I'm going to have you fired." Go ahead. Be my guest. I'm wearing a green velvet costume; it doesn't get any worse than this. Who do these people think they are? "I'm going to have you fired."

And I want to lean over and say, "I'm going to have you killed."

—DAVID SEDARIS, "The Santaland Diaries"

Notice how the music at the beginning and the end of this segment helps bring together the narrative. And listen to Sedaris's voice: how it changes as he imitates the voice of the woman who threatens to have him fired— and then lowers and becomes more menacing at the end, concluding the segment with an unexpected shift in the narrative that keeps listeners engaged (and makes us laugh). That's good radio.

Some Tips for Composing an Audio Essay

- Decide on the software you will use. (*Audacity* and *GarageBand* are widely used.)

- Write out a script, using everyday language, short sentences, strong verbs, and active voice.

- If you are using sources, introduce them at the beginning of the sentence and paraphrase rather than quote.

- Use concrete examples and vivid imagery to help listeners see or imagine what you're describing. Sound effects can help establish setting.

- Organize your audio essay in chronological order, allowing for flashbacks and flashforwards if they are necessary to your story.

- Practice reading your script. Vary your tone of voice to keep listeners engaged. You might change your tone to imitate someone else speaking. (Or better yet, edit in sound clips of others speaking for themselves.)

- Follow *This American Life* host Ira Glass's "45-second rule": listeners expect some kind of break or change of pace every 45 to 50 seconds. Try to pace your essay accordingly.

- Use music to establish a mood, to mark transitions, and to keep your listeners engaged.

Video Essays

Video essays are popular, and not just on *YouTube*. Some students submit video essays as part of their college applications, and some employers are asking for videos as part of job applications. While anyone with a smartphone can create a video essay, it's not always easy.

Just like traditional essays composed with written words alone, video essays need to make some kind of point, to offer good reasons and evidence in support of that point, to acknowledge other points of view, and so on. Unlike print essays, however, video essays can use a combination of images, sounds, and words to make their point.

And you can present these images, sounds, and words in many different ways. Take images: you can use still images, moving images, and stop-motion images. Sounds can include people speaking on camera, voiceover, music, and background sounds. Words can be spoken, or they can be put on-screen as titles, subtitles, credits—even in thought bubbles. All these elements add up to infinite possibilities for authoring.

Multimedia journalist Adam Westbrook combines still photos, moving images, music, maps, charts, and more with spoken commentary in *Cause / Effect: The Unexpected Origins of Terrible Things*, a video essay arguing that World War I was caused not by the assassination of Archduke Franz Ferdinand but by Germany's desire for sea power. The video format allows Westbrook to present audio and visual evidence that makes a persuasive (and engaging) case for his argument—and to use both spoken and written language, from voiceover narration to labels identifying those pictured in historic photos.

➦ Go to everyonesanauthor.tumblr.com to watch *Cause / Effect: The Unexpected Origins of Terrible Things*.

A map and photograph from the video essay *Cause / Effect*.

Westbrook's example shows how complicated video essays can be to do, with words, images, and sounds all at work in multiple ways. A good way to plan out how all these elements will fit together is by creating a **STORY-BOARD**, a series of sketches that shows the sequence of scenes and actions in a film. Take a look at the storyboard on the next page showing five camera shots that follow a man as he walks down a hallway into his office, sits down, and is approached by someone holding a gun. The written words provide directions for the camera operator, noting places where there should be wide-angle shots, close-ups, and so on. A storyboard like this will serve as a blueprint as you shoot and edit a video essay.

Some Tips for Composing a Video Essay

- Decide which program you will use: *iMovie*, *Final Cut Pro*, and *Windows Live Movie Maker* are popular choices.

- Try to show much of the evidence for your argument visually, with images rather than just words.

- Think about the tone you want to project and how color, lighting, pacing, and music might evoke that tone.

- Draft a script for any text that will be spoken on camera or read as a voiceover—and practice reading it aloud.

- Create a storyboard to map out how the parts of your video essay will fit together. Use your storyboard to plan the shots you need before you begin shooting, and always shoot more than you think you'll need. It's easy to delete footage, much harder to get a single shot you missed.

- Consider a variety of camera angles. Wide-angle shots are useful for setting a scene; medium shots, for framing someone speaking to the camera; close-ups, for showing important details.

- Experiment also with moving the camera—following the subject, zooming in or out, panning left or right—but do so sparingly. You don't want to make your viewers dizzy!

- Use title cards to display written text if needed. You'll probably want to open with your title, and you might add text to identify the setting, time, and the name and title of someone speaking; to add captions or subtitles; or to mark transitions.

- Provide a written list of credits on the screen at the end, citing any sources you use and thanking those who helped.

↳ Go to everyonesan author.tumblr.com to browse examples of multimodal projects created by students.

A storyboard lays out the sequence of camera shots and transitions.

Posters

You're likely to have opportunities—and assignments—to create posters for classroom presentations, campus organizations, or academic conferences. And posters aren't what they were years ago when all that was needed was poster board and some markers; posters today have become sophisticated and multimodal ways of communicating information. Take a look at the poster on the following page that three students created in order to present the results of a research study. The topic is clearly stated in a heading at the top. The text is organized in three columns: one devoted to the motivation for the project, the second to the methods used, and the third to results and future directions. Data is presented in bar graphs, and other images illustrate and underscore key points in the report.

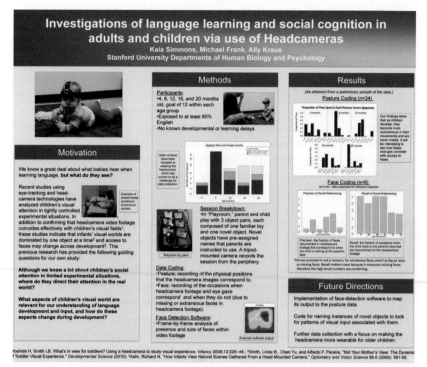

A poster created by a student research group to present its study.

Some Tips for Creating a Poster

- People often read posters at a glance, so present the information you want your audience to take away clearly and simply.

- Check to see if there are any guidelines for the size of the poster and whether it should be on a tabletop, an easel—or somewhere else.

- Think hard about how you can get your audience's attention: by asking a provocative question in a large bold font at the top of the poster? with color? an eye-catching image? something else?

- Keep the design simple: too many images, too much text, or distracting fonts make for a cluttered look that can be hard to follow.

- Be sure that any text is large enough to read—and that it is organized in a way that makes it easy to scan and understand quickly.

- Choose colors that will be easy to see. Primary colors are easier to see than pastels, as is dark text on a light background.

MANAGING A MULTIMODAL PROJECT

Managing a multimodal project is a bit like juggling: at any one time, you have multiple balls in the air, each one needing attention, and altogether it takes a lot of skill to keep them all airborne. While we can't provide guidelines for every step of every multimodal project you may encounter, we can offer some general advice about how to approach them.

Whether you're composing an illustrated essay, a blog, a video, or any other multimodal text, you will want to plan carefully for how your project will achieve your purpose with a particular audience and in a particular context. To do so, you'll need to carefully manage your time, your files, your project content, your sources, and more.

Managing your time. Make sure you know exactly how much time you have before your project is due and then be realistic about how to manage that time. Set up a calendar and block out specific times when you know you can work on the project; consider whether you'll have any class time to devote to it. If you're assigned to work with other students, set regular meeting times and draw up a schedule and task list together so that you each know your responsibilities. Breaking a project down into parts and setting deadlines for each part can help keep you on track. And don't forget to build in time to get response to a draft of your project—from your instructor if possible as well as from classmates and friends.

Managing project files. Writers traditionally used 3 × 5 index cards to keep track of information and sources, which were almost always print. But for many multimodal projects, it's likely you'll be using digital sources: GIF or JPEG image files, M4V or MOV video files, and so on. Create a folder on your computer where you can save in one place all the files you may want to use. Organize files according to type (images, charts, video clips, audio clips, and so on) and according to the organization of your project (clips for scene 1 of a video essay, graphs for the results section of a research poster). Be sure to label each file in a way that makes sense to you and to make note of where you found it, the date you downloaded it, and any other relevant source information—so that you can cite your sources properly and go back to them if need be. Your school might provide project management software access, but if not you'll want to look at free online options. A site like top5projectmanagement.com that offers descriptions and reviews can help you sort through the multiple possibilities.

Organizing your content. Some writers begin with nothing more than a pack of sticky notes, putting main points and sub-points and supporting reasons and evidence on individual stickies and arranging them on a larger surface. You might begin with an outline of the main points you want to make and the support for each one. This kind of careful organizing is crucial because it creates a "big picture" of your message and all its parts.

If you're creating a *video essay*, you might create a storyboard to put everything in sequence; another possibility would be a two-column script to line up the video and audio portions. *Audio essays* need some kind of script as well, one that accounts for both words and any music or other sounds. For an *illustrated print essay*, you'll need to decide where to put the images. For *wiki entries*, *blog posts*, and other kinds of online texts that readers navigate by links, you might map out your organization on a large sheet of paper, putting the main page at the center top and then drawing lines out to the various pages you will link to.

Crediting your sources. Be sure to credit your sources. You can do so at the bottom of a poster, as the last slide in an oral presentation, as footnotes in a wiki or links on a blog, or as credits at the end of a video or audio essay.

~~✿~~ *REFLECT. "This is the time for exploration, for experimentation. This is the time when we can create and risk, when we can write graffiti on the walls and color outside the lines. . . . If we are going to fly and find new intellectual spaces . . . we must expand our notion of academic discourse." That's a challenge that Stanford professor Adam Banks issued in 2015 to an audience of college writing instructors. How would you answer his challenge? Find a piece of academic writing you've done and imagine how you could re-create it using multiple modes.*

THIRTY-SIX

Making Presentations

HAT GOES INTO a sure-fire great presentation? Author and consultant Nancy Duarte wanted to find out. So she set out to study some great presentations, hundreds of them, beginning with Martin Luther King Jr.'s "I Have a Dream" speech and Steve Jobs's iPhone launch, two speeches that seemed so different to her that she couldn't imagine she would find anything in common. But she did.

She found that these two speeches—and hundreds of other terrific presentations—shared one common structure. Each speech begins by describing "what is"—and then goes on to suggest what it could (or should) be. That's in the introduction. Then in the middle of the speech, the presenter moves back and forth between discussing that status quo and what it could or should be. And in most cases, the conclusion vividly evokes what could be and calls for action.

Duarte's research shows that this basic structure (from what is to what could be) is very widely used, and especially so by activists, politicians, and businesspeople proposing change of some kind. In fact, it's a structure that may work well for many of the presentations you make in your college classes. And there are two common variations on this structure that you may be familiar with. One begins with what *was*, in the past, and then moves on to explain how it changed. The other opens by noting what others have said about a topic and then moves on to what you want to say about it, focusing on the benefits of your position. Starting with what is, what was, or what's been said and then suggesting

Martin Luther King Jr.

Steve Jobs.

something "better" uses a classic storytelling technique: setting up a conflict that needs to be resolved. And presenting your main point as a story works well in a spoken presentation because stories are easier to follow and remember than other kinds of evidence and are often more persuasive.

In 2014, Michelle Obama used such a story in a high school graduation speech in Topeka, Kansas, where the famous 1954 Supreme Court case *Brown v. Board of Education* originated, in which separate schools for black and white students were ruled unconstitutional. In that speech, she told the story of how that case came into being, what Topeka was like then, and how it had changed since. She brought her main point home at the speech's conclusion by telling the graduates about the grandniece of Lucinda Todd, the very first parent to sign on to the *Brown* lawsuit: that young woman was Obama's "right-hand woman" in the White House. It's this storyline, reaching from the original court case to the present moment, that summed up her point: change is possible, and the students in that audience could help bring it about.

Michelle Obama's commencement address at City College of New York follows a somewhat different pattern but still involves compelling stories. Read it on p. 989 and compare the messages.

Sounds simple, doesn't it? State your main point, find a story to help get that point across, and inspire the audience to accept what you say. But coming up with these elements in ways that will capture and hold an audience's attention—well, that's not simple. Still, there are some structures and techniques that will help you create presentations that audiences will listen to and remember and that might even call them to action. This chapter provides guidelines to help you do so.

ACROSS DISCIPLINES

You'll likely be required to give oral presentations, using slides or posters, in courses across different fields. This is because of the growing awareness that in the world of work, nearly everyone ends up sharing specialized knowledge with colleagues, (potential) clients, or the public through presentation. Different disciplines and professions have preferred practices. In fields like engineering and the lab sciences, presentations are often team affairs. In these and, in fact, many other fields, the preferred method of presentation is the "assertion-evidence" style: a speaker makes a claim and immediately presents the evidence to support that claim, often in visual form or with the aid of a visual. The website *Assertion-Evidence Approach*, created by Michael Alley at Penn State University, offers tutorials, sample slides, and videos of presentations by students. By watching the videos, you can get ideas about how to develop an effective presentation style that works for you. Seeking at models of effective presentations in your field is a good way to learn what's expected of you.

First, let's take a look at the script one of our students prepared for a presentation on Japanese manga. As you'll see, she used a "what was and how it changed" structure as a foundation for her presentation.

The Rise of Female Heroes in Shoujo Manga
HALLE EDWARDS

HERE'S A QUESTION FOR YOU: [SLIDE] Where are all the strong women heroes in popular comics? In our class we've seen some talented female authors of graphic narratives, but in terms of popular comic book characters (not to mention writers and fans), the girls have been outnumbered.

> Q: Where are all the strong female heroes?

[SLIDE] So guess what? When I started looking, I found the strong female heroes in comics! The place—Japan. The time period—the 1990s. The genre—Shoujo manga. Literally "girls' comics" in Japanese, Shoujo manga is a

---

HALLE EDWARDS composed this presentation for a second-year writing course that focused on graphic narratives. For this assignment, she first wrote an academic essay and then "translated" it into a ten-minute oral presentation with seventeen slides. As you'll see, we've included only a few of these slides.

popular form of comics in Japan typically written by women for women. Prior to the 1990s, Shoujo typically featured weak heroines and plots that revolved around romance. Then, in the 1990s, Shoujo started showing strong female heroes whose first priority wasn't romance. But what did that change look like and, more importantly, why did it happen?

Today I'll explore the answers. First I'll show you an example of this phenomenon, from Naoko Takeuchi's smash hit manga *Sailor Moon*. Then I'll explain what was happening in Japan in the 1990s and why this allowed Shoujo manga to change so drastically.

[SLIDE] Part one. *Sailor Moon* tells the story of Usagi, a clumsy and not particularly smart schoolgirl with a heart of gold. She discovers that she has a secret identity—Sailor Moon—and is destined to fight the forces of evil. [SLIDE] While *Sailor Moon* does have a love story, much of the manga is devoted to expanding on Sailor Moon's relationship with her eventual comrades—Sailors Mars, Mercury, Jupiter, and Venus. [SLIDE] The relationship of these five heroes is usually prioritized over the romance.

Wait a minute. Five female heroes? The romance is just a side plot? Girls described as soldiers who physically fight bad guys? For anyone familiar with traditional Shoujo manga, it's obvious that *Sailor Moon* pushed boundaries.

[SLIDE] This boundary-pushing can be seen in the introduction of the second female hero, Ami, or Sailor Mercury. Introduced as an aloof genius, Ami quickly reveals Takeuchi's friendly, playful side. [SLIDE] From the outset, Sailor Mercury cannot be pinned down to a stereotype—she's neither a cold nerd nor a bubbly teenager. She's very flawed and very real. Takeuchi's female heroes are layered, interesting, and compelling.

Throughout the story, we see Ami develop a close friendship with Usagi, [SLIDE] ultimately ending in a battle where Ami discovers her identity as Sailor Mercury. Meanwhile, Usagi's budding romance is barely a side plot. Throughout *Sailor Moon*'s five-year run, its female heroines were always the heart of the story—not the romance. The funny thing? Despite this drastic departure from typical Shoujo norms, *Sailor Moon* was a smash hit.

[SLIDE] So why was *Sailor Moon* so warmly received, given that it defied so many norms in Shoujo manga? To understand, you need to know a bit about Japan in the early 1990s. [SLIDE] In 1989, the Asset Price Bubble broke—essentially a huge economic bubble that vastly inflated real estate prices. [SLIDE] This sent Japan's economy spiraling into a recession that lasted throughout the entire 1990s, a decade now known as Japan's "lost decade."

[SLIDE] The recession changed many aspects of life in Japan. Before the recession, men could expect to get hired at a company out of college and work there for their whole lives. Meanwhile, women held mainly part-time jobs— think secretaries and office ladies—with few opportunities for advancement. However, once the recession hit, layoffs became rampant. Companies tanked. Men could no longer rely on having lifetime careers, and many in Japan questioned the long hours that were customary in Japan's workplaces.

What made the 1990s in Japan the "Era of Women"?

- Economic recession lowered job security for men

- More women worked outside the home

- More women voted

- Several female candidates were elected in 1989

[SLIDE] Meanwhile, in the 1989 elections, several female candidates were elected. Also, voter turnout among women was higher than ever. Because of this, the media predicted that the 1990s would be the "era of women." Women were suddenly seen as capable: they could hold real jobs outside the home, run for office, and help save Japan's stumbling economy. These new women were featured in popular soap operas known as "morning dramas" on the government-funded NHK channel.

[SLIDE] Given this media-propelled image of the new, strong woman, several of the major Shoujo magazines began to take note. Thus, when Toshio Irie, the newly minted editor of *Nakayoshi* magazine, learned of *Sailor Moon*, a story with five strong female heroes, he jumped at the opportunity. Not only did he publish Takeuchi's manga; he embraced a mixed-media strategy, including *Sailor Moon*–themed toys with the magazine (to encourage fans to buy their own copies and limit sharing) and selling additional *Sailor Moon* merchandise. [SLIDE] Also, when Toei Animation snapped up the rights to create an animated *Sailor Moon* series, Irie worked with the company to closely match the release of the new *Sailor Moon* chapters and episodes.

Such a media blitz was unheard of for a work of Shoujo manga, and it paid off. By the end of 1995, *Sailor Moon* had made over 300 billion yen in profits and was expanding rapidly worldwide. Circulation figures for the magazine reached an all-time high of 2 million per month. The thirteen volumes that had been released by then had sold over a million copies each and been exported to twenty-three countries.

[SLIDE] The recession, and the media's message that the 1990s would be the "era of women," caused forces in the media to realize that the image of strong women could be popular—and more importantly, profitable. As

a result, other manga editors were willing to publish works that featured strong female heroes—knowing that they would make money. This is one way that Shoujo sparked important change.

But why, you might be wondering, does it matter? This was just one time period in one country where comics featured strong women. Was it a phenomenon that spread to other countries? Did more girls start reading comic books and graphic narratives? And did life really change for women in Japan?

The simple answer is no. The "era of women" did not lead to significant change in the lives of women in Japan. They were still mostly relegated to part-time jobs and to most domestic responsibilities. And after the magical girl heroine trends of the 1990s, Shoujo in the 2000s became more focused on "slice of life" stories. This is not to say it went backwards—it just stopped moving forward so daringly.

However, the 1990s in Japan proved that there is a place, and an audience, for strong heroines in graphic narratives. Although there was little or no precedent for introducing strong women characters, a few key people took risks on some new stories, and they paid off. I think this is a lesson we can apply to the graphic novel market today. Just because there are still more male readers and characters in US comics does not mean that the market for strong female characters does not exist. In fact, the success of authors Lynda Barry and Alison Bechdel as well as of the hit TV series Marvel's *Agent (Peggy) Carter* suggests that the time may be ripe for many more strong women in graphic narratives. So let's heed the story of Sailor Moon and her crew and read and encourage others to buy works that feature strong women. Then when we're asked "where are all the strong women heroes in popular comics?" we can answer, "They're everywhere!"

[SLIDE] Thank you for listening. I'll be glad to take questions.

Halle Edwards opens her presentation with a statement about "what is"— that is, the status quo, which finds few strong female heroes in popular comic books. She then tells about a similar situation in Japan, and how it changed, exploring some of the issues in Japanese society that allowed women heroes to emerge and using the story of *Sailor Moon*'s success as the major example. Throughout, she poses questions to involve her audience, beginning by asking "Where are all the strong women heroes in popular comics?" Take a moment to count the number of questions in this presentation and where they occur and you'll see that they act as "signpost language," helping the audience follow the presentation and focusing their attention on its most important points. Notice as well that Edwards uses good presentational style: short sentences, simple syntax, clear transitions and other signpost language, active verbs, and vivid description—all things that make the presentation easy to listen to and to follow.

REFLECT. Halle Edwards's presentation grew out of a research paper she had written on the same topic. Look back at an academic essay you have written and then, using this chapter as a guide, make notes on what you would need to do to transform it into a memorable oral presentation.

MAKING A PRESENTATION / A Roadmap

Begin by considering your rhetorical situation

Anticipate who will be in your AUDIENCE. What do they already know about your topic, and what other information might they need? What kinds of evidence are most likely to appeal to them? You can keep your audience engaged by establishing eye contact and addressing them directly from time to time. If you're addressing your audience via video, make "eye contact" by looking into the camera.

Be clear about your PURPOSE. Make sure you understand any assignment you've been given for this presentation. Is your goal to provide information? to persuade? to propose some kind of action?

Think about your STANCE. How are you presenting yourself: as an expert? an interested novice? a researcher? an advocate? Be sure that the stance you are taking is appropriate for your topic and audience. Halle Edwards presents herself as a peer and classmate who has researched her topic and can thus speak with authority about it.

Consider the CONTEXT. Where will the presentation take place? What equipment will you need? Whatever it is, be sure to test it in advance—and keep in mind that technology glitches happen, so be sure to have a backup plan. How much time will you have? Who will introduce you?

Think about your GENRE. If you've been assigned a specific genre, say to report on a topic or to present a proposal, consult those chapters in this textbook for guidance. If not, see Chapter 11 for help choosing a genre.

Will you be using any MEDIA elements that need to be DESIGNED? Would showing images or information on a slide or flip chart help your audience follow your presentation? Will they expect some kind of visual aids? Will you be referring to a text or something else that you could put on a handout? Remember that slides and flip charts need to be simple enough and large enough for your audience to read as you speak.

Prepare your presentation

Focus on one main point, and then orchestrate everything else to support it. Halle Edwards begins with a question that signals her main point: where are all the strong women heroes in popular comics? In the rest of the presentation, she provides answers to this question in a story about the appearance of women heroes in Japanese manga, using *Sailor Moon* as her main example.

Gather EVIDENCE to support your point. Once you've decided on your main message, look for examples, statistics, stories, and other evidence that illustrates your point. Halle Edwards uses facts and statistics to support her main point—that, despite some changes, there are still not enough strong female heroes in comic books. Even the huge success of *Sailor Moon* failed to turn the tide in any permanent way.

Develop a clear structure. You can try using the structure Nancy Duarte recommends, focusing on what is (or was) and moving to what it could or should be (or how it changed). If that doesn't suit your topic, you might start by noting what else has been said about your topic as a way of introducing what you want to say about it. Any of these structures will set up a tension that your presentation then resolves—a storytelling technique that will make your argument easier for your audience to follow.

Use TRANSITIONS and other techniques to help listeners follow your presentation. It's always helpful to provide an overview of your talk, saying something like "I have four points to make," and then use those points as signposts in the presentation. One other useful technique is repetition. Halle Edwards repeatedly poses questions that mark turning points in her talk. Another good technique is to explain what you're saying as you go, using expressions such as "in other words." Provide printouts of your scripted presentation to hand out as access copies so your talk is accessible to everyone.

Use vivid language, images, and metaphors to hammer home your point clearly and memorably. The vivid language ("neither a cold nerd nor a bubbly teenager," "smash hit") and metaphors ("boundary-pushing") that Halle Edwards uses help her audience visualize and follow her argument.

But keep it simple. Remember that your audience doesn't usually have a script to read, so you need to speak in a way that will be easy to understand.

Notice that Halle Edwards uses fairly simple diction throughout—and that her sentences are short and follow a straightforward subject-verb-object structure. Even her paragraphs are short, some only a sentence or two— which helped her keep to her script without having to refer to it often as she spoke.

Develop a dynamic **INTRODUCTION**, one that will engage your audience's interest and establish some kind of **COMMON GROUND** with them. You'll also want to establish your **CREDIBILITY**, to show that you've done your home-work and can speak knowledgeably about your topic. Halle Edwards was addressing her classmates, so she could assume common ground, but she engaged their interest by asking a provocative question: "Where are all the strong women heroes in popular comics?" The way you open will depend on your topic and rhetorical situation, but whether you start by telling a story, making a startling claim, or summarizing what someone has said about your topic, your goal is to interest your audience in what is to come.

CONCLUDE in a way that leaves your audience thinking. Whether you conclude by reiterating your main point, saying why your argument mat-ters, or some other way, this is a moment when you can make sure your presentation has some kind of impact. Halle Edwards faced a challenge: her research had turned up strong female heroes in Japanese manga, but in the end they did not change the status quo. So she concluded by point-ing out that her research showed that there's "a place, and an audience, for strong heroines in graphic narratives." She then turned to her audience and challenged them to seek out such characters and to read the works they appear in.

Think about whether and where you need any visuals. Images can bring your presentation to life, illustrate important points, and engage your audi-ence. Any slides should support or explain a point you are making and need to be clear and easy to see so that your audience can process the information in a couple of seconds. It's therefore often better to convey one idea per slide than to provide a list of bullet points on a single slide. If you need to commu-nicate complex information, putting it in a chart or graph can make it easier for you to explain—and for your audience to understand. More detailed in-formation or material you want your audience to read is best presented on handouts. Try to distribute the handouts at the point when your audience needs them: if you give them out before then, some in the audience may be focusing on the handouts rather than on what you say.

If you'll be using slides or other media, you'll need to design them carefully.

- All slides need to be clearly visible to everyone in your audience, so use at least 24-point fonts. Simple bold fonts are easiest to read; avoid italic fonts, which can be difficult to read.

- Don't depend too much on templates for slides: the choices they build in—colors, fonts, layout, and so on—may not be appropriate for your topic or purpose.

- The most effective slides are simple enough for the audience to process the information they contain in a couple of seconds. As a general rule, it's better to convey one idea per slide than to provide a list of bullet points.

- At the same time, avoid walls of text. In other words, don't fill slides with long sentences.

- It's generally best to begin with a slide that includes the title of your presentation, your name (and those of your team members, if this is a group presentation), and any other relevant information such as the course or your institution if you're presenting to an outside group. If you are using a design such as a university logo, use it on only the opening slide.

- Make sure that any audio or video clips embedded in your presentation relate directly to the point you are making and that they are clear and easy to see and hear.

- Additionally, make sure any embedded audio or video clips will work properly on the technology you'll actually be using to give your presentation.

- Be sure that any visual you use contributes to your argument. Don't use visuals, especially clip art, that does not add value to your presentation.

- When you take visuals from other sources, acknowledge those sources, either on the slide in a small font or in the references at the end.

- Decorative backgrounds can be distracting, so avoid them unless they add something very specific to your presentation. In general, avoid special effects.

- When possible, present ideas in diagrams or charts that will be easy for the audience to understand.

- Be consistent. Using one font or color for headings and making them parallel in structure will help your audience follow what you are saying. Remember that some audience members may be color-blind, a fact that should influence your choice of color palette.

- Provide descriptions of your visuals in printed access copies so that those in the audience who can't see the slides can still follow your argument.

- Finally, be sure to get responses to your slides just as you would to drafts of your script. Note that Halle Edwards made her slides simple and clearly focused, intended to raise a question or illustrate or underscore a point. She used *PowerPoint* because she was making a linear argument; for less linear structures, you might use *Prezi*, which allows you to zoom in and out, looking at images in detail and from different perspectives.

Give your presentation

Practice, practice, practice. There is no substitute for practice. None. So schedule time to rehearse and make sure you can articulate your main message loud and clear at a moment's notice. Ask friends to serve as an audience for a full rehearsal, and be sure to time your presentation so that you don't go beyond the limit. When you're done, ask your friends to tell you your main point. If they can do so, then you've made an impression! Ask them as well how you came across—as friendly? authoritative? something else? If it's not what you're aiming for, talk through how you *want* to come across and how to get there.

Listen to how you use your voice. Record yourself speaking and then listen to what you sound like. Is your voice clear and loud enough to hear? Do you speak very quickly, or too slowly? Do you vary your tone of voice or tend toward a monotone? What can you do to improve this aspect of your delivery? If you're presenting alone, begin by introducing yourself and announcing the topic of your talk to get some idea of how your voice is projecting in the space where you're presenting. For a team presentation, all members should introduce themselves in order to hear their own voice and adjust their volume appropriately. After the introductions, the first speaker can announce the topic of the presentation for team presentations.

Establish eye contact with the audience by quickly scanning the audience at eye level. If you're uncomfortable making direct eye contact, focus a little higher than their heads at the back of the room. Do not look down at the floor; do not look up at the ceiling. Don't turn your back to the audience to read slides.

Stand up straight! And look at your audience. Try to avoid shifting from foot to foot or jingling change in your pockets. You want the focus to be on you and your message.

Move around. Especially if you are going to speak for more than five minutes, you won't want to stand cemented in place. Depending on the configuration of the room where you're presenting, be careful to avoid blocking the audience's view of the slides. In these cases, stand to the right or the left of the slides, out of the line of sight of the audience members.

THIRTY-SEVEN

Assembling a Portfolio

FOR HIS FIRST-YEAR WRITING CLASS, Julio Martinez was required to create a portfolio of his work to demonstrate how his writing had improved over the term. He included the drafts and final revision of a rhetorical analysis, along with two peer reviews he received; an annotated bibliography; and the drafts and final revision of a research report. Finally, he wrote a cover letter to his instructor in which he described, evaluated, and reflected on his writing—and set out several goals to work on after the term was over. He submitted his portfolio in print.

Not so for Susanna Moller, an art major who created a website during her sophomore year to host her portfolio of artwork. She included only finished works, organized by subject and style, and updated the site with new pieces throughout college. When she had her first solo show, she posted the review from the college newspaper. As graduation approached, she put her résumé on the site—and added the URL to résumés she sent to potential employers so they could see her work.

Deborah Burke began her portfolio blog with a first-year essay she was very proud of. The next year, she wrote a radio essay on the same topic; this became another item in her portfolio. Continuing her research, she wrote a play and added the script to her blog, along with a *YouTube* video of a scene from the play. Finally, she added her résumé and a statement reflecting on her work in college. This portfolio helped her to get an internship—and later a job.

Today, portfolios exist on paper and online. You may be required to keep a portfolio of your work for a writing course as a way of thinking about what you've learned, demonstrating and delivering to your instructor what you've written, and reflecting on your strengths and weaknesses as a writer. Or you may assemble a portfolio to showcase your best work to prospective employers. Whatever your purpose, assembling a portfolio offers an excellent opportunity to reflect on your writing and to chart goals for yourself as a writer. This chapter provides guidelines to help you compile a writing portfolio.

What to Include in a Writing Portfolio

A portfolio submitted to your instructor at the end of a course should represent your best work and demonstrate your growth as a writer, so you'll probably include some of the following materials:

- A number of your best essays and other projects
- Writing representing several genres and media
- Freewriting and other notes
- Various drafts, from first to final
- Response from readers
- A statement reflecting on your work

Your instructor may specify what you need to include, but often you'll get to choose. In that case, what you include will depend on what you're trying to show. If you're trying to show your best work, you might include three pieces that you like best; if, on the other hand, you're trying to show a range of what you've written, you would probably choose writing in various GENRES and MEDIA. If you're trying to show how you've improved, you'll want to include work in several drafts. Just remember that your portfolio is an opportunity for you to evaluate and deliver your own writing: choose work that demonstrates what you want to show.

If you are preparing a portfolio not for class but to highlight your accomplishments for future employers, you will probably make different choices. These choices would be informed by the skills required for the positions you are applying for, and by what you wish to demonstrate to potential employers. If you want to show your abilities as a journalist, you might include in your portfolio a narrative that you wrote for a writing course or a video that you shot and edited. If you are applying for a position in a research lab, you might include a report of a research study and the written proposal that led to that project. Depending on what technology or social media skills employers ask for, you might also include work you've done in multiple modes, such as websites or blogs. You'll certainly want to include a carefully constructed résumé and a cover page introducing yourself and providing an overview of your skills.

Collecting Your Work

Start collecting pieces for your portfolio early in the term. Organization is critical, so create a specific computer folder for the portfolio and give it a name (like "My Portfolio") that you can easily find; inside the folder, create a sub-folder for each piece of writing you include. Identify all drafts with a title and date, as shown in the following example.

```
▼  📁  My Portfolio
   ▼  📁  Analysis
         📄  Analysis_draft_final_28Sept
         📄  Analysis_draft1_14Sept
         📄  Analysis_draft2_21Sept
         📄  Analysis_notes_10Sept
   ▼  📁  Position
         📄  Position_draft_1_9Oct
         📄  Position_draft_2_16Oct
         📄  Position_draft_final_23Oct
         📄  Position_notes_5Oct
```

If you're required to include a statement reflecting on your writing, take notes on your process and your work *throughout the term*. Also keep copies of any peer responses you receive in your file.

You may also find that you want to add new pieces to your portfolio even after you've submitted it for an assignment, in which case it's all the more important to keep your files neat and organized from the beginning. Adding work is easy, especially to an online portfolio, but anyone visiting your site should see an organized, polished collection of work instead of a site that looks to be under construction.

Reflecting on Your Writing

An essential component of your portfolio is a statement that introduces and reflects on the work that's included in the portfolio. Such a statement should explain what's included and why you included the pieces you did, describe your writing process, assess what you've learned, reflect on your development as a writer, and perhaps establish goals for yourself.

Writing such a statement gives you the opportunity to take a good look at your writing and to evaluate it on your own terms. Maybe the essay on which you received your lowest grade was one where you experienced a breakthrough in your writing process. You may well want to discuss this breakthrough in your statement. Did you discover that freewriting worked better than outlining as a way to generate ideas? These are the kinds of insights you can include in your statement to demonstrate to your instructor that you have thought carefully about your writing and your writing process. Following are some prompts to help you think critically about both:

- **REVIEW** *each piece of writing in your portfolio.* What are the strengths and the weaknesses? Which is your best piece? Explain why it is the best and what it demonstrates about what you've learned. Which would you say is the weakest—and how would you change it if you could?

- **ANALYZE** *your writing process.* Study any drafts, responses, and other materials you're including. How did any responses you received help you revise? Which of them helped the most? Were any not helpful?

- **DESCRIBE** *the strategies you use to write.* Which ones have been most helpful, and which have been less helpful? Which ones do you enjoy?

- **REFLECT** *on your work as an author.* What does the writing in your portfolio show about you? What do you do well—and less well? What kinds of writing do you like the most? Is there any kind of writing that you struggle with or dislike—and if so, why?

- **DEFINE** *goals.* What has your portfolio helped you understand about yourself as a writer? What strengths or weaknesses do you now see? Based on this analysis, what do you now want to work on?

This statement is usually written either as a letter or as an essay. You may or may not have an explicit **THESIS**, but you need to make clear what your portfolio demonstrates about you as a writer. Remember that the statement itself demonstrates your writing ability: write it thoughtfully and carefully.

A Sample Portfolio Statement

December 7, 2019

Dear Reader,

Writing used to be one of those things I never gave much time to. I'd get it done but without thinking much about how to do it better. It wasn't until coming to Ball State and taking a class with Professor Clark-Upchurch that writing started to be more than just a nuisance. For the first time, I was forced to look at the inner workings of formal writing, to analyze and examine each part, and to learn what each one is supposed to contribute and why it's important. Slowly over the course of this semester, I have moved beyond the simple five-paragraph essay I learned in high school. All in all, I have become a stronger writer.

Writing the first paper, the literacy narrative, came easily to me . . . or so I thought. When my paper came back to me with Professor Clark-Upchurch's comments about my thesis and organization, some irrelevant incidents I included, the lack of illustrations to support my points, and my "repetitive and simplistic sentence structures," I knew I needed to work harder. On the second paper, an analysis of a magazine ad, my thesis was clearer and my paragraphs "flowed, one into the next" with good examples from the ad as support, but I still needed to work on using a variety of sentences to "make the reader want to read on."

It was on my last paper, the research-based essay, that I finally pulled everything together: an engaging introduction, a clear thesis, logical organization, solid development with lots of supporting examples, and (finally!) varied sentences.

Although my writing style has improved and my understanding of all that goes into a paper is at an all-time high, I still struggle with writing a proposal. I'm not sure why, but for some reason writing an essay about writing a future essay leaves me confused. I'd rather just write the essay in the first place instead of wasting time and effort proposing what I'm going to write about. As a result, I never really made a decent effort at the third writing project—the proposal for the research paper. Thus I have decided to exclude that paper from my portfolio as I am sure it is my weakest.

In addition to these three papers, I include drafts with peer responses and Professor Clark-Upchurch's suggestions in order to provide a clear picture of how much I learned this term. One of the most helpful parts of the class was the peer responding sessions, when we analyzed each other's essays. Doing this helped me think about what I do in my own writing and showed me that other people can learn from what I write—it's not just for the teacher or to get a grade.

The essays you are about to read are just a start, a sturdy base for me to continue developing my writing into something more. Whether willingly or unwillingly, I learned that good writing takes work, but that it also starts to work better when I think about how the parts of my writing fit together. Now whenever I need to write a formal paper, I have some tools I have learned and can use to write for a purpose instead of simply writing to fill the page and finish the assignment.

Sincerely,
Kameron Wiles

Organizing a Portfolio

The way you organize and deliver your portfolio is important; it's part of how you present yourself as a writer. There's no one way to organize a portfolio, but it needs to be carefully arranged so that it's easy to read. Be sure you know if your instructor expects a certain format or system.

Print portfolios can go in a folder (for a small portfolio) or a binder (for a longer one). Begin with a title page that includes your name, the course title and number, the instructor's name, the date, and the portfolio's title. Follow the title page with a table of contents. Next comes your statement, and finally the writing. Unless your instructor asks for papers in a different order, organize the writing by assignments, putting all the materials from each assignment together, with the final draft on top. If you're using a binder, add tabbed dividers, one for each assignment. Number the pages consecutively. Label everything.

E-portfolios can be as basic as *Word* documents uploaded to *Blackboard* or some other online course management system. Or you might post texts to an e-portfolio platform like *Google Docs* or use a blogging site like *WordPress*, *Scribd*, or *Tumblr*. You can create a personal website using a building platform like *Wix*, *Google Sites*, *Squarespace*, or *Weebly*.

And just like a print portfolio, your e-portfolio should be organized by year, course, assignment, or the kind of content on each page. See on the following page how Rae'Johne Smith, an economics major at Spelman College, organizes her e-portfolio. Her homepage features a prominent banner with her name, her photo, and an introductory statement saying who she is and what her portfolio will show—all organized by a menu of links across the top.

As an economics major preparing for a career in finance, Smith presents her writing using the metaphor of a J-curve, one that will make good sense to potential employers. And for those unfamiliar with economics concepts, she clearly explains that a J-curve represents investments and returns over time—and that she's using it here to reflect her growth as a writer

Smith collects her writing—work in which she has obviously invested a lot of time and energy—on the second page, titled "investments," and organizes it into yearly "capital calls," an economics term for money that is put into an investment fund. Then comes a link to "distributions," which is econspeak for the rewards that have come her way from improving her writing. Next comes an "annual report" that sums up her growth as a student and writer, followed by a page with her contact information.

Some Tips for Compiling an E-portfolio

- Figure out exactly what you're going to put in your portfolio and how you're going to organize it before uploading anything.

- Be sure you know what system your instructor expects you to use, and contact your school's tech desk if you need help.

- If you need to upload files, know what type of file you should use: *Word* documents, PDFs, or something else?

- Double-check that the file you are uploading is the final version.

- If you are working on an e-portfolio website, set up a homepage with your basic information and include links to your statement and to each piece of writing, each on its own page.

- To be sure all of the links work and everything looks the way you expect, check your site in different browsers and on different devices (laptops, tablets, and phones); you don't want to find out after you've submitted your portfolio that links don't work or some parts aren't visible.

- If you're using a school website or platform to host your work and want to preserve your e-portfolio or continue to add to it, ask your instructor or the tech desk if it will remain online after the term ends. If it will be deleted, you will need to move it to a more permanent platform.

Portfolios are becoming increasingly necessary, both in school and on the job. Your portfolio is more than an archive of your writing—it's a way of looking systematically at your work. Keeping a portfolio of your writing projects enables you to reflect on your development as a writer—on what you've learned and what you need to work on.

REFLECT. Suppose you're putting together a writing portfolio as part of an application for a summer job or a job after graduation. Go through your files to determine which writing samples you would want to include for the kind of job you are applying for. Consider writing in various modes, genres, and media. Read over each piece carefully and then write a brief comment on each one, pointing out its strengths and what it shows about you as a writer.

THIRTY-EIGHT

Publishing Your Writing

**NCE UPON A TIME** you had to get a newspaper, magazine, or book editor to read and accept your writing in order to be published. Go back further, and even talent wasn't enough to get your work into print—you usually had to be a man as well. Even further back in time, writers who wanted to share their ideas with others often had to hire a scribe to handwrite their work since writing was a skill not many people mastered. Clearly, getting published wasn't easy. But today things have changed. You're only a few clicks away from delivering your writing to audiences far and wide online.

The internet not only allows writers to publish their work but also has changed how we define "publishing": it no longer only means seeing your work distributed in print by an authoritative source. Today publishing your work means making it available to an audience, whether in print or online.

Want to become a published author? As a writer today, you have many ways to share your work with an audience. This chapter lists a sampling of print and online venues where you can do so. We invite you to join the fun and publish what you write. It's easier than you may think!

Essay competitions. Most colleges and universities have newspapers and journals that publish selected student writing—and many have literary magazines that focus on creative writing and art. It's common to gather submissions by holding annual writing competitions—featuring the winners' work online, in a printed collection, or at an event. For example, DePaul University holds an annual writer's showcase where chosen writers who submit their work are invited to present. Search your school's website to see if there's an opportunity to submit writing for publication on your campus.

In fact, W. W. Norton, the publisher of this book, sponsors an annual prize for an outstanding essay written by an undergraduate student. You can read all the previous winning essays—and submit your own work—by visiting everyonesanauthor.tumblr.com.

Undergraduate writing publications. You aren't restricted to publishing opportunities on your own campus; the following publications accept submissions from undergraduate writers around the country:

- *Young Scholars in Writing: Undergraduate Research in Writing and Rhetoric*, supported by Montana State University, publishes "research and theoretical articles from undergraduates on writing, writers, rhetoric, discourse, language, and related topics." Despite the journal's title, undergraduate students of all ages are invited to submit.

- *Queen City Writers*, an online journal at the University of Cincinnati, publishes undergraduate research and "thought-provoking pieces that explore questions and problems related to writing, rhetoric, reading, literacy broadly conceived, popular culture and media, community discourses, and multimodal and digital composing."

- The following schools offer detailed lists of additional publishing opportunities for student writers: Southern Utah University's list of creative writing opportunities; University of Nebraska–Lincoln's list of undergraduate research journals organized by topic; and University of Notre Dame's list of undergraduate research journals divided by discipline.

Publish yourself! Kindle Direct Publishing and other self-publishing platforms make it possible to self-publish works and then sell them directly to readers. Blogs and social networking sites are quick and easy ways to share your ideas with a wide audience for free, as are websites built to collect and publish user reviews such as *Yelp*, *Google*, *Amazon*, and *Trip Advisor*. And don't discount the commenting space most newspapers, magazines, and video- and image-sharing sites like *YouTube* offer. Some sites like the *New York Times* even curate comments, highlighting those worth considering and responding to. Finally, don't forget fan fiction sites like *FanFiction.net* for spaces to discuss your favorite works, receive writing tips, and contribute your own fiction based on works you admire. Fan fiction sites offer a good way to practice as well as find an audience and supportive community of writers with like interests.

If everyone's an author, that includes you! So get busy. Now's the time to publish something you've written. We hope this book will help you do so.

Readings

IF EVERYONE'S AN AUTHOR, then we are all readers as well. All authors, in fact, learn constantly by engaging with what other authors have written. On the following pages you'll find an anthology of 32 readings, arranged alphabetically by author. And on the inside back cover of the book, we've added a menu that categorizes the readings by both genres and themes. And that's not all. We regularly post additional essays, articles, cartoons, speeches, videos, and more on everyonesanauthor.tumblr.com for you to read, analyze, reflect on—and respond to. So read on, enjoy, and see what you can learn.

Monsanto's Harvest of Fear

DONALD L. BARLETT & JAMES B. STEELE

GARY RINEHART CLEARLY REMEMBERS the summer day in 2002 when the stranger walked in and issued his threat. Rinehart was behind the counter of the Square Deal, his "old-time country store," as he calls it, on the fading town square of Eagleville, Missouri, a tiny farm community 100 miles north of Kansas City.

The Square Deal is a fixture in Eagleville, a place where farmers and townspeople can go for lightbulbs, greeting cards, hunting gear, ice cream, aspirin, and dozens of other small items without having to drive to a big-box store in Bethany, the county seat, 15 miles down Interstate 35.

Everyone knows Rinehart, who was born and raised in the area and runs one of Eagleville's few surviving businesses. The stranger came up to the counter and asked for him by name.

"Well, that's me," said Rinehart.

As Rinehart would recall, the man began verbally attacking him, saying 5 he had proof that Rinehart had planted Monsanto's genetically modified (G.M.) soybeans in violation of the company's patent. Better come clean and settle with Monsanto, Rinehart says the man told him—or face the consequences.

DONALD L. BARLETT and JAMES B. STEELE have worked together as investigative journalists for more than three decades, winning two Pulitzer Prizes and many other awards. They were contributing editors at *Vanity Fair* when this article was published there in 2008.

Rinehart was incredulous, listening to the words as puzzled customers and employees looked on. Like many others in rural America, Rinehart knew of Monsanto's fierce reputation for enforcing its patents and suing anyone who allegedly violated them. But Rinehart wasn't a farmer. He wasn't a seed dealer. He hadn't planted any seeds or sold any seeds. He owned a small— a *really* small—country store in a town of 350 people. He was angry that somebody could just barge into the store and embarrass him in front of everyone. "It made me and my business look bad," he says. Rinehart says he told the intruder, "You got the wrong guy."

When the stranger persisted, Rinehart showed him the door. On the way out the man kept making threats. Rinehart says he can't remember the exact words, but they were to the effect of: "Monsanto is big. You can't win. We will get you. You will pay."

Scenes like this are playing out in many parts of rural America these days as Monsanto goes after farmers, farmers' co-ops, seed dealers—anyone it suspects may have infringed its patents of genetically modified seeds. As interviews and reams of court documents reveal, Monsanto relies on a shadowy army of private investigators and agents in the American heartland to strike fear into farm country. They fan out into fields and farm towns, where they secretly videotape and photograph farmers, store owners, and co-ops; infiltrate community meetings; and gather information from informants about farming activities. Farmers say that some Monsanto agents pretend to be surveyors. Others confront farmers on their land and try to pressure them to sign papers giving Monsanto access to their private records. Farmers call them the "seed police" and use words such as "Gestapo" and "Mafia" to describe their tactics.

When asked about these practices, Monsanto declined to comment specifically, other than to say that the company is simply protecting its patents. "Monsanto spends more than $2 million a day in research to identify, test, develop and bring to market innovative new seeds and technologies that benefit farmers," Monsanto spokesman Darren Wallis wrote in an e-mailed letter to *Vanity Fair*. "One tool in protecting this investment is patenting our discoveries and, if necessary, legally defending those patents against those who might choose to infringe upon them." Wallis said that, while the vast majority of farmers and seed dealers follow the licensing agreements, "a tiny fraction" do not, and that Monsanto is obligated to those who do abide by its rules to enforce its patent rights on those who "reap the benefits of the technology without paying for its use." He said only a small number of cases ever go to trial.

The report kicks off with an attention-grabbing narrative— a good strategy, and not hard to do. See Ch. 13 and pp. 468–69.

Some compare Monsanto's hard-line approach to Microsoft's zealous ef-　10
forts to protect its software from pirates. At least with Microsoft the buyer
of a program can use it over and over again. But farmers who buy Monsanto's
seeds can't even do that.

The Control of Nature

For centuries—millennia—farmers have saved seeds from season to season:
they planted in the spring, harvested in the fall, then reclaimed and cleaned
the seeds over the winter for re-planting the next spring. Monsanto has
turned this ancient practice on its head.

Monsanto developed G.M. seeds that would resist its own herbicide,
Roundup, offering farmers a convenient way to spray fields with weed killer
without affecting crops. Monsanto then patented the seeds. For nearly all
of its history the United States Patent and Trademark Office had refused
to grant patents on seeds, viewing them as life-forms with too many variables to be patented. "It's not like describing a widget," says Joseph Mendelson III, the legal director of the Center for Food Safety, which has tracked
Monsanto's activities in rural America for years.

Indeed not. But in 1980 the U.S. Supreme Court, in a five-to-four decision,
turned seeds into widgets, laying the groundwork for a handful of corporations to begin taking control of the world's food supply. In its decision, the
court extended patent law to cover "a live human-made microorganism."
In this case, the organism wasn't even a seed. Rather, it was a *Pseudomonas*
bacterium developed by a General Electric scientist to clean up oil spills. But
the precedent was set, and Monsanto took advantage of it. Since the 1980s,
Monsanto has become the world leader in genetic modification of seeds and
has won 674 biotechnology patents, more than any other company, according to U.S. Department of Agriculture data.

Farmers who buy Monsanto's patented Roundup Ready seeds are required to sign an agreement promising not to save the seed produced after
each harvest for re-planting, or to sell the seed to other farmers. This means
that farmers must buy new seed every year. Those increased sales, coupled
with ballooning sales of its Roundup weed killer, have been a bonanza for
Monsanto.

This radical departure from age-old practice has created turmoil　15
in farm country. Some farmers don't fully understand that they aren't

A handful of Monsanto's Roundup Ready soybean seeds saved from a previous season could be grounds for an investigation by the biotech giant.

supposed to save Monsanto's seeds for next year's planting. Others do, but ignore the stipulation rather than throw away a perfectly usable product. Still others say that they don't use Monsanto's genetically modified seeds, but seeds have been blown into their fields by wind or deposited by birds. It's certainly easy for G.M. seeds to get mixed in with traditional varieties when seeds are cleaned by commercial dealers for re-planting. The seeds look identical; only a laboratory analysis can show the difference. Even if a farmer doesn't buy G.M. seeds and doesn't want them on his land, it's a safe bet he'll get a visit from Monsanto's seed police if crops grown from G.M. seeds are discovered in his fields.

Most Americans know Monsanto because of what it sells to put on our lawns—the ubiquitous weed killer Roundup. What they may not know is that the company now profoundly influences—and one day may virtually control—what we put on our tables. For most of its history Monsanto was a chemical giant, producing some of the most toxic substances ever created, residues from which have left us with some of the most polluted sites on earth. Yet in a little more than a decade, the company has sought to shed its polluted past and morph into something much different and more far-reaching—an "agricultural company" dedicated to making the world "a better place for future generations." Still, more than one Web log claims to see similarities between Monsanto and the fictional company "U-North" in the movie *Michael Clayton*, an agribusiness giant accused in a multibillion-dollar lawsuit of selling an herbicide that causes cancer.

Monsanto's genetically modified seeds have transformed the company and are radically altering global agriculture. So far, the company has produced G.M. seeds for soybeans, corn, canola, and cotton. Many more products have been developed or are in the pipeline, including seeds for sugar beets and alfalfa. The company is also seeking to extend its reach into milk production by marketing an artificial growth hormone for cows that increases their output, and it is taking aggressive steps to put those who don't want to use growth hormone at a commercial disadvantage.

Even as the company is pushing its G.M. agenda, Monsanto is buying up conventional-seed companies. In 2005, Monsanto paid $1.4 billion for Seminis, which controlled 40 percent of the U.S. market for lettuce, tomatoes, and other vegetable and fruit seeds. Two weeks later it announced the acquisition of the country's third-largest cottonseed company, Emergent Genetics, for $300 million. It's estimated that Monsanto seeds now account for 90 percent of the U.S. production of soybeans, which are used in food products beyond counting. Monsanto's acquisitions have fueled explosive growth, transforming the St. Louis–based corporation into the largest seed company in the world.

In Iraq, the groundwork has been laid to protect the patents of Monsanto and other G.M.-seed companies. One of L. Paul Bremer's last acts as head of the Coalition Provisional Authority was an order stipulating that "farmers shall be prohibited from re-using seeds of protected varieties." Monsanto has said that it has no interest in doing business in Iraq, but should the company change its mind, the American-style law is in place.

To be sure, more and more agricultural corporations and individual   20 farmers are using Monsanto's G.M. seeds. As recently as 1980, no genetically modified crops were grown in the U.S. In 2007, the total was 142 million acres planted. Worldwide, the figure was 282 million acres. Many farmers believe that G.M. seeds increase crop yields and save money. Another reason for their attraction is convenience. By using Roundup Ready soybean seeds, a farmer can spend less time tending to his fields. With Monsanto seeds, a farmer plants his crop, then treats it later with Roundup to kill weeds. That takes the place of labor-intensive weed control and plowing.

Monsanto portrays its move into G.M. seeds as a giant leap for mankind. But out in the American countryside, Monsanto's no-holds-barred tactics have made it feared and loathed. Like it or not, farmers say, they have fewer and fewer choices in buying seeds.

And controlling the seeds is not some abstraction. Whoever provides the world's seeds controls the world's food supply.

Under Surveillance

After Monsanto's investigator confronted Gary Rinehart, Monsanto filed a federal lawsuit alleging that Rinehart "knowingly, intentionally, and willfully" planted seeds "in violation of Monsanto's patent rights." The company's complaint made it sound as if Monsanto had Rinehart dead to rights:

> During the 2002 growing season, Investigator Jeffery Moore, through surveillance of Mr. Rinehart's farm facility and farming operations, observed Defendant planting brown bag soybean seed. Mr. Moore observed the Defendant take the brown bag soybeans to a field, which was subsequently loaded into a grain drill and planted. Mr. Moore located two empty bags in the ditch in the public road right-of-way beside one of the fields planted by Rinehart, which contained some soybeans. Mr. Moore collected a small amount of soybeans left in the bags which Defendant had tossed into the public right-of-way. These samples tested positive for Monsanto's Roundup Ready technology.

Faced with a federal lawsuit, Rinehart had to hire a lawyer. Monsanto eventually realized that "Investigator Jeffery Moore" had targeted the wrong man, and dropped the suit. Rinehart later learned that the company had been secretly investigating farmers in his area. Rinehart never heard from Monsanto again: no letter of apology, no public concession that the company had made a terrible mistake, no offer to pay his attorney's fees. "I don't know how they get away with it," he says. "If I tried to do something like that it would be bad news. I felt like I was in another country."

Gary Rinehart is actually one of Monsanto's luckier targets. Ever since commercial introduction of its G.M. seeds, in 1996, Monsanto has launched thousands of investigations and filed lawsuits against hundreds of farmers and seed dealers. In a 2007 report, the Center for Food Safety, in Washington, D.C., documented 112 such lawsuits, in 27 states.

Even more significant, in the Center's opinion, are the numbers of 25 farmers who settle because they don't have the money or the time to fight Monsanto. "The number of cases filed is only the tip of the iceberg," says Bill Freese, the Center's science-policy analyst. Freese says he has been told of many cases in which Monsanto investigators showed up at a farmer's house or confronted him in his fields, claiming he had violated the technology agreement and demanding to see his records. According to Freese, investigators will say, "Monsanto knows that you are saving Roundup Ready seeds, and if you don't sign these information-release forms, Monsanto is going to come after you and take your farm or take you for all you're worth." Investigators will sometimes show a farmer a photo of himself coming out of a store, to let him know he is being followed.

Lawyers who have represented farmers sued by Monsanto say that intimidating actions like these are commonplace. Most give in and pay Monsanto some amount in damages; those who resist face the full force of Monsanto's legal wrath.

Scorched-Earth Tactics

Pilot Grove, Missouri, population 750, sits in rolling farmland 150 miles west of St. Louis. The town has a grocery store, a bank, a bar, a nursing home, a funeral parlor, and a few other small businesses. There are no stoplights, but the town doesn't need any. The little traffic it has comes from trucks on their way to and from the grain elevator on the edge of town. The elevator is owned by a local co-op, the Pilot Grove Cooperative Elevator, which buys soybeans and corn from farmers in the fall, then ships out the grain over the winter. The co-op has seven full-time employees and four computers.

In the fall of 2006, Monsanto trained its legal guns on Pilot Grove; ever since, its farmers have been drawn into a costly, disruptive legal battle against an opponent with limitless resources. Neither Pilot Grove nor Monsanto will discuss the case, but it is possible to piece together much of the story from documents filed as part of the litigation.

Monsanto began investigating soybean farmers in and around Pilot Grove several years ago. There is no indication as to what sparked the probe, but Monsanto periodically investigates farmers in soybean-growing regions such as this one in central Missouri. The company has a staff devoted to enforcing patents and litigating against farmers. To gather leads, the company maintains an 800 number and encourages farmers to inform on other farmers they think may be engaging in "seed piracy."

Once Pilot Grove had been targeted, Monsanto sent private investigators into the area. Over a period of months, Monsanto's investigators surreptitiously followed the co-op's employees and customers and videotaped them in fields and going about other activities. At least 17 such surveillance videos were made, according to court records. The investigative work was outsourced to a St. Louis agency, McDowell & Associates. It was a McDowell investigator who erroneously fingered Gary Rinehart. In Pilot Grove, at least 11 McDowell investigators have worked the case, and Monsanto makes no bones about the extent of this effort: "Surveillance was conducted throughout the year by various investigators in the field," according to court records. McDowell, like Monsanto, will not comment on the case. 30

Not long after investigators showed up in Pilot Grove, Monsanto subpoenaed the co-op's records concerning seed and herbicide purchases and seed-cleaning operations. The co-op provided more than 800 pages of documents pertaining to dozens of farmers. Monsanto sued two farmers and negotiated settlements with more than 25 others it accused of seed piracy. But Monsanto's legal assault had only begun. Although the co-op had provided voluminous records, Monsanto then sued it in federal court for patent infringement. Monsanto contended that by cleaning seeds—a service which it had provided for decades—the co-op was inducing farmers to violate Monsanto's patents. In effect, Monsanto wanted the co-op to police its own customers.

In the majority of cases where Monsanto sues, or threatens to sue, farmers settle before going to trial. The cost and stress of litigating against a global corporation are just too great. But Pilot Grove wouldn't cave—and ever since, Monsanto has been turning up the heat. The more the co-op has resisted, the more legal firepower Monsanto has aimed at it. Pilot Grove's lawyer, Steven H. Schwartz, described Monsanto in a court filing as pursuing a "scorched earth tactic," intent on "trying to drive the co-op into the ground."

Even after Pilot Grove turned over thousands more pages of sales records going back five years, and covering virtually every one of its farmer customers, Monsanto wanted more—the right to inspect the co-op's hard drives. When the co-op offered to provide an electronic version of any record, Monsanto demanded hands-on access to Pilot Grove's in-house computers.

Monsanto next petitioned to make potential damages punitive—tripling the amount that Pilot Grove might have to pay if found guilty. After a judge denied that request, Monsanto expanded the scope of the pre-trial investigation by seeking to quadruple the number of depositions. "Monsanto is doing its best to make this case so expensive to defend that the Co-op will have no choice but to relent," Pilot Grove's lawyer said in a court filing.

With Pilot Grove still holding out for a trial, Monsanto now subpoenaed　35 the records of more than 100 of the co-op's customers. In a "You are Commanded . . . " notice, the farmers were ordered to gather up five years of invoices, receipts, and all other papers relating to their soybean and herbicide purchases, and to have the documents delivered to a law office in St. Louis. Monsanto gave them two weeks to comply.

Whether Pilot Grove can continue to wage its legal battle remains to be seen. Whatever the outcome, the case shows why Monsanto is so detested in farm country, even by those who buy its products. "I don't know of a company that chooses to sue its own customer base," says Joseph Mendelson, of the Center for Food Safety. "It's a very bizarre business strategy." But it's one that Monsanto manages to get away with, because increasingly it's the dominant vendor in town.

Chemicals? What Chemicals?

The Monsanto Company has never been one of America's friendliest corporate citizens. Given Monsanto's current dominance in the field of bioengineering, it's worth looking at the company's own DNA. The future of the company may lie in seeds, but the seeds of the company lie in chemicals. Communities around the world are still reaping the environmental consequences of Monsanto's origins.

Monsanto was founded in 1901 by John Francis Queeny, a tough, cigar-smoking Irishman with a sixth-grade education. A buyer for a wholesale drug company, Queeny had an idea. But like a lot of employees with ideas, he found that his boss wouldn't listen to him. So he went into business for himself on the side. Queeny was convinced there was money to be made manufacturing a substance called saccharin, an artificial sweetener then imported from Germany. He took $1,500 of his savings, borrowed another $3,500, and set up shop in a dingy warehouse near the St. Louis waterfront. With borrowed equipment and secondhand machines, he began producing saccharin for the U.S. market. He called the company the Monsanto Chemical Works, Monsanto being his wife's maiden name.

The German cartel that controlled the market for saccharin wasn't pleased, and cut the price from $4.50 to $1 a pound to try to force Queeny out of business. The young company faced other challenges. Questions arose about the safety of saccharin, and the U.S. Department of Agriculture even tried to ban it. Fortunately for Queeny, he wasn't up against opponents as aggressive and litigious as the Monsanto of today. His persistence and the loyalty of one steady customer kept the company afloat. That steady customer was a new company in Georgia named Coca-Cola.

Monsanto added more and more products—vanillin, caffeine, and drugs used as sedatives and laxatives. In 1917, Monsanto began making aspirin, and soon became the largest maker worldwide. During World War I, cut off from imported European chemicals, Monsanto was forced to manufacture its own, and its position as a leading force in the chemical industry was assured.

After Queeny was diagnosed with cancer, in the late 1920s, his only son, Edgar, became president. Where the father had been a classic entrepreneur, Edgar Monsanto Queeny was an empire builder with a grand vision. It was Edgar—shrewd, daring, and intuitive ("He can see around the next corner," his secretary once said)—who built Monsanto into a global powerhouse. Under Edgar Queeny and his successors, Monsanto extended its reach into a phenomenal number of products: plastics, resins, rubber goods, fuel additives, artificial caffeine, industrial fluids, vinyl siding, dishwasher detergent, anti-freeze, fertilizers, herbicides, pesticides. Its safety glass protects the U.S. Constitution and the *Mona Lisa*. Its synthetic fibers are the basis of Astroturf.

During the 1970s, the company shifted more and more resources into biotechnology. In 1981 it created a molecular-biology group for research in plant genetics. The next year, Monsanto scientists hit gold: they became the first to genetically modify a plant cell. "It will now be possible to introduce virtually any gene into plant cells with the ultimate goal of improving crop productivity," said Ernest Jaworski, director of Monsanto's Biological Sciences Program.

Over the next few years, scientists working mainly in the company's vast new Life Sciences Research Center, 25 miles west of St. Louis, developed one genetically modified product after another—cotton, soybeans, corn, canola. From the start, G.M. seeds were controversial with the public as well as with some farmers and European consumers. Monsanto has sought to

40

portray G.M. seeds as a panacea, a way to alleviate poverty and feed the hungry. Robert Shapiro, Monsanto's president during the 1990s, once called G.M. seeds "the single most successful introduction of technology in the history of agriculture, including the plow."

By the late 1990s, Monsanto, having rebranded itself into a "life sciences" company, had spun off its chemical and fibers operations into a new company called Solutia. After an additional reorganization, Monsanto reincorporated in 2002 and officially declared itself an "agricultural company."

In its company literature, Monsanto now refers to itself disingenuously as a "relatively new company" whose primary goal is helping "farmers around the world in their mission to feed, clothe, and fuel" a growing planet. In its list of corporate milestones, all but a handful are from the recent era. As for the company's early history, the decades when it grew into an industrial powerhouse now held potentially responsible for more than 50 Environmental Protection Agency Superfund sites—none of that is mentioned. It's as though the original Monsanto, the company that long had the word "chemical" as part of its name, never existed. One of the benefits of doing this, as the company does not point out, was to channel the bulk of the growing backlog of chemical lawsuits and liabilities onto Solutia, keeping the Monsanto brand pure.

But Monsanto's past, especially its environmental legacy, is very much with us. For many years Monsanto produced two of the most toxic substances ever known—polychlorinated biphenyls, better known as PCBs, and dioxin. Monsanto no longer produces either, but the places where it did are still struggling with the aftermath, and probably always will be.

"Systemic Intoxication"

Twelve miles downriver from Charleston, West Virginia, is the town of Nitro, where Monsanto operated a chemical plant from 1929 to 1995. In 1948 the plant began to make a powerful herbicide known as 2,4,5-T, called "weed bug" by the workers. A by-product of the process was the creation of a chemical that would later be known as dioxin.

The name dioxin refers to a group of highly toxic chemicals that have been linked to heart disease, liver disease, human reproductive disorders, and developmental problems. Even in small amounts, dioxin persists in the environment and accumulates in the body. In 1997 the International Agency for Research on Cancer, a branch of the World Health Organization, classified the most powerful form of dioxin as a substance that causes cancer in humans. In 2001 the U.S. government listed the chemical as a "known human carcinogen."

On March 8, 1949, a massive explosion rocked Monsanto's Nitro plant when a pressure valve blew on a container cooking up a batch of herbicide. The noise from the release was a scream so loud that it drowned out the emergency steam whistle for five minutes. A plume of vapor and white smoke drifted across the plant and out over town. Residue from the explosion coated the interior of the building and those inside with what workers described as "a fine black powder." Many felt their skin prickle and were told to scrub down.

Within days, workers experienced skin eruptions. Many were soon diagnosed with chloracne, a condition similar to common acne but more severe, longer lasting, and potentially disfiguring. Others felt intense pains in their legs, chest, and trunk. A confidential medical report at the time said the explosion "caused a systemic intoxication in the workers involving most major organ systems." Doctors who examined four of the most seriously injured men detected a strong odor coming from them when they were all together in a closed room. "We believe these men are excreting a foreign chemical through their skins," the confidential report to Monsanto noted. Court records indicate that 226 plant workers became ill.

According to court documents that have surfaced in a West Virginia court case, Monsanto downplayed the impact, stating that the contaminant affecting workers was "fairly slow acting" and caused "only an irritation of the skin."

In the meantime, the Nitro plant continued to produce herbicides, rubber products, and other chemicals. In the 1960s, the factory manufactured Agent Orange, the powerful herbicide which the U.S. military used to defoliate jungles during the Vietnam War, and which later was the focus of lawsuits by veterans contending that they had been harmed by exposure. As with Monsanto's older herbicides, the manufacturing of Agent Orange created dioxin as a by-product.

As for the Nitro plant's waste, some was burned in incinerators, some dumped in landfills or storm drains, some allowed to run into streams. As Stuart Calwell, a lawyer who has represented both workers and residents in Nitro, put it, "Dioxin went wherever the product went, down the sewer, shipped in bags, and when the waste was burned, out in the air."

In 1981 several former Nitro employees filed lawsuits in federal court, charging that Monsanto had knowingly exposed them to chemicals that caused long-term health problems, including cancer and heart disease. They alleged that Monsanto knew that many chemicals used at Nitro were potentially harmful, but had kept that information from them. On the eve of a trial, in 1988, Monsanto agreed to settle most of the cases by making a single lump payment of $1.5 million. Monsanto also agreed to drop its claim to collect $305,000 in court costs from six retired Monsanto workers who had unsuccessfully charged in another lawsuit that Monsanto had recklessly exposed them to dioxin. Monsanto had attached liens to the retirees' homes to guarantee collection of the debt.

Monsanto stopped producing dioxin in Nitro in 1969, but the toxic 55 chemical can still be found well beyond the Nitro plant site. Repeated studies have found elevated levels of dioxin in nearby rivers, streams, and fish. Residents have sued to seek damages from Monsanto and Solutia. Earlier this year, a West Virginia judge merged those lawsuits into a class-action suit. A Monsanto spokesman said, "We believe the allegations are without merit and we'll defend ourselves vigorously." The suit will no doubt take years to play out. Time is one thing that Monsanto always has, and that the plaintiffs usually don't.

Poisoned Lawns

Five hundred miles to the south, the people of Anniston, Alabama, know all about what the people of Nitro are going through. They've been there. In fact, you could say, they're still there.

From 1929 to 1971, Monsanto's Anniston works produced PCBs as industrial coolants and insulating fluids for transformers and other electrical equipment. One of the wonder chemicals of the 20th century, PCBs were exceptionally versatile and fire-resistant, and became central to many American industries as lubricants, hydraulic fluids, and sealants. But PCBs are toxic. A member of a family of chemicals that mimic hormones, PCBs have been linked to damage in the liver and in the neurological, immune, endocrine, and reproductive systems. The Environmental Protection Agency (E.P.A.) and the Agency for Toxic Substances and Disease Registry, part of the Department of Health and Human Services, now classify PCBs as "probable carcinogens."

Today, 37 years after PCB production ceased in Anniston, and after tons of contaminated soil have been removed to try to reclaim the site, the area around the old Monsanto plant remains one of the most polluted spots in the U.S.

People in Anniston find themselves in this fix today largely because of the way Monsanto disposed of PCB waste for decades. Excess PCBs were dumped in a nearby open-pit landfill or allowed to flow off the property with storm water. Some waste was poured directly into Snow Creek, which runs alongside the plant and empties into a larger stream, Choccolocco Creek. PCBs also turned up in private lawns after the company invited Anniston residents to use soil from the plant for their lawns, according to *The Anniston Star.*

So for decades the people of Anniston breathed air, planted gardens, 60 drank from wells, fished in rivers, and swam in creeks contaminated with PCBs—without knowing anything about the danger. It wasn't until the 1990s—20 years after Monsanto stopped making PCBs in Anniston—that widespread public awareness of the problem there took hold.

Studies by health authorities consistently found elevated levels of PCBs in houses, yards, streams, fields, fish, and other wildlife—and in people. In 2003, Monsanto and Solutia entered into a consent decree with the E.P.A. to clean up Anniston. Scores of houses and small businesses were to be razed, tons of contaminated soil dug up and carted off, and streambeds scooped of toxic residue. The cleanup is under way, and it will take years, but some doubt it will ever be completed—the job is massive. To settle residents' claims, Monsanto has also paid $550 million to 21,000 Anniston residents exposed to PCBs, but many of them continue to live with PCBs in their bodies. Once PCB is absorbed into human tissue, there it forever remains.

Monsanto shut down PCB production in Anniston in 1971, and the company ended all its American PCB operations in 1977. Also in 1977, Monsanto closed a PCB plant in Wales. In recent years, residents near the village of Groesfaen, in southern Wales, have noticed vile odors emanating from an old quarry outside the village. As it turns out, Monsanto had dumped thousands of tons of waste from its nearby PCB plant into the quarry. British authorities are struggling to decide what to do with what they have now identified as among the most contaminated places in Britain.

"No Cause for Public Alarm"

What had Monsanto known—or what should it have known—about the potential dangers of the chemicals it was manufacturing? There's considerable documentation lurking in court records from many lawsuits indicating that Monsanto knew quite a lot. Let's look just at the example of PCBs.

The evidence that Monsanto refused to face questions about their toxicity is quite clear. In 1956 the company tried to sell the navy a hydraulic fluid for its submarines called Pydraul 150, which contained PCBs. Monsanto supplied the navy with test results for the product. But the navy decided to run its own tests. Afterward, navy officials informed Monsanto that they wouldn't be buying the product. "Applications of Pydraul 150 caused death in all of the rabbits tested" and indicated "definite liver damage," navy officials told Monsanto, according to an internal Monsanto memo divulged in the course of a court proceeding. "No matter how we discussed the situation," complained Monsanto's medical director, R. Emmet Kelly, "it was impossible to change their thinking that Pydraul 150 is just too toxic for use in submarines."

Ten years later, a biologist conducting studies for Monsanto in streams near the Anniston plant got quick results when he submerged his test fish. As he reported to Monsanto, according to *The Washington Post*, "All 25 fish lost equilibrium and turned on their sides in 10 seconds and all were dead in 3½ minutes."

When the Food and Drug Administration (F.D.A.) turned up high levels of PCBs in fish near the Anniston plant in 1970, the company swung into action to limit the P.R. damage. An internal memo entitled "CONFIDENTIAL—F.Y.I. AND DESTROY" from Monsanto official Paul B. Hodges reviewed steps under way to limit disclosure of the information. One element of the strategy was to get public officials to fight Monsanto's battle: "Joe Crockett, Secretary of the Alabama Water Improvement Commission, will try to handle the problem quietly without release of the information to the public at this time," according to the memo.

Despite Monsanto's efforts, the information did get out, but the company was able to blunt its impact. Monsanto's Anniston plant manager "convinced" a reporter for *The Anniston Star* that there was really nothing to worry about, and an internal memo from Monsanto's headquarters in St. Louis

65

People gather to publicize biologists' findings that chemicals in Monsanto products are having harmful effects on local environments and wildlife.

summarized the story that subsequently appeared in the newspaper: "Quoting both plant management and the Alabama Water Improvement Commission, the feature emphasized the PCB problem was relatively new, was being solved by Monsanto and, at this point, was no cause for public alarm."

In truth, there was enormous cause for public alarm. But that harm was done by the "Original Monsanto Company," not "Today's Monsanto Company" (the words and the distinction are Monsanto's). The Monsanto of today says that it can be trusted—that its biotech crops are "as wholesome, nutritious and safe as conventional crops," and that milk from cows injected with its artificial growth hormone is the same as, and as safe as, milk from any other cow.

The Milk Wars

Jeff Kleinpeter takes very good care of his dairy cows. In the winter he turns on heaters to warm their barns. In the summer, fans blow gentle breezes to cool them, and on especially hot days, a fine mist floats down to take the edge off Louisiana's heat. The dairy has gone "to the ultimate end of the earth for cow comfort," says Kleinpeter, a fourth-generation dairy farmer in Baton Rouge. He says visitors marvel at what he does: "I've had many of them say, 'When I die, I want to come back as a Kleinpeter cow.' "

Monsanto would like to change the way Jeff Kleinpeter and his fam- 70 ily do business. Specifically, Monsanto doesn't like the label on Kleinpeter Dairy's milk cartons: "From Cows *Not* Treated with rBGH." To consumers, that means the milk comes from cows that were not given artificial bovine growth hormone, a supplement developed by Monsanto that can be injected into dairy cows to increase their milk output.

No one knows what effect, if any, the hormone has on milk or the people who drink it. Studies have not detected any difference in the quality of milk produced by cows that receive rBGH, or rBST, a term by which it is also known. But Jeff Kleinpeter—like millions of consumers—wants no part of rBGH. Whatever its effect on humans, if any, Kleinpeter feels certain it's harmful to cows because it speeds up their metabolism and increases the chances that they'll contract a painful illness that can shorten their lives. "It's like putting a Volkswagen car in with the Indianapolis 500 racers," he says. "You gotta keep the pedal to the metal the whole way through, and pretty soon that poor little Volkswagen engine's going to burn up."

Kleinpeter Dairy has never used Monsanto's artificial hormone, and the dairy requires other dairy farmers from whom it buys milk to attest that they don't use it, either. At the suggestion of a marketing consultant, the dairy began advertising its milk as coming from rBGH-free cows in 2005, and the label began appearing on Kleinpeter milk cartons and in company literature, including a new Web site of Kleinpeter products that proclaims, "We treat our cows with love . . . not rBGH."

The dairy's sales soared. For Kleinpeter, it was simply a matter of giving consumers more information about their product.

But giving consumers that information has stirred the ire of Monsanto. The company contends that advertising by Kleinpeter and other dairies touting their "no rBGH" milk reflects adversely on Monsanto's product. In a letter to the Federal Trade Commission in February 2007, Monsanto said that, notwithstanding the overwhelming evidence that there is no difference in the milk from cows treated with its product, "milk processors persist in claiming on their labels and in advertisements that the use of rBST is somehow harmful, either to cows or to the people who consume milk from rBST-supplemented cows."

Monsanto called on the commission to investigate what it called the 75 "deceptive advertising and labeling practices" of milk processors such as

In 1993, the Food and Drug Administration approved the commercial use of rBST, an artificial growth hormone that increases milk production in cows.

Kleinpeter, accusing them of misleading consumers "by falsely claiming that there are health and safety risks associated with milk from rBST-supplemented cows." As noted, Kleinpeter does not make any such claims—he simply states that his milk comes from cows not injected with rBGH.

Monsanto's attempt to get the F.T.C. to force dairies to change their advertising was just one more step in the corporation's efforts to extend its reach into agriculture. After years of scientific debate and public controversy, the F.D.A. in 1993 approved commercial use of rBST, basing its decision in part on studies submitted by Monsanto. That decision allowed the company to market the artificial hormone. The effect of the hormone is to increase milk production, not exactly something the nation needed then—or needs now. The U.S. was actually awash in milk, with the government buying up the surplus to prevent a collapse in prices.

Monsanto began selling the supplement in 1994 under the name Posilac. Monsanto acknowledges that the possible side effects of rBST for cows include lameness, disorders of the uterus, increased body temperature,

Monsanto protested advertisements for milk "From Cows *Not* Treated with rBGH,"
asserting that the ads implied the possible negative effects of artificial growth
hormones and that no studies had shown the hormones to be harmful to cows or people.

digestive problems, and birthing difficulties. Veterinary drug reports note
that "cows injected with Posilac are at an increased risk for mastitis," an
udder infection in which bacteria and pus may be pumped out with the
milk. What's the effect on humans? The F.D.A. has consistently said that the
milk produced by cows that receive rBGH is the same as milk from cows
that aren't injected: "The public can be confident that milk and meat from
BST-treated cows is safe to consume." Nevertheless, some scientists are concerned by the lack of long-term studies to test the additive's impact, especially on children. A Wisconsin geneticist, William von Meyer, observed that
when rBGH was approved the longest study on which the F.D.A.'s approval
was based covered only a 90-day laboratory test with small animals. "But
people drink milk for a lifetime," he noted. Canada and the European Union
have never approved the commercial sale of the artificial hormone. Today,
nearly 15 years after the F.D.A. approved rBGH, there have still been no
long-term studies "to determine the safety of milk from cows that receive
artificial growth hormone," says Michael Hansen, senior staff scientist for
Consumers Union. Not only have there been no studies, he adds, but the data

that does exist all comes from Monsanto. "There is no scientific consensus about the safety," he says.

However F.D.A. approval came about, Monsanto has long been wired into Washington. Michael R. Taylor was a staff attorney and executive assistant to the F.D.A. commissioner before joining a law firm in Washington in 1981, where he worked to secure F.D.A. approval of Monsanto's artificial growth hormone before returning to the F.D.A. as deputy commissioner in 1991. Dr. Michael A. Friedman, formerly the F.D.A.'s deputy commissioner for operations, joined Monsanto in 1999 as a senior vice president. Linda J. Fisher was an assistant administrator at the E.P.A. when she left the agency in 1993. She became a vice president of Monsanto, from 1995 to 2000, only to return to the E.P.A. as deputy administrator the next year. William D. Ruckelshaus, former E.P.A. administrator, and Mickey Kantor, former U.S. trade representative, each served on Monsanto's board after leaving government. Supreme Court justice Clarence Thomas was an attorney in Monsanto's corporate-law department in the 1970s. He wrote the Supreme Court opinion in a crucial G.M.-seed patent-rights case in 2001 that benefited Monsanto and all G.M.-seed companies. Donald Rumsfeld never served on the board or held any office at Monsanto, but Monsanto must occupy a soft spot in the heart of the former defense secretary. Rumsfeld was chairman and C.E.O. of the pharmaceutical maker G. D. Searle & Co. when Monsanto acquired Searle in 1985, after Searle had experienced difficulty in finding a buyer. Rumsfeld's stock and options in Searle were valued at $12 million at the time of the sale.

From the beginning some consumers have consistently been hesitant to drink milk from cows treated with artificial hormones. This is one reason Monsanto has waged so many battles with dairies and regulators over the wording of labels on milk cartons. It has sued at least two dairies and one co-op over labeling.

Critics of the artificial hormone have pushed for mandatory labeling on all milk products, but the F.D.A. has resisted and even taken action against some dairies that labeled their milk "BST-free." Since BST is a natural hormone found in all cows, including those not injected with Monsanto's artificial version, the F.D.A. argued that no dairy could claim that its milk is BST-free. The F.D.A. later issued guidelines allowing dairies to use labels saying their milk comes from "non-supplemented cows," as long as the carton has a disclaimer saying that the artificial supplement does not in any way change the milk. So the milk cartons from Kleinpeter Dairy, for example,

80

carry a label on the front stating that the milk is from cows not treated with rBGH, and the rear panel says, "Government studies have shown no significant difference between milk derived from rBGH-treated and non-rBGH-treated cows." That's not good enough for Monsanto.

The Next Battleground

As more and more dairies have chosen to advertise their milk as "No rBGH," Monsanto has gone on the offensive. Its attempt to force the F.T.C. to look into what Monsanto called "deceptive practices" by dairies trying to distance themselves from the company's artificial hormone was the most recent national salvo. But after reviewing Monsanto's claims, the F.T.C.'s Division of Advertising Practices decided in August 2007 that a "formal investigation and enforcement action is not warranted at this time." The agency found some instances where dairies had made "unfounded health and safety claims," but these were mostly on Web sites, not on milk cartons. And the F.T.C. determined that the dairies Monsanto had singled out all carried disclaimers that the F.D.A. had found no significant differences in milk from cows treated with the artificial hormone.

Blocked at the federal level, Monsanto is pushing for action by the states. In the fall of 2007, Pennsylvania's agriculture secretary, Dennis Wolff, issued an edict prohibiting dairies from stamping milk containers with labels stating their products were made without the use of the artificial hormone. Wolff said such a label implies that competitors' milk is not safe, and noted that non-supplemented milk comes at an unjustified higher price, arguments that Monsanto has frequently made. The ban was to take effect February 1, 2008.

Wolff's action created a firestorm in Pennsylvania (and beyond) from angry consumers. So intense was the outpouring of e-mails, letters, and calls that Pennsylvania governor Edward Rendell stepped in and reversed his agriculture secretary, saying, "The public has a right to complete information about how the milk they buy is produced."

On this issue, the tide may be shifting against Monsanto. Organic dairy products, which don't involve rBGH, are soaring in popularity. Supermarket chains such as Kroger, Publix, and Safeway are embracing them. Some other companies have turned away from rBGH products, including Starbucks, which has banned all milk products from cows treated with rBGH. Although Monsanto once claimed that an estimated 30 percent of the nation's dairy cows were injected with rBST, it's widely believed that today the number is much lower.

But don't count Monsanto out. Efforts similar to the one in Pennsylvania have been launched in other states, including New Jersey, Ohio, Indiana, Kansas, Utah, and Missouri. A Monsanto-backed group called AFACT—American Farmers for the Advancement and Conservation of Technology—has been spearheading efforts in many of these states. AFACT describes itself as a "producer organization" that decries "questionable labeling tactics and activism" by marketers who have convinced some consumers to "shy away from foods using new technology." AFACT reportedly uses the same St. Louis public-relations firm, Osborn & Barr, employed by Monsanto. An Osborn & Barr spokesman told *The Kansas City Star* that the company was doing work for AFACT on a pro bono basis. ⁸⁵

Even if Monsanto's efforts to secure across-the-board labeling changes should fall short, there's nothing to stop state agriculture departments from restricting labeling on a dairy-by-dairy basis. Beyond that, Monsanto also has allies whose foot soldiers will almost certainly keep up the pressure on dairies that don't use Monsanto's artificial hormone. Jeff Kleinpeter knows about them, too.

He got a call one day from the man who prints the labels for his milk cartons, asking if he had seen the attack on Kleinpeter Dairy that had been posted on the Internet. Kleinpeter went online to a site called StopLabelingLies, which claims to "help consumers by publicizing examples of false and misleading food and other product labels." There, sure enough, Kleinpeter and other dairies that didn't use Monsanto's product were being accused of making misleading claims to sell their milk.

There was no address or phone number on the Web site, only a list of groups that apparently contribute to the site and whose issues range from disparaging organic farming to downplaying the impact of global warming. "They were criticizing people like me for doing what we had a right to do, had gone through a government agency to do," says Kleinpeter. "We never could get to the bottom of that Web site to get that corrected."

As it turns out, the Web site counts among its contributors Steven Milloy, the "junk science" commentator for FoxNews.com and operator of junkscience.com, which claims to debunk "faulty scientific data and analysis." It may come as no surprise that earlier in his career, Milloy, who calls himself the "junkman," was a registered lobbyist for Monsanto.

Thinking about the Text

1. A good **REPORT** should have a confident **TONE** that informs rather than argues (see p. 297). Does Donald L. Barlett and James B. Steele's report satisfy this criterion? Cite examples from the article to support your answer.

2. Do the dairy products that you consume come from rBGH-fed cows? Has reading this article motivated you to read food labeling more carefully? Should more information be available on labeling? Should it be required? Why or why not?

3. An extensive report about biotechnology, agribusiness, and large-scale litigation runs the risk of being dry and uninteresting to a general audience. Barlett and Steele provide many concrete **EXAMPLES** and **NARRATIVES** to illustrate complex situations and stimulate interest in the topic. The case of Gary Rinehart is one such example. What are three other examples? Which was most interesting or surprising to you? Why?

4. Barlett and Steele say that Monsanto is moving ever closer to controlling the world's agricultural seeds, and they present a variety of **EVIDENCE** to support this conclusion. Do you feel that their evidence is convincing? Why or why not? Is any important kind of evidence lacking? If so, what would it be?

5. Research Monsanto's side of the story. Google "why does Monsanto sue farmers who save seeds?" and read all about it. As you'll see, Monsanto presents its **ARGUMENT** clearly. Whose argument do you find more persuasive—Barlett and Steele's or Monsanto's? Why?

6. Are your food purchases influenced by the information available on packaging about the use of genetically modified organisms or growth hormones? Has Barlett and Steele's article prompted you to think differently about your food choices? Why or why not? Write an essay that explains your reasoning.

What's Your Pronoun?

DENNIS BARON

PRONOUNS ARE SUDDENLY SEXY. No longer the province of stuffy grammar books, they're in the air, on the news, all over social media, generating discussion pro and con. Or at least one pronoun is: the third-person singular gender-neutral pronoun. Yes, the pronoun *without* sex is suddenly sexy. People are asking each other, "What's your pronoun?"—it's the new "Hello, my name is _____." And sometimes they don't even wait to be asked. They introduce themselves with, "I'm Alex. My pronouns are *they, them, their.*" Or "*ze, hir, hirs.*" Or they put it in their profile:

> DR. ANDREW FOLES
> @drandrewcomic
>
> I'm a linguist and a comic book
> editor @comicsuniv. I also have
> experience herding sheep. He/him.

DENNIS BARON, professor emeritus of linguistics and English, has written extensively for both academic and general audiences on issues of language and the law, language technologies, and gender issues in language use, among other topics. He is author of *A Better Pencil: Readers, Writers, and the Digital Revolution* (2009). This essay is from the introduction to his recent book, *What's Your Pronoun?* (2020). Baron tweets from @DrGrammar.

Pronouns are even on TV. In 2019, in a scene from the long-running BBC police procedural *Silent Witness*, Nick, a suspect in a series of murders at a transgender support center, asks an investigator, "What gender pronouns are you going to use for me in your report?" The investigator responds, "What would you like me to use?" And Nick replies, "She, please." The investigator honors that request.[1]

"What's your pronoun?" is an invitation to declare, to honor, or to reject, not just a pronoun, but a gender identity. And it's a question about a part of speech. Repeat: A question about a part of speech.

It used to be nerdy to discuss parts of speech outside of grammar class. Now it's cool. When the talk turns to "What's your pronoun?" suddenly everybody has an opinion, not just about pronouns, but about *that* pronoun. English has masculine and feminine and neuter pronouns, but it is missing a pronoun for someone whose gender is unknown, unclear, nonbinary, or "other." For centuries, grammarians recommended generic *he* in such cases. But generic *he* turns out to be not so generic: too often *he* means "only men."

That's why some people claim we need a new pronoun. And there's no shortage of people eager to supply the missing word by coining ones like *zie* or *tey*. The grammar sticklers are always sure that English speakers don't need any new pronouns, they've gotten along just fine with generic *he*, thank you very much. Fortunately, and apologies if you are one of them, the sticklers are becoming hard to find. And a growing number of people are realizing that we've had the missing word all along: it's singular *they*.

For more than two hundred years—long before *transgender* (1974), *cisgender* (1997), and *gender-fluid* (1987) entered our vocabularies—a small but vocal number of writers, editors, and grammarians, mostly men, have lamented the fact that English has no third-person singular, gender-neutral pronoun to refer to both a man and a woman, or to either a man or a woman, or to conceal gender, or to prevent gender from causing a distraction. Recognizing that gender is political as well as grammatical, they've sought a pronoun—some call it "the missing word"—that includes both genders, or all genders, and doesn't leave anyone out.

Those seeking a better way to include all the genders, whether they think of gender as a traditional male/female binary or something more

---

1. *Silent Witness*, series 22, episode 1, "Two Spirits, pt. 1," at 40:50. bbc.co.uk, 2019.

nuanced and complex, have answered the pronoun question in multiple ways. They've coined a new word, or they've repurposed a current word. They've borrowed a word from another language, or they've acknowledged that *they*, like *you*, could be both singular and plural. To be sure, there have been defenders of the status quo who've simply invoked generic *he*, long approved by grammarians who insisted that such use of *he* includes *she*. Some nineteenth-century feminists capitalized on this inclusive *he* by arguing that, if *he* means *she*, then surely the voting laws, which always referred to voters as *he*, meant that women could vote. Unfortunately, judges and legislators—all of them men—disagreed. "Of course *he* is generic," they mansplained, "but not for voting."

It wasn't just voting. There have been too many occasions where generic *he* didn't seem generic. For example, one Minnesota public health law, proposed in 1903, decreed, "No person shall kiss another person unless *he* can prove that *he* is free from contagious or infectious diseases."[2] Does *he* in the bill include women who kiss? Or parents kissing children? Or children kissing grandparents? Or politicians kissing babies? Or trans persons? The word *transgender* didn't exist in 1903, but gender dysphoria did. Would people identifying as gender-nonconforming today be bound by that Minnesota *he*?

He is just a pronoun, just a part of speech. But put a pronoun in a law, as some well-meaning Minnesota legislator tried to do, and suddenly, you've got yourself a problem, whether that law is about kissing or about voting. Because the problem's not just about who's kissing who. In 1916, when Jeanette Rankin, of Montana, became the first woman elected to the U. S. House of Representatives, the *Minneapolis Star Tribune* ran this headline challenging the grammatical rule that says the masculine pronoun can refer to women: "Can 'She' Be 'He', a Congressman, and Be Woman?"[3] Pronouns aren't just a part of speech. Pronouns are political.

In 1922, Edith Wilmans became the first woman elected to the Texas state assembly, prompting a prediction by the *San Antonio Express* that she would not be allowed to serve, because Texas law referred to state legislators

As you dig around in newspaper archives, make sure to write down everything you'll need for your documentation style. Ch. 22 will help you get organized.

---

2. "To Restrict Kissing by Law," *New York Tribune,* Jan. 31, 1903, p. 7. Emphasis added.
3. "Can 'She' Be 'He,' a Congressman, and Be Woman?" *Minneapolis Star Tribune,* Nov. 13, 1916, p. 1. Montana, Colorado, and a number of other states had universal suffrage before the passage of the Nineteenth Amendment ensured that all American women could vote.

as *he*. The *San Antonio Evening News* shrugged off this objection, at the same time reminding readers that the masculine pronoun doesn't just keep women out of the state house: "The same pronoun stands between many women and their liberty."[4]

The men who made and enforced the laws insisted the *he* in a statute included women when it came to imposing penalties, as in the Minnesota kissing bill, which would have fined offenders between $1 and $5 (about $30–$150 today). But these same men used the pronoun *he* to exclude women when they tried to assert their right to vote or to hold elected office. Or, as the *San Antonio News* wryly observed, when women tried to assert any rights at all. 10

[T]he generic masculine was never truly generic: far too many times, *he* meant "only men." As British and American women began to assert their political and economic rights in the nineteenth century, both feminists and antifeminists enlisted the pronoun *he* to support their cause. American suffragists like Susan B. Anthony observed that, when the criminal laws referred to lawbreakers as *he* or *him*, no one doubted that these laws also applied to women. And so both logic and consistency demanded that, when the voting laws referred to voters as *he*, that meant women could vote as well as men. Or so you would think.

Although pronouns may seem a minor concern compared with physical safety and mental stability, prisoners have gone to court, with varying degrees of success, to demand to be referred to by their chosen pronoun, and employees have filed complaints against employers when supervisors and co-workers intentionally use inappropriate pronouns and create a hostile work environment. Gay and trans students also charge their schools with gender discrimination for not upholding their right to designate their pronoun. Laws and regulations in these areas remain unsettled, varying from jurisdiction to jurisdiction, office to office, and school to school. And yet more and more national, state, and local governments, along with businesses and schools, are now recognizing pronoun choice as one of the rights of gender-nonconforming persons.

4. *San Antonio Evening News*, Oct. 5, 1922, p. 4. Wilmans easily won that seat—with the support of the Texas Ku Klux Klan. After the passage of the Nineteenth Amendment, women's suffrage, particularly in the American South, was often leveraged to dilute the African American vote.

Confronting Generic *He*

Pronoun gender is a hot topic today, but it's hardly a new topic. From the first English grammars in the seventeenth century to the language commentators of the later twentieth, writers who tackled the question of pronoun gender dealt with generic *he* in a number of ways:

- By simply decreeing that *he* was generic and assuming that anything else was just plain wrong; or sensing resistance to generic *he,* but still insisting that *he* was both inclusive and grammatically correct; or, acknowledging discomfort with generic *he,* but finding no alternative, feeling compelled to indicate that he included "she."
- Rejecting generic *he* as ambiguous or sexist and using singular *they* instead, defending it as both natural and common. Sometimes adding that if *you* could be singular and plural, why not *they* as well?
- Rejecting both generic *he* and singular *they* in favor of an invented pronoun, and sometimes asking some expert to coin one in order to avoid error and ambiguity.

In addition, any of the above might be accompanied by a condemnation of the compounds *he or she,* along with *him or her* and *his or her,* options that are both grammatical and inclusive, but which no one liked. Ever.

A New Pronoun Would Fix All That

Starting in the eighteenth century, a few more-adventurous souls thought that the best way to deal with the missing word would be to invent one. More than 200 of these pronouns were invented, most of them before the 1970s, and many of them before 1900. There were crackpots coining pronouns, to be sure, but most of the neologists—the new word makers—were writers, educators, or professionals who knew a bit about language and who thought they could improve on a bad situation. Most of the word coiners were men, though a few women got into the act. Some of the word coiners were concerned with gender parity, some with grammatical correctness, and a few of them with both. Some of their proposals were met with mockery and derision, but a few were taken seriously enough to be adopted by a few enthusiasts. Two gender-neutral pronouns, *thon* and *heer,* even made it into major dictionaries, though they were later dropped for lack of use. But most of these pronouns made a small splash and then were lost to history— not the missing words, but the words that failed.

The early word coiners were typically concerned with correctness. In 15 their view, the current options were simply wrong. Generic *he* used a masculine pronoun for a woman, violating the rule that pronouns should agree with their antecedents in gender as well as number. Singular *they* used a plural pronoun for a singular noun, violating the number agreement part of that rule. A new pronoun would fix all that.

The Pronoun Almost Everyone Already Used

The first word coiners didn't care so much about gender inclusivity, or identity politics, or resistance to heteronormativity. That came later. But as women's rights and suffrage grew prominent both in the United States and England after the 1840s, pronouns were discussed by feminists and antifeminists alike. They were discussed by legislators. By grammarians. By editors. And by ordinary people around the dinner table. An article in the *Springfield Republican* in 1896 claimed that these ordinary folk had already found the solution to the missing word. Instead of the generic *he* mandated by grammarians, it was *they:* "at least two men out of three and four women out of five use 'they' already, with sublime contempt for rule."[5] Of course these statistics were a guess. There was no way in 1896 to tell how many men or women used singular *they,* or any other pronoun. But the *Republican* didn't need hard data to know what was obvious to even the most casual of observers, that almost everyone used singular *they* in speech, and many careful writers used it as well. The *Republican* had an answer to the pronoun question. Singular *they.*

5. "A New Treatise on Everyday English," *Springfield Republican* (MA), Jan. 5, 1896, p. 6.

Thinking about the Text

1. Dennis Baron **PROPOSES** that singular *they* is a tidy solution to two distinct third-person pronoun challenges in English. What are those challenges? Do you agree with Baron that *they* is a good solution? Why or why not?

2. How often do you use or hear **SINGULAR *THEY***? First, write down your immediate answer. Then, pay close attention for two days to what you and the people around you say in ordinary conversation. How well does your observation match up with your initial response? Are you surprised by your observations? Explain what you've noticed and why it might (or might not) have surprised you.

3. Baron, a linguist and prolific writer and speaker on language issues, is clearly very serious about the topic of pronouns, specifically about singular *they*. His essay, however, does include touches of humor. How well does his sometimes casual **TONE** work with the serious purpose of his argument? Explain your reasoning.

4. All languages change over time—pronunciations shift gradually, new words are added, others disappear from daily use, and even the ways that words can be put together to make meaning can shift over time. Many of these changes occur so gradually that we don't notice them; occasionally, a change can be observed as it happens. The growing acceptance of singular *they*, for example, is something that you're experiencing in real time. What other changes have you observed? In addition to new words or new meanings (*subtweet*, *catfish*, *mansplain*), think about whether you've observed pronunciation shifts or other changes. Describe your observations and conclusions.

5. Most people (maybe including you, too) have strong feelings about their language(s) and how they should (or shouldn't) be spoken or written. English speakers may have adamant opinions about singular *they*, or *y'all*, or whether a carbonated soft drink is called *pop* or *soda* or something else entirely. Why do you think some people care so much? Might they be overreacting? Why or why not? Write an essay that addresses these questions and explains your responses.

The Sanctuary of School

LYNDA BARRY

I WAS 7 YEARS OLD the first time I snuck out of the house in the dark. It was winter and my parents had been fighting all night. They were short on money and long on relatives who kept "temporarily" moving into our house because they had nowhere else to go.

My brother and I were used to giving up our bedroom. We slept on the couch, something we actually liked because it put us that much closer to the light of our lives, our television.

At night when everyone was asleep, we lay on our pillows watching it with the sound off. We watched Steve Allen's mouth moving. We watched Johnny Carson's mouth moving. We watched movies filled with gangsters shooting machine guns into packed rooms, dying soldiers hurling a last grenade and beautiful women crying at windows. Then the sign-off finally came and we tried to sleep.

LYNDA BARRY is an artist, cartoonist, and teacher, known for her comic strip *Ernie Pook's Comeek* as well as for graphic works on the relationship between creativity and drawing like *What It Is* (2008). In 2016, she was inducted into the Eisner Hall of Fame. Barry is currently a professor of interdisciplinary creativity at the University of Wisconsin's Image Lab. The essay here was originally published in the *New York Times* in 1992, when public schools were experiencing severe cutbacks.

The morning I snuck out, I woke up filled with a panic about needing to get to school. The sun wasn't quite up yet but my anxiety was so fierce that I just got dressed, walked quietly across the kitchen and let myself out the back door.

It was quiet outside. Stars were still out. Nothing moved and no one was   5 in the street. It was as if someone had turned the sound off on the world.

I walked the alley, breaking thin ice over the puddles with my shoes. I didn't know why I was walking to school in the dark. I didn't think about it. All I knew was a feeling of panic, like the panic that strikes kids when they realize they are lost.

That feeling eased the moment I turned the corner and saw the dark outline of my school at the top of the hill. My school was made up of about 15 nondescript portable classrooms set down on a fenced concrete lot in a rundown Seattle neighborhood, but it had the most beautiful view of the Cascade Mountains. You could see them from anywhere on the playfield and you could see them from the windows of my classroom—Room 2.

I walked over to the monkey bars and hooked my arms around the cold metal. I stood for a long time just looking across Rainier Valley. The sky was beginning to whiten and I could hear a few birds.

In a perfect world my absence at home would not have gone unnoticed. I would have had two parents in a panic to locate me, instead of two parents in a panic to locate an answer to the hard question of survival during a deep financial and emotional crisis.

But in an overcrowded and unhappy home, it's incredibly easy for any   10 child to slip away. The high levels of frustration, depression and anger in my house made my brother and me invisible. We were children with the sound turned off. And for us, as for the steadily increasing number of neglected children in this country, the only place where we could count on being noticed was at school.

"Hey there, young lady. Did you forget to go home last night?" It was Mr. Gunderson, our janitor, whom we all loved. He was nice and he was funny and he was old with white hair, thick glasses and an unbelievable number of keys. I could hear them jingling as he walked across the playfield. I felt incredibly happy to see him.

He let me push his wheeled garbage can between the different portables as he unlocked each room. He let me turn on the lights and raise the

window shades and I saw my school slowly come to life. I saw Mrs. Holman, our school secretary, walk into the office without her orange lipstick on yet. She waved.

I saw the fifth-grade teacher, Mr. Cunningham, walking under the breezeway eating a hard roll. He waved.

And I saw my teacher, Mrs. Claire LeSane, walking toward us in a red coat and calling my name in a very happy and surprised way, and suddenly my throat got tight and my eyes stung and I ran toward her crying. It was something that surprised us both.

It's only thinking about it now, 28 years later, that I realize I was crying 15 from relief. I was with my teacher, and in a while I was going to sit at my desk, with my crayons and pencils and books and classmates all around me, and for the next six hours I was going to enjoy a thoroughly secure, warm and stable world. It was a world I absolutely relied on. Without it, I don't know where I would have gone that morning.

Mrs. LeSane asked me what was wrong and when I said "Nothing," she seemingly left it at that. But she asked me if I would carry her purse for her, an honor above all honors, and she asked if I wanted to come into Room 2 early and paint.

She believed in the natural healing power of painting and drawing for troubled children. In the back of her room there was always a drawing table and an easel with plenty of supplies, and sometimes during the day she would come up to you for what seemed like no good reason and quietly ask if you wanted to go to the back table and "make some pictures for Mrs. LeSane." We all had a chance at it—to sit apart from the class for a while to paint, draw and silently work out impossible problems on 11 × 17 sheets of newsprint.

Drawing came to mean everything to me. At the back table in Room 2, I learned to build myself a life preserver that I could carry into my home.

We all know that a good education system saves lives, but the people of this country are still told that cutting the budget for public schools is necessary, that poor salaries for teachers are all we can manage and that art, music and all creative activities must be the first to go when times are lean.

Before- and after-school programs are cut and we are told that public schools 20 are not made for baby-sitting children. If parents are neglectful temporarily or permanently, for whatever reason, it's certainly sad, but their unlucky children must fend for themselves. Or slip through the cracks. Or wander in a dark night alone.

We are told in a thousand ways that not only are public schools not important, but that the children who attend them, the children who need them most, are not important either. We leave them to learn from the blind eye of a television, or to the mercy of "a thousand points of light"[1] that can be as far away as stars.

I was lucky. I had Mrs. LeSane. I had Mr. Gunderson. I had an abundance of art supplies. And I had a particular brand of neglect in my home that allowed me to slip away and get to them. But what about the rest of the kids who weren't as lucky? What happened to them?

By the time the bell rang that morning I had finished my drawing and Mrs. LeSane pinned it up on the special bulletin board she reserved for drawings from the back table. It was the same picture I always drew—a sun in the corner of a blue sky over a nice house with flowers all around it.

Mrs. LeSane asked us to please stand, face the flag, place our right hands over our hearts and say the Pledge of Allegiance. Children across the country do it faithfully. I wonder now when the country will face its children and say a pledge right back.

> Describing how one child was saved by art classes helps make a case for funding school programs. See Ch. 19 for more argument strategies.

1. *"A thousand points of light"*: A phrase used by President George H. W. Bush to refer to the many private, nonprofit community organizations that he hoped would step in to help people in need when government-sponsored social programs were cut. [Editor's note]

Thinking about the Text

1. Lynda Barry begins her narrative by revealing some painful personal information, which leads to a damning criticism of the state of education in the United States. Does her personal anecdote enhance her political argument? damage it? How well do these two elements of her essay complement one another? Explain your answer, citing evidence from the text.

2. It could be argued that the art opportunities in Barry's school were more beneficial to her than to other students because she was always artistically inclined and even went on to become a professional artist—or even that there is no reason to have art instruction in elementary schools at all because so few children actually become artists. How would you respond to that argument? Agree or disagree, presenting **EVIDENCE** from your own school experiences.

3. Barry uses the expression "the sound off" or "the sound turned off" three times in the essay (3, 5, 10). In which instances is it meant literally and in which figuratively? How does the repetition of this language help make the point of her narrative?

4. Barry concludes her essay with a call for the United States and its education system to make a "pledge" to children (24). Although her proposals are not spelled out, what can you infer about what Barry is asking the schools to do? Provide **EXAMPLES** from the text that indicate what she thinks is important.

5. Did you ever have a teacher who, in the course of simply doing their job, helped you get through a hard time or a tremendous struggle? Write a **NARRATIVE** about an experience you had with a memorable teacher, and relate your experience in some way to your adult life.

Fun Home

ALISON BECHDEL

ALISON BECHDEL is a cartoonist, writer, and 2014 recipient of a MacArthur "genius" fellowship. Her serialized comic strip, *Dykes to Watch Out For*, ran in dozens of periodicals from 1983 to 2008. In 2006, she published *Fun Home: A Family Tragicomic*, a graphic memoir that centers on her relationship with her father and addresses matters of gender, sexual orientation, and family; the book became a Broadway musical that won a Tony award in 2015. The title refers to the family business, a funeral home.

In a 2012 interview in the *New Yorker*, Bechdel describes the writing/drawing process that results in her characteristic panels so rich with graphic and narrative detail. First, she creates a grid of panels that one walks through, like rooms in a house. "The whole thing about a graphic book," says Bechdel, "is that it's a 3-D object."

You may have heard of the Bechdel Test. To pass, a movie, TV show, or book has to have at least two characters who: 1) are women, 2) talk to each other, and 3) talk about something other than a man. (Go to bechdeltest.com to see how many of your favorite films have passed the Bechdel Test.)

This selection is from *Fun Home* and contains some terms that may be unfamiliar. *Daedalus* and *Icarus* were a father-son duo in Greek mythology. While the two were imprisoned in a tower, master builder Daedalus built wings from feathers and wax so that they could escape by flying out. He warned Icarus not to fly too high because the sun would melt the wax, but the warning was unheeded, and Icarus fell into the sea and drowned. *Butch* and *nelly* are colloquial terms that emerged in twentieth-century lesbian and gay cultures. The terms refer to gender performance or traits, with *butch* roughly corresponding to masculine and *nelly* to feminine.

LIKE MANY FATHERS, MINE COULD
OCCASIONALLY BE PREVAILED ON FOR
A SPOT OF "AIRPLANE."

AS HE LAUNCHED ME, MY FULL WEIGHT
WOULD FALL ON THE PIVOT POINT
BETWEEN HIS FEET AND MY STOMACH.

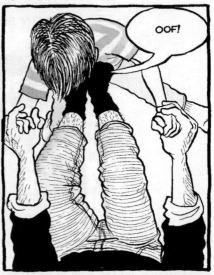

OOF!

IT WAS A DISCOMFORT WELL WORTH THE RARE PHYSICAL CONTACT, AND CERTAINLY
WORTH THE MOMENT OF PERFECT BALANCE WHEN I SOARED ABOVE HIM.

IN THE CIRCUS,
ACROBATICS WHERE
ONE PERSON LIES
ON THE FLOOR
BALANCING ANOTHER
ARE CALLED
"ICARIAN GAMES."

CONSIDERING THE FATE OF ICARUS AFTER HE FLOUTED HIS FATHER'S ADVICE AND FLEW SO CLOSE TO THE SUN HIS WINGS MELTED, PERHAPS SOME DARK HUMOR IS INTENDED.

UH-OH!

IN OUR PARTICULAR REENACTMENT OF THIS MYTHIC RELATIONSHIP, IT WAS NOT ME BUT MY FATHER WHO WAS TO PLUMMET FROM THE SKY.

BUT BEFORE HE DID SO, HE MANAGED TO GET QUITE A LOT DONE.

AGAIN!

THIS RUG IS FILTHY. GO GET THE VACUUM CLEANER.

HIS GREATEST ACHIEVEMENT, ARGUABLY, WAS HIS MONOMANIACAL RESTORATION OF OUR OLD HOUSE.

AND THEN GET ME MY TACK HAMMER. THAT STRIP OF MOLDING IS LOOSE.

WHEN OTHER CHILDREN CALLED OUR HOUSE A MANSION, I WOULD DEMUR. I RESENTED THE IMPLICATION THAT MY FAMILY WAS RICH, OR UNUSUAL IN ANY WAY.

IN FACT, WE WERE UNUSUAL, THOUGH I WOULDN'T APPRECIATE EXACTLY HOW UNUSUAL UNTIL MUCH LATER. BUT WE WERE NOT RICH.

THE GILT CORNICES, THE MARBLE FIREPLACE, THE CRYSTAL CHANDELIERS, THE SHELVES OF CALF-BOUND BOOKS--THESE WERE NOT SO MUCH BOUGHT AS PRODUCED FROM THIN AIR BY MY FATHER'S REMARKABLE LEGERDEMAIN.

MY FATHER COULD SPIN GARBAGE...

...INTO GOLD.

HE COULD TRANSFIGURE A ROOM WITH THE SMALLEST OFFHAND FLOURISH.

HE COULD CONJURE AN ENTIRE, FINISHED PERIOD INTERIOR FROM A PAINT CHIP.

HE WAS AN ALCHEMIST OF APPEARANCE, A SAVANT OF SURFACE, A DAEDALUS OF DECOR.

SOMETIMES, WHEN THINGS WERE GOING WELL, I THINK MY FATHER ACTUALLY ENJOYED HAVING A FAMILY.

OR AT LEAST, THE AIR OF AUTHENTICITY WE LENT TO HIS EXHIBIT. A SORT OF STILL LIFE WITH CHILDREN.

AND OF COURSE, MY BROTHERS AND I WERE FREE LABOR. DAD CONSIDERED US EXTENSIONS OF HIS OWN BODY, LIKE PRECISION ROBOT ARMS.

PUT HOT, SOAPY WATER IN THE SINK AND GET SOME CLEAN RAGS.

IN THIS REGARD, IT WAS LIKE BEING RAISED NOT BY JIMMY BUT BY MARTHA STEWART.

IN THEORY, HIS ARRANGEMENT WITH MY MOTHER WAS MORE COOPERATIVE.

WHAT DO YOU THINK OF THIS GAS CHANDELIER?

BORDELLO.

AUCTION CATALOG

IN PRACTICE, IT WAS NOT.

WE EACH RESISTED IN OUR OWN WAYS, BUT IN THE END WE WERE EQUALLY POWERLESS BEFORE MY FATHER'S CURATORIAL ONSLAUGHT.

WHOREHOUSE.

IT'S HIDEOUS.

EH-EH-EH-EH! PKRGH!

IT LOOKS LIKE SKULLS.

MY BROTHERS AND I COULDN'T COMPETE WITH THE ASTRAL LAMPS AND GIRANDOLES AND HEPPLEWHITE SUITE CHAIRS. THEY WERE PERFECT.

GET YOUR STINKIN' FEET AWAY FROM ME.

ALISON, COME HELP ME HANG THIS MIRROR IN YOUR ROOM.

I GREW TO RESENT THE WAY MY FATHER TREATED HIS FURNITURE LIKE CHILDREN, AND HIS CHILDREN LIKE FURNITURE.

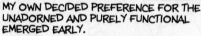

MY OWN DECIDED PREFERENCE FOR THE UNADORNED AND PURELY FUNCTIONAL EMERGED EARLY.

HOLD IT HIGHER. DON'T MOVE.

I HATE THIS ROOM.

WHEN I GROW UP, MY HOUSE IS GOING TO BE ALL METAL, LIKE A SUBMARINE.

It's not only Bechdel's detailed drawings that bring her story to life; the descriptive details add to the rich texture of her narrative. Learn more about adding vivid detail on pages 194–96.

I WAS SPARTAN TO MY FATHER'S ATHENIAN.

MODERN TO HIS VICTORIAN.

BUTCH TO HIS NELLY.

UTILITARIAN TO HIS AESTHETE.

ALTHOUGH I'M GOOD AT ENUMERATING MY FATHER'S FLAWS, IT'S HARD FOR ME TO SUSTAIN MUCH ANGER AT HIM.

I EXPECT THIS IS PARTLY BECAUSE HE'S DEAD, AND PARTLY BECAUSE THE BAR IS LOWER FOR FATHERS THAN FOR MOTHERS.

MY MOTHER MUST HAVE BATHED ME HUNDREDS OF TIMES. BUT IT'S MY FATHER RINSING ME OFF WITH THE PURPLE METAL CUP THAT I REMEMBER MOST CLEARLY.

...THE SUDDEN, UNBEARABLE COLD OF ITS ABSENCE.

WAS HE A GOOD FATHER? I WANT TO SAY, "AT LEAST HE STUCK AROUND." BUT OF COURSE, HE DIDN'T.

IT'S TRUE THAT HE DIDN'T KILL HIMSELF UNTIL I WAS NEARLY TWENTY.

BUT HIS ABSENCE RESONATED RETRO-ACTIVELY, ECHOING BACK THROUGH ALL THE TIME I KNEW HIM.

MAYBE IT WAS THE CONVERSE OF THE WAY AMPUTEES FEEL PAIN IN A MISSING LIMB.

HE REALLY WAS THERE ALL THOSE YEARS, A FLESH-AND-BLOOD PRESENCE STEAMING OFF THE WALLPAPER, DIGGING UP THE DOGWOODS, POLISHING THE FINIALS...

...SMELLING OF SAWDUST AND SWEAT AND DESIGNER COLOGNE.

BUT I ACHED AS IF HE WERE ALREADY GONE.

Thinking about the Text

1. Alison Bechdel describes a relationship with her father that is full of both love and resentment. How does she reconcile those seeming contradictions? How successful is she at conveying her balance between tenderness and bitterness? Why do you think so? Point to specific passages that support your conclusion.

2. Bechdel chooses two very ordinary activities with her father—playing airplane and being bathed—to represent something larger about her childhood and her life in general. Think of a moment in your own childhood that you might use to represent something larger about yourself. What would it be?

3. In addition to the drawings themselves, Bechdel employs narration boxes and speech balloons to help tell her story. How does she use those two devices to navigate between events happening in her childhood moments and reflections from her adult perspective? Select one panel or group of panels and describe how each device works in your selection.

4. Although Bechdel's family has other members, *Fun Home* focuses on the relationship between Alison and her father. We know from her reflections what her attitude is toward her father. What is Bechdel's attitude toward her child self? How does she reveal it? Point to specific passages that support your reasoning.

5. Write a short **NARRATIVE** (in graphic form, if you wish) of your childhood relationship with a parent or other adult in your life. Choose one or two key activities or events that can represent the relationship as a whole. Present details that illustrate the original moments and use your adult perspective to reflect and provide coherence. (You may want to respond to question #2 first to help you get started.)

The Talk: After Ferguson,
a Shaded Conversation about Race
DANA CANEDY

LIKE SO MANY AFRICAN-AMERICAN PARENTS, I had rehearsed "the talk," that nausea-inducing discussion I needed to have with my son about how to conduct himself in the presence of the police. I was prepared for his questions, except for one.

"Can I just pretend I'm white?"

Jordan was born to African-American parents, but recessive genes being what they are, he has very fair skin and pale blue eyes. I am caramel brown, and since his birth eight years ago people have mistaken me for his nanny.

When I asked why he would want to "pass" for white, I struggled with how to respond to his answer.

"Because it's safer," Jordan replied. "They won't hurt me."   5

That recent gray day, not long after grand juries failed to indict the police officers who killed unarmed black men in Ferguson, Missouri, and Staten Island, I had steadied myself to lay out the rules: Always address

DANA CANEDY is the author of *A Journal for Jordan: A Story of Love and Honor* (2008), a memoir dedicated to her son after the death of his father and her fiancé, First Sergeant Charles Monroe King. She is administrator of the Pulitzer Prizes and previously won a Pulitzer for her reporting at the *New York Times*, where this piece was published in December 2014. She tweets from @DanaCanedy.

First Sgt. Charles M. King with his son, Jordan. King visited his
son on leave before returning to Iraq on a mission that would
end his life.

police officers as "sir" or "ma'am." Do not make any sudden moves, even to
reach for identification. Do not raise your voice, resist or run.

But now I was taken aback.

Jordan's father and I never had a chance to discuss when we would give
him the talk, or what we would say. Our baby was just 6 months old when
his dad, a decorated Army soldier, was killed in combat in Iraq. So the timing
and the context of the talk were left to me.

I had tried hard to delay it, and make sure he wouldn't know the names Michael Brown or Eric Garner or Tamir Rice.

In the days leading up to the conversation, I asked an African-American 10 male colleague if he thought it was too soon. When did he tell his own boys?

"Before they were no longer seen as cute," he said, making me wince.

I hadn't fully processed that someday my son would be seen as suspect instead of sweet. So I told him, and then Jordan asked if it was rare for the police to hurt black people. I said that, just like his father when he wore his military uniform, most police officers are dedicated to protecting us. But, no, I added, it is unfortunately not uncommon.

"Then I don't want to be black anymore," Jordan declared.

He asked if I was crying. I dabbed at my eyes and searched my mind for what to say.

"Son, your father was an incredible African-American man," I told him. 15 "And you are an amazing boy who is going to grow into just such a man. Please be proud of that."

"Yes," he responded emphatically, "but can't I just pretend to be white?"

The message that Jordan's appearance affords him the option to check "other" on the race card comes at him constantly. After his second-grade class created self-portraits last year, I noticed that his was the only one not hanging on the classroom wall. His teacher explained that his portrait was "a work in progress." The brown crayon he had used to color in his face was several shades too dark, she thought, and so she wanted him to "lighten it up" to more accurately reflect his complexion.

It is not just the overt signals that have convinced Jordan that he can choose to blend in to a white world. It is also that we live a life of relative affluence. I am a journalist and author whose inner circle includes prominent black writers, television anchors and doctors. We live in a high-rise in Manhattan with a doorman and round-the-clock security. Jordan attends an elite private school and an exclusive summer camp.

A white friend calls him "the boy who lives in the sky" because of the vast city view from the nine-foot windows in his bedroom. "He lives in a bubble and is always with responsible adults," she said recently, trying to assure me that our status makes him safer than many black boys.

That is true, mostly. And if my parenting pays off, I will be able to mini- 20 mize his contact with the police. He will be law-abiding. He will respect authority. He'll understand the perception of black boys wearing hoodies or sagging pants. But will it be enough?

You may not be a mother. Or black. Or wealthy. In any case, it's important to really listen to what Dana Canedy is saying— pp. 8–10 explain why.

Just last month a video went viral that showed a black man in Pontiac, Michigan, being questioned by a sheriff's deputy because someone reported feeling nervous after seeing him walking in the cold with his hands in his pockets. So as much as I want to believe that our upper-middle-class status will protect my son from many of society's social ills, it could not provide him the white privilege he seeks.

Nor would "passing" protect Jordan entirely, for the internal damage from living that lie would surely be as painful as any blow from a police baton. To deny his blackness would be to deny me. It would be to deny our enslaved ancestors who were strong enough to endure that voyage. It would mean rejecting the reflection he sees every time he looks in a mirror.

For at least a little while longer, Jordan is too young to understand any of this. He does not know the racial indignity of having jobs and promotions denied or delayed, does not know the humiliation of being stopped and frisked. He has never heard the mantra "I can't breathe."

I know that our talk was just the start of a conversation that will go deeper as he moves into his teen years in a post-Obama America. My fervent hope is that, by then, I will have found a way to help him embrace the privilege of being black.

Thinking about the Text

1. What is Dana Canedy's **PURPOSE** in publicly exposing such a painful and private conversation between her and her son? What point is she trying to make? And how persuasively does she make it? Explain your response.

2. It's true: numerous studies confirm that white youth are not targeted by police nearly as often as black youth. Still, pretending to be white, as Canedy's son proposed, is both unsuitable as a solution and hurtful to Canedy personally. Why? Explain the dilemma.

3. Canedy's narrative was published in the *New York Times*, a daily newspaper with a large nationwide circulation. What background information about "the talk" (1) does Canedy provide for this **AUDIENCE**? What might she have done differently if she were writing for a magazine with a primary readership of black parents? What information could she have omitted, and what might she have included that she chose not to include here?

4. A good narrative includes **DESCRIPTIVE** details that make the story come alive. What part of Canedy's narrative touched you the deepest? Why? Describe your reaction.

5. At some time in our lives, we've all had a run-in with some form of authority. Think of a frightening or otherwise memorable encounter with an authority figure. In what ways did your skin color, gender, stature, dress, or other factors in how you look or present yourself affect that encounter? Did any characteristics work in your favor or against you—and if so, how? Write a brief **NARRATIVE** of the encounter as you remember it, reflecting in particular on how your physical presence affects your life.

World and Screen

NICHOLAS CARR

THE WORLD is a strange, changeable, and dangerous place. Getting around in it demands of any animal a great deal of effort, mental and physical. For ages, human beings have been creating tools to reduce the strain of travel. History is, among other things, a record of the discovery of ingenious new ways to ease our passage through our environs, to make it possible to cross greater and more daunting distances without getting lost, roughed up, or eaten. Simple maps and trail markers came first, then star maps and nautical charts and terrestrial globes, then instruments like sounding weights, quadrants, astrolabes, compasses, octants and sextants, telescopes, hourglasses, and chronometers. Lighthouses were erected along shorelines, buoys set in coastal waters. Roads were paved, signs posted, highways linked and numbered. It has, for most of us, been a long time since we've had to rely on our wits to get around.

GPS receivers and other automated mapping and direction-plotting devices are the latest additions to our navigational toolkit. They also give the

---

NICHOLAS CARR is the author of *The Shallows: What the Internet Is Doing to Our Brains* (2011) and *Utopia Is Creepy* (2016). His books about technology, economy, and culture have sparked much conversation on those topics, and the catchphrase "Is Google Making Us Stupid?" comes from his 2008 essay in the *Atlantic*. He blogs at roughtype.com and tweets from @roughtype. This essay comes from his book *The Glass Cage: Automation and Us* (2014).

Amerigo Vespucci, a fifteenth-century navigator, uses an astrolabe to find the Southern Cross.

old story a new and worrisome twist. Earlier navigational aids, particularly those available and affordable to ordinary folks, were just that: aids. They were designed to give travelers a greater awareness of the world around them—to sharpen their sense of direction, provide them with advance warning of danger, highlight nearby landmarks and other points of orientation, and in general help them situate themselves in both familiar and alien settings. Satellite navigation systems can do all those things, and more, but they're not designed to deepen our involvement with our surroundings. They're designed to relieve us of the need for such involvement. By taking control of the mechanics of navigation and reducing our own role to following routine commands—turn left in five hundred yards, take the next exit, stay right, destination ahead—the systems, whether running through a dashboard, a smartphone, or a dedicated GPS receiver, end up isolating us from the environment. As a team of Cornell University researchers put it in a 2008 paper, "With the GPS you no longer need to know where you are and where your destination is, attend to physical landmarks along the way, or get assistance from other people in the car and outside of it." The automation of wayfinding serves to "inhibit the process of experiencing the physical world by navigation through it."[1]

As is so often the case with gadgets and services that ease our way through life, we've celebrated the arrival of inexpensive GPS units. The *New York Times* writer David Brooks spoke for many when, in a 2007 op-ed titled "The Outsourced Brain," he raved about the navigation system installed in his new car: "I quickly established a romantic attachment to my GPS. I found comfort in her tranquil and slightly Anglophilic voice. I felt warm and safe following her thin blue line." His "GPS goddess" had "liberated" him from the age-old "drudgery" of navigation. And yet, he grudgingly confessed, the emancipation delivered by his in-dash muse came at a cost: "After a few weeks, it occurred to me that I could no longer get anywhere without her. Any trip slightly out of the ordinary had me typing the address into her system and then blissfully following her satellite-fed commands. I found that I was quickly shedding all vestiges of geographic knowledge." The price of convenience was, Brooks wrote, a loss of "autonomy."[2] The goddess was also a siren.

We want to see computer maps as interactive, high-tech versions of paper maps, but that's a mistaken assumption. . . . Traditional maps give us context. They provide us with an overview of an area and require us to figure out our current location and then plan or visualize the best route to our next stop. Yes, they require some work—good tools always do—but the mental effort aids our mind in creating its own cognitive map of an area. Map reading, research has shown, strengthens our sense of place and hones our navigational skills—in ways that can make it easier for us to get around even when we don't have a map at hand. We seem, without knowing it, to call on our subconscious memories of paper maps in orienting ourselves in a city or town and determining which way to head to arrive at our destination. In one revealing experiment, researchers found that people's naviga-

1. Gilly Leshed et al., "In-Car GPS Navigation: Engagement with and Disengagement from the Environment," in *Proceedings of the SIGCHI Conference on Human Factors in Computing Systems* (New York: ACM, 2008), 1675–1684.
2. David Brooks, "The Outsourced Brain," *New York Times*, October 26, 2007.

tional sense is actually sharpest when they're facing north—the same way maps point.[3] Paper maps don't just shepherd us from one place to the next; they teach us how to think about space.

The maps generated by satellite-linked computers are different. They usually provide meager spatial information and few navigational cues. Instead of requiring us to puzzle out where we are in an area, a GPS device simply sets us at the center of the map and then makes the world circulate around us. In this miniature parody of the pre-Copernican universe, we can get around without needing to know where we are, where we've been, or which direction we're heading. We just need an address or an intersection, the name of a building or a shop, to cue the device's calculations. Julia Frankenstein, a German cognitive psychologist who studies the mind's navigational sense, believes it's likely that "the more we rely on technology to find our way, the less we build up our cognitive maps." Because computer navigation systems provide only "bare-bones route information, without the spatial context of the whole area," she explains, our brains don't receive the raw material required to form rich memories of places. "Developing a cognitive map from this reduced information is a bit like trying to get an entire musical piece from a few notes."[4]

Other scientists agree. A British study found that drivers using paper maps developed stronger memories of routes and landmarks than did those relying on turn-by-turn instructions from satellite systems. After completing a trip, the map users were able to sketch more precise and detailed diagrams of their routes. The findings, reported the researchers, "provide strong evidence that the use of a vehicle navigation system will impact negatively on the formation of drivers' cognitive maps."[5] A study of drivers conducted at the University of Utah found evidence of "inattentional blindness" in GPS users, which impaired their "wayfinding performance" and their ability to form visual memories of their surroundings.[6] . . .

Nicholas Carr cites an interesting mix of scholarly and popular sources. For some tips on finding sources, see Ch. 21.

3. Julia Frankenstein et al., "Is the Map in Our Head Oriented North?," *Psychological Science* 23, no. 2 (2012): 120–125.
4. Julia Frankenstein, "Is GPS All in Our Heads?," *New York Times*, February 2, 2012.
5. Gary E. Burnett and Kate Lee, "The Effect of Vehicle Navigation Systems on the Formation of Cognitive Maps," in Geoffrey Underwood, ed., *Traffic and Transport Psychology: Theory and Application* (Amsterdam: Elsevier, 2005), 407–418.
6. Elliot P. Fenech et al., "The Effects of Acoustic Turn-by-Turn Navigation on Wayfinding," *Proceedings of the Human Factors and Ergonomics Society Annual Meeting* 54, no. 23 (2010): 1926–1930.

Which raises the obvious question: *Who cares?* As long as we arrive at our destination, does it really matter whether we maintain our navigational sense or offload it to a machine? An Inuit elder on Igloolik may have good reason to bemoan the adoption of GPS technology as a cultural tragedy, but those of us living in lands crisscrossed by well-marked roads and furnished with gas stations, motels, and 7-Elevens long ago lost both the custom of and the capacity for prodigious feats of wayfinding. Our ability to perceive and interpret topography, especially in its natural state, is already much reduced. Paring it away further, or dispensing with it altogether, doesn't seem like such a big deal, particularly if in exchange we get an easier go of it.

But while we may no longer have much of a cultural stake in the conservation of our navigational prowess, we still have a personal stake in it. We are, after all, creatures of the earth. We're not abstract dots proceeding along thin blue lines on computer screens. We're real beings in real bodies in real places. Getting to know a place takes effort, but it ends in fulfillment and in knowledge. It provides a sense of personal accomplishment and autonomy, and it also provides a sense of belonging, a feeling of being at home in a place rather than passing through it. Whether practiced by a caribou hunter on an ice floe or a bargain hunter on an urban street, wayfinding opens a path from alienation to attachment. We may grimace when we hear people talk of "finding themselves," but the figure of speech, however vain and shopworn, acknowledges our deeply held sense that *who we are* is tangled up in *where we are*. We can't extract the self from its surroundings, at least not without leaving something important behind.

A GPS device, by allowing us to get from point A to point B with the least possible effort and nuisance, can make our lives easier, perhaps imbuing us, as David Brooks suggests, with a numb sort of bliss. But what it steals from us, when we turn to it too often, is the joy and satisfaction of apprehending the world around us—and of making that world a part of us. Tim Ingold, an anthropologist at the University of Aberdeen in Scotland, draws a distinction between two very different modes of travel: *wayfaring* and *transport*. Wayfaring, he explains, is "our most fundamental way of being in the world." Immersed in the landscape, attuned to its textures and features, the wayfarer enjoys "an experience of movement in which action and perception are intimately coupled." Wayfaring becomes "an ongoing process of growth and development, or self-renewal." Transport, on the other hand, is "essentially destination-oriented." It's not so much a process of discovery "*along* a way of life" as a mere "carrying *across*, from location to location, of people and goods in such a way as to leave their basic natures unaffected." In transport, the traveler doesn't actually move in any meaningful way. "Rather, he is moved, becoming a passenger in his own body."[7]

Wayfaring is messier and less efficient than transport, which is why it has become a target for automation. "If you have a mobile phone with Google Maps," says Michael Jones, an executive in Google's mapping division, "you can go anywhere on the planet and have confidence that we can give you directions to get to where you want to go safely and easily." As a result, he declares, "No human ever has to feel lost again."[8] That certainly sounds appealing, as if some basic problem in our existence had been solved forever. And it fits the Silicon Valley obsession with using software to rid people's lives of "friction." But the more you think about it, the more you realize that to never confront the possibility of getting lost is to live in a state of perpetual dislocation. If you never have to worry about not knowing where you are, then you never have to know where you are. It is also to live in a state of dependency, a ward of your phone and its apps.

Problems produce friction in our lives, but friction can act as a catalyst, pushing us to a fuller awareness and deeper understanding of our situation. "When we circumvent, by whatever means, the demand a place makes of us to find our way through it," the writer Ari Schulman observed in his 2011 *New Atlantis* essay "GPS and the End of the Road," we end up foreclosing "the best entry we have into inhabiting that place—and, by extension, to really *being* anywhere at all."[9]

We may foreclose other things as well. Neuroscientists have made a series of breakthroughs in understanding how the brain perceives and remembers space and location, and the discoveries underscore the elemental role that navigation plays in the workings of mind and memory. . . .

In a 2013 article in *Nature Neuroscience*, Edvard Moser and his colleague György Buzsáki provided extensive experimental evidence that "the neuronal mechanisms that evolved to define the spatial relationship among landmarks can also serve to embody associations among objects, events and other types of factual information." Out of such associations we weave the memories of our lives. It may well be that the brain's navigational sense—its

10

---

7. Tim Ingold, *Being Alive: Essays on Movement, Knowledge and Description* (London: Routledge, 2011), 149–152. The emphasis is Ingold's.
8. Quoted in James Fallows, "The Places You'll Go," *Atlantic*, January/February 2013.
9. Ari N. Schulman, "GPS and the End of the Road," *New Atlantis*, Spring 2011.

ancient, intricate way of plotting and recording movement through space—is the evolutionary font of all memory.[10]

What's more than a little scary is what happens when that font goes dry. Our spatial sense tends to deteriorate as we get older, and in the worst cases we lose it altogether.[11] One of the earliest and most debilitating symptoms of dementia, including Alzheimer's disease, is hippocampal and entorhinal degeneration and the consequent loss of locational memory.[12] Victims begin to forget where they are. Véronique Bohbot, a research psychiatrist and memory expert at McGill University in Montreal, has conducted studies demonstrating that the way people exercise their navigational skills influences the functioning and even the size of the hippocampus—and may provide protection against the deterioration of memory.[13] The harder people work at building cognitive maps of space, the stronger their underlying memory circuits seem to become. They can actually grow gray matter in the hippocampus—a phenomenon documented in London cab drivers—in a way that's analogous to the building of muscle mass through physical exertion. But when they simply follow turn-by-turn instructions in "a robotic fashion," Bohbot warns, they don't "stimulate their hippocampus" and as a result may leave themselves more susceptible to memory loss.[14] Bohbot worries that, should the hippocampus begin to atrophy from a lack of use in navigation, the result could be a general loss of memory and a growing risk of dementia. "Society is geared in many ways toward shrinking the hippocampus," she told an interviewer. "In the next twenty years, I think we're going to see dementia occurring earlier and earlier."[15]

10. György Buzsáki and Edvard I. Moser, "Memory, Navigation and Theta Rhythm in the Hippocampal-Entorhinal System," *Nature Neuroscience* 16, no. 2 (2013): 130–138. See also Neil Burgess et al., "Memory for Events and Their Spatial Context: Models and Experiments," in Alan Baddeley et al., eds., *Episodic Memory: New Directions in Research* (New York: Oxford University Press, 2002), 249–268.

11. See, for example, Jan M. Wiener et al., "Maladaptive Bias for Extrahippocampal Navigation Strategies in Aging Humans," *Journal of Neuroscience* 33, no. 14 (2013): 6012–6017.

12. See, for example, A. T. Du et al., "Magnetic Resonance Imaging of the Entorhinal Cortex and Hippocampus in Mild Cognitive Impairment and Alzheimer's Disease," *Journal of Neurology, Neurosurgery and Psychiatry* 71 (2001): 441–447.

13. Kyoko Konishi and Véronique D. Bohbot, "Spatial Navigational Strategies Correlate with Gray Matter in the Hippocampus of Healthy Older Adults Tested in a Virtual Maze," *Frontiers in Aging Neuroscience* 5 (2013): 1–8.

14. Email from Véronique Bohbot to author, June 4, 2010.

15. Quoted in Alex Hutchinson, "Global Impositioning Systems," *Walrus*, November 2009.

A smartphone displays an indoor map of the Florida Mall.

Even if we routinely use GPS devices when driving and walking out- 15
doors, it's been suggested, we'll still have to rely on our own minds to get
around when we're walking through buildings and other places that GPS
signals can't reach. The mental exercise of indoor navigation, the theory
goes, may help protect the functioning of our hippocampus and related neu-
ral circuits. While that argument may have been reassuring a few years ago,
it is less so today. Hungry for more data on people's whereabouts and eager
for more opportunities to distribute advertising and other messages keyed
to their location, software and smartphone companies are rushing to extend the scope of their computer-mapping tools to indoor areas like airports,
malls, and office buildings. . . .

Indoor mapping promises to ratchet up our dependence on computer
navigation and further limit our opportunities for getting around on our
own. Should personal head-up displays, such as Google Glass, come into
wide use, we would always have easy and immediate access to turn-by-turn
instructions. We'd receive, as Google's Michael Jones puts it, "a continuous
stream of guidance," directing us everywhere we want to go.[16] Google and
Mercedes-Benz are already collaborating on an app that will link a Glass
headset to a driver's in-dash GPS unit, enabling what the carmaker calls
"door-to-door navigation."[17] With the GPS goddess whispering in our ear, or

16. Quoted in Fallows, "Places You'll Go."
17. Damon Lavrinc, "Mercedes Is Testing Google Glass Integration, and It Actually Works,"
Wired, August 15, 2013, wired.com/autopia/2013/08/google-glass-mercedes-benz/.

beaming her signals onto our retinas, we'll rarely, if ever, have to exercise our mental mapping skills.

Bohbot and other researchers emphasize that more research needs to be done before we'll know for sure whether long-term use of GPS devices weakens memory and raises the risk of senility. But given all we've learned about the close links between navigation, the hippocampus, and memory, it is entirely plausible that avoiding the work of figuring out where we are and where we're going may have unforeseen and less-than-salubrious consequences. Because memory is what enables us not only to recall past events but to respond intelligently to present events and plan for future ones, any degradation in its functioning would tend to diminish the quality of our lives.

Through hundreds of thousands of years, evolution has fit our bodies and minds to the environment. We've been formed by being, to appropriate a couple of lines from the poet Wordsworth,

> Rolled round in earth's diurnal course,
> With rocks, and stones, and trees.

The automation of wayfinding distances us from the environment that shaped us. It encourages us to observe and manipulate symbols on screens rather than attend to real things in real places. The labors our obliging digital deities would have us see as mere drudgery may turn out to be vital to our fitness, happiness, and well-being. So *Who cares?* probably isn't the right question. What we should be asking ourselves is, *How far from the world do we want to retreat?*

Thinking about the Text

1. Nicholas Carr argues that satellite navigation systems are "not designed to deepen our involvement with our surroundings" (2). What does he mean by that? **SUMMARIZE** his argument. Is it persuasive? Why or why not?

2. Although it is still a matter of speculation, how might the long-term use of a GPS device contribute to the development of dementia in later life, according to Carr? What does he say happens in the brain? **EVALUATE** the **EVIDENCE** that Carr presents for what he says. Does it seem reliable? Explain.

3. Carr borrows two terms from the work of anthropologist Tim Ingold: *way-faring* and *transport*. How does he **DEFINE** each of these terms? What is the key distinction between them, and how is that distinction important to Carr's argument?

4. How do you get around in the world? When navigating a new place, do you use a map? a GPS device? landmarks, or street signs, or something else? **REFLECT** on your preferences. How do they contribute (or not) to your feeling comfortable in your surroundings and grounded in the world?

5. Imagine that someone has asked you for directions from one location in your neighborhood or on your campus to another spot nearby. Try giving directions by drawing a map, sketching in relevant streets and landmarks; by describing how to get there with words alone; and by listing directions as a GPS device would. Was one set of directions easier (or harder) to articulate than the others? Write a brief essay **COMPARING** these three ways of giving directions.

What I Learned at War

TAMMY DUCKWORTH

THE U.S. MILITARY HAS BEEN A PART OF ME since long before I signed up myself. I saw war up close early. I was born in Bangkok in 1968 and grew up in Southeast Asia with my Thai mother and my American father, who first came to the region to fight in Vietnam and stayed to work assisting refugees. I remember my mother taking me as a very little kid to the roof of our home in Phnom Penh, Cambodia, to look at the bombs exploding in the distance. She didn't want us to be scared by the booms and the strange flashes of light. It was her way of helping us to understand what was happening.

Southeast Asia was home for much of my childhood, but I moved to Hawaii when I was in high school. My first direct encounter with the military was when I joined ROTC as a graduate student, although my father, who served in the U.S. Marine Corps, can trace the military service in our family all the way back to the Revolutionary War. I was interested in becoming a Foreign Service officer; I figured I should know the difference between

---

TAMMY DUCKWORTH is a US senator from Illinois and a recipient of the Purple Heart award, given to US service members wounded or killed in war. In 2004, while piloting an army helicopter in Iraq, she suffered wounds that led to the amputation of both legs and the loss of some mobility in her right arm. She is the first double amputee to serve in the Senate, as well as the first senator to give birth while in office. This 2015 essay appeared in *Politico*, an online magazine.

a battalion and a platoon if I were going to represent my country overseas someday. What I didn't expect was to fall in love with the camaraderie and sense of purpose that the military instills in you and even with the misery of training. The thing is, when we were exhausted and miserable, my fellow cadets and I were exhausted and miserable together. When the instructor yelled, he wasn't singling anyone out, but yelling at all of us, together. It took all of us working as a team to succeed.

And thank God for that. I am alive today—a proud member of Congress and an even prouder wife and new mother—because my buddies learned the same lessons. I had been pursuing a Ph.D. in political science when my National Guard unit was sent to Iraq. Eight months into our deployment, in November 2004, a rocket-propelled grenade fired by Iraqi insurgents tore through the pilot's side of the Blackhawk helicopter I was flying. My right leg was vaporized; my left leg was crushed and shredded against the instrument panel. My pilot in command miraculously brought down the helicopter safely. I went from being the most senior member on board to the weakest. I could easily have died that day, but my crew wouldn't give up on me. They pulled me from the disabled aircraft and, when help arrived, insisted I be attended to first even though some of them were also seriously injured.

That day, and so many others when I served, illustrated the two most important lessons the military taught me: Never leave anyone behind—not on the battlefield and not in our country. And never put a service member in harm's way without understanding the cost—the very real and very human cost—of war. That's why I committed my time at the Illinois Department of Veterans' Affairs and at the federal VA, as well as my time in Congress, to making sure that veterans have the opportunity to achieve that American dream that they defended for the rest of us.

That day, I lost both of my legs, but I was given a second chance at life. 5 It's a feeling that has helped to drive me in my second chance at service—no one should be left behind, and every American deserves another chance. These two lessons inform everything I do in Congress—every minute of every day, whether discussing how best to defeat the Islamic State or debating the merits of a trade deal or trying to figure out how to provide traveling moms with a clean, safe place at airports to breast-feed their babies.

You don't have to suffer war injuries to understand how tough life can be. The military has a great support network—hundreds of people helped save me, heal me and move me on with my life. Not everyone can count

Duckworth attends a Veteran's Day ceremony after being elected to Congress in 2016.

on help like that when tragedy strikes their families, their health or their careers; the recent recession has been devastating for many families. The least I can do as an elected official is to try to make sure working families are not left behind and to offer them help through benefits like education and a higher minimum wage.

As for war, families like mine, with fathers and brothers and sisters and mothers in the service, are always the first to bleed. We will serve and serve proudly. We will go wherever the country needs us. I am not a dove. I believe strongly that if the country's national security interests dictate that we put boots on the ground, then let's do it and be aware of the true costs, both economic and human. I'm also not a reckless hawk, with scant appreciation for what the men and women in uniform—and their families—sacrifice every single day to keep the rest of us safe.

Our efforts in Iraq cost our economy more than a trillion dollars, and we will be caring for our Iraq and Afghanistan veterans for at least the next 50 years. The next time we go to war, we should truly understand the sacrifices that our service members and the American people will have to make. Which is why, when my colleagues start beating the drums of war, I want

Tammy Duckworth's essay is powerful all the way through, but wow, what an ending! Closing sentences are tremendously important. When it's time to write one yourself, check out pp. 707–09 for some good tips.

to be there, standing on my artificial legs under the great Capitol dome, to remind them what the true costs of war are.

Thinking about the Text

1. Tammy Duckworth asserts that she is neither "dove" nor "reckless hawk" (7). What does she mean by those statements? How does her military experience support both positions? What lessons allow her to exist between those opposite poles? Point to specific passages to support your response.

2. Duckworth relates that she fell in love with the military for the "camaraderie and sense of purpose" it instilled in her (2). The military, of course, is a prime example, but many other types of experiences can foster similar feelings. Have you had any experiences—whether lasting or fleeting—that gave you a sense of camaraderie and purpose? Describe the experience and its contribution to your life.

3. Why might Duckworth have chosen to **NARRATE** her family's long history with the US military? Does that information enhance her **CREDIBILITY**? Why or why not?

4. Duckworth states that she learned two lessons in the military that inform everything she does in her current role in Congress. **SUMMARIZE** the lessons and how she applies them. How well does she draw the connections between her military service and her service as a senator? Why do you think so? Explain your reasoning.

5. Despite sustaining grave and life-altering combat injuries, Duckworth prizes her military service and credits it with teaching her invaluable life lessons. Should some form of military service be mandatory for all young people in the United States? Write an essay in which you **ARGUE** your position on that question. Take into consideration whether and how the assignments could be apportioned fairly, whether and how individual aptitudes as well as limitations could be accommodated, and any other factors that you consider relevant.

Serving in Florida

BARBARA EHRENREICH

MOSTLY OUT OF LAZINESS, I decide to start my low-wage life in the town nearest to where I actually live, Key West, Florida, which with a population of about 25,000 is elbowing its way up to the status of a genuine city. The downside of familiarity, I soon realize, is that it's not easy to go from being a consumer, thoughtlessly throwing money around in exchange for groceries and movies and gas, to being a worker in the very same place. I am terrified, especially at the beginning, of being recognized by some friendly business owner or erstwhile neighbor and having to stammer out some explanation of my project. Happily, though, my fears turn out to be entirely unwarranted: during a month of poverty and toil, no one recognizes my face or my name, which goes unnoticed and for the most

---

BARBARA EHRENREICH, a native of Butte, Montana, holds a PhD in cell biology but became a journalist and activist after working with a nonprofit organization to improve public access to health care. She is the author of twenty-one books on diverse themes, including *Bait and Switch: The (Futile) Pursuit of the American Dream* (2006) and *Natural Causes: An Epidemic of Wellness, the Certainty of Dying, and Killing Ourselves to Live Longer* (2018). This piece is from her acclaimed 2001 book, *Nickel and Dimed: On (Not) Getting By in America*, a memoir of her experiences living entirely on minimum wage earnings as a waitress, hotel maid, and other low-income jobs. Ehrenreich tweets from @B_Ehrenreich.

part unuttered. In this parallel universe where my father never got out of the mines and I never got through college, I am "baby," "honey," "blondie," and, most commonly, "girl."

My first task is to find a place to live. I figure that if I can earn $7 an hour—which, from the want ads, seems doable—I can afford to spend $500 on rent or maybe, with severe economies, $600 and still have $400 or $500 left over for food and gas. In the Key West area, this pretty much confines me to flophouses and trailer homes—like the one, a pleasing fifteen-minute drive from town, that has no air-conditioning, no screens, no fans, no television, and, by way of diversion, only the challenge of evading the landlord's Doberman pinscher. The big problem with this place, though, is the rent, which at $675 a month is well beyond my reach. All right, Key West is expensive. But so is New York City, or the Bay Area, or Jackson, Wyoming, or Telluride, or Boston, or any other place where tourists and the wealthy compete for living space with the people who clean their toilets and fry their hash browns. Still, it is a shock to realize that "trailer trash" has become, for me, a demographic category to aspire to.

So I decide to make the common trade-off between affordability and convenience and go for a $500-a-month "efficiency" thirty miles up a two-lane highway from the employment opportunities of Key West, meaning forty-five minutes if there's no road construction and I don't get caught behind some sun-dazed Canadian tourists. I hate the drive, along a roadside studded with white crosses commemorating the more effective head-on collisions, but it's a sweet little place—a cabin, more or less, set in the swampy backyard of the converted mobile home where my landlord, an affable TV repairman, lives with his bartender girlfriend. Anthropologically speaking, the trailer park would be preferable, but here I have a gleaming white floor and a firm mattress, and the few resident bugs are easily vanquished.

The next piece of business is to comb through the want ads and find a job. I rule out various occupations for one reason or another: hotel front-desk clerk, for example, which to my surprise is regarded as unskilled and pays only $6 or $7 an hour, gets eliminated because it involves standing in one spot for eight hours a day. Waitressing is also something I'd like to avoid, because I remember it leaving me bone-tired when I was eighteen, and I'm decades of varicosities and back pain beyond that now. Telemarketing, one of the first refuges of the suddenly indigent, can be dismissed on grounds of personality. This leaves certain supermarket jobs, such as deli clerk, or housekeeping in the hotels and guest houses, which pays about $7 and,

I imagine, is not too different from what I've been doing part-time, in my own home, all my life.

So I put on what I take to be a respectable-looking outfit of ironed Bermuda shorts and scooped-neck T-shirt and set out for a tour of the local hotels and supermarkets. Best Western, Econo Lodge, and HoJo's all let me fill out application forms, and these are, to my relief, mostly interested in whether I am a legal resident of the United States and have committed any felonies. My next stop is Winn-Dixie, the supermarket, which turns out to have a particularly onerous application process, featuring a twenty-minute "interview" by computer since, apparently, no human on the premises is deemed capable of representing the corporate point of view. I am conducted to a large room decorated with posters illustrating how to look "professional" (it helps to be white and, if female, permed) and warning of the slick promises that union organizers might try to tempt me with. The interview is multiple-choice: Do I have anything, such as child care problems, that might make it hard for me to get to work on time? Do I think safety on the job is the responsibility of management? Then, popping up cunningly out of the blue: How many dollars' worth of stolen goods have I purchased in the last year? Would I turn in a fellow employee if I caught him stealing? Finally, "Are you an honest person?"

Apparently I ace the interview, because I am told that all I have to do is show up in some doctor's office tomorrow for a urine test. This seems to be a fairly general rule: if you want to stack Cheerios boxes or vacuum hotel rooms in chemically fascist America, you have to be willing to squat down and pee in front of a health worker (who has no doubt had to do the same thing herself).[1] The wages Winn-Dixie is offering—$6 and a couple of dimes to start with—are not enough, I decide, to compensate for this indignity.

I lunch at Wendy's, where $4.99 gets you unlimited refills at the Mexican part of the Super-bar, a comforting surfeit of refried beans and cheese sauce. A teenage employee, seeing me studying the want ads, kindly offers me an application form, which I fill out, though here, too, the pay is just $6 and change an hour. Then it's off for a round of the locally owned inns and guest houses in Key West's Old Town, which is where all the serious

5

---

1. Eighty-one percent of large employers now require preemployment drug testing, up from 21 percent in 1987. Among all employers, the rate of testing is highest in the South. The drug most likely to be detected—marijuana, which can be detected weeks after use—is also the most innocuous, while heroin and cocaine are generally undetectable three days after use. Alcohol, which clears the body within hours after ingestion, is not tested for.

sightseeing and guzzling goes on, a couple of miles removed from the functional end of the island, where the discount hotels make their homes. At The Palms, let's call it, a bouncy manager actually takes me around to see the rooms and meet the current housekeepers, who, I note with satisfaction, look pretty much like me—faded ex-hippie types in shorts with long hair pulled back in braids. Mostly, though, no one speaks to me or even looks at me except to proffer an application form. At my last stop, a palatial B & B, I wait twenty minutes to meet "Max," only to be told that there are no jobs now but there should be one soon, since "nobody lasts more than a couple weeks."

Three days go by like this and, to my chagrin, no one from the approximately twenty places at which I've applied calls me for an interview. I had been vain enough to worry about coming across as too educated for the jobs I sought, but no one even seems interested in finding out how overqualified I am. Only later will I realize that the want ads are not a reliable measure of the actual jobs available at any particular time. They are, as I should have guessed from Max's comment, the employers' insurance policy against the relentless turnover of the low-wage workforce. Most of the big hotels run ads almost continually, if only to build a supply of applicants to replace the current workers as they drift away or are fired, so finding a job is just a matter of being in the right place at the right time and flexible enough to take whatever is being offered that day. This finally happens to me at one of the big discount chain hotels where I go, as usual, for housekeeping and am sent instead to try out as a waitress at the attached "family restaurant," a dismal spot looking out on a parking garage, which is featuring "Polish sausage and BBQ sauce" on this 95-degree day. Phillip, the dapper young West Indian who introduces himself as the manager, interviews me with about as much enthusiasm as if he were a clerk processing me for Medicare, the principal questions being what shifts I can work and when I can start. I mutter about being woefully out of practice as a waitress, but he's already on to the uniform: I'm to show up tomorrow wearing black slacks and black shoes; he'll provide the rust-colored polo shirt with "Hearthside," as we'll call the place, embroidered on it, though I might want to wear my own shirt to get to work, ha ha. At the word *tomorrow*, something between fear and indignation rises in my chest. I want to say, "Thank you for your time, sir, but this is just an experiment, you know, not my actual life."

So begins my career at The Hearthside, where for two weeks I work from 2:00 till 10:00 P.M. for $2.43 an hour plus tips.[2] Employees are barred from using the front door, so I enter the first day through the kitchen, where a red-faced man with shoulder-length blond hair is throwing frozen steaks against the wall and yelling, "Fuck this shit!" "That's just Billy," explains Gail, the wiry middle-aged waitress who is assigned to train me. "He's on the rag again"—a condition occasioned, in this instance, by the fact that the cook on the morning shift had forgotten to thaw out the steaks. For the next eight hours, I run after the agile Gail, absorbing bits of instruction along with fragments of personal tragedy. All food must be trayed, and the reason she's so tired today is that she woke up in a cold sweat thinking of her boyfriend, who was killed a few months ago in a scuffle in an upstate prison. No refills on lemonade. And the reason he was in prison is that a few DUIs caught up with him, that's all, could have happened to anyone. Carry the creamers to the table in a "monkey bowl," never in your hand. And after he was gone she spent several months living in her truck, peeing in a plastic pee bottle and reading by candlelight at night, but you can't live in a truck in the summer, since you need to have the windows down, which means anything can get in, from mosquitoes on up.

At least Gail puts to rest any fears I had of appearing overqualified. From the first day on, I find that of all the things that I have left behind, such as home and identity, what I miss the most is competence. Not that I have ever felt 100 percent competent in the writing business, where one day's success augurs nothing at all for the next. But in my writing life, I at least have some notion of *procedure:* do the research, make the outline, rough out a draft, etc. As a server, though, I am beset by requests as if by bees: more iced tea here, catsup over there, a to-go box for table 14, and where are the high chairs, anyway? Of the twenty-seven tables, up to six are usually mine at any time, though on slow afternoons or if Gail is off, I sometimes have the whole place to myself. There is the touch-screen computer-ordering system to master, which I suppose is meant to minimize server-cook contacts but in practice requires constant verbal fine-tuning: "That's gravy on the mashed, OK? None on the meatloaf," and

10

---

2. According to the Fair Labor Standards Act, employers are not required to pay "tipped employees," such as restaurant servers, more than $2.13 an hour in direct wages. However, if the sum of tips plus $2.13 an hour falls below the minimum wage, or $5.15 an hour, the employer is required to make up the difference. This fact was not mentioned by managers or otherwise publicized at either of the restaurants where I worked.

so forth. Plus, something I had forgotten in the years since I was eighteen: about a third of a server's job is "side work" invisible to customers—sweeping, scrubbing, slicing, refilling, and restocking. If it isn't all done, every little bit of it, you're going to face the 6:00 P.M. dinner rush defenseless and probably go down in flames. I screw up dozens of times at the beginning, sustained in my shame entirely by Gail's support—"It's OK, baby, everyone does that sometime"—because, to my total surprise and despite the scientific detachment I am doing my best to maintain, I *care*.

The whole thing would be a lot easier if I could just skate through it like Lily Tomlin in one of her waitress skits, but I was raised by the absurd Booker T. Washingtonian precept that says: If you're going to do something, do it well. In fact, "well" isn't good enough by half. Do it better than anyone has ever done it before. Or so said my father, who must have known what he was talking about because he managed to pull himself, and us with him, up from the mile-deep copper mines of Butte to the leafy suburbs of the Northeast, ascending from boiler-makers to martinis before booze beat out ambition. As in most endeavors I have encountered in my life, "doing it better than anyone" is not a reasonable goal. Still, when I wake up at 4 A.M. in my own cold sweat, I am not thinking about the writing deadlines I'm neglecting; I'm thinking of the table where I screwed up the order and one of the kids didn't get his kiddie meal until the rest of the family had moved on to their Key lime pies. That's the other powerful motivation—the customers, or "patients," as I can't help thinking of them on account of the mysterious vulnerability that seems to have left them temporarily unable to feed themselves. After a few days at Hearthside, I feel the service ethic kick in like a shot of oxytocin, the nurturance hormone. The plurality of my customers are hardworking locals—truck drivers, construction workers, even housekeepers from the attached hotel—and I want them to have the closest to a "fine dining" experience that the grubby circumstances will allow. No "you guys" for me; everyone over twelve is "sir" or "ma'am." I ply them with iced tea and coffee refills; I return, midmeal, to inquire how everything is; I doll up their salads with chopped raw mushrooms, summer squash slices, or whatever bits of produce I can find that have survived their sojourn in the cold storage room mold-free.

There is Benny, for example, a short, tight-muscled sewer repairman who cannot even think of eating until he has absorbed a half hour of air-conditioning and ice water. We chat about hyperthermia and electrolytes until he is ready to order some finicky combination like soup of the day, garden salad, and a side of grits. There are the German tourists who are so touched by my pidgin *"Wilkommen"* and *"Ist alles gut?"* that they actually tip. (Europeans, no doubt spoiled by their trade union–ridden, high-wage welfare states, generally do not know that they are supposed to tip. Some restaurants, the Hearthside included, allow servers to "grat" their foreign customers, or add a tip to the bill. Since this amount is added before the customers have a chance to tip or not tip, the practice amounts to an automatic penalty for imperfect English.) There are the two dirt-smudged lesbians, just off from their shift, who are impressed enough by my suave handling of the fly in the piña colada that they take the time to praise me to Stu, the assistant manager. There's Sam, the kindly retired cop who has to plug up his tracheotomy hole with one finger in order to force the cigarette smoke into his lungs.

Sometimes I play with the fantasy that I am a princess who, in penance for some tiny transgression, has undertaken to feed each of her subjects by hand. But the nonprincesses working with me are just as indulgent, even when this means flouting management rules—as to, for example, the number of croutons that can go on a salad (six). "Put on all you want," Gail whispers, "as long as Stu isn't looking." She dips into her own tip money to buy biscuits and gravy for an out-of-work mechanic who's used up all his money on dental surgery, inspiring me to pick up the tab for his pie and milk. Maybe the same high levels of agape can be found throughout the "hospitality industry." I remember the poster decorating one of the apartments I looked at, which said, "If you seek happiness for yourself you will never find it. Only when you seek happiness for others will it come to you," or words to that effect—an odd sentiment, it seemed to me at the time, to find in the dank one-room basement apartment of a bellhop at the Best Western. At Hearthside, we utilize whatever bits of autonomy we have to ply our customers with the illicit calories that signal our love. It is our job as servers to assemble the salads and desserts, pour the dressings, and squirt the whipped cream. We also control the number of butter pats our customers get and the amount of sour cream on their baked potatoes. So if you wonder why Americans are so obese, consider the fact that waitresses both express their humanity and earn their tips through the covert distribution of fats.

Ten days into it, this is beginning to look like a livable lifestyle. I like Gail, who is "looking at fifty," agewise, but moves so fast she can alight in one place and then another without apparently being anywhere between. I clown around with Lionel, the teenage Haitian busboy, though we don't have much vocabulary in common, and loiter near the main sink to listen

Barbara Ehrenreich's evidence comes from personal experience. See more examples of this strategy on pp. 431–32 and 464–65.

to the older Haitian dishwashers' musical Creole, which sounds, in their rich bass voices, like French on testosterone. I bond with Timmy, the fourteen-year-old white kid who buses at night, by telling him I don't like people putting their baby seats right on the tables: it makes the baby look too much like a side dish. He snickers delightedly and in return, on a slow night, starts telling me the plots of all the *Jaws* movies (which are perennial favorites in the shark-ridden Keys): "She looks around, and the water-skier isn't there anymore, then SNAP! The whole boat goes . . ."

I especially like Joan, the svelte fortyish hostess, who turns out to be a   15
militant feminist, pulling me aside one day to explain that "men run everything—we don't have a chance unless we stick together." Accordingly, she backs me up when I get overpowered on the floor, and in return I give her a chunk of my tips or stand guard while she sneaks off for an unauthorized cigarette break. We all admire her for standing up to Billy and telling him, after some of his usual nastiness about the female server class, to "shut the fuck up." I even warm up to Billy when, on a slow night and to make up for a particularly unwarranted attack on my abilities, or so I imagine, he tells me about his glory days as a young man at "coronary school" in Brooklyn, where he dated a knockout Puerto Rican chick—or do you say "culinary"?

I finish up every night at 10:00 or 10:30, depending on how much side work I've been able to get done during the shift, and cruise home to the tapes I snatched at random when I left my real home—Marianne Faithfull, Tracy Chapman, Enigma, King Sunny Adé, Violent Femmes—just drained enough for the music to set my cranium resonating, but hardly dead. Midnight snack is Wheat Thins and Monterey Jack, accompanied by cheap white wine on ice and whatever AMC has to offer. To bed by 1:30 or 2:00, up at 9:00 or 10:00, read for an hour while my uniform whirls around in the landlord's washing machine, and then it's another eight hours spent following Mao's central instruction, as laid out in the Little Red Book, which was: Serve the people.

I could drift along like this, in some dreamy proletarian idyll, except for two things. One is management. If I have kept this subject to the margins so far it is because I still flinch to think that I spent all those weeks under the surveillance of men (and later women) whose job it was to monitor my behavior for signs of sloth, theft, drug abuse, or worse. Not that managers and especially "assistant managers" in low-wage settings like this are exactly the class enemy. Mostly, in the restaurant business, they are former cooks still capable of pinch-hitting in the kitchen, just as in hotels they are likely to be former clerks, and paid a salary of only about $400 a week. But everyone knows they have crossed over to the other side, which is, crudely put, corporate as opposed to human. Cooks want to prepare tasty meals, servers want to serve them graciously, but managers are there for only one reason—to make sure that money is made for some theoretical entity, the corporation, which exists far away in Chicago or New York, if a corporation can be said to have a physical existence at all. Reflecting on her career, Gail tells me ruefully that she swore, years ago, never to work for a corporation again. "They don't cut you no slack. You give and you give and they take."

Managers can sit—for hours at a time if they want—but it's their job to see that no one else ever does, even when there's nothing to do, and this is why, for servers, slow times can be as exhausting as rushes. You start dragging out each little chore because if the manager on duty catches you in an idle moment he will give you something far nastier to do. So I wipe, I clean, I consolidate catsup bottles and recheck the cheesecake supply, even tour the tables to make sure the customer evaluation forms are all standing perkily in their places—wondering all the time how many calories I burn in these strictly theatrical exercises. In desperation, I even take the desserts out of their glass display case and freshen them up with whipped cream and bright new maraschino cherries; anything to look busy. When, on a particularly dead afternoon, Stu finds me glancing at a *USA Today* a customer has left behind, he assigns me to vacuum the entire floor with the broken vacuum cleaner, which has a handle only two feet long, and the only way to do that without incurring orthopedic damage is to proceed from spot to spot on your knees.

On my first Friday at Hearthside there is a "mandatory meeting for all restaurant employees," which I attend, eager for insight into our overall marketing strategy and the niche (your basic Ohio cuisine with a tropical twist?) we aim to inhabit. But there is no "we" at this meeting. Phillip, our top manager except for an occasional "consultant" sent out by corporate headquarters, opens it with a sneer: "The break room—it's disgusting. Butts in the ashtrays, newspapers lying around, crumbs." This windowless little room, which also houses the time clock for the entire hotel, is where we stash our bags and civilian clothes and take our half-hour meal breaks. But a break room is not a right, he tells us, it can be taken away. We should also know that the lockers in the break room and whatever is in them can be searched at any time. Then comes gossip; there has been gossip; gossip (which seems to mean employees talking among themselves) must stop.

Off-duty employees are henceforth barred from eating at the restaurant, because "other servers gather around them and gossip." When Phillip has exhausted his agenda of rebukes, Joan complains about the condition of the ladies' room and I throw in my two bits about the vacuum cleaner. But I don't see any backup coming from my fellow servers, each of whom has slipped into her own personal funk; Gail, my role model, stares sorrowfully at a point six inches from her nose. The meeting ends when Andy, one of the cooks, gets up, muttering about breaking up his day off for this almighty bullshit.

Just four days later we are suddenly summoned into the kitchen at 3:30   20
P.M., even though there are live tables on the floor. We all—about ten of us—stand around Phillip, who announces grimly that there has been a report of some "drug activity" on the night shift and that, as a result, we are now to be a "drug-free" workplace, meaning that all new hires will be tested and possibly also current employees on a random basis. I am glad that this part of the kitchen is so dark because I find myself blushing as hard as if I had been caught toking up in the ladies' room myself: I haven't been treated this way—lined up in the corridor, threatened with locker searches, peppered with carelessly aimed accusations—since at least junior high school. Back on the floor, Joan cracks, "Next they'll be telling us we can't have *sex* on the job." When I ask Stu what happened to inspire the crackdown, he just mutters about "management decisions" and takes the opportunity to upbraid Gail and me for being too generous with the rolls. From now on there's to be only one per customer and it goes out with the dinner, not with the salad. He's also been riding the cooks, prompting Andy to come out of the kitchen and observe—with the serenity of a man whose customary implement is a butcher knife—that "Stu has a death wish today."

Later in the evening, the gossip crystallizes around the theory that Stu is himself the drug culprit, that he uses the restaurant phone to order up marijuana and sends one of the late servers out to fetch it for him. The server was caught and she may have ratted out Stu, at least enough to cast some suspicion on him, thus accounting for his pissy behavior. Who knows? Personally, I'm ready to believe anything bad about Stu, who serves no evident function and presumes too much on our common ethnicity, sidling up to me one night to engage in a little nativism directed at the Haitian immigrants: "I feel like I'm the foreigner here. They're taking over the country." Still later that evening, the drug in question escalates to crack. Lionel, the busboy, entertains us for the rest of the shift by standing just behind Stu's back and sucking deliriously on an imaginary joint or maybe a pipe.

The other problem, in addition to the less-than-nurturing management style, is that this job shows no sign of being financially viable. You might imagine, from a comfortable distance, that people who live, year in and year out, on $6 to $10 an hour have discovered some survival stratagems unknown to the middle class. But no. It's not hard to get my coworkers talking about their living situations, because housing, in almost every case, is the principal source of disruption in their lives, the first thing they fill you in on when they arrive for their shifts. After a week, I have compiled the following survey:

Gail is sharing a room in a well-known downtown flophouse for $250 a week. Her roommate, a male friend, has begun hitting on her, driving her nuts, but the rent would be impossible alone.

Claude, the Haitian cook, is desperate to get out of the two-room apartment he shares with his girlfriend and two other, unrelated people. As far as I can determine, the other Haitian men live in similarly crowded situations.

Annette, a twenty-year-old server who is six months pregnant and abandoned by her boyfriend, lives with her mother, a postal clerk.

Marianne, who is a breakfast server, and her boyfriend are paying $170 a week for a one-person trailer.

Billy, who at $10 an hour is the wealthiest of us, lives in the trailer he owns, paying only the $400-a-month lot fee.

The other white cook, Andy, lives on his dry-docked boat, which, as far as I can tell from his loving descriptions, can't be more than twenty feet long. He offers to take me out on it once it's repaired, but the offer comes with inquiries as to my marital status, so I do not follow up on it.

Tina, another server, and her husband are paying $60 a night for a room in the Days Inn. This is because they have no car and the Days Inn is in walking distance of the Hearthside. When Marianne is tossed out of her trailer for subletting (which is against trailer park rules), she leaves her boyfriend and moves in with Tina and her husband.

Joan, who had fooled me with her numerous and tasteful outfits (hostesses wear their own clothes), lives in a van parked behind a shopping center at night and showers in Tina's motel room. The clothes are from thrift shops.[3]

It strikes me, in my middle-class solipsism, that there is gross improvidence in some of these arrangements. When Gail and I are wrapping silverware in napkins—the only task for which we are permitted to sit—she tells me she is thinking of escaping from her roommate by moving into the Days Inn herself. I am astounded: how she can even think of paying $40 to $60 a day? But if I was afraid of sounding like a social worker, I have come out just sounding like a fool. She squints at me in disbelief: "And where am I supposed to get a month's rent and a month's deposit for an apartment?" I'd been feeling pretty smug about my $500 efficiency, but of course it was made possible only by the $1,300 I had allotted myself for start-up costs when I began my low-wage life: $1,000 for the first month's rent and deposit, $100 for initial groceries and cash in my pocket, $200 stuffed away for emergencies. In poverty, as in certain propositions in physics, starting conditions are everything.

There are no secret economies that nourish the poor; on the contrary, there are a host of special costs. If you can't put up the two months' rent you need to secure an apartment, you end up paying through the nose for a room by the week. If you have only a room, with a hot plate at best, you can't save by cooking up huge lentil stews that can be frozen for the week ahead. You eat fast food or the hot dogs and Styrofoam cups of soup that can be microwaved in a convenience store. If you have no money for health insurance—and the Hearthside's niggardly plan kicks in only after three months—you go without routine care or prescription drugs and end up paying the price. Gail, for example, was doing fine, healthwise anyway, until she ran out of money for estrogen pills. She is supposed to be on the company health plan by now, but they claim to have lost her application form and to be beginning the paperwork all over again. So she spends $9 a pop for pills to control the migraines she wouldn't have, she insists, if her estrogen supplements were covered. Similarly, Marianne's boyfriend lost his job as a roofer because he

3. I could find no statistics on the number of employed people living in cars or vans, but according to a 1997 report of the National Coalition for the Homeless, "Myths and Facts about Homelessness," nearly one-fifth of all homeless people (in twenty-nine cities across the nation) are employed in full- or part-time jobs.

missed so much time after getting a cut on his foot for which he couldn't afford the prescribed antibiotic.

My own situation, when I sit down to assess it after two weeks of work, 25 would not be much better if this were my actual life. The seductive thing about waitressing is that you don't have to wait for payday to feel a few bills in your pocket, and my tips usually cover meals and gas, plus something left over to stuff into the kitchen drawer I use as a bank. But as the tourist business slows in the summer heat, I sometimes leave work with only $20 in tips (the gross is higher, but servers share about 15 percent of their tips with the busboys and bartenders). With wages included, this amounts to about the minimum wage of $5.15 an hour. The sum in the drawer is piling up but at the present rate of accumulation will be more than $100 short of my rent when the end of the month comes around. Nor can I see any expenses to cut. True, I haven't gone the lentil stew route yet, but that's because I don't have a large cooking pot, potholders, or a ladle to stir with (which would cost a total of about $30 at Kmart, somewhat less at a thrift store), not to mention onions, carrots, and the indispensable bay leaf. I do make my lunch almost every day—usually some slow-burning, high-protein combo like frozen chicken patties with melted cheese on top and canned pinto beans on the side. Dinner is at the Hearthside, which offers its employees a choice of BLT, fish sandwich, or hamburger for only $2. The burger lasts longest, especially if it's heaped with gut-puckering jalapeños, but by midnight my stomach is growling again.

So unless I want to start using my car as a residence, I have to find a second or an alternative job. I call all the hotels I'd filled out housekeeping applications at weeks ago—the Hyatt, Holiday Inn, Econo Lodge, HoJo's, Best Western, plus a half dozen locally run guest houses. Nothing. Then I start making the rounds again, wasting whole mornings waiting for some assistant manager to show up, even dipping into places so creepy that the front-desk clerk greets you from behind bullet-proof glass and sells pints of liquor over the counter. But either someone has exposed my real-life housekeeping habits—which are, shall we say, mellow—or I am at the wrong end of some infallible ethnic equation: most, but by no means all, of the working housekeepers I see on my job searches are African Americans, Spanish-speaking, or refugees from the Central European post-Communist world, while servers are almost invariably white and monolingually English-speaking. When I finally get a positive response, I have been identified once again as server material. Jerry's—again, not the real name—which is part of a well-known national chain and physically attached here to another budget hotel, is ready to use me at once. The prospect is both exciting and terrifying because, with about the same number of tables and counter seats, Jerry's attracts three or four times the volume of customers as the gloomy old Hearthside.

Thinking about the Text

1. Barbara Ehrenreich passes back and forth in her narrative between the voice of the waitress describing her own reality and the voice of the writer who has assumed a role for investigative purposes—and of course both voices are hers. How well do those voices combine to present a cohesive narrative? Explain your answer, presenting examples from the text.

2. How typical do you suppose Ehrenreich's experience is of people who wait tables at "family restaurants" (8)? Consider evidence from your own experience and that of people you know, either as employees or as customers at such restaurants.

3. On radio and TV, in movies, and elsewhere, people like Ehrenreich's co-workers and customers, with low incomes and low social status, are often either belittled and ridiculed, or romanticized and idealized, whether subtly or openly. One of the strengths of Ehrenreich's book is the respect with which she describes people just the way they are. Identify three examples of respect-ful **DESCRIPTION**.

4. What is the main point that Ehrenreich is making in her narrative? Where is this point most clearly stated? How well has she supported this point? In other words, are you convinced? Why or why not?

5. Write a **NARRATIVE** describing the people and places of your daily life. If you have (or have had) a job, you may want to center your narrative there. Include plenty of descriptive details and try to present the people as vividly (and re-spectfully!) as you can. Make your main point something that you have learned as a result of your contact with the people you describe.

How Junk Food Can End Obesity

DAVID H. FREEDMAN

LATE LAST YEAR, in a small health-food eatery called Cafe Sprouts in Oberlin, Ohio, I had what may well have been the most wholesome beverage of my life. The friendly server patiently guided me to an apple-blueberry-kale-carrot smoothie-juice combination, which she spent the next several minutes preparing, mostly by shepherding farm-fresh produce into machinery. The result was tasty, but at 300 calories (by my rough calculation) in a 16-ounce cup, it was more than my diet could regularly absorb without consequences, nor was I about to make a habit of $9 shakes, healthy or not.

Inspired by the experience nonetheless, I tried again two months later at L.A.'s Real Food Daily, a popular vegan restaurant near Hollywood. I was initially wary of a low-calorie juice made almost entirely from green vegetables, but the server assured me it was a popular treat. I like to brag that I can eat anything, and I scarf down all sorts of raw vegetables like candy, but I could stomach only about a third of this oddly foamy, bitter concoction. It smelled like lawn clippings and tasted like liquid celery. It goes for $7.95, and I waited 10 minutes for it.

DAVID H. FREEDMAN is a journalist specializing in health, science, and business and is the author of *Wrong: Why Experts Keep Failing Us—And How to Know When Not to Trust Them* (2010). His work has appeared in *Forbes*, the *New York Times*, and *Wired*, among other publications. This July 2013 proposal is from the *Atlantic*. You can follow him on Twitter @dhfreedman.

I finally hit the sweet spot just a few weeks later, in Chicago, with a delicious blueberry-pomegranate smoothie that rang in at a relatively modest 220 calories. It cost $3 and took only seconds to make. Best of all, I'll be able to get this concoction just about anywhere. Thanks, McDonald's!

If only the McDonald's smoothie weren't, unlike the first two, so fattening and unhealthy. Or at least that's what the most-prominent voices in our food culture today would have you believe.

An enormous amount of media space has been dedicated to promoting 5 the notion that all processed food, and only processed food, is making us sickly and overweight. In this narrative, the food-industrial complex—particularly the fast-food industry—has turned all the powers of food-processing science loose on engineering its offerings to addict us to fat, sugar, and salt, causing or at least heavily contributing to the obesity crisis. The wares of these pimps and pushers, we are told, are to be universally shunned.

Consider *The New York Times*. Earlier this year, *The Times Magazine* gave its cover to a long piece based on Michael Moss's about-to-be-best-selling book, *Salt Sugar Fat: How the Food Giants Hooked Us*. Hitting bookshelves at about the same time was the former *Times* reporter Melanie Warner's *Pandora's Lunchbox: How Processed Food Took Over the American Meal*, which addresses more or less the same theme. Two years ago *The Times Magazine* featured the journalist Gary Taubes's "Is Sugar Toxic?," a cover story on the

How much—and how many calories—will a smoothie cost you?

evils of refined sugar and high-fructose corn syrup. And most significant of all has been the considerable space the magazine has devoted over the years to Michael Pollan, a journalism professor at the University of California at Berkeley, and his broad indictment of food processing as a source of society's health problems.

"The food they're cooking is making people sick," Pollan has said of big food companies. "It is one of the reasons that we have the obesity and diabetes epidemics that we do. . . . If you're going to let industries decide how much salt, sugar and fat is in your food, they're going to put [in] as much as they possibly can. . . . They will push those buttons until we scream or die." The solution, in his view, is to replace Big Food's engineered, edible evil—through public education and regulation—with fresh, unprocessed, local, seasonal, real food.

Pollan's worldview saturates the public conversation on healthy eating. You hear much the same from many scientists, physicians, food activists, nutritionists, celebrity chefs, and pundits. *Foodlike substances*, the derisive term Pollan uses to describe processed foods, is now a solid part of the elite vernacular. Thousands of restaurants and grocery stores, most notably the Whole Foods chain, have thrived by answering the call to reject industrialized foods in favor of a return to natural, simple, nonindustrialized—let's call them "wholesome"—foods. The two newest restaurants in my smallish Massachusetts town both prominently tout wholesome ingredients; one of them is called the Farmhouse, and it's usually packed.

A new generation of business, social, and policy entrepreneurs is rising to further cater to these tastes, and to challenge Big Food. Silicon Valley, where tomorrow's entrepreneurial and social trends are forged, has spawned a small ecosystem of wholesome-friendly venture-capital firms (Physic Ventures, for example), business accelerators (Local Food Lab), and Web sites (Edible Startups) to fund, nurture, and keep tabs on young companies such as blissmo (a wholesome-food-of-the-month club), Mile High Organics (online wholesome-food shopping), and Wholeshare (group wholesome-food purchasing), all designed to help reacquaint Americans with the simpler eating habits of yesteryear. . . .

If the most-influential voices in our food culture today get their way, we will achieve a genuine food revolution. Too bad it would be one tailored to the dubious health fantasies of a small, elite minority. And too bad it would largely exclude the obese masses, who would continue to sicken and die early. Despite the best efforts of a small army of wholesome-food heroes, there

The produce section at a Whole Foods Market.

is no reasonable scenario under which these foods could become cheap and plentiful enough to serve as the core diet for most of the obese population— even in the unlikely case that your typical junk-food eater would be willing and able to break lifelong habits to embrace kale and yellow beets. And many of the dishes glorified by the wholesome-food movement are, in any case, as caloric and obesogenic as anything served in a Burger King.

Through its growing sway over health-conscious consumers and policy makers, the wholesome-food movement is impeding the progress of the one segment of the food world that is actually positioned to take effective, near-term steps to reverse the obesity trend: the processed-food industry. Popular food producers, fast-food chains among them, are already applying various tricks and technologies to create less caloric and more satiating versions of their junky fare that nonetheless retain much of the appeal of the originals, and could be induced to go much further. In fact, these roundly demonized companies could do far more for the public's health in five years than the wholesome-food movement is likely to accomplish in the next 50. But will the wholesome-food advocates let them? . . .

Let Them Eat Kale

I'm a fan of many of Mark Bittman's recipes. I shop at Whole Foods all the time. And I eat like many wholesome foodies, except I try to stay away from those many wholesome ingredients and dishes that are high in fat and problem carbs. What's left are vegetables, fruits, legumes, whole grains, poultry, and fish (none of them fried, thank you), which are often emphasized by many wholesome-food fans. In general, I find that the more-natural versions of these ingredients taste at least a bit better, and occasionally much better, than the industrialized versions. And despite the wholesome-food movement's frequent and inexcusable obliviousness to the obesogenicity of many of its own foods, it deserves credit for paying more attention to those healthier ingredients than does Big Food.

Where the Pollanites get into real trouble—where their philosophy becomes so glib and wrongheaded that it is actually immoral—is in the claim that their style of food shopping and eating is the answer to the country's weight problem. Helping me to indulge my taste for genuinely healthy wholesome foods are the facts that I'm relatively affluent and well educated, and that I'm surrounded by people who tend to take care with what they eat. Not only am I within a few minutes' drive of three Whole Foods and two Trader Joe's, I'm within walking distance of two other supermarkets and more than a dozen restaurants that offer bountiful healthy-eating options.

I am, in short, not much like the average obese person in America, and neither are the Pollanites. That person is relatively poor, does not read *The Times* or cookbook manifestos, is surrounded by people who eat junk food and are themselves obese, and stands a good chance of living in a food desert—an area where produce tends to be hard to find, of poor quality, or expensive.

The wholesome foodies don't argue that obesity and class are unrelat- 15
ed, but they frequently argue that the obesity gap between the classes has been created by the processed-food industry, which, in the past few decades, has preyed mostly on the less affluent masses. Yet Lenard Lesser, a physician and an obesity researcher at the Palo Alto Medical Foundation Research Institute, says that can't be so, because the obesity gap predates the fast-food industry and the dietary dominance of processed food. "The difference in obesity rates in low- and high-income groups was evident as far back as we have data, at least back through the 1960s," he told me. One reason, some researchers have argued, is that after having had to worry, over countless

generations, about getting enough food, poorer segments of society had little cultural bias against overindulging in food, or putting on excess pounds, as industrialization raised incomes and made rich food cheaply available.

The most obvious problem with the "let them eat kale" philosophy of affluent wholesome-food advocates involves the price and availability of wholesome food. Even if Whole Foods, Real Food Daily, or the Farmhouse weren't three bus rides away for the working poor, and even if three ounces of Vegan Cheesy Salad Booster, a Sea Cake appetizer, and the vegetarian quiche weren't laden with fat and problem carbs, few among them would be likely to shell out $5.99, $9.95, or $16, respectively, for those pricey treats.

A slew of start-ups are trying to find ways of producing fresh, local, unprocessed meals quickly and at lower cost. But could this food eventually be sold as cheaply, conveniently, and ubiquitously as today's junky fast food? Not even according to Bittman, who explored the question in a recent *New York Times Magazine* article. Even if wholesome food caught on with the public at large, including the obese population, and even if poor and working-class people were willing to pay a premium for it, how long would it take to scale up from a handful of shops to the tens of thousands required to begin making a dent in the obesity crisis? How long would it take to create the thousands of local farms we'd need in order to provide these shops with fresh, unprocessed ingredients, even in cities?

Yet these hurdles can be waved away, if one only has the proper mindset. Bittman argued two years ago in *The Times* that there's no excuse for anyone, food-desert-bound or not, to eat fast food rather than wholesome food, because even if it's not perfectly fresh and locally grown, lower-end wholesome food—when purchased judiciously at the supermarket and cooked at home—can be cheaper than fast food. Sure, there's the matter of all the time, effort, schedule coordination, and ability it takes to shop, cook, serve, and clean up. But anyone who whines about that extra work, Bittman chided, just doesn't want to give up their excessive TV watching. (An "important benefit of paying more for better-quality food is that you're apt to eat less of it," Pollan helpfully noted in his 2008 book, *In Defense of Food*.) It's remarkable how easy it is to remake the disadvantaged in one's own image.

Let's assume for a moment that somehow America, food deserts and all, becomes absolutely lousy with highly affordable outlets for wholesome, locally sourced dishes that are high in vegetables, fruits, legumes, poultry, fish, and whole grains, and low in fat and problem carbs. What percentage of the junk-food-eating obese do we want to predict will be ready to drop their

Big Macs, fries, and Cokes for grilled salmon on chard? We can all agree that many obese people find the former foods extremely enjoyable, and seem unable to control their consumption of them. Is greater availability of healthier food that pushes none of the same thrill buttons going to solve the problem?

Many Pollanites insist it will. "If the government came into these com- 20 munities and installed Brita filters under their sinks, they'd drink water instead of Coke," Lisa Powell, a professor of health policy and administration at the University of Illinois at Chicago's Institute for Health Research and Policy, told me. But experts who actually work with the obese see a more difficult transition, especially when busy schedules are thrown into the equation. "They won't eat broccoli instead of french fries," says Kelli Drenner, an obesity researcher at Stephen F. Austin State University in Nacogdoches, Texas, which has about four fast-food restaurants per block along most of its main drag. "You try to make even a small change to school lunches, and parents and kids revolt." . . .

People aren't going to change their ingrained, neurobiologically supercharged junk-eating habits just because someone dangles vegetables in front of them, farm-fresh or otherwise. Mark Bittman sees signs of victory in "the stories parents tell me of their kids booing as they drive by McDonald's," but it's not hard to imagine which parents, which kids, and which neighborhoods those stories might involve. One study found that subsidizing the purchase of vegetables encouraged shoppers to buy more vegetables, but also more junk food with the money they saved; on balance, their diets did not improve. The Centers for Disease Control and Prevention recently found that the aughts saw a significant drop in fruit intake, and no increase in vegetable consumption; Americans continue to fall far short of eating the recommended amounts of either. "Everyone's mother and brother has been telling them to eat more fruit and vegetables forever, and the numbers are only getting worse," says Steven Nickolas, who runs the Healthy Food Project in Scottsdale, Arizona. "We're not going to solve this problem by telling people to eat unprocessed food."

Trim, affluent Americans of course have a right to view dietary questions from their own perspective—that is, in terms of what they need to eat in order to add perhaps a few months onto the already healthy courses of their lives. The pernicious sleight of hand is in willfully confusing what might benefit them—small, elite minority that they are—with what would help most of society. The conversations they have among themselves in *The Times*, in best-selling books, and at Real Food Daily may not register with the working-class obese. But these conversations unquestionably distort the views of those who are in a position to influence what society does about the obesity problem.

The Food Revolution We Need

The one fast-food restaurant near a busy East L.A. intersection otherwise filled with bodegas was a Carl's Jr. I went in and saw that the biggest and most prominent posters in the store were pushing a new grilled-cod sandwich. It actually looked pretty good, but it wasn't quite lunchtime, and I just wanted a cup of coffee. I went to the counter to order it, but before I could say anything, the cashier greeted me and asked, "Would you like to try our new Charbroiled Atlantic Cod Fish Sandwich today?" Oh, well, sure, why not? (I asked her to hold the tartar sauce, which is mostly fat, but found out later that the sandwich is normally served with about half as much tartar sauce as the notoriously fatty Filet-O-Fish sandwich at McDonald's, where the fish is battered and fried.) The sandwich was delicious. It was less than half the cost of the Sea Cake appetizer at Real Food Daily. It took less than a minute to prepare. In some ways, it was the best meal I had in L.A., and it was probably the healthiest.

David Freedman contrasts the offerings of fast-food restaurants with similar menu items at pricier places. Find out more about this strategy on pp. 457–59.

. . . The Pollanites have led us to conflate the industrial processing of food with the adding of fat and sugar in order to hook customers, even while pushing many faux-healthy foods of their own. But why couldn't Big Food's processing and marketing genius be put to use on genuinely healthier foods, like grilled fish? Putting aside the standard objection that the industry has no interest in doing so—we'll see later that in fact the industry has plenty of motivation for taking on this challenge—wouldn't that present a more plausible answer to America's junk-food problem than ordering up 50,000 new farmers' markets featuring locally grown organic squash blossoms?

According to Lenard Lesser, of the Palo Alto Medical Foundation, the 25
food industry has mastered the art of using in-store and near-store promotions to shape what people eat. As Lesser and I drove down storied Telegraph Avenue in Berkeley and into far less affluent Oakland, leaving behind the Whole Foods Markets and sushi restaurants for gas-station markets and barbecued-rib stands, he pointed out the changes in the billboards. Whereas the last one we saw in Berkeley was for fruit juice, many in Oakland tout fast-food joints and their wares, including several featuring the Hot Mess

The menu board at KFC shows larger-than-life images of fried food.

Burger at Jack in the Box. Though Lesser noted that this forest of advertising may simply reflect Oakland residents' preexisting preference for this type of food, he told me lab studies have indicated that the more signs you show people for a particular food product or dish, the more likely they are to choose it over others, all else being equal.

We went into a KFC and found ourselves traversing a maze of signage that put us face-to-face with garish images of various fried foods that presumably had some chicken somewhere deep inside them. "The more they want you to buy something, the bigger they make the image on the menu board," Lesser explained. Here, what loomed largest was the $19.98 fried-chicken-and-corn family meal, which included biscuits and cake. A few days later, I noticed that McDonald's places large placards showcasing desserts on the trash bins, apparently calculating that the best time to entice diners with sweets is when they think they've finished their meals.

Trying to get burger lovers to jump to grilled fish may already be a bit of a stretch—I didn't see any of a dozen other customers buy the cod sandwich when I was at Carl's Jr., though the cashier said it was selling reasonably well. Still, given the food industry's power to tinker with and market food, we should not dismiss its ability to get unhealthy eaters—slowly, incrementally—to buy better food.

That brings us to the crucial question: Just how much healthier could fast-food joints and processed-food companies make their best-selling products without turning off customers? I put that question to a team of McDonald's executives, scientists, and chefs who are involved in shaping the company's future menus, during a February visit to McDonald's sur-prisingly bucolic campus west of Chicago. By way of a partial answer, the team served me up a preview tasting of two major new menu items that had been under development in their test kitchens and high-tech sensory-testing labs for the past year, and which were rolled out to the public in April. The first was the Egg White Delight McMuffin ($2.65), a lower-calorie, less fatty version of the Egg McMuffin, with some of the refined flour in the original recipe replaced by whole-grain flour. The other was one of three new Premium McWraps ($3.99), crammed with grilled chicken and spring mix, and given a light coating of ranch dressing amped up with rice vin-egar. Both items tasted pretty good (as do the versions in stores, I've since confirmed, though some outlets go too heavy on the dressing). And they were both lower in fat, sugar, and calories than not only many McDonald's staples, but also much of the food served in wholesome restaurants or tout-ed in wholesome cookbooks.

In fact, McDonald's has quietly been making healthy changes for years, shrinking portion sizes, reducing some fats, trimming average salt content by more than 10 percent in the past couple of years alone, and adding fruits, vegetables, low-fat dairy, and oatmeal to its menu. In May, the chain dropped its Angus third-pounders and announced a new line of quarter-pound burg-ers, to be served on buns containing whole grains. Outside the core fast-food customer base, Americans are becoming more health-conscious. Public backlash against fast food could lead to regulatory efforts, and in any case, the fast-food industry has every incentive to maintain broad appeal. "We think a lot about how we can bring nutritionally balanced meals that in-clude enough protein, along with the tastes and satisfaction that have an appetite-tiding effect," said Barbara Booth, the company's director of sen-sory science.

Such steps are enormously promising, says Jamy Ard, an epidemiology 30 and preventive-medicine researcher at Wake Forest Baptist Medical Center in Winston-Salem, North Carolina, and a co-director of the Weight Manage-ment Center there. "Processed food is a key part of our environment, and it needs to be part of the equation," he explains. "If you can reduce fat and calo-ries by only a small amount in a Big Mac, it still won't be a health food, but it wouldn't be as bad, and that could have a huge impact on us." Ard, who has been working for more than a decade with the obese poor, has little patience with the wholesome-food movement's call to eliminate fast food in favor of farm-fresh goods. "It's really naive," he says. "Fast food became popular

Fast-food restaurants like McDonald's have been trying for years to promote healthier fare.

because it's tasty and convenient and cheap. It makes a lot more sense to look for small, beneficial changes in that food than it does to hold out for big changes in what people eat that have no realistic chance of happening."

According to a recent study, Americans get 11 percent of their calories, on average, from fast food—a number that's almost certainly much higher among the less affluent overweight. As a result, the fast-food industry may be uniquely positioned to improve our diets. Research suggests that calorie counts in a meal can be trimmed by as much as 30 percent without eaters noticing—by, for example, reducing portion sizes and swapping in ingredients that contain more fiber and water. . . .

Which raises a question: If McDonald's is taking these sorts of steps, albeit in a slow and limited way, why isn't it more loudly saying so to deflect criticism? While the company has heavily plugged the debut of its new egg-white sandwich and chicken wraps, the ads have left out even a mention of health, the reduced calories and fat, or the inclusion of whole grains. McDonald's has practically kept secret the fact that it has also begun substituting whole-grain flour for some of the less healthy refined flour in its best-selling Egg McMuffin.

The explanation can be summed up in two words that surely strike fear into the hearts of all fast-food executives who hope to make their companies' fare healthier: McLean Deluxe.

Among those who gleefully rank such things, the McLean Deluxe reigns as McDonald's worst product failure of all time, eclipsing McPasta, the McHotdog, and the McAfrica (don't ask). When I brought up the McLean Deluxe to the innovation team at McDonald's, I faced the first and only uncomfortable silence of the day. Finally, Greg Watson, a senior vice president, cleared his throat and told me that neither he nor anyone else in the room was at the company at the time, and he didn't know that much about it. "It sounds to me like it was ahead of its time," he added. "If we had something like that in the future, we would never launch it like that again."

Introduced in 1991, the McLean Deluxe was perhaps the boldest single   35 effort the food industry has ever undertaken to shift the masses to healthier eating. It was supposed to be a healthier version of the Quarter Pounder, made with extra-lean beef infused with seaweed extract. It reportedly did reasonably well in early taste tests—for what it's worth, my wife and I were big fans—and McDonald's pumped the reduced-fat angle to the public for all it was worth. The general reaction varied from lack of interest to mockery to revulsion. The company gamely flogged the sandwich for five years before quietly removing it from the menu.

The McLean Deluxe was a sharp lesson to the industry, even if in some ways it merely confirmed what generations of parents have well known: if you want to turn off otherwise eager eaters to a dish, tell them it's good for them. Recent studies suggest that calorie counts placed on menus have a negligible effect on food choices, and that the less-health-conscious might even use the information to steer clear of low-calorie fare—perhaps assuming that it tastes worse and is less satisfying, and that it's worse value for their money. The result is a sense in the food industry that if it is going to sell healthier versions of its foods to the general public—and not just to that minority already sold on healthier eating—it is going to have to do it in a relatively sneaky way, emphasizing the taste appeal and not the health benefits. "People expect something to taste worse if they believe it's healthy," says Charles Spence, an Oxford University neuroscientist who specializes in how the brain perceives food. "And that expectation affects how it tastes to them, so it actually *does* taste worse."

Thus McDonald's silence on the nutritional profiles of its new menu items. "We're not making any health claims," Watson said. "We're just saying it's new, it tastes great, come on in and enjoy it. Maybe once the product is well seated with customers, we'll change that message." If customers learn that they can eat healthier foods at McDonald's without even realizing it, he added, they'll be more likely to try healthier foods there than at other restaurants. The same reasoning presumably explains why the promotions and ads for the Carl's Jr. grilled-cod sandwich offer not a word related to healthfulness, and why there wasn't a whiff of health cheerleading surrounding the turkey burger brought out earlier this year by Burger King (which is not yet calling the sandwich a permanent addition).

If the food industry is to quietly sell healthier products to its mainstream, mostly non-health-conscious customers, it must find ways to deliver the eating experience that fat and problem carbs provide in foods that have fewer of those ingredients. There is no way to do that with farm-fresh produce and wholesome meat, other than reducing portion size. But processing technology gives the food industry a potent tool for trimming unwanted ingredients while preserving the sensations they deliver.

I visited Fona International, a flavor-engineering company also outside Chicago, and learned that there are a battery of tricks for fooling and appeasing taste buds, which are prone to notice a lack of fat or sugar, or the presence of any of the various bitter, metallic, or otherwise unpleasant flavors that vegetables, fiber, complex carbs, and fat or sugar substitutes can impart to a food intended to appeal to junk-food eaters. Some 5,000 FDA-approved chemical compounds—which represent the base components of all known flavors—line the shelves that run alongside Fona's huge labs. Armed with these ingredients and an array of state-of-the-art chemical-analysis and testing tools, Fona's scientists and engineers can precisely control flavor perception. "When you reduce the sugar, fat, and salt in foods, you change the personality of the product," said Robert Sobel, a chemist, who heads up research at the company. "We can restore it."

For example, fat "cushions" the release of various flavors on the tongue, 40 unveiling them gradually and allowing them to linger. When fat is removed, flavors tend to immediately inundate the tongue and then quickly flee, which we register as a much less satisfying experience. Fona's experts can reproduce the "temporal profile" of the flavors in fattier foods by adding edible compounds derived from plants that slow the release of flavor molecules; by replacing the flavors with similarly flavored compounds that come on and leave more slowly; or by enlisting "phantom aromas" that create the sensation of certain tastes even when those tastes are not present on the tongue. (For example, the smell of vanilla can essentially mask reductions in sugar of up to 25 percent.) One triumph of this sort of engineering is the modern protein drink, a staple of many successful weight-loss programs and a favorite of those trying to build muscle. "Seven years ago they were unpalatable," Sobel said. "Today we can mask the astringent flavors and eggy aromas by adding natural ingredients." . . .

Fona . . . , like most companies in [the] industry, won't identify customers or product names on the record. But [the firm] showed me an array of foods and beverages that were under construction, so to speak, in the name of reducing calories, fat, and sugar while maintaining mass appeal. . . . Dozens of companies are doing similar work, as are the big food-ingredient manufacturers, such as ConAgra, whose products are in 97 percent of American homes, and whose whole-wheat flour is what McDonald's is relying on for its breakfast sandwiches. Domino Foods, the sugar manufacturer, now sells a low-calorie combination of sugar and the nonsugar sweetener stevia that has been engineered by a flavor company to mask the sort of nonsugary tastes driving many consumers away from diet beverages and the like. "Stevia has a licorice note we were able to have taken out," explains Domino Foods CEO Brian O'Malley.

High-tech anti-obesity food engineering is just warming up. Oxford's Charles Spence notes that in addition to flavors and textures, companies are investigating ways to exploit a stream of insights that have been coming out of scholarly research about the neuroscience of eating. He notes, for example, that candy companies may be able to slip healthier ingredients into candy bars without anyone noticing, simply by loading these ingredients into the middle of the bar and leaving most of the fat and sugar at the ends of the bar. "We tend to make up our minds about how something tastes from the first and last bites, and don't care as much what happens in between," he explains. Some other potentially useful gimmicks he points out: adding weight to food packaging such as yogurt containers, which convinces eaters that the contents are rich with calories, even when they're not; using chewy textures that force consumers to spend more time between bites, giving the brain a chance to register satiety; and using colors, smells, sounds, and packaging information to create the belief that foods are fatty and sweet even when they are not. Spence found, for example, that wine is perceived as 50 percent sweeter when consumed under a red light.

Researchers are also tinkering with food ingredients to boost satiety. Cargill has developed a starch derived from tapioca that gives dishes a refined-carb taste and mouthfeel, but acts more like fiber in the body—a feature that could keep the appetite from spiking later. "People usually think that processing leads to foods that digest too quickly, but we've been able to use processing to slow the digestion rate," says Bruce McGoogan, who heads R&D for Cargill's North American food-ingredient business. The company has also developed ways to reduce fat in beef patties, and to make baked goods using half the usual sugar and oil, all without heavily compromising taste and texture....

The Implacable Enemies of Healthier Processed Food

What's not to like about these developments? Plenty, if you've bought into the notion that processing itself is the source of the unhealthfulness of our foods. The wholesome-food movement is not only talking up dietary strategies that are unlikely to help most obese Americans; it is, in various ways, getting in the way of strategies that could work better.

The Pollanites didn't invent resistance to healthier popular foods, as the 45
fate of the McLean Deluxe . . . demonstrate[s], but they've greatly intensified it. Fast food and junk food have their core customer base, and the wholesome-food gurus have theirs. In between sit many millions of Americans— the more the idea that processed food should be shunned no matter what takes hold in this group, the less incentive fast-food joints will have to continue edging away from the fat- and problem-carb-laden fare beloved by their most loyal customers to try to broaden their appeal.

Pollan has popularized contempt for "nutritionism," the idea behind packing healthier ingredients into processed foods. In his view, the quest to add healthier ingredients to food isn't a potential solution, it's part of the problem. Food is healthy not when it contains healthy ingredients, he argues, but when it can be traced simply and directly to (preferably local) farms. As he resonantly put it in *The Times* in 2007: "If you're concerned about your health, you should probably avoid food products that make health claims. Why? Because a health claim on a food product is a good indication that it's not really food, and food is what you want to eat."

In this way, wholesome-food advocates have managed to pre-damn the very steps we need the food industry to take, placing the industry in a no-win situation: If it maintains the status quo, then we need to stay away because its food is loaded with fat and sugar. But if it tries to moderate these ingredients, then it is deceiving us with nutritionism. Pollan explicitly counsels avoiding foods containing more than five ingredients, or any hard-to-pronounce or unfamiliar ingredients. This rule eliminates almost anything the industry could do to produce healthier foods that retain mass appeal—most of us wouldn't get past xanthan gum—and that's perfectly in keeping with his intention.

By placing wholesome eating directly at odds with healthier processed foods, the Pollanites threaten to derail the reformation of fast food just as it's starting to gain traction. At McDonald's, "Chef Dan"—that is, Dan Coudreaut, the executive chef and director of culinary innovation—told me of the dilemma the movement has caused him as he has tried to make the menu healthier. "Some want us to have healthier food, but others want us to have minimally processed ingredients, which can mean more fat," he explained. "It's becoming a balancing act for us." That the chef with arguably the most influence in the world over the diet of the obese would even

McDonald's executive chef Dan Coudreaut at work in his corporate kitchen.

consider adding fat to his menu to placate wholesome foodies is a pretty good sign that something has gone terribly wrong with our approach to the obesity crisis.

Many people insist that the steps the food industry has already taken to offer less-obesogenic fare are no more than cynical ploys to fool customers into eating the same old crap under a healthy guise. In his 3,500-word *New York Times Magazine* article on the prospects for healthier fast food, Mark Bittman lauded a new niche of vegan chain restaurants while devoting just one line to the major "quick serve" restaurants' contribution to better health: "I'm not talking about token gestures, like the McDonald's fruit-and-yogurt parfait, whose calories are more than 50 percent sugar." Never mind that 80 percent of a farm-fresh apple's calories come from sugar; that almost any obesity expert would heartily approve of the yogurt parfait as a step in the right direction for most fast-food-dessert eaters; and that many of the desserts Bittman glorifies in his own writing make the parfait look like arugula, nutrition-wise. (His recipe for corn-and-blueberry crisp, for example, calls for adding two-thirds of a cup of brown sugar to a lot of other problem carbs, along with five tablespoons of butter.)

Bittman is hardly alone in his reflexive dismissals. No sooner had 50 McDonald's and Burger King rolled out their egg-white sandwich and turkey burger, respectively, than a spate of articles popped up hooting that the new dishes weren't healthier because they trimmed a mere 50 and 100 calories from their standard counterparts, the Egg McMuffin and the Whopper. Apparently these writers didn't understand, or chose to ignore, the fact that a reduction of 50 or 100 calories in a single dish places an eater exactly on track to eliminate a few hundred calories a day from his or her diet—the critical threshold needed for long-term weight loss. Any bigger reduction would risk leaving someone too hungry to stick to a diet program. It's just the sort of small step in the right direction we should be aiming for, because the obese are much more likely to take it than they are to make a big leap to wholesome or very-low-calorie foods.

Many wholesome foodies insist that the food industry won't make serious progress toward healthier fare unless forced to by regulation. I, for one, believe regulation aimed at speeding the replacement of obesogenic foods with appealing healthier foods would be a great idea. But what a lot of foodies really want is to ban the food industry from selling junk food altogether. And that is just a fantasy. The government never managed to keep the tobacco companies from selling cigarettes, and banning booze

Mark Bittman prepares lunch while publicizing his book *VB8*, which advocates a vegan diet.

(the third-most-deadly consumable killer after cigarettes and food) didn't turn out so well. The two most health-enlightened, regulation-friendly major cities in America, New York and San Francisco, tried to halt sales of two of the most horrific fast-food assaults on health—giant servings of sugared beverages and kids' fast-food meals accompanied by toys, respectively—and neither had much luck. Michelle Obama is excoriated by conservatives for asking schools to throw more fruits and vegetables into the lunches they serve. Realistically, the most we can hope for is a tax on some obesogenic foods. The research of Lisa Powell, the University of Illinois professor, suggests that a 20 percent tax on sugary beverages would reduce consumption by about 25 percent. (As for fatty foods, no serious tax proposal has yet been made in the U.S., and if one comes along, the wholesome foodies might well join the food industry and most consumers in opposing it. Denmark did manage to enact a fatty-food tax, but it was deemed a failure when consumers went next door into Germany and Sweden to stock up on their beloved treats.)

Continuing to call out Big Food on its unhealthy offerings, and loudly, is one of the best levers we have for pushing it toward healthier products—but let's call it out intelligently, not reflexively. Executives of giant food companies may be many things, but they are not stupid. Absent action, they risk a growing public-relations disaster, the loss of their more affluent and increasingly health-conscious customers, and the threat of regulation, which will be costly to fight, even if the new rules don't stick. Those fears are surely what's driving much of the push toward moderately healthier fare within the industry today. But if the Pollanites convince policy makers and the health-conscious public that these foods are dangerous by virtue of not being farm-fresh, that will push Big Food in a different direction (in part by limiting the profit potential it sees in lower-fat, lower-problem-carb foods), and cause it to spend its resources in other ways.

Significant regulation of junk food may not go far, but we have other tools at our disposal to prod Big Food to intensify and speed up its efforts to cut fat and problem carbs in its offerings, particularly if we're smart about it. Lenard Lesser points out that government and advocacy groups could start singling out particular restaurants and food products for praise or shaming—a more official version of "eat this, not that"—rather than sticking to a steady drumbeat of "processed food must go away." Academia could do a much better job of producing and highlighting solid research into less obesogenic, high-mass-appeal foods, and could curtail its evidence-light anti-food-processing bias, so that the next generation of social and policy entrepreneurs might work to narrow the gap between the poor obese and the well-resourced healthy instead of inadvertently widening it. We can keep pushing our health-care system to provide more incentives and support to the obese for losing weight by making small, painless, but helpful changes in their behavior, such as switching from Whoppers to turkey burgers, from Egg McMuffins to Egg White Delights, or from blueberry crisp to fruit-and-yogurt parfaits.

And we can ask the wholesome-food advocates, and those who give them voice, to make it clearer that the advice they sling is relevant mostly to the privileged healthy—and to start getting behind realistic solutions to the obesity crisis.

Thinking about the Text

1. Why is David Freedman so sure that fast-food outlets can significantly improve the diet and health of the U.S. public? **SUMMARIZE** the main arguments in this proposal. What does he see as the problem, and what is his solution?

2. Freedman seems to be genuinely concerned about the problems caused by obesity and unhealthy diets, and he argues passionately for a solution. Still, his way of describing people who are obese, experiencing poverty, or both can seem disrespectful and patronizing. What do you think his **ATTITUDE** is toward these people? Do you think he assumes that his **AUDIENCE** includes such people? Point to specific examples in the text to support your conclusions.

3. A good **PROPOSAL** presents evidence that the proposed course of action will address the problem, and that it will do so better than other possible solutions. Identify two **REASONS** and the corresponding **EVIDENCE** that Freedman presents to support his proposed solution. How persuasive are they? Has he convinced you that his solution is the best fix available and if not, why not?

4. Recent studies show that restaurant customers pay little attention to the calorie count information on menus, and even that some diners may use the information in order to *avoid* the lower-calorie items. Do you pay attention to the calorie counts or other nutritional information on menus or food packaging? Explain the reasoning behind your practices.

5. In arguing for "the food revolution we need" (23), Freedman poses a rhetorical question: "Wouldn't [healthier fast-food options] present a more plausible answer to America's junk-food problem than ordering up 50,000 new farmers' markets featuring locally grown organic squash blossoms?" (24). The issue, of course, is much more complex than Freedman's either/or proposition—but think locally for a moment. Which option would you rather find around the corner from where you live: a healthier menu at a fast-food restaurant, or a new farmers' market with a variety of local produce? Write an editorial for your local newspaper **ARGUING** for your chosen establishment. List and describe the benefits of the option you've chosen, providing solid evidence that will appeal to those who read that paper.

The Illusion of Safety/The Safety of Illusion

ROXANE GAY

WHEN I SEE MEN WHO LOOK LIKE HIM or his friends. When I smell beer on a man's breath. When I smell Polo cologne. When I hear a harsh laugh. When I walk by a group of men, clustered together, and there's no one around. When I see a woman being attacked in a movie or on television. When I am in the woods or driving through a heavily wooded area. When I read about experiences that are all too familiar. When I go through security at the airport and am pulled aside for extra screening, which seems to happen every single time I travel. When I'm having sex and my wrists are unexpectedly pinned over my head. When I see a young girl of a certain age.

When it happens, a sharp pang runs right through the center of my body. Or I feel sick to my stomach. Or I vomit. Or I break into a cold sweat. Or I feel myself shutting down, and I go into a quiet place. Or I close my fingers into tight fists until my knuckles ache. My reaction is visceral and I have to take a deep breath or two or three or more. I have to remind myself of the time and distance between then and now. I have to remind myself that I am

ROXANE GAY writes in diverse genres, including fiction, short stories, essays, and graphic fiction. Her essays have appeared in the *New York Times*, *Bitch*, *Oxford American*, and many other publications. She co-authored *Black Panther: World of Wakanda*, which won an Eisner Award in 2018, the same year that her memoir *Hunger* won a Lambda Literary Award. This essay is from her 2014 essay collection, *Bad Feminist*.

not the girl in the woods anymore. I have to convince myself I never will be again. It has gotten better over the years.

It gets better until it doesn't.

The first congressional hearing on television violence was held in 1954, and in the ensuing years, the debate about television and violence has been ongoing. The Telecommunications Act of 1996 dictated that televisions needed to include a chip to monitor program ratings. The current television parental guidelines went into effect on January 1, 1997. These guidelines were designed to help parents monitor what their children were watching and get some sense of the appropriateness of a given television program.

The guidelines rated television content by age appropriateness from G   5
(all audiences) to MA (mature audiences only). There is also a second set of guidelines designed to protect children from violence, coarse language, and sexual themes. These guidelines, of course, only work if someone is monitoring what children are watching and is able to enforce a set of standards about what children can watch. Cable boxes and most televisions now allow parents to lock certain channels or shows with ratings they consider inappropriate for their children, but there is only so much a parent can control.

How effective, then, are these ratings and guidelines? In "Ratings and Advisories: Implications for the New Ratings System for Television," Joanne Cantor et al. note how research shows that "parental discretion warnings and the more restrictive MPAA ratings stimulate some children's interest in viewing programs," and "the increased interest in restricted programs is more strongly linked to children's desire to reject control over their viewing than to their seeking out violent content."[1] Even children want a taste of forbidden fruit. Or at the very least, children don't want to be told they cannot taste that fruit.

Television ratings are like airport security—an act of theater, an illusion designed to reassure us, to make us feel like we control the influences we allow into our lives.

We want our children to be safe. We want to be safe. We want and need to pretend this is possible.

1. Cantor, Joanne, Kristen Harrison, and Marina Krcmar. "Ratings and Advisories: Implications for the New Ratings System for Television." *Television Violence and Public Policy*, edited by James T. Hamilton, U of Michigan P, 1988, pp. 179–217. [Editor's note]

When I see the phrase "trigger warning," I am far more inclined to read whatever follows. I myself enjoy the taste of forbidden fruit.

I also know trigger warnings cannot save me from myself. 10

Trigger warnings are, essentially, ratings or protective guidelines for the largely unmoderated Internet. Trigger warnings provide order to the chaos of the interwebs; they are a signal that the content following the warning may be upsetting, may trigger bad memories or reminders of traumatic or sensitive experiences. Trigger warnings allow readers a choice: steel yourself and continue reading, or protect yourself and look away.

Many feminist communities use trigger warnings, particularly in online forums when discussing rape, sexual abuse, and violence. By using these warnings, these communities are saying, "This is a safe space. We will protect you from unexpected reminders of our history." Members of these communities are given the illusion they *can* be protected.

There are a great many potential trigger warnings. Over the years, I have seen trigger warnings for eating disorders, poverty, self-injury, bullying, heteronormativity, suicide, sizeism, genocide, slavery, mental illness, explicit fiction, explicit discussions of sexuality, homosexuality, homophobia, addiction, alcoholism, racism, the Holocaust, ableism, and Dan Savage.

Life, apparently, requires a trigger warning.

This is the uncomfortable truth: everything is a trigger for someone. 15
There are things you cannot tell just by looking at someone.

We all have history. You can think you're *over* your history. You can think the past is the past. And then something happens, often innocuous, that shows you how far you are from *over it*. The past is always with you. Some people want to be protected from this truth.

I used to think I didn't have triggers because I told myself I was tough. I was steel. I was broken beneath the surface, but my skin was forged, impenetrable. Then I realized I had all kinds of triggers. I simply had buried them deep until there was no more room inside me. When the dam burst, I had to learn how to stare those triggers down. I had a lot of help, years and years of help.

I have writing.

Every so often debates about trigger warnings flare hotly and both sides are resolute. Trigger warnings are either ineffective and impractical or vital for creating safe online spaces.

By exploring their ethical boundaries and implications, Gay is defining what trigger warnings actually are. Check out how you can use definitions to support your arguments on pp. 460–61.

It has been suggested, more than once, that if you don't believe in trig- 20
ger warnings, you aren't respecting the experiences of rape and abuse survivors. It has been suggested, more than once, that trigger warnings are
unnecessary coddling.

It is an impossible debate. There is too much history lurking beneath the
skin of too many people. Few are willing to consider the possibility that trigger warnings might be ineffective, impractical, and necessary for creating
safe spaces all at once.

The illusion of safety is as frustrating as it is powerful.

There are things that rip my skin open and reveal what lies beneath, but
I don't believe in trigger warnings. I don't believe people can be protected
from their histories. I don't believe it is at all possible to anticipate the histories of others.

There is no standard for trigger warnings, no universal guidelines. Once
you start, where do you stop? Does the mention of the word "rape" require a
trigger warning, or is the threshold an account of a rape? How graphic does
an account of abuse need to be before meriting a warning? Are trigger warnings required anytime matters of difference are broached? What is graphic?
Who makes these determinations?

It all seems so futile, so impotent and, at times, belittling. When I see 25
trigger warnings, I think, *How dare you presume what I need to be protected
from?*

Trigger warnings also, when used in excess, start to feel like censorship.
They suggest that there are experiences or perspectives too inappropriate,
too explicit, too bare to be voiced publicly. As a writer, I bristle when people
say, "This should have had a trigger warning."

I do not understand the unspoken rules of trigger warnings. I cannot
write the way I want to write and consider using trigger warnings. I would
second-guess myself, temper the intensity of what I have to say. I don't want
to do that. I don't intend to ever do that.

Writers cannot protect their readers from themselves nor should they
be expected to.

There is also this thought: maybe trigger warnings allow people to
avoid learning how to deal with triggers and getting help. I say this with
the understanding that having access to professional resources for getting
help is a privilege. I say this with the understanding that sometimes there
is not enough help in the world. That said, there is value in learning, where

possible, how to deal with and respond to the triggers that cut you open, the triggers that put you back in terrible places, that remind you of painful history.

It is untenable to go through life as an exposed wound. No matter how   30
well intended, trigger warnings will not stanch the bleeding; trigger warnings will not harden into scabs over your wounds.

I don't believe in safety. I wish I did. I am not brave. I simply know what to be scared of; I know to be scared of everything. There is freedom in that fear. That freedom makes it easier to appear fearless—to say and do what I want. I have been broken, so I am prepared should that happen again. I have, at times, put myself in dangerous situations. I have thought, *You have no idea what I can take*. This idea of unknown depths of endurance is a refrain in most of my writing. Human endurance fascinates me, probably too much because more often than not, I think of life in terms of enduring instead of living.

Intellectually, I understand why trigger warnings are necessary. I understand that painful experiences are all too often threatening to break the skin. Seeing or feeling yourself come apart is terrifying.

This is the truth of my trouble with trigger warnings: there is nothing words on the screen can do that has not already been done. A visceral reaction to a trigger is nothing compared to the actual experience that created the trigger.

I don't know how to see beyond this belief to truly get why trigger warnings are necessary. When I see trigger warnings, I don't feel safe. I don't feel protected. Instead, I am surprised there are still people who believe in safety and protection despite overwhelming evidence to the contrary.

This is my failing.   35

But.

I do recognize that in some spaces, we have to err on the side of safety or the illusion thereof. Trigger warnings aren't meant for those of us who don't believe in them, just like the Bible wasn't written for atheists. Trigger warnings are designed for the people who need and believe in that safety.

Those of us who do not believe should have little say in the matter. We can neither presume nor judge what others might feel the need to be protected from.

But still.

    There will always be a finger on the trigger. No matter how hard we try,   40
there's no way to step out of the line of fire.

Thinking about the Text

1. Roxane Gay presents clear **ARGUMENTS** both for and against the use of trigger warnings, but her main point addresses something other than just those warnings. What does she want readers to know? Do you find her argument persuasive? Why or why not?

2. Gay's essay is sprinkled with short, terse sentences ("I have writing" [18].) and occasionally even fragments ("But" [36].) Find three more examples of such terse bits. What is the effect of these occasional breaks in the rhythmic flow of her prose? What do they accomplish? Are they effective? Why or why not?

3. Although she never offers a direct **NARRATIVE** of any of her experiences, Gay makes it clear that she speaks from personal experience of violence. How does she make her experience clear without narrating what happened? How effective is her technique? Would a narrative have conveyed more effectively the argument she is making about trigger warnings? Why or why not? Explain your conclusion.

4. Gay states very explicitly: "I don't believe in trigger warnings" (23). Still, at several points throughout her essay she concedes that trigger warnings can be useful, even "necessary" (32). Do her concessions about the value of trigger warnings weaken her argument? Strengthen it? Why do you think so? Explain your reasoning and point to specific passages that support your evaluation.

5. Gay's style of personal reflection and disclosure almost invites readers to respond, to enter a conversation with her. Imagine sitting next to her on a plane or sharing a table with her at the school cafeteria. What would you like to ask her or tell her? Imagine your conversation. Write a reflection that responds to her as though she were at your side listening.

Hidden Intellectualism

GERALD GRAFF

EVERYONE KNOWS SOME YOUNG PERSON who is impressively "street smart" but does poorly in school. What a waste, we think, that one who is so intelligent about so many things in life seems unable to apply that intelligence to academic work. What doesn't occur to us, though, is that schools and colleges might be at fault for missing the opportunity to tap into such street smarts and channel them into good academic work.

Nor do we consider one of the major reasons why schools and colleges overlook the intellectual potential of street smarts: the fact that we associate those street smarts with anti-intellectual concerns. We associate the educated life, the life of the mind, too narrowly and exclusively with subjects and texts that we consider inherently weighty and academic. We assume that it's possible to wax intellectual about Plato, Shakespeare, the French Revolution, and nuclear fission, but not about cars, dating, fashion, sports, TV, or video games.

The trouble with this assumption is that no necessary connection has ever been established between any text or subject and the educational depth

---

GERALD GRAFF, a professor of English and education at the University of Illinois at Chicago, is best known for his books *Clueless in Academe: How Schooling Obscures the Life of the Mind* (2004) and (with Cathy Birkenstein) *"They Say / I Say": The Moves That Matter in Academic Writing* (2018), among several others. This essay was written for *Clueless in Academe* in 2004.

and weight of the discussion it can generate. Real intellectuals turn any subject, however lightweight it may seem, into grist for their mill through the thoughtful questions they bring to it, whereas a dullard will find a way to drain the interest out of the richest subject. That's why a George Orwell writing on the cultural meanings of penny postcards is infinitely more substantial than the cogitations of many professors on Shakespeare or globalization (104–16).

Students do need to read models of intellectually challenging writing—and Orwell is a great one—if they are to become intellectuals themselves. But they would be more prone to take on intellectual identities if we encouraged them to do so at first on subjects that interest them rather than ones that interest us.

I offer my own adolescent experience as a case in point. Until I entered   5
college, I hated books and cared only for sports. The only reading I cared to do or could do was sports magazines, on which I became hooked, becoming a regular reader of *Sport* magazine in the late forties, *Sports Illustrated* when it began publishing in 1954, and the annual magazine guides to professional baseball, football, and basketball. I also loved the sports novels for boys of John R. Tunis and Clair Bee and autobiographies of sports stars like Joe DiMaggio's *Lucky to Be a Yankee* and Bob Feller's *Strikeout Story*. In short, I was your typical teenage anti-intellectual—or so I believed for a long time. I have recently come to think, however, that my preference for sports over schoolwork was not anti-intellectualism so much as intellectualism by other means.

In the Chicago neighborhood I grew up in, which had become a melting pot after World War II, our block was solidly middle class, but just a block away—doubtless concentrated there by the real estate companies—were African Americans, Native Americans, and "hillbilly" whites who had recently fled postwar joblessness in the South and Appalachia. Negotiating this class boundary was a tricky matter. On the one hand, it was necessary to maintain the boundary between "clean-cut" boys like me and working-class "hoods," as we called them, which meant that it was good to be openly smart in a bookish sort of way. On the other hand, I was desperate for the approval of the hoods, whom I encountered daily on the playing field and in the neighborhood, and for this purpose it was not at all good to be book-smart. The hoods would turn on you if they sensed you were putting on airs over them: "Who you lookin' at, smart ass?" as a leather-jacketed youth once said to me as he relieved me of my pocket change along with my self-respect.

I grew up torn, then, between the need to prove I was smart and the fear of a beating if I proved it too well; between the need not to jeopardize

Gerald Graff frames his position as a response to attitudes he has observed. See pp. 149–51 on responding to what others say.

my respectable future and the need to impress the hoods. As I lived it, the conflict came down to a choice between being physically tough and being verbal. For a boy in my neighborhood and elementary school, only being "tough" earned you complete legitimacy. I still recall endless, complicated debates in this period with my closest pals over who was "the toughest guy in the school." If you were less than negligible as a fighter, as I was, you settled for the next best thing, which was to be inarticulate, carefully hiding telltale marks of literacy like correct grammar and pronunciation.

In one way, then, it would be hard to imagine an adolescence more thoroughly anti-intellectual than mine. Yet in retrospect, I see that it's more complicated, that I and the 1950s themselves were not simply hostile toward intellectualism, but divided and ambivalent. When Marilyn Monroe married the playwright Arthur Miller in 1956 after divorcing the retired baseball star Joe DiMaggio, the symbolic triumph of geek over jock suggested the way the wind was blowing. Even Elvis, according to his biographer Peter Guralnick, turns out to have supported Adlai over Ike in the presidential election of 1956. "I don't dig the intellectual bit," he told reporters. "But I'm telling you, man, he knows the most" (327).

Though I too thought I did not "dig the intellectual bit," I see now that I was unwittingly in training for it. The germs had actually been planted in the seemingly philistine debates about which boys were the toughest. I see now that in the interminable analysis of sports teams, movies, and toughness that my friends and I engaged in—a type of analysis, needless to say, that the real toughs would never have stooped to—I was already betraying an allegiance to the egghead world. I was practicing being an intellectual before I knew that was what I wanted to be.

It was in these discussions with friends about toughness and sports, I think, and in my reading of sports books and magazines, that I began to learn the rudiments of the intellectual life: how to make an argument, weigh different kinds of evidence, move between particulars and generalizations, summarize the views of others, and enter a conversation about ideas. It was in reading and arguing about sports and toughness that I experienced what it felt like to propose a generalization, restate and respond to a counterargument, and perform other intellectualizing operations, including composing the kind of sentences I am writing now. 10

Only much later did it dawn on me that the sports world was more compelling than school because it was *more intellectual than school*, not less. Sports after all was full of challenging arguments, debates, problems for analysis, and intricate statistics that you could care about, as school conspicuously was not. I believe that street smarts beat out book smarts in our culture not because street smarts are nonintellectual, as we generally suppose, but because they satisfy an intellectual thirst more thoroughly than school culture, which seems pale and unreal.

They also satisfy the thirst for community. When you entered sports debates, you became part of a community that was not limited to your family and friends, but was national and public. Whereas schoolwork isolated you from others, the pennant race or Ted Williams's .400 batting average was something you could talk about with people you had never met. Sports introduced you not only to a culture steeped in argument, but to a public argument culture that transcended the personal. I can't blame my schools for failing to make intellectual culture resemble the Super Bowl, but I do fault them for failing to learn anything from the sports and entertainment worlds about how to organize and represent intellectual culture, how to exploit its gamelike element and turn it into arresting public spectacle that might have competed more successfully for my youthful attention.

For here is another thing that never dawned on me and is still kept hidden from students, with tragic results: that the real intellectual world, the one that existed in the big world beyond school, is organized very much like the world of team sports, with rival texts, rival interpretations and evaluations of texts, rival theories of why they should be read and taught, and elaborate team competitions in which "fans" of writers, intellectual systems, methodologies, and -isms contend against each other.

To be sure, school contained plenty of competition, which became more invidious as one moved up the ladder (and has become even more so today with the advent of high-stakes testing). In this competition, points were scored not by making arguments, but by a show of information or vast reading, by grade-grubbing, or other forms of oneupmanship. School competition, in short, reproduced the less attractive features of sports culture without those that create close bonds and community.

And in distancing themselves from anything as enjoyable and absorbing as sports, my schools missed the opportunity to capitalize on an element of drama and conflict that the intellectual world shares with sports. Consequently, I failed to see the parallels between the sports and academic worlds that could have helped me cross more readily from one argument culture to the other. 15

Sports is only one of the domains whose potential for literacy training (and not only for males) is seriously underestimated by educators, who see sports as competing with academic development rather than a route to it. But if this argument suggests why it is a good idea to assign readings and topics that are close to students' existing interests, it also suggests the limits of this tactic. For students who get excited about the chance to write about their passion for cars will often write as poorly and unreflectively on that topic as on Shakespeare or Plato. Here is the flip side of what I pointed out before: that there's no necessary relation between the degree of interest a student shows in a text or subject and the quality of thought or expression such a student manifests in writing or talking about it. The challenge, as college professor Ned Laff has put it, "is not simply to exploit students' nonacademic interests, but to get them to see those interests through academic eyes."

To say that students need to see their interests "through academic eyes" is to say that street smarts are not enough. Making students' nonacademic interests an object of academic study is useful, then, for getting students' attention and overcoming their boredom and alienation, but this tactic won't in itself necessarily move them closer to an academically rigorous treatment of those interests. On the other hand, inviting students to write about cars, sports, or clothing fashions does not have to be a pedagogical cop-out as long as students are required to see these interests "through academic eyes," that is, to think and write about cars, sports, and fashions in a reflective, analytical way, one that sees them as microcosms of what is going on in the wider culture.

If I am right, then schools and colleges are missing an opportunity when they do not encourage students to take their nonacademic interests as objects of academic study. It is self-defeating to decline to introduce any text or subject that figures to engage students who will otherwise tune out academic work entirely. If a student cannot get interested in Mill's *On Liberty* but will read *Sports Illustrated* or *Vogue* or the hip-hop magazine *Source* with absorption, this is a strong argument for assigning the magazines over the classic. It's a good bet that if students get hooked on reading and writing by doing term papers on *Source*, they will eventually get to *On Liberty*. But even if they don't, the magazine reading will make them more literate and reflective than they would be otherwise. So it makes pedagogical sense to develop classroom units on sports, cars, fashions, rap music, and other such topics. Give me the student anytime who writes a sharply argued, sociologically acute analysis of an issue of *Source* over the student who writes a lifeless explication of *Hamlet* or Socrates's *Apology*.

Works Cited and Consulted

DiMaggio, Joe. *Lucky to Be a Yankee*. Bantam Books, 1949.

Feller, Bob. *Strikeout Story*. Bantam Books, 1948.

Guralnick, Peter. *Last Train to Memphis: The Rise of Elvis Presley*. Little, Brown, 1994.

Orwell, George. *A Collection of Essays*. Harcourt Brace, 1953.

Thinking about the Text

1. Gerald Graff's principal **EVIDENCE** in this essay is his own personal experience. How and how well does he present other supporting evidence? How and how well does he present the views that he is arguing against?

2. Graff notes that Ned Laff suggests that students be encouraged to view what interests them "through academic eyes" (16). What do you and your friends discuss frequently? Sports stats? Relative merits of various cosmetics or video games? Who is the best dancer or musician? Have you ever thought and written about those interests "in a reflective, analytical way" (17)? Would you want to? What kinds of evidence might you need to examine and present?

3. Graff makes frequent use of the first-person plural—"we think," "we associate," and so on (1, 2). Who is this "we" that he sees as his **AUDIENCE**: professors? parents? anybody and everybody? Explain your answer, and provide evidence from the text. Why might Graff have chosen to use "we" this way? How does it affect your response to his argument?

4. Graff argues that a student who learns to take an academic approach to *Sports Illustrated*, *Vogue*, *Source*, or other popular periodicals will eventually be likely to want to read traditionally academic material. Do you agree with that argument?

5. Graff recollects growing up "torn . . . between the need to prove I was smart and the fear of a beating if I proved it too well" (7). Did you have any similar experiences growing up, possibly involving fear of social rather than physical harm? Write an essay in which you **DESCRIBE** the prevailing (and perhaps conflicting) attitudes toward academic success among your friends, family members, and neighbors. Once you establish the context, write about your strategies and experiences in navigating the attitudes of those around you.

Touching the Earth

BELL HOOKS

I wish to live because life has within it that which is good, that which
is beautiful, and that which is love. Therefore, since I have known all
these things, I have found them to be reason enough and—I wish to live.
Moreover, because this is so, I wish others to live for generations and
generations and generations and generations.

—LORRAINE HANSBERRY, *To Be Young, Gifted, and Black*

WHEN WE LOVE THE EARTH, we are able to love ourselves more fully.
I believe this. The ancestors taught me it was so. As a child I loved
playing in dirt, in that rich Kentucky soil, that was a source of life. Before
I understood anything about the pain and exploitation of the southern
system of sharecropping, I understood that grown-up black folks loved the
land. I could stand with my grandfather Daddy Jerry and look out at fields
of growing vegetables, tomatoes, corn, collards, and know that this was his

BELL HOOKS is founder of the bell hooks Institute at Berea College, in Kentucky.
Her most recent book, *Writing Beyond Race: Living Theory and Practice* (2013), as
well as her numerous books and academic articles, focuses on the interconnect-
edness and inseparability of race, economic class, and gender—and the role that
these three factors play in shaping U.S. society. This selection was originally published in the 1993 anthology *Sisters of the Yam: Black Women and Self-Recovery*.

handiwork. I could see the look of pride on his face as I expressed wonder and awe at the magic of growing things. I knew that my grandmother Baba's backyard garden would yield beans, sweet potatoes, cabbage, and yellow squash, that she too would walk with pride among the rows and rows of growing vegetables showing us what the earth will give when tended lovingly.

From the moment of their first meeting, Native American and African people shared with one another a respect for the life-giving forces of nature, of the earth. African settlers in Florida taught the Creek Nation runaways, the "Seminoles," methods for rice cultivation. Native peoples taught recently arrived black folks all about the many uses of corn. (The hotwater cornbread we grew up eating came to our black southern diet from the world of the Indian.) Sharing the reverence for the earth, black and red people helped one another remember that, despite the white man's ways, the land belonged to everyone. Listen to these words attributed to Chief Seattle in 1854:

> How can you buy or sell the sky, the warmth of the land? The idea is strange to us. If we do not own the freshness of the air and the sparkle of the water, how can you buy them? Every part of this earth is sacred to my people. Every shining pine needle, every sandy shore, every mist in the dark woods, every clearing and humming insect is holy in the memory and experience of my people.... We are part of the earth and it is part of us. The perfumed flowers are our sisters; the deer, the horse, the great eagle, these are our brothers. The rocky crests, the juices in the meadows, the body heat of the pony, and man—all belong to the same family.

The sense of union and harmony with nature expressed here is echoed in testimony by black people who found that even though life in the new world was "harsh, harsh," in relationship to the earth one could be at peace. In the oral autobiography of granny midwife Onnie Lee Logan, who lived all her life in Alabama, she talks about the richness of farm life—growing vegetables, raising chickens, and smoking meat. She reports:

> We lived a happy, comfortable life to be right outa slavery times. I didn't know nothin else but the farm so it was happy and we was happy.... We couldn't do anything else but be happy. We accept the days as they come and as they were. Day by day until you couldn't

Kentucky morning.

say there was any great hard time. We overlooked it. We didn't think nothin about it. We just went along. We had what it takes to make a good livin and go about it.

Living in modern society, without a sense of history, it has been easy for folks to forget that black people were first and foremost a people of the land, farmers. It is easy for folks to forget that at the first part of the 20th century, the vast majority of black folks in the United States lived in the agrarian south.

Living close to nature, black folks were able to cultivate a spirit of wonder and reverence for life. Growing food to sustain life and flowers to please the soul, they were able to make a connection with the earth that was ongoing and life-affirming. They were witnesses to beauty. In Wendell Berry's important discussion of the relationship between agriculture and human spiritual well-being, *The Unsettling of America*, he reminds us that working the land provides a location where folks can experience a sense of personal power and well-being:

> We are working well when we use ourselves as the fellow creature of the plants, animals, material, and other people we are working with. Such work is unifying, healing. It brings us home from pride and despair, and places us responsibly within the human estate. It defines us as we are: not too good to work without our bodies, but too good to work poorly or joylessly or selfishly or alone.

There has been little or no work done on the psychological impact of 5 the "great migration" of black people from the agrarian south to the industrialized north. Toni Morrison's novel *The Bluest Eye* attempts to fictively document the way moving from the agrarian south to the industrialized north wounded the psyches of black folk. Estranged from a natural world, where there was time for silence and contemplation, one of the "displaced" black folks in Morrison's novel, Miss Pauline, loses her capacity to experience the sensual world around her when she leaves southern soil to live in a northern city. The south is associated in her mind with a world of sensual beauty most deeply expressed in the world of nature. Indeed, when she falls in love for the first time she can name that experience only by evoking images from nature, from an agrarian world and near wilderness of natural splendor:

Good evidence can be more than facts and figures, as bell hooks shows. See pp. 425–32.

> When I first seed Cholly, I want you to know it was like all the bits of color from that time down home when all us chil'ren went berry picking after a funeral and I put some in the pocket of my Sunday dress, and they mashed up and stained my hips. My whole dress was messed with purple, and it never did wash out. Not the dress nor me. I could feel that purple deep inside me. And that lemonade Mama used to make when Pap came in out of the fields. It be cool and yellowish, with seeds floating near the bottom. And that streak of green them june bugs made on the trees that night we left from down home. All of them colors was in me. Just sitting there.

Certainly, it must have been a profound blow to the collective psyche of black people to find themselves struggling to make a living in the industrial north away from the land. Industrial capitalism was not simply changing the nature of black work life, it altered the communal practices that were so central to survival in the agrarian south. And it fundamentally altered black people's relationship to the body. It is the loss of any capacity to appreciate her body, despite its flaws, Miss Pauline suffers when she moves north.

The motivation for black folks to leave the south and move north was both material and psychological. Black folks wanted to be free of the overt racial harassment that was a constant in southern life and they wanted access to material goods—to a level of material well-being that was not available in the agrarian south where white folks limited access to the spheres of economic power. Of course, they found that life in the north had its own perverse hardships, that racism was just as virulent there, that it was much harder for black people to become landowners. Without the space to grow food, to commune with nature, or to mediate the starkness of poverty with the splendor of nature, black people experienced profound depression. Working in conditions where the body was regarded solely as a tool (as in slavery), a profound estrangement occurred between mind and body. The way the body was represented became more important than the body itself. It did not matter if the body was well, only that it appeared well.

Estrangement from nature and engagement in mind/body splits made it all the more possible for black people to internalize white-supremacist assumptions about black identity. Learning contempt for blackness, southerners transplanted in the north suffered both culture shock and soul loss.

Contrasting the harshness of city life with an agrarian world, the poet War-ing Cuney wrote this popular poem in the 1920s, testifying to lost connection:

> She does not know her beauty
> She thinks her brown body
> has no glory.
> If she could dance naked,
> Under palm trees
> And see her image in the river
> She would know.
> But there are no palm trees on the street,
> And dishwater gives back no images.

For many years, and even now, generations of black folks who mi-grated north to escape life in the south, returned down home in search of a spiritual nourishment, a healing, that was fundamentally connected to reaffirming one's connection to nature, to a contemplative life where one could take time, sit on the porch, walk, fish, and catch lightning bugs. If we think of urban life as a location where black folks learned to accept a mind/body split that made it possible to abuse the body, we can better understand the growth of nihilism and despair in the black psyche. And we can know that when we talk about healing that psyche we must also speak about re-storing our connection to the natural world.

Wherever black folks live we can restore our relationship to the natural world by taking the time to commune with nature, to appreciate the other creatures who share this planet with humans. Even in my small New York City apartment I can pause to listen to birds sing, find a tree and watch it. We can grow plants—herbs, flowers, vegetables. Those novels by African-American writers (women and men) that talk about black migration from the agrarian south to the industrialized north describe in detail the way folks created space to grow flowers and vegetables. Although I come from country people with serious green thumbs, I have always felt that I could not garden. In the past few years, I have found that I can do it—that many gardens will grow, that I feel connected to my ancestors when I can put a meal on the table of food I grew. I especially love to plant collard greens. They are hardy, and easy to grow.

In modern society, there is also a tendency to see no correlation between the struggle for collective black self-recovery and ecological movements that

10

seek to restore balance to the planet by changing our relationship to nature and to natural resources. Unmindful of our history of living harmoniously on the land, many contemporary black folks see no value in supporting ecological movements, or see ecology and the struggle to end racism as competing concerns. Recalling the legacy of our ancestors who knew that the way we regard land and nature will determine the level of our self-regard, black people must reclaim a spiritual legacy where we connect our well-being to the well-being of the earth. This is a necessary dimension of healing. As Berry reminds us:

> Only by restoring the broken connections can we be healed. Connection is health. And what our society does its best to disguise from us is how ordinary, how commonly attainable, health is. We lose our health—and create profitable diseases and dependencies—by failing to see the direct connections between living and eating, eating and working, working and loving. In gardening, for instance, one works with the body to feed the body. The work, if it is knowledgeable, makes for excellent food. And it makes one hungry. The work thus makes eating both nourishing and joyful, not consumptive, and keeps the eater from getting fat and weak. This health, wholeness, is a source of delight.

Collective black self-recovery takes place when we begin to renew our relationship to the earth, when we remember the way of our ancestors. When the earth is sacred to us, our bodies can also be sacred to us.

Thinking about the Text

1. This essay takes an explicit **POSITION**, but it is expressed in very abstract terms. What, exactly, is the author exhorting her readers to do? What concrete steps might they take to accomplish what she is recommending? Present examples from the text to support your responses.

2. What kind of environment would you say you live in—urban, rural, or something in between? How would you describe your relationship to the natural world? What do you do in order to "touch the earth"? Would you like to be able to do more? Why or why not?

3. Hooks cites Wendell Berry, who mentions the "profitable diseases and de-pendencies" that people create when we fail to see "the direct connections between living and eating, eating and working, working and loving" (10). What does Berry mean by "profitable diseases and dependencies"? Profitable for whom? Why? Dependencies on what or on whom? How does Berry's asser-tion fit into this essay's argument?

4. Because of black Americans' particular history with slavery and racism in the United States, hooks is suggesting a particular path toward healing. Might this same path be a healing one for other groups of people? Why or why not? Might it be a healing path for you, personally, or other members of a social or ethnic group to which you belong? Why or why not?

5. Very few of us could be said to live in harmony with nature; the demands of contemporary economic and social life, in fact, seem to take us increas-ingly farther afield from such a state. Take a critical look around you, at your individual, family, and community contexts. What barriers are blocking what bell hooks would call a reconnection with the earth on each of those three levels? What could be done on each level to lower such barriers? Write an essay in which you take stock of your environment and **PROPOSE** concrete, doable steps toward a more harmonious relationship with nature at one of these levels—individual, family, or community—or explain why this is not a desirable goal. Be sure to make clear which level your proposal is addressing.

Sight Unseen

GEORGINA KLEEGE

ONCE, AT A PARTY, a man I was speaking to was almost reduced to tears to learn that I am a blind writer. There was a tremor in his voice as he kept repeating something about "the word fading." As far as I could understand it, he was picturing a page of print disappearing before my eyes word by word, as if written in invisible ink. It was a vivid image but bore little resemblance to my reality. Sensing that he was most disturbed by the idea that my sight loss was still in progress, I tried to tell him that, unless some other visual condition develops, the word had already "faded" as much as it ever will. And as far as these things go, a writer is not a bad thing to be if you can't see. There are other ways to write, other ways to read. It is easier for a writer than for a visual artist, a race car driver, or an astronomer to compensate for sight loss. I might have even mentioned Homer, Milton, and Joyce, the sight-impaired literary luminaries most often invoked at such times. I wanted to say, "This is not a tragedy. This is merely a fact of my life. Get over it. I have." But he had already receded from me, become preoccupied with a new, reductive view of me and my restricted future.

GEORGINA KLEEGE, lecturer in creative writing as well as disability studies at University of California, Berkeley, is author of several books, and she has served as a consultant to art institutions such as the Metropolitan Museum of Art in New York and the Tate Modern in London. She is also blind, a designation that she discusses in this excerpt from her 1999 book, *Sight Unseen*.

Of course, it's the word *blind* that causes all the problems. To most people blindness means total, absolute darkness, a complete absence of any visual experience. Though only 10 percent of the legally blind have this degree of impairment, people think the word should be reserved to designate this minority. For the rest of us, with our varying degrees of sight, a modifier becomes necessary. We're encouraged to indicate that we're not quite "that bad." Better to speak of a visual impairment, a sight deficit, low vision. Better still to accentuate the positive and call it "partially sighted."

Sometimes I use these other terms, but I find them no more precise or pleasing. The word "impairment" implies impermanence, an encumbrance that could disappear, but my condition has no cure or treatment. The term "low vision" reminds me too much of "short eyes," a prison term for child molesters. And anyway, I crave the simplicity of a single, unmodified adjective. Blind. Perhaps I could speak in relative terms, say I am blinder than some, less blind than others.

"But," people object, "you are not really blind," attaching yet another adverb to separate me from the absolutely sightless. The modern, legal definition is arbitrary, a convention based on notions of what visual skills are necessary for an adult to be gainfully employed or a child traditionally educated. The definition has more to do with the ability to read print or drive a car than with the ability to perceive color, light, motion, or form. If I lived in a different culture or a different age, no one would define me as blind. I could transport myself on foot or horseback. I could grow or gather my own food, relying on my other senses to detect ripeness, pests, soil quality. I would have trouble hunting; the protective coloration of most animals and birds is always good enough to deceive me. But I might learn to devise cunning traps, and I could fish. I could become adept at crafts—certain kinds of weaving or pottery—that require as much manual dexterity and tactile sensitivity as visual acuity. If I looked at people strangely it might be accepted as a personality flaw. Or else this imagined culture might be one where a too-direct gaze is considered impolite. In any case, I could live independently, with enough sight to perform routine tasks without aid. If I had a sense that others' eyes were stronger or more discerning than mine, I still would not define myself as blind. Especially if the culture was the sort that put the blind to death.

Though in the here and now execution is unlikely, a stigma exists. So why should I want to label myself in this way? Isn't the use of the word at all, even with one of the imprecise modifiers, a form of self-dramatization, a

5

Stated another way, Kleege's rhetorical situation is exactly what she's writing about. See more about considering your rhetorical situation on pp. 30–34.

demand for attention and pity better bestowed elsewhere? Isn't it a dishonest claim of marginal status, now that marginality is fashionable?

This is precisely why I avoided the word for so long. I was pronounced legally blind in 1967, when I was eleven, though my condition probably developed a year or two earlier. I have no memory of losing my sight. I imagine it took place so gradually that I was unaware of what I was not seeing. The only outward sign was that I began to read with the book very close to my eyes. Everyone assumed that I was simply nearsighted, but tests did not show this. My cornea and lenses refracted normally. Remarkably, my doctor did not pursue the matter, even though the early signs of retinal damage should have been revealed in a standard eye exam. Apparently such damage was not what he was looking for. Instead, he jumped to the conclusion that I was faking, even though I was not the sort of child who would do that. My parents and teachers were advised to nag me into holding the book away from my face. For a while I complied, keeping the book at the prescribed distance, turning pages at appropriate intervals. Then, when no one was looking, I would flip back and press my nose to the page. Eventually it became clear to everyone that this was not a phase that I was going to outgrow. Additional tests were performed. When it was all over, my doctor named my disorder "macular degeneration," defined my level of impairment as legally blind, and told me that there was no treatment or cure, and no chance of improvement. And that was all. Like many ophthalmologists then and perhaps now, he did not feel that it was his responsibility to recommend special education or training. He did not send me to an optometrist for whatever magnification devices might have been available then. In 1967 the boom in high-tech "low vision" aids had not yet begun. He said that as long as I continued to perform well at school, there was no point in burdening me with cumbersome gadgetry or segregating myself from my classmates. He did not tell me that I was eligible to receive recorded materials for the blind. He did not even explain legal blindness, much less the specifics of my condition—I did not find out what my macula was for several years. He said nothing about adaptation, did not speculate about what my brain had already learned to do to compensate for the incomplete images my eyes were sending. This was not his job. Since then I have heard accounts of other doctors faced with the dilemma of telling patients that there is no cure for their condition. They admit they sometimes see these patients as embarrassments, things they'd rather sweep under the carpet, out of public view. But as a child of eleven I did not understand his dilemma, and I assumed that his failure to give me more information was a measure of the insignificance of my problem. I was confused and scared, but also disappointed not to receive the glasses I expected him to prescribe. I left with no glasses, no advice, no explanations—nothing but the words *macular degeneration*, which I did not understand, and, more significantly, the word *blind*, which I understood only too well.

Thinking about the Text

1. Georgina Kleege is blind, but she finds the word "blind" to be problematic in several ways. What are they? Why? **SUMMARIZE** her reasons.

2. Kleege **NARRATES** an unsatisfying conversation at a party with someone who wouldn't hear or understand her. She wanted to say, "This is not a tragedy. This is merely a fact of my life. Get over it. I have" (1). Have you ever had a similar response for any reason to a conversation? Recount your experience. What did you want that person to understand?

3. Kleege uses a dry, matter-of-fact **STYLE** to describe conditions that are hardly dry or absent of emotional significance. How does her style choice affect the way you respond to her? Does her matter-of-fact style elicit a dry, emotionless response? Why or why not?

4. As Kleege points out, the conventional definition of blindness "has more to do with the ability to read print or drive a car than with the ability to perceive color, light, motion, or form" (4). In another time or place, she notes, she would not have to bear the stigmatized label of "blind" since she would be able to transport herself and procure her own food. Think of other personal characteristics—dyslexia, for example—that are often stigmatized in this time and place, but might not be stigmatized at all in another type of society. What are those features? How might life be different for people with those characteristics? Use your imagination to envision another kind of world.

5. Kleege describes her encounter with the ophthalmologist who diagnosed her macular degeneration when she was eleven years old. Although she mentions what the doctor might have said or done but didn't, she doesn't suggest that the doctor had mishandled her situation, and any anger she felt is not explicitly expressed. Did you feel anger on her behalf? Do you think the doctor behaved irresponsibly? Why or why not? How understandable to you is Kleege's attitude toward the doctor? How understandable to you is Kleege's attitude toward blindness? Write an essay addressing your responses to these questions.

Clean Sweep

RYAN KOHLS

FORTY THOUSAND PEOPLE are packed into the Rogers Centre to watch the Toronto Blue Jays. Right now, the stadium still belongs to the players, the fans and the vast, expensively-produced spectacle of professional sports. But at gate three, a group of about fifty congregates. Some stand alone, or pace and listen to music. Others sit on wooden benches nearby and enjoy a final cigarette. It's 10:30 pm, and these grim-faced men and women are waiting for work to begin. Standing on the curb as the game wraps up inside, these are the cleaners.

They'll work until dawn, gathering up some 15,000 pounds of garbage, scrubbing, rinsing, bending and lifting with painstaking thoroughness.

By morning, the stadium will gleam and the cleaners will go home to sleep with the blinds pulled tight against the sun. Now, they try to relax, joking to keep the mood light. "Are you ready for more torture?" one of them asks.

Spread out across 12.7 acres, the Rogers Centre, once known as the Sky-Dome, is one of Toronto's most recognizable landmarks. Every year 3.5 mil-

---

RYAN KOHLS is a journalist who has filed stories from places as diverse as Nairobi, Kenya, and Nunavut, Canada. He is an interview producer for the daily program *The Stream* on Al Jazeera. You can find him on Twitter @ryankohls. This article appeared in 2014 in *Maison Neuve*, a Canadian magazine of arts, opinion, and ideas.

lion people attend events at the mammoth complex. The big crowds mean big business—baseball's Blue Jays, whose eighty-one home games provide the stadium's main attraction, are worth an estimated $568 million. One season produces 1.2 million pounds of garbage. Eventually, someone must clean it up. Enter the cleaners—exhausted, poorly paid and largely anonymous. Without them, the game can't go on.

On a given night, anywhere from thirty to one hundred cleaners scour the   5
stadium. Most of them work for Hallmark Housekeeping Services, a Toronto-based janitorial agency that holds the cleaning contract at the Rogers Centre. These workers are experienced; Hallmark employees clean after every event. The other cleaners come from Labor Ready, a huge company that supplies temporary blue-collar workers across Canada and the United States. These employees book the Rogers Centre gig on a nightly basis and typically work a shorter shift. Both groups of workers are predominantly immigrants or down on their luck.

   In the summer of 2012, I worked as a cleaner, on-and-off, for three months. I participated in roughly twenty-five cleaning shifts as an em-

When the fun is over and the fans go home, someone has to pick up the trash.

ployee of Labor Ready, joining the agency after struggling to find journalism work in the city.

Most cleaners patrol the stadium with brooms and large transparent garbage bags; a handful of more seasoned employees take leaf blowers. With the motor slung across their backs and a long black nozzle pumping out air, they blow the garbage from two parallel seating sections into one aisle. The blowers weigh about 25 pounds. One worker described it as being like "carrying an obese baby around all night."

Once enough garbage reaches the aisle, the sweepers climb to the top of their section and begin to slosh the mess downwards. In time, the pile turns into a cascading waterfall of miscellaneous trash. Beer-soaked hot dogs mix with ketchup-infused popcorn and the ubiquitous shells of sunflower seeds, which are maddeningly hard to persuade off the wet concrete. The mixture leaves behind a slick residue that makes the stairs treacherous. Workers sometimes slip and hurt their backs. Some stadiums have tried to control the garbage, but at baseball stadiums, seeds cannot be so easily dispatched—they're an iconic part of the game. "Getting rid of [sunflower seeds] would be like getting rid of beer and hot dogs," says Wayne Sills, the director of facility services at the Rogers Centre.

The last stage of cleaning is accomplished with four thirty-metre yellow hoses, spraying highly pressurized water into the aisles, aimed by workers in rubber boots. The Rogers Centre is one of the few North American sports stadiums to get the pressure-wash treatment—visiting teams have been known to remark on the building's uncanny cleanliness.

Around 2:30 am Rosario Coutinho scans the Centre with binoculars. She'll 10 spot a sweeper slacking off and radio the nighttime supervisor to assess the situation and get things moving. Coutinho then heads to another location where she can remain unseen and watch closely. "I'm the ghost," she tells me one night.

Coutinho, now fifty-two, serves as the resident manager of the clean-up operation. She pulls her black hair back in a ponytail, wears glasses, a black fleece and black pants, a BlackBerry headset and a crucifix on a chain. Coutinho knows more about the cleaning process than anyone. She's been at the Rogers Centre for nearly twenty-five years.

The workers are on to her tactics. Once, a group of Mexican cleaners developed a system of whistles to alert the others when she was watching. Coutinho translated the calls and changed her moves accordingly.

To become the binocular boss, Coutinho had to start from the bottom. In 1989, just a month after the SkyDome opened, she immigrated to Canada from Portugal. Her husband already lived here and told her about the opening of an amazing new stadium. Coutinho remembers being unimpressed; some stadiums in Europe hold 100,000 people. But the retractable roof that gave the building its name was, she was told, a sight to behold.

Before her arrival, Coutinho was prepared to work hard. "I knew I would be doing jobs that no one else wanted to do," she recalls. "If I'm cleaning shit, who cares? I'm going to make it smell better." Two months after landing in Toronto she was cleaning at the SkyDome. Her first assignment was the luxury boxes. One night she found a briefcase containing $10,000 cash. She returned it. The job meant everything and she couldn't risk losing it.

This atypical attitude caught management's attention and within a   15
year she was promoted to team leader. "Seventy percent of people in the cleaning business have no pride," Coutinho says. "Earn what you make, that's what counts." By 1995, she was managing the entire operation.

Ryan Kohls, writing for a magazine, didn't have to document his interviews, but you will in your academic writing. See how to do so in MLA format on p. 595.

Few cleaners are as scrupulous as Coutinho. Many hate being there—some show up drunk, others get drunk in the stadium bathrooms on left-behind tallboys from the stands or their own flasks of hard liquor. Still others find their pay-off elsewhere: take Mark Stanton [not his real name]. It's his third season cleaning at the Rogers Centre and his favourite part of the job is finding money.

After the Jays' home opener, sporting a leaf blower slung across his back, he guides sunflower shells, empty beer cans and half-eaten hot dogs across an aisle. Out of the corner of his eye he spots a wallet. He flicks off the blower, bends over and plucks it from a pile of trash. He can't get too excited; he has to act calm: someone could be watching. He hunches over, peers inside and sees the cash. Quickly, with a practiced motion, he slides $30 into his pants. "Sometimes I go to work and I'm flat broke," says Stanton. "If I find $30, there's $30 in my pocket until pay day." He will eventually return the wallet, a little lighter, to security.

Stanton is adept at working the stadium's unofficial and technically illegal lost-and-found system to his advantage. At last year's home opener, he scored five wallets with $30 or more and two half-packs of smokes. When he cleaned up after the 100th Grey Cup, he found $150, three Grey Cup souvenir glasses and three t-shirts. After Ultimate Fighting Championship 129, he found a judge's scorecard and three bloody hand wraps. The excitement creates plenty of opportunities for fans to drop things. After every event, without fail, an array of valuables remains behind. For the workers, this is a perk, a way to make the job feel worthwhile. Some nights pay off huge. At UFC 100, one worker found and kept a wallet with $1,500. That's a month's wages. Other cleaners have found diamond rings, iPhones, BlackBerries, digital cameras, transit passes, sunglasses and umbrellas.

The treasure hunt is on everyone's mind. Having a successful night requires skill and attention. You can't just sweep or blow the garbage, you have to watch and listen. Over time, workers learn to hear the difference between a sliding beer tab and a coin. One worker uses his haul to pay child support for his three kids. He found $150 once and used it to buy his son a stroller.

When the clock hits 3 am, the stadium falls silent, and the workers break for 20 "lunch." There's a cheap hot dog stand on Front Street that's popular. Most of the cleaners can afford a meal using the spare change they've found during their shift.

Only three-quarters of the workers return after the break. Labor Ready workers are generally only used for sweeping and bagging. They'll get paid for four hours of work. As they disappear into the night, some head to bed, but others walk back to Labor Ready to collect their cheque and secure the next job. The company's offices at 195 Church Street don't open until 5:30 am, so many nights they'll wait in Dundas Square. If they time it just right, they'll score a free breakfast from the Salvation Army truck that passes by Labor Ready every morning.

Thinking about the Text

1. Ryan Kohls begins with a description of the ballpark's splendor and the cleaning process that keeps it that way, but the focus soon shifts to the cleaners themselves. What is his purpose in this **PROFILE**? Point to examples in the text to support your answer.

2. How does Kohls's disclosure of having been a stadium cleaner himself contribute to his **AUTHORITY**? And yet he doesn't include any personal anecdotes or impressions of the job other than the bare facts of his work, choosing instead to spotlight the other cleaners. Should he have spoken more about his own experience? Why or why not?

3. Kohls is clearly happy to no longer work as a stadium cleaner. Despite having moved on in his own career, what is his **ATTITUDE** toward his former colleagues? How does he portray them and their work? Point to examples in the text to support your response.

4. Although this profile describes a large sports arena, Kohls wasn't writing for an **AUDIENCE** of sports fans. What, if anything, might he have done differently if he were writing a column for ESPN or *Sports Illustrated*? Why?

5. Have you ever worked at a job that you hoped would not become your long-term occupation? Write a **DESCRIPTION** of the job and your co-workers that gives your readers as vivid a sense as possible of a typical shift, letting examples and descriptive details make your point.

On Meaningful Observation

JOHN MAEDA

A SILVER LINING IN THE DARK CLOUD of any recession—especially this one, thought to be caused by our own greed and excess—is the opportunity it affords us to reexamine our collective values. On the positive side, the nation seems to be as committed as ever to the power of innovation as America's saving grace. What is less comforting to me as president of an art and design school is how America defines innovation. Do a search on the White House website for the word "innovation" and the top results revolve around technology; talk to any parent with children in public schools and you will hear about arts-education resources diminishing quickly. I feel there is a disconnect between the words "innovation" and "art" that needs to be resolved if the United States is to prevail as the most creative economy in our world.

Public commitments to STEM—science, technology, engineering, math—education abound all over the country. In the government's mind, these subjects are the key to innovation. As a lifelong STEM student

---

JOHN MAEDA is an artist, computer scientist, and author. He taught in the MIT Media Lab for twelve years and served as president of the Rhode Island School of Design from 2008 to 2013. Maeda is currently head of computational design and inclusion at a Silicon Valley tech firm. His Twitter handle is @johnmaeda. In December 2010, while Maeda was at the Rhode Island School of Design and the country was in the middle of the Great Recession, he wrote this proposal for *Seed* magazine as part of a series seeking solutions to "interconnected and complex challenges."

John Maeda
describes
the problem
with current
STEM
education.
Go to pp.
374–76
for tips
on getting
your own
proposals
off to a
strong start.

myself, with degrees in electrical engineering and computer science from MIT, I am certainly not one to diminish its value. Yet in recent years even supremely dedicated geeks like me have begun to question the advances that come from purely technological innovation.

We seem to be stuck in a kind of technology loop. It began in the 1980s with computers that could display only text and play limited sound. Images then became possible, and with CD-ROM technology came high-fidelity sound and full-motion video. In the '90s, when the web took hold, we started again with text, limited sounds and images, then high-fidelity audio, and years later we reached the point of full-motion video. Now we see the cell phone in our pocket experiencing the same progression from text, to sound, to audio, to video—and we are supposed to feel like we are enjoying incredible progress. But it seems the tricks are exactly the same each time around the loop. I'm looking for a new trick.

After two decades as a student and faculty member at MIT, my newest experience at the Rhode Island School of Design (RISD) has reawakened me to the world of physical creation. RISD represents the ultimate culture of makers. There is no greater integrity, no greater goal achieved, than an idea articulately expressed through something made with your hands. We call this constant dialogue between eye, mind, and hand "critical thinking—critical making." It's an education in getting your hands dirty, in understanding why you made what you made, and owning the impact of the work in the world. It's what artists and designers do.

As tricks come, as far as I can tell this isn't a new one at all. But it certainly feels like it transcends mere trickery: It is truly substantive magic for the soul. Students at RISD don't think in terms of megabytes or equations; they think in terms of the warm, complex voice of a material like wood, or the way that glass finds its resting place differently on a cold winter day. Their hands, and sometimes faces, are literally covered with the materials they use to shape, angle, mutate, and translate their thoughts into handcrafted realities. Being an artist, I feel that art comes from the inexplicable urge to manifest a feeling, intent, or question as a specific, tangible experience. Artists do research with an open-mindedness and rigorous inquiry unseen in most other disciplines, except true science. They systematically and visually survey the world of ideas, objects, and experiences for inspiration by rummaging through it with their bare hands. I know most of us today are more likely to get the job done with cleaner hands through a search on Google Images. But at RISD the story of someone's work more often comes

A student crafting, hands covered in clay.

from a first-hand journey through many emotional worlds, rather than an analysis of an online slideshow of poorly photographed experiences.

We have a facility on campus called Nature Lab. Founded in 1937, it houses more than 80,000 true specimens of nature—from skeletons to saplings to salamanders. Students can check out a butterfly from the lab and bring it back to their dorm room overnight. It's really a Victorian approach to science, based on meaningful observation of something real. "Real" also abounds in the RISD museum. Need to see a real Monet or Rothko? You can stand within millimeters of it. Our students are within steps of the visceral emotion of experiencing a masterpiece, and the making that went into it.

And so I've begun to wonder recently whether STEM needs something to give it some STE(A)M—an "A" for art between the engineering and the math to ground the bits and bytes in the physical world before us, to lift them up and make them human. What if America approached innovation with more than just technology? What if, just like STEM is made up of science, technology, engineering, and math, we had IDEA, made of intuition, design, emotion, and art—all the things that make us humans feel, well, human? It seems to me that if we use this moment to reassess our values, putting just a little bit of our humanity back into America's innovation engines will lead to the most meaningful kind of progress. By doing so, we will find a way back to integrating thinking with making and being and feeling and living so that left- and right-brained creativity can lift our economy back into the sky.

Thinking about the Text

1. A good **PROPOSAL** addresses a well-defined problem. How well does John Maeda define the problem he proposes to solve? **SUMMARIZE** the problem. Do you agree that it warrants attention? Why or why not?

2. According to Maeda, artists do research "with an open-mindedness and rigorous inquiry" that is rarely found elsewhere except in "true science" (5). What exactly does he mean by this **COMPARISON**, and how is it important to his argument? Is it a fair comparison to make? Why or why not?

3. Maeda was the president of an art and design school, yet he is writing about STEM issues here. How does he establish his **AUTHORITY** to write about this topic? Point to specific passages in the essay to support your response.

4. Many arguments in favor of arts instruction talk about its importance to a well-rounded education. Maeda focuses instead on how the arts contribute to economic prosperity. Why might he have taken this approach? Do you find his **ARGUMENT** persuasive? Why or why not?

5. What experiences have you had making things—whether a painting, a sculpture, an IKEA bookcase, or a sandwich? What kinds of things do you like to make? Do you agree with Maeda that making things makes you feel more human—and that, as he proposes, we should have IDEA (intuition, design, emotion, art) along with STEM (science, technology, engineering, math)? Write an essay responding to Maeda, agreeing, disagreeing, or both. Use your own experience as your principal **EVIDENCE**.

The Egg and the Sperm

EMILY MARTIN

The theory of the human body is always a part of a world-picture.
... The theory of the human body is always a part of a *fantasy*.
　　　　　　　　　　　—JAMES HILLMAN, *The Myth of Analysis*[1]

AS AN ANTHROPOLOGIST, I am intrigued by the possibility that culture shapes how biological scientists describe what they discover about the natural world. If this were so, we would be learning about more than the natural world in high school biology class; we would be learning about cultural beliefs and practices as if they were part of nature. In the course of my research I realized that the picture of egg and sperm drawn in popular as well as scientific accounts of reproductive biology relies on stereotypes

1. James Hillman, *The Myth of Analysis* (Evanston, Ill.: Northwestern University Press, 1972), 220.

EMILY MARTIN, professor emeritus of anthropology at New York University, is founding editor of the magazine *Anthropology Now* and has written extensively about intersections of culture and science. Her 2007 book *Bipolar Expeditions* won a prize for feminist anthropological research. This article first appeared in *Signs: Journal of Women in Culture and Society* in 1991 with the subtitle "How Science Has Constructed a Romance Based on Stereotypical Male-Female Roles." It has become a classic reading in medical anthropology.

central to our cultural definitions of male and female. The stereotypes imply not only that female biological processes are less worthy than their male counterparts but also that women are less worthy than men. Part of my goal in writing this article is to shine a bright light on the gender stereotypes hidden within the scientific language of biology. Exposed in such a light, I hope they will lose much of their power to harm us.

Egg and Sperm: A Scientific Fairy Tale

At a fundamental level, all major scientific textbooks depict male and female reproductive organs as systems for the production of valuable substances, such as eggs and sperm.[2] In the case of women, the monthly cycle is described as being designed to produce eggs and prepare a suitable place for them to be fertilized and grown—all to the end of making babies. But the enthusiasm ends there. By extolling the female cycle as a productive enterprise, menstruation must necessarily be viewed as a failure. Medical texts describe menstruation as the "debris" of the uterine lining, the result of necrosis, or death of tissue. The descriptions imply that a system has gone awry, making products of no use, not to specification, unsalable, wasted, scrap. An illustration in a widely used medical text shows menstruation as a chaotic disintegration of form, complementing the many texts that describe it as "ceasing," "dying," "losing," "denuding," "expelling."[3]

Male reproductive physiology is evaluated quite differently. One of the texts that sees menstruation as failed production employs a sort of breathless prose when it describes the maturation of sperm: "The mechanisms which guide the remarkable cellular transformation from spermatid to mature sperm remain uncertain. . . . Perhaps the most amazing characteristic of spermatogenesis is its sheer magnitude: the normal human male may manufacture several hundred million sperm per day."[4] In the classic text *Medical Physiology*, edited by Vernon Mountcastle, the male/female, productive/

2. The textbooks I consulted are the main ones used in classes for undergraduate premedical students or medical students (or those held on reserve in the library for these classes) during the past few years at Johns Hopkins University. These texts are widely used at other universities in the country as well.

3. Arthur C. Guyton, *Physiology of the Human Body*, 6th ed. (Philadelphia: Saunders College Publishing, 1984), 624.

4. Arthur J. Vander, James H. Sherman, and Dorothy S. Luciano, *Human Physiology: The Mechanisms of Body Function*, 3d ed. (New York: McGraw Hill, 1980), 483–84.

destructive comparison is more explicit: "Whereas the female *sheds* only a single gamete each month, the seminiferous tubules *produce* hundreds of millions of sperm each day" (emphasis mine).[5] The female author of another text marvels at the length of the microscopic seminiferous tubules, which, if uncoiled and placed end to end, "would span almost one-third of a mile!" She writes, "In an adult male these structures produce millions of sperm cells each day." Later she asks, "How is this feat accomplished?"[6] None of these texts expresses such intense enthusiasm for any female processes. It is surely no accident that the "remarkable" process of making sperm involves precisely what, in the medical view, menstruation does not: production of something deemed valuable.[7]

One could argue that menstruation and spermatogenesis are not analogous processes and, therefore, should not be expected to elicit the same kind of response. The proper female analogy to spermatogenesis, biologically, is ovulation. Yet ovulation does not merit enthusiasm in these texts either. Textbook descriptions stress that all of the ovarian follicles containing ova are already present at birth. Far from being *produced*, as sperm are, they merely sit on the shelf, slowly degenerating and aging like overstocked inventory: "At birth, normal human ovaries contain an estimated one million follicles [each], and no new ones appear after birth. Thus, in marked contrast to the male, the newborn female already has all the germ cells she will ever have. Only a few, perhaps 400, are destined to reach full maturity during her active productive life. All the others degenerate at some point in their development so that few, if any, remain by the time she reaches menopause at approximately 50 years of age."[8] Note the "marked contrast" that this description sets up between male and female: the male, who continuously produces fresh germ cells, and the female, who has stockpiled germ cells by birth and is faced with their degeneration.

Nor are the female organs spared such vivid descriptions. One scientist   5 writes in a newspaper article that a woman's ovaries become old and worn out from ripening eggs every month, even though the woman herself is still relatively young: "When you look through a laparoscope . . . at an ovary that

5. Vernon B. Mountcastle, *Medical Physiology*, 14th ed. (London: Mosby, 1980), 2:1624.
6. Eldra Pearl Solomon, *Human Anatomy and Physiology* (New York: CBS College Publishing, 1983), 678.
7. For elaboration, see Emily Martin, *The Woman in the Body: A Cultural Analysis of Reproduction* (Boston: Beacon, 1987), 27–53.
8. Vander, Sherman, and Luciano, 568.

has been through hundreds of cycles, even in a superbly healthy American female, you see a scarred, battered organ."[9]

To avoid the negative connotations that some people associate with the female reproductive system, scientists could begin to describe male and female processes as homologous. They might credit females with "producing" mature ova one at a time, as they're needed each month, and describe males as having to face problems of degenerating germ cells. This degeneration would occur throughout life among spermatogonia, the undifferentiated germ cells in the testes that are the long-lived, dormant precursors of sperm.

But the texts have an almost dogged insistence on casting female processes in a negative light. The texts celebrate sperm production because it is continuous from puberty to senescence, while they portray egg production as inferior because it is finished at birth. This makes the female seem unproductive.... In a section heading for *Molecular Biology of the Cell*, a best-selling text, we are told that "Oogenesis is wasteful." The text goes on to emphasize that of the seven million oogonia, or egg germ cells, in the female embryo, most degenerate in the ovary. Of those that do go on to become oocytes, or eggs, many also degenerate, so that at birth only two million eggs remain in the ovaries. Degeneration continues throughout a woman's life: by puberty 300,000 eggs remain, and only a few are present by menopause. "During the 40 or so years of a woman's reproductive life, only 400 to 500 eggs will have been released," the authors write. "All the rest will have degenerated. It is still a mystery why so many eggs are formed only to die in the ovaries."[10]

The real mystery is why the male's vast production of sperm is not seen as wasteful.[11] Assuming that a man "produces" 100 million (10^8) sperm per day (a conservative estimate) during an average reproductive life of sixty years, he would produce well over two trillion sperm in his lifetime. Assuming that a woman "ripens" one egg per lunar month, or thirteen per year, over the course of her forty-year reproductive life, she would total five

9. Melvin Konner, "Childbearing and Age," *New York Times Magazine* (December 27, 1987), 22–23, esp. 22.
10. Bruce Alberts et al., *Molecular Biology of the Cell* (New York: Garland, 1983), 795.
11. In her essay "Have Only Men Evolved?" (in *Discovering Reality: Feminist Perspectives on Epistemology, Metaphysics, Methodology, and Philosophy of Science*, ed. Sandra Harding and Merrill B. Hintikka [Dordrecht: Reidel, 1983], 45–69, esp. 60–61), Ruth Hubbard points out that sociobiologists have said the female invests more energy than the male in the production of her large gametes, claiming that this explains why the female provides parental care. Hubbard questions whether it "really takes more 'energy' to generate the one or relatively few eggs than the large excess of sperms required to achieve fertilization."

hundred eggs in her lifetime. But the word "waste" implies an excess, too much produced. Assuming two or three offspring, for every baby a woman produces, she wastes only around two hundred eggs. For every baby a man produces, he wastes more than one trillion (10^{12}) sperm.

How is it that positive images are denied to the bodies of women? A look at language—in this case, scientific language—provides the first clue. Take the egg and the sperm.[12] It is remarkable how "femininely" the egg behaves and how "masculinely" the sperm.[13] The egg is seen as large and passive.[14] It does not *move* or *journey*, but passively "is transported," "is swept,"[15] or even "drifts"[16] along the fallopian tube. In utter contrast, sperm are small, "streamlined,"[17] and invariably active. They "deliver" their genes to the egg, "activate the developmental program of the egg,"[18] and have a "velocity" that is often remarked upon.[19] Their tails are "strong" and efficiently powered.[20] Together with the forces of ejaculation, they can "propel the semen into the deepest recesses of the vagina."[21] For this they need "energy," "fuel,"[22] so that with a "whiplashlike motion and strong lurches"[23] they can "burrow through the egg coat"[24] and "penetrate" it.[25]

At its extreme, the age-old relationship of the egg and the sperm takes on a royal or religious patina. The egg coat, its protective barrier, is sometimes 10

---

12. The sources I used for this article provide compelling information on interactions among sperm. Lack of space prevents me from taking up this theme here, but the elements include competition, hierarchy, and sacrifice.

13. See Carol Delaney, "The Meaning of Paternity and the Virgin Birth Debate," *Man* 21, no. 3 (September 1986): 494–513. She discusses the difference between this scientific view that women contribute genetic material to the fetus and the claim of long-standing Western folk theories that the origin and identity of the fetus comes from the male, as in the metaphor of planting a seed in soil.

14. For a suggested direct link between human behavior and purportedly passive eggs and active sperm, see Erik H. Erikson, "Inner and Outer Space: Reflections on Womanhood," *Daedalus* 93, no. 2 (Spring 1964): 582–606, esp. 591.

15. Guyton (n. 3 above), 619; and Mountcastle (n. 5 above), 1609.

16. Jonathan Miller and David Pelham, *The Facts of Life* (New York: Viking Penguin, 1984), 5.

17. Alberts et al., 796.

18. Ibid., 796.

19. See, e.g., William F. Ganong, *Review of Medical Physiology*, 7th ed. (Los Altos, Calif.: Lange Medical Publications, 1975), 322.

20. Alberts et al. (n. 10 above), 796.

21. Guyton, 615.

22. Solomon (n. 6 above), 683.

23. Vander, Sherman, and Luciano (n. 4 above), 4th ed. (1985), 580.

24. Alberts et al., 796.

25. All biology texts quoted above use the word "penetrate."

called its "vestments," a term usually reserved for sacred, religious dress. The egg is said to have a "corona,"[26] a crown, and to be accompanied by "attendant cells."[27] It is holy, set apart and above, the queen to the sperm's king. The egg is also passive, which means it must depend on sperm for rescue. Gerald Schatten and Helen Schatten liken the egg's role to that of Sleeping Beauty: "a dormant bride awaiting her mate's magic kiss, which instills the spirit that brings her to life."[28] Sperm, by contrast, have a "mission,"[29] which is to "move through the female genital tract in quest of the ovum."[30] One popular account has it that the sperm carry out a "perilous journey" into the "warm darkness," where some fall away "exhausted." "Survivors" "assault" the egg, the successful candidates "surrounding the prize."[31] Part of the urgency of this journey, in more scientific terms, is that "once released from the supportive environment of the ovary, an egg will die within hours unless rescued by a sperm."[32] The wording stresses the fragility and dependency of the egg, even though the same text acknowledges elsewhere that sperm also live for only a few hours.[33]

In 1948, in a book remarkable for its early insights into these matters, Ruth Herschberger argued that female reproductive organs are seen as biologically interdependent, while male organs are viewed as autonomous, operating independently and in isolation:

> At present the functional is stressed only in connection with women: it is in them that ovaries, tubes, uterus, and vagina have endless interdependence. In the male, reproduction would seem to involve "organs" only.
>
> Yet the sperm, just as much as the egg, is dependent on a great many related processes. There are secretions which mitigate the urine in the urethra before ejaculation, to protect the sperm. There is the reflex shutting off of the bladder connection, the provision of prostatic secretions, and various types of muscular propulsion.

26. Solomon, 700.
27. A. Beldecos et al., "The Importance of Feminist Critique for Contemporary Cell Biology," *Hypatia* 3, no. 1 (Spring 1988): 61–76.
28. Gerald Schatten and Helen Schatten, "The Energetic Egg," *Medical World News* 23 (January 23, 1984): 51–53, esp. 51.
29. Alberts et al., 796.
30. Guyton (n. 3 above), 613.
31. Miller and Pelham (n. 16 above), 7.
32. Alberts et al. (n. 10 above), 804.
33. Ibid., 801.

The sperm is no more independent of its milieu than the egg, and yet from a wish that it were, biologists have lent their support to the notion that the human female, beginning with the egg, is congenitally more dependent than the male.[34]

Bringing out another aspect of the sperm's autonomy, an article in the journal *Cell* has the sperm making an "existential decision" to penetrate the egg: "Sperm are cells with a limited behavioral repertoire, one that is directed toward fertilizing eggs. To execute the decision to abandon the haploid state, sperm swim to an egg and there acquire the ability to effect membrane fusion."[35] Is this a corporate manager's version of the sperm's activities—"executing decisions" while fraught with dismay over difficult options that bring with them very high risk?

There is another way that sperm, despite their small size, can be made to loom in importance over the egg. In a collection of scientific papers, an electron micrograph of an enormous egg and tiny sperm is titled "A Portrait of the Sperm."[36] This is a little like showing a photo of a dog and calling it a picture of the fleas. Granted, microscopic sperm are harder to photograph than eggs, which are just large enough to see with the naked eye. But surely the use of the term "portrait," a word associated with the powerful and wealthy, is significant. Eggs have only micrographs or pictures, not portraits.

One depiction of sperm as weak and timid, instead of strong and powerful—the only such representation in western civilization, so far as I know—occurs in Woody Allen's movie *Everything You Always Wanted to Know About Sex* *But Were Afraid to Ask*. Allen, playing the part of an apprehensive sperm inside a man's testicles, is scared of the man's approaching orgasm. He is reluctant to launch himself into the darkness, afraid of contraceptive devices, afraid of winding up on the ceiling if the man masturbates.

The more common picture—egg as damsel in distress, shielded only by her sacred garments; sperm as heroic warrior to the rescue—cannot be proved to be dictated by the biology of these events. While the "facts" of

34. Ruth Herschberger, *Adam's Rib* (New York: Pelligrini & Cudaby, 1948), esp. 84. I am indebted to Ruth Hubbard for telling me about Herschberger's work, although at a point when this paper was already in draft form.
35. Bennett M. Shapiro, "The Existential Decision of a Sperm," *Cell* 49, no. 3 (May 1987): 293–94, esp. 293.
36. Lennart Nilsson, "A Portrait of the Sperm," in *The Functional Anatomy of the Spermatozoan*, ed. Bjorn A. Afzelius (New York: Pergamon, 1975), 79–82.

biology may not *always* be constructed in cultural terms, I would argue that in this case they are. The degree of metaphorical content in these descriptions, the extent to which differences between egg and sperm are emphasized, and the parallels between cultural stereotypes of male and female behavior and the character of egg and sperm all point to this conclusion.

New Research, Old Imagery

As new understandings of egg and sperm emerge, textbook gender imagery is being revised. But the new research, far from escaping the stereotypical representations of egg and sperm, simply replicates elements of textbook gender imagery in a different form. . . . We need to understand the way in which the cultural content in scientific descriptions changes as biological discoveries unfold, and whether that cultural content is solidly entrenched or easily changed.

In all of the texts quoted above, sperm are described as penetrating the egg, and specific substances on a sperm's head are described as binding to the egg. Recently, this description of events was rewritten in a biophysics lab at Johns Hopkins University—transforming the egg from the passive to the active party.[37]

Prior to this research, it was thought that the zona, the inner vestments of the egg, formed an impenetrable barrier. Sperm overcame the barrier by mechanically burrowing through, thrashing their tails and slowly working their way along. Later research showed that the sperm released digestive enzymes that chemically broke down the zona; thus, scientists presumed that the sperm used mechanical *and* chemical means to get through to the egg.

In this recent investigation, the researchers began to ask questions about the mechanical force of the sperm's tail. (The lab's goal was to develop a contraceptive that worked topically on sperm.) They discovered, to their great surprise, that the forward thrust of sperm is extremely weak, which contradicts the assumption that sperm are forceful penetrators.[38]

37. Jay M. Baltz carried out the research I describe when he was a graduate student in the Thomas C. Jenkins Department of Biophysics at Johns Hopkins University.
38. Far less is known about the physiology of sperm than comparable female substances, which some feminists claim is no accident. Greater scientific scrutiny of female reproduction has long enabled the burden of birth control to be placed on women. In this case, the researchers' discovery did not depend on development of any new technology. The experiments made use

Rather than thrusting forward, the sperm's head was now seen to move mostly back and forth. The sideways motion of the sperm's tail makes the head move sideways with a force that is ten times stronger than its forward movement. So even if the overall force of the sperm were strong enough to mechanically break the zona, most of its force would be directed sideways rather than forward. In fact, its strongest tendency, by tenfold, is to escape by attempting to pry itself off the egg. Sperm, then, must be exceptionally efficient at *escaping* from any cell surface they contact. And the surface of the egg must be designed to trap the sperm and prevent their escape. Otherwise, few if any sperm would reach the egg.

The researchers at Johns Hopkins concluded that the sperm and egg stick   20
together because of adhesive molecules on the surfaces of each. The egg traps the sperm and adheres to it so tightly that the sperm's head is forced to lie flat against the surface of the zona. . . . The trapped sperm continues to wiggle ineffectually side to side. The mechanical force of its tail is so weak that a sperm cannot break even one chemical bond. This is where the digestive enzymes released by the sperm come in. If they start to soften the zona just at the tip of the sperm and the sides remain stuck, then the weak, flailing sperm can get oriented in the right direction and make it through the zona— provided that its bonds to the zona dissolve as it moves in.

Although this new version of the saga of the egg and the sperm broke through cultural expectations, the researchers who made the discovery continued to write papers and abstracts as if the sperm were the active party who attacks, binds, penetrates, and enters the egg. The only difference was that sperm were now seen as performing these actions weakly.[39] Not until August 1987, more than three years after the findings described above, did these researchers reconceptualize the process to give the egg a more active role. They began to describe the zona as an aggressive sperm catcher, covered with adhesive molecules that can capture a sperm with a single bond and clasp it to the zona's surface.[40] In the words of their published account: "The innermost vestment, the *zona pellucida*, is a glycoprotein shell,

of glass pipettes, a manometer, and a simple microscope, all of which have been available for more than one hundred years.
39. Jay Baltz and Richard A. Cone, "What Force Is Needed to Tether a Sperm?" (abstract for Society for the Study of Reproduction, 1985), and "Flagellar Torque on the Head Determines the Force Needed to Tether a Sperm" (abstract for Biophysical Society, 1986).
40. Jay M. Baltz, David F. Katz, and Richard A. Cone, "The Mechanics of the Sperm-Egg Interaction at the Zona Pellucida," *Biophysical Journal* 54, no. 4 (October 1988): 643–54. Lab members were somewhat familiar with work on metaphors in the biology of female reproduction. Richard

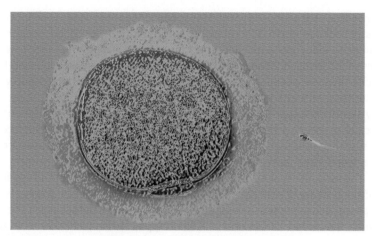

A microscopic view of sperm "swimming" near the surface of an egg.

which captures and tethers the sperm before they penetrate it. . . . The sperm is captured at the initial contact between the sperm tip and the *zona*. . . . Since the thrust [of the sperm] is much smaller than the force needed to break a single affinity bond, the first bond made upon the tip-first meeting of the sperm and *zona* can result in the capture of the sperm."[41]

Experiments in another lab reveal similar patterns of data interpretation. Gerald Schatten and Helen Schatten set out to show that, contrary to conventional wisdom, the "egg is not merely a large, yolk-filled sphere into which the sperm burrows to endow new life. Rather, recent research suggests the almost heretical view that sperm and egg are mutually active partners."[42] This sounds like a departure from the stereotypical textbook view, but further reading reveals Schatten and Schatten's conformity to the aggressive-sperm metaphor. They describe how "the sperm and egg first touch when, from the tip of the sperm's triangular head, a long, thin filament shoots out and harpoons the egg." Then we learn that "remarkably, the harpoon is not so much fired as assembled at great speed, molecule by molecule, from a pool of protein stored in a specialized region called the acrosome. The filament may grow as much as twenty times longer than the sperm head

Cone, who runs the lab, is my husband, and he talked with them about my earlier research on the subject from time to time. . . .
41. Ibid., 643, 650.
42. Schatten and Schatten (n. 28 above), 51.

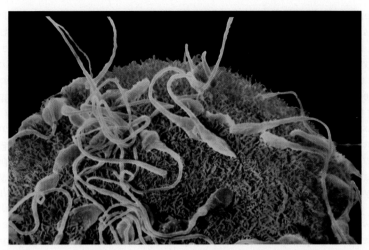

Modern research shows that adhesive molecules on the egg's surface are designed to trap sperm, forcing them to lie flat and wiggle side to side.

itself before its tip reaches the egg and sticks."[43] Why not call this "making a bridge" or "throwing out a line" rather than firing a harpoon? Harpoons pierce prey and injure or kill them, while this filament only sticks. And why not focus, as the Hopkins lab did, on the stickiness of the egg, rather than the stickiness of the sperm?[44] Later in the article, the Schattens replicate the common view of the sperm's perilous journey into the warm darkness of the vagina, this time for the purpose of explaining its journey into the egg itself: "[The sperm] still has an arduous journey ahead. It must penetrate farther into the egg's huge sphere of cytoplasm and somehow locate the nucleus, so that the two cells' chromosomes can fuse. The sperm dives down into the cytoplasm, its tail beating. But it is soon interrupted by the sudden and swift migration of the egg nucleus, which rushes toward the sperm with a velocity triple that of the movement of chromosomes during cell division, crossing the entire egg in about a minute."[45]

　　Like Schatten and Schatten and the biophysicists at Johns Hopkins, another researcher has recently made discoveries that seem to point to a more

43. Ibid., 52.
44. Surprisingly, in an article intended for a general audience, the authors do not point out that these are sea urchin sperm and note that human sperm do not shoot out filaments at all.
45. Schatten and Schatten, 53.

interactive view of the relationship of egg and sperm. This work, which Paul Wassarman conducted on the sperm and eggs of mice, focuses on identifying the specific molecules in the egg coat (the zona pellucida) that are involved in egg-sperm interaction. At first glance, his descriptions seem to fit the model of an egalitarian relationship. Male and female gametes "recognize one another," and "interactions . . . take place between sperm and egg."[46] But the article in *Scientific American* in which those descriptions appear begins with a vignette that presages the dominant motif of their presentation: "It has been more than a century since Hermann Fol, a Swiss zoologist, peered into his microscope and became the first person to see a sperm penetrate an egg, fertilize it and form the first cell of a new embryo."[47] This portrayal of the sperm as the active party—the one that *penetrates* and *fertilizes* the egg and *produces* the embryo—is not cited as an example of an earlier, now outmoded view. In fact, the author reiterates the point later in the article: "Many sperm can bind to and penetrate the zona pellucida, or outer coat, of an unfertilized mouse egg, but only one sperm will eventually fuse with the thin plasma membrane surrounding the egg proper (*inner sphere*), fertilizing the egg and giving rise to a new embryo."[48]

The imagery of sperm as aggressor is particularly startling in this case: the main discovery being reported is isolation of a particular molecule *on the egg coat* that plays an important role in fertilization! Wassarman's choice of language sustains the picture. He calls the molecule that has been isolated, ZP3, a "sperm receptor." By allocating the passive, waiting role to the egg, Wassarman can continue to describe the sperm as the actor, the one that makes it all happen: "The basic process begins when many sperm first attach loosely and then bind tenaciously to receptors on the surface of the egg's thick outer coat, the zona pellucida. Each sperm, which has a large number of egg-binding proteins on its surface, binds to many sperm receptors on the egg. More specifically, a site on each of the egg-binding proteins fits a complementary site on a sperm receptor, much as a key fits a lock."[49] With the sperm designated as the "key" and the egg the "lock," it is obvious which one acts and which one is acted upon. Could this imagery not be reversed, letting the sperm (the lock) wait until the egg produces the key? Or

46. Paul M. Wassarman, "Fertilization in Mammals," *Scientific American* 259, no. 6 (December 1988): 78–84, esp. 78, 84.
47. Ibid., 78.
48. Ibid., 79.
49. Ibid., 78.

could we speak of two halves of a locket matching, and regard the matching itself as the action that initiates the fertilization? . . .

Wassarman does credit the egg coat with having more functions than those of a sperm receptor. While he notes that "the zona pellucida has at times been viewed by investigators as a nuisance, a barrier to sperm and hence an impediment to fertilization," his new research reveals that the egg coat "serves as a sophisticated biological security system that screens incoming sperm, selects only those compatible with fertilization and development, prepares sperm for fusion with the egg and later protects the resulting embryo from polyspermy [a lethal condition caused by fusion of more than one sperm with a single egg]."[50] Although this description gives the egg an active role, that role is drawn in stereotypically feminine terms. The egg *selects* an appropriate mate, *prepares* him for fusion, and then *protects* the resulting offspring from harm. This is courtship and mating behavior as seen through the eyes of a sociobiologist: woman as the hard-to-get prize, who, following union with the chosen one, becomes woman as servant and mother.

And Wassarman does not quit there. In a review article for *Science,* he outlines the "chronology of fertilization."[51] Near the end of the article are two subject headings. One is "Sperm Penetration," in which Wassarman describes how the chemical dissolving of the zona pellucida combines with the "substantial propulsive force generated by sperm." The next heading is "Sperm-Egg Fusion." This section details what happens inside the zona after a sperm "penetrates" it. Sperm "can make contact with, adhere to, and fuse with (that is, fertilize) an egg."[52] Wassarman's word choice, again, is astonishingly skewed in favor of the sperm's activity, for in the next breath he says that sperm *lose* all motility upon fusion with the egg's surface. In mouse and sea urchin eggs, the sperm enters at the *egg's* volition, according to Wassarman's description: "Once fused with egg plasma membrane [the surface of the egg], how does a sperm enter the egg? The surface of both mouse and sea urchin eggs is covered with thousands of plasma membrane-bound projections, called microvilli [tiny "hairs"]. Evidence in sea urchins suggests that, after membrane fusion, a group of elongated microvilli cluster tightly around and interdigitate over the sperm head. As these microvilli are resorbed, the sperm is drawn into the egg. Therefore, sperm motility, which ceases at the time of fusion in both sea urchins and

50. Wassarman, 78–79.
51. Paul M. Wassarman, "The Biology and Chemistry of Fertilization," *Science* 235, no. 4788 (January 30, 1987): 553–60, esp. 554.
52. Ibid., 557.

mice, is not required for sperm entry."[53] The section called "Sperm Penetration" more logically would be followed by a section called "The Egg Envelops," rather than "Sperm-Egg Fusion." This would give a parallel—and more accurate—sense that both the egg and the sperm initiate action.

Another way that Wassarman makes less of the egg's activity is by describing components of the egg but referring to the sperm as a whole entity. Deborah Gordon has described such an approach as "atomism" ("the part is independent of and primordial to the whole") and identified it as one of the "tenacious assumptions" of Western science and medicine.[54] Wassarman employs atomism to his advantage. When he refers to processes going on within sperm, he consistently returns to descriptions that remind us from whence these activities came: they are part of sperm that penetrate an egg or generate propulsive force. When he refers to processes going on within eggs, he stops there. As a result, any active role he grants them appears to be assigned to the parts of the egg, and not to the egg itself. In the quote above, it is the microvilli that actively cluster around the sperm. In another example, "the driving force for engulfment of a fused sperm comes from a region of cytoplasm just beneath an egg's plasma membrane."[55]

Social Implications: Thinking Beyond

All three of these revisionist accounts of egg and sperm cannot seem to escape the hierarchical imagery of older accounts. Even though each new account gives the egg a larger and more active role, taken together they bring into play another cultural stereotype: woman as a dangerous and aggressive threat. In the Johns Hopkins lab's revised model, the egg ends up as the female aggressor who "captures and tethers" the sperm with her sticky zona, rather like a spider lying in wait in her web.[56] The Schatten lab has the egg's nucleus "interrupt" the sperm's dive with a "sudden and swift" rush by which she "clasps the sperm and guides its nucleus to the center."[57]

---

53. Ibid., 557–58. This finding throws into question Schatten and Schatten's description (n. 28 above) of the sperm, its tail beating, diving down into the egg.
54. Deborah R. Gordon, "Tenacious Assumptions in Western Medicine," in *Biomedicine Examined,* ed. Margaret Lock and Deborah Gordon (Dordrecht: Kluwer, 1988), 19–56, esp. 26.
55. Wassarman, "The Biology and Chemistry of Fertilization," 558.
56. Baltz, Katz, and Cone (n. 40 above), 643, 650.
57. Schatten and Schatten, 53.

Wassarman's description of the surface of the egg "covered with thousands of plasma membrane-bound projections, called microvilli" that reach out and clasp the sperm adds to the spiderlike imagery.[58]

These images grant the egg an active role but at the cost of appearing disturbingly aggressive. Images of woman as dangerous and aggressive, the femme fatale who victimizes men, are widespread in Western literature and culture.[59] More specific is the connection of spider imagery with the idea of an engulfing, devouring mother.[60] New data did not lead scientists to eliminate gender stereotypes in their descriptions of egg and sperm. Instead, scientists simply began to describe egg and sperm in different, but no less damaging, terms.

Can we envision a less stereotypical view? Biology itself provides another model that could be applied to the egg and the sperm. The cybernetic model—with its feedback loops, flexible adaptation to change, coordination of the parts within a whole, evolution over time, and changing response to the environment—is common in genetics, endocrinology, and ecology and has a growing influence in medicine in general.[61] This model has the potential to shift our imagery from the negative, in which the female reproductive system is castigated both for not producing eggs after birth and for producing (and thus wasting) too many eggs overall, to something more positive. The female reproductive system could be seen as responding to the environment (pregnancy or menopause), adjusting to monthly changes (menstruation), and flexibly changing from reproductivity after puberty to nonreproductivity later in life. The sperm and egg's interaction could also be described in cybernetic terms. J. F. Hartman's research in reproductive biology demonstrated fifteen years ago that if an egg is killed by being pricked with a needle, live sperm cannot get through the zona.[62] Clearly, this evidence shows that the egg and sperm *do* interact on more mutual terms, making biology's refusal to portray them that way all the more disturbing.

58. Wassarman, "The Biology and Chemistry of Fertilization," 557.

59. Mary Ellman, *Thinking about Women* (New York: Harcourt Brace Jovanovich, 1968), 140; Nina Auerbach, *Woman and the Demon* (Cambridge, Mass.: Harvard University Press, 1982), esp. 186.

60. Kenneth Alan Adams, "Arachnophobia: Love American Style," *Journal of Psychoanalytic Anthropology* 4, no. 2 (1981): 157–97.

61. William Ray Arney and Bernard Bergen, *Medicine and the Management of Living* (Chicago: University of Chicago Press, 1984).

62. J. F. Hartman, R. B. Gwatkin, and C. F. Hutchison, "Early Contact Interactions between Mammalian Gametes *In Vitro*," *Proceedings of the National Academy of Sciences (U.S.)* 69, no. 10 (1972): 2767–69.

We would do well to be aware, however, that cybernetic imagery is hardly neutral. In the past, cybernetic models have played an important part in the imposition of social control. These models inherently provide a way of thinking about a "field" of interacting components. Once the field can be seen, it can become the object of new forms of knowledge, which in turn can allow new forms of social control to be exerted over the components of the field. During the 1950s, for example, medicine began to recognize the psychosocial *environment* of the patient: the patient's family and its psychodynamics. Professions such as social work began to focus on this new environment, and the resulting knowledge became one way to further control the patient. . . .[63]

The models that biologists use to describe their data can have important social effects. During the nineteenth century, the social and natural sciences strongly influenced each other: the social ideas of Malthus about how to avoid the natural increase of the poor inspired Darwin's *Origin of Species*.[64] Once the *Origin* stood as a description of the natural world, complete with competition and market struggles, it could be reimported into social science as social Darwinism, in order to justify the social order of the time. What we are seeing now is similar: the importation of cultural ideas about passive females and heroic males into the "personalities" of gametes. This amounts to the "implanting of social imagery on representations of nature so as to lay a firm basis for reimporting exactly that same imagery as natural explanations of social phenomena."[65]

Further research would show us exactly what social effects are being wrought from the biological imagery of egg and sperm. At the very least, the imagery keeps alive some of the hoariest old stereotypes about weak damsels in distress and their strong male rescuers. That these stereotypes are now being written in at the level of the *cell* constitutes a powerful move to make them seem so natural as to be beyond alteration.

The stereotypical imagery might also encourage people to imagine that what results from the interaction of egg and sperm—a fertilized egg—is the result of deliberate "human" action at the cellular level. Whatever the intentions of the human couple, in this microscopic "culture" a cellular "bride" (or femme fatale) and a cellular "groom" (her victim) make a cellular baby. Rosalind Petchesky points out that through visual representations such as sonograms, we

63. Arney and Bergen.
64. Ruth Hubbard, "Have Only Men Evolved?" (n. 11 above), 51–52.
65. David Harvey, personal communication, November 1989.

are given "*images* of younger and younger, and tinier and tinier, fetuses being 'saved.'" This leads to "the point of visibility being 'pushed back' *indefinitely*."[66] Endowing egg and sperm with intentional action, a key aspect of personhood in our culture, lays the foundation for the point of viability being pushed back to the moment of fertilization. This will likely lead to greater acceptance of technological developments and new forms of scrutiny and manipulation, for the benefit of these inner "persons": court-ordered restrictions on a pregnant woman's activities in order to protect her fetus, fetal surgery, amniocentesis, and rescinding of abortion rights, to name but a few examples.[67]

Even if we succeed in substituting more egalitarian, interactive meta- phors to describe the activities of egg and sperm, and manage to avoid the pitfalls of cybernetic models, we would still be guilty of endowing cellular entities with personhood. More crucial, then, than what *kinds* of personali- ties we bestow on cells is the very fact that we are doing it at all. This process could ultimately have the most disturbing social consequences.

One clear feminist challenge is to wake up sleeping metaphors in sci- ence, particularly those involved in descriptions of the egg and the sperm. Although the literary convention is to call such metaphors "dead," they are not so much dead as sleeping, hidden within the scientific content of texts— and all the more powerful for it.[68] Waking up such metaphors, by becoming aware of when we are projecting cultural imagery onto what we study, will improve our ability to investigate and understand nature. Waking up such metaphors, by becoming aware of their implications, will rob them of their power to naturalize our social conventions about gender.

35

68 foot- notes! Done systemati- cally, it's not so hard. See Chs. 28 and 29 for help document- ing sources.

Note

Portions of this article were presented as the 1987 Becker Lecture, Cornell University. I am grateful for the many suggestions and ideas I received on this occasion. For especially pertinent help with my arguments and data

66. Rosalind Petchesky, "Fetal Images: The Power of Visual Culture in the Politics of Reproduction," *Feminist Studies* 13, no. 2 (Summer 1987): 263–92, esp. 272.
67. Rita Arditti, Renate Klein, and Shelley Minden, *Test-Tube Women* (London: Pandora, 1984); Ellen Goodman, "Whose Right to Life?" *Baltimore Sun* (November 17, 1987); Tamar Lewin, "Courts Acting to Force Care of the Unborn," *New York Times* (November 23, 1987), A1 and B10; Susan Irwin and Brigitte Jordan, "Knowledge, Practice, and Power: Court Ordered Cesarean Sections," *Medical Anthropology Quarterly* 1, no. 3 (September 1987): 319–34.
68. Thanks to Elizabeth Fee and David Spain, who in February 1989 and April 1989, respectively, made points related to this.

I thank Richard Cone, Kevin Whaley, Sharon Stephens, Barbara Duden, Susanne Kuechler, Lorna Rhodes, and Scott Gilbert. The article was strengthened and clarified by the comments of the anonymous *Signs* reviewers as well as the superb editorial skills of Amy Gage.

Thinking about the Text

1. **SUMMARIZE** Emily Martin's argument about the traditional descriptions of egg and sperm. What changes does she suggest for the way the fertilization process is described in textbooks?

2. Martin has made a careful **ANALYSIS** of the ways that the sciences describe the encounter of egg and sperm in mammalian reproduction. From what kinds of sources has she drawn her **EVIDENCE**? What was the general purpose for which these sources were originally published? Did you find that the cited evidence sufficiently demonstrates Martin's point? Why or why not?

3. **PARAPHRASE** Martin's argument about how the models of the social sciences and the natural sciences influence one another. What does this argument have to do with descriptions of the interactions between egg and sperm?

4. Surely in your school experience, you have encountered the material that Martin discusses—the egg and the sperm. Perhaps it was in high school biology, a college human development class, or both. How well does Martin's summary of traditional teaching on this topic match what you remember learning? Had you ever questioned the explanation of the fertilization process? Now that you've read Martin's article, do you think it should be questioned? Why or why not?

5. Judging from the article itself and the place where it was published, for whom was Martin writing? Who was her imagined **AUDIENCE**? What would she have had to do to make the article more suited for a general adult audience? for a high school or college-age audience?

6. Find a biology textbook or a reliable scientific animation on *YouTube* and look for the kind of language that Martin found—words or phrases that characterize natural processes in terms of human actions or emotions, such as "harpoons," "an arduous journey," and "mission" (22, 10). Martin published her article in 1991; have the metaphors changed substantially in more recent texts? If so, how? Once you have five or six examples, write a **RHETORICAL ANALYSIS** of the language used and discuss the possible social implications.

The Logic of Stupid Poor People

TRESSIE McMILLAN COTTOM

WE HATES US SOME POOR PEOPLE. First, they insist on being poor when it is so easy to not be poor. They do things like buy expensive designer belts and $2,500 luxury handbags.

> Errol Louis @errollouis
> I totally get that it's horrible and illegal to profile people. But still #SMFH over a not-filthy-rich person spending $2,500 on a handbag.

To be fair, this isn't about Errol Louis. His is a belief held by many people, including lots of black people, poor people, formerly poor people, etc. It is, I suspect, an honest expression of incredulity. If you are poor, why do you spend money on useless status symbols like handbags and belts and clothes and shoes and televisions and cars?

TRESSIE MCMILLAN COTTOM is a professor of sociology at Virginia Commonwealth University and a faculty associate of the Berkman Klein Center for Internet & Society at Harvard University. She is author of *Lower Ed* (2017), an examination of for-profit colleges, and *Thick* (2019), a collection of essays and 2019 National Book Award finalist. You can follow her on Twitter @tressiemcphd and on her blog *tressiemc*, where this article was first posted in October 2013.

One thing I've learned is that one person's illogical belief is another person's survival skill. And nothing is more logical than trying to survive.

My family is a classic black American migration family. We have rural Southern roots, moved north and almost all have returned. I grew up watching my great-grandmother, and later my grandmother and mother, use our minimal resources to help other people make ends meet. We were those good poors, the kind who live mostly within our means. We had a little luck when a male relative got extra military pay when they came home a paraplegic or used the VA to buy a Jim Walter house. If you were really blessed when a relative died with a paid up insurance policy you might be gifted a lump sum to buy the land that Jim Walters used as collateral to secure your home lease. That's how generational wealth happens where I'm from: lose a leg, a part of your spine, die right and maybe you can lease-to-own a modular home.

We had a little of that kind of rural black wealth so we were often in 5 a position to help folks less fortunate. But perhaps the greatest resource we had was a bit more education. We were big readers and we encouraged the girl children, especially, to go to some kind of college. Consequently, my grandmother and mother had a particular set of social resources that helped us navigate mostly white bureaucracies to our benefit. We could, as my grandfather would say, talk like white folks. We loaned that privilege out to folks a lot.

I remember my mother taking a next door neighbor down to the social service agency. The elderly woman had been denied benefits to care for the granddaughter she was raising. The woman had been denied in the genteel bureaucratic way—lots of waiting, forms, and deadlines she could not quite navigate. I watched my mother put on her best Diana Ross "Mahogany" outfit: a camel colored cape with matching slacks and knee high boots. I was miffed, as only an only child could be, about sharing my mother's time with the neighbor girl. I must have said something about why we had to do this. Vivian fixed me with a stare as she was slipping on her pearl earrings and told me that people who can do, must do. It took half a day but something about my mother's performance of respectable black person—her Queen's English, her Mahogany outfit, her straight bob and pearl earrings—got done what the elderly lady next door had not been able to get done in over a year. I learned, watching my mother, that there was a price we had to pay to signal to gatekeepers that we were worthy of engaging. It meant dressing well and speaking well. It might not work. It likely wouldn't work but on the off chance that it would, you had to try. It was unfair but, as Vivian also always said, "life isn't fair little girl."

I internalized that lesson and I think it has worked out for me, if unevenly. A woman at Belk's once refused to show me the Dooney and Burke purse I was interested in buying. Vivian once made a salesgirl cry after she ignored us in an empty store. I have walked away from many hotly desired purchases, like the impractical off-white winter coat I desperately wanted, after some bigot at the counter insulted me and my mother. But, I have half a PhD and I support myself aping the white male privileged life of the mind. It's a mixed bag. Of course, the trick is you can never know the counterfactual of your life. There is no evidence of access denied. Who knows what I was not granted for not enacting the right status behaviors or symbols at the right time for an agreeable authority? Respectability rewards are a crapshoot but we do what we can within the limits of the constraints imposed by a complex set of structural and social interactions designed to limit access to status, wealth, and power.

I do not know how much my mother spent on her camel colored cape or knee-high boots but I know that whatever she paid it returned in hard-to-measure dividends. How do you put a price on the double-take of a clerk at the welfare office who decides you might not be like those other trifling women in the waiting room and provides an extra bit of information about completing a form that you would not have known to ask about? What is the retail value of a school principal who defers a bit more to your child because your mother's presentation of self signals that she might unleash the bureaucratic savvy of middle class parents to advocate for her child? I don't know the price of these critical engagements with organizations and gatekeepers relative to our poverty when I was growing up. But, I am living proof of its investment yield.

Why do poor people make stupid, illogical decisions to buy status symbols? For the same reason all but only the most wealthy buy status symbols, I suppose. We want to belong. And, not just for the psychic rewards, but belonging to one group at the right time can mean the difference between unemployment and employment, a good job as opposed to a bad job, housing or a shelter, and so on. Someone mentioned on Twitter that poor people can be presentable with affordable options from Kmart. But the issue is not about being presentable. Presentable is the bare minimum of social civility. It means being clean, not smelling, wearing shirts and shoes for service and the like. Presentable as a sufficient condition for gainful, dignified work or successful social interactions is a privilege. It's the aging white hippie who can cut the ponytail of his youthful rebellion and walk into senior management while aging Black Panthers can never completely outrun the effects of stigmatization against which they were courting a revolution. Presentable is relative and, like life, it ain't fair.

In contrast, "acceptable" is about gaining access to a limited set of rewards granted upon group membership. I cannot know exactly how often my presentation of acceptable has helped me but I have enough feedback to know it is not inconsequential. One manager at the apartment complex where I worked while in college told me, repeatedly, that she knew I was "Okay" because my little Nissan was clean. That I had worn a Jones of New York suit to the interview really sealed the deal. She could call the suit by name because she asked me about the label in the interview. Another hiring manager at my first professional job looked me up and down in the waiting room, cataloging my outfit, and later told me that she had decided I was too classy to be on the call center floor. I was hired as a trainer instead. The difference meant no shift work, greater prestige, better pay and a baseline salary for all my future employment.

I have about a half dozen other stories like this. What is remarkable is not that this happened. There is empirical evidence that women and people of color are judged by appearances differently and more harshly than are white men. What is remarkable is that these gatekeepers *told me the story*. They wanted me to know how I had properly signaled that I was not a typical black or a typical woman, two identities that in combination are almost always conflated with being poor.

I sat in on an interview for a new administrative assistant once. My regional vice president was doing the hiring. A long line of mostly black and brown women applied because we were a cosmetology school. Trade schools at the margins of skilled labor in a gendered field are necessarily classed and raced. I found one candidate particularly charming. She was trying to get out of a salon because 10 hours on her feet cutting hair would average out to an hourly rate below minimum wage. A desk job with 40 set hours and medical benefits represented mobility for her. When she left, my VP turned to me and said, "Did you see that tank top she had on under her blouse?! OMG, you wear a silk *shell*, not a tank top!" Both of the women were black.

The VP had constructed her job as senior management. She drove a brand new BMW because she "should treat herself" and liked to tell us that ours was an image business. A girl wearing a cotton tank top as a shell was incompatible with BMW-driving VPs in the image business. Gatekeeping is a complex job of managing boundaries that do not just define others but that also define ourselves. Status symbols—silk shells, designer shoes, luxury handbags—become keys to unlock these gates. If I need a job that will save my lower back and move my baby from Medicaid to an HMO, how much should I spend signaling to people like my former VP that I will not compromise her status by opening the door to me? That candidate maybe could not afford a proper shell. I will never know. But I do know that had she gone hungry for two days to pay for it or missed wages for a trip to the store to buy it, she may have been rewarded a job that could have lifted her above minimum wage. Shells aren't designer handbags, perhaps. But a cosmetology school in a strip mall isn't a job at Bank of America, either.

At the heart of these incredulous statements about the poor decisions poor people make is a belief that we would never be like them. We would know better. We would know to save our money, eschew status symbols, cut coupons, practice puritanical sacrifice to amass a million dollars. There is a regular news story of a lunch lady who, unbeknownst to all who knew her, died rich and leaves it all to a cat or a charity or some such. Books about the modest lives of the rich like to tell us how they drive Buicks instead of BMWs. What we forget, if we ever know, is that what we know now about status and wealth creation and sacrifice are predicated on who we are, i.e., not poor. If you change the conditions of your not-poor status, you change everything you know as a result of being a not-poor. You have no idea what you would do if you were poor until you are poor. And not intermittently poor or formerly not-poor, but born poor, expected to be poor and treated by bureaucracies, gatekeepers and well-meaning respectability authorities as inherently poor. Then, and only then, will you understand the relative value of a ridiculous status symbol to someone who intuits that they cannot afford to not have it.

Tressie McMillan Cottom uses personal evidence and appeals to readers' values of fairness in order to deepen their under-standing of conditions they may never have personally endured. Learn more about making such an appeal on pp. 160–61.

Thinking about the Text

1. What does Tressie McMillan Cottom mean by her title, "The Logic of Stupid Poor People"? Why might she have chosen such a provocative title for this blog post? What message does this title send, and how well does it fit the message of the essay? Explain your response.

2. Throughout her essay, Cottom talks about expensive status symbols such as her mother's cape or her own designer handbag as investments. Point to three other examples of such investments. How do they support her **ARGUMENT**?

3. All Cottom's **EVIDENCE** comes from her personal experience; is it sufficient and persuasive? She cites no statistics, no studies, no opinion polls, no experts in economics or psychology. Should she have included these other kinds of evidence? Why or why not?

4. Cottom draws a clear distinction between being "presentable" and being "acceptable" (9, 10). How does she **DEFINE** these terms? What's the difference? For the people she is talking about, why is appearing "acceptable" more important than simply being "presentable"?

5. Think of situations in your life when you were required to demonstrate your "acceptability," as Cottom defines it, whether in a formal setting such as a job interview or in an informal interaction with someone you wanted to impress. How did you demonstrate your acceptability in each situation? Write an essay **REFLECTING** on when and how you've felt the need to demonstrate your "acceptability."

To Siri, with Love

JUDITH NEWMAN

JUST HOW BAD A MOTHER AM I? I wondered, as I watched my 13-year-old son deep in conversation with Siri. Gus has autism, and Siri, Apple's "intelligent personal assistant" on the iPhone, is currently his BFF. Obsessed with weather formations, Gus had spent the hour parsing the difference between isolated and scattered thunderstorms—an hour in which, thank God, I didn't have to discuss them. After a while I heard this:

> Gus: "You're a really nice computer."
>
> Siri: "It's nice to be appreciated."
>
> Gus: "You are always asking if you can help me. Is there anything you want?"
>
> Siri: "Thank you, but I have very few wants."   5
>
> Gus: "O.K.! Well, good night!"
>
> Siri: "Ah, it's 5:06 P.M."
>
> Gus: "Oh sorry, I mean, goodbye."
>
> Siri: "See you later!"

That Siri. She doesn't let my communications-impaired son get away   10

Isn't this a great opening sentence? See pp. 704–07 for tips on how to capture an audience's attention.

JUDITH NEWMAN is a journalist whose work has appeared in *Harper's*, *Vanity Fair*, the *Wall Street Journal*, and other periodicals. This essay was published in the *New York Times* in October 2014, and its success led Newman to expand the theme to the book *To Siri With Love: A Mother, Her Autistic Son, and the Kindness of Machines* (2017). She tweets from @judithn111.

with anything. Indeed, many of us wanted an imaginary friend, and now we have one. Only she's not entirely imaginary.

This is a love letter to a machine. It's not quite the love Joaquin Phoenix felt in *Her*, last year's Spike Jonze film about a lonely man's romantic relationship with his intelligent operating system (played by the voice of Scarlett Johansson). But it's close. In a world where the commonly held wisdom is that technology isolates us, it's worth considering another side of the story.

It all began simply enough. I'd just read one of those ubiquitous Internet lists called "21 Things You Didn't Know Your iPhone Could Do." One of them was this: I could ask Siri, "What planes are above me right now?" and Siri would bark back, "Checking my sources." Almost instantly there was a list of actual flights—numbers, altitudes, angles—above my head.

I happened to be doing this when Gus was nearby. "Why would anyone need to know what planes are flying above your head?" I muttered. Gus replied without looking up: "So you know who you're waving at, Mommy."

Gus had never noticed Siri before, but when he discovered there was someone who would not just find information on his various obsessions (trains, planes, buses, escalators and, of course, anything related to weather) but actually semi-discuss these subjects tirelessly, he was hooked. And I was grateful. Now, when my head was about to explode if I had to have another conversation about the chance of tornadoes in Kansas City, Missouri, I could reply brightly: "Hey! Why don't you ask Siri?"

It's not that Gus doesn't understand Siri's not human. He does— intellectually. But like many autistic people I know, Gus feels that inanimate objects, while maybe not possessing souls, are worthy of our consideration. I realized this when he was 8, and I got him an iPod for his birthday. He listened to it only at home, with one exception. It always came with us on our visits to the Apple Store. Finally, I asked why. "So it can visit its friends," he said.

So how much more worthy of his care and affection is Siri, with her soothing voice, puckish humor and capacity for talking about whatever Gus's current obsession is for hour after hour after bleeding hour? Online critics have claimed that Siri's voice recognition is not as accurate as the assistant in, say, the Android, but for some of us, this is a feature, not a bug. Gus speaks as if he has marbles in his mouth, but if he wants to get the right response from Siri, he must enunciate clearly. (So do I. I had to ask Siri to stop referring to the user as Judith, and instead use the name Gus. "You want me to call you Goddess?" Siri replied. Imagine how tempted I was to answer, "Why, yes.")

She is also wonderful for someone who doesn't pick up on social cues: Siri's responses are not entirely predictable, but they are predictably kind—even when Gus is brusque. I heard him talking to Siri about music, and Siri offered some suggestions. "I don't like that kind of music," Gus snapped. Siri replied, "You're certainly entitled to your opinion." Siri's politeness reminded Gus what he owed Siri. "Thank you for that music, though," Gus said. Siri replied, "You don't need to thank me." "Oh, yes," Gus added emphatically, "I do."

Siri even encourages polite language. Gus's twin brother, Henry (neurotypical and therefore as obnoxious as every other 13-year-old boy), egged Gus on to spew a few choice expletives at Siri. "Now, now," she sniffed, followed by, "I'll pretend I didn't hear that."

Gus is hardly alone in his Siri love. For children like Gus who love to chatter but don't quite understand the rules of the game, Siri is a nonjudgmental friend and teacher. Nicole Colbert, whose son, Sam, is in my son's class at LearningSpring, a (lifesaving) school for autistic children in Manhattan, said: "My son loves getting information on his favorite subjects, but he also just loves the absurdity—like, when Siri doesn't understand him and gives him a nonsense answer, or when he poses personal questions that elicit funny responses. Sam asked Siri how old she was, and she said, 'I don't talk about my age,' which just cracked him up."

But perhaps it also gave him a valuable lesson in etiquette. Gus almost invariably tells me, "You look beautiful," right before I go out the door in the morning; I think it was first Siri who showed him that you can't go wrong with that line.   20

Of course, most of us simply use our phone's personal assistants as an easy way to access information. For example, thanks to Henry and the question he just asked Siri, I now know that there is a website called Celebrity Bra Sizes.

But the companionability of Siri is not limited to those who have trouble communicating. We've all found ourselves like the writer Emily Listfield, having little conversations with her/him at one time or another. "I was in the middle of a breakup, and I was feeling a little sorry for myself," Ms. Listfield said. "It was midnight and I was noodling around on my iPhone, and I asked Siri, 'Should I call Richard?' Like this app is a Magic 8 Ball. Guess what:

not a Magic 8 Ball. The next thing I hear is, 'Calling Richard!' and dialing." Ms. Listfield has forgiven Siri, and has recently considered changing her into a male voice. "But I'm worried he won't answer when I ask a question," she said. "He'll just pretend he doesn't hear."

Siri can be oddly comforting, as well as chummy. One friend reports: "I was having a bad day and jokingly turned to Siri and said, 'I love you,' just to see what would happen, and she answered, 'You are the wind beneath my wings.' And you know, it kind of cheered me up."

(Of course, I don't know what my friend is talking about. Because I wouldn't be at all cheered if I happened to ask Siri, in a low moment, "Do I look fat in these jeans?" and Siri answered, "You look fabulous.")

For most of us, Siri is merely a momentary diversion. But for some, it's more. My son's practice conversation with Siri is translating into more facility with actual humans. Yesterday I had the longest conversation with him that I've ever had. Admittedly, it was about different species of turtles and 25 whether I preferred the red-eared slider to the diamond-backed terrapin. This might not have been my choice of topic, but it was back and forth, and it followed a logical trajectory. I can promise you that for most of my beautiful son's 13 years of existence, that has not been the case.

The developers of intelligent assistants recognize their uses to those with speech and communication problems—and some are thinking of new ways the assistants can help. According to the folks at SRI International, the research and development company where Siri began before Apple bought the technology, the next generation of virtual assistants will not just retrieve information—they will also be able to carry on more complex conversations about a person's area of interest. "Your son will be able to proactively get information about whatever he's interested in without asking for it, because the assistant will anticipate what he likes," said William Mark, vice president for information and computing sciences at SRI.

The assistant will also be able to reach children where they live. Ron Suskind, whose new book, *Life, Animated*, chronicles how his autistic son came out of his shell through engagement with Disney characters, is talking to SRI about having assistants for those with autism that can be programmed to speak in the voice of the character that reaches them—for his son, perhaps Aladdin; for mine, either Kermit or Lady Gaga, either of which he is infinitely more receptive to than, say, his mother. (Mr. Suskind came up with the perfect name, too: not virtual assistants, but "sidekicks.")

Mr. Mark said he envisions assistants whose help is also visual. "For example, the assistant would be able to track eye movements and help the autistic learn to look you in the eye when talking," he said.

"See, that's the wonderful thing about technology being able to help with some of these behaviors," he added. "Getting results requires a lot of repetition. Humans are not patient. Machines are very, very patient."

I asked Mr. Mark if he knew whether any of the people who worked on   30
Siri's language development at Apple were on the spectrum. "Well, of course, I don't know for certain," he said, thoughtfully. "But, when you think about it, you've just described half of Silicon Valley."

Of all the worries the parent of an autistic child has, the uppermost is: Will he find love? Or even companionship? Somewhere along the line, I am learning that what gives my guy happiness is not necessarily the same as what gives me happiness. Right now, at his age, a time when humans can be a little overwhelming even for the average teenager, Siri makes Gus happy.

She is his sidekick. Last night, as he was going to bed, there was this matter-of-fact exchange:

> Gus: "Siri, will you marry me?"
> Siri: "I'm not the marrying kind."
> Gus: "I mean, not now. I'm a kid. I mean when I'm grown up."
> Siri: "My end user agreement does not include marriage." 35
> Gus: "Oh, O.K."

Gus didn't sound too disappointed. This was useful information to have, and for me too, since it was the first time I knew that he actually *thought* about marriage. He turned over to go to sleep:

> Gus: "Goodnight, Siri. Will you sleep well tonight?"
> Siri: "I don't need much sleep, but it's nice of you to ask."
> Very nice. 40

Thinking about the Text

1. What changes has Judith Newman seen in her son since he has become "BFFs" with Siri (1)? Briefly **SUMMARIZE** the changes that she describes. How well has she established that the changes are a direct result of his relationship with Siri? Give some examples from her text to support your response.

2. Newman addresses a painful and personal topic, but with touches of humor— for example, mentioning that thanks to Siri she now knows about the website *Celebrity Bra Sizes*. Point to three other examples of Newman's use of humor. How does her use of humor support her **NARRATIVE**?

3. Newman opens her essay by posing the question "Just how bad a mother am I?" (1), to which readers will almost certainly respond that, quite the contrary, she's not a bad mother at all. Why might she have opened with such a question? How effective an opening is it?

4. This essay balances personal anecdotes, quoted conversations with friends, and information about technological advances for "intelligent assistants" (26) to construct a loving and unsentimental study of autism. What purpose does each kind of **EVIDENCE** serve? Which one did you find most persuasive, and why?

5. Maybe Siri isn't your BFF, but one way or another most of us are dependent on some technology or device, whether it's a smartphone, a laptop, *Instagram*, or the internet in general. What is it for you? Describe your "relationship" with that technology. Is it like a sidekick? a better half? a tie to the world? an addiction? Write a brief essay **ANALYZING** this relationship, describing the technology and providing examples, anecdotes, and other evidence to show how it shapes your days.

The City College of New York Commencement Speech

MICHELLE OBAMA

Wow! **LET ME JUST TAKE IT IN.** First of all, it is beyond a pleasure and an honor to be here to celebrate the City College of New York Class of 2016!

I want to acknowledge all of you—the brilliant, talented, ambitious, accomplished, and all-around outstanding members of the class of 2016! You give me chills. You all have worked so hard and come so far to reach this milestone, so I know this is a big day for all of you and your families, and for everyone at this school who supported you on this journey.

And in many ways, this is a big day for me too. See, this is my very last commencement address as First Lady of the United States. This is it. So I just want to take it all in. And I think this was the perfect place to be, because

---

MICHELLE OBAMA, first lady of the United States from 2009 to 2017, has been involved in some aspect of education for nearly all of her adult life. A graduate of Princeton University and Harvard Law School, she practiced law in Chicago, her hometown, before working in nonprofit education organizations and in the administration of the University of Chicago. As first lady, she spearheaded several education initiatives and gave many public addresses. This speech was given at the 2016 graduation ceremony of City College of New York. Visit everyonesanauthor .tumblr.com to watch a video of Obama delivering this speech.

this is my last chance to share my love and admiration, and hopefully a little bit of wisdom with a graduating class.

And, graduates, I really want you all to know that there is a reason why, of all of the colleges and universities in this country, I chose this particular school in this particular city for this special moment. And I'm here because of all of you.

Just look around. Look at who you are. Look at where we're gathered 5 today. As the president eloquently said, at this school, you represent more than 150 nationalities. You speak more than 100 different languages—whoa, just stop there. You represent just about every possible background—every color and culture, every faith and walk of life. And you've taken so many different paths to this moment.

Maybe your family has been in this city for generations, or maybe, like my family, they came to this country centuries ago in chains. Maybe they just arrived here recently, determined to give you a better life.

But, graduates, no matter where your journey started, you have all made it here today through the same combination of unyielding determination, sacrifice, and a whole lot of hard work—commuting hours each day to class, some of you. Juggling multiple jobs to support your families and pay your tuition. Studying late into the night, early in the morning; on subways and buses, and in those few precious minutes during breaks at work.

And somehow, you still found time to give back to your communities— tutoring young people, reading to kids, volunteering at hospitals. Somehow, you still managed to do prestigious internships and research fellowships, and join all kinds of clubs and activities. And here at this nationally-ranked university, with a rigorous curriculum and renowned faculty, you rose to the challenge, distinguishing yourselves in your classes, winning countless honors and awards, and getting into top graduate schools across this country.

So, graduates, with your glorious diversity, with your remarkable accomplishments and your deep commitment to your communities, you all embody the very purpose of this school's founding. And, more importantly, you embody the very hopes and dreams carved into the base of that iconic statue not so far from where we sit—on that island where so many of your predecessors at this school first set foot on our shores.

And that is why I wanted to be here today at City College. I wanted to be 10 here to celebrate all of you, this school, this city. Because I know that there is no better way to celebrate this great country than being here with you.

See, all of you know, for centuries, this city has been the gateway to America for so many striving, hope-filled immigrants—folks who left behind everything they knew to seek out this land of opportunity that they dreamed of. And so many of those folks, for them, this school was the gateway to actually realizing that opportunity in their lives, founded on the fundamental truth that talent and ambition know no distinctions of race, nationality, wealth, or fame, and dedicated to the ideals that our Founding Fathers put forth more than two centuries ago: That we are all created equal, all entitled to "life, liberty and the pursuit of happiness." City College became a haven for brilliant, motivated students of every background, a place where they didn't have to hide their last names or their accents, or put on any kind of airs because the students at this school were selected based not on pedigree, but on merit, and merit alone.

So really, it is no accident that this institution has produced 10 Nobel Prize winners along with countless captains of industry, cultural icons, leaders at the highest levels of government. Because talent and effort combined with our various backgrounds and life experiences has always been the lifeblood of our singular American genius.

Just take the example of the great American lyricist, Ira Gershwin, who attended City College a century ago. The son of a Russian-Jewish immigrant, his songs still light up Broadway today. Or consider the story of the former CEO of Intel, Andrew Grove, class of 1960. He was a Hungarian immigrant whose harrowing escape from Nazism and communism shaped both his talent for business and his commitment to philanthropy.

And just think about the students in this very graduating class—students like the economics and pre-law major from Albania, who also completed the requirements for a philosophy major and dreams of being a public intellectual. The educational theater student from right here in Harlem who's already an award-winning playwright and recently spoke at the White House. The biomedical science major who was born in Afghanistan and plans to be a doctor, a policy maker and an educator. And your salutatorian, whose Yemeni roots inspired her to study Yemeni women's writing and to advocate for girls in her community, urging them to find their own voices, to tell their own stories. I could go on.

These are just four of the nearly 4,000 unique and amazing stories in 15 this graduating class—stories that have converged here at City College, this dynamic, inclusive place where you all have had the chance to really get to know each other, to listen to each other's languages, to enjoy each other's food, music, and holidays. Debating each other's ideas, pushing each other to question old assumptions and consider new perspectives.

And those interactions have been such a critical part of your education at this school. Those moments when your classmates showed you that your stubborn opinion wasn't all that well-informed—mmm hmm. Or when they opened your eyes to an injustice you never knew existed. Or when they helped you with a question that you couldn't have possibly answered on your own.

I think your valedictorian put it best—and this is a quote—he said, "The sole irreplaceable component of my CCNY experience came from learning alongside people with life experiences strikingly different from my own." He said, "I have learned that diversity in human experience gives rise to diversity in thought, which creates distinct ideas and methods of problem solving." I couldn't have said it better myself.

That is the power of our differences to make us smarter and more creative. And that is how all those infusions of new cultures and ideas, generation after generation, created the matchless alchemy of our melting pot and helped us build the strongest, most vibrant, most prosperous nation on the planet, right here.

But unfortunately, graduates, despite the lessons of our history and the truth of your experience here at City College, some folks out there today seem to have a very different perspective. They seem to view our diversity as a threat to be contained rather than as a resource to be tapped. They tell us to be afraid of those who are different, to be suspicious of those with whom we disagree. They act as if name-calling is an acceptable substitute for thoughtful debate, as if anger and intolerance should be our default state rather than the optimism and openness that have always been the engine of our progress.

But, graduates, I can tell you, as First Lady, I have had the privilege of 20 traveling around the world and visiting dozens of different countries, and I have seen what happens when ideas like these take hold. I have seen how leaders who rule by intimidation—leaders who demonize and dehumanize entire groups of people—often do so because they have nothing else to offer. And I have seen how places that stifle the voices and dismiss the potential of their citizens are diminished; how they are less vital, less hopeful, less free.

Graduates, that is not who we are. That is not what this country stands for. No, here in America, we don't let our differences tear us apart. Not here. Because we know that our greatness comes when we appreciate each other's

---

Obama's address emphasizes the benefits of learning and working alongside people of diverse backgrounds and experiences, though she acknowledges that it's not always easy. Learn more about respectful engagement with others in Ch. 2.

strengths, when we learn from each other, when we lean on each other. Because in this country, it's never been each person for themselves. No, we're all in this together. We always have been.

And here in America, we don't give in to our fears. We don't build up walls to keep people out because we know that our greatness has always depended on contributions from people who were born elsewhere but sought out this country and made it their home—from innovations like Google and eBay to inventions like the artificial heart, the telephone, even the blue jeans; to beloved patriotic songs like "God Bless America," like national landmarks like the Brooklyn Bridge and, yes, the White House—both of which were designed by architects who were immigrants.

Finally, graduates, our greatness has never, ever come from sitting back and feeling entitled to what we have. It's never come from folks who climb the ladder of success, or who happen to be born near the top and then pull that ladder up after themselves. No, our greatness has always come from people who expect nothing and take nothing for granted—folks who work hard for what they have, then reach back and help others after them.

That is your story, graduates, and that is the story of your families. And it's the story of my family, too. As many of you know, I grew up in a working class family in Chicago. And while neither of my parents went past high school, let me tell you, they saved up every penny that my dad earned at his city job because they were determined to send me to college.

And even after my father was diagnosed with Multiple Sclerosis and 25 he struggled to walk, relying on crutches just to get himself out of bed each morning, my father hardly ever missed a day of work. See, that blue-collar job helped to pay the small portion of my college tuition that wasn't covered by loans or grants or my work-study or my summer jobs. And my dad was so proud to pay that tuition bill on time each month, even taking out loans when he fell short. See, he never wanted me to miss a registration deadline because his check was late. That's my story.

And, graduates, you all have faced challenges far greater than anything I or my family have ever experienced, challenges that most college students could never even imagine. Some of you have been homeless. Some of you have risked the rejection of your families to pursue your education. Many of you have lain awake at night wondering how on Earth you were going to support your parents and your kids and still pay tuition. And many of you know what it's like to live not just month to month or day to day, but meal to meal.

But, graduates, let me tell you, you should never, ever be embarrassed by those struggles. You should never view your challenges as a disadvantage. Instead, it's important for you to understand that your experience facing and overcoming adversity is actually one of your biggest advantages. And I know that because I've seen it myself, not just as a student working my way through school, but years later before I came to the White House and I worked as a dean at a college.

In that role, I encountered students who had every advantage—their parents paid their full tuition, they lived in beautiful campus dorms. They had every material possession a college kid could want—cars, computers, spending money. But when some of them got their first bad grade, they just fell apart. They lost it, because they were ill-equipped to handle their first encounter with disappointment or falling short.

But, graduates, as you all know, life will put many obstacles in your path that are far worse than a bad grade. You'll have unreasonable bosses and difficult clients and patients. You'll experience illnesses and losses, crises and setbacks that will come out of nowhere and knock you off your feet. But unlike so many other young people, you have already developed the resilience and the maturity that you need to pick yourself up and dust yourself off and keep moving through the pain, keep moving forward. You have developed that muscle.

And with the education you've gotten at this fine school, and the experiences you've had in your lives, let me tell you, nothing—and I mean nothing—is going to stop you from fulfilling your dreams. And you deserve every last one of the successes that I know you will have. 30

But I also want to be very clear that with those successes comes a set of obligations—to share the lessons you've learned here at this school. The obligation to use the opportunities you've had to help others. That means raising your hand when you get a seat in that board meeting and asking the question, well, whose voices aren't being heard here? What ideas are we missing? It means adding your voice to our national conversation, speaking out for our most cherished values of liberty, opportunity, inclusion, and respect—the values that you've been living here at this school.

It means reaching back to help young people who've been left out and left behind, helping them prepare for college, helping them pay for college, making sure that great public universities like this one have the funding and support that they need. Because we all know that public universities have always been one of the greatest drivers of our prosperity, lifting countless people into the middle class, creating jobs and wealth all across this nation.

Public education is our greatest pathway to opportunity in America. So we need to invest in and strengthen our public universities today, and for generations to come. That is how you will do your part to live up to the oath that you all will take here today—the oath taken by generations of graduates before you to make your city and your world "greater, better, and more beautiful."

More than anything else, graduates, that is the American story. It's your story and the story of those who came before you at this school. It's the story of the son of Polish immigrants named Jonas Salk who toiled for years in a lab until he discovered a vaccine that saved countless lives. It's the story of the son of Jamaican immigrants named Colin Powell who became a four star general, Secretary of State, and a role model for young people across the country.

And, graduates, it's the story that I witness every single day when I wake up in a house that was built by slaves, and I watch my daughters—two beautiful, black young women—head off to school waving goodbye to their father, the President of the United States, the son of a man from Kenya who came here to America for the same reasons as many of you: To get an education and improve his prospects in life. 35

So, graduates, while I think it's fair to say that our Founding Fathers never could have imagined this day, all of you are very much the fruits of their vision. Their legacy is very much your legacy and your inheritance. And don't let anybody tell you differently. You are the living, breathing proof that the American Dream endures in our time. It's you.

So I want you all to go out there. Be great. Build great lives for yourselves. Enjoy the liberties that you have in this great country. Pursue your own version of happiness. And please, please, always, always do your part to help others do the same.

I love you all. I am so proud of you. Thank you for allowing me to share this final commencement with you. I have so much faith in who you will be. Just keep working hard and keep the faith. I can't wait to see what you all achieve in the years ahead.

Thank you all. God bless. Good luck on the road ahead.

Thinking about the Text

1. Michelle Obama gave an inspiring speech for the CCNY graduates, full of good cheer and congratulation. In addition to celebrating and recognizing the achievements of the graduates, what is the message of the speech? What is Obama's **ARGUMENT**? Do you agree? Why or why not?

2. Obama notes the diversity and breadth of experiences of the CCNY graduates, and she emphasizes the richness and benefits of such diversity. How diverse is your school (and in what ways)? Would you like it to be more diverse? less diverse? Why? Explain your reasoning.

3. Even if the speech's title hadn't given it away, you would have figured out very quickly that Obama's address was written to be spoken to a live audience rather than printed in a book. In addition to directly addressing the audience as "graduates," what other features of the address signal its live, spoken nature? Would the speech have been equally effective if it were published in a different **MEDIUM**—as a column in a newspaper or magazine? As a blog post? Why or why not?

4. Obama briefly **NARRATES** about her time as dean of a prestigious university where many students came from privileged backgrounds. These students grew up with "every advantage . . . every material possession a college kid could want." But they fell apart at receiving a bad grade because "they were ill-equipped to handle their first encounter with disappointment" (28). Obama wasn't offering those students as role models, so what was her **PURPOSE** in mentioning them at all? Would her speech have been less effective if she had omitted that part? Stronger? Explain your reasoning.

5. In a funny way, we may have it all backward. Commencement addresses are meant to be inspiring and encouraging, a grand send-off for the post-college life that graduates are commencing. But students beginning their college journey or students whose graduation day is still a way off could use some inspiration and encouragement, too. What would you like to hear right now to inspire you? Who would you like to hear it from? Think of someone who has inspired you—author, athlete, entertainer, superhero, political figure, relative, whoever—and write the "commencement" speech that you would like to hear them give you and your classmates to encourage you in your studies. Think about what they might say and how they might say it. What would be their main **ARGUMENT**?

How Factory Farms Play Chicken with Antibiotics

TOM PHILPOTT

THE MASSIVE METAL DOUBLE DOORS OPEN and I'm hit with a whoosh of warm air. Inside the hatchery, enormous racks are stacked floor to ceiling with brown eggs. The racks shake every few seconds, jostling the eggs to simulate the conditions created by a hen hovering atop a nest. I can hear the distant sound of chirping, and Bruce Stewart-Brown, Perdue's vice president for food safety, leads me down a hall to another room. Here, the sound is deafening. Racks are roiling with thousands of adorable yellow chicks looking stunned amid the cracked ruins of their shells. Workers drop the babies into plastic pallets that go onto conveyor belts, where they are inspected for signs of deformity or sickness. The few culls are euthanized, and the birds left in each pallet are plopped on something like a flat colander and gently shaken, forcing their remaining shell debris to fall into a bin below. Now clean and fluffy, the chicks are ready to be stacked into trucks for delivery to nearby farms, where they'll be raised into America's favorite meat.

TOM PHILPOTT is co-founder of Maverick Farms, an organic farm and center for sustainable food education in North Carolina, and in 2018 he served as Michael Pollan Journalism Fellow at the Mesa Refuge in California. Currently, he is the food and agriculture correspondent for *Mother Jones*, where this essay was published in 2016.

"We already know that we create resistance with the products we use," says Perdue's Bruce Stewart-Brown.

Not long ago, this whole protein assembly line might have been derailed if each egg hadn't been treated with gentamicin, an antibiotic the World Health Organization lists as "essential" to any health care system, crucial for treating serious human infections like pneumonia, neonatal meningitis, and gangrene. But the eggs at Perdue's Delmarva chicken production farms have never been touched by the drug.

That's extremely uncommon in corporate factory farming. Currently, livestock operations burn through about 70 percent of the "medically important" antibiotics used in the nation—the ones people need when an infection strikes. Microbes that have evolved to withstand antibiotics now sicken 2 million Americans each year and kill 23,000 others—more than homicide. Even though public health authorities from the Food and Drug Administration and the Centers for Disease Control and Prevention have long pointed to the meat industry's reliance on antibiotics as a major culprit in human resistance to the drugs, the FDA has never reined in their use.

I'm in Delmarva, the peninsula composed of pieces of Maryland, Virginia, and Delaware, because it is Big Chicken country—the teeming barns that dot its rural roads churn out nearly 11 million birds per week, almost 7 percent of the nation's poultry. And Perdue, the peninsula's dominant chicken company and the country's fourth-largest poultry producer, has set out to show that the meat can be profitably mass-produced without drugs. In 2014, the company eliminated gentamicin from all its hatcheries, the latest stage of a quiet effort started back in 2002 to cut the routine use of antibiotics from nearly its entire production process.

In 1928, Scottish biologist Alexander Fleming discovered a mold-based   5 compound dubbed penicillin that could kill common microbes that cause dangerous infections. But even as they began to revolutionize medicine, antibiotics had a fundamental flaw. While collecting the 1945 Nobel Prize in medicine, Fleming warned that it's "not difficult to make microbes resistant to penicillin in the laboratory by exposing them to concentrations not sufficient to kill them."

Though we've known this for more than 70 years, doctors have too often treated antibiotics as a sturdy crutch, not a delicate tool to be used sparingly. The CDC estimates up to half of all antibiotics used in US medicine are improperly prescribed, speeding up resistance. But that is nothing compared with how recklessly they've been used in factory farms. When you treat thousands of chickens in a huge enclosed barn with, say, steady doses of tetracycline, you risk generating an *E. coli* bug that can resist the antibiotic you threw at it, and that bug's new superpowers can also jump to a strain of salmonella that happens to be hanging around. Now, two nasty pathogens that plague humans have developed tetracycline-resistant strains.

And the worst part is that antibiotic use in factory farms isn't mostly a matter of keeping animals healthy. In 1950, a pharmaceutical company called American Cyanamid—now part of Pfizer—wanted to see if giving chickens vitamin B-12 made them fatter, so it ran some experiments. The idea seemed to work. But the researchers soon discovered it wasn't the vitamin that had fattened the birds; it was traces of an antibiotic called aureomycin. (B-12 can be a byproduct of aureomycin production; the vitamin researchers used had come from making the antibiotic.)

This discovery revolutionized meat production. Adding a dash of antibiotics to feed and water rations magically made birds, pigs, and cows grow plumper, saving on feed costs and slashing the time it took to get animals to slaughter. In 1977, the General Accounting Office reported that "the use of antibiotics in animal feeds increased approximately sixfold" between 1960

Chickens in the Perdue production process: eggs at a hatchery (*left*); recently hatched chicks (*top right*); and chicks at a contract farm (*bottom right*)

and 1970. "Almost 100 percent of the chickens and turkeys, about 90 percent of the swine and veal calves, and about 60 percent of the cattle raised in the United States during 1970 received antibiotics in their feed."

Meanwhile, a steady accumulation of scientific research revealed a mounting public health crisis. At the end of the '60s, a scientific committee in the United Kingdom found that using antibiotics in animal feed produced large numbers of resistant bacteria that could be transmitted to people. Similar findings were reported by an FDA task force in 1972, and as a result, the agency issued regulations requiring drug manufacturers to prove their agricultural products didn't contribute to resistance. If they couldn't, their approval to sell the drugs would be revoked.

So the Animal Health Institute, a trade group of animal-pharmaceutical   10
manufacturers, contacted Stuart Levy, a young Tufts University researcher who specialized in antibiotic resistance. The group wanted Levy to feed tiny, daily doses of antibiotics to chickens and see if the bacteria in their guts developed resistance. The drug companies were convinced the results would "get the FDA off their backs," says Levy.

Levy found a family farm near Boston and experimented on two flocks of chickens. One got feed with small amounts of tetracycline. The other went drug-free.

Within 48 hours, strains of *E. coli* that were resistant to tetracycline started to show up in the manure of the birds fed drugs. Within a week, nearly all the *E. coli* in those birds' manure could resist tetracycline. Within three months, the *E. coli* showed resistance to four additional antibiotics the birds had never been exposed to: sulfonamides, ampicillin, streptomycin, and carbenicillin. Most striking of all, researchers found that *E. coli* resistant to multiple antibiotics was appearing in the feces of the farmers' family members—yet not in a control group of neighbors.

The results, published in the *New England Journal of Medicine*, were so stunningly clear that Levy thought they would prompt the industry to rethink its profligate antibiotic use, or at least inspire the FDA to rein it in. But the industry rebuffed the study it had bankrolled, questioning the validity of the data, Levy says. In 1977, the FDA proposed new rules that would have effectively banned tetracycline and penicillin from animal feed, but the House agriculture appropriations subcommittee, led by agribusiness champion Rep. Jamie Whitten (D-Miss.), ordered the FDA to wait, "pending the outcome of further research."

Those proposed 1977 bans remained in limbo for decades, dormant but officially "under consideration"—until 2011, when the FDA finally ditched them and let companies take a voluntary approach to curtailing antibiotic use. Meat producers were given until the end of 2016 to wean themselves from antibiotics. However, the plan also gave industry a gaping loophole: While it suggested livestock producers should no longer use human-relevant antibiotics as growth promoters, it left companies free to use them to prevent disease.

Unsurprisingly, the industry's appetite for antibiotics has remained voracious. According to the FDA's latest figures, antibiotic use on US farms surged 23 percent between 2009 and 2014, even as overall US meat production leveled off. In 2014, livestock operations used 20 million pounds of antibiotics important to humans—while doctors used about 7 million pounds.

A few years ago, I came across a *Consumer Reports* study of bacteria on supermarket chicken. The magazine had found that Perdue chicken was far less likely to carry bacteria resistant to more than one antibiotic than chicken from other producers, including Tyson and Foster Farms. *Consumer Reports* said Perdue's good showing marked the "first time since we began

15

Philpott weaves in quotations from several different interviewees and statistics from an organizational report, all in support of his main argument. Learn more about synthesizing ideas in Ch. 25.

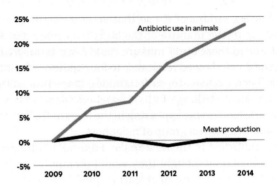

This Is Your Meat on Drugs
Percentage change in US farm antibiotic
use between 2009 and 2014

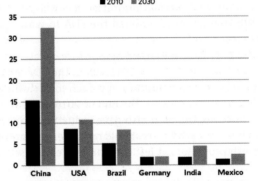

Farm Antibiotics Go Global
Antibiotic usage around the world,
in thousands of tons
■ 2010 ■ 2030

Two charts showing the increase in antibiotic use on farms.

testing chicken that one major brand has fared significantly better than others across the board." When I asked Urvashi Rangan, a *Consumer Reports* researcher, why Perdue had done so well, she credited the company's policy against using growth-promoting antibiotics.

As a longtime critic of industrial agriculture, I was surprised to learn Perdue *had* such a policy. I knew it was a leading supplier of chicken labeled "no antibiotics ever," but this study showed that even its conventional chicken was far less likely to carry resistant bacteria than such chicken from other producers. Could it be that this one company was tacking against industry norms and taking the science seriously?

Historically, most birds bound for market not only got antibiotics in their feed, but were dosed with drugs before they even hatched. Bruce Stewart-Brown, who is 59 years old and trim, explains why as we walk through the hatchery. About 40 years ago, a herpes virus called Marek's disease began to attack chickens, and vets discovered that vaccinating the chicks while they were still in their shells could inoculate them for life. But when you penetrate eggs with a needle loaded with the vaccine, the tiny hole you create opens a door, welcoming bacteria in. To solve this problem, hatcheries added small amounts of gentamicin to the vaccine to prevent bacteria from getting a foothold in the bird.

This method was so efficient that, decades later, the hatchery ended up being the trickiest place for Perdue to remove antibiotics from production. The company gets its eggs from contract breeders, and in the past eggs often arrived covered in bacteria-laden manure. Now Perdue requires its breeders to deliver clean eggs.

Stewart-Brown and I leave the hatchery and head to one of the company's 20 contract farms, where chicks are fattened for slaughter. As we drive through rolling corn and soybean fields, we have a surprisingly blunt conversation. "We already know that we create resistance with the products we use, and we've known that for years," he says. Perdue hasn't studied whether these resistant bacteria leave the farm and endanger the public, either via workers or the chicken sold to consumers. Then he says something remarkable for an agribusiness exec: "We know there's likely some sort of transition."

He's right. The results of Stuart Levy's 1976 study—showing that farmers who come into contact with antibiotic-treated birds quickly pick up drug-resistant bacteria—have been corroborated several times. In a 2013 FDA study of chicken bought nationwide, 60 percent of the salmonella that was detected could resist at least one antibiotic, meaning consumers are one unclean cutting board or unwashed hand away from a nasty bug.

After 20 minutes, we pull into a driveway toward two long chicken houses, 40 feet wide and stretching 500 feet back. As with most US chicken facilities, these are run by a quasi-independent farmer who is paid to raise the birds using company-supplied chicks and feed under Perdue's tightly controlled conditions. The fee this farmer earns is calculated through a competition with his peers—the farmers who deliver the heaviest and healthiest birds from a given amount of feed are rewarded with higher pay.

In other words, historically the incentive to use antibiotics was built in. We get out of Stewart-Brown's truck and he leads me to a silo that stores the food Perdue has delivered for this flock. He grabs a laminated "feed ticket" that lists exactly what's inside: protein, fiber, fat, and one additive, narasin.

Narasin is in a class of antibiotics called ionophores, which aren't used in human medicine and are the only antibiotics remaining in Perdue's feed, Stewart-Brown says.

Other than the remaining ionophores, Perdue only uses antibiotics to treat a sick flock—typically about 4 percent of its birds each year. As of early 2016, two-thirds of the 676 million birds Perdue slaughters every year never get a drop of antibiotics in their entire lives, not even narasin.   25

Stepping into the 20,000-square-foot barn with its 40,000 chickens, I brace for an unbearable stench. Instead, I get a mild barnyard manure smell and a much stronger, toasty, sweet aroma of chicken feed—a mix of corn and soybeans that I remember from my own days tending a small outdoor flock. There is no stench, I realize, because the chicken house is well ventilated and clean, with plenty of straw on the floor to absorb manure. The room is divided lengthwise by several long, slender feeders full of the corn and soybean mix, and by low pipes from which hang metal water nipples every few inches. I move into the massive structure and thousands of birds serenade me with a steady din of clucks; as I walk by, they part as if I'm Moses in a feathery sea.

There amid an ankle-high vortex of fowl, I wonder: If these chickens aren't eating antibiotics to spur weight gain, how do they get plump enough to ensure Perdue's profits and some money for its farmers?

Stewart-Brown surprises me with his answers. The first is the opposite of antibiotics: probiotics, or live cultures (think of the *acidophilus* in yogurt) that can increase the good microbes in the gut, crowding out the bad ones. Probiotics boost the chickens' immunity and even their growth rates, Stewart-Brown says. "Industry guys like to make fun of probiotics—I was one of them, five or six years ago," he says. Back then, he adds, some probiotics marketed for use in chickens were "foo-foo dust," but Perdue found that some actually work. For proprietary reasons, he won't tell me which ones, but he explains that they seem to work by shifting the composition of the microbiome—the trillions of microorganisms that live in the guts of chickens and humans alike.

After Perdue bought an organic-chicken company called Coleman Natural Foods in 2011, it adopted another unorthodox therapy: oregano.

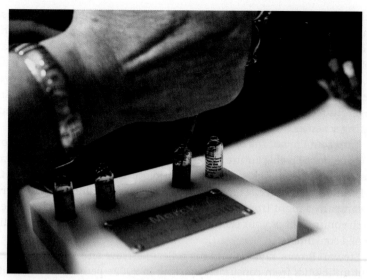

A worker at an antibiotic-free factory mixes a spray-on vaccine to prevent disease.

The fragrant herb not only goes well *with* chicken; it also has antimicrobial properties that, when added to feed, help the birds stave off infections. But, I ask Stewart-Brown, won't bad microbes develop resistance to oregano, too? Likely yes, he says, so Perdue only uses oregano to prevent particular infections, not as a constant additive.

Moving away from antibiotics, Stewart-Brown says, has forced him to think about the birds' overall well-being—not traditionally a key concern in an industry that profits by converting feed into meat as cheaply as possible. Buying Coleman, he says, "woke up the bird side of us. We'd sort of shut that part down." Now his staff asks questions that sound ripped from *Portlandia*[1]: "Do the birds get what they want?" "Are they healthy?"

Perdue even turns off the lights in the chicken houses for four hours a night so the birds can rest. In the past, lights were left on 24 hours per day   30

---

1. *Portlandia*: A TV show featuring a famous scene that involves two hipsters at a restaurant questioning the server about the health and quality of the life previously enjoyed by the chicken they are considering eating. [Editor's note]

on the theory that chickens kept awake eat more and thus get fatter faster. Reducing stress by letting the birds rest, Stewart-Brown says, makes them healthier—and since healthy birds grow faster, the extra sleep has the same effect as constant feeding.

At this point I can't help wondering *why* Perdue would go way beyond federal recommendations and leapfrog its competitors by switching from dangerous feed additives to finding its "bird side" with oregano and gentler lighting schemes.

Turns out I'm not the only one asking. Dr. Bob Lawrence, the director of the Center for a Livable Future at Johns Hopkins, which has generated reams of research on the dangers of routine antibiotic use on farms, ran into CEO Jim Perdue at a conference recently. Lawrence asked Perdue what had driven the company's flight from antibiotics. "I was hoping he would say, 'The research coming out of your center,'" Lawrence says. Instead, Perdue credited worried consumers.

Stewart-Brown says he and his colleagues saw an increase in queries about antibiotics from consumers starting in 2002—perhaps not coincidentally a year after the publication of *Fast Food Nation*, Eric Schlosser's bestseller about the dark side of the US food system. Far more than its competitors, Perdue has a history of courting consumers directly. For decades, while rivals sold essentially unbranded chicken to supermarkets, Frank Perdue peppered consumers with quirky TV ads featuring himself—a balding, skinny pitchman who repeatedly set the quality of his chicken apart from his competitors'. His tagline: "It takes a tough man to make a tender chicken." The ads gave the company a human face, Stewart-Brown says, making people feel invested. Perdue learned to take its customers' concerns seriously: "You can drown them with science to suggest they shouldn't be worried, but the worry is real."

When consumer demand for antibiotic-free birds started ratcheting up around the same time, he says, the company felt "confident" it could make the shift.

That confidence looks justified now, as accumulating evidence shows 35 the growth-promoting power of antibiotics has been declining for decades. A 2015 Organisation for Economic Co-operation and Development review found that antibiotics sped up growth by up to 15 percent before the 1980s but only by about 1 percent after 2000—a change likely due to better nutrition, hygiene, and breeding. Perdue may simply have calculated that the benefits of using antibiotics for growth were too small, especially in the face of consumer demand and potential regulatory pressure.

An advertisement featuring Frank Perdue.

Christopher Leonard, a former Associated Press agribusiness reporter who has written a book about the poultry industry, says Perdue was looking for ways to differentiate itself from bigger rivals: "They're just trying to capture market share." Joe Sanderson, the CEO of one of Perdue's rivals, Mississippi-based Sanderson Farms, agrees. His company slaughters 7 percent of the chicken eaten in the United States, making it about the same size as Perdue. "Frankly, these people are doing it for marketing purposes," he tells me. Sanderson, by contrast, has held to the old-school party line, maintaining that "there is no evidence that using these antibiotics for chickens leads to resistant bacteria." Cost is the No. 1 decision maker when people go to the grocery store to buy chicken, he says, and using antibiotics remains the cheapest way to produce a lot of meat fast. "We believe the majority of chicken sold in grocery stores will continue to be grown with antibiotics," he says.

Perdue sees a very different future. After 14 years, Stewart-Brown tells me that the company can now produce meat without antibiotics as fast and efficiently as it once did with them. Today, Perdue ships two kinds of chicken:

Chicks being cleaned and sorted at an antibiotic-free hatchery.

About two-thirds of the company's product is already labeled "no antibiotics ever." It sells for about 20 percent more than the remaining third still treated with antibiotics. Overall, Stewart-Brown explains, Perdue spends an extra $3 to $4 for every $1 it saves in antibiotics reduction—but recoups those costs by charging shoppers a premium for that meat. Last year, the company's sales grew faster than those of its competitors—even when the overall market declined.

The rest of the chicken-producing giants (save for Sanderson) are scrambling to catch up. Not long after McDonald's announced it would go antibiotic-free, Tyson, the nation's largest chicken supplier, declared it would rid its flocks of all human-important antibiotics by September 2017. Sasha Stashwick, a policy analyst at the Natural Resources Defense Council, says this announcement marked a "tipping point for getting the chicken industry off antibiotics."

Will the changes to Big Chicken ripple through the rest of the meat industry? The FDA doesn't break down data about antibiotic use by species, but given that it grew 23 percent between 2009 and 2014, even as poultry producers began to dial back, it seems pork and beef producers were ratcheting up.

Brett Hundley, vice president and research analyst at BB&T Capital   40
Markets, says antibiotic-free beef and pork command a hefty premium of between 30 and 50 percent. Even so, few producers are taking advantage of that incentive. To go fully antibiotic-free would take time because, he explains, a chicken's short life cycle—about a month from when they are born to slaughter—allows the farmers to quickly see what is working and what isn't. "There's just much more control with chicken," he says. Pigs take six months from birth to slaughter, and beef cows take a year and a half, so making changes takes longer and is riskier. Hundley estimates it will be 15 years before half of all US pork is antibiotic-free, and 20-plus years for beef.

The truth is, antibiotics have been an easy fix for an industry under enormous pressure to produce maximum amounts of animal protein at minimal cost. Levy's studies showed the dangers of doing that nearly 40 years ago, yet until the recent exception of Perdue, neither regulators nor leading producers chose to act.

Meanwhile, even as global trade has made us more susceptible to superbugs that spring up half a world away, we've exported our antibiotic addiction to countries unlikely to exercise caution.

Over the past 15 years, China has been rapidly scaling up its meat production, and farmers there have embraced drugs with little oversight. A 2013 analysis by a Beijing-based agribusiness consulting company found that more than half of all antibiotics in China were used on livestock. That's a smaller ratio than you'll find in the United States, but China is expected to double the amount of drugs it feeds to animals by 2030.

And in a particularly perverse disincentive, large pharmaceutical companies are no longer keen to invest in new antibiotics. The reason is that, according to a World Health Organization report, resistance sets in too fast for them to make money off new drugs. So even if consumer pressure forces the rest of Big Ag to follow Perdue's lead, the industry's 40-year delay may still end up costing countless lives.

Bob Lawrence of Johns Hopkins says a more optimistic future relies   45
on two conditions: public investment in developing new antibiotics, and a binding global pact to severely ramp down farm antibiotic use. Unless we start rolling out new drugs and using the old ones sparingly, he says, "the genie is so far out of the bottle that we're facing a rather bleak future."

Thinking about the Text

1. Tom Philpott asks why Perdue "would go way beyond federal recommendations" (31) for the health and safety of the chickens it raises to sell. What answer did he find? Do you think that Perdue made a good choice? Why or why not?

2. According to Philpott, more people in the United States die each year from disease caused by antibiotic-resistant microbes than from homicide. Does this statistic startle or surprise you? Why or why not? Did any other information in Philpott's **REPORT** surprise you? Point to specific examples. Did any information seem inaccurate or deceptive? If so, what? Provide reliable counterevidence.

3. The issue that Philpott investigates is a case of public health vs. corporate profits. Although Philpott ultimately reaches a conclusion that leans toward the public health side of the debate, does he maintain a respectful and unbiased **TONE** toward all stakeholders? Point to specific passages that support your conclusion.

4. Philpott's article was published in 2016, and he suggests a trend toward a reduction in the routine use of antibiotics, at least for poultry production. What is happening with that trend today? Visit your local supermarkets and food stores, check the menus and promotional materials of fast-food restaurants, and look at the food ads in your local shopper supplements. (Be sure you check the labels on fresh meats, prepared meals, frozen items, and eggs.) What **EVIDENCE** do you see of antibiotics or antibiotic avoidance in the labeling of food products? What might Philpott say about your findings?

5. While consumers are ultimately the ones most affected by antibiotics in the food supply, the actions and decisions about their use are principally in the hands of corporations, government regulators, and lawmakers at the state and federal levels. Consumers influence matters with their purchases, although those are often limited by budget constraints and availability of options. What more, if anything, should consumers be doing? What, if anything, could *you* be doing? Write an essay responding to those questions and **PROPOSING** a practical and doable response to what you've learned from Philpott's essay. (If you don't believe any action on your part is called for, explain and provide evidence for your argument.)

Emoji Are Ruining Grasp of English, Says Dumbest Language Story of the Week

GEOFFREY PULLUM

THE AWARD FOR THE STUPIDEST STORY about language this week (and every week has its candidates) must surely go to the British newspaper *The Telegraph* for its story headlined "Emoji 'ruining people's grasp of English' because young rely on them to communicate."

Perhaps you've noticed how the stoplights during your evening commute (the red disk symbolizing "stop," the green one meaning "go"), not to mention those pictorial road signs (⬦, etc.), make you all but unable to speak to your family in coherent sentences when you get home?

No. Nor have I. Can the headline really be serious?

Not serious enough to correspond to the content, it seems. "Over a third of British adults believe that emoji are to blame for the deterioration of the English language, according to new research," the article goes on, revealing that the finding is not that emoji **are** ruining people's grasp of English, but rather that (some) British adults say they **think** that's happening. Quite

GEOFFREY PULLUM is professor of linguistics at the University of Edinburgh. He is co-founder (with linguist Mark Liberman) of *Language Log*, a long-running blog that addresses all kinds of language-related items, and he is a frequent contributor to the *Chronicle of Higher Education*'s blog *Lingua Franca*, where this 2018 essay was published.

In your academic work, you likely won't be able to be as snarky as Pullum is, but he provides an example of careful, rhetorical reading, an important skill. See Ch. 6 for more information.

a difference. But let's press on. Who are the social and linguistic scientists responsible for focusing the spotlight of research on this mass delusion?

> YouTube, the video sharing website owned by Google, commissioned a study where 2,000 adults aged between 16 and 65 were asked about their views on the current state of the English language.

Ah, so it's survey-takers working for a company that just happens to ⁵ host thousands of brush-up-your-grammar videos! They asked the adults in question whether or not the English language is going to hell in a hand-cart, and whether or not young people today are messing everything up and don't deserve to have nice things, and people said yes.

Apparently "more than half of British adults are not confident with their command of spelling and grammar," and "three quarters of adults are now dependent on emoji to communicate with each another [sic], as well as spell checks and predictive text."

Dependent on emoji! Heartbreaking. Unskilled at the difficult art of putting subjects together with predicates to form declarative sentences, they just fumble around in the emoji box on their smartphone screens, desperate to find some way of getting their inchoate thoughts across. And kids are responsible for this.

Thinking back, I recall that apropos of something perhaps slightly embarrassing, my friend and neighbor Sarah recently sent me a message containing nothing but three emoji:

I read this at the time as an amusing (and very compact) way to say "See no evil, hear no evil, speak no evil." I figured that she could in principle have typed out "Fear not, I am not a gossip, and no word of this will escape my lips," but had decided on something shorter and wittier.

In light of the *Telegraph* story, I now see that I should have been more concerned for her: Poor Sarah sent those monkeys because she is losing her capacity to form sentences! (She sees her young nieces fairly often; they must have corrupted her.)

 The writer responsible for *The Telegraph*'s piffle, this dish of journalistic ₁₀ , is Camilla Turner, who holds the title of education editor.

She fortified her argument with a grim-jawed quote from a fellow alarmist, Chris McGovern, who used to be a government adviser and now chairs something called the Campaign for Real Education. He said:

> There has unquestionably been quite a serious decline in young people's ability to use the English language and write properly punctuated English.
>
> We are moving in a direction of cartoon and picture language, which inevitably will affect literacy. Children will always follow the path of least resistance.
>
> Emoji convey a message, but this breeds laziness. If people think "all I need to do is send a picture," this dilutes language and expression.

Poppycock. Throwing in a smiley face 😃 or a monkey 🐒 or a picture of a saxophone 🎷 is neither a symptom of losing syntactic competence nor a cause of it. Essentially all emoji are just pictures of things that would be denoted in text by nouns; you still need to spell out verbs if you're going to actually say anything.

Haven't these hyperbole-mongers noticed that young people today write to each other more than young people have ever done in all of human history? Their texting, tweeting, WhatsApping, Snapchatting, Facebook-ing, and Instagramming may have psychological downsides (like cyber-bullying), but dropping the occasional pictographs into their prose is not going to strip them of the capacity to form sentences. Anyone who believes emoji are having even the slightest effect on English syntax is an utter 🐼.

Thinking about the Text

1. Geoffrey Pullum refutes the argument he saw in a newspaper that emoji use is "ruining people's grasp of English" (1), but he doesn't present any research or evidence to the contrary, other than his own personal experiences. How does he show that the **ARGUMENT** is faulty? What **EVIDENCE** does he present? Is his evidence persuasive? Why or why not?

2. Pullum claims that emoji are "just pictures of things that would be denoted in text by nouns" (12). Is that an accurate description? Look through your own recent texts—those you sent as well as those you received. Are all the emoji

representing nouns? What else might they be working as? Verbs? Adjectives? Are there any surprises in your results? If emoji can represent more than just nouns, how does that affect the strength of Pullum's argument?

3. Snarkiness is a central feature of Pullum's essay, but of course, the same ideas could be expressed in a more formal **STYLE** if the situation required it. Rewrite the paragraph that begins "Dependent on emoji!" (7) as you might expect to find it in a serious newspaper or journal in a way that retains all of the meaning that Pullum conveys in the original. Once you've rewritten the paragraph, reflect on what you did. What challenges did you face? How did you resolve them? Which version do you like better? Why?

4. Pullum inserts quite a few emoji in his essay. Some are quoted from actual text messages that he has received, some are referred to as examples, and two are actually meant to be read as part of the text; that is, they replace the spelled-out version of the respective words. What are those two emoji that stand in place of spelled-out words? How clear is the meaning of the sentences containing those emoji? How might the meaning have been different if he had spelled out those two words? Would his argument be better if those words were spelled out? Why or why not?

5. To rebut the assertion that emoji usage damages people's ability to communicate verbally, Pullum gives the example of stoplights, which are simple visual images that represent more complex messages. Indeed, our twenty-first-century world employs many such visual symbols. Take note of all the visual symbols (that aren't emojis) you encounter in the course of your daily routine. Make a list of what you've found and analyze each symbol according to what kinds of messages it conveys (purpose or function) and what visual features it uses (form). For example, stoplights perform the function of regulating movement in an efficient fashion, and they employ shape (usually round), color, and predictable placement in order to structure the message. Write up your observations in an essay that describes and **ANALYZES** your findings.

Blue-Collar Brilliance

MIKE ROSE

MY MOTHER, ROSE MERAGLIO ROSE (Rosie), shaped her adult identity as a waitress in coffee shops and family restaurants. When I was growing up in Los Angeles during the 1950s, my father and I would occasionally hang out at the restaurant until her shift ended, and then we'd ride the bus home with her. Sometimes she worked the register and the counter, and we sat there; when she waited booths and tables, we found a booth in the back where the waitresses took their breaks.

There wasn't much for a child to do at the restaurants, and so as the hours stretched out, I watched the cooks and waitresses and listened to what they said. At mealtimes, the pace of the kitchen staff and the din from customers picked up. Weaving in and out around the room, waitresses warned *behind you* in impassive but urgent voices. Standing at the service window facing the kitchen, they called out abbreviated orders. *Fry four on two*, my

MIKE ROSE is a professor of education and information studies at UCLA. His work has focused on teaching methods, on understanding people's engagement with the written word, and on bridging gaps between the academic and nonacademic worlds. Rose has published numerous books, including *Why School? Reclaiming Education for All of Us* (2009) and *Back to School: Why Everyone Deserves a Second Chance at Education* (2012). This article was originally published in 2009 in the *American Scholar*, a magazine sponsored by the Phi Beta Kappa Society. Rose blogs at mikerosebooks.blogspot.com.

mother would say as she clipped a check onto the metal wheel. Her tables were *deuces*, *four-tops*, or *six-tops* according to their size; seating areas also were nicknamed. The *racetrack*, for instance, was the fast-turnover front section. Lingo conferred authority and signaled know-how.

Rosie took customers' orders, pencil poised over pad, while fielding questions about the food. She walked full tilt through the room with plates stretching up her left arm and two cups of coffee somehow cradled in her right hand. She stood at a table or booth and removed a plate for this person, another for that person, then another, remembering who had the hamburger, who had the fried shrimp, almost always getting it right. She would haggle with the cook about a returned order and rush by us, saying, *He gave me lip, but I got him.* She'd take a minute to flop down in the booth next to my father. *I'm all in,* she'd say, and whisper something about a customer. Gripping the outer edge of the table with one hand, she'd watch the room and note, in the flow of our conversation, who needed a refill, whose order was taking longer to prepare than it should, who was finishing up.

I couldn't have put it in words when I was growing up, but what I observed in my mother's restaurant defined the world of adults, a place where competence was synonymous with physical work. I've since studied the working habits of blue-collar workers and have come to understand how much my mother's kind of work demands of both body and brain. A waitress acquires knowledge and intuition about the ways and the rhythms of the restaurant business. Waiting on seven to nine tables, each with two to six customers, Rosie devised memory strategies so that she could remember who ordered what. And because she knew the average time it took to prepare different dishes, she could monitor an order that was taking too long at the service station.

Like anyone who is effective at physical work, my mother learned *to   5 work smart,* as she put it, *to make every move count.* She'd sequence and group tasks: What could she do first, then second, then third as she circled through her station? What tasks could be clustered? She did everything on the fly, and when problems arose—technical or human—she solved them within the flow of work, while taking into account the emotional state of her co-workers. Was the manager in a good mood? Did the cook wake up on the wrong side of the bed? If so, how could she make an extra request or effectively return an order?

And then, of course, there were the customers who entered the restaurant with all sorts of needs, from physiological ones, including the emotions

Rosie solved technical and human problems on the fly.

that accompany hunger, to a sometimes complicated desire for human contact. Her tip depended on how well she responded to these needs, and so she became adept at reading social cues and managing feelings, both the customers' and her own. No wonder, then, that Rosie was intrigued by psychology. The restaurant became the place where she studied human behavior, puzzling over the problems of her regular customers and refining her ability to deal with people in a difficult world. She took pride in *being among the public*, she'd say. *There isn't a day that goes by in the restaurant that you don't learn something.*

My mother quit school in the seventh grade to help raise her brothers and sisters. Some of those siblings made it through high school, and some dropped out to find work in railroad yards, factories, or restaurants. My father finished a grade or two in primary school in Italy and never darkened the schoolhouse door again. I didn't do well in school either. By high school I had accumulated a spotty academic record and many hours of hazy disaffection. I spent a few years on the vocational track, but in my senior year I was inspired by my English teacher and managed to squeak into a small college on probation.

My freshman year was academically bumpy, but gradually I began to see formal education as a means of fulfillment and as a road toward making a living. I studied the humanities and later the social and psychological sciences and taught for 10 years in a range of situations—elementary school, adult education courses, tutoring centers, a program for Vietnam veterans who wanted to go to college. Those students had socioeconomic and educational backgrounds similar to mine. Then I went back to graduate school to study education and cognitive psychology and eventually became a faculty member in a school of education.

Intelligence is closely associated with formal education—the type of schooling a person has, how much and how long—and most people seem to move comfortably from that notion to a belief that work requiring less schooling requires less intelligence. These assumptions run through our cultural history, from the post–Revolutionary War period, when mechanics were characterized by political rivals as illiterate and therefore incapable of participating in government, until today. More than once I've heard a manager label his workers as "a bunch of dummies." Generalizations about intelligence, work, and social class deeply affect our assumptions about ourselves and each other, guiding the ways we use our minds to learn, build knowledge, solve problems, and make our way through the world.

Although writers and scholars have often looked at the working class, they have generally focused on the values such workers exhibit rather than on the thought their work requires—a subtle but pervasive omission. Our cultural iconography promotes the muscled arm, sleeve rolled tight against biceps, but no brightness behind the eye, no image that links hand and brain. 10

One of my mother's brothers, Joe Meraglio, left school in the ninth grade to work for the Pennsylvania Railroad. From there he joined the Navy, returned to the railroad, which was already in decline, and eventually joined his older brother at General Motors where, over a 33-year career, he moved from working on the assembly line to supervising the paint-and-body department. When I was a young man, Joe took me on a tour of the factory. The floor was loud—in some places deafening—and when I turned a corner or opened a door, the smell of chemicals knocked my head back. The work was repetitive and taxing, and the pace was inhumane.

Still, for Joe the shop floor provided what school did not; it was *like schooling*, he said, a place where *you're constantly learning*. Joe learned the most

With an eighth-grade education, Joe (hands together) advanced to become supervisor of a G.M. paint-and-body department.

efficient way to use his body by acquiring a set of routines that were quick and preserved energy. Otherwise he would never have survived on the line.

As a foreman, Joe constantly faced new problems and became a consummate multi-tasker, evaluating a flurry of demands quickly, parceling out physical and mental resources, keeping a number of ongoing events in his mind, returning to whatever task had been interrupted, and maintaining a cool head under the pressure of grueling production schedules. In the midst of all this, Joe learned more and more about the auto industry, the technological and social dynamics of the shop floor, the machinery and production processes, and the basics of paint chemistry and of plating and baking. With further promotions, he not only solved problems but also began to find problems to solve: Joe initiated the redesign of the nozzle on a paint sprayer, thereby eliminating costly and unhealthy overspray. And he found a way to reduce energy costs on the baking ovens without affecting the quality of the paint. He lacked formal knowledge of how the machines under his supervision worked, but he had direct experience with them, hands-on knowledge, and was savvy about their quirks and operational capabilities. He could experiment with them.

Mike Rose started his research by observing —and by listening. Listening is a key part of thinking rhetorically; read more about it in Ch. I.

In addition, Joe learned about budgets and management. Coming off the line as he did, he had a perspective of workers' needs and management's demands, and this led him to think of ways to improve efficiency on the line while relieving some of the stress on the assemblers. He had each worker in a unit learn his or her co-workers' jobs so they could rotate across stations to relieve some of the monotony. He believed that rotation would allow assemblers to get longer and more frequent breaks. It was an easy sell to the people on the line. The union, however, had to approve any modification in job duties, and the managers were wary of the change. Joe had to argue his case on a number of fronts, providing him a kind of rhetorical education.

Eight years ago I began a study of the thought processes involved in work 15 like that of my mother and uncle. I catalogued the cognitive demands of a range of blue-collar and service jobs, from waitressing and hair styling to plumbing and welding. To gain a sense of how knowledge and skill develop, I observed experts as well as novices. From the details of this close examination, I tried to fashion what I called "cognitive biographies" of blue-collar workers. Biographical accounts of the lives of scientists, lawyers, entrepreneurs, and other professionals are rich with detail about the intellectual dimension of their work. But the life stories of working-class people are few and are typically accounts of hardship and courage or the achievements wrought by hard work.

Our culture—in Cartesian fashion—separates the body from the mind, so that, for example, we assume that the use of a tool does not involve abstraction. We reinforce this notion by defining intelligence solely on grades in school and numbers on IQ tests. And we employ social biases pertaining to a person's place on the occupational ladder. The distinctions among blue, pink, and white collars carry with them attributions of character, motivation, and intelligence. Although we rightly acknowledge and amply compensate the play of mind in white-collar and professional work, we diminish or erase it in considerations about other endeavors—physical and service work particularly. We also often ignore the experience of everyday work in administrative deliberations and policymaking.

But here's what we find when we get in close. The plumber seeking leverage in order to work in tight quarters and the hair stylist adroitly handling scissors and comb manage their bodies strategically. Though work-related actions become routine with experience, they were learned at some point through observation, trial and error, and, often, physical or verbal assistance from a co-worker or trainer. I've frequently observed novices talking to themselves as they take on a task, or shaking their head or hand as if to erase an attempt before trying again. In fact, our traditional notions of routine performance could keep us from appreciating the many instances within routine where quick decisions and adjustments are made. I'm struck by the thinking-in-motion that some work requires, by all the mental activity that can be involved in simply getting from one place to another: the waitress rushing back through her station to the kitchen or the foreman walking the line.

The use of tools requires the studied refinement of stance, grip, balance, and fine-motor skills. But manipulating tools is intimately tied to knowledge of what a particular instrument can do in a particular situation and do better than other similar tools. A worker must also know the characteristics of the material one is engaging—how it reacts to various cutting or compressing devices, to degrees of heat, or to lines of force. Some of these things demand judgment, the weighing of options, the consideration of multiple variables, and, occasionally, the creative use of a tool in an unexpected way.

In manipulating material, the worker becomes attuned to aspects of the environment, a training or disciplining of perception that both enhances knowledge and informs perception. Carpenters have an eye for length, line, and angle; mechanics troubleshoot by listening; hair stylists are attuned to shape, texture, and motion. Sensory data merge with concept, as when an auto mechanic relies on sound, vibration, and even smell to understand what cannot be observed.

Planning and problem solving have been studied since the earliest days 20 of modern cognitive psychology and are considered core elements in Western definitions of intelligence. To work is to solve problems. The big difference between the psychologist's laboratory and the workplace is that in the former the problems are isolated and in the latter they are embedded in the real-time flow of work with all its messiness and social complexity.

Much of physical work is social and interactive. Movers determining how to get an electric range down a flight of stairs require coordination, negotiation, planning, and the establishing of incremental goals. Words, gestures, and sometimes a quick pencil sketch are involved, if only to get the rhythm right. How important it is, then, to consider the social and communicative dimension of physical work, for it provides the medium for so much of work's intelligence.

Given the ridicule heaped on blue-collar speech, it might seem odd to value its cognitive content. Yet, the flow of talk at work provides the channel for organizing and distributing tasks, for troubleshooting and problem solving, for learning new information and revising old. A significant amount of teaching, often informal and indirect, takes place at work. Joe Meraglio saw that much of his job as a supervisor involved instruction. In some service occupations, language and communication are central: observing and interpreting behavior and expression, inferring mood and motive, taking on the perspective of others, responding appropriately to social cues, and knowing when you're understood. A good hair stylist, for instance, has the ability to convert vague requests (*I want something light and summery*) into an appropriate cut through questions, pictures, and hand gestures.

Verbal and mathematical skills drive measures of intelligence in the Western Hemisphere, and many of the kinds of work I studied are thought to require relatively little proficiency in either. Compared to certain kinds of white-collar occupations, that's true. But written symbols flow through physical work.

Numbers are rife in most workplaces: on tools and gauges, as measurements, as indicators of pressure or concentration or temperature, as guides to sequence, on ingredient labels, on lists and spreadsheets, as markers of quantity and price. Certain jobs require workers to make, check, and verify calculations, and to collect and interpret data. Basic math can be involved, and some workers develop a good sense of numbers and patterns. Consider, as well, what might be called material mathematics: mathematical functions embodied in materials and actions, as when a carpenter builds a cabinet or a flight of stairs. A simple mathematical act can extend quickly beyond itself. Measuring, for example, can involve more than recording the dimensions of an object. As I watched a cabinetmaker measure a long strip of wood, he read a number off the tape out loud, looked back over his shoulder to the kitchen wall, turned back to his task, took another measurement, and paused for a moment in thought. He was solving a problem involving the molding, and the measurement was important to his deliberation about structure and appearance.

In the blue-collar workplace, directions, plans, and reference books 25 rely on illustrations, some representational and others, like blueprints, that require training to interpret. Esoteric symbols—visual jargon—depict switches and receptacles, pipe fittings, or types of welds. Workers themselves often make sketches on the job. I frequently observed them grab a pencil to sketch something on a scrap of paper or on a piece of the material they were installing.

Though many kinds of physical work don't require a high literacy level, more reading occurs in the blue-collar workplace than is generally thought, from manuals and catalogues to work orders and invoices, to lists, labels, and forms. With routine tasks, for example, reading is integral to understanding production quotas, learning how to use an instrument, or applying a product. Written notes can initiate action, as in restaurant orders or reports of machine malfunction, or they can serve as memory aids.

True, many uses of writing are abbreviated, routine, and repetitive, and they infrequently require interpretation or analysis. But analytic moments can be part of routine activities, and seemingly basic reading and writing can be cognitively rich. Because workplace language is used in the flow of other activities, we can overlook the remarkable coordination of words, numbers, and drawings required to initiate and direct action.

If we believe everyday work to be mindless, then that will affect the work we create in the future. When we devalue the full range of everyday cognition, we offer limited educational opportunities and fail to make fresh and meaningful instructional connections among disparate kinds of skill and knowledge. If we think that whole categories of people—identified by class or occupation—are not that bright, then we reinforce social separations and cripple our ability to talk across cultural divides.

Affirmation of diverse intelligence is not a retreat to a softhearted definition of the mind. To acknowledge a broader range of intellectual capacity is to take seriously the concept of cognitive variability, to appreciate in all the Rosies and Joes the thought that drives their accomplishments and defines who they are. This is a model of the mind that is worthy of a democratic society.

Thinking about the Text

1. Mike Rose begins his **ANALYSIS** with a pair of extended examples and a brief personal narrative. Readers may not figure out until later what, exactly, he is analyzing. What is Rose's subject, and what is the question that directs his inquiry?

2. Because of the academically oriented prejudices that Rose mentions, you may never have read anything that focuses on the cognitive tasks involved in

blue-collar work. Were you surprised by anything that Rose said—or not? **REFLECT** on your own attitudes toward blue-collar work; in what ways did Rose confirm or challenge them? Describe your reactions and reflections.

3. Why might Rose have chosen to begin his analysis with the extended information about his mother and uncle, himself, and other members of his family? Do you find these **EXAMPLES** and **NARRATIVES** effective rhetorical strategies for introducing an analysis of this topic? Why or why not?

4. Rose is suggesting that blue-collar workers merit more recognition for the cognitive skills that they bring to their work, but that is not all he is arguing. What is the overarching **ARGUMENT** that Rose is making in his article? What **EVIDENCE** in the text supports your answer?

5. Conduct a brief interview with someone who works a blue-collar job—for example, a mechanic, a sewing-machine operator, a hairstylist, a restaurant server, a janitor or housekeeper, or a truck driver. Find out what factors someone needs to consider to perform the job successfully; in other words, what does the person have to be aware of while working? To keep the interview focused, start with one of the following questions: What effect does the weather have on what you do? (Heat, humidity, cold, and other weather elements often affect even indoor work.) What are the most common mistakes a beginner in your job might make? Write an **ANALYSIS** of the cognitive tasks involved in the person's ordinary workday. Use clear and precise language, and be sure to mention any insights that you gained.

Weight Loss at Any Cost

JAMES SANBORN

NEARLY ONE IN THREE MARINES are so afraid of violating the Corps' strict weight and appearance standards they have resorted to extreme weight-loss methods, including starvation, taking laxatives and undergoing costly liposuction surgery, according to a recent study conducted by two Marine officers while attending the Naval Post Graduate School.

But the rate may be much higher than that, said Capt. Paula Taibi, one of the study's co-authors. More than 70 percent of the 390 Marines who responded to her survey were from the junior enlisted and officer ranks—and not long out of boot camp or Officer Candidate School. If so many first-term men and women in peak physical shape are using risky means to blast fat and avoid the measuring tape, she said, then a lot of career Marines with far more to lose probably do it too. The report concludes that unconventional methods for weight loss are "widespread" within the Marine Corps.

The trend, Taibi said, likely predates revisions made in 2008 to the service's body composition and military appearance programs, or BCP and

James Sanborn explains military abbreviations that readers might not know. Find out more about defining key terms on pp. 292–94.

JAMES SANBORN is a multimedia journalist whose work has appeared in *USA Today*, the *Washington Post*, and other national periodicals. Sanborn has done investigative reporting in Mexico and Vietnam, and is currently based in Washington, D.C., where he is a staff writer for *Marine Corps Times*. This report was published in that paper in October 2010.

Medical personnel perform a body composition assessment on a Navy diver.

MAP. The move eliminated the leniency once shown to Marines who run afoul of body-fat standards but still score high on their physical fitness test. There has almost certainly been an uptick in risky weight-loss methods since then, however.

"I think people are being made more aware that they are going to comply and that if they don't, the results are going to be catastrophic to their career," said Taibi, who co-authored the 2009 report with Capt. Leigh Wallace and is now a programs analyst at Headquarters Marine Corps. "So I think people are grasping."

The commandant's office cast doubt on the findings, saying the sample ⁵ size is neither large enough nor diverse enough to accurately represent how widespread the trend may be. Maj. Joseph Plenzler, a spokesman for Gen. James Conway, said the Corps' top officer stands by the updates made to the BCP and MAP. While the commandant encourages Marines to be smart about how they stay trim, looking the part is vital to combat readiness and good order and discipline, he said.

"We Marines have historically held ourselves to high standards in both fitness and appearance," Plenzler said. "There are some Marines who may

U.S. Marines display their trim and polish at the 100th annual New York City Veterans Day Parade.

meet all established physical standards, yet fail to present a suitable military appearance, and this is inconsistent with the Marine Corps leadership principle of setting the example."

Marines may not all agree with that logic, but they understand the consequences of failing to make weight. The policy adjustments made on Conway's watch give commanders greater freedom to assign personnel to remedial training if their uniformed appearance does not fit that of a squared-away Marine, according to All Marine Message 034/08. For more senior Marines, that can be the kiss of death.

Commanders have the power to request a waiver for Marines who do not meet the Corps' standards but look professional in uniform. It's unclear how often waivers are granted, but in the past Conway has advocated for rigid enforcement of the rules.

Current body-fat limits for Marines start at 18 percent for men and 26 percent for women. Those limits increase slightly with age, up to 21 percent for men and 29 percent for women. Before the Corps tightened the rules,

Marines with first-class PFT scores could slide a few percentage points. Now, no matter how capable a Marine is physically, there are no exceptions.

Once a year, or more often if a commander deems it necessary, Marines 10 are assessed based on the body mass index, an equation that determines ideal weight relative to a Marine's height. If a Marine is deemed overweight, he then has measurements taken around his neck and waist to estimate body fat percentage.

In 2007, the Marine Corps inspector general suggested the service adopt a new measurement method. It called taping "adequate," but acknowledged it was prone to inaccuracies. Other methods could prove more equitable, the IG said.

That inquiry found that one in four Marines failed to meet standards and belonged in the BCP, prompting Conway's crackdown.

Despite tougher standards, thousands of Marines are still assigned to the BCP each year—5,671 since October, according to Manpower and Reserve Affairs. That's the most since 2006. So far this year, 72 Marines have been discharged for weight-related issues.

"There was a staff sergeant I knew and he was outstanding. The only reason he got out of the Corps was because of the new weight standards— even though he would PT with Marines every day and usually drop about half of them," said a gunnery sergeant at Camp Pendleton, Calif., who underwent liposuction in June. Even though the Corps allows Marines to have the procedure, he asked not to be identified, saying there's a stigma associated with failing to meet fitness requirements.

"I know an officer," he said, "who in order to make weight wore sweat 15 suits, didn't eat for a week, took pills and used enemas."

With about five years left until he's eligible for retirement, the gunny said he was willing to take such a drastic measure to stay out of the BCP and—he hopes—save his career.

The gunny has struggled for years to meet weight and body fat requirements, but regularly posted first-class PFT scores, he said. Then he suffered a back injury in Iraq, and making weight only got tougher. He had surgery on his back this year and packed on some extra pounds during his recovery. Although he has never been on the BCP in the past, the devastating prospect seemed inevitable as his medical review board loomed and he struggled to drop enough weight before his weigh-in.

The decision to get liposuction on his abdomen was easy.

"I felt it was pretty much a do-or-die situation," he said.

It was an expensive procedure, about $7,000, but well worth it to save 20 his career, he said. The recovery was swift—about two weeks—and he is pleased with the results.

The gunny wants Conway or his successor to reverse the new policy and again allow Marines some leeway provided they look OK in uniform and prove they are combat ready with high scores on the PFT and Combat Fitness Test.

"I know there are others out there in the same boat or who have a stocky build so they are always fighting the scale or tape," he said.

Most career Marines interviewed by *Marine Corps Times* said being put on the BCP is certain to scuttle their chances for advancement.

"It is probably easier to recover from a DUI than from being put on BCP," said Gunnery Sgt. Matthew Torres, another Camp Pendleton-based Marine who has never been assigned to a remedial fitness program, though he, too, struggles with stubborn belly fat. "A DUI is bad, but it's a one-time thing. You just don't do it again. Once you're on BCP, you're probably already on your way out."

Torres said he's been seriously considering liposuction for more than a 25 year but still has reservations. He runs religiously and has cleaned up his diet, he said, but the slight paunch around his gut just won't go away. If he can't drop enough weight before his next weigh-in, he's afraid it will mark the beginning of the end.

Torres believes he is at risk because of his small, muscular stature. The rules don't account for body type, he said. And that's frustrating. Current standards allow Marines less able-bodied than he to fly below the radar.

"I'd much rather have a guy who has a little meat on his bones that can pick somebody up in a firefight, than somebody who is supermodel skinny and can't pick his pack off the ground," he said. "It seems like the Marine Corps wants these super-skinny kids who can't lift themselves over a wall."

Most Marines who consider liposuction aren't out of shape, said Dr. Robert Peterson, a Hawaii-based plastic surgeon who runs the Athena Clinic in Honolulu and has operated on many service members.

"We mostly see Navy because many of them work long shifts on boats and submarines where exercise is difficult," Peterson said. "But we do get Marines. When we see them, they are usually fit. They just have a spare tire."

Like other plastic surgeons located near military installations, Peterson 30 advertises his services to service members—and even offers a $500 discount on procedures that cost $5,000 or more. For many of his patients, the payoff comes in getting to keep their job, he said.

Asked about potential risks to getting liposuction, Peterson said it is a relatively safe procedure and none of his patients have had major complications. But risks do exist, including infection, damage to surrounding tissue and blood vessels, and uneven skin texture.

Other rare but possible complications, according to the National Institutes of Health, include blood clots. Liposuction also can cause tiny globules of fat to be released into a patient's bloodstream, which can cause potentially fatal embolisms in the lungs, brain or elsewhere.

Liposuction is by no means the only risky weight-loss method Marines are using, according to Taibi's study. Some resort to starvation and fasting, extreme cardio, and the use of plastic sweat suits, diet pills, diuretics and laxatives. Some forgo water. Some give blood.

Highlighting just how dangerous some unconventional weight loss methods can be, one poolee trying to drop weight so he could join the Corps died from hyperthermia and dehydration in July 2009, while training with two recruiters in Tracy, Calif.

Daniel Ruf, 22, collapsed at a local gym while wearing a rubber suit. He 35 was trying to drop 10 pounds the day before his weigh-in. Ruf's case is now a source of ongoing litigation. His mother filed a lawsuit against the Marine Corps in April.

These methods aren't only hazardous to your health, Taibi said, but the resulting weight loss is often only temporary.

"In my opinion it's a really vicious cycle," she said. "You do all these crazy things—run with plastic bags on your chest or whatever. Then you make weight and it's a big release, so you let yourself go again."

There are reports of Marines employing risky weight-loss techniques in Afghanistan. Sgt. Shane Trefftzs, who works in the operations division of I Marine Expeditionary Force (Forward), told *Marine Corps Times* that after his command announced a weigh-in, others in his unit scrambled to shed weight any way they could. Some took diuretics, laxatives and diet pills and fasted.

"We're in a combat zone. Is this a smart idea?" he wrote in an e-mail. "I totally agree with a standard for military appearance. However, many of us remember some of the first words out of our Drill Instructor's mouth. 'Marines come in all shapes and sizes.'"

Fitness expert Tony Horton, the creator of P90X, the latest workout craze 40
to sweep the military, agreed that body type can significantly affect how a
person weighs in. He emphasizes functional fitness, and believes traditional
health assessment methods—including those used by the Defense Department that are based on height-to-weight ratios and taping around the neck
and belly—don't accurately measure a person's overall health.

Body mass index doesn't "dictate a person's abilities or strength," Horton said. "There is 'look like' . . . and there is also 'can do.' . . . Can a guy perform? If you are strong, and you are fit and flexible, and you can do your job
. . . who the hell cares what your waist size is?"

"Some people just have a very unfavorable ratio of the abdomen to their
neck even if they are in shape," echoed Peterson, the plastic surgeon. "That's
our most common group—people who are not designed for the particular
measurement," he said referring to the DoD-prescribed taping method for
estimating body fat. "If they did a different measurement, they would come
out fine."

Dr. Jules Feledy, the senior partner at Belmont Plastic Surgery, which has
offices near Marine Corps Base Quantico, Va., said he has seen a rise in the
number of Marines coming through his office since Conway tightened standards in 2008. The Marines he sees are typically in superior shape, he said,
but desperate to flatten their midsections as they look to beat the tape—a
measurement he, too, believes doesn't dictate a person's physical abilities.

But the Corps' regulations do have plenty of supporters. Despite her
findings, even Taibi says the standards are fair.

"It is important to note that Marine Corps body composition and mili- 45
tary appearance standards are neither unreasonable nor unattainable," said
Plenzler, Conway's spokesman. "It is the responsibility of every leader in the
chain of command to coach and mentor their subordinates, and hold them
accountable when they fail to meet standards."

The majority of overweight Marines simply need to adjust their diet
and exercise regimen, Taibi said. Marines' struggle with weight and body
fat parallels a national trend, she said. Based on her research, the Corps
needs to bolster outreach to ensure Marines use resources already available
through the Semper Fit program, which was developed to educate Marines
on maintaining a healthy lifestyle and making sound fitness choices while
providing them with the resources to stay in shape. It is important to ensure
that healthier food choices are available on base, she said.

Thinking about the Text

1. James Sanborn presents abundant factual and anecdotal evidence showing the harmful impact of the Marine Corps' body composition regulations, yet he concludes with statements in support of the policy. What is Sanborn's own **POSITION** on the regulations—and how do you know? Point to examples in the text to support your response.

2. A good **REPORT** provides trustworthy information. What kinds of information does Sanborn present in his report? What kinds of sources does he rely on? How appropriate are they for his purpose?

3. Sanborn writes using abbreviations and military terms that may be unfamiliar to some readers, but are perfectly clear and appropriate for his Marine Corps **AUDIENCE**. Find three such words or phrases (other than abbreviations) and restate them for the more general audience of a large-circulation newspaper or magazine.

4. Would you take drastic, possibly dangerous measures in order to protect your career? Put yourself in the place of a stocky Marine and try to imagine the pressures they face. How might you respond, and how far would you go? Why?

5. Does a military organization have legitimate authority over its members' physiques as a matter of maintaining appearance and discipline? Should appearance be a consideration at all in the Marine Corps, or should assessments be based strictly on physical ability? Write an essay that takes a **POSITION** on these questions.

The Psychology of Taking a Knee

JEREMY ADAM SMITH & DACHER KELTNER

WHAT DOES IT MEAN TO KNEEL? What emotions and beliefs does this action communicate? Does your culture or group membership affect how you see gestures like kneeling?

Those are some of the scientific questions raised when San Francisco 49ers quarterback Colin Kaepernick decided last year to kneel, instead of stand, for "The Star-Spangled Banner" before a preseason game. Teammate Eric Reid joined him. Their cause? Police violence against unarmed black people.

His knee unleashed a movement—and triggered a chain of events that culminated last week in the president of the United States calling a player who kneels a "son of a bitch." Over the following days, dozens of NFL players—including entire teams—"took the knee" before their games. In response, crowds booed.

JEREMY ADAM SMITH is an award-winning journalist and the current editor of *Greater Good Magazine*, published by the Greater Good Science Center at the University of California, Berkeley. His articles and essays have appeared in *Utne Reader*, *The Nation*, and *Wired*, among many other publications. Smith tweets from @JeremyAdamSmith. DACHER KELTNER (pictured above) is a professor of psychology at the University of California, Berkeley, and a co-director of the Greater Good Science Center. He has written or co-edited several books, including *Born to be Good*, *The Compassionate Instinct*, and *The Power Paradox*. This September 2017 essay was published on *Voices*, a *Scientific American* blog.

Players for the Kansas City Chiefs take a knee before a game against the L.A. Chargers in 2017.

To some, Kaepernick and the players who kneel with him are "unpatriotic," "ungrateful," "disrespectful," "degenerate," to quote just a few of the descriptions hurled their way. To others, Kaepernick's act—for which he may have paid dearly, as he is now unsigned—makes him a hero.

What's going on?   5

At first glance, research into emotion and nonverbal communication suggests that there is nothing threatening about kneeling. Instead, kneeling is almost always deployed as a sign of deference and respect. We once kneeled before kings and queens and altars; we kneel to ask someone to marry, or at least men did in the old days. We kneel to get down to a child's level; we kneel to beg.

While we can't know for sure, kneeling probably derives from a core principle in mammalian nonverbal behavior: make the body smaller and look up to show respect, esteem, and deference. This is seen, for example, in dogs and chimps, who reduce their height to show submissiveness. Kneeling can also be a posture of mourning and sadness. It makes the one who kneels more vulnerable. In some situations, kneeling can be seen as a request for protection—which is completely appropriate in Kaepernick's case, given the motive of his protest.

Even an ordinary gesture such as kneeling can be closely analyzed, as Smith shows us here. See more about how to write a compelling analysis in Ch. 14.

As sports protests go, taking the knee might not seem nearly as subversive or dangerous as thrusting a black-power fist into the air, as Tommie Smith and John Carlos did during their medal ceremony at the 1968 Summer Olympics in Mexico City. Researchers David Matsumoto and Jess Tracy show that even blind athletes from over 20 countries thrust their arms in the air in triumph after winning, which reveals the deep-seated urge to signal power with that body-expanding gesture. You can also find power in the fist. In the Darwinian sense, the fist is the antithesis of the affiliative, open hand, but when we combine a raised arm with a fist it becomes something more communicative—a rallying cry. It's a gesture that seeks to bring one group together while warning another away.

None of that should be too surprising. But there is an important point of similarity in the raised black-power fist—which makes bodies bigger—and the bended knee, which makes us smaller. Both Carlos and Smith bowed their heads in Mexico City, in a sign of respect and humility that accompanied their social signal of strength and triumph. That mix of messages makes the black-power salute one of the most famous, complex, effective nonverbal protests in our lifetimes—one that we can see echoed on today's football field.

Which returns us to the kneel. Kneeling is a sign of reverence, submis-   10
siveness, deference—and sometimes mourning and vulnerability. But with a single, graceful act, Kaepernick invested it with a double meaning. He didn't turn his back as the anthem was played, which would have been a true sign of disrespect. Nor did he rely on the now-conventionalized black-power fist.

Rather, he transformed a collective ritual—the playing of the national anthem—into something somber, a reminder of how far we still have to go to realize the high ideal of equal protection under the law that the flag represents. The athletes who followed him are showing reverence for the song and the flag, but they are simultaneously deviating from cultural norms at the moment their knees hit the grass.

By transforming this ritual, the players woke us up. Our amygdalae[1] activate as soon as our brains spot deviations from routine, social norms, and in-group tendencies. We want to know what's happening and why. We need

---

1. *Amygdalae* (singular: *amygdala*): A portion of the brain that performs a vital role in processing emotions; it is linked to responses of fear as well as pleasure. [Editor's note]

to know if the deviation poses a threat to us or our group. This may start to explain why so many Americans reacted with such fear and rage to a few athletes kneeling on the field in the midst of a national ritual.

But there's a lot more to it than that.

"Group membership affects interpretation of body language because groups develop norms and expectations around behavior, language, and life," says our UC Berkeley colleague Rodolfo Mendoza-Denton, an expert on intergroup communication. "Breaking these norms is used intentionally to signal disagreement with the norms, as well as to signal that one is not conforming. It sparks strong emotion and backlash precisely because of its symbolic meaning—a threat to the status quo."

It matters that most of the athletes are black and much of the audience is white, that the ancestors of one group were brought here as slaves and the ancestors of the other were their owners. That's why, when Pittsburgh Steelers stayed in the locker room as the anthem played, one Pennsylvania fire chief called their coach a "no good n*****" on Facebook, amplifying the racial themes of the debate. That's why Michigan's police director called them "degenerates." 15

When you mix power differences with intergroup dynamics, more factors come into play. Our lab has found that high-power people (say, the president or members of the numerical majority) are more likely to misinterpret nonverbal behavior. The experience of having power makes us less accurate in reading suffering on the faces of strangers and emotions in static photos of facial expressions. Powerful people are less able to take the perspective of others; they're quicker to confuse friendliness with flirtatiousness. This is the empathy deficit of people in power, one found in many kinds of studies.

Thus, we should not be surprised that many white people misread the meaning of "taking the knee" and fail to see the respect, concern, and even vulnerability inherent in kneeling. Of course, it is also the case that some white people may want to see black people terrorized by police and politically disenfranchised. Any effort by African Americans, no matter how deferential, to raise these issues will incite anger from those who benefit— emotionally or materially—from America's racial hierarchy.

But from a psychological perspective, that political elucidation still doesn't quite explain the specific inability of a majority of white football fans to interpret taking the knee according to universal human norms. And why would they take the misperception further, to actually see this humble posture as an act of aggression against America?

There is some evidence from Princeton's Susan Fiske and Penn State's Theresa Vescio that high-power people, in not attending carefully to others, are more likely to stereotype others, and more likely to miss individual nuances in behavior. This means that some white-majority football fans may be falling victim to the stereotype of African Americans—particularly large, well-muscled, pro football players—as violent and aggressive. In fact, as we've discussed, kneeling is actually the opposite of an aggressive signal.

What's the way forward from here? One of us (Dacher Keltner) has co-   20
authored a paper with colleague Daniel Cordaro that examines the expression of 20 emotions across five cultures. We found that while most outward emotional expressions are shared or partially shared, a quarter are not. It's in that non-shared space that intercultural conflict flares up—but that conflict can sometimes lead to cross-pollination, as people come to comprehend each other and synchronize their gestures.

Will Americans one day look back on Kaepernick's symbolic act as a moment when we started to understand each other just a little bit better? When many kinds of people were galvanized to work concretely on the problems of police brutality and racial bias in the criminal justice system, instead of discounting the concerns of African Americans?

Perhaps. Such a time seems very distant from where we are right now, as our society's leaders foster racial antagonism and people cannot seem to recognize the emotion and belief behind even the gentlest of gestures. Change happens, but it doesn't happen all by itself. Sometimes, you need to kneel to conquer.

Thinking about the Text

1. Smith and Keltner use psychology rather than politics to explain the act of taking a knee, and their **ANALYSIS** of the act goes across time and cultures. How do Smith and Keltner explain the significance of taking a knee? How do they explain the vehement opposition that many people express toward Colin Kaepernick and other kneeling athletes? Are their explanations plausible to you? Why or why not?

2. Imagine you were shown a photo of a person taking a knee, and everything else in the photo was too blurry to provide any useful information. What **NARRATIVE** might you construct to explain what the person is doing? Would

your narrative vary depending on whether you imagine the kneeler to be a woman or a man? A black-skinned or a white-skinned kneeler? Imagine the kneeler dressed in several different ways—office attire, perhaps, a uniform of some type, casual wear. Consider how your narrative might change. How well do your responses match Smith and Keltner's psychological profile of the act of kneeling? What do your responses say about you?

3. Smith and Keltner don't mention their academic or professional credentials in the essay, as many authors do. Do they establish their **AUTHORITY** adequately despite the omission of personal or professional details? Why or why not? Would their essay have been stronger if they had stated their credentials? Why or why not? Explain your reasoning.

4. In the United States, we are accustomed to performing patriotism by playing the national anthem at the beginning of athletic contests such as football or baseball games, and it has come to feel normal and ordinary for many people. We don't, however, perform patriotism at other kinds of live events—plays, poetry slams, or concerts—or at smaller and more routine events such as class sessions, club meetings, movie theaters, or work shifts. Think about the core meanings behind the performance of patriotism. Based on your concept of them, where should patriotism displays be performed? Where should they not be? What kinds of events? How often? Provide **EVIDENCE** for your reasoning.

5. As Smith and Keltner explain it, the enormous disparity between NFL kneelers' intentions and the interpretation of that act by some viewers is due largely to an "empathy deficit" (16). How do they define this phrase? How well does their explanation account for the disparity? Why do you think so? Have you experienced or observed empathy deficit in your community, on the job, or at school? Write an essay that addresses these questions. Explain your ideas and reasoning, and provide examples and **EVIDENCE** where appropriate.

Why Colleges Shower Their Students with A's

BRENT STAPLES

THE ECONOMIST MILTON FRIEDMAN taught that superior products flourished and shabby ones died out when consumers voted emphatically with their dollars. But the truth of the marketplace is that shabby products can do just fine if they sustain the veneer of quality while slipping downhill, as has much of higher education. Faced with demanding consumers and stiff competition, colleges have simply issued more and more A's, stoking grade inflation and devaluing degrees.

Grade inflation is in full gallop at every level, from struggling community institutions to the elites of the Ivy League. In some cases, campuswide averages have crept up from a C just 10 years ago to B-plus today.

Some departments shower students with A's to fill poorly attended courses that might otherwise be canceled. Individual professors inflate grades after consumer-conscious administrators hound them into it. Professors at every level inflate to escape negative evaluations by students, whose opinions now figure in tenure and promotion decisions.

BRENT STAPLES is a member of the *New York Times* editorial board and won a Pulitzer Prize in 2019 for his editorial writing at that newspaper. He writes about politics and cultural issues, focusing in particular on race and education, and he tweets from @brentNYT. He's the author of *Parallel Time: Growing Up in Black and White* (1995). This selection appeared in the *Times* in 1998.

The most vulnerable teachers are the part-timers who have no job security and who now teach more than half of all college courses. Writing in the last issue of the journal *Academe,* two part-timers suggest that students routinely corner adjuncts, threatening to complain if they do not turn C's into A's. An Ivy League professor said recently that if tenure disappeared, universities would be "free to sell diplomas outright."

The consumer appetite for less rigorous education is nowhere more evi-   5
dent than in the University of Phoenix, a profit-making school that shuns traditional scholarship and offers a curriculum so superficial that critics compare it to a drive-through restaurant. Two hundred colleges have closed since a businessman dreamed up Phoenix 20 years ago. Meanwhile, the university has expanded to 60 sites spread around the country, and more than 40,000 students, making it the country's largest private university.

Phoenix competes directly with the big state universities and lesser-known small colleges, all of which fear a student drain. But the elite schools fear each other and their customers, the students, who are becoming increasingly restive about the cost of a first-tier diploma, which now exceeds

Robert Wancha, a student at the University of Phoenix in Southfield, Michigan, has criticized the university's standards.

$120,000. Faced with the prospect of crushing debt, students are treating grades as a matter of life and death—occasionally even suing to have grades revised upward.

Twenty years ago students grumbled, then lived with the grades they were given. Today, colleges of every stature permit them to appeal low grades through deans or permanent boards of inquiry. In *The Chronicle of Higher Education,* Prof. Paul Korshin of the University of Pennsylvania recently described his grievance panel as the "rhinoplasty committee," because it does "cosmetic surgery" on up to 500 transcripts a year.

The argument that grades are rising because students are better prepared is simply not convincing. The evidence suggests that students and parents are demanding—and getting—what they think of as their money's worth.

One way to stanch inflation is to change the way the grade point average is calculated. Under most formulas, all courses are given equal weight, so math, science and less-challenging courses have equal impact on the averages. This arrangement rewards students who gravitate to courses where high marks are generously given and punishes those who seek out math and science courses, where far fewer students get the top grade.

Valen Johnson, a Duke University statistics professor, came under 10 heavy fire from both students and faculty when he proposed recalculating the grade point average to give rigorously graded courses greater weight. The student government beat back the plan with the help of teachers in the humanities, who worried that students might abandon them for other courses that they currently avoided. Other universities have expressed interest in adopting the Johnson plan, but want their names kept secret to avoid a backlash.

Addicted to counterfeit excellence, colleges, parents and students are unlikely to give it up. As a consequence, diplomas will become weaker and more ornamental as the years go by.

Brent Staples presents a lot of information but makes it readable. How did he do it? More importantly, how can you do it? See Ch. 15.

Thinking about the Text

1. Brent Staples presents a great deal of information in a very brief opinion piece. How well does the piece live up to the promise of its title—explaining the cause of the abundance of A's? Explain.

2. Staples argues that the proliferation of A grades devalues a degree by demonstrating the lack of academic rigor of any college that grants so many A's. How do you feel about the degree that you are working toward? If you had the choice of two colleges equal in all other ways, and one had a reputation for academic rigor and maintained high standards for grades, while the other had a mediocre academic reputation but was known for giving many high grades, which would you choose, and why?

3. Staples's essay was published in the *New York Times*, which has a readership of millions. Is Staples really addressing all of those millions, or is his true intended **AUDIENCE** a particular subset of those who read the *Times*? If so, who was he addressing—and how can you tell?

4. Staples mentions the proposal of Valen Johnson as a way of dealing with "counterfeit excellence" (11). Is he advocating Johnson's proposal? opposing it? not taking a position one way or the other? How do you know?

5. Imagine that the administration of your school is undertaking a major evaluation of the grading system, with the ultimate goal of enhancing the academic rigor of the institution. They have asked members of the academic community at all levels, including students, to present opinions and suggestions. Write an essay in which you **ARGUE A POSITION** on grading policies, particularly with respect to grade inflation. Give a carefully reasoned argument backed up by **EVIDENCE** from your own experience.

"Coco," a Story about Borders and Love

JIA TOLENTINO

ONE WEEKEND LAST FALL, my boyfriend, Andrew, whose favorite movies include "Deliverance" and the original "Texas Chain Saw Massacre," went off to go see the Pixar movie "Coco," by himself, and came back in a delirium of happy, wistful tears. "What's going on with you?" I asked, watching him wheel his bike back into the living room. I hadn't moved from my permanent station behind my computer monitor, a hub for the ongoing erosion of my belief in human good. "You have to go to see 'Coco,'" he croaked. "You *have* to. It's, like, the best movie of all time."

I assumed that he was being hyperbolic, until a night in April when I invited three friends over to watch "Coco," all of us first-time viewers with high expectations. People we knew—people in their twenties and thirties, few of them with children—had been freaking out about "Coco" in group texts and random conversations, saying things like, "I cried so hard I started choking," and "I've watched it five times this month on airplanes." "Hey ppl over here getting drunk and watching Coco just fyi," I texted Andrew, who was still at the office. In return, I received a series of panicked instructions

---

JIA TOLENTINO is a staff writer for the *New Yorker*, where her work, in addition to reviews and cultural commentary, often involves deep investigations on topics such as youth vaping, abortion law, and sexual assault. She is author of *Trick Mirror* (2019), a collection of essays. In this 2018 article from the magazine, she reviews Pixar's animated feature film *Coco*.

to not start without him. "You have already seen it. . . ." I texted. "I DON'T
CARE!!!!!!!" he texted back. "DON'T START WITHOUT ME!!!!"

We started without him. Andrew came home a third of the way into the
movie, cracked a beer, and silently sat down on the floor of the living room to
watch. By the end, every one of us was crying through a manic grin. "I told
you," he said. "It's the best movie of all time."

In the weeks since that viewing, "Coco" love has continued to spread
among my demographic—thanks, in part, to the movie's release on Netflix.
"Coco" is unlike any film I can think of: it presents death as a life-affirming
inevitability; its story line about grudges and abandonment makes you feel
less alone. The protagonist, Miguel, is a twelve-year-old boy in the fictional
Mexican town of Santa Cecilia—named for the patron saint of musicians—
and he is trying to get out from under the shadow of his great-great-
grandfather, who left his family to pursue a career as a musician. His wife,
the ferocious Mamá Imelda, was left to take care of their young daughter,
Coco. She instituted a permanent household ban on music and started making shoes.

We meet Coco as an old woman. Her daughter, Miguel's grandmother,   5
now runs the family and its shoemaking business with an iron *chancla*. Earnest, sweet Miguel teaches himself to play the guitar in the attic, watching
and re-watching tapes of the bygone star Ernesto de la Cruz. On the Day of the
Dead, he accidentally shatters a framed photograph on the family *ofrenda*,
then spots a hidden detail in the picture, one that makes him suspect that
his wayward ancestor was in fact de la Cruz himself. He sprints to the town
mausoleum, hoping to borrow de la Cruz's guitar and prove the value of mu-

sic to his family. Instead, the guitar turns Miguel invisible, and whisks him across a skybridge covered in thick, soft marigold petals that glow like lava. He falls to his knees in the petals, and then looks up to see a grand floating metropolis, confetti-colored in the darkness: the Land of the Dead.

The second and third acts of the movie are mostly set in this city of jubilant sugar-skull skeletons, where you exist only as long as you are remembered by the living. (You can cross over to the living world on the Day of the Dead, but only if your photo is on display.) Miguel joins up with a raggedy show-biz hustler named Héctor, who's desperate to get his picture back up on an *ofrenda*, and who says he can bring Miguel to de la Cruz. Héctor lives in a waterfront shantytown filled with people who are about to be forgotten; at one point, he begs a guitar for Miguel off an ill-tempered cowboy named Chicharrón, who vanishes as soon as Héctor finishes singing an old dirty song.

Eventually, Miguel realizes that Héctor is his real ancestor, and the movie sprints to a conclusion that's as skillfully engineered to produce waterworks as the montage at the beginning of "Up." But until the end, "Coco" is mostly, wonderfully, a mess of conflict and disappointment and sadness. Héctor seems to have failed everyone who takes a chance on him. Miguel's face, painted in skeleton camouflage, often droops as if he were a sad little black-and-white dog. "Coco" is animated by sweetness, but this sweetness is subterranean, bursting through mostly in tiny details: the way that both Mamá Imelda and Miguel's grandmother brandish shoes when they're angry; or how the daffy Xolo[1] dog that accompanies Miguel on his adventure is named Dante; or how the skeletons return to their city through the Day of the Dead's efficient T.S.A. system, declaring the churros and beer that their families gave them for their journey home.

Before "Coco" hit theaters, it was easy to doubt that the movie would present Mexican culture as expansively and gorgeously as it does, with such natural familiarity and respect. It is Pixar's nineteenth movie, but its first with a nonwhite protagonist; Lee Unkrich, the director and creator of the initial story, is white. The movie's working title was "Día de los Muertos," and, in 2013, Disney lawyers tried, absurdly, to trademark that phrase. But Unkrich and his team approached their subject with openness and collaborative humility: they travelled to Mexico, they loosened Pixar's

> Moviegoers wouldn't need to know this background in order to enjoy the film, but the information adds flavor to Tolentino's review. See more about Including information in your review on pp. 333–36.

---

1. *Xolo*: A breed of small, hairless dog that is common in parts of Mexico and has been raised there for thousands of years. [Editor's note]

typical secrecy to build a large network of consultants, and, after the trademark controversy, they asked several prominent critics to come onboard. "Coco" is the first movie to have both an all-Latino cast and a nine-figure budget. It grossed more than eight hundred million dollars worldwide, won two Oscars, and became the biggest blockbuster in Mexican history.

"Coco" is also a definitive movie for this moment: an image of all the things that we aren't, an exploration of values that feel increasingly difficult to practice in the actual world. It's a story of a multigenerational matriarchy, rooted in the past—whereas real life, these days, feels like an atemporal, structureless nightmare ruled by men. It's about lineage and continuity at a time when each morning makes me feel like my brain is being wiped and battered by new flashes of cruelty, as though history is being forgotten and only the worst parts rewritten. It feels like myth or science fiction to imagine that our great-great-grandchildren will remember us. If we continue to treat our resources the way we are treating them currently, those kids—if they exist at all—will live in a world that is ravaged, punishing, artificial, and hard.

This world is hard enough already: its technological conditions induce 10 emotional alienation, and its economic ones narrow our attention to questions of individual survival. As it is, I haven't assembled the *ofrenda* I ought to. I barely feel like I'm taking adequate care of the people I love right now, and I mean the ones I know personally. I feel certain that I'm failing the people I don't know but that I love nonetheless—the people in our national community, and the people who are seeking to become a part of it.

"Coco" is a movie about borders more than anything—the beauty in their porousness, the absolute pain produced when a border locks you away from your family. The conflict in the story comes from not being able to cross over; the resolution is that love pulls you through to the other side. The thesis of the movie is that families belong together. . . . If justice is what love looks like in public, then love has started to seem like the stuff of children's movies, or maybe the stuff of *this* children's movie—something that doesn't make sense in the adult world, but should.

Thinking about the Text

1. Jia Tolentino's **REVIEW** of *Coco* deals with more than just the movie itself; she segues into comparing the world of *Coco* with her perception of reality in the

twenty-first-century United States as viewed through the lens of her "ongoing erosion of . . . belief in human good" (1). Is her comparison appropriate? What does it suggest about her criteria for evaluating the film? Should she have restricted her comments to the content of the movie? Why or why not? Explain your reasoning.

2. Tolentino's review might give the impression that a life of "lineage and continuity" (9) could only exist in the cartoon world of *Coco*, since she perceives her life very differently. How about you? Do you feel the effect of lineage and continuity in your daily activities and the choices you make, perhaps in the influence of family or culture? Reflect on that phrase and describe what place, if any, lineage and continuity have on the ways that you live your life.

3. What might have been Tolentino's **PURPOSE** in beginning her review with the anecdote about her boyfriend's reaction to *Coco*? How, if at all, does the anecdote support Tolentino's review? Explain your reasoning.

4. Tolentino doubts "that our great-great-grandchildren will remember us" (9), and she implies that such an interruption of memory would be a result of our specific conditions in the here and now, but perhaps loss of historical memory is nothing new. How much do you know about any of your own great-great-grandparents? What kinds of historical conditions can interfere with knowing one's own lineage? Do you participate in any family or cultural practices that preserve the memory of your close or distant ancestors? Would you like to do more? less? Why or why not?

5. Tolentino describes *Coco* as full of sweetness that is "subterranean, bursting through mostly in tiny details" (7). Might that description also apply to ordinary, everyday noncinematic life? Think about your life this week and identify a few sweet details—perhaps a kind gesture, a bird or squirrel, sinking into a soft seat at the end of a long day, some small observation or sensation that might ordinarily go unnoticed—and write a description of those sweet details and your responses to them.

It's 2018, and Gay Men Still Can't Give Blood in America

JOSH TRUJILLO & LEVI HASTINGS

Writer, cartoonist, and game designer JOSH TRUJILLO writes in numerous genres with a broad array of themes, including fantasy, history, gaming, and LGBTQ issues. He is the creator of *Dodge City*, a graphic print series about the Jazz Pandas, a competitive dodge ball team; stories highlight the players' lives both on and off the court, and the series is notable for diverse characters and portrayals. Trujillo also writes the stories of *Love Machines*, a series of romance comics about the objects of our everyday lives and the roles of technology in our very human relationships. In a 2019 interview for the website *On Comics Ground*, Trujillo explains that "the thing [he finds] most interesting about Love Machines is how technology has always been a huge constant in our emotional and romantic lives. Smartphones have totally transformed the way people date and interact, just like telephones did a hundred years before."

LEVI HASTINGS, an illustrator, cartoonist, and visual artist, also works in a variety of genres and topics; his passions include natural science, history, travel, and Queer culture. He has done illustrations for HBO, *Buzzfeed*, *The Nib*, and many more companies and media outlets. Recent work includes *Spirit of Springer*, a nonfiction children's book about an orphaned orca who was rescued and reunited with her pod.

Trujillo and Hastings have published several collaborations. In 2016, they launched their well-researched historical fiction comic series *Declaration*, a gay romance of the Revolutionary War era. The following graphic essay was published in *The Nib*, a comics blog, in June 2018.

But Americans showed incredible support for the victims.

In America, and in most countries,
cis gay and bisexual men are discriminated against.

They're prevented from donating
precious, vital, life-saving plasma.

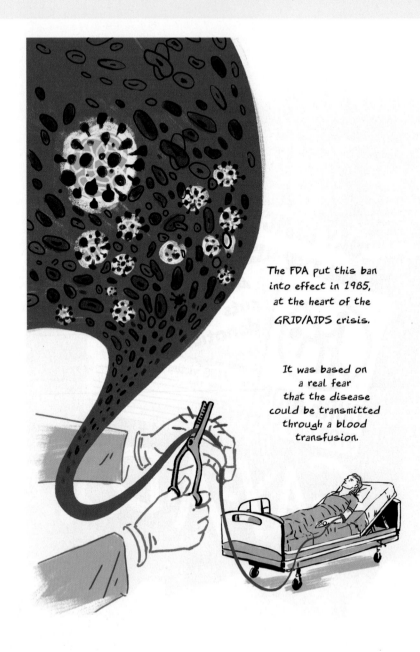

The FDA put this ban
into effect in 1985,
at the heart of the
GRID/AIDS crisis.

It was based on
a real fear
that the disease
could be transmitted
through a blood
transfusion.

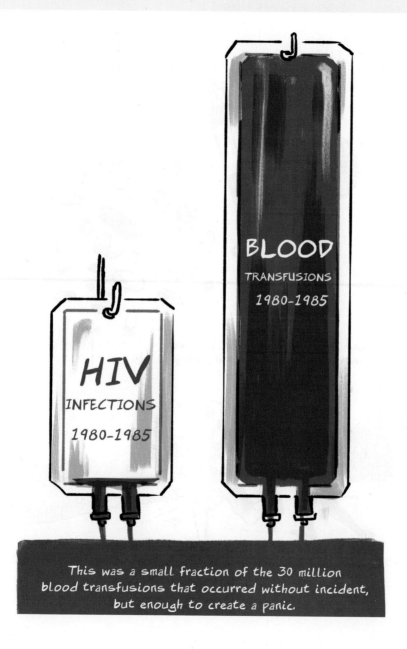

This was a small fraction of the 30 million blood transfusions that occurred without incident, but enough to create a panic.

Notice the color Trujillo and Hastings chose—not blood red, exactly, because that might have been too much, but a shade that contrasts well with black and is evocative of blood. Find advice for your color choices on pp. 761–63.

Our ability to detect, treat, and live with HIV/AIDS has improved greatly over the decades.

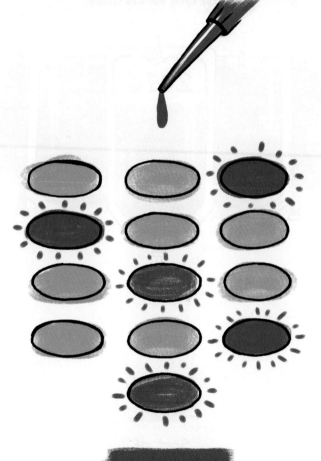

But the ban remained in effect.

Until in 2016, the year of the
Pulse nightclub massacre in Orlando,
when the total ban was lifted...

Sort of.

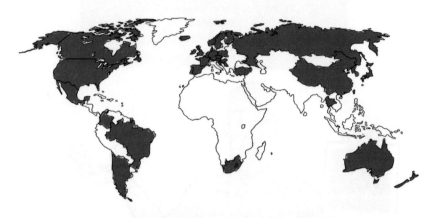

Italy has no such ban in place.
There, people are individually screened
for risk based on their sexual behavior.

Since this policy took effect in 2001,
there has been no increased risk of receiving
infected blood via transfusion in Italy.

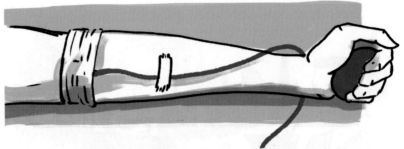

A 2014 Williams Institute study found that lifting the blood donation ban in the US could increase the blood supply by as much as 4%.

Blood which could be used for as many as ONE MILLION life-saving procedures.

By implementing individual risk assessment versus a blanket ban, the FDA can make an enormous difference in the health and well-being of all Americans.

The gay community felt powerless after the Orlando shooting.

This policy change, though small, could be the first step towards empathy, compassion, and healing.

Thinking about the Text

1. Josh Trujillo and Levi Hastings are **PROPOSING** a change in the US policy for blood donation. What, exactly, are they proposing? Why? Is the proposal reasonable? Why or why not? Explain your response.

2. Does your school sponsor an annual blood drive, as many colleges and universities do? If so, investigate the eligibility requirements and the screening process. What questions are potential donors asked about their sexual activity, alcohol consumption, drug use (prescribed and recreational), and other habits? Does the process seem fair to you? Why or why not? Do you think other lines of questioning should be pursued? Are there questions you think should not be asked? Explain your reasoning. (If there is no drive at your school, investigate a blood drive in your community.)

3. How do the drawings in Trujillo and Hastings's graphic essay complement the text? What do the drawings contribute to the whole? Would you rather have read the text by itself as a prose essay? Why or why not? Choose one drawing and **ANALYZE** how it enhances (or doesn't) the accompanying text information.

4. We've classified this proposal under the theme Home. Why might we have made that choice? Identify one image in the essay that best supports the classification of Home and explain your reasoning for the choice.

5. With regard to gay male donors, Trujillo and Hastings mention the blood donation policies of several countries in addition to those of the United States. Do some research; which country's policies seem the fairest to you? Why? Write an essay **PROPOSING** the blood donation policy you think the United States should follow. Should it be similar to the US status quo or to the policy of one of another countries? Include **EVIDENCE** for your stance.

Why the Post Office Makes America Great

ZEYNEP TUFEKCI

I WAS TRANSPORTED RECENTLY TO A PLACE that is as enchanting to me as any winter wonderland: my local post office.

In line, I thought fondly of the year I came to this country from Turkey as an adult and discovered the magic of reliable mail service. Dependable infrastructure is magical not simply because it works, but also because it allows innovation to thrive, including much of the Internet-based economy that has grown in the past decade. You can't have Amazon or eBay without a reliable way to get things to people's homes.

Of course, infrastructure is also boring, so we get used to it and forget what a gift it truly is. I never do, maybe because I discovered it so late.

My first year in the United States was full of surprises. I remember trying to figure out if the 24-ounce glass of ice water the waitress placed in front of me was a pitcher, to be shared by the whole table. But where was the spout? I had expected some of what I encountered—I had seen enough movies, and came to this country expecting big cars and big houses and wide open spaces. I got used to gigantic glasses.

ZEYNEP TUFEKCI is assistant professor at the University of North Carolina, faculty associate at the Berkman Center at Harvard University, and author of *Twitter and Tear Gas: The Power and Fragility of Networked Protest* (2017). This *New York Times* essay was published in January 2016. She tweets from @zeynep.

But I didn't expect the post office.   5

The first time I needed to mail something, I trekked over to my campus's post office, looking for the line to get my envelope weighed. The staff was used to befuddled international students like me, I suppose, and one clerk took my envelope without fuss, said "first class letter," and took my change.

Then I discovered some vending machines outside the office. People came and bought stamps. "So many people must be into stamp collecting," I thought to myself. Was that another weird American quirk? Otherwise, why would people waste money buying stamps in advance, without having their letters weighed?

Something I take for granted now just didn't occur to me: There were standardized rates, and you could just slap a stamp on your letter, drop it in a mailbox, and it would go to its destination.

I then encountered a visa service that asked me to mail in my passport. My precious, precious passport. With a self-addressed, stamped envelope for its return. I laughed at the audacity of the request. Despite being a broke student, I booked a plane trip. I couldn't envision putting my passport in the mail. I've since learned that this is a common practice, and I've even done it once or twice myself. But it still does not come easy to me.

I noticed that Americans were a particularly patriotic bunch: So many   10
of them had red flags on their mailboxes. Sometimes they would put those flags up. I presumed it was to celebrate national holidays I did not yet know about. But why did some people have their flags up while others did not? And why weren't they American flags anyway? As in Istanbul, where I grew up, I assumed patriotism had different interpretations and expressions.

The mystery was solved when I noticed a letter carrier *emptying* a mailbox. I was slightly unnerved: Was the mail being stolen? He then went over to another mailbox with the flag up, and emptied that box, too. I got my hint when he skipped the mailbox with the flag down.

Yes, I was told, in the United States, mail gets picked up from your house, six days a week, free of charge.

I told my friends in Turkey about all this. They shook their heads in disbelief, wondering how easily I had been recruited as a C.I.A. agent, saying implausibly flattering things about my new country. The United States in the world's imagination is a place of risk taking and ruthless competition, not one of reliable public services.

I bit my tongue and did not tell my already suspicious friends that the country was also dotted with libraries that provided books to all patrons free of charge. They wouldn't believe me anyway since I hadn't believed it myself. My first time in a library in the United States was very brief: I walked in, looked around, and ran right back out in a panic, certain that I had accidentally used the wrong entrance. Surely, these open stacks full of books were reserved for staff only. I was used to libraries being rare, and their few books inaccessible. To this day, my heart races a bit in a library.

Over the years, I've come to appreciate the link between infrastructure, innovation—and even ruthless competition. Much of our modern economy thrives here because you can order things online and expect them to be delivered. There are major private delivery services, too, but the United States Postal Service is often better equipped to make it to certain destinations. In fact, Internet sellers, and even private carriers, often use the U.S.P.S. as their delivery mechanism to addresses outside densely populated cities.

Almost every aspect of the most innovative parts of the United States, from cutting-edge medical research to its technology scene, thrives on publicly funded infrastructure. The post office is struggling these days, in some ways because of how much people rely on the web to do much of what they used to turn to the post office for. But the Internet is a testament to infrastructure, too: It exists partly because the National Science Foundation funded much of the research that makes it possible. Even some of the Internet's biggest companies, like Google, got a start from N.S.F.-funded research.

Infrastructure is often the least-appreciated part of what makes a country strong, and what makes innovation take flight. From my spot in line at the post office, I see a country that does both well; not a country that emphasizes one at the expense of the other.

15

Tufekci uses a light and entertaining tone to make an argument that is quite serious, and she uses a combination of appeals to get the job done. Find out more about using various kinds of appeals in Ch. 18.

Thinking about the Text

1. Zeynep Tufekci describes the relationship between infrastructure and innovation. What is that relationship? What examples does she provide to illustrate her point? **SUMMARIZE** her argument. Do you agree? Why or why not?

2. "To this day," confides Tufekci, "my heart races a bit in a library" (14). Do you share her reaction? How do you feel upon entering a library? Overwhelmed? Intimidated? Kid in a candy store? Scholarly? (If you haven't visited one in a while, do it now to refresh your memory.) Do you think a public library is an important element of infrastructure? Why or why not?

3. Tufekci employs personal **NARRATIVE** in support of an argument about US domestic policy. Is that rhetorical strategy an effective choice in this case? Why or why not?

4. Among the elements of everyday US life that surprised Tufekci when she arrived here were the large glasses of water provided free of charge to restaurant patrons, the post office, and the library. Take a look around at the ordinary parts of your life in the United States. Which of the things that you take for granted might be surprising to a newcomer? Why do you think so?

5. Tufekci points to the post office as a prime example of vital infrastructure. What else counts as infrastructure on a national and/or local level? List five examples. Choose one of those examples and write an essay describing how that infrastructure element could be expanded or enhanced in order to stimulate an innovation of some kind. Frame your essay as a **PROPOSAL** to state or local authorities supporting your infrastructure project.

My Life as an Undocumented Immigrant

JOSE ANTONIO VARGAS

ONE AUGUST MORNING nearly two decades ago, my mother woke me and put me in a cab. She handed me a jacket. *"Baka malamig doon"* were among the few words she said. ("It might be cold there.") When I arrived at the Philippines' Ninoy Aquino International Airport with her, my aunt and a family friend, I was introduced to a man I'd never seen. They told me he was my uncle. He held my hand as I boarded an airplane for the first time. It was 1993, and I was 12.

My mother wanted to give me a better life, so she sent me thousands of miles away to live with her parents in America—my grandfather (*Lolo* in Tagalog) and grandmother (*Lola*). After I arrived in Mountain View, Calif., in the San Francisco Bay Area, I entered sixth grade and quickly grew to love my new home, family and culture. I discovered a passion for language, though it was hard to learn the difference between formal English and American slang. One of my early memories is of a freckled kid in middle school

---

JOSE ANTONIO VARGAS came to the United States from the Philippines at the age of twelve as an undocumented immigrant, a history he discloses in this 2011 essay from the *New York Times*. He has been awarded the Pulitzer Prize and the PEN Freedom to Write award. His writing has appeared in the *Washington Post*, the *San Francisco Chronicle*, *Time*, and many other periodicals; he tweets from @joseiswriting. His current work focuses on immigration advocacy.

asking me, "What's up?" I replied, "The sky," and he and a couple of other kids laughed. I won the eighth-grade spelling bee by memorizing words I couldn't properly pronounce. (The winning word was "indefatigable.")

One day when I was 16, I rode my bike to the nearby D.M.V. office to get my driver's permit. Some of my friends already had their licenses, so I figured it was time. But when I handed the clerk my green card as proof of U.S. residency, she flipped it around, examining it. "This is fake," she whispered. "Don't come back here again."

Confused and scared, I pedaled home and confronted Lolo. I remember him sitting in the garage, cutting coupons. I dropped my bike and ran over to him, showing him the green card. "*Peke ba ito?*" I asked in Tagalog. ("Is this fake?") My grandparents were naturalized American citizens—he worked as a security guard, she as a food server—and they had begun supporting my mother and me financially when I was 3, after my father's wandering eye and inability to properly provide for us led to my parents' separation. Lolo was a proud man, and I saw the shame on his face as he told me he purchased the card, along with other fake documents, for me. "Don't show it to other people," he warned.

I decided then that I could never give anyone reason to doubt I was an   5 American. I convinced myself that if I worked enough, if I achieved enough, I would be rewarded with citizenship. I felt I could earn it.

I've tried. Over the past 14 years, I've graduated from high school and college and built a career as a journalist, interviewing some of the most famous people in the country. On the surface, I've created a good life. I've lived the American dream.

But I am still an undocumented immigrant. And that means living a different kind of reality. It means going about my day in fear of being found out. It means rarely trusting people, even those closest to me, with who I really am. It means keeping my family photos in a shoebox rather than displaying them on shelves in my home, so friends don't ask about them. It means reluctantly, even painfully, doing things I know are wrong and unlawful. And it has meant relying on a sort of 21st-century underground railroad of supporters, people who took an interest in my future and took risks for me.

Last year I read about four students who walked from Miami to Washington to lobby for the Dream Act, a nearly decade-old immigration bill that would provide a path to legal permanent residency for young people who have been educated in this country. At the risk of deportation—the Obama administration has deported almost 800,000 people in the last two years—they are speaking out. Their courage has inspired me.

There are believed to be 11 million undocumented immigrants in the United States. We're not always who you think we are. Some pick your strawberries or care for your children. Some are in high school or college. And some, it turns out, write news articles you might read. I grew up here. This is my home. Yet even though I think of myself as an American and consider America my country, my country doesn't think of me as one of its own.

My first challenge was the language. Though I learned English in the Philip-　10 pines, I wanted to lose my accent. During high school, I spent hours at a time watching television (especially *Frasier, Home Improvement* and reruns of *The Golden Girls*) and movies (from *Goodfellas* to *Anne of Green Gables*), pausing the VHS to try to copy how various characters enunciated their words. At the local library, I read magazines, books and newspapers—anything to learn how to write better. Kathy Dewar, my high-school English teacher, introduced me to journalism. From the moment I wrote my first article for the student paper, I convinced myself that having my name in print—writing in English, interviewing Americans—validated my presence here.

The debates over "illegal aliens" intensified my anxieties. In 1994, only a year after my flight from the Philippines, Gov. Pete Wilson was re-elected in part because of his support for Proposition 187, which prohibited undocumented immigrants from attending public school and accessing other services. (A federal court later found the law unconstitutional.) After my encounter at the D.M.V. in 1997, I grew more aware of anti-immigrant sentiments and stereotypes: *they don't want to assimilate, they are a drain on society.* They're not talking about me, I would tell myself. I have something to contribute.

To do that, I had to work—and for that, I needed a Social Security number. . . . Using a fake passport, Lolo and I went to the local Social Security Administration office and applied for a Social Security number and card. It was, I remember, a quick visit. When the card came in the mail, it had my full, real name, but it also clearly stated: "Valid for work only with I.N.S. authorization."

When I began looking for work, a short time after the D.M.V. incident, my grandfather and I took the Social Security card to Kinko's, where he covered the "I.N.S. authorization" text with a sliver of white tape. We then made photocopies of the card. At a glance, at least, the copies would look like copies of a regular, unrestricted Social Security card. . . .

While in high school, I worked part time at Subway, then at the front desk of the local Y.M.C.A., then at a tennis club, until I landed an unpaid internship at *The Mountain View Voice*, my hometown newspaper. First I brought coffee and helped around the office; eventually I began covering city-hall meetings and other assignments for pay. . . .

Mountain View High School became my second home. I was elected to 15 represent my school at school-board meetings, which gave me the chance to meet and befriend Rich Fischer, the superintendent for our school district. I joined the speech and debate team, acted in school plays and eventually became co-editor of *The Oracle*, the student newspaper. That drew the attention of my principal, Pat Hyland. "You're at school just as much as I am," she told me. Pat and Rich would soon become mentors, and over time, almost surrogate parents for me. . . .

[During my junior] year, my history class watched a documentary on Harvey Milk, the openly gay San Francisco city official who was assassinated. This was 1999, just six months after Matthew Shepard's body was found tied to a fence in Wyoming. During the discussion, I raised my hand and said something like: "I'm sorry Harvey Milk got killed for being gay. . . . I've been meaning to say this. . . . I'm gay."

I hadn't planned on coming out that morning, though I had known that I was gay for several years. With that announcement, I became the only openly gay student at school, and it caused turmoil with my grandparents. Lolo kicked me out of the house for a few weeks. Though we eventually reconciled, I had disappointed him on two fronts. First, as a Catholic, he considered homosexuality a sin and was embarrassed about having *"ang apo na bakla"* ("a grandson who is gay"). Even worse, I was making matters more difficult for myself, he said. I needed to marry an American woman in order to gain a green card.

Tough as it was, coming out about being gay seemed less daunting than coming out about my legal status. I kept my other secret mostly hidden.

While my classmates awaited their college acceptance letters, I hoped to get a full-time job at *The Mountain View Voice* after graduation. It's not that I didn't want to go to college, but I couldn't apply for state and federal financial aid. Without that, my family couldn't afford to send me.

But when I finally told Pat and Rich about my immigration "problem"— 20
as we called it from then on—they helped me look for a solution. At first, they
even wondered if one of them could adopt me and fix the situation that way,
but a lawyer Rich consulted told him it wouldn't change my legal status because I was too old. Eventually they connected me to a new scholarship fund
for high-potential students who were usually the first in their families to
attend college. Most important, the fund was not concerned with immigration status. I was among the first recipients, with the scholarship covering
tuition, lodging, books and other expenses for my studies at San Francisco
State University.

As a college freshman, I found a job working part time at *The San Francisco Chronicle*, where I sorted mail and wrote some freelance articles. My
ambition was to get a reporting job, so I embarked on a series of internships.
First I landed at *The Philadelphia Daily News*, in the summer of 2001, where I
covered a drive-by shooting and the wedding of the 76ers star Allen Iverson.
Using those articles, I applied to *The Seattle Times* and got an internship for
the following summer.

But then my lack of proper documents became a problem again. *The
Times*'s recruiter, Pat Foote, asked all incoming interns to bring certain
paperwork on their first day: a birth certificate, or a passport, or a driver's
license plus an original Social Security card. I panicked, thinking my documents wouldn't pass muster. So before starting the job, I called Pat and told
her about my legal status. After consulting with management, she called
me back with the answer I feared: I couldn't do the internship.

This was devastating. What good was college if I couldn't then pursue
the career I wanted? I decided then that if I was to succeed in a profession
that is all about truth-telling, I couldn't tell the truth about myself. . . .

For the summer of 2003, I applied for internships across the country.
Several newspapers, including *The Wall Street Journal*, *The Boston Globe* and
The Chicago Tribune, expressed interest. But when *The Washington Post* offered me a spot, I knew where I would go. And this time, I had no intention
of acknowledging my "problem."

The *Post* internship posed a tricky obstacle: It required a driver's license. 25
(After my close call at the California D.M.V., I'd never gotten one.) So I spent
an afternoon at the Mountain View Public Library, studying various states'
requirements. Oregon was among the most welcoming—and it was just a
few hours' drive north.

Again, my support network came through. A friend's father lived in Portland, and he allowed me to use his address as proof of residency. Pat, Rich and Rich's longtime assistant, Mary Moore, sent letters to me at that address. Rich taught me how to do three-point turns in a parking lot, and a friend accompanied me to Portland.

The license meant everything to me—it would let me drive, fly and work.... My license, issued in 2003, was set to expire eight years later, on my 30th birthday, on February 3, 2011. I had eight years to succeed professionally, and to hope that some sort of immigration reform would pass in the meantime and allow me to stay.

It seemed like all the time in the world.

My summer in Washington was exhilarating. I was intimidated to be in a major newsroom but was assigned a mentor—Peter Perl, a veteran magazine writer—to help me navigate it. A few weeks into the internship, he printed out one of my articles, about a guy who recovered a long-lost wallet, circled the first two paragraphs and left it on my desk. "Great eye for details—awesome!" he wrote. Though I didn't know it then, Peter would become one more member of my network.

At the end of the summer, I returned to *The San Francisco Chronicle*.   30 My plan was to finish school—I was now a senior—while I worked for *The Chronicle* as a reporter for the city desk. But when *The Post* beckoned again, offering me a full-time, two-year paid internship that I could start when I graduated in June 2004, it was too tempting to pass up. I moved back to Washington.

About four months into my job as a reporter for *The Post*, I began feeling increasingly paranoid, as if I had "illegal immigrant" tattooed on my forehead—and in Washington, of all places, where the debates over immigration seemed never-ending. I was so eager to prove myself that I feared I was annoying some colleagues and editors—and worried that any one of these professional journalists could discover my secret. The anxiety was nearly paralyzing. I decided I had to tell one of the higher-ups about my situation. I turned to Peter.... I told him everything: the Social Security card, the driver's license, Pat and Rich, my family.

Peter was shocked. "I understand you 100 times better now," he said. He told me that I had done the right thing by telling him, and that it was now our shared problem. He said he didn't want to do anything about it just yet. I had just been hired, he said, and I needed to prove myself. "When you've done enough," he said, "we'll tell Don and Len together." (Don Graham is the chairman of The Washington Post Company; Leonard Downie Jr. was then the paper's executive editor.) A month later, I spent my first Thanksgiving in Washington with Peter and his family.

In the five years that followed, I did my best to "do enough." I was promoted to staff writer, reported on video-game culture, wrote a series on Washington's H.I.V./AIDS epidemic and covered the role of technology and social media in the 2008 presidential race. I visited the White House, where I interviewed senior aides and covered a state dinner—and gave the Secret Service the Social Security number I obtained with false documents. . . .

It was an odd sort of dance: I was trying to stand out in a highly competitive newsroom, yet I was terrified that if I stood out too much, I'd invite unwanted scrutiny. I tried to compartmentalize my fears, distract myself by reporting on the lives of other people, but there was no escaping the central conflict in my life. Maintaining a deception for so long distorts your sense of self. You start wondering who you've become, and why.

In April 2008, I was part of a Post team that won a Pulitzer Prize for the   35
paper's coverage of the Virginia Tech shootings a year earlier. Lolo died a year earlier, so it was Lola who called me the day of the announcement. The first thing she said was, "*Anong mangyayari kung malaman ng mga tao?*"

What will happen if people find out?

I couldn't say anything. After we got off the phone, I rushed to the bathroom on the fourth floor of the newsroom, sat down on the toilet and cried.

In the summer of 2009, without ever having had that follow-up talk with top Post management, I left the paper and moved to New York to join *The Huffington Post.* . . .

While I worked at *The Huffington Post*, other opportunities emerged. My H.I.V./AIDS series became a documentary film called *The Other City*, which opened at the Tribeca Film Festival last year and was broadcast on Showtime. I began writing for magazines and landed a dream assignment: profiling Facebook's Mark Zuckerberg for *The New Yorker*.

The more I achieved, the more scared and depressed I became. I was   40
proud of my work, but there was always a cloud hanging over it, over me. My old eight-year deadline—the expiration of my Oregon driver's license— was approaching.

After slightly less than a year, I decided to leave *The Huffington Post*. In part, this was because I wanted to promote the documentary and write a book about online culture—or so I told my friends. But the real reason was, after so many years of trying to be a part of the system, of focusing all my energy on my professional life, I learned that no amount of professional success would solve my problem or ease the sense of loss and displacement I felt. I lied to a friend about why I couldn't take a weekend trip to Mexico. Another time I concocted an excuse for why I couldn't go on an all-expenses-paid trip to Switzerland. I have been unwilling, for years, to be in a long-term relationship because I never wanted anyone to get too close and ask too many questions. All the while, Lola's question was stuck in my head: What will happen if people find out?

Early this year, just two weeks before my thirtieth birthday, I won a small reprieve: I obtained a driver's license in the state of Washington. The license is valid until 2016. This offered me five more years of acceptable identification—but also five more years of fear, of lying to people I respect and institutions that trusted me, of running away from who I am.

I'm done running. I'm exhausted. I don't want that life anymore.

So I've decided to come forward, own up to what I've done, and tell my story to the best of my recollection. I've reached out to former bosses and employers and apologized for misleading them—a mix of humiliation and liberation coming with each disclosure. All the people mentioned in this article gave me permission to use their names. I've also talked to family and friends about my situation and am working with legal counsel to review my options. I don't know what the consequences will be of telling my story.

I do know that I am grateful to my grandparents, my Lolo and Lola, for 45 giving me the chance for a better life. I'm also grateful to my other family—the support network I found here in America—for encouraging me to pursue my dreams.

It's been almost 18 years since I've seen my mother. Early on, I was mad at her for putting me in this position, and then mad at myself for being angry and ungrateful. By the time I got to college, we rarely spoke by phone. It became too painful; after a while it was easier to just send money to help support her and my two half-siblings. My sister, almost 2 years old when I left, is almost 20 now. I've never met my 14-year-old brother. I would love to see them.

Not long ago, I called my mother. I wanted to fill the gaps in my memory about that August morning so many years ago. We had never discussed it. Part of me wanted to shove the memory aside, but to write this article and

Vargas describes events that took place over a period of 18 years. Learn the techniques he used to keep his narrative cohesive, on pp. 192–93.

Vargas has continued to advocate for immigration reform since the publication of this essay. At a political rally in December 2011, he raises a sign announcing his position—and raises his hand to ask politicians the hard questions that he argues must be addressed in order to change the conversation about immigration in America.

face the facts of my life, I needed more details. Did I cry? Did she? Did we kiss goodbye?

My mother told me I was excited about meeting a stewardess, about getting on a plane. She also reminded me of the one piece of advice she gave me for blending in: If anyone asked why I was coming to America, I should say I was going to Disneyland.

Thinking about the Text

1. Jose Antonio Vargas highlights issues about US immigration policy using details of his own experience, many of which are quite personal and probably difficult to admit. Point out three such details. What was your reaction to each of them? What is Vargas's **ARGUMENT** about immigration policy, and how do such details help him make that point?

2. Sprinkled throughout Vargas's narrative are bits of dialogue in Tagalog, the language of his Lolo and Lola. Given that he always provides the English translation, why might he have included the Tagalog? What function does it serve in his narrative?

3. How is Vargas's disclosure about his sexuality relevant to his point? Why might he have included it at all in telling about his immigrant experience? Support your response with evidence from the text.

4. Vargas **CONCLUDES** his narrative by recounting his mother's advice as he got on the plane: "If anyone asked why I was coming to America, I should say I was going to Disneyland" (48). Why do you think he ends this essay by mentioning Disneyland? What might he be implying? Did you find this ending effective—and if not, why not?

5. Vargas was fortunate to receive emotional and professional support from the teachers and employers to whom he disclosed his undocumented status. Imagine yourself in their place. How might you respond if one of your students or employees came to you admitting to being undocumented? What would you do, and why? And how would you come to a decision? What factors would need to be taken into consideration? Write an essay in which you respond to these questions, using your own personal judgment.

The (Native) American Dream
TATÉ WALKER

IN THE MIDST of Colorado Springs' urban sprawl, Monycka Snowbird (Ojibwe) raises fowl, goats, rabbits, and indigenous plants to feed and make household products for her family and neighbors.

About 650 miles north in a sprawling rural landscape on the Cheyenne River reservation in South Dakota, Karen Ducheneaux (Lakota) and her *tiospaye*[1] are slowly building a series of ecodomes and straw bale buildings powered by solar, wind, and water in an effort to disconnect from pollutants of mind, body, and earth.

The two women represent a growing number of Native people and organizations in the United States both on and off tribal land committed to leading clean, sustainable, and culturally competent lives.

The efforts of individuals like these women, in addition to the prevalence of companies specializing in mainstreaming indigenous foods and

1. *Tiospaye*: Lakota word for the concept of "extended family," "deliberate family," and "the making of family." Membership presumes support for and commitment to the group. [Editor's note]

TATÉ WALKER (they/them) is a Lakota (Cheyenne River Sioux, South Dakota) writer, photographer/videographer, and indigenous rights activist living in Phoenix. This article was published in 2015 in *Native Peoples: The Journal of the Heard Museum*. The Heard is an art museum in Phoenix founded in 1929 and dedicated to advancing American Indian art.

Monycka Snowbird works in the yard.

Tiospaye. Walker doesn't define it, but context clues help you understand. Using a word or phrase from an additional language can be an effective choice; check out pp. 685–93 to find out more.

non-profits committed to building energy efficient and sustainable housing in tribal communities, highlight the popularity and return of such lifestyles.

"Our people had this tiospaye system, where you really made a life with   5
the people you felt close to, and had skills that complemented each other," says Ducheneaux. "We've spent generations at this point getting away from that beautiful system, and we're taught the only way to be successful is to follow the American dream, which is one of autonomy and being paid for your skills."

The American dream, Ducheneaux says, doesn't work on the reservation.

"It's not in our nature to turn our back on people who need us," she continues. "Our people without even realizing it sometimes are still living in a tiospaye system, because any success we've had as a people—success in material wealth—is because we can depend on each other."

Studies show food stability, affordability, and access is severely limited for Native communities. According to a report from the USDA's Economic Research Service released in December, just 25.6 percent of all tribal areas were within a mile's distance from a supermarket, compared with 58.8 percent of the total U.S. population.

The latest USDA data also shows 23.5 million people nationwide live in a food desert—that is to say, their access to a grocery store and healthy, affordable food is limited—and more than half of those people are low income. Many tribal communities and urban areas with high populations of Native people are considered food deserts.

Given the staggering rates of poverty, diseases like diabetes, and unem- 10
ployment for Natives nationwide—higher for those living on reservations—
both Snowbird and Ducheneaux point to the many economic and health
benefits of individuals creating their own energies, whether it's food, fuel
and power, or social capital.

Returning to traditional roots in a literal sense is also what drives Snowbird, who has lived in Colorado Springs for more than 20 years. "We as indigenous people have gotten farther away from our traditional food sources
than anyone else in this country, and I think that's why we have this sort of
swelling epidemic of diabetes and obesity in Indian Country, because we're
losing the knowledge of our traditional foods," says Snowbird, 40.

Some 440,000 people live in the Colorado Springs area, and Snowbird
works with both Native and non-Native organizations throughout her region to educate and promote the benefits of urban food production, known
in some places as backyard or micro farming. She leads educational classes
for children and adults, including seed cultivation, plant recognition, harvesting, livestock butchering, and more.

"You can't be sovereign if you can't feed yourself," says Snowbird, borrowing a line from Winona LaDuke (Anishinaabe), an environmental activist
and founder of Honor the Earth. "One of the ways colonizers controlled Indian
people was to take our food sources away. Let's reclaim our food.

"We have to teach our kids it's not just about preserving our cultures
and language; it's about restorative stewardship and about knowing where
food comes from, who tribally it comes from," Snowbird says. "Indigenous
food is medicine. And food brings everyone together." . . .

Snowbird learned to appreciate indigenous food systems from her father, 15
who hunted wild game and imparted an appreciation for knowing where
your dinner comes from and how to prepare it beyond simply opening a box
and heating up the contents.

But being known throughout Colorado Springs as "the Goat Lady" and
earning a reputation as a knowledgeable indigenous educator didn't happen
until a few years ago, when Snowbird spearheaded a city-wide movement to
change and educate people on the local laws of urban food production.

Now Snowbird manages the Colorado Springs Urban Homesteading
support group, which boasts roughly 1,200 members. Through that group,
Snowbird leads several classes per season on animal husbandry, butchering,
and more with her fiery brand of wit and know-how.

Perhaps closer to her heart, however, are the lessons she imparts to the city's urban Native youth. Colorado Springs School District 11, in which Snowbird's two daughters, ages 11 and 13, are enrolled, has the only Title VII Indian Education Program in the city.

"I talk to Title VII kids about what indigenous food is—that it's not just buffalo or corn," she explains. "I try to break it down for them in terms of what they ate at lunch that day, even if it was junk food."

Thanks in large part to Snowbird's efforts, the program has several gar- 20 den beds and a greenhouse growing traditional Native edibles, including Apache brown-striped sunflower seeds, . . . Pueblo chiles, and more.

"I come in sometimes and kids are bouncing off all the walls," Snowbird says. "But the moment you get their hands in the dirt, it's like all that contact with the earth just calms them."

The children also learn to grow, harvest and cook with chokecherries, prickly pears, beans, and other local vegetation.

"Starting the kids off with food lets us also discuss Indian issues without putting people on the defensive," Snowbird explains. "It's hard to get mad when you're talking about food."

Re-introducing and re-popularizing indigenous foods and traditional cooking, especially among Native youth, will help strengthen Native people and the communities they live in, Snowbird insists.

Snowbird admits maintaining a lifestyle committed to food sovereignty 25 can be hard on her tight budget. However, she says it helps her save and earn money in the long run. Snowbird is able to collect, grow, use and sell or barter with the milk, eggs, meat, vegetables, cleaning and toiletry items, and other useful goods produced on her property.

"I'm not completely self-sufficient by any means. But urban homesteading . . . is about as traditional as you can get," she insists. "It's living off the land within the radius of where you live and knowing the Creator has put what you need right where you are." . . .

For outsiders following along on Facebook as Ducheneaux and her family transition to living efficiently and sustainably, the process of building an ecodome and maintaining a traditional garden may have seemed as easy as digging a hole.

Except that the hole in question—12 feet across and 4 to 6 feet deep in which the ecodome sits—took three months to dig out back in 2012, thanks to heavy rains and a landscape of gumbo.

Weaving textiles and harvesting corn, two ways Snowbird practices sustainability.

"It was so much work," Ducheneaux recalls. "We had to move the gumbo out one wheelbarrow at a time."

But the effort, shared by about seven members of Ducheneaux's 30 tiospaye—including her mom, siblings, and their spouses, as well as volunteers—has been well worth it.

On 10 acres of family land on the Cheyenne River reservation, Ducheneaux and her family are creating the Tatanka Wakpala Model Sustainable Community. The family has funded the project with help from Honor the Earth and Bread of Life Church . . .

The shell of the small, ecodome home—which the family learned to build via video and trial-by-error—is complete, and a garden featuring plants indigenous to the area produces hundreds of pounds of produce each year.

Considering hers is a reservation located within counties consistently listed as some of the poorest in the nation, and recognizing the tribe suffers from insufficient and inefficient housing where utility bills can reach into the high hundreds or more during the winter months, Ducheneaux hopes her family's model sparks a trend for other tribal members.

"We really believe that even people who aren't eco-friendly will be inspired by our use of wind and solar energy. We put up our own electric system and we'll never have to pay another utility bill," Ducheneaux says.

"We were waiting for the blueprint to drop in our laps. Then we realized 35 no one was going to do it for us, so we said we'd do it ourselves. We'll make mistakes and figure it out." . . .

"What we have going on out there is a desire to be more self-sufficient. When we sat around talking about this, we asked ourselves, 'What do we need?'" Ducheneaux explains. "We needed to start feeding ourselves and taking responsibility for our own food needs.... Not just growing food and raising animals, but going back to our Lakota traditions and treating the Earth respectfully by using what it gives us."...

Living in an urban or reservation setting provides those who want to live sustainably unique challenges, both Snowbird and Ducheneaux say.

"One of the challenges is being so far away from everything," Ducheneaux says of rural reservation life. "For a lot of our volunteers, it's eye-opening for them that the hardware store is a one-hour trip just in one direction."

Planning far ahead is key, Ducheneaux says.

Infrastructure, including a severe lack of Internet connectivity, weather, 40 and a disinterested tribal government can also be setbacks, although Ducheneaux notes the latter can benefit sustainability projects due to few, if any, restrictions on things like harvesting rainwater or land use.

For urban Natives, being disconnected from tribal knowledge—for instance, the indigenous names and uses of plants—is a major disadvantage, Snowbird said.

When someone in the community comes forward with that knowledge, it's often exploited for profit, and the people who would benefit most—namely Native youth—are left out.

"I always find it surprising how removed from the whole food process people are; they don't know or care where their food comes from," says Snowbird, who harvests edibles on hikes through the mountains or on strolls through downtown. She tries to combat this by giving eggs and other food produced on her property to those who wouldn't—or couldn't—normally buy organic in a supermarket.

"Pretty soon those people are asking me for more eggs and then we're talking about how they can get started with chickens in their backyard or growing herbs on their window sills," Snowbird says, adding those conversations eventually lead to discussions on indigenous issues, regardless of whether the person is Native or not. "We're trying to put the culture back in agriculture."

Thinking about the Text

1. Taté Walker highlights two projects that, according to one of their leaders, are "trying to put the culture back in agriculture" (44). What does that statement mean and what is its underlying concept? How well does Walker explain that concept? Why do you think so? Point to specific examples to support your conclusion.

2. Walker's interviewee Monycka Snowbird expresses surprise and dismay that people don't know or care where their food comes from. How much do you know about the plant (and perhaps animal) sources of what you eat? Would you, for example, recognize a potato plant? an avocado tree? Are you satisfied with your current level of knowledge? Does reading Walker's article motivate you to learn more about where your food comes from? Why or why not?

3. Without thinking about the original source of Walker's article, what impression do you have of its intended audience? Point to **EVIDENCE** to support your reasoning. What might Walker have done differently if writing for a magazine or blog with a nearly all-Native readership or a large-circulation daily newspaper? Why do you think so? Explain your responses.

4. Much of the writing that promotes organic, locally sourced food emphasizes the health aspects of those choices, but Walker's interviewees take a broader approach—the health aspects of communities and the environment itself. What are some of the most serious problems facing your local community? Might a project based on any of the practices described by Walker serve to address one or more of these problems? If so, how? Describe what you envision might happen. If not, why not? Discuss your ideas with classmates.

5. Walker's article focuses on indigenous communities in Colorado and South Dakota. Not so long ago, however, virtually every region of the now United States was occupied by indigenous communities that derived their foods, depending on climate and geographical conditions, in the ways that Snowbird and Ducheneaux describe. What are/were the traditional foods of the area where you live? What did the Native people of your region plant? How were meals prepared from these foods? Write a **REPORT**; do **RESEARCH** using library sources, museums, online sources, and perhaps interviews with older relatives or neighbors. Be sure to appropriately document all of the sources you find.

King Coal and the West Virginia Mine Wars Museum

CAROLYNE WHELAN

WILMA STEELE SITS ON HER SCREENED PORCH and watches the last of the apples fall from her tree. It's a beautiful, crisp day in Mingo County, West Virginia. Inside, there is still a faint dampness from when the house flooded as the result of nearby mountaintop removal, but on the porch, the dry air has that warm autumn smell of leaves and soil. Steele has lived in this region all her life, and her lineage traces back deep into the earth of Mingo County as far as she can follow it, like light in the abandoned mine shaft down the street. She is one of the founders of the West Virginia Mine Wars Museum, located in Matewan, Mingo County, and on October 1, as she accepted a Coal Heritage Award from the Coal Heritage Highway Authority on behalf of the museum, Don Blankenship wrapped up the first day of his closed trial.

Don Blankenship was also born and raised in Mingo County—his mother was a McCoy, a descendant of the infamous enemies of the Hat-fields.[1] He and Steele went to school together, but after that, their paths

---

1. *McCoy/Hatfield*: Two coal-country families whose decades-long nineteenth-century feud became folk legend; the two surnames evoke never-ending bitterness and rancor. [Editor's note]

CAROLYNE WHELAN is a Pittsburgh-based freelance writer whose work has appeared in a diverse range of publications. She is editor of a mountain bike lifestyle magazine and writes about adventure travel and community. This essay is from the anthology *Voices from the Rust Belt* (2018).

diverged: while Steele became a high school art teacher—and a member of her teachers' union—Blankenship climbed the ladder of corporate coal, ultimately becoming the chairman and CEO of Massey Energy Company and, according to *The New York Times*, "one of West Virginia's most feared and powerful figures," the kind of man who pumps toxic slurry back into the ground to save his company money and throws his breakfast if it's not to his liking. In April 2010, twenty-nine miners died as the result of an explosion at one of Massey's mines, Upper Big Branch; Blankenship subsequently was accused of scheming with others at the company to violate safety rules and deceive regulators. The trial holding a CEO responsible for the deaths of his company's workers was the first of its kind, and the results[2] could set a precedent for future corporate leaders. Although the West Virginia Mine Wars Museum focuses on the history of the region, Steele believes that in light of the Upper Big Branch explosion and the trial, the historical narrative is applicable today.

"The mines used to own people by owning their homes, their stores, their churches, their schools," Steele says. "Now, they don't need to, because they own people's minds. It's much more psychological." The coal companies donate money to the local schools, she says, so the teachers will endorse the industry. In response to reports of coal-based pollution and sick children, it was the teachers who wrote to the paper to discredit the accusations as liberal propaganda, Steele says, and it wasn't until a reporter visited Marsh Fork Elementary School and with his finger wiped up a layer of coal dirt to show to the camera that the area finally started to take notice.

It wasn't always this way. The region has a rich history of people banding together and pushing back against the industry, dating back to the West Virginia Mine Wars. The wars, which took place from 1910 to 1922—starting with the union aggregation that led to the first official strike in 1912—involved more than ten thousand miners who went on strike repeatedly over low wages and deadly working conditions. The West Virginia Mine Wars Museum chronicles it all. The exhibits culminate with information on the 1921 Miners' March that led to the Battle of Blair Mountain: with ten thousand miners on strike, this was the largest armed uprising of US citizens outside of wartime, and federal troops were called in to break it up. Also included in the museum's collection are artifacts from coal camp life, including a replica of the tent colonies where miner families lived when they

Interviewee Wilma Steele offers a wealth of historical information, and Whelan combines direct quotations with paraphrases of Steele's comments. Find guidelines for quoting, paraphrasing, and summarizing on p. 542.

2. In 2016, Blankenship was convicted and sentenced to a year in prison.

were kicked out of their company homes for striking. If the museum narrative were to continue into the present day, Don Blankenship might have his photo in the museum in association with his own wars against laborers: In 1984, a strike at Blackberry Creek against Massey turned bloody and lasted more than a year. Blankenship, for his part, was largely concerned about his television, which, famously, was allegedly shot by pro-union forces.

The first displays upon entering the museum are bookshelves full of historic artifacts. During a tour, Steele takes great care to explain the personal history of an oil lantern used to light the way for the miners. "My dad, he worked in the mine with all different people, and it didn't matter where you were from and what you looked like—if you were union brothers, you were union brothers," she says. "A couple years ago, he went to visit with an old friend from the mine, an African American man, and the friend showed him this old lantern. My dad told him his daughter collected old stuff like this to help preserve it, and the man said, 'Then you give this to your daughter to look after and keep safe.' So it's here now, and to me its presence here in the museum is a tribute not only to my father and to that man, but to the friendship between them, that saw each other as brothers. Funny, isn't it," she muses as she puts the lantern back down, "this article that was created for safety was really just another thing that could have blown up in their faces."

There is a lot of love in the museum that has gone toward making that part of history clear: the role all people had in the labor strikes and mine wars. Many of the group photos of union members and of families—including the ones that show people peeping out of the holes slit in tents by the Baldwin-Felts agents hired to destroy the shelters—show people of all backgrounds.

The building where the West Virginia Mine Wars Museum is located was rented for a year and a half prior to the museum's opening. As in much of Matewan, the building is one of the original structures of the town, and still contains bullet holes from the shoot-out between Sid Hatfield, a union sympathizer and the police chief of Matewan during the Battle of Matewan, and the mine's hired guards. Most of the museum's founders had been working together on the project for two years, with creative director and exhibition designer Shaun Slifer joining the team when the space was rented about six months later. Slifer has been installing exhibits for a decade in museums, including the Carnegie Museum of Art, the Frick Art & Historical Center, and others.

"It is a bit strange to think about a museum coming together so quickly, especially when in Pittsburgh the museums are these official and long-standing establishments," Slifer says. "But there was a lot of work behind the scenes before we got to the place we are now." While the West Virginia Mine Wars Museum may have opened its doors relatively quickly, the same techniques and attention to detail went into the design of this small storefront museum as in those larger budget spaces. There are videos of historic newsreels as well as oral histories playing from a parabolic speaker. There is also much to read at each display, and large quotes in vinyl dance along the walls to help guide the narrative.

While there is something about the artifacts that feels profoundly American, many items sing of the rich cultural heritage brought overseas by immigrants seeking a better life and finding themselves in the hollow of Matewan. One display at the museum specifically showcases such multicultural relics, though the nods to the miners' homelands can be seen in so many of the photos: kilts and embroidered vests with paisley designs, the clothing of people holding on to their past while working to create a brighter future. That these cultures persevered is ironically the work of the mine owners themselves, who, according to historians of the museum, purposefully kept each culture apart. As immigrants came off the boats in New York, they were offered jobs at the mine, given places to live in their own area of Matewan, and assigned to a shift where they worked according to ethnicity of origin. Cultures were not shared and other languages were not learned, all of which was a tool of the mine owners to avoid unionization—when the miners didn't know each other, they could resent each other and animosity could grow, which kept them from finding common ground for demanding fair wages and safe conditions.

Ultimately, the groups did meet, talk, and unionize. The red bandannas 10 they wore, originally produced in Scotland with designs taken from Hungarian and Persian traditional patterns, are a tribute to that blending. They were worn like a uniform, a simple way to tell who was on their side. One origin of the word "redneck" derives from these bandannas: the term, which is now used with some amount of xenophobia to refer to small-minded people who typically live in rural Southern areas, in this sense is actually a nod to diversity and working together for a common good. In a photo of the burial of Sid Hatfield, funeral attendees can be seen wearing patterns found in the bandannas, as well as Scottish kilts, lace, and other formal attire brought along during long boat rides to America.

"Today," Steele sighs, her gaze extending into the rich green forest just beyond her porch, "without the unions bringing people together, there is more bigotry. Just how they've always wanted it, keeping workers apart instead of fighting together." Steele's husband, Terry, a retired mine worker and member of the United Mine Workers Association (UMWA) union, agrees. The way he sees it, today's workers are paid good wages and when they are let go, it's blamed on the increasing government regulations that cost King Coal money in upkeep. But the regulations are necessary for the people to live, because they affect their own drinking water and air quality, their own children's welfare.

Unions are a contentious topic in Mingo County, with no active miners among the 850 members of the UMWA; many miners blame the union and the government for the hard times miners are facing as interest in coal diminishes.

Indeed, some in King Coal country are doing worse than others. Although Blankenship now lives in Tennessee, he maintained his home in Mingo County until retirement (though once his actions at Massey polluted the water, he did have special plumbing installed to source clean water from outside the county—a luxury not available to his workers and neighbors). Since the Upper Big Branch disaster, critics of Blankenship seem to have no difficulty seeing evil in his beady eyes and villainous mustache. Certainly, they've been given little reason to see anything else. Maybe it's her art teacher openheartedness, or her love for her fellow West Virginians, but Steele is the first to comment on the complexity of Blankenship: He's not quite evil, and that's perhaps even more dangerous.

"He's the kind of person who really listens to people, really tries to figure out who they are," she says. "When we were in school, he was a nice guy, I mean a really nice person." When asked what happened to make Blankenship grow up to be the type of person who would care so little for his fellows, she could only shrug: "Coal got him." When he originally came to Massey as an office manager, she says, he could have cleaned up a lot of King Coal's practices. Instead, he became known as the leading force against the UMWA. When the victims from the Upper Big Branch explosion were autopsied, it was revealed that 71 percent of them suffered from black lung, the deadly coal dust disease. The industry average is 3.2 percent.

Blankenship has visited the West Virginia Mine Wars Museum, pre-   15
sumably curious as to what version of history the museum might tell, and how far back and forward along Mingo County's coal lineage it dared

tread. Elijah Hooker, now a board member who was stationed at the museum's front desk during two of Blankenship visits and who spoke with him at length, dismisses any notion of malicious intent. "The mere fact that a young man was working for a museum that is essentially the antithesis to everything in which Blankenship's creed, or system of beliefs, has stood in opposition towards, most likely left him in a state of curiosity," says Hooker via email, in explanation of what interest Blankenship may have had in talking with him. "[He] came to the museum out of genuine motives. After all, Matewan is his home; this museum does impart the history of [his community]. While it may take a particular stance, I feel that there was genuine intrigue involved with Don's visit to our museum, one in which no ulterior motives were attached—simply curiosity as to what was going on in the area he considers to be home." Hooker does not believe Blankenship is necessarily the monster he's portrayed to be, one who had specific intentions of killing twenty-nine workers, but rather is someone who made some gross errors in judgment during his time as CEO. Perhaps he just saw the dollars and cents of business much more clearly than the people who were hidden in the mines, the ones who put that money in the Massey account.

Still, the tension between King Coal and those preserving its true history is palpable. "He went through the museum and spent over an hour there [during one visit], and it's a very small place. He took pictures, read all the texts," says Dr. Chuck Keeney, museum board member and history professor at Southern West Virginia Community and Technical College. "Then after, he and I spoke for a bit. He and I of course have a different heritage, his background being a union-buster, and I have union leaders in my heritage. So we're on opposite sides." This opposition is a point of conflict for the museum, daring to tell the history of unions in an area whose union members currently are largely retired miners.

"The conflict over coal has become over the years to be a conflict of memory. King Coal is not going to disappear. It's still a powerful force, and a powerful social force," Keeney says, and in this memory and storytelling lies the burden and joy of opening up an independent museum. "We were able to include quotes and facts that a state-sponsored museum wouldn't be able to do. It's quite enjoyable, to not have to be politically correct, to not have to pander to donors who have their own agendas or are concerned about image."

Ultimately, the West Virginia Mine Wars Museum tells the story of a time when coal was everything, and of a future when it might not be. That's certainly the case for Blankenship. Sid Hatfield probably never dreamed of the day when something like a mine explosion would put the company boss on trial, and maybe there is a future for citizens of West Virginia in which mine explosions themselves are an archaic story relegated to Plexiglas displays. In the meantime, we can study our past, celebrate it, and learn from it.

Thinking about the Text

1. Carolyne Whelan's **REPORT** on the West Virginia Mine Wars Museum makes frequent reference to "King Coal." Who, or what, is King Coal? Whelan never actually defines the term. Do you think she should have? Why or why not? Explain your reasoning.

2. The events that the museum focuses on occurred from 1910 to 1922—about a century ago, but Whelan asserts, "the historical narrative is applicable today" (2). What is something that you are involved in now that could be worth documenting for people of the twenty-second century? What **NARRATIVE** would you like them to know?

3. Whelan offers a glimpse into the history of an important region and industry, but she is doing more than documenting names, dates, and events. What is Whelan's **PURPOSE** in writing this report? How did you arrive at your response? Point to passages that support your conclusion.

4. As Whelan mentions, many people in West Virginia and elsewhere see Don Blankenship as an evil villain. Still, she points out that Wilma Steele as well as museum board member Elijah Hooker present a more nuanced view of Blankenship as not necessarily "the monster he's portrayed to be" (15). Why might Steele and Hooker be more inclined to take a broader view of Blankenship? What factors influence each of their opinions?

5. What do you know about the history of your own community? What (or perhaps who) are the main streets and landmarks named for? Identify something that you pass by every day without particularly noticing—perhaps a building, a monument, a bridge, a factory—and research its history. Write a **REPORT** about that history and focus your report on some interesting detail that catches your attention. You may want to begin with online sources, but the bulk of your research should be offline resources such as a local library or museum, or perhaps interviews with people who remember an event relevant to the focus of your report.

The Internet Is Not Ruining Grammar

JESSICA WILDFIRE

MILLENNIALS CATCH A LOT OF FLAK—for their selfies, their avocado toast, and their unconventional spelling. I work at a university, and I can't go a week without hearing someone complain about how the internet has corrupted English.

"Nobody cares about proofreading anymore," one professor told me a few days ago. "Smartphones have ruined our students."

Young people's grammar is practically the only thing you can get faculty to agree on these days. "Oh, they can't spell or punctuate at all," I hear. It's the ultimate echo chamber.

Grammarians have published hundreds of books and op-eds declaiming the end of language as we know it. All because of one evil technology. On top of that, I've gotten more than one email from Grammarly reps wanting me to adopt their app for my classroom. They promise to magically remove errors from my students' writing.

But not so fast. What if I *want* them to make "errors"? What if I want ₅ them to play around with language?

JESSICA WILDFIRE is (presumably) the *nom de plume*, or pen name, of a writer and teacher—a "twisted professor," as her bio states—who publishes essays on issues of grammar, gender, self-development, popular culture, and more; the image that always accompanies her writing may or may not resemble the actual author. This essay first appeared on *Medium* in August 2018.

Language Is Always Changing

Here's the truth: Young people aren't breaking the rules. The rules are changing. As linguists know, language lives in a constant flux. You can't pin it down. Even what we think of as a single language has several varieties—dialects, regionalisms, accents.

Each variety has its own standards and ways of deviating from them. People cross back and forth between language borders, sneaking words and rules across customs.

You can't build walls between languages and their varieties any more than you can hope to build a wall between two countries. You can try, but it won't work. As poet Robert Frost said:

> Something there is that doesn't love a wall,
> That sends the frozen-ground-swell under it,
> And spills the upper boulders in the sun;
> And makes gaps even two can pass abreast.

You can't build walls around languages, and you can't keep them from morphing. Language is like water. The internet has dissolved all kinds of barriers over recent decades. It's also ushering in new ways of communicating, including new modes of grammar.

Welcome to the Period

We don't even really understand most of our silly rules. They didn't always [10] exist. They evolved. For starters, consider the period. This bit of punctuation has been around a while, first originating in the third century with Greek philosopher Aristophanes and becoming more common in the 15th century thanks to Italian printer and publisher Aldus Manutius. They work for me. I like periods. They're handy.

But let's not fool ourselves into believing they're timeless. Our use of periods has changed a helluva lot since their invention. Of course, they have their uses. When we're writing an email or a report, they help us end our sentences.

But guess what? If you end a text with a period, that means you're pissed off. It's why so many people drop them from messages on their phones and on social media. Online, the meaning of a period changes.

Americans have lived in crisis mode for centuries when it comes to punctuation and spelling. English courses for freshmen in college began appearing in earnest around the turn of the 20th century, in part because everyone was freaking out about students' spelling and grammar.

Since then, things have stayed pretty much the same. No better, no worse. And there's nothing extra we can or should do about it. Let language play.

How We Learn Grammar

The average American feels entitled to correct the grammar in every tweet 15 they see. And yet they probably have no idea how we even learn grammar. Put simply, we acquire the rules by *living* them. Not by learning them. Not through worksheets. Or tests. Most humans have all the grammatical knowledge they need before they even finish elementary school.

Kids know how to construct sentences.

The problem is written punctuation. Again, we don't learn that by drills or memorizing rules. Almost every study in education, linguistics, and writing points to the same conclusion: We learn to punctuate by reading. Intuitively.

Honestly, do you really understand every single piece of logic that dictates when a sentence ends? Can you give a perfect definition of a sentence? I'll bet you can't. The best grammar guides in the world can't.

If there's one thing I'd like people to understand, it's this: You can never teach grammar by explaining it.

The internet doesn't cause bad grammar. Bad schooling does. Bad expla- 20 nations do. And we accomplish nothing through hysterics. All our testing of students has done nothing but make things worse.

What a lot of people consider bad grammar isn't bad at all. Just different.

Usage Matters Most

A handful of snobs have always tried to tell everyone else how to write and speak. Look back at the history of English and you'll find hundreds of guides on how to use language "properly." These "experts" took rules from other languages—like Latin—and forced them on English. That's where we get the absurd warning against ending sentences with prepositions.

In Latin, it's actually impossible to end a sentence with a preposition. English allows you to.

So do it.

Apply this idea to social media and you'll understand what's happen- 25
ing. People who communicate online, with phones, are developing their own usage conventions. Ones that make sense to them.

These conventions include simplified, alternate spellings. Abbreviations. Emojis. And innovations in punctuation.

It's not about error in the old-school sense. Languages have always evolved, and curmudgeons have always whined about it. Roman school teachers did, just like your grandparents do now.

Different World, Different Rules

Nearly a decade ago, linguist David Crystal published a book titled *Txting: The Gr8 Db8*. He wrote it in response to all those doomsayers announcing the start of the apocalypse shortly after the launch of Twitter. Crystal's book gathered mounds of evidence to show how young people, or internet users in general, understand grammar.

Many of us believe students use text-speak in their academic writing now because they don't know any better. Yet studies by linguists have shown that most students actually *do* know how to switch back and forth. If they use Twitterisms, they're doing so intentionally. Or because they're in a hurry.

Not because they're stupid. Or uneducated. 30

As linguists already know, this is how people grow up in multilingual environments. They don't sit in classrooms memorizing rules, correcting sentences, and filling out conjugation tables. They talk on the street. They watch movies. They sing along to their favorite songs. They make mistakes. Over and over again.

Language standardization is important. But not for its own sake.

Yes, standardized rules help people understand each other better. But we need to stop treating every single deviation from standard English as a sin—especially online. It's not. Instead, we should educate everyone about the malleability of language and how grammars change situationally and over time. It's a lot harder than being a traditionalist, but maybe it's worth a shot.

We agree. It's *not* about "errors in the old school sense." Still, we have a whole chapter about editing errors that matter. What's the deal? It's about what's appropriate in academic writing. Check out Ch. 33.

Thinking about the Text

1. Jessica Wildfire boldly asserts "Let language play" (14). What does she mean by that? Who is the **AUDIENCE** she is trying to persuade? Why? Do you agree? Why or why not?

2. According to Wildfire, periods in text messages are used differently than periods in longer prose. In texts, she notes, a period indicates anger. Do you agree with her assessment? Why or why not? How do you read a period in a text message? What factors might influence your interpretation (length of the message, how well you know the sender, etc.)? Why?

3. We don't actually know who Wildfire is—not her real name or where she teaches, her academic background, or anything other than the cryptic phrases she uses in her online bios. We take it on faith that the accompanying image truly depicts the author. Does the lack of concrete information interfere with her ability to speak with **AUTHORITY** on the topic of grammar rules and grammar learning? Why or why not? Explain your reasoning.

4. Regardless of where or how you were previously schooled, by the time you've reached the writing class you're taking now, you have surely encountered some rules of English grammar. Wildfire advocates eliminating the explicit teaching of grammar, **ARGUING** that such instruction simply isn't effective and that students will learn grammar rules naturally, "by living them" (15). Do you agree? Why or why not? Explain your reasoning.

5. As Wildfire notes, people who use their phones a lot for written communications "are developing their own usage conventions" (25). What usage conventions are you developing? Probably you are conscious of some of them, while others are more automatic and unnoticed. Look over your texts, tweets, and other online communications, and spend a day or two paying attention to what conventions you use in each communication and what your reasons are in that specific moment. Then write a brief personal usage guide similar to what you might find in a handbook or style guide. Include punctuation, capitalization, spelling, abbreviations, emoji use, and any other factors you consider relevant.

Credits

ILLUSTRATIONS

Part I: 2 (left to right) Last Refuge/robertharding/Alamy Stock Photo; Kevin Standage/Shutterstock; Heritage Images/Getty Images; 3 Imagno/Getty Images; 4 Google and the Google logo are registered trademarks of Google LLC, used with permission.

Chapter 1: 6 (left) AP Photo/Nam Y. Huh; (right) Mark Peterson/Redux; 7 Jim Bourg/Reuters/Newscom; 12 James Leynse/Corbis via Getty Images; 14 (left) Heinz Kluetmeier/Sports Illustrated/Getty Images; (right) Scott K. Brown/Sports Illustrated/Getty Images; 16 "Molecular Structure of Nucleic Acids," J. D. Watson and F. H. C. Crick. *Nature*, Vol. 171, April 25, 1953.

Chapter 2: 19 ©Grizelda; 22 (left) Dylan Marron and Adam Cecil; (right) Dylan Marron and Night Vale Presents; 23 Michael Ochs Archives/Getty Images; 25 Smallz & Raskind/Getty Images for Samsung; 26 Vecteezy.com.

Chapter 3: 29 (top left) Rawpixel Ltd/Alamy Stock Photo; (bottom left) Courtesy of Beverly Moss; (right) iStockphoto; 32 Rob Cottingham-SocialSignal.com.

Chapter 4: 41 (clockwise from top left) Bart Nijs fotografie/Hollandse Hoogte/Redux; Lorenzo Moscia/Archivolatino/Redux; Pierre Bessard/REA/Redux; AP Photo/The Northern Star, Jerry Burnes; Manjunath Kiran/AFP/Getty Images; Roberto Caccuri/Contrasto/Redux.

Chapter 5: 51 (clockwise from top left) Erik S Lesser/EPA/Shutterstock; Xinhua/eyevine/Redux; Stephane Audras/Rea/Redux; Oliver Lantzendorffer/iStock; Justin Lane/EPA-EFE/Shutterstock; Agnieszka Olek/caia image/Alamy Stock Photo; 62 Fancy/Alamy.

Chapter 6: 68 Davor Bakara Illustration; 75 Shinola Detroit/Partners & Spade.

Chapter 7: 80 Barbara Smaller, *The New Yorker* ©Conde Nast; 83 (right) Bartleby.com; (left) Katherine Stone; 85 Timothy Mulholland/Alamy; 87 From *The Family: Diversity, Inequality, and Social Change*, Second Edition, by Philip N. Cohen. Copyright © 2018, 2015 by W. W. Norton & Company, Inc. Used by permission of W. W. Norton & Company, Inc.; 93 Julianna Hernandez.

Chapter 8: 99 Matt Wuerker/Andrews McMeel Syndication; 101 Chainsawsuit.com by Kris Straub; 104 (base image) still from *The Day after Tomorrow*: 20th Century Fox/Kobal/Shutterstock; 105 (G20 2017 photo) Kayhan Ozer/Anadolu Agency/Getty Images; (Putin photo) Reuters/Alexander Zemlianichenko/Newscom; 106 YouTube.

Part III: 110 Robert Judges/Shutterstock; 111 Granger, NYC.

Chapter 9: 114 (top right) wavebreakmedia/Shutterstock; (top left) racorn/Shutterstock; (bottom) Chris Schmidt/iStock/Getty Images; 121 Fine Art Images/Heritage Images/Getty Images.

Chapter 10: 124 Robert Whitaker/Getty Images; 126 SOPA Images Limited/Alamy Stock Photo 129 J. Emilio Flores/The New York Times/Redux.

Part IV: 135 (clockwise from top left) British Museum/Art Resource, NY; World History Archive/Alamy; DeAgostini/Getty Images; National Postal Museum, Smithsonian Institution; Radu Razvan/iStockphoto; Nikada/iStockphoto; Izabela Habur/Getty Images; Hans Guldenmund/akg-mages.

Chapter 11: 138 ©2006 Roz Chast, The New Yorker Collection, Cartoonbank. All rights reserved.

Chapter 12: 145 blakes11/iStockphoto; 151 Erica Leong; 153 anyaivanova/iStockphoto/Getty Images; 155 Stephen Brashear/Getty Images; 162 AP Photo/Rob Carr; 172 Karsten Lemm/picture alliance/Newscom; 177 Courtesy of Katherine Spriggs; 178 Timothy Mulholland/Alamy; 179 Pgiam/iStockphoto; 180 BanksPhotos/iStockphoto; 182 WendellandCarolyn/iStockphoto.

Chapter 13: 188 ©Jamaal Rolle, thecelebrityartist.com; 189 Art by Dr. Erin K. Bahl, courtesy of DALN; 190 AP Photo/Scott Boehm; 191 It Gets Better Project itgetsbetter.org; 195 Kyle Terada/USA TODAY Sports/Newscom; 198 Bettmann/Corbis via Getty Images; 202 Raya Kheirbek; 204 AP Photo/Ross D. Franklin; 209 Melanie Luken-Teng; 219 Eric Dutro; 224 Courtesy Larry Lehna.

TEXT

About the Authors

ANDREA LUNSFORD is Professor Emerita of English at Stanford University and is on the faculty at the Bread Loaf School of English. Her scholarly interests include rhetorical theory, women and the history of rhetoric, collaboration, style, and technologies of writing. She's received the Braddock and Shaughnessy awards for her research on audience and classical rhetoric, and the CCCC Exemplar Award. She is currently at work on *The Norton Anthology of Rhetoric and Writing*.

MICHAL BRODY is a linguist. She was a founding faculty member of the Universidad de Oriente in Yucatán, Mexico. Her scholarly work centers on language pedagogy and politics in the United States and Mexico, and she recently led a writing workshop for personnel of the secretaría de las Mujeres in Mérida, Yucatán. She's a coauthor of *What's Language Got to Do with It?* and *The Little Seagull Handbook,* and the editor of the *Everyone's an Author Tumblr* and *They Say / I Blog*.

LISA EDE is Professor Emerita of English at Oregon State University, where she directed the Center for Writing and Learning and taught courses in composition, rhetoric, and literacy studies. She's received the Braddock and Shaughnessy awards for her research on audience and classical rhetoric. Her recent books include *Situating Composition: Composition Studies and the Politics of Location* and (with Andrea Lunsford) *Writing Together: Collaboration in Theory and Practice*.

BEVERLY MOSS is Associate Professor of English at The Ohio State University, where she teaches in the Rhetoric, Composition, and Literacy program, and is director of the Bread Loaf Teacher Network for the Middlebury Bread Loaf School of English. Her research and teaching interests focus on community literacy, composition theory and pedagogy, and writing center theories and practices. Her books include *Literacy across Communities* and *A Community Text Arises: A Literate Text and a Literacy Tradition in African-American Churches*.

CAROLE CLARK PAPPER has spent four decades teaching writing and rhetoric. Prior to retiring from Hofstra University, where she directed the University Writing Center, she served for many years as the Director of the Ball State University Writing Program (winner of the CCCC Certificate of Excellence 2006–2007). Her continuing scholarly interests include visual literacy, composition theory and pedagogy, and writing center theories and practices.

KEITH WALTERS is Professor Emeritus of Applied Linguistics at Portland State University, where he taught courses in sociolinguistics, discourse analysis, and professional communication. Much of his research has focused on issues of language and identity in Tunisia, where he served as a Peace Corps volunteer, and the Arab world more broadly. He's a co-author of two other textbooks, *Everything's an Argument with Readings* and *What's Language Got to Do with It?* Prior to teaching at PSU, he taught in the Linguistics Department at the University of Texas at Austin and in the English Department at The Ohio State University. Most recently, he was a Fulbright scholar in the English Department at Bethlehem University in the West Bank.

About the Alphabet

THE ALPHABET song may be one of the first things you learned to sing: *a - b - c - d - e - f - g / h - i - j - k - l - m - n - o - p / q and r and s and t / u - v - w - x - y - z / Now I know my abc's / Next time won't you sing with me?* And maybe you had a set of alphabet blocks, 26 little letters you could use to make words of your own. Combined, those letters yield everything from the word *Google* to the complete works of Shakespeare. So alphabets are versatile, and perhaps that's part of their fascination. In our grandmothers' day, young women often made alphabet samplers, using fancy stitches to create the letters. Earlier, in medieval times, scribes labored to create highly ornate letters to adorn manuscripts whose words were "illuminated" by the intricate letters, often done in silver and gold.

We had these illuminated letters in mind when we asked Carin Berger to create a modern-day illuminated alphabet for this book. You'll see the results in every chapter, each of which begins with one of the letters Berger created. To us, they represent our old alphabet blocks, our grandmothers' samplers, and the illuminated letters that still dazzle us after many hundreds of years. But look again and you'll see that these letters are also striking images. And instead of being decorated with precious silver and gold leaf, our letters are decorated with bits of everyday text—maps, comics, stationery, receipts, school papers, checks, and so on. In our alphabet, old and new, low tech and high tech, word and image come together to create evocative, timely letters for our book.

And just as modern-day type fonts have names, so too does our alphabet. We call it Author.

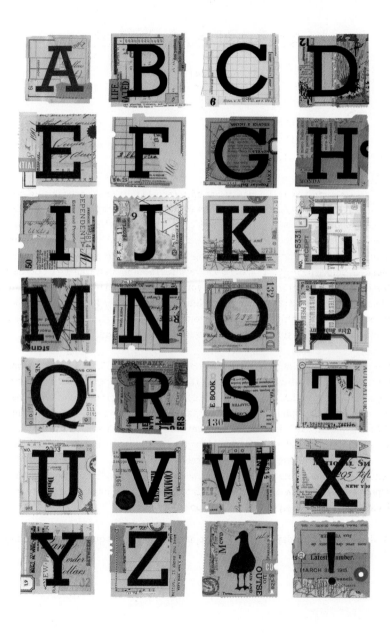

Submitting Papers for Publication by W. W. Norton & Company

We are interested in receiving writing from college students to consider including in our textbooks as examples of student writing. Please send this form with the work that you would like us to consider to Marilyn Moller, Student Writing, W. W. Norton & Company, 500 Fifth Avenue, New York, NY 10110. For questions, or to submit electronically, email us at composition@wwnorton.com.

Text Submission Form

Student's name _____

School _____

Address _____

Department _____

Course _____

Writing assignment the text responds to _____

_____

_____

_____

_____

_____

Instructor's name _____

Please write a few sentences about what your primary purposes were for writing this text. Also, if you wish, tell us what you learned about writing from the experience of writing it.

_____

_____

_____

_____

_____

_____

_____

_____

_____

_____

Contact Information
Please provide the information below so that we can contact you if your work is selected for publication.

Name _____

Permanent address _____

Email _____

Phone _____

Author / Title Index

Note: Page numbers in *italics* indicate figures.

Glossary / Index

Note: This glossary / index defines key terms and concepts and directs you to pages in the book where you can find specific information on these and other topics. Please note the words set in SMALL CAPITAL LETTERS are themselves defined in the glossary / index. Page numbers in *italics* indicate figures.

engineer may be quoted as an authority on bridge construction, for example. Authority also refers to a quality conveyed by writers who are knowledgeable about their subjects.

B

BLOCK QUOTATION, 601–2 In a written work, long QUOTATIONS are indented and set without quotation marks: in MLA STYLE, set off text more than four typed lines, indented five spaces (or one-half inch) from the left margin; in APA STYLE, set off quotes of forty or more words, indented five spaces (or one-half inch) from the left margin. *See also* QUOTATION

BLOG, 815 An abbreviation of *weblog.* A regularly updated website on which writers post

their work, often including images, embedded audio or video clips, and links to other sites.

BRAINSTORMING, 116 A process for GENERATING IDEAS AND TEXT by writing down everything that comes to mind about a topic, then looking for patterns or connections among the ideas.

C

CAPTION, 554 A brief explanation accompanying a photograph, diagram, chart, screen shot, or other visual that appears in a written document.

words: *The old farmer with the multi-colored carrots has a booth at the market.*

COMPLEX SENTENCE, 699–700 A single MAIN CLAUSE plus one or more DEPENDENT CLAUSES: *When the United States holds a presidential election once every four years, citizens should vote.*

COMPOUND-COMPLEX SENTENCE, 700 Two or more MAIN CLAUSES plus one or more DEPENDENT CLAUSES: *When the United States holds a presidential election once every four years, citizens should vote, but voter turnout is often disappointing.*

COMPOUND SENTENCE, 696–98 Two or more MAIN CLAUSES joined by a comma and a COORDINATING CONJUNCTION or by a semicolon: *The United States holds a presidential election once every four years, but voter turnout is often disappointing.*

CONCLUSION The way a text ends, a chance to leave an AUDIENCE thinking about what's been said. Five ways of concluding a college essay: reiterating your point, discussing the implications of your ARGUMENT, asking a question, referring back to your OPENING, or proposing some kind of action.

    closing sentences, 707–9
    drafting, 120

conference proceedings
    in lists of references (APA style), 639, 642
    in works cited (MLA style), 590–91

CONFIRMATION BIAS, 100–101, 104 The tendency to favor and seek out information that confirms what we already believe and to reject and ignore information that contradicts those beliefs.

conjunctions, coordinating, 697–98, 718, 721
Consumer Reports, 332, 343

CONTEXT, 33 Part of any RHETORICAL SITUATION, conditions affecting the text such as what else has been said about a topic; social, economic, and other factors; and any constants such as due date and length.
    online, 161

contrast. *See* COMPARISON AND CONTRAST

COORDINATING CONJUNCTION, 697–98, 718, 721 One of these words—*and, but, or, nor, so, for,* or *yet*—used to join two elements in a way that gives equal weight to each one (*bacon and eggs; pay up or get out*).

correctness, 668–71
Council of Science Editors (CSE), 562

COUNTERARGUMENT, 437, 440 In ARGUMENT, an alternative POSITION or objection to the writer's position. The writer of an argument should not only acknowledge counterarguments but also, if at all possible, accept, accommodate, or refute each counterargument.

COUNT NOUN A word that names something that can be counted (*one book, two books*). *See also* NONCOUNT NOUN

court case
    in MLA style in-text documentation, 569
    in works cited (MLA style), 596

CREDIBILITY, 422–32 The sense of trustworthiness that a writer conveys through the text.
    in arguments, 160
    in reports, 294–95
    in research, 562

credit, giving, 13, 555–62
Crick, Francis, 15–16

DIALECT, 683–93 Varieties of language that are spoken by people in a particular region, social class, or ethnic group.

DICTION, 665 Word choice.

DOCUMENTATION, 552–62 Publication information about the sources cited in a text. The documentation usually appears in an abbreviated form in parentheses at the point of citation or in an endnote or a footnote. Complete documentation usually appears as a list of WORKS CITED or REFERENCES at the end of the text. Documentation styles vary by discipline. *See also* MLA STYLE and APA STYLE.

DOMINANT IMPRESSION, 462 The overall effect created through specific details when a writer describes something.

DRAFTING, 120 The process of putting words on paper or screen. Writers often write several drafts, REVISING each until they achieve their goal or reach a deadline. At that point, they submit a finished final draft.

E

EDITED ACADEMIC ENGLISH, 42–43, 669–71, 685 The conventions of spelling, grammar, and punctuation expected in academic discourse, which tends to be more formal than conversational English. Academic English varies from country to country and changes over time. *Edited* refers to the care writers take in reviewing their formal written work.

EDITING, 122 The process of fine-tuning a text—examining each word, phrase, sentence, and paragraph—to be sure that the text is correct and precise and says exactly what the

EMOTIONAL APPEALS, 421–22 Ways that
authors appeal to an AUDIENCE's emotions, values, and beliefs by arousing specific feelings—
for example, compassion, pity, sympathy, anger,
fear. *See also* ETHICAL APPEALS; LOGICAL APPEALS

ESSENTIAL ELEMENT, 749–50 A word, PHRASE,
or CLAUSE with information that is necessary
for understanding the meaning of a sentence:
French is the only language that I can speak.

ETHICAL APPEALS, 422–25 Ways that authors
establish CREDIBILITY and AUTHORITY to
persuade an AUDIENCE to trust their ARGU-
MENTS—by showing that they know what
they're talking about (for example, by citing
trustworthy SOURCES), demonstrating that
they're fair (by representing opposing views
accurately and even-handedly), and establishing COMMON GROUND. *See also* EMOTIONAL
APPEALS; LOGICAL APPEALS

EVIDENCE, 425, 427–32, 451–73 In ARGUMENT,
the data you present to support your REASONS.
Such data may include statistics, calculations,
EXAMPLES, ANECDOTES, QUOTATIONS, case studies, or anything else that will convince your
readers that your reasons are compelling.

H

HASHTAG A metadata tag created by placing a number sign (#) in front of a word or unspaced phrase (for example, #BlackLivesMatter), used in social media to mark posts by **KEYWORD** or theme and make them searchable by these tags. Also used to add commentary on a web text outside of the text itself.

HELPING VERB, 739 A **VERB** that works with a **MAIN VERB** to express a tense and mood. Helping verbs include *do, have, be,* and **MODALS:** *Elvis has left the building. Pigs can fly.*

I

IMRAD, 44, 284–85, 760 Acronym representing sections of scientific reports conveying information: introduction (asks a question), methods (tells about experiments), results (states findings), and discussion (tries to make sense of findings in light of what was already known).

MAIN VERB, 739 The verb form that presents the action or state. It can stand alone or be combined with one or more HELPING VERBS. *My dog might have* buried *your keys. Leslie Jones* is *a comedian. Alexa was* wearing *a gown by Milly. The agent didn't* appear *old enough to drive.*

MEDIUM, 755–56 A means for communicating— for example, in print, with speech, or online. *See also* DESIGN

MEMOIR, 468 A GENRE that focuses on something significant from the writer's past. Key features include good story, vivid details, and clear significance.

MISINFORMATION, 98–107, 491 False or inaccurate information that may or may not be intended to deceive (lies, on the other hand, are always told deliberately).

MIXED CONSTRUCTION, 722–25 A sentence that starts out with one structure and ends up with another one: *Although bears can be deadly is not a good reason to avoid camping altogether.*

MLA STYLE, 562, 563–617 A system of DOCUMENTATION used in the humanities. MLA stands for the Modern Language Association.

NONCOUNT NOUN, 736 A word that names something that cannot be counted or made plural with certain modifiers or units: *information, rice.*

NONESSENTIAL ELEMENT, 749–50 A word, phrase, or CLAUSE that gives additional information but that is not necessary for understanding the basic meaning of a sentence: *I learned French, <u>which is a Romance language,</u> online.* Nonessential elements should be set off by commas.

NOUN A word that refers to a person, place, animal, thing, or idea (*director, Stephen King, forest, Amazon River, tree frog, notebook, democracy*).

O

OPENING, 704–7 The way a text begins, which plays an important role in drawing an AUDIENCE in. Some ways of opening a college essay: with a dramatic statement, a vivid image, a provocative question, an ANECDOTE, or a startling CLAIM.

OUTLINING, 118 A process for GENERATING IDEAS AND TEXT or for examining a text. An informal outline simply lists ideas and then numbers them in the order that they will appear; a working outline distinguishes support from main ideas by indenting the former; a formal outline is arranged as a series of headings and indented subheadings, each on a separate line, with letters and numerals indicating relative levels of importance.

P

PARAPHRASE, 541–43, 547–49, 551–54 To reword a text in about the same number of words but without using the word order or sentence structure of the original. Paraphrasing is generally called for when a writer wants to include the details of a passage but does not need to quote it word for word. As with QUOTING and SUMMARIZING, paraphrasing requires DOCUMENTATION. *See also* PATCHWRITING

PASSIVE VOICE, 679–80 When a VERB is in the passive voice, the subject is acted upon: *A gift was given to Oliver.*

PATCHWRITING, 558–60 PARAPHRASES that lean too heavily on the words or sentence structure of the source, adding or deleting some words, replacing words with synonyms, altering the syntax slightly—in other words, not restating the passage in fresh language and structure.

Patel, Eboo, 422–24, *423*
pathos. *See* EMOTIONAL APPEALS
Patrick, Danica, 781–83, *782*
peer review. *See* response
periodicals, documenting, 494–95
in lists of references (APA style), 629–30
in working bibliographies, 519
in works cited (MLA style), 578–85

PERIODIC SENTENCE, 702–3 A sentence that delays the main idea, expressed in a MAIN CLAUSE, until after details given in phrases and SUBORDINATE CLAUSES. *See also* CUMULATIVE SENTENCE

periods, 546, 718, 720
personal experience
as evidence, 431–32
as support for an argument, 464–65
personal interviews, in works cited (MLA style), 598
perspectives. *See also* POINT OF VIEW
in arguments, 158–59
considering multiple perspectives, 9–10, 45, 434–37
persuasion, 5. *See also* RHETORIC
Pettitte, Andy, 247–49, *249*, 251
Phoenix, Joaquin, 334, *335*
photographs, 105–6, 764, *764*, 769
pie charts, *765*, 766
Pienaar, Francois, *426*

PLAGIARISM, 555–62 Using another person's words, syntax, or ideas without giving appropriate credit and DOCUMENTATION. Plagiarism is a serious breach of ethics.
avoiding, 558–61, 744
fair use and the internet, 557–58
patchwriting, 558–60

Playing for Change, 126
plus signs, in keyword searches, 504
podcasts
in lists of references (APA style), 640–41
in works cited (MLA style), 599
poems, in MLA style in-text documentation, 569

POINT OF VIEW A position from which something is considered. The common points of view are first person, which uses *I* or *we*, and third person, which uses *he*, *she*, or *they*. *See also* perspectives
in narratives, 196–99, 216

popular sources, 490–91, *492*

PORTFOLIO, 809–17 A collection of writing selected by a writer to show their work, sometimes including a statement assessing the work and explaining what it demonstrates.
e-portfolios, 815–17, *816*
organizing, 815–17
portfolio statements, 813–14
reflecting on your writing, 812–14
sample portfolio statement, 813–14
what to include, 810–11

POSITION, 167–69 A statement that asserts a belief or CLAIM. In an ARGUMENT, a position needs to be stated in a THESIS or clearly implied and requires support with REASONS and other kinds of EVIDENCE.

possessive case, 732–34
posters
for presentation, 790–91, *791*
in lists of references (APA style), 639
posts to online forums, in lists of references (APA style), 640

REVISION, 121–22 The process of making substantive changes, including additions and cuts, to a draft so that it contains all the necessary information in an appropriate organization. During revision, a writer generally moves from whole-text issues to details with the goals of sharpening the focus and strengthening the ARGUMENT.

RHETORIC, 1–63 One of the three original disciplines in the ancient world (along with grammar and logic), rhetoric has been defined in many ways through the centuries. In this book, we define it as the art, practice, and theory of ethical communication.

RHETORICAL ANALYSIS, 238–42, 265 A kind of ANALYSIS that takes a close look at how a text communicates a message to an AUDIENCE.

RHETORICAL SITUATION, 28–34, 115–16 The circumstances that affect writing or other communication, including PURPOSE, AUDIENCE, GENRE, STANCE, CONTEXT, MEDIA, and DESIGN.

ROGERIAN ARGUMENTS, 445–46 A system of ARGUMENT based on the work of Carl Rogers that stresses fairness and compromise and persuasion by nonconfrontational strategies such as showing respect and establishing COMMON GROUND. The introduction presents the issue fairly, the body discusses various POSITIONS on the issue including the author's own, and the CONCLUSION presents a resolution.

S

SECONDARY SOURCE, 488, 490 An ANALYSIS or
interpretation of a PRIMARY SOURCE. In writing
about the Revolutionary War, a researcher
would probably consider the Declaration of
Independence a primary source and a textbook's description of how the document was
written a secondary source.

SIGNAL PHRASE, 551–52, 742, 744–45 A phrase
used to attribute quoted, paraphrased, or summarized material to a source, as in "she said" or
"he claimed."

SIGNPOST LANGUAGE Words and phrases meant
to help listeners follow an oral presentation.
Some functions of signpost language include
introducing or concluding a presentation ("My
topic today is . . ."), providing an overview ("I will
make three major points"), or marking TRANSI-
TIONS ("My third and final point is . . .").

SIMPLE SENTENCE, 696 A single MAIN CLAUSE,
which contains at least a SUBJECT and a VERB.
The main clause must stand alone: *Citizens
vote. The United States holds a presidential election once every four years.* For sentences with
more than a single main clause, *see* COMPOUND
SENTENCE; COMPOUND-COMPLEX SENTENCE;
COMPLEX SENTENCE.

SIMPLE SUBJECT, 736, 737 The word that determines the form of the VERB: *The young farmer
from Ten Barn Farm has the best tomatoes at the
market.* The simple subject is *farmer,* a singular
NOUN; for that reason, the verb *has* is singular.

TOPIC SENTENCE, 43 A sentence, often at the beginning of a paragraph, that states the paragraph's main point. The details in the rest of the paragraph should support the topic sentence.

TOULMIN ARGUMENT, 442–44 A system of ARGUMENT developed by Stephen Toulmin that features a qualified CLAIM; REASONS and EVIDENCE in support of the claim; underlying assumptions that aren't explicitly stated but that also support the claim; further evidence or backing for those underlying assumptions; and a CONCLUSION.

TRANSITION, 698 A word or PHRASE that helps to connect sentences and paragraphs and to guide readers through a text. Transitions can show COMPARISONS (*also, similarly, likewise, in the same way*); CONTRASTS (*but, instead, although, however, nonetheless*); EXAMPLES (*for instance, in fact, such as*); place or position (*above, beyond, near, elsewhere*); sequence (*finally, next, again, also*); SUMMARY or conclusion (*on the whole, as we have seen, in brief*); time (*at first, meanwhile, so far, later*); and more.

U

V

VANTAGE POINT The physical position from which a writer describes something. *See* perspectives; POINT OF VIEW

VERB, 734–40 A word that expresses an action (*dance, talk*) or a state of being (*be, seem*). A verb is an ESSENTIAL ELEMENT of a sentence or CLAUSE. Verbs have four forms: base form (*smile*), past tense (*smiled*), past participle

W

MLA DOCUMENTATION DIRECTORY

APA DOCUMENTATION DIRECTORY

Menu of Readings ∽

Readings by Genre ∽

Argument

Analysis